REDESCRIBING THE GOSPEL OF MARK

EARLY CHRISTIANITY AND ITS LITERATURE

David G. Horrell, General Editor

Number 22

REDESCRIBING THE GOSPEL OF MARK

Edited by

Barry S. Crawford and Merrill P. Miller

SBL PRESS

 **PRESS**

Atlanta

Copyright © 2017 by SBL Press

Library of Congress Cataloging-in-Publication Data

Names: Crawford, Barry S., editor. | Miller, Merrill P., editor.
Title: Redescribing the Gospel of Mark / edited by Barry S. Crawford and Merrill P. Miller.
Description: Atlanta : SBL Press, 2017. | Series: Early Christianity and its literature ; Number 22 | Includes bibliographical references and index.
Identifiers: LCCN 2016056524 (print) | LCCN 2016057451 (ebook) | ISBN 9781628371635 (paperback) | ISBN 9780884142041 (hardcover) | ISBN 9780884142034 (ebook)
Subjects: LCSH: Bible. Mark—Criticism, interpretation, etc.
Classification: LCC BS2585.53 .R434 2017 (print) | LCC BS2585.53 (ebook) | DDC 226.3/06—dc23
LC record available at https://lccn.loc.gov/2016056524

Printed on acid-free paper.

CONTENTS

Acknowledgments..vii

Abbreviations..ix

Introduction
    Barry S. Crawford... 1

Conjectures on Conjunctures and Other Matters: Three Essays
    Jonathan Z. Smith..17

The Markan Site
    Jonathan Z. Smith..99

Cartwheels: Or on Not Staying Upside Down Too Long
    Burton L. Mack..127

On Smith, On Myth, On Mark
    William E. Arnal..145

Markan Grapplings
    Christopher R. Matthews...169

The Spyglass and Kaleidoscope: From a Levantine Coign of
    Vantage
    Burton L. Mack..181

The Social Logic of the Gospel of Mark: Cultural Persistence
    and Social Escape in a Postwar Time
    Merrill P. Miller 207

Mark, War, and Creative Imagination
 William E. Arnal...401

Q and the "Big Bang" Theory of Christian Origins
 Robyn Faith Walsh...483

Ancient Myths and Modern Theories of Christian Origins: The
 Consultation (1995–1997) and Seminar (1998–2003) in
 Retrospect with Attention to Successor Groups and a
 Recommendation
 Barry S. Crawford and Merrill P. Miller...535

Bibliography...575

Contributors..647

Index of Ancient Texts...649

Index of Modern Authors...664

Index of Subjects..672

Acknowledgments

Our thanks to David Horrell, series editor, and the anonymous readers for accepting this volume for publication, and to Nicole Tilford, Bob Buller, and the entire staff of SBL Press for their assistance throughout the publication process.

A special word of thanks to Sharon Urban and Sue Taylor-Owens at Washburn University, whose kindness, patience, and, above all, word processing expertise rescued the present volume on numerous occasions. We also wish to express our gratitude to Yoram and Gabriel Miller. Your timely interventions and your heavy lifting continually kept the project on course. And Abby Aron, this book may have little to do with your own third-grade book project, "Jonathan's Spooky Adventures," but thank you for persistently inquiring about the progress of our book, even though it could not be imagined as a graphic novel.

We recognize the contributions of our indexers to the benefit of readers of the volume: for the index of ancient texts, Ian Brown, University of Toronto, and for the index of subjects, Katherine Koopman of Koopman Information Services.

To Bill Arnal, Erin Roberts, and all the current and future participants in the SBL Redescribing project, it is you we had especially in mind while writing the concluding chapter of the volume. The book is dedicated to Sherwood D. Miller, in loving memory.

Abbreviations

Primary Sources

X	Monacensis, tenth century CE
Ψ	Athous Lavrensis, eighth–ninth century CE
א	Sinaiticus, fourth century CE
1 En.	1 Enoch (Ethiopic Apocalypse)
2 Bar.	2 Baruch (Syriac Apocalypse)
3 Bar.	3 Baruch (Greek Apocalypse)
4 Bar.	4 Baruch (Paraleipomena Jeremiou)
A	Alexandrinus, fifth century CE
Avot R. Nat.	Avot of Rabbi Nathan
Avod. Zar.	Avodah Zarah
Abr.	Philo, *De Abrahamo*
Abst.	Porphyry, *De abstinentia*
Acts Pet.	Acts of Peter
Ag. Ap.	Josephus, *Against Apion*
Alex.	Plutarch, *Alexander*
Ann.	Tacitus, *Annales*
Ant.	Josephus, *Jewish Antiquities*
As. Mos.	Assumption of Moses
Apol.	Tertullian, *Apologeticus*
Bib. hist.	Diodorus Siculus, *Bibliotheca historica*
B	Vaticanus, fourth century CE
b.	Babylonian Talmud
C	Ephraaemi Rescriptus, fifth century CE
Conf.	Philo, *De confusione linguarum*
Contempl.	Philo, *De vita contempliva*
D	Beza, fifth century CE
Deipn.	Athenaeus, *Deipnosophistae*
Descr.	Pausanias, *Graeciae descriptio*

Dial.	Tacitus, *Dialogus de oratoribus*
Diatr.	Epictetus, *Diatribai* (*Dissertationes*)
Dion.	Nonnus, *Dionysiaca*
Dom.	Suetonius, *Domitianus*
Edict.	Justinian, *Edicta* / *The Digest*
Ep.	Pliny the Younger, *Epistulae*
Ep.	Seneca, *Epistulae morales*
Ex. quaest. Rom.	Augustine, *Expositio quarumdam quaestionum in epistula ad Romanos*
Fab.	Phaedrus, *Fabulae*
Flacc.	Philo, *In Flaccum*
Fug.	Philo, *De fuga et inventione*
Geogr.	Strabo, *Geographica*
Giṭ.	Giṭṭin
Gos. Thom.	Gospel of Thomas
Hal.	Hallah
Hist.	Herodian, *Historia*; Herodotus, *Historiae*; Tacitus, *Historiae*
Hist. Rom.	Dio Cassius, *Historia Romana*
Ign. *Eph.*	Ignatius, *To the Ephesians*
J.W.	Josephus, *Jewish War*/*Judean War*
Jub.	Jubilees
Ketub.	Ketubbot
Lam. Rab.	Lamentations Rabbah
Legat.	Philo, *Legatio ad Gaium*
Life	Josephus, *The Life*
LXX	Septuagint
m.	Mishnah
Mos.	Philo, *De vita Mosis*
MT	Masoretic Text
Mut.	Philo, *De mutatione nominum*
Nav.	Lucian, *Navigium*
Nero	Suetonius, *Nero*
Noct. Att.	Aulus Gellius, *Attic Nights*
Od.	Homer, *Odyssey*
Opif.	Philo, *De opificio mundi*
Philops.	Lucian, *Philopseudes*
Praep. ev.	Eusebius, *Preparatio evangelica*
Prec. ger. rei publ.	Plutarch, *Praecepta gerendae rei publicae*

Prov.	Philo, *De providentia*
Pun.	Silius Italicus, *Punica*
QG	Philo, *Questiones et solutiones in Genesin*
Rerum nat.	Lucretius, *De rerum natura*
Resp.	Plato, *Respublica*
Shabb.	Shabbat
Satry.	Petronius, *Satyricon*
Sib. Or.	Sibylline Oracles
Somn.	Philo, *De somniis*
Spec.	Philo, *De specialibus legibus*
Syr.	Appian, *Syriaca*
Syr. d.	Lucian, *De Syria dea*
t.	Tosefta
T. Levi	Testament of Levi
Tranq.	Seneca, *De tranquillitate animi*
V. Procli	Marinus, *Vita Procli*
Vita	Josephus, *The Life*

Secondary Sources

AB	Anchor Bible
ABD	*Anchor Bible Dictionary.* Edited by David Noel Freedman. 6 vols. New York: Doubleday, 1992.
AcBib	Academia Biblica
AGJU	Arbeiten zur Geschichte des Antiken Judentums und des Urchristentums
AJP	*American Journal of Philology*
AJSR	*Association for Jewish Studies Review*
ANRW	*Aufstieg und Niedergang der römischen Welt: Geschichte und Kultur Roms im Spiegel der neueren Forschung.* Part 2, *Principat.* Edited by Hildegard Temporini and Wolfgang Haase. Berlin: de Gruyter, 1972–.
AOS	American Oriental Series
AR	*Archiv für Religionswissenschaft*
ATLA	American Theological Library Association
BAGD	Bauer, Walter, William F. Arndt, F. Wilbur Gingrich, and Frederick W. Danker, *and Other Early Christian Literature.* 3rd ed. Chicago: University of Chicago Press, 2000.

BBB	Bonner Biblische Beiträge
BCSSR	*Bulletin of the Council of Societies for the Study of Religion*
BETL	Bibliotheca Ephemeridum Theologicarum Lovaniensium
BFCT	Beiträge zur Förderung christlicher Theologie
Bib	*Biblica*
Bib. hist.	Diodorus Siculus, *Bibliotheca historica*
BibInt	Bible Interpretation Series
BibSem	The Biblical Seminar
BJS	Brown Judaic Studies
BSGRT	Bibliotheca scriptorum Graecorum et Romanorum Teubneriana
BTB	*Biblical Theology Bulletin*
BTS	Biblical Tools and Studies
BZNW	Beihefte zur Zeitschrift für die neutestamentliche Wissenschaft
CB	Cultura Bibica
CBQ	*Catholic Biblical Quarterly*
CIG	*Corpus Inscriptionum Graecarum*. Edited by August Böckh. 4 vols. Berlin: Reimer, 1828–1877.
CIJ	*Corpus Inscriptionum Judaicarum*. Edited by Jean-Baptiste Frey. 2 vols. Rome: Pontifical Biblical Institute, 1936–1952.
CIL	*Corpus Inscriptionum Latinarum*. Berlin, 1862–
CIS	*Corpus Inscriptionum Semiticarum*. Paris, 1881
ConBNT	Coniectanea Neotestamentica or Coniectanea Biblica: New Testament Series
CP	*Classical Philology*
CPJ	*Corpus Papyrorum Judaicarum*. Edited by Victor A. Tcherikover. 3 vols. Cambridge: Harvard University Press, 1957–1964.
CRINT	Compendia Rerum Iudaicarum ad Novum Testamentum
CSHJ	Chicago Studies in the History of Judaism
DDD	*Dictionary of Deities and Demons in the Bible*. Edited by Karel van der Toorn, Bob Becking, and Pieter W. van der Horst. Leiden: Brill, 1995. 2nd rev. ed. Grand Rapids: Eerdmans, 1999.

DSD	*Dead Sea Discoveries*
ECL	Early Christianity and Its Literature
EPRO	Etudes préliminaires aux religions orientales dans l'empire romain
FGH	*Die Fragmente der griechischen Historikor.* By Felix Jacoby. Leiden: Brill, 1954–1964.
FHG	*Fragmenta Historicorum Graecorum.* Edited by C. Müller and T. Müller. 5 vols. Paris: Didot, 1841–1870.
Historia	*Historia: Zeitschrift für alte Geschichte*
HR	*History of Religions*
HRCS	Hatch, Edwin, and Henry A Redpath. *Concordance to the Septuagint and Other Greek Versions of the Old Testament.* 2 vols. Oxford: Clarendon, 1897. 2nd ed. Grand Rapids: Baker, 1988.
HSCP	*Harvard Studies in Classical Philology*
HTR	*Harvard Theological Review*
HTS	Harvard Theological Studies
HUCA	*Hebrew Union College Annual*
ID	*Inscriptions de Délos.* Edited by Félix Dürrbach, Pierre Roussel, Marcel Launey, André Plasart, and Jacques Couprey. Paris: Académie des inscriptions & belles-lettres, 1926–.
IG	*Inscriptiones Graecae. Editio Minor.* Berlin: de Gruyter, 1924–
IGRR	*Inscriptiones graecae ad res romanas pertinentes auctoritate et impensis academiae inscriptionum et litterarum humaniorum collectae et editae.* Edited by René Cagnat. Reprints from the collection of the University of Toronto Libraries. Toronto: University of Toronto Libraries, 1901.
ILS	*Inscriptiones Latinae Selectae.* 3 vols. Edited by Hermann Dessau. Berlin: Berolini Apud Weidmannos, 1892–1916.
JAAR	*Journal of the American Academy of Religion*
JAJ	*Journal of Ancient Judaism*
JBL	*Journal of Biblical Literature*
JECS	*Journal of Early Christian Studies*
JGRChJ	*Journal of Greco-Roman Christianity and Judaism*
JJS	*Journal of Jewish Studies*

JQR	*Jewish Quarterly Review*
JR	*Journal of Religion*
JRS	*Journal of Roman Studies*
JSJ	*Journal for the Study of Judaism in the Persian, Hellenistic, and Roman Periods*
JSJSup	Supplements to the Journal for the Study of Judaism in the Persian, Hellenistic, and Roman Periods
JSNT	*Journal for the Study of the New Testament*
JSNTSup	Journal for the Study of the New Testament Supplement Series
JSOT	*Journal for the Study of the Old Testament*
JSOTSup	Journal for the Study of the Old Testament Supplement Series
JSPSup	Journal for the Study of the Pseudepigrapha Supplement Series
Jud	*Judaica*
KAI	*Kanaanäische und aramäische Inschriften.* Herbert Donner and Wolfgang Röllig. 2nd ed. Weisbaden: Harrassowitz, 1966–1969.
KlPauly	*Der kleine Pauly: Lexikon der Antike.* Edited by Konrat Ziegler and Walther Sontheimer. 5 vols. Munich: Deutscher Taschenbuch Verlag, 1964–1975.
LASBF	*Liber Annuus Studii Biblici Franciscani*
LCL	Loeb Classical Library
LHBOTS	Library of Hebrew Bible/Old Testament Studies
LNTS	Library of New Testament Studies
LSJ	Liddell, Henry George, Robert Scott, Henry Stuart Jones. *A Greek-English Lexicon.* 9th ed. with revised supplement. Oxford: Clarendon, 1996.
LSTS	Library of Second Temple Studies
MTSR	*Method and Theory in the Study of Religion*
MTSRSup	Supplements to Method and Theory in the Study of Religion
NA[27]	*Novum Testamentum Graece.* Edited by Eberhard Nestle, Erwin Nestle, and Kurt Aland. 27th ed. Stuttgart: Deutsche Bibelstiftung, 1993.
Neot	*Neotestamentica*
NovTSup	Supplements to Novum Testamentum
NRSV	New Revised Standard Version

NTL	New Testament Library
NTS	*New Testament Studies*
Numen	*Numen: International Review for the History of Religions*
OED	*Oxford English Dictionary: Being a Corrected Re-issue with an Introduction, Supplement, and Bibliography of A New English Dictionary on Historical Principles.* Edited by James A. H. and Murray R. W. Burchfield. Oxford: Clarendon Press, 1933.
OGIS	*Orientis Graeci Inscriptiones Selectae.* Edited by Wilhelm Dittenberger. 2 vols. Leipzig: Hirzel, 1903–1905.
PGL	*Patristic Greek Lexicon.* Edited by Geoffrey W. H. Lampe. Oxford: Clarendon, 1961.
PL	Patrologia Latina [= *Patrologiae Cursus Completus*: Series Latina]. Edited by Jacques-Paul Migne. 217 vols. Paris: Migne, 1844–1855.
Proof	*Prooftexts: A Journal of Jewish Literary History*
PW	*Paulys Real-Encyclopädie der classischen Altertumswissenschaft.* New ed. by Georg Wissowa and Wilhelm Kroll. 50 vols. in 84 parts. Stuttgart: Metzler & Druckenmüller, 1894–1980.
RBL	*Review of Biblical Literature*
RBS	Resources for Biblical Study
RE	*Realencyklopädie für protestantische Theologie und Kirche*
RevPhil	*Revue de philology*
RHR	*Revue del'historie des religions*
RlA	*Reallexicon der Assyriologie.* Edited by Erich Ebeling et al. Berlin: de Gruyter, 1928–.
RSV	Revised Standard Version
RVV	Religionsgeschichtliche Versuche und Vorarbeiten
SBL	Society of Biblical Literature
SBLSP	Society of Biblical Literature Seminar Papers
SBLStBL	Society of Biblical Literature Studies in Biblical Literature
SBLTT	Society of Biblical Literature Texts and Translations
SBT	Studies in Biblical Theology
SCJ	Studies in Christianity and Judaism / Études sur le christianisme et le judaïsme
Semeia	*Semeia*

SemeiaSt	Semeia Studies
SFSHJ	South Florida Studies in the History of Judaism
SHR	Studies in the History of Religions
SJLA	Studies in Judaism in Late Antiquity
SR	*Studies in Religion*
SSEJC	Studies in Scripture in Early Judaism and Christianity
ST	*Studia Theologica*
StBibLit	Studies in Biblical Literature
STDJ	Studies on the Texts of the Desert of Judah
SVTP	Studia in Veteris Testamenti Pseudepigraphica
SymS	Symposium Series
TANZ	Texte und Arbeiten zum neutestamentliche Zeitalter
TAPA	*Transactions of the American Philological Association*
TDNT	*Theological Dictionary of the New Testament*. Edited by Gerhard Kittel and Gerhard Friedrich. Translated by Geoffrey W. Bromiley. 10 vols. Grand Rapids: Eerdmans, 1964–1976.
TJT	*Toronto Journal of Theology*
TSAJ	Texte und Studien zum antiken Judentum
TUGAL	Texte und Untersuchungen zur Geschichte der altchristlichen Literatur
UBS3	*The Greek New Testament*. Edited by Kurt Aland et al. in cooperation with the Institute for New Testament Textual Research. 3rd ed. New York: United Bible Societies, 1975.
WGRWSup	Writings from the Greco-Roman World Supplement Series
WUNT	Wissenschaftliche Untersuchungen zum Neuen Testament
ZNW	*Zeitschrift für die neutestamentliche Wissenschaft und die Kunde der älteren Kirche*

Introduction

Barry S. Crawford

This is the third of a three-volume series of studies by members of the Society of Biblical Literature's Consultation (1995–1997), then Seminar (1998–2003), on Ancient Myths and Modern Theories of Christian Origins, both concerned with redescribing the beginnings of Christianity as religion, that is, with theories and methods developed in the social sciences and related areas for studying religious phenomena of various sorts and geographical locations, not just the specific literature, beliefs, and practices of early Christians. The work of the consultation and seminar did not end, however, with the completion of the seminar's term in 2003. Its project of redescription was continued by two successor program units, the Redescribing Early Christianity Group (2007–2012) and the current Redescribing Early Christianity Seminar, begun in 2013.

The primary purpose of the seminar (and earlier consultation) was twofold: to offer a redescription of Christian origins and to construct or contribute to a general theory of religion engendering explanations of the rise and development of Christianity accessible and coherent to colleagues in academic disciplines not generally known for describing religion in terms of volcanic eruptions of the numinous or transformative personal experiences. This would mean, of course, that the dominant paradigm, or master narrative, of Christian beginnings, as found in the gospels (most notably Luke) and the book of Acts, and subsequently enshrined in Eusebius's *Ecclesiastical History*, should not simply be translated into historical descriptions. There are indications already in the New Testament that locating Christian beginnings in a unilinear generative impulse grounded in the experience, intentions, and fate of Jesus and his earliest followers and reaching as far as the second, third, and even fourth centuries, is fantasy, not history. What is needed instead, and what the project has attempted to provide, is a *re*description based on careful attention to social and anthropological perspectives and models.

The primary motivation for embarking on this redescription project was to test the provocative proposals on Christian origins offered by Burton L. Mack in his groundbreaking work, *A Myth of Innocence*.[1] From its inception, the project was also—and continues to be—fundamentally indebted to the foundational work of Jonathan Z. Smith and was fortunate to have his participation throughout its first incarnation, from the inaugural meeting of the consultation in 1995 until the closing session of the Ancient Myths Seminar in 2003.[2] Both the consultation and seminar sought to apply Smith's approach and methods to various social locations and their literary productions (or, as project participants called them, "sites") in early Christianity, some for which there is solid historical and textual evidence (such as Paul's group[s] in Corinth), some which have to be reconstructed (such as the early Jesus schools). The general procedure for the project was to problematize consensus views, identify unexamined scholarly assumptions and categories, recontextualize and redescribe key data, and account for the nature and impact of central primary texts in earliest Christianity in categories and terms derived from, and hence compatible with, contemporary social and anthropological theory. In the first volume of the series, *Redescribing Christian Origins*,[3] papers from the consultation and seminar focus on such sites as the Q Gospel and the Gospel of Thomas, a possible Jesus school in Jerusalem, and a pre-Pauline *Christos* association. As its title indicates, the second volume, *Redescribing Paul and the Corinthians*,[4] deals exclusively with Paul and his church(es) in Corinth, as seen especially in 1 Corinthians.

Over the course of its life, the seminar (and consultation) has been guided by two terms, both ultimately derived from Mack's *Myth of Innocence*, that have served as the principal operating categories of its investigations. These

---

1. Burton L. Mack, *A Myth of Innocence: Mark and Christian Origins* (Philadelphia: Fortress, 1988; repr. with new preface, Minneapolis: Fortress, 2006).

2. Smith's work is vast. For a helpful introduction to it, see *Relating Religion: Essays in the study of Religion* (Chicago: University of Chicago Press, 2004), especially the introductory essay, "When the Chips Are Down," 1–60.

3. Ron Cameron and Merrill P. Miller, eds., *Redescribing Christian Origins*, SymS 28 (Atlanta: Society of Biblical Literature, 2004).

4. Ron Cameron and Merrill P. Miller, eds., *Redescribing Paul and the Corinthians*, ECL 5 (Atlanta: Society of Biblical Literature, 2011).

terms are *mythmaking*—the imaginative construction of a unifying picture of the past dealing with a situation having links to the present—and *social formation*—the shared values, hierarchies, codes, interactions, and interests of group life. The pressing issue that has followed the project throughout the course of its deliberations is the question of the interrelationship, intersection, or "nexus" of these two categories. Participants in the project have discovered that the correlation between mythmaking and social formation is not as simple and straightforward as once thought.

This realization was underscored by Smith's two papers, which head the other pieces in the present volume. Most of the papers in this volume are revised and edited versions of the papers presented in the seminar sessions at the Society of Biblical Literature Annual Meetings in 2002–2003. Besides this introduction and the concluding chapter in the volume, two other papers are much more recent: the paper by Merrill P. Miller, written between 2013–2015, and the paper by Robyn Faith Walsh, written in the summer of 2015. Smith's paper, "Conjectures on Conjunctures and Other Matters: Three Essays," is his opening response to the assignment given him by the seminar's steering committee, as it turned its attention to explore the connection between mythmaking and social formation in the Gospel of Mark. Echoing a caution he voiced in the first volume with his "Metareflection" at the end of the book,[5] Smith observes that "the overarching problematic of our work" is formulating "the nexus between social formation and mythmaking," and that the pressing challenge before the seminar "will be to avoid formulations which see the one as the dependent variable of the other, or which see the one as congruent to the other."[6] Toward this end, Smith invokes the work of Marshall Sahlins on what happens to indigenous cultures—to their mythmaking capabilities and social networks—in collisions with colonial powers. Sahlins's model, however, applies primarily to the initial phases of contact between radically different cultures. The Markan context was one of long-standing Roman colonial occupation in which a mix of subordinate eastern Mediterranean cultures had been engaged in transactions with each other—and with colonial authorities—for some time. In such a situation, to imagine confrontations between divergent cultures suddenly brought together will not suffice. In

---

5. See Jonathan Z. Smith, "*Dayyeinu*," in Cameron and Miller, *Redescribing Christian Origins*, 483–87.

6. See Smith, "Conjectures on Conjunctures and Other Matters," 59 in this volume.

an ancient Levantine context, it is better to look for more typical "endog-enous events" or intracultural "incidents." In the third section of the first essay, Smith translates Sahlins's categories into his own language to clarify the "second-order discourse" of his own analysis. He prefers "situational incongruity as it presents itself to thought" over Sahlins's "conjuncture" not only to describe native responses to external colonial interventions wherever they may occur but especially to denote the sorts of intracultural "incidents" (Smith's favored term) more typical of longer-term relations among peoples of the ancient Levant; in place of Sahlins's "reproduction," he uses "experimental application" for mechanisms of cultural continuity and persistence; and, with some hesitation, he proposes the term "rectifi-cation" for Sahlins's "transformation" to designate processes altering native structures in reaction to cultural disjunctions.[7]

Smith's second paper, "The Markan Site," focuses on the *setting* rather than the text of Mark. It also addresses the anxiety of some seminar par-ticipants, based on concerns already expressed in "Conjectures on Con-junctures," over whether Sahlins's categories (now translated into Smith's terminology) are in fact relevant to the Gospel of Mark. Smith there-fore begins his essay with Nicholas Thomas's work, especially his more theoretical monograph, *Out of Time*,[8] where in chapter 8 Thomas prof-fers a critique of Sahlins's model, allowing Smith to imagine other pos-sible responses to colonial pressures and other instances of intracultural change.[9] On this basis, Smith proposes a locus for Mark on the south Syrian coast, perhaps in Tyre, where for a century or so a vibrant mélange of ethnicities and cultures, including Judeans and others identifying with Israel, variously contended with Roman imperial power and policies—and with each other. In the one Markan text Smith examines at some length, the narrative of the Syro-Phoenician woman in Mark 7:24–30, such a context seems clearly in view. Smith's construction of the Markan site suggests that what we have in Mark is a *bios* of a Galilean sage com-posed in what Smith calls a "Levantine Judean association" to serve as a model for working out its own identity and purpose as it negotiated the complexities of relationships with other ethnic and cultural groups in the region and with Rome.

---

7. Ibid., 72.

8. Nicholas Thomas, *Out of Time: History and Evolution in Anthropological Dis-course*, 2nd ed. (Ann Arbor: University of Michigan Press, 1996).

9. Ibid., 102–16.

Smith's two papers dominated discussion in the seminar's sessions on Mark. Three formal responses to his work, also circulated prior to the meeting, are included in this volume. Mack's "Cartwheels: Or On Not Staying Upside Down Too Long" provides a helpful summary of Smith's major contributions to the seminar's Markan redescription project, together with a roster of questions to help set the agenda for its deliberations. Mack observes that Smith, in his "Conjectures on Conjunctures" paper, has articulated the principal conceptual issues facing the seminar, the most important of which is the problem of formulating more adequately the nexus of mythmaking and social formation. Smith has also, with the aid of Sahlins's work, set forth his own social theory within the context of the history of scholarship in this area. Moreover, Mack emphasizes that in his "Markan Site" paper Smith offers a thick description of a social location or "site," which may serve as the basis for a redescription of a mythic text like the Gospel of Mark.

The agenda Mack envisioned for the seminar's discussions include a range of issues and questions to be explored, two of which he himself takes up in his analysis of Mark's literary production in a separate essay later in the volume: (1) the reasons for linking Mark's *bios* with a persecution plot and martyrology and the problem(s) to which this was thought to be the solution; and (2) why write a *bios* in the first place, and what is its social logic? The latter question is also addressed in Miller's paper in this volume.

William E. Arnal's "On Smith, On Myth, On Mark" issues a caution to seminar members about becoming too preoccupied with theorizing for its own sake and neglecting the equally important task of redescribing the Gospel of Mark and other key sites in early Christianity. As essential as they are, Smith's musings on theory must be judged in terms of their usefulness in helping us arrive at a picture of Christian beginnings different from the mythical Lukan-Eusebian paradigm, which has dominated New Testament scholarship to the present day. As to the question of whether Smith's two foundational papers do this, Arnal answers with a definite yes.

Arnal begins with a distinction Smith draws in "Conjectures on Conjunctures" between two modes or frames of language and myth: (1) the *communicative* and (2) the *rhetorical.* The communicative uses unconscious grammatical and syntactical structures for everyday communication or for unquestioned worldviews or understandings of existence. The rhetorical consciously manipulates "pre-positioned resources of language and story" for purposes of persuasion, usually with specific situations in view.[10] Arnal explores the consequences and implications of his "hunch" (as he calls it, though it is more of a conviction, really) that much of ancient Christian material, including Mark, is far more rhetorical than communicative, though Arnal does not neglect the communicative frame of the Markan myth in his own essay on Mark. Following Smith, Arnal locates Mark in post-70 Syria or Phoenicia, addressing critical ethnic issues generated by the Roman-Judean war. For Arnal, however, Mark was composed *very soon* after the war (70–75 CE), in a situation of *crisis* in which one's ethnic identity had become a matter of life and death. In his major essay in this volume, Arnal explores in detail how the Markan narrative, with its image of Jesus as a perpetually displaced and wandering outsider, addresses and resolves the ethnic turmoil generated in the immediate aftermath of Rome's brutal suppression of the Jewish revolt.

In his brief but provocative review, "Markan Grapplings," Christopher R. Matthews calls attention to possible ambiguities or aporias in Smith's theoretical program that may require further clarification. These uncertainties typically involve subtle distinctions Smith makes among categories and terms critical to his theoretical approach.[11] With regard to a particularly crucial distinction in Smith's theorizing, especially pertinent is Matthews's question as to whether the story of the Syro-Phoenician woman (Mark 7:24–30) is better understood in terms of an *inter*cultural event rather than an *intra*cultural event, as Smith proposes. Or is it the case, Matthews suggests, that the Syro-Phoenician woman is a hybrid—or at least an ambiguous—narrative, requiring an intermediate category or term designating a situation in which the *inter*cultural-*intra*cultural boundaries are obscured? Identifying the precise cultural and social location for the Gospel of Mark, a notoriously knotty problem, has been a major preoccupation of the seminar and, as the attention devoted to the topic in the present volume indicates, a challenge central to its task of redescription. Readers of this volume will obviously note that a south Syrian location for the Gospel of Mark has not been argued vis-à-vis other possible locations, such as Galilee, Antioch, Rome, Alexandria, though a Syrian location has certainly had its advocates. Rather, Smith's focus on the Phoenician coast is *stipulated as plausible*, following the considerations of Mack in *Myth of*

---

10. Smith, "Conjectures on Conjunctures," 68.

11. Matthews also cites Mack's observation in "Cartwheels" that Smith has not completely demonstrated how such terms as "incident," "incongruity," "mythmaking," and other key categories of his are applicable to Mark. See Mack, "Cartwheels," 135.

Innocence, in order to explore its significance for a redescription of the Gospel of Mark in context. All of the papers of the volume have found it useful to keep Smith's Levantine ethnography in view.

The papers in the remainder of the book are also responses to Smith's leading essays but, with the partial exception of Mack's piece, not in any formal sense as focused assessments of his work. Rather, building on Smith's proposals, they represent independent forays into the Gospel of Mark, its context, composition, and project, as part of the seminar's Markan redescription project. In "The Spyglass and Kaleidescope: From a Levantine Coign of Vantage," Mack wants to see how Smith's postulation of a south Syrian context for Mark affects the analysis of the gospel. Not only is it possible to imagine Mark in the setting Smith posits, Mack argues, but placing Mark in this area of the Levant, outside of the traditional Galilee-Jerusalem axis, helps to clarify formerly problematic aspects of the narrative, such as the presence of Pharisees as Jesus's opponents in pre-70 Galilee and synagogues as venues for Jesus's teaching. Such details, if composed in a south Syrian location, reinforce the notion that Mark is a work of imaginative fiction and lead us to inquire not about their historical referents but about their *function* in the narrative. They enable us to see that Jesus's debates with Pharisees, typically in synagogues, repeatedly engage issues of *purity*, a major ethnic marker the discussion of which would be especially appropriate for working out complex ethnic relations toward the end of the first century in the multicultural world of southern Syria. Both Mack and Miller find the idea of the Galilee-Jerusalem axis of the narrative conceived as a single land to make sense retrospectively in this time frame in a location somewhat removed from the narrative setting of the gospel. Moreover, Smith's Syrian ethnography allows the social logic of Mark's narrative to be toned down from the apocalyptic resolution presented in a *Myth of Innocence* and to emerge in more complex ways.

For Mack, the most important interpretive advantage afforded by Smith's Syrian ethnography is that it clears the ground for a proper assessment of Mark's construction of a *bios*-martyr myth. According to Mack, Mark is an origin myth for a "Levantine Judean association" (Smith's term) finding its way and working things out among the layered cultures in southern Syria in the wake of the Roman-Judean war. It combines the *bios* genre with the myth of the martyr's noble death to show that its current way of life—what it says and does—is grounded in the words and deeds of a worthy sage from the recent past who died for the truth of his teachings, thus confirming the validity of his instruction for virtuous living. But for

Mack, the Jesus figure in Mark is not only a martyr; he is a royal figure, a "'king' capable of being compared imaginatively to the divine king of the new city (or even imperium) they were now to call their home."[12]

Miller's "The Social Logic of the Gospel of Mark: Cultural Persistence and Social Escape in a Postwar Time" is a sustained analysis of the nature and purpose of Mark's narrative project in conversation with many scholars of Mark's Gospel, the writings of Josephus, apocalypses, and other writings of the Greco-Roman world, and in debate with scholars about the fallout from the war in the last decades of the first century. Miller's analysis offers an array of factors bearing on an understanding of Mark's project: Smith's Syrian ethnography; Mack's literary and rhetorical analysis of the Gospel of Mark; hindsight as foresight in Josephus's *Judean War*;[13] the Roman regional project of ending the rule of client kings in favor of direct Roman rule in its eastern provinces, together with the social integration of their native peoples and its particularly crushing impact politically, culturally, and symbolically on the Roman province of Judea because of the war; the loss of influence of Judeans in regional politics in competition with other cultural and political formations and ethnicities as a consequence of the failed revolt; the effect of Flavian propaganda and policy after the war; and the imposition of the *fiscus Iudaicus* on the reputation and marking of Jews as Roman subjects.

---

12. "Spyglass," 205.

13. For clarification, references to Josephus's *Judean War* rather than the more common *Jewish War*, along with references to the Roman-Judean war in this introduction and in the concluding paper of the volume, follow the practice of Miller's paper in this volume. There he presents his rationale for the translation of *Ioudaios/Ioudaioi* in English as well as for general references to Jews or Judeans ("The Social Logic of the Gospel of Mark," 207–10 with nn. 1–3). It should be noted that Miller's criteria for instances where he uses "Judean" as a noun or adjective are not based on the practice or rationale of the current Brill English translation and commentary of Josephus's works under the general editorship of Steve Mason. In fact, Miller refers to Jews far more often than to Judeans. His criteria for the choice of English terms is largely indebted to considerations presented in Michael L. Satlow, "Jew or Judean?," in *"The One Who Sows Bountifully": Essays in Honor of Stanley K. Stowers*, ed. Caroline Johnson Hodge et al., BSJ 356 (Providence, RI: Brown Judaic Studies, 2013), 165–75, and in Cynthia Baker, "A Jew by Any Other Name?," *JAJ* 2 (2011): 153–80. Other contributors to this volume follow their own criteria or rationale in these matters without having made them explicit in their papers.

Miller argues that Mark 13 is not constructed to be read from a single vantage point but with different questions in view. In his judgment, Mark's less overtly historicized references to the destruction of the temple than those offered by the writers of Matthew and Luke are not an indication of a date much closer to the war but are characteristics of Markan style throughout the narrative. He suggests a date in the 80s CE, with time to reflect on the fallout from the war. Persecution in Mark is seen in a number of different ways: discursively, as a model for clarification and as a position negotiated in a cultural field; socially, as a local phenomenon in flouting expected social roles and as the consequence of a broader Roman concern to control the activities of unauthorized religious specialists. Although Miller rejects the idea that the Gospel of Mark represents a major cultural shift vis-à-vis Q and other Jesus traditions (which is not to say that there is no cultural shift at all), it is not primarily the content of Jewish cultural beliefs and practices to which he calls attention in characterizing Mark's project as a strategy in cultural persistence. It is rather the degree to which fantasy is invoked—the imaginative lengths to which the writer goes to outwit the constraints imposed by the Judean defeat and the greater Roman presence—in order to account for and even to take advantage of political and social marginalization and humiliation at the end of centuries of imperial support of the Judean temple, the decimation of the Judean ruling class, and the transformation of the Roman province of Judea into diaspora.

Miller adopts John Kloppenborg's characterization of Mark's Gospel as a dual narrative of the death of Jesus and the destruction of the temple.[14] However, on Miller's analysis, the death of Jesus and the destruction of the temple are linked in two different ways: as parallel events marked by human and divine abandonment, identifying a commonality in loss; and as antagonistic events in which the passion of Jesus serves as a substitute story with which to identify, a story of loss, humiliation, and death, though not defeat, in time marking a counter-memorialization over against the destruction of the temple; a story of leaving, evoking the fantasy of exemption and social escape from self-identification as Jews subjected to Rome in the particularly humiliating circumstances following a failed revolt. The construction of Mark's Gospel, linking the death of Jesus with an event

---

14. John S. Kloppenborg, "*Evocatio deorum* and the Date of Mark," *JBL* 124 (2005): 449.

affecting the city, temple, people, and land, gives epic proportion to this single death by association with sacred history and the realities of imperial power. It casts the narrative itself as an exercise in cultural persistence, a particular instance of mythmaking aimed at rectifying a situation of incongruity by imaginative labor, shielding the announcement of God's reign and the labor on its behalf from vulnerability through disaffection and disavowal. In this way it is not unlike the concerns of other Jewish writings of the late first and early second centuries addressing cultural survival and reclamation in the aftermath of the first Roman-Judean war.

In his introduction to the essay, Miller sets out some of the theoretical ground for a dialectical reading of the social logic of Mark's Gospel as a project aimed at both cultural persistence and social escape. Such a reading must reject essentialized notions of identity as *assumed* viable analytical tools and/or entities in the world, whether they are those of the contemporary or the ancient world. There are more flexible concepts for understanding processes of social formation and the multiple circumstances and ways in which identification as Jews and resistance to identification as Jews might be performed by the same individuals or within a particular group.

Unlike the other studies of Mark in this volume, which focus on the nature and meaning of Mark's mythmaking and its significance for the social formation it connotes, Arnal's essay, "Mark, War, and Creative Imagination," deals mainly with the *composition* of the gospel—the process by which it was constructed. Arnal offers a series of finely tuned examinations of selected Markan texts, including the cursing of the fig tree (Mark 11:12–14; 20–21), the disturbance in the temple (Mark 11:15–19), material relating to John the Baptist (with special attention to Jesus's baptism, Mark 1:9–11), various episodes in the passion narrative (the triumphal entry [Mark 11:1–10], the Gethsemane story [Mark 14:32–42], and the Lord's Supper scene [Mark 14:22–25]), and, finally, the parable of the tenants (Mark 11:1–12). From these, Arnal demonstrates "just how creative a product [Mark's] 'Gospel' really is"[15] by showing that Mark has in each instance invented key stories in the plotline of Jesus's career, using prepositioned elements consisting for the most part of sayings of Jesus (the authenticity of which is of absolutely no interest to Arnal), the Jewish scriptures (in LXX form), and various events from Mark's own time. The parable of the tenants presents a special case in that Mark, by inserting

---

15. Arnal, "Mark, War, and Creative Imagination," 405.

imagery from Isaiah's song of the vineyard (Isa 5:1–7), has transformed the parable into an allegory providing the template for Mark's entire narrative, "incorporating the whole sweep of epic and gospel into a single brief account."[16] Following Ronald Hock, Arnal shows that the sequence of John and Jesus corresponds to the slave and the son in the parable of the tenants based on a typical social event in agrarian societies.[17] According to Arnal, the allegorization of the parable did not follow from Mark's narrative scheme but generated that scheme.

Broader matters concerning Mark's mythmaking, together with Arnal's proposal regarding the identity of Mark's readers, are briefly addressed in the paper's concluding section, "Some Tentative Conclusions and Suggestions." Here Arnal observes that Mark's preoccupation with the temple's destruction and its connection with Jesus's death signals a date for Mark's composition very soon after 70 CE and in a region directly affected by it, though the precise location cannot be determined. Interest in ethnic relations between Galilee and Phoenicia and depictions of various *dramatis personae* (especially Simon of Cyrene, who enters Jerusalem "from the country") suggest that Mark was written for "doubly displaced" Jews: those who came from their original homelands to Jerusalem, were uprooted by the Roman-Judean war, and traveled north to resettle in Syria-Galilee. According to Arnal, this "situational incongruity" of uprootedness and double-displacement was thought through and explained by Mark in terms of another narrative, in which the Son of God came to what should have been his home in Jerusalem, was rejected there, and, after an act of "staggering Roman violence … returned to his true home and so resumed his true identity."[18]

Although Walsh's paper, "Q and the 'Big Bang' Theory of Christian Origins," focuses on Q rather than Mark, it offers much both to the present volume and to the ongoing redescription project of the seminar and its two successor groups. Her observations on the production of literature in the ancient Hellenistic world, for example, apply as well to Mark and other gospels as they do to Q or to any literary work of that era. In two

---

16. Ibid., 466.
17. Ronald F. Hock, "Social Experience and the Beginning of the Gospel of Mark," in *Reimagining Christian Origins: A Colloquium Honoring Burton L. Mack*, ed. Elizabeth A. Castelli and Hal Taussig (Valley Forge, PA: Trinity Press International, 1996), 311–26.
18. Arnal, "Mark, War, and Creative Imagination," 481.

interrelated areas, especially, Walsh's study proffers insights critical to a reassessment of Mark: (1) the nature of the gospel's authorship and (2) the audience to which it was directed.

With regard to the gospel's authorship, Walsh presents a compelling case that authors of early Christian texts, such as Q and the Gospel of Mark, were literate specialists, as were, for example, the classical authors Virgil or Philodemus, though not as skilled or accomplished. As such, they composed their works for other like-minded individuals, and they were not simply conduits for the collective interests or concerns of a group, a view Walsh ascribes to the late eighteenth- and early nineteenth-century Romantic movement's conception of the author/genius as voice of the spirit and memories of the *Volk*. In his *A Myth of Innocence*, which initially inspired the work of the seminar, the volumes it spawned, and its successor groups, Mack described Mark in similar terms, though without rehearsing Romanticism's possible influence. For Mack, Mark was "an authorial, intellectual achievement … open to discourse with other intellectuals,"[19] an assessment of the gospel that Arnal recently cited as formative for much of his own scholarship and "more radical in its implications than some of the book's other, more famous contentions."[20]

Examination of the nature of authorship in the Greco-Roman world raises the closely related question of the intended audience of ancient literary productions, like Q and Mark's Gospel. Here Walsh, following Stanley Stowers, explodes the long-standing notion among New Testament scholars that early Christian literature, such as Q and Mark, was necessarily representative of the beliefs and practices of tightly bounded religious communities.[21] Since we know that the writing of literature was the prerogative of elite literate specialists who circulated their writings among networks of other writers and intellectuals, Walsh wonders why we should think of the author of Q—or, in our case, Mark—behaving any differently. The conclusion that Walsh draws from her study, then, is that Mark was composed by an elite literary producer in the aftermath of the Roman-Judean war, using his writing to work things out with regard to the meaning and purpose of the conflict in a context of major symbolic change. In a time of

19. Mack, *Myth of Innocence*, 321–23.

20. Review essay roundtable on *A Myth of Innocence: Mark and Christian Origins*, by Burton L. Mack, *JAAR* 83 (2015): 837.

21. See Stanley K. Stowers, "The Concept of 'Community' and the History of Early Christianity," *MTSR* 23 (2011): 238–56.

"cosmic paranoia," Mark constructed the figure of Jesus as "the hero-that-succeeded … in escaping" the destroyed locative order.[22] Mark presented his ideas, in the form of his narrative, to a network of other authors and consumers of ancient literature.

The volume concludes with a retrospective by the editors on what we think we have learned from the consultation and seminar, and what we have continued to learn from the successor program units and related work. We describe the older seminar in terms of its reflexive location in the broader field of religion, its major operative categories and their rectifications in the course of the work, the differences among the members of the seminar with respect both to strategies of redescription and to social theory and historical analysis, and we include an account of some of our fundamental agreements. The editors view the current volume as an example of continuing revision rather than a trajectory of cumulative successes. At the end, we offer a recommendation about where we might go from here based on a brief evaluation of the strengths and limitations of the older seminar relative to the successor groups, in conjunction with a proposal for studying the history of early Christianity as an example of ancient Mediterranean and West Asian religion.

While the papers in the volume are for the most part not in direct dialogue with each other—or in accord with one another on certain issues—there are, as noted in the preceding description of the volume's concluding retrospect (and prospect), important common working assumptions and agreements among them in their independent forays into the task of redescribing the Gospel of Mark (and Q) that arise from the collaborative work of the two previous seminar volumes and influences from the successor groups. To begin with, members of the seminar and its successor groups are generally agreed that the work in the first volume of the series has contributed in significant ways toward problematizing the dominant paradigm or master narrative (the "Big Bang" theory) of Christian origins as an accurate representation of how things actually began. As described above, this explanation posits a dramatic beginning and miraculous expansion and development of what was later to become the Christian religion. Regardless of their differences on other matters, participants in

---

22. The reference is to Jonathan Z. Smith, "The Influence of Symbols upon Social Change: A Place on Which to Stand," in *Map Is Not Territory: Studies in the History of Religions,* SJLA 23 (Leiden: Brill, 1978; Chicago: University of Chicago Press, 1993), 138–39.

the redescription project are at one in holding that this way of accounting for Christian origins is completely inadequate and must not be reinscribed as history. In this connection, it should also be noted that in the present volume studies of Mark (and Q) are conducted in the absence of anything that can be labeled as "Christianity."

For the independent papers on Mark (those by Mack, Miller, and Arnal), the work of Smith in "Conjectures on Conjunctures" is foundational, especially when it comes to constructing a context for Mark's narrative. In various ways, all three operate with Smith's categories of "experimental application," "situational incongruity," and "rectification." In this connection, Mack's categories of "social formation" and "mythmaking" are also instrumental for the independent papers on Mark, especially in light of Smith's category of situational incongruity, which has to be constructed in order to specify the processes of mythmaking and social formation in any given instance. Smith's "Markan Site" paper presented the seminar participants with the challenge of imagining the writing of Mark's Gospel in a Levantine multi-ethnic milieu of more long-term and typical relations among peoples with an extended history of interactions with each other and with imperial regimes, "a permanent site of pre-modern (as well as modern) imperialisms and colonialisms, with its attendant patterns of emigration and immigration, of resistance and adjustment, of subjugation and entrepreneurial initiative."[23] On this basis, and while bracketing the military and political context of the Roman-Judean war and the fallout from the war (though remarking on incidents of ethnic conflict and violence), Smith shows us the difference this setting makes for imagining the kinds of social interests, issues, and questions the writing of the gospel could respond to and engender. The paper is especially significant for the redescription project of this volume in calling attention to the construction of difference, particularly in matters of ethnicity, purity, native and foreign among related peoples. That Arnal (in the last section of his paper), Miller and Walsh—and Mack, too, for that matter—have written papers that do not bracket but take serious account of the war and its aftermath in constructing a "situation" addressed by Mark's narrative project is justified on the basis of material from Thomas, which is cited by Smith in his first two pages of the "Markan Site."

---

23. Smith, "The Markan Site," 104.

Widespread agreement exists on a number of issues related to the production and intended audience of the Gospel of Mark—and, for Walsh's contribution, of the sayings gospel Q. Both Mark and Q are viewed as products of literate circles, as the works of actual *authors*, rather than the transcription of communal oral tradition. In Mark's case, we have a work of creative *fiction* written not for a bounded Christian community with "a deep social and mental coherence, a commonality of mind and practice"[24] but for a network of other literate specialists of similar skills and interests. While other major papers, besides the paper by Walsh, do not necessarily limit a Markan circle to a network of literate specialists or eliminate the possibility of some audience/s of non-literates, they are consistent with an emphasis on the primacy of the sort of social formation Walsh's paper has in view. With regard to dating Mark's composition, participants in the redescription project, like many New Testament scholars, consider Mark to be a post-70 CE document, written in the aftermath of the Roman-Judean war. Mack and Miller, however, place the gospel further out from the conflict, in the 80s, perhaps even later. According to Miller, Mark comes from a time in which the task at hand is dealing with the *consequences* of the war, and it makes a different kind of sense when set in this context rather than in the context of the war itself. A post-70 CE date is also put forward by Walsh for the composition of Q, which she argues for while rejecting appeals to theories of the document's stratification or complex redactional history.

Finally, on two matters typically emphasized in characterizations of Mark's narrative project, the writers in this volume part company. First, the papers of Arnal, Mack, and Miller detect no interest on Mark's part in distinguishing separate missionary campaigns among Jews and gentiles and, following Smith, explicitly reject a Pauline binary as an appropriate formulation for issues of ethnic identifications in Mark in its Levantine setting. Second, and most importantly, the papers in this volume find little, if any, evidence of the apocalyptic fervor—or hysteria—which otherwise figures so prominently in scholarly treatments of Mark's project. Two other matters of agreement in the papers are also significant. The writer of Mark is intent on presenting Jesus as a figure of epic importance, and his narrative can be read as an instance of epic revision. All of the papers would also agree with an observation of Arnal in an essay outside this volume on

---

24. Stowers, "Concept of 'Community,' " 238–39.

the legacy of the Gospel of Mark, even if there are some differences in how Mark's own project is thought to be related to this legacy: The writing of a gospel narrative, the earliest of the canonical gospel narratives, has meant that "Christianity's foundational gesture is not to be found in Jesus, but in the *story* of Jesus."[25]

---

25. William E. Arnal, "What Branches Grow Out of This Stony Rubbish? Christian Origins and the Study of Religion," *SR* 39 (2010): 557, emphasis original.

Conjectures on Conjunctures
and Other Matters: Three Essays

Jonathan Z. Smith

Man has always been thinking equally well.
— Claude Lévi-Strauss, "The Structural Study of Myth."

It is vain to seek a reality that is at once of a cultural order and cannot be translated in terms of intellectual activity. For individuals and social groups, in struggling against each other, transforming nature, or organizing their life in common, bring into play a system of concepts which is never the only possible one and which defines the very form of their actions. At this level, the distinction between infrastructure and superstructure disappears, for economic, social, and political relations, like the theories that account for them in a given society, are just as much products of the mind.
— Lucien Sebag, *Marxisme et Structuralisme*

Fieldwork, the distinctive procedural hallmark of the anthropological enterprise, became an unquestioned professional requirement during the decades of sociocultural anthropology's "classical period," roughly 1925 to 1960. For our purposes, the major consequence of this is a presentism characteristic of much ethnographic reporting: the society as observed at the time of the fieldworker's interaction with it. While this presentism raises large conceptual questions,[1] its practical result with respect to theory was a strong bias against the historical in dominant approaches, whether the latter was functionalism or structuralism (to name but two, all but opposite options). In addition to reflecting contemporary practice,

---

1. Perhaps the most influential of these has been Johannes Fabian, *Time and the Other: How Anthropology Makes Its Object* (New York: Columbia University Press, 1983).

such an attitude was thoroughly congruent with older (at times, still lingering) "evolutionary" assumptions about "timeless savages," as well as with romantic notions of a "pristine field." Read today, there is something almost quaint about the heated debates over the fairly modest proposals set forth in E. E. Evans-Pritchard's classic lectures, "Social Anthropology: Past and Present" (1950) and "Anthropology and History" (1961),[2] which called for a redress of the imbalance.

I state this at the outset to make it plain that, despite more recent engagements of the one field with the other (or of cooperative ventures, such as those strongly advocated by Marcel Detienne),[3] there is nothing natural about the relations between anthropology and history. They have to be conceptualized, and this requires, among other things, translating each in terms of the other. One cannot simply lift the data, procedure, or theory of the one and transport it to the other.

At our seminar sessions held in Denver in 2001, I briefly touched on the possible contributions one stage in the ongoing work of Marshall Sahlins might make to our work. I chose him because he is a major American anthropologist, early known for his pioneering work in economic and political anthropology.[4] He is prepared equally to work in a highly

---

2. E. E. Evans-Pritchard, "Social Anthropology: Past and Present," in *Social Anthropology and Other Essays* (Glencoe, IL: Free Press, 1962), 146–51, Evans-Pritchard, "Anthropology and History," in *Social Anthropology and Other Essays*, 172–91.

3. Marcel Detienne, *Comparer l'incomparable* (Paris: Éditions du Seuil, 2000).

4. Marshall Sahlins, "Differentiation by Adaptation in Polynesian Societies," *Journal of the Polynesian Society* 66 (1957): 291–300; Sahlins, *Social Stratification in Polynesia*, Monographs of the American Ethnological Society 29 (Seattle: University of Washington Press, 1958); Sahlins, "Political Power and the Economy in Primitive Society," in *Essays in the Science of Culture in Honor of Leslie White*, ed. G. E. Dole and R. L. Carneiro (New York: Crowell, 1960), 390–415; Sahlins, "Production, Distribution and Power in a Primitive Society," in *Selected Papers of the Fifth International Congress of Anthropological and Ethnological Societies*, ed. A. F. C. Wallace (Philadelphia: University of Pennsylvania Press, 1960), 495–500; Sahlins, "The Segmentary Lineage: An Organization of Predatory Expansion," *American Anthropologist* 63 (1961): 322–45; Sahlins, "Remarks on Social Structure in Southeast Asia," *Journal of the Polynesian Society* 72 (1963): 39–50; Sahlins, "On the Ideology and Composition of Descent Groups," *Man* 65 (1965): 104–7; Sahlins, "Economic Anthropology and Anthropological Economics," *Social Science Information* 8 (1969): 13–33; Sahlins, *Stone Age Economics* (Chicago: Aldine-Atherton, 1972); Sahlins, "Culture as Protein and Profit," review of *Cannibals and Kings*, by Marvin Harris, *New York Review of Books*, 23 November 1978, 45–53; Sahlins, "Hierarchy and Humanity in Polynesia,"

focused field situation, in Turkey and, especially, in Fiji, October 1954–
August 1955,[5] or in a broadly comparative manner.[6] He is a first-rate archi-
val historian, and he has written extensively on what he terms "historical
ethnography."[7] In each of these areas, as well as others, he has persistently

---

in *Transformations of Polynesian Culture*, ed. A. Hooper and J. Huntsman (Auckland:
Polynesian Society, 1985), 195–217; Sahlins, "Cery Cery Fuckabede," *American Ethnologist* 20 (1993): 848–67.

5. Marshall Sahlins, "Esoteric Efflorescence on Easter Island," *American Anthro-
pologist* 57 (1955): 1045–52; Sahlins, "Land Use and Extended Family in Moala, Fiji,"
American Anthropologist 59 (1957): 449–63; Sahlins, *Moala: Culture and Nature on a
Fijian Island* (Ann Arbor: University of Michigan Press, 1962).

6. Sahlins, *Social Stratification in Polynesia*; Sahlins, *Tribesmen,* Foundations of
Modern Anthropology Series (Englewood Cliffs, NJ: Prentice-Hall, 1968); Sahlins,
Stone Age Economics, 41–148; Sahlins, "Colors and Cultures," in *Culture in Practice:
Selected Essays* (New York: Zone Books, 2000), 139–62.

I am not clear that I can convey the excitement I felt as a graduate student beginning to focus on comparison as my topic when I read, then, the first footnote to Sahlins's 1963 essay, "Poor Man, Rich Man, Big-Man, Chief: Political Types in Melanesia
and Polynesia," *Comparative Studies in Society and History* 5 (1963): 285–303; repr. as
pages 71–93 in *Culture in Practice*: "The comparative method so far followed in this
research has involved reading the monographs and taking notes. I don't think I originated the method, but I would like to christen it 'The Method of Uncontrolled Comparison'.… The two forms [of leadership] are abstracted sociological types. Anyone
conversant with the anthropological literature of the South Pacific knows there are
important variants of the types, as well as exceptional political forms not fully treated
here. All would agree that consideration of the variations and exceptions is necessary
and desirable. Yet there is pleasure too, and some intellectual reward, in discovering
the broad patterns. To (social) scientifically justify my pleasure, I could have referred
to the pictures drawn of Melanesian big-men and Polynesian chiefs as 'models' or as
'ideal types.' If that is all that is needed to confer respectability on the paper, may the
reader have it his way" (89 n. 1). (Sahlin's discomfort with "The Method of Uncontrolled Comparison" is a witty reference to Fred Eggan's much-cited 1953 Presidential Paper for the American Anthropological Association, later published as "Social
Anthropology and the Method of Controlled Comparison," *American Anthropologist*
NS 56 [1964]: 743–63). To have Sahlins speak of his "pleasure" in the comparative
enterprise in a context where comparison was widely abjured was utterly liberating.

7. Marshall Sahlins and Dorothy B. Barrière, eds., "William Richards on Hawaiian
Culture and Political Conditions of the Islands in 1841," *Hawaiian Journal of History*
7 (1973): 18–40; Sahlins, "The Apotheosis of Captain Cook," *Kroeber Anthropological
Society Papers* 53–54 (1979): 1–31; Sahlins, *Historical Metaphors and Mythical Reali-
ties: Structure in the Early History of the Sandwich Islands Kingdom,* Association for
Social Anthropology in Oceania Special Publications 1 (Ann Arbor: University of

raised issues of theory[8] with some attention to both Marxism and structuralism.[9] In particular, I called attention to his reflections on the relations
between "reproduction" and "transformation" in the context of a "structure of conjuncture"[10] as, perhaps, engaging what would be strong formulations of our more implicit theoretical divergences. In a similar vein, I
also noted in my "Metareflection" (distributed to members of the seminar
in 2001 and published in our first volume of papers) the usefulness of Sahlins in avoiding formulations on the relations of mythmaking and social
formation, which see "the one as the dependent variable of the other, or
which see the one as congruent to the other."[11] It should be stressed that

---

Michigan Press, 1981); Sahlins, "Raw Women, Cooked Men, and Other 'Great Things'
of the Fiji Islands," in *The Ethnography of Cannibalism*, ed. P. Brown and D. Tuzin
(Washington, DC: Society for Psychological Anthropology, 1983), 72–93; Sahlins,
Islands of History (Chicago: University of Chicago Press, 1985); Sahlins, "War in the
Fiji Islands: The Force of Custom, and the Custom of Force," in *International Ethics
in the Nuclear Age*, ed. R. J. Myers, Ethics and Foreign Policy Series 4 (Lanham, MD:
University Press of America, 1987), 299–328; Sahlins, "Deserted Islands of History: A
Reply to Jonathan Friedman," *Critique of Anthropology* 8 (1988): 41–51; Sahlins, "Cap-
tain Cook at Hawaii," *Journal of the Polynesian Society* 98 (1989): 371–423; Sahlins,
"The Political Economy of Grandeur in Hawaii from 1810 to 1830," in *Culture through
Time: Anthropological Approaches*, ed. E. Ohnuki-Tierney (Stanford, CA: Stanford
University Press, 1990), 26–56; Sahlins, *Historical Ethnography*, vol. 1 of *Anahulu:
The Anthropology of History in the Kingdom of Hawaii*, by Patrick Vinton Kirch and
Marshall Sahlins (Chicago: University of Chicago Press, 1992); Sahlins, *How "Natives"
Think: About Captain Cook, for Example* (Chicago: University of Chicago Press, 1995);
Sahlins, "Comments," *Current Anthropology* 38 (1997): 272–76; Sahlins, *Culture in
Practice*, 271–76, 293–351.

8. Marshall Sahlins, "Evolution: Specific and General," in *Evolution and Culture*,
ed. Marshall Sahlins and E. R. Service (Ann Arbor: University of Michigan Press,
1960), 12–44; Sahlins, "Culture and Environment: The Study of Cultural Ecology," in
Horizons of Anthropology, ed. S. Tax (Chicago: Aldine, 1964), 215–31; Sahlins, *Culture
and Practical Reason* (Chicago: University of Chicago Press, 1976); Sahlins, *The Use
and Abuse of Biology: An Anthropological Critique of Sociobiology* (Ann Arbor: University of Michigan Press, 1976).

9. See, especially, Marshall Sahlins, "On the Delphic Writings of Claude Lévi-
Strauss," *Scientific American* 214 (1966): 131–36; Sahlins, "Economic Anthropology
and Anthropological Economics"; Sahlins, *Stone Age Economics*, 149–83; Sahlins,
Culture and Practical Reason; Sahlins, "Comment," *Current Anthropology* 17 (1976):
298–300; Sahlins, "Raw Women, Cooked Men."

10. Sahlins, *Historical Metaphors and Mythical Realities*.

11. Jonathan Z. Smith, "*Dayyeinu*," in *Redescribing Christian Origins*, ed. Ron Cameron and Merrill P. Miller, SymS 28 (Atlanta: Society of Biblical Literature, 2004), 486.

Sahlins himself has gone on to other topics, briefly to an engagement with symbolic anthropology,[12] before turning to questions of globalization and theoretical issues with respect to agency.[13]

I was asked to carry these reflections into our next seminar sessions, held in Toronto in 2002. I propose to characterize and engage Sahlins's understanding of "conjuncture" in essay 1, saving "reproduction" and "transformation" for essay 2. I shall conclude, in essay 3, with a translation of Sahlins's terminology into language more congruent with my own work. Finally, each of these three privileged terms in Sahlins has a significant prehistory, which I will discuss in an appendix, below.

---

12. Sahlins, *Culture and Practical Reason*; Sahlins, "Colors and Colors," 139–62.

13. Marshall Sahlins, "The Economics of Develop-Man in the Pacific," *Res* 21 (1992): 13–25; Sahlins, "Two or Three Things That I Know about Culture," *Journal of the Royal Anthropological Institute* NS 5 (1999): 399–421; Sahlins, *Culture in Practice*, 353–413, 415–69, 471–500, 501–26, 527–83; Sahlins, *Apologies to Thucydides: Understanding History as Culture and Vice Versa* (Chicago: University of Chicago Press, 2004).

I should at this point issue a "disclosure" which is, in fact, a "disclaimer." Sahlins and I have been colleagues at the University of Chicago for most of our respective academic careers. While I have read Sahlins since college days, and with considerable eagerness since 1963 (see n. 6 above)—his work (Marshall Sahlins, "The Social Life of Monkeys, Apes, and Primitive Men," in *Readings in Anthropology*, ed. M. H. Fried, 2 vols. [New York: Crowell, 1959], 2:186–99) was introduced to me in an anthropology course I took at Columbia University in 1959 with Morton H. Fried, which emphasized the cultural materialist anthropologies associated with Leslie White and his students at the University of Michigan—Sahlins and I have only a nodding relationship as we pass each other on campus. We have spoken together but once, for two minutes in an elevator, when I congratulated him on the recent publication of his selected essays, *Culture in Practice*. While I have occasionally alluded to Sahlins in lectures and taught him in an introductory college class, I do not think I have ever cited him in print before 2004 ("*Dayyeinu*," 486 nn. 9–10; cf. Jonathan Z. Smith, "Re: Corinthians," in *Relating Religion: Essays in the Study of Religion* [Chicago: University of Chicago Press, 2004], 347, 358 n. 35; repr. pages 17–34 in *Redescribing Paul and the Corinthians*, ed. Ron Cameron and Merrill P. Miller, ECL 5 [Atlanta: Society of Biblical Literature, 2011], 28 n. 38). My use of him in the context of our seminar sessions in Denver was, as implied above, entirely tactical, as a perhaps useful example. As it appeared to have served this purpose, I have framed some of my discussion in this paper in terms of Sahlins's works.

Essay 1. Sahlins: Conjuncture

1.

Special attention ought to be paid to zones and periods where contact took place between societies and cultures traditionally in the domain of history on the one hand and ethnology [on] the other. In other words, the study of acculturations should make it possible to clarify the relative positions of the ethnological and the historical. In particular, the historian will be interested in knowing to what extent and under what conditions the terminology and problematics of acculturation may be extended to the study of internal acculturations within a given society.

— Jacques Le Goff, "L'historien et l'homme quotidien"

Sahlins's interest in a term such as "conjuncture" must be seen in the broader context of a revision of American anthropological theory, beginning in the early 1960s, by a strong, though diverse group of cultural materialists who, among other achievements, redirected attention to economic and political anthropology and to a renewed interest in thick historical projects. For our purposes, one of the significant theoretical revisions was directed at the notion of "culture" in historical processes. As a summary statement, take the opening pages of Eric Wolf's instant classic, *Europe and the People without History*:

The central assertion of this book is that the world of humankind constitutes a manifold, a totality of interconnected processes, and [that] inquiries that disassemble this totality into bits and then fail to reassemble it falsify reality. Concepts like "nation," "society," and "culture" name bits and threaten to turn names into things. Only by understanding these names as bundles of relationships, and by placing them back into the field from which they were abstracted, can we hope to avoid misleading inferences and increase our share of understanding.... By turning names into things we create false models of reality. By endowing nations, societies, or cultures with the qualities of internally homogenous and externally distinctive and bounded objects, we create a model of the world as a global pool hall in which the entities spin off each other like so many hard and round billiard balls. Thus it becomes easy to sort the world into differently colored balls.... The habit of treating named entities such as Iroquois, Greece, Persia, or the United States as fixed entities opposed to one another by stable internal architecture and external boundaries interferes with our ability to understand their mutual encounter and confrontation. Indeed, this tendency has made it difficult to understand all such encounters and confrontations.[14]

One consequence of rejecting the billiard-ball notion of "hard" cultures glancing off one another was a discomfort with the usual term "contact" as descriptive of intercultural relations. Contact seemed to deny what one early participant in this revisionary enterprise argued, a notion of societies and cultures as "open systems ... inextricably involved with other aggregates, near and far, in weblike, netlike connections."[15] "Encounters" or "connections" are but two of the replacement terms for "contact."[16] "Conjuncture" is another candidate.

Although Sahlins, in his early work, unproblematically employs "contact,"[17] in his mature historiographical work "[structure of the] conjuncture" replaces "contact."[18] The word "conjuncture" was both resident and resonant in Paris by the time Sahlins was there, working as a guest researcher in Lévi-Strauss's institute in the heady years, 1967–1969. It has a genealogy that extends in two different directions: to Braudel and to Althusser. Sahlins is clearly aware of both[19] (see appendix below). He offers

---

14. Eric. R. Wolf, *Europe and the People without History* (Berkeley: University of California Press, 1982), 3, 6, 7.

15. Alexander Lesser, "Social Fields and the Evolution of Society," *Southwestern Journal of Anthropology* 17 (1961): 42. See also Wolf, *Europe and the People Without History*, 15.

16. See the discussion of alternative terms by Robin Torrence and Anne Clarke, "Negotiating Difference: Practice Makes Theory for Contemporary Archaeology in Oceania," in *The Archaeology of Difference: Negotiating Cross-Cultural Engagements in Oceania*, ed. Robin Torrence and Anne Clarke, One World Archaeology 35 (London: Routledge, 2000), 12–16. They focus on "contact," "encounter," and "engagement."

17. E.g., Sahlins, *Moala*, 14–18, and passim.

18. Sahlins, *Historical Metaphors and Mythical Realities*, 33, 35, 38, 48, 50, 54, 72; but note "acculturation" (vii, 30) and "situations of culture contact" (68). The latter expression is also used in Sahlins, *Islands of History*, xiv, xvii, 67, 125 n. 11, 127, 152–54; Sahlins, *Historical Ethnography*, 67–76, 132, 161.

19. Braudel first appears in Sahlins in a fairly glancing manner (*Historical Metaphors and Mythical Realities*, 8; cf. the subtitle to ch. 2). He later takes pains to distinguish his usage from Braudel's (Sahlins, *Islands of History*, xiv, 125 n. 11; Sahlins, *Culture in Practice*, 295), although close associates have, at times, linked their usages (Patrick Vinton Kirch, *The Archeaology of History*, vol. 2 of *Anahulu: The Anthropology of the Kingdom of Hawaii*, by Patrick Vinton Kirch and Marshall Sahlins [Chicago: University of Chicago Press, 1992], 25).

Sahlins refers to Althusser in his early collection, *Stone Age Economics*. His use of Althusser (and Balibar) is more sustained in later work, especially *Culture and Practical Reason*. Although Althusser uses the term "structure(s) of the/a conjuncture" (see, e.g., Louis Althusser, *For Marx*, trans. Ben Brewster [London: Allen Lane, 1969], 179; Louis Althusser and Etienne Balibar, *Reading Capital*, trans. B. Brewster [London: NLB, 1970], 33)—unlike Braudel, who quite sharply distinguishes conjuncture and structure—Sahlins, to the best of my knowledge, has never explicitly associated his use of "conjuncture" with its massive deployment in Althusser. For the systemic roles of conjuncture in both Braudel and Althusser, see the appendix, below.

While "conjuncture" occurs in a seemingly Althusserian sense in Sahlins's *Stone Age Economics*, 87, it is worth detailing its first persistent deployment in a historical context in Sahlins's *Historical Metaphors and Mythical Realities* to gain a sense of its semantic range. Interestingly, to the best of my knowledge, the term first makes an appearance in the third chapter on transformation. In the previous chapter on reproduction, as well as in the preface, Sahlins uses the more traditional terminology of "acculturation" (vii, 30). When the term "conjuncture" is first introduced, it is in a statement of Sahlins's agendum: "My aim is to demonstrate such historical uses of structural theory. I examine a certain interplay between pragmatic 'structures of the conjuncture' and the received cultural order [i.e., reproduction], as mediated by the constituted interests of the historical actors" (33). The linkage of conjuncture with "pragmatic" is clarified in the next occurrence: "Nothing guarantees that the situations encountered in practice will stereotypically [i.e., reproduction] follow from the cultural categories by which the circumstances are interpreted and acted upon. Practice, rather, has its own dynamics—a 'structure of the conjuncture'—which meaningfully defines the persons and the objects that are parties to it. And these contextual values, if unlike the definitions culturally presupposed [i.e., if not reproductive], have the capacity then of working back on the conventional values [i.e., transformation]" (35). It is the relations of actors in a "situation … of culture contact" (68), in an "event" (50), when the template of the received cultural order of these relations proves incapable of being "stereotypic reproduction" (6), that these relations are reconfigured, are transformed. If conjuncture is the situation, the structure of the conjuncture is the transformed formation of the set of relations between the actors. This is best exemplified in relations of exchange/trade. "Commercial exchange has its own sociology: this is what I mean by a 'structure of the conjuncture'.… The exchange signifies a 'between' relation, sociologically distinct from the inclusion implied by Polynesian conceptions.… Hawaiian men thus passed in practice from one kind of integration with foreigners to another. Their womenfolk were following a similar course, although in a different mode" (38). "The engagement of different categories of Hawaiian society … to the foreigners … was traditionally motivated.… In this sense, Hawaiian culture would reproduce itself as history. Its tendency was to encompass the advent of Europeans within the system as constituted, thus to integrate circumstance as structure and make of the event a version of itself. But in the event, the project of cultural reproduction failed. For again, the pragmatics had its own dynamics: relationships that defeated both intention and convention. The complex of exchanges that developed between Hawaiians and Europeans, the structure of the

a third position, conceived, especially, as a corrective to some anthropological understandings of the implications of Lévi-Strauss, with a curious hybrid nomenclature, "the structure of the conjuncture," conjoining structure and historical "event."

Lévi-Strauss was not alone in perceiving a tension between structure and some understandings of history. What for Saussure were two methodological standpoints, synchrony and diachrony, have been converted, in some of Lévi-Strauss's formulations, into opposing forces with synchrony attempting to repair itself from the perturbations of diachrony. Ethnologized, this becomes the controversial distinction between "cool" and "hot" societies.[20] From the point of view of structure, Lévi-Strauss's clearest and most persistent exemplum has to do with clan divisions and

---

conjuncture, brought the former into uncharacteristic conditions of internal conflict and contradiction. Their differential connections with Europeans thereby endowed their own relationships to each other with novel functional content. This is structural transformation. The values acquired in practice return to structure as new relationships between its categories" (50; cf. 41, 48).

The structure of conjuncture is, always, a structure of practice. It is, for this reason, that the dynamics of reproduction and transformation are a part of any culture's social and historical experience—whether or not the processes are motivated by intercultural conjuncture. This is most explicit in the last two paragraphs of Sahlins's work (72), but is perhaps better formulated, earlier, with respect to a particular example: "Taken together, the set of transformations mediated by tabu suggests a permanent dialectic of structure and practice. Revised in practice, in relations of the conjuncture, the categories return to the cultural order in altered relationships to each other. But then, responding to structural change in the cultural order, the relations of the conjuncture change from one historical moment to the next" (54).

20. Claude Lévi-Strauss, *The Savage Mind*, The Nature of Human Society Series, trans. John Weightman and Doreen Weightman (Chicago: University of Chicago Press, 1966), 233–34: "I have suggested elsewhere that the clumsy distinction between 'peoples without history' and others could with advantage be replaced by a distinction between what for convenience I called 'cold' and 'hot' societies: the former seeking, by the institutions they give themselves, to annul the possible effects of historical factors on their equilibrium and continuity in a quasi-automatic fashion; the latter resolutely internalizing the historical process and making it the moving power of their development." Cf. Lévi-Strauss, "The Scope of Anthropology," in vol. 2 of *Structural Anthropology*, trans. Monique Layton (New York: Basic Books, 1963), 2:29–30; and G. Charbonnier's 1959 interviews published as *Conversations with Claude Lévi-Strauss*, trans. John Weightman and Doreen Weightman (London: Cape, 1969), 32–42. For the purposes of this seminar, it is useful to see a comparison between "cold societies" and what Sahlins describes as mechanisms of reproduction, and "hot societies" and Sah-

the "logic of totemic classifications." He offers an "only slightly imaginary example":

Suppose that a tribe was once divided into three clans ... :

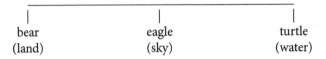

| bear | eagle | turtle |
| (land) | (sky) | (water) |

Suppose further that demographic changes led to the extinction of the bear clan and an increase in the population of the turtle clan and that, as a result, the turtle clan split into two sub-clans.... The old structure will disappear completely and be replaced by a structure of this type:

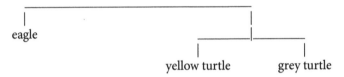

eagle

yellow turtle   grey turtle

It can be seen ... that demographic evolution can shatter the structure but that if the structural orientation survives the shock, it has, after each upheaval, several means of re-establishing a system, which may not be identical with the earlier one but is at least formally of the same type.[21]

Here the structure has maintained three divisions, even though now they stand in a relationship of subordination rather than of equivalence, and even though the trichotomous relations between land/sky/water have been "lost" to "two successive dichotomies; between sky and water and then between yellow and grey."

Lévi-Strauss goes on to remind us that this "system rested on myths of creation and origin and permeated the entire ritual." Even if demographic change perturbs the immediate clan system, "this upheaval will not have immediate repercussions on all planes." Eventually, "the myths and rites will change, but only with a time-lag."[22] He continues:

---

lins's mechanisms of transformation. But note that, in Sahlins, these two mechanisms are internal to any given society, and not a principle of classification between societies.

21. Lévi-Strauss, *Savage Mind*, 67–68.

22. Ibid., 68.

If, for the sake of argument, we suppose an initial point at which the set of systems was precisely adjusted, then this network of systems will react to any change affecting one of its parts like a motor with a feed-back device: governed (in both senses of the word) by its previous harmony, it will direct the discordant mechanism towards an equilibrium which will be at any rate a compromise between the old state of affairs and the confusion brought in from the outside.[23]

It is revealing at this point to compare an analogous case from Sahlins's Fijian ethnography. Regardless of particular affiliations, the Fijians divide themselves into a dual organization of land-people and sea-people.[24] The land-people (sometimes termed animal-people) are associated with the original settlers and are agriculturalists who would be unsuccessful without the chiefs whose *mana* guarantees fertility. For this reason, the chiefs have rights over the produce of the land, especially first fruits. The sea-people, characterized as fishermen, are associated with the ruling chiefs who originally came to the island from elsewhere. They are bound to the land-people, especially through their women; the chiefs were given the first-born daughters of the indigenous people.[25]

A difference of social groups corresponds to the distinction of land and sea on the geographic plane, itself an instance of a general spatial differentiation of interior and peripheral, correlated with the oppositions of indigenous and foreign, earlier and later, even animal and cultural;

23. Ibid., 68–69. Compare my critical treatment of a similar example from the Winnebago with Lévi-Strauss in Jonathan Z. Smith, *To Take Place: Toward Theory in Ritual*, CSHJ (Chicago: University of Chicago Press, 1987), 43, 143–45 n. 100. With reference to the latter, in the context of Sahlins's discussion of Fiji, note that there is a long-standing anthropological tradition of comparing Fijian and Winnebago social organizations. See Arthur Maurice Hocart, *Kings and Councillors: An Essay in the Comparative Anatomy of Human Society* (Cairo: P. Barbey, 1936; repr., ed. R. Needham, Chicago: University of Chicago Press, 1970), 103: "There is a remarkable similarity between the Fijian and Winnebago organization." See further Sahlins, *Culture and Practical Reason*, 46–47 n. 34.

24. I should note that Lévi-Strauss has briefly treated the Polynesian two moieties of sea-people/land-people with quite different interests. See Claude Lévi-Strauss, "From Mythical Possibility to Social Existence," in *The View from Afar*, trans. Joachim Neugroschel and Phoebe Hoss (New York: Basic Books, 1985), esp. 158–61; this is a translation of Lévi-Strauss's essay, "De la possibilité mythique à l'existence sociale," *Le Débat* 19 (1982): 96–120, which I have not seen.

25. Sahlins, *Moala*, 298–300, 360–61; Sahlins, *Culture and Practical Reason*, 24–29.

the same groups again are inferior and superior politically, ritual and secular functionally.[26]

But there are historical and demographical problems:

> The village of Nuku ... has the usual dual organization of land and sea sections, although strictly speaking there has never been a single Land group in the community. Nuku was founded in the latter part of the nineteenth century exclusively by master fishers attached to the chiefs, Sea People par excellence who had migrated from the capital village of Navucinimasi and ulteriorly from the islands of Gau and Bau.[27]

In this, one notes a certain resemblance to the Paao system.[28] To continue:

> Yet by the local conception, certain Nuku groups were Land People. If one suggests to Nuku villagers—as I often did—that all the local groups are Sea People, this is readily admitted. But it will also be explained that one body of the people was first to come to Nuku from the chief's village, that they *receive* the fish from the sea and are warriors (*bati*) for the later groups; that is, they are "Land" in relation to the true Sea People who arrived afterward.[29]

Sahlins employs this example to make a number of analytic moves related to Lévi-Strauss (explicitly), but yet with a different set of nuances and interests from Lévi-Strauss. First, the more Lévi-Straussian formulation:

> This example is especially capital for its disclosure of the mechanism of cultural reproduction in the face of a historical disconformity. Mutilated by history, the moiety system is recreated by the transposition of symbolic correspondences from related domains to the population remaining. A dual division of groups into "Land" and "Sea" is restored by a congruent contrast between original and immigrant peoples.[30]

26. Sahlins, *Culture and Practical Reason*, 24.
27. Ibid., 41.
28. Sahlins, *Historical Metaphors and Mythical Realities*, 9–11.
29. Sahlins, *Culture and Practical Reason*, 41, emphasis original.
30. Ibid., 41–42.

Second, one that echoes Lévi-Strauss's point about a "network of systems … not all of which are equally vulnerable to demographic changes."[31] But here, Sahlins introduces his persistent interest in practice:

> Yet such is merely the mechanics of the process. More fundamental is the fact that the moiety opposition is always present in village life, even in the absence of its historical existence, because the distinction between Land People and Sea People is continually *practiced* in a thousand details of rite and myth, domestic and public life…. Land and sea compose a necessary axis of virtually every group and activity. The social duality is not only conceived; it is lived.[32]

Finally, Sahlins's analytic point, gaining a structural understanding of history:

> There is no escaping the contradiction of a village at once composed of Land People and Sea People, and yet of Sea People alone. The point is of potential significance to a dynamic theory of structure…. In the Nuku case, the opposition of structure and event is overcome, but at the cost of a social complication which denies the structure even as it is confirmed. One dualism negates the other, is placed across the other, and it seems reasonable to suppose that any system will discover limits to its ability to thus accumulate historical contradictions, or at least that it will become vulnerable to some transformation.[33]

Note the analytic progression here. What began as an "apposite example of 'stereotypic reproduction,'" an exemplum that is "especially capital for its disclosure of the mechanism of cultural reproduction in the face of a historical discontinuity," is now, by virtue of that very labor of reproduction, at the brink of a necessary "transformation."[34] Sahlins need only signal a theoretical caution lest he be misunderstood:

> From a naturalistic perspective these [occasions of contradiction/transformation] would appear to be the "adaptive" moments. But in fact structure remains the beginning of historical wisdom. History is not simply an opening into something new—let alone something more

---

31. Lévi-Strauss, *Savage Mind*, 68.
32. Sahlins, *Culture and Practical Reason*, 42, emphasis original.
33. Ibid.
34. Ibid., 41, 42.

practical.... The change may also be a closure: a definitive selection of only one of the permutations latent in any given structure.... The general point is that where there is such structural contradiction there is also historical direction.[35]

I have given these two examples to make two quite different points: one is general, and one is an attempt to inform the work of our seminar. In contrasting the two analogous cases in Lévi-Strauss and in Sahlins, I have hoped to suggest ways in which Sahlins modified a mode of structuralism to be more responsive to the historical while not relaxing a commitment to the analytical priority of structure. For our seminar, I have wanted to stress that the "contradiction" in each of the examples was entirely intracultural.

2

In the steering committee's communications to me concerning this assignment, there was anxiety with respect to the applicability of a Sahlins-type model to the Markan site. With respect to the Corinthians, as well as the New Guinean analogy, there was an "encounter" situation—natives and intruders—which allowed us to play between a "double set of systems," introducing categories such as translation, incongruity, and misunderstanding.[36] This seemed much like the "conjuncture" in Sahlins's privileged example of the Hawaiians and the British/Captain Cook. In their communication, the steering committee noted, not at all inaccurately, "we won't have that advantage in working with Mark." But Sahlins claims that, while the analysis is clarified by a conjuncture, it is not limited to such a case: "Such a confrontation of cultures affords a privileged occasion for seeing very common types of historical change *en clair*. The general statements I derive about historical processes do not require conditions of intercultural contact."[37] Again:

---

35. Ibid., 42, 45.

36. See Ron Cameron and Merrill P. Miller, "Introducing Paul and the Corinthians," in Cameron and Miller, *Redescribing Paul and the Corinthians*, 15; cf. 1, 10–11. The New Guinean analogy is discussed with respect to the Corinthians in Smith, "Re: Corinthians," 21–28, 32–33 with n. 45.

37. Sahlins, *Historical Metaphors and Mythical Realities*, vii; Sahlins quotes this second sentence in a later work to make this same point (*Culture in Practice*, 276 n. 1).

Such effects as transformation and reproduction are maximally dis-
tinguishable in situations of culture contact, although the processes
involved are by no means unique to these situations. For here, in the
clash of cultural understandings and interests, both change and resistance to change are themselves historic issues.... Still, all these processes
are occurring in the same general way within any society, independently
of radical differences in culture, so long as actors with partially distinct
concepts and projects relate their actions to each other.[38]

Despite the attention paid to it, "conjuncture" may prove something of
a red herring. "Transformation" and "reproduction," along with action/
practice, are, in fact, the more crucial elements. With respect to the work
of the seminar, I am far more concerned as to whether we can gain a sufficiently thick behavioral description from the Markan site, what Sahlins
has described as "the interested action of historic agents, including the
microsociology of their interaction."[39] My anxiety at this point is ameliorated, to some degree, by Sahlins's description of "all these processes" that
occur "in the same general way within any society" omitted in the quotation above (signaled by the ellipses). Sahlins wrote of the intercultural
conjuncture: "People are criticizing each other. Besides, their different
interpretations of the same events also criticize each other, and so allow
us a proper sense of the cultural relativity of the event and the responses
to it."[40] He then offers the translation of this into an intracultural occasion
(quoted above), yielding the enabling clause, which permits him to claim
generality "so long as actors with partially distinct concepts and projects
relate their actions to each other." Both the intercultural and the intracultural formulations sound like not unfamiliar projects to this seminar
(although the historian, to no small degree, loses the observer's ability to
discern that people, in the course of their daily activities, often do not
behave the way they say they behave, or say they ought to behave. The
capacity to observe this incongruity, this difference, this gap, stands at the
heart of the anthropologist's claimed privilege of interpretation—recall
my example, in "Re: Corinthians," of Sumbanese sacrificial meat.).[41]

38. Sahlins, *Historical Metaphors and Mythical Realities*, 68.
39. Sahlins, *Islands of History*, xiv.
40. Sahlins, *Historical Metaphors and Mythical Realities*, 68.
41. Smith, "Re: Corinthians," 19–20.

Besides, in a most important 1991 essay, "The Return of the Event, Again," Sahlins offers us a major theoretical assist. After arguing that the "too-simple dualism of 'event' and 'structure' is causing conceptual problems," Sahlins reconceives the question as consisting of three terms, "happenings, structures, and events—in which the event is the relation between the other two":

> While events emanating from natural or foreign causes can show this complexity *en clair*, endogenous events, developing within a given historical order, are constructed in the same general way. They likewise involve a work of cultural signification, which can be similarly described as the appropriation of local phenomena that have their own reasons *in* and *as* an existing cultural-historical scheme. Let us simply substitute *incident* for *happening* in the above argument about exogenous events: an endogenous event is a relation between an incident and a structure.[42]

The potential utility of Sahlins for the seminar, then, will have to be framed in terms of the "event" relations between "incident" and "structure" in the Markan site, rather than in terms of the "event" relations between "conjuncture" and "structure."

Note should be taken of one of Sahlins's most recent works, published after our seminar sessions, *Apologies to Thucydides: Understanding History as Culture and Vice Versa*. While retaining a focus on "structures and contingencies of the conjuncture," in this work Sahlins rarely employs the terminology of "reproduction" and "transformation,"[43] but rather focuses his attention on the issue of agency,[44] a persistent feature throughout his writings but one previously left relatively untheorized. Here, "agency" is defined as "individual action ... interventions that affect the history of social collectivities, thus specifically 'historical agency.' I do not argue for or against 'agency' in the sense of one's personal responsibility for one's actions ... inasmuch as my position is that the complex biographical determinations of the individuality of history-making persons are not

---

42. Marshall Sahlins, "The Return of the Event, Again: With Reflections on the Beginnings of the Great Fijian War of 1843 to 1855 between the Kingdoms of Bau and Rewa," in *Culture in Practice*, 300–301, emphasis original.

43. E.g., Sahlins, *Apologies to Thucydides*, 291.

44. Ibid., esp. 125–93, 277–92.

specified by the larger structures of the conjuncture that authorize and realize his or her social effects."[45]

In this book, Sahlins makes a distinction between "two polar types" of agency, "systemic" and "conjunctural" agency, the former described as those individuals "systemically authorized to make history by their command position in a structural order designed to realize their will," with Napolean and the sacred kings of Fiji his most frequent examples. The opposite type, "conjunctural agency," occurs when individuals have "greatness thrust upon them by their position in a certain situation, a structure of the conjuncture that makes what they do fateful for the larger society."[46] For the latter, his most extended example is Elián Gonzalez and his relatives, which "features the construction of conjunctural agency."[47]

What is of most importance for the seminar is that the Gonzalez affair provides a detailed example of an "incident" as an "endogenous event," a formulation I appealed to above in answering our steering committee's question as to whether Sahlins could be deployed in an intracultural situation such as Mark, while granting his applicability to an intercultural site such as Corinth.[48]

In his formulations on agency, Sahlins claims a theoretical assist from Jean-Paul Sartre's *Search for a Method*, notably Sartre's "notion that societies live out historically the idiosyncrasies of the individuals in whom they personify themselves, leading to a renewed emphasis on the relations of 'structure' to 'contingency.'"[49]It is the third part of Sartre's essay devoted to "la méthode progressive-régressive"[50] that is of most importance to Sahlins, a Sartrean meditation which takes its starting

---

45. Ibid., 155 n. 1.

46. Ibid., 10, 155.

47. Ibid., 166–93; this is a revised and extended version of Marshall Sahlins, "The Iconization of Elián Gonzalez: The Making of National History by Family Melodrama," *Criterion: A Publication of the University of Chicago Divinity School* 42 (2003): 2–13.

48. See, especially, Sahlins, *Apologies to Thucydides*, 186–87, which he labels a "break … for an anthropological reflection on order in culture."

49. Ibid., 10, 152–57.

50. Jean-Paul Sartre, *Theorie des ensembles pratiques*, vol. 1 of *Critique de la raison dialectique, précedé de questions de méthode*, Bibliothèque des idées (Paris: Gallimard, 1960), 60–111, esp. 60–63, 84–89; Sarte, *Search for a Method*, trans. Hazel E. Barnes (New York: Vintage Books, 1968), 85–166, esp. 85–90, 128–40; translation of *Questions de method*, the prefatory essay in vol. 1 of *Critique de la raison dialectique* (Paris: Gallimard, 1960).

point from a passage in Plekhanov on Napolean "which has always made me laugh"[51]—perhaps a unique response in Plekhanov's reception history. Sahlins cites from Sartre's Method "a golden paragraph on the dialectics of structure and agency, a passage that has been for me a capital statement on this issue":[52]

> We must go further [beyond the question of the "ambiguity of the event"] and consider in each case the role of the individual in the historic event. For this role is not defined once and for all: it is the structure of the groups considered which determines it in each case. Thereby, without entirely eliminating contingency, we restore it to its limits and its rationality. The group bestows its power and its efficacy upon the individuals whom it has made and who have made it in turn, whose irreducible particularity is one way of living universality. [In his quotation, Sahlins omits Sartre's next sentence: "Through the individual the group looks back on itself and finds itself again in the particular opaqueness of life as well as in the universality of its struggle."] Or rather, this universality takes on the face, the body, the voice of the leaders which it has given itself; thus the event itself, while a collective apparatus, is more or less marked with individual signs; persons are reflected in it [the event] to the same extent that the conditions of conflict and the structures of the group have permitted them to be personalized.[53]

Essay 2. Sahlins: Reproduction and Transformation

If, as we have said, the conceptual scheme governs and defines practices [*les pratiques*], it is because these [practices] … which the ethnologist studies as discrete realities … are not to be confused with praxis [*la praxis*] which … constitutes the fundamental totality for the human sciences. Marxism, if not Marx himself, has too often reasoned as though practices derived directly [*découlaient immédiatement*] from praxis. Without questioning the undoubted primacy of infrastructure, we believe that a mediator always interposes itself [or: interpolates itself, *s'intercale*] between praxis and practices, this [mediator] is the conceptual scheme by the operation of which matter and form, both the one and the other

---

51. Sarte, *Search for Method*, 85; cf. Sahlins, *Apologies to Thucydides*, 156.
52. Sahlins, *Apologies to Thucydides*, 156–57.
53. Sartre, *Questions de méthode*, 84, in vol. 1 of *Critique de la raison dialectique*; Sarte, *Search for a Method*, 130.

deprived of any independent existence, are realized as structures, that is to say, as entities which are both empirical and intelligible.
— Claude Lévi-Strauss, *La pensée sauvage*

1.

Every people ultimately come from somewhere else; nowhere more so than on islands. Islands may be insular; they are not, thereby, insulated. As one recent work reminds us, beaches are not only sites for arrivals but also for departures.[54] This is especially true for the complex, settlement patterns of the Pacific islands, ultimately from Southeast Asia, in waves of successive water crossings. It is a prehistory long known in its mythical encodings; one that is still being archaeologically deciphered.[55]

In such a setting, and paying attention to etymologies, no one is "autochthonous," "aboriginal," "indigenous," or "native." Yet the myths and traditions from Fiji and Hawaii that Sahlins summarizes as patterns

54. Greg Dening, *Islands and Beaches: Discourse on a Silent Land, Marquesas 1774–1880* (Honolulu: University of Hawaii Press, 1980). Cf. James Clifford, "Traveling Cultures," in *Cultural Studies*, ed. Lawrence Grossberg, Cary Nelson, and Paula Treichler (New York: Routledge, 1992), 96–116, esp. 100; repr. in James Clifford, *Routes: Travel and Translation in the Late Twentieth Century* (Cambridge: Harvard University Press, 1997), 17–46, esp. 24.

55. For the present, the standard history remains Geoffrey Irwin, *The Prehistoric Exploration and Colonization of the Pacific* (Cambridge: Cambridge University Press, 1992); cf. Irwin, "The Colonization of the Pacific: Chronological, Navigational and Social Issues," *Journal of the Polynesian Society* 107 (1998): 111–44. Irwin's studies replace Peter Bellwood, *Man's Conquest of the Pacific: The Prehistory of Southeast Asia and Oceania* (Auckland: Collins, 1978). For the present state of the question, see the useful review by Matthew Spriggs, "Pacific Archaeologies: Contested Ground in the Construction of Pacific History," *Journal of Pacific History* 34 (1999): 109–21. New archaeological data becomes regularly available. These may be tracked in journals such as *Archaeology and Physical Anthropology in Oceania* 1–15 (1966–1980), retitled *Archaeology in Oceania* 16– (1981–). These materials, nearly to date, have been stunningly synthesized in Patrick Vinton Kirch, *On the Road of the Winds: An Archaeological History of the Pacific Islands before European Contact* (Berkeley: University of California Press, 2000). On the specific issue of journeying, see the symposium published in Marshall I. Weisler, ed., *Prehistoric Long-Distance Interaction in Oceania: An Interdisciplinary Approach*, New Zealand Archaeological Association Monograph 21 (Auckland: New Zealand Archaeological Association, 1997). For the myths, see Sahlins, *How "Natives" Think*, 120 n. 2: "As is well known, generally throughout Polynesia gods and people originate in an overseas land."

for "reproduction" all focus on oppositional sets between indigenous and outsiders—land-people/sea-people—which are "translated" (in one of Lévi-Strauss's senses of "transformation" [see appendix, below]) into other codes, ranging from the ritual cycles of Lono and Ku, to the opposition of the mackerel to the bonito fishing seasons.[56] In both societies, the outsider (the "stranger king")[57] becomes politically dominant at the expense of the indigenous. In this old mythic history of outside/inside, relations were prepositioned to make intelligible (if not desirable) the new conjunctural encounter of the Hawaiians and the British. Furthermore, in the traditions of both Fiji and Hawaii, the native chiefs' daughters become the wives of the outsider new kings in a form of mediation.[58]

---

56. Sahlins, *Historical Metaphors and Mythical Realities*, 10–12.

57. See Sahlins, *Islands of History*, 73–103.

58. Sahlins, *Moala*, 298–300, 360–61; Sahlins, *Culture and Practical Reason*, 24–29; Sahlins, "The State of the Art in Social/Cultural Anthropology: Search for an Object," in *Perspectives on Anthropology*, ed. A. F. C. Wallace, John Lawrence Angel, and Richard Fox, Special Publications of the American Anthropological Association 10 (Washington, DC: American Anthropological Association, 1977), 23–30; Sahlins, *Historical Metaphors and Mythical Realities*, 11–12, 16.

The Fijian pattern is based on Sahlins's fieldwork and influenced by the careful mapping of such oppositional structures in Arthur M. Hocart, *The Northern States of Fiji*, Royal Anthropological Institute of Great Britain and Ireland, Occasional Publication, 11 (London: Royal Anthropological Institute of Great Britain and Ireland, 1952), 27–49. The Hawaiian mythic pattern is, largely, dependent on the researches of Abraham Fornander, *An Account of the Polynesian Race, Its Origin and Migrations and the Ancient History of the Hawaiian People to the Times of Kamchamcha I*, 3 vols. (London: Trübner, Ludgate Hill, 1878–1880; repr., Rutland, VT; Tokyo: Charles E. Tuttle, 1969); Thomas G. Thrum, ed., *The Fornander Collection of Hawaiian Antiquities and Folk-Lore*, Memoirs of the Bernice Pauahi Bishop Museum 4–6 (Honolulu: Bishop Museum Press, 1916–1920).

There is a problem with Fornander's data going well beyond the usual complaints about his ethnic and diffusionary preoccupations (e.g., that the Hawaiians were "Arians" with "Cushite," "Chaldaeo-Arabic," and "Dravidian" influences [Fornander, *Account of the Polynesian Race*, 2:1–2]). It centers on Fornander's Epoch IV, beginning ca. 1100 CE (*Account of the Polynesian Race*, 2:6–7, 58–69). Irving Goldman, *Ancient Polynesian Society* (Chicago: University of Chicago Press, 1970), 205–7, puts the problem succinctly: This period "was called by Fornander the 'Migratory Period' on the assumption that foreign invasions had upset the earlier calm. The evidence for foreign invasions is not actually in the traditions—which describe only internal dissensions—but is a shrewd deduction made by Fornander, who believed that invading chiefs had conquered an indigenous folk and reduced them to the status of commoners," even though "the published traditions do not actually speak of any change in the condition of the commoners; this must be deduced from references to chiefly prerogatives." This was also, "Fornander believes," a period when the "great departmental deities, Kane, Ku and Lono had replaced in importance the local ancestral gods." Likewise, Goldman quotes Fornander's "surmise" that human sacrifice was also instituted in this period, as there are no indications in traditions concerning prior periods, "though they [human sacrifices] may have existed."

Sahlins maintains some aspects of this reconstruction with an appeal to comparative data. There is a "general Polynesian—or indeed Austronesian—distinction between immigrant chiefs and indigenous people" (*Historical Ethnography*, 17; see further, among other works, Sahlins, *Islands of History*, 73–103, for the pattern in Fiji; Sahlins, *Islands of History*, 104–35, for Hawaii; as well as the important Polynesian comparative footnote in Sahlins, *How "Natives" Think*, 120 n. 2).

I would note that Sahlins also points to a difference at the level of mythmaking between Polynesian cosmology (the Maori are the privileged example) and Hawaiian myth (*Historical Metaphors and Mythical Realities*, 12–17; cf. Sahlins, "Hierarchy and Humanity in Polynesia," 195–217; Sahlins, *How "Natives" Think*, 25). In part he does so by appealing to Georges Dumézil's important argument that Indo-European cosmic myth (e.g., Indic) is, in some Indo-European traditions (e.g., Roman), transformed to historical epics, "*du mythe au roman*" (see Georges Dumézil, *Mythe et epopee*, 4 vols. [Paris: Gallimard, 1968–1973]). Sahlins suggests an analogous transformation. "Rather than an account of the differentiation of elementary constituents of the universe [as in the Maori, in Hawaii], it tells of the differentiations that make the human order…. Polynesian cosmogony becomes Hawaiian sociology" (*Historical Metaphors and Mythical Realities*, 15). However, it is important to note what Dumézil maintains in the preface to his four-volume study devoted to this transformation. He writes of the "decisive progress" he made in the 1950s: "the day that I realized … that the tripartite ideology was not necessarily accompanied, in the life of a society, by a *real* tripartition of that society, as is the case following the Indian model; on the contrary, I recognized that, wherever one could establish its presence, [the ideology] is nothing (or is no longer, or perhaps never was [anything]) but an ideal and, at the same time, a means of analyzing, of interpreting the forces which are responsible for the course of the world and of human life" (*Mythe et épopée*, 1:15, emphasis original [my translation]; cf. Smith, *To Take Place*, 41, 142 n. 88).

Sahlins's lengthiest deployment of an analogous understanding with respect to the Hawaiian legends of pre-/post-invasion rulership occurs, to the best of my recollection, in *Historical Ethnography*. It is a most important passage, which I abbreviate here: "On the eastern side of Kaiaka Bay … there stood, in ancient times, a royal temple of a distinctive kind, called Kapukapuakea. According to tradition, it had a significance different from the *heiau* (temples) of human sacrifice…. The contrast seems all the greater since nothing remains of Kapukapuakea: it is just a memory, perhaps an invention…. The ruins of these *heiau* survived into the twentieth century to be described by archaeologists … whereas Kapukapuakea's remains, being mythical, belong to ethnography…. It was the site where the good chief, Ma'ilikukahi, of ancient royal stock, was installed by the priests as king of O'ahu…. Polynesianists will recognize the tradi-

These archaic traditions of a past "conjuncture," which may serve as patterns for "reproduction" in a new conjuncture, themselves encompass a "transformation." The outsider was transformed into the powerful insider; the peripheral became central, displacing the previous center to the periphery.

As discussed above (in essay 1), this model is in dialogue, primarily, with Lévi-Strauss's *La pensée sauvage*[59] (a title that should be more strictly translated as *Savage Thought*, recalling that Lévi-Strauss is here punning between *la pensée sauvage* as a "wild pansy," and *la pensée sauvage* as "savage thought," as both the photograph of *Viola tricolor* on the French dust jacket and the appendix—untranslated in the English—on the folk symbolism of the wild pansy make plain. For an English reader, if this pun be known, it recalls Ophelia's "pansies, that's for thoughts" in Shakespeare's *Hamlet* 4.5, lines 177–178.). This is not the context to review the complex question of Lévi-Strauss and history—one often polemically simplified by his opponents—but only to juxtapose Lévi-Strauss at two or three points

---

tion.... If the ceremonial practices of historic times establish the rule of a king metaphorically identified with the god, in olden days the king was the god himself. Along with this transformation goes a correlated distinction between the modern king and the mythical—human sacrifice.... It is a structure of the *longue durée*: the paradigmatic opposition between the original king of sacred descent and legitimate succession on one side, and on the other the violent stranger and usurper who seizes power through the sacrifice of his predecessor and maintains it by offerings of the corpses of his adversaries.... Here are legendary versions of cosmic origins.... The legendary associations of these haunts articulate a continuing social self-consciousness.... They represent a deep faultline in the existing structure, a cleavage between the local people and their parvenu rulers that cannot be directly expressed yet will be all too clearly revealed in the course of historic events.... The landscape and its legends thus inscribe a criticism of the existing regime.... Places and names evoke an alternative society: older, truer, and more directly related to the people.... Kindly kings who made kinsmen of commoners.... The nostalgic alternative is not conceived as an egalitarian society.... It remains chief-centered, hierarchical. Still the good society was organized for the people, if not by them.... In the society portrayed by traditional narratives—as in the historic society of early modern times—the paramount chief distributed the control of lands among his chiefs and people according to rank.... Utopian, however, from the perspective of historical society were practices by which the common people were related as kinsmen to the paramount *ali'i* and the rules that enjoined everyone to life off their own production (Sahlins, *Historical Ethnography*, 21–25).

59. Claude Lévi-Strauss, *La pensée sauvage* (Paris: Plon, 1962). I cite here the English translation, *The Savage Mind*.

to the agendum of Sahlins. One can easily cite passages in Lévi-Strauss, which emphasize the dualism. For example, "there is a constantly repeated battle between synchrony and diachrony from which it seems that diachrony must emerge victorious every time";[60] or a passage that comes close to Sahlins's critique of the notion of "stereotypic reproduction," "cool societies" are those which seek "to annul the possible effects of historical factors on their equilibrium and continuity in a quasi-automatic fashion."[61] But these must be balanced over against other passages in which Lévi-Strauss relates what Sahlins terms reproduction and transformation in a more complex, dialectical fashion. One formulation raises the question of ideology, to be discussed below:

> Do mythical representations correspond to an actual structure [*une structure actuelle* carries the double sense of "real structure" and "present structure," absent in the English] which models social and religious practices or do they translate only the congealed image by means of which native philosophers give themselves the illusion of fixing a reality which escapes them?[62]

Another formulation, with its language of "relations of opposition, correlation, or analogy," is, in principle, translatable into Sahlins's model:

> The antinomy which some believe they have detected between history and system would seem to be present … only if we were not aware of the dynamic relation between the two aspects. [In a note to this sentence Lévi-Strauss adds that "these two notions are of value only as limiting cases."] There is room between them for a diachronic and non-arbitrary construction providing a transition from one to the other. Starting from a binary opposition, which affords the simplest possible example of a system, this construction proceeds by the aggregation, at each of the two poles, of new terms, chosen because they stand in relations of opposition, correlation, or analogy to it. It does not, however, follow from this that the relations in question have to be homogeneous.[63]

---

60. Lévi-Strauss, *Savage Mind*, 155.
61. Ibid., 234.
62. Ibid., 231.
63. Ibid., 161.

Both of these latter passages, the one by raising the issue of ideology, the other of relations, are summarized by Lévi-Strauss's comment, elsewhere, concerning a social effort at rediscovering "an ideal homologous relationship" between infra- and superstructures.[64]

In relation to Lévi-Strauss, I would summarize the thrust of Sahlins's understanding of his three central terms as follows: if *reproduction* represents a mechanism for maintaining continuity[65] and *conjuncture* a

---

64. Claude Lévi-Strauss, "Postscript to Chapter XV ['Social Structure']," in vol 1 of *Structural Anthropology*, trans. Claire Jacobson and Brooke Grundfest Schoeps (New York: Basic Books, 1963), 1:334. The passage (333–34) is quoted more extensively as the epigraph to the section on "transformation" in the appendix, below.

65. Sahlins uses "reproduction" in several senses. In his earlier work it can carry the Marxist sense of relations between production and reproduction (e.g., *Culture and Practical Reason*, 133, 147), or the equally Marxist anthropological meaning of small-scale societies reproducing themselves (e.g., *Stone Age Economics*, 84; *Culture and Practical Reason*, 41, 48, 147). However, in *Culture and Practical Reason*, Sahlins begins to use the term in the sense that will come to dominate his works devoted to "structural history," although not paired with "transformation" (see n. 67 below). Thus, he links "stereotypic reproduction" with "cultural reproduction in the face of a historical disconformity" (*Culture and Practical Reason*, 41), speaking of the "reconstruction of structure at the expense of event" (42). See the discussion of the Marxist senses of "reproduction" in the appendix, below. Sahlins wittily distinguishes from the structuralist: "structuralism is not so much a theory of simple reproduction as it has been a theory of structures that so reproduce" (21).

There is also a brief account in the appendix below of the association of "stereotypic" with reproduction. I should note that, in my own unpublished work on ritual, I have been helped by P. Zumthor's work on topoi ("Topique et tradition," *Poétique* 2 [1971]: 354–65), where he associates the stereotypical with the work of tradition in the "total culture" as opposed to single texts, and compares it to Lévi-Strauss on bricolage. Because the type is "reutilizable indefinitely within different contexts," this demonstrates tradition's capacity to be, at one and the same time, both an agent of passivity and a struggle against passivity. That is to say, the stereotype can be, at one and the same time, a mechanical reproduction or a stimulus to conceptual development (read: transformative).

In Sahlins's 1976 lecture, "The State of the Art in Social/Cultural Anthropology"—which is a condensation of some of the theoretical sections of *Culture and Practical Reason*—Sahlins introduces both the Fijian moiety distinction of land- and sea-people and its disconfirmation in practice (23–24 [see above, essay 1]) as well as the example of Captain Cook (24–30), employing for the latter the term "structure of the conjuncture" (24 [here, curiously modifying it as "the Saussurean-like structure of the conjuncture"], 27, 29). In the Fijian case, he argues: "As for stereotypic reproduction, strictly speaking, it does not occur … the process is as much reconstruction as reproduction, necessarily creating changes in the relative functional values of preexisting categories and oppositions" (23). In the case of Hawaii, reproduction is represented in more structuralist terminology: "a process by which an indigenous order produces both permutations of itself and a system of historic action" (24); "situational permutation of a complex structure" (25); etc. And while the pair reproduction/transformation does not occur, the "role of structure" is contrasted with "the ultimate problem of transformation" (27).

It is in *Historical Metaphors and Mythical Realities* that the term "reproduction" takes on gravity. The first reference implicitly sets up the contrast with "transformation" and shifts the location of reproduction from a Marxist context to a (critical perspective on a) structuralist position, requiring, therefore, that Sahlins concomitantly vary the usual structuralist context and understanding of "transformation'" (see the appendix below, 92–98, as well as n. 67 below). Within structuralism, as Sahlins depicts it, "action entered into account only as it represented the working out of an established order, the 'stereotypic reproduction' (Godelier's phrase) of existing cultural categories…. The event thus enters culture as an instance of a received category" (6–7). This is immediately associated with Braudel's *longue durée* (8; cf. the subtitle to ch. 2).

In the chapter devoted to "Reproduction: Structures of the Long Run" (9–32), the term, in fact, rarely occurs (the most notable exception being the "capacity of Hawaiian culture to reproduce itself as history," 12). Rather, the notion is expressed through synonymous formulations—"Hawaiian history often repeats itself, since only the second time is it an event. The first time it is myth" (9); "incidents … were in many respects historical metaphors of a mythical reality" (11); Cook was the "historical image of a mythical theory" (17); the "capacity to encompass historical circumstances within received relationships" (29); cf. "encompass … within the system as constituted," (50); and, later in ch. 3, "the legendary and historical stories … are paradigmatic" (60)— before returning briefly to the term "reproduction" ("reproduced a customary distinction," 29; "the reproduction of the traditional structure," 32).

There are interesting reformulations of "reproduction" in Sahlins's subsequent essays, for example, "the *calcul sauvage* seems to share with its more famous cousin (*la pensée sauvage*) a great capacity to neutralize the events that beset it…. Everything happened as if nothing happened: as if there could be no history, as there could be no unexpected event, no happening, not already provided for" (*Islands of History*, 30–31); "every such reproduction of the categories is not the same. Every reproduction of culture is an alteration, insofar as in action, the categories by which a present world is orchestrated pick up some novel empirical content" (144). It is, perhaps, of significance that Sahlins can write a lengthy detailed essay, "Captain Cook at Hawaii," without featuring the terminology of "reproduction," "transformation," or "structure of the conjuncture." Sahlins describes this essay as "the most extensive and best documented article I have published about Cook as an actualization of Lono" (*How "Natives" Think*, 3).

A moment from a Sahlins's after-dinner speech may serve as well as an after-footnote logion: "What else can one say … except that some people have all the luck? When Europeans invent their traditions, with the Turks at the gates, it is a genuine cultural rebirth, the beginnings of a progressive future. When other people do it, it is

situation of disjunction,[66] then *transformation* becomes a mechanism for incorporating the disjunction in a way that alters the structure/category previously reproduced.[67] But such a set of formulations raises several questions. I focus, first, on the understanding of "reproduction."

---

a sign of cultural decadence, a factitious recuperation, which can only bring forth the simulacra of a dead past" (Sahlins, *Waiting for Foucault, Still*, 4th ed. [Chicago: Prickly Paradigm Press, 2002], 4).

66. I have discussed Sahlins's notion of conjuncture in essay 1, above, as well as in the section on the genealogy of "conjuncture" in the appendix, below.

67. As noted above (n. 65), Sahlins does not pair "reproduction" with "transformation" in *Culture and Practical Reason*. There are, to the best of my knowledge, only two occurrences of "transformation" in the work: one is the Marxist sense of "transformation of the economic base and, consequently, more or less rapid transformation of the 'entire immense superstructure'" (5); the other is a purely structuralist sense, "a permutation of the correlations … this transformation is accompanied by a series of others" (43); the latter is synonymous with similar observations of "transposition" or "transferred" (42, 44).

In Sahlins's lecture "The State of the Art in Social/Cultural Anthropology," which developed both the language of "reproduction" and "stereotypic reproduction," "transformation" is relatively underdeveloped, being, more often than not, signaled by terms such as "shifts" (23, 25); yet Sahlins is prepared to speak of "the ultimate problem of transformation" (27) without returning to the phrase. The closest he comes to a definition is the following: "Again we have to do with a structure of the conjuncture, a motivated encoding of the pragmatic situation which in turn orders its course, and in the functional values thus gained reorders also itself. We should not, then, be content to confine the symbolic to the realm of thought, for it is equally the system of action. What seems to be a mere opposition of logic becomes, through the appropriation of circumstance as significance, a true force of reason: contrast transformed into motion by the thermodynamics of the symbolic" (30).

It is therefore to *Historical Metaphors and Mythical Realities* that one must turn for the first, systematic account of transformation—now, by chapter titles alone, explicitly juxtaposed to reproduction (9, 33, 67; cf. "permutation [rather] than a transformation," 64). The alternative term seems to be "revalued" (35, 70; cf. "revised," 53). Transformation is when the "received system … enter[s] into a dialectic with practice," and there is "interplay between pragmatic 'structures of the conjuncture' and the received cultural order, as mediated by the constituted interests of the historical actors" (33). "Categories" are "redefined" and "the effects become systemic" (37). The predicate of transformation is that, in the conjuncture, "the project of cultural reproduction failed," yielding to "internal conflict and contradiction" (50). "At the extreme, what began as reproduction ends as transformation" (67; cf. "the transformation of a culture is a mode of its reproduction," *Islands of History*, 138). The "differential connections with Europeans … endowed" the Hawaiians' "relationships to each other

(1) In what ways is Sahlins's (strong) notion of reproduction in a historical situation different from the common (and somewhat weaker) notion of historical correspondence? Take an example I used in a 1975 essay, reprinted in *Map Is Not Territory*, when writing of scribal wisdom:

> For the scribe, if events have significance largely in terms of their precedent, then the same text may be used to describe two widely separated historical events so long as their pattern, their 'value' was perceived to be the same. For example, one of the great monuments of Sumerian literary composition is the "Lament over the Destruction of Sumer and Ur," a work composed c. 2100 BC bewailing the invasion of the Guti in 2500 BC…. The same text was recopied in 287–286 BC bewailing the destructive acts of the Hellenistic monarch, Antigonus. The same text is, at one and the same time, a Sumerian "original" religious expression and a Hellenistic Babylonian "original" religious expression. (The notion of "late copy" must be abandoned in such instances.) The Guti invasion provided a pattern for interpreting all acts of foreign invasion and domination in Babylonia in the same way as the Hyksos invasion provided a pattern for the Egyptian.[68]

---

with novel functional content. This is structural transformation. The values acquired in practice return to structure as new relationships between its categories," a process that is potentially continual (*Historical Metaphors and Mythical Realities*, 50; cf. 54).

As with "reproduction" (see n. 65 above), so with "transformation." The subsequent reflections on Hawaiian tradition yield some striking reformulations of Sahlins's position, perhaps most interestingly: "The performative and prescriptive structures … have different historicities…. The performative orders tend to assimilate themselves to contingent circumstances; whereas, the prescriptive rather assimilate the circumstances to themselves" (*How "Natives" Think*, xii; cf. 27–28).

As above, so here too, let me end this note by allowing Sahlins the last, and his latest, word: "Empirical contradictions of categorical expectations do not simply remove all the cultural traces of their lives from people's minds, restoring them to neonatal specimens now ready to become Lockean sensationalist philosophers. Which is why there is history, and not the dead hand of 'reality'" (*How "Natives" Think*, 249)—a sentiment echoed more forcefully in Sahlins, *Waiting for Foucault*, 7: "One of the current arguments against the coherence of cultures and the possibility of doing any kind of systematic ethnography is that, like a certain famous philosophical river, cultures are always changing. Such is the flux that one can never step into the same culture twice. Yet unless identity and consistency were symbolically imposed on social practices, as also on rivers, and not only by anthropologists but by the people, there could be no intelligibility or even sanity, let alone society. So to paraphrase John Barth, reality is a nice place to visit (philosophically), but no one ever lived there."

68. Jonathan Z. Smith, "Wisdom and Apocalyptic," in *Religious Syncretism in*

I balk at terming such a pattern for interpretation a "reproduction," even in this case where the texts are the same. (Compare the multiple referents in European discourse about the "Huns" or contemporary political rhetoric about avoiding "another Munich" or "another Vietnam.") Is the intention, in such utterances, to make a (strong) statement "A is B," or the (weaker) statement that "A resembles B"?

(2) Such formulae appear to be part of a set of broader rhetorical, historicizing devices, the *paradeigma* or *exemplum*, the *eikôn* or *imago*, the *typos* or *figura*,[69] all of which may be grouped together under Ernst Robert Curtius's term "the exemplary figure."[70] (I think here of George Cary's masterwork, *The Medieval Alexander*, which focuses on the exemplary role of the figure of Alexander, as well as incidents from the biographical legends of Alexander, in medieval moralists, theologians and mystics, books of exempla, sermons, and in secular writers.)[71] Common to each of these devices is that they refuse a logic of identity in favor of a logic of relations.

Antiquity: Essays in Conversation with Geo Widengren, ed. B. A. Pearson, Series on Formative Contemporary Thinkers 1 (Missoula, MT: Scholars Press, 1975), 136–37; repr. in, *Map Is Not Territory: Studies in the History of Religions*, SJLA 23 (Leiden: Brill, 1978; Chicago: University of Chicago Press, 1993), 71–72.

69. See, among others, Joseph A. Mosher, *The Exemplum in the Early Religious and Didactic Literature of England* (New York: Columbia University Press, 1911); Jean Thiébaut Welter, *L'Exemplum dans la littérature religieuse et didactique du moyen âge* (Paris: Occitania, 1927); Hildegard Kornhardt, "Exemplum: Eine bedeutungsgeschichtliche Studie" (PhD diss., Göttingen, 1936); Erich Auerbach, "Figura," *Archivum Romanicum* 22 (1938): 436–89; Leonhard Goppelt, *Typos: Die typologische Deutung des Alten Testaments in Neuen*, BFCT 2/43 (Gütersloh: Bertelsmann, 1939; repr., Darmstadt: Wissenschaftliche Buchgesellschaft, 1973); Goppelt, "τύπος, κτλ.," *TDNT* 8:246–59; Earl Roy Miner, ed., *Literary Uses of Typology: From the Late Middle Ages to the Present* (Princeton: Princeton University Press, 1977); William M. A. Grimaldi, *Aristotle: Rhetoric I; A Commentary* (New York: Fordham University Press, 1980), see esp. the appendix; Paul J. Korshin, *Typologies in England, 1650–1820* (Princeton: Princeton University Press, 1982). My interest in this topic was first aroused by Moses Gaster, *The Exempla of the Rabbis: Being a Collection of Exempla, Apologues, and Tales Culled from Hebrew Manuscripts and Rare Hebrew Books* (London: Asia Publishing, 1924; repr., New York: Ktav, 1968).

70. Ernst Robert Curtius, *European Literature and the Latin Middle Ages*, trans. W. R. Trask (Princeton: Bollingen Foundation, 1953), 57–61.

71. George Cary, *The Medieval Alexander*, ed. D. J. A. Ross (Cambridge: Cambridge University Press, 1956), esp. 77–274.

(3) With respect to the logic of identity, the problem raised in question (2) is a different matter from that of a formulation such as "Cook is Lono," a sentence Sahlins carefully refrains from penning. Rather, drawing upon Hawaiian theology, he employs expressions such as "figuration"[72] or "the principle of historical representation or incarnation."[73] From quite a different perspective, that of ritual logic, Valerio Valeri, author of a classic study on kingship and sacrifice in ancient Hawaii, and Sahlins's colleague at the University of Chicago until Valeri's untimely death, writes, "Cook could not simply be Lono, he had to become Lono by first being connected with Kunoakea. Apparently, only his transformation could fully establish his identity as the god of the Makahiki—that is, establish it in a ritually controlled way, not as an unmediated and uncontrolled fact."[74]

(4) At several junctures, Sahlins employs or implies a proportional format such as:

Europeans : Hawaiians in general : : Hawaiian chiefs : commoners[75]

Might this diagram be rewritten—following Saussure's well-known dictum, "*dans la langue il n'y a que des différences*"[76]—as one of difference

---

72. Sahlins, *Historical Metaphors and Mythical Realities*, 12.

73. Ibid., 16; cf. Sahlins, *How "Natives" Think*, 198 n. 1.

74. Valerio Valeri, "The Transformation of a Transformation: A Structural Essay on an Aspect of Hawaiian History, 1809 to 1819," in *Clio in Oceania: Toward a Historical Anthropology*, ed. Aletta Biersack (Washington, DC: Smithsonian Institution Press, 1991), 134. I cannot stress too highly the historiographic and theoretical importance of Valeri's larger work, *Kingship and Sacrifice: Ritual and Society in Ancient Hawaii*, trans. P. Wissing (Chicago: University of Chicago Press, 1985). For those students of early Christianities of long memory, one observation alone is worth the price of admission: after commenting that vegetable offerings are "of course ... not in the least accounted for by [René] Girard's theory," Valeri goes on to note that "decomposition, which marks the separation from the human and visible world, seems thus a more general and perhaps more important element than the violent act of killing, which is present only in animal and human sacrifices" (69).

75. E.g., Sahlins, *Historical Metaphors and Mythical Realities*, 10; cf. the longer proportional formula that would result from combining 11–12 and 53.

76. Ferdinand de Saussure, *Cours de linguistique générale*, ed. T. de Mauro (Paris: Payot, 1984), 166.

in relations, as in Lévi-Strauss,[77] rather than as an equivalence between the items related? Such a rewriting would yield:

(ethnic system)   Europeans =/= Hawaiians in general
                                          |
(political system)   Hawaiian chiefs =/= commoners

"The system would be profoundly altered," Lévi-Strauss argues,[78] if it were rewritten:

Europeans =/= Hawaiians in general
      | |
Hawaiian chiefs =/= commoners

thus placing the relations between the terms rather than between the relations. Sahlins, at times, skirts this "alteration."

(5) One wonders, as well, whether the relationships between the two systems might be better described as translation-transformations (see appendix, below) or even as systemic substitutions. (To give an example building on Saussure's analogy that if chess "pieces made of ivory are substituted for pieces made of wood, the change makes no difference to the system. But if the number of pieces is diminished or increased, that is a change which profoundly affects the 'grammar' of the game."[79] In my example, if I were to lose one of the Queens in a Saussurean chess set, I could substitute any object for it, from a penny to a slice of pizza, as long as it maintained the same relations of difference with respect to the "moves" of a Queen as different from the moves of other pieces.)

---

77. See, most famously, Lévi-Strauss's diagram of "a homology between *two systems of differences*" (*Savage Mind*, 115, emphasis original). This is not, of course, to deny the presence of proportional formulae in Lévi-Strauss. See, e.g., Lévi-Strauss, *The Raw and the Cooked*, vol. 1 of *Mythologiques*, trans. John Weightman and Doreen Weightman (New York: Harper & Row, 1969), 130, 136, 190–91, 246, 256, 277–78, 289. Lévi-Strauss's consistent terminology for such formulae is "equivalence" or "equation."

78. Lévi-Strauss, *La pensée sauvage*, 152.

79. Ferdinand de Saussure, *Course in General Linguistics*, ed. C. Bally, A. Sechehaye, and A. Riedlinger, trans. R. Harris (La Salle, IL: Open Court, 1986), 23; cf. 88: "A state of the board in chess corresponds exactly to the state of the language. The value of the chess pieces depends on their position upon the chess board, just as in the language each term has its value through its contrast with all the other terms."

2.

Of far more interest to the seminar, at our sessions in Denver, was Sahlins's mechanism of "transformation," which provoked discussion of categories such as "incongruency" and "translation."

Let me introduce Sahlins's "transformation" in an oblique manner. Michel de Certeau, in a posthumously published (unsuccessful) 1978 proposal to the Centre nationale de la recherche scientifique, wrote:

> Since these [travel] accounts enter into the more general category of a science of the Other or "heterology," it is important to ask, starting from Brazilian sources in particular, from the confrontation of different documents: a) how the specificity of another society, for example, that of the Tupi, resisted occidental codifications; b) how the fragments of a particular historicity of other societies (with, notably, differing relations to time, to space, and so on), elements capable of inscribing those societies within a duration, a memory, and a space of their own, were first brought into use; c) how, in the text of the ethnographic project, oriented initially toward reduction and preservation, are irreducible details (sounds, "words," singularities) insinuated as faults in the discourse of comprehension, so that the travel narrative presented the kind of organization that Freud posited in ordinary language: a system in which indices of an unconscious, that Other of the conscience, emerge in *lapsus* or witticisms. The history of voyages would especially lend itself to this analysis by tolerating or privileging as an "event" that which makes an exception to the interpretive codes.[80]

---

80. Michel de Certeau, "Travel Narratives of the French to Brazil: Sixteenth to Eighteenth Centuries," *Representations* 33 (1991): 223. Note that Sahlins quotes a portion of Certeau's text, given as item "c" above (*How "Natives" Think*, 118).

I have used Certeau to make one sort of point with reference to "transformation" in Sahlins; permit me to use the Certeau quotation to make one other. Certeau refers to the Brazilian Tupi tribe in Certeau, "Ethno-graphie, l'oralité, ou l'espace d l'autre: Léry," in *L'Écriture de l'histoire*, 2nd ed. (Paris: Gallimard, 1993), 215–48. This reference no doubt occurs because of his classic study of Jean de Léry's 1578 account of the Tupi, *History of a Voyage to the Land of Brazil*, Latin American Literature and Culture 6, trans. J. Whatley (Berkeley: University of California Press, 1990); trans. of *Histoire d'un voyage en la terre du Brésil* (La Rochelle: Antoine Chuppin, 1578). This reference called to mind a contemporary of Léry, André Thevet, who published a first account of the Tupinamba in his spectacularly successful *Les singularitez de la France Antartique, autremont nommée Amerique* (Paris: Heritiers de Maurice de la Porte, 1557). In a second, far less popular work, *La cosmographie universelle d'André Thevet, Cosmo-*

Note that here Certeau writes entirely from the perspective of European apprehension. Sahlins, by contrast, analyzing the response of both parties, in the "event" of a "conjuncture," revises Certeau's "faults," "lapse(s)," and "exception(s)" into "transformation."[81]

Clearly, it is transformation within a "situation" that bears the burden of Sahlins's sense of the thickness of historical events and processes. Although the word is of structuralist pedigree (see appendix, below), it is Sahlins's intent to counter-distinguish it from the sense it bears in Lévi-Strauss when the latter titles a chapter of *The Savage Mind*, "Systems of Transformations," and gives, as his first definition, "codes suitable for conveying messages which can be transposed into other codes."[82] In a conscious inversion, what Lévi-Strauss terms "transformation," Sahlins terms "reproduction."

---

graphe du Roy, de deux voyages par luy faits aux Indes Australes, et Occidentales (Paris: Pierre L'Huillier et Guillaume Chaudière, 1575), book 21, chs. 4–6, Thevet recorded a Tupi myth, which, some fifty years after first contact between the Tupi and the French and Portugese, incorporated the Europeans into a traditional Tupi anthropogony. Alfred Métraux prepared a critical edition of the myth in *La religion des Tupinamba et ses rapports avec celles des autres tribus tupi-guarani*, Bibliothèque de l'école des hautes études, Sciences religieuses 45 (Paris: E. Leroux, 1928); cf. Métraux, "The Tupinamba," in *The Tropical Forest Tribes*, vol. 3 of *Handbook of South American Indians*, ed. J. H. Steward (Washington, DC: Smithsonian Institution, Bureau of American Ethnology, Bulletin 143, 1946–1949), esp. 131–33; Métraux, "Twin Heroes in South American Mythology," *Journal of American Folklore* 59 (1946): 114–23. This myth, in turn, forms a central text for Lévi-Strauss in *The Story of Lynx*, trans. C. Tihanyi (Chicago: University of Chicago Press, 1995), 43–63, which should be read as a structuralist counterpoint to Sahlins's *Historical Metaphors and Mythical Realities* on the Hawaiians. For a quite different sort of meditation, see the extended studies on "Gurani metaphysics" in Pierre Clastres, "De l'un sans multiple," in *La société contra l'état* (Paris: Editions de Minuit, 1974), 146–51; Clastres, *Le grande parler: Mythes et chants sacrées des Indiens Gurani* (Paris: Editions du Seuil, 1974).

81. For Sahlins's usage, see n. 67 above.

82. Lévi-Strauss, *Savage Mind*, 75. Lévi-Strauss's most complex usage in his chapter on "Systems of Transformations" is analogous to the transformations with a geo-historical set, illustrated with reference to South America in appendix, below. "We see therefore that going from the Aranda to the Warramunga, one passes from a system with a collective mythology (multiplicity of ancestors) but an individualized ritual to the reverse system of an individualized mythology but a collective ritual.... All these transformations could be systematically set out" (87–88).

There are issues with Sahlins's notion of transformation to which I shall want to return. Here, I lift out only two matters, both with respect to Sahlins's semiotic frame.

(1) For Sahlins, it is Saussure on *système* and *état*, as related to the distinctions between *langue/parole*, synchrony/diachrony, that has had those pernicious effects, when taken over into cultural anthropology, that the thoroughly non-Saussurean term "transformation" is designed to address. (To judge from the indispensable *Lexique de la terminologie Saussurienne*, "transformation" bears no technical sense in Saussure; its few occurrences carry the quite ordinary meaning associated with "alteration" and "changement.")[83] Sahlins writes:

> Language can be analyzed as a structure only insofar as it is considered as a *state*, its elements standing in the temporal order of simultaneity.... From the perspective of a system of signs, the changes to which it submits will appear fortuitous. The only *system* consists in the way these historical materials are interrelated at any given time or state of the language.[84]

Here, he appears to be paraphrasing Saussure's best-known chess analogy, one made with respect to the question of the systematicity of the *état de langue*, which is the focus of Sahlins's concerns:

> A state of the board in chess corresponds exactly to the state of the language.... The system is only ever a temporary one. It is true that the values also depend ultimately upon one invariable set of conventions, the rules of the game, which exist before the beginning of the game and remain in force after each move. The rules, fixed once for all, also exist in the linguistic case.... Finally, in order to pass from one stable condition to another, or, in our terminology, from one synchronic state to another, moving one piece is all that is needed. There is no general upheaval. That is the counterpart of the diachronic fact.... For in the case of chess (a) one piece only is moved at a time. Similarly, linguistic

---

83. Rudolf Engler, *Lexique de la terminologie Saussurienne* (Utrecht; Anvers: Het Spectrum, 1968), s.v. "transformation"; cf. s.v. "altération," and s "changement." Engler is the editor of the *Edition critique du "Cours de linguistique générale" de F. de Saussure* (Wiesbaden: Otto Harrassowitz, 1967), 1–3. In his *Lexique*, Engler builds on the "Lexique de la terminologie" in the magisterial work by Robert Godel, *Les sources manuscrites du cours de linguistique générale de F. de Saussure* (Geneva: Droz, 1957; Paris: Minard, 1957), 252–81.

84. Sahlins, *Historical Metaphors and Mythical Realities*, 4, emphasis original.

changes affect isolated elements only. (b) In spite of that the move has a repercussion on the entire system. It is impossible for the player to foresee where its consequences will end.... It is exactly the same where a language is concerned.[85]

The question that may fairly be asked is whether Sahlins's quarrel is with Saussure or with appropriations of his thought (especially within varieties of structuralism associated with aspects of Lévi-Strauss's thought). After all, in the passage just quoted, an "event"—"moving one piece," "no general upheaval" required—is sufficient to have "a repercussion on the entire system," such that it is "impossible ... to foresee where its consequences will end."

I would want to go further and assert a position argued elsewhere.[86] Saussure, in proposing the distinction between *langue* and *parole*, is proposing the construction of two theoretical objects, as distinct from empirical objects of study;[87] *langue* serves as the disciplinary horizon for general linguistics, *parole* serves as the disciplinary horizon for specialized or historical linguistics. But I would want to revisit the familiar correlation of this distinction with that between synchrony and diachrony. Accepting the arguments of the Southwest Neo-Kantian school on an analogous dichotomy (nomothetic/idiographic), synchronic and diachronic are alternative modes of considering the same phenomenon. It is a methodological distinction, not a distinction between different objects—let alone, as in some formula-

85. Saussure, *Course in General Linguistics*, 88.

86. See, especially, Jonathan Z. Smith, "A Twice-Told Tale: The History of the History of Religions' History," *Numen* 48 (2001): 142–43 with n. 20; repr. in *Relating Religion*, 369–70 with n. 20, citing the discussion and references in Smith, *To Take Place*, 33–34 nn. 48–51. I have made the same argument with respect to the relations of morphology to history in Smith, "Acknowledgments: Morphology and History in Mircea Eliade's *Patterns in Comparative Religion* (1949–1999), Part 1: The Work and Its Contexts," *HR* 39 (2000): 329–30; repr. in *Relating Religion*, 72–73.

87. Beginning with the definitive ch. 3, sec. 1 in Saussure, *Cours de linguistique générale*, Saussure consistently employs "le langage" to name the empirical object of linguistic studies, carefully distinguishing this term from "la langue." For example, *Cours de linguistique générale*, 25: "Mais, qu'est-ce que la langue? Pour nous, elle ne se confond pas avec le langage." See further the citations, especially from the student manuscript MS 3283, in Engler, *Lexique de la terminologie Saussurienne*, s.v. "langage" and "langue."

tions, two rival forces in human culture which Sahlins's dialectical formulation of reproduction/transformation is designed, in part, to address.[88]

To return to Saussure's chess analogy, it is the same chess game as an object that is in view whether one asks the diachronic question as to the history of the game,[89] or synchronically grasps the current "state of play." That is why, in both of these activities, Saussure frames the distinction from the point of view of the observer (or investigator): "Any one who has followed the whole game has not the least advantage over a passer-by who happens to look at the game at that particular moment."[90]

(2) In the passage quoted above, Saussure concedes one dissimilarity in his *langue*/chess analogy: "In chess, the player intends to make his moves, and to have some effect upon the system. In a language, on the contrary, there is no premeditation. Its pieces are moved, or rather modified, spontaneously and fortuitously." This raises questions as to Sahlins's interest in praxis, agency, and motivation. Here, I want only to place transformation within this context.

Let me call attention to two passages, one from the conclusion, one from the introduction, which frame Sahlins's Hawaiian example. In each, the dynamics of conjuncture/reproduction, transformation/action are translated into a theoretical language: in the first instance, into a materialist discourse; in the second, into a linguistic discourse which, significantly, shifts from a Saussurean to a Peircean understanding of signs. In the first translation, Sahlins writes:

> Action begins and ends in structure: begins in the projects of people as social beings, to end by absorption of the effects in a cultural practico-inert. Yet in the interim the categories may be functionally displaced, their respective positional values altered; hence, by definition, a new structural order is in place.[91]

---

88. See, especially, Sahlins, *Historical Metaphors and Mythical Realities*, 67–68: "Even the apparently extreme processes of culture-in-history we have been discussing, reproduction and transformation, are they truly—i.e., phenomenally—distinct? Clearly they are analytically separable.... At the least, all structural transformation involves structural reproduction, if not also the other way around."

89. Saussure, *Course in General Linguistics*, 23.

90. Ibid., 88.

91. Sahlins, *Historical Metaphors and Mythical Realities*, 72.

It is the use of the Sartrean coinage, "practico-inert," that is troubling. In Sahlins's formulation, transformation as praxis is an "interim" affair, fated to be "absorbed" in counter-praxis.[92]

In the second instance, Sahlins seeks to rectify what he takes to be a purely structuralist position:

> In speech is History made. Here signs are set in various and contingent relationships according to people's instrumental purposes—purposes of course that are socially constituted even as they may be individually variable. Signs thus take on functional and implicational values in a project of action.... They are subjected to analysis and recombination, from which arise unprecedented forms and meanings (metaphors, for

---

92. It is not possible to clarify what Sahlins understands by the term "practico-inert." It occurs, to the best of my recollection, only in this passage, and Sahlins provides neither a definition nor a citation. "Practico-inert" was coined and first introduced by Sartre in the "Conclusion" to the *Questions de methode* (*Search for a Method*, 173). It becomes an important term in the English translation of the first volume of the *Critique de la raison dialectique*, where book 1 is entitled "From Individual Praxis to the Practico-Inert," and is massively deployed in the 1985 unfinished second volume, *The Intelligibility of History*, vol. 2 of *Critique of Dialectical Reason*, ed. Arlette Elkaïm-Sartre, trans. Quintin Hoare (New York: Verso, 1991). The *Critique* was addressed by Lévi-Strauss in the final chapter of *Savage Mind*. Sahlins (in *Culture and Practical Reason* and in *Islands of History*) refers only to the prefatory *Search for a Method*, which would have provided him with no definition of the term. It would be beyond the scope of this essay to review the scores of references to "practico-inert" listed in the indices to Sartre's two volumes. For our purposes, it is sufficient to cite Thomas R. Flynn's characterization: "The practico-inert functions as anti-praxis or anti-dialectic, making history possible and rendering any overarching master dialectic impossible. The practico-inert is the locus of scarcity, that simple but transcendental fact that there are not enough material goods to go around, of material objectivity [in Hegel's sense of "objective spirit"; see *Critique* 1:665–67], and of the permanence of human endeavors in their 'solid' state as institutions, traditions, artifacts, and the like (what Sartre terms 'worked matter'). Yet the same practico-inert by its sheer material recalcitrance blocks the success of any superdialectic. It is never fully subsumable into a non-inertial form. Hence in the *Critique* it dissipates practical unities, hardens spontaneity into habit, reverses or deflects projects with its counter-finality, and functions generally as the antithesis of freedom" ("Mediated Reciprocity and the Genius of the Third," in *The Philosophy of Jean-Paul Sartre*, ed. P. A. Schilpp, The Library of Living Philosophers 16 [La Salle, IL: Open Court, 1981], 349). In addition, one should certainly note Sartre's astounding definition, in *L'Idiot de la famille*, 3 vols. (Paris: Gallimard, 1971–1973), 3:44 (my translation): "The objective mind—in a specific society at a given period—is none other than 'Culture' as practico-inert"!

example). Above all, in speech people bring signs into indexical relationships with the objects of their projects.... In the event, speech brings signs into "new" contexts of use, entailing contradictions which must be in turn encompassed by the system.[93]

Does not this language about speech replicate the dynamics of conjuncture/reproduction/transformation/practice? If practice is "the sign in action, as opposed to its position in structure,"[94] if "the dialectics of history" are "powered by disconformities between conventional values and intentional values, between intersubjective meanings and subjective interests, between symbolic sense and symbolic reference"[95]—then how does one evaluate actions? Of more gravity, in the colonial system named "conjuncture" by Sahlins, how do "signs in action" enable resistance as a mode of response different from both reproduction and transformation? A rebellion, a revolution is not the same as a "cultural performance," understood as a "semiotics of identity."[96]

---

93. Sahlins, *Historical Metaphors and Mythical Realities*, 5–6; cf. 69–70.

94. Ibid., 68.

95. Ibid., 72.

96. In writing that Sahlins shifts from a Saussurean to a Peircean understanding of signs, I focus attention on Sahlins's statement, "in speech people bring signs into indexical relationships with the objects of their projects" (*Historical Metaphors and Mythical Realities*, 5–6). As is well known, in Peirce, an "indexical sign" differs from a "symbol" in that the relation between sign and signified does not rest on convention, and differs from an "icon" in that the relation does not rest on similarity, but rather on a direct, causal relation in the way that smoke is an index of fire, or a weathervane an index of the wind's direction. In more contemporary language one might say that indexical signs function in analog fashion, presuming a direct (physical, causal) connection between sign and object. In Peircean terminology, an index is a "sinsign" in that it is "an actual existent thing or event which is a sign," and its object, a "dicisign," which "for its interpretant is a sign of actual existence." Thus an index "is a real thing or fact which is a sign of its object by virtue of being connected with it as a matter of fact" (Charles S. Peirce, *Collected Papers*, ed. Charles Hartshorne and Paul Weiss, 6 vols. [Cambridge: Harvard University Press, 1931–1958], 2:245–51; 4:447, 538; see the more available and less expensive collection in Justus Buchler, ed., *Philosophical Writings of Peirce* [New York: Dover, 1955], 101–3). These characteristics of the indexical sign allow Sahlins to emphasize the corrigibility of signs insofar as the common understanding of signs is "as the names of things." When "the world" does "not conform to the presuppositions by which some people talk about it," this indexical relation—although Sahlins does not specifically limit his formulation to indexical signs—allows them to "potentially revise the general conceptual values of linguistic

Let me be clear at this point. I am not uncomfortable with Sahlins's position, though I would have framed it somewhat differently. After all, I concluded one of my conjunctural essays:

> The myth of Hainuwele is an application of this archaic mythologem to a new, cargo situation.... The setting of the tale is not the mythic "once upon a time" but, rather, the painful, post-European "here and now." The Ceramese myth of Hainuwele does not solve the problem, overcome the incongruity, or resolve the tension. Rather, it results in thought. It is a testing of the adequacy and applicability of traditional patterns and categories to new situations and data in the hopes of achieving rectification.... To be sure ... the white man was not brought into conformity with native categories; he still fails to recognize a moral claim of reciprocity. But this is not how we judge success in matters of science. We judge harshly those who have abandoned the novel and the incongruous to a realm outside of the confines of understanding, and we value those who (even though failing) stubbornly make the attempt at achieving intelligibility, at achieving rectification of either the data or the model.[97]

Nevertheless, it seemed of some use to make plain what is entailed in an acceptance of Sahlins's model.[98]

---

terms and relations by reference to a world" (Sahlins, *Historical Metaphors and Mythical Realities*, 6).

In the text above I invoked Milton Singer's term "cultural performance" because Singer, a long-time colleague of Sahlins at Chicago, both introduced Peirce to, and "translated" his formulations for anthropology. See Milton Singer, *Man's Glassy Essence: Explorations in Semiotic Anthropology* (Bloomington: Indiana University Press, 1984), who coined the phrase "cultural performance" and dwells on its relation to Peirce's semiotics.

97. Jonathan Z. Smith, "A Pearl of Great Price and a Cargo of Yams: A Study in Situational Incongruity," *HR* 16 (1976): 18–19; repr. in *Imagining Religion: From Babylon to Jonestown*, CSHJ (Chicago: University of Chicago Press, 1982), 100–101.

98. Compare Sahlins, "The State of the Art in Social/Cultural Anthropology," 30: "We should not, then, be content to confine the symbolic to the realm of thought, for it is equally a system of action. What seems to be a mere opposition of logic, becomes, through the appropriation of circumstance as significance, a true force of reason, contrast transformed into motion by a thermodynamics of the symbolic."

Essay 3. In His Own Voice

In the previous essay I signaled a set of issues that need to be addressed, in my own voice, by way of clarifying some of the turns in our seminar sessions in Denver, as well as speaking to several questions addressed to me by the steering committee as an assignment for our subsequent sessions in Toronto.

Let me begin by stating the obvious: with respect to matters of theory and method, as with other human activities, everyone is situated in a basic topography of near and far. For myself, listing the loci of the "near" in a rough chronology of influence, they would be what has come to be called Austro-Marxism (especially as associated with Max Adler); the Baden or Southern or Southwestern School (especially Heinrich Rickert) and the Marburg School (especially Ernst Cassirer) within German Neo-Kantianisms; German biological morphology (as developed from Goethe in the eighteenth and nineteenth centuries); formalist understandings of language (ranging from Saussure to some Soviet theoreticians); and the French tradition of social thought (ranging from Émile Durkheim and Marcel Mauss to Claude Lévi-Strauss and Louis Dumont)—each read and thought about in terms of the other. What each of these has in common is some form of Neo-Kantianism.[99] Then, too, as is the case in such locative

---

99. Perhaps the most interesting of the recent number of works on German Neo-Kantianism is Klaus Christian Köhnke, *Entstehung und Aufstieg des Neukantianismus: Die deutsche Universitätsphilosophie zwischen Idealismus und Positivismus* (Frankfurt: Suhrkamp, 1986). I know of nothing comparable for French Neo-Kantianism.

In some of the traditions listed, their Neo-Kantianism is self-evident; others, perhaps, require some clarification.

(1) The Austro-Marxist thinkers (some of whom were associated with the Marburg School) are responsible for an entire subgenre of literature linking together Kant and Marx, ranging from Karl Vorländer, *Kant und Marx: Ein Beitrag zur Philosophie des Sozialismus* (Tübingen: Mohr, 1911), to Max Adler, *Kant und der Marxismus* (Berlin: E. Laub, 1925). From the point of view of the human sciences, it is Adler's works that are most suggestive. See, especially, Adler, *Das Soziologie in Kants Erkenntniskritik: Ein Beitrag zur Auseinandersetzung zwischen Naturalismus und Kritizismus* (Vienna: Verlag der Wiener Volksbuchhandlung, 1924); Adler, *Soziologie des Marxismus*, 2 vols. (Vienna: Europa Verlag, 1930–32), now reprinted with the addition of a previously unpublished third volume, 3 vols. (Vienna: Europa Verlag, 1964); Adler, *Ausgewählte Schriften*, ed. A. Pfabigan and N. Leser, Quellen und Studien zur österreichischen Geistesgeschichte im 19. und 20. Jahrhundert 2 (Vienna: Österreichischer Bundesverlag, 1981). The collection of brief texts in English translation, *Austro-Marxism*, trans.

activities, the near determines the far. As with Israel and Canaan, or Paul and other apostles, one always works hardest at counter-distinguishing oneself from those who, from some other perspective, would be judged,

---

Tom Bottomore and Patrick Goode (London: Oxford University Press, 1978), rather downplays the Neo-Kantianism.

(2) In the case of biological morphology, there is a more complex pedigree. In its classical eighteenth- and early nineteenth-century forms, morphology is largely an interaction between Goethe and Romantic *Naturphilosophie*. However, in the late nineteenth century, the Baden Neo-Kantians became important to morphology in its struggle against evolutionary theories. For this combination, see, among others, Hans Driesch, *Die Biologie als selbständige Grundwissenschaft: Eine kritische Studie* (Leipzig: W. Engelmann, 1893); Driesch, *The Science and Philosophy of the Organism*, 2nd ed. (London: Black, 1928). For me, Ernst Cassirer has been a major influence on the understanding of biological morphology and on the relations between biological and cultural morphologies. See, among other works, Cassirer, "Structuralism in Modern Linguistics," *Word: Journal of the Linguistic Circle of New York* 1 (1945): 99–120; Cassirer, *The Problem of Knowledge: Philosophy, Science and History since Hegel*, trans. W. H. Woglom and C. W. Hendel (New Haven: Yale University Press, 1950), 118–26; Cassirer, *The Logic of the Humanities*, trans. C. S. Howe (New Haven: Yale University Press, 1960), 117–81; cf. the new translation, *The Logic of the Cultural Sciences: Five Studies*, trans. S. G. Lofts, foreword by Donald Phillip Verene (New Haven: Yale University Press, 2000), 56–102.

(3) While the Neo-Kantianism of Durkheim and the French Durkheimian tradition has never been questioned—it is, by the way, a tradition that persistently positions itself, implicitly or explicitly, with respect to Marx—this connection has recently been the subject of investigation by philosophically sophisticated scholars of Durkheim and Mauss. See, among others, Steven Collins, "Categories, Concepts or Predicaments? Remarks on Mauss's Use of Philosophical Terminology," in *The Category of the Person: Anthropology, Philosophy, History*, ed. Michael Carrithers, Steven Collins, and Steven Lukes (Cambridge: Cambridge University Press, 1985), 46–82; Terry F. Godlove Jr., *Religion, Interpretation and Diversity of Belief: The Framework Model from Kant to Durkheim to Davidson* (Cambridge: Cambridge University Press, 1989); cf. Godlove, "Is 'Space' a Concept? Kant, Durkheim and French Neo-Kantianism," *Journal of the History of the Behavioral Sciences* 32 (1966): 441–55.

(4) One of the interesting (although admittedly minor) developments in scholarship on the history of ideas has been emphasis on the influence of Neo-Kantianism on Soviet linguists and literary-critical theorists. This has led, among other unexpected results, to the charge that Bakhtin, at several critical junctures in his writings, plagiarized Cassirer! See Brian Poole, "Bakhtin and Cassirer: The Philosophical Origins of Bakhtin's Carnival Messianism," *The South Atlantic Quarterly* 97 (1998): 537–78.

I should note one influence not subsumable under the rubric of Neo-Kantianism, my long-standing obligation to the 'Scottish Institutionalists' who first framed the Enlightenment project of reason in sociological terms.

for all practical purposes, to be the same. For this reason, some forms of materialist thought were early objects of distancing. Later, in thinking through issues in the study of religion, the "far" became a variety of approaches that may be loosely linked together under the rubrics of phenomenological and hermeneutic enterprises.

Two chief consequences follow from this litany. One is a commitment to what has been termed, chiefly by its critics, a "framework theory of knowledge," largely the result of an anthropological, social, and linguistic translation of Kantianism, most often associated, in its initial formulations, with Durkheim and his sociology of knowledge.[100] The other is an insistence on the cognitive power of tension.[101]

The first commitment plays the role of a workaday assumption as to "what is the case," leading to an overarching interest in interpreting cultural data in terms of thought and language, and an abiding suspicion of arguments from "experience," as well as a marked disinterest in individualistic formulations of agency, interest, or motivation.

The second interest has been an object of persistent engagement in an attempt to frame a more labile model of difference: in intellectual and

---

100. On the framework theory, see Godlove, *Religion, Interpretation and Diversity of Belief*, who points to the central problem of the framework theory as expressed by Émile Durkheim (61): "But if the categories at first do not more than translate social states, does it not follow that they can be applied to the rest of nature only as metaphors? If their purpose is merely to express social things, it would seem that they could be extended to other realms only by convention. Thus insofar as they serve us in conceiving the physical or biological world, they can only have the value of artificial symbols—useful perhaps, but with no connection to reality" (*The Elementary Forms of Religious Life*, trans. K. E. Fields [New York: Free Press, 1995], 17). Sahlins consistently refers to this theme in Durkheim (e.g., *Culture and Practical Reason*, 116; "The State of the Art in Social/Cultural Anthropology," 15; *Historical Metaphors and Mythical Realities*, 67).

101. I have chosen the term "tension" to avoid the others, embedded in quite particular philosophical traditions. I owe my interest in the concept of tension to my teacher, Martin Foss, *Symbol and Metaphor in Human Experience* (Princeton: Princeton University Press, 1949), who uses it in a Hegelian fashion, to describe metaphor "as a process of tension and energy, manifested in the process of language, not in a single word" (61). Foss's usage needs to be distinguished from the better-known formulation of poetry as tension in Allen Tate, "Tension in Poetry," *The Southern Review* (1938): 101–15; repr. in *Essays of Four Decades* (Wilmington, DE: ISI Books, 1999), 56–71; cf. Tate, *On the Limits of Poetry* (New York: Swallow Press/William Morrow, 1948), 82–84.

historical settings, deploying terms such as "gap," "incongruity," or "displacement"; in anthropological constructions, attempting typologies of
"difference" or "diverse kinds" in conscious avoidance of the language of
the "other" (let alone, the "Other"); in second-order disciplinary discourse,
stressing explanation as translation, models as requiring difference from
what they model lest they be paraphrases, and comparison as an analogical
project across difference. Translated into procedural terms, the question
becomes one of working at the possibilities for a responsible integration
of morphological and historical studies, with analogical comparison as the
privileged site for negotiating these two, often opposed, projects.[102]

---

102. Let me indicate only some basic references for the various sorts of workings
with difference enumerated in this paragraph.

(1) On incongruity as a theoretical concept, especially in relation to myth in historical settings, see n. 105 below.

(2) On the anthropological plottings of difference, see Jonathan Z. Smith, "What
a Difference a Difference Makes," in *"To See Ourselves as Others See Us": Christians,
Jews, "Others" in Late Antiquity*, ed. J. Neusner and E. S. Frerichs, Scholars Press Studies in the Humanities (Chico, CA: Scholars Press, 1985), 3–48; repr. in *Relating Religion*, 251–302; Smith, "Differential Equations: On Constructing the Other," in *Relating
Religion*, 230–50; Smith, "Close Encounters of Diverse Kinds," in *Religion and Cultural
Studies*, ed. S. L. Mizruchi (Princeton: Princeton University Press, 2001), 3–21; repr.
in *Relating Religion*, 303–22.

(3) On difference, translation, explanation, and models (a topic first strongly
advanced at our first Consultation on Ancient Myths and Modern Theories of Christian Origins, held in Philadelphia in 1995), see Smith, "Social Formations of Early
Christianities: A Response to Ron Cameron and Burton Mack," *MTSR* 8 (1996): 271–
78; Smith, "Bible and Religion," *BCSSR* 29 (2000): 87–93; repr. in *Relating Religion*,
197–214; Smith, "A Twice-Told Tale," 131–46; repr. in *Relating Religion*, 362–74; Smith,
"Religion Up and Down, Out and In," in *Sacred Time, Sacred Place: Archaeology and
the Religion of Israel*, ed. B. M. Gittlen (Winona Lake, IN: Eisenbrauns, 2002), 3–10.

(4) On comparison and analogy, see Smith, "*Adde Parvum Parvo Magnus Acervus
Erit*," *HR* 11 (1971): 67–90; repr. in *Map Is Not Territory*, 240–64; Smith, "In Compari-
son a Magic Dwells," in *Imagining Religion*, 19–35, 139–41; Smith, *Drudgery Divine:
On the Comparison of Early Christianities and the Religions of Late Antiquity*, Jordan
Lectures in Comparative Religion 14 (London: School of Oriental and African Stud-
ies, University of London; Chicago: University of Chicago Press, 1990), esp. 36–53;
Smith, "The 'End' of Comparison: Redescription and Rectification," in *A Magic Still
Dwells: Comparative Religion in the Postmodern Age*, ed. Kimberley C. Patton and Ben-
jamin C. Ray (Berkeley: University of California Press, 2000), 237–41.

(5) On morphology and history, see Smith, "Acknowledgments: Morphology
and History in Mircea Eliade's *Patterns in Comparative Religion* (1949–1999), Part 1,"
315–31; repr. in *Relating Religion*, 61–79; Smith, "Acknowledgments: Morphology and

With this much by way of background, I want to turn to one of my assignments from the steering committee, to clarify my statement in *"Dayyeinu"* as to the overarching problematic of our work being that of formulating "the nexus between mythmaking and social formation," as well as the accompanying caution: "The challenge, here, will be to avoid formulations which see the one as the dependent variable of the other, or which see the one as congruent to the other."[103]

Let me begin with a word. Given what I have said above with respect to an attempt to rectify explanation in terms of translation, when I use the term "nexus" it is in its classical sense of "association," "interwoven," "bound together" (as in the wonderful, and sadly obsolete, adjective "nexible"—a word I have waited decades to be able to use in print), and not in its later nineteenth-century causal sense. That is to say, while there may be necessary relations, these are not necessarily causal ones.[104]

What is in common to both of my cautions with respect to formulating the nexus between social formation and mythmaking is a rejection of the notion of the myth as mirror: whether that which is reflected be

---

History in Mircea Eliade's *Patterns in Comparative Religion* (1949–1999), Part 2: The Texture of the Work," *HR* 39 (2000): 332–51; repr., pages 80–100 in *Relating Religion*.

103. Smith, *"Dayyeinu,"* 486.

104. While he is not a figure I am accustomed to appealing to, I resonate with a passage (unfortunately, available to me only in English translation) from Michel Foucault's 1963 literary-critical piece discussing the relations of Robbe-Grillet's novels to those of Sollers, Thibaudeau, and Baudry: "It was not a question of deciding on originalities, but of establishing from one work to another, a visible relation, namable in each of its elements, which would not be of the order of resemblance (with the whole series of badly thought out and frankly unthinkable notions of influence and imitation), nor of the order of replacement (of succession, development …): a relation such that the works might define each other against, beside and at a distance from each other, taking support at the same time from their difference and their simultaneity, and defining, without privilege or culmination, the scope of a *network* (Michel Foucault, "Distance, Aspect, Origin," in *The Tel Quel Reader*, ed. and trans. Patrick Ffrench and Roland-François Lack [London: Routledge, 1998], 102, emphasis original).

With an appropriate translation from literary texts to social events, Foucault's "network" is very much the sort of nexus I have in mind. (By the way, in support of the notion that "conjuncture" became a term, in French texts of the late 1960s and 1970s, all but evacuated of specific connotation, see Foucault, *Discipline and Punish: The Birth of the Prison*, trans. Alan Sheridan [New York: Pantheon, 1977], 55, where the term "historical conjuncture" simply refers to the co-occurrence of continued public executions alongside the increase in rigor of the 1670 Ordinance on criminal justice.)

expressed as social situation (as some functionalisms as well as the seminar has sometimes formulated it), infrastructure (as in some materialisms), or as divine archetypes (as in Mircea Eliade). Clearly my own interest in tension, in incongruency, would resist a replication model.[105]

---

105. In the development of my work, I place considerable emphasis on the 1974 inaugural lecture for the William Benton Professorship of Religion and the Human Sciences in the College of the University of Chicago (Jonathan Z. Smith, "Map Is Not Territory," in *Map Is Not Territory*, 289–309), which self-consciously signaled a turn from an attempt to test the limits of an accommodation to the sort of enterprise associated with Eliade, particularly with respect to the category of "sacred space" in the course of which I had developed the locative/utopian distinction, to "a new set of concerns with the incongruous which will preoccupy me in future research" (Smith, *Map Is Not Territory*, xv). While often using Adolf Jensen as a stalking horse for Eliade on the issue of an ontological replication, I turned to the more general question as to the consequences of accepting, within mythic materials or within scholarly approaches to the study of myth, a "conservative, ideological element" which lays "prime emphasis upon congruency and conformity, whether it be expressed through phenomenological descriptions of repetition, functionalist descriptions of feedback mechanisms or structuralist descriptions of mediation. Therefore it has seemed to me of some value, in my own work, to explore the dimensions of incongruity that exist in religious materials. For I do believe that religion is, among other things, an intellectual activity—and, to play upon Paul Ricoeur's well-known phrase, it is the perception of incongruity that gives rise to thought" ("Map Is Not Territory," 293–94, paraphrasing Ricoeur's formulation, "le symbole donne à penser," in *Finitude et culpabilité: La symbolique du mal*, vol. 2.2 of *Philosophie de la volonté*, Philosophie de l'esprit [Paris: Aubier, 1960], 324). It is probably appropriate to note that I took classes with Ricoeur in college. In those more phenomenological days, 1955–1960, he may well have had more influence on me than I presently recognize. Certainly, given my interest in metaphoric "tension" (see n. 102 above), his own approach to the same topic had an attraction. It may well have been from Ricoeur—either in conversations once he joined the faculty at the University of Chicago or from Ricoeur's, *The Rule of Metaphor*, trans. R. Czerny, K. McLaughlin, and J. Costello (Toronto: University of Toronto Press, 1977), 239–46; translation of *La métaphore vive* (Paris: Seuil, 1975)—that I first learned of the use of the term "redescription" in relation to metaphors and models (see Mary B. Hesse, "The Explanatory Function of Metaphor," in *Models and Analogies in Science* [Notre Dame: University of Notre Dame Press, 1966], 157–77; cf. Max Black, "Models and Archetypes," in *Models and Metaphors: Studies in Language and Philosophy* [Ithaca, NY: Cornell University Press, 1962], 219–43, esp. 236–38) that has loomed so large in my work, although with an expanded range of meanings, since my 1977 lecture "Sacred Persistence: Toward a Redescription of Canon," in vol. 1 of *Approaches to Ancient Judaism: Theory and Practice*, ed. William S. Green, BJS 1 (Missoula, MT: Scholars Press, 1978), 11–28; repr. and rev. pages 36–52 in *Imagining Religion*.

For myself, any confidence I might have once had in an understanding of myth as congruent (or, for that matter, in the more often asserted congruence of ritual to myth) was decisively broken in 1960 when I first read Lévi-Strauss's "Four Winnebago Myths"—a text that remains his most accessible treatment of a set of myths. In that essay he wrote:

> Since the publication of Boas's *Tsimshian Mythology*, anthropologists have often simply assumed that a full correlation exists between the myths of a given society and its culture.... It does not follow that whenever a social pattern is alluded to in a myth this pattern must correspond to something real.... There must be, and there is, a correspondence between the unconscious meaning of a myth—the problem it tries to solve—and the conscious content it makes use of to reach that end, i.e., the plot. However, this correspondence is not necessarily an exact reproduction; it can also appear as a logical transformation.... We may be confronted with the pattern of a nonexistent society ... even one contrary to the Winnebago traditional pattern.[106]

To return to my 1974 inaugural lecture, "Map Is Not Territory," I would direct the reader to those passages in which I insist that "there is no pristine myth; there is only application"; that "myth is (to slightly emend Gilbert Ryle's well-known formulation) a self-conscious category mistake. That is to say, the incongruity of myth is not an error, it is the very source of its power. Or (to borrow Kenneth Burke's definition of the proverb) a myth is a 'strategy for dealing with a situation' " (299, citing Kenneth Burke, *The Philosophy of Literary Form: Studies in Symbolic Action*, rev. ed. [New York: Vintage Books, 1957], 256, emphasis omitted); I also make the comparison between jokes and riddles ("Map Is Not Territory," 300–302); and I go on to deploy a set of exempla that defined my research agendum for nearly a decade: "primitive classification," ritualized incongruity, the diviner's basket, Mediterranean materials, "hunting magic," "myths of rupture," and Hainuwele (including a version [307–8] of the paragraph quoted above, at the conclusion of essay 2), before concluding: "myth is best conceived ... as a limited collection of elements with a fixed range of cultural meanings which are applied, thought with, worked with, experimented with in particular situations. That the power of myth depends upon the play between the applicability and inapplicability of a given element in the myth to a given experiential situation.... [Some] traditions are more closely akin to the joke in that they neither deny nor flee from disjunction, but allow the incongruous elements to stand. They suggest that symbolism, myth, ritual, repetition, transcendence are all incapable of overcoming disjunction. They seek, rather, to play between the incongruities and to provide an occasion for thought" (308–9). The majority of these items were developed, with appropriate ethnographic and historical detail, in *Imagining Religion*, which largely contains essays researched and written between 1974 and 1980.

106. Claude Lévi-Strauss, "Four Winnebago Myths: A Structural Sketch," in

What this liberating passage seemed to suggest, at the time, was that the relations in myth are within myth; we need not turn to external relations, whether these be in nature, in society, or within other cultural formations. (For this reason, as I turned to writing my dissertation on James George Frazer, I kept over my desk, as a motto, Lévi-Strauss's critical sentence from *La pensée sauvage*: "L'erreur de Mannhardt et de l'école naturaliste fut de croire que les phénomènes naturels sont *ce que* le mythes cherchent à expliquer: alors qu'ils sont plutôt ce *au moyen de quoi* les mythes cherchent à expliquer des réalités qui ne sont pas elles-mêmes d'ordre naturel, mais logique.")[107] To state a Sahlins's sort of concern, this

---

Culture in History: Essays in Honor of Paul Radin, ed. Stanley Diamond (New York: Columbia University Press, 1960), 351–62; repr. pages 198–210 (passage quoted, 203–4) in vol. 2 of *Structural Anthropology*.

Since Lévi-Strauss mentions Boas's Tsimshian materials, recall Lévi-Strauss's best-known treatment of them in which he argues that "when we move on to the sociological aspects … it is not a question of an accurate documentary picture of the reality of native life, but a sort of counterpoint which seems sometimes to be in harmony with this reality, and sometimes to part from it in order to rejoin it again" (Lévi-Strauss, "The Story of Asdiwal," in *Structural Anthropology*, 2:155; trans. of *La Geste d'Asdiwal* [Paris: Imprimerie Nationale, 1958]); that "the myth is certainly related to given facts, but not as a *representation* of them. The relationship is of a dialectic kind, and the institutions described in the myths can be the very opposite of the real institutions" (2:172, emphasis original); and finally, in one of his more important statements, that "such [mythical] speculations, in the last analysis, do not seek to depict what is real, but to justify the shortcomings of reality, since the extreme positions are only *imagined* in order to show that they are *untenable*. This step, which is fitting for mythical thought, implies an admission … that the social facts when thus examined are marred by an insurmountable contradiction. A contradiction which … society cannot understand and prefers to forget" (2:173, emphasis original).

Years later, Lévi-Strauss argued in retrospect, in response to criticisms of his 1958 essay, that Asdiwal "makes a point of transposing every aspect of social reality in a paradoxical perspective," and that "the empiricism of our critics prevents them from interpreting the mythic motifs as functions of each other.… They claim to see in them mere reflections of actual social conditions" ("Asdiwal Revisited, 1972–3," in *Anthropology and Myth: Lectures, 1951–1982*, trans. R. Willis [Oxford: Blackwell, 1987], 97, 99).

Lévi-Strauss has a second (1982) revisiting of Asdiwal, in the course of which he juxtaposes Asdiwal to the Polynesian land-people/sea-people opposition (Lévi-Strauss, "From Mythical Possibility to Social Existence," in *The View from Afar*, 157–75).

107. Lévi-Strauss, *La pensée sauvage*, 138, emphasis original; cf. the English translation in *Savage Mind*, 95.

might suggest that reproduction and transformation are activities within myth, rather than mechanisms for interaction with a situation where action modifies myth.

Now, I would know better and, with the benefit of both hindsight and Lévi-Strauss's *Mythologiques*, state more precisely that the relations are between myths (for Lévi-Strauss, these would be ethno-geographically related or adjacent, and thus, in my sort of terminology, have homological rather than analogical relations), and that the other relations (for example, natural, cultural formations) are translations between codes, operations summarized by the term "transformations." (See appendix, below.)

What I did not pay attention to, then, in the passage just quoted from "Four Winnebago Myths," but which may now help us clarify the issue at hand, is the word "unconscious." I took it, correctly, I think, to be reflecting usage within the Durkheimian tradition (and, for that matter, the Saussurean) as a means of emphasizing the social rather than the individual, for which language, above all, was the model.[108]

But there are other senses of "unconscious" in Lévi-Strauss, accompanied by a concomitant shift in the language of incongruency.[109] Where there is "contradiction" there is active unconsciousness. This is to the fore, for example, in Lévi-Strauss's discussions of myths of dual organizations which suggest egalitarian structures, but which, in fact, conceal triadic hierarchical structures, which I took up in *To Take Place*.[110] Such contradictions, as Hans H. Penner has shrewdly observed, may, in other modes

---

108. One might compare here Sahlins's formulation, which includes a pragmatics (part of which I cited in "*Dayyeinu*," 486 n. 9): "The sign is determined as a concept by its differential relation to other signs in the collective symbolic scheme. On the other hand, the sign represents a differential interest to various subjects according to its place in their specific life schemes. 'Interest' and 'sense' (or 'meaning') are two sides of the same thing, the sign, as related respectively to persons and to other signs. *Yet my interest in something is not the same as its sense*" (Sahlins, *Historical Metaphors and Mythical Realities*, 68–69, emphasis original).

109. The discussion of "unconscious" in Lévi-Strauss in Marcel Hénaff, *Claude Lévi-Strauss and the Making of Structural Anthropology*, trans. Mary Baker (Minneapolis: University of Minnesota Press, 1998), 94–119, is a major contribution.

110. Smith, *To Take Place*, 40–45, 142–46, where the question of "ideology" is briefly raised. For another formulation in Lévi-Strauss, see his comment in "The Story of Asdiwal," cited above, n. 106: "The social facts when thus examined are marred by an insurmountable contradiction. A contradiction which … society cannot understand and prefers to forget" (*Structural Anthropology*, 2:173).

of discourse, give rise to the question of myth as "ideology"[111]—a word

---

111. See Hans H. Penner, ed., *Teaching Lévi-Strauss*, Teaching Religious Studies 1 (Atlanta: Scholars Press, 1998), 10. Commenting on Lévi-Strauss's statement that "the purpose of myth is to provide a logical model capable of overcoming a contradiction (an impossible achievement if, as it happens, the contradiction is real)" ("The Structural Study of Myth," 1:229), Penner observes: "Given what Lévi-Strauss has published, the 'real' in this statement refers to the political/economic infrastructure of a society. Thus if the content of a myth contradicts (or is in opposition to) that actual infrastructure of a society (as it usually does) then the myth will never resolve its purpose but will continue to transform itself into never ending sets of contradictions and oppositions. This is, of course, the classic formulation of ideology that we find in Marx" (*Teaching Lévi Strauss*, 10; cf. the similar statement in Penner, *Impasse and Resolution: A Critique of the Study of Religion*, Toronto Studies in Religion 8 [New York: Peter Lang, 1989], 159–60).

Without raising the question as to how Lévi-Strauss would respond to Penner's translation—see the passage quoted as an epigraph to essay 2 from Lévi-Strauss, *La pensée sauvage*, 173 (and compare the standard English translation in *Savage Mind*, 130)—I am not comfortable with Penner's use of the Marxist distinction. Rather than debating the issue on my own terms, for the purposes of this paper, I will affirm Sahlins, who uses the passage from *La pensée sauvage*, 173, in the context of his discussion of the "venerable conflict" as to "whether the cultural order is to be conceived as the codification of man's actual purposeful and pragmatic action; or whether, conversely, human action in the world is to be understood as mediated by the cultural design, which gives order at once to practical experience, customary practice, and the relationship between the two. The difference is not trivial, nor will it be resolved by the happy academic conclusion that the answer lies somewhere in between, or even on both sides (i.e., dialectically)…. The opposition therefore cannot be compromised … the relation can only be an encompassment." Sahlins continues: Lévi-Strauss's conceptual scheme is "the very *organization* of material production; analyzing it, we are in the economic base itself. Its presence there dissolves the classic antinomies of infrastructure and superstructure, the one considered "material" the other "conceptual." Of course, it does not dissolve the "material" as such. But the so-called material causes must be, *in that capacity*, the product of a symbolic system…. The general determinations of praxis are subject to the specific formulations of culture; that is, of an order that enjoys, by its own properties as a symbolic system, a fundamental autonomy" (*Culture and Practical Reason*, 55–57, emphasis original; compare Sahlins's strong statement on cultural autonomy in Sahlins, *Use and Abuse of Biology*, x–xii).

Within one understanding of Marxism, there would be no strain with respect to both Lévi-Strauss's and Sahlins's translation of the relations of infrastructure/superstructure (if "intellectual" be substituted for "symbolic"). I would compare these quotations from Lévi-Strauss and Sahlins to one of Adler's persistent themes: "Economic phenomena are never 'material' in the materialist sense, but have precisely a 'mental' character" (*Soziologie des Marxismus*, 1:118; cf. Adler, *Marx als Denker: Zum 25 Todes-*

I have largely refrained from employing as a technical term in my own work, precisely because of its polysemy in contemporary usage. Of the formulations most useful in the present context, one would argue that myth resembles ideology when the latter is understood as a suppression (repression) of contradictions; the other would see myth as an ideological formation interpolated between the subject and its proper object of cognition.[112]

---

jahre von Karl Marx [Berlin: Buchhandlung Vorwärts, 1908], 8 [my translation]). I am well aware that others would sharply disagree.

112. This is not the context in which to launch a general discussion of ideology. My formulation of two senses of ideology in the context of a congruence notion of mirroring has been largely influenced by Pierre Macherey, "Lenin, Critic of Tolstoy: The Image in the Mirror," in *A Theory of Literary Production*, trans. Geoffrey Wall (London: Routledge & Kegan Paul, 1978), 105–35. This is a different matter from Richard Rorty's general critique of a mirror epistemology in relation to what he terms a "pragmatic theory of knowledge" (*Philosophy and the Mirror of Nature* [Princeton: Princeton University Press, 1979]).

For the purposes of this paper, I would only note the irony that "ideology," in many of its contemporary usages, has come to mean the opposite of what it denoted when it was coined. (This is by no means a unique phenomenon in philosophical discourse. Think of the all but total reversals of meaning of "individual" and "subjective"/"objective" so brilliantly chronicled by Raymond Williams in *Keywords: A Vocabulary of Culture and Society* [Oxford: Oxford University Press, 1976], 133–36, 259–64). When coined, at the time of the French Revolution, by the Lockean philosopher, Antoine Louis Claude Destutt Comte de Tracy in the opening pages of *Élements d'idéologie* (Paris: Courcier, 1801), incorporated as parts 2–5 of his collection, *Projet d'éléments d'idéologie à l'usage des écoles centrales de la République française* (Paris: Pierre Didot, 1801–1815), it meant the "science of ideas," with "ideas" understood as a direct result of "sensations" of an external world, in contradistinction to "metaphysics," which was the result of "imagination." In later usage, "ideology" has often taken on Destutt de Tracy's sense of "imagination," that which is interposed between the world-as-it-is and the world-as-thought. For those of us committed to a framework theory of knowledge, this "interposition" is positive, though it needs to be framed in terms of a social epistemology rather than in terms of Destutt de Tracy's individual epistemology. (Williams's otherwise important treatment of "ideology" [*Keywords*, 126–30] is insufficient in its reading of Destutt de Tracy; in this respect, only, see Hans Barth, *Truth and Ideology*, trans. F. Lilge [Berkeley: University of California Press, 1976], 1–8. I regret that I have not been able to obtain Patrick Quentin, *Les origines de l'idéologie* [Paris: Economica, 1987].)

Note that while Marx, in Paris in 1844–1845, read and abstracted parts 4 and 5 of Destutt de Tracy's *Projet*, the *Traité de la volonté et de ses effects* (Karl Marx and Friedrich Engels, *Collected Works*, 50 vols., trans. Richard Dixon et al. [New York: International Publishers, 1975–2004], 3:217, 288, 318; 4:33; 5:228–29)—possibly in

Even more helpful to our question, I think, are two remarkable essays that Lévi-Strauss published in *Festschriften* in 1971 and which are now reprinted consecutively in *Structural Anthropology*. Although the first interests me more, as it focuses on the Hidatsa, the subject of Lévi-Strauss's most important interpretation of a ritual,[113] the second essay is more directly relevant, in which he distinguishes three sorts of "transformations." It is the third form that is most suggestive. While the other two (considered as an ethno-geographical set; see appendix below) either maintain or reduce the number of translations into diverse codes, the third, the Cree, takes a different path in relation to the "fact" that they, unlike their neighbors, had "very early … established friendly relations with the French and the English." Here, the transformation appears conscious, it is a "manipulation meant to make the myth fit an aspect of their history":

> The Tsimshian were trying to justify an order they wished to retain unchanged by a tradition the origin of which they dismissed as lost in the dawn of time. The Cree adapted the same myth to recent history, with the manifest intention of justifying a development in the making and of validating one of its possible orientations—collaboration with the white man—among others left open to them. The story of the Tsimshian legend is imaginary…. That of the Cree myth refers to real events…. Thus, a myth which is transformed in passing from tribe to tribe finally exhausts itself—without disappearing, for all of that. Two paths still remain open: that of fictional elaboration, and that of reactivation with a view to legitimizing history. This history, in its turn, may be of two

---

the context of his close relationship with, and subsequent harsh criticism of, Pierre-Joseph Proudhon—I can recall no instance where Marx relates "ideology" to Destutt de Tracy's formulations, although it is in this same period that Marx and Engels first employ the term, in *The German Ideology*, ed. David Riazanov (Moscow: Marx-Engels Institute, 1932) (written November 1845–August 1846), which sarcastically quotes Destutt de Tracy as part of the critique of Max Stirner as "St. Max" (*Collected Works*, 5:228–29).

113. In my unpublished work on ritual, Lévi-Strauss's interpretation of the Hidatsa eagle hunt, in the context of his Hidatsa ethnography, has been crucial. Listing the treatments in chronological order, see the report on his 1959–1960 seminar at the Collège de France in *Anthropology and Myth*, 217–20; Lévi-Strauss, *Savage Mind*, 48–53; Lévi-Strauss, *The Origin of Table Manners*, trans. John Weightman and Doreen Weightman (Chicago: University of Chicago press, 1978), 296–97; Lévi-Strauss, "Relations of Symmetry Between Rituals and Myths of Neighboring Peoples," in *Structural Anthropology*, 2:238–55.

types: retrospective, to found a traditional order on a distant past; or prospective, to make this past the beginning of a future which is starting to take shape.[114]

This last observation, as to unconscious/conscious by Lévi-Strauss, provides what is needed, from my perspective, to begin the answer to the steering committee's question as to the nexus between mythmaking and social formation. Insofar as mythmaking is a linguistic activity, it is both a human and a social activity. In this sense it is correctly viewed as generated by, organized by, structures that are largely unconscious in the sense specified above. This lack of consciousness extends beyond grammar and transformations to the level of worldview. To use a well-known example, the correlation of the first-person pronoun with subjectivity (even, individuality) is an unconscious extension from the linguistic world to the social world, the "second environment" in which we largely dwell.[115] Insofar as we think with stories—the parallel means we have of "making sense" alongside discursive reason—the structures and processes of sense-making share in this unconscious extension. This is a quotidian activity; it

---

114. Lévi-Strauss, "How Myths Die," in *Structural Anthropology*, 2:267–68. To this notion of historical "exhaustion" must be juxtaposed a more internalized sort of formulation; compare: "Now something irreversible occurs ... the mythic substance allows its internal principles of organization to seep away. Its structural content is diminished. Whereas at the beginning the transformations were vigorous, by the end they have become quite feeble.... [Codes] which before functioned visibly, are now reduced to a state of latency; and the structure deteriorates into seriality. The deterioration begins when oppositional structures give way to reduplicative structures: the successive episodes all follow the same pattern. And the deterioration ends at the point where reduplication replaces structure.... The myth, having nothing more to say, or very little, can only continue by dint of self-repetition" (Lévi-Strauss, *Origin of Table Manners*, 129).

115. In this example, I refer to the series of articles on the pronoun and subject by Émile Benveniste, *Problems in General Linguistics*, trans. M. E. Meek (Coral Gables: University of Miami Press, 1971); trans. of vol. 1 of *Problèmes de linguistique générale* (Paris: Gallimard, 1966–1974), 195–204, 217–30, and passim. Note that Benveniste relates the "I" primarily to discourse; other modes of speech eliminate the subject, most particularly, historical narrative. "We shall define historical narration as the mode of utterance that excludes every 'autobiographical' linguistic form. The historian will never say 'je' or 'tu' or 'maintenant,' because he will never make use of the formal apparatus of discourse, which resides primarily in the relationship of the persons 'je : tu.' Hence we shall find only the forms of the 'third person' in a historical narrative strictly followed" (*Problems in General Linguistics*, 206–7).

requires no "crisis" for its generation.[116] To put it bluntly, as long as we are social, as long as we speak, there will be myth; its presence requires no special explanation. Theories as to the origins of myth are always motivated by, and depend on, a critique of myth.

It is a different case when we shift from a communicative to a rhetorical frame, that is to say, when we seek to persuade or convince, usually with respect to some "situation." Here, we consciously deploy the "pre-positioned" resources of language and story (as in Lévi-Strauss's Cree example). An account of such rhetoric must balance the already-present frameworks with the particular "occasion," as well as the audience(s). Such an understanding applies to texts such as the Gospel of Mark as it does to other mythic texts I have analyzed elsewhere, such as *Enuma elish*, Hainuwele, and the Io cosmogony.[117]

In either case, as students of myth know full well as they practice their craft, whether it be Lévi-Strauss's ethno-geographic sets or the parallel printing of the Synoptic Gospels, our chief access to the mythmaking processes of thinking with stories is comparison among (all) the versions—not in a juridical process of evaluating conflicting testimonies (the process undertaken by nineteenth-century Roman historians and carried over into New Testament scholarship) that results in a "harmony" rather than a "synopsis," but rather one of letting the differences stand. (There will be dispute as to the significance of the differences, ranging from a generative sense of the play of permutation and combination to the detection of interests, which will need to be clarified at the level of second-order discourse.)

---

116. In the response I gave at our first consultation on Ancient Myths and Modern Theories of Christian Origins, I cautioned against reliance on a crisis/response model: "Beyond the well-known problems with defining 'crisis' (see Barkun, and the difficulty with demonstrating that a given response is both sufficient *and* necessary), there remains the issue that the crisis is as much a construct, is as contained by discourse and representation, as is the response. (See, already, Aberle, 1962)" (Smith, "Social Formations of Early Christianities," 274, emphasis original). I would give the same caution today. (The references in the quotation are to Michael Barkun, *Disaster and the Millennium* [New Haven: Yale University Press, 1974]; David Aberle, "A Note on Relative Deprivation Theory as Applied to Millenarian and Other Cult Movements," in *Millennial Dreams in Action*, ed. S. L. Thrupp [The Hague: Mouton, 1962], 209–14.)

117. See the treatment of these texts in Smith, "Wisdom and Apocalyptic," 137–40; repr. in *Map Is Not Territory* 72–74; Smith, "A Pearl of Great Price and a Cargo of Yams," 1–11, 11–19 (repr. in *Imagining Religion*, 90–96, 96–101); Smith, "Map Is Not Territory," 302–7; Smith, "The Unknown God: Myth in History," in *Imagining Religion*, 66–89.

As a provisional conclusion to this lengthy three-part response to the steering committee's queries, and in the interests of enabling the processes of clarifying second-order discourse, I would attempt to translate some of Sahlins into my sort of language, with the assistance of Lévi-Strauss.

As a first approximation, reading Sahlins from the point of view of Smith, what is termed "conjuncture" I would replace by "*situational incongruity*" as it presents itself to thought.[118] Rather than "reproduction," I would speak of "experimental application."[119]

---

118. In nn. 118–20 I want to locate the terms I am using to translate Sahlins within their context in my own work. "What is termed 'conjuncture' I would replace by '*situational incongruity*' as it presents itself to thought." While this compound phrase occurs rarely in my written work—but see the subtitle to my essay "A Pearl of Great Price and a Cargo of Yams: A Study in Situational Incongruity"—the linkage of "incongruous" and "situation" abounds, especially in essays of the 1970s. Therefore, each term must be treated, to some degree, separately.

From one point of view, the term "situation" may mean no more than historical context, and is so occasionally used. But, one such association gives a clue to what 'situation' signifies. As stated in n. 105 above, I place considerable emphasis on the 1974 inaugural lecture. There, I state, "(to borrow Kenneth Burke's definition of the proverb) a myth is a 'strategy for dealing with a situation'" ("Map Is Not Territory," 299). Let me say that while I applauded Burke's defense of "strategy" against his critics who found it "suggesting an overly conscious procedure," I deliberately misread his understanding of situation. For Burke, "situation" is that which is "typical and recurrent in a given social structure"; "many of the 'typical, recurrent situations' are not peculiar to our own civilization at all," and in this sense they could "even be" said to be "timeless" (Burke, *Philosophy of Literary Form*, 256–60, emphasis omitted). I gave the word more of a Sartrean turn, as a "condition" in which one finds oneself, which calls forth a "project" or an "action." (While "situation" in this sense is the focus of the powerful opening chapter of part 4 of Jean-Paul Sartre, *L'être et le néant: Essai d'ontologie phénoménologique* [Paris: Gallimard, 1943], 507–642, for my purpose, thinking of the linguistic project of myth, the analogous analysis in "Qu'est-ce que la littérature?," which makes up the bulk of Sartre's *Situations II: Qu'est-ce que la littérature?* [Paris: Gallimard, 1948], 2:55–330; rev. and enl. by Arlette Elkaïm-Sartre in *Situations III: Littérature et engagement* [Paris: Gallimard, 2013], 9–267, is more apropos.) "Situation" is a historical setting of "incongruity" between cultural norms and expectations and historical reality which calls forth *thought* as well as action. In its situation, this understanding of "situation" was an attempt to begin to get at notions of myth as a-historical, cyclical, or archetypal—a set of strongly held positions at the time. Thus, I say in the introduction to *Imagining Religion*: "I hold that there is *no privilege* to myth…. [Myths] must be understood primarily as texts in context, specific acts of communication between specified individuals, at specific points in time and space, about specifiable subjects. Kenneth Burke's definition of a proverb as a 'strategy for dealing with a situation' provides an important insight when extended to these materials. For the historian of religion, the task then becomes one of imagining the "situation," of constructing the context.... For there is no primordium—it is all history" (xiii, emphasis original). For this emphasis on the "specificity" of myth, I would refer the reader to Smith, "Unknown God," researched and written from 1970–1980, which remains my favorite piece of work.

While I glancingly employ this sense of "situation" in a 1970 publication, noting that "insufficient attention has been paid ... to [European] 'Cargo' as disruptive of [native systems of] equivalence and place, and the requirement of some system of exchange in order to rectify this situation" (Smith, "Influence of Symbols upon Social Change: A Place on Which to Stand," *Worship* 44 [1970]: 471; repr. in *Map Is Not Territory*, 142), it is in my inaugural lecture ("Map Is Not Territory") that I begin to employ the term as part of an understanding of myth and ritual. In that lecture, I use "situation" in two senses, the first being the one indicated above. Thus I write of the diviner seeking a fit between "the structure" and the "client's situation" (300), of an "incongruity between the expectation and the actuality" (301), of "the indigenous situation [which] is rendered problematic by the incongruous presence of the white man" (302), most closely to the proposed formulation, of "a native strategy for dealing with a new, incongruous situation, a strategy that thinks with indigenous elements" (304), of a "non-traditional situation," and the question of a "mythic precedent for this situation" (306–7). In the majority of instances, in the lecture, I refer to this as "the cargo situation" (305, 306, 307).

It is in this context that I introduce in the lecture a second sense of "situation" with the formula, "a 'cargo situation' without a cargo cult" (304). This sort of formulation is frequently applied to Mediterranean materials where I distinguish between a situation and a literature or movement: "an *apocalyptic situation*, though not necessarily [an] apocalyptic literature" (Smith, "Wisdom and Apocalyptic," 137, emphasis original; cf. 139–40, 154–55; repr. in *Map Is Not Territory*, 72, cf. 74, 86, and passim). While the distinction is different, the understanding is the same: it is a novel "situation" caused by outsiders which leads to significant changes, such as the "cessation of native kingship" which raises the question of the "typological" applicability of old patterns to the new situation ("Wisdom and Apocalyptic," 155, 136–37; repr. in *Map Is Not Territory*, 86, 71–72).

These same patterns of usages persist in my essays in Smith, "The Bare Facts of Ritual," *HR* 20 (1980): 123; repr. in *Imagining Religion*, 62; Smith, "Unknown God," 66, 80, 83, 87; Smith, "A Pearl of Great Price and a Cargo of Yams," 1–2, 7–8, 14–15, 18; repr. in *Imagining Religion*, 90, 94, 98, 100.

119. I have suggested "experimental application" as a translation for Sahlins's "reproduction." Here, I want self-consciously to avoid all of the implications latent in this word from the Marxist description of the Indian village community, as well as Godelier's critical description of structuralism in terms of "stereotypic reproduction." What is at stake, initially, is a rejection of the sort of formulation, such as Stanner's, of aboriginal life as a "one-possibility thing," leading to the notion of a lack of critical thought ("Map Is Not Territory," 297, citing W. E. H. Stanner, "The Dreaming," in

Reader in Comparative Religion: An Anthropological Approach, ed. William A. Lessa and Evan Z. Vogt [New York: Harper & Row, 1965], 161, 166).

It should be noted that this is the first time, to the best of my recollection, I have joined together two central terms in my lexicon, "experiment" and "application." Let me take up each one separately. I have already cited the key text from "A Pearl of Great Price and a Cargo of Yams," 18–19; repr. in *Imagining Religion*, 100–101, at the conclusion of essay 2. Let me quote it here from its slightly earlier form in my inaugural lecture: "The Ceramese myth of Hainuwele or the Tangu tale of the Two Brothers does not solve the dilemma, overcome the incongruity or resolve the tension. Rather it provides the native with an occasion for thought. It is a testing of the adequacy and applicability of native categories to new situations and data. As such, it is preeminently a rational and rationalizing enterprise, an instance of an experimental method. The experiment was a failure. The white man was not brought into conformity with native categories, he still fails to recognize a moral claim of reciprocity. But this is not how we judge the success of a science. We judge harshly those who have abandoned the novel and the incongruous to a realm outside of the confines of understanding and we value those who (even though failing) stubbornly make the attempt at achieving intelligibility, who have chosen the long, hard road of understanding.... Myth is best conceived not as a primordium, but rather as a limited collection of elements with a fixed range of cultural meanings which are applied, thought with, worked with, experimented with in particular situations. ("Map Is Not Territory," 307–8)

In contrast to the way in which Sahlins sometimes presents his case, I want to insist on a critical perception available at the outset in a setting of "situational incongruity," which leads to a testing of the fit/no fit of established patterns of thought; and I want to insist that this is the everyday way in which people work with their myths, not one confined to moments of extraordinary tension.

In the last sentence of the passage just quoted, I wrote of "meanings which are applied"—but this does not begin to hint at the theoretical resonance of the term "application" in conjunction with myth. I noted above that in the late 1960s through the mid-1970s I often used Adolf Jensen as a stalking horse for Eliade on the issue of ontological replication (see n. 105 above). For Jensen, truth lay in a primordial moment of ontic "seizure," as I explain: "All subsequent 'formulations' and 'concretizations' are reinterpretations of this primal experience and are termed by Jensen, 'applications'—a pejorative word in his lexicon" (Smith, "Sacred Persistence," 16, 17; repr. in *Imagining Religion*, 42, cf. 42–43, citing Adolf E. Jensen, *Myth and Cult among Primitive Peoples* [Chicago: University of Chicago Press, 1963], 5–6, 66, 171, 174, 176, 194; see also, among other references, Smith, "Good News Is No News: Aretalogy and Gospel," in *Christianity, Judaism and Other Greco-Roman Cults: Studies for Morton Smith at Sixty*, ed. Jacob Neusner, 4 vols., SJLA 12 [Leiden: Brill, 1975], 1:37–38; repr. in *Map Is Not Territory*, 205–6; Smith., "Map Is Not Territory," 299, 303–4). "Seizure" was primary; "application," secondary. Ontology was primary; the anthropological, especially the linguistic, was a "depletion." Such a position was, for me at the time, the enemy of enemies leading, in its most extreme forms, to an antihuman anthropology of silence before The Sacred. (See the anecdote of Eliade in what I believe to be the last time I returned to Jensen, in Smith, "A Slip in Time Saves Nine: Prestigious Origins

It is Sahlins's understanding of the term "transformation" that causes me more difficulty, let alone all of its varied senses (catalogued in both essay 2, above, and the appendix, below). While recalling that thought is as much an activity as action, I still want a less instrumental (though no less interested) sense than Sahlins often allows. With some hesitation, I would propose the term "rectification."[120]

Again," in *Chronotypes: The Construction of Time*, ed. J. Bender and D. E. Wellbery [Stanford, CA: Stanford University Press, 1991], 233 n. 15; cf. 72–74 for my treatment of both Jensen and Eliade.) In an "in-your-face" stratagem, I adopted "application" as one of my most valued terms. (See Smith, "No Need to Travel to the Indies: Judaism and the Study of Religion," in *Take Judaism, for Example: Studies toward the Comparison of Religions*, ed. Jacob Neusner, CSHJ [Chicago: University of Chicago Press, 1983], 223–24, where, after summarizing Jensen, I insist that, "in culture, there is no text, it is all commentary; that there is no primordium, it is all history; that all is application" [224]. Parts of this essay served as a rough draft for the "Introduction" to *Imagining Religion*, xi–xiii.)

In my work, application carries a range of meanings from the testing of the appropriateness of a received category (as in the quotation from "Map Is Not Territory," 308), to a pressing of the appropriateness through "rationalizing" (307; cf. "rationalization, accommodation, and adjustment," in Smith, "Bare Facts of Ritual," 123; repr. in *Imagining Religion*, 62), casuistry ("there is an almost casuistic dimension ... which may be best described as 'application'" ["A Pearl of Great Price and a Cargo of Yams," 19; repr. in *Imagining Religion*, 101]), "exegetical ingenuity" ("Sacred Persistence," 14–18, 26; repr. in *Imagining Religion*, 39–44, 52—this latter is an element in a theory of culture which still retains prime importance for my work), or the "commonplace, commonsense resolutions in practice" discussed in Smith, "Re: Corinthians," 4. The paradigm case for "application" is the African diviner's basket ("Map Is Not Territory," 300; "Sacred Persistence," 25–27; repr. in *Imagining Religion*, 50–52), one of my central analogies to myth.

120. "Rectification" is used in two different contexts in my work. The first, and actually later, usage is the sense familiar to the seminar, that one of the aims of a "redescriptive" project is a rectification of scholarly categories. (I think I first used the term in this sense in *To Take Place*, 103.) This sense owes not a little to the Chinese philosophical project of the "rectification of the names" (Burton Watson, *Hsün Tzu: Basic Writings* [New York: Columbia University Press, 1963], 139–56; cf. *The Analects of Confucius*, 13.3, as well as to Burton L. Mack's "redescription" of my work at our first Consultation on Ancient Myths and Modern Theories of Christian Origins ("On Redescribing Christian Origins," *MTSR* 8 [1996]: 256–59; repr. in *The Christian Myth: Origins, Logic, and Legacy* [New York: Continuum, 2001], 70–74; cf. Smith, "The 'End' of Comparison," 239).

The earlier sense, "rectification" in relation to myth, is the one I appeal to here, particularly as developed in "A Pearl of Great Price and a Cargo of Yams" with respect to the "cargo situation." (The importance of rectification in this essay, to me, was signaled on several occasions, e.g., "Map Is Not Territory," 308 n. 21; "The Domestication of Sacrifice," 194 n. 7). The defining sentence is with respect to both the Babylonian

Appendix: Some Words about Words: "Conjuncture," "Reproduction,"
"Transformation

1. "Conjuncture"

Read "conjuncture," one thinks "conjunction"; read "conjunction," one thinks "and," that indeclinable little word, "empty" in itself, that links parts or elements of speech from which it most frequently gains significance by clarifying their relations.[121]

As a word conjuncture/conjunction seems odd—almost pleonastic. Whether in Latin or in English, it doubles the relation. Conjunct or con-join brings together (*con*) that which has already been joined (*iungere*). The prefix, con-, in this formation, does not seem to modify the relation as it does in ad-junct/ad-join, dis-junct/dis-join, in-junction/en-join, re-junction/re-join, subjunction/sub-join.[122]

Akitu ritual and the myth of Hainuwele, that in these two documents, confronting a "situation" through devices of "application," "this incongruity is surprising in light of past precedents; but that it may only be addressed, worked with, and perhaps even overcome in terms of these same precedents. I have suggested that both of these texts have in common the attempt at rectification" ("A Pearl of Great Price and a Cargo of Yams," 19; repr. in *Imagining Religion*, 101). It is the attempt to "correct" a situation, in thought if not in fact, in terms of traditional resources that, themselves, may well be modified in the process (8–9, 16–18; repr. in *Imagining Religion*, 94–95, 99–100).

Set in a different context, rectification is reinterpretation of tradition, in the sense that has motivated most of my studies in Mediterranean religions in late antiquity. To cite a 1976 statement, reiterated in 1988: "A central preoccupation of all my work has come to be the notion that, regardless of whether we are studying texts from literate or non-literate cultures, we are dealing with *historical processes of reinterpretation*, with *tradition*. That, for a given group at a given time to choose this or that way of interpreting their tradition is to opt for a particular way of relating themselves to their historical past and their social present" (*Map Is Not Territory*, xi, emphasis original; cf., *Drudgery Divine*, 106–7). It is, in the sense I've learned from Cassirer (but also from Marx and Heidegger), the "work" that culture does (see "Influence of Symbols upon Social Change," 472; repr. in *Map Is Not Territory*, 144; "Unknown God," 89; cf. ritual as "a quite ordinary mode of human social labor," in Smith, "The Domestication of Sacrifice," in *Violent Origins: Walter Burkert, René Girard, and Jonathan Z. Smith on Ritual Killing and Cultural Formation*, ed. Robert G. Hamerton-Kelly [Stanford, CA: Stanford University Press, 1987], 198).

121. See Tesnière, below.

122. Note that the English "conjuncture" is derived from the French *conjuncture* which in Old French [1164] has the earlier form, *conjointure*. See Algirdas Julien Grei-

Of the several meanings of "conjuncture" listed in the *OED*, the *Dictionary* gives as "the only current sense" the definition, "a meeting of circumstances or events; a particular state of affairs, esp. of a critical nature; a juncture, crisis."[123] From my perspective, what is important about the definition is the notion of "a meeting," in *The Century Dictionary and Cyclopedia*, the defining term is "an association," in *The American Heritage Dictionary* (4th ed.), "a combination," in Éliane de Wilde's and Philippe Roberts-Jones's *Le dictionnaire des peintres belges du XIVe siècle à nos jours* a "rencontre des circonstances"—none of these carry any necessary sense of causality.[124] As with arguments from concomitant variation, conjuncture may invite causal speculation, it neither requires nor establishes it. In my work, which employs the term, "situation," rather than "conjuncture," "nexus" is used in its older associative sense with the same strictures.

1.1. Braudel

> Events are like the foam on the surface of the great waves of conjuncture, underlying which are structures, which change almost imperceptibly at a much slower pace.
> —Georges Duby, *L'histoire continue*

In 1949, in his preface to the first edition of *The Mediterranean and the Mediterranean World in the Age of Philip II*, Fernand Braudel wrote, "the final effort then is to dissect history [*arrives a une decomposition de l'histoire*] into various planes, or, to put it another way, to divide historical time into geographical time, social time, and individual time." These three times are further characterized. Geographical time is "a history whose passage is almost imperceptible, that of man in relationship to his environment," it is an "almost timeless history," a history of "constant repetition, ever-

---

mas, *Dictionnaire de l'ancien français jusqu'au milieu du XIVe siècle*, 2nd ed. (Paris: Larousse, 1968), s.v. "conjoindre."

123. *OED*, s.v. "conjuncture."

124. See *The Century Dictionary and Cyclopedia: The Century Dictionary Prepared under the Superintendence of William Dwight Whitney; Revised and Enlarged under the Superintendence of Benjamin E. Smith* (New York: Arkose, 2015); *The American Heritage Dictionary of the English Language*, 4th ed. (Boston: Houghton Mifflin, 2006); Éliane de Wilde and Philippe Roberts-Jones, ed., *Le dictionnaire des peintres belges du XIVe siècle à nos jours* (Brussels: La Renaissance du Livre, 1995). Cited by Sahlins, *Islands of History*, 125 n. ll.

recurring cycles." The second time, "the time of social history," "the history of groups and groupings," is a time with "slow but perceptible rhythms." The third time, is that of a "history of events" [*l'histoire événementielle*] "a scale not of man but of men," events which are "surface disturbances, crests of foam that the tides of history carry on their strong backs," a history of "brief, rapid, nervous fluctuations."[125] In subsequent writings, this rather impressionistic division became a full-blown typology.

Although there were earlier formulations, the best known, and most widely cited, is Braudel's classic 1958 article, "History and the Social Sciences, The *Longue duree*."[126] Here, the first sort of time is labeled a "history to be measured in centuries, even of the very long time span, of the *longue durée*," while the second form of time is now termed a history of "conjunctures," of "cyclical" movements which lay "open large sections of the past, ten, twenty, fifty years at a stretch." The third form of time remains that of "the individual and the event."[127] In Braudel's account, the notion of the "conjuncture" largely derives from economic historians, who work with "a new kind of historical narrative ... of the conjuncture, of the cycle, and even of the 'intercycle' covering a decade, a quarter of a century and, at the outside, the half-century of Kondratiev's classic cycle."[128]

In Braudel's article, "structure" is clearly aligned not with conjuncture but with the *longue durée*; "structures" can be "stable elements for an infinite number of generations."[129] This is made most explicit in an earlier article on economic history, here, "*histoire structurale* ("structural history") [is] less in opposition to the history of events (*événementielle*) than to the history of

125. Fernand Braudel, "Preface to the First Edition," in *The Mediterranean and The Mediterranean World in the Age of Philip II*, trans. Siân Reynolds, 2nd ed. (New York: Harper & Row, 1972), 1:20–21.

126. Braudel, "History and the Social Sciences, The *Longue Duree*," in *On History*, trans. S. Matthews (Chicago: University of Chicago Press, 1980), 25–54; trans. of "Histoire et sciences sociales: La longue durée," *Annales, Economies, Sociétés, Civilisations* 13 (1958): 725–53.

127. Ibid., 27.

128. Ibid., 29; cf. Braudel, *The Perspective of the World*, vol. 3 of *Civilization & Capitalism 15th–18th Century*, trans. Siân Reynolds (New York: Harper & Row, 1984), 71–73, 82–85. (It is not irrelevant to note that the French title of this volume is *Le Temps du Monde* [Paris: A. Colin, 1979]). Note should be taken of the important critical study of Braudel's prime example, Gaston Imbert, *Des Mouvements de lonque durée Kondratieff* [Aix-en-Provence: La Pensée université, 1959].

129. Braudel, "History and the Social Sciences," 31.

conjunctures."[130] This sort of language is incorporated in the second (1966) edition of Braudel's *The Mediterranean*, where structure is the "permanent," the "slow-moving"; conjuncture is the "ephemeral," the "fast."[131]

1.2. Althusser

> There will always be Althusserians of the conjuncture and Althusserians of the structure.
> —Étienne Balibar, "L'objet d'Althusser"

> This brings up the problem of the conjuncture, of the always specific conditions that make a change of structure possible.
> —Maurice Godelier, *Rationalité et irrationalité en économie*

There is a sense, of course, in which Jeremy Hawthorne's witty observation is correct within certain circles: "Conjuncture seems to have risen and fallen in concord with the changing authority of Louis Althusser."[132] Surely it is a long-standing, much-used term in Althusser's lexicon, sometimes descending almost into self-parody as when he deploys it five times in the space of a brief 1967 passage of fifty words:

> As the Introduction shows, this conjuncture is, first, the theoretical and ideological conjuncture in France, more particularly the present conjuncture in the French Communist Party and in French philosophy. But as well as this peculiarly French conjuncture, it is also the present ideological and theoretical conjuncture in the inter-national Communist movement.[133]

---

130. Braudel, "Toward a Historical Economics," in *On History*, 87; cf. Braudel, "History and Sociology," in *On History*, 74, "over and above the '*recitatif*' of the conjuncture, structural history, or the history of the *longue durée*, inquires into whole centuries at a time; "the *longue durée* is the endless, inexhaustible history of structures and groups of structures" (75); or, again, in a review (1963), "I even suspect that Pierre Chaunu consciously preferred the conjunctural narrative, closer as it is to history as it is lived, and easier to grasp ... than structural history, which can be observed only in the abstraction of the *longue durée*" (*On History*, 93).

131. Braudel, *Mediterranean and the Mediterranean World*, 1:353; cf. 2:1244, "I am by temperment a 'structuralist,' little tempted by the event, or even by the short-term conjuncture which is after all merely a grouping of events in the same area."

132. Jeremy Hawthorne, "Conjuncture," in *A Concise Glossary of Contemporary Literary Theory*, 2nd ed. (London: Edward Arnold, 1994), 124.

133. Louis Althusser, "To My English Readers," in Althusser, *For Marx*, trans.

Used this way, as Althusser suggests,[134] "conjuncture" goes back to a Leninist notion, expressed with an apparent variety of terms (I do not read Russian): "combination," "situation," "merger," "conjuncture," "transition," "interlacing"—most particularly by Lenin as he addressed, from Switzerland in March, 1917, the "first stage of this first revolution, namely, of the Russian revolution of March 1, 1917."[135]

> There are no miracles in nature or history, but every abrupt turn in history, and this applies to every revolution, unfolds such unexpected and specific combinations of forms of struggle and alignment of forces of the contestants, that to the lay mind there is much that must appear miraculous.[136]

> That the revolution succeeded so quickly and—seemingly, at the first superficial glance—*so* radically, is only due to the fact that, as a result of an extremely unique historical situation, *absolutely dissimilar currents*, *absolutely heterogeneous* class interests, *absolutely contrary* political and social strivings have merged, and in a strikingly 'harmonious' fashion.[137]

> The conflict of these three forces determines the situation that has now arisen, a situation that is *transitional* from the first stage of the revolution to the second. The antagonism between the first and second force is not profound, the result *solely* of the present conjuncture of circumstances, of the abrupt turn of events in the imperialist war.[138]

> We shall explain the peculiarity of the present situation which is a transition.... The proletariat, using the *peculiarities* of the present transition situation, can and will proceed.[139]

Ben Brewster (London: Allen Lane, 1969); repr. New York: Vintage Books, 1970; repr. London: NLB, 1977; repr., London: Verso, 1979], 9–10 (pagination identical in each printing). This text is, obviously lacking in the French original, *Pour Marx*, Théorie 1 (Paris: F. Maspero, 1965). For a more generalized frequent usage, see Althusser's 1966 essay, "Conjoncture philosophique et récherche philosophique marxiste," in *Écrits philosophiques et politiques*, ed. F. Matheron (Paris: Stock: IMEC, 1994–1995], 2:394–415.

134. Althusser, *For Marx*, 177 n. 13.

135. Vladimir Il'ich Lenin, "Letters from Afar: First Letter; The First Stage of the First Revolution," in vol. 2 of *Selected Works*, 2nd rev. ed. [Moscow: Progress, 1967], 1–10.

136. Ibid., 1.

137. Ibid., 5.

138. Ibid., 7–8.

139. Ibid., 9–10. Compare the stronger formulations written a month later [April, 1917] after Lenin's arrival in Petrograd; not cited by Althusser: "The Bolshevik slogans

In such passages, "conjuncture" bears a primarily intracultural connotation. As Althusser states, Lenin "was not acting on Imperialism in general, he was acting on the concrete of the Russian situation, of the Russian conjuncture."[140] Later, "This is what is irreplaceable in Lenin's texts: the analysis of a structure of a *conjuncture* ... which political action was able to transform ... between February and October, 1917."[141]

To summarize, Althusser's conclusions on conjuncture, as represented in the 1962–1963 essays, are reprinted in *For Marx*. As Althusser reads Lenin in the passages quoted above, the issue of 1917 stands in tension with Marx's understanding of "contradiction," in classic formulations such as that in the preface to the 1859 *Critique of Political Economy*. In Russia, at the time of the Revolution, the "contradiction" (or "conflict") between the forces of material production and the system of social relations (more strictly, "the relations of production" [Produktionsverhältnisse]) represented in class antagonisms was insufficient to produce a revolution.[142] In Althusser's analysis of Lenin's analysis, this fundamental antagonism must "fuse" with other systemic contradictions, the fusion taking on its own character. This fusion, this conjuncture, as a totality determines, even as it is determined by the various levels of the "social formation." For this reason, borrowing a term from Freud, it is "overdetermined." For Althusser, this model, first applied by Lenin in a revolutionary situation, can be generalized. Any society, as a totality and in its various levels, is "governed" by the states of relations in and between these levels which develop, at varying

----

and ideas in general have been fully corroborated by history; but *concretely,* things have shaped *differently* from what could have been anticipated (by anyone): they are more original, more peculiar, more variegated.... It has *already* turned out differently; an extremely original, novel, and unprecedented interlacing ... has already taken place" (Vladimir Il'ich Lenin, "Letters on Tactics," in *The April Theses* [Moscow: Foreign Languages Publishing House, 1951], 20, 22, all emphases in the original).

140. Althusser, *For Marx*, 178.

141. Ibid., 179; note this early occurrence of the phrase, "structure of a conjuncture."

142. "No social order is ever destroyed before all the productive forces for which it is sufficient have been developed, and new superior relations of production never replace older ones before the material conditions for their existence have matured within the framework of the old society" (Karl Marx, *A Contribution to the Critique of Political Economy*, ed. M. Dobb, trans. S. W. Ryanzanskaya [Moscow: Progress Publishers, 1970] 20–21).

rates, "semi-autonomously" in terms of their own internal mechanisms, as well as being affected, to varying degrees, by each other.[143]

Second, what Althusser and Lenin have in common in these analyses is their orientation to seizing the "current moment," the "present situation," for action. The most generalized use of conjuncture in Althusser denotes the union of theory and practice in such a situation.[144]

"Conjuncture" is not the only term Althusser uses to characterize this "situation." With reference to the same pages in Lenin's "Letters from Afar," Althusser uses a more active (and revolutionary) term. He speaks of an "accumulation of contradictions" which lead to a "revolutionary rupture," a "ruptural principle," a "vast accumulation of contradictions comes to play *in the same court,* some of which are radically heterogeneous—of different origins, different sense, different *levels* and *points* of application—but which nevertheless merge into a ruptural unity."[145] Elsewhere, Althusser employs the more generalized term, "encounter."[146]

---

143. This is a summary of the relevant aspects in Althusser, "Contradiction and Overdetermination," (1962) in *For Marx*, 87–116, and "On the Marxist Dialectic" (1963) in *For Marx*, 161–218. Compare Althusser's own summary formulation of these two articles in Althusser and Balibar, *Reading Capital*, 97. For the historiographical implications, see below.

144. This is one of the grand themes of Althusser's 1972 lecture, revised throughout the 1980's, "Machiavel et nous," in Althusser, *Écrits philosophiques et politiques*, 2:42–161; now available in English translation, *Machiavelli and Us*, ed. F. Matheron, trans. with an introduction by Gregory Elliot (London: Verso, 1999); see especially the formulations on pp. 17–19, 28, 45, 66; cf. the appended 1977 lecture, "Machiavelli's Solitude," 127.

145. Althusser, *For Marx*, 99–101. The term *coupure/rupture* was developed from its usage in Gaston Bachelard's work on the history of scientific thought by Althusser's student, Pierre Macherey with respect to Marx. See Macherey, "À propos de la rupture," *La Nouvelle Critique* (1965): 136–40; Macherey, "A propos du processus d'exposition du 'Capital': Le travail des concepts," in *Lire le Capital*, by Louis Althusser, Jacques Rancière, and Pierre Macherey 2 vols., Théorie 2–3 (Paris: Maspero, 1965), 213–56; I cite *Lire le Capital*, É. Balibar et P. Bravo Gala, eds., 3rd ed., Quadrige 186 (Paris: PUF, 1996), 201–44, esp. pp. 220, 230, 244. Note that the English translation, Louis Althusser and Étienne Balibar, *Reading Capital*, omits the essays by Roger Establet, Pierre Macherey, and Jacques Ranciere. For Althusser's acknowledgement of Macherey, see *Reading Capital*, 30 n. ll; 46 n. 24; 50. See also Althusser's "Letter to the Translator," in *Reading Capital*, 323–24, and "break, epistemological" in the glossary of *Reading Capital*, 309–10.

146. See, among others, *Machiavelli and Us*, 15, 74–80. See further, below.

But already, there is a certain complexity. A "historical situation" characterized by a concatenation of forces (a "combination," "alignment," "merger," "conjunction") that was unexpected ("miraculous," "extremely unique," "peculiarity"), almost as if by chance ("the result solely of the present conjuncture of circumstances," "of the abrupt turn of events"—see the final point on Althusser, below), all the more surprising in that these forces are oppositional ("absolutely dissimilar," "absolutely heterogeneous," "absolutely contrary"). The Leninist "present conjuncture" is in disequilibrium, it is a "transition."[147] This introduces a set of historiographical problems.

"Conventional" Marxist analysis (especially as practiced during the Stalinist period) would argue for a direct relation of base/superstructure, and appeal to a teleological notion of "necessary contradictions." For example, treating exactly the same phenomena as Lenin in his "Letters from Afar" and "Letters on Tactics," Stalin, in the "Foundations of Leninism" (April, 1924), restates Lenin. After describing three "contradictions inherent" in imperialism, Stalin writes:

> The historical significance of the great war, the imperialist war, was (among other things) that it concentrated these conflicts and brought them simultaneously into play, thus facilitating and accelerating the revolutionary battles of the proletariat. In other words, the growth of imperialism not only made the revolution a practical necessity, it has also created conditions favourable to an immediate onslaught on the strongholds of capitalism.[148]

---

147. Compare Balibar's "Elements for a Theory of Transition," in *Reading Capital*, 273–309, which treats and deploys all of the key terms in Sahlins's, *Historical Metaphors and Mythical Realities*, i.e., "reproduction," "transformation," "conjuncture," and "structure."

148. Joseph Stalin, *Foundations of Leninism: Lectures Delivered at the Sverdlow University in the Beginning of April 1924; A New Translation* (London: Lawrence & Wishart, 1924), 82; cf., Stalin, *The Road to Power* (New York: International Publishers, 1939), 9–10 (August, 1917), 28–29 (September, 1917); Stalin, *On Lenin* (Moscow: Foreign Languages Publishing House, 1950), 55–56 (September, 1927). See also the notorious textbook, Stalin and the Commission of Central Committee of the C.P.S.U., eds. (but generally attributed to Stalin), *History of the Communist Party of the Soviet Union, Bolsheviks: Short Course* (New York: International Publishers, 1939), 180–87, which quotes from Lenin's "Letters from Afar" and "Letters on Tactics," but ignores his analysis. History presents the theoretical basis of the Stalinist understanding of dialectical and historical materialism (102–31); this section is, in fact, a revised form

Given this "conventional" understanding of Marxism, the lineaments of Althusser's revisionary project are plain. Focusing only on those elements central to understanding "conjuncture" and translating them into historiographical terms, if, with Althusser, a "social formation" is understood as a complex whole consisting of "semi-autonomous" practices, then these practices will have differential developments. Conjuncture is when these different times coincide, being, thus, "overdetermined."

When this sort of analysis is explicitly applied to historiographic issues, it leads, among other consequences, to Althusser's criticism of Braudel, that while Braudel, and other *Annales* historians

> *observe that there are* different times in history, varieties of time, long times, medium times and short times, and … are content to note their interferences as so many products of their intersection; they do not … relate these varieties as so many *variations* to the structure of the whole although the latter directly governs the production of these variations; rather, they are tempted to relate these varieties, as so many variants measurable by their duration, to ordinary time itself.[149]

Finally, note a more general thesis concerning conjuncture, which is entirely Althusser's. (It has little direct relevance to the seminar's interest in Sahlins). On the basis of the published materials, it remains difficult to interpret.

In 1966, in previously unpublished fragment, Althusser writes, in a cryptic formulation, of a doubleness—chance/structure:

> 1. Theory of the encounter or conjunction (= genesis…) (cf. Epicurus, clinamen, Cournot), chance, etc., pre-cipitation, coagulation. 2. Theory of the *conjuncture* (= structure) … philosophy as general theory of the *conjuncture* (= conjunction).[150]

---

of the theory section in *Stalin, Anarchism or Socialism?* (Moscow: Foreign Languages Publishing House, 1950).

149. Althusser and Balibar, *Reading Capital*, 96, emphasis original. For the purpose of the seminar, further analysis of the historiographic sections in *Reading Capital* is not required (Althusser, 92–144; Balibar, 199–308), nor is there any new development of the concept of conjuncture. In *Reading Capital*, conjuncture is employed frequently as a general term for a fusion of "practices" that leads to a transformation/ revolution/reversal; see, e.g., 45, 115 n. 11, 141, 185, even allowing the formulation, "personal conjuncture," 50.

150. Passage quoted by François Matheron, "Presentation," in Althusser, *Écrits*

While it is dangerous to interpret such a fragment, there is a set of resonant words.[151] Taken together, they seem to forecast an important theme developed in the 1980's in works such as "The Subterranean Current of the Materialism of the Encounter" (drafted in 1982), which announces, in its notorious opening, that:

> My essential thesis (is) the *existence of a materialist tradition almost completely unrecognized* in the history of philosophy ... *a materialism of the encounter*, hence of the aleatory and of contingency, which is opposed ... to the various registered materialisms, including the materialism commonly attributed to Marx, Engels, and Lenin, which, like every materialism in the rationalist tradition, is a materialism of necessity and teleology.[152]

1.3. Tesnière

In my unpublished work on language-like ritual systems, I have been more influenced by a different perspective on conjunction, one that is less historicistic, more structural and linguistic—the "dependency grammar" associated with Lucien Tesnière.[153] As these interests are remote from those of

philosophiques et politiques (Paris: Le Livre de Poche, 1990), 1:21; Matheron, introduction to *Écrits Philosophiques et politiques*; Louis Althusser, *The Spectre of Hegel: Early Writings* (London: Blackwell, 1997; London: Verso, 1997), 10. Matheron goes on immediately to cite a similar phrase among Althusser's manuscript notes on Pierre Macherey, *A Theory of Literary Production*, trans. Geoffrey Wall (London: Routledge & Kegan Paul, 1978): "Theory of the clinamen. First theory of the encounter!"

151. For example, the clinamen as the chance "swerve" taken by atoms in Epicurus's revision of Democritus [Lucretius, *Rerum nat.* 2.21–293]; Antoine Augustin Cournot [1801–1877] who gave to chance an equal role to that of necessity in both physical and human events (Antoine Augustin Cournot, *Exposition de la théorie des chances et des probabilités* [Paris: L. Hachette, 1843]; cf. Jean de la Harpe, *De l'ordre et du hasard: Le réalisme critique d'Antoine Augustin Cournot*, Mémoires de l'Université de Neuchâtel 9 [Neuchâtel: Université de Neuchâtel, 1936]).

152. Louis Althusser, "Le courant souterrain du matérialisme de la rencontre," in Althusser, *Ecrits philosophiques et politiques*, 1:539–40.

153. Lucien Tesnière, *Esquisse d'une syntaxe structurale* (Paris: C. Klincksieck, 1953); Tesnière, *Éléments de syntaxe structurale* (Paris: C. Klincksieck, 1959). See further, Helmut Schumacher and Norbert Trautz, "Bibliographie zur Valenz und Dependenz," in *Untersuchungen zur Verbvalenz: Eine Dokumentation über die Arbeit an einem deutschen Valenzlexikon*, ed. Helmut Schumacher (Tübingen: Narr, 1976), 317–43.

the seminar, let me briefly define his terminology. In a significant alteration of the assumptions associated with the French Port-Royal grammarian tradition, Tesnière proposes that syntactic relations are paradigmatic relations of "dependency" where one element "governs" the others in a hierarchy (objectified in a tree-diagram) regardless of syntagmatic order (subject/predicate), which formed the basis for the Port-Royal investigations. "Connection" is the representation of these hierarchical, logical relations. Connection is made usefully more complex by two further relations, "junction" and "translation." A junction is where syntactic elements that serve the same syntactic function are joined by "empty words" (such as the conjunctions, "and," "or"), which have a strictly syntactic rather than a semantic function; while translation (often a preposition) alters the syntactic function.[154]

1.4. Conclusions: "Conjuncture"

(1) Despite Sahlins's appeal to "the celebrated 'structures of the *longue durée*,'"[155] his own usage directly challenges Braudel. Sahlins conjoins "structure" and "conjuncture," Braudel has these terms in opposition. Measured from the standpoint of duration (recall Althusser's critique of Braudel at just this point[156]), while both conjuncture and the *longue durée* are opposed to the "event," conjuncture is relatively short-term, as opposed to the long-term. Sahlins clarifies both the difference to Braudel as well as his notion of "structure" when linked to conjuncture in an important note to his 1982 Frazer Lecture, "Captain James Cook; or, the Dying God,"[157] although, counter to what Sahlins appears to suggest, in the second sentence, *I* have not found the phrase, "the structure of the conjuncture" in Braudel, nor do I think he could have written it as it would contain,

---

154. I should note, though I find it less fruitful, that A. J. Greimas has been much influenced by Tesnière, although he radically reformulates Tesnière's system in terms of both syntagmatics and semantics. See, for example, A. J. Greimas and Joseph Courtés, *Semiotics and Language: An Analytical Dictionary*, trans. L. Crist et al., Advances in Semiotics (Bloomington: Indiana University Press, 1982), s.v. "conjunction" and s.v. "junction."

155. See Sahlins, *Historical Metaphors and Mythic Realities*, 8. The French quotation is from Braudel, "Histoire et sciences sociales."

156. Althusser, *Reading Capital*, 96.

157. Sahlins, *Islands of History*, 125 n. 11.

from his perspective, a contradiction. Sahlins writes, in response to some reviews of Sahlins, *Historical Metaphors and Mythical Realities* that:

> I have not used the notion of a conjunctural structure in the Braudelian sense.… Braudel's "structure of the conjuncture" refers to relations of some intermediate duration—as opposed to the *longue durée* on the one hand and the event on the other—such as capitalist economic cycles. My own use is more literal (*conjoncture*, "*Situation qui résulte d'une recontre de circonstances*" [Robert]), and while definitely *événmentielle* allows more than Braudel does for the structuration of the situation, a "structure of the conjuncture" in this sense is a situational set of relations, crystallized from the operative cultural categories and the actors' interests.… Like Giddens (1976) notion of social action, it is subject to the double structural determination of intentions grounded in a cultural scheme and the unintended consequences arising from recuperation in other projects and schemes.[158]

I take up both Sahlins definitions of the "structure of the conjuncture" in Sahlins, "Captain James Cook: Or, the Dying God" (which clarifies the usage in Sahlins, *Historical Metaphors and Mythic Realities*).[159]

(2) Althusser is a more difficult case. Sahlins never explicitly relates his use of "conjuncture" to Althusser's, even though Althusser occasionally uses the formulation associated with Sahlins: "structure(s) of a/the conjuncture." More suggestively, Sahlins uses an Althusserian-style vocabulary when writing of the intracultural effects of change on structure. (It may be significant that such vocabulary does not occur in Sahlins's analyses of intercultural encounter.) For example, in the course of the Fijian case cited above (part 1), Sahlins observes that the fact that the "established" system "survives a variety of historical attacks only means that it has not yet met the decisive one—the one that over-determines its own contradictions to release the future already prefigured."[160] Where they differ is that in Althusser's most historicistic formulations, the "contradictions" are the result of the uneven development of semi-autonomous systems, whereas

---

158. Ibid.

159. See Sahlins, "Captain James Cook: Or The Dying God," in *Islands of History*, 104–35; Sahlins, *Historical Metaphors and Mythic Realities*. See also Sahlins, *Cultural in Practice: Selected Essays* (New York: Zone Books, 2000), 295, 300–1) in part 1 above and his focus on agency in part 2 above.

160. Sahlins, *Culture and Practical Reason*, 43.

in Sahlins "contradiction" is, most fundamentally, within the logic of the system itself: "Complimentary yet unequal, symmetrical but asymmetrical, Fijian dualism contains an endemic contradiction, a conflict … of reciprocity and hierarchy."[161] This structural contradiction is exacerbated by contingency, resulting, in the Fijian example, in a disjunction between the structured system and demographic fact. This disjunction may be absorbed into the system (reproduction) or result in transformation or radical change. "The general point *is* that where there is … structural contradiction there is also historical direction."[162]

Given my contrast between Althusser's and Sahlins's use of "contradiction," I should note the one instance I can recall in Sahlins where this distinction seems to have been relaxed, in his important two-part essay on "The Domestic Mode of Production":[163]

> The three elements of the DMP [the Domestic Mode of Production] … are systematically interrelated. Not only is each in reciprocal bond with the others, but each by its own modesty of scale is adapted to the nature of the others. Let any one of these elements show an unusual inclination to develop, it meets from the others the increasing resistance of an incompatability. The normal systemic resolution of this tension is restoration of the status quo ("negative feedback"). Only in the event of an historic conjuncture of additional and external contradictions ("overdetermination") would the crisis pass over into destruction and transformation![164]

While this seems to be related to Sahlins's general Marxist perspective on contradiction (see the paragraph immediately above), the vocabulary here is sufficiently distinctive to suggest a direct influence from Althusser.[165]

(3) While perhaps influenced by Althusser, Sahlins's use of the "structure of the conjuncture" must be taken as his own coinage. While the point is developed more fully in essay 2 above, I would only wish for a more

---

161. Ibid., 43.

162. Ibid., 45.

163. Sahlins, "The Domestic Mode of Production," in *Stone Age Economics* (Chicago: Aldine-Atherton, 1972), 41–148.

164. Ibid., 87.

165. Althusser's *Pour Marx* [*For Marx*] as well as Althusser and Balibar *Lire le Capital* [*Reading Capital*] are cited in the general bibliography to Sahlins, *Stone Age Economics*. *Lire le Capital* is referenced (76 n. 26) or quoted (126 n. 11, 135 n. 18) in the two parts of the essay but not with reference to conjuncture.

transitive formulation, something like "structuring a conjuncture" or the "structuration of a conjuncture."[166] I take this to be a friendly amendment.

2. "Reproduction"

> This reproduction is at the same time necessarily new production and the destruction of the old form.
> —Karl Marx, *Grundrisse: Foundations of the Critique of Political Economy*

> No system exists or can reproduce itself than within definite limits, by way of transformations that are compatible with the unintentional properties of its inner structures.
> —Godelier, *Rationalité et irrationalité en economie*

"Reproduction" has both a set of common meanings and specialized usages in a variety of disciplines and intellectual traditions. The semantic field we are concerned with may be limited to Marxist discourse.

(1) "Reproduction" is a dominant term (linked with "production") in Marxist discourse. From chapter twenty-five, "Simple Reproduction," in the seventh part of the first volume of *Capital*, with its pregnant formulation, "every social process of production is, at the same time, a process of reproduction,"[167] through the complex third part of the second volume, "The Reproduction and Circulation of the Aggregate Social Capital,"[168] reproduction is one of *Capital*'s central themes. Here, reproduction represents the possibility of continued production achieved through exploitative mechanisms such as the reinvestment of accumulated surplus.

(2) In the third volume of *Capital*, building on the *Grundrisse* and the preface to *A Contribution to the Critique of Political Economy*,[169] Marx expands "reproduction" to include parallel structures necessary to, but

---

166. Cf. Sahlins, "Captain James Cook: Or the Dying God," 125 n. 11: "structuration of the situation."

167. Karl Marx, *Capital: A Critique of Political Economy*, ed. Friedrich Engels, trans. Samuel Moore and Edward Aveling, revised and amplified by E. Untermann (New York: Modern Library, 1906), 1:620.

168. Marx, *Capital*, 2:351–523.

169. Karl Marx, *Grundrisse der Kritik der Politischen Ökonomie* (Berlin: Dietz, 1953); Marx, *A Contribution to the Critique of Political Economy*, ed. M. Dobb; trans. S. W. Ryanzanskaya (Moscow: Progress, 1970).

different from, those of production at the level of "superstructure." This understanding of reproduction is developed by Étienne Balibar.[170] Taken from the economic to the political sphere, "reproduction" is an equally central term in some of Althusser's best known work, especially his 1970 essay, "Ideology and Ideological State Apparatuses: Notes Toward an Investigation."[171] Unlike "conjuncture," this is a road that need not be traveled.

(3) There is a second general Marxist use of the term "reproduction" occurring chiefly in the section from the *Grundrisse* entitled, "Formen die der Kapitalistischen Produktion vorhergehen,"[172] which was enormously influential on Marxist anthropologists, including Sahlins. Here, reproduction is used in almost a contrary manner to sense (1) above, insofar as both simple extended reproduction is associated with surplus value. Without employing the term, the fundamental definition and contrast is given as referring to tribal societies: "The purpose of this labour is not the creation of value ... its purpose is the maintenance of the owner and his family as well as of the communal body as a whole."[173] Even in early settlements, relations of humans to the earth "is naive; they regard themselves as its communal proprietors, and as those of the community which produces and reproduces itself by living labour."[174] Taken this way, "reproduction" shades over into a procreative and demographic function.[175] This demographic sense of "reproduction" has been much enlarged by contemporary Marxist anthropologists working on tribal society, most famously by Claude Meillassoux's analysis of cereal horticulture in pre-colonial Africa.[176]

---

170. See his contribution in Althusser and Balibar, *Reading Capital*, 254–72 and passim.

171. See Louis Althusser, "Ideology and Ideological State Apparatuses: Notes Toward an Investigation," in *Lenin and Philosophy and Other Essays* (New York: NLB, 1971), 127–86.

172. See Marx, "Formen die der Kapitalistischen Produktion vorhergehen," in *Grundrisse der Kritik der Politischen Ökonomie*, 375–413. This section was translated into English before the entire work. It was introduced by the distinguished British Marxist historian, E. J. Hobsbawm. See Karl Marx, *Pre-capitalist Economic Formations*, ed. E. J. Hobsbawm, trans. J. Cohen (New York: International Publishers, 1965).

173. Marx, *Pre-capitalist Economic Formations*, 68.

174. Ibid., 69.

175. See, e.g., ibid., 82–83.

176. See Claude Meillassoux, *Maidens, Meal and Money: Capitalism and the Domestic Economy* (Cambridge: Cambridge University Press, 1981).

Meillassoux is critical of Sahlins ("The Domestic Mode of Production,"
parts 1–2 in *Stone Age Economics*) for its lack of historical concreteness.[177]
Meillassoux argues that the social structure of the agriculturalists is built
upon "the relations of production insofar as these emerge from the economic constraints imposed by agricultural activity—undertaken under
conditions defined by the level of productive powers—and upon relations
of reproduction necessary to perpetuate the productive cell." This requires
a "control of women" more primary than "authority gained through the
material management of subsistence."[178]

(4) For Sahlins, as well as for other anthropologists influenced by
Marx, there is a narrower sense to the term, associated with Marx's writings on pre-capitalist social and economic formations, which may, but
need not necessarily, entail Marx's controversial formulation of the "Asiatic mode of production." This is, to borrow the useful formulations of
Levine and Wright, a formation "in which no mechanisms exist for translating an incompatability between forces and relations of production into
a contradiction.... A contradiction implies that a stable reproduction of a
structure is impossible, that there are endogenously generated imperatives
for change." In the absence of such imperatives, there is "permanent stagnation," a replicating reproduction.[179]

For anthropologists, it is the formations related to "village community," or "community system" that carry the most interest. Marx signals his
interest in the exceptional quality of the social formation represented by
the village structure of the Indian community early on in the first chapter
of *Capital*. The "division of labour is a necessary condition for the production of commodities, but it does not follow conversely, that the production
of commodities is a necessary condition for the division of labour. In the

177. Ibid., 38.
178. Ibid., 45. See further Meillassoux, "From Reproduction to Production:
A Marxist Approach to Economic Anthropology," *Economy and Society* 1 (1972):
93–105. Other Marxist anthropologists (as well as feminist theoreticians) have subjected Meillassoux to sharp criticism. See the remarks and bibliography in Donald L.
Donham, *History, Power, Ideology: Central Issues in Marxism and Anthropology*, rev.
ed. (Berkeley: University of California Press, 1999), 77–83.
179. Andrew Levine and Erik Olin Wright, "Rationality and Class Struggle," in
Marxist Theory, ed. Alex Callinicos, Oxford Readings in Politics and Government
(Oxford: Oxford University Press, 1989), 17–41, esp. 40; see further, Anne M. Bailey
and Josep R. Llobera, "The Asiatic Mode of Production, An Annotated Bibliography,"
Critique of Anthropology 2 (1974): 95–107; 4–5 (1975): 165–76.

primitive Indian community there is a social division of labour, without production of commodities."[180] However, the classic locus is in the section on division of labor in the first volume of *Capital*, where Marx writes of "those earlier forms of society in which the separation of trades has been spontaneously developed, then crystallized, and finally made permanent by law."[181] Marx gives as his prime example, "those small and extremely ancient Indian communities, some of which have continued down to this day" which "are based on the possession in common of the land, on the blending of agriculture and handicrafts, and on an unalterable division of labour, which serves, when ever a new community is started, as a plan and a scheme ready cut and dried."[182] This picture of an ancestral template gives rise to the anthropological sense of "reproduction" as Marx concludes his description:

> The simplicity of the organization for production in these self-sufficing communities that constantly reproduce themselves in the same form, and when accidentally destroyed, spring up again on the spot and with the same name—this simplicity supplies the key to the secret of the unchangeableness of Asiatic societies, an unchangeableness in such striking contrast with the constant dissolution and refounding of Asiatic States, and the never-ceasing changes of dynasty. The structure of the economic elements of society remains untouched by the storm-clouds of the political sky.[183]

---

180. Marx, *Capital*, 1:49.

181. Ibid., 1:392.

182. Ibid.

183. Ibid., 1:393–94; cf. ibid., 3:773–74, where, describing an analogous situation of "primitive or undeveloped" societies, Marx describes them as being in a state of "constant reproduction," which achieves stability "by mere repetition of their very reproduction." This passage is not only quoted by Sahlins (*Culture and Practical Reason*, 48) but also by Lévi-Strauss (*Structural Anthropology*, 1:336), who, after all, wrote his master's thesis on *Les postulats philosophiques du matérialisms historique*.

See further Marx's remarks on the Indian "village system" in the 1853 *New York Daily Tribune* columns (Karl Marx and Friedrich Engels, *Collected Works*, trans. Richard Dixon, 50 vols. (New York: International Publishers, 1975–2004), 12:127–32: "these small stereotyped forms of social organization" (12:131); and "a society whose framework was built on a sort of equilibrium" (12:18). See also Marx's *Letter to Engels* (June 14, 1853), which writes of Indian villages "each of which possessed a completely separate organization and formed a little world in itself.... [For the English] the breaking up of these stereotyped forms was the sine qua non for Europeanization" (in Karl

Marx's continuing interest in the "Indian community" is indicated by his lengthy extracts, made late in his life, from John B. Phear.[184] Ironically, Phear's method may, itself, be described as a mode of "stereotypic reproduction." Krader writes: "Phear's work is a detailed although generalized account of village life in what is today Bangla Desh, the region with which he was most familiar. His method was to describe a 'type specimen' of a village which existed nowhere but whose conditions of life were presumed to be reproduced in many parts of the region at that time."[185]

There are several thorny issues in which the "Indian community" becomes directly or indirectly implicated which are fortunately remote from the interests of the seminar, and thus need to be, here, simply listed. (1) The question of the "Asiatic mode of production" has been alluded to/ above. (2) The question as to whether Marx and Engels differed in the general historiography, and, more particularly, on issues attendant to the question of "primitive communism." (3) Most central for a Marxist anthropology (and rising chiefly from Engels), the question as to how kinship systems in "primitive" societies be understood. While the relations entailed in the reproduction of human beings are clearly material, is a kinship system a "mode of material production," or is it a "superstructural," "ideological phenomenon"? The fact that, in the case of kinship systems, the answer appears to be both raises problems for the usual construction of the relations of base to superstructure. Take for example the following criticism of Maurice Godelier in a 1975 study of a Tamil Indian village by the Swedish Marxist anthropologists, Gören Djurfeldt and Staffan Lindberg: "We have been unable to follow Godelier when he interprets infrastructure as a functional distinction. This allows him to say that in primitive societies kinship functions as infrastructure.... If this is to mean that 'kinship is thus here both infrastructure and superstructure' ... then

Marx and Friedrich Engels, *Selected Correspondence*, ed. S. Ryazanskaya, trans. I. Lasker, 2nd ed. [Moscow: Progress Publishers, 1965], 85, 86).

184. See John B. Phear, *The Aryan Village in India and Ceylon* (London: Macmillan, 1880). Marx's extracts are preserved as *Notebook* B 146, pages 128–55 (1880–1881, now at the International Institute for Social History) as transcribed in Lawrence Krader, ed., *The Ethnological Notebooks of Karl Marx: Studies of Morgan, Phear, Maine, Lubbock*, Quellen und Untersuchungen zur Geschichte der deutschen und österreichischen Arbeiterbewegung NS 3 (Assen: Van Gorcum, 1972).

185. Lawrence Krader, "The Ethnological Notebooks of Karl Marx: A Commentary," in *Toward a Marxist Anthropology: Problems and Perspectives*, ed. S. Diamond, World Anthropology (The Hague: Mouton, 1979), 157.

the material content of the infrastructure is lost, and with it, an essential element of historical materialism."[186]

(5) An additional note. Sahlins not only employs the term "reproduction" but also uses the phrase, first in a 1976 lecture, "stereotypic reproduction" which he attributes to "Godelier 1972."[187] Godelier's phrase, which Sahlins returns to with some persistence,[188] apparently referred critically to structuralism. Sahlins writes, "Structuralism would then be innocent of any temporal knowledge save that of 'stereotypic reproduction' (Godelier 1972).... As for stereotypic reproduction, strictly speaking it does not occur."[189] Sahlins states, in response to criticism by Gananath Obeyesekere:[190]

> I introduced this phrase (coined by Maurice Godelier) into the discussion of Hawaiian history in order to repudiate it as an appropriate description of cultural practice.... Since 1977, I have repeatedly adopted the phrase "stereotypical reproduction" as a negative characterization of the ahistorical disposition of a certain structuralism.... "Stereotypic reproduction" has long been cited by me as a defect of classical structuralist theory.[191]

I think, in general, Sahlins is correct. But there are, at least, two other instances (beyond the "partial exception" he notes).[192] These occur in two sentences which immediately precede and follow his citation of the pas-

---

186. Gören Djurfeldt and Staffan Lindberg, *Behind Poverty: The Social Formation in a Tamil Village*, Scandinavian Institute of Asian Studies Monograph Series 22 (London: Curzon Press, 1975), 27.

187. Sahlins, "State of Art in Social/Cultural Anthropology," 22–23; cf. Sahlins, *How "Natives" Think*, 246–47, where he gives a history of his usage of the term.

188. E.g., Sahlins, Culture and Practical Reason, 41, 48.

189. Sahlins, "The State of Art in Social/Cultural Anthropology," 22, 23. I should add that *I* am citing Sahlins's representation of Godelier's meaning because, with some chagrin, I must confess that I have read the referenced Godelier work, both in the French original, Maurice Godelier, *Rationalité et irrationalité en économie*, and in English translation, *Rationality and Irrationality in Economics*, trans. B. Pearce (New York: Monthly Review Press, 1972; London: NLB, 1972), several times without being able to spot the phrase.

190. Gananath Obeyesekere, *The Apotheosis of Captain Cook: European Mythmaking in the Pacific* (Princeton: Princeton: Princeton University Press, 1992), 55, 58, 59, 98, 168.

191. Sahlins, *How "Natives" Think*, 246; cf. 243–51.

192. See ibid., 246.

sage from Marx's *Capital*,[193] quoted above, which speaks of "these self-sufficing communities that constantly reproduce themselves in the same form" (recalling that in the additional descriptions of the Indian village system by Marx, quoted above, Marx twice uses the word "stereotyped" when writing of their "forms of social organization"). Sahlins comments, "Marx was clearly aware of the ability of archaic societies to structure the circumstances of history. The passage from *Capital* on the permanence of Indian village communities is a classic statement of 'stereotypic reproduction.'" Again, following the quotation from Marx, "Marx recognized the stereotypic reproduction of Asiatic communities, although by comparison with a modern anthropology his theory of it does not seem powerful."[194] Earlier, after presenting the issue of the sea people and land people in Nuku, discussed in part 1 of the paper above, Sahlins writes, "This is an apposite example of 'stereotypic reproduction' in Godelier's [1972 (1966)] phrase. The example is especially capital for its disclosure of the mechanism of cultural reproduction in the face of a historical disconformity,"[195] even though he does state, later in the same paragraph, that "such is merely the mechanics of the process."[196]

3. "Transformation"

> If we grant, following Marxian thought, that infrastructures and super-structures are made up of multiple levels and that there are various types of transformations from one level to another, it becomes possible ... to characterize different types of societies in terms of the types of transformations which occur with them. These types of transformations amount to formulas showing the number, magnitude, direction, and order of the convolutions that must be unraveled ... in order to uncover (logically, not normatively) an ideal homologous relationship between the different structural levels.
> —Claude Lévi-Strauss, *Structural Anthropology*

Although "transformation" has more technical usages than "reproduction," its genealogy is less complex. Sahlins clearly takes the term from Lévi-Strauss, though not its understanding.

---

193. Marx, *Capital*, 1:392–94.
194. Sahlins, *Culture and Practical Reason*, 48.
195. Ibid., 41.
196. Ibid., 42.

(1) Lévi-Strauss has been uncommonly clear as to its source in his thought. What was implied by some pages in *The Naked Man*,[197] towards the conclusion of the "Finale" to his vast four-volume *Mythologiques*,[198] is made explicit in his response to questions by Didier Eribon, published in French under the evocative title, *The Near and the Far*,[199] and in English translation under the more prosaic title, *Conversations with Claude Lévi-Strauss*.[200] Here, Lévi-Strauss affirms that the idea of transformation in his thought is neither derived from logic or linguistics, but rather from biological morphology, in particular, D'Arcy Wentworth Thompson, *On Growth and Form*.[201]

> I found it [the idea of transformation] in a work that played a decisive role for me and that I read during the war while I was in the United States: *On Growth and Form* in two volumes, by D'Arcy Wentworth Thompson, which was first published in 1917. The author, a Scottish naturalist (I inadvertently wrote "English" in *The Naked Man*), interpreted the visible differences between species, or between animal or vegetable organs in the same genera, as transformations. This was an illumination for me, particularly since I was soon to notice that this way of seeing was part of a long tradition: behind Thompson was Goethe's botany, and behind Goethe, Albrecht Durer and his *Treatise on the Proportions of the Human Body*.[202]

> Another itinerary, better known to historians of ideas, has brought us to the notion of transformation in linguistics; perhaps it also began with Goethe and came down to us by way of William von Humboldt and Baudoin de Courtenay. Whatever the area under consideration, the moment

197. Claude Lévi-Strauss, *The Naked Man*, trans. John Weightman and Doreen Weightman (New York: Harper & Row, 1981).

198. Claude Lévi-Strauss, *Mythologiques*, 4 vols. (Paris: Plon, 1964–1971).

199. Claude Lévi-Strauss and Didier Eribon, *De prés et de loin* (Paris: O. Jacob, 1988).

200. Claude Lévi-Strauss and Didier Eribon, *Conversations with Claude Lévi-Strauss*, trans. P. Wissing (Chicago: University of Chicago Press 1991).

201. D'Arcy Wentworth Thompson, *On Growth and Form*, new ed. (Cambridge: Cambridge University Press, 1942). Lévi-Strauss references a two-volume edition that is unknown to me.

202. See Stephen Jay Gould's fascinating critical, yet appreciative, engagement with D'Arcy Thompson's *Growth and Form* in his recently published masterwork, *The Structure of Evolutionary Theory* (Cambridge: Harvard University Press, 2002), 1181–1208.

one tries to account for diversity by the different ways elements can be combined, the notion of transformation arises.[203]

In *The Naked Man,* Lévi-Strauss gives more specifics as to Thompson's enterprise, citing particular page references and reproducing several of Thompson's drawings. From this it is apparent that Lévi-Strauss's interest in Thompson largely focused on the concluding chapter, "On the Theory of Transformations, or The Comparison of Related Forms,"[204] where Thompson seeks to demonstrate that if selected plant or animal bodies—taken as a "type"—are plotted on Cartesian coordinates, it will be found that when these are systematically distorted through various operations, this yields forms of species related to the original plotted species. Lévi-Strauss does not focus on Thompson's overall project of mathematizing every aspect of living form (to take an example, almost at random, that the arrangement of spirals in the cones of the Norway spruce conforms to the Fibonacci numerical series.[205] Lévi-Strauss writes that Thompson:

> showed that by varying the parameters of a system of coordinates, it is possible, by means of a series of continuous transitions, to move from one living form to another, and, with the help of an algebraic function, to deduce the outlines or external differences ... which make it possible to distinguish at a glance, from their shape, two or more kinds of leaves,

---

203. Lévi-Strauss and Eribon, *Conversations,* 113–14. (The brief history of ideas Lévi-Strauss offers in this passage is not without interest.) Thompson cites Dürer in his *Growth and Form* and reproduces several of his drawings (see 1053–55 and notes). I suspect Lévi-Strauss may have been also influenced by Ernst Cassirer whose article, "Structuralism in Modern Linguistics," appeared in the journal *Word: Journal of the Linguistic Circle of New York* of which Lévi-Strauss was one of the editors. The thesis of the article is that structuralism in linguistics is analogous to morphology in biology. This article forms a pair with Lévi-Strauss's "L'Analyse structurale en linguistique et en anthropologie," *Word: Journal of the Linguistic Circle of New York* 1 (1945): 33–53, which announced Lévi-Strauss's decisive move to the linguistic analogy in his work. In this, he was clearly most influenced by his colleague at New York's *Ecole libre des hautes etudes* [the 'University in Exile'], Roman Jakobson; see Lévi-Strauss's preface to *Six Lectures on Sound and Meaning,* by Roman Jakobson, trans. J. Mepham (Cambridge: MIT Press, 1978), xi–xxvi.

204. Thompson, *On Growth and Form,* 1026–95.

205. Ibid., 922–24.

flowers, shells or bones, or even whole animals, provided the creatures concerned belong to the same botanical or zoological class.[206]

Viewed from one perspective, as the reference to Goethe suggests, Lévi-Strauss's focus on transformation harks back to a morphological understanding of transformation as "metamorphosis."[207] D'Arcy Thompson's mathematization of the morphological project allowed Lévi-Strauss to formulate transformation as a set of algebraic operations represented, best, by the "*Table des symbols*," which stands at the close of each of the four volumes of *Mythologiques*.[208]

(2) Viewed from another perspective, transformation is a process of "translation" from one code or system to another analogous to that of signs in semiotic systems: "The property of a system of signs is to be transformable, in other words translatable, into the language of another system with the help of substitutions."[209] This becomes, again with specific reference to Goethe's metamorphosis, a definition of structure.

> An arrangement is structured which meets but two conditions: that it be a system ruled by an internal cohesiveness and that this cohesiveness, inaccessible to observation in an isolated system, be revealed in a study of transformations through which similar properties are recognized in apparently different systems. As Goethe wrote: "All forms are

---

206. Lévi-Strauss, *Naked Man*, 676–77 and figure 39 (which combines in a single plate Thompson's figures in *Growth and Form*, 1062–64), 517–26. See also Lévi-Strauss's use of *Growth and Form*, 1032, in polemics with Georges Gurvitch in "Postscript to Chapter XV ['Social Structure']," 328.

In connection with D'Arcy Thompson's notion of algebraic "distortion" as part of his morphological project, you may want to compare the remarks on Belon's morphological distortion in my "Metareflection," "*Dayyeinu*," 484–85 n. 4. Note that Thompson presumes an intra-generic distortion; Belon, an inter-generic operation.

207. See Smith, "Acknowledgments: Morphology and History, Part 1," 318–28.

208. See Lévi-Strauss, *Mythologiques*, 1:348, 2:408, 3:422, 4:622. These have been transposed to the beginning of each of the volumes in their English translation, *Introduction to a Science of Mythology*, trans. John Weightman and Doreen Weightman (New York: Harper & Row; London: Jonathan Cape Limited, 1969–1981), 1:xiii; 2:9; 3:11; 4:9. They are similar to the formula announced in the 1955 article, "Structural Study of Myth," 228.

209. Lévi-Strauss, *Structural Anthropology*, 2:19.

similar, and none is like the others. So that their chorus points the way to a hidden law."[210]

Or, in short form, "in the anthropological sense of the term, structure is defined as the totality formed of relations between elements of a system and of their transformations."[211] And yet again:

> The task I have undertaken ... consists in proving that myths which are not alike, or in which the similarities seem at first glance to be accidental, can nevertheless display an identical structure and belong to the same group of transformations. It is not, then, a question of listing common features, but of demonstrating that, in spite of their differences, and perhaps even because of them, myths which seem at first to present no similarities, proceed according to the same principles and originate from a group of operations.[212]

(3) From the perspective of the interests of our seminar, this latter sort of argument is most interesting when it is historically formulated, as, for example in Lévi-Strauss's second of his three "rules" of myth interpretation: "A myth must never be interpreted individually, but in its relationship to other myths which, taken together, constitute a transformation group."[213] It must be granted that, in such formulations, Lévi-Strauss offers a primarily spatialized sense of history, largely through the employment, especially in the case of the Americas, of diffusion.[214]

In Lévi-Strauss's *Mythologiques*, this methodological procedure becomes one of the overarching themes of the four volumes.

---

210. Ibid.

211. Lévi-Strauss, *Anthropology and Myth*, 169.

212. Lévi-Strauss, The *Origin of Table Manners*, vol. 3 of Weightman and Weightman, *Introduction to a Science of Mythology*, 200.

213. Lévi-Strauss, *Structural Anthropology*, 2:65.

214. For Kant, this would be termed "natural history." As a result of this sort of history taking into account of "wanderings," natural history "would in all likelihood reinterpret a large number of apparently distinct types into varieties of the same species." See Immanuel Kant, "Von den verschiedenen Racen der Menschen," in *Gesammelte Schriften* (Berlin: G. Reimer, 1902–1983]), 2:434. The latter comment by Kant is a succinct description of Lévi-Strauss's enterprise in *Mythologiques*. See further, Smith, "Acknowledgments: Morphology and History, Part 1," 328.

I shall take as my starting point one myth, originating from one community, and shall analyze it, referring first of all to the ethnographic context and then to other myths belonging to the same community. Gradually broadening the field of inquiry, I shall then move on to myths from neighboring societies, after previously placing them, too, in their ethnographic context. Step by step, I shall proceed to more remote communities but only after authentic links of a historical or geographic nature have been established with them or can reasonably be assumed to exist.[215]

Levi-Strauss insists that, although the method for interpreting the myths will be "structural analysis," the resulting "set," the resulting "transformation groups," will show that "in spite of its formal approach, structural analysis establishes the validity of ethnographic and historical interpretations" of the peoples from whom the myths were recorded.[216]

While the particular analysis of myths and their relations will demonstrate transformations (sense 1) of elements, viewed in terms of tribal relations established historically, there is a set of overall transformations (sense 2) between the ethnically located group of myths. These transformations may be expressed, for the raw and the cooked, in terms of three transformation formulae[217] or in summary prose descriptions, such as those offered of the same set in Levi-Strauss's summaries of his seminar lectures for 1961–1962, and 1962–1963:

It is demonstrated that in the group so formed, the Tupi myths exemplify the most thorough going transformation: the crucial opposition is that between cooking, formerly a secret known only to the carrion-eaters, and putrefaction that they are nowadays reduced to consuming. The Ge, however, displace the opposition to one between cooked food and its consumption in the raw state, which is the present condition of the original master of fire, the jaguar. Within this system, the Bororo myths appear to hesitate between the two extreme formulations.[218]

In the myths of central Brazil, the problem of the Nature-Culture transition was most often illustrated by the story of the invention, discovery

---

215. Lévi-Strauss, *Raw and the Cooked*, 1.
216. Ibid., 9.
217. Lévi-Strauss, *From Honey to Ashes*, vol. 2 of Weightman and Weightman, *Introduction to a Science of Mythology*, 26–27.
218. Lévi-Strauss, *Anthropology and Myth*, 40.

or obtaining of cooking fire. This mythical theme, particularly well exemplified among the central and eastern Ge, has been traced, in a southwesterly direction to the Bororo, through a double transformation at once sociological and technological. Effectively, the Ge myths are transformed among the Bororo into myths of the origin of water. At the same time, a sociological pattern found at the basis of the Ge myths in the form of a conflict between two brothers-in-law, is found in the corresponding Bororo myth as a conflict between father and son.[219]

(4) Sahlins's interest in the term, "transformation," clearly reflects his serious, critical engagement with Levi-Strauss, but as with the other terms discussed in this appendix, Sahlins has creatively reconfigured its meaning. Sahlin's use of "transformation" in relation to "reproduction" in a "structure of conjuncture" does not employ any of the three senses of "transformation" in Levi-Strauss as described above.[220]

---

219. Ibid., 41. Compare the more general statement of the enterprise of *Mythologiques* in Levi-Strauss's seminar lectures for 1967–1968 (ibid., 56).

220. For Sahlins's use of the term, see part 2 above.

The Markan Site

Jonathan Z. Smith

Among the various Oceanic specialists who have remarked on Marshall Sahlins's work, Nicholas Thomas, at the Australian National University, is perhaps the most interesting, both in his particular studies, as represented by *Entangled Objects: Exchange, Material Culture, and Colonialism in the Pacific*, and in his more theoretical work, *Out of Time: History and Evolution in Anthropological Discourse*.[1] In the latter, Thomas develops the argument that Sahlins's mechanisms of reproduction/transformation, which stress "the creative dynamics of the indigenous cultural scheme," entail "a particular power relation which could exist only at a certain phase of colonial history, namely the period between initial contact and the establishment of formal metropolitan rule or some form of disruptive occupation." In such a moment:

---

1. Nicholas Thomas, *Entangled Objects: Exchange, Material Culture, and Colonialism in the Pacific* (Cambridge: Harvard University Press, 1991); Thomas, *Out of Time: History and Evolution in Anthropological Discourse*, Cambridge Studies in Social Anthropology 67 (Cambridge: Cambridge University Press, 1989; 2nd ed., Ann Arbor: University of Michigan Press, 1996). See also, with particular relevance to the issues Thomas raises here, Thomas, *Marquesan Societies: Inequality and Political Transformation in Eastern Polynesia* (Oxford: Clarendon, 1990); Thomas, "Partial Texts: Representation, Colonialism and Agency in Pacific History," *Journal of Pacific History* 25 (1990): 139–58; Thomas, "Against Ethnography," *Cultural Anthropology* 6 (1991): 306–22; Thomas, "Historical Anthropology and the Politics of Critique," *Pacific Studies* 15 (1992): 142–58; Thomas, "Substantivization and Anthropological Discourse: The Transformation of Practices into Institutions in Neotraditional Pacific Societies," in *History and Tradition in Melanesian Anthropology*, ed. James G. Carrier, Studies in Melanesian Anthropology 10 (Berkeley: University of California Press, 1992), 64–85; Thomas, "The Inversion of Tradition," American *Ethnologist* 19 (1992): 213–32; Thomas, *Colonialism's Culture: Anthropology, Travel, and Government* (Princeton: Princeton University Press, 1994); Thomas, *In Oceania: Visions, Artifacts, Histories* (Durham, NC: Duke University Press, 1997).

Connections with foreigners were ... manipulated and willingly reproduced, rather than imposed. There was space under these circumstances
for precisely the sort of innovative meanings discussed by Sahlins. Since
foreign links actually tended to be positively valued, the logic of meanings was extended to encompass and in some sense appropriate selected
aspects of what was foreign.

By contrast:

The properties of a formal colonial situation in which administrative
rule is asserted, or one in which intruders dispossess natives for land
or labour, are of course very different. It is one thing to speak of a performative culture order which assimilates to itself contingencies, and
quite another for a people to find their leaders powerless, themselves
landless, and their crucial ritual practices proscribed. Such people will
find the "working misunderstandings" which sometimes operate so creatively in the inter-enactment of cultural structure do not in fact work....
The Cook/Lono case is thus only a model for a certain class of historical changes. Such processes perhaps took place more in the Pacific than
on colonized continents, because the insular nature of Pacific societies
provided some defence against disruption, and gave greater space to
indigenous manipulation of relatively manageable colonial intrusions....
But there came a time in each place—perhaps in a few places it is still to
come—when these incursions ceased to be manageable. The histories
subsequent to that time cannot be seen in terms of the increments and
extensions of an indigenous cultural logic. The stream of outside offerings ceases to be a matter of contingent events which internal structure
selectively receives and accommodates, and the structural aspect of what
is external itself impinges on the local system and its contingencies.[2]

Here we might anticipate a series of stratagems, from manipulation and
inversion to conflict and rebellion.[3]

---

2. Thomas, *Out of Time*, 111–14.

3. Thomas has been particularly interested in "manipulation." See the general
statement in ibid., 111–13, and the multiple examples in *Entangled Objects*.

I find Thomas's remarks on "inversion," in *Out of Time*, 113–14, particularly suggestive: "Sometimes the dominated people half-adopt the colonizer's representations,
even if they invert them and positively assert whatever the dominant culture denigrates.
Thus, in what have become 'traditional' communities in parts of modern Hawaii, the
virtues of gift-giving, reciprocity and egalitarianism in interaction are stressed, not
because such practices really reflect anything that has persisted since former times,

In the Papua New Guinea case (as well as in Sahlins's Hawaiian example), which was compared to the Corinthian situation at the meetings of the seminar held in Denver in 2001, the times were comparable. In both instances, there was a relatively recent intrusion. Hence, Thomas's model would predict "working misunderstandings," with, as in Sahlins, the possibility of creative relations between the twin projects of reproduction and transformation affecting both sides of the relationship. The Levantine coast, the topic of the seminar's sessions held in Toronto in 2002, appears to have a quite different history.

1.

If Phoenicia bore you, who will find fault?
—Zenodotus the Stoic

If I am a Syrian, what wonder?
Stranger, we dwell in one country—the cosmos.
—Meleager of Gadara

One who acquires [land] in Syria is like one who acquires [land] in the outskirts of Jerusalem.
—m. Hal. 4:11

---

but precisely because sharing and parity reverse the rules of the external monetized world, in which such communities are poor and marginal.... It can be argued that this type of oppositional cultural expression is very widespread in both colonial and non-colonial situations ... that, for instance, many of the singular features of hunter-gatherer societies derive not from pristine simplicity but rather from the facts of their 'encapsulation' by threatening and potentially dominant groups dependent on other forms of production. In these situations, historical relations must be constitutive rather than contingent." See, further, Thomas, "Inversion of Tradition"; and Marshall Sahlins, "Cery Cery Fuckabede," *American Ethnologist* 20 (1993): 848–67.

After all, the narratives of Cook's voyages contain as many notices of violence and resistance at initial contact. For this reason, for example, Fiji was named "the Savage Island" by Cook (James Cook, *The Voyage of the Resolution and Adventure 1772–1775*, vol. 2 of *The Journals of Captain James Cook*, ed. J. C. Beaglehole and R. A. Skelton [Cambridge: The Hakluyt Society at the University Press, 1955–1974], 434–37). Indeed, the indigenous myth of the foreign conquering chiefs (the "stranger kings") on which Sahlins relies is surely an ambivalent account which can lead as much to active "nativistic" resistance as to "reproduction." See, among others, Alan Howard, "Cannibal Chiefs and the Charter for Rebellion in Rotuman Myth," *Pacific Studies* 10 (1986): 1–27.

The money mentioned by the Torah is always Tyrian money. What is
Tyrian money? It is Jerusalem money.
—t. Ketub. 12.6

If we accept a Markan locus on the south Syrian coast, then matters there
may be supposed to have been quite different from Corinth.[4] Because of
its strategic value with respect to both overland and sea trade, the Levant

---

4. Leaving aside the notorious problem of the geographical and political definition of "Syria," I presume, for the purposes of this paper, that our primary locale is the
coastal region extending from Ptolemais to Sidon, including major sites such as Tyre
as well as smaller ones such as Umm el-Ammed, Kafir Yassif, Ekdippa (Akhzib), and
those clustered at the "Ladder of Tyre."

Clearly the larger region of Northern Galilee and Southwestern Syria Phoenicia
is likewise entailed, especially the set of port cities near Haifa, including 'Athlit and
Dor(a). For myself, if the focus of one of the seminar's concerns is ethnic conflict and
identity formation, Caesarea (Strato's Tower) would be a more tempting target area, if
only on the basis of the Josephus data. See, for example, the discussion of the conflict
reported in Josephus, *J.W.* 2.13.7 §266–270 and *Ant.* 20.8.7 §173–178 in Shaye J. D.
Cohen, *The Beginnings of Jewishness: Boundaries, Varieties, Uncertainties*, Hellenistic
Culture and Society 31 (Berkeley: University of California Press, 1999), 15–16; and
compare Fergus Millar, *The Roman Near East, 31 BC–AD 337* (Cambridge: Harvard
University Press, 1993), 356–57. See also, among other Caesarean conflicts, Josephus,
J.W. 2.14.4–5 §284–292; 2.18.1 §457–458; 2.21.8–10 §632–646; 3.9.7–8 §445–461,
some of which have parallels in Josephus, *Life* 17–22 §87–107; 53–55 §271–286; 65
§340–345; and compare the odd formulation concerning some of these conflicts in
Emil Schürer, *The History of the Jewish People in the Age of Jesus Christ (175 B.C.—A.D.
135)*, rev. and ed. Geza Vermes, Fergus Millar, and Martin Goodman (Edinburgh:
T&T Clark, 1973–1979), 2:117 with n. 168. Lee I. Levine, *Caesarea under Roman Rule*,
SJLA 7 (Leiden: Brill, 1975) remains the most useful overview.

Even this more expansive characterization remains, in my opinion, too Judea-
centric. After all, the Persian period already saw the granting of alternating Sidonian
and Tyrean hegemony over the coastal region as far south as Ashkelon (see Pseudo-
Scylax, *Periplus*) as part of a wider, Achaemenid, trans-Mediterranean stratagem for
constraining Greek naval activity. This policy accounts for the later Hellenistic (ca.
210–112 BCE) graves at Marisa (Maresha), the provincial capital of the hyparchy
of Idumaea, which show that "Sidonian, Idumean, and Jewish families were living
together, using the same tombs, and together being hellenized" (Erwin R. Goodenough, *Jewish Symbols in the Greco-Roman Period*, 13 vols., Bollingen Series 37 [New
York: Pantheon, 1953–1968], 1:74; cf. John P. Peters and Hermann Thiersch, *The
Painted Tombs in the Necropolis of Marissa*, ed. S. A. Cook [London: Committee of the
Palestine Exploration Fund, 1905]; Schürer, *History of the Jewish People*, 2:4–5 n. 8,
with further bibliography)—including the grave (tomb A) and epitaph (*OGIS* 593) of

has always been contested space, a region, at most, of client-kings not of kingdoms, endlessly encompassed in the larger schemes of greater powers:

Apollophanes, son of Sesmaios, the *arxas* (chief) of the Sidonians in Marisa for thirty-three years. Marisa was destroyed by the Parthians in 40 BCE.

The same policy accounts for the fame of Ashkelon as a center of temples and cults of Syrian deities. (See already Herodotus, *Hist.* 1.105; cf. Schürer, *History of the Jewish People*, 2:31–32 with nn. 8–16.) Note the incorporation of Ashkelon in the Semiramis myth in Diodorus Siculus 2.4.2–6 (Paul-Louis van Berg, *Corpus Cultus Deae Syriae*, Series Études préliminaires aux religions orientales dans l'empire romain 28 [Leiden: Brill, 1972–] ,1. 2:13–36). The Diodorus citation recounts the relations of Atargatis to fish, the fish lake at Ashkelon, and the Syrian prohibition with respect to eating fish.

The Syrian prohibition was as proverbial in Greco-Roman literature as Jewish pork abstention (see the convenient short list in Austin M. Harmon's note to Lucian, *Syr. d.* 45 [LCL 4:398–99 n. 1]; Porphyry, *Abst.* 2.61 mentions first the Syrians' fish avoidance, then the Jews' pork avoidance). Perhaps the most interesting treatment occurs as part of the lengthy (largely alphabetical) discussion of fish in books 7 and 8 (in part) of Athenaeus's *Deipnosophistae*, a section which exhibits a piscine learning that rivals F. J. Dölger's. The reference (*Deipn.* 8.37, 346c–e; van Berg, *Corpus Cultus Deae Syriae*, 1.1: no. 109) includes citations from Antipater of Tarsus (Hans von Arnim, *Stoicorum Veterum Fragmenta* [Leipzig: Teubner, 1903–1924], 3:257, no. 64); Mnaseas (of Patara?) (*FHG* 3:155, no. 32); and Xanthus the Lydian (*FGrHist* 765; van Berg, *Corpus Cultus Deae Syriae*, 1.2:97–110). Cf. Philo's report of the prohibition against catching or eating doves in Ashkelon (*Prov.* 2.64).

On the matter of Judea-centrism, we should bear in mind the shrewd observations and questions of John M. G. Barclay, *Jews in the Mediterranean Diaspora from Alexander to Trajan (323 BCE–117 CE)* (Edinburgh: T&T Clark, 1996), 243 (cf. n. 28), while prescinding from some of his assumptions: "The chequered history of the [Syro-Palestinian] region and the continual expansion and contraction of what could be considered 'Jewish' territory make it particularly difficult here to distinguish between 'homeland' and 'Diaspora.' When large numbers of Jews settled in the Greek coastal cities, could they consider these as properly 'Jewish,' even 'holy land,' or were they, in such a Hellenized environment, in the 'Diaspora'? At different points in time, one might have given different answers to this question, depending on whether the city in question was under Greek/Roman control, or in the power of Alexander Jannaeus or Herod the Great. But even under Jewish rulers, the Greek history, constitution and ambience of such cities made the question difficult to answer, and … such ambiguities could become the cause of strife between Jews and non-Jews. For our purposes, it seems best to include in our study not only those Jews who lived in Syrian cities which were always outside Jewish control (e.g. Antioch, Damascus, Tyre, Sidon, Ptolemais) but also those who resided in the Hellenistic cities of the coastal plain, the Decapolis and Peraea, where the majority of the population was gentile and the cultural environment was predominantly Syro-Hellenistic." Keeping such questions fluid is one of the important features of Fergus Millar's work (*The Roman Near East*) on the region.

Egypt and Mesopotamia (as well as the Hittites), Greece and Persia, Ptol-
emies and Seleucids, Rome and Parthia, Roman and Byzantine Christianities, Sassanians and Islam—not to mention lesser powers such as the
Nabataeans or Armenians.[5] As with the Oceanic islands of our seminar's
sessions in Denver, the Levantine coast has been not only a place of the
arrival of others but also a site for departures, from the Phoenicians of
the archaic period to the famed *Syri negotiatores* of the Roman era. From
this perspective, the Levant must be seen, above all, as a permanent site
of premodern (as well as modern) imperialisms and colonialisms, with
its attendant patterns of emigration and immigration, of resistance and
adjustment, of subjugation and entrepreneurial initiative, played out on
a range of social locales from that of the individual and familial to that of
the civic and regional.

One consequence of this is that the notion of "native," of "indigenous,"
as routinely applied by anthropology is inapplicable. "Native," within such
a context, is as much a strategically constructed category as is "outsider"—
often a project in the manufacture of difference (a process already appar-

---

5. See, for example, Arnold J. Toynbee, *A Study of History*, 12 vols. (London:
Oxford University Press, 1934–1961), 8:93–94: "This summary recapitulation of Syria's political history brings out the fact that, over a span of four thousand years—from
the twenty-first century BC to the twentieth century of the Christian Era—the usual
political fate of Syria had been to find herself included in the dominions of some universal state. Even when one of these oecumenical empires embracing Syria had broken
up, Syria's destiny, as often as not, had been immediately to be annexed entire to some
other empire of the same kind.... Even at times when Syria had not been included
as a whole within the frontiers of some single empire, her most frequent alternative
fate had been to be partitioned between two empires embracing other regions besides
their portions of Syrian territory.... The intervals during which Syria had been under
the sovereignty of local Syrian states had been few and far between.... The degree
to which Syria's political history has been dominated by her geographical location at
a meeting-point of natural thoroughfares was the more impressive, considering that
Syria's physical structure was inimical to the imperialism to which Syria had usually
been subject, while it was favorable to the *Kleinstaaterei* in which she had so seldom
been free to indulge in.... If Syria's geographical location had insulated her from the
outer world, as Nature had insulated New Guinea, instead of exposing her ...to the
play of external influences and pressures from all quarters of the compass, her physi-
ography ...would have imposed on her, as her normal regime, a political decentraliza-
tion which the political effects of her location had precluded on all but four occasions
in her history during the last four thousand years."

ent in the heavily valenced, imagined relations of "Canaanites" to "Israel-ites" in the largely Persian period narratives in the Hebrew Bible).

Let me begin an exploration of the Markan site at a seemingly remote locale, Puteoli (older Greek name, Dicaearchia; New Testament Greek, Potioloi; Italian, Pozzuoli), a major Campanian port city on the north shore of the Bay of Naples, five miles west of the city of Naples. I do so not because Agrippa (Philo, *Flacc.* 27), Antipas (Josephus, *Ant.* 18.7.2 §248), the anonymous Pseudo-Alexander (Josephus, *J.W.* 2.7.1 §104), Philo and his fellow emissaries (*Legat.* 185), Paul (Acts 28:13–14),[6] or, in other traditions, Peter (Acts Pet. 5–6) and Josephus (*Life* 16), among others, all stopped here, but because it tells us something of importance about Levantine religion.[7]

Puteoli's central manufacturing, trading, and transport roles in the wider trans-Mediterranean economy guaranteed the presence of a wide diversity of folk and their religions,[8] most especially, given the triangle of

---

6. The reference in Acts 28:14 to Paul's meeting with the *adelphoi* in Puteoli has been important in the Neapolitan Catholic interest in establishing an already existent Christian church in the region. Such interests gain expression in a collective volume issued to commemorate the nineteenth centennial of Paul's stop.

7. Compare the strategic use of the same chief texts from Puteoli at the beginning of ch. 5, "The Path to Rome," in Arthur Darby Nock, *Conversion: The Old and New in Religion from Alexander the Great to Augustine of Hippo* (Oxford: Oxford University Press, 1933), 66. Cf. L. Michael White, *Building God's House in the Roman World: Architectural Adaptation among Pagans, Jews, and Christians*, vol. 1 of *The Social Origins of Christian Architecture*, HTS 42 (Valley Forge, PA: Trinity Press International, 1990), 31–32.

8. Among the varied folk, with the exception of Egyptians and Syrians (see below, nn. 10–15): (1) Spaniards (Martin Percival Charlesworth, *Trade Routes and Commerce of the Roman Empire*, 2nd ed. [Cambridge: University Press, 1926], 154); (2) North Africans, Oea (*CIL* 10.1684); (3) Ethiopians (Dio Cassius, *Hist. Rom.* 62.63.3; see Frank Martin Snowden Jr., *Blacks in Antiquity: Ethiopians in the Greco-Roman Experience* [Cambridge: Harvard University Press, 1970], 163); (4) Judeans (Josephus, *Ant.* 17.12.1 §328; *J.W.* 2.7.1 §104).

For various religious items: (1) Cybele: three statues; one ex-voto lamp; religious association(s): Dendrophores, Cernophores, Religiosi (V. Tam Tinh Tran, *Le culte des divinités en Campanie en dehors de Pompei, de stables et d'Herculanum*, EPRO 27 [Leiden: Brill, 1972], 86–88, 100–113); (2) Dedication to Sol Invictus as "*Gen(io) col(oniae)*" (*CIL* 10.1591; Tran, *Le culte des divinités*, 182).

At the other end, note the presence of Campanian bronzes in Kolhapur, India, most likely shipped from Puteoli (Richard Daniel de Puma, "The Roman Bronzes from Kolhapur," in *Rome and India: The Ancient Sea Trade*, ed. V. Begley and R. D. de Puma

trade (Egypt, the Levant or Asia Minor, Italy),[9] Egyptians,[10] and Syrians.[11]

[Madison, WI: University of Wisconsin Press, 1991], 82–112, esp. 100–101). The close similarity of some of these pieces to the bronze horde from the Masada region which Yigael Yadin identifies as being of Southern Italian manufacture, in the second half of the first century CE (*The Finds from the Bar-Kokhba Period in the Cave of Letters* [Jerusalem: Israel Exploration Society, 1963], 42–83), gives some chronological reference. See also the sigillata stamp *RVFIO* from Arikamedu, which appears to be of Puteolian manufacture (Howard Comfort, "Terra Sigillata at Arikamedu," in *Rome and India*, esp. 141, 150 nn. 32–33; cf., in general, R. E. M. Wheeler, A. Ghosh, and K. Deva, "Arikamedu: An Indo-Roman Trading Station on the East Coast of India," *Ancient India* 2 [1946], 17–124). The anonymous *Periplus of the Erythraean Sea*, trans. and ed. G.W. B. Huntingford (London: The Hakluyt Society, 1980), 49, has a splendid portrait of the import and export goods available at Bauggaza.

The most remote commodity at Puteoli was silk. Ultimately from China, it was largely carried by land caravan to the Mediterranean coast. Syrian Antioch was an important destination. Alternatively, it would be carried by caravan to India, shipped through the Indian Ocean to Egyptian ports on the Red Sea, then to Tyre or Antioch. The silk would be reprocessed in Syria or Egypt—Tyre was a major center of this industry—before being shipped to Rome, through Puteoli. (Note Domitian's construction of a warehouse complex in Rome for the storage of silk and spices in conjunction with improving and shortening the road between Puteoli and Rome in 92 CE). See, in general, Geoffrey Francis Hudson, *Europe and China: A Survey of Their Relations from the Earliest Times to 1800* (London: E. Arnold, 1931), esp. 77–86; Luce Boulnois, *La route de la soie* (Paris: Arthaud, 1963); John Ferguson, "China and Rome," *ANRW* 9.2:581–603; M. G. Rashke, "New Studies in Roman Commerce," *ANRW* 9.2:604–1361, with a cartographic appendix. See, now, reports of the new finds at Berenike in Egypt, with the important supposition that "artifacts at the site indicated that the [Indian Ocean] ships might have been built in India and were probably crewed by Indians" (John Noble Wilford, "Under Centuries of Sand, a Trading Hub," *New York Times*, July 9, 2002, sec. D: 1 and 9).

9. For the triangular route, see Lucian, *Navigium*, and the study by Lionel Casson, "The Isis and Her Voyage," *TAPA* 81 (1950): 43–56; cf. Nelson Glueck, *Deities and Dolphins: The Story of the Nabataeans* (London: Cassell, 1965), 378.

10. The route from Alexandria to Puteoli by way of Asia Minor or the Levant was the dominant mode of transshipment (Strabo, *Geogr.* 17.1.7); for this reason, both the data for the presence of Egyptians and for Egyptian religion in Puteoli is extensive. See, among others, Michel Malaise, *Inventaire préliminaire des documents égyptiens découverts en Italie*, EPRO 21 (Leiden: Brill, 1972), 284–91; Malaise, *Les conditions de pénétration et de diffusion des cultes égyptiens en Italie*, EPRO 22 (Leiden: Brill, 1972), 523 s.v. Pouzzoles; Tran, *Le culte des divinités*, 3–27, 49–63.

11. The Syrian artifacts recovered at Puteoli, besides those discussed in the text above (see also nn. 12–15, below), include: (1) a portal with a reference to an "order" of I. O. M. Heliopolitanus proposing the restoration of his temple (*ILS* 4289; Tran, *Le*

Our interest focuses on a small group of Greek Syro-Phoenician texts from Puteoli together with a few related Levantine texts:

(1) The first Puteolian text, dated May 79 CE, concerns the transportation of a statue of the god of Sarepta by boat from the port of Tyre to Puteoli:

> In the consulship of Lucius Caese[nnius] and Publius Calvisius in the year 204 according to the Tyrian reckoning, on the eleventh of Arte-mision, the [ho]ly god of [S]arepta came from Tyre by ship to Puteoli, brought by a member of the Elim by the [command of the god]. (*OGIS* 594)[12]

---

culte des divinités, 147); (2) two inscriptions recording priests of I. O. M. Heliopolitanus (*ILS* 4290; Tran, *Le culte des divinités*, 147–49); (3) an inscription concerning a burial plot controlled by a religious corporation of Jupiter Heliopolitanus (*CIL* 10.1579; *ILS* 4291; Tran, *Le culte des divinités*, 149–50); (4) an inscription of 116 CE concerning the *cultores Iovis Heliopolitani berytenses qui Puteolis consistunt* (*CIL* 10.1634; Tran, *Le culte des divinités*, 150); (5) an honorific inscription for a priest of Jupiter Damascenus (*CIL* 10.1576; Tran, *Le culte des divinités*, 151–52); (6) a dedication to the Dea Syria (*CIL* 10.1554; Tran, *Le culte des divinités*, 158); (7) an inscription commemorating a taurobolium in honor of Venus Caelestis dated October 134 (*CIL* 10.1596; Tran, *Le culte des divinités*, 159–60, with an important critical and bibliographical discussion; cf. Robert Duthoy, *The Taurobolium: Its Evolution and Terminology*, EPRO 10 [Leiden: Brill, 1959], 125 and no. 50); (8) a record of an offering to Venus Caelestis (*CIL* 10.1598; Tran, *Le culte des divinités*, 161); and (9) the dedication of a temple to Venus Caelestis (Tran, *Le culte des divinités*, 161–63). Note also the Nabataean materials relating to Dusares (Tran, *Le culte des divinités*, 141–47).

12. There are several problems in the history of the discussion of this text (largely summarized in Tran, *Le culte des divinités*, 156–58). Several are caused by lacunae. The first is the restoration of [..]*ios* [S]*arepteno*[s]. Some scholars have restored the first word as [*Hê*]*lios*, leading to an understanding of the second word as *Araptenos* on the basis of an alleged solar cult in Arefa/Araphat/Arphas in Lebanon. C. C. Torrey's notice of an inscription in the Yale Babylonian Collection from Syria ("The Exiled God Sarepta," *Berytus* 9 [1948–1949]: 45–49), which refers to the *theos hagios Sareptênos* (and appears to refer to the same transfer of the god) makes this restoration unlikely. A third inscription "to the holy god of Sarepta" on a stone from Sarafand makes the Sareptian reading certain (James B. Pritchard, *Recovering Sarepta, A Phoenician City: Excavations at Sarafand, Lebanon, 1969–1974 by the University Museum of the University of Pennsylvania* [Princeton: Princeton University Press, 1978], 44–45 with fig. 16).

The second problem is the word *elim*. The name is obviously the Semitic plural, "gods." Is this the proper name of an individual or of a guild of cult functionaries? I have followed the latter understanding.

The third problem is the Latin subinscription: *Pro sal(ute) Imp(eratoris) Domitiani Aug(usti) ... l(ocus) c(oncessus) d(ecreto) [d(ecurionum)]*. As the Greek text is

(2) In 1948–1949, C. C. Torrey published a votive tablet, now in the
Yale Babylonian Collection, reported to be of Syrian provenance: "To the
holy god of Sarepta, a fellow traveler (*synekdêmos*) has set up this votive
offering." Torrey suggests that this is a "voice from the other end—the
beginning—of the voyage of the Phoenician party through the Mediterranean," understanding the "party" as being either a group of emigrants or
exiles from Sarepta.[13]

(3) The second text from Puteoli appears to be a dedication to Baal-
Melqart. The surviving Greek portion of the inscription consists of the
standard praise formula for Tyre: "Tyre, holy and inviolable, a[nd autonomous metropolis] of Phoenicia and the cities [of Coele Syria] to god, holy
and august…" (*CIL* 10.1601; *IGRR* 419).[14]

(4) The third text from Puteoli, nearly a century later than the Sarepta
text, is better known. It contains both a letter written by the commercial
agency of the Tyrians at Puteoli to Tyre (July 174 CE) and an extract
from the minutes of the meeting of the council at Tyre (December 174
CE) in response:

> Letter written to the city of Tyre, the sacred, inviolable and autonomous
> metropolis of Phoenicia and of other cities, and leader of the fleet. To the
> chief magistrates, council, and people of their sovereign native city, from
> those (Tyrians) resident in Puteoli. Greetings.

> By the gods and the Fortune of our lord the Emperor. As you know,
> there are many commercial stations in Puteoli other than ours, but ours
> excels the others both in its organization and in its grandeur. Formerly,
> this upkeep was financed by the Tyrians residing in Puteoli who were
> numerous and wealthy, but now this upkeep has devolved on us, who
> are few in number, and since we pay the expenses for the sacrifices and
> rituals to our ancestral gods consecrated here in their temples, we do
> not have the funds to pay the station's yearly rent of 100,000 denarii,

---

dated to 79 CE, and Domitian did not assume power until late 81, the text is later than
the arrival of the statue and the Sareptian group.

13. Torrey, "Exiled God of Sarepta." I would take the term *synekdêmos* (written,
as is typical in inscriptions, *synegdêmos*) not as "fellow exile" but in its more usual
sense of "fellow traveler" (e.g., *OGIS* 494 [Miletus, second century CE]), as in the Latin
comes. Given the situation, it might carry the sense cited by Liddell and Scott (*LSJ*, s.v.
συνέκδημος 1706a), on the basis of *IG* 12(8).186, 9 (Samothrace, first century BCE),
of a group of private persons accompanying a public mission.

14. Tran, *Le culte des divinités*, 152–53.

as in addition the expenses of the feast where the oxen are sacrificed have been imposed on us. For this reason we beg you to provide for the station's continued existence which will continue only if you undertake responsibility for payment of the 100,000 denarii annual rent. As to the other expenses, including those incurred to repair the station for the birthday festival of our lord the Emperor, we have placed this on our account so as to not impose upon the city (of Tyre) so heavy an expense. We remind you also that, unlike that which is the case with the station in the sovereign city of Rome, the station here (Puteoli) receives no contributions either from shipowners or from merchants. We therefore appeal to you, it rests with you to deal with this matter. Written in Puteoli, July 23, in the counsulship of Gallus and Flaccus Cornelius. (*OGIS* 595; *IG* 14.830; *IGRR* 1.421)

The "extract from the minutes of the meeting of the council session held December 8, 174, Callicrates Pausanias presiding" that follows is chiefly an extraordinarily close paraphrase of "the letter of the Tyrians who had the agency at Puteoli, the letter being delivered by one of them, Laches." After the reading one council member, Philocles, son of Diodorus, reported that "the Tyrians who have the station in Rome" have always, "by custom," provided the rent funds from their receipts to the Tyrians of Puteoli. The council decided that this latter practice will continue.[15]

What broader generalizations do these Puteolian texts suggest? The first Puteolian text (no. 1) concerns a locative deity, bearing only a toponym as his name, *theos hagios Sareptênos*.[16] Yet its placement at Puteoli

---

15. There are a large number of passing references to this inscription in the scholarly literature. The most important items, along with a text and French translation, are provided in Tran, *Le culte des divinités*, 153–56; cf. 136–37. I have freely adapted, above, both this French translation and the English translation in Naphtali Lewis and Meyer Reinhold, eds., *The Empire*, vol. 2 of *Roman Civilization: Selected Readings*, Records of Civilization, Sources and Studies 45 (New York: Columbia University Press, 1955), 196–97.

16. While names consisting of a deity + toponym are well known in Syro-Phoenician literature (especially in association with Baal, e.g., Baal of Sidon [*KAI* 14, 60], Baal of Tyre [*KAI* 47]), metonymical constructions with the toponym alone are not unknown. See the biblical parallel, Baal of Peor (Num 25:3, 5), who could simply be termed Peor (Num 25:18 [twice]; cf. 31:16). Compare Sidonian coins through the first century CE bearing the legend, "of Sidon (the) goddess" (Millar, *Roman Near East*, 286). Employing a more generic geographical category, see the widespread titulature for Baalat/Atargatis as the *Syria thea* of the Greek inscriptions or the *dea Syria* of the Roman. The latter is often contracted as *Dasyria* (e.g., *CIL* 10.1554), *Iasura* (Franz

indicates that a locative deity has become a deity of anywhere. It is a "fellow traveler" (no. 2) with those who accompany it on the sea journey from Sarepta to Puteoli; its departure from the one, and its arrival at the other site are both memorialized. Its mode of transport is not unfamiliar. As with the well-known instances of Sarapis's transfer from Sinope to Alexandria, or from Egypt to Delos; the stone of Cybele from Pessinus to Rome; or the lesser known but more relevant tradition of the transport of a statue of Herakles from Tyre to Erythrae (Pausanias, *Descr.* 7.5.5–9), it is a lithic object, an image or an aniconic stone, that serves as the means of conveyance in response to the expressed will of the deity. As with these, Sarepta is accompanied by a native cult functionary ("one of the *Elim*," text no. 1). Meanwhile, its cult continues in its home city (Yale votive tablet, text no. 2).[17]

The phenomenon of enlarging the scope of a locative deity's range to that of anywhere is clearly associated with trade, with emigrants and their attendant associations (see already the fourth century BCE *koinon tôn Sidôniôn* at Piraeus devoted to the Baal of Sidon, *KAI* 60). Perhaps the most successful enlargement, in terms of both duration and dispersion, was the Tyrian linkage of the locative Melqart (*mlk-qrt*, "king of the city"; *mlqrt b r*, "Melqart in Tyre"; *b'l r*, "Lord of Tyre") with Herakles, the traveling deity *sans pareil*.[18] What I do not find in the southern Levantine region with

Cumont, *The Oriental Religions in Roman Paganism* [New York: Dover, 1956], 104), or named simply as *Syria* (*CIL* 3.10393).

17. With n. 13 above.

18. The association is already in Herodotus, *Hist.* 2.44; at the other end of the time scale, see the elaborate description of Tyre in Nonnus, *Dion.* 40.311–580, including Dionysos's invocation of Herakles-Melqart (lines 369–410), followed by a theophany (lines 411–580). The synchronism in Josephus, *Ant.* 8.5.3 §146, following Menander of Ephesus, guarantees the tradition in Judea in our time period.

The importance of Herakles in Syria from Tyre to Dura, ranging in date, iconographically, from the three Palestinian Persian period statues of Herakles (Palestine Archaeological Museum, *Gallery Book: Persian, Hellenistic, Roman, and Byzantine Periods* [Jerusalem; Palestine Archaeological Museum, 1943], nos. 759–61) to the presence of at least thirty images of Herakles in both temples and private houses at Dura (Susan B. Downey, *The Heracles Sculpture*. Final Report 3.1.1 of *The Excavations at Dura-Europos Conducted by Yale University and the French Academy of Inscriptions and Letters*, ed. C. Bradford Welles [New Haven: Dura-Europos Publications, 1969]; cf. Henri Seyrig, "Heracles-Nergal," *Syria* 24 [1944]: 77 n. 4) raises the question as to the degree to which the complex strands of the Hellenistic Herakles, important in Greco-Roman, Jewish (especially Philo, *Legat.* 78–79, 81, 90–93), and Christian texts

which we are concerned is the transformation of a god of anywhere to a god of everywhere such as is associated with Baal (Bel) Shamim, especially at Palmyra (invoked as Zeus in the Greek inscriptions from Palmyra), but not, apparently, with the Baal Shamin/Zeus equivalence at Tyre.[19]

The third text from Puteoli (no. 4) focuses not so much on divinity as it does on the fiscal problems of a commercial association of Tyrians in Puteoli (one of a group of such stations, for example, Rome). What it suggests are a number of important features: (1) The long-standing Levantine pattern of internationalism (for example, Carthage in relation to Tyre as in Diodorus Siculus, *Bib. hist.* 17.4.3; 20.14.1–2) persists with its complex interrelationships, responsibilities, and loyalties between the homeland and emigrant communities, as well as among the emigrant communities; (2) supported by a considerable translocal network of communication (in this case, both personal and written). (3) With respect to the homeland, the Tyrians maintain temples (note the plural) in Puteoli with "sacrifices and rituals" devoted to their "ancestral gods."[20] (4) This continuation of homeland practices occurred alongside active religious relations with the encompassing imperial culture. Text no. 4 specifies participation in a (civic) ox sacrifice feast as well as in the festival for the imperial birthday. (5) There is no hint that, thereby, the members of the "station" have lost their identities as Tyrians. That is to say, I see no clear indication of the shift that Shaye J. D. Cohen has shrewdly observed with respect to associations on Delos:

> The corporations of the Egyptians and Syrians on Delos and elsewhere in the Hellenistic age underwent a similar development [to that predicated in the revised edition of Schürer of associations in Judea].

---

and iconography were incorporated into the figure of Melqart-Herakles, especially in the Levant.

The Hellenistic Herakles is the only mythological figure whose comparison to aspects of the Christ myth remains, for me, interesting; see below, n. 31).

19. For Baal Shamin at Palmyra, see the review of the materials in Javier Teixidor, *The Pagan God: Popular Religion in the Greco-Roman Near East* (Princeton: Princeton University Press,1977), 130–35; cf. 135–38. For Baal Shamin/Zeus at Tyre, see Henri Seyrig, "Antiquités syriennes 83: Les grands dieux de Tyr à l'époque grecque et romaine," *Syria* 40 (1963): 19–20. I have deliberately abstained from the thorny question of (Theos) Hypsistos in Syrian traditions (Franz Cumont, "Ὕψιστος," PW 9:444–50; and Carsten Colpe, "Hypsistos," *KlPauly* 2:1291–92, provide useful summaries).

20. See n. 11 for other Syro-Phoenician religious data from Puteoli.

Originally ethnic in character, they gradually were redefined in religious terms. Thus the worshipers of Isis in Greece about 300 BCE called themselves "Egyptians," presumably because they were ethnic Egyptians, but by the second century BCE on Delos they had redefined themselves as the nonethnic association of "Isiasts." Other Egyptian Gods on Delos (Sarapis, Osiris, Anoubis) also had clubs of devotees (Sarapiasts, Osiriasts, Anoubiasts). Similarly, the Syrians in Delos originally called themselves "the association of the Syrian club members … whom the Goddess has assembled"; as the worship of the Goddess attracted Alexandrians, Athenians, Italians, and other non-Syrians—that is, as the association lost its ethnic character—they dropped the name "Syrians." They called themselves "the worshipers." It is not clear if the Phoenicians too broadened their base as did the Syrians; the associations of the Herakleistai and Poseidoniastai [on Delos] seem to have remained ethnic.[21]

(Rather than see Mark's "association" in terms of Jewish/gentile relations, it might be useful to ask whether it might be a group at the beginnings [?] of making an analogous transition.)

This said, taking the set of four texts quoted above, one is led to the most general sort of conclusion. In every way southwestern coastal Syria participated in the characteristic late antique patterns of religious persistence and change with respect to both homeland and diaspora features of domestic, civic, and temple-based cult; with respect to both priesthoods and associations; and with respect to the native preservation, as well as the translation into Greek, of old mythologies along with the development of new mythic traditions ranging from cosmogonies to royal ideologies.

To put this in another fashion, at the level of religious patterns, Syro-Phoenician religious phenomena are thoroughly comparable, in important respects, to what is frequently predicated of Judean religious phenomena. There are, of course, particular local histories which lead now to a marking, now to a relaxing, of constructed cultural boundaries, but these incidents ought not, in the main, inform any attempt at generalization concerning a coastal region that is, essentially, a "contact zone."

---

21. Cohen, *Beginnings of Jewishness*, 80 with n. 36.

2.

In southern Syria a local god by the name of Theandrites [earlier, The-andrios] bore in his own name a theological problem that the Christians thought they had created themselves. Theandrites means quite simply "The God-Man." His cult can be traced back for centuries in the fer-tile plain of the Hawrân, and his devotees can be found as far afield as North Africa.... But Theandrites was not only a local god, he was inter-national too.... The significance of a god-man deity in an indigenous cult of Semitic paganism scarcely needs underscoring. But the failure to notice him on the part of scholars of the early Christian church is almost culpable.
—G. W. Bowersock, *Hellenism in Late Antiquity*

By way of a conclusion to my 1992 tribute to Wilfred Cantwell Smith, I remarked,

The diversities between religions have never struck me as particularly interesting. They are sheerly different; nothing more needs to be said. But the diversities within religious traditions who understand themselves in some sense to be the "same," or between traditions who understand themselves in some sense to be related are differences which, at the very least, are potentially consequential. For, while these sorts of differences often lead to violence or to mutual anathematizing, they are the sorts of differences which most often lead to thought.[22]

---

22. Jonathan Z. Smith, "Scriptures and Histories (An Essay in Honor of Wilfred Cantwell Smith)," *MTSR* 4 (1992): 104–5. Cf. Smith, "*Adde Parvum Parvo Magnus Acervus Erit*," *HR* 11 (1971): 69; repr. in *Map Is Not Territory: Studies in the History of Religions*, SJLA 23 (Leiden: Brill, 1978; Chicago: University of Chicago Press, 1993), 242, where the category of "TOO-MUCH-LIKE-US" is introduced as one of the four spec-ifications of the "WE/THEY" duality. In Smith, "Differential Equations: On Construct-ing the Other," in *Relating Religion: Essays in the Study of Religion* (Chicago: University of Chicago Press, 2004), 245, the issue is reformulated: "The issue of difference as a mode of both culturally encoding and decoding, of maintaining and relativizing inter-nal as well as external distinctions, raises the last point, the observation that, rather than the remote 'other' being perceived as problematic and/or dangerous, it is the proximate 'other,' the near neighbor, who is most troublesome. That is to say, while difference or 'otherness' may be perceived as being either LIKE-US or NOT-LIKE-US, it becomes most problematic when it is TOO-MUCH-LIKE-US or when it claims to BE-US. It is here that the real urgency of theories of the 'other' emerges, called forth not so much by a requirement to place difference, but rather by an effort to situate ourselves.

As with Canaanites in the biblical creation of cultural boundaries or with the Samaritans for Judeans in the Greco-Roman period, this is particularly the case when ideological categories such as originality, dependence, and deviation are at stake. Thus it comes as no surprise that, with the exception of issues relating to Roman imperial sacra in Jerusalem (for example, Josephus, *J.W.* 2.9.2–3 §§169–174; *Ant.* 18.3.1 §§55–59), understood as "other,"[23] one of the longer narratives in Josephus's account of incidents leading up to the Roman-Jewish War is devoted to a conflict of the "near," one between Galileans and Samaritans in Gema, spreading to Jerusalem, and leading, ultimately, to the exile of Cumanus, Claudius's procurator in Judea (*J.W.* 2.12.3–7 §§232–246; *Ant.* 20.6.1–3 §§119–136).

This is not the setting in which to enter into the lengthy controversy over the identity of the people known as Samaritans in the Greco-Roman period. In their self-representation on Delos, they are "Israelites who contribute their offerings to the holy temple Argarizin [Gerazim]." They understand themselves to differ from the *Ioudaioi* in *genos* and *ethê* (Josephus, *Ant.* 12.5.5 §261), even though foreigners perceive them to share the same practices and to be their kin (*Ant.* 12.5.5 §260). While Josephus offers several vignettes of the intermural hostility between Samaritans and Judeans, an incident such as the alleged Samaritan attempt to pollute the Jerusalem temple testifies, at the same time, to the fact that, at first sight, Samaritans and Judeans are indistinguishable (*Ant.* 18.2.2 §§29–30; note the possible lacuna in the Greek text). The dramatic effort to prove the Samaritan side of the intracultural Jerusalem/Gerazim dispute (*Ant.* 12.1.1 §10; 13.3.4 §74; cf. John 4:20) was sufficient to result in a violent encounter between Samaritans and Roman troops under Pilate (*Ant.* 18.4.1 §§85–

This, then, is not a matter of the 'far' but preeminently of the 'near.' The deepest intellectual issues are not based upon perceptions of alterity, but, rather, of similarity, at times, even, of identity."

23. As Elias Bickerman, *Der Gott der Makkabäer: Untersuchungen über Sinn und Ursprung der Makkabäischen Erhebung* (Berlin: Schocken Verlag, 1937), ably demonstrates for Seleucid Jerusalem such symbols are by no means unambiguously evaluated as "other." The ambiguity is evident in the limited opposition to Herod's golden eagle on the doorway to the Temple in Jerusalem (Josephus, *J.W.* 1.33.2–4 §648–655 and *Ant.* 17.6.2–3 §149–157).

On the matter of images in relation to loci other than the temple, see the shrewd observation by R. Meyer that resistance to them depends on accepting the Pharisaic extension of sanctity from the cultic to the domestic sphere ("Die Figurendarstellung in der Kunst der späthellenistischen Zeit," *Jud* 5 [1949]: 12–13).

87; cf. the even more disastrous encounter under Vespasian, *J. W.* 3.7.32 §§307–315).

In Josephus's rendition of a letter addressed by the Samaritans in 166 BCE to Antiochus Epiphanes, organized by Josephus as a conscious counterpoint to the Judean experience with the same monarch (*Ant.* 12.5.5 §257), the Samaritans famously are represented as naming themselves "the Sidonians in Shechem" (*Ant.* 12.5.5 §258), as being "Sidonians by origin" (*Ant.* 12.5.5 §260). In the complex of new *origines gentium* myths this cuts both ways. For the Seleucids, the Samaritans being Sidonians means they are Phoenicians; for the Judeans, the same identification could be taken to mean the Samaritans are Canaanites—the former bearing a positive valence, the latter a negative one (see Josephus, *J. W.* 6.10.1 §439; in the Mishnah and the Tosefta any non-Israelitic slave is an *'eved Kena'ani*).[24]

---

24. Cf. Josephus, *J. W.* 1.2.6 §62–63 and *Ant.* 13.9.1 §255–256 for the destruction of the Samaritan temple at Gerazim (a "copy of the Temple in Jerusalem"; cf. *Ant.* 11.8.4 §322–24) in association with Hyrcanus's campaign at Shechem, a campaign also associated with the forced circumcision and "conversion" of the Idumaeans. (Cf. the circumcision of the eponymous Shechem in Gen 34:14–18, with far from the promised results.) Josephus, in a polemic ethnic identification, here terms the Samaritans "Cuthaeans" (*Ant.* 11.7.2 §302; cf. the Cuthaean transportation to Samaria, *Ant.* 9.14.3 §288). As with its biblical role representing the Northern Kingdom, Shechem serves here as a sign of the proximate other (and a powerful religious rival to Jerusalem); see, among others, the hexameters by Theodotus on Shechem, whether the author be a Judean or a Samaritan (Carl R. Holladay, ed., *Poets,* vol. 2 of *Fragments from Hellenistic Jewish Authors,* SBLTT 30 [Atlanta: Scholars Press, 1989], 51–204, with rich notes and bibliography)—reinforced by the mention of both Samaritans/Cuthaeans and Idumaeans.

The most provocative study of the Samaritan traditions remains Hans Gerhard Kippenberg, *Garizim und Synagoge: Traditionsgeschichtliche Untersuchung zur samaritanischen Religion der aramäischen Periode,* RVV 30 (Berlin: de Gruyter, 1971).

While my emphasis in interpreting the Samaritans' self-identification as Sidonians in Josephus, *Ant.* 12.5.5 §257–264 is different, I am entirely dependent here on the lexical materials reviewed in Elias Bickerman's brilliant article, "Un document relatif à la persécution d'Antiochus IV Epiphane," *RHR* 115 (1937): 188–221; cf. Martin Hengel, *Judaism and Hellenism: Studies in Their Encounter in Palestine during the Early Hellenistic Period,* trans. J. Bowden, 2 vols. (Philadelphia: Fortress, 1974), 2:195 n. 233; Morton Smith, *Palestinian Parties and Politics that Shaped the Old Testament,* 2nd ed. (London: SCM, 1987), 143–45. My general framework is dependent on Bickerman's classic article, "*Origines Gentium,*" *CP* 47 (1952): 65–81. It is not without significance that, except for the Tyrian identification of Melqart with Herakles, it is Sidon that provides Bickerman with his most specific Syro-Phoenician examples of the pattern

I assume some such situation of thought and conflict about differences, which are interesting (or troublesome) within a general perception of similarity to be the case in the Levant—whether of the tenth century BCE or the first century CE. After all, the varied sorts of folk all speak some Northwest Semitic language (that is, one of the Syro-Palestinian languages). In much of the region in our period, Aramaic and Greek serve as common media of communication. To take the two taxic indicators of

---

(74). I note as a curiosity the first-century tradition in Pompeius Trogus (*apud* Marcus Juniamus Justinus, *Epitoma historiarum Philippicarum Pompei Trogi: Accedunt prologi in Pompeium Trogum,* ed. Franz Rühl and Otto Seel, 2nd ed. [Stuttgart: Teubner, 1972], 36.2.1); van Berg, *Corpus Cultus Deae Syriae,* 1.1: no. 64; cf. 1.2:111–12) that the "Jews were originally from Damascus, the most illustrious city in Syria." The source here may well be Nicolas of Damascus (*apud* Josephus, *Ant.* 1.7.2 §159–160; and Eusebius, *Praep. ev.* 9.16.417C).

The issue of Canaanite/Sidonian/Phoenician is, of course, far more complex, both as a historical matter and within the Greco-Roman ethnohistories. From the Judean side, the notice of Gen 10:15, "Canaan became the father of Sidon" (MT, LXX), is the obvious starting point. I take it that this lies behind the textual variation between the *sperma Chanaan* and the *sperma Sidōnos* in Sus 56. Canaan/Canaanite is occasionally translated as Phoenicia/Phoenician in the LXX, but in relatively insignificant passages without apparent pattern (HRCS 3:155); cf. Matt 15:22 which alters the Syro-Phoenician woman of Mark 7:26 to a Canaanite woman (see the conclusion to this paper, below), both agreeing on the location in the region of Tyre and Sidon (Mark 7:24, 31; Matt 15:21; a variant reading of Mark 7:26 reads a Syrian woman rather than a Syro-Phoenician). Perhaps of more interest is the LXX translation of Sidon as Phoenicia (Isa 23:2) and of Sidonians as Phoenicians (Deut 3:9). On the Samaritan (?) side, Pseudo-Eupolemus persistently uses Phoenicia/Phoenicians for Canaan/Canaanites (Carl R. Holladay, ed., *Historians,* vol. 1 of *Fragments from Hellenistic Jewish Authors,* SBLTT 20 (Chico, CA: Scholars Press, 1983), 181 n. 13]). See, further, n. 41 below.

The Idumaeans present an interesting parallel. Judean texts emphasize their forced conversion as the result of a military defeat (e.g., Josephus, *Ant.* 13.9.1 §257–258; Strabo, *Geogr.* 16.2.34, represents it as a voluntary departure from the Nabataeans); Ptolemy of Ascalon (?) notes their compulsory circumcision but gives them a more prestigious pedigree: they were "Syrians and Phoenicians" (*FGrHist* 199; Menahem Stern, ed., *Greek and Latin Authors on Jews and Judaism,* 3 vols. [Jerusalem: Israel Academy of Sciences and Humanities, 1974–1984], no. 146; Schürer, *History of the Jewish People,* 1:27–28). Enlarging their pedigree, and making them equivalent in prestige to the Judeans, Alexander Polyhistor has Judah and Idumaea as the children of the "Syrian" Semiramis (*FGrHist* 273; Stern, *Greek and Latin Authors,* no. 53); the two sons of Semiramis are well known in Greek reports (especially in Ktesias), but this appears to be a unique identification). It should be noted that the citations of Ptolemy and Alexander Polyhistor occur in late schools.

most interest to outsiders, circumcision was widely practiced throughout the region (already in third millennium BCE western Syria)[25] and some form of pork avoidance (more usually cultic rather than domestic) was common.[26] Both practices persist well into the Greco-Roman period.

The histories of these peoples were intertwined for centuries (one need think only of Tyre and Jerusalem),[27] and these histories were subjected to continual processes of reinterpretation in light of present conditions and perceptions of the directionality and valence of the interrelationships. The

---

25. See, already, Herodotus, *Hist.* 2.104, which lists the Phoenicians (except those in contact with Greeks; cf. Ezek 32:30 for the claim that the Sidonians were uncircumcised), the Palestinian Syrians (despite Josephus, *Ant.* 8.10.3 §262; *Ag. Ap.* 1.22 §169–171; and Diodorus Siculus, *Bib. hist.* 1.28, there is no need to confine this reference to the Judeans), the Syrians who live near the Thermodon and Parthenius rivers, the Macrones, as well as the Colchians, Egyptians, and Ethiopians who are considered by Herodotus to be the originators of the custom. As Jack M. Sasson has convincingly argued, the practice is a West Semitic-Syrian one, as early as the third millennium BCE ("Circumcision in the Ancient Near East," *JBL* 85 [1966]: 473–76). The mythic presence of circumcision in Philo of Byblos (*FGrHist* 790 F 2) suggests its persistence in the Roman period, surely until Hadrian's prohibition. The practice "officially" returns with Elagabalus in 218 CE (Dio Cassius, *Hist. Rom.* 80.11.1). Note that the ethnographic catalogues in Jewish texts such as Jer 9:24–25 and Philo, *QG* 3.48, omit the Syro-Phoenician, but add the Arabian tribes.

26. See, among other loci, *CIL* 5.4242; Herodian, *Hist.* 5.6.9; Silius Italicus, *Pun.* 3.21–26; Porphyry, *Abst.* 1.14, as well as the discussion in Denis van Berchem, "Sanctuaires d'Hercule-Melqart: Contribution à l'étude de l'expansion phénicienne en Mediterranée," *Syria* 44 (1967): 86–90, 99–100. See also the statue on Delos of Astartê Palaistinê Aphroditê Ourania, donated by an individual from Ashkelon, containing the well-known inscription, "It is unlawful to offer any part of a goat, pig or cow" (*ID* 2305; André Plassart, *Les sanctuaires et les cultes du Mont Cynthe*, Exploration archéologique de Délos 11 [Paris: E. de Boccard, 1928], 287).

27. One must begin with the blunt observation by Herbert Niehr, "The Rise of YHWH in Judahite and Israelite Religion: Methodological and Religio-Historical Aspects," in *The Triumph of Elohim: From Yahwisms to Judaisms*, ed. D. V. Edelman (Grand Rapids: Eerdmans, 1996), 53 with n. 26: "Since Judah became a state only during the 8th century BCE, historians must reckon with the existence of a modest Judahite chiefdom before that time which was politically and economically dependent on Tyre"; cf. J. K. Kuan, "Third Kingdoms 5.1 and Israelite-Tyrian Relations during the Reign of Solomon," *JSOT* 46 (1990): 31–46. The most impressive literary reflections of the relationship to Tyre in the Hebrew Bible are the oracles against Tyre in Isa 23 and Ezek 26–28 (both with interpolations). It has been suggested that Ezek 27:12–24 quotes a Tyrian poem (Maria Eugenia Aubet, *The Phoenicians and the West: Politics, Colonies, and Trade* [Cambridge: Cambridge University Press, 1993], 98–99).

several Judean and Phoenician versions of the relations of Solomon and Hiram are sufficient to make this point.[28]

There have been religious relationships as well, ranging, on the Judean side, from the experiment by the Jerusalem "Hellenizers" with an essentially Syro-Phoenician cult of Zeus Olympias/Baal Shamen (2 Macc 6:2), as well as the Judean delegation with funds to sacrifice at the Tyrian festival of Herakles-Melqart (2 Macc 4:18–20), to a possible Roman era mixed cult of Sabaoth Adonai in Sidon (*CIJ* 875–876); on the Syrian side, such interrelationships include those Syrians' wives who had associated themselves with some form of Judaism (Josephus, *J. W.* 2.20.2 §§559–560).

For these reasons, I see no need to confine Mark's relations only to a Jewish setting. I can imagine equally "heady," as well as heated, conversations with Syro-Phoenicians (and, for that matter, with Samaritans, Idumaeans, and Nabataeans) about questions of religious interest which might come to inform discourse in Mark's Levantine Judean association. If one violates an item in the purity code, is confession required?[29] Is a meal in an association subject to the same scruples as a meal in a temple?[30]

---

28. While the differences between the Deuteronomistic and the Chronicler historical narratives are not without interest, the most elaborated reinterpretation is surely Eupolemus, frg. 2 (Holladay, *Historians*, 114–31, 138–52), especially in the treatment of Erich S. Gruen, *Heritage and Hellenism: The Reinvention of Jewish Tradition* (Berkeley: University of California Press, 1998), 143–46, with bibliography. The Phoenician traditions are reported and interacted with in Josephus, *Ag. Ap.* 1.17–18 §107–127; *Ant.* 8.2.6–9 §50–60; 8.4.6–8.6.1 §127–154. See Ben Zion Wacholder, *Eupolemus: A Study of Judaeo-Greek Literature* (Cincinnati: Hebrew Union College-Jewish Institute of Religion, 1975), 217–23; H. Jacob Katzenstein, *The History of Tyre: From the Beginning of the Second Millenium B.C.E until the Fall of the Neo-Babylonian Empire in 538 B.C.E.* (Jerusalem: Schocken Institute for Jewish Research, 1973), 77–115.

29. See Raffaele Pettazzoni, "La confession des péchés en Syrie aux époques préchrétiennes," in vol. 1 of *Mélanges syriens offerts à Monsier René Dussaud*, Bibliothèque archéologique et historique 30 (Paris: Geuthner, 1939), 1:197–202.

30. As is often noted, "dining-rooms were a special feature of Syrian temples" (Arthur Darby Nock, "Religious Symbols and Symbolism II," in *Arthur Darby Nock: Essays on Religion and the Ancient World*, ed. Zeph Stewart, [Oxford: Clarendon, 1972], 2:905); "in Syria, even a little rural shrine might have five separate rooms for eating" (Ramsay MacMullen, *Paganism in the Roman Empire* [New Haven: Yale University Press, 1981], 37, citing Jean Starcky, "Autour d'une dédicace palmyrénienne à Sadrafa et à Du'anat," *Syria* 26 [1949]: 43–85, esp. 62). Any number of temple inscriptions mention *triklinia* or other elements of feasting in association with Syro-Phoenician deities and cults (e.g., *IGRR* 3.1045, 1533; *CIL* 3.4789, 79545; 6.30931, 8750–8751;

What happened in Sidon a generation ago that resulted in the "fraud" of the revenant, Pseudo-Alexander (Josephus, *J.W.* 2.7.1–2 §§101–110; *Ant.* 17.12.1–2 §§324–338)? How does Herakles assuming the form of a slave relate to his being a model for kingship?[31] Who is Theandrites?[32] What

---

10.1590; 11.696; see also Ernest Will, "Cultes et salles de banquet dans les cultes de la Grèce et de l'Empire romain," in *De l'Euphrate au Rhin: Aspects de l'hellenisation et de la romanisation du Proche-Orient* [Beirut: Institut Français D'Archéologie du Proche-Orient, 1995], 393–402). On the other hand, meals are a major focus of religious associations, both in their native and their emigrant form (e.g., *OGIS* 591 at Delos). At times, these come together; see, for example, the *marzeah* association room (*smk'*) in the northern angle of the Baal Shamin temple court in Palmyra (Paul Collart and Jacques Vicari, *Le sanctuaire de Baalshamin à Palmyre: Topographie et architecture*, 2 vols., Bibliotheca Helvetica Romana 10 [Neuchâtel: Paul Attinger, 1969], 1:63–65; Teixidor, *Pagan God*, 132–35).

I am tempted to suggest, from a later period, that proximity to the plethora of dining halls in the Dura temples may have prompted the Hebrew halakhic liturgical fragment from the Dura Jewish association (i.e., the synagogue) focused on permitted and forbidden animal food. See Charles Bradford Welles, Robert O. Fink, and J. Frank Gilliam, eds., *The Parchments and Papyri: The Excavations at Dura Europos*, Final Report 5.1 (New Haven: Yale University Press, 1959), no. 11.

Note that the issues treated here in nn. 30–31 would have particular relevance to matters of mutual assessment between any other form of Jewish association and the Pharisaic *havurah*, which (following Jacob Neusner) I understand to be (pre-70 CE) largely concerned with an association of lay folk undertaking to eat in a domestic setting following the dietary rules appropriate to priests' meals. See Jacob Neusner, *Fellowship in Judasim: The First Century and Today* (London: Valentine, Mitchell, 1963), 22–40; revised in Neusner, *From Politics to Piety: The Emergence of Pharisaic Judaism* (Englewood Cliffs, NJ: Prentice-Hall, 1973), 83–90.

31. I have in mind particularly the materials in Ragnar Hoïstad, *Cynic Hero and Cynic King: Studies in the Cynic Conception of Man* (Lund: Bloms, 1948). See also, on Herakles and kingship, Andrew Runni Anderson, "Heracles and His Successors," *HSCP* 39 (1928): 7–58; J. Tondriau, "Héracles, Héraclides et autres émules du héros," *Annali di Instituto Lombardo, Scienza e lettere* 83 (1950): 397–406; Wilhelm Derichs, "Herakles, Vorbild des Herrschers in der Antike" (PhD diss., University of Cologne, 1951). For the philosophical mythologization, see also R. Friedrich Pfister, "Herakles und Christus," *AR* 34 (1937): 42–60; Herbert Jennings Rose, "Heracles and the Gospels," *HTR* 31 (1938): 113–42; Robert Schilling, "L'Hercule romain et la réforme religieuse d'Auguste," *RevPhil* 16 (1942): 31–57; Gilbert Murray, "Heracles 'The Best of Men,'" in *Greek Studies* (Oxford: Clarendon Press, 1946), 106–26; B. M. Marti, "L'Hercule sur l'Oeta," *Revue des études latines* 27 (1949): 189–210; Marcel Simon, *Hercule et le Christianisme* (Paris: Les Belles Lettres, 1955); and, most usefully, David E. Aune, "Heracles and Christ: Heracles Imagery in the Christology of Early Christi-

price did you get for your olive oil?[33] Are there problems with the Tyrian mint?[34] What are the Romans up to? What will it mean for us? The similarities these questions presume, and the differences that would be noted, become occasions for marking boundaries.

It is in this context that I appreciated Burton L. Mack's effort in *A Myth of Innocence* (chapters 1 and 7) to speak of "synagogue reform," "meal practices" in the context, especially, of the pronouncement stories, and to relate these, in Mark, to a "failure" of the "reform."[35] I am persuaded by the theoretical contributions of Nicholas Thomas and Marshall Sahlins that it is not only cosmic events, but also small incidents that are provocative for thought about similarities and differences, the near and the far, especially with respect to "proximate others."[36] For example, in Josephus's account of

anity," in *Greeks, Romans, and Christians: Essays in Honor of Abraham J. Malherbe*, ed. David L. Balch, Everett Ferguson, and Wayne Meeks (Minneapolis: Fortress, 1990), 3–19; cf. Aune, "Herakles," *DDD*, 402–5. See above, n. 18.

32. On Theandrios/Theandrites, see Dominique Sourdel, *Les cultes du Hauran à l'époque romaine*, Institut Français d'Archéologie de Beyrouth, Bibliothèque archéologique et historique 53 (Paris: Geuthner, 1952), 78–81; G. W. Bowersock, "An Arabian Trinity," *HTR* 79 (1986): 17–21; cf. Bowersock, *Hellenism in Late Antiquity*, 4, 18; Schürer, *History of the Jewish People*, 2:42 n. 76. Inscriptions: William Henry Waddington, *Inscriptions grecques et latines de Syrie* (Paris: Didot, 1870; repr. Rome, 1968): 2046, 2374a (= *CIG* 4609, addenda, p. 1181), 2481; Enno Littman, David Magee Jr., and Duane Reed Stuart, eds., *Greek and Latin Inscriptions in Syria: Div. 3, Sect. A; Southern Syria*, Publications of the Princeton Archaeological Expedition to Syria in 1904–5 and 1909 (Leiden: Brill, 1907–1921): 693, 763; *ILS*: 4349; Robert C. Gregg and Dan Urman, *Jews, Pagans, and Christians in the Golan Heights: Greek and Other Inscriptions of the Roman and Byzantine Eras*, SFSHJ 140 (Atlanta: Scholars Press, 1996), 147. The god seems to have been important to late empire Neo-Platonic philosophers, especially Proclus (Marinus, *V. Procli* 19).

Later Theandros appears as a Christian name in Qoureye near Bostra (Waddington, *Inscriptions grecques et latines de Syrie*, 1905) and as Christian theological term (*PGL*, s.v. θεανδρίτης and θεανδρικός).

33. See Zeev Safrai, *The Economy of Roman Palestine* (London: Routledge, 1994), 122–27 et passim.

34. John S. Kloppenborg, *Excavating Q: The History and Setting of the Sayings Gospel* (Edinburgh: T&T Clark, 2000; repr., Minneapolis: Fortress, 2000), 173, n. 9 has a useful catalogue of finds of Tyrian coins in North Galilee.

35. Burton L. Mack, *A Myth of Innocence: Mark and Christian Origins* (Philadelphia: Fortress, 1988; repr. with new preface, Minneapolis: Fortress, 2006).

36. In emphasizing little incidents, I am gaining a further assist from Thomas, *Out of Time*, 84–85, who writes of the need for a different sort of historiographical

the antecedents of the Roman-Jewish War, these might include the construction of a building on land adjacent to a synagogue which resulted in narrowing the passage between the two buildings, leading to both a small Jewish insurrection and a small act of Caesarean desecration (*J.W.* 2.14.4–5 §§284–292); an armed dispute over civic ancestry (*J.W.* 2.13.7 §§266–270;[37] or the massacres of Judeans in which closely associated Syro-Phoenician cities participated differently—Tyre joining, Sidon abstaining (*J.W.* 2.18.5 §§477–479).[38] Each of these would be occasions for thought.

Within Mark, such thought comes to focus in 7:24–30, the narrative of the Syro-Phoenician woman which is concerned with a well-known Syrian religious practice, exorcism (Lucian, *Philops.* 16). Together with 7:31, the Markan redactional frame contains one of the denser concentrations of Levantine topography in the New Testament: a circuit of the outer northern limits of Jesus's loci of activity. As is well known, the narrative has been identified as pre-Markan, one of a double miracle chain, paired with Jairus's daughter (Mark 5:21–23, 35–43) and the woman with the flow of blood (Mark 5:25–34), and associated with Elijah traditions.[39]

Many understandings of the pericope of the Syro-Phoenician woman appear, to me, overdetermined by its Matthean redaction (Matt 15:21–28). While both agree on the locale of the encounter, the Tyrian-Sidonian coastal region (Mark 7:24 [some manuscripts have Tyre only] // Matt 15:21), the alteration of the woman's identification from being a "Greek,

---

inquiry which understands that native accounts may "reflect the absent causes in the living group: happenings which shape practice and arrangements, but which are not known or spoken of." I relate this to my discussion of Sahlins's "incidents" in intracultural situations in my seminar paper, "Conjectures on Conjunctures and Other Matters," in this volume, 30–34.

37. See Cohen, *Beginnings of Jewishness*, 15–16.

38. As it does not involve relations with Syro-Phoenicians, I regretfully exclude the incident of the Roman soldier's fart (Josephus, *J.W.* 2.12.1 §224–227). There is nothing in Josephus's account of the post-70 aftermath that would allow one to gauge the impact on the coastal region. The route of Titus's triumphal procession organizes Josephus's narration in *J.W.* 7: from Jerusalem to Caesarea (*J.W.* 7.2–3 §36–37), then to Berytus (*J.W.* 7.3.1 §39), followed by a journey "through a number of Syrian towns" (*J.W.* 7.5.1 §96) to Antioch which becomes the focus of Josephus's narrative (esp. *J.W.* 7.5.2 §100–111).

39. Paul J. Achtemeier, "Toward the Isolation of Pre-Markan Miracle Catenae," *JBL* 89 (1970): 287–88.

a Syro-Phoenician by birth" (Mark 7:26)[40] to a "Canaanite … from that region" (Matt 15:22) places her within a differently valenced pedigree, that of a traditional proximate other.[41] The entire Matthean narrative expansion (Matt 15:22b–24), her address to Jesus as "Lord, Son of David," his disciples' rejection of her, Jesus's response invoking his being sent "only to the lost sheep of the house of Israel"—all invoke the ancient biblical contestation between "the house of Israel" and Canaan concentrated in, but not limited to, the Deuteronomistic conquest myth. Furthermore, the identification itself is mythic; no first-century Levantine, to the best of my knowledge, would identify her- or himself as a Canaanite.[42] The "children" in Jesus's harsh saying (Matt 15:26) have to be the "house of Israel" as, probably, does the "master" in Matthew's version of the woman's rejoinder. It is an ethnic insider/outsider conflict, resolved only by the woman's "faith" (Matt 15:28a), which results in one of Jesus's long-range healings.

Shorn of the Matthean reinterpretation, the Markan narrative is far less definite, far more edgy. It suggests a relationship presently being experimented with, rather than one definitively settled in the distant past. The woman's initial response of *proskynêsis* (Mark 7:25c, admittedly, *prospiptein*) obviates the need for noting the woman's faith. The successful response to her petition depends entirely, as best as I can see, on her clever rejoinder to Jesus's saying. Her identification as a "Hellene [*hellēnis*], a Syro-Phoenician by birth" (7:26) is both a cultural and an ethnic designation that carries prestige in the Levant.[43] It marks her as a proximate other with which relations are possible, unencumbered by an epic past. The referent of "children" is less explicit; but the exclusionary sense divined by Matthew in the term is surely not present. The Markan "first" in "let the children be fed first" (7:27) raises possibilities by suggesting that others

---

40. Note the variant, "a Syrian women."

41. See n. 25.

42. Unless speaking Phoenician (but see Millar, *Roman Near East*, 274–75, 290, et passim). The most often cited example of the term is the Phoenician text on the third century BCE coinage (Beirut mint) from Laodicea ad Mare; *l:dk>sbkncn*, translated into Greek as *Laodikeia he en Phoinike* (*RlA*, 5:354), which demonstrates the persistence of the term *kncn* in Semitic languages, but its replacement by "Phoenicia" in Greek. The fourth century CE report of Augustine, *Exp. quaest. Rom.* 13 [PL 35:2096]), that the Carthaginians, when questioned "in Phoenician" termed themselves Chanani makes the same point. For other examples, see Zellig S. Harris, *A Grammar of the Phoenician Language*, AOS 8 (New Haven: American Oriental Society, 1936), 7.

43. See, again, n. 26.

may be fed second or later. (I assume, with Paul Achtemeier, that *proton* is part of Mark's redaction.[44]) At the very least, while lacking commensality, the matter of a (positive) relationship is left open.

I am tempted to make a further suggestion with reference to the Elijah-Elisha echoes postulated for this episode. Beyond Q 10:13–15, which to some degree damns Tyre and Sidon with faint praise, and the geographical listing of Mark 3:7–8, which largely signifies "every one," the only other topographical reference of note to the Levant is in the special Lukan narrative 4:16–30, especially verses 25–27, with its mention of both the widow of Sarepta and Naaman the Syrian, the one miraculously fed by Elijah during a Samaritan drought and famine (1 Kgs 17:8–16), the other healed by Elisha of leprosy in a most complex narrative (2 Kgs 5:1–27)—with the point made that Elijah and Elisha were sent to "no one" in Israel, "but only" to these Syro-Phoenicians. (The sphere of Elijah's activity largely borders on what will become Syro-Phoenicia, culminating in the contest with the priests of Baal at Mount Carmel [1 Kgs 18:20–40] and marked by controversy with King Ahab's Phoenician wife, Jezebel, the "daughter of King Ethbaal of the Sidonians" [1 Kgs 16:31].) The point here is not well captured by general phrases such as the "gentile mission." Rather, the passage suggests some original (Jewish?) interest in collecting precedents for positive Levantine relations, carried over, perhaps by Syrian Christians, in Luke's time.

I note, as well, the presence among the wall paintings in the Dura synagogue of three Elijah scenes: Elijah's feeding of the widow, along with the contest at Carmel, is depicted on the south wall; Elijah's revival of the Sareptan widow's son (1 Kgs 17:17–24) is on the west wall.[45] This juxtaposition—both Sarepta incidents, positive; the Carmel conflict, negative—might suggest a continued Syrian Jewish interest in experimenting with, in mapping and exploring, Syro-Phoenician relations.

It remains only to relate the above to some of the agenda of the seminar in terms of other elements in the Markan site. It seems to me that

---

44. Achtemeier, "Toward the Isolation of Pre-Markan Miracle Catenae," 287.

45. Carl H. Kraeling, *The Synagogue: The Excavations at Dura-Europos Conducted by the Yale University and the French Academy of Inscriptions and Letters*, Final Report 8.1 (New Haven: Yale University Press, 1956), 134–50; Goodenough, *Jewish Symbols in the Greco-Roman Period*, 1–13; Goodenough, *Symbolism in the Dura Synagogue*, vols. 9–11 in *Jewish Symbols in the Greco-Roman Period*, Bollingen Series 37 (New York: Pantheon, 1964), 9:227–37; 10:148–59; 11: plates VIII and XV, figures 335, 340–42.

Q-type Jesus teachings and some forms of non-Pauline Christ traditions are available pre-70 CE. Levantine philosophical interests (as conveniently documented by Martin Hengel)[46] would be sufficient to suggest an audience for the former; mythologies associated with Herakles-Melqart are sufficient for the latter.[47]

The presence of Pharisees in Galilee pre-70 is difficult enough to establish, let alone for the Syro-Phoenician area. I suppose, on the analogy of the rabbinic move after the Second Jewish War, that one might imagine some Pharisaic movement north post-70. The destruction of the temple would have removed the urgency of a focus on a domestic setting for their purity concerns, and if we presume their continued existence, then the formation of associations which might bring them into conflict with other sorts of associations such as synagogues is plausible. While the Pharisaic concern would be entirely with intra-Judean relations, I have suggested that the relations of purity in associations to those of temples would be a matter of interest to both Syro-Phoenicians and Levantine Jews;[48] the destruction of the temple would seem to encourage experimentation with respect to the taxonomies of purity and forbidden things. (While later in date, see the well-known anecdote of Rabbi Gamaliel and Proklos the philosopher [son of Philosophos] in the Bath of Aphrodite in Ptolemais [m. ʿAbod. Zar. 3:4].)

Apocalyptic traditions are the ones most difficult to account for within a Levantine context. While there are clearly occasional instances of rebellion and resistance, largely in the context of the decline of Seleucid power (Dio Cassius, *Hist. Rom.* 54.7.6 may be an exception), I can think of no native Syrian apocalypse analogous to those of Egypt or Iran. Perhaps this is due, at least in part, to the lack of strong native kingship or of strong ideologies of the same.

The Judean linkage of apocalypse and temple destruction/profanation appears distinctive in the region. (It is prominent in Egyptian traditions.) While there are historical and theological reflections as well as some connection to a restoration through the agency of a redeeming figure (the *Taheb*), I know of no Samaritan apocalypse in response to the second century BCE destruction of the temple on Gerazim until some mythic

---

46. Hengel, *Judaism and Hellenism*, 1:83–88.
47. See n. 32.
48. See n. 31.

elements are developed in medieval texts.[49] Nor is there any sign that Syrians interpreted in an apocalyptic fashion the results of a widespread earthquake, during the reign of Claudius, which destroyed, among other locales, the temples of Artemis, Area, and Herakles in Antioch.[50]

I am intrigued by the arguments of some scholars for locating the Jewish redaction of the fourth Sibylline Oracle (4.1–48, 102–92), framing an earlier anti-Macedonian oracle (4.49–101) of unknown date and provenance, in southern Syria or the Transjordan, ca. 80 CE. The fact that this text appears to reject in principle all temple worship as impiety (4.8–11, 24–30), including that of the temple in Jerusalem (4.115–119), resulting in its destruction by the Romans (4.115–116, 125–127), makes it an interesting point of comparison with the Markan construction.

---

49. See the convenient summary in John MacDonald, *The Theology of the Samaritans*, NTL (London: SCM, 1964), 364–71; see the discussion of first through fourth century traditions in Wayne A. Meeks, *The Prophet-King: Moses Traditions and the Johannine Christology*, NovTSup 14 (Leiden: Brill, 1967), 246–50. As noted above (114–15), Josephus, *Ant* 18.85–87, is evidence for a Samaritan nativistic movement at Gerazim; see further, Marilyn F. Collins, "The Hidden Vessels in Samaritan Traditions," *JSJ* 3 (1972): 97–116.

50. Glanville Downey, *A History of Antioch in Syria: From Seleucus to the Arab Conquest* (Princeton: Princeton University Press, 1961), 196.

Cartwheels:
Or On Not Staying Upside Down Too Long

Burton L. Mack

Pre- and Re-

While I know that there are no originary events, no replications, that all moments of construal are reinterpretation or redescription of reinterpretations and redescriptions, there are times when knowing the pre-re-moments help in explaining the re-re-moments. This seems to be one of those pre-pre-re-re cases. What the seminar does not know, but I know full well, is that, trading letters, papers, phone calls, and memos with Jonathan Z. Smith in the course of what he has called receiving his "assignment" from the executive committee, has had me doing cartwheels all summer long. Willi Braun has written to say that receiving Smith's "dossiers" has "adrenalized and overwhelmed" him at the same time. But what if you saw these dossiers as only the final version of Smith's many "assignments" to me, and that in effect I had innocently asked for them? My "Heady Stuff" paper needed some qualifications.[1] And our categories of "social formation" and "mythmaking" needed a lot of redefinition, if we wanted to move on to Mark with theories of "conjuncture," "reproduction," and "transformation" as the frame.

It was Merrill Miller who thought it time to get more specific about the ways in which category definition and social theory were impinging upon our seminar projects of redescription. He noted Smith's "nexus" statement in his "Metareflection" and his challenge for more precision in the way in which some of our "second-order" categories were being used (such

---

1. Burton L. Mack, "Heady Stuff in the Mile High City," paper presented at the Ancient Myths and Modern Theories of Christian Origins Seminar, December 2001.

as "ethnicity" and "epic").[2] Miller also noted my reference to Sahlins's "structures of conjuncture" in "Heady Stuff" and my suggestion that we see it as a more responsible way of getting "social formation" and "myth-making" together than I had yet been able to do. I used the term "mecha-nism," thinking of the dynamics Sahlins described for the way in which the changes took place in both social and cultural systems in his analysis of the Cook/Lono chapter of Hawaiian colonial history. Miller wanted to know if each of us could say more about "nexus" and "mechanism," especially in light of the problem we would have with the redescription of a social set-ting for Mark.

The two papers Smith has written for seminar discussion are his response to Miller's queries and my own suggestion that it might be time for the seminar to engage Smith's "agendum" directly in relation to the seminar's own project. The "Conjectures" paper is Smith's way of (1) posi-tioning his own social theory within the histories of scholarly discourse, (2) using Sahlins's work as an entrée to those histories (since the seminar had already found his references to Sahlins productive), and (3) focusing upon conceptual issues pertinent to the seminar's project.[3] His paper on Mark, on the other hand, serves (1) as a Smithian "e.g." for the "applica-tion" of Smith's social theory (of "situation") to one of the seminar's "sites," as well as (2) an experiment in method for the location and redescription of a mythic text.[4] It is a response, not only to the challenge that we explore starting with social situation instead of the logic of a myth, but also that a situation needs to be described in such a way that the dynamics of rela-tions and changes in behavior and thinking are imaginable. With that in mind, I would like now to make a few observations about the papers.

Conjuncture and Situation

In his Denver paper ("Re: Corinthians"), Smith referred to Sahlins's *His-torical Metaphors and Mythical Realities* as analogy to his own description of a postcolonial chapter of history in Papua New Guinea, which he then

---

2. The reference is to Jonathan Z. Smith, "*Dayyeinu,*" in *Redescribing Christian Origins*, ed. Ron Cameron and Merrill P. Miller, SymS 28 (Atlanta: Society of Biblical Literature, 2004), 483–87.

3. See Jonathan Z. Smith, "Conjectures on Conjunctures and Other Matters: Three Essays" (in this volume).

4. Jonathan Z. Smith, "The Markan Site" (in this volume).

used as analogy for his redescription of Paul's encounter with the Corinthians.[5] As a result we were able to reimagine the dynamics of the cross-cultural "mythmaking" and social behavioral moments in the Corinthian situation much differently than before. Smith apparently took note of our response to his reference to Sahlins's terminology and decided to start with Sahlins as a way to introduce his (Smith's) own history of conceptual refinements in a dynamic social anthropology with structural, linguistic, and intellectual components. I note the care with which the pedigrees for Sahlins and his terminologies are traced and explained. I note Smith's agreements with and/or appreciations for Sahlins's thought as social theorist and historian. I also note the ways in which Smith interweaves his own interests and thinking into the explications, debates, and genealogical histories of Sahlins's thinking about culture and history.

These Smithian construals of Sahlins's work are of importance, not only as explications of Smith's own "agendum" but also as his address to me and the seminar on issues of category formation pertinent to our project. There is the modification of Marxist theories of reproduction by including concepts of structure, history, and transformation. There is the delight and intellectual advance resulting from setting up "uncontrolled" comparisons, working with cross-cultural analogies, and striving for generalizations. There is the distinction between intercultural and intracultural situations and events. There is also the development of language to distinguish intracultural events ("incidents") from intercultural events ("conjunctures"). Taking the last distinction as an example of Smith's address to the seminar, "conjuncture" may well continue to be helpful for describing the Paul-Corinthian situation, but it can no longer serve this purpose for the Markan. (I note that, while Smith makes this point in his "Conjectures" paper, he reserves a critical discussion of the reasons for it, proposed by Nicholas Thomas,[6] for the introduction to the Mark paper.)

---

5. See Jonathan Z. Smith, "Re: Corinthians," in *Relating Religion: Essays in the Study of Religion* (Chicago: University of Chicago Press, 2004), 340–61; repr. in *Redescribing Paul and the Corinthians*, ed. Ron Cameron and Merrill P. Miller, ECL 5 (Atlanta: Society of Biblical Literature, 2011), 17–34; Marshall Sahlins, *Historical Metaphors and Mythical Realities: Structure in the Early History of the Sandwich Islands Kingdom*, Association for Social Anthropology in Oceania Special Publications 1 (Ann Arbor: University of Michigan Press, 1981).

6. Nicholas Thomas, "Histories Structured and Unstructured," in *Out of Time: History and Evolution in Anthropological Discourse*, 2nd ed. (Ann Arbor: University of Michigan Press, 1996), 102–16.

But then, Smith moves from discussions of Sahlins on Lévi-Strauss, since Lévi-Strauss along with Althusser seems to have been an important thinker for Sahlins's discourse, to Smith on Lévi-Strauss in order to trace the introduction into the discussion of conceptual features Smith wants to highlight for himself and for us. These include the grounding of structuralist thought in biological morphology and linguistics, the effect of these streams of discourse on the notion of "transformation," and the resulting shift in anthropology to emphasize thought, logic, and the intelligibility of myths and mythmaking. It is at this point that Smith can use Lévi-Strauss as his dialogue partner for the clarification of his own interests in (1) myth as a conceptual scheme mediating a dialectical relationship between infra- and superstructures, (2) structure as a system of relations, (3) relations as marked by differences, (4) thinking as the result of working with two systems of differences, and (5) mythmaking as generated by "unconscious" structures.

In course, Smith's own project on method and theory of comparison comes into view. Since his interest in comparison is grounded in a social and intellectual anthropology and aimed at bringing anthropology and history together in the redescription of a social "e.g.," whether a myth, ritual, event, or situation, it is not surprising that his discussions of (in effect) "social formation" and "mythmaking" à la Sahlins, Lévi-Strauss, and the scholarly discourses they represent finally come to a "translation" of it all "In His Own Voice."[7] What we have here is "let it rip" explication of Smith's own "agendum," phrased now in terms of a set of concepts that we can use to refine our own categories and project. I am sure we have all taken note of those places where Smith "translates" Sahlins's terminology by replacing "conjuncture" with "'situational incongruity' as it presents itself to thought," "reproduction" with "experimental application," and "transformation" with "rectification."[8] With that we should be ready to revisit the Levantine as the site for imagining a social situation within which Mark may have been addressed and to which Mark may have been written.

Rectifications

Having had the seminar's project in mind all along while reading both the "Conjectures" and "Markan Site" papers, the question of our categories

---

7. See essay 3 in "Conjectures on Conjunctures."
8. See "Conjectures on Conjunctures," 69–72.

for site selection, text analysis, and doing redescription has never been far away. What follows are a few observations on the way in which Smith's papers address this issue as I see it.

The overarching categories with which we have been working are, of course, *social formation* and *mythmaking*. It is now clear that my earlier "hand and glove" metaphor was not helpful for this relationship because it did not sufficiently guard against the traditional "mirror" or "reflection" definitions of myth and society (or ritual). While such definitions were never intended when making the case for locating a text at the intersection of social formation and mythmaking, Smith's caution can be taken as a challenge to be much more specific about the (noncausal, nonreflective) "nexus" that lets us use these terms together to describe a situation. This means, as well, that our off-handed use of the term *site*, after it has served its first-level function of suggesting a location for such an intersection, needs to be redescribed as a "situation" and fleshed out in terms of social, historical, and cultural indices that mark it as an occasion for thought. Thus the relationship between *social formation* and *mythmaking* calls for careful handling of the dynamic, reciprocal impingements of the multiple systems that structure a society and its culture at a given point of its history.

If, then, the notions associated with the traditional imagination of a novel organic community, cell, or (heaven forbid) church have influenced the way in which we have understood the *social formation* we seek when setting up a site, these notions now need to be toned down if not erased completely. That is because a description of the social "situation" in general will only be adequate if the "already constituted" social identities, configurations, and practices are part of the picture, and the people in mind are given a place among other peoples in the expansive horizons of cultural contexts, constraints, and worldviews that will define the occasion for thought. This does not mean that another "association" may not have formed around "new" ideas, teachings, or interests. But the notion of a (brand) new "community" that appeared with the early Christians (concerned with distinctive identity and sense of "mission") has always frustrated such a social anthropology as ours. The traditional Christian notion of "conversion," for example, entails a complete shift of identity on the part of the individual via response to a novel address about a singular event and experience. To parry the ghosts of such an imagination of Christian origins I have been much impressed with Smith's reference to Eytan Bercovitch's concept of "the creativity of multiplicity" among the Atbalmin who were able to live in (negotiate) several worlds ("landscapes") at the same time.[9] One of the results of this was the fact that, as Bercovitch put it, "What was indigenous in Atbalmin Christianity ... was ... not so much how they were Christian but how they were both Christian and non-Christian at the same time."[10] For Christian origins, this would mean that questions about *ethnicity*, Mediterranean modes of self-*identity*, and Smith's helpful classification of types of religion in terms of orientation to locations ("here, there, and anywhere" which can equal "home," "land," and/or "diaspora," all of which are terms already on our table) become features not only of the social landscape in general but of the particular social formations within which we seek to set particular myths.[11]

As for *myth*, we now can see how very important it is to guard against any descriptions or formulations that might allow for the old "mirror" or "reflection" function of myth to keep shining through. We are learning that there are not only gaps between myths (as cultural systems) and societies (as structures of practices), but also lags in the changes between patterns of practices and their mythic rationalizations. If we want to tackle a moment of myth*making* we need to distinguish between myths already in place, those that belong to the immediate prehistory of a people's tradition or culture, and their transformations in the process of being reimagined or conceived.

It is here that the "intersection" between social formation and myth*making* can now be made more precise. If the "situation" presents an occasion for thought because of some "incongruity" between "expectations" and the reality of social histories, mythmaking is one of the ways in which the problem can be addressed ("rectified in thought if not in action"). It will not be the only way, for change in practices may well precede attempts to "elaborate" or "manipulate" mythic materials in the interest of justifying changes or legitimizing resistance. That being the case, it may be very difficult to identify the specific "event" (whether as "conjuncture" or "incident," intercultural or intracultural) that triggers a mythmaking moment. But questions about the social and cultural circumstances that occasion the

---

9. See Eytan Bercovitch, "The Altar of Sin: Social Multiplicity and Christian Conversion among a New Guinea People," in *Religion and Cultural Studies*, ed. Susan L. Mizruchi (Princeton: Princeton University Press, 2001), 211–35.

10. Bercovitch, "Altar of Sin," 228; cited by Smith, "Re: Corinthians," 345.

11. The reference is to Jonathan Z. Smith, "Here, There, and Anywhere," in *Relating Religion*, 323–39.

construction of a new mythic construal (such as Mark) are still the right questions to ask, as are questions about what I have been calling a myth's "social logic."

As an aside, I would like to explore the possibility of linking my notion of *social interests* to Smith's elaboration of Lévi-Strauss's concept of the (social) "unconscious." In both of their references, as I see it, the intention has been to acknowledge (if not account for) the way in which a culture's myths affect the way in which a people automatically look at their world ("worldview") without necessarily realizing its cultural construction; thus both "work" at the level of the social "unconscious." The term I have often used for this phenomenon is "mentality," which I have understood as a mode of thinking taken for granted by a people because of rootage in the systems of signs and patterns of practices that structure their culture.

I have not used the term "unconscious" for this, but I find the concept of the "social unconscious" in Smith (à la Lévi-Strauss) intriguing as a way to guard against certain misunderstandings and criticisms of "mythmaking" as if it were a thoroughly conscious activity or enterprise. I now want to note that my intention in moving from "mentality" to "social interests" in the course of the seminar's project was precisely an attempt to theorize the always already social "logics" and "interests" of all the systems of signs and patterns of practices that structure human societies and locate them *at the substrate of this level of the social "unconscious."* I do have serious misgivings about the terms "the unconscious" and "the human mind" as Lévi-Strauss uses them and Marcel Hénaff conceptualizes them because these terms lead so easily to a reification of "intelligibility" that does not contrast sufficiently with other notions of the unconscious, the preconscious, and transcendent structural entities.[12] It is precisely this concept of "the mind" as "the unconscious" that Hénaff uses to argue for the advance Lévi-Strauss makes over nineteenth century concepts of "society" as being prior to individual identities, psychologies, and capacities for thinking (including a critique of Durkheim and Mauss at this point).[13]

I find this unfortunate, for I want to see the "logic" of the "principles" that structure human societies (for example, "reciprocity," "dual organization," "incest prohibition," "atomic family unit," and so forth, from

---

12. Marcel Hénaff, *Claude Lévi-Strauss and the Making of Structural Anthropology*, trans. Mary Baker (Minneapolis: University of Minnesota Press, 1998), 94–119. Referred to by Smith, "Conjectures on Conjunctures," 63 n. 109.

13. Hénaff, *Claude Lévi-Strauss*, 116.

Lévi-Strauss, and "modes of classification," "marking difference," and "comparison" à la Smith) as the result of experiments with social relations, interests, and construals in the first place. I want to think that what we call the "logic" or "intelligibility" of the human and natural worlds (whether at the level of unconscious grammars of intelligibility or at the conscious level of making sense of social relations, situations, and human manipulations of the natural order) are the products of the ways in which social "agreements" and cultural "constructions" have been worked out in the course of living together, eventually to be taken for granted as accepted, that is, "understood" as the way things are and work. Note that if the "principles" of "the human mind" in Lévi-Strauss are set in motion, it is not difficult to imagine human experimentation with "relations," "differences," "consequences," "classifications," and so forth, all of which are the hallmarks both of social practices and thinking. In some such way, my notion of "social interests" was intended to be taken at the level of "prior," "unconscious" social grammars in the interest of defining the "already socially constituted" as itself a human, cultural construction. I realize that my notion of "social interests" begs the question of the "origin" of those interests, but no more so than predicating something called "the unconscious" or "the human mind" in order to name the prior and objective structure of intelligibility (logic) that guarantees the distinction between social "principles" and natural "laws." I know that it is a tautology to say that social interests are the basis for systems of signs and patterns of practices that structure society. (Hénaff would find this argument sufficient for throwing the concept out as the product of an unsophisticated naiveté.) But it keeps the imagination focused on the dynamics of social life and thought at the several levels of awareness this discourse has asked us to acknowledge in ways that concepts of "the unconscious mind" do not.

But enough. I may have to give up on the term "interests" simply because it is so automatically taken in reference to conscious, if not self-conscious motivations for action or thought, something very much different than what I have had in mind for a social theory of cultural constructions. But in the meantime I will keep "social interests" as a candidate for rectification that has not yet been challenged as such.

The Levant

Smith's description of the people of the Levant in the time of Mark's composition is a tour de force when compared with the usual expectations about a site description for a New Testament text. It is also a powerful application (or in some ways a preparation for the application) of his theory paper to a particular social "situation." He has not completely spelled out the ways in which "incident," "incongruity," "mythmaking," and "rectifying situations or construals in thought if not in action" (a gloss, not a direct quotation) apply to Mark (leaving that for us to discuss). But he has painted a picture of the social situation and history of the Levant that can make a difference in our reading of Mark if only we can situate it there. What we see is a documentation for a detailed picture of the Levant as a particular district within the larger Greco-Roman world with specifically local features that, however, do not keep the peoples there from thinking of themselves and behaving as citizens of the empire. Temples, gods, goddesses, shrines, priests, festivals, special days, civic celebrations, modes of production and marketing, all look pretty much as if these peoples had been ordinary citizens of the larger Mediterranean world for a long, long time. Then, within that district, there are many "ethnic" distinctions among peoples who nevertheless have much in common (for example: Northwest Semitic languages, avoidance of pork, circumcision, temple-state models for urban temple centers without real temple states or kings, trade and funerary associations, trading stations in the "diaspora," mechanisms for maintaining networks and identities as distinct peoples without threatening working relations with other peoples throughout the ecumene, and so forth). The point is that "ethnic" differences may ride on small markers, and that the resulting picture of cross-boundary relations and practices does not look like a pool game.

The zingers, of course, are the points Smith makes about *ethnicity*, the little ways in which groups with similar ethnicities marked their differences from one another, and how the peoples of the Levant may have related to (and thought about) Judea and Jerusalem. It looks like the messy history of marking ethnic distinctions in the Levant cannot be rectified by the simple correlation of "Jew" and "Judea." It is very important, I think, to note that what we have called "ethnicities" (with whatever set of connotations for more precise definition) was referred to in practice by the people themselves more as a matter of extraction from a place, whether "land" (Egypt, Babylonia, Greece, Syria, Idumea, etc.) or "city" (Rome, Carthage, Corinth, etc.), than by reference to other ways of marking social identity. But as Miller has reminded me, these "extractions" were only labels, and they do not tell us about all of the other ways in which social identities were marked. Smith's description of the "Tyrians" and their investments in

Tyrian identification while living in a much larger world is very thought provoking. It rings true as an example of Bercovitch's ethnography with its emphasis on the many "landscapes" within which the Atbalmin found simultaneous orientation. It also underscores the importance of the differences Smith finds in the ways in which "religion" was practiced when located "here, there, or anywhere."

The one very interesting exception to this mode of marking cultural identity (focused on place and placement) is Smith's reference to Shaye Cohen's work on the associations at Delos.[14] In some cases, but not the Tyrian, it seems that people from several "ethnic" extractions, belonging to the same religious association for a generation or so, began to identify themselves by reference to the patron deity (for example, the "Isiasts"). I am wondering about other ways as well to mark ethnic identities, some of which we may well want to discuss, such as "epic" revision. I would say we have some work to do reconceiving our category of *ethnicity* and relating it to the assumed problems of identity in early Christian groups. Since ethnicity was and is a cultural construction, and not a matter merely of "extraction," Paul's "Jew/gentile" question turns out not to be very helpful. Paul may not have been the only Jew or Jewish Christian interested in talking to gentiles about thinking of themselves as belonging to "Israel," but it is looking less and less certain that his notions of Christian identity, mission, and the conversion of the gentiles were typical for the times or that they actually worked the way he wanted. Paul is the problem, not the clue to imagining Christian origins, and has been all along, from our work on Q and the Gospel of Thomas to the *christos*/Christ cult question, the Corinthian situation, and now Mark.

Mark according to Smith

Smith plops Mark down in this Levantine situation. It is post-70 CE in time but without the crisis mood for Jews usually associated by modern scholars with the destruction of the temple. It is nevertheless a "situation" in which "incidents" are imaginable that could (and did) create "incongruities" in terms of group identity and the marking of differences between and among ethnic and other groupings. Features of the Markan composi-

---

14. Shaye J. D. Cohen, *The Beginnings of Jewishness: Boundaries, Varieties, Uncertainties*, Hellenistic Culture and Society 31 (Berkeley: University of California Press, 1999), 80 with n. 36. See Smith, "The Markan Site," 111–12.

tion that fit quite easily into the Levantine situation are: purity concerns, meal protocol, Q-type teachings, pronouncement stories, martyr myth, a fascination with royal ideology, and the way in which the pericope of the Syro-Phoenician woman addresses ethnic differences. Smith notes that the prominent role of the Pharisees in Mark, as well as the apocalyptic/ temple frame, is more difficult to account for in this situation. But he nevertheless suggests a long list of critical questions about social codes and history that he can imagine as topics for "heady and heated debates" with others on the part of what he calls Mark's " Levantine Judean association." Some of these are not much different in kind than discussions these peoples may have had about Pharisees, Jerusalem, and apocalyptic histories. What a relief. No high drama needed. No cosmic revelations breaking through. Just social formation and mythmaking in the interest of a Jesus school marking some differences in the Levant, post-70. (Might I add that it was also a relief to me that Smith did not make anything this time around of his earlier essay on the gospels where Jesus was explained as a "divine man," an example of the exceptional human figure whom readers of Greco-Roman aretalogies might want to "meet" and "imitate," but, of course, could not, thus marking difference and calling for thought.[15] I think I see ways of handling that description as well as this present one, but I am glad—or am I just hoping?—that I do not have to do both of them in the same set of discussions.)

Mack on Mark

So now let me say what I think about our chances of making some sense of Mark's mythmaking. Some may remember the way I imagined the problems I saw Mark addressing in *A Myth of Innocence*.[16] There was the war and the confusions I thought it created for all forms of Judaism and the early Jesus movements. There was the debate with the Pharisees that had not gone well about what to think about the codes of clean/unclean. There were also the Pauline Christians with a cult of the Christ as a divine presence who were creating an embarrassment for level-headed Jews. I

15. See Jonathan Z. Smith, "Good News Is No News: Aretalogy and Gospel," in *Map Is Not Territory: Studies in the History of Religions*, SJLA 23 (Leiden: Brill, 1978; Chicago: University of Chicago Press, 1993), 190–207.

16. Burton L. Mack, *A Myth of Innocence: Mark and Christian Origins* (Philadelphia: Fortress, 1988; repr. with new preface, 2006).

thought Mark was trying to make the most of a recent separation from some kind of Pharisaic association for which his Jesus school was hardly prepared, exacerbated by the postwar confusions in general about belonging to "Israel" now that the temple was no longer there. He saw a way to do this by means of a clever, if difficult, requisition of the Christ myth (martyrology) and supper ritual for his "passion narrative" even while downplaying their cultic functions.

That was fifteen years ago. In the meantime, and especially in the course of the seminar's work, I now see things differently. The post-70 CE situation will have to be construed apart from the crisis/response model I naively had in mind. The debate with the Pharisees will have to be rethought in terms of competing school traditions and associations instead of as a "failed synagogue reform movement." The use of the "Christ cult" as a foil for Mark's martyr myth in narrative form will have to be dropped. The reasons for this are (1) that my erstwhile imagination of a Christ cult has not weathered well the work of the seminar on *christos*, the "Christ myth," and the Pauline "communities"; (2) the probability that the term *christos* emerged in a Jesus school or association before it was linked to a martyrology or used as a cognomen for Jesus; and (3) that the supper text in 1 Corinthians, which I thought of in terms of a ritualized meal and which I saw as the intertextual link between Paul and Mark, is now better described as a myth of origins in which the founder of an association or school, understood to have been martyred for his teachings, gets to come to speech on the occasion (as martyrs in the Greek tradition regularly were imagined to do, even though in this scene Jesus addresses his followers instead of the tyrant) in order to explain to his followers that his martyrdom was actually "for them," that is, for the "cause" of the association even though it was yet to be formed. The grotesqueness of the scene and its convoluted logic underscore the difficulties of such mythmaking for these Jesus associations. It is not much different in its violation of standard narrative logics than Mark's story of the crucifixion. My change of view of the Pauline foil does not mean that Mark may not have known about such texts and concepts, for the intertextuality of his gospel is very rich and wide ranging. But it does mean that I do not need to use Paul or the "Christ cult" usually thought to be documented in his letters as the counterpoint to Mark. The reasons Mark may have had for composing his gospel as he did will have to be found elsewhere.

That said, I see no reason to question the narrative logic of Mark's Gospel as I was able to work it out in *A Myth of Innocence*. It is a refinement of the social logic that can now be entertained. Having toned down the overly dramatic atmosphere in which Mark's production was once understood, we are still left with a most interesting set of indices about the social situation with which to ask about the sense of its composition. What would be wrong with imagining a Jesus school in the Levant with forty years of elaborated teaching materials in hand, having formed an association, but seeing themselves and their teachings still as a compatible component of the "social cohesion" (Miller's term) we have to posit for the Galilee before the war? Miller has noted the lack of reference to the temple in the early Jesus materials as if it were taken for granted as an overarching presence of political and religious control even in Galilee despite the mix of peoples and interests living together there. There is a striking similarity between the social situation of the Galilee and that of the Levant in terms of Smith's emphasis upon the long history of hegemonies and their lack of kings and temple-states. I am not sure whether "social cohesion" helps with the way in which orientation to the Jerusalem temple gets bouncy, not only already in adjacent Samaria, but especially as one moves farther away. I do take note of Smith's reference to Barclay's point about the difficulty of distinguishing between "homeland" and "diaspora" in these lands because of the "continual expansion and contraction of what could be considered 'Jewish' territory."[17] But I see no reason not to apply the criteria of Smith's "here, there, anywhere" typology to Mark in Levantine context. This is especially so because he and Miller have used the homeland-diaspora distinction to such great advantage when engaging the heightened symbolic and mythic value of Jerusalem precisely for those at a distance from it, that is, in the diaspora. Why not imagine that, for Mark and his Jesus school, Galilee was still a kind of homeplace, a land of origin, even if there were no actual locations that the association could identify as the "home," "city," "temple," or "land of extraction" from which it derived. The very absence of such could have been a feature that worked both to clarify their identity as a people of "anywhere" even as it posed problems for myths of origin and the identification of places that could put them solidly somewhere in the real world. Most of the peculiarities of early Christian myths and social formations can be viewed as attempts to enhance and define the importance of a school tradition that did *not* have features of identification common for

---

17. John M. G. Barclay, *Jews in the Mediterranean Diaspora from Alexander to Trajan (323 BCE–117 CE)* (Edinburgh: T&T Clark, 1996), 243 (cf. n. 28). See Smith, "The Markan Site," 103 n. 4.

other peoples, associations, and societies of the time. There was no home-place in customary terms; their founder teacher could not be imagined as a successor to the traditions of Greek schools; they apparently did not know of a location for their founder's tomb; and, as for the location of their social ideal, the kingdom of God, they had to go cosmic.

If we dare think such thoughts, the debates with the Pharisees that surface in the Jesus materials in Q and Mark do not need to be taken as evidence for the presence of Pharisees in the synagogues of the Levant (much less Galilee!). Mark's fiction of Jesus's encounter with the temple authorities in Jerusalem need not be taken as evidence for the historicity of the event or as a problem for the location of Mark and his Jesus association. The point is that, since the temple had been taken for granted as part of the social-political structures that provided "cohesion" for all of these peoples, including the Jesus people, and since the temple was now destroyed, what to make of the new situation was a problem no matter what conception a group may have had to imagine social cohesion in terms of a sovereign power that guaranteed its structures. The question we need to ask about Mark is not for the reasons for a sudden shift to apocalyptic in order to imagine a future for the kingdom of God. That is easy, especially now that we do not have to see Mark grabbing for straws in a situation of political hysteria. Neither is the question difficult about why Mark, in the Levant, would want to imagine Jesus in Galilee and Jerusalem, in conflict with institutions there instead of providing instructions for the future association he intended for his followers. This is especially so if the destruction of the temple "would have removed the urgency of a focus on a domestic setting for their purity concerns," and other concerns, we might add.[18]

The really interesting question has to do with the observation that, whereas the temple(-state) had been taken for granted all this while, and perhaps even valued highly as the guarantee of social cohesion (among the few references to the temple in the Jesus traditions about Mark's time there are some that take the form of mourning or lament), Mark's story says that it was Jesus (or the consequences of the conflict between Jesus and the temple) that brought it down. That is a flip that bears scrutiny and calls for explanation. Smith is right to see the fourth Sibylline oracle as an analogue. Could it really be that Mark had already entertained the audacious notion that the destruction of the temple made possible a revision of the

---

18. Smith, "The Markan Site," 124.

ending of the *epic* of Israel, one that now might end with Jesus in charge and give his Jesus association a place at the table in the larger scheme of things? Does "the" epic of Israel not have to be more than a collection of past "precedents"? Does it not count as myth? Can we not see Mark's mythmaking taking the form of epic-revision? Can Mark's "divine man" not be compared with other "ideal figures" of the time, rather than only with Greek gods and heroes? It is clear that Mark's characterization of Jesus from the very first of the story is that of a "divine man," but what about the way in which he engages all of the social levels, offices, and landscapes in the course of his march to the "throne" as "king"? Can that not be the way in which Mark is packing his ideal figure with collective, structural, social, and functional features in the same way as all of the Jewish intellectuals of the time had been doing and would continue to do? The way I put it in my earlier studies of this literature, the bigger than life images of ideal kings, priests, prophets, and teachers, some embellishments of already known and named figures, such as Moses, others unnamed and floating only in the imagination, such as in the T. Levi 18, were actually compact, collective anthropological images of *social* configurations for the purpose of thinking about a present problematic social and political situation in terms of ideals constructed from the epic. The strategy was to "lift" the "ideal" from some selected epic "precedent" as counterpoint to the present situation and thus throw light upon it, whether of critique or of legitimation. Could we not use Lévi-Strauss's method for making a "set" of all the many ways in which the epic of Israel was configured and retold in the literatures of the time, and come up with something like the structure and logic of "the" epic of Israel? Could that epic not look more and more like an ingenious interweaving of all "orders of reality" of significance within the horizons of these people, a marvelous register of a cultural system and its transformations through time, a mythic reservoir of social-historical images set within a comprehensive worldscape in which all of the peoples, natural environments, and cosmic containments were available for the work of doing comparisons, thinking critically, and reinventing the social shape of the people with both feet on solid ground even in times when that ground was shaking? What if Mark was born and bred in the heady and heated atmosphere of this Jewish discourse, a discourse accustomed to mythmaking in the interest of social critique, an intellectual tradition of amazingly poignant production both before and after the Roman-Jewish war? What then? Why, we would not have to ask anymore "How (the historical) Jesus became the Christ, the Son of God, as portrayed in the gospels." We would want to ask more about Mark, this kind of mythmaking, ideal figures, and the funny ways in which a Jewish intellectual in a Jesus school (of all things) tried to think clearly about the consequences of the destruction of the temple for the post-temple future of the "Jewish" people with the teachings of Jesus ringing in his ears. But enough.

Agenda

It remains to list a set of questions as suggestions for setting our agenda for discussion. Some are questions I would like to ask Smith, others are issues we might use to make some progress in making sense of Mark as mythmaking. The questions follow:

(1) How does Smith's inter/intracultural distinction help us describe the events and cultural precedents for Mark and his situation? He has said that Sahlins's category of "conjuncture" may be a "red herring." If by that he wants to highlight the difference between a situation of "balanced" misunderstandings between two very different cultures on the occasion of the first phase of encounter (as in Hawaii) and the layered history of cultures in the Levant, well and good. But to move quickly to the inter/intracultural distinction and then apply it to the difference between Mark (in the Levant) and Paul (at Corinth) raises all kinds of questions about the significance of the many layers of social history and cultural construals evident in the Levant. Within which cultural traditions should Mark be placed in order to look for "incidents" instead of "conjunctures" as the events of significance for the occasion? And which cultural traditions would have given rise to "expectations" for which the social situation was seen as incongruous? And from which cultural traditions would it have been "natural" (that is, in keeping with his "intracultural" orientation) to engage in mythmaking activity?

(2) As for Smith's understanding of mythmaking, we might want to ask about the distinctions he makes (in conversations with Lévi-Strauss) among such terms as myth, mythmaking, ideology, rhetorical manipulation, and fictional elaboration, as well as about his references to the terms conscious and unconscious in relation to the way in which myth is "generated" in the first place. It might be important to know, for instance, whether Smith thinks of Mark's mythmaking as fictional elaboration or as rhetorical manipulation in the interest of making legitimate a problematic history.

(3) As for the critique of the "mirror" analogy for the function of myth, we might want to ask how then a myth "applies to," "addresses," or

"solves the problem of" a social situation? We can note the ways in which Smith's own studies of mythmaking (Hainuwele, the Maori's Io myth) and ritual invention ("Bare Facts," the hypothetical tiger's drink) consciously "reflect" (and "reflect upon") their social situations. How does this differ from mirror theories of the relation of myth to society?[19]

(4) How can we understand a martyr myth to have emerged within the Jesus schools? For what reasons? As a "solution" to what problem, incongruity, or event?

(5) In relation to Smith's reference to the Herakles-Melqart mythology and the royal ideology of the Sidonians, can we imagine them as analogies to Mark, or may they have been part of the cultural traditions that interested Mark and that he reinterprets? Is this the place to look for Mark's characterization of Jesus as a royal figure? If we note a "Jewish" ambivalence toward the category of the king and its prominence in subsequent Christian mythologies, does Mark represent an early step in the parting of the ways?

(6) Why a *bios* at all? Is not the writing of a *bios*, no matter of what generic class, a striking feature of Mark's mythmaking? Can it be accounted for in terms of response to his situation and, if so, with what consequence for his listeners/readers? What was the situation? What was the problem? What was the "social logic" of the *bios* that addressed this situation? What do you get when you dare to think of the origin of your association that way?

---

19. See Smith, "Conjectures on Conjunctures," 59–60, 66–68. The reference to "Bare Facts" alludes to Smith, "The Bare Facts of Ritual," in *Imagining Religion: From Babylon to Jonestown* (Chicago: University of Chicago Press, 1982), 53–65.

On Smith, on Myth, on Mark*

William E. Arnal

Theoretical Issues: Prolegomena

It is extraordinarily difficult to find a place from which to respond adequately to Jonathan Z. Smith's tour de force on the ways in which Marshall Sahlins's conceptual apparatus may assist the work of this seminar. I will, therefore, simply use Smith's massive papers as a launching pad for some of my own concerns, without making the futile attempt to do these papers justice thereby.

Musings on the Role of Theory

As a preliminary matter, I note that I find myself increasingly ambivalent about the role of theory in the study of religion. On the one hand, I have long maintained—implicitly in my work and explicitly to my students— that it is impossible to approach any subject matter (never mind one as slippery as "religion") without a conceptual framework for processing the data it presents. Even simple description requires a theoretical basis for the selection and representation of the data embodied in the "original." So it is always better to be cognizant of, and explicit about, the theoretical framework that must necessarily be applied in any investigation of anything, if only to make one's conclusions the more transparent, and, perhaps, a little more internally consistent.

---

* This paper was originally written in 2002 directly in response to Jonathan Z. Smith's paper, "Conjectures on Conjunctures and Other Matters: Three Essays," which he presented to the Seminar on Ancient Myths and Modern Theories of Christian Origins at the annual meeting of the Society of Biblical Literature in Toronto in November, 2002.

On the other hand, I have noticed that far too much of the theoretical work in our field, including some of my own theoretical questings, takes the form of an almost metaphysical concern with some form of higher truth, with what is "really the case." In such a mode, theory turns out to be little more than a kind of secular theology. It also tends to come detached from its ostensible subject matter and to inhabit an ethereal world that is in fact precisely *theoretical.* Our field, the study of religion, remains plagued by a bifurcation between theory and "substantive" work, a bifurcation that ensures both that too many investigations of actual phenomena are theoretically naive (or at best opaque) and that too many theoretical inquiries are ungrounded in, or fail to refer to, actual data.[1]

By contrast theory should operate (in general) as something of a tool, either a way of achieving some sort of handle on a problematic array of data or as a framework for relating diverse phenomena and indicating how those phenomena should be treated. Specifically for the purposes of this seminar, theory should therefore serve to guide us to specific insights into the origins of the Jesus movements and, even more precisely, should give us whatever intellectual leverage we need to produce a picture, or set of pictures, of the earliest Jesus people that differs substantially from the Lukan-Eusebian mythic presentation still taken for granted by most scholarship today.

I want to stress that this observation is not in any way intended as a criticism of Smith's work or his papers for this year's sessions. One of the most striking features of Smith's entire body of work, as well as his contributions to our seminar, is the precision with which he combines and balances theoretical and substantive concerns, conceptual and concrete conclusions (reflected also in the exhaustive nature of Smith's mastery of both the concepts and the data addressed in any particular investigation). Burton L. Mack's work, as well, to a large degree reflected in the agenda (and even the name) of this seminar, has also aimed to bring theory to bear on actual data—the literary remains of the earliest Jesus people—to a degree unusual in "Christian origins."[2]

---

1. So also William E. Arnal, "Approaches to the Study of Religion: Introducing Graduate Students to Religious Studies," *MTSR* 11 (1999): 107–18; Arnal, "Black Holes, Theory, and the Study of Religion," *SR* 30 (2001): 209–14.

2. The usual approach seems to adopt a rather unreflective "common sense" approach to its subject matter or to introduce "theory" only in the service of various

My point, rather, is that, whatever theoretical conversations we engage in, we need to be very careful not to get sidetracked into a futile effort to work out in detail a "theory of everything" that all of us can assent to in all its details. Our theoretical debates, I think, must remain focused on—and in the end be judged in terms of—their utility for assisting us in constructing a plausible and genuinely different picture of key moments of the early Jesus movements. Indeed, I am inclined to go a little further. I do not think that the almost-perfect balance Smith's scholarship has achieved in terms of theory and data is an appropriate goal for us, as a group, to aspire to. Our interest remains "ancient myths and modern theories *of Christian origins*," not simply "myths and theories" or "myths and theories of religion." Our work as a seminar, in other words, could in the end be wholly successful, even if we never achieve any consensus among ourselves on, say, what myth is, or how it relates to social formation, or even what a social formation is. Rather, if we manage, in spite of such differences, to arrive at a reconstruction of Christian origins that is genuinely different from, and more coherent than, the traditional picture that still seems to set the parameters for the historically thinkable even in the most scholarly treatments of Jesus and his earliest "followers," we will have succeeded.

But I must qualify these assertions. I am not saying that theory is or should be unimportant to us. Nor do I think I would support a theoretical opportunism or "ad hoc-ism" in which the only theoretical criterion is utility, without respect to accuracy or consistency. My point is simply that this seminar's theorizing probably ought to be a means rather than an end. I continue to view Willi Braun's and my formulation of our "Theses on Key Terms" as instrumental in precisely this sense.[3] My goal, at any rate, was not necessarily to convince the participants in this seminar of the perfect, detailed, and overarching accuracy of my own understandings of society, culture, ideology, religion, and so on, so much as it was to help us avoid formulations that would lead us away from, or prevent us from attaining to, a viable and significantly different view of the object of our inquiries.[4]

---

kinds of hermeneutics, often as little more than a rationale for (re-)theologizing the discourse.

3. William E. Arnal and Willi Braun, "Social Formation and Mythmaking: Theses on Key Terms," in *Redescribing Christian Origins*, ed. Ron Cameron and Merrill P. Miller, SymS 28 (Atlanta: Society of Biblical Literature, 2004), 459–67.

4. Hence the concerted criticism in "Social Formation and Mythmaking" of what I took to be a potential idealism in some of the seminar's formulations. I recognized

By these standards, Smith's theoretical forays in "Conjectures on Conjectures" will need to be assessed mainly in terms of the kind of leverage they might give us for approaching the Gospel of Mark, rather than in terms of any detailed assent to them in principle. The fundamental question for our discussions must be, "has Smith's paper given us some effective tools and occasion to sharpen those we already possess?" For what it's worth, I think the answer is yes.

Ancient Theories and Modern Myths

I also note, as a further preliminary matter, Smith's opening quotation for his paper, Claude Lévi-Strauss's famous insistence that "man has always been thinking equally well."[5] This conviction appears to have been of major import for Lévi-Strauss's own project, elucidating precisely the sensibility and intelligence behind the apparent grotesqueries of kinship structures, totems, myths, masks, and so on. This same conviction appears to me to have played a foundational role in much of Smith's work as well, as his opening with this quotation underscores. According to such a view, myth (as well as some other aspects of behavior or intellection that we refer to as "religious") is not to be relegated to the realm of fantasy or the

---

then and continue to insist on the typological (rather than essential) character of the ideal/material dichotomy; so also Smith, in his opening quotation for his "Conjectures on Conjectures" paper from Lucien Sebag, *Marxisme et Structuralisme* (Paris: Payot, 1964), 193: "The distinction between infrastructure and superstructure disappears, for economic, social, and political relations, like the theories that account for them in a given society, are just as much products of the mind" (see "Conjectures on Conjectures," 17, in this volume.) As Braun and I wrote: "It is probably an idealist fallacy to regard ideas and discourse as something other than a component (analytically speaking) of the material framework in which they operate.... There need not be anything idealist about ideas, in which case any dichotomy between ideas and material forces is itself idealist! But *for our purposes here, and as a corrective*, it is worth viewing those material social manifestations that present themselves as nonmaterial to be effects, if only for the sake of conceptual clarity" ("Social Formation and Mythmaking," 465, emphasis added). My insistence on the causal priority of "material" to "ideal" phenomena—offered in the face of my own recognition of the artificiality of the distinction—was in part a function of the conviction that the traditional picture of Christian origins relies upon an implicit idealist theory of history and that, to whatever extent we persisted in adhering to such a perspective, it would be that much harder to escape from the confines of the traditional view in any decisive way.

5. See Smith, "Conjectures on Conjectures," 17.

"primitive mind" or some other form of intellectual failure; it is not a "disease of language"; it does not even represent a distinct type of thought at odds from the everyday ways in which we all, as human beings, apprehend and make sense of the world. Rather, myth is a rational (if not necessarily lucid) articulation of systems of classification and a form of experimentation with those classifications, their boundaries, and their implications; it is a mental expression of the sensible, assimilable, humanly accessible character of the world. According to such a view, myth*making* is never a singular activity. Myths as such are not made; they are always already there, and they are altered, manipulated, toyed with, in the service of sometimes quite quotidian efforts to retrench, redefine, or experiment with the intelligibility of the human universe.

Such a view relates to my own persistent tendency to see a strange parallelism between what we as a group are actually doing, and what the ancient Jesus people whom we discuss were doing. One way to understand this parallelism is provided to us by the view of myth articulated above. "Their" mythmaking was none other than some form of socially contextualized theorizing about social context. It was an effort to shape and modify myths already-given to meet, somehow, a social situation that was deemed to have changed enough (however much—or little—that may be) or to have required enough thinking about to merit the intellectual labor that went into adjusting the patchwork of mythic elements available to and of concern to the mythmakers in question. The Gospel of Mark, in short, if understood in these terms, can be called an ancient myth of Christian origins, but it is also an ancient *theory*—a theory of Mark's social world and its sensibility (the details of which remain to be determined).

By the same token, our own modern theories could be viewed as myths. What are we doing if not taking the pieces of an already-extant myth and rearranging them, combining them with other cultural fragments in novel ways, assembling them into a new pattern that makes more sense to us? The "Christian myth" itself is but a modern assemblage of more ancient fragments, worked over and over for almost 2000 years. For most of us, they have been worked over yet again into the mythic novelty of the "historical-critical method" as it has been taught to us. Indeed, it seems to be this more modern myth—the critical scholarly reconstruction of Christian origins, which we do not think has gone far enough—that we are really seeking to engage and, it is hoped, to "correct." Is not our "theory" precisely bricolage, precisely the combination of one with another, of new myths with old, Marx with Mark, Sahlins with Paul? Are we not engaging in this mythmaking precisely as a rationalization for, expression of, and experimentation with, a novel social form: this very seminar? This new social form, moreover, as well as its attendant myths, appears to have been brought into being as a result of—no surprise—a "conjuncture," if we wish to use Sahlins's terminology, or a "situational incongruity," if we wish to use Smith's. That conjuncture or situational incongruity is, of course, the "secularization" (for lack of a better term) of the discourse on the New Testament, and thus the novel social situation in which a subject matter from one arena (the seminary) is brought into contact with the methods and expectations of another arena (the secular humanities or, perhaps for some of us, the social sciences).[6]

In Sum

All of this is open-ended musing, but there are a couple of conclusions that I would insist upon. The first is that we, this seminar, have set for ourselves the project of understanding "Christian origins" in a different way; we have not set ourselves the task of theorizing religion, or for that matter, of theorizing culture, in any comprehensive way. Any attempt to define the role of theory for this group, therefore, must begin with this limitation. We may differ on "how much" theory is "enough" for the task we have set for ourselves, but we should at least be clear on what that task is. The second conclusion is that we need to be somewhat self-conscious about the extent to which our own theorizing duplicates the "ancient theories" of the objects of our investigations. There is nothing wrong with this in and of itself. But I think it is useful to bear this in mind, in order to resist the corollary tendency to limit to a projection of the details of our own myth-making situation the kinds of situations and mythmaking agenda that early Christian groups may have engaged in. In particular, I think that our tendency to stress the voluntary, intellectual, and experimental character of ancient Christian social formations may be little more than a reflection

---

6. This conjuncture, this intra-cultural meeting of two (sub)cultures, has all kinds of disturbing implications, not all of them methodological or theoretical. One that I have felt particularly keenly is that of *relevance*. One need not question the value of meticulous study of works that are canonical, and thus are models for faith and practice. Once these texts have been abstracted from an ecclesiastical context, however, it becomes rather difficult to explain the importance of a life devoted to their analysis.

of the voluntary, intellectual, and experimental character of our seminar.[7] It is not that some or even all of these ancient groups may not actually have been precisely as we are predisposed to make them, but it is important to recognize that we do have this predisposition, in the interests of our own mythmaking, and that it has the potential to distort our conclusions.

Theory: Conjunctures with Smith and Sahlins

As a piece with my insistence that our task here is not to develop a theory of culture in general but to adopt what critical tools will assist us in coming to a new understanding of "Christian Origins"—and, at this point, the Gospel of Mark in particular—I will attempt only a very limited engagement with Smith on theoretical matters. My comments concern two main issues: (1) the intellectualist character of the approach to myth discussed by Smith and (2) the question of the nexus between mythmaking and social formation.

Intellectualism

The theoretical framework articulated in Smith's "Conjectures on Conjunctures" paper is not, so far as I can tell, one that I would describe as *idealist*. Ideas are not presented by him as giving birth to themselves but as being generated and modified by people in specific contexts: ideas are products of historical agents. But I *would* describe his approach to myth as intellectualist.[8] If I understand him correctly, Smith is saying that myth is to be understood as a mental, or better, communicative operation aimed at resolving or otherwise treating, precisely, conceptual (that is, mental and/ or communicative) conundrums. Conceptual schemes—of which myths are a part—serve to structure (and thus render intelligible) praxis. *Tensions*

---

7. My use of the word "reflection" here is not intended to invoke a reflection theory of the myth-social formation nexus. What I have in mind, rather, are the limitations imposed on the imagination by the boundaries of one's own particular historical context.

8. I am using *intellectualist* descriptively, rather than as a label. I am not suggesting an affinity with Müller, Spencer, Tylor, Frazer, or others who "theorized that the idea of religion sprang from rational inferences based on individual human experiences of oneself or the world" (Brian Morris, *Anthropological Studies of Religion* [Cambridge: Cambridge University Press, 1987], 106).

between actual circumstances and the conceptual schemes used to mediate them—tensions which cannot be understood solely in either intellectual or material/pragmatic terms but only as a combination of the two—are occasions for thought. They are motivations for creative engagement with the conceptual schemata in question. I think this formulation admirably helps to clarify what is accomplished by mythmaking in the first place. I also appreciate (and take to heart) the clarification Smith offers about the referents of myth: "What this liberating passage [from Lévi-Strauss's "Four Winnebago Myths"] seemed to suggest, at the time, was that the relations in myth are within myth; we need not turn to external relations.... Now, I would know better and, with the benefit of both hindsight and Lévi-Strauss's *Mythologiques*, state more precisely that the relations are between myths."[9] A given myth refers not to itself, not to society, but to other myths.

As I understand it, this assertion in no way denies a relationship between myths and sociohistorical "events," but it specifies that the myths themselves (and/or the elements therein) do not refer directly or specifically to those events but engage with them (in whatever fashion) by referring *among themselves*. Thus, in the case of the Markan myth, we should seek first not a direct relation between individual Markan mythologoumena and some social reality (even though, in fact, such a linkage almost certainly exists[10]), but rather should look at the ways in which Mark's myth is itself a reference to, modification of, engagement with, a myth or set

---

9. Smith, "Conjectures on Conjunctures," 62–63. Smith's reference is to Claude Lévi-Strauss, "Four Winnebago Myths: A Structural Sketch," in *Culture in History: Essays in Honor of Paul Radin*, ed. Stanley Diamond (New York: Columbia University Press, 1960), 351–62.

10. I say this because I do not want to throw away our ability to make inferences from a text to its social situation, even if we adopt wholesale the theory of myth that I am attempting here to abstract from Smith's paper. Markan *mythic* references to the temple, for instance, should be understood according to this view as engagements with other cultural references to the temple, rather than to the temple itself and its (presumed) recent destruction. But it is not to be doubted, I think, that these references to the temple's destruction allow us to infer the fact of the temple's recent destruction. The case is even more apparent in the Matthean and Lukan "predictions" (see Matt 22:7; Luke 21:20, 24). In each case, a myth (the Markan material) is being modified in order to comment on another myth (either the import of Jesus's death, in Matthew, or [perhaps] the role of the gentiles, in Luke). But in each case the quite reasonable inference can be made from these "predictions" that both of the authors were aware of the factual destruction of the Jerusalem temple.

of mythologoumena that were now, for Mark, somehow ineffectual with respect to his situation and so somehow stimulated creative thought.[11] Thus, most obviously, Mark's references to Jesus are not to be understood as referring, ultimately, to the real historical person of Jesus at all, a point I think we all recognize. But—and this is important—these images of Jesus also do not refer to, say, Mark's own historical circumstances. They refer, rather, to other images of Jesus, or Herakles, or Theandrites, or to kingship ideologies, or to "ancient theories" about the temple, and so on.[12] It is the relations between these images that in turn interact in some way with the socio-historical circumstances in which Mark found himself.[13]

There is, however, an important complication, touched on in passing by Smith, which I think deserves some of our attention. After describing the communicative and/or intellectual function of myth in some detail and dealing with its "unconscious" aspects, Smith states at the end of his third and last theoretical essay:

> It is a different case when we shift from a communicative to a rhetorical frame, that is to say, when we seek to persuade or convince, usually with respect to some "situation." Here, we consciously deploy the "pre-positioned" resources of language and story.... An account of such rhetoric must balance the already-present frameworks with the particular "occasion," as well as the audience(s). Such an understanding applies to texts such as the Gospel of Mark as it does to other mythic texts I have analyzed elsewhere.[14]

---

11. Note that such an approach may be best served by describing that historical situation as fully as possible, more or less independently of the agenda of the text in question. This is precisely the approach endeavoured by the steering committee this year, in its request that Smith describe the Markan "site" without necessarily going into detail about the actual Markan myth. See Smith, "The Markan Site," in this volume. Thus the theoretical hunches of the steering committee appear to have meshed nicely with the basic theory of myth being articulated by Smith in "Conjectures on Conjunctures."

12. As an interesting application of the idea that Mark is in some respects a mythic rejoinder to ancient theories about temples, see John S. Kloppenborg, "*Evocatio Deorum* and the Date of Mark," *JBL* 124 (2005): 419–50.

13. A further clarification or qualification: I say this without meaning to imply that the sociohistorical events in question be of any momentous proportions. Smith stresses, rightly in my view, that "this is the everyday way in which people work with their myths, not one confined to moments of extraordinary tension" (Smith, "Conjectures on Conjunctures," 71 n. 119).

14. Ibid., 68.

This description—and especially its invocation of a distinction between "communication" and "rhetoric"—puzzled and intrigued me. After reading it over several times, I decided to take the "difference" here (as in, "it is a *different* case") as a departure from the *unconscious* character of linguistic structures. Smith appears to be saying that myth, as a human and social "thinking with stories," can be "organized by structures that are largely unconscious" like linguistic activity itself.[15] Grammar is a "largely unconscious" linguistic structure; so also may be the structures that organize worldview. What is *different* about a rhetorical frame, then, seems to be the *consciousness* that is brought to bear on both its construction *and* its relation to the "real" world. This makes sense to me: communication may seek little more than understanding, but rhetoric definitely seeks to *persuade* and, presumably, to make that persuasion effective in action.

But I cannot help but wonder what other consequences might emerge from this distinction, what other differences it encodes, and whether it has some bearing on Smith's basic understanding of myth. Are we to regard myth, theoretically articulated as above, as limited to communicative frames, and therefore to regard this theoretical articulation as inapplicable to rhetorical frames? I am not sure. But given that a rhetorical performance is most definitely and self-consciously related to a very precise context and has as its goal some sort of actual engagement with that context in order to effect some change in it, it strikes me as reasonable enough to conclude that at least one possible difference between a communicative and a rhetorical situation rests with the referents of each. If we follow Smith, following Lévi-Strauss, a (communicative) myth relates to other myths. Do Smith's comments quoted above—practically his final word in this paper—allow for a (rhetorical) myth to relate *directly* to a "situation"? And if indeed this rhetorical understanding does apply to Mark, as Smith explicitly states, why focus so much attention on the "communicative" aspects of myth?

Of course, the difference between a communicative and a rhetorical situation may not so much inhere in the situation itself as be a function of our interpretive frameworks, a matter of emphasis or perspective, as with synchronic versus diachronic.[16] But this generates its own questions.

---

15. Ibid., 67.

16. Ibid., 50: "Synchronic and diachronic are alternative modes of considering the same phenomenon. It is a methodological distinction, not a distinction between different objects."

Is Smith suggesting the applicability of a quite different understanding of the relation of mythic elements to their social context *alongside* the one he (apparently) prefers? Just how are we to understand rhetoric? It seems clear to me that there are forms of discourse that are conceived *as* social actions and that have or aim to have direct social consequences—forensic speech being the most obvious and blatantly rhetorical example. How are we to untangle communicative mythmaking from the rhetorical deployment of myth, whether this is conceived as a methodological or substantive distinction? My own hunch is that a great deal of the ancient Christian material is much more "rhetorical" than "communicative" (I am thinking here most especially of the clearly persuasive character of the traditions of the "Jesus schools," most obviously manifest in Q). At the very least, it quite thoroughly mixes mythic material with overtly hortatory concerns. We therefore need to establish what relationship our theories of myth have to this other material.

More generally, it needs to be stressed that, in spite of the name of this seminar, *myth* is not the only form of expression we encounter in ancient Christian writings. That, for example, Mark's basic story of Jesus—even many of its details—or Paul's central account of a crucified Christ vindicated by God are properly understood as myth is clear enough. But one of the striking features of the ancient Christian literature to which we have access is precisely its witch's brew of mythologoumena alongside community instructions, quotidian notices, hortatory rhetoric, exegesis, and so on.[17] It is worth asking, therefore, to what extent a theory of, precisely, *myth* is likely to elucidate the whole range of ancient Christian concerns to

---

17. Regarding quotidian notices, I have in mind the sort of thing we encounter, e.g., in 1 Cor 16:12: "As for our brother Apollos, I strongly urged him to visit you with the other brethren, but it was not at all his will to come now. He will come when he has the opportunity." Note, however, that seemingly quotidian notices of this sort can in fact have a mythmaking function. An example is 2 Tim 4:13: "When you come, bring the cloak that I left with Carpus at Troas, also the books, and above all the parchments." The fact that Paul did not write this letter means that this line must have some *literary* or imaginative function rather than its apparent literal sense. If this function is only to provide verisimilitude to the letter as a whole, this is still a mythmaking move. And the intention could be much more involved than this: "Paul's" concern here with books and parchments implicitly casts him as an authoritative writer (presumably, of letters), which shores up the authorizing fiction undergirding the Pastorals as a set. On this issue, see William A. Richards, *Difference and Distance in Post-Pauline Christianity: An Epistolary Analysis of the Pastorals*, StBibLit 44 (New York: Lang, 2002).

which these various texts attest. The focus of our attention has tended to be myth, and this is certainly the main thrust of Smith's paper.[18] But myth is not all there is. There is action and ritual, buying and selling, apostasy and martyrdom, life and death—the whole range of behaviors, practices, and performances that make up life and make up history. In short, I think that even were we to understand myth perfectly, there would be a great deal more to be resolved about ancient Christianity or even about the ancient Christian writings available to us.

Nexus

To start into the slippery subject matter of the nexus between myth and social formation, however, it seems that Smith is hinting that myth plays a much more central role in history than my comments above would imply. Smith appears in places to suggest that myth is itself precisely what gives intelligibility to social praxis. He begins his second essay with a quotation from Lévi-Strauss in which conceptual schemata (exemplified in myth) form a crucial part of the overarching social order, which is itself partially comprised of this conceptual apparatus:

> We believe that a mediator always interposes itself [or: interpolates itself, s'intercale] between praxis and practices, this [mediator] is the conceptual scheme by the operation of which matter and form, both the one and the other deprived of any independent existence, are realized as structures, that is to say, as entities which are both empirical and intelligible.[19]

Sahlins does something similar in his concept of the "event." As described by Smith, Sahlins attempts to clarify and elaborate the relation between event and structure by establishing a three-fold typology of happenings (or incidents), structures, and events. An "event" is the relation between a "happening" or "incident," conceived as raw circumstance, and the conceptual structures through which existence is made intelligible.[20] Either

---

18. Though this is not the only thrust of his paper. See below for some discussion of the possible implications of Smith's "Conjectures on Conjunctures" for a broader theory of *history*.

19. Smith, "Conjectures on Conjunctures," 48-49, quoting Lévi-Strauss, *La Pensée sauvage* (Paris: Plon, 1962). The insertions in square brackets are Smith's.

20. Smith, "Conjectures on Conjunctures," 32.

formulation means that human actors do not interact with sheer materiality, nor with social forces as given, nor with practices as such, but with and in terms of extant conceptualizations that give shape to these factors. Human beings act and interact with the world, but they are not precisely interacting with raw happening or raw matter. Rather, they interact with these items in a universe always-already conceived as intelligible.[21]

Such a view has as one of its implications a broadening of the social import of myth. Myth, if one follows Sahlins's notion of "event," is already present and active even in practice, even in the most quotidian exchanges. As a mediating force, it is inextricably intertwined with both broad social forces and structures, on the one hand, and individual occurrences, on the other. It is the link between them. To be more precise, myth is *one* form or *one* expression of such mediating conceptualizations, and so while myth as such may not be omnipresent in social activity, the kind of thinking that it represents is.[22] We have moved, then, from a theory of myth to a much broader theory of society and history. "Structures" are not now simply to be understood as conceptual arrangements but as a kind of social organizational principle, a reality that spans ideas and practices. It would be inappropriate to regard this conception to be idealist, since it asserts the essential unity of "ideal" and "material" phenomena and since it is simply a way of asserting that the social world is experienced as intelligible.

To some degree this makes sense to me, and certainly vitiates my criticism, above, that our real subject matter is more than simply myth. For according to this view, no social behaviors, no historical "events," can be understood apart from their intelligibility for their actors, any more than they can be understood apart from their material context. But I am still somewhat hesitant. This insistence on the pervasive and social character of structure is rendered *historical* by Sahlins by means of his understanding of *mechanisms of transformation*. The reproduction of structures is not taken by Sahlins to be an ahistorical or antihistorical activity (apparently contra Lévi-Strauss and his "cold" societies), but a function of *tension* between

---

21. See Marshall Sahlins, *Islands of History* (Chicago: University of Chicago Press, 1985), 153–54. Sahlins stresses, as well, that the raw happening always to some degree *pushes back* against the structures through which it is made intelligible, thus perpetually transforming those structures; see ibid., 144–45, 149.

22. As Sahlins explains: "We know the world as logical instances of cultural classes: 'Captain Cook is a god.' It is not that, as some have believed, we have a 'need' to classify. Formal classification is an intrinsic condition of symbolic action" (ibid., 146).

historical happening and extant structure.[23] As the structure is reproduced in the face of this tension, it is also altered in the process. History involves the selection and/or transmutation of a particular structural permutation and so, *inter alia*, the rejection of alternative permutations. Thus "where there is … structural contradiction there is also historical direction."[24] Or again: "Action begins and ends in structure: begins in the projects of people as social beings, to end by absorption in a cultural practico-inert."[25] Thus, as Smith says, "Sahlins modified a mode of structuralism to be more responsive to the historical while not relaxing a commitment to the analytical priority of structure."[26]

My difficulty here is that such a view, while certainly making sense of the nexus between social formation and mythmaking and while certainly providing a historical dimension to an essentially structural understanding of both society and myth, appears to me to have the *potential* to reduce history to little more than the alteration of mythic structures. If I have read Smith correctly, and he Sahlins, history is itself embodied in the mechanisms of reproduction and transformation, which should be understood quite broadly as involving both social and conceptual aspects, each in fact inextricable from the other. One must be careful and vigilant, however, not to allow this formulation to drift, in its application, in the idealist direction of viewing history as a series of alterations in ideas. In other words, if we are to use Sahlins's conceptualizations of reproduction

---

23. Ibid., 138, 143–46, 148–49.

24. Smith, "Conjectures on Conjunctures," 30, quoting Sahlins, *Culture and Practical Reason* (Chicago: University of Chicago Press, 1976), 45.

25. Smith, "Conjectures on Conjunctures," 51, quoting Sahlins, *Historical Metaphors and Mythic Realities: Structure in the Early History of the Sandwich Islands Kingdom*, Association for Social Anthropology in Oceania Special Publications 1 (Ann Arbor: University of Michigan Press, 1981), 72. Smith's difficulties with the term "practico-inert" as used here (see "Conjectures on Conjunctures," 52 n. 92) are a bit of a puzzle to me. Sahlins's phrasing suggests to me a "rough and ready," almost metaphoric, application of the Sartrean concept, extracted from its existentialist context (in which it signifies precisely the *resistance* of the world "as given" to the individual creative projects of the existential human person), as simply "matter in which past praxis is embodied" (Jean-Paul Sartre, *Theory of Practical Ensembles*, vol. 1 of *Critique of Dialectical Reason*, ed. Jonathan Rée, trans. Alan Sheridan-Smith, rev. ed. [New York: Verso, 1976], 829; cf. 67, 71, and esp. 318–21). It thus offers a convenient designation for the structural absorption of historical "event," as well as the "push-back" against concepts provided by raw event.

26. Smith, "Conjectures on Conjunctures," 30.

and transformation, we must take care to bear in mind that what is being reproduced and/or transformed is the whole structure of social praxis, and not just a set of ideas (much less a set of ideas which in their turn directly transform social praxis).[27]

I also note that while this formulation of historical process does go some considerable way to answering my criticism of a too-focused obsession with myth and myth alone, it does not offer much of a rejoinder to my comments about rhetoric, which have their own implications for historical change. One almost gets the impression from Smith and Sahlins that historical change only happens automatically or accidentally. Things proceed apace and are rendered intelligible, and then something comes along—an incursion from another cultural complex, an unpredictable demographic change, an unaccounted-for new phenomenon—that requires the structure somehow to adjust itself in order to render the novelty intelligible. I am too much of a (vulgar?) Marxist to find this a compelling account of all processes of historical change. Conceptual structures do not simply render things intelligible. They also infuse them with value; they are *interested* and advantage certain persons, types of persons, types of behavior over against others. Is it not then equally important to view structural change in terms of the dynamics of opposition inherent to any given social structure? Should we not insist on the conscious *rhetorical* alteration of structure, for advantage, for exploitation and repression, for resistance and revolt, alongside the *communicative* alteration of structure to incorporate "accidental" change?[28]

The example offered by Smith of Sahlins's treatment of the Fijian sea-people/land-people categorization is a case in point.[29] We may understand the imposition of this system of classification in a locale in which it does

---

27. It is also worth stressing once again that it makes most sense to view the distinction between "reproduction" and "transformation"—like that of communicative vs. rhetorical and synchronic vs. diachronic, noted above—as a matter of approach or emphasis, rather than something inhering in the "event" itself. Every "reproduction" is a transformation of sorts, at the very least applying an "old" structure to a "new" happening. And every transformation is a reproduction of sorts, insofar as it operates in terms of the very system of intelligibility that it transforms.

28. So also Smith, "Conjectures on Conjunctures," 53: "In the colonial system named 'conjuncture' by Sahlins, how do 'signs in action' enable resistance as a mode of response different from both reproduction and transformation? A rebellion, a revolution is not the same as a 'cultural performance,' understood as a 'semiotics of identity.' "

29. Ibid., 27–30.

not "really" exist (that is, it has no historical basis) as the imposition of a conceptual system onto an "accidental" set of circumstances (the existence on a particular island of individuals who are *all* "sea-people") in order to invest those circumstances with an intelligibility they would not otherwise possess. But we can *also* understand this example in terms of the opportunistic importation of a structure of intelligibility from another context in order to rationalize an interested action (namely, the domination of one group of "sea people" by another); or, perhaps, to erect an analogy (dominated sea people are analogous to land people) deliberately in order to persuade someone of something: whether that the dominated sea people should submit or that there ought to be a dimension of reciprocity implied by the domination, etc. Perhaps, again, this is not so much a criticism of Sahlins's model as it is a preference on my part for a certain kind of emphasis or perspective.

As a final theoretical point, I return to a matter that has concerned me since my very first participation in this Seminar and is one of the issues on which I have disagreed somewhat with Mack's reconstruction of Christian origins. I do not think that it is most helpful for us to imagine the development of the Jesus movements, or even of the New Testament myth, primarily in terms of *internal* reactions to, and developments within, a "Christian" sociality.[30] By contrast, I have thought that one of the best ways to provide a viable alternative to the Christian myth is to resist this frankly reifying approach and to focus instead on the synchronic relations between a given set of Christian mythmaking activities and the historical circumstances in which those activities take place. Thus a given Christian conception—say, Jesus as an apocalyptic preacher as found in Q^2—is best understood (for our purposes) not in terms of where the apocalyptic traditions recounted in Q^2 came from but in terms of what they accomplish for the purveyors of that material.

At first glance, it may seem that the theoretical position articulated by Smith, and especially the insistence that myths signify with respect to other myths, militates against my insistence on the utility of an *external* (to the Christian "movement" itself, that is) orientation. But I think perhaps just the opposite is true. In the examples given by Smith and by Sahlins,

---

30. This was a point emphasized in William E. Arnal, "Why Q Failed: From Ideological Project to Group Formation," in Cameron and Miller, *Redescribing Christian Origins*, 67–87; and emphasized again in Arnal and Braun, "Social Formation and Mythmaking" (especially 462–67, nn. 3, 4, 5, 7, 8, 10, 13).

what we do *not* seem to see in mythic reproduction *or* transformation is a simple "development" of ideas. Rather, external "happenings" of one sort or another are assimilated into conceptual structures, which had not initially accounted for them; in short, "happenings" are made into "events." What helps us understand the reproductions and transformations are precisely those previously-unassimilable (or, at least, unassimilated) happenings and their impact on the system in question.[31] So sociohistorical happenings are central to an explanation of any mythic system. And there is no necessity in this approach that the relations between myths be relations between the *same* myths. That is, the examples given by Smith and Sahlins, and Smith's own discussion of the Markan site, do not provide a model that requires us to privilege Jesus-myths as the "objects" to which other Jesus-myths relate. First, the approach as articulated does not predict *what* myths will serve as the points of reference; the whole cultural milieu provides the deposit of raw materials that may be used in any mythmaking activity. Second, as already noted, mythmaking as an act of reproduction and/or transformation is at least partly a response to external "happenings" apart from which they are not properly understood. Thus Sahlins's model, it seems to me, actually offers some support for a point I have been making all along.

The Markan Myth

The Gospel of Mark, a huge contribution to the development of "the Christian myth," requires a more sustained examination than is possible here, particularly in terms of (1) its transformation of the Jesus traditions into a narrative; and (2) its subsequent reception and—through the vehicle of its appropriation by Matthew, Luke, and John—*massive* influence on the shape of all subsequent Christian mythmaking. Both of these topics require extended treatment on their own but cannot be treated here. My intention in what follows is simply—and briefly—to engage what I regard to be more the interesting and/or problematic features of Smith's papers as they apply to the Gospel of Mark, and particularly to focus on the issue of ethnicity and crisis.

---

31. I stress again, as does Smith, the quotidian character of such "happenings." The "intrusions" that generate reproduction/transformation by no means need be momentous in and of themselves.

Generalities

First, however, a handful of general comments. The theoretical tools that Smith gives us in his extended "Conjectures on Conjunctures" essays suggest their own approach to the Gospel of Mark. It would be useful to see precisely what such an approach, comprehensively applied, would look like. So far as I can tell, such an approach would require us to seek, on the one hand, to relate Mark's myth to the extant mythic structures to which it refers (these would, of course, need to be identified); and on the other hand, to describe the context which occasions these "rectifications." At least conceptually (if not methodologically), these operations are to be kept separate. Smith's paper suggests, again, that myth is not best understood in terms of the relations between mythologoumena and social details, but in the relations *among* myths, and the relation of those relations to a "situational incongruity."[32] Moreover, judging from both his theoretical comments in the "Conjectures on Conjunctures" paper, and his actual investigation into "the Markan site," an application of Smith's approach would also refer in *both* of its operations to a context broader than the traditions of the Christian groups already-extant in Mark's own time. It would seek, instead, to relate Mark's myths to other, non-"Christian" but contemporary and shared, cultural traditions; and then to relate both to a shared context.[33] Finally, it would seek to determine what in that context had provided the "incongruity," the "occasion for thought," that stimulated reproductive or transformative (or experimental or rectifying) mythmaking activity. Such an approach would be both theoretically coherent and extraordinarily useful as a clarification of the way we ought to be inquiring into the Markan Gospel and its mythmaking activity.

---

32. See Smith, "Conjectures on Conjunctures," 69–73, where he "translates" Sahlins's terminology into his own, with "situational incongruity" approximating "conjuncture," "experimental application" for "reproduction," and, more hesitantly, "rectification" for "transformation."

33. This is an important point. A corollary of both Smith's "Conjectures on Conjunctures" paper and his work on the Markan site is that the various cultural products of a given context are available and shared among and between groupings within that context. A Jesus-person, then, has available to him or her various other cultural artifacts; likewise, outsiders may borrow freely from the cultural products of Jesus-people and use them to whatever ends they may see fit.

Ethnicity and Crisis

On the more specific matter of the substance of Smith's description of the Markan site, it is impossible not to be struck by the degree to which it is focused on questions of ethnic identity and the relations between ethnic entities, however constructed. That these matters are of major concern to Mark is not to be doubted. Not only does the story of the Syro-Phoenician woman (Mark 7:24–30) address such matters directly, but one can also see ethnic dimensions and import in most of Mark's other dominant concerns: purity, the temple, the role of Jesus as king, and so on. Moreover, it constitutes a *major* step forward for us that Smith has conceptualized these inter-ethnic and intra-ethnic issues in terms of the general multiethnic situation of the Levant, including its long-standing lack of political autonomy, rather than in terms of an over-determined Jew-gentile distinction. In Smith's reconstruction, we are dealing with a real situation, as really experienced by the author of Mark,[34] rather than an abstract and unsituated "theological belief" about the differences between Jews and gentiles. We have moved, in this account, from the imaginative and hermetically sealed "biblical" world to the real social world in which Mark lived.

But I would want, in the case of Mark, to nudge the ethnic concerns with which Mark is struggling more in the direction of a *crisis* than Smith, apparently, would prefer. This is not because of any theoretical disagreement with Smith's point that mythmaking is, or can be, a quotidian activity. But if indeed we maintain—as I think we should—that Mark is a Syrian or Syro-Phoenician product from the period immediately after the Jewish War (say, 70–75 CE or so), then I think that we must recognize that the war situation itself made ethnic identity and relationships (particularly as they pertained to the ethnic construct of Judean/Jew) a matter of pressing—even life-and-death—concern. Josephus recounts a number of instances in which the context of war brought ethnic relationships—including those that had been, or should have been, normalized long in the past—to such a crisis that deadly riots and inter-ethnic warfare ensued. As just one example among many, Josephus writes:

---

34. Provided, of course, that a setting on the Levantine coast in the immediate post-Jewish War period is the correct one for Mark. I am assuming, here and in what follows, that it is.

Thus far the Jews had been faced with aliens only, but when they invaded Scythopolis they found their own nation in arms against them; for the Jews in this district ranged themselves on the side of the Sycthopolitans, and, regarding their own security as more important than the ties of blood, met their own countrymen in battle. However, this excess of ardour brought them under suspicion: the people of Scythopolis feared that the Jews might attack the city by night and inflict upon them some grave disaster, in order to make amends to their brethren for their defection. They, therefore, ordered them if they wished to confirm their allegiance and demonstrate their fidelity to their foreign allies, to betake themselves and their families to the adjoining grove. The Jews obeyed these orders, suspecting nothing. For two days the Scythopolitans made no move, in order to lull them into security, but on the third night, watching their opportunity when some were off their guard, and others asleep, they slaughtered them all to the number of upward of thirteen thousand and pillaged all their possessions.[35]

Taking into account the standard Josephan penchant for exaggeration, we nonetheless have, here and elsewhere, strong evidence that the events of the war problematized both intra- and interethnic relationships to a considerable degree, and often with very dramatic consequences.

I would additionally suggest the following further analogies.[36]

(1) The town in which I grew up, about an hour's drive west of Toronto, used to be named Berlin. In a small downtown park there was a bust of Kaiser Wilhelm II. In 1916, after a series of anti-German outbursts across Canada, and some two years after Canada, along with Great Britain, had declared war on Germany, the city council voted to change the name of the town to Kitchener.[37] During the same period, a small mob attacked the

---

35. Josephus, *J.W.* 2.18.3 §§466–468 (Thackeray, LCL). Cf. Josephus, *J.W.* 2.20.2 §§559–561; *Vita* 25–27.

36. The first two of these examples appeal to me a great deal, mostly because they concern places with which I am intimately familiar, and they mix a sense of history and of event with the quotidian events and settings of my own life. But they exemplify phenomena—interethnic violence in wartime or war-like situations—that can be illustrated by a great many more, and more "world-historical," episodes.

37. See W. V. Uttley, *A History of Kitchener, Ontario* (Waterloo, ON: Chronicle, 1937), 409. This text, the only "history" of the town that I was able to uncover easily, is a locally published piece of civic boosterism and therefore lacks reference to less prominent (and certainly more unpleasant) episodes of anti-German sentiment during the period from 1914–1918.

bust of the Kaiser and tossed it into a pond.[38] The image was replaced with a statue of Queen Victoria, which, like the name Kitchener, remains to this day. On a Sunday morning in 1916, likewise, a detachment of soldiers stationed in a camp outside the city marched into town, to a Lutheran church on King Street (which still sits right beside my old high school), dragged the minister from the pulpit, and forced him to kiss the Union Jack.[39]

(2) In Toronto, about a forty-five-minute walk from the Convention Centre, the site of the 2002 meeting of our seminar, at the intersection of Bloor and Christie streets, there is a small park known as Christie Pits. In 1933, on the evening of 16 August, there was an anti-Semitic riot in the park (then known as Willowvale Park).[40] A contemporary newspaper account rather breathlessly describes it thus:

> Widespread disorder raged over the vast area of Toronto streets for hours last night when rioting broke out following the display of a swastika emblem on a white quilt at a baseball game in Willowvale Park. In the disturbance which flared up like a spark among tinder, scores were injured; five were removed to hospital. Lead pipes, baseball bats, broom-handles and clubs were freely used. Police at times were almost overwhelmed or out-numbered; reserves were called out and batons were drawn. Long after midnight the reserves were still patrolling the affected area as groups of rioters armed with broom-handles hid in alleys or made sorties therefrom to beat up foes. The disturbance became largely racial in character, bands of Gentiles and of Jews apparently taking up opposing sides in the battle. So far as could be deemed, no arrests took place arising from the disorders, the police apparently devoting their major attention to breaking up the several serious melees which developed, in which hundreds appeared to be fighting at once. More than 8,000 per-

---

38. Citizenship and Immigration, Canada's official (government) web page, states that: "Southwest of Toronto, in Berlin, Ontario, a prosperous city where persons of German ancestry made up three-quarters of the population, anti-German feeling ran so high that a statue [actually, a bust] of Kaiser Wilhelm was pulled down and heaved into the lake in Victoria Park. In 1916, the city's name was changed to Kitchener" (http://tinyurl.com/SBL4520e).

39. This episode is known to me through oral accounts from long-time Kitchener residents. I assume that they could be verified by checking the microfilm archives of the *Kitchener-Waterloo Record*, but I have not undertaken to do so. The event is not mentioned in Uttley, *History of Kitchener*, for obvious reasons.

40. There is at least one whole book devoted to this episode: Cyril H. Levitt and William Shaffir, *The Riot at Christie Pits* (Toronto: Lester & Orpen Dennys, 1987).

sons were involved or enmeshed in the disturbances shortly after they
began. One Jewish youth was struck over the head with a baseball bat,
dozens of others received less serious injuries, fist fights and free-for-
alls raged all over the park, police billies were used and for half an hour
the situation threatened to get out of hand [!]. Cries of "The Swastika!
The Swastika!" rose in various parts of the park as soon as the taunting
emblem made its appearance. In one confused mass, in sections of the
crowd, more than 3,000 surged across the park and over the hill toward
the emblem. Fighting broke out as Jews recognized Gentiles.[41]

(3) In our own time, we see for instance attacks on Muslim—or even
"Muslim-appearing"—Americans in response to the events of September 11, 2001.[42] The October 2002 "Beltway Sniper" attacks in the Washington DC area, as well as the media response to them, may also reflect
something of the complicated (and dangerous) state of Muslim identity in
the United States (as well as its interaction with other issues of American
ethnic identity).[43]

(4) An example more historically prominent still, and perhaps most
telling of the lot, is found in the famous antidraft riots that occurred in
New York City during the American Civil War. The Union government

---

41. *The Toronto Daily Mail and Empire*, 17 August 1933, quoted in toto in Levitt
and Shaffir, *Riot at Christie Pits*, 18–19. I have eliminated the newspaper-style para-
graphing of the original.

42. See, e.g., "Anatomy of a Hate Crime," in Newsweek (http://tinyurl.com/
SBL4520d): "Nationwide, there have been more than 300 acts—or threats—of violence
against those presumed to be Arab or Muslim, according to the American Arab Anti-
Discrimination Committee in Washington. These include cases of mistaken identity,
such as a Sikh gas-station owner who was shot dead in Mesa, Ariz., by a man who
apparently thought his turban meant he was a Muslim. Near Los Angeles last week,
an Egyptian-born grocer, a Christian, was shot dead in his store, an attack the FBI is
treating as a hate crime. 'It's people lashing out at what they think of as TV Arabs,' says
Hussein Ibish, a spokesman for the committee."

43. I refer here both to general American perceptions of how Islam relates to
ethnicity and "American-ness" and to the attitudes of Muslim Americans regarding
their standing and identity within the United States. The problem is, of course, also
current in Canada. In the case of the Washington-area sniper, it is very difficult to sort
out what motivations served as background to the crimes. A case could be made that
they were religiously motivated (the shooter appears to have been a convert to Islam)
or ethnically motivated (the shooter was black) or motivated by nothing other than
hope for financial gain (the shooter apparently sent extortionary notes toward the end
of his spree).

had introduced the incredibly unpopular Enrollment and Conscription Act in March of 1863. The implementation of the Act recognized the extant military precedents of "substitution" and "commutation": a draftee could avoid actual military service by producing a substitute to serve in his stead or by paying a $300 "commutation fee." This escape-hatch for the wealthy, alongside allegations of regional and political bias in the application of the draft,[44] the military misfortunes of the North, and the decreasing popularity of the war since the Emancipation Proclamation,[45] engendered bitter resentment.

This resentment manifested itself most vividly in New York City on 13–15 July, when the first implementation of the draft provoked three days of rioting in which hundreds of people were killed.[46] The intrinsic unfairness of the draft, the fact that New York City tended to strong Democratic sympathies, and the sense that Irish immigrants were being drafted for a war that was not really their concern all guaranteed that conscription would be badly received in New York. But as the violence escalated, it also began to focus more and more on black Americans, becoming, in the end, an antiblack, as much as an anticonscription, riot.[47]

What is striking here is the strange constellation of ethnic charge and counter-charge. George Templeton Strong, in his diary, lamented the antiblack orientation of the riots while simultaneously vilifying the Irish immigrants who he felt were responsible for the riots: "A black man hanged … for no offense but that of Nigritude.… [No wonder St. Patrick drove all the venomous vermin out of Ireland! Its biped mammalians supply that island its full average share of creatures that crawl and eat dirt and poison every community they infest. Vipers were superfluous. But] my own theory is that St. Patrick's campaign against the snakes is a Popish delusion. They

---

44. On the Union draft, see Peter J. Parish, *The American Civil War* (New York: Holmes & Meier, 1975), 142, 500.

45. Apparently many northerners were more inclined to fight for the unity of the nation than for the emancipation of southern slaves. The Emancipation Proclamation, promulgated on 1 January, 1863, made it appear as though the war were being fought to end slavery, and thus ostensibly involved the loss of white lives for a black cause.

46. Property damage from the riots was estimated at the time to be approximately two million dollars. My information about the riots is mainly drawn from Parish, *American Civil War*, 501.

47. See the unscholarly but vivid description in James McCague, *The Second Rebellion: The Story of the New York City Draft Riots of 1863* (New York: Dial, 1968), 93–94.

perished of biting the Irish people."[48] Parish sums up the overall situation as one of "nativist prejudice against the immigrant, immigrant fear of the Negro, class antagonism, and narrow partisanship."[49]

The Civil War exacerbated, and was exacerbated by, webs of ambiguous and conflicting American identities, including ethnic identities, and this eventually spilled over into strange and violent events like the New York City draft riots. The ideal self-identification for citizens of the Union was as loyal, over against seditious (and perhaps as northern over southern). But other identifications were possible as well: Republican versus Democrat (leading to the fragmentation of the Democratic party, depending on its allegiance to, or rejection of, a Union currently governed by Republicans), wealthy versus poor, white versus black, immigrant versus established, and Protestant versus Catholic (compare with Strong's comments on the "Popish" Irish).

In sum, the fact that Mark concerns himself with matters of ethnic identities and definitions in, we presume, a context overshadowed by the Jewish War and its effects suggests that something rather more momentous than quotidian "experimentation" with myth is going on here. Josephus directly attests to some of the ethnicity-related furor that accompanied the war, and the analogies suggested above likewise imply a pervasive tendency to revisit matters of ethnic relations in war or war-like situations. I am therefore more inclined than Smith is to look for a crisis setting to account for the "situational incongruities" or "conjunctures" that stimulate Mark's myth-making interest in ethnicity. Indeed, it may be that the *extreme* character of Mark's situation helps account for the *extreme* character of his "transformations."

---

48. George Templeton Strong, *The Civil War 1860–1865*, vol. 3 of *The Diary of George Templeton Strong*, ed. Allan Nevins and Milton Halsey Thomas (New York: Octagon Books, 1974), 337, 343. The material outside of the square brackets is quoted in Parish, *The American Civil War*, 501; the additional material, within the square brackets, is provided for context.

49. Ibid., 501.

Markan Grapplings

Christopher R. Matthews

"This," Belbo said, "would explain why Dee paid so much attention to those royal cartographers. It was not to discover the 'true' form of the earth, but to reconstruct, among all the mistaken maps, the one right map, the one of use to him."

"Not bad, not bad at all," Diotallevi said. "To arrive at the truth through the painstaking reconstruction of a false text."

— Umberto Eco, *Foucault's Pendulum*

My agreement with the steering committee for this paper was to offer reflections on aspects of the other papers prepared for our sessions in Toronto. Both Burton L. Mack and William E. Arnal have responded in some detail to Jonathan Z. Smith's extensive work that allows the seminar to conceptualize a theoretical grappling hook for the recovery of the "submerged" Markan situation. Mack's and Arnal's coverage of Smith's contributions has allowed me the luxury of focusing on some of the issues that they have raised from my own perspective. I am in complete accord with Arnal's sentiments, expressed at the outset of his paper, regarding the challenge of crafting an adequate response to Smith's essays. But, in fact, Arnal has done a fine job of interacting with Smith's presentations, and he advances a number of important questions and concerns that merit our attention. I am sympathetic to his call in the first section of his paper that we should keep our focus on acquiring the theoretical tools most useful for the task of redescribing "the key moments of earliest Christianity" (even though the question of "how much theory is enough" remains). I agree with him that Smith has "given us some effective tools and occasion to sharpen those we already possess."[1] His treatment of the distinction

---

1. William E. Arnal, "On Smith, on Myth, on Mark," 148, in this volume.

between "communication" and "rhetoric,"[2] which grows out of Smith's discussion of the "nexus between mythmaking and social formation,"[3] raises what I take to be the crucial issue of the different relations of mythmaking to its social context that apply in situations of "unconscious" sensemaking versus situations of "conscious" manipulation. Arnal also makes a nice case, complete with comparative exempla, to push ethnic concerns as they surface in Mark "more in the direction of a *crisis* than Smith."[4] I had noted while reading Smith's papers what I thought might be a "tension" between an "insistence on the cognitive power of tension,"[5] on the one hand, and the opposition of "quotidian activity" to "crisis,"[6] on the other (although "crisis," in fact, is not banned in the latter passage but is simply not "required"). Finally, I cannot but agree that it would be useful to see Smith's theoretical tools applied comprehensively to Mark,[7] which brings to mind Mack's wry comment that Smith "has not completely spelled out the ways in which 'incident,' 'incongruity,' 'mythmaking,' and 'rectifying situations or construals in thought if not in action' … apply to Mark (leaving that for us to discuss)."[8] But Mack immediately goes on to affirm that Smith "has painted a picture of the social situation and history of the Levant that can make a difference in our reading of Mark," with the proviso: "if only we can situate it there."[9]

The Markan Intercultural/Intracultural Situation

Allow me to segue to the first question on Mack's agenda, listed at the end of "Cartwheels,"[10] and ask: When the grappling hook catches on Mark 7:24–30, 31, should we imagine that we are in touch with a narrative that has sprouted from an intracultural or an intercultural social situation? As

---

2. Ibid., 153–55.

3. Jonathan Z. Smith, "Conjectures on Conjunctures and Other Matters: Three Essays," 67, in this volume.

4. Arnal, "On Smith, on Myth, on Mark," 163, emphasis original.

5. Smith, "Conjectures on Conjunctures," 57.

6. Ibid., 67–68.

7. Arnal, "On Smith, on Myth, on Mark," 162.

8. Mack, "Cartwheels: Or on Not Staying Upside Down Too Long," 135, in this volume.

9. Ibid.

10. Ibid., 142.

Smith makes clear at the outset of his "Markan Site" essay,[11] the circumstances of a Levantine Markan situation may be presumed to have been quite different from those of the "encounter" situation at Corinth. For, given the fate of the Levant as a site of successive "imperialisms and colonialisms," there " 'native' ... is as much a strategically constructed category as is 'outsider'—often a project in the manufacture of difference."[12] In his treatment of Marshall Sahlins's terminology in his "Conjectures on Conjunctures" paper, Smith had already observed that "the potential utility of Sahlins for the seminar ... will have to be framed in terms of the 'event' relations between 'incident' and 'structure' in the Markan site, rather than in terms of the 'event' relations between 'conjuncture' and 'structure.' "[13] As we have all learned, "conjuncture" marks an intercultural event and "incident" marks an intracultural event. But as Smith stresses with reference to Sahlins's own clarifying comments on his analytical model, even though it is true that situations of intercultural contact (conjuncture) offer "a privileged occasion for seeing very common types of historical change *en clair*,"[14] the fact remains that "all these [historical] processes are occurring in the same general way within any society, independently of radical differences in culture, so long as actors with partially distinct concepts and projects relate their actions to each other."[15] At this point Smith suggests that " 'conjuncture' may prove something of a red herring. 'Transformation' and 'reproduction,' along with action/practice, are, in fact, the more crucial elements."[16]

The employment of this terminology raises some questions (for me at least—perhaps sent off the path by the red herring) with respect to the analytical fit we can achieve in the case of the Markan situation. Given the distinctiveness of the portion of the Markan text before us ("one of the denser concentrations of Levantine topography in the New Testament"

---

11. Smith, "The Markan Site," 102, in this volume.

12. Ibid.," 104.

13. Smith, "Conjectures on Conjunctures," 32.

14. Marshall Sahlins, *Historical Metaphors and Mythical Realities: Structure in the Early History of the Sandwich Islands Kingdom*, Association for Social Anthropology in Oceania Special Publications 1 (Ann Arbor: University of Michigan Press, 1981), vii; cited in Smith, "Conjectures on Conjunctures," 30.

15. Sahlins, *Historical Metaphors and Mythical Realities*, 68; cited in Smith, "Conjectures on Conjunctures," 31.

16. Smith, "Conjectures on Conjunctures," 31.

that marks "the outer northern limits of Jesus's loci of activity"[17]) and
the characterization of the Syro-Phoenician coastal region as a "contact
zone,"[18] does not the story of the Syro-Phoenician woman exemplify a
"conjuncture" (an intercultural event/situation) rather than an "incident"
(an intracultural event/situation)? (I somewhat opportunistically take
advantage of "contact zone" as an entrée to Sahlins's employment of "conjuncture," which replaces his earlier use of "contact.") To opt for the intracultural side of the equation as a clear choice is seemingly complicated by
several factors. First, there is the identification of the narrative in Mark
7:24–30 as pre-Markan. What does it mean for Mark if the "situational
incongruity" that is the topic of this narrative comes in the form of a tradition? One possibility is that it has come to Mark from "outside." Yet we
still might suppose that its status as "tradition" does not disqualify it from
being considered as a piece drawn from, say, "forty years of elaborated
teaching materials in hand."[19] If the latter is even remotely the case, and
we suppose that the Jesus school in question has been in the Levant all
this time, the presence of this narrative in its current form seems to suggest a considerable period of "experimentation" (or, more conservatively,
stasis) with regard to relations between the Markan group and certain
"proximate others." That is to say that the narrative appears to indicate a
situation short of "transformation" or "rectification."

Unless I have completely misconstrued the variables here, the second
complicating factor is contained in Mack's "questions about the significance of the many layers of social history and cultural construals evident
in the Levant."[20] He poses the difficult query: "Within which cultural traditions should Mark be placed in order to look for 'incidents' instead of 'conjunctures' as the events of significance for the occasion?" The "many layers
of social history and cultural construals evident in the Levant" appear,
to me at least, to introduce an extra measure of complexity in thinking
about how "Smith's inter/intracultural distinction help[s] us describe the
events and cultural precedents for Mark and his situation."[21] The problem
can be ameliorated, I suppose, simply by taking it for granted that any
intracultural situation will be many-layered, as in the present case of the

---

17. Smith, "The Markan Site," 121.
18. Ibid., 112.
19. Mack, "Cartwheels," 139.
20. Ibid., 142.
21. Ibid.

Levant where we posit a "situation of thought and conflict about differences, which are interesting (or troublesome) within a general perception of similarity,"[22] giving full weight to the centuries-long intertwining of the historical and religious circumstances of the people of the Levant.[23] So, when we grant that there is "no need to confine Mark's relations only to a Jewish setting,"[24] does that assume that now the Levant functions as intracultural territory? As the boundaries of what constitutes an intracultural situation expand, does the line between intracultural and intercultural shift? How far would we have to go before Paul among the Corinthians is also an intracultural situation (after all, Paul is not really comparable to the British in Hawaii, not least because he has nothing more than rhetoric to support what might very loosely be called his colonizing activity)? Is it possible that Mark should be imagined to be composed of some combination of "conjunctures" and "incidents"? Or is some intermediate term needed to specify a subcultural situation that blurs the larger intercultural/intracultural distinction? The narrative of the Syro-Phoenician woman appears to stand out as an ambiguous case with respect to the application of the terminology we are trying out.

As Mack notes, "there is a striking similarity between the social situation of the Galilee and that of the Levant in terms of Smith's emphasis upon the long history of hegemonies and their lack of kings and temple-states."[25] I notice that at least in Smith's description of "a Markan locus on the south Syrian coast,"[26] "the larger region of Northern Galilee and Southwestern Syria Phoenicia is likewise entailed."[27] But if we choose to operate with the assumption that Mark is not physically located in Galilee, the notion that somehow "Galilee was still a kind of homeplace"[28] might suggest that Mark's group could be distinguished from those proximate others in the Levant and thus in some sense be culturally, if not geographically, adjacent to them. The situation might be somewhat analogous to the Tyrians in Puteoli, who retain their identities as Tyrians,[29] although for Mark's group

---

22. Smith, "The Markan Site," 116.
23. Ibid., 117.
24. Ibid., 118.
25. Mack, "Cartwheels," 139.
26. Smith, "The Markan Site," 102.
27. Ibid., 102 n. 4.
28. Mack, "Cartwheels," 139.
29. Smith, "The Markan Site," 111.

there is the problem of the lack of "features of identification common for other peoples, associations, and societies of the time."[30] Yet the latter situation would also signal the Markan group's difference (or peculiarity) with respect to others in the region. Even so, we can probably assume in the case of Mark's group and its neighbors that the correspondences in the overarching cultural context in which they lived would allow (or ensure) that "small incidents that are provocative for thought about similarities and differences"[31] would ensue eventually. But the form in which we find the story of the Syro-Phoenician woman incorporated into Mark (together with the lack of additional exempla of the same category—contact, experimentation, negotiation with proximate others) seems to indicate that the Markan group remains stuck somewhere between "reproduction" and "transformation" with respect to the interrelations this narrative may be symbolically advocating.[32] I confess that it is not clear to me how to imagine the operation of "reproduction"/"experimental application" and "transformation"/"rectification" in the Levant in relation to the multitude of local histories found there. Do we not have to conceive of multiple cultural layers, each of which is concerned with its own tasks of reproduction and transformation, even while influencing and being influenced by the sum total of all impinging events? It is at this point that Smith's "anxiety" about "whether we can gain a sufficiently thick behavioral description from the Markan site" becomes troubling for me.[33]

Myth and Mythmaking

In his deliberations and reflections on Smith's various discussions of myth, Arnal raises questions about the "communicative" versus the "rhetorical"

---

30. Mack, "Cartwheels," 139–40.

31. Smith, "The Markan Site," 120.

32. Without gainsaying Arnal's relation of the distinction between "reproduction" and "transformation" (Arnal, "On Smith, on Myth, on Mark," 157–59) to Smith's observation that "synchronic and diachronic are alternative modes of considering the same phenomenon" ("Conjectures on Conjunctures," 50), I believe my concern here still holds insofar as I am looking for a descriptive label that seems to be missing in terms of making the analysis more precise.

33. Smith, "Conjectures on Conjunctures," 31. How do we put ourselves in a position to responsibly engage in the "careful handling of the dynamic, reciprocal impingements of the multiple systems that structure a society and its culture at a given point of its history" (Mack, "Cartwheels," 131)?

frame of myth, the relation of these different frames to the characterization "conscious" or "unconscious," the "broadening of the social import of
myth,"[34] and "the *potential* [of Sahlins's modified structuralism?] to reduce
history to little more than the alteration of mythic structures."[35] Although
I am in need of gaining better clarity on all of these issues, I will venture a
few observations in order to work my way around to the topics of mythmaking and social interests. Arnal wonders whether "we [are] to regard
myth ... as limited to communicative frames, and ... as inapplicable to
rhetorical frames,"[36] insofar as the latter are "self-consciously related to
a very precise context" and seek "actual engagement with that context in
order to effect some change in it."[37] But some of Smith's statements about
the situational nature of myth would appear to disallow Arnal's conclusion that "one possible difference between a communicative and a rhetorical situation rests with the referents of each," insofar as a "communicative
myth" relates to other myths, while a "rhetorical myth" relates directly to a
"situation."[38] Allow me to complicate this conclusion by noting Smith's discussion of the term "situation" with the following citation from his earlier
work: "[Myths] must be understood primarily as texts in context, specific
acts of communication between specified individuals, at specific points in
time and space, about specifiable subjects.... For the historian of religion,
the task then becomes one of imagining the 'situation,' of constructing the
context.... For there is no primordium—it is all history."[39] To this let me
add yet another quotation that is pertinent to this topic: "Myth is best conceived not as a primordium, but rather as a limited collection of elements
with a fixed range of cultural meanings which are applied, thought with,
worked with, experimented with in particular situations."[40] Smith immediately follows this quotation with the following statement: "In contrast
to the way in which Sahlins sometimes presents his case, I want to insist

---

34. Arnal, "On Smith, on Myth, on Mark," 153–57.

35. Ibid., 158, emphasis original.

36. Ibid., 154.

37. Ibid.

38. Ibid.

39. Smith, *Imagining Religion: From Babylon to Jonestown*, CSHJ (Chicago: University of Chicago Press, 1982), xiii, cited in "Conjectures on Conjunctures," 70 n.
118.

40. Smith, "Map is Not Territory," in *Map Is Not Territory: Studies in the History
of Religions*, SJLA 23 (Leiden: Brill, 1978; Chicago: University of Chicago Press, 1993),
308, cited in "Conjectures on Conjunctures," 71 n. 119.

on a critical perception available at the outset in a setting of 'situational incongruity,' which leads to a testing of the fit/no fit of established patterns of thought; and I want to insist that this is the everyday way in which people work with their myths, not one confined to moments of extraordinary tension."[41] The relation of myth to situation in these citations seems to complicate Arnal's attempt to work out the difference between communication and rhetoric. It also seems to blur a distinction between the conscious and unconscious functions of myth. To approach this dilemma from another vantage point, permit me to cartwheel over to Mack.

In the context of his discussion of myth and social interests, Mack identifies the concept of the "social unconscious" to be "intriguing as a way to guard against certain misunderstandings and criticisms of 'mythmaking' as if it were a *thoroughly* conscious activity or enterprise."[42] Much of the mythmaking that concerns us, however, does appear to be conceived of as conscious. The comprehensive "mythic reservoir" of "the epic of Israel" available to Mark is apparently accessible through intellectual activity: "What if Mark was born and bred in the heady and heated atmosphere of this Jewish discourse, a discourse accustomed to mythmaking in the interest of social critique, an intellectual tradition of amazingly poignant production both before and after the Roman-Jewish war?"[43] While supposing that the addition of the verbal element "making" to "myth" must mark a difference from the employment of "myth" alone, it seems as though Mack's use of "myth*making*" encompasses both the communicative and the rhetorical aspects of myth, precisely those features that have caused us (or at least me) difficulty in the discussion above. It is almost as if the conscious and unconscious poles of mythmaking somehow allow it to serve (in a kind of double duty) as the " 'intersection' between social formation and myth*making*." For, "if we want to tackle a moment of myth*making* we need to distinguish between myths already in place, those that belong to the immediate prehistory of a people's tradition and culture [the unconscious pole], and their transformations in the process of being reimagined or conceived [the conscious pole]").[44] Mack himself identifies one of Smith's interests (in dialogue with Claude Lévi-Strauss) as "myth-

---

41. Ibid.
42. Mack, "Cartwheels," 133, emphasis added.
43. Ibid., 141.
44. Ibid., 132, emphasis original.

making as generated by 'unconscious' structures."[45] It is precisely in the context of his discussion of the treatment of the unconscious/conscious by Lévi-Strauss that Smith turns to the "question as to the nexus between mythmaking and social formation," about which he immediately comments: "Insofar as mythmaking is a linguistic activity, it is both a human and a social activity. In this sense it is correctly viewed as generated by, organized by structures that are largely unconscious in the sense specified above. This lack of consciousness extends beyond grammar and transformations to the level of worldview."[46] It is shortly after making this point that Smith informs us of the "different case when we shift from a communicative to a rhetorical frame."[47]

There appears to be a polyvalence in the terminology we are working with that might require "rectification." Although Mack has reserved final judgment as to whether rectification is in order for the term "social interests," it does seem that a certain amount of schooling is required to realize that "social interests" are "to be taken at the level of 'prior,' 'unconscious' social grammars in the interest of defining the 'already socially constituted' as itself a human, cultural construction."[48] But whether "social interests" are any more or less problematic than the rest of the terminology we are working with is still an open question for me.

Stromata

Kingdom

Why the focus on the kingdom of God in the early strata of the Jesus schools? As Smith notes, "Because of its strategic value ... the Levant has always been contested space, a region, at most, of client-kings not of kingdoms, endlessly encompassed in the larger schemes of greater powers.... The Levant must be seen, above all, as a permanent site of premodern ... imperialisms and colonialisms."[49] It would be remarkable if the political history of the Levant and its surroundings did not assure an ever-present unconscious fatigue with respect to this "long history of hegemonies." In

---

45. Ibid., 130.
46. Smith, "Conjectures on Conjunctures," 67.
47. Ibid., 68.
48. Mack, "Cartwheels," 134.
49. Smith, "The Markan Site," 102–4.

such a context a mythic appeal to a kingdom of God would be a most "attractive" counterpoint to the incongruity presented by reality.

Paul

I prescind from any comment on Paul or the "Christ cult" in connection with their status as a foil for Mark. But I would offer a gloss to Mack's judgment that "it is looking less and less certain that [Paul's] notions of Christian identity, mission, and the conversion of the gentiles were typical for the times or that they actually worked the way he wanted. Paul is the problem, not the clue to imagining Christian origins, and has been all along, from our work on Q and the Gospel of Thomas to the *christos*/Christ cult question, the Corinthian situation, and now Mark."[50] Even if Paul's notions were untypical and worked contrary to his expectations, nevertheless, not only is his activity at least contemporary with our other sources, we also have to contend with the fact that there are successors (the Deuteropaulinists and Luke, among others) who carry on even while working their various rectifications.

Confiscation

Smith's description of the redactional presentation of "the outer northern limits of Jesus's loci of activity"[51] in Mark 7 reminded me of some geographical maneuvers in Acts that also feature the eastern Mediterranean coastline (unfortunately only as far north as Caesarea). According to Acts 8:40, after his miraculous transportation from the scene of his encounter with an Ethiopian, Philip finds himself at Azotus/Ashdod (about twenty miles northeast of Gaza) and proceeds up the coast to Caesarea, preaching the gospel in all the towns along the way. Curiously, according to Acts 9:32–10:48, this is precisely the area where Peter will soon enjoy his greatest missionary success. As Julius Wellhausen had already noted: "Es befremdet aber, dass er [Peter] dabei wiederum den Spuren des Philippus folgt, durch gewisse Städte der palästinischen Küstengegend bis nach Cäsarea, gerade wie er es in Samarien getan hat."[52] Whether Luke's motives in framing this relation are benign or otherwise, the itineraries of these

---

50. Mack, "Cartwheels," 136.
51. Smith, "The Markan Site," 121.
52. Julius Wellhausen, *Kritische Analyse der Apostelgeschichte*, Abhandlungen der

figures seemingly suggest that certain territories that formerly had been "under the sway" of Philip now pass to Peter. Perhaps Mark 7:24, 31 (as also 3:7–8) also seeks to signal some analogous assimilation with regard to territory and presents the appeal through the figure of Jesus himself. But, truth be told, "confiscation" appears to be over-the-top as a descriptor for what's going on in Acts, since Philip's fate is not consistent with the Long Goodbye of the practico-inert. Instead of the Big Sleep, he emerges just where we should expect him, in Caesarea, to serve as Paul's host (Acts 21:8) on the latter's way to an appointment in Jerusalem.

Proximate Others and Gentiles at Caesarea

On the basis of the echoes to the Elijah and Elisha cycles intertextually "recognized" in the account of the Syro-Phoenician woman (1 Kgs 17:8–24; 2 Kgs 4:18–37), Smith notes another appeal to these ancient biblical precedents in the special Lukan material at Luke 4:25–27 (1 Kgs 17:8–16; 2 Kgs 5:1–27). He suggests that the Lukan appropriation of these verses in support of the notion of a "gentile mission" obscures some "original (Jewish?) interest in collecting precedents for positive Levantine relations, carried over, perhaps by Syrian Christians, in Luke's time."[53] There is at least one other place in Luke's work where intertextual associations with Elijah traditions are worth mentioning in the current discussion, namely in the account of Philip's encounter with the Ethiopian in Acts 8:26–40, which contains echoes of 1 Kgs 18 and 2 Kgs 2.[54] In scholarship this particular Philip story is often juxtaposed with the legend of the conversion of Cornelius at Caesarea in Acts 10:1–11:18 as an example of competing traditional stories that seek to record the "first conversion" of a gentile.[55]

---

königlichen Gesellschaft der Wissenschaften zu Göttingen, Philologisch-historische Klasse, NS 15/2 (Berlin: Weidmann, 1914), 18.

53. Smith, "The Markan Site," 123.

54. See, e.g., Étienne Trocmé, *Le 'livre des Actes' et l'histoire*, Études d'histoire et de philosophie religieuses 45 (Paris: Presses Universitaires de France, 1957), 180; Ernst Haenchen, *The Acts of the Apostles: A Commentary*, trans. Bernard Noble and Gerald Shinn, under the supervision of Hugh Anderson and revised by R. McL. Wilson (Philadelphia: Westminster, 1971), 310–13; see also Thomas L. Brodie, "Towards Unraveling the Rhetorical Imitation of Sources in Acts: 2 Kgs 5 as One Component of Acts 8,9–40," *Bib* 67 (1986): 41–67, although I find his notion of the imitation process to be too mechanical.

55. See, e.g., Haenchen, *Acts of the Apostles*, 315: "The story of the eunuch is the

But leaving that issue aside, I simply want to underscore what appears to be evidence of Luke's access to a variety of elaborated traditions connected with Caesarea that play a significant role in Acts. It may not be far-fetched to imagine that he comes into contact with a piece such as Luke 4:25–27 in this same context.[56]

Hellenistic parallel to Luke's account of the first Gentile-conversion by Peter: its parallel—and rival."

56. On Caesarea, see Smith, "The Markan Site," 102 n. 4.

The Spyglass and the Kaleidoscope:
From a Levantine Coign of Vantage*

Burton L. Mack

Introduction

The meetings of the seminar on Ancient Myths and Modern Theories of Christian Origins, held in Toronto, produced several challenges to our categories of social formation and mythmaking. We had asked Jonathan Z. Smith to consider the Levant as a social setting for the Gospel of Mark. Merrill P. Miller had *Jesus and the Village Scribes*[1] in mind, where William E. Arnal set the text of the Sayings Gospel Q aside while he worked out a social description of the Galilee as the setting into which Q could then be placed. So we asked Smith if something like that might be done with the Levant and Mark and whether he thought it might have merit as a way to address the seminar's interest in bringing "social formation" and "mythmaking" together. We all knew that the Markan text was notoriously difficult to place. But apparently he thought our suggestion was worth a try. Without discussing directly the problem of locating Mark (anywhere) in the Roman world, or even mentioning the traditional arguments for considering the Levant as a plausible option, Smith painted a picture of the social fabric and history of the Levant with particular focus upon Tyre

---

* This is a revised version of a paper that was presented at our seminar sessions held in Atlanta in 2003. It is based, in part, on an earlier debriefing paper, "Cartwheels," in this volume, which was written in response to the two papers by Jonathan Z. Smith in this volume: "Conjectures on Conjunctures and Other Matters: Three Essays," and "The Markan Site"; these were presented at our seminar sessions held in Toronto in 2002.

1. William E. Arnal, *Jesus and the Village Scribes: Galilean Conflicts and the Setting of Q* (Minneapolis: Fortress, 2001).

without any reference to Mark and only afterward raised some questions about the possibilities and problems of placing Mark in that context. In course, and without directly mentioning the strategy, that is, the steering committee's query/suggestion about inverting the usual practice of looking for and at a setting mainly through windows provided by the text, Smith took his "assignment" as an opportunity to tease many of the issues in method and theory with which the seminar has been struggling. Thus, instead of scanning the Levantine social scape for "associations," "schools," ethnic enclaves, or "communities" that might bear resemblance to a Markan group as we might have tried to imagine it from the text, he cited the range of data available for constructing a large picture of the practices, institutions, and mentalities of the Levantine peoples and used Tyre as a privileged "e.g." This in effect asked us not only to set aside the Markan text while reconstructing a social setting but also to expand the parameters of that social setting far beyond the usual preoccupations with the pictures of synagogues, Pharisees, priests, and scribes in Galilee and Jerusalem given with the text. We were also being asked to set aside the images of disciples, followers, and smaller groups customarily in mind for the Jesus movements when trying to imagine the Markan "community."

This proposal is fair, strategic, and fully appropriate for advancing the seminar's project. It is designed to provide a fairly data-rich social setting that can then be used as a lens or frame through which to ask about Mark in relation to people living in the first century rather than only in relation to an imagined insular and insulated religious enclave. Testing the "fit" or problems with this setting for the Markan text need not be thought of only in terms of arguments for its plausible historical location. We are not unaware of other proposals, such as Rome, Alexandria, and northern Syria. But in these cases too, supposing one wanted to be as responsible as we would like to be about theorizing the reflexivity of social situation and mythmaking, a similar painting of the social picture for each of these other locations would have to be made in order to ask how the text may have come to be written in such a setting, or how it may have sounded when read. So although the Levantine setting is hypothetical, it is at least plausible (and, I do think, more probable than others that have been suggested). But irrespective of that issue, by making a serious attempt to place Mark in that setting we are in effect encouraged to sharpen our critical questions and analytical categories. The setting provides us with some wonderfully contiguous, if not contingent, indices for comparing features of the social realities of the Levant with the social, "historical," and mythic narrative worlds projected by the text. I need not emphasize that, without the control of such a setting, not only the "narrative world" of Mark's *bios*, but even the "social" and "historical" worlds it describes are quickly and easily taken up into the standard Christian imagination and interpretation of Christian origins. That being the case, I think it important that the seminar work through the challenge Smith has presented to us.

I would like to see for myself, at least, if I can follow Smith's strategy well enough and long enough to see some of the changes called for in my own erstwhile views of Mark's mythmaking. To do this I will have to sum up what I have been able to make of Smith's Tyrian ethnography and discussion of Mark in that context. But I also want to say how I see the difference it makes for interpreting Mark, especially in regard to questions about the reasons for Mark's construction of a *bios*-martyr myth, and what we might then say about our categories of mythmaking and social formation.

A Tyrian Ethnography

By focusing on Tyre, a center of civilization comes into view located just outside the Jerusalem-Galilee axis. It is this axis that has always framed the way in which Mark and its social situation have been interpreted. Thus, spending some scholarly time on the Syrian seacoast city of Tyre is bound to bring pressure to bear, not only on the customary readings of Mark, but also on the way in which the Jerusalem-Galilee axis has appeared to scholars interested mainly in the gospels. It is welcomed pressure. Instead of imagining the peoples of the Levant confronted with the tensions created by the Hellenization of their age-old Semitic traditions, building up to crisis proportions in Judea where the last holdout temple-state on the ancient Near Eastern model was fatally compromised by the Greeks and finally destroyed by the Romans in a world-historical event (hardly a parody of my own erstwhile infelicitous descriptions of the crucial "event"), we catch sight of people going about their business before and after the war in a multicultural world, taking for granted their identities as citizens of a city with roots in an illustrious history of fully functional social, political, and cultural structures, practices, and productions. Lest we forget the point of it all, the Tyrians were a Semitic people, sharing with other peoples of the Levant such markers of identity as northwest Semitic language, the practice of circumcision, temple-city centers, shrines and temple memorialization of outlying places of historic and legendary significance, calendars of religious feasts and festivals, and so on. Thus the differences among these peoples—including Idumaeans, Nabataeans, Judeans, Samaritans, Galileans, southern Syrians (with noteworthy differences among Tyrians, Sidonians, and other city dwellers along the coast), northern Syrians, and so forth—will have to be seen in the way each constructed or settled upon variations in the overall common pattern.

Tyre was not a temple-state on the ancient Near Eastern large-scale model as we (and I) have imagined that model, with priests and kings presiding over a twofold system of hierarchies in control of peoples and extensive lands, but it did have a temple, a history of kings, and influence (control?) over its hinterland peoples and villages. Nor was it a polis recently founded by the Seleucids. It was an ancient Canaanite/Phoenician "mother city" that had produced colonies throughout the western Mediterranean, controlled sea trade for centuries, developed an alphabet and writing, produced schools and intellectuals, and survived many conquests and challenges by foreign powers and interests (including the armies of Nebuchadnezzar and Alexander). Even now in the first century under Roman occupation of the Levant, Tyre was an independent city, "sacred, inviolate, autonomous," self-governed on the Hellenistic model (with a *boulê*), minting its own coins (with its own siglum and depicting the head of Melqart, instead of the Roman emperor), producing philosophers and jurists (of Roman law!), while continuing to cultivate links to its own Phoenician history. Smith's review of the exchange of letters between the Tyrians of Puteoli and Tyre extends this history of independent self-confidence and self-identification well towards the end of the second century. What can we learn from this?

Well, it does seem that the markers of importance for self-identification in the Levant may have to be ranked a bit differently than we have been assuming. We see a people who were apparently able to negotiate, accommodate, and assimilate layers of cultural and structural impingements without threatening what it meant to be a Tyrian. While what it meant to be a Tyrian must have included some of the markers we have associated with the term "ethnicity"—land, lineage, language, history, purity rules, temples, and gods—all seemed to have been subsumed in the social formations and cultural configurations of the city itself, that is, their city. Thus Greek had apparently eclipsed the northwest Semitic Phoenician before the Roman period, and during the Roman period Latin also came to be taken for granted. The city was protected by its patron god, of course, but there were also other gods and temples located there. And in the case of Tyre's patron deity, it was recognized both as Melqart (the Semitic Baal or king of the city) and as Herakles (the Hellenistic "hero" of power and philanthropy). So what we seem to have here is an "ethnic identity" controlled by the social structure and practices of a city within which multiple cultural traditions and more particular "ethnicities" could be accommodated and managed (or "negotiated," to use Smith's term). As for the way in which Tyrians handled their relations to other peoples and centers of power, they took their place within the larger Roman world as a matter of course, establishing "stations" ("associations"?) in other lands and cities as well as accepting and honoring patronage as a Roman *colonia* when offered at the end of the second century.

This is a remarkably different picture of a Semitic people's response to the social and political history of the Levant during the Greco-Roman period from that determined by our customary reconstructions of the machinations in Jerusalem. Since Smith has emphasized the similarities (and long-standing patterns of exchange) among the many peoples of the Levant before going on to explore the significance of partial differences of constructed "ethnic" markings and the way in which smallish "incidents" of conflict could get out of hand, the point must be that, not only do many of our categories need more precision ("ethnicity," "association," "identity," "social formation," "social interests," etc.), but also the social and political histories customary for imagining the "events" in Judea and beyond may well be reconsidered. What if we removed Mark's story as a window onto that history? What if Josephus's description of the tensions that built up to account for the revolt was an exaggerated construction in retrospect? What if James S. McLaren is right, and the war was triggered by a series of accidents instead of pieties pressed to the breaking point?[2] What then? Then we would have to redescribe the investments at stake in the many interests that seem to have been active in the histories of the peoples of the Levant, including Judeans, during the first century.

Smith has included a few observations about the way Judeans fit into the Levantine picture. The stories of trade, exchange, intermarriage, conquest, land ownership, estate economies, and the use of "international" coinage (the Tyrian shekel) correlate nicely with recent studies

---

2. James S. McLaren, *Turbulent Times? Josephus and Scholarship on Judaea in the First Century CE*, JSPSup 29 (Sheffield: Sheffield Academic, 1998).

by "Old Testament" scholars of the history of Jerusalem and the invention of "Israel's" epic history during the Hellenistic period.[3] It is important not to lose sight of the fact that the "kings," priests, and people of Jerusalem/Judea developed a distinctive social and cultural formation during this period, structured as a temple-state and marked by concern for self-identification and an outpouring of intellectual energy both in Jerusalem and diaspora associations. But here, as well as throughout the Levant, the post-Alexander Hellenes and the Romans marked the horizon of the larger worlds in need of negotiation. We are being asked, I think, to see the Judeans and their history of negotiating relations with all of their "others" more as a variant among the other Semitic peoples of the Levant, and less a peculiar (much less a "unique") social configuration as has been customary in biblical scholarship. Smith did not emphasize the presence of Hellenes and Hellenistic institutions in the Levant, but this set of social and cultural features needs also to be in mind as we turn to Mark.

Situating Mark

Smith uses the pericope about the Syro-Phoenician woman (Mark 7:24–30) to suggest the author's familiarity with and interest in relating to peoples along the southern Syrian seacoast. It is a telling observation, for, in distinction from all of the other geographical indicators in Mark, most of which are set in Galilee and Jerusalem and are tightly woven into the narrative plot and setting of the story, this one makes its point by being exceptional. The marks of its distinctiveness are not limited to its geographical and social location. The pericope is a *chreia* (or "pronouncement story"), the form of which highlights a winning response to a difficult challenge. In all of the many other pronouncement stories in Mark, Jesus is the winner (usually when challenged by Pharisees or dumb disciples) and he gets the last word. This is the only pronouncement story in which he is bested. It has been called a "double *chreia*" because there are two exchanges of riposte. The woman wins because she successfully meets the challenge of

---

3. See especially Mario Liverani, *Israel's History and the History of Israel*, trans. Chiara Peri and Philip R. Davies, Bible World (London: Equinox, 2005). Cf. Ron Cameron and Merrill P. Miller, "Introduction: Ancient Myths and Modern Theories of Christian Origins," in *Redescribing Christian Origins*, ed. Ron Cameron and Merrill P. Miller, SymS 28 (Atlanta: Society of Biblical Literature, 2004), 16 n. 41.

Jesus's first response. Noteworthy as well is that the pericope combines the genres of miracle story and *chreia*, much like the first and last stories in the first chain of pronouncement stories (Mark 2:1–3:6).[4] This is a fine indication of authorial invention and intention. So the question can certainly be asked in this case, differently than in the case of the other stories set in Galilee and Judea, why the author was interested in having Jesus encounter a Syro-Phoenician? Smith's point is that the story is about a situation in which different "ethnic" identities were seen as "negotiable" by the author and his "school" (my term). The story marks the woman "as a proximate other with which relations are possible."[5] This is elaborated by an exploration of rather long-standing "Jewish" (Judean) interests in "collecting precedents for positive Levantine relations."[6] I think that is right and will want to say more about Mark in the context of Judean-Levantine relations below.

But first, Smith also lists a number of other ways in which Mark might well be understood in a Levantine context. He mentions "Q-type Jesus teachings"[7] to which I would want to add the Cynic-like features of the pronouncement stories, as well as the Markan characterization of Jesus as a kind of teacher, both perfectly imaginable for Tyre and other cities with traditions of Hellenic and Hellenistic philosophical schools. The purity concerns under discussion in the pronouncement stories and elsewhere in the narrative are also of a kind characteristic for peoples of the Levant, especially those concerns associated with temples. It would also be possible to think of a number of other practices mentioned by Smith in passing as helpful in situating Mark. Meal protocol, *marzeah* rituals and rooms, ideologies of kingship, the construction of epic histories (e.g., Philo of Byblos), and so forth can all be seen as features of a social and cultural setting that may have been familiar to Mark without necessary appeal to specifically Judean practices. Smith also lists a number of topics for "heady" and "heated" conversations that "Mark's Levantine Judean association" could as easily have had with Syro-Phoenicians as with others in Galilee

---

4. See Burton L. Mack, *A Myth of Innocence: Mark and Christian Origins* (Philadelphia: Fortress, 1988; repr. with new preface, Minneapolis: Fortress, 2006), 197, 216, 239, 381.

5. Jonathan Z. Smith, "The Markan Site," 122.

6. Ibid., 123.

7. Ibid., 123–24.

and Judea.[8] The list includes topics such as violations of purity and what to do about them; the difference between meal scruples for home and temple practices; discussions of events (Pseudo-Alexander's fraud, what the Romans are up to); exploring symbols (Theandrites) and myths (e.g., of Herakles as a model for kingship); as well as the cost of olive oil and problems with the Tyrian mint.

This reconstruction of a Levantine ethos makes it possible to imagine the author of Mark at work in such a setting, taking the larger social picture for granted even while casting his narrative of Jesus almost entirely along the Jerusalem-Galilee axis. At first this experiment in locating Mark seems to surface as many problems for interpretation as it does possibilities. Smith lists the incidence of synagogues, Pharisees, and the relation of apocalyptic to the Jerusalem temple as problems. It is true that we know of no synagogues as Mark describes them, either in Galilee or southern Syria, before the second or third centuries. We no longer think that the Pharisees played any important role in the emergence of these ("Diaspora") institutions, and we are not even sure of the Pharisees being a recognizable social presence in Galilee, much less Syria before the war. As for apocalyptic, it points to an interest in the fate of a temple unlikely for Levantines. Nevertheless, these problematic items do not preclude the possibility of the author's location in the Levant, outside of Galilee and/or Judea. These items are already problematic as features of the story set in Galilee and Jerusalem before the war no matter where the author is located. They are actually less problematic as features of a story constructed after the war and in another location, for then one can see that they belong to the author's imagination and reconstruction of times and places before the war not of his own experience. This means that, whatever the author knew about synagogues farther afield, however the author learned about Pharisees and their imagined challenge to Jesus and his followers, and why ever he wanted to cast his story of Jesus and the temple in apocalyptic terms, he has to be seen as bringing together social and historical figures and events that did not belong together at the time his story is set and that need not be together in the social situation in which this author was actually working. Thus, they are not really problematic features of a narrative created in a southern Syrian location. They actually can be seen as additional confirmation of the mythic or fictional construction of the narrative. As a matter

8. Ibid., 118–20.

of fact, the fictional and imaginative aspects of these features of Mark's story can easily be turned to advantage, if he is located in southern Syria. That is because this particular configuration of what Smith has called "the near and the far"[9] allows us to use this distance of the author in time and place from the events storied in his narrative to better work out the logic of the story including the (historical) fictions. I am thinking here, not only of Smith's typology of the "here," "there," and "anywhere" locations of significance for religious centers and practices.[10] I am also impressed by Miller's application of a Smithian axiom to this locative theory in order to clarify the reasons behind Paul's interest in Jerusalem as reported in Galatians.[11] The axiom was, in effect, that the (symbolic) importance of the homeland temple ("there") is enhanced for those living in the Diaspora. I'll come back later to how this might work in the case of a Levantine Mark.

A second consideration having to do with a Levantine location for Mark has also become important for me. Not having been convinced that the annexation of Idumea, Samaria, and Galilee by the Hasmoneans was an entirely joyful homecoming for the peoples living in those lands, I imagine the relations of Idumea, Samaria, Galilee, and southern Syria to Jerusalem each with a slightly different valence in terms of their distance (and, of course, their historically different experiences) from Judea. Thus I imagine the author of Mark, now located in southern Syria, to be in a situation both "near" and "far" from both Galilee (a kind of "there" for the origins of the Jesus school or "traditions") and Jerusalem (the political and religious center of importance for Galilee before the war). I need only assume that the author was interested in the rationale for some configuration of a Jesus school in southern Syria after the Roman-Jewish war in order to get started with a set of observations on how that location helps to explain the particular rationalization he came up with. I need not fuss in advance with the question of whether it was the teachings of Jesus or the persons who espoused them who had migrated from Galilee, or whether the "school" to which the author belonged had formed its own "associa-

---

9. Ibid.

10. Jonathan Z. Smith, *Relating Religion: Essays in the Study of Religion* (Chicago: University of Chicago Press, 2004), 323–39.

11. Merrill P. Miller, "Antioch, Paul, and Jerusalem: Diaspora Myths of Origins in the Homeland," in Cameron and Miller, *Redescribing Christian Origins*, 177–235; cf., Ron Cameron, "Introduction to the Papers from the First Year of the Seminar," in Cameron and Miller, *Redescribing Christian Origins*, 152–55.

tion" or network of families, or carried on in tandem to other social venues (such as synagogue, Levantine Judean association, or even an association of Pharisees). The point is that the slightly removed location from Hasmonean territory, negotiating relations after the war with Romans, Levantine "cousins," Judean Pharisees (or Pharisaic teachings), and perhaps (still) Galilean siblings and Tyrian hinterland friends and families, allows us to explore the "social logic" of the Markan narrative from quite a different perspective from that traditional to New Testament scholarship.

Mark in Context

A Little Help From the Pharisees

Having argued for placing Mark in this social and intellectual setting, I want now to elaborate on the point just made about turning the problematic features of the narrative to interpretive advantage. If we temporarily set aside the historical questions about the Pharisees (problematic in Galilee, the synagogues, and in general) and ask instead about their function in the Markan narrative, it is fairly clear that they play the role of antagonist on issues of purity and authority. The issues span a spectrum touching upon questions of ritual purity, moral purity, and social relations governed by the temple's system of authorization regarding status and practices. If we use the term *purity* in its broadest sense to encompass this spectrum of issues, it means that the essential issues under debate in the mind of the author have to do with purity and authority. If we notice that the temple priests begin to play the role of antagonist toward the end of the narrative but that the issue is the same, namely, purity, now in relation to the sanctity of the temple, one can hardly avoid the conclusion that questions of purity as defined by the Pharisees and the temple priests were issues of some importance for the author. Although Jesus as the protagonist of the story counters with rhetorical arguments, putdowns, and irony, it is not too difficult to imagine that debates about these issues may not always have been so cleanly and easily settled in the discussions that must have taken place in the author's mind and/or Jesus school. The questions about purity, that is, must have been real issues in many forums, not only those having to do with the teachings of Jesus. That is because purity codes had been defined by the temple system, and with the temple no longer there, the practice of purity in the domestic sphere would have lost its authorizing institution, if not its model. One can imagine that everyone who had lived under the temple's rule, including Judeans, Galileans, Jesus people, "Pharisees," priests, and other client groups, would have been involved in discussing and experimenting with practices no longer authorized by the temple-state. This observation does not tell us when and where a branch of the Jesus school may have encountered real live Pharisees, before or after the war, who may have taken exception to their views and behavior. But it does tell us that issues of social propriety and teachings (perhaps even issues of recognition, identity, and formation) could have focused on adjudicating definitions of purity in discussion with other groups and that the adjudication was taking place among groups or schools of thought that saw themselves related to one another ethnically. That is because purity rules were "ethnic" markers, and the particular set of purity concerns taken seriously on both sides of the debate in Mark's story were Judean. So what we have to recognize is that the situation reflected in this Markan window has to be described as a family quarrel about where and how to draw the lines between relatives who must have seen themselves as very close siblings or cousins experimenting with alternate teachings. That both of these groups must have taken the Judean temple-state for granted is also clear. The teachings of the Pharisees can be seen as a kind of translation of the temple's purity codes; the teachings of these Jesus people can be seen as a kind of translation of the temple's social and theocratic ideologies.

If so, the move from Galilee to southern Syria does not indicate any kind of "mission," much less a "mission to the gentiles." This is a terribly important observation to keep in mind, for it marks a most significant contrast to the Pauline formulation of the "Christ message." A recent study by Caroline Johnson Hodge demonstrates just how pivotal the notion of a mission to the gentiles was for all of Paul's thinking.[12] Her thesis is largely persuasive, namely, that ideologies of lineage, patriliny, kinship, and ethnicity common for much of the Greco-Roman world were taken for granted by Paul and used to create what Stanley K. Stowers has called, in personal correspondence, "a myth of kinship and futuristic fantasies." With a discussion of these ideologies in place, Johnson Hodge is able to account for the Abraham-faithfulness/Christ-faithfulness "lineage" (in a way much better than I had imagined in my critique of Paul's argument in

---

12. Caroline Johnson Hodge, *If Sons, Then Heirs: A Study of Kinship and Ethnicity in the Letters of Paul* (New York: Oxford University Press, 2007).

Galatians in *Who Wrote the New Testament?*).[13] She is also able to work out
Paul's myth of "aggregate ethnic manipulation" for the gentiles. In course,
Johnson Hodge can explain much of the curious terminology, phraseology,
and conceptuality of Paul's discourse. The message, moreover, is clearly
put forth as a solution to the "problem" of gentiles being accepted by the
Judean god as part of his family (Israel). This is not the place to discuss the
fine points of Johnson Hodge's thesis or the oddities of Paul's mythmaking. My reference to it is intended to remind us of (1) Paul's division of all
ethnic differences into the single opposition between "Jew" and "gentile,"
(2) the ways in which these notions of "ethnicity" were basic for Paul's
gospel, and (3) how Paul's gospel has been taken as the standard articulation of what all of early Christianity was about. The point is that the discussion of the markers of "ethnicity" in Mark is *not* about the problem of
the gentiles, does not seek a mythic solution to such a problem of exclusion from "Israel," does not demand conversion by means of accepting a
Christ myth, and thus does not need to manipulate genealogical lineages
in order to entertain a future for the Jesus school as belonging to Israel.

In the "Cartwheels" paper I wrote that "Paul is the problem, not the
clue to imagining Christian origins."[14] I want now to underscore that
statement in the light of Johnson Hodge's thesis and Smith's implicit challenge to our use of the term "ethnicity" as a general category for social
self-identity in both the Jesus movements and the Pauline assemblies.
The term as defined by Paul's "Judean/gentile" contrast is not relevant for
Mark. There is no "gentile problem" addressed in Mark (or in the earlier
Jesus traditions). This does not mean that issues relating to "ethnic identity" are not important for Mark. Indeed, the major set of issues has to do
with social behavior appropriate for what Smith has called "Mark's Levantine Judean association."[15] But the parties involved belong already to the
"family," and the issues are not spelled out in terms of ethnic divisions that
need to be overcome.

Thus the appearance of the Pharisees in Mark is not a problem for a
Levantine location. It appears, as a matter of fact, that the debate with the
Pharisees is settled now, if ever it was a real confrontation; it is a thing of
the past. The issues of the debate are still vividly in mind, however, and

---

13. Burton L. Mack, *Who Wrote the New Testament? The Making of the Christian
Myth* (San Francisco: HarperSanFrancisco, 1995), 113–21.
14. Mack, "Cartwheels: Or On Not Staying Upside Down Too Long," 136.
15. Smith, "Markan Site," 118.

the results of the debate, namely, the decision of the Jesus people to reject Pharisaic rules, are apparently regarded as definitional. Thus these stories serve to confirm the appropriateness of the southern Syrian seacoast as a place where purity concerns would still have to be debated, without, however, calling into fundamental question other ethnic markers (such as homeland, kinship, language, rituals, cultural ethos, social behavior, and so forth). As in most other references to the Pharisees in the literature of the period, in Mark they represent a kind of party or school of thought. Such a school of thought could be taken seriously and discussed without actual encounter, and, judging from the range of stereotypes possible for the Pharisees (in Q, Gospel of Thomas, Matthew, Luke, and Josephus), it would have been easy to set them up as straw men in a set of Jesus *chreiai*.

But What about the Synagogue?

Just as in the case of the Pharisees, the appearance of synagogues in the narrative does not need to be taken historically (with respect to the time of Jesus in Galilee) or as a mirror of the author's own situation. The problem, rather, is that the author does know about synagogues as a place for gathering, instruction, and debate, and, since the use of this setting is pointed and thematic, the author assumed that listeners/readers also would know about them. If only for this reason, it might be best to consider a somewhat later dating for Mark than has been usual. A later dating, say toward the very end of the first century, would make it possible to see not only how the author could easily have gathered up information about what we now see as separate problematic aspects of his conjoined social descriptions, but also how he could have gotten away with the fiction of it all having taken place in Galilee and Judea forty years before the war. Either way, however, sooner or later after the war, the place of the synagogues in the story can be turned away from the problematic into the advantageous in our quest for a social location for Mark. That is because meeting in synagogues and houses is a narrative theme of some significance in the story. Since it does not take much of a twitch for our spyglass to act like a kaleidoscope, it is not too difficult to turn it ever so slightly and catch different glimpses of what Smith called Mark's "Levantine Judean association." The scene can change with each twist of the glass and the peoples from Galilee, Judea, and southern Syria step in and out, debating the school traditions associated with Jesus and the Pharisees, and trying desperately to imagine the future of the people of the "kingdom of God" that Jesus had talked about and the temple represented. There is also just a touch of interest in movement from synagogue to house to agora and back again, as if these (Markan) Jesus people had not (yet, if ever?) settled into an association with definitive borders and identity of their own. So out with my earlier description of a "synagogue *reform* movement,"[16] and on to people from Galilee and perhaps from Judea interested still in the teachings of Jesus but having to figure out how in the world they could still be thought relevant to a world without the temple. This does mean that for these Jesus people the teachings of Jesus had not been understood as a critique of the temple system and a program to substitute something else. Judging from other variants of the Jesus traditions (Q, for example), the temple had apparently been taken for granted by the Jesus people as a fixture in their social and cultural landscape until its destruction brought forth various kinds of consternation and rationalization. I see no reason to doubt that the Jesus people had taken their "citizenship" in the Jerusalem temple-state of the Hasmonean period for granted. Now that the temple was no longer there, the question of orientation to the "landscapes" of the larger world would need to be discussed and debated. It may well be that some parting of the ways had occurred between the Jesus people and the "synagogue" (Mark 13:9), but if so it is not clear what the destruction of the temple or the debates with the Pharisees may have had to do with it.

Why Then the Apocalypse?

If we stick with Smith's definition of the social situation to which an apocalyptic imagination was addressed, namely the wrong king on the throne and the consequential pollution of a people's land and temple,[17] it seems clear that the New Testament texts regularly classified as "apocalyptic" should not count. Most can be accounted for as the employment of this or that feature of an apocalyptic scenario in the interest of arguing for some other mythic claim to be taken seriously. In most cases, the apocalyptic

---

16. Mack, *Myth of Innocence*, 94–96, 192–207, emphasis added; cf. 101, 107, 125–26, 166, 226–27, 239, 244, 280–81, 316–21, 326–27, 355; Mack, "A Myth of Innocence at Sea," *Continuum* 1 (1991): 147–51.

17. See Jonathan Z. Smith, "Wisdom and Apocalyptic," in *Map Is Not Territory: Studies in the History of Religions*, SJLA 23 (Leiden: Brill, 1978; Chicago: University of Chicago Press, 1993), 67–87; Smith, "A Pearl of Great Price and a Cargo of Yams: A Study in Situational Incongruity," in *Imagining Religion: From Babylon to Jonestown*, CSHJ (Chicago: University of Chicago Press, 1982), 90–101.

scenario merely functions as a threat for not taking the claim seriously. In no case is this eschatological threat anchored in a response to "an apocalyptic situation," much less dependent upon or derived from the other more fundamental mythic claims themselves. Paul's eschatological threats and apocalyptic finales are rather loosely tacked on to his *kerygma*, not derived from it. In Q, both the eschatological promise and threat of judgment function in support of the seriousness with which individuals should take the teachings of Jesus.[18] Thus, among early "Christian" texts, it is only in Mark where an apocalyptic situation is described at all, and there it is turned on its head. The Markan apocalypse does not tell of the pollution of the land by foreign invaders and the eventual restoration of valid royalty and the temple service. Instead, it assumes the past destruction of the temple to have been a judgment upon it provoked by Jesus, and the eschatological resolution to be an appearance of Jesus and his kingdom. Interestingly, Mark's employment of apocalyptic themes, in distinction from most of the other borrowings from the genre of apocalyptic in early Christian literature, does not seem to be motivated by the need to threaten a final judgment upon the ungodly. It is the "disciples" who are warned about the consequences of not staying true to ("following") the teachings of Jesus.

I do like Smith's suggestion about comparing Mark with the fourth Sibylline Oracle at the point of attitudes toward the temple's destruction, namely that it was deserved. The reason this comparison helps is because at least one other text written by a "Jewish" intellectual entertained a thought somewhat similar to Mark's, although Mark is very cagey at the point of whether the temple "deserved" its destruction at the hand of the Romans, and Mark leaves it to the imagination of the reader to think that it was "caused" by the temple's rejection of Jesus. Nevertheless, if the fourth Sibylline Oracle can be placed in southern Syria ca. 80 CE, we might have what Smith has referred to as a "pre-positioned" element, namely a feature of the social and cultural landscape of the Levant in the company of which Mark's story need not be seen as all that novel.[19]

Thus the Markan employment of apocalyptic was hardly occasioned by a direct and dramatic experience of the Roman-Jewish war. That means that the social location we are considering, at a distance from Jerusalem in geography, time, and social demarcation, makes it possible to

---

18. See Burton L. Mack, *The Lost Gospel: The Book of Q and Christian Origins* (San Francisco: HarperSanFrancisco, 1993), 133–34.

19. Jonathan Z. Smith, "Conjectures on Conjunctures," 36, 68.

tone down the problems of historiography and ask instead about the logic of Mark's mythmaking.

Mark's *Bios* and the Martyr Myth

The really important question to ask about Mark's mythmaking is why he wrote a *bios* at all. The question about how he managed that is also important but not nearly so difficult as to account for the rather elaborate narrative itself and the reasons for writing it. It is clear that calling this narrative a *bios* is not quite accurate, of course. The attempts to identify its genre as a *bios*, or for that matter as a history, a novel, a martyrology, or a cult legend, have all helped to identify particular features of the story that would have been recognizable as belonging to this or that genre. But none has been able to come up with a generic template to tell us how such a narrative as Mark's story worked, what it was for, and why, then, it was written. The question is especially important in light of the fact that neither the pre-Markan Jesus traditions nor the Pauline discourses appear to have needed the kind of story Mark composed.

I would like to try my hand at suggesting a solution to this question, and, as you might suspect, I find it quite helpful to think of the author located in southern Syria. I imagine the author working with a large number of resources: the Jesus school traditions, Levantine commonplaces about teachers, kings, and heroes, Jewish and Hellenistic martyrologies, Jewish epic literature, rich material both textual and discursive having to do with the Roman-Jewish war, the destruction of the temple, and especially what to make of the Galilee-Judea linkage now that the temple was in ruins. I would like to start with a few remarks about several items in the author's list of resources and how they fit into the composition, saving the question of why such was imagined until later.

Although it is clear that the Markan intellectual milieu had put its own spin on materials belonging to the Jesus school and its traditions, it is helpful, I think, to imagine these materials with roots still understood to be Galilean. Q-type teachings material would be part of that resource, even though not surfacing as such in the narrative. (As you know, I have argued that Mark knew the Q material.[20]) The various castings of Jesus

---

20. See Burton L. Mack, "Q and the Gospel of Mark: Revising Christian Origins," *Semeia* 55 (1991): 15–39; cf. Mack, *Myth of Innocence*, 59, 84, 170–71, 197–98, 204–5, 319–20, 323–24.

as a teacher would also have been taken for granted in Jesus school traditions, even though the kind of teacher Jesus turns out to be in Mark's *bios* is certainly an odd revision of the earlier pictures. The pronouncement stories in Mark may well be taken as a "development" within a Jesus school that had come to focus on debates with itself and the traditions of the Pharisees over questions of purity. Since it appears that the author used these stories thematically, and in fact revised several,[21] the development they represent within a Jesus school may have been rather recent. The chains of divine man stories ("miracle" stories) are a bit more difficult to place on a path from Galilee to Syria. Their interest in epic precedents set in (northern) Israel speaks for Galilean roots, as might also the descriptions of the people (unclean in the view of temple personnel) in need of help. But all of that, plus their divine man characterization, could easily be imagined as appropriate for a Syrian provenance as well. In any case, a number of developments have to be acknowledged within the Jesus school(s) before and/or during Mark's time, developments he could take for granted in the writing of his *bios*. Finding links between the teachings of Jesus and the epic traditions of Israel were features of these traditions, and, as Miller has helped us see, it is highly probable that Jesus as a founder figure for the Jesus school(s) had been imagined as their *christos* (or teacher for the times "anointed" by God). It should be emphasized that, according to Miller's work on the *christos* designation in the pre-Markan Jesus traditions,[22] it was not linked to a martyr myth, much less to the logic of Paul's Christ myth. Thus there is much about the shape of the Jesus materials at Mark's disposal that can easily be imagined for a Jesus school residing in southern Syria.

Three additional resources need now to be discussed for which the southern Syrian location is even more conducive. They are (1) post-war perspectival information about Galileans and the war, (2) the function and destiny of mythic figures of sovereign and heroic stature (such as Melqart-Herakles), and (3) martyrologies. Taking the last first, reference need be made only to the number of recent studies on the ideology of martyrdom, stories of persons who died the "noble death," and their prevalence during

---

21. See Mack, *Myth of Innocence*, 172–207.

22. Merrill P. Miller, "The Problem of the Origins of a Messianic Conception of Jesus," in Cameron and Miller, *Redescribing Christian Origins*, 301–35; Miller, "The Anointed Jesus," in Cameron and Miller, *Redescribing Christian Origins*, 375–415.

this period throughout the Greco-Roman world.[23] While there is no particular reason for a fascination with or the generation of martyr myths in
southern Syria, one can imagine a conducive atmosphere for rehearsals of
noble deaths after the war created by the recent histories and mix of Seleucids, Maccabees, and Romans, as well as the kind of stories about Judean
defenders and defectors told by Josephus. The point would be to see Mark's
story of Jesus's confrontation of the temple authorities generated in the
context of these histories, rather than as a narrative elaboration of Paul's
Christ myth. The contrast is in reality most striking. The Christ myth
reduced the several elements of a martyrology to two essentials without
narrative embellishment: Jesus was (1) faithful unto death, (2) for a cause.
To this was added a vindication by God (raised from the dead). The logic
of this myth (for the "cause" Paul had in mind, namely the "vindication" of
the gentiles) rode on the concentration of motivations limited to Jesus and
God. This logic would have been ruined by any narrative elaboration as a
martyrology in which the motivations and actions involved in confrontation with opposing human forces were customary. Mark's story not only
lets these motivations and actions surface, they actually carry the story
along as a studied theme. This means that Mark's martyr myth should not
be interpreted according to Paul's Christ myth, as modern scholars tend to
do.[24] The logic of Mark's martyr myth is quite different from Paul's Christ
myth, and I'll try to spell it out below. But first, all of the "resources" have
to be lined out.

I have been taken by Smith's reference to Herakles as a well-known
mythic figure of significance for Tyre, one that might bear comparison
with Mark's portrayal of Jesus. The points of comparison are intriguing.
Herakles was popular as a symbol of strength while undergoing trials. His
trials were also allegorized by Stoics and Cynics in order to create models
of the ideal king. The ideal king was invariably set over against the tyrant,
the image of sovereign power gone wrong. In distinction from other Greek
heroes, Herakles was not associated with a particular district or lineage,
did not have a local tomb. In the popular imagination, Herakles could be
found anywhere, and he was available for merger with other heroes (The-

23. See David Seeley, *The Noble Death: Graeco-Roman Martyrology and Paul's Concept of Salvation*, JSNTSup 28 (Sheffield: Sheffield Academic, 1990).

24. See Burton L. Mack, "Rereading the Christ Myth: Paul's Gospel and the Christ Cult Question," in *Redescribing Paul and the Corinthians*, ed. Ron Cameron and Mer-rill P. Miller, ECL 5 (Atlanta: Society of Biblical Literature, 2011), 35–73.

seus), kings (many Roman emperors), localized king-deities (Melqart), and other founder-teachers (Moses at Dura-Europos). The story about the way he ended his life (mounting a funeral pyre for burning instead of waiting for the poison of a treachery to have its effect) was often interpreted as a noble death. As a matter of fact, it is quite important to realize that the concept of the noble death included suicide as well as unflinching behavior when confronted by the sword. One can see how the people of Tyre, familiar as they must have been with the stories of Herakles, may have responded to Mark's story of Jesus's decision to confront the authorities in Jerusalem knowing what his fate would be. It would also not be difficult to imagine that the author was familiar with the stories of Herakles, and that they influenced the way in which he constructed his story of Jesus.

It is obvious that the author was successful in weaving together many different kinds of material. But the most important materials, thematically and for the overall impression of the narrative as story, are (1) the way in which the Jesus materials are woven together to create a kind of *bios* in Galilee, and (2) the way in which a martyr myth plots the ending of the *bios* in Jerusalem. It is the combination of *bios* and martyr myth against the background of Galilee and Jerusalem that makes most sense as a story invented after the war by Jesus school people at some remove, say in southern Syria. Why? Because the story requires the postwar retrospective as a lens to grant credibility to the prehistory it narrates, and the prehistory it narrates works well only if the settings for the *bios* and martyrdom are imagined as a single "land," governed by a single system of temple related officials and institutions, and inhabited by people all of whom understand themselves to be living under the arc of the temple system. Thus the story collapses the difference between Galilee and Judea on purpose, just as it collapses the differences among scribes, Pharisees, priests, high priests, and Herodians when joined in the plot against Jesus. And yet, even though the events of the war must be in mind, the destruction of the temple is not mourned, described, dramatized, or celebrated in any way. Only in the apocalyptic discourse in Mark 13 does language appear that might be compared with other Jewish literature in response to the event (Josephus, 4 Ezra, 2 Baruch). Even there the rumble of wars and rumors of wars appear mainly as a touch of credibility viewed from a distance, not intended to preempt the real and significant ending of the story yet to be told.

This means, I think, that the author had to come to terms with the fact of the temple's end, and he found a way to put a construction on it that allowed his Jesus school to continue thinking of itself as okay in the larger scheme of things, that is, as a people whose "kingdom" was able to encompass the larger horizon of the multicultural world in which they now found themselves. This takes seriously the above analysis of the Jesus people and their history of debate with the Pharisees. It means that they had taken the temple system for granted as the overarching world within which they had experimented with lifestyle changes and kingdom of God concepts in the school of Jesus. That had apparently worked quite well until they ran into debates with "the Pharisees." As a result of that encounter/discussion, if not before, it would have become necessary to realize that they were experimenting with only one way among other options of living as a citizen of the temple-state centered in Jerusalem. Suppose, then, that the temple's destruction came as a surprise, an unwanted, unexpected event that, while not directly threatening the Jesus people or school, removed their point of orientation for anchoring their mythology of the kingdom of God in a place with epic history (Smith's "there"). The resulting disorientation, though not generated by having taken sides in any pro/anti-temple movements, would still have been unnerving. The fact that the temple was no longer there could be taken advantage of, not only to acknowledge the challenge its demise introduced to the rationale of the Jesus people but also to account for the very origins of the Jesus movement now imagined self-servingly as a challenge to the temple system. This, at any rate, is apparently what the author worked out.

The costs of the particular myth Mark came up with were therefore very high. Not only did it mean that the temple system deserved to be destroyed by the Romans, a possible if rather brutal and fantastic conclusion, especially if proffered by a Jesus school. It also meant that the manifestation of the kingdom of God, exactly the program in which the Jesus people were interested and active, would no longer have a frame of reference for comparison and definition, that is, means of being obvious in the practices of an association and discourse of a school. What "kingdom of God" meant in the teachings of Jesus and the practices of the Jesus school could no longer be just a "translation" of the temple's social and theocratic ideologies; it would have to function now as a completely transcendent and imaginary ideal. Thus, the "kingdom of God" would no longer be visible. It would no longer benefit from human labors or visible manifestations. It would become a "seed growing secretly" and a "mystery" known only to those with eyes to see. As for the time when it would finally become visible, a heavenly rupture of divine glory and power would have to occur.

So why the *bios*-martyr myth? It was one author's answer to a situation rife with multiple incongruities challenging the traditions of a Jesus school hardly formed or sure of itself as an association on its own. The answer can be called a myth of origins, for it packs all of the later features of the school, its teachings as they had developed, and its self-understanding vis-à-vis other associations and peoples into a story of their inauguration. This is classic mythmaking in the genre of myths of origin. It corresponds to a mode of intellection designed to comprehend the relations among several fundamental factors that play some role in the construction of a social complex by painting an originary scenario for analysis. From the many myths of origin documented in ethnography, through Rousseau's noble savage, Kierkegaard's teacher with disciples secondhand, Freud's original Oedipal event, Jensen's root-crop murder, Girard's original scapegoat, and Burkert's first return from the hunt, the strategy has been the same. Critics have always countered with the observation that the intellectual has cheated, that the subsequent effects of the imagined moment have been slipped in as features of the setting prior to the moment imagined to account for them. But that is precisely what a myth of origin must do. A myth of origin always cheats if viewed as an account of causation. It should rather be seen as the manipulation of a complex set of factors to form a scene in which a single set of relations can be studied in motion. I recall Smith's discussion of ritual as a "mode of paying attention" (with reference to Lévi-Strauss's observation about ritual as a "parcelling out" of details), as well as Smith's observations on the effect of miniatures (e.g., of temples and Easter tombs), namely as a way to comprehend in smaller, more manageable scale the larger whole that is too large and complex to grasp in a single sighting.[25] Both of these examples have as their point the importance of thought and deliberation in the construction of religious artifacts and practices. I would like to suggest the same for myths of origin, and especially now for Mark's narrative. Note the links created by having Jesus say what your school has recently been teaching, suggesting that the temple was always more important as a frame of reference for your ideas than you may have realized, erasing the differences between Galilee and Judea as a way to enhance the large-scale

---

25. See Jonathan Z. Smith, "The Domestication of Sacrifice," in *Violent Origins: Walter Burkert, René Girard, and Jonathan Z. Smith on Ritual Killing and Cultural Formation*, ed. Robert G. Hamerton-Kelly (Stanford, CA: Stanford University Press, 1987), 191–205; repr. in Smith, *Relating Religion*, 145–59; Smith, *To Take Place: Toward Theory in Ritual*, CSHJ (Chicago: University of Chicago Press, 1987), esp. 103–17, 174–79.

relevance of the "new teaching with authority," devising a plot to imagine how the temple authorities may be imagined to have taken note of Jesus's teachings, constructing a martyr myth as if Jesus died nobly for the truth of his teachings, thus showing his teachings to be valid for virtuous living and dying, packing in a host of ironies to let the reader understand more than those in the story (and those in the present who may not understand as well), and ending the story with the promise of a future for the Jesus people as vague but surely as certain as the promise of a future for Jesus had to be. No wonder the founder-teacher had to be upgraded to some kind of divine man or son of God! What a story.

I would not think Mark's story was an immediate success in or out of his Levantine Judean association. But it certainly may have raised eyebrows and, because it hangs together as a story, may well have become the basis for debate, joking, discussion, and yes, some new insights that may have emerged in the teasing about the place of the Jesus school in the southern Syrian world, insights that could have settled in over time as acceptable notions. Overkill? Of course. Community sustaining? No. But if we read this material as it must have been read, namely retrospectively through the lens of events created by the war, in drafts at different times, and participating in the lively discussions of negotiated differences going on in the Levant late in the first century, it may not have sounded as singularly dramatic as later Christian readings have imagined it. The mood of apocalyptic apparently passed, if ever there had been such a mood, thus letting Mark's story be read and revised by later writers in Jesus schools much more confident of their places in the world.

Social Formation and Mythmaking?

Miller asked me to conclude my reflections on a Levantine location for Mark by saying how I understood its effect upon the categories we have been using for our redescription project, namely *social formation* and *mythmaking*. In particular, he wanted to know whether Smith's discussion of his own categories for method and theory in describing the social and intellectual aspects of myths and rituals had helped us redefine our own project. Miller's questions are fair, especially since Smith's papers on Mark and the Levantine setting were his response to our pointed request that he help us with our category formations. The answer, then, in general is "Yes, much has been learned about being more precise in our use of these categories." On the other hand, being more precise turns out to be more a matter of spelling out the dynamics of processes and reflexive relations imagined for each category in relation to the other, rather than questioning the validity or helpfulness of the two as such. There was certainly a large measure of generalization and naiveté in our use of these terms at the beginning of the project. But it was not wrongheaded and they did serve us well in our plan to resituate and interrogate texts of some importance for our attempt to revise the traditional imagination of Christian origins. What happened was not that we failed to redescribe the social logic of these texts as myths or to reimagine the various social locations as formations that invited rationalization. The problems we kept running into were (1) that we had no theory to account for or analyze the linkage between the two (a "mechanism" to explain the reflexive relation between social formation and mythmaking); (2) that without a theory of social formation we often got caught with descriptions that were too simple, organic, and insular, rather than ways of sustaining group interests while belonging to more complex social configurations that required negotiation; and (3) that without a theory of mythmaking, we had to rely on rhetorical analyses that exposed only the interests of the mythmaker, not those of the social group addressed. Smith's papers and seminar discussions have pressed us to shift our focus on all three fronts. Social formations, always already complex with many centers of interests in dynamic relations to one another, change slowly and by degrees. Social formations are not insular units bouncing off one another like billiard balls. The Christian notion of "conversion" or "new community formation" turns out to be completely inappropriate for Christian origins, even for Paul and his "congregations." As for mythmaking, we have learned to be more careful about the ways in which various kinds of authorization, factors of credibility, and reasons for the entertainment or acceptance of a mythic notion impinge upon the process. Smith's cautions about the many ways in which changing situations and interests impinge upon the mechanisms of transformation/rectification and reproduction/experimental application finally bring us to a thorough reconsideration of the situational context for imagining the processes of social formation and mythmaking. Instead of assuming dramatic events at the social level or shocking ideas at the level of myth that "trigger" the processes of mythmaking and social formation, we now have "'situational incongruity' as it presents itself to thought."[26]

---

26. Smith, "Conjectures on Conjunctures," 69, emphasis original.

I would say we have made progress on all three fronts. Placing Mark in the Levant turns out to be the best exercise yet in a redescription that actually brings social formation and mythmaking together. It is true that the mythmaking part of this project is still the stronger lead, as it has always been. But in this case it has been possible to analyze it in greater detail simply because of its location in southern Syria and the ways in which snippets of inference from the text about the social history of Mark's Jesus school can be imagined to fit into that larger setting. And in that setting, the "situational incongruity" that calls for some mythmaking can be reconstructed as a set of interrelated impingements upon a Jesus school which can easily be understood to have created questions for the group. I am afraid that I may not have satisfied Smith's desire to distinguish sharply between "incident" and "event" as types of change that can create a situation of incongruity. This distinction was intended to address my delight in Marshall Sahlins's description of the "conjuncture" of cultures in the history of Captain Cook and the Hawaiians, a description I took as a way to imagine the mechanisms of "reproduction" and "transformation" in application to my notions of social formation and mythmaking.[27] Smith's caution was that Sahlins's "conjuncture" was limited to a clash of two very different cultures, and that significant changes could take place in many other ways including intracultural "incidents" that created "situations of incongruity" calling for thought. The point is well-taken, and I have been especially thankful for his reference to Nicholas Thomas's observation that Sahlins's description of the reproductions/transformations that took place during Cook's visits to Hawaii could be generalized only for a very brief period of new cross-cultural encounters.[28] The point of application, of course, is to the ingrained tendency in Markan studies to highlight the Roman-Jewish war as the dramatic event that triggered the writing of the Markan myth. I readily confess to having described Mark's situation and motivation this way in *A Myth of Innocence*. But now, having situated Mark in the Levant and having considered the many social issues and relations addressed by the myth in keeping with Smith's definition of "incidents" and his definition of myth as the way in which a situation of incongruity can be solved

---

27. Marshall Sahlins, *Historical Metaphors and Mythical Realities: Structure in the Early History of the Sandwich Islands Kingdom*, Association for Social Anthropology in Oceania Special Publications 1 (Ann Arbor: University of Michigan Press, 1981).

28. Nicholas Thomas, *Out of Time: History and Evolution in Anthropological Discourse*, 2nd ed. (Ann Arbor: University of Michigan Press, 1996), 111–14.

"in thought if not in fact,"[29] I have not been able to delete the postwar situation as an important factor in the set of incongruities addressed by the myth. I have, however, been able to tone down the sense of dramatic "event" and immediacy, precisely by thinking of Mark at home in southern Syria, removed somewhat from the war in time and place, and by revisiting the text and its logic which now look more like a myth of origin to be consulted at leisure than an apocalyptic tractate with urgent instructions for a time of uncertainty and hysteria. I imagine this "myth of origin" to be an author's occasional piece, not growing out of a sense of great urgency, whether the author's own or that of his group. So not only have the notions of cultural clash and dramatic event been toned down in the description of the situational incongruities of the Markan setting; the concept of social formation as that of a cell or community has also shifted to more recognizably normal groupings of family networks, "schools," and "associations." The notion of myth as a shared story of importance for a group's common identity has shifted in order to make room for intellectual experimentation, discussion, and disagreement, as well as time lags that can introduce both deletions and revisions. If so, I would say, we have a real redescription on our hands. The Gospel of Mark turns out to be a myth of origin for a "Levantine Judean association" that cultivates the teachings of Jesus as a way of taking their place in the Diaspora of the larger Roman world after the war. No enclave. No Christ myth. No Christ cult. No congregation in need of justification. No mission. Rather, a group or network of Galilean-Judeans rethinking the "kingdom of God" in a situation of multiple incongruities without a temple "there" in Jerusalem any more but with a "king" capable of being compared imaginatively to the divine king of the new city (or even imperium) they were now to call their home.

---

29. Smith, "Conjectures on Conjunctures," 72 n. 120; cf. 60–61 n. 105; 69–73 nn. 118–20; and see Smith, "Map Is Not Territory," in *Map Is Not Territory*, 299–300, 307–8; Smith, "A Pearl of Great Price," 94–95, 99–101.

The Social Logic of the Gospel of Mark:
Cultural Persistence and Social Escape
in a Postwar Time*

Merrill P. Miller

1. Introduction

This introduction is not intended as a summary of the ten sections of the main body of the paper to follow, though for convenience, given the length of the paper, I list the sections of the paper and their inclusive pages at the end of the introduction. Having completed the paper, it appeared to me that some of the theoretical and analytical influences on positions taken in the paper had not been sufficiently spelled out, in particular the problems of "ethnicity," "identity," and "community" as analytical terms. There were studies that had influenced my thinking in preparing the paper which needed description and highlighting, especially those of Rogers Brubaker on "identity without groups," Nathanael Andrade on ancient Syrian identity, and Eric Stewart on Markan geography and spatial concepts. Some issues of terminology also needed clarification, for example, translations of *Ioudaioi* and *Ioudaismos*, "Judaism" as a religion, my preference for referring to "followers of Jesus" rather than "Christians" and to Mark's

---

* I am hardly the only writer on Mark who argues for a post-70 date for the composition of this gospel, though my dating of ca. 80–85 is later than most advocates of a postdestruction date. However, my particular contention is that dating the Gospel of Mark after the destruction of the Jerusalem temple has not resulted in exploiting a postdestruction context for the interpretation of the writer's project in any way that is comparable to the other canonical gospels. The reasons for this mostly have to do with exploiting the Gospel of Mark for purposes determined by its modern position as the earliest canonical gospel. See below, section 3: Making a Difference on the Date of Mark, 254–62.

"readers" rather than "hearers" and "audience." Several concepts that are central to my construction of Mark's "project" as a response to political and cultural loss in the wake of the destruction of the temple are also previewed here: "cultural persistence," "social escape," "exemption." I briefly address here my reasons for viewing Mark as a written composition rather than a product of oral composition and performance. Because I have not addressed directly questions of Jewish purity practices in the body of the paper, I recognized the necessity here of at least presenting several contributions to recent discussions of Mark 7:1–23, especially in order to question what I regard as oversimplified conclusions about the social interests and social circles of Mark's Gospel. I judged that it was better to handle the matters taken up here more fully in an introduction than as items scattered in footnotes throughout the paper.

The English translation of Greek *Ioudaios/Ioudaioi* and equivalent terms in Latin, Hebrew, and Aramaic concerns not only how to conceive *Ioudaioi* in relation to other peoples in the ancient Mediterranean world but also has a bearing on the usage of words like "identity," "ethnicity," and "community" as analytical terms in the study of ancient as well as in the study of modern societies. "*Ioudaios*" as an ethnic term is ambiguous in the Greco-Roman world. As Michael Satlow has written, "'Ethnicity' as a category for understanding ancient Jewish identity is no less problematic than religion. Ἰουδαῖος is neither a 'religious' nor an 'ethnic' term. It is also not usefully understood as a hybrid of the two. It is, rather, largely a flexible, ethnographic trope—a term that, like the modern 'Jew' or 'Jews,' is inherently ambiguous."[1] Unlike the ancient languages, English has two words that could translate *Ioudaios*, and therefore some choice is necessary. In my view, a choice must also take into account that many elements treated as typical markers of "ethnic identity"—birth, descent, geography,

---

1. Michael L. Satlow, "Jew or Judaean?," in "*The One Who Sows Bountifully*": *Essays in Honor of Stanley K. Stowers*, ed. Caroline Johnson Hodge et al., BJS 356 (Providence, RI: Brown Judaic Studies, 2013), 167. Focusing on Greek writers from the second century BCE to the second century CE, Satlow concludes, "Most Greek and Roman ethnographers who mention Ἰουδαῖοι treat them like Istrians or Siceli, a population with its own political structure located within a particular territory; this comes closest to what we would translate as 'Judaean.' For ancient ethnographers who focused more attention on the Ἰουδαῖοι, though, 'ethnicity' was hardly a stable category. The writers themselves … manipulated it for their own ends; this is how the Idumaeans can both be and not be part of the ἔθνος of the Ἰουδαῖοι…. This is also a construction of ἔθνος that privileges ancestral customs and thus can sever ἔθνος from γένος" (174–75).

ancestral traditions and customs—are not equally in view, or necessarily in view at all, in particular instances of the term, and this is not to mention when the issue in view pertains to disputed boundaries of belonging and the various mechanisms of in-migration, including "conversion." I have generally referred to "Jews" rather than "Judeans" in this paper, since in English usage I think the more ambiguous term is usually preferable to a primary focus on a particular territory (Judea, whether referring to the district around Jerusalem or to the Roman province of Judea/Palestine) carried by the *English* term.[2] In instances where geographical place of origin and/or the political organization and policies of the ruling class of the territory are primarily in view, I have translated or referred to "Judean/s" and also where the emphasis in context requires distinguishing Judeans in Judea/Palestine from Jews of the diaspora or Judeans from Galileans and Idumeans.

I do not believe that there is any substantive theoretical or analytical gain in limiting the translation of *Ioudaioi* to "Judeans," or in referencing them as "Judeans," until some point in the period of the Second Temple or in the period of late antiquity. Nor do I believe that any contemporary moral, social, and historical concern is unambiguously served by the attempt to distinguish ancient Judeans from modern Jews, whether it is the interest of arresting modern anti-Judaism and anti-Semitism in translating references to *Ioudaioi* in New Testament texts, or it is the interest of averting Christian supersessionist readings of ancient Judaism. Cynthia Baker has shown that it is unhelpful in both theoretical and historical terms to move from using "Judean" to using "Jew" based on historical changes or on religious innovations emerging from the time of the Israelite nation to the rabbinic movement of late antiquity. These changes do

---

2. For this reason I cannot agree with the way in which John M. G. Barclay argues for "Judean" rather than "Jew" as the more appropriate translation of *Ioudaios* in Josephus's work, *Against Apion*, by highlighting the range of ethnic characteristics featured in the document, including land, while seeming by implication to limit the appropriate context for "Jew" to instances where religious commitment is the primary focus, as though "Jew" is exclusively or even predominantly a religious rather than ethnic term. On the contrary, in current English usage, the term "Judean" has a far more limited range than the term "Jew" (John M .G. Barclay, "Constructing Judean Identity after 70 CE: A Study of Josephus's *Against Apion*," in *Identity and Interaction in the Ancient Mediterranean: Jews, Christians and Others; Essays in Honour of Stephen G. Wilson*, ed. Zeba A. Crook and Philip A. Harland, New Testament Monographs 18 (Sheffield: Sheffield Phoenix, 2007), 99–112.

not mark clear boundaries dividing ethnicity from religion in such a way that would justify the exclusive use of "Judean" for an earlier time when ethnic identity would apply, while relegating the use of "Jew" for a later time when religious identity would apply. "There was no evolution from 'ethnic Judaeans' to 'religious Jews.'"[3]

Since it is common in modern scholarship to refer to the ancestral laws, customs, and traditions of the Jews as "Judaism," I have not avoided the term altogether, obviously when I am citing a scholar who uses it, but also when discussing the work of other scholars who commonly refer to "Judaism." As a translation of *Ioudaismos/Iudaismus* in the few instances in antiquity in which it appears in Jewish texts, and in several early Christian texts, it is misleading, as Steve Mason has demonstrated.[4] It is found far

---

3. Cynthia Baker, "A 'Jew' by Any Other Name?," *JAJ* 2 (2011): 178. While Baker acknowledges that "'Judaean' can undoubtedly be a pedagogically powerful intervention in a world and academy deeply influenced by Christian tropes" (178), she observes that "the heightened trend in employment of the term 'Judaeans' to signify an earlier 'ethnic group,' in contradistinction to later 'Jews,' moves in the opposite direction. Not only does it misrepresent the semantic range of the term 'Jews' ... but it carries the implication that the 'Judaeans' of antiquity were, in fact, *superseded* by the Church's theologically constituted 'Jews'" (177). Nor did mechanisms of assimilation turn Judeans into Jews, "however framed or ritualized (as covenant, marriage, alliance, or conversion)," for they "in no way abrogated the narratives of ancestry, kinship, shared history, and the like that make *yehudim/Ioudaioi* 'ethnic.'" Nor did *Ioudaioi* exclude ethnic combinations—"Idumean *Ioudaioi*, Alexandrian *Ioudaioi*, and Elephantine Aramean *yehuda'i* being three significant ancient examples—and it seems, in some contexts, to have been treated as a kind of 'superethnos' like '*Hellenos*,' albeit on a much smaller scale" (175). Baker's essay is organized around the debate on these matters epitomized in the work of Shaye Cohen, Joseph Blenkinsopp, Marc Zvi Brettler, and Steve Mason. For bibliography on the debate, including other significant contributions, see ibid., 153, n. 1.

4. Steve Mason, "Jews, Judaeans, Judaizing, Judaism: Problems of Categorization in Ancient History," *JSJ* 38 (2007): 457–512. Where the word appears several times in the Maccabean literature, in Galatians, and in Ignatius of Antioch, it is more appropriately translated "Judaizing," and associated with a rhetoric urging movement from X to Y, or imploring adherence to Y as opposed to X, rather than taking it as an abstract term signifying an entire culture, legal system, or religion (460–70, and see 476–80 for discussion of the two Greek inscriptions in which the word is found). Similarly, James Pasto translates 2 Macc 2:21; 8:1; 14:38; and 4 Macc 4:26, "collaborating with the Judeans," "being loyal to the Judeans." The same intention holds with the use of the term *Hellenismos* in the Maccabean literature (James Pasto, "The Origin, Expansion and Impact of the Hasmoneans in Light of Comparative Ethnographic Studies [and

more frequently in Christian literature beginning in the third century in the pejorative sense of a system of obsolete beliefs and practices to which Jews inexplicably continue to hold or as a Christian interpellation in the interest of early Christian self-definition, though not without mutual effect on both Jews and Christians.[5]

Apart from the validity of "Judaizing" rather than "Judaism" as a translation of *Ioudaismos* in the instances cited by Mason, the claim that "Judaism" is too much of an anachronism to be descriptively useful in ancient contexts (because religion did not exist as a native category disembedded from family, political institutions, legal systems, and wider cultural complexes) is countered by Seth Schwartz on the grounds that "religion can be salvaged as a heuristic concept if we mean by it: the practices (including cognitive ones) which constitute people's relations to their god(s)."[6] Similarly, Schwartz argues against a tendency, admittedly less in vogue today than in the last decades of the previous century, to underscore the variety of expressions of Judaism by referring to plural "Judaisms." For Schwartz, the emphasis on agency at the expense of structure is particularly unfortunate in periods of ancient Judaism "when the argument can be made … that the tendency towards unification and integration was actually theirs … and not merely an artifact of unenlightened modern scholarly intervention: structural-functionalism would be needed to account for this very fact, but agency-oriented theory would then address the limitations of

---

Outside of Its Nineteenth-Century Context]," in *Second Temple Studies III: Studies in Politics, Class and Material Culture*, ed. Philip R. Davies and John M. Halligan, JSOT-Sup 340 [London: Sheffield Academic, 2002], 172–75).

5. Daniel Boyarin, *Borderlines: The Partition of Judaeo-Christianity* (Philadelphia: University of Pennsylvania Press, 2004).

6. Seth Schwartz, "How Many Judaisms Were There? A Critique of Neusner and Smith on Definition and Mason and Boyarin on Categorization," *JAJ* 2 (2011): 230. Schwartz maintains that too exclusive a focus on validity in categorization to the exclusion of utility is unhelpful (229). On religion's disembedding, he responds sceptically, "How, exactly, are we meant to pin down the moment of religion's disembedding? Indeed, why should we think that there even was such a moment—as opposed to a process?" Schwartz argues instead "that the Jews [in antiquity] were always suspended between ethnicity and religion, and that the different moments of absolute discontinuity observed by Cohen and Boyarin were in reality small tectonic jolts, and not in themselves moments in which entirely new socio-discursive realities came into existence" (230).

the tendency to integration."[7] As the reader will see in the course of the paper, I have drawn in significant ways on Schwartz's revisionist account of the impact of successive imperialisms on Jewish society, especially on the political and cultural divide distinguishing Palestinian Jewish society of the period of the Second Temple from the society of the second and third centuries.[8] Schwartz's emphasis on an ideological core, one torah, one temple, one God, is useful as a heuristic to account for tendencies of integration during the Second Temple period, especially in comparison with subsequent periods and does not obscure the heterogeneity of thought and practice, the ways in which Jews negotiated the ideological core. However, it is another question whether an ideological core should be made an organizing principle of Jewish society across some eight centuries of history.[9] Moreover, the problem is not just a proper accounting of structure and agency, or of ideology and practice in the study of society, but rather the tendency to use the same terms in analysis to describe both social processes and entities in the world.[10]

---

7. Ibid., 220. As the most influential exponents of the view of plural "Judaisms," Schwartz cites the work of Jacob Neusner, and for theoretical reflections, Jonathan Z. Smith, "Fences and Neighbors: Some Contours of Early Judaism," in *Imagining Religion: From Babylon to Jonestown*, CHSJ (Chicago: University of Chicago Press, 1982), 1–18.

8. Seth Schwartz, *Imperialism and Jewish Society, 200 B.C.E. to 640 C.E.* (Princeton: Princeton University Press, 2001). For a similar view, see James Pasto, "The Origin, Expansion and Impact of the Hasmoneans," 183: "It is primarily in the pre-70 CE period that strong and central Jewish institutions (temple, army, bureaucracy) came into being and flourished, and therefore, it is *primarily in this period that we would expect to find a normative big tradition … not in the post-70 period* when centralized Jewish institutions declined."

9. See below, n. 218.

10. In the essay, "How Many Judaisms Were There?," some of Schwartz's formulations of the problem are themselves problematic. Citing the work of Lester Grabbe and Neusner as examples of the undertheorization of diversity in the study of ancient Judaism in the period of the Second Temple, Schwartz ignores or misses a conception which they share. The descriptions are different, to be sure, Grabbe emphasizing a variety of sectarian, millenarian and revolutionary movements, which nonetheless "were all part of a single ideological and social entity," while Neusner argues for "the nearly monadic self-enclosure of the various Judaisms" (ibid., 212). But both share the conception of a single entity in the world, whether it is the single ideological and social entity of "Judaism" or the monadic self-enclosure of "Judaisms." In the second half of the essay treating Mason and Boyarin, some of the formulations also seem overdrawn. To contend that Jews and Egyptians were not viewed either by themselves or by out-

The sociologist and ethnographer who has most trenchantly critiqued this tendency in the study of contemporary societies is Rogers Brubaker in a collection of essays.[11] In the introduction to the collection, Brubaker describes the two main targets of the essays. The first is "groupism": "the tendency to take bounded groups as fundamental units of analysis (and basic constituents of the social world)." As he explains, it is not a question of banning groups from the study of ethnicity. "Bounded and solidary groups are one modality of ethnicity.... But they are only one modality. 'Groupness' is a variable, not a constant; it cannot be presupposed.... [Ethnicity] works not only, or even especially, in and through bounded groups, but in and through categories, schemas, encounters, identifications, languages, stories, institutions, organizations, networks, and events."[12] The second target he refers to as "complacent and clichéd constructivism," a symptom of which is that constructivist and groupist language is often casually conjoined.[13] The key term, "identity" is scrutinized for its "hard"

---

siders as comparable ethnic groups is surely an over generalization (cf. Cynthia M. Baker, "'From Every Nation under Heaven': Jewish Ethnicities in the Greco-Roman World," in *Prejudice and Christian Beginnings: Investigating Race, Gender, and Ethnicity in Early Christian Studies*, ed. Laura Nasrallah and Elisabeth Schüssler Fiorenza [Minneapolis: Fortress, 2009], 79–99, esp. 98). The question is from whose standpoint, under what circumstances, and for what purposes they were viewed variously as alike and unlike. Moreover, it is one thing to argue for the practical and theoretical usefulness of differentiating religious phenomena from other kinds of phenomena in society, including other cultural phenomena, on the grounds of a *monothetic* definition of religion of the sort proposed by Schwartz. It is another thing to conceive of a religion, Judaism, as an entity in the world. Schwartz's emphasis on the need to take account of self-consciousness regarding boundaries between groups in social description is legitimate, but such boundary making runs the gamut from strict genealogical and ritual conceptions (see Matthew Thiessen, *Contesting Conversion: Genealogy, Circumcision, and Identity in Ancient Judaism and Christianity* (New York: Oxford University Press, 2011) to conceptions of political and military alliances and hyphenated ethnicities. Moreover, it hardly makes problematic Smith's *polythetic* approach to taxonomies of Judaism in the article cited above, n. 7, where the interest is not monadic self-enclosed systems but facilitating comparisons that problematize the capacity of functionalist explanations of society and eschew essentializing descriptions of boundaries.

11. Rogers Brubaker, *Ethnicity without Groups* (Cambridge: Harvard University Press, 2004).

12. Ibid., 2, 3–4.

13. Ibid., 3. Thinking the social world in substantialist concepts (Bourdieu) "has proved surprisingly robust. It has managed to withstand a quarter century of constructivist theorizing in the social sciences ... sustained critique of reification in

and "soft" uses in contemporary politics and social analysis and found to be problematic and not absolutely indispensable as an analytical term, however significant its role has been in the making of particular claims.[14] The problem is that it does both too much work and too little, and its use as a term of analysis and as a term of practice are often insufficiently distinguished.[15] Strong, essentialist uses of the term emphasize sameness over time and persons, a noninstrumental, deep, abiding condition of social being capable of producing social and political action and strong bounded groups. Weak uses of "identity" stress its evanescence, the product of multiple and shifting discourses, something fragmented, unstable, constructed and negotiated, and also compromises the commonsense meaning of the term.[16] Brubaker proposes that a set of less congested, more flexible terms can do the theoretical work better.[17]

---

anthropology ... influential and destabilizing contributions of feminist, post-structuralist, post-modernist, and other theories, and even widespread acknowledgment, in principle, that 'cultures,' 'communities,' 'tribes,' 'races,' 'nations' and 'ethnic groups' are not bounded wholes" (3). The essays in the volume are committed to "disaggregated modes of analysis" without espousing "ontological or methodological individualism. The alternative to the substantialist idiom of bounded groups is not an idiom of individual choice, but rather (as Bourdieu never tired of emphasizing) a relational, processual, and dynamic analytical language" (3).

14. The essay "Beyond 'Identity'" is chapter 2, written with Frederick Cooper.

15. Ibid., 32.

16. Ibid., 33–41.

17. Ibid., 41–48: "Identification" and "categorization" derived from verbs inviting specification of agents without presupposing internal sameness and bounded groupness; "self-understanding" and "social location," along with "self-representation" and "self-identification," dispositional terms that can be conceptualized in a noninstrumental manner without presupposing a modern Western unitary entity and not restricted to situations of stability or flux; "commonality," "connectedness," "groupness," which point to sharing a common attribute and to relational ties, which do not necessarily engender groupness but which in combination can be linked to a strong sense of belonging together characteristic of large-scale collectivities. The point is to develop a theoretical vocabulary that helps "to distinguish instances of strongly binding, vehemently felt groupness from more loosely structured, weakly constraining forms of affinity and affiliation" (48). Brubaker's chapter 3, "Ethnicity as Cognition," written with Mara Loveman and Peter Stamatov, explores the development of the "cognitive turn" in the human sciences and resources "for conceptualizing perspectives on the world rather than entities in the world, while at the same time helping to explain the tenacious hold of groupist ways of thinking and practice" (4–5).

I have at least tried to gesture in the direction of the theoretical proposals of Brubaker's work in this paper by avoiding the assumption that certain labels like "Jews" and "Christians," "Jewish Christians" and "gentile Christians" reference strongly bounded groups and essentialist identities rather than perspectives, categorizing, self-and collective-identifications and representations, commonalities, connections, strategies, interests, markings, and modes of affiliation. It is not that strongly bounded groups and foundational identities should be ruled out in the study of early Christianity or of Greco-Roman and late antique Judaism, any more than in the study of contemporary societies, but that they are often taken as givens rather than justified, confusing the invoking of groupism in order to evoke groups and effect social formation with the actual existence of strongly bounded entities in the social world. The term that is most misleading in this respect in the study of Christian formation, especially with respect to the earliest evidence, is "community."[18] It is not possible to avoid entirely conflating processes of social formation with groupism and essentialist identity in the study of ancient societies for the practical reason that to a greater degree than is the case in contemporary studies, one inevitably uses concepts and models intended for analysis to fill in gaps in the data as well.[19] Moreover, it is obvious that one cannot simply override labels and concepts that one finds problematic when citing and discussing the work of other scholars. In general throughout the paper I have referred to "followers of Jesus." This avoids constantly referring to "Christians" (except where the term is used in the primary sources or where a longer time frame is in view), as though the label represented bounded groups, a primary sense of belonging and exclusive mode of identification, and a firm set of unifying and distinguishing characteristics; or referring to "Jewish Christians" and "gentile Christians," as though the labels presupposed different social formations, mutually exclusive ethnic identifications, or guaranteed a distinctive set of practices and social locations.[20] Reference to followers of

---

18. See Stanley K. Stowers, "The Concept of 'Community' and the History of Early Christianity," *MTSR* 23 (2011): 238–56; and see below, 224–25 with nn. 35–39.

19. The point has been made by Schwartz, *Imperialism and Jewish Society*, 4.

20. Moreover, such labels tend to highlight religious, cultural, and ethnic categories in contexts where other categories of identification and boundary making are more salient, such as status, education, gender, language, age, disability, insiders and outsiders; see Halvor Moxnes, "Identity in Jesus' Galilee—From Ethnicity to Locative Intersectionality," *BibInt* 18 (2010): 390–416. On the variability of designations and

Jesus also allows me to think of the interests, activities, and circumstances of those who can be classified usefully as independent religious specialists without foreclosing on factors of social formation, existing social contexts, and groups.[21] Not that "followers of Jesus" is without problems. This is not just because it is vague, but because it presupposes a level of commitment, affiliation, and discipleship that I do not intend as a limit on those whom the writer of Mark might have considered his closest circle, or whom he had in view as a target audience, or succeeded in attracting for reasons and interests not encompassed by affiliation and discipleship.[22]

---

modes of identifying in Greco-Roman Palestine, see Joseph Geiger, "Language, Culture and Identity in Ancient Palestine," in *Greek Romans and Roman Greeks: Studies in Cultural Intervention*, ed. Erik Nis Ostenfeld, Aarhus Studies in Mediterranean Antiquity 3 (Aarhus: Aarhus University Press, 2002), 233–46: "There were no hard and fast rules for identifying and designating 'the other'. Identifying him was accomplished according to the circumstances and needs of the occasion." Given the succession of empires and the movements of peoples that swept across the region from Babylonian and Persian empires to the Roman conquest, "multiple and complex identities may have been almost the rule, rather than the exception ... [and] call up the image of the kaleidoscope rather than that of the mosaic" (242). And see, Burton L. Mack, "The Spyglass and Kaleidoscope: From a Levantine Coign of Vantage" (in this volume). On the demography of Galilee, see Milton Moreland, "The Inhabitants of Galilee in the Hellenistic and Early Roman Periods: Probes into the Archaeological and Literary Evidence," in *Religion, Ethnicity, and Identity in Ancient Galilee*, ed. Jürgen Zangenberg, Harold W. Attridge, and Dale Martin, WUNT 210 (Tübingen: Mohr Siebeck, 2007), 133–59. On questions of regional and temporal perspectives, how to account for the increase of the Jewish population of Galilee in the Hasmonean and early Roman periods, the extent of a type of material culture in Galilee associated with Jewish purity rituals, and what "Jewish" explains for identifying the majority of the inhabitants of early Roman Galilee, Moreland differs significantly from the survey of Mark A. Chancey, "The Ethnicities of Galileans," in *Galilee in the Late Second Temple and Mishnaic Periods*, ed. David A. Fiensy and James Riley Strange (Minneapolis: Fortress, 2014), 1:112–28.

21. For the classification and theorizing of independent religious specialists as a neglected category in the study of the emergence of Christianity, see the work of Heidi Wendt referenced below, n. 191.

22. Only occasionally does the label, "followers of Jesus," refer to characters in Mark's narrative; my general, much more typical, use is not intended to mirror Mark's narrative world. I intend the label to be vague, and so its use does not distinguish the extent, degree, or reasons for individual or collective interest in communication about Jesus or the level of commitment within different kinds of social formations. Nor does it differentiate the possible relations of religious specialists to existing groups or to forming groups—all matters which I presuppose are in fact significant

The usefulness of Brubaker's theoretical work for the study of an ancient society is demonstrated in the study of Greco-Roman Syria by Nathanael Andrade.[23] Despite the word "identity" in the title of the book, Andrade, following Brubaker, adopts terms such as "identification" and "performances," arguing that "ethnicity is a mode of cognition and categorical framing, not necessarily a group implementing mass organized action."[24] While drawing on postcolonial concepts, Andrade also exposes their problematics. In application to ancient Syria they are often used to situate provincials ambiguously between the immutable binary systems of the Greeks and the purely indigenous, thereby tending to reinstate the views both of certain Greek intellectual elites who regarded Syrian Greekness as barbarian and many modern Roman historians who argue that there was no Syrian culture in the Roman imperial period.[25] According to Andrade's historical narrative, Roman imperial policy, unlike either the Seleucids or the Parthians, created a civic-political context in which ethnic Syrians along with other ethnic Near Eastern peoples were given citizenship and incorporated into a Greek peer-polity network composed of regional Greek *poleis*. Citizenship did not mean that one governed as members of the *bouletai* of these *poleis*, but that one identified with the *poleis* and peer-polity network in ways that reshaped expressions of both

---

distinctions in the social world. Indeed, the label is not meant to exclude those whose primary interest may simply be in the rhetorical figure of Jesus in Mark's Gospel. It is intended to include people who had some sort of interest in the sayings, deeds, and fate of Jesus of Nazareth and/or connections with those who practiced and communicated in the name of Jesus in distinction from the myriad others who had no such interests or connections.

23. Nathanael J. Andrade, *Syrian Identity in the Greco-Roman World* (Cambridge: Cambridge University Press, 2013).

24. Ibid., 4–5 n. 14. "Following Cooper and Brubaker ... I generally refrain from using the word 'identity'" (5 n. 16).

25. Ibid., 10–14, 29. Andrade maintains that scholars have located Greek or Syrian culture (or its lack) in the wrong place, in classical Greek forms and in continuous pre-Hellenistic Near Eastern forms, and then posit mixture, boundary crossing, third space rather than recognizing the variety of idioms in which Syrian identification could be expressed. "[Syrians] could transform Greek idioms into Syrian culture and experience them as part of authentic Syrian expression." They did not have "to anchor their Syrian identification strictly in Syrian ethnic genealogy and Aramaic use or else disavow any social significance to being Syrian." They could "posit links to a collective Aramean or Assyrian past without cultivating idioms continuously transmitted from pre-Hellenistic periods (even if Jews did so articulately)" (14–15).

Greekness and Syrianness.[26] For considerations attendant on locating
the Gospel of Mark in a post-70 setting of southern Syria,[27] Andrade has
highlighted the generally different ways in which Jews and Syrians framed
their social and cultural identities and underscores the Roman imperial
contribution to conflict among provincials, especially in the cities within
and surrounding the Roman province of Judea,[28] and the very different
consequences for Jews and Syrians of Roman policies of social integration
of provincial populations.[29]

---

26. Ibid., 15–18, 22. "Even as citizens (*politai*) of Greek polities exerted less control of governance, they still constituted vital audiences for elite civic counselors" (22).
In part 1 of the book, Andrade traces the Roman imperial preconditions for the emergence of a variety of expressions of Greekness and Syrianness from the second century
BCE to the first century CE in the changing conditions of regional civic contexts. Parts
2 and 3 treat the first to third centuries CE.

27. While a southern Syrian provenance for the Gospel of Mark does seem to
me more likely than either Rome or Alexandria, among other contenders, I have not
attempted in this paper to argue against other positions on locale or to make the reference to place of composition more specific. In planning for sessions and papers on the
Markan site, members of the seminar found no strong reasons to counter the observations of Burton Mack in *A Myth of Innocence: Mark and Christian Origins* (Philadelphia: Fortress, 1988; repr., Minneapolis: Fortress, 2006), 315–18, for suggesting
Phoenician coastal cities, Tyre, Sidon, or Byblos, as good candidates with appropriate
cultural resources and traditions to account for the intellectual labor of the Gospel
of Mark and for evidence in the gospel of the troubled history of Judea. Smith has
"run" with Mack's proposal in his paper "The Markan Site" (in this volume), though
his Levantine "ethnography" is not limited to urban centers of the Phoenician coast.
A Phoenician coast urban setting does imply that the almost exclusively rural settings
of the gospel narrative are not evidence of the location of the writer, for example, in
satellite villages of a Phoenician city or in contiguous rural areas of a "greater Galilee."
But neither should we suppose that the Gospel of Mark is the work of only a single
individual or that the resources, circles, or experience of the writer are limited to a
particular urban setting. One advantage of a Phoenician coastal city is that connections and communications between such a city and Rome and Alexandria are not
difficult to imagine.

28. Andrade has devoted an essay to the subject elsewhere, "Ambiguity, Violence,
and Community in the Cities of Judaea and Syria," *Historia* 59 (2010): 342–70. For
a more detailed account of regional competition and conflict as the decisive factor
in motivating Judeans to go to war, see Steve Mason, "Why Did Judaeans Go to War
with Rome in 66–67 CE? Realist-Regional Perspectives," in *Jews and Christians in the
First and Second Centuries: How to Write Their History*, ed. Peter J. Tomson and Joshua
Schwartz, CRINT 13 (Leiden: Brill, 2014), 126–206; and see below, n. 171.

29. "Because violence between Greeks [aka Syrians] and Jews contributed to the

I have avoided slashing every reference to Mark's "readers" with "hearers" or "audience." I mostly refer to readers, by which I mean the first or intended real readers I posit as part of the effort of historical contextualization of the composition and reception of Mark rather than the ideal readers constructed by the narrative. Referencing real readers or a real author (Mark by name, according to tradition and convention) who are not directly known necessarily entails taking account of such narrative constructions, whether they are oriented to intrinsic conceptions of author, or text, or reader, without supposing that such constructions deliver a social world external to the text, though every text has one, just as identifying and interpreting phenomena intrinsic to the text and labeling it the ideal author and reader entail the judgments of real readers and real performers.[30] It is not a question of dismissing problems of circular reasoning or of being paralyzed by them, but of recognizing a degree of autonomy between text and context, authors and readers, performers and audience, whose relations cannot be represented without imagination. Indeed, the effort to treat with a measure of independence a range of issues bearing on the construction and description of an early post-70 context in the region of southern Syria (including Palestine), on the one side, and engaging a

---

first Jewish revolt's regional dimensions, Judea's integration into the Roman provincial system was indeed turbulent. But after the revolt, the territories of greater Judea and southern Syria were more firmly embedded in the Roman provinces of Syria and Judea, even if Agrippa II maintained territory some decades afterward.... In Judea and Syria, the Jews, with their unique scriptural tradition, their 'ancestral laws,' and their veneration of the Jewish temple of Jerusalem, were perhaps the foremost victims of Greek city-states' integrative features.... When this spate of local violence and confrontations reached the level of regional revolt, Roman legions sacked Jerusalem and ravaged the Jewish temple, thereby destroying a symbol of Jewish self-perception and community that had hindered integration into Roman imperial and Greek civic structures.... Yet, amid such social tensions, violence, and cultural destruction, the production of 'Greek' and 'Syrian' as intersecting modes of civic performance for the next two centuries constituted the basis for social cohesion in Roman Syria.... As this happened, the Roman administration and its agents governed Syria, Judea, and adjacent territories through their negotiations with civic councils (*boulai*), not client kings" (Andrade, *Syrian Identity*, 120–21).

30. For the different hermeneutic goals of author- text- and reader- oriented narrative criticism, see Mark Allan Powell, "Narrative Criticism: The Emergence of a Prominent Reading Strategy," in *Mark as Story: Retrospect and Prospect*, ed. Kelly R. Iverson and Christopher W. Skinner, RBS 65 (Atlanta: Society of Biblical Literature, 2011), 19–43.

variety of issues in the study of Mark's Gospel, on the other—precisely because reading text and context in relation to each other is not just a challenge but finally a necessity of historical study of the emergence and achievement of a written narrative composition—accounts in large part for the unusual length of this paper. The decision to refer to readers is not intended to deny the complex relations and interfacing of oral and scribal practices in the world of the Markan text or to discount oral practices that attend the composition, reproduction, reading, and reception of a written text in societies in which the literate skills required for narrative writing are highly specialized and most of the population is nonliterate. Rather, it is my view that the Gospel of Mark is not an epiphenomenon or secondary product of purely oral composition, performance, and accumulation and that its literary characteristics cannot be accounted for without presupposing chirographic intervention in oral practices.[31] Mark's narrative entails

31. Cf. Antoinette Wire, "Mark: News as Tradition," in *The Interface of Orality and Writing*, ed. Annette Weissenrieder and Robert B. Coote, WUNT 260 (Tübingen: Mohr Siebeck, 2010), 52–70. Wire sees the writer of Mark as the transcriber of stories produced and guarded by favorite storytellers, who were capable of bringing together stories told and retold continuously amid crises and scatterings across a span of some forty years. Mark is a scribe drawn back from mission when the Jerusalem church flees or Mary (Acts 12:12) dies, or, alternatively, when the story told by Galilean women becomes known in Greek-speaking cities (69–70). For Wire, the Gospel of Mark does not constitute a genre but an integration of story patterns of conflict and the prophet's sign (55–66). The repetition of these patterns, their integration, and their snowballing effects are not evidence of a unified literary achievement but of the interests of successive storytellers (63). In my judgment, it does not work to take the very evidence of literary design, of response to a history of disappointing results or failed expectations (Mark 4:13), or of interests that make the Jesus figure uncontainable within typical social roles, and attribute all of this to reinterpretations of a prophet's signs (64), or to the difference between the historical reticence of Jesus and the exuberance of storytellers baffled by the traditional reticence of the prophet (60–61). It is a different matter when one is attributing these tensions to purely intrinsic elements of the narrative, for example, the tension between the voice of the narrative figure, Jesus, and the voice of the narrator, as exemplified in the work of Elizabeth Struthers Malbon, *Mark's Jesus: Characterization as Narrative Christology* (Waco, TX: Baylor University Press, 2009). I find it difficult to move from Wire's achievement in *Holy Lives, Holy Deaths: A Close Hearing of Early Jewish Storytellers*, SBLStBL 1 (Atlanta: Society of Biblical Literature, 2002), where the contextualizing of Jesus materials in a range of Jewish story types, motifs, and storytelling works precisely because the question of interventions marking "Christian" beginnings as a historical phenomenon is not in the picture, to the more recent project, *The Case for Mark Composed in*

literary skills and ambition beyond those of sayings collections and brief narratives (the influences of oral practices on the composition of Mark notwithstanding)[32] and presupposes the existence of chirographs, however few at first, pointing to the gospel as something to be regarded also as a prestige object.[33] Mark's project points to circles of friends and collaborators that included a network of readers who were consumers precisely of

---

Performance, Biblical Performance Criticism 3 (Eugene, OR: Cascade, 2011), where it is not only the capacities and sustainability of oral performance that are on stage but the singular figure of Jesus, and storytelling as a collective project of communities devoted exclusively to him. The alternative does not require one to imagine the composition let alone the "publication" of the Gospel of Mark as the mental or physical labor of a single individual. For some helpful considerations on the sorts of people that might constitute some of Mark's closest circle in this connection, see Pieter J. J. Botha, "'Publishing' a Gospel: Notes on Historical Constraints to Gospel Criticism," in Weissenrieder and Coote, *Interface of Orality and Writing*, 335–52.

32. "Granted that the Gospel of Mark, like much ancient writing, was intended to be recycled into oral performance, is it oral-traditional literature in the sense conjectured by Albert Lord?… a transcript of oral performance?" (Werner H. Kelber, "The Oral-Scribal-Memorial Arts of Communication in Early Christianity," in *Jesus, the Voice, and the Text: Beyond the Oral and the Written Gospel*, ed. Tom Thatcher [Waco, TX: Baylor University Press, 2008], 250, responding to Joanna Dewey in the same volume, "The Gospel of Mark as Oral Hermeneutic," 71–87). "Do we not see here [in Mark] the beginning of a circumspectly drawn literary construction? Are there not interconnections between parts, and arching thematic constructions that have overriding effect on oral units? In short, is it truly conceivable that the Gospel of Mark's scribal composition did not take advantage of some potentialities inherent in the chirographic medium?" (Kelber, "Oral-Scribal-Memorial Arts," 250).

33. For Robert B. Coote, "Scripture and the Writer of Mark," in Weissenrieder and Coote, *Interface of Orality and Writing*, 363–78, Mark is not a raconteur or rhapsode. "The writer may have been an itinerant … but if so he was an itinerant Jewish scribe, who once journeyed to town or village assemblies which were without benefit of Scripture texts, and now to comparable assemblies of followers of Jesus" (374). That Mark could presumably tell his story orally does not make it inevitable that he belonged to circles that produced such stories. "Partly he wrote it because that's what he did, write, and because there was a status, a power, in texts as such, a 'formidable object'.… But I think the main answer is: to *fix* his story as an ironic story" (377, emphasis original). For Chris Keith the presence of manuscripts as prestige cultural artifacts is the main point in considering the significance of the Gospel of Mark for the emergence of a Christian book culture, because the presence of a manuscript is the emblem of the status and identity of a community ("Early Christian Book Culture and the Emergence of the First Written Gospel," in *Mark, Manuscripts, and Monotheism: Essays in Honor of Larry W. Hurtado*, ed. Chris Keith and Dieter T. Roth, LNTS 528

writings and wanted and were able to consult written texts for comparison, reference, and interpretation, as well as readers capable of recitation and performance for target audiences.[34]

[London: Bloomsbury, 2015], 22–39). For further references to the emergence of a Christian book culture, see below, n. 385.

34. Again Kelber: "Notwithstanding their oral roots and function, chirographs transcribed and stabilized language in ways oral speech never could and opened it to visual inspection and unceasing efforts at interpretation" (Werner Kelber, "The Oral and the Written Gospel: Fourteen Years Afterward," in *Imprints, Voiceprints, and Footprints of Memory: Collected Essays of Werner H. Kelber*, RBS 74 [Atlanta: Society of Biblical Literature, 2013], 181). I have cited Kelber here and above, n. 32, in isolation from his thesis that the Gospel of Mark represents a *Traditionsbruch*, a rupture with tradition, occasioned by what proved to be utterly failed expectations in the wake of the catastrophe of 70 among leaders of the Jerusalem church, who are viewed by Kelber as the primary oral authorities and agents in the construction of memories and traditions of Jesus, and whose failure and passing from the scene are negotiated in the gospel in the negative roles of the disciples, the family of Jesus, and Christian prophets (ibid., 182–84; and see Kelber, "Oral-Scribal-Memorial Arts," 251; also Kelber, "The Works of Memory: Christian Origins as Mnemohistory," in Kelber, *Imprints, Voiceprints, and Footprints of Memory*, 289–91; and see below, n. 105) In turn, Kelber has taken the thesis and produced an oeuvre on media and memory, a communications history of early Christianity. He attributes Markan composition to a reservoir of memories not a well-stocked library and has been a consistent critic of the influences of print media on gospel scholarship and of linear, evolutionary conceptions of tradition formation in the practice of form and redaction criticism. While I see the consequences of 70 as a context or environment of political, cultural, and symbolic loss and spend much of this paper constructing a "situation" (in Smith's sense of "situational incongruity" calling forth efforts of rectification in thought and practice; see J. Z. Smith, "Conjectures on Conjunctures and Other Matters: Three Essays," 69 n. 118, in this volume), which I set in relation to a range of issues in the study of Mark's Gospel, I do not take this situation as constituting a rupture internal to a Jesus movement either with respect to the centrality of Jerusalem in the formation of early Jesus traditions, supposedly bringing to an end the christology of oral tradents, or with regard to a crisis created by the passing of a foundation generation and the intervention of a written text on an antecedent oral tradition (see below, n. 105). Coote's conception of the function of Markan irony is similar to Kelber's conception of Mark as representative of a *Traditionsbruch*. In the wake of the Roman crushing of the revolt, Mark countered the foundational story and expectations of a Jerusalem church hierarchy by drawing on the biblical latter prophets as earlier witnesses to the reality that the happy ending of Israel's salvation-story was not the end of the story (Coote, "Scripture and the Writer of Mark," 369–71, 377–78). But the thesis of a Markan rewriting of an already foundational Christian story stemming from Jerusalem seems to me unfounded with respect to the sources of early Jesus traditions and overdrawn with reference to situations and responses of

followers of Jesus at the outbreak of the Judean revolt. Turning to deuteronomistic traditions and the latter prophets in the aftermath of the sack of Jerusalem and the destruction of the temple is exactly what other Jewish writers did, even if not in the same ways. Furthermore, Markan irony strikes me as more complex and multifaceted in relation to a post-70 context than such a thesis allows.

For a theory of oral communication that challenges some of Kelber's conceptions, a theory that takes its starting point not from the presence of the voice of Jesus in face-to-face communication but from the absence of Jesus, a nondialogical, nonreciprocal model with the messenger as archtype of distant communication, see Kristina Dronsch and Annette Weissenrieder, "A Theory of the Message for New Testament Writings or Communicating the Words of Jesus: From Angelos to Euangelion," in Weissenrieder and Coote, *Interface of Orality and Writing*, 205–35: "With Peters we want to suggest a change of perspective, namely that dialogues based on 'a continuous process of adjustment of language to communal expectations, of social to linguistic realities' [Kelber, *Oral and Written Gospel*, 92] forms rather the exception than the rule" (208), referring to J. Durham Peters, *Speaking into the Air: A History of the Idea of Communication* (Chicago: University of Chicago Press, 1999). "In this perspective it is to be considered that a large part of the communication is not dialogue centered but a communication situation that is simply without reciprocity" ("A Theory of the Message," 211). Keith's critique of Kelber has to do with what Keith calls "the oral-preference perspective" of Kelber and others in conceptualizing the significance of Mark's textualization of the Jesus tradition: "the emergence of the first written Gospel is understood against a backdrop of ancient orality rather than ancient book culture" (Keith, "Early Christian Book Culture," 34). Stated elsewhere, "Scholars (including Kelber) still routinely overlook the significance of Mark's Gospel as a physical artifact, preferring instead to focus upon texts' effects upon oral tradition or the manners in which texts still function like oral tradition" (Chris Keith, "Prolegomena on the Textualization of Mark's Gospel: Manuscript Culture, the Extended Situation, and the Emergence of the Written Gospel," in *Memory and Identity in Ancient Judaism and Early Christianity: A Conversation with Barry Schwartz*, ed. Tom Thatcher, SemeiaSt 78 (Atlanta: SBL Press, 2014), 168. Keith advocates a "*Wirkungsgeschichte* perspective" to Mark's textualization (162). He does not reject Jan Assmann's notion of a *Traditionsbruch*, a crisis of "communicative memory" at around the forty-year mark, or the possibility that Mark is responding to some trauma, the crucifixion, the Neronian persecution, 70 CE, the death of the first generation of apostles, but holds that it is incomplete (173–74). Instead, he appeals to Assmann's concept of the *zerdehnte Situation*, "the expanded context" (175–76). The crucial matter does not lie in displacement of oral tradition or in initiating a different process of memory and identity construction but rather in breaking the communicative constraints of orality, "since the tradition's audience is no longer confined to those who are physically present before the author/performer/messenger" (176; note also in response to some of Keith's proposals the sociologist Barry Schwartz's critical remarks on Assmann's concepts of *Traditionsbruch* and *zerdehnte Situation* ["Harvest," in Thatcher, *Memory and Identity*, 323–24, 335]).

While the work on orality and rhetoric in recent decades has vigor-
ously exposed the influences of print media on methods of study and conceptions of tradition formation in early Christianity, what has not been sufficiently registered is the extent to which notions of oral folk community
in form criticism and of solidary communities of believers in redaction
criticism continue to be presupposed in the proposals and accounts of the
oral biosphere of early Christianity. This is the idea of community "as a
deep social and mental coherence, a commonality in mind and practice,"
writes Stanley Stowers.[35] He traces the influence of ideas of communal
creativity and authorship in the study of the gospels to the nineteenth-century Romantic movement. Form criticism and redaction criticism "fleshed
out the German Romantic equation of unique historical experience, language, tradition and *Volk* in terms of unique Christian communities."[36]
Durkheimian inspired functionalist conceptions of society as an organic
whole further contributed to "community" as an explanatory assumption.[37]
As Stowers demonstrates, the liabilities of an unexamined conception of
community are many. It is unusable as an analytic concept in social theory
and often serves as a romantic theological conception while parading as
social description. It occludes the evidence of partial and selective acceptance of messages and practices and ignores the difficulty of acquisition
and consistent influence of specialized knowledges across broad domains
of life. It posits a tight fit between the message and the audience, whereas a

---

35. Stowers, "The Concept of 'Community,'" 238. The critique of such conceptions of community, and indeed of some applications of social memory theory, is at
the center of Robyn Walsh's alternative proposal to account for Q and gospel narratives as products of writers in a social network of other writers rather than as products
of oral communities or of oral traditions. For Walsh the problems associated with
form and redaction criticism are not occasioned by the influences of print media on
scholarship but by the influences of a Romantic tradition of nineteenth and twentieth
century scholarship on Christian origins (see "Q and the 'Big Bang' Theory of Christian Origins," in this volume).

36. Stowers, "The Concept of 'Community,'" 240. Further development and critique of this tradition of scholarship is presented in Walsh, "Q and the 'Big Bang'
Theory," esp. 491–504.

37. Stowers, "The Concept of 'Community,'" 242. This conception and analytic
assumption of community has been equally influential in the study of Paul's churches.
For a critique and set of alternative conceptions of intervention, recognition, interest,
and mixed reception, see the essays in Ron Cameron and Merrill P. Miller, eds., *Redescribing Paul and the Corinthians*, ECL 5 (Atlanta: Society of Biblical Literature, 2011).

rhetorical and artistic semi-autonomy responding to audiences in creative ways would be more common. Most of all, it limits the kinds of social formations used in the explanation of early Christianity.[38] Imagining that the gospels were written for Christian communities everywhere only makes matters worse, substituting "a coherent trans-empire entity" for a tightly bounded local community in order to account for any evidence of teaching and writing about Jesus Christ.[39]

In recent decades the burgeoning field of social memory studies has also found application in early Christian studies.[40] Here too the idea of communities registering deep social and mental commonalities is posited as the context and source of social memory work engendering identity formation in early Christianity. Real communities are precisely communities of memory constantly rehearsing their constitutive memories. However, the problems of application—at least to begin with—are not those of relating personal memory to the frameworks of sociality in which they

---

38. Stowers, "The Concept of 'Community,'" 245–50. In addition to households, "why should formations such as neighborhoods, merchant networks, patterns of social connection based on religious places, artisan networks, religious entrepreneurial-consumer relations and networks, circles of slave friends, linked levels of social domination, coalitions of friendship and enmity, age and gender sets, many sorts of markets, patterns and practices of ethnic identification and non-ethnic identification … not be important for the social explanation of early Christianity?" (249–50).

39. Ibid., 253. Stowers advocates in particular taking account of networks of literate and specialized culture producers (250); and see Stowers, "The Religion of Plant and Animal Offerings Versus the Religion of Meanings, Essences and Textual Mysteries," in *Ancient Mediterranean Sacrifice: Images, Acts, Meanings*, ed. Jennifer Wright Knust and Zsuzsanna Várhelyi (Oxford: Oxford University Press, 2011), 35–56; Stowers, "Kinds of Myth, Meals, and Power: Paul and the Corinthians," in Cameron and Miller, *Redescribing Paul and the Corinthians*, 105–49. In her paper in this volume, Walsh presents evidence to show that a writer's primary interests, values, and social relationships are shared within a network of literate culture producers and not within a religious association. She maintains that this is the case where the writings explore religious subjects, and even if the writer participates in such an association ("Q and the 'Big Bang' Theory," 509–10). For a similar proposal regarding the primary interests, social networks and values of Gospel writers, see Richard Last, "The Social Relationships of Gospel Writers: New Insights from Inscriptions Commending Greek Historiographers," *JSNT* 37 (2015): 223–52.

40. See esp. the essays collected in Alan Kirk and Tom Thatcher, eds., *Memory, Tradition, and Text: Uses of the Past in Early Christianity*, SemeiaSt 52 (Atlanta: Society of Biblical Literature, 2005); in Thatcher, *Memory and Identity*; and in Kelber, *Imprints, Voiceprints, and Footprints of Memory*.

are formed (Maurice Halbwachs), or of balancing presentist perspectives against the weight of available pasts, or avoiding the reification of collective memory, or even the issue of time lapse between the experience of trauma and finding a commonplace in tradition for the construction of memory as a heuristic.[41] The initial problem is to imagine whose memories we are talking about and then to consider all the sorts of interferences, disruptions, dislocations, and failures—not to mention contestations, competitions, diverse interests, translations and misunderstandings—attendant on the formation of collective memories, which too often tend to be imagined as continuous, linear processes of communication. The contexts in which communication about Jesus went on were not necessarily primary loci of memory or identity for many of those who had interests and reasons to participate. Nor did the targeted contexts of memory entrepreneurs, whether in Jerusalem, in Galilean villages, or in Greco-Roman urban centers of the eastern Mediterranean, bring together a captive audience.[42] As a

---

41. See Alan Kirk's introductory essay, "Social and Cultural Memory," in Kirk and Thatcher, *Memory, Tradition, and Text*, 1–24. Reference to the formative work of Maurice Halbwachs on social memory and to Aleida and Jan Assmann on cultural memory can be found in Kirk's essay. In the same volume, see Arthur J. Dewey, "The Locus for Death: Social Memory and the Passion Narratives," 119–28; and see Werner H. Kelber, "The Works of Memory," in *Imprints, Voiceprints, and Footprints*, 265–96; see also, Jeffrey K. Olick, "Products, Processes, and Practices: A Non-reificatory Approach to Collective Memory," *BTB* 36 (2006): 5–14.

42. For Corinth, see Jonathan Z. Smith, "Re: Corinthians," in *Relating Religion: Essays in the Study of Religion* (Chicago: University of Chicago Press, 2004), 340–61; repr. in Cameron and Miller, *Redescribing Paul and the Corinthians*, 17–34. For Galilean villages, see Milton Moreland, "The Galilean Response to Earliest Christianity: A Cross-Cultural Study of the Subsistence Ethic," in *Religion and Society in Roman Palestine: Old Questions, New Approaches*, ed. Douglas R. Edwards (London: Routledge, 2004), 37–48; Moreland, "The Jesus Movement in the Villages of Roman Galilee: Archaeology, Q, and Modern Anthropological Theory," in *Oral Performance, Popular Tradition, and Hidden Transcript in Q*, ed. Richard A. Horsley, SemeiaSt 60 (Atlanta: Society of Biblical Literature, 2006), 159–80; John Kloppenborg, "Q, Bethsaida, Khorazin and Capernaum," in *Q in Context II: Social Setting and Archeological Background of the Sayings Source*, ed. Markus Tiwald, BBB 173 (Göttingen: V&R Unipress; Bonn: Bonn University Press, 2015), 61–90. On the failure of Q to survive as a text, apart from the question of the appeal of its message in its formative context, see William E. Arnal, "Why Q Failed: From Ideological Project to Group Formation," in Cameron and Miller, *Redescribing Christian Origins*, 67–87, from a Marxist materialist perspective; and from the perspective of evolutionary biology and the cognitive science of religion, see Petri Luomanen, "From Mark and Q to Matthew: An Experiment

matter of historical beginnings, we cannot formulate "Christian" groups or "Christian" social memory as anything but interventions in already existing social formations and collective memories. The latter too would be subject to appropriation and manipulation but would exhibit resistance to reinvention as well.[43] Access to biblical texts, to Jewish cultural memory, to prepositioned elements of tradition, and to communicative memories

---

in Evolutionary Analysis," in *Mark and Matthew II: Comparative Readings; Reception History, Cultural Hermeneutics, and Theology*, ed. Eve-Marie Becker and Anders Runesson, WUNT 304 (Tübingen: Mohr Siebeck, 2013), 37–73.

43. In a contemporary context, Brubaker acknowledges the important work on social memory from a constructivist perspective, but cautions, citing Michael Schudson, "The Present in the Past versus the Past in the Present," *Communication* 11 (1989): 107, "The past is in some respects, and under some circumstances, highly resistant to efforts to make it over" (Brubaker with Margit Feischmidt, "1848 in 1998: The Politics of Commemoration in Hungary, Romania, and Slovakia," in Brubaker, *Ethnicity without Groups*, 162). Similarly, but with a sustained critique of the constructivist position on social memory theory, see Barry Schwartz, "Christian Origins: Historical Truth and Social Memory," in Kirk and Thatcher, *Memory, Tradition, and Text*, 43–56, and Schwartz, "Where There's Smoke, There's Fire," in Thatcher, *Memory and Identity*, 7–37. However, with respect to evaluating claims about the development of Christian social memory and identity, it is pertinent to ask, when and where is it that one actually sees smoke rather than fog? Are the smoke signals seen by followers of Jesus only evidence of fires lit by other followers of Jesus? Keith's pertinent observations on the significance of manuscripts as prestige objects for community identity and status in terms of the *Wirkungsgeschichte* of Markan textuality are also tied to, indeed belong to, the *Wirkungsgeschichte* of the historical Jesus. Thus, different views of Jesus's literacy in the early textual evidence are also to be explained by reference to Jesus's practice (see Keith, *Jesus' Literacy: Scribal Culture and the Teacher from Galilee*, LNTS 413 (London: T&T Clark, 2011). Here, it seems that an evolutionary model of history operates with the notion of a continuous development of primary communities of belief and practice devoted exclusively to Jesus and traceable as a history of effects to the historical Jesus. The point is that Brubaker in studying the "memory projects" associated with the 150th anniversary of the revolutions of 1848 in contemporary Hungary, Slovakia, and Romania has been able to draw on rich comparative materials, on the discourses of memory entrepreneurs and the perspectives of ordinary people, and consider the factors impinging on the resonance or lack of resonance of these projects. On the problematics of the postmodern "memory turn" in historical studies, see Kerwin Lee Klein, "On the Emergence of Memory in Historical Discourse," *Representations* 69 (2000): 127–50. "The clustering of quasi-religious terms around *memory* suggests some conclusions about the effects of our new key word.... It is no accident that our sudden fascination with memory goes hand in hand with postmodern reckonings of history as the marching blackboot and of historical consciousness as an oppressive fic-

of Jesus of Nazareth, which should not be assumed to be either homogeneous or continuous, do not of themselves explain how or why a variety of entrepreneurial culture producers made this Jesus a focal figure of their practices and writings.

I have found it useful not to draw a sharp divide between the transformative and reproductive sides of social memory and cultural practice on the grounds that Jonathan Z. Smith has spelled out in his paper in this volume on the work of Marshall Sahlins.[44] The malleable potential of social memory is not without constraints and the reproduction of memories and cultural practice is not without invention. With respect to the Gospel of Mark as a project of social memory and cultural practice, I have adopted a concept of "cultural persistence," which I have drawn from the work of Steven Weitzman.[45] His argument is that Jews, like other peoples in the midst of imperial powers, occupied a position of relative weakness and responded to situations of increasing constraints in their ability to control or effect cultural survival. Regardless of how one evaluates particular tactics as factors in accounting for Jewish cultural survival, Weitzman, relying on the notion of the "arts of the weak" in the work of Michel de Certeau,[46] demonstrates the range and ingenuity of tactics employed by Jews of the Second Temple period, in sharp contrast to the notion of inertia to characterize Jewish responses to cultural challenges and threats. Unlike biological survival, the struggle for cultural survival is not constrained by reality in the same way; but the tactics that must be generated in response to changes unfavorable to survival are analogous to the struggle for biological survival.[47] Weitzman has in view in particular the survival of Jewish

---

tion. Memory can come to the fore in an age of historiographic crisis precisely because it figures as a therapeutic alternative to historical discourse" (145, emphasis original).

44. "Conjectures on Conjunctures," and Smith's own preference for a less instrumental but more strategic set of terms in essay 3.

45. Steven Weitzman, *Surviving Sacrilege: Cultural Persistence in Jewish Antiquity* (Cambridge: Harvard University Press, 2005).

46. Michel de Certeau, *The Practice of Everyday Life*, trans. Steven Rendall (Berkeley: University of California Press, 1984), 35–36.

47. Weitzman, *Surviving Sacrilege*, 4–7, 11, 160–61. I need to stress at the outset that my use of Weitzman's concept is not concerned only, or even primarily, with the content of a culture, though that is of course not excluded, but with the strategies and imaginative labor necessary to find appropriate expression for cultural survival under circumstances of increasing external constraint; see below, nn. 177 and 353. For contemporary colonial regimes on the same topic of external constraints on native

ritual and the survival of the cult both before and after the destruction of the temple. It may seem patently counterintuitive to associate the Gospel of Mark with the idea of Jewish cultural persistence. I am not saying that the goals are the same—preserving Jewish ritual and some imagination of a still existing temple cult or its revival. But Weitzman shows that tactics range from appeasement and symbiosis, to resistance, to flight, concealment, and deflection, and include flights of fancy and magical practices. Indeed, it is clear that Jesus's actions in the temple and the parable of the tenants are intended to pose a threat to the Jerusalem establishment as guardians of the temple cult. But themes that are driven by the announcement of the kingdom of God and the coming of the Son of Man, the presence throughout Mark of scriptural idioms and texts, and mimetic writing drawing on biblical intertexts and figures of biblical lore are not superficial features of the gospel text nor can they be relegated to pre-Markan sources. The Gospel of Mark does not represent a seismic cultural shift from a biblical, Jewish cultural matrix to a Greco-Roman, gentile cultural matrix, as though these were somehow discrete entities in any case.[48] At the same time, I do not view the Gospel of Mark exclusively from the perspective of cultural persistence. I also take account of what I see as polemical aims, a discursive effort to convey a notion of "exemption" from the consequences of the recent Roman intervention and the end of centuries of imperial support of the temple and a native mediating class. I see the plot of Mark

---

responses, see Smith, "The Markan Site," 100, citing Nicolas Thomas, *Out of Time: History and Evolution in Anthropological Discourse*, 2nd ed. (Ann Arbor: University of Michigan Press, 1996), 111–14.

48. This is the view of Dennis R. MacDonald, reiterated in connection with his reconstruction of Q (Q+) and presented as an alternative solution to the Synoptic problem in *Two Shipwrecked Gospels: The Logoi of Jesus and Papias' Exposition of Logia about the Lord*, ECL 8 (Atlanta: Society of Biblical Literature, 2012), 541: "Mark's imitation of Homer was not merely a literary adjustment to Christian tradition; it was a seismic cultural shift. The world of the *Logoi of Jesus*, though Hellenized, was Palestinian and Jewish; its intertexts were almost exclusively biblical. By imitating Greek poetry, Mark transformed his protagonist into a rival of Greek heroes and gods." While I find this description far too onesided and stated as though we must think of cultures as discreet, bounded entities in the world, I agree that Mark also has in view Jesus's trumping the traditional heroes of the Greco-Roman world. For a similar critique of a "billiard ball" conception of cultures, see Smith's long citation to this effect from Eric R. Wolf's *Europe and the People Without History* in "Conjectures on Conjunctures," 22–23.

linking the death of Jesus and the destruction of the temple from both perspectives: cultural persistence and social escape. Similarly, the only way it makes sense to me to contend that the writer of Mark is responding to a situation of political, cultural, and symbolic loss in the wake of a failed revolt is to recognize how the "crisis" is also created for positioning a Jesus narrative in an enlarged political and cultural framework.[49]

With regard to Markan geography and spatial concepts, it seems to me quite wrong conceptually to suppose that the Markan author has emplotted a Jewish mission that is expanded territorially into a gentile mission and has incorporated into this "turn to the gentiles" scenes depicting the rejection of Jewish purity rituals, food laws, and table fellowship (Mark 7:1–30).[50] The more appropriate description of the totality of spaces in

---

49. On "crisis/response," see Smith, "Conjectures on Conjunctures," 68 n. 116. I have followed Weitzman in referring to "cultural persistence" rather than "religious persistence." This is not because I think religious data cannot be distinguished from other sorts of cultural data and theorized, or because "Judaism" cannot be a useful heuristic in the analysis of Jewish society in antiquity, but mainly as a matter of acknowledging the embeddedness of religious data in institutions comprising a larger social, political, and cultural matrix in the ancient world.

50. Mark describes the crowds that come to Jesus from a distance by reference to regions not in terms of ethnicity (3:7–8). Are those who come from Idumea, from beyond the Jordan, and the region around Tyre Jews or gentiles? Mark's Gospel does not clearly mark out population enclaves or administrative zones. Nor are the Tyrian hinterland and the region of the Decapolis appropriately described as "gentile territories." Gerd Theissen calls attention to the fact that these areas also included a significant population of Jews. Yet Theissen maintains that Mark has given a whole new meaning to Jesus's own itinerary by turning Jesus's movements into journeys that initiate a gentile mission. The only evidence Theissen gives for this is Mark 7:19b, which may be a later gloss, and may not be a judgment about the food laws of Leviticus in any case (Theissen, *The Gospels in Context: Social and Political History in the Synoptic Tradition*, trans. Linda M. Maloney [Minneapolis: Fortress, 1991], 68). The only time Mark makes explicit reference to Jews and non-Jews as distinguished ethnicities is in the two pericopes comprising Mark 7:1–30 (excluding the Roman capital charge against Jesus), and in both cases particular practices are in view. But do "all the Jews" (*Ioudaioi*) who, like the Pharisees, wash their hands before meals (7:3) refer to "Judeans" in distinction from Galileans and diaspora Jews? And when Mark describes the woman who comes to Jesus in a house in the region of Tyre begging Jesus to exorcise her daughter's demon and identifies her as a Ἑλληνίς, Συροφοινίκισσα τῷ γένει, are we to understand that she is an ethnic Greek "born outside the homeland"? (using "Syro-Phoenician" as a geopolitical label for her place of birth and domicile; see Alan H. Cadwallader, *Beyond the Word of a Woman: Recovering the Bodies of*

which Jesus is active in Mark is "the single land of Jesus," irrespective of particular population enclaves, which in any case were peoples who had lived under the arc of the Jerusalem temple system or in close proximity to its influence. Jesus's powers are active in all of them (the notable exception, though still with qualification, is his home town, Mark 6:5, and even this is not an exception with respect to his discursive powers).[51] There

---

the Syrophoenician Women [Adelaide, Australia: ATF Press, 2008], 122). Or is she to be understood as a "Hellenized Phoenician," with "Greek" signifying language and cultural identification? (Theissen, *Gospels in Context*, 70). Or does "Greek" refer to "civic status" and "Syrophoenician" to "provincial affiliation, ethnicity, language, or cultural attributes"? (Andrade, *Syrian Identity*, 110). Or is she just a gentile? Matthew describes her as the quintessential biblical "other," a "Canaanite woman" (15:22). See Smith's observations on the different implications of these descriptions in Mark and Matthew ("The Markan Site," 121–23), which could be read as a response to Joseph Geiger's musings: "One wonders how the authors of the Gospels could have known so much about the woman or why they cared to provide us with the information, since the exact description of a Hellenized native in such terms, as in Mark, is rare if not unique; the only fact of relevance to the story is that she is a gentile" ("The Jew and the Other: Doubtful and Multiple Identities in the Roman Empire," in *Jewish Identities in Antiquity: Studies in Memory of Menahem Stern*, ed. Lee I. Levine and Daniel R. Schwartz [Tübingen: Mohr Siebeck, 2009], 139). In any case, the exorcism of a Syro-Phoenician woman's daughter does not make a gentile mission. If the issue of the pericope is relations with ethnic others, both the Markan and Matthean versions are illustrative, in different ways to be sure, of Smith's conception of constructing the other in situations of near-near relations, one of the major points of his Levantine ethnography in "The Markan Site" (see Jonathan Z. Smith, "Differential Equations: On Constructing the Other," in *Relating Religion*, 230–50). The two-part description of the woman in Mark is the more surprising, if the issues addressed in the scene are principally those of gender and the actions and conditions pertinent to the place of women at the table rather than those of ethnicity, proximate neighbors, regional economic conflict, mission, or even the word of a woman. The case for such a reading has been made especially by Cadwallader, *Beyond the Word of a Woman*. Hal Taussig also sees debate about women's power in early groups of followers of Jesus as the main issue, but takes Mark's view to represent a more compromised position (see Taussig, "Dealing under the Table: Ritual Negotiation of Woman's Power in the Syro-Phoenician Woman Pericope," in *Reimagining Christian Origins: A Colloquium Honoring Burton L. Mack*, ed. Elizabeth A. Castelli and Hal Taussig [Valley Forge, PA: Trinity Press International, 1996], 264–79).

51. For the settings of Mark's *bios* and martyrdom as a single "land," see Mack, "The Spyglass and Kaleidoscope," 199. Conceivably, with respect to Mark 3:7–8 and the conflict of authority at the center of the Markan plot, the single land of Jesus is imagined as the Judean temple state, the region around Tyre and Sidon marking a

are no particular ethnic indicators in the healing of the deaf and dumb man in Mark 7:31–37, other than that it takes place in the Decapolis, and it is hardly conclusive that we are to think of the second feeding miracle as having occurred on the eastern side of the Sea of Galilee, since Mark 8:10 does not refer to crossing to the other side but to landing the boat in the region of Dalmanutha. If we take account of events that appear to occur in the region of the Golan from Mark 8:22 to 9:29, there are no consistent markers suggesting that regions to the north and east of Galilee are conceived by the writer as the locale of a mission to gentiles or that make it appropriate to suppose that Mark thinks of the peoples in view as encompassed by a Jew/gentile totalizing binary. A perspective taking seriously intracultural relations and patterns of interaction of the *longue durée* makes it more appropriate to imagine the south Levant as a region of hyphenated and aggregated ethnicities organized mainly around changing and hybrid patterns of practice associated with the dominant institutions of family, temple, city, and empire.[52] The writer of Mark has ignored for the most part the actual cultural diversity and ethnic hybridity of the region, letting markers of identification depend exclusively on the response to Jesus, on the one hand, and, on the other, opposing the practices of Jesus to those identified with the temple and its authorities and to those associated with the *archein tōn ethnōn* (10:42–44).[53] So, as Stewart has shown by applying models of spatiality to the data of Mark,[54] it is neither the conception of a gentile mission plotted on an east-west axis nor the opposition of Galilee to Jerusalem on a north-south axis that dominates Mark's concept of space. Rather, it is the opposition between spaces representing civiliz-

border area and Samaria conspicuously not mentioned; whereas, in a passage suggesting a circuitous journey of Jesus to the north and east, Mark 7:31, the writer may imagine the single land of Jesus as the Roman province of Syria.

52. With respect to the incorporation of non-Judean districts into the Hasmonean *ethnos* of the *Ioudaioi*, a pattern of conquest cum integration may have imitated Roman patterns, but integration was not merely a political phenomenon. It was aided by centuries of cultural and religious ties and economic strategies and interactions within the region; see Schwartz, *Imperialism and Jewish Society*, 39, and on the incorporation of Idumea in particular, Pasto, "Origin, Expansion, and Impact of the Hasmoneans," 197.

53. For Mark 10:42–44 as an example of inversion in colonized settings, see the remarks of Smith, "The Markan Site," 100 with n. 3, citing Thomas.

54. Eric C. Stewart, *Gathered around Jesus: An Alternative Spatial Practice in the Gospel of Mark* (Cambridge: James Clarke, 2009), 179–219.

ing centers: synagogues, houses, temple and city, which in Mark become the sites of unclean spirits and of surveillance of Jesus and his disciples, and the spaces representing threats to civilization: the typical haunts of demons and other special dangers, borderland territories, wilderness and desert, the sea, and the mountain, which in Mark become places of refuge from surveillance and places where epiphanies occur and kingdom teaching and practice are most effective.[55] Like the emperor or an itinerant philosopher, Jesus is a centripetal force, a traveling center, drawing disciples and crowds from the civilized center to gather around him.[56]

---

55. Referring to a study by Roy D. Kotansky, "Jesus and Heracles in Cádiz (τὰ Γάδειρα): Death, Myth, and Monsters at the 'Straits of Gibraltar' (Mark 4:35–5:43)," in *Ancient and Modern Perspectives on the Bible and Culture: Essays in Honor of Hans Dieter Betz*, ed. Adela Yarbro Collins, Scholars Press Homage Series 22 [Atlanta: Scholars Press, 1998], 160–229), Stewart acknowledges that Mark's text (or its pre-Markan source) "alludes to the tradition of seafarers arriving in strange and distant lands.... There are many common elements between the stories of sea travel discussed in chapter four and this Markan unit. The disciples and Jesus are threatened with shipwreck and death (4:37–38) and land on a distant shore in which the 'natives' behave in an uncivilized fashion—living among the tombs and in the mountains (5:2–5)" (Stewart, *Gathered around Jesus*, 182–83).

56. Stewart's study is a major contribution to the social theorizing of space in the ancient Mediterranean world. Its application to Mark with reference especially to the opposition of civilized and uncivilized spaces encoding social practices and power relations is also an important contribution to the study of Mark. But I do not agree with Stewart that the Jesus of Mark's Gospel controls the physical space of the very institutions of civilization, the synagogue and temple, whose leaders oppose him (*Gathered around Jesus*, 191). While Jesus acts with power within their spaces, in the long run he leaves them. Indeed, he does not control the spaces of refuge and is finally arrested in one of them (Mark 14:32–50). Stewart's conclusion that the old spaces of civilization with their practices must be destroyed before a pure space embodying the practices of the kingdom can be created is hardly a happy thought (ibid, 219). Stewart's reading of Jesus's opposition to the purity system is likewise overdrawn. One can even propose that the purity system associated with the civilized space of the temple has a striking parallel to being gathered around Jesus, and not without irony, as an instance of "the thinking of the temple" (see Francis Schmidt, *How the Temple Thinks: Identity and Social Cohesion in Ancient Judaism*, trans. J. Edward Crowley, BibSem 78 [Sheffield: Sheffield Academic, 2001]). Being gathered around Jesus is hardly an unmixed blessing, esp. for those who are most closely gathered around him in Mark, i.e., the disciples. Viewing Jesus as an alternative to the inclusive classification system represented by the temple and purity, one finds a hierarchy and a leveling of statuses in both. With respect to status leveling, just as sooner or later and most of the time, ordinary people contract ritual impurity, so most of the time the crowds will be in a state

The reading of Mark 7:15, 19b as declarations rejecting biblical food laws rather than specific purity practices (e.g., hand washing before meals), and the description of Jewish ritual practices presumably for the benefit of those unfamiliar with them (Mark 7:3–4, absent in Matthew) are generally taken as evidence of the gentile audience of Mark's Gospel and the rejection by gentile followers of Jesus of any imposition of Jewish practice with regard to forbidden foods. But anyone who has followed the literature on Mark 7:1–23 will know that matters are more complicated. Neither matters of theory or practice, nor the tradition-history of the passage are settled.[57] The issue of hand washing and Jesus's response (vv. 1–8, the purity of hands at mealtime) seem to many completely disconnected from the issue Jesus addresses to the crowd and privately to the disciples (vv. 14–23, the purity of foods, *kashrut*). But John Poirier has argued for the essential unity of verses 1–5 (excluding vv. 3–4) and verses 14–23 on the grounds that the Pharisees' practice of washing their hands before meals was concerned precisely with the fear of ingesting impurity in the act of eating. On Poirier's analysis, the context for this is not the imitation at common meals of priestly practice in the temple but the concern for a state

---

of incomprehension because they are given parables, that is, riddles, by Jesus. But it is okay because an appropriate distance is presupposed, even if the crowds are gathered around Jesus. And it seems somehow easier for unnamed minor characters to make an appropriate response to Jesus in Mark, even though their responses carry less weight for the plot of the narrative. With regard to status hierarchy, even if inverted in Mark, those who are closest to the sources of divine presence are most vulnerable to status degradation, at least temporarily—priests in the case of the temple, those who have received the mystery of the kingdom of God in the case of the disciples in Mark. Of course, outright opposition to Jesus's authority is a different matter than simple failure to understand Jesus's identity or God's plan, just as grievous sins are a different matter than ritual defilement. But it is also the case that purity practices are by no means exclusively associated with the temple in the first century CE, as will be clear below.

57. On theories of purity from a functionalist and symbolic approach, distinguishing three distinct systems: food laws, contact and contagion, and serious sins, see Jonathan Klawans, *Impurity and Sin in Ancient Judaism* (Oxford: Oxford University Press, 2000), and from a psycho-biological approach emphasizing the emotions of disgust and fear and theorizing Klawans's distinct systems as overlapping systems, see Thomas Kazen, *Issues of Impurity in Early Judaism*, ConBNT 45 (Winona Lake, IN: Eisenbrauns, 2010), 13–40: "A common denominator for various uses of purity language can be found in a negative emotional response to threatening stimuli, a reaction of disgust towards revolting or objectionable substances and towards states associated with such substances, or towards behaviour evoking similar feelings" (18).

of ritual purity in connection with a regimen of prayer and torah study, following a diaspora Jewish model.[58] Yair Furstenberg links the Jewish ritual practice to a matrix of standard practice of table etiquette in the Greco-Roman world. "Hand washing was not originally a priestly custom; rather it was a product of everyday normative behaviour in a society that indeed held purity as a significant cultural category.... Hand washing in the *halakhic* realm should be understood similarly to how it is understood in accepted table etiquette, namely, as a method for dispelling pollution from the body."[59] According to Furstenberg, not only does hand washing originate outside the biblical Levitical system but the Pharisees and early rabbis were operating from different principles than those of the Levitical system on the direction of pollution: food and liquids contaminating people and vessels rather than people and vessels contaminating foods and liquids as in the biblical system. Thus, Furstenberg understands the first limb of Mark 7:15 to be rejecting the ingestion of impurity and the second limb to be upholding the Levitical system regarding the impurity of substances that exit the body, "menstruation, seminal discharges of different kinds, parturient blood discharge and saliva." Furstenberg acknowledges that the force of Jesus's statement "lies in its ability simultaneously to rise to a moral level, which Jesus reveals to his disciples in the interpretation of the *mashal*."[60] An implication of this reading is that Mark 7:19b, "declaring all foods clean," would refer to the elimination of foods as a source of contamination of the body and not a permission to eat foods forbidden in the Pentateuch.[61]

---

58. John C. Poirier, "Why Did the Pharisees Wash Their Hands?," *JJS* 47 (1996): 217–33: "The Pharisees' concern was analogous to modern table etiquette—that one must guard against ingesting impurity—but with a concern for a truly ritual (= religiously incapacitating) sort of defilement" (227).

59. Yair Furstenberg, "Defilement Penetrating the Body: A New Understanding of Contamination in Mark 7:15," *NTS* 54 (2008): 193–94. Furstenberg compares Jesus in Mark 7 and Diogenes in Diogenes Laertius, *Lives* 6.61) both purging food, dismissing the popular fear of ingesting pollution (194 n. 51).

60. Furstenberg, "Defilement Penetrating the Body," 194–95, 198.

61. As noted also by Daniel Boyarin, following Furstenberg, *The Jewish Gospels: The Story of the Jewish Christ* (New York: The New Press, 2012), 117–21. Kazen, *Issues of Impurity*, 131–32, rejects Furstenberg's reading of Mark 7, mainly on the grounds of lack of evidence that the historical Jesus regarded the human body as "the primary source of impurity and transmitter of bodily contact-contagion," and because the distinction between biblical and *halakhic* principles would not have been nearly as clear

Is it really justified simply to assume that the only way to account for Mark's enumeration of the purity practices of the Pharisees and "all the Jews" is to conclude that he is informing a gentile audience about practices unknown to them? (Mark 7:2–3). The description is an exaggeration whether one translates πάντες οἱ Ἰουδαῖοι "all the Judeans" or "all the Jews" (v. 3). This Johannine-sounding phrase is most likely associated with the expansion of purity beyond the temple and temple-related practices in the first century.[62] What may actually be unknown to Mark's audience is the reference to "the tradition of the elders" (v. 3), which may have been unfamiliar to many Jews as well as others in his audience. Mark has supplied an explanation. By doing so he has also anticipated the charge of the Pharisees and scribes, which is formulated specifically with reference to "the tradition of the elders" (v. 5), and in a way that seems calculated more for ridicule and polemic aimed at Jewish scrupulousness than for information

---

as Furstenberg presents it (132). In Kazen's view, Jewish purity practices were of no interest to the writer of the gospel except as a set-up for the distinction between outer and inner purity and issues of commensality between Jewish and gentile believers in Christ. However, he also observes that Mark 7:19b does not necessarily mean that the Markan audience is discussing whether to eat pork or not (127–28). Kazen argues that Mark 7:15 in the context of the historical Jesus should be understood as a *relative* distinction reflecting a Semitic dialectic negation, "not so much as," or "rather," thus prioritizing moral purity over ritual purity in a manner similar to Hos 6:6. If this is correct, it would appear that the contribution of the writer of Mark to the tradition is hardly distinctive, since there is nothing to contradict this reading from a Markan perspective. It is equally clear that the writer of Mark accepts the distinction between human tradition and divine commandment, even if this distinction also belongs to a prior stage of the tradition (123–30; Kazen's argument in this section is mainly in debate with James G. Crossley, *The Date of Mark's Gospel: Insights from the Law in Earliest Christianity*, JSNTSup 266 [London: T&T Clark, 2004]). Like most others, Kazen regards the listing of Jewish purity practices in Mark 7:2–3 as a clear indication that Mark is offering explanations for practices unknown to a gentile audience (Kazen, *Issues of Impurity*, 119 n. 34). This conclusion is surely unwarranted, at least for the practice of washing hands before meals. Kazen does not dispute the view of Furstenberg that this Jewish ritual arises from the practice of common table etiquette in the Greco-Roman world. An audience would not have to know anything about the separate susceptibility of hands to impurity (and vv. 2–3 give no such details, in any case) to be utterly unsurprised that Jews, like many others in the Greco-Roman world, wash their hands before meals.

62. For an account of expansionist Jewish purity practice in the first century, see Thomas Kazen, *Jesus and Purity Halakhah: Was Jesus Indifferent to Impurity?*, rev. ed., ConBNT 38 (Winona Lake, IN: Eisenbrauns, 2010), 60–88.

(vv. 3–4), anticipating as well that Jesus will respond not with an answer but with a counter-charge formulated precisely as observance of human tradition designed to circumvent the commandment of God (vv. 6–13).[63]

Evaluating the position of Mark 7:1–23 on purity in early Jesus traditions must also take account of the Q saying (Matt 23:25–26 // Luke 11:39–41) and its parallel in the Gos. Thom. 89, referring to washing utensils (in this case, "the cup") and conceptualized as an issue of "outside" and "inside." Risto Uro sees the three extant versions as significant variants, each with "its own peculiar perspective and hermeneutic horizon."[64] The Thomasine version, closer to Luke than to Matthew but shorter, clearly has as its hermeneutic horizon a rejection of common Jewish practices. Uro comments: "The Thomasine group is not engaged in a direct conflict with Pharisaic Judaism and the rabbis but rather with Jewish-Christian groups in which all or many of the important Jewish identity-markers discussed in *Thomas* were being practised."[65] The importance of taking account of the Gospel of Thomas, a collection of sayings also originating in Syria, for perspective on Mark 7:1–23 is even clearer in connection with the parallel between Mark 7:15 // Matt 15:11 and Gos. Thom.14.5. This saying of Jesus, the only address to the crowd in this unit in Mark and Matthew, is not only enigmatic but potentially very troublesome for any sort of nego-

---

63. See Burton Mack, *Myth of Innocence*, 189–92, setting out the unit as an elaboration of a *chreia* reworked from an original Cynic-like *chreia*. "The introduction was necessary in order to shift the objection away from Jesus and back onto the Pharisees. The problem now is not that Jesus and his disciples do not wash, but that the Pharisees do. In the shift, the basis for Pharisaic law is specified as the 'tradition of the elders'" (191).

64. Risto Uro, "Washing the Outside of the Cup: *Gos. Thom.* 89 and Synoptic Parallels," in *From Quest to Q: Festschrift James M. Robinson*, ed. Jón Ma. Ásgeirsson, Kristina de Troyer, and Marvin W. Meyer, BETL 146 (Leuven: Leuven University Press, 2000), 318. He interprets Luke 11:41 with its reference to almsgiving making "all things clean" as a general statement comparable to Rom 14:20 and Mark 7:19: "Luke clearly echoes the Markan story in 7, 1–23 … [which] also slides from the issue of washing … to a more general statement about unclean food" (314). It is also important to understand, as Uro observes, that the relative priority of inner to outer purity is not a difference between a "nonactual" metaphorical purity and "actual" ritual purity. Both belong to conceptions of purity that overlap. Jesus's explanation to the disciples is "medical," a kind of decontamination process (Mark 7:19a): unclean foods cannot defile because they do not reach the heart (310–11, 317). Again, this is hardly reason to assume that Mark 7:19b must refer to permitting the eating of foods forbidden in the Pentateuch.

65. Ibid., 320.

tiation with Jewish practices. If taken as an independent Cynic-like *chreia* and understood as an absolute rather than relative distinction, it can be considered a rejection of both ritual washings and dietary laws.[66] By comparison, Mark has hedged such an interpretation of the saying intended for a general audience by staging a private controversy, condemning the Pharisees for violation of God's commandments, and offering a private explanation to disciples featuring a statement about what happens to food over against the array of behaviors that really defile.[67] "Early Christians were often at pains to argue about purity codes."[68] But there is no reason to suppose that other Jews and non-Jews did not also debate these and other disputed matters.[69]

Index of the remaining sections of the paper:
2. The Gospel of Mark in a Levantine Cultural Milieu and the First Roman-Judean War (239–54)
3. Making a Difference on the Date of Mark (254–62)
4. Two Jesuses and the Portents of Doom (262–66)
5. The Death of Jesus and the Destruction of the Temple in Mark (266–75)
6. Mark 13 and the War Generation (275–302)
7. The Consequences of a Failed Revolt (302–21)

---

66. See above, 235 with n. 59 and above, n. 63.

67. See John Horman, *A Common Written Greek Source for Mark and Thomas*, SCJ 20 (Waterloo, ON: Wilfrid Laurier University Press, 2011), 92–96, 182–83.

68. Uro, "Washing the Outside of the Cup," 316, adding, "One need only refer to Paul's curious explanation that food offered to idols does not pollute those who have 'knowledge' but corrupts (or pollutes) the *syneidesis* of those who do not have *gnosis* (1 Cor 8, 7–12), or Mark's rationale that unclean food does not really pollute a person since it does not enter his heart but 'goes out into the sewer' (Mark 7, 19)" (316–17).

69. Commenting on Josephus's account of the conversion of Izates of Adiabene when at first he followed the advice of Ananias to the effect that adhering to the ancestral practices of Jews was more authoritative than circumcision (*Ant.* 20.2.4 §§41–42), Hayim Lapin writes, "This, from a contemporary of the author of Acts about an older contemporary of Paul, suggests the possibility that debates over proselytizing, circumcision, and belonging as described in Acts for first-century Christian groups may well have been 'intra-Jewish' debates that also occurred in other Jewish communities" (Lapin, "Post-70 Judaism in Judea and the Near East," in *The Cambridge History of Religions in the Ancient World: From the Hellenistic Age to Late Antiquity*, ed. William Adler, vol. 2 of *The Cambridge History of Religions in the Ancient World*, ed. Michelle Renee Saltzman [Cambridge: Cambridge University Press, 2013], 122).

8. Responses to the Destruction: Apocalypses, Related Writings, and Josephus (322–35)
9. The *Fiscus Iudaicus* and the Parting of the Ways? (335–53)
10. The *Fiscus Iudaicus* and Narratives of Victimization, Freedom, and Escape (354–73)
11. Conclusion: The Social Logic of Mark's Dual Narrative (373–99)

2. The Gospel of Mark in a Levantine Cultural Milieu and the First Roman-Judean War

In an article highlighting the Greco-Roman Levantine milieu of the Gospel of Mark, Richard C. Miller has set the empty tomb story in an array of Greek and Roman translation stories and argues that the closing scene in Mark exhibits typical features of translation fables, most especially, the vanished body. The scene should not be understood in relation to a narrower Judaic conception of resurrection but interpreted in terms that would register in its broader Mediterranean milieu. Unlike the way in which a translation fable might be marked in an interlude in biography or history, Mark does not report "a *sui generis* historic moment"; instead, "Mark renders his hero-sage within the standing mythographic tradition of the 'translation fable,' thus by *interpretatio graeca et romana* elevating him to the rank of the classical Mediterranean demigod."[70]

According to Miller, Mark's narrative as a whole is typical of Greco-Roman literature with respect to its literary conventions, cultural codes, and semiotic inventory and differs from predecessors and contemporaries in this domain "by means of generic reconstitution, conventional variation, and superficial regional attire."[71] "Read as part of this broader cultural-literary domain, Mark applies indigenous cultural coloring … weaving it with Near Eastern motifs …; or, at other moments, Mark has with ingenuous superficiality assigned Palestinian nomenclature and cultural flourish."[72] Though Mark's narrative resides most comfortably "at and often beyond the conventional outskirts of early Judaism" and "comes bracketed within a playful mode of fable," it is nevertheless in Miller's esti-

---

70. Richard C. Miller, "Mark's Empty Tomb and Other Translation Fables in Classical Antiquity," *JBL* 129 (2010): 776.

71. Ibid., 761.

72. Ibid., 760.

mation a hybridic literary text, one which is also "critically engaging Palestinian Judaisms…, revealing a narrative composed and consumed by an external society."[73] In sum,

> Mark's metanarrative articulates sociocultural unrest in the Greek East in the wake of a regional, provoked conflict with Rome, a conflict, according to Josephus, brought on by the very points of perceived Jewish obstinance derided and scorned throughout Mark's narration. Though Mark's story is set in Palestine, one may better classify Mark as Mediterranean, Levantine literature aimed at the registration of sociocritical positions within a region of cultural-political upheaval, that is, ca. the 70 c.e. demolition of Jerusalem.[74]

Miller's regional and cultural location of the Gospel of Mark in the Hellenistic Levant and broad classification of it as Mediterranean, Levantine literature seems to me on target. That Mark features topoi, generic markings, and literary techniques familiar from Greek literature written in the early Roman period has repeatedly been demonstrated. Such a broad description would not exclude Jewish writings from Palestine and the Levant in any case. But Miller's view that the knowledge of biblical figures and topoi assumed of Mark's readers is superficial, that is, "content well within the common Mediterranean public domain"[75] such as the legendary ascensions of Moses and Elijah, is too minimal, and in fact is quite misleading. The narrative exhibits a significant level of Jewish enculturation with respect to the use of the Septuagint and familiarity with stories featuring biblical figures. Even supposing that there were some readers whose knowledge of Greek biblical texts was virtually limited to the few explicitly cited in Mark, it would be obvious even to them that these texts

---

73. Ibid., 770, 776, 771.

74. Ibid., 771, pointing to Antioch on the Orontes as a typical Levantine city exemplifying the cosmopolitan, cultural hybridity appropriate as a site of Mark's composition. Miller refers in particular to the Romulus fable, not just for comparison with Mark, but in order to set the Markan reception trajectory in the other canonical Gospels in a development that also featured the optional component of translated "appearance" tradition (772–74; for bibliography, 774 nn. 26–27). For a recent study of the tradition history of the disappearance and appearance traditions viewed as independent traditions that gradually merged, see Daniel A. Smith, *Revisiting the Empty Tomb: The Early History of Easter* (Minneapolis: Fortress, 2010).

75. Miller, "Mark's Empty Tomb," 771 n. 23.

carry a formal authority and belong to the cultural codes of the Markan narrative universe.[76] A recent study argues that Mark is indeed an example of Greco-Roman mimetic writing, but that the narratives of Elijah and Elisha in 1 and 2 Kings have a better case as sources at the macrolevel of the Markan narrative than do those from the Greek classical canon.[77]

The range of scholarly views put forward on the generic classification of Mark further complicates determination of the cultural ambience, social location, and purpose of the narrative. The gospel has been identified not only as one or another type of Greco-Roman biography, including memorabilia and aretalogy,[78] but has also been described as a parody

---

76. Moreover, knowledge of central biblical traditions and institutionalized Jewish practices are not necessarily a gauge of the range of interests in matters pertaining to Jews or in the kinds of expertise associated with Jews.

77. Adam Winn, *Mark and the Elijah-Elisha Narrative: Considering the Practice of Greco-Roman Imitation in the Search for Markan Source Material* (Eugene, OR: Pickwick, 2010). I take contemporary studies of Markan mimetic composition to be at least an index of what a reader could possibly identify or imagine of classical and biblical stories alluded to in the Markan narrative, and thus an index of the cultural hybridity of the author and the range and complexity of intended or imagined readers. For examples from the Greek classical tradition, see Dennis R. MacDonald, *The Homeric Epics and the Gospel of Mark* (New Haven: Yale University Press, 2000). For the biblical tradition, see Wolfgang Roth, *Hebrew Gospel: Cracking the Code of Mark* (Oak Park, IL: Meyer-Stone Books, 1988). For Mark as Palestinian haggada, see Roger David Aus, *The Stilling of the Storm: Studies in Early Palestinian Judaic Tradition*, International Studies in Formative Christianity and Judaism (Binghamton, NY: Global Publications, Binghamton University, 2000); Aus, *My Name Is "Legion": Palestinian Judaic Traditions in Mark 5:1–20 and Other Gospel Texts*, Studies in Judaism (Lanham, MD: University Press of America, 2003); Aus, *"Caught in the Act," Walking on the Sea, and the Release of Barabbas Revisited*, SFSHJ157 (Atlanta: Scholars Press, 1998); Aus, *Feeding the Five Thousand: Studies in the Judaic Background of Mk 6:30–44 par. and John 6:1–15*, Studies in Judaism (Lanham, MD: University Press of America, 2010). For a general thesis on the formation of the New Testament as an intertextual development, see Thomas L. Brodie, *The Birthing of the New Testament: The Intertextual Development of the New Testament Writings*, New Testament Monographs 1 (Sheffield: Sheffield Phoenix, 2004).

78. R. A. Burridge, *What Are the Gospels? A Comparison with Graeco-Roman Biography*, 2nd ed. (Grand Rapids: Eerdmans, 2004); for Mark and memorabilia, Vernon K. Robbins, *Jesus the Teacher: A Socio-rhetorical Interpretation of Mark* (Philadelphia: Fortress, 1984); and for aretalogy, Lawrence M. Wills, *The Quest of the Historical Gospel: Mark, John, and the Origins of the Gospel Genre* (London: Routledge, 1997). For a different estimate of the significance of Jesus as a figure of aretalogy, see Jonathan Z. Smith, "Good News Is No News: Aretalogy and Gospel," in *Map Is Not*

of the genre.[79] Mark has been associated with prophetic biography[80] and classified with Greco-Roman novels,[81] with Jewish novels,[82] and with

Territory: Studies in the History of Religions, SJLA 23 (Leiden: Brill, 1978; repr. Chicago: University of Chicago Press, 1993), 190–207.

79. David E. Aune, "Genre Theory and the Genre-Function of Mark and Matthew," in *Mark and Matthew I: Comparative Readings; Understanding the Earliest Gospels in Their First-Century Settings*, ed. Eve-Marie Becker and Anders Runesson, WUNT 271 (Tübingen: Mohr Siebeck, 2011), 145–75. "The Gospel of Mark appears to have been written *in reaction to* Greco-Roman biography rather than as a simple emulation of it. That is, Mark can be understood as an intentional *parody* of the hierarchy of values that typically characterized Greco-Roman biography" (168, emphasis original). Aune refers to a broad definition of parody that would include serious writing (169), citing Simon Dentith, *Parody* (London: Routledge, 2000), 9: "Parody includes any cultural practice which provides a relatively polemical allusive imitation of another cultural production or practice." Compare Gerd Theissen's conception of Mark as "a biography with a public claim," that is, a Greco-Roman genre reshaped from a tradition of prophetic books (Gerd Theissen, *The New Testament: A Literary History*, trans. Linda M. Maloney [Minneapolis: Fortress, 2012], 53–54).

80. Klaus Baltzer, *Die Biographie der Propheten* (Neukirchen-Vluyn: Neukirchener Verlag, 1975).

81. Mary Ann Tolbert, *Sowing the Gospel: Mark's World in Literary-Historical Perspective* (Minneapolis: Fortress, 1989). Similar patterns of sequencing narrative and contrasting world views of the Greek novel and the Gospel of Mark are highlighted in Rob Starner, *Kingdom of Power, Power of Kingdom: The Opposing World Views of Mark and Chariton* (Eugene, OR: Pickwick, 2011). The collection of essays in Ronald F. Hock, J. Bradley Chance, and Judith Perkins, eds., *Ancient Fiction and Early Christian Narrative*, SymS 6 (Atlanta: Scholars Press, 1998) includes two essays comparing the Gospel of Mark and the Life of Aesop: Richard I. Pervo, "A Nihilist Fabula: Introducing the *Life of Aesop*," 77–120, and Whitney Shiner, "Creating Plot in Episodic Narratives: *The Life of Aesop* and the Gospel of Mark," 155–76. Recent interest in the comparison of Aesop and Mark is occasioned by the fact that both are closer to each other in style, social location, and antiestablishment values than either is to the more culturally dominant Greco-Roman biography. Moreover, the use of the Semitic Story of Ahiqar in the Aesop Romance also provides a link to Jewish novels; see Lawrence M. Wills, *The Jewish Novel in the Ancient World* (Ithaca, NY: Cornell University Press, 1995). But the insights drawn from such comparisons can be quite disparate. Compare Wills's description of the Aesop narrative, and his reconstructed narrative underlying Mark and John as hero stories designed to legitimate the cult of the hero (*Quest of the Historical Gospel*, 10, 177–78), with Pervo's analysis of the Aesop figure as an antihero who "has no belief in immortality and no desire to perish as a glorious martyr, scapegoat, or victim of injustice." His postmortem fate is thus "the absolute final irony." "The post-ultimate irony is that this anti-hero was heroized after his death" ("Nihilist Fabula," 115, 118, 117). This is not necessarily a judgment on Wills's thesis regarding

Greco-Roman and biblical historiography.[83] One implication of these clas-

---

Mark and John. Even though I am not persuaded by Wills's thesis of an earlier narrative common to Mark and John legitimating the cult of the hero, it may still be the case that the author of Mark was influenced by the sort of hero figure in conflict with his people that Wills has in view. David Watson, who thinks both Mark and Aesop can be considered aretalogical, novelistic biographies, differentiates the goals of their critique of elite social values. He sees the Gospel of Mark having the reform of society in view far more than the Life of Aesop. This judgment seems to depend largely on his estimate of the different social significance of their endings and the demands made on those of higher social standing among their readers (David F. Watson, "The *Life of Aesop* and the Gospel of Mark: Two Ancient Approaches to Elite Values," *JBL* 129 [2010]: 699–716).

82. Michael E. Vines, *The Problem of Markan Genre: The Gospel of Mark and the Jewish Novel*, AcBib 3 (Atlanta: Society of Biblical Literature, 2002).

83. Eve-Marie Becker, *Das Markus-Evangelium im Rahmen antiker Historiographie*, WUNT 194 (Tübingen: Mohr Siebeck, 2006); Becker, "The Gospel of Mark in the Context of Ancient Historiography," in *The Function of Ancient Historiography in Biblical and Cognate Studies*, ed. Patricia G. Kirkpatrick and Timothy Goltz, LHBOTS 489 (New York: T&T Clark, 2008), 124–134; Adela Yarbro Collins, *Mark: A Commentary*, Hermeneia (Minneapolis: Fortress, 2007), 33–44. Collins classifies Mark as historical monograph (42) having an affinity to the didactic type of ancient biography (33). The classification of Mark with ancient historiography is mainly predicated on the use of sources in a continuous narrative, the variety of kinds of materials that can be included in the genre, and various ways in which ancient historiography can invoke a transcendent perspective on events. "The question of the attitude of the author of Mark to such elements [as the miraculous] is difficult to discern. It may be that he believed that the mighty deeds of Jesus were historical events. Alternatively, he may have seen them as figurative expressions of the role and power of Jesus" (41). Accordingly, when ancient historiography is viewed as a mimetic genre the question of evaluating historical reliability in a modern sense is not determinative of its literary classification (35–36). In that case, one might ask how much the Gospel of Mark's historical reliability differs from "an historical novel, the fictional biography of a presumably historical individual" (Pervo, "Nihilist Fabula," 82).

The issue of the veracity of a history in the Greco-Roman world can be seen as a pressing problem for Josephus, who had to find a way to argue for the veracity of the *Antiquities,* and thus for the antiquity of the Jews, despite his dealing with temporal periods that would be associated with myth and not history in a Greek historiographical tradition. The move he makes of appealing to prophets and divinely revealed truth would hardly be recognized in that tradition (*Ag. Ap.* 1.7–8 §§37–38); see John M. G. Barclay, "Judean Historiography in Rome: Josephus and History in *Contra Apionem* Book 1," in *Josephus and Jewish History in Flavian Rome and Beyond*, ed. Joseph Sievers and Gaia Lembi, JSJSup 104 (Leiden: Brill, 2005), 29–43: "Josephus's provocative claim is that this Judean tradition stands not as a radical alternative to the

sifications is the relationship of each to classical and biblical epic. Michael Vines believes that for the author of Mark biography would have been the wrong genre "to challenge the dominant 'epic' traditions of Judaism." With respect to mounting this challenge Mark is closer to Menippean satire.[84] *Aesop* too can be viewed as a parody of epic. "Insofar as the romance is epic it parodies epic by presenting a hero more like Thersites than Achilles."[85] Classifying Mark as history has suggested a quite different relationship to biblical epic. For example, Adela Yarbro Collins sees Mark as a continuation of biblical epic: "He continues Israelite and Jewish ethnic sacred history and illustrates the fulfillment of the universalist tendency in Israelite and Jewish literature through the extension of the revitalization movement begun by John and Jesus to the gentiles."[86] Finally, though Mark's narrative cannot be classified as an apocalypse it is generally thought to be governed by an apocalyptic world view, exemplified in Jesus's programmatic announcement of the kingdom of God, in the periodization of time and divinely determined course of events,[87] in a discourse focused on a

---

mainstream historiographical tradition, but as a variant within it, even as its supreme exemplar of accuracy and truth" (42). Barclay draws on postcolonial theory to assess the significance of Josephus's appeal to prophetic authority for authenticating claims to historical truth in *Contra Apionem*. For a different assessment, which sees Josephus playing down an appeal to prophetic revelation in *Contra Apionem* and drawing on the methods of Roman rhetorical education for making his case on the basis of historical plausibility rather than historical certainty, see Robert G. Hall, "Josephus, *Contra Apionem* and Historical Inquiry in the Roman Rhetorical Schools," in *Josephus' Contra Apionem: Studies in Its Character and Context with a Latin Concordance to the Portion Missing in Greek*, ed. Louis H. Feldman and John R. Levison, AGJU 34 (Leiden: Brill, 1996), 229–49. However, Hall acknowledges that Josephus "probably never abandons his Jewish predilection for certainty grounded in revelation" (249 n. 26).

84. Vines, *Problem of Markan Genre*, 131–42. Yet this cannot be the whole story of the gospel's relationship to biblical epic, since in Vines's own estimation Mark is closest to the Jewish novel, despite the fact that these novels have a decidedly affirmative relationship to the pieties of biblical epic (144–60).

85. Pervo, "Nihilist Fabula," 119.

86. Collins, *Mark*, 43.

87. "Mark's notion of an eschatological fulfillment, of course, has its origin in the prophetic books of the Old Testament or Jewish Bible. His overall conception of history, however, with its notion of a fixed divine plan (8:31; 13:7, 20; 14:36, 49) and its incipient periodization … is due to the influence of apocalyptic tradition and literature" (ibid.). But writing history as prophecy is not an innovation of the Persian or Hellenistic periods, nor is it limited to the apocalyptic genre. It goes back to scribes of the ancient Near East combining local historiographic traditions and mantic prac-

time of tribulation (Mark 13),[88] and in elements of mystery, concealment, and revelation.[89] Not only does the Gospel of Mark incorporate features

---

tices, a combination expressed independently in different genres and historical periods and cutting across the genre identified as apocalypse in biblical studies, as demonstrated by Matthew Neujahr, *Predicting the Past in the Ancient Near East: Mantic Historiography in Ancient Mesopotamia, Judah, and the Mediterranean World*, BJS 354 (Providence, RI: Brown Judaic Studies, 2012).

88. Christopher Rowland, "The Parting of the Ways: The Evidence of Jewish and Christian Apocalyptic and Mystical Material," in *Jews and Christians: The Parting of the Ways A.D. 70 to 135; The Second Durham-Tübingen Research Symposium*, ed. James D. G. Dunn, (Grand Rapids: Eerdmans, 1999), 213–37: "In comparison with the more extended accounts of the coming of the new age to be found in other material both Christian and Jewish the synoptic discourses concentrate on the period of strife and tribulation leading up to the coming of the son of man. What happens thereafter is not explored" (230–31).

89. Among scholars who argue for the unity of the themes associated with the so-called messianic secret, three approaches may be noted here. Gerd Theissen, "Die pragmatische Bedeutung der Geheimnismotive im Markusevangelium: Ein wisssenssoziologischer Versuch," in *Secrecy and Concealment: Studies in the History of Mediterranean and Near Eastern Religions*, ed. Hans G. Kippenberg and Guy G. Stroumsa, SHR 65 (Leiden: Brill, 1995), 225–45, maintains that the function of the secret is to protect the group. Like Jesus, the disciples may legitimately conceal their identities when they are endangered, but they are warned that this will not be possible in the long run and when confronted and challenged, like Jesus, they must bear witness and risk death. "Diese darf Jesu in dem Sinne 'nachfolgen', dass sie zunächst mit gutem Gewissen 'geheim' bleibt. Ihre 'Täten' werden bekannt, ihre eigentliche Identität aber darf vom Geheimnis geschützt werden. Langfristig aber ist es für Christen unvermeidlich, dass sie sich zu ihrer Identität öffentlich bekennen und wie Jesus das Martyrium riskieren" (244). Adopting a history of religions approach, Adela Yarbro Collins, "Messianic Secret and the Gospel of Mark: Secrecy in Jewish Apocalypticism, the Hellenistic Mystery Religions, and Magic," in *Rending the Veil: Concealment and Secrecy in the History of Religions*, ed. Elliot R. Wolfson (Chappaqua, NY: Seven Bridges Press, 1999), 11–30, stresses reverence for the divine, vulnerability of the sacra or the message to ridicule and profanation, and control of access. The tension between revelation and secrecy is resolved "by the felicitous description of the Gospel of Mark by Martin Dibelius as a series of secret epiphanies" (24). The book by David F. Watson, *Honor among Christians: The Cultural Key to the Messianic Secret* (Minneapolis: Fortress, 2010) examines the significance of secrecy in the ancient Mediterranean world and concludes that the passages in Mark described in this way are not examples of secrecy regarding the identity of Jesus but express the inversion of the ancient Mediterranean-wide values of honor and shame. Passages in Mark which have seemed to contradict the secrecy motif are not contradictions but simply inconsistencies amounting to a

of more than one Greco-Roman and biblical genre, but it does so in a manner that is not clearly determined by any single genre.

What seems to me to be most provocative in Miller's essay and deserving of a more extended discussion is his description of the polemical aim of Mark, what one might think of as the author's project: "aimed at the registration of sociocritical positions within a region of cultural-political upheaval" in the wake of the Roman-Judean war. "Jesus thus becomes the literary vehicle and emblem of a charged socio-political-religious response to an obstinate, broken Jewish revolt against Rome; he serves as a literary-cultural *evocatio sacrorum*, an instrument functioning to delineate and extract the best of a (regionally perceived) failed religious civilization."[90] On this account one might imagine that the Roman siege practice of *evocatio deorum*, which may have been performed at the beginning of the siege in 70 CE,[91] and the triumphal procession in Rome in 71 CE, and the reestablishing of the *pax deorum* in 75 CE,[92] were not just expressions of Roman piety operating in the crushing of a locally inspired and implemented revolt or the propaganda of a new imperial family, but incorporated a regional judgment on an entire religious civilization as well. The Flavians in fact did not transfer the god of the Jerusalem temple to a better home in Rome[93] or reestablish the Judean cult in Jerusalem, but according to Miller's description they also did not prevent the author of Mark from extracting (or should we say "transporting") the best of a failed religious civilization.

Miller's description at points is too redolent of a later Christian literary tradition and Christian imperial propaganda with respect to

---

recognition that the honor-shame system, though its values can be inverted, cannot be escaped, and so can also be used to illustrate other important themes.

90. Miller, "Mark's Empty Tomb," 771.

91. See John S. Kloppenborg, "*Evocatio deorum* and the Date of Mark," *JBL* 124 (2005): 419–50, concluding, "Without actually describing the *evocatio* ritual, Josephus leaves sufficient hints in his account that it probably was performed" (444).

92. The newly constructed Temple of Peace, where the gold vessels taken from the Jerusalem temple were deposited, was dedicated in 75 CE.

93. The ritual practice of *evocatio* may not always have involved the transport of the deity to Rome. See Kloppenborg, "*Evocatio deorem*," 440–41, citing Gabriella Gustaffson, *Evocatio Deorem: Historical and Mythical Interpretations of Ritualised Conquests in the Expansion of Ancient Rome*, Acta Universitatis Upsaliensis Historia Religionum 16 (Uppsala: Uppsala Universitet, 2000), 80.

the obsolescence of "Judaism."[94] Furthermore, Miller's contention that "the very points of perceived Jewish obstinance" provoking the conflict with Rome is attested by both Mark and Josephus is misleading in both cases.[95] For Mark, Judean leaders, whoever they were thought to be, brought disaster not because they provoked a war with Rome but because they opposed Jesus and were therefore thieves and corrupt. For Josephus, one should not confuse his situation and views in Rome in the 70s, 80s, and 90s with his position and behavior in Jerusalem and Galilee in 66–67. Josephus's claim that it was tyrants, bandits, and prophets bent on undermining a reasonable process of integration into the empire and not members of the ruling class that broke with Rome and prosecuted the war is a later apologetic for his own class. It was in the dynamics of factionalism among the Judean elite to which Josephus belonged that a coalition was formed with sufficient resources and stability to violate the status quo, begin the hostilities, establish a functioning political entity independent of Rome, and take steps to defend it, though Josephus has certainly sought to conceal this (*J. W.* 2.17.2–10, 19.5–20.1, 20.4 §§408–456, 533–556, 566–568; *Life* 17–23).[96] Far from equating the destruction

---

94. "The supersessionist claim is, quite simply, that Christianity had made its parent obsolete, having taken over all that was good about it" (Tessa Rajak, "The Greek Bible Translations among Jews in the Second Century CE," in *Jewish Identities in Antiquity: Studies in Memory of Menahem Stern*, ed. Lee I. Levine and Daniel R. Schwartz, TSAJ 130 [Tübingen: Mohr Siebeck, 2009], 323, arguing against the standard scholarly narrative on Greek Bible translations post-70 CE).

95. Miller, "Mark's Empty Tomb," 771 with n. 22.

96. "Josephus was of course at pains in his history precisely to deny this participation in the revolt by his own class. He portrays his friends as moderate leaders who tried to provide a stable government for Jerusalem while negotiating for an agreement with Rome.... The ruling class *might* have chosen to behave in this way. Mediation between the people and Rome was indeed its natural function. Even the *attitude* of moderation ascribed to it by Josephus was probably often real. Nonetheless, I believe that the historian's apologetic must be rejected in its entirety, for the revolutionary *actions* taken by many members of the ruling class are too well documented to deny" (Martin Goodman, *The Ruling Class of Judaea: The Origins of the Jewish Revolt Against Rome A.D. 66–70* [Cambridge: Cambridge University Press, 1987], 167, emphasis original). The later prosecution of the war was not led by bandits, prophets, or messiahs, but by factions of the Judean ruling class. "It can safely be asserted that *all* the prominent figures who proposed themselves as national leaders between A.D. 50 and A.D. 70 were derived from the old ruling class" (Goodman, *Ruling Class of Judaea*, 206, emphasis original). In comments to reviews of his book, Goodman conceded that this may not have been

of the temple with the perception of a failed Jewish civilization, Josephus

---

the case with the final leader of the revolt, Simon b. Gioras (see Goodman, "Current Scholarship on the First Revolt," in *The First Jewish Revolt: Archaeology, History, and Ideology*, ed. Andrea M. Berlin and J. Andrew Overman [London: Routledge, 2002], 18. James McLaren links Josephus directly to the priests who participated in the decision to cease the sacrifices offered in the temple on behalf of Rome as well as to those appointed for the defense of Galilee. Josephus's apparent foresight of the disaster that would surely result from a decision to go to war against Rome was not an expression of his attitudes and behavior in 66 and 67, but the benefit of a historical perspective and understanding shaped by the defeat in Galilee, the opportunity and decision to save his own life, the fall of Jerusalem and destruction of the temple, and his situation in Rome. From the angle of hindsight Josephus's commentaries on events are not simply lies to cover up the actions of a rebel turned lackey; nor can his behavior be squared with that of a provincial aristocrat who had always acted in the interest of avoiding a military clash with Rome. From hindsight he learned that his initial views and behavior had been wrong. According to McLaren, actively participating in a rebellion against Rome and finding a way to live with Rome required no major change of principles on the part of Josephus. They were consistent with the principle that God intended the Jews to live as a free people under the rule of priests, and with the principle that God was in control of the well being of people and the course of events (James S. McLaren, "Delving into the Dark Side: Josephus' Foresight as Hindsight," in *Making History: Josephus and Historical Method*, ed. Zuleika Rodgers, JSJSup 110 [Leiden: Brill, 2007], 49–67, esp. 50–53 with nn. 6–8, including McLaren's observations on Josephus's references to Ananus b. Ananus [*J. W.* 2.22.1 §651; 4.5.2 §§320–321], and why descriptions of events and actions should take precedence over descriptions of intentions and motivations). Josephus's hindsight also comes through in places where he has chosen to be silent, for example, "his silence regarding the capture of the Roman standards in 66 C.E., and his silence regarding the argument in favour of ceasing to offer sacrifices on behalf of the Romans." But hindsight is occasionally bracketed in brief asides in later writings, as for example in *Life* 348, where Josephus remarks on the failure of Sepphoris to provide assistance to a besieged Jerusalem when the "common temple of all was at risk of coming under the authority of the enemy" ("Delving into the Dark Side, 64, citing the translation of Steve Mason, *Life of Josephus*, vol. 9 of *Flavius Josephus: Translation and Commentary* [Leiden: Brill, 2001], 142). In an earlier essay, McLaren argued that Josephus made Judas the Galilean the ideological scapegoat for the slogan, "No master but God," a slogan that supported not fanatic insurgents but the ruling class in taking the measures that established an independent state in 66. The ideology can still be seen reflected in Josephus's view of the ideal polity of the rule of God through a priestly aristocracy (*Ag. Ap.* 2.17, 22 §§164–165, 184–187) but has been presented in an apologetic framework aimed at divorcing it utterly from the doctrine of the rebels (McLaren, "Constructing Judaean History in the Diaspora: Josephus's Accounts of Judas," in *Negotiating Diaspora: Jewish Strategies in the Roman Empire*, ed. John M. G. Barclay, LSTS 45 [London: T&T Clark, 2004], 90–108).

in Rome is an apologist for Roman rule *and* for that very civilization and its priestly aristocracy, while he blames the whole affair of the war and its outcome on lower class Roman officials and miscreant rebels.[97] In the face of accusations of misanthropy directed at Jews (*Ag. Ap.* 2.15, 34, 37 §§148, 236, 258), Josephus appeals to the admirable and unmatched devotion of Jews to their laws (*Ag. Ap.* 1.8 §§42–43; 2.38, 39 §§272, 277) and counters that Jews accept non-Jews who wish to adopt their customs and to live under their laws (*Ag. Ap.* 2.29, 37 §§209–210, 261) and that social separation for the sake of protecting cultural goods from being exposed to contempt or indifference is a virtue recognized and practiced by other peoples as well (*Ag. Ap.* 2.37–38 §§255–270, 209–210). Josephus may always have expected, or at least have hoped, that the temple cult in Jerusalem would soon be restored (*Ag. Ap.* 2.24 §§193–194).[98]

Nevertheless, I am in fundamental agreement with Miller that we should locate Mark's literary project in a region of cultural-political upheaval in the wake of a provoked war with Rome, responding to shrinking cultural and political options following the failure to secure either a successful polity of integration mediated by a Judean elite approved by Rome or greater autonomy for an enduring Judean state by that same Judean elite. A regional animus among non-Judean ethnic populations of southern Syria, especially in urban centers bordering the Roman province of Judea, threatened by what was perceived as Judean regional aggression, along with a mutual interest in reestablishing workable relations with neighbors and urgent calls by some Jews for stricter adherence to teachings promoting social separation should all be kept in view.[99] In the wake

---

97. This is not to deny that in the face of the destruction there were Jews who despaired of the power of a deity unable or unwilling to protect the deity's own temple and people and concluded that loyalty to erstwhile family practices, to Jewish institutions and traditions, had become incredible. For these Jews–and there may have been many–one might speak of the perception of a failed civilization. The problem of course is that the traces of such Jews are hardly visible if at all. For possible evidence of disaffected Jews, see below, n. 223.

98. Goodman, *Ruling Class of Judaea*, 232; Goodman, *Rome and Jerusalem: The Clash of Ancient Civilizations* (New York: Knopf, 2007), 426; and see Steven Weitzman, *Surviving Sacrilege*, 94–95, on the significance of the precedents cited by Josephus in the *Antiquities* of foreign rulers returning plundered temple vessels and helping rebuild the temple (11.1.3, 5.1 §§12–18, 123–130; 12.2.5, 3.3 §§40–84, 138–144).

99. Josephus describes in vivid terms and no doubt exaggerated scale the mutual slaughter of Jews and Syrians (often referred to as Greeks by Josephus) in the cities of

of a decimated Judean ruling class, and with no intention on Rome's part
to install others as native mediators of a semi-autonomous Judea,[100] those
who were exponents of particular teachings claiming religious expertise

---

the coastal plain, the Decapolis, and Syria in 66, in the time between the destruction
of the Roman garrison in Jerusalem and the setting out of the Roman general Cestius
Gallus from Antioch (*J.W.* 2.18.1–5 §§457–480; *Life* 25), and after the defeat of Cestius
Gallus outside Jerusalem (*J.W.* 2.20.2 §§560–561). The extremity of the situation for
Jews in most of these cities (Antioch, Sidon, Apamea, and Gerasa are noted as exceptions) is evident in that Jews who showed no revolutionary intentions were not spared,
and despite the fact that each city had its Jewish sympathizers ("Judaizers," as Josephus
refers to them, *J.W.* 2.18.2 §463). In Damascus, even the circumstance that most of
the wives of those plotting against the Jews had "converted to Judaism" did not save
the Jews of that city (*J.W.* 2.20.2 §§560–561 [Thackeray, LCL]). Josephus also reports
a change of fortune for Jews in Antioch from the time Vespasian arrived in Syria to
prosecute the war. Jews had large numbers of Greeks attracted to their religious practices in Antioch (*J.W.* 7.3.3 §45). The atmosphere changed dramatically when the son
of a Jewish magistrate in the city charged Jews with a plot to burn down the city. These
suspicions, which already infuriated the masses and had led to consigning some of the
accused to the flames and subjecting others to a test of sacrifice "after the manner of
the Greeks" (*J.W.* 7.3.3 §50 [Thackeray, LCL]), were exacerbated when later a fire did
break out burning down much of the center of the city. Accusations against the Jews
were investigated and proved false, but the climate did not improve (*J.W.* 7.3.4 §§54–
62). In 70, after the destruction of the Jerusalem temple when Titus came to Antioch
on his way to Egypt and return to Rome, the senate and people of Antioch petitioned
him to expel the Jews from the city, which he refused saying, "But their own country
to which, as Jews, they ought in that case to be banished, has been destroyed, and no
other place would now receive them" (*J.W.* 7.5.2 §109 [Thackeray, LCL]). Josephus
makes the further point that Titus also refused to revoke the right of Jews to their own
practices (*J.W.* 7.5.2 §§110–111). Whether this mutual hostility extends back to bitter
memories of Hasmonean expansion, it clearly was fueled by the prospects and circumstances of war in the region. But this is not the only picture Josephus presents of relations between Jews and Syrians. He also remarks about the especially large numbers
of Jews in Syria where the proximity of the countries has resulted in a more normal
intermingling (*J.W.* 7.3.3 §43) and where Jews and Syrians live side by side in several
of the villages of Agrippa II's kingdom (*J.W.* 3.3.5 §58).

   100. See Schwartz, *Imperialism and Jewish Society*, 111, and below, n. 103; Goodman, *Ruling Class of Judaea*, 231–33; Goodman, *Rome and Jerusalem*, 436–39; Goodman, *State and Society in Roman Galilee, A.D. 132–212*, 2nd ed. (London: Vallentine
Mitchell, 2000), xi–xii; and Junghwa Choi, *Jewish Leadership in Roman Palestine from
70 CE to 135 CE*, AGJU 83 (Leiden: Brill, 2013), 206–7, contra David Goodblatt, *The
Monarchic Principle: Studies in Jewish Self-Government in Antiquity* (Tübingen: Mohr
Siebeck, 1994), 219–20.

of one sort or another could continue to press their claims and programs,[101]

---

101. "That Pharisees, Sadducees and Essenes were still the main philosophies of Judaism in the nineties CE was of course explicitly asserted by Josephus in the *Antiquities* and in his *Vita*, and there is no reason whatsoever to read his account of the present state of Judaism as an historical report on Jewish philosophies which had ceased to exist" (Martin Goodman, "Religious Variety and the Temple in the Late Second Temple Period and its Aftermath," *JJS* 60 [2009]: 212). What had ceased was the "public stage on which such variety was visible" (211); see also, Goodman, "Sadducees and Essenes after 70 CE," in *Crossing the Boundaries: Essays in Biblical Interpretation in Honour of Michael D. Goulder*, ed. S. E. Porter, Paul Joyce and David E. Orton (Leiden: Brill, 1994), 347–56; repr. in Goodman, *Judaism in the Roman World: Collected Essays*, AGJU 66 (Leiden: Brill, 2007), 153–62.

It is unlikely that the continued presence of these "sects" or the beginnings of the formation of rabbinic teacher-disciple circles had any formal authority or jurisdiction in determining the civic law of the province of Judea or its environs, and perhaps not much influence on private religious practice either, in the wake of the destruction of the temple. In this connection, see Schwartz, *Imperialism and Jewish Society*, 103–61. Schwartz presents a minimalist reading of the rabbinic evidence for the place of the rabbis in Jewish society in the second and third centuries. He is not alone in this view, see Catherine Hezser, *The Social Structure of the Rabbinic Movement in Roman Palestine*, TSAJ 66 (Tübingen: Mohr Siebeck,1997); Shaye J. D. Cohen, "The Place of the Rabbi in Jewish Society of the Second Century," in *The Galilee in Late Antiquity*, ed. Lee I. Levine (New York: Jewish Theological Seminary, 1992), 157–73; Cohen, "The Rabbi in Second-Century Jewish Society," in *The Cambridge History of Judaism: The Early Roman Period*, ed. W. Horbury, W. D. Davies, and John Sturdy, vol. 3 of *The Cambridge History of Judaism*, ed. W. D. Davies and Louis Finkelstein (Cambridge: Cambridge University Press, 1999), 922–90, esp. 967–71: "In sum, the rabbis did not control the religious and civil life of second-century Palestinian Jewry" (971); Goodman, *State and Society in Roman Galilee*, 93–118; Choi, *Jewish Leadership in Roman Palestine*, 187–89; cf. Hayim Lapin, *Rabbis as Romans: The Rabbinic Movement in Palestine 100–400 C.E.* (Oxford: Oxford University Press, 2012), 38, "Traditions about the earliest phases and the prehistory of the rabbinic movement are already part of a project of retrospection.... Throughout our period, Rabbis were not a leadership group, but rather a coterie of like-minded inventors and transmitters of tradition. To the extent that we can say anything about Rabbis as a movement in the late first and early second centuries, their concerns are too specific, too bound up with matters of primary interest to pietists and ritual specialists, and quite possibly too 'sectarian' in orientation, to address the needs of anyone but a small group of committed members." Lapin considers some complex relationship with pre-70 Pharisees to be likely, but his emphasis is clearly on the embeddedness of the rabbinic movement in the changed circumstances of provincialization in the second and third centuries. There is something of a consensus that has emerged. In his review of books by Nicole Belayche, Seth Schwartz, and Daniel Boyarin, Stuart S. Miller acknowledges, though perhaps more

but Roman administration would now dominate in the region,[102] and

---

as a concession, "Certainly in the last quarter century, there has been an increased realization, both in Israel and in the United States, that the rabbis are only part of the larger story of Roman Palestine" (Stuart S. Miller, "Review Essay: Roman Imperialism, Jewish Self-Definition, and Rabbinic Society: Belayche's *Iudaea-Palaestina*, Schwartz's *Imperialism and Jewish Society*, and Boyarin's *Border Lines* Reconsidered," *AJSR* 31 [2007]: 337; and see Miller, *Sages and Commoners in Late Antique 'Erez Israel: A Philological Inquiry into Local Traditions in Talmud Yerushalmi*, TSAJ 111 [Tübingen: Mohr Siebeck, 2006]). Cf. Daniel R. Schwartz, "Introduction: Was 70 CE a Watershed in Jewish History? Three Stages of Modern Scholarship, and a Renewed Effort," in *Was 70 CE a Watershed in Jewish History? On Jews and Judaism before and after the Destruction of the Second Temple*, ed. Daniel R. Schwartz and Zeev Weiss in collaboration with Ruth A. Clements, AGJU 78 (Leiden: Brill, 2012), 1–19. The material evidence of continued practice of what is sometimes referred to as "household Judaism" after 70 should not be ignored, see Joshua Schwartz, "Yavne Revisited: Jewish 'Survival' in the Wake of the War of Destruction," in Tomson and Schwartz, *Jews and Christians in the First and Second Centuries*, 238–52, esp. 249–52, reflecting the views of Andrea Berlin, "Jewish Life before the Revolt: The Archaeological Evidence," *JSJ* 36 (2005): 417–70. However, in some respects this evidence of Jewish practice post-70 suggests a mirror image of what Seth Schwartz in *Imperialism and Jewish Society*, 40–42, 50–52, 71–73, has argued regarding continued private religious practices, in contrast to the organization and character of public spaces, among non-Judean ethnic groups incorporated under Hasmonean rule. In an earlier essay Schwartz compared the Hellenization of Palestine in the third and second centuries BCE, Judaization under the Hasmoneans in the second and first centuries BCE, Christianization in the fourth and fifth centuries and Islamicization in the seventh and eighth, and argued, "They all ... produced temporarily a gulf between public and private which served as the mechanism for preservation of elements of the older cultural systems, and, as the gulf narrowed, as the norms of public and the practices of private life were inevitably contaminated, for the incorporation and naturalization of old elements in the new systems" (Seth Schwartz, "The Hellenization of Jerusalem and Shechem," in *Jews in a Graeco-Roman World*, ed. Martin Goodman (Oxford: Oxford University Press, 1998), 38. The gulf was weaker in the case of Hellenization because the Macedonians, while patronizing Greek urban culture in the cities of the Near East had not, like the Romans later, "utilized this newly created urban culture as a way of holding their empire together" (ibid., 45; see above, 217–18).

102. Under the heading, "Vespasian: A New Near Eastern Empire," Fergus Millar writes: "Judaea became a one-legion province governed by a senator of praetorian rank, Commagene ceased to be a dependent kingdom and became part of the province of Syria, as (it seems clear) did the kingdom of Sohaemus of Emesa ... and Palmyra, whatever its relation to the province before, was now clearly tied to it.... It was at this moment, in the 70s, that after nearly a century and a half the Roman presence in the Near East ceased to be a bridgehead and came to resemble an integrated provincial and

traditional village landowners and local urban councilors would be in demand apart from priests and retainers authorized by a Jerusalem establishment.[103] For some who were familiar with sayings attributed to Jesus

---

military system.… Fragmentary as our evidence is, we can observe both an intensification and a considerable geographical expansion of the Roman presence. An important aspect of both was the replacement of royal rule … by Roman provincial rule. Two further stages of this process were soon to follow: the absorption of the kingdom of Agrippa II and then that of Nabataea" (Millar, *The Roman Near East, 31 BC–AD 337* [Cambridge: Harvard University Press, 1994], 80, 90).

103. "With the outbreak of the Jewish revolt against Rome in 66 C.E., five centuries of imperial support for the Temple, the Torah, and their human representatives, the priests and scribes, came to an end.… Throughout the Near East in the late first and early second centuries the emperors were replacing quasi-autonomous local rulers, the 'client kings,' with Roman officials, establishing 'colonies' (cities with more or less Greco-Roman constitutions and in some cases a citizen body that also enjoyed Roman citizenship and so favorable tax status), imposing direct taxation, and introducing judges (primarily the governors and their staff) who ruled by complicated, largely ad hoc mixtures of Roman, Greco-oriental, and local law" (Schwartz, *Imperialism and Jewish Society*, 105–06). For a different view, see Joan E. Taylor, *The Essenes, the Scrolls, and the Dead Sea* (Oxford: Oxford University Press, 2012). Taylor interprets the three *haireseis* of Josephus, the Pharisees, Essenes, and Sadducees, not as philosophical schools, but as schools of legal interpretation, i.e., legal societies. Taylor seems to me to conflate the public role of certain individuals Josephus identifies by these labels with the formal juridical authority of these "societies" as such. Her view that Rome gave formal sanction to Jewish law as the law of the land between 70 and 135, and that these legal societies provided the authorized leadership (170) also conflates different issues. The influence of Pharisees and Essenes on "a purity-focused Jewish life post-Temple" (169) is one thing; juridical authority in private and civic law is another. The relationship of Roman law in the province and the local indigenous private law operative in the evidence from the Babatha and Salome Komaise archives from the Dead Sea border areas of the Roman provinces of Arabia and Judea in the early second century is complex and disputed. But one cannot appeal to the documents of these archives for evidence of the functioning of Jewish courts in this area because there is none (see below, n. 222, on the archives). Furthermore, to judge from Josephus's descriptions of the philosophical and theological views of Pharisees, Essenes, and Sadducees, one cannot view these "societies" as strictly schools of legal interpretation; see Jonathan Klawans, *Josephus and the Theologies of Ancient Judaism* (Oxford: Oxford University Press, 2012). In his study of the models of Jewish leadership in the period 70–135 CE, Choi underlines the politically dependent nature of learned leadership before the destruction of the temple; afterwards, under direct Roman rule, there simply was no political basis to support a role of leadership (*Jewish Leadership in Roman Palestine*, 89–92, 186–89).

or who were tradents of Jesus traditions, a time for a more ambitious cultural production had come, beyond local oral and written traditions of the teachings and healings of Jesus, and not limited to the practices and goals of other itinerant entrepreneurs engaged in demonstrations of the divine *pneuma* of a prophetic or cosmic Christ—a time to imagine Jesus of Nazareth in his own time in an enlarged political frame now that Roman military power had been experienced up close, and to rethink his place in relation to an epic scriptural frame now that there was no temple there. The story of Jesus from the beginning would of course have to be set in a time when there was still a temple there.

3. Making a Difference on the Date of Mark

Miller does not give a specific date for the writing of Mark, but it is clear that the destruction of Jerusalem is presupposed. His reference to the social-political-religious critique registered by the Gospel of Mark is nevertheless focused on the radical separatist tendencies of a prewar Judaism that led to what is seen as an altogether unnecessary war. This focus on prewar conditions, on Mark's knowledge of conditions in Judea (and/or in Syria or Rome) during the war, especially messianic and apocalyptic expectations evoked by the war, and on persecution or the threat of persecution experienced by followers of Jesus in the years 66–74 encompassing the war is typical of Markan scholarship. Even for those who think the gospel was most likely written after the destruction of the temple, the significance of the event is focused on its relation to the coming of the Son of Man. The concerns of the author and his readers prove to be hardly different than they are for those who think the gospel was written before the destruction of the temple.[104] This is not to mention influence on the dating of Mark that

---

104. So, for example, Theissen, *The Gospels in Context*, 258–71, suggests a date "probably after the capture of the temple in August 70 and before all military activities and events in the immediate aftermath of the war had ceased" (271). But the only point that Theissen makes requiring a post-August 70 date for the composition of Mark depends on his interpretation of Mark 13:14 as a reuse by the author of a prophecy dating back 30 years to the time of Caligula's threatened placement of his statue in the temple. The text in its Markan context is said to refer to the threat that Rome would establish a cult on the site of the destroyed temple (259–60, 262–64). Otherwise, most of the evidence Theissen brings could be accommodated to a pre-August 70 date. There is no direct evidence for such a Roman intention just after 70, although such fears do seem realistic enough, especially if one is thinking of a cult for the use

of Roman soldiers of the *legio X Fretensis* now headquartered in Jerusalem. But the main concern of the Romans in the early 70s was clearly pacification of the region. In any case, the major point for Theissen is to show that "Mark's Gospel is marked by the proximity of war, both in its chronology and in its content" (271; but also see below, n. 106). Joel Marcus, *Mark 1–8: A New Translation with Introduction and Commentary*, AB 27 (New Haven: Yale University Press, 2000), 39, assigns dates as early as 69 and as late as 74–75 (see also, Marcus, "The Jewish War and the *Sitz im Leben* of Mark," *JBL* 111 [1992]: 441–62, where he specifies a date shortly after the destruction of the temple in 70 [460]). But all of the evidence that Marcus draws on to situate the writing of Mark refer to events or circumstances that are prior to the war or during the war, and do not have to presuppose the destruction of the temple. Brian J. Incigneri, *The Gospel to the Romans: The Setting and Rhetoric of Mark's Gospel*, BibInt 65 (Leiden: Brill, 2004), has constructed an elaborate, multifaceted argument to demonstrate that Mark was written for the situation of Christians in Rome in 71, shortly after Titus's return and the victory procession in Rome. However, despite the postdestruction date, what is clearly most important for understanding the situation is what Incigneri describes as the experience of trauma and continued threat hanging over Christians in Rome in the wake of the Neronian persecution. The Flavian propaganda marking the end of the civil struggles in Rome and the end of the war in Judea are thought to have made the situation even more alarming, especially for Jewish Christians in Rome. H. N. Roskam, *The Purpose of the Gospel of Mark in Its Historical and Social Context*, NovTSup 114 (Leiden: Brill, 2004), takes a strong position on a postdestruction date early in the 70s in her reading of Mark 13 (81–94). But her view that Mark is an apologetic for the nonpolitical aims of Jesus in a situation of persecution of a Markan community in Galilee is linked to an assumption about a Jewish leadership concerned to keep the peace and turn troublemakers over to prevent violent responses from the Romans. Apart from situations in Alexandria and in Cyrene just after 70, the evidence for Jewish leaders taking initiative against individuals viewed as troublemakers comes from situations prior to the war and the destruction of the temple. After 70, Rome did not recognize any Judean leadership with authority to represent the native population across the province, and Roman officials were now directly responsible for affairs in the province of Judea, including Galilee, apart from the territory along the western side of the lake still part of Agrippa II's mostly non-Jewish realm. Moreover, what Josephus highlights in the mid-60s at the time of the threat of war and the beginning of hostilities is the plight of Jews in Syrian cities, even if they demonstrated their lack of sympathy for the war in Judea. Apologetics did not help. While pacification of the region would have been a major Roman concern after the sacking of Jerusalem and the destruction of the temple, there is no evidence of persecution of Jews in Galilee by Roman officials after the war. Roskam herself acknowledges that we can only speak of Mark's perception or expectation of persecution. Nor "does Mark make plain precisely why the Christian faith provokes persecution" (73). (See Zeba Crook, a review of *The Gospel to the Romans: The Setting and Rhetoric of Mark's Gospel*, by Brian J. Incigneri, and *The Purpose of the Gospel of Mark in Its Historical and Social Context*, by H. N. Roskam, *RBL* [2006]: http://tinyurl.com/SBL4520a). In sum, a predestruction or post-destruction date has made little difference in the formulation of the issues to which

stems from research aimed at uncovering Mark's sources and evidence for the historical Jesus. But if one supposes that the destruction of the temple is an event of the past for Mark, why should one necessarily suppose a date very close to 70? Why not suppose 80–85? To propose a date a decade later than 70–75 is not to exclude the use of sources that go back before the war. Nor is it to deny that the years that span the war are within the purview of the author and significant for Mark 13 and Mark's Gospel as a whole or to reject the dependence of Matthew and Luke on Mark. It is rather to suggest that Mark's more contemporizing and urgent presentation of war-time scenarios is not evidence that the general context and issues for the writer and his readers are significantly different than they are for the more distanced and historicized presentations of Matthew and Luke. I maintain that the generative context of these issues was contention over responses to the physical devastation and displacement created by the war, the loss of the political and cultural center of Jewish society, and with it a much weakened position in regional struggles with neighbors, the further dominance of the province of Syria in the region, the increased Roman presence in the eastern provinces and direct military rule in Palestine, the social stigma of defeat in war, and Flavian propaganda and policy. In particular, I am proposing that the plot of Mark's story reflects the author's decision to link the death of Jesus and the destruction of the temple.[105] Mark's com-

---

Mark's Gospel was responding, as long as the suggested dates fall within the span of the war years, 66–74, with issues revolving around messianic and apocalyptic expectations and persecution or the threat of persecution viewed as the primary concerns of the Markan context.

105. In *The Kingdom in Mark: A New Place and a New Time* (Philadelphia: Fortress, 1974), Kelber also views the destruction of Jerusalem and the temple as a major impetus for the composition of Mark's Gospel and treats the linking of the death of Jesus and the destruction of the temple as a central theme. But in this book and in subsequent writings, Kelber understands the Markan plot as a response not only to the trauma of the destruction but also in the context of a *traditionsbruch*, an internal rupture within the Jesus movement in response to the trauma of Jesus's death and the demise of the oral tradents (of the Jerusalem church) who before 70 had shaped the memory tradition of the earliest community. Kelber comments on his approach to the passion narrative: "My own work on Mark's passion narrative proceeded from the issue of trauma. As controlled as the plot appears on the surface, it struggles with the dreadful task of absorbing Jesus' execution, the destruction of the temple (a theme closely intertwined with Jesus' own story), and the demise of the disciples" ("The Oral-Scribal-Memorial Arts," 256). By way of contrast, I am not inclined to associate Mark's passion narrative with the memory work of an author or a community suffering three

position constructs this entanglement in the interest of what we from our greater distance can think of as a particular response to a postdestruction era. Thus, my intention in proposing a somewhat later date for Mark is a change of perspective in conceptualizing the social interests and social logic of the writing. Not the gospel's relation to sources whose origin preceded the war, nor its reflection only on the time of the war, but the Gospel of Mark as a response in a neighboring area of Syria to the *consequences* of a failed policy of Roman-Judean collaboration and a failed Judean revolt.[106]

---

traumas (however, for more on Mark and trauma, see below, nn. 187, 189, and 381). Rather, I would appeal to the rhetorical strategies for rectifying situational incongruity of an author operating in a broader cultural climate. Nor would I describe the relationship of the death of Jesus and the destruction of the temple in Mark as exclusively causal, as Kelber seems to do, even if he also acknowledges that Jesus cannot be the agent of destruction as expressed in Mark 14:58 and 15:29: "Jesus anticipated, even precipitated, the temple conflagration, and in part it was in the process of his mission against the temple that he was destroyed himself" (Kelber, "The Oral-Scribal-Memorial Arts," 258); cf. Kelber, "Conclusion: From Passion Narrative to Gospel," in *The Passion in Mark: Studies on Mark 14–16*, ed. Werner H. Kelber (Philadelphia: Fortress, 1976), 171.

106. In *The Religion of the Earliest Churches: Creating a Symbolic World*, trans. John Bowden (Minneapolis: Fortress, 1999), Gerd Theissen attributes a much more significant role to the destruction of the temple in accounting for Mark's Gospel (in comparison to the treatment in his earlier work, *The Gospels in Context*). He states explicitly, "Certainly the destruction of the temple was one of the factors prompting the composition of the oldest Gospel." However, this is tied directly to the fulfillment of Jesus's prophecy of the destruction of the temple. "Would not this confirmation lead to reflection on his message generally, and necessarily call attention to his past history—and not just to the one who would come in a future parousia?" Christians mourned the destruction of the temple but experienced it as confirmation of Jesus's message. In a similar way, Theissen argues that the destruction brings about the creation of a ritual sign system independent of Judaism. "After the loss of the temple it was even more necessary than before to lay a foundation for their own ritual system," thus the significance of baptism and eucharist and the distancing from Jewish rituals in Mark. In each case, the new occasion presented by the destruction is seen by Theissen to be linked not just to Mark's literary construction of the past but to an earlier history (173). It is the same for Jesus's divine status. The earliest gospel message was that Jesus's divinity was proclaimed as an act of God, the resurrection. Mark retrojects this status back to Jesus's lifetime, but though he lets his divinity be seen within the narrative, it is only accepted without qualification by the character of God in the narrative (172). It is not surprising that Theissen observes that this assessment of Mark's Gospel "would change only a little" if it was written immediately before 70 in anticipation of the temple's destruction (353 n. 15). It is hard to imagine both mourning the temple's

Positions on the date of Mark mostly come down to judgments about Mark 13 as the only evidence that is relevant for dating the gospel, especially Jesus's prophecy of the destruction of the temple in verse 2bc, οὐ μὴ ἀφεθῇ ὧδε λίθος ἐπὶ λίθον ὃς οὐ μὴ καταλυθῇ, a saying that clearly could not have been transmitted without an appropriate context. Mark's editorial hand is generally acknowledged by commentators in the formulation of 13:1–2, so unlike what is often argued on other passages in Mark 13, these verses cannot be thought to preserve a pre-Markan tradition that has been left unchanged. Moreover, as John Kloppenborg has shown, verse 2bc is not just a general prediction of the destruction of the temple, but a specific formulation of destruction which reflects the knowledge of the Roman ritual of *evocatio*, the calling out of the tutelary deity from a temple before the temple and city are devoted to destruction (*devotio*) and its inhabitants killed or taken captive.[107] Mark 13:2bc is a prophecy of *devotio*, presupposing an earlier ritual of *evocatio* "as part of the toolkit of Roman siege tactics."[108] The specificity of the prophecy and its conformity to what actually happened give the impression that it has been formulated after the event.[109] However, Kloppenborg's conclusion that this impression is in fact the case is not based on the close conformity of the prophecy to the event.

---

destruction and putting a new ritual system in its place immediately after or even before the event without overdetermining the outcome on the basis of its continuity with the past of the historical Jesus and the earliest Christians.

107. Kloppenborg, "*Evocatio deorum*," 434–41. On evidence of Markan redaction of the framework of 13:1–2ab, see pp. 429, 447 with nn. 32, 84. Referencing Gustafsson's work (*Evocatio Deorum*, 80; see above, n. 93), Kloppenborg notes, "From the Roman standpoint…, the *evocatio* did not necessarily imply transport to Rome" (Kloppenborg, "*Evocatio deorum*," 449 n. 89).

108. Kloppenborg, "*Evocatio deorum*," 441. Kloppenborg believes that Josephus gives an indication that the ritual was performed when he tells the rebels that "the Deity has fled from the holy places and taken his stand on the side of those with whom you are now at war" (443, citing *J.W.* 5.9.4 §412). The long historical harangue which Josephus directs at the rebels, while he is dodging their missiles, is presented of course not as confirmation of the Roman theology of *evocatio deorum*, but as impending doom from the Deuteronomistic perspective of judgment for their own crimes against the Deity.

109. Regarding the position of those who argue that the prophecy does not conform to the event, Kloppenborg counters that the argument "seems needlessly pedantic. Titus's destruction of Jerusalem was thorough and Josephus's own statement [*J.W.* 7.1.1 §1] suggests that Mark 13:2 would have served as a generally credible summary of what occurred" (ibid., 432).

In fact, he believes that Mark 13:2 is a recasting of Q 13:35a, ἰδοὺ ἀφίεται ὑμῖν ὁ οἶκος ὑμῶν. "Mark 13:2 presupposes what Q 13:35a states expressly, that the deity has abandoned the 'house' (= temple)."[110] Both sayings could have circulated prior to the destruction of the temple. Rather, his conclusion is based on considerations of the difference "between omens and rituals that (allegedly) occurred before the events, and their literary and historiographic use in narrative."[111] Whatever might have been expected or performed in the context of the Roman-Judean war, or in the expectation of war, the act of narration, and the values, ideologies, and themes represented therein, depended on knowledge of the realization of these expectations. Though Mark is not expressing Rome's ideology of empire, his narration of Jesus's prophecy of destruction "is better seen as a retrospective comment on that destruction, just as the uses of omens, portents, and reports of the desertion of towns by their tutelary deities serve as topoi of Roman historiography."[112] Kloppenborg's reasoning here seems to me the most persuasive argument for a post-70 dating of the Gospel of Mark. Connecting the life and death of Jesus some forty years earlier with the destruction of the temple, and not only by way of a prophecy, set that life and death in relation to a widely known about, even notorious, event, that is, on a world historical stage.

This conclusion does not amount to dismissing a text like Q 13:35a or the evocation of destruction in the early 60s by the peasant prophet, Jesus ben Hananiah, in the story told by Josephus (*J.W.* 6.5.3 §§300–309), as postfactum rationalizations. According to Kloppenborg, "one can surmise that anyone who had knowledge of the practices of *evocatio* and *devotio* … could have concluded from the events, say, of 66–69 CE, that the total destruction of the temple would not only be possible, but would be a nearly inevitable consequence of war."[113] I agree that one cannot exclude the possibility of such prophecies on the grounds that the destruction of the temple was completely unforeseeable. But, as we have already seen, to suppose that prophecies of destruction were generated by a sense of the nearly inevitable consequence of war with Rome is misleading to the

---

110. Two other texts have also been suggested as the source for Mark 13:2: Mark 14:58 and Luke 19:43–44a.

111. Kloppenborg, "*Evocatio deorum*," 446.

112. Ibid., 449. Similarly, William E. Arnal, "Mark, War, and Creative Imagination," 475 n. 206 (in this volume), drawing on Kloppenborg, "*Evocatio deorum*."

113. Kloppenborg, "*Evocatio deorum*," 442.

extent that it uncritically reproduces Josephus's own view of the matter in the *Judean War*. "Josephus has told us all the reasons why the Jews should not have gone to war with the Romans.... The message is clear: it was a war in which the Jews were doomed from the start."[114]

---

114. James S. McLaren, "Going to War against Rome: The Motivation of the Jewish Rebels," in *The Jewish Revolt against Rome: Interdisciplinary Perspectives*, ed. Mladen Popović, JSJSup 154 (Leiden: Brill, 2011), 129. This essay represents McLaren's first attempt to follow up the theme of his earlier book regarding the central problem for modern historians' use of Josephus: the larger interpretative framework of his writings. See McLaren, *Turbulent Times? Josephus and Scholarship on Judaea in the First Century CE*, JSPSup 29 (Sheffield: Sheffield Academic, 1998). He does not seek to provide a neutral perspective in describing the decision to go to war but to present it from the perspective of those who supported the decision as a war of independence (129 n. 1). He builds on the work of David M. Rhoads, *Israel in Revolution 6–74 C.E.: A Political History Based on the Writings of Josephus* (Philadelphia: Fortress, 1976), who approached the motivation of the Jewish combatants by reversing Josephus's polemic, but McLaren seeks to extract further information from Josephus by attending to the series of actions taken by the combatants early in the war and assessing the repeated references to "freedom" in the *Judean War* (133–41). The main focus of the essay is on what can be learned from the material remains of the war: documents and coins (142–49). The minting of its own coins is especially significant to McLaren: "The ability to mint coinage was the domain of Rome to allocate.... The decision to start minting coinage for use in the new state symbolised an end to dependence on foreign coinage, a rejection of Rome" (148). McLaren's description of the motivation of the rebels to create an independent state is problematic in some ways, since it can imply a notion of political sovereignty more appropriate for the modern world of nations than for the world of provincials in an ancient empire. As Weitzman has argued in distinguishing the conditions of modern nationalism from the political goals that come to expression in the world depicted in 2 Maccabees, the story shows "how the Jews and their temple achieved what many other cities were after in this period: the Seleucids' recognition of their temple's inviolability; release from taxes and other obligations; the right to mint coins; and permission to publically declare themselves 'free'" (Steven Weitzman, "On the Political Relevance of Antiquity: A Response to David Goodblatt's *Elements of Ancient Jewish Nationalism*," *Jewish Social Studies: History, Culture, Society* 14 [2008], 171). The fact that in our case factions of the Judean elite acted on their own both to commence military hostilities against Rome and to establish a new political status in defiance of Rome does not mean that we should think of the goal as political sovereignty in a world of modern nations rather than the achievement ultimately of recognition of a new and heightened status and place within the empire, that is, an increase in autonomy. Indeed, in another essay, McLaren himself has asked the reader to imagine "the type of narrative Josephus would construct if the revolt had concluded with increased Jewish autonomy" ("Delving into the Dark Side," 66). For a view of the

Common to the discussion of why a seemingly forlorn war was entered into has been the enduring influence of Josephus' interpretative framework.… However, the material remains from the war highlight the importance of not allowing the post-war reconstruction of Josephus to control our investigation.… In hindsight, for Josephus there was good reason to view the war as a futile cause and there was also a convenience in being able to blame it on misguided radical hopes of divine assistance.[115]

Not only does the evidence suggest that ending the sacrifices in the temple on behalf of Rome was a considered decision bringing together a number of factions in Jerusalem and followed by a series of actions designed to establish a state in defiance of Rome and to defend it, but there were also reasons later in the war to suppose that Rome was not inclined to undertake a siege of Jerusalem. The slow progress of the war in 68 and 69 from the point of view of an immediate threat to Jerusalem could have been seen as uncertainty about the prosecution of the war in Judea because of the civil war in Rome and Vespasian's preoccupation with the principate. Even the brutality of Rome's pacification of Galilee and the Judean countryside, razing towns and killing and enslaving many noncombatants, could have been seen, perhaps correctly, by those in Jerusalem engaged in a struggle for power and popular support, as terror tactics intended to bring about submission without having to engage in a siege of Jerusalem. None of the civil strife in Jerusalem was about whether the war was worth pursuing.[116] The continuation of the temple service uninterrupted until

---

motivations to go to war with Rome having less to do with defiance of Rome than with the weakening of the position of Judeans in competition and conflict with neighbors in the region, see Mason, "Why Did Judaeans Go to War with Rome in 66–67 CE?" Further on the causes of the war, see below, n. 171.

115. McLaren, "Going to War against Rome," 151. "As much as Josephus has encouraged us to do so, there is no need to seek distinctive factors, such as extremist ideologies or radical aspirations or hopes of divine assistance, in order to explain the decision to go to war in 66 C.E. Like many other people that have started a war, the Jews were simply optimistic that they would succeed.… They were not the first group of people in history to make that assessment nor were they last to think they would win a war that was eventually lost" (153).

116. "Confirmation that the ruling class remained deeply involved to the end may be found in Titus' attitude to the Jews after the war. His triumph was held for a victory over *all* Judaea, not just a rebellious section or class of the population. The Judaean ruling class was deprived of its land and power. Many were crucified or enslaved, and all survivors (and all Jews outside Judaea) were subjected to the ignominy of the *fiscus*

the last days of the war also suggests cooperation among the factions and their supporters. The Passover pilgrims in 70 who ended being caught up in the siege (*J. W.* 6.421) does not suggest an anticipation of the destruction of the temple and the city even at that late date, let alone its inevitability.[117]

> The rebels certainly did not expect to fail. Even in A.D. 70 a success-ful siege seemed impossible. With vast food supplies if they had been carefully rationed, the population could last out for years. The Romans outside the walls suffered from a lack of water and some of them even deserted to the Jews (Cassius Dio 65.5.2–4). Even less in A.D. 66 could anyone reasonably have expected the vigour and disregard for the lives of his troops with which Titus captured the city by direct assault: in con-trast to his father or Cestius Gallus, Titus was spurred on to victory by the sudden need of his family, so unexpectedly raised to the principate, to win a famous triumph to glorify their name.[118]

4. Two Jesuses and the Portents of Doom

There is no more portentous expression of doom than Josephus's story of the prophet Jesus ben Hananiah. But the prophet and his oracle are not so much an expression of the inevitability of war with Rome and its out-come. Rather, the initial setting of the story in 62, four years before the war began, "when the city was enjoying profound peace and prosperity" (*J. W.* 6.5.3 §300), suggests the topos of the true prophet who warns of doom in conditions that seem to forecast the opposite, in contrast to the false prophet who deceives the people with promises of deliverance even as the temple is burning, carrying to a climax of deception and destruction the work of many false prophets who had deceived the people throughout the period (*J. W.* 6.5.2 §§285–286). The people believed the messages of the false prophets and ignored the fearful portents that had occurred (6.5.3 §§288–300), the last of which Josephus reports as the story of Jesus ben Hananiah and his daily repeated dirge over seven years until finally he was killed during the siege by a stone hurled from a catapult (6.5.3 §§300–309). This Jesus too had been arrested by some of the leading citizens, received

---

Iudaicus, regardless of their economic or social background" (Goodman, *Ruling Class of Judaea*, 200–201).

117. Ibid., 176–83.
118. Ibid., 177–78.

blows, and was brought to the Roman governor, who had him scourged and then released, judging him to be a maniac.

In a monograph comparing the story of Jesus of Nazareth in Jerusalem and the story of Jesus ben Hananiah in Jerusalem, Ted Weeden Sr. has occasion to draw on Kloppenborg's discussion of the Roman ritual of *evocatio* to argue that Josephus has himself composed the series of portents and prodigies as a theology of *evocatio*, obviously not in order to demonstrate the effectiveness of the Roman ritual, but to show that God had decided to abandon the temple because of the tyranny, false prophecy, and bloodshed of the rebels. The final portent, the oracle of Jesus-Ananias (Weeden's shortened form for Jesus ben Hananiah) against the city, the temple, and the people represents the *devotio*.[119] Thus, Weeden does not view the oracle of Jesus-Ananias as a real warning in the early 60s "regarding the precarious political situation of Jerusalem" but as an invention of Josephus, who saw both the prophet and himself as a latter-day Jeremiah.[120]

Weeden's discussion of *evocatio deorum* comes in the epilogue of his monograph, the main text of which was presented to members of the

---

119. Theodore J. Weeden Sr., "Two Jesuses, Jesus of Nazareth and Jesus of Jerusalem: Provocative Parallels and Imaginative Imitation," *Forum* NS 6 (2003): 137–332. Weeden discusses the entire composition of Josephus's digression (*J.W.* 6.5.2–4 §§285–315), labeling 6.5.2–3 §§285–288, the Deuteronomistic introduction; 6.5.3 §§289–299, the *evocatio*; 6.5.3 §§300–309, the *devotio*; and 6.5.4 §§310–315, the Deuteronomistic conclusion (313–18). Josephus's list of prodigies overlap with those found in Tacitus, *Hist.* 5.13. In accepting the view that Tacitus is dependent on Josephus for the overlap, Weeden is following the arguments of Tessa Rajak, *Josephus: The Historian and His Society* (London: Duckworth, 1983), 193–94 with n. 18, and Steve Mason, "Josephus, Daniel and the Flavian House," in *Josephus and the History of the Greco-Roman Period: Essays in Memory of Morton Smith*, ed. F. Parente and J. Sievers (Leiden: Brill, 1994), 188–89; and see Mason's full discussion of Josephus's account of his surrender, his knowledge of Daniel 7, the ambiguous oracle found in the sacred writings (*J.W.* 6.5.4 §§312–315), and Tacitus's reference to the oracle (*Hist.* 5.13), ibid., 184–90.

120. Weeden, "Two Jesuses," 300–4, 309–12, 318–25. The words in quotations are cited by Weeden (313) from Kloppenborg, "*Evocatio deorum*," 442. Weeden is by no means the first scholar to recognize Josephus's personal identification with the figure of Jeremiah (300). Even Josephus's account of the death of Jesus-Ananias is suspiciously close to his description of the circumstances of his own near-death experience (*J.W.* 5.13.3 §§541–542; 5.9.3 §362). One can make as strong a case for Josephus's identification with Daniel (see Klawans, *Josephus and the Theologies of Ancient Judaism*, 193–94).

Jesus Seminar in October, 2003.[121] The original form of the argument was
that the Q redactor (Q 13:34–35), the authors of Mark, Luke, and John,
independent of each other, all drew on the oracle of Jesus-Ananias from
a story transmitted orally as part of the lore about the war.[122] Moreover,
according to Weeden, both stories belonged to the genre of the persecuted
righteous/innocent one, a wisdom tale which included vindication.[123] The
story circulated after the war, and Weeden's main thesis is that the Jewish
and Roman trials found in the gospels, as well as parallels in other scenes
in Jerusalem, are examples of the practice of literary mimesis based on
the story of Jesus-Ananias.[124] Weeden's response to a criticism that it was
unlikely that an obscure peasant would serve as a model for mimesis rather
than a well known biblical prophet like Jeremiah occasioned a revision of
the thesis found in the epilogue.[125] There he makes the case that all these
texts have been influenced by the biblical figure of Jeremiah, including
Jesus-Ananias.[126] Josephus created the figure of Jesus-Ananias to serve as a
kind of alter ego in patterning both the prophet and himself after the figure
of Jeremiah.[127] So, Weeden concludes that the New Testament texts are all
directly dependent on the text of Josephus. In an addendum to the main
body of the text, he had argued for Caesarea Philippi as the most likely
place to locate Mark.[128] Now, in the epilogue, he makes a case for Mark's
access to book 6 of *Judean War* through the channels of Agrippa II and the
Jewish community in that city. This would mean that the Gospel of Mark
and the redaction of Q could not have been written before the early 80s.[129]

Weeden has presented an impressive list of parallels between Jesus of
Nazareth in Jerusalem and Jesus-Ananias in Jerusalem in a Greco-Roman
environment in which the penchant for mimetic writing was a central
feature of literary production.[130] The original thesis argued for an orally

---

121. Weeden, "Two Jesuses," 287–332 (the epilogue).
122. Ibid., 137–276, the main body of the text.
123. Ibid., 161–66.
124. Ibid., 272–76.
125. Ibid., 287–88.
126. Ibid., 289–309.
127. Ibid., 309–325.
128. Ibid., 277–86.
129. Ibid. 325–32; for the date, see 328 with n. 78.
130. Ibid., 138–52. On the methodological criteria for determining Greco-Roman
textual *mimesis*, see ibid., 189–91, following criteria developed by MacDonald, *The Homeric Epics and the Gospel of Mark*, 4–9.

transmitted story, a piece of lore about Jerusalem and the war, circulating after the war.[131] On the basis of this thesis, we have to imagine that the redactor of Q, the authors of Mark, Luke, and John had independent access to this story with no other evidence of its circulation outside the text of Josephus.[132] To imagine this, one has to suppose wide circulation of the story, which would probably mean that there were different versions. Yet, much of Weeden's argument for dependence requires the particular details of Josephus's text.[133] The reworking of the thesis to demonstrate that all of these texts have made use of LXX Jeremiah I consider to be the firmest part of the thesis. But to an extent, this very demonstration weakens the argument of direct dependence on Josephus's story of Jesus-Ananias, including Q 13:35a, which could have used LXX Jer 12:7a, Ἐγκαταλέλοιπα τὸν οἶκόν μου, ἀφῆκα τὴν κληρονομίαν μου, as a model. Weeden's appeal to five parallels between Mark's Jesus and Josephus's Jesus-Ananias that cannot be accounted for on the basis of conventional penal processes can all be explained, I think, on the basis of independent access to Jeremiah.[134] Obviously, what cannot be explained by appeal to Jeremiah is the transfer to Roman authority in both texts, but just here one encounters a crucial Markan verb not encountered in the Jesus-Ananias account.[135] In any case, the Jesus-Ananias tale and the Markan passion narrative both are said to draw on the wisdom story of the righteous/innocent one, which features many examples of endangerment from a foreign empire. I find persuasive Weeden's case for Josephus as the creator of the portents and prodigies, including the last portent, the one regarding Jesus-Ananias. Portents regularly accompany wars, and sometimes are imagined and used in order to boost the morale of troops or noncombatants caught up in the conflict. But they are often found in literary works, including histories, and, as Kloppenborg maintains, their value as a literary topos presupposes retrospective reflection.[136] I am less persuaded by Weeden's argument for independent access to book 6 of the *Judean War*. One wonders why Matthew shows no independent access to the Jesus-Ananias story, even

---

131. Weeden, "Two Jesuses," 188–89.
132. See ibid., 200–201.
133. The criteria for determining *mimesis* work better where written texts are accessible.
134. See Weeden, "Two Jesuses," 159–60.
135. On *paradidonai* in Mark, see Mack, *Myth of Innocence*, 298–99, 304–5.
136. See above, 259.

though his gospel has the strongest links to Jeremiah,[137] while the Gospel of John, apparently without dependency on Jeremiah,[138] shows parallels to the story of Jesus-Ananias. Luke has the strongest case, because unlike Mark and John, Luke-Acts may show dependence on Josephus in other materials.[139] On Mark's access to book 6 of the *Judean War* in Caesarea Philippi among Herodians, Pharisees, and an observant Jewish community, one might ask why Mark would be inclined to believe what he read in the work of a Jerusalem priest, or why he would have an interest or opportunity to look into material presumably thought to support the interests of Herodians and Pharisees, who are projected back into the Galilee of Jesus as his opponents.[140]

5. The Death of Jesus and the Destruction of the Temple in Mark

Although I believe there are reasons to doubt that any of these oracles (Q 13:35a, Mark 13:2, the oracle of Jesus ben Hananiah) circulated prior to the destruction of the temple and that expressions of the inevitability of the outcome of the decision to go to war with Rome are more appropriately viewed as expressions of the certainty of hindsight, combining mantic and historiographic practices, I am in complete agreement with Kloppenborg's assessment of the significance of Mark 13:2 in Mark's narrative: "Mark 13:2 reflects the distinctive perspective of Mark, who created a 'dual narrative' that related the fate of Jesus at the hands of his priestly opponents and Pilate's soldiers, and the fate of the temple and its city."[141] The bracketing of Jesus's disruption in the temple (11:15–19) with the cursing of the fig tree (11:12–21, 27–34), the fate of the tenants in the parable (12:1–12), the darkening of the sky and tearing of the temple's veil (15:33, 38) as Jesus

137. Weeden, "Two Jesuses," 306.
138. Ibid., 307 n. 47.
139. Ibid., 211 n. 5.
140. Ibid., 331. On the Herodians as Essenes, see Taylor, *The Essenes, the Scrolls, the Dead Sea*, 109–30.
141. Kloppenborg, "*Evocatio deorum*," 449. By citing Kloppenborg's description of the Markan plot as a dual narrative, I do not intend to suggest a two-level narrative, as some scholars have interpreted the Gospel of John. The scenes in Mark are not consistently coded with a significance for Jesus's time and a significance for the time and circumstances of the writer and his readers. It is rather a question of characterizing and accounting for the fated intersection of the death of Jesus and a future event of geopolitical significance.

dies on the cross are all omens of the coming destruction. "In this way Mark creates a narrative in which the fate of Jesus is correlated with the destruction of the temple."[142] I would maintain that the entire plot of the gospel is constructed with this correlation in view.[143] The death of Jesus seals the fate of the temple and with it the fate of the Jerusalem and temple elite who reject his authority and seek his death. The rending of the temple curtain is surely to be understood in connection with Jesus's prophecy of the destruction of the temple.[144] But the rending, whether read as a cosmic disclosure linked to the disclosure at Jesus's baptism,[145] or seen as a sign of vindication of Jesus's judgment on the temple authorities,[146] or imagined as an *evocatio sacrorum*,[147] also signifies that the torn social fabric of

---

142. Ibid.

143. Jesus's entrance into Galilee begins with the teaching event in the synagogue of Capernaum (Mark 1:21–28); his entrance into Jerusalem begins with the teaching event of the temple cleansing (11:15–18). The first round of teaching in Galilee ends with the plot to destroy Jesus (Mark 3:6); the second round of teaching in Jerusalem ends with the destruction of the tenants in the parable (12:9) and the prophecy of the temple's destruction (13:2). See Mack, *Myth of Innocence*, 273–75. The temple act not only functions as the provocation for the arrest of Jesus; it is also "pivotal to the integration of all three narrative themes [formed in earlier parts of the narrative]: the crowds, the leaders, and the disciples" (275).

144. Ibid., "The anti-temple theme is present in much of the material. It is the reason for the taunts and the focus of the miracles. Jesus' death is the sign of the end of the temple's time. The rending of the temple curtain anticipates the destruction of the temple in 70 C.E. There is no other sense to be made of the concentration of suggestions than that the reader associate the two events" (297).

145. Kloppenborg, "*Evocatio deorum*," 428 n. 30: "The uses of ἐσχίσθη (*passivum divinum*) and ἀπ᾽ ἄνωθεν ἕως κάτω point to God's judgment and action. The conjunction of σχίζειν and the confession of Jesus as 'son of God' (15:39) recall the baptismal scene (1:9–11)." Jesus's final cry and expiration effecting the tearing of the temple curtain has also been viewed as a kind of exorcism: "So the symbolism at the crucifixion is compounded of both cosmic myth and inverted exorcism. The exit of God's spirit from Jesus and the world is marked by a prodigy signifying destruction" (Mack, *Myth of Innocence*, 287). For an analysis of the rich connections between the baptism, transfiguration, and crucifixion scenes in Mark, see Arnal, "Mark, War, and Creative Imagination," 415–24. The argument for identifying the temple curtain in Mark 15:38 as the outer curtain of the temple and not the inner curtain is not as strong as Arnal supposes, basing himself on the views of David Ulansey, "The Heavenly Veil Torn: Mark's Cosmic *Inclusio*," *JBL* 110 (1991): 124–25; cf. Collins, *Mark*, 759–64.

146. Weeden, "Two Jesuses," 206–7 with n. 30.

147. Miller, "Mark's Empty Tomb," 771.

Jewish society represented by the destruction of the temple corresponds to the torn social fabric of a kingdom society represented by the flight of the disciples and the destruction of the body of Jesus.[148] The death of Jesus and the destruction of the temple in Mark are therefore parallel as well as intersecting events.

The importance is not that Mark's story necessarily represents the earliest instance of connecting the two events. The *Sophia* oracles, Q 11:49–51; 13:34–35 // Matt 23:34–39, make a similar connection. But Q never refers directly to Jesus's death, never singles it out as the reason for judgment (see also Q 6:22–23). The condemnation of this generation in Q and the fate of Jerusalem and the temple are represented as the culmination of a long history of rejecting God's messengers, including the Q messengers themselves. Viewing Jesus's death as the death of a prophet makes it a particular instance, even if climactic, of a general pattern, not a death for the benefit of others or a model for emulation. Thus in Q 14:27, where we might suppose Jesus's death is in view as a model of endurance, the reference is not to following Jesus by enduring rejection in the line of the prophets but to taking up one's cross. The same is true of the narrative functions of the wisdom tale in Q.[149] "The elements of the wisdom

---

148. It does not signify access, as some have maintained, but abandonment, and is accompanied by a series of omens that signify destruction. "The ripping of such prominent social fabric as that which constitutes the robes of the high priest and the curtain of the temple is the shredding of what holds the society together. Things are literally coming apart at the seams." Which curtain is referred to may be unknown. "What we know is that a major boundary of the dwelling place of God has ripped in two and thus ceased to serve as a boundary, at the very moment that Jesus' bodily boundaries are likewise rendered defunct." (Nicole Wilkinson Duran, *The Power of Disorder: Ritual Elements in Mark's Passion Narrative*, LNTS 378 [London: T&T Clark, 2008], 119–20). Collins, *Mark*, 763–64, rejects the type of connection between Mark 1:10 and 15:38 suggested above, n. 145, maintaining that the phrase, "the heavens torn apart," in 1:10 reflects Isa 69:19b MT and that both 1:10 and 15:38 should be viewed as a "nontraditional theophany" (764). I see little to recommend this view in distinction from a judgment theme in 15:38 and in favor of a view of some sort of new access to the divine presence. Collins's interpretation here seems to me mostly dependent on her view that the torn temple curtain of this scene was the climactic scene of a pre-Markan passion narrative. The pre-Markan source did not contain a temple theme (626); see below, n. 347.

149. In his Harvard dissertation, published in 1972, George Nickelsburg identified an existing genre consisting of eighteen functions which he labeled "The Wisdom Tale" or "The Story of the Persecution and Exaltation/Vindication of the Righteous."

tale refer not exclusively to Jesus' fate but *generally* to the Q people and to the sages and prophets who preceded them."[150] In the parable of the tenants Mark too identifies the death of Jesus as the climax of a history of rejection and murder of the prophets. But unlike Q the death of Jesus is plotted in Mark's passion narrative. The passion narrative in Mark is not a historicizing of the kerygma. Rather, the predictions of the passion in

---

He traced the performances of the genre in Gen 37–50; Ahiqar; Dan 3 and 6; Susanna; Wis 2; 4–5; 3 Maccabees; and 2 Macc 7. Most of the examples focus on an individual or individuals, but the suffering righteous can also be identified collectively as in Wisdom of Solomon and some of the psalms of lament (George W. E. Nickelsburg, *Resurrection, Immortality and Eternal Life in Intertestamental Judaism*, HTS 26 [Cambridge: Harvard University Press, 1972]). In his later article, "The Genre and Function of the Markan Passion Narrative," *HTR* 73 (1980): 153–84, Nickelsburg added three more functions and analyzed Mark's passion narrative as another performance of the genre. It is interesting to note that with the exception of Mark and 2 Macc 7, all other examples of the genre discussed by Nickelsburg are set in the diaspora and concern both external and internal threats to the integrity of Jewish existence arising in the context of a minority community in foreign lands. In contrast to the theme of the violent fate of the prophets, which mostly functions as a theodicy of judgment in a situation of disaster that has befallen the Jewish people, the goal of the wisdom tale is the rescue (also after death) and vindication of the innocent sufferer, a theodicy of salvation for the individual or the collective, and sometimes for the whole community. Punishment is also a narrative function in the wisdom tale both as an aspect of the vindication of the suffering righteous and as a contrast between the fate of the righteous and the fate of the wicked. For a different view of the genre of the passion narrative, see Adela Yarbro Collins, "The Genre of the Passion Narrative," *ST* 47 (1993): 3–28; Collins, *Mark*, 627–39. Collins maintains that Mark's passion narrative and a pre-Markan passion narrative are both adaptations of the death of famous persons (Gr. τελευτή; Lat. *exitus illustrium virorum*). Kelber rejects the view of a literary genre in favor of the suffering righteous as a wide-ranging motif, following the research of Lothar Ruppert in the 1970s, drawn on as "a memory place" by the Markan author (Werner H. Kelber, "Memory and Violence, or: Genealogies of Remembering [In Memory of Edith Wyschogrod]," in *Imprints, Voiceprints, and Footprints*, 358–59).

150. John S. Kloppenborg, *Excavating Q: The History and Setting of the Sayings Gospel* (Edinburgh: T&T Clark; Minneapolis: Fortress, 2000), 373, emphasis original. "When one asks, is there any reason to suppose that Q knows a pre-Markan passion account or a salvific interpretation of Jesus' death, the answer must be, no. This is because at the numerous points where Q might have borrowed from either the individualistic reading of the wisdom tale or its rich texture of the Psalms of the Righteous Sufferer or from the passion kerygma's salvific construal of Jesus' death, *it consistently fails to do so*" (374, emphasis original).

Mark 8–10 are "a script for writing an account of Jesus' death as a geopolitical event."[151]

In his 1980 article, "The Genre and Function of the Markan Passion Narrative," Nickelsburg called attention to the disjunctive relationship between elements focused on christology and elements focused on the temple theme in the passion narrative, precisely where these elements are juxtaposed. For example, in the trial before the chief priests and the whole Sanhedrin, Jesus is accused of threatening to destroy the temple, but it is narrated as a false accusation and is not the grounds on which Jesus is condemned. Those grounds have to do with the christological titles central to the Markan narrative (14:62). Thus, the taunt directed at Jesus on the cross regarding the threat to destroy the temple (15:29–30) cannot function as an ordeal because it has nothing to do with what Jesus himself claims in Mark, while the taunt of the chief priests and scribes which follows in verses 31–32 does represent the narrative function of ordeal because it picks up one of the titles of honor Jesus has expressly acknowledged. The tearing of the temple veil is followed by the centurion's acclamation, but it appears to be triggered by the manner in which Jesus dies, not by the tearing of the curtain of the temple (vv. 38–39). The christological motif is consistent and continuous in the passion narrative; the temple motif is broken and contradictory. Nickelsburg concluded on the basis of these observations and others that a pre-Markan passion narrative had connected Jesus's role as rejected and exalted Messiah with a new era in which the present temple would be replaced by an eschatological temple or by the community of Jesus's followers as a new temple. Mark rewrote the narrative because he wanted to dissociate the christological claims from any miracles having to do with the temple.[152]

In his monograph, Weeden has commented at length on this disjunction observed by Nickelsburg and others and its resolution in terms of a pre-Markan passion narrative. Weeden agrees that there is a pre-Markan passion narrative written in the genre of the wisdom tale. For Weeden of course that pre-Markan story is not "Christian" but Jewish, the story told by Josephus about Jesus-Ananias. It is the influence of that story that accounts for the presence of the temple-destruction saying in the trial before the chief priests and Sanhedrin. Moreover, the antitemple theme

---

151. Mack, *Myth of Innocence*, 280.
152. Nickelsburg, "Markan Passion Narrative," 176–84.

is consistent with Mark's own viewpoint. But for Weeden this only highlights the illogic of the way it is introduced and indeed the illogic of the
entire scene:

> Mark narrates at the opening of the trial what is totally unexpected and
> contradictory to his story line up to that point. Mark states the follow-
> ing (14:55): "Now the chief priests and the whole council [Sanhedrin]
> sought testimony against Jesus to put him to death; *but they found none.*"
> That latter statement is logically, by virtue of Mark's story line to that
> point, incredible.... What about their own charges against Jesus for his
> provocative act and proclamation in the temple that led them to want
> to arrest him in the first place?... The paradox deepens. While the high
> priest pursues the issue of the temple charge brought against Jesus, that
> charge apparently does not rise to the level of condemnation in the
> mind of the high priest. However, when the high priest poses the *entirely
> unmotivated and certainly unexpected* christological question to Jesus,
> "Are you the Christ, the Son of the Blessed?, and Jesus answers affirma-
> tively, all 'hell' breaks loose (emphasis original).[153]

Weeden's answer to the illogic of the trial is the actual experience of Mark's
readers:

> But for Mark it was not sufficient just to replace the anti-temple motif of
> Jesus' opposition to the temple cult with a christological confession and
> resultant 'christological charge' against Jesus. Mark's primary purpose
> which led him to produce this contradictory and disjunctive narrative
> of revisionist history—that which was to replace the putative cause of
> Jesus' arrest and death, his provocative act and saying against the temple
> cult and the temple establishment authorities—was to make Jesus' chris-
> tological confession as the cause for Jesus' rejection and sentence to
> death. With that objective in mind, Mark created Jesus' experience at the
> Jewish trial as mirrored reflection of the Christian preachers' experience
> of persecution by Jewish authorities for 'blasphemous' witness to Jesus as
> God's crucified and exalted Messiah.[154]

To bring the point home, Weeden then arranges a synchrony of some thirteen features of Jesus's prophecy of persecution to which disciples of Jesus
will be subject (13:9–13) and their parallels suffered by Jesus in the Gospel

---

153. Weeden, "Two Jesuses," 174–75.
154. Ibid., 175.

of Mark.[155] "Thus, in the fictive creation of Jesus' trial before the Sanhedrin, Mark anachronistically applied to Jesus the experience of Christians persecuted for their proclaiming of the gospel."[156]

It seems to me that these observations of Nickelsburg and Weeden regarding the disjuncture in Mark between the antitemple theme and the christology can be reduced to the fact that the grounds of the conspiracy to arrest Jesus in order to put him to death are not the grounds on which he is condemned to death and executed. But lurking behind the observed literary problems in Mark's construction of the trial are also assumptions about the "real historical facts" of the death of Jesus and the persecution of "Christians" by Jews. "Mark was the first Christian of record to attribute Jesus' death to Jesus' christological claim for himself rather than his provocations against the temple cult and its authorities, the provocations which were likely the real cause of his death."[157] Suddenly we are dealing not with a narrative problem but with a historical problem. The same is true for Mark 13:9–13. If Mark did not get the grounds for Jesus's execution right, he certainly must have gotten right the causes of persecution of Jesus's followers in his own time. But if we stick with the literary construction, these matters are not all that difficult.

The hearsay about Jesus destroying the temple (14: 58) is in fact false as formulated and false with respect to what has occurred to this point in Mark's narrative. A parable told against the temple authorities (12:1–12) and a prophecy of the destruction of the temple (13:2) is not a first person claim to destroy the temple and build another. Even the prophecy itself has been made privately to four of Jesus's disciples and not publicly. Moreover, the tearing of the temple curtain as Jesus expires is presented as an omen and the agent in the passive voice is God (15:38). Yes, Jesus's death can be seen as having sealed the fate of the temple from the perspective of knowing what happened in 70. But the implication for Mark's readers is also that the threats and warnings were not heeded. Something similar can be said about the persecution of Jesus and what the disciples are to expect in 13:9–13. The literary implications are the reverse of what Weeden presents. In the context of Mark's narrative, the correlations point to Jesus's experience as a model. How the story may engage its readers in a postdestruction setting, and whether the story reflects the specific experiences or

---

155. Ibid., 176–77.
156. Ibid., 177. For the entire discussion, 161–77.
157. Ibid.

immediate circumstances of its readers are two different matters that may be mutually illuminating precisely in their difference. In that case Jesus as model for the prophesied suffering of the disciples may function as a way to bring clarity to a much more varied and unfocused range of experiences of Mark's readers.[158]

What is most surprising about Weeden's discussion is that it ignores his own hypothesis. If the story of Jesus-Ananias is the hypotext for Mark's hypertext, we should attend to the fact that in the former case woes directed against Jerusalem, the temple, and the people resulted in arrest and physical abuse (immediately, unlike in the case of Jesus in the gospels). But when brought to the Roman governor, he was flogged and released (again, unlike in the case of Jesus in the gospels), because he was deemed not to be a threat, merely insane. According to the story, Jesus-Ananias continued in this vein for seven years and was never executed. It is true that Mark has an interest in making christology the ground of Jesus's execution, and so the high priest must demand that Jesus tell him whether what only "Christians" believe is true.[159] That is Markan irony. But I think it is also the case that in composing the scene the author is aware that what makes good literary sense as motivations leading to Jesus's arrest might not work very well in accounting for a Roman crucifixion. On just the charge alone of being an annoying prophet, Pilate might be thought likely to release him, as Albinus did in the story of Jesus-Ananias, or to tell the high priest and the council to take care of the matter themselves (cf. John 19:6, and see how the ironies pile up in the verses that follow).[160] My point

---

158. See below, 292–93.

159. Cf. Mack, *Myth of Innocence*, 295.

160. We do have Josephus's account of the execution of James by the high priest without consulting Rome in a situation in which the newly appointed governor had not yet arrived. In Josephus's account, convening the Sanhedrin without the governor's consent is a matter of blame. (*Ant.* 20.9.1 §§200–202). If, hypothetically, the governor had been there and given his consent for convening the Sanhedrin, would James still have suffered a Jewish form of execution? The author of Luke-Acts has no problem imagining the Sanhedrin convening in the case of Stephen, hearing false witnesses raise the accusation about Jesus as temple destroyer (Acts 6:13–14a, here rather than in the trial of Jesus in Luke), and having Stephen stoned to death (or letting him be stoned to death) without involving the Roman authorities in any way. The Jews still stone the messengers of God, who in this case happens to be the first "Christian" martyr. See Shelly Matthews, *Perfect Martyr: The Stoning of Stephen and the Construction of Christian Identity* (Oxford: Oxford University Press, 2010).

here is that Mark's trial scenes are not just a matter of the author's christological interests or of the ironies he builds around Jesus as Messiah and
Son of God in Pilate's questioning of Jesus and in the mocking and taunts.
It is also a matter of accounting for the execution of Jesus by making the
charge not only ironic but one that can also be understood to have occasioned a Roman execution, the charge of sedition, insurrection. The field
of signification of Jesus's death is thereby enlarged beyond that of the death
of a prophet who is put to death by his own people.[161] There are only a few
things that seem relatively clear about formulations of the temple saying.
Where Jesus is the agent of the threat to destroy the temple (Mark 14:58
and Acts 6:14a), the threat is explicitly stated to be false testimony. It is not
any the less a false accusation as part of the taunt in Mark 15:29–30. In the
trial scene in Matthew, the saying is not explicitly stated to be false, but the
context is clearly one of seeking false testimony (26:59–61). Moreover, the
saying itself is not formulated as a direct threat, but as a claim to power
(cf. John 19:10) and, unlike Mark, does not include the phrases "made
with hands ... not made with hands." The formulation in Gos. Thom. 71
refers to "house" and in the context of that gospel is very unlikely to have
any direct association with the temple in Jerusalem.[162] I do not think that

---

161. I want to be clear that I am referring to the appropriateness of the charge,
"King of the Jews," in the case of a Roman public execution, not how and why Jesus
actually met his death. See Paula Fredriksen, "Gospel Chronologies, the Scene in the
Temple, and the Crucifixion of Jesus," in *Redefining First-Century Jewish and Christian
Identities: Essays in Honor of Ed Parish Sanders*, ed. Fabian E. Udoh et al., Christianity
and Judaism in Antiquity Series 16 (Notre Dame: University of Notre Dame Press,
2008), 246–82: "If Pilate had seriously thought that Jesus were politically dangerous
in the way that crucifixion implies, more than Jesus would have died, and certainly
the community of his followers would not have been able to set up in Jerusalem, evidently unmolested by Rome for the six years or so that Pilate remained in office" (251,
emphasis original); cf. Merrill P. Miller, " 'Beginning from Jerusalem ...': Re-examining Canon and Consensus," *Journal of Higher Criticism* 2 (1995): 3–30. Other popular
Jewish charismatic figures who were armed and/or who had very large followings are
not analogous cases. The followers were wiped out along with the leaders (Fredriksen, "Gospel Chronologies," 251). John the Baptist does not provide an analogy, even
though he is executed and his followers are not. "The analogue to Antipas's execution
of John—off-stage, separated from any followers, in the socially and politically controlled environment of a prison—would have been a similarly off-stage execution of
Jesus.... *No amount of religious tension between Jesus and the priests can account for
Pilate's decision to kill Jesus by crucifixion*" (255, emphasis original).

162. For a discussion of the Gos.Thom. 71, see Ron Cameron, "Ancient Myths

Mark 14:58 can be taken to imply that though it is false in the context in which it is presented, it is true with respect to the transfer of divine presence from the temple in Jerusalem to the followers of Jesus. If we think of the agency of the future Son of Man as judge rather than the agency of the earthly Jesus, there is no connection with the building of another temple or another kind of temple in sayings attributed to Jesus. If we are thinking of "destroying" and "building" and "three days" as having reference to the death and resurrection of Jesus, we note that in the Gospel of John it is necessary to make the reference explicit, after a typical Johannine misdirection to Jesus's audience, including the disciples (2:18–22). In order to make the comparison the statement is not formulated as a threat with Jesus as the agent. In my judgment, the most that could be inferred from the particular Markan formulation of the false accusation in 14:58 is a deliberate intention to exclude a hope constructed around the expectation of divine intervention in the building of a new temple. When one attempts to reconstruct a tradition history of the temple saying apart from particular formulations in literary contexts, the possibilities of meaning and reference are too varied to be particularly helpful.

Those who survived the war had seen Roman power up close or had heard stories about the demonstration of that power in the Roman province of Judea. From that vantage point the capital offence inscribed on the cross is an especially mocking accusation. But in the gospels the scene with Pilate also shows that Rome is not in charge. In order to get that to register, the Judean ruling class destroyed in the war whose remnants were now bereft of power would take one for the team, so to speak. The writer of the Gospel of John had his own way of stating the point (19:11). For the adherents of a powerful god in defeat, protecting the reputation of the god is an index of cultural persistence, as well as of personal investments and social interests, for the writer of the Gospel of Mark as much as for other Jews.

6. Mark 13 and the War Generation

As he leaves the temple, Jesus responds to a disciple's admiration of the grandeur of the temple by prophesying its utter destruction. On the

---

and Modern Theories of the *Gospel of Thomas* and Christian Origins," in Cameron and Miller, *Redescribing Christian Origins*, 93–98.

Mount of Olives overlooking the temple, Jesus is asked privately by four disciples when this will be, presumably referring to the destruction of the temple, but the question is elaborated by asking about the sign when "all these things" are about to be accomplished (13:1–4). In the discourse that follows, at the point where the four are assured that "all these things" will happen before the passing of this generation (13:30), they have been warned not to be led astray: many will come in Jesus's name making false claims (13:6), there will be wars and rumors of wars, earthquakes and famines, all of which must take place, but these signs are only the beginning of the birth pangs (13:7–8). They are warned about persecutions by authorities and betrayals by family members which they must endure to the end, as the gospel must first be preached to all nations (13:9–13). It will be a time of the worst suffering in the history of the creation and will include the desecration of the temple and the command to flee Judea. Mercifully, the suffering will be shortened by God for the sake of the elect, or no one would be saved. In these conditions they must beware of false messiahs and false prophets and the signs and omens they perform which, were it possible, would lead astray even the elect (13:14–23). Only after that suffering will the Son of Man come with great glory accompanied by cosmic signs and gather his elect (13:24–27). Just as they know from the fig tree the sign that summer is near, so, when they see "these things" happening, they know that he (it?)[163] is near, at the gates (13:28–29). Then, at the conclusion of the discourse, Jesus tells the four that no one but God knows the day or the hour, when the time will come. It will be like the master who leaves the house with his slaves in charge and no one knows the time of his return. No one should be caught by surprise but carry on and keep alert. Everyone should take this to heart and keep awake (13:32–37).

One might well be puzzled by mixed messages; indeed, one might wonder whether the destruction of the temple is referenced at all in this discourse. Some problems of interpretation of Mark 13 may be occasioned by the assumption that only one perspective or a single issue is at stake for his readers. Mark's readers, though obviously not the same as the audience of Jesus's discourse, are nonetheless often assumed to include at least some at the upper limit of Jesus's own generation and many whose period of flourishing was a decade or two before the war and included the war

---

163. I assume the masculine pronoun is intended on the grounds that what precedes and what follows has reference to the coming of the Son of Man.

years (66–74). My proposed dating suggests a slight shift, thinking of Mark's contemporaries as a generation that survived the war years and were already affected by the consequences and uncertainties occasioned by Roman policy without a temple in Jerusalem, after some six centuries of almost uninterrupted functioning of the temple under the canopy of foreign empires. While we can think of them as belonging to the war generation, there is an important difference for contemporaries who are not living in the immediate traumas of the war years at the time of the composition of Mark but in a time of reflection arising from the display of Roman power in the region and Judean defeat. Readers of Mark faced with living in situations arising as a consequence of the war may be as much in need of precedents for understanding the times and its challenges as in exact correspondences between Jesus's discourse and the events of 66–70. After all, the apocalypses written around the end of the first century cope with the destruction of the city and temple in 70 CE by setting their protagonists in the ruins of the temple and the exile of Babylon of 586 BCE.

The discourse of Jesus in Mark 13 is framed by his prophecy of the destruction of the temple and the events leading to his arrest and execution. But Mark 13:14 instructs the reader to take note, reflect on, and possibly explain to an audience words drawn from Dan 9:27 (found as well in Dan 11:31; 12:11; and in 1 Macc 1:54) referring not to the destruction of the temple but to its desecration by Antiochus Epiphanies in 167 BCE. There the "abomination of desolation" is identified as the foreign altar and sacrifices carried out in the Jerusalem temple. In Mark the reference is apparently to the desecrater himself (ἑστηκώς, masc. pf. ptc.), perhaps, as some have suggested, referring to the Roman general when he stood with his soldiers in the court of the temple and they sacrificed to their standards and hailed Titus as emperor (Josephus, *J.W.* 6.6.1 §316), though the perfect participle suggests a continuing state. Much more difficult as a reference to conditions in Jerusalem in August 70 is the exhortation for those in Judea to flee to the hills. Flight from Jerusalem at this point was clearly impossible at this time and hardly possible from elsewhere in Judea. Moreover, the fear of flight in the winter obviously does not fit the date of the destruction.[164] Admittedly, all of these issues can be resolved

---

164. Marcus ("Jewish War," 454–55) takes Mark 13:14 to refer to the occupation of the temple by Eleazar b. Simon in the winter of 67–68 and the profanation of the temple with blood described and condemned by Josephus (*J.W.* 4.3.10 §§182–183). This would make more sense of the exhortation to flee Judea and the concern

more or less satisfactorily by assuming that Mark is working with an earlier source, perhaps from the period of Caligula's plan to have a statue
of himself installed in the temple, or possibly in the 60s as an anticipation that conflict with Rome would end in the desecration of the temple.
This seems to me a more likely anticipation of the consequences of the
revolt in the 60s, even after the war had begun, than the destruction of the
temple. But even if Mark is using a source, the question remains why he
did not rework the source at this point (13:14–18). Luke clearly reworked
Mark here by eliminating the reference to Daniel and flight in winter and
replacing it with armies surrounding Jerusalem (21:20–24).[165]

I believe there are two reasons for Mark's retention or choice of an
act of desecration to signal explicitly for the reader's understanding in
a discourse presumably concerned with events surrounding the destruction of the temple in 70. The first is to draw attention to an event of the
past for comparison with the situation described in 13:14–20, a situation

---

expressed over flight in the winter. However, aside from ignoring Josephus's polemical
aims in his description of internal conflicts among those who continued to prosecute
the war, there is also the question whether profanation by blood shed in the temple
precincts by Judeans would come to mind in connection with a phrase associated with
gentile profanation of the temple by means of an altar and sacrifices. Marcus has also
seen in Jesus's allusion to Jer 7:11 in Mark 11:17b a condemnation of the Zealot leaders, but in the context of Jesus's temple act, the allusion to Jer 7:11 is more likely to be
associated with commercial activity in the temple.

165. Matt 24:15–20 is more difficult to assess. Daniel is specifically cited as the
source for "the abomination of desolation standing in the holy place" (ἑστός ἐν τόπῳ
ἁγίῳ). Kloppenborg points to the placement of 24:14 referring to the full evangelization of the nations before the end comes as evidence that 24:15–20 has a more remote
event of the future in view having nothing specifically to do with the destruction of the
temple ("*Evocation deorum*," 426 n. 24). Matthew appears to be even more elusive than
Mark on locating the destruction of the temple in Jesus's discourse. In Matthew, following Jesus's prophecy of the destruction of the temple, the disciples ask Jesus when
this will be, and elaborate with the further question, "and what will be the sign of your
coming and of the end of the age" (24:3). Nevertheless, the intention to suggest a more
distant event in Mark 13:14–18 cannot be excluded in assessing the discourse in Mark.
Although not as clearly placed, Mark too refers to the evangelization of all nations
(13:10) and implies in context that one cannot expect persecution to cease as long as
the gospel is preached, and so one must endure to the end. There is no reason to think
Mark does not imagine the proclamation of the gospel to all nations to extend into the
future of his readers. Fear of Roman sacrifice at the ruins of the temple by its soldiers
and other Roman settlers in the area can be imagined long before the building of Aelia
Capitolina in the second century, as Theissen has suggested (see above, n. 104).

which features desecration, flight, and great distress. We should recall that 1 Maccabees describes a period of distress not only with reference to the desecrating altar and sacrifices of the Seleucids and their supporters but also in the description of a broader attack on the city and its people. Prior to the establishment of the garrison in Jerusalem and the eventual sacrilege on the altar of burnt offering in 167 BCE, the Seleucid forces destroyed many people, plundered the city, set it aflame, tore down houses and surrounding walls, and took women and children captive (1 Macc 1:29–32). In the *ex eventu* prophecy of Dan 9, the abomination of desolation (v. 27) follows a reference to the destruction of the city and sanctuary (v. 26). Thus, drawing attention to an act of desecration in the words of Dan 9:27 need not be divorced from an event of destruction of city and temple. The urgency of flight from Judea to the hills in winter may also be reminiscent of the flight of Mattathias from Modein after the persecution spread to the towns of Judea: "Then he [Mattathias] and his sons fled to the hills [εἰς τὰ ὄρη, just as in Mark 13:14] and left all that they had in the town" (1 Macc 2:28; cf. Mark 13:15–16).[166] The point of such an allusion in Mark 13:14 seems to be to underscore a different outcome. In this case it would not be a flight to organize resistance in the wilderness of Judea but to escape with one's life. Surely, this would be a last escape route. Escape in the future would require a different kind of flight. Both in Daniel and in Mark the time of suffering is described in unprecedented terms, in Daniel, "a time of tribulation such as never occurred before until that time" (LXX Dan 12:1; cf. Theodotion and MT); in Mark, "a tribulation, such as has never occurred since the beginning of creation that God created until now, and never will again" (13:19). Thus, the Seleucid-Maccabean conflict as precedent for Mark 13:14–20 calls for the reader to associate the destruction of the temple with desecration, to see in the flight an opposition to its precedent, one that signifies the end of armed resistance and, perhaps, even of routes of escape, in effect, magnifying the suffering of this time beyond its precedent.[167]

---

166. The season in which this flight took place is not specified, but it could be thought to be winter given the dates referred to in 1 Macc 1:54, 59.

167. The question then would not be merely what Mark knows about the circumstances of the destruction of Jerusalem and the temple, as though we must assume that he does not know what the writer of Luke's Gospel knows (19:43–44; 21:20–24), because he wrote before the actual destruction of the temple took place. Even if Mark is using earlier sources, he is writing *ex eventu* prophecy in a manner influenced espe-

Calling attention to an act of desecration for purposes of comparison with the memory of an earlier period of suffering is not the only way
to account for a text that seems unfamiliar with the circumstances of the
destruction of the temple in 70. A second reason may have been to serve
as an ironic commentary on the outcome of what the author took to be the
reason for Jerusalem to have gone to war with Rome. He would have been
right, at least in part, to have thought so. There is a fairly long list of incidents reported by Josephus from the beginning of Roman rule in Palestine
of what were regarded as violations of the sanctity of the temple, inappropriate Roman oversight of the temple, and misappropriations of temple
treasure, despite what in other respects could be regarded as a workable
and advantageous accommodation over 130 years.[168] Josephus reports
Pompey's entry into the innermost part of the sanctuary, the holy of holies,
after he captured Jerusalem (*J.W.* 1.7.6 §§152–153; *Ant.* 14.4.4 §§71–73).
Josephus takes pains to tell his reader that in no way did Pompey plunder
the sanctuary, and that he gave orders to have it cleansed. Yet Josephus
describes the penetration by foreigners of the place allowed entry only to
the high priest, the viewing by foreign eyes of its objects, as the calamity
that most affected the nation at the time of civil war and the beginning of
Roman rule in Palestine.[169] Ten years later, the governor of Syria, Crassus,

---

cially by the book of Daniel, though presented in the genre of a farewell discourse, and
drawing on a literary technique utilized in scribal compositions ranging from ancient
Assyria, Babylonia, Judea, Egypt to the hellenized Mediterranean that combines local
historiographic traditions and mantic practices (Neujahr, *Predicting the Past*, and see
above, n. 87). But it is still a question of how he wants to depict the events and for what
purpose, not merely how transparent his description is to what actually occurred.

168. Having told of a Jew who had once saved the life of King Ptolemy Philopa-
tor, even the author of 3 Maccabees thought the most fitting way to initiate the tales of
horror and humor for Egyptian Jews was to have the king come to Jerusalem and be so
impressed with the temple in Jerusalem that he desires a view of the inner sanctuary.
When he is refused on the grounds that it would be a violation of sacred law, he does
not desist. To paraphrase the king, "Even so, why the hell shouldn't I get to see the holy
of holies" (1:9–15).

169. See ch. 4, "Optical Elusions," in Weitzman, *Surviving Sacrilege*, 79–95, on
Roman *scoptophilia* and the use of the Greco-Roman rhetorical devices, *ekphrasis* and
enargeia, by Philo and Josephus as literary expressions of the aspiration to prevent foreign eyes from seeing what was forbidden. The techniques were not merely imitations
of well known rhetorical practice but were designed to stimulate aesthetic pleasure in
descriptions of those parts of the temple permitted to foreign entry and foreign gaze,
while stressing absence and invisibility in descriptions of those parts into which entry

does plunder the temple to finance his expedition against the Parthians (*J.W.* 1.8.8 §179; *Ant.* 14.7.1 §§105–109). The temple treasury was plundered by the procurator, Sabinus, and by Roman soldiers in the upheavals of 4 BCE (*J.W.* 2.3.3 §50; *Ant.* 17.10.2 §264). Pilate introduced Roman standards into Jerusalem and confiscated temple funds to build an aqueduct, resulting in riots and large numbers of dead (*J.W.* 2.9.2–4 §§169–177). When Rome took control of the administration of the province in 6 CE, they held the vestments of the high priest in the Antonia fortress and controlled the appointments of high priests. Though control of the vestments was returned to the priests after Pilate was recalled (*Ant.* 18.4.3 §§90–95), the matter was still at issue after the death of Agrippa I (*Ant.* 20.1.1–2 §§6–14). The Caligula affair has occasioned three major accounts: *J.W.* 2.10.1–5 §§184–203; *Ant.* 18.8.1–8 §§257–309; Philo, *Legat.* 200–373. Neither the motive of Caligula in ordering his statue to be installed in the temple, nor how the affair ended are completely clear because of differences in the accounts. Though it can be disputed that the motive was to establish a place for the imperial cult in the temple and, if necessary, to go to war to do it, the affair demonstrated to Jews at the very least just how vulnerable the center of Jewish culture could be under Roman rule. According to James McLaren, the decision to rebel in 66 was "not so much that something Roman was perceived to be taking over, as it was that some Jews, including Galileans, believed Rome failed to recognize that the temple was off limits and that it did not belong to them."[170] He continues, "Therefore, when Florus demanded in 66 C.E. that the arrears in tax were to be paid

---

and sight were forbidden. Such tactics were intended to evoke the sort of observation Josephus records of Titus when he contemplates saving the temple, "inasmuch as it would be an ornament to the empire if it stood" (*J.W.* 6.4.3 §241). The tactic failed of course, visibly, in the triumphal procession in Rome after the war, and even more, ironically, in the subsequent construction of the Arch of Titus. Describing the scene depicted on the structure dedicated in 81, Weitzman notes, "What appears to be an unmediated glimpse of the vessels is anything but, the panel directing the eye's movements by foregrounding parts of the scene and obscuring others in darkness. In a cruel twist, the scene projects the negative image of the Temple as portrayed by Jews, thrusting its unseen contents into the illuminated foreground while erasing its visible exterior from view" (94).

170. James S. McLaren, "Searching for Rome and the Imperial Cult in Galilee: Reassessing Galilee-Rome Relations (63 B.C.E. to 70 C.E.)," in *Rome and Religion: A Cross-Disciplinary Dialogue on the Imperial Cult*, ed. Jeffrey Brodd and Jonathan L. Reed, WGRWSup 5 (Atlanta: Society of Biblical Literature, 2011), 128.

out of temple funds, his action could be viewed as simply another part of a larger narrative of Roman behavior and poor decision making. The crucial difference on this occasion was that a sufficient number of Jews with the necessary power decided to take action to control their fate, putting into practice the ideology of 'serving God alone' by ensuring that the temple was the property of God."[171]

---

171. Ibid., 129. "For the rebels, [Florus's demand that the shortfall in taxes be paid from the temple] … was not an issue of the negotiation process breaking down, nor was it a gradual or rapid encroachment by Rome. What Florus had done was to ignore totally that the temple was Jewish, not Roman" (128 n. 49). Mason sees interethnic regional rivalry much more than a breakdown of bilateral relations between Romans and Judeans, or Roman overreach in connection with the Jerusalem temple, as the motivation for the Judeans to have gone to war with Rome ("Why Did Judaeans Go to War with Rome in 66–67 CE?"). Judeans turned to self-help when Roman support of their regional interests, which had mostly been forthcoming in the past, failed in connection with the Judean bid to recognize their claims in Caesarea in an increasingly dangerous alliance to Judean influence and interests of a Roman equestrian governor in Caesarea and Samarian interests represented by Samarian auxiliary troops in Caesarea and Jerusalem. But Mason does not dismiss the significance of Florus's actions in connection with the rivalry in Caesarea: "That Samarian-Caesarean axis, directed by a governor focused on financial exploitation of the Judaeans, best explains why the failure of the Judaeans' effort to remake Caesarea with higher Roman support was so urgent, and why its dismissal was so catastrophic. It left no options except radical self-help" (ibid., 202). It is difficult to disentangle Roman-Judean bilateral relations from inter-ethnic regional rivalries. Mason points out that the Jerusalem response of refusing gifts from gentiles was generic and not aimed exclusively at Rome and that the legends on the Jerusalem shekels from 66 may have been aimed more at the Tyrian currency which portrayed the Phoenician god Melkart and declared " 'Tyre the holy and inviolable'. As is well known, the first Jerusalem shekels were produced from 66, just when the Tyrian currency [used in the Jerusalem temple] disappears" (ibid., 203–4). On the history of the Roman-Judean War, see now Steve Mason, *A History of the Jewish War, A.D. 66–74* (New York: Cambridge University Press, 2016). Nathanael Andrade also takes as a starting point for analyzing the significance of violence in regional rivalries in southern Syria the statements of Josephus in the *Judean War* and in *Antiquities* regarding the rival claims in Caesarea ("Ambiguity, Violence, and Community in the Cities of Judaea and Syria"). But his perspective is somewhat different. The populations of southern Syria, including Jews, were heterogeneous with respect to ethnic origins as well as to cultural affinities. The significance of Josephus's apparent interchangeable references to Syrians and Greeks has to do with the fact that rivalry was focused on solidifying the dominant citizen population and polity to be recognized in civic urban spaces and their cultic topographies. When Roman imperial intervention extended citizen privileges to Near Easterners in Greek city-states, "the terms Greek and Syrian could be used to describe intersecting civic categories, not mutually exclusive ethnic ones" (ibid., 353).

Objects from the temple survived its destruction, but not under Judean control. In his chapter entitled, "Flights of Fancy," Weitzman explores two more techniques aimed at cultural survival under the radar of Roman rule: effecting relocation of the temple by metonymy, by physical association relocating something from which the cult could in time be revived, and by metaphor, by resemblance imagining the transfer of the qualities of one object to the other.[172] On the use of metonymy, Weitzman discusses the Copper Scroll from Qumran as a third option, different from the direct attempt of the Samaritans to recover the cult objects believed to be hidden by Moses, and different from the hope of recovery of hidden cult objects with God's help in the future. On the use of metaphor, he presents examples such as the temple at Leontopolis, thought by some to have been built on the model of the Jerusalem temple, the community as temple at Qumran, and the heavenly temple of late first-century CE apocalyptic texts.

> Thinking metonymically—concentrating the Temple's identity in portable, concealable symbols—a Jew could slip the Temple cult under the surface of reality, keeping it in safekeeping for the time being. Thinking metaphorically—creating a double of the Temple—a Jew could move

---

The conflict was over rival polities identifying civic space and heterogeneous ethnicities were expressed in identification with civic performances. Thus, ethnic rivalry was an expression of differences in polities and material culture dominant in civic space and not strictly divisions created by ethnic origins or personal cultural affinities. One of the civic performances most devastating but also most potent in solidifying civic identity and perpetuating narratives of ethnic rivalry was violence. The coins minted in Jerusalem proclaiming Jerusalem's inviolability were matched, so to speak, by coins minted by Greek authorities in the early stages of the revolt. "These coins also deviated significantly from previous issues by innovatively depicting Greek deities as defending their civic-cultic landscapes" (ibid., 363). Despite the efforts of Herodian dynasts and Roman administration to create recognized civic terrains as "Greek" or "Jewish," "Hasmonean conquest, Roman intervention, and Herodian rule had raised ambiguities about civic identities and topographies. These ambiguities stimulated violence" (ibid., 362). The Roman suppression of the revolt not only destroyed the central institution of a Judean polity in the region, it resolved these ambiguities and strengthened Greek civic polities wherever these polities had been contested or threatened by Jews in the region.

172. Weitzman, ch. 5 of *Surviving Sacrilege*, 96–117, with reference to Jonathan Z. Smith, *To Take Place: Toward Theory in Ritual* (Chicago: University of Chicago Press, 1997), 86–88; Steven Fine, *This Holy Place: On the Sanctity of the Synagogue during the Greco-Roman Period* (Notre Dame: University of Notre Dame Press, 1997), 49–55, 79–94, 132–34; and Stanley Tambiah, *Culture, Thought and Social Action: An Anthropological Perspective* (Cambridge: Harvard University Press, 1985), 35–37.

it to safer territory or turn the Temple itself into an expendable copy. Both techniques rely on "flights of fancy" but at their core … is a survival instinct responding to reality, the impulse of a people threatened by Roman predation, greatly constrained in their ability to hide or flee in any literal sense, but moved to take flight nonetheless.[173]

If we think about Mark 13 and the narrative which contains it as a response to cultural loss at a time when the consequences of the failure of both accommodation and military adventure had begun to set in, then the farewell discourse of Jesus and the story of the beginning of the gospel can also be thought of as a flight of fancy responding to a survival instinct. The use of *ex eventu* prophecy, particularly after military defeat, as a tactic of the weak(er) for conveying a fatalistic conception of history is completely understandable in a region like the southern Levant whose peoples had lived for over a millennium in the shadow of empires.[174] In this case, however, it is not the survival of the temple as the focal point of a culture that is in view. It is the survival of the kingdom Jesus announces and the strategic concealing of the locus of the kingdom in order to imagine its ultimate appearance, in a story that highlights misrecognition and demands acceptance of loss and humiliation. Mark's Gospel has its own way of preventing the outsider from taking over, in this case by viewing the people of the kingdom, the followers of Jesus, as the ultimate outsider (Mark 13:13a). But again in its own way the story is also the refusal of a perception of Jewish society imposed by Roman power and now by Flavian policy. The author of Mark, perhaps always closer himself to synagogues than to the temple in Jerusalem, could imagine Jesus in a teaching moment demanding recognition that the temple was to be a house of prayer for all nations (11:17a). The prophet Isaiah in a visionary moment had said so on behalf of those formerly excluded from the temple (Isa 56:7). These were to be received as faithful proselytes not intruders.[175] In

---

173. Weitzman, Surviving Sacrilege, 114.

174. See Smith, "The Markan Site," and Neujahr, *Predicting the Past*, 249: "The key for understanding this shared, cross-cultural interest in mixing literary reflections of native mantic practices with historiographic traditions is an issue of historical circumstance. The loss of native political autonomy, particularly in the face of military defeat, led scribes to fuse predictive traditions to a fatalistic notion of history that culminates in redemption and ultimate supremacy of the scribe and his audience."

175. It is unlikely that Jesus's words in Mark 11:17 are condemning the practice of animal sacrifice itself. For a thorough study of the whole issue based on clearly dis-

Mark's time the effort to keep the powerful intruder out had ended in disaster. A different social formation might be imagined, one invested in dissemination of the word and in acts of transformation, which despite the risks of many failures might here and there achieve surprising results (Mark 4:3–9, 14–20) and keep the powerful intruder at bay.[176] In this way,

---

tinguishing cultural practices: on the one hand, the actual practice of offering animals on the altar and, on the other, debate among literate cultural critics about ideas of proper sacrifice, its meaning and efficacy, see Daniel C. Ullucci, *The Christian Rejection of Animal Sacrifice* (Oxford: Oxford University Press, 2012). Klawans suggests the most plausible interpretation of Jesus's temple act in Mark 11:15–16 is protest against the poor having to pay for their own sacrifices (see Jonathan Klawans, *Purity, Sacrifice, and the Temple: Symbolism and Supersessionism in the Study of Ancient Judaism* [Oxford: Oxford University Press, 2006], 236–40). Ullucci rejects this proposal not only on the grounds that it presupposes the historicity of the event, but also that precisely on those grounds the protest would be irrelevant, considering the costs to poor pilgrims of reaching Jerusalem on the festival (*Christian Rejection of Animal Sacrifice*, 81 with n. 78); rather, Ullucci argues, the issue of the pericope is the quite common objection to too close an association of economic exchange with sacrificial exchange, thus corrupting a proper understanding of reciprocity as the hallmark of the latter (81–82). In addition to the Isaiah and Jeremiah texts, Mark 11:17 may also recall the removal of foreign influence from Jerusalem at the beginning of the war, and if so, the issue of control of temple finances between Rome and the Judean priestly elite, a memory of the real contention over whether it was a Roman or Jewish temple. On the issue of gentile sacrifice in the Jerusalem temple and an interpretation of the logic of different positions taken in 66, see Daniel R. Schwartz, "On Sacrifice by Gentiles in the Temple of Jerusalem," in *Studies in the Jewish Background of Christianity* (Tübingen: Mohr Siebeck, 1992), 102–16.

176. See Anders Runesson, "Was There a Christian Mission before the Fourth Century? Problematizing Common Ideas about Early Christianity and the Beginnings of Modern Mission," in *The Making of Christianity: Conflicts, Contacts, and Constructions; Essays in Honor of Bengt Holmberg*, ed. Magnus Zetterholm and Samuel Byrskog, CB 47 (Winona Lake, IN: Eisenbrauns, 2012), 205–47. Runesson regards virtually all efforts to influence as proselytizing mission, whether it is in the private, semi-public, or public spheres, reversing the procedure of Martin Goodman, *Mission and Conversion: Proselytizing in the Religious History of the Roman Empire* (Oxford: Clarendon, 1994). "I would still use 'mission' in the sense of *the intent and/or strategies used to influence others, passively or actively, to change their views and/or their behavior*" (Runesson, "Was There a Christian Mission," 213, emphasis original). Runesson includes Roman military conquest and empire building as forms of proselytizing mission, identifying political boundaries and the domain of the Roman gods (235). Accordingly, the proclamation of the gospel to all nations is a form of counter-colonialism, expanding the God of Israel's domain by other means (238–43). This conception, however, does

the Gospel of Mark can also be thought of as a response to sacrilege, a project of cultural persistence.[177]

Since the coming of the Son of Man is said to occur after the tribulation described in the preceding verses (13:24), it appears to be separated from the events associated with the period of unprecedented suffering. Yet, according to what follows in 13:28–29, the coming of the Son of Man seems to follow closely on "these things" described in 13:5–23. The question then is whether the coming of the Son of Man is included in "all these things" that are to take place before this generation has passed away (13:30). The answer would seem to be that the coming of the Son of Man, even if it is to be distinguished from events described as bringing about unprecedented suffering, is nonetheless to occur in "those [same] days" predicted in Jesus's discourse (13:19, 24). Since it is usually thought that the Gospel of Mark was written shortly before or shortly after 70, it is imagined that the coming of the Son of Man is anticipated as a deliverance or vindication to occur immediately in the wake of the shortened days of unprecedented suffering. In order not to be misled or to experience disappointment in the midst of this heightened apocalyptic enthusiasm, Jesus informs the disciples that no one knows exactly the day or hour of the coming of the Son of Man, and so one must keep awake and watch for it. There are several problems not accounted for in this scenario. The first is that reference to "this generation" (13:30) is a collective label in Mark and Q, a negative characterization of the present generation which deserves and will receive God's punishment (Mark 8:12; 8:38; 9:19). The coming of the Son of Man as an event occurring within the time frame of this generation must be an event that is appropriate to what "this generation" can expect. In Mark 13:26, "Then *they* will see the Son of Man coming in clouds with great

---

need to be tailored to reality. While the rhetoric and imagination is often imperial in scope, the sphere of competition for cultural capital for followers of Jesus in the first few centuries marks out a far more restricted field of interaction and goals than direct competition with the empire or with imperial elites. This is not to deny the pertinence of a theo-political imagination or rule out real concerns about potential intervention by local provincial and Roman officials.

177. Again, by "cultural persistence" I am not referring primarily to a continuity of content of beliefs and practices, but to a certain persistent imagination and strategies characteristic of social life and ongoing processes of social identification in circumstances of increasing external constraints; see above, 228–29 with n. 47. Cf. Jonathan Z. Smith, "Sacred Persistence: Toward a Redescription of Canon," in Smith, *Imagining Religion*, 36–52.

power and glory," despite the fact that it is the disciples who are addressed throughout the discourse. In Mark 14:62 Jesus, addressing the Sanhedrin, says, "*you* will see the Son of Man ... coming with the clouds of heaven." In Mark 8:38, "those who are ashamed of me and my words in this adulterous and sinful generation, of *them* the Son of Man will be ashamed when he comes in the glory of his father with the holy angels" (emphasis added). Since those who will see the Son of Man coming in the clouds with great power and glory in 13:26 are not the disciples but those who will see their vindication, one cannot limit the event of his coming to the sending out of angels to gather the elect in 13:27, even if one thinks of 13:26–27 as essentially an event of vindication. The vindication implies a divine judgment of those who "will see," and be the objects of shame.[178] Even in Dan 7:13 the picture of one in human likeness coming with the clouds of heaven to the Ancient of Days to receive dominion and kingship is surrounded by the aura of God's judgment of political entities hostile to his people (Dan 7:9–10, 22). In Mark, those who will see God's judgment are clearly the Jerusalem ruling class, particularly the temple elite, who prosecuted Jesus, and in Mark's own time, prosecuted the war.

A second problem is that Jesus's farewell discourse cannot be clarified merely in terms of a temporal sequence of events. The two parables that conclude the address, the fig tree (vv. 28–29) and the householder on a journey (vv. 34–36), have different implications about what is at stake. The first parable, pointing to a process in nature, implies that signs reveal a sequence from which one can know with certainty what time it is, what is about to happen. It is the time of the signs. Jesus has told the disciples everything in advance, so they must stay alert for the signs, most especially because there are signs that lead astray (13:23). But for this generation the signs are all negative (cf. Mark 8:12). Insofar as the coming of the Son of Man is an event of this generation it is the culmination or outcome of all these preceding negative signs, accompanied by appropriate cosmic phenomena, from which only the elect, those who endure to the end, will be gathered and protected. The second parable, drawn from everyday social life, implies not a reading of signs but a way of living that is not taken by surprise. One knows what to expect—and it is not earthly disasters or heavenly disasters—but not when. There are no signs to be read. If then the return of the master is also an analogy for the coming of

---

178. For the same motif, see Wis 5:2; Rev 11:12; 1 En. 62:3–5.

the Son of Man, the parousia cannot be thought of as a deliverance based on the endurance of persecution and suffering and proper attention to the signs. Here, the parousia is about watching for a home coming, a return for which one cannot prepare by heeding signs and enduring suffering. There is uncertainty about the time but it does not matter as long as one stays awake, as long as one is steady on the job. Thinking the master is not coming and going to sleep may mean punishment when the master comes, but it is because one has been caught by surprise. This is not simply a continuation of the foregoing, a difference between knowing that all these things will occur in this generation (v. 30) but not knowing the precise day or hour (v. 32). The parables that conclude the farewell discourse imply different ways of thinking about the coming of the Son of Man and different ways of registering what may be important in the time of Mark's readers.

I have highlighted the difference between the two closing parables in Mark 13 because it also bears on the issue of unfulfilled prophecy, which is often thought to be central in accounting for the composition of Mark 13. The parable of the householder on a journey should be related to material in Q found in Luke 17 and Matt 24. This is one of the loci in Mark 13 where Matthew combines Mark and Q. Matthew 24:37–42 // Q 17:26–27, 30, 34–35 also likens the coming of the Son of Man to an unanticipated event (of the past) that suddenly overwhelms without signs of its coming. The difference from Mark's closing parable is that the event in Q presupposes a universal catastrophe. The coming of the Son of Man is like lightning lighting up the sky from one end to the other (Q 17:24). Matti Myllykoski has argued on the basis of this Q apocalypse that the final redaction of Q presupposed a different situation after the terrible turbulence of the war years.[179]

> Observations on the Q passages … have led me to conclude that the author of Q largely used sayings material that was produced during the critical years of the Jewish War. However, the situation of his community was already different. The situation described in Q 17 presupposes peaceful conditions.… Some groups in the Jesus movement interpreted

---

179. Matti Myllykoski, "The Social History of Q and the Jewish War," in *Symbols and Strata: Essays on the Sayings Gospel Q*, ed. Risto Uro, Publications of the Finnish Exegetical Society 65 (Helsinki: The Finnish Exegetical Society; Göttingen: Vandenhoeck & Ruprecht, 1996), 143–99, esp. 185–99. For other passages in Q that may belong to a postdestruction setting, whatever their ultimate origin, see below, n. 351.

the war as a link in the chain of events that would lead to the second coming of Jesus as the Son of Man. The Q people who proclaimed the judgment of "this generation" did not have to explain prophecies that had failed. At the time the Q document was written, presumably around 75 C.E., they continued to expect the entirely unpredictable day of final judgment and deliverance.[180]

According to Myllykoski, passages in Mark, such as 13:21–23, 32; 14:57–59, can all be explained as Markan redaction of traditional material "which interpreted the destruction of the temple as a sign of the immediate coming of the Son of Man." It is Mark's revision of what proved to be a false prophecy. Nonetheless, Myllykoski believes that the Markan redaction is earlier than the Q redaction, because Mark 13 is written in a situation in which "the war is still actual."[181] Mark may have revised materials based on what proved to be failed prophecies in connection with the destruction of the temple. But in my view that only indicates that Mark's Gospel postdates the destruction of the temple. It does not say what the farewell discourse of Jesus in Mark 13 was intended to communicate to postdestruction readers. Moreover, Myllykoski's conclusions about the time and situation of the Q apocalypse make it surprising that he fails to note that Mark 13 closes with a parable that also presupposes that the coming of the Son of Man will be without warning. There will be no signs.

If Mark 13:32–37 is a fundamentally different way of imagining the parousia from what precedes, it does not mean that 13:5–31 cannot be read as prophecy fulfilled. Mark has not simply abandoned a sinking ship, as if prophecies associated with the coming of the Son of Man in "this generation" have failed. The omens and signs in 13:21–23 are of course deceptions that lead astray because they imagine an earthly deliverer, whereas the Son of Man reveals himself from heaven. If "this generation" in 13:30 is understood as a temporal boundary relative to the disciples to whom Jesus speaks and to followers in the generation following Jesus's death, then the coming of the Son of Man is also an event of the past for Mark's readers on my proposed dating of the gospel. It is quite possible to

---

180. Ibid., 199. Myllykoski argues that the main redaction of Q, which emphasizes the utter rejection of "this generation," is best accounted for on the grounds of what the Q community suffered during the war years as followers of Jesus who proclaimed a message of repentance in his name. I have a different view of the suffering that followers of Jesus may have encountered during the war; see below, 292–93.

181. Ibid., 193, 196.

read 13:24–27 as phenomena symbolic of the chaos of temporal events of war and destruction and the gathering of the elect as an appropriate topos following such events. Thomas R. Hatina has demonstrated this, drawing on a variety of biblical passages.[182] However, unlike Hatina, I consider it important and deliberate that in formulating verses 24–27, Mark prescinds from any direct statement of the Son of Man as the agent of destruction. The primary biblical passages drawn on by Hatina to demonstrate this usage of cosmic phenomena are passages, including Dan 7, in which God's judgment is against a foreign nation, not against Israel or an empowered religious elite. Moreover, the agent of the destruction of the tenants in Mark 12:1–12 is God. Mark is as reticent to attribute agency to the Son of Man in the destruction of Jerusalem and the temple as he is to attribute such agency to the earthly Jesus, conceivably both for reasons of historical sensibilities and for reasons internal to the tensions between the voices in the narrative regarding the authentication of claims to divine status and

---

182. In a chapter entitled "The Vindication of the Kingdom: Isaiah 13.10; 34:4; Daniel 7.13; Zechariah 2.10 and Deuteronomy 30.4 in Mark 13.24–27," Hatina argues for the plausibility of relating Mark 13:24–27, and the entirety of Mark 13, to the war and the destruction of the temple as events of the recent past (Thomas R. Hatina, *In Search of a Context: The Function of Scripture in Mark's Narrative*, JSNTSup 232, SSEJC 8 [London: Sheffield Academic, 2002], 325–73. On this reading the "gathering" topos may reflect Mark 13:10 or simply imply self-construction as aliens and exiles. Knowing that much of the Jerusalem elite had been destroyed, including many priests, and that their remnants had lost their position of power, it could seem to some survivors, i.e., to those not ashamed of Jesus's words "in this evil and adulterous generation," that the kingdom of God as judgment had come with power (Mark 8:38–9:1). However, if Mark 9:1 is related to the parousia, the connection seems to be mediated by its relationship to the scene which follows, the transfiguration (Mark 9:2–8). On the transfiguration as a scene bearing all the symbols of the manifestation of divinity, symbols which were the "cultural common coin in the ancient Mediterranean world," see M. David Litwa, *Iesus Deus: The Early Christian Depiction of Jesus as a Mediterranean God* (Minneapolis: Fortress, 2014), 120–21. "The Jews did not borrow these symbols from the Greeks, nor did Hellenes plagiarize the Hebrew Scriptures. Such symbols were not the proper possession of any particular ethnicity or subculture in the Mediterranean world. From Spain to Palestine, they formed a kind of *koine* signifying manifest divinity" (122). One feature common to such scenes, the offer of worship, I would qualify because it is deflected here, if not regarded as inappropriate, not only because Jesus's sonship outranks Moses and Elijah, but because the teaching which Peter has already heard (Mark 8:31) and which he and the other disciples are now to heed as divine instruction is not about Jesus's manifest divinity but about his suffering, execution and resurrection.

the attribution of ultimate agency to any agent other than God.[183] But the coming of the Son of Man is an event of judgment, just as the death of Jesus seals the fate of the temple. Just as verses 24–27 can be accommodated to the issue to which *ex eventu* prophecy speaks, so can these verses be separated from what precedes and what follows, partly on structural grounds, but mainly on the grounds that the cosmic phenomena are understood on a scale that exceeds temporal events and point to the parousia as the end of the age.[184] For that matter, it has also been argued that Jesus's discourse does not address the fall of Jerusalem and the destruction of the temple at all, on the grounds that the change of scene from the temple (vv. 1–2) to the Mount of Olives (v. 3) implies a change of subject, so that the private teaching of Jesus addressing the two-part question of his four

---

183. See Malbon, *Mark's Jesus*, and Theissen, *Religion of the Earliest Churches*, 172. I also differ from Hatina in holding that Mark 13:32–35 does not belong to this reading of Mark 13. Hatina rejects the proposal of R. T. France, *Jesus and the Old Testament: His Application of Old Testament Passages to Himself and His Mission* (Downers Grove, IL: InterVarsity Press, 1971), 231–32, to separate these verses, which France argued concern the parousia, from vv. 5–31 concerned with the fall of Jerusalem, on the grounds that France's appeal to the phrase "about that day or hour" and to the Son's lack of knowledge in v. 32 are not strong enough to signal that a different event is in view in vv. 32–37 (Hatina, *In Search of a Context*, 347–48). My argument is different. Even though both the fig tree and the householder on a journey function as *parenesis*, their lessons and dispositions are opposites. The one is drawn from nature and concerns the utter certainty and predictability of a sequence of events, so one should pay attention to the signs, endure, and not be led astray by false hopes; the other is drawn from social life and concerns the utter uncertainty and unpredictability of the timing of an event that can therefore take you completely by surprise and find you asleep, so one should stay alert and be prepared, for there are no signs. The *parenesis* of the one is based on what is made known on the strength of the prophetic witness; the *parenesis* of the other is based on what cannot be made known even on the strength of the prophetic witness. It is not a question of different events that are involved, the fall of Jerusalem and destruction of the temple, on the one hand, and the parousia of the Son of Man and final judgment, on the other, but of different readings that Jesus's discourse invites.

184. As Hatina acknowledges is the case in Jewish pseudepigraphal literature, citing As. Mos. 10:1–10, 4 Ezra 5:4–5, and passages from 1 Enoch, Jubilees, and the Testament of the Twelve Patriarchs (*In Search of a Context*, 362–63 with n. 128). On possible parallels between Mark 13:24–27 and 1 Thess 4:15–17, see Adela Yarbro Collins, "Composition and Performance in Mark 13," in *A Wandering Galilean: Essays in Honour of Seán Freyne*, ed. Zuleika Rodgers with Margaret Daly-Denton and Anne Fitzpatrick McKinley, JSJSup 132 (Leiden: Brill, 2009), 548–50.

disciples does not have reference to Jesus's prophecy of the destruction of the temple but to the parousia and the end of the age.[185] Finally, the parousia is represented in very different ways in verses 24–27 than in verses 32–37 (the parable and the close of the discourse). But you cannot have it all these ways is the objection. But why not? It depends what question is addressed to Jesus's discourse. Jesus's credibility as a diviner of geopolitical events in a time of turmoil is one question. What to be thinking and doing in the new normal is another. The scope of the coming reign of God is still another. If Mark 13 is just transparent enough to discern *ex eventu* prophecy in Jesus's discourse, the writer of the discourse and the gospel seems to have counted more on keeping his readers busy. Then as now, he was right.

Mark 13 expands story time beyond the plotted time of Jesus's earthly life and accommodates different readings of the discourse. However, the farewell address is itself an episode within the unfolding of the narrative and replicates a pattern seen earlier in the story in which public action is followed by private teaching (4:1–20; 7:1–23; 9:14–29; 10:1–12). It also anticipates in an ironic way what is to come in the story, especially as it concerns Jesus's fate and its relationship to the theme of discipleship (14:32–42, 43–52, 61–62, 66–72; 16:1–8). Thus, plotted time and story time relate to each other not just as a sequential unfolding of events but as a pattern repeated in sequences of events. What happens to John the Baptist happens to Jesus, and what happens to Jesus will happen to the disciples. The time of Jesus then is not merely sequential but paradigmatic. From this perspective, the time of Jesus's audience (including "all" in 13:37) and the time of Mark's are constructed with reference to the narrative time of the earthly Jesus. The response of Jesus to persecution serves as a model to which the disciples in the story fail to conform, thus functioning as a negative example. Mark's readers are urged to respond in their own time in identification with Jesus rather than with the disciples in the story.

It is misleading to suppose that there must be a close fit between a prophecy of persecution to be suffered by the disciples of Jesus in Mark 13: 9–13 and the actual circumstances or expectations of followers of Jesus, including those of Mark's own circles at the time of writing. Some followers of Jesus may have suffered during the war years, but probably for the same reasons that others suffered, depending on their proximity to

---

185. On this reading, συντελέω in v. 4 is understood to refer to the end of the age, as explicitly in Matt 24:3.

the hostilities, participation or nonparticipation, sympathy with the war or antagonism to it, entrapment in local hysteria, hatreds, ethnic conflicts, and old grudges, rather than because of any particular set of practices or beliefs related to self-identification as followers of Jesus. We should not expect that all followers of Jesus found themselves in the same circumstances, made the same choices, or held the same attitudes toward the revolt. To imagine there was a single position on the war among those close enough to be affected by it is to imagine tightly bounded social and ideological communities with forms of centralized leadership.[186] In short, Jesus's warnings that persecutions will come because of him and for the sake of the gospel more likely function for his readers to place suffering on a stage appropriate to Mark's story of Jesus and bring clarity to what were otherwise more diffused circumstances and reasons for any actual suffering experienced by followers of Jesus in connection with the war. The model works precisely because it is different from the range of situations and occasions it seeks to focus and clarify.[187]

In Mark, discipleship is virtually defined by reference to taking up one's cross, suffering rejection, enduring hardship, facing death for the sake of Jesus and the gospel. This strong theme, highlighted and set in counterpoint by the characterization of the disciples as Jesus's closest followers who nonetheless do not to get it and who fail in Jesus's hour of persecution and suffering, together with what seems a lack of resolution of the discipleship theme and the apparent urgency of issues expressed in Jesus's farewell address in Mark 13, have been taken as evidence of the conditions that pertained at the time of the writing of Mark's Gospel. The narrative addresses those who are being severely tested by persecution or by the imminent threat of persecution having to do with their proclamation of the gospel in a climate of eschatological excitement created by rumors

---

186. See above, 224–25.

187. "Imagination is intrinsic to the very process of representation. It seizes upon an inchoate experience from life, and forms it, through association, condensation, and aesthetic creation, into some specific shape," Jeffrey C. Alexander, "Toward a Theory of Cultural Trauma," in *Cultural Trauma and Collective Identity*, by Jeffrey C. Alexander et al. (Berkeley: University of California Press, 2004), 9, paraphrasing Durkheim on religious imagination in *Elementary Forms of Religious Life*. Furthermore, it is not only readers with an interest in participation in a particular religious formation that have to be taken into account. The theme of discipleship with patterns of imitation and hardship could attract the interest of readers for reasons intrinsic to the way in which the theme is developed in Mark.

of war and the outbreak of the Judean revolt. I am arguing instead that warnings of persecution in Mark belong to a model of discipleship concerned with the construction of a usable social identity not with a community traumatized by persecution.[188] The stylistic effect of immediacy

---

188. Incigneri, *Gospel to the Romans*, 208–52, 314–66, presents what seems to me on the whole to be implausible when he imagines Mark creating a match between a text set in a different time and place and the details of a specific situation, and writing it in less than a year under the kinds of pressures attributed to the writer and his community in Rome in 71. Admittedly, there are some plausible connections, but the match is so detailed one might think the Gospel of Mark was the story of Roman Christians in 71. Also implausible in my judgment is Incigneri's view of Mark's intention to join two aims: to prepare the community for an ordeal of suffering and persecution which is imminent and virtually certain to come with the new Flavian ruler, and at the same time to motivate members of the community to forgive those who had earlier failed the community (with reference to the disciples in the gospel, and even to Judas, which is surely a stretch). Moreover, on Incigneri's reading, the writer sought to achieve both of these aims among people already highly traumatized from the Neronian persecution. Is it wrong to suspect that such people would actually need therapy to deal with the Gospel of Mark on this reading? Roskam, *Purpose of Mark*, presents the thesis that Mark was written in Galilee as an *apologia* to Roman authorities in the province shortly after the war to demonstrate that followers of Jesus were not a politically subversive element in society, because Jesus had no political ambitions. While it is surely plausible to suppose that Galileans in general would have been aware of the increased Roman military presence after the war and Rome's intention to ensure the pacification of the province, it seems to me that such a demonstration was unnecessary in one sense and ineffective or even counterproductive in another. Followers of Jesus were not organized for the purpose and obviously had no power to challenge Roman rule directly or hinder Roman pacification of the province of Judea, including Galilee. Being perceived to be socially perverse, however, could sometimes get you in trouble with authorities. In such eventualities, a story about a provincial prophet and exorcist executed by Rome who was to return soon as Son of God to trump all earthly authority, a story linked to ancient prophecies being read and circulated by people operating independently of recognized authorities, was more likely to be incriminating than an effective *apologia*. Those who went about as religious specialists doing the works of Jesus in his name, healings and exorcisms, or spreading his teachings and telling stories about him, could come under surveillance and suffer punishments merely on the grounds that they were unauthorized (see below, n. 191, the work of Heidi Wendt on independent religious specialists).

To make a different but related point, the destruction of the temple gave the writer the opportunity to enhance earlier claims and portraits of Jesus by relating his story of Jesus, who was active a generation earlier, to a much more politically charged context of Judean revolt and Roman power. With respect to the construction of a for-

and urgency in Jesus's discourse has more typically produced historical assumptions about the circumstances and experiences of Mark's readers than readerly assumptions about the attractions of the narrative.[189] These

midable social identity, suspicion of subversion did not pose as much of a threat as anonymity did among a people now subjected to Rome in the most direct and forceful way. The followers of Jesus were not to be ignored, which was probably often the case. They were not nobodies. They were hated by all (Mark 13:13a); see Benjamin H. Dunning, *Aliens and Sojourners: Self as Other in Early Christianity* (Philadelphia: University of Pennsylvania Press, 2009), 112–13, referencing Julia Kristeva, *Strangers to Ourselves*, trans. Leon S. Roudiez (New York: Columbia University Press, 1991), 39. Explaining early Christian representation of "alien identity" in Bourdieuian terms, Dunning writes, "Positioning oneself in a relationship of alienation to a cultural field is itself a practice within that field.... There is no place to stand outside the various fields of culture from which a group can make these claims—there is only rhetoric to this effect" (113). With respect to the representation of persecution, the Gospel of Mark is also staking out a position within a cultural field, while employing a rhetoric that represents it as a given of discipleship.

189. For example, Duran, *Power of Disorder*, 122, writes: "Mark's task is, so far as we know, to make a story—to gather meaning—out of events experienced as meaningless trauma. Like other attempts to make sense of especially chaotic moments in existence, his gospel must remain close to his intended readers' experience of trauma and senselessness, or it will be dismissed as incredible. Any attempt to make order from what has been experienced as chaos—to literally bring some kind of life out of the tomb, as Mark does—must retain a proximity to the chaos that is its raw material. Ritual, largely through its groundedness in bodily experience, works in Mark's Passion to keep us close to the process of making order from chaos, a process that is not complete before the story begins, but occurs within the course of its telling. It seems to me that Mark imagines readers who would have no way of understanding Matthew's church-building or the reassuring calm of Luke, much less the philosophical musings of John—for such attitudes require a degree of confidence in a normal, continuous future that Mark's gospel lacks." In the context of Duran's discernment of ritual elements in Mark's passion narrative, this powerful statement seems to me to express a sensibility that is shared by many scholars focused on the experience of reading or hearing Mark's story of Jesus. I would want to qualify this sensibility. On the one hand, there is a suggestion that order and chaos, meaning and meaninglessness, are polar opposites when in fact they cannot be represented without being relative to each other. On the other hand, a less naturalistic theory of trauma would hold that what is important for a collective view of trauma is a process of representation that is dependent on many factors. "For traumas to emerge at the level of the collectivity, social crises must become cultural crises. Events are one thing, representations of these events quite another. Trauma is not the result of a group experiencing pain. It is the result of this acute discomfort entering into the core of the collectivity's sense of identity" (Alexander, "Theory of Cultural Trauma," 10; for more on Mark and trauma, see below, n.

attractions may have more to do with accruing capital in a cultural field than with existential pressures and threats.[190] Though literary ambition and appeal to a certain cadre of readers may only be one of the aims of Mark's narrative project, such interests at play in a subfield of literate culture producers should not be dismissed on grounds that they are at odds with the use of the narrative as a tool of recruitment, or as a tool of social identification, or as a platform for convening followers and entertaining interpretations and debate. These uses themselves depend on the success of the literary strategies employed for attracting interest in the story itself.

I am not saying that followers of Jesus experienced no conflicts and no responses that could be described or perceived as persecution.[191] What

---

381). In any case, I am not convinced of Duran's unified imagination of Mark's readers. Should we really suppose that Mark's readers, even those whom he envisioned as such, were in similar situations during the war and were all similarly traumatized? Should we even suppose that all his intended readers were self-identified as followers of Jesus? As to the intelligibility of Matthew, Luke, and John for Mark's readers, the latter after all include the writers of at least two of these gospels, who, like Mark's more immediate circles, are likely to have found Mark's Gospel useful, engaging, and demanding, inviting further imagination, even if that also meant it was ripe for clarification, correction, and, yes, perhaps displacement. Nor do I believe one can determine the date of composition on the basis of Duran's observations. The apocalypses of 4 Ezra and 2 Baruch contain moving laments over the destruction of the first temple. Even if we suppose that these reflect in some measure poignant moments of mourning rooted in genuine grief, a reliving of painful experience in the immediate aftermath of the destruction of the second temple, this clearly does not mean that these texts were written immediately after the war and that the representation of mourning is not for its effect in the context of writings written some decades later.

190. On fields and cultural production in the study of early Christianity, and on proposals regarding the primary interests, social relationships and values of gospel writers, see the essays by Stanley Stowers, Robyn Walsh, and Richard Last, above, n. 39.

191. The work of Heidi Wendt is opening up for exploration and theorization a subcategory of religious agents. In a realm of religious activity particularly neglected in the study of early Jewish and Christian formation, and generally undertheorized, Wendt is showing the importance of freelance specialists and their often ethnically coded skills and offerings for understanding mechanisms of the spread of new forms of religion, without invoking Jewish proselytizing and Christian mission as exceptional categories, and for explaining the reasons and consequences of Roman regulation of this category of religious agent, including, though not singling out, those who were Jews or Christians. She argues that expulsions of Jews from Rome in the first century, usually thought to have included the wider Jewish community, were actually

might have been known in Markan circles about imprisonment and execution of earlier followers of Jesus? On the basis of the literary evidence available, and taking it at face value, it involves individuals in their capacities
as leading actors. But we do not have any clear or detailed explanations of
the causes of Stephen's death, or the death of the apostle James in Acts, or
the motivations for the execution of James the brother of Jesus in Josephus.
How much of the circumstances and causes of the executions of Peter and
Paul were available, even presuming the later traditions are reliable? Even
in Syria, Mark and his circles could have known about the fate suffered
by Christians in Rome under Nero some fifteen to twenty years earlier on
my proposed dating of Mark. The event as a collective scapegoating, at
least as it is described by Tacitus, would hardly make for ennobling sentiments. It would not be easy to construct the victims as martyrs. The label
"Christian" was probably coined as an outsider term of opprobrium, but
how would the label and the reference to Christ have come to the attention
of authorities in an urban center if not, at least in the first instance, from
having been informed about followers of Jesus from people in a position

---

directed against unaffiliated specialists in Jewish religious practices (Heidi Wendt,
"*Iudaica Romana*: A Rereading of Judean Expulsions from Rome," *JAJ* 6 [2015]:
97–126). She sees the spread of Jewish practices and Christian formations as much
an effect as a cause of Roman regulation and punishment. The impetus for discourses
of martyrdom is not primarily conflict with Rome, but competition for authenticity among religious specialists to support claims for the efficacy of their offerings
and accrue cultural capital (Wendt, "*Ea Superstione*: Christian Martyrdom and the
Religion of Freelance Experts," *JRS* 105 [2015]: 1–20). Wendt does not set this subcategory of religious agent in absolute contrast to other religious actors and forms of
religious activity. In an unpublished paper, she writes, "If we examine the activities
of independent specialists in other [non-Judean] forms of ethnic religion … we learn
that some formed networks with one another, while others attempted to establish
groups with regular contours and institutional characteristics, and others still inter-
faced with existing religious groups or institutions" (Wendt, "*Interpres Legum*: Judean
Diviners in the Early Roman Empire" [paper presented at the Annual Meeting of
the Society of Biblical Literature, Chicago, 19 November 2012], 20). It is interesting
to observe that Mark 9:38–40 indicates that the writer is aware of the category of
unauthorized freelancers who are not regarded as followers. Mark 9:41 shows he is
also familiar with the genitive of *Christos* as an expression of identification applied
to the disciples. Wendt is setting Christian formation and its regulation in a broader
comparative context of ancient Mediterranean religion in the periods of the early
and high Roman Empire. See now Heidi Wendt, *At the Temple Gates: The Religion of
Freelance Experts in the Roman Empire* (New York: Oxford University Press, 2016).

to know them because they were family members, neighbors, associates in
crafts or trade, clients, and perhaps, if not synagogue members or associates themselves, at least known to them? This means that knowledge of
their presence in Rome would not have come about initially through surveillance of their activities by Roman authorities. To civic authorities in
Antioch or Rome, would followers of Jesus have been clearly distinguish-
able from Jews were it not for the label "Christian?" Would it have made
any difference to them, except in circumstances of intragroup disputes or
entrepreneurial activities among non-Jews that created local grievances
and public disturbances? Exposure arose at first in more intimate circles,
and not directly from the initiative of authorities.[192] Even in connection

192. I would insist on this point, even if the label *Christianos/Christianus* was first
used by Roman authorities; see David G. Horrell, "The Label Χριστιανός: 1 Peter 4:16
and the Formation of Christian Identity," *JBL* 126 (2007): 362–67. I am not convinced
by Horrell's linking of the situation implied in 1 Peter with the situation depicted in
Pliny's correspondence with Trajan dated to ca. 111–112 (*Ep.* 10.96–97). While it is
not impossible that the suffering described in 1 Peter could have included prosecution
and execution, I do not see anything in the letter that makes this the most plausible
conclusion to reach (ibid., 370–76). The significance of 1 Peter as evidence of insider
adoption of an outsider term of stigma and therefore as evidence of its use as a term
of collective belonging, that is, vis-á-vis a hostile world, should perhaps be acknowledged, but with several qualifications, I think. First, I doubt that we would see even
a first instance of this if it were actually the case that Roman or local officials were
regularly prosecuting and executing followers of Jesus as a special target of Roman and
provincial policy. First Peter 4 represents the prospect of reversing the outsider social
verdict, as Horrell has observed (ibid., 380). Second, the term may also function to
reinforce self-identification as aliens and exiles (1 Pet 2:11–12). Third, it seems to me
correct to conclude that widespread use of the term "Christian" as a term of belonging
prior to writers such as Ignatius, Polycarp, and Diognetus is belied by the absence of
such evidence in the New Testament writings (ibid., 361). My emphasis on the more
intimate circles and circumstances of potential exposure of the activities of followers
of Jesus to Roman surveillance and prosecution is not intended to discount Roman
administrative efforts to control and suppress the activities of unauthorized religious
specialists. "Roman tactics for isolating, examining and punishing Christians were
already well rehearsed in earlier and ongoing proscriptions or expulsions of *magi*,
astrologers, seers, prophets, other varieties of diviners, and philosophers, *inter alios*"
(Wendt, "*Ea Superstitione*," 2). Moreover, "The evidence for their activities suggests
that from the early decades of the imperial period they grew increasingly influential,
more diverse with respect to the skills or methods in which they claimed expertise,
and more assorted in the ethnic coding of their wisdom and practices.... The same
period witnessed an escalation in both the frequency and severity of efforts intended

with the fire in Rome, authorities would have required informants in order to isolate and carry out a collective scapegoating of Christians.[193] So what would these grievances have been about, if not about expectations regarding appropriate social roles and one's loyalties, or at least the perception of one's loyalties, and about what were believed to be concomitant threats to social well being. With respect to corporate punishment by Jews, we have Paul's own reference to being beaten in synagogues (2 Cor 11:24). For this to have occurred, he would have had to identify himself as a Jew, submit to punishment, and been viewed by synagogue authorities as engaging in activities threatening to the well being of Jewish groups in urban centers. Even if 1 Thess 2:14–16 is not authentic or if comparison with the experience of persecution of followers of Jesus in Judea in verse 14 is an example of an invented tradition, the passage probably informs us correctly that the issue for Paul was a response to his preaching to gentiles, at least potentially resulting in the renunciation of traditional gods and breaking with practices and social networks taken for granted as essential to maintain family loyalties and civic order.[194] For more established Jewish groups,

---

to counteract specialist influence, particularly throughout the first century c.e."(ibid., 4). Although I have more of a sense of these Roman measures and edicts as ad hoc than does Wendt, there is certainly a range of evidence to show that examination and punishment by Roman officials often occurred in situations of competition between religious specialists (ibid., 13–15). See the discussion of Roman religious policy, especially as directed toward freelance religious specialists and uncontrolled spread of oracles, in James B. Rives, *Religion in the Roman Empire*, Blackwell Ancient Religions (Malden, MA: Blackwell, 2007), 187–90. Since one can see certain patterns of response as well as the effect of precedents over time, the expression Rives uses to characterize Roman religious policy, "ad hoc 'policies,'" (191), taking account that they were mostly reactive, may be the most appropriate description.

193. The exact relation of this collective punishment under Nero to the fire or to the charge of arson is not clear. Unlike Tacitus (*Ann.* 15.44), Suetonius's briefer account does not describe the types of punishment inflicted, nor relate the actions taken against Christians to the fire but to a broader sweep of social behavior judged inimical to good order that included actions against charioteers and expulsion of pantomime actors (*Nero*, 16.2).

194. 1 Thess 2:14–16 as an example of Paul inventing a tradition for the edification and encouragement of his Thessalonians is argued by Sarah Rollens, "Inventing Tradition in Thessalonica: The Appropriation of the Past in 1 Thessalonians 2:14–16," *BTB* 46 (2016): 123–32. On the persecution of Paul by Jews, see Martin Goodman, "The Persecution of Paul by Diaspora Jews," in *Judaism in the Roman World*, 145–52. Cf. William E. Arnal, who sees Paul's message and activities as exposing the arbitrari-

there were good local political reasons to be more circumspect and not approve unauthorized activities promoting what could be construed as Jewish practices and beliefs among non-Jews and certainly not to advertise them as a strategy to bring about the end of the age.[195] The potential

---

ness of the unspoken rules of family and ethnic well being taken for granted in the Roman imperial world ("Doxa, Heresy, and Self-Construction: The Pauline *Ekklēsiai* and the Boundaries of Urban Identities," in *Heresy and Identity in Late Antiquity*, ed. Eduard Iricinschi and Holger M. Zellentin, TSAJ 119 [Tübingen: Mohr Siebeck, 2008], 50–101): "One might surmise that the motivation for *Jewish* persecution of *Paul* (and Paul alone) is precisely the threat his message poses to the *modus vivendi* that allows such subcultures to continue to exist meaningfully under foreign domination. The problem is not that Paul threatens particularistic Jewish pride by 'allowing' Gentiles to participate in Jewish identity …; it is that Paul threatens continued Jewish existence as such by seeking to extend this identity beyond the parameters *allowed* by Rome" (98, emphasis original; see below, n. 195).

195. Or, as has been argued by Arnal in the case of Paul, to promote them as a strategy to subvert *doxa*, the taken for granted within a given social formation, "the universe of the undiscussed" ("Doxa, Heresy, and Self-Construction," 56, citing Pierre Bourdieu, *Outline of a Theory of Practice*, Cambridge Studies in Social and Cultural Anthropology, trans. R. Nice [Cambridge: Cambridge University Press, 1972], 168). In this case, it is the *doxa* of Roman political hegemony, there being no discourse available to challenge the subordination of all ethnic groups to one ethnic group, all cities of the empire to one city, thus reproducing in the name of family, civic, and ethnic well being the universality of the one ethnic group, the one city ("Doxa, Heresy, and Self-Construction," 64–75). In this article, Arnal takes up recent efforts to redefine heresy as a sociological rather than exclusively ideological or religious phenomenon. By deploying a particular model of Bourdieu's formulation of the relationship of orthodoxy and heresy to *doxa*, Arnal is able to show that *heresy* can be understood "as a departure from some elements of *doxa*" with orthodoxy now occupying a position of "explicit retrenchment of a challenged doxa," instead of the more typical notion of orthodoxy as the "*dominant representation* of doxa," and thus the precondition both temporally and conceptually of heterodoxy (58–59, emphasis original). In this formulation, heresy is seen as radically subversive, arising without a concomitant orthodoxy, dissolving doxa as such by forcing it to become articulate, to become an orthodoxy. It is in these terms that Arnal sees Paul's discourse and practice to be disruptive of the structures of Roman imperial hegemony. Paul constructs his largely gentile *ekklēsiai* as "artificial Jews" (citing Wayne A. Meeks, "Corinthian Christians as Artificial Aliens," in *Paul Beyond the Judaism/Hellenism Divide*, ed. Troels Engberg-Pedersen [Louisville: Westminster John Knox, 2001], 129–38), that is, as communities "unrooted in actual familial identity and so uncontained by fractional ethnicity" (97), thus creating a "violation of the taken-for-granted norm of *Roman universality*, or of the ostensibly non-ethnic character of Roman identity, and its replacement with a contradictory and

danger of official intervention resulting from such activities was doubtless

---

subversive notion of *Jewish* universality," seen with special clarity, Arnal suggests, in Paul's "collection for the saints" (96, emphasis original). Since Arnal acknowledges that the phenomena he describes in this article are mainly discursive, that Paul "did not liberate anyone from its [Rome's] real domination" (even though Paul's community organizing is the only reason his words have survived, 101), indeed, "that Paul is not interested in human social reform, at least not of the society at large outside of his *ekklēsiai*, but expects some kind of divinely-initiated transformation of the world" and encourages his adherents "to live quietly and set positive examples for outsiders ... and not engage in open rebellion against the civic authorities" (86, n. 101)—for these reasons we might take Paul's self-and-community constructions to have the same import as Dunning's characterization of alien identity in 1 Peter: an effort to construct an exceptional identity while acting in completely ordinary ways (*Aliens and Sojourners*, 12; see above, n. 188). However, on Arnal's redescription of heresy, Paul's discourse is not simply "an identity-creating gesture." Its very possibility presupposes the contradictions that arise in the course of sustaining the doxic exceptionalism of Roman universalism, especially for those among his addressees who have lost viable networks of family and ethnic connections (100). "Here heresy is not invoked to make selves *or* mark others (101, emphasis original). Rather, "by imputing an essentially Jewish identity to the displaced of the empire, Paul and his adherents called into question the unspoken doxa of the imperial order and so became heretics and were persecuted as such" (100). With respect to the persecution of Paul's gentile adherents, it seems to me that Arnal comes closer to an explanation when he refers to the import of Pauline exclusivity, the repudiation of the gods as "an overt repudiation of the authority or jurisdiction of civic institutions" (96), rather than supposing that occasions of persecution arose because Pauline social formations appeared to hold a self-conception that could not be assimilated to the doxa of Roman universalism, a conception of heresy that Arnal himself notes functions at a more subliminal level than heterodoxy (60–61; 82–83).The preconditions for heresy as an intervention in doxa are more likely to have registered for Romans in the functioning of the Jerusalem cult (see below, 308–9). To Paul, participation in non-Judaic cult was not something meaningless for his gentiles in Christ but a participation with demons (taking account of 1 Cor 10:14–22, contra Arnal's reading of 1 Cor 8 [97]). In Paul's discourse, it is not a question of making even a fractional place for the cultural and ethnic formations of the gentiles; there is no place at all. The circumstances accounting for persecution of gentile adherents of Paul are most likely to have been occasioned in the first instance by tensions in family, neighborhood, work place, and associations relating to the violation of expected social roles, which then may sometimes have escalated in public disruptions or have come to the attention of civic and imperial authorities and been subject to punishment as unauthorized activities of individuals and their social formations. For critical exposure of the *doxa* of classical Greek performances of the second Sophistic by the Syrian writers, Lucian of Samosata, Justin Martyr, and Tatian, see Andrade's illuminating discussion in chs. 9 and 10, *Syrian Identity*, 261–313.

known to Mark and his readers and may have some relationship to the reading and pertinence of the persecutions prophesied in Mark 13:9–13. But they do not need to reflect an imminent collective threat, daily experience, or past persecution in order to account for their place in Mark's story.

7. The Consequences of a Failed Revolt

Roman retaliation for the revolt, not uncharacteristically, was severe. But this does not refer merely to the thoroughness of the military operations in Jerusalem, and later at Masada, once the temple was in flames, or to the numbers taken captive and sold into slavery, or executed in victory celebrations enroute to Rome. In this case Rome's victory over a rebellious province was also linked to the legitimation of a new imperial dynasty in Rome. Over the next decade the center of Rome was changed with monuments celebrating the end of the civil wars of 68–69, an anti-Neronian populous theme, and the victory over Judea.[196] The rebuilding of the temple of Jupiter Capitoline, burned during the civil wars, was immediately undertaken by Vespasian, financed with the funds collected by the *fiscus Iudaicus*, the treasury for the tax imposed on all Jews throughout the empire after the war. The building of the Temple of Peace was also undertaken immediately and completed in 75, housing among the many monuments brought to the temple for public view also the menorah and table of the shewbread taken from the Jerusalem temple and paraded in the triumphal procession of 71 as described by Josephus (*J.W.* 7.5.4–6 §§123–157). The Torah scroll and temple curtains also included in the procession were kept in Vespasian's palace. The monumental amphitheater, the Colosseum, now known to have originally named Vespasian as builder and paid for from the spoils of war, more than likely an indirect reference to the Judean war, was opened in 80 under Titus.[197] The latter's prominence in the victory in Judea was certainly not forgotten as displayed by the Arch of Titus, occupying a place of prominence, and dedicated in 81 with an inscription magnifying his achievement by the obviously false boast that no king or commander before him had ever conquered the city of Jerusalem. The

---

196. See Fergus Millar, "Last Year in Jerusalem: Monuments of the Jewish War in Rome," in *Flavius Josephus and Flavian Rome*, ed. Jonathan Edmondson, Steve Mason, and James Rives (Oxford: Oxford University Press, 2005), 101–28.

197. Ibid., 117–19.

surviving Arch of Titus, completed after his death, contains no reference to war or victory but is unmistakably related to the victory in the famous relief depicting the temple vessels. As Fergus Millar summarizes, "On any interpretation, the theme of the defeat of the Jews and the destruction of Jerusalem, coinciding with the need for self-assertion on the part of a new dynasty, and with the need to establish an emphatic public contrast with Nero, left a remarkable imprint on the evolution of public monuments in Imperial Rome."[198]

The Flavian monuments tell us the extent of the new dynasty's need to exploit the victory for propaganda purposes and the lengths to which they were prepared to go in order to advertise the legitimacy and benefits of Flavian rule. The humiliation of Judea was also given expression in the *Iudaea capta* coins, still issued in 85 in Domitian's reign, especially those depicting the disgraced Judea as a subjugated woman. However, it has been argued that it is only the comparative abundance of evidence preserved by Jews and Christians that leads to conclusions that Jews were more anti-Roman, more difficult to govern, more prone to revolt, and more religiously or ideologically committed to national independence than other peoples. Martin Goodman has made this point in several publications.[199] In his major work comparing Jewish and Roman civilizations, he has argued that there were no structural incompatibilities between Jews and the Roman state that could explain the fate of the Jews after 70, nor could the culmination of the war itself have been anticipated: "The destruction of Jerusalem in 70 was the product of no long-term policy on either side. It had come about through a combination of accidents, most of them unrelated in origin to the conflict: the death of Nero, leading to Vespasian's bid for power in Rome and Titus' quest for the propaganda coup of a rapid conquest of Jerusalem, and the devastating effect in the summer heat of a firebrand thrown by a soldier into the

---

198. Ibid., 127.

199. Martin Goodman, "Opponents of Rome: Jews and Others," in *Images of Empire*, ed. Loveday Alexander, JSOTSup 122 (Sheffield: JSOT Press, 1991), 222–38; Goodman, "Jews, Greeks, Romans," in *Jews in a Graeco-Roman World*, ed. Martin Goodman (Oxford: Oxford University Press, 1998), 3–14; Goodman, "Current Scholarship on the First Revolt," 20–21. On revolts in the Roman empire, see S. L. Dyson, "Native Revolts in the Roman Empire," *Historia* 20 (1971): 239–74, and Greg Woolf, "Provincial Revolts in the Early Roman Empire," in Popović, *Jewish Revolt against Rome*, 27–44.

Temple of God."[200] Yet Goodman has been one of the strongest proponents of the unprecedented severity of the Roman response to the Jews
after 70. The Roman victory was not merely over Judea, but over Judaism. It was not typical of Rome to parade victory over foreign gods. It
would not have been without precedent to have incorporated the worship of the God of Jerusalem into the religious rites of Rome rather than
to have held captive as museum pieces symbols of the God of the Jews,
advertising that the cult of this god had come to an end.[201] "In the eyes of

---

200. Goodman, *Rome and Jerusalem*, 423. In his earlier book on the Judean
revolt, *The Ruling Class of Judaea*, Goodman had also called attention to contingencies that had occasioned a full scale war and its outcome. But more than in the recent
book he had also analyzed social, cultural, and economic factors as underlying causes
that clearly amounted to structural incompatibilities between the Roman state and the
Jews, especially the problems generated by the difference between Roman qualifications of wealth and property for an elite with whom they would negotiate as interme-
diaries of the provincial population and Jewish sensibilities about the intellectual and
religious qualifications of a ruling class they would acknowledge as legitimate. See
Seth Schwartz, "*Sunt Lachrymae Rerum*," review of Goodman, *Rome and Jerusalem*,
JQR 99 (2009): 56–64, and James Carleton Paget, "After 70 and All That: A Response
to Martin Goodman's *Rome and Jerusalem*," *JSNT* 31(2009): 339–65. In addition to
high regard for the work and some substantive critique, both Schwartz and Paget call
attention to the contrast between Goodman's earlier book and *Rome and Jerusalem*.

201. Goodman, *Rome and Jerusalem*, 431–32; see also, Jodi Magness, "The Arch
of Titus at Rome and the Fate of the God of Israel," *JJS* 59 (2008): 201–17, and Philip
S. Esler, "God's Honour and Rome's Triumph: Responses to the Fall of Jerusalem
in 70 CE in Three Jewish Apocalypses," in *Modeling Early Christianity*, ed. Philip S.
Esler (London: Routledge, 1995), 239–58. Heidi Wendt explores the significance of
the Roman triumph from a different angle, suggesting that it also worked to create
interest in Judaica, at least in Rome. "In the wake of the Flavian triumph, the copy of
the law … that Josephus describes being paraded on a *ferculum* as the culmination of
items despoiled from the Jerusalem temple (*J.W.* 7.150) was either incorporated into
the civic collection of prophetic corpora that also included the *Sibylline Oracles*, or at
least might have been thought to be part of this collection" (Heidi Wendt, "'Entrusted
with the Oracles of God': The Fate of the Judean Writings in Flavian Rome," in *A
Most Reliable Witness: Essays in Honor of Ross Shepard Kraemer*, ed. Susan Ashbrook
Harvey et al., BJS 358 [Providence, RI: Brown University Press, 2015], 101). Wendt
suggests that "the triumphal introduction of Judean writings to Rome resulted not
in their removal to the imperial palace as war booty but rather in their incorporation
into the amalgam of prophecies curated within the temple of Apollo Palatinus" (107).
"The considerable attention drawn to Judea in Flavian ideology, monuments, and even
romantic entanglements likely amplified interest in Judaica among Roman audiences,
even as the negative consequences of the war—the destruction and despoliation of

ordinary pagans, such actions were most naturally interpreted as the end of worship of the Jewish God."[202] Rome could have recognized the thoroughness of its victory and reestablished the mediating position of the remnants of the Judean elite, in particular, the high priests and other elite who had escaped to the Roman side (Josephus, *J.W.* 6.2.2 §§113–115), or even more plausibly rewarded the loyalty of Agrippa II by appointing him as a client king over Judea.[203] Rebuilding on a modest scale a

---

the temples in Jerusalem and Leontopolis, local conflicts, the *fiscus iudaicus*—exacted considerable tolls on provincial and diaspora Judean populations" (106–7).

202. Martin Goodman, "The *Fiscus Iudaicus* and Gentile Attitudes to Judaism in Flavian Rome," in Edmondson et al., *Flavius Josephus and Flavian Rome*, 170. Paget, "After 70 and All That," questions in a number of ways whether the evidence supports Goodman's thesis that the Roman response to the revolt was intended to signify the end of Judaism.

203. Goodman, *Rome and Jerusalem*, 436–38. Goodman acknowledges that Agrippa II may have had no particular interest in ruling a Judea in ruins and had better prospects in Rome (437). For a different view of the reason Agrippa II was not made king after the war, see Daniel R. Schwartz, "Herodians and *Ioudaioi* in Flavian Rome," in Edmondson et al., *Flavius Josephus and Flavian Rome*, 63–78. Schwartz presents the view that after 70 Rome no longer thought of *Ioudaia* as the territory of *Ioudaioi* and increasingly referred to it as Idumea or Palestina, even before formally renaming the province with the foundation of Aelia Capitolina. Kings ruled territories. This presupposes, as Schwartz argues, that Agrippa II would not have accepted Idumea as the name of his territory, despite his own origins, for he considered himself a *Ioudaios*. Schwartz's argument seems problematic, since the Roman province was still called Judea and the client kings, Herod and Agrippa I, had ruled over more than just the territory of Judea. Equally problematic in my judgment is Schwartz's argument that Josephus in the *Judean War* held out the possibility that Agrippa II might become Rome's client in Judea but by the writing of the *Antiquities* he had concluded that there was no need for a king of Judea, since *Ioudaioi* were now to be defined by relation to religion rather than place. In addition to this problematic dichotomy, the continuing importance of the Hebrew Bible or the LXX and other Greek translations as sources of authority for Jewish ideology and practice must take into account that biblical texts were also sources for the centrality of Jerusalem, the temple, and the land. The much more direct answer to not rewarding Agrippa's loyalty and eligibility as a ruler over Judea was Rome's military strategy to strengthen its eastern frontier against Parthia, which gave political advantage to direct Roman rule through city councils, village councils, new *coloniae*, and military rule, what Junghwa Choi has called a change "from right person to right system" (*Jewish Leadership in Roman Palestine*, 117–51, esp. 137–46). Lesser Armenia and Commagene were annexed in the early 70s, while Batanea, Trachonitis, and Auranitis were taken from Agrippa II and the kingdom of Chalcis was annexed in the early to mid-90s. "Now with the benefit of hindsight, *none*

temple that had burned down would hardly have been unprecedented. "A small building for the Holy of Holies, an altar, and markers to delineate the perimeters of sacred ground, would suffice, provided that they were all in the correct place in Jerusalem. The most onerous task would be to clear the site of rubble. There were plenty of priests of good pedigree still alive able to fulfil their functions—of whom not the least well known was Josephus himself."[204] Instead, Judea was placed under what was virtually military rule with the Tenth Legion, one of the insignias of which was the wild boar, stationed in Jerusalem.[205] For good measure, the temple of Onias at Leontopolis was also closed down immediately after the war. What was most ironic about not reestablishing the cult in Jerusalem was that it meant that the primary symbol of Jewish loyalty to the empire, the daily sacrifices offered on behalf of the emperor and the Roman people, and temple sacrifice, the one practice Jews had in common with religious practice throughout the Roman world, no longer had any place. Instead, all Jews wherever they lived in regions and cities of the empire, the overwhelming majority of whom had no involvement in the war whatever, were subjected to the payment of a tax. Was the initial transfer of the Jerusalem temple tax to the temple of Jupiter in Rome also an invitation to Jews to transfer allegiance to the superior power of the supreme Roman god, Jupiter?[206] In any case, the imposition of the tax entailed a public reorientation from Jerusalem to Rome. What Jews had formerly collected for Jerusalem was now collected for Rome.

Goodman believes that there is a direct connection between the failure to allow the reestablishment of the Jerusalem cult and the outbreak of hostilities in Egypt, Cyrene, Cyprus, and Mesopotamia in 115–117.[207] The revolt in Judea in 132–135 under the leadership of Shimʿon bar Kosiba is seen as a response to the establishment of *colonia Aelia Capitolina* rather than the occasion of its establishment as retaliation.[208] Goodman rejects

---

of the annexed kingdoms *were restored* after 70 CE, which supports the Roman tendency to direct Roman rule, the 'right system' " (161–62, emphasis original). Finally, in 106 CE the kingdom of Nabatea was annexed.

204. Goodman, *Rome and Jerusalem*, 427.

205. Ibid., 432, 438–39.

206. Ibid., 433; Magness, "Arch of Titus," 207–9.

207. Martin Goodman, "The Temple in First-Century CE Judaism," in *Judaism in the Roman World*, 47–58; Goodman, *Rome and Jerusalem*, 443, 457–58.

208. Goodman, *Rome and Jerusalem*, 464–65.

the view, in my opinion correctly, that there was an easy transition for Jews to nonsacrificial forms of religious practice: "There is not a shred of evidence that any ordinary Jew at this time thought of the cessation of sacrifices as desirable. On the contrary, all Jews were waiting impatiently for God to be worshipped properly again, 'speedily, in our days.'"[209] But Goodman's only way of accounting for the severity of the Roman response is the legitimation and propaganda needs of all three Flavian emperors and, after the brief reign of Nerva, the continuation of the policy through Trajan, because of his father's service to the Flavians in the war as commander of the Tenth Legion from 67–69 and his prominence after the war under Flavian patronage.[210] Though it came some 17 years after Trajan had put down the hostilities of 115–117, the end of Judea as the homeland of the Jews under Hadrian was already in sight.

> The symbolic transfer of the Jews' annual tribute from the Temple of the Jewish God to the temple of Jupiter Capitolinus in Rome had now gone one stage further. Now in Jerusalem, too, Jupiter Capitolinus was to dominate the new Roman city, ideologically, if not physically, displacing once and for all the cult of the Jews. Thus was the suppression of the revolt under Trajan linked to the foundation of Aelia Capitolina and, in turn, to the outbreak of a further terrible war in 132.[211]

Goodman's thesis of the severity of the Roman response to Jews and Judaism after 70 needs some significant qualification, for at the very least one also has to account for the fact that Roman policy clearly did not intend to abolish all Jewish practice, since the very practices most associated with the distinctiveness of the Jews were not targeted by any imperial policy aimed exclusively at them, and were even upheld on occasion in instances of hostility of local elites to their continuation, for example, in Antioch and Alexandria (Josephus, *J.W.* 7.5.2 §§100–111; *Ant.* 12.3.1 §§121–124).[212] Goodman is correct to emphasize the religious and not

---

209. Ibid., 427–28.
210. Ibid., 449–52.
211. Ibid., 464.
212. For the situation of Jews and followers of Jesus in Antioch after the war, see Warren Carter, "Matthew: Empire, Synagogues, and Horizontal Violence," in Becker and Runesson, *Mark and Matthew I*, 284–85. Paget, "After 70 and All That," correctly underscores the lack of any evidence of large-scale Roman reprisals against Jewish diaspora populations, but seems to me to miss the implications of the imposition of

narrowly political dimension of Roman policy after the war, but it was the
Jerusalem cult that was the target. James Rives has put the aims of Roman
policy in a more appropriate framework.[213] Even if there was some basis
for Josephus to have maintained that Titus was not from the start of the
siege bent on destroying the temple, the actions that followed in Rome
from 71, "taken together, constitute what we may reasonably describe as
a policy.... It is important to stress that this policy concerned the Temple
not simply as a building, a potential fortress for rebels, but as the cultic
centre of the Jews: its goal was apparently the permanent abolition of the
Jewish sacrificial cult."[214] Rives explains that the problem from a Roman
imperial perspective regarding religious practices of provincials would
not have been customs and usages of Jews as an ethnic group, even if
these were often described with terms signifying cultic practices, nor with
wisdom or philosophical conceptions of the divine, nor with local Jewish
associations. These were all associated with individuals and families and
with local ethnic associations maintaining ties with ancestral deities. It
was rather what a Vespasian would have identified as the anomalous organization of the civic cult of the Jews. This was more than the concern that
the temple of a major provincial city could become the focus of a regional
nationalism directed against Roman interests, especially on the occasion
of major festivals. It was rather a problem of a potential rivalry with Rome:

---

the *fiscus Iudaicus*, regarding it as "an anomaly and may be best explained by the fact
that all Jews had paid this tax before the revolt" (354). The *fiscus* was not the same as
the temple tax, not just with respect to the goal of the collection but in terms of the liability of all members of a family and the period of time of liability. Nor were the kinds
of sanctions for nonpayment the same. Even if Vespasian's primary motivation was
financial, is it really plausible to suppose that diaspora Jews who had no involvement
in the war would have thought that the tax amounted to a simple transfer of funds
in the absence of a central Jewish cultic site rather than a tax imposed on account of
a Judean revolt against Rome? How many Jews paid the temple tax, and would no
record of paying it have counted as nonliability for the Roman imposed tax? For the
view that Vespasian's motives were primarily financial, see Paul Foster, "Vespasian,
Nerva, Jesus, and the *Fiscus Judaicus*," in *Israel's God and Rebecca's Children: Christology and Community in Early Judaism and Christianity. Essays in Honor of Larry W.
Hurtado and Alan F. Segal*, ed. David B. Capes et al. (Waco, TX: Baylor University
Press, 2007), 306–9.
    213. James Rives, "Flavian Religious Policy and the Destruction of the Jerusalem
Temple," in Edmondson et al., *Flavius Josephus and Flavian Rome*, 145–66.
    214. Ibid., 154.

Although other immigrant groups maintained their devotion to ancestral cults, that of the Jews went much further by excluding any participation in local cults. Moreover, their ties to the ancestral cult centre were more formally organized than those of other diaspora groups.... The temple functioned ... as a civic cult, but the people whom it bound together were not the inhabitants of a single city or region. From Vespasian's point of view, this anomalous organization would have made the Jews to some extent a shadow *civitas*, a people who identified themselves primarily not with the city in which they lived nor even with Rome, but with Jerusalem and its cult. Jerusalem would thus have appeared as a kind of rival to Rome, the only other city whose "citizens", so to speak, were scattered throughout the empire.[215]

Rives concludes that the assumption of the emperor Vespasian that the loss of their civic cult would facilitate the Jews' integration in their local urban environments and the assumption of the priest Josephus that temple and torah must again be integrated were incompatible. The role of scriptures and law continued to provide a source of collective identity for Jews without the temple cult, and the Flavian policy continued because it made sense from the perspective of the Roman elite regarding normative religious practice and from the point of view of imperial interests of integration of local populations.[216] In the long run, Flavian policy and its

---

215. Ibid., 163. The expanse of the Jewish diaspora was in fact beyond the boundaries of the Roman empire. Rives has not discounted other explanations for Flavian decisions and actions after the war, in particular, financial straits as a consequence of Nero's extravagance and the need to rebuild after the civil wars, and ideological needs of the new dynasty, requiring the suppression of the Jerusalem cult and the transfer of both attributes and revenues of the Jewish god to the Roman god, a representation in celebration, in stone, and in policy of the foundation myth of the dynasty (155–56).

216. Ibid., 165–66. Paget, "After 70 and All That," is not fully persuaded by Rives's explanation: It could be countered "that the view of Judaism he attributes to Vespasian is overly sophisticated, and that the failure of the Diaspora to participate in the revolt ... would not have encouraged Vespasian to arrive at a view of the temple as a potentially dangerous civic cult" (351). But Rives's explanation is offered precisely as a recognition that required no detailed or sophisticated knowledge of Jewish practices and organization but simply a difference from ordinary elite Roman perceptions of the appropriate place of civic cults under Roman rule. Even though it is reasonable to question whether there was some specific point at which the Flavian dynasty made a conscious decision to permanently end the Jerusalem cult, Rives's explanation of the kind of thinking and interests that would have made the Jerusalem cult appear anomalous seems to me a crucial consideration in accounting for the fact that the cult

continuation in the reigns of Trajan and Hadrian may have been quite successful, for, as Rives notes, it has been argued that the majority of Palestinian Jews in the second and third centuries did in fact become more integrated into Roman imperial society.[217] "In the second and third centuries, the 'Jewish' cities of Palestine and the larger villages in their vicinity were normal participants in the urban culture of the Roman east, a culture that was suffused with pagan religiosity. This participation was not forced on the cities by the emperor but was in part the response of city elites to conditions created by the end of Jewish autonomy and the imposition of direct Roman rule, among other factors."[218]

was not reestablished in the period between 70 and 132, despite what many Jews probably did continue to hope for in that period. Moreover, Rives's explanation correlates with the end of Roman support of a mediating Judean elite, and more generally with Roman interests in facilitating conditions for the integration of provincial populations in the eastern cities and regions of the empire. Cf. Andrade, "Ambiguity, Violence and Community in the Cities of Judaea and Syria," 358 n. 50: "I emphasize that outbreaks of violence were part of a 'civic' struggle because I believe that violent factions conceived of their conflict as one between different civic orders (*politeiai*) with their cults, not necessarily different 'religious systems.'" Andrade refers to the essay of Rives we are discussing and concludes that the Romans "may have conceived of the Jewish cult as a civic one whose 'citizens' inhabited the far reaches of the Roman empire. In this sense, the Flavians' destruction of the Jewish temple could have been a calculated strategy to integrate Jews into a Roman imperial system" (ibid.). One might appeal to fear of a rebuilt Jerusalem temple serving again as a fortress for revolt, but such a fear as the grounds for not reestablishing the cult in Jerusalem cuts both ways: as a preventive measure, but also as an incentive to further revolt.

217. Rives, "Flavian Religious Policy," 164 n. 29; the reference is to Seth Schwartz in particular, *Imperialism and Jewish Society*, 129–61.

218. Schwartz, *Imperialism and Jewish Society*, 158. While the magnitude of Schwartz's revisionist history has been widely acknowledged, his description of the collapse of the ideological matrix of Judaism ("Judaism shattered," "Jewish society disintegrated," 175) in the second and third centuries and its re-emergence in Jewish communities of Palestine in the fifth and sixth centuries (described mostly as an appropriation of a Christian model, "repackaged Christianity," 179) has not gone unchallenged. For several full-length reviews with both positive assessments and substantive critiques, see Fergus Millar, "Transformations of Judaism and Graeco-Roman Rule: Responses to Seth Schwartz's *Imperialism and Jewish Society*," *JJS* 57 (2006): 139–58; Stuart S. Miller, "Roman Imperialism, Jewish Self-Definition, and Rabbinic Society," *AJSR* 31 (2007): 336–50; Michael L. Satlow, "A History of the Jews or Judaism: On Seth Schwartz's *Imperialism and Jewish Society, 200 B.C.E. to 640 C.E.*," *JQR* 95 (2005): 151–62; Yaron Eliav, "The Matrix of Ancient Judaism," *Proof* 24 (2004): 116–28; and see also, Adiel Schremer, "The Religious Orientation of Non-Rabbis in Second-Century

Palestine: A Rabbinic Perspective," in *"Follow the Wise": Studies in Jewish History and Culture in Honor of Lee I. Levine*, ed. Zeev Weiss et al. (Winona Lake, IN: Eisenbrauns, 2010), 319–41. Schwartz's case for the paganization of the Jewish population of Palestine at this time does not rest exclusively on the absence of Jewish markings of the material artifacts, or on an assessment of the water installations of Sepphoris having no special ritual significance, or on playing down the significance of the necropolis of Beth Shearim, as some have alleged (Eliav, "Matrix," 121–23; Miller, "Roman Imperialism," 340–41, 348–49). Given the fact that Syria Palaestina was now an imperial province with two Roman legions and settled veterans, that Jews were not now the majority population of the province, that Jewish practices were no longer supported by a Roman authorized elite for the Jewish population of the province as a whole, and given the extent of Roman initiative and support of urbanization and success in coopting local elites, the attraction of Jews to politically dominant Greco-Roman and Semitic pagan cultural forms and religious practices should not be surprising. What is more surprising is that "a traditionalizing, primordialist Jewish movement arose in Palestine after the suppression of two revolts against Rome" (Lapin, *Rabbis as Romans*, 10), which included "the generation or compilation of a massive work in Hebrew [the Mishnah] ... devoted in part to the memory of the Temple and for the rest to the disputed rules as to how to conduct a Jewish life in an environment in which pagans were ever-present" (Millar, "Transformations of Judaism," 149). "In late antiquity as in other periods, we may miss truly significant developments if we take ethnic or religious identity (in our case, 'Jewishness') as historical givens" (Lapin, *Rabbis as Romans*, 35). However, as Satlow points out, for all of Schwartz's revisionism there is a strong traditionalist element in his approach to Jewish identity, which he tends to equate with "Judaism" understood as the ideological core of one torah, one temple, one God ("Jews or Judaism," 157, 159). Although Schwartz uses the concept effectively in my judgment as a heuristic to take account of factors of integration, symbolic prestige, and power relations obtaining in the Second Temple period in contrast to later periods, his employment of the core ideology as the organizing principle for identifying expressions of "Judaism" throughout the long expanse of time covered in the book lends itself to problematic abstraction. If this core ideology is not to be equated with how Jews thought and acted, as Schwartz himself emphasizes for the Second Temple period, and if even then "'*torah*' *was a series of negotiations between an authoritative but opaque text and various sets of traditional but not fully authorized practice*" (*Imperialism and Jewish Society*, 68, emphasis original), why should negotiations by Jews of traditional concepts and practices not remain the operative principle in the following period in Palestine, even when the results amounted to quite different performances under the constraints and pressures of a set of changed relations between the imperial authority and their Jewish subjects? Note that Schwartz's taxonomy of the Jewish population in the second and third centuries, even along an ideological continuum, suggests a greater heterogeneity than some of his generalizations would seem to allow (176). Furthermore, Schwartz himself sees that without presupposing some forms of Jewish identification in the second and third centuries apart from the rabbis, one could not account for the new expressions of the core ideology in the subsequent period of a Christian empire, especially since the rabbis are not central to this emergence on

The Flavians announced the Judean defeat to the world, and not just to those who lived in Rome or those who traveled regularly to Rome.[219]

Schwartz's analysis (240, 259). With the publication of Andrade's *Syrian Identity*, one also needs to consider whether the very success of a Roman imperial policy of integration of provincials through identification with a network of Greek cities effected also for urban Jews of the province a range of expressions of "Greek" and "Jew," "Syrian" and "Jew," just as with "Greek" and "Syrian," which were dependent neither on adherence to an ideological core nor on a fundamental polarity but on intersecting modes of civic performance (see above, 217–18 with nn. 25–26, 29). Note Schwartz's own remark about most Palestinian Jews in the second and third centuries being Jews in the way that Lucian of Samosata was a Syrian (*Imperialism and Jewish Society*, 15). As Satlow concludes, "The interesting and useful question focuses not on 'Judaism' but on Jews" ("Jews or Judaism," 161). One must also take account of evidence of ongoing Jewish subcultures not focused in particular on Palestine but easily ignored by equating "Judaism" with an ideological core for which only the rabbis can qualify as carriers in the second and third centuries; for examples, see Annette Yoshiko Reed, "Rabbis, 'Jewish Christians', and Other Late Antique Jews: Reflections on the Fate of Judaism (s) after 70 C.E.," in *The Changing Face of Judaism, Christianity, and Other Greco-Roman Religions in Antiquity*, ed. Ian H. Henderson and Gerbern S. Oegema with the assistance of Sara Parks Ricker, Studien zu den Jüdischen Schriften aus hellenistisch-römischer Zeit 2 (Gütersloh: Gütersloher Verlagshaus, 2006), 323–46, and David Frankfurter, "Beyond 'Jewish Christianity': Continuing Religious Sub-Cultures of the Second and Third Centuries and Their Documents," in *The Ways That Never Parted: Jews and Christians in Late Antiquity and the Early Middle Ages*, ed. Adam H. Becker and Annette Yoshiko Reed (Minneapolis: Fortress, 2007), 131–43.

219. Avi Avidov has argued in his study of the systemic structural factors creating Jewish marginality that while the Flavians announced the Judean defeat to the world, Roman imperial policy had worked against the social integration of Jews long before the revolt of 66 and the effects of Flavian policy (*Not Reckoned among Nations: The Origins of the So-Called "Jewish Question" in Roman Antiquity*, TSAJ 128 (Tübingen: Mohr Siebeck, 2009). Avidov maintains that cultural assimilation, degrees of economic well being, and legal standing are not adequate indices of social integration, the willingness and ability to perform expected social roles leading to political integration (166). His argument depends on making the case that Roman patronage did not work to create deep networks of patronage linking center and periphery in Judean society either in Palestine or the diaspora as it was intended in Roman imperial society. The argument entails a critique of pan-Mediterranean views of patronage, interpreting every relationship that is not strictly horizontal as an example of patronage, including its application in New Testament studies (147–56, 150–52). For a much more detailed critique of the same, see Erlend D. MacGillivray, "Re-evaluating Patronage and Reciprocity in Antiquity and New Testament Studies," *JGRCHJ* 6 (2009): 37–81. Seth Schwartz has taken up the issue in *Were the Jews a Mediterranean Society? Reciprocity and Solidarity in Ancient Judaism* (Princeton: Princeton University Press, 2010).

If you had visited Rome only several times during the 70s and 80s, you might have come to associate the changing face of the city with the Judean defeat and talked about it back home. If you lived in a provincial city of the Roman East in which there was a sizable Jewish population, you might have remarked about Jews still sending funds abroad, but to Rome not Jerusalem. If you lived in regions outside the territory of Judea, but in parts of the Roman province of Judea and in surrounding regions of Syria heavily populated by Jews, you may have welcomed or bemoaned the end of public deference shown to representatives of the Jerusalem establishment, welcomed or bemoaned the increased Roman presence, and gotten accustomed to no longer being inconvenienced or benefitted by Jewish pilgrims on their way to Jerusalem for a festival. More would be reminded of the Judean defeat from the circulation of *Iudaea capta* coins, minted again in the mid-80s. Was it only in Alexandria and Antioch after the war that there was an expectation that Rome would accede upon request to abolishing their rights (Josephus, *J.W.* 7.5.2 §§110–111; *Ant.* 12.3.1 §§121–124; *Ag. Ap.* 2.4 §§38–39)? Would it not have seemed surprising to some in the Roman East who had a reason to take note (and not only to a priest like Josephus or to Jews in particular) that the Flavians had made an example of the Jews but apparently had no intention of interfering with their peculiar practices? Perhaps some would surmise that Rome stood to lose a hefty source of annual income from the Jewish tax were they to take steps to interfere with Jewish practices to the point of weakening their communal institutions throughout the empire. Before the war the sanctions bearing on Jews who did not pay the temple tax were social; the

---

He has also critiqued the application of "mediterraneanism" in Hebrew Bible studies (23–24 n. 9). While Avidov's case for the mal-integration of Jews is controversial, esp. with respect to diaspora Jewish social formations in cities of the Eastern provinces of the Roman empire, it does point up the possibility that Rome would have eventually exercised greater control of the Jerusalem temple, curbed its reach, and created incentives producing conditions in Palestine similar to those that obtained in the second and third centuries, even if the ruling class of Judea had taken a different course and there had been no revolts, given the policy of establishing direct Roman administration in territories of client kings in the Roman East beginning in the last decades of the first century CE. But as it turned out, it was in conditions of political, cultural, and symbolic loss in the wake of a failed revolt that created the pressures and attractions of deeper modes of integration of Jewish populations in Roman provincial societies in the region of south Syria, and therefore also created new challenges and pressures on strategies of cultural persistence.

sanctions on Jews who did not pay the tax to Rome were also material and punitive. The tax paid to Rome was a far heavier financial burden, since liability applied not only to male Jews between the ages of twenty to fifty but to children from the age of three, women at least to age sixty-two, and slaves, which also meant that the tax rolls would have to be regularly updated.[220] The Judean defeat was to be paid for by all Jews annually. Would it really have said nothing about perceptions of Jewish collective identity that all Jews were liable to pay a tax to Rome irrespective of their relationship to the war, presumably even those who had fought against the rebels?[221]

Direct Roman rule also introduced changes in the legal status of the local population:

> They [Roman rulers] did not recognize the autonomy of the local population (except, of course, of the citizen bodies of Greek cities, in a very tenuous way), and they did not appoint intermediaries between the 'natives' and themselves—the main characteristics of the old client-kingship system, which by the later first century was an unambiguous failure.... To be sure, the government did nothing to prevent Jews from patronizing their legal experts for advice and arbitration. Yet by failing to recognize their jurisdiction, they made them effectively powerless to compete with the Roman courts and the arbitration of Jewish city councillors and landowners for most purposes.[222]

---

220. For general references to the *fiscus Iudaicus*, see Josephus, *J.W.* 7.6.6 §218; Cassius Dio, *Hist. Rom.* 65.7.2. The information on the liability of members of Jewish families besides male Jews comes from Jewish tax receipts on *ostraka* from the town of Apollinopolis Magna (Edfu) in Egypt covering the years 71/72 to 116 (*CPJ* 2.160–229), and from two preserved papyri from Egypt at Arsinoë from the year 73 and at Karanis from 145/6 or 167/8 (*CPJ* 2.421, 460). The Arsinoë papyrus from early in Vespasian's reign refers to those who had to undergo an *epikrisis*, examination, referring to women and children who were now liable for the Jewish tax and had to be added to the Jewish men. The *fiscus Iudaicus* is discussed in detail below, sections 9 and 10.

221. James Rives distinguishes between the possible effect of the tax on the corporate identity of the Jews and Vespasian's own motivations "to link the Jews to Rome and its god" ("Flavian Policy and the Jerusalem Temple," 164, n. 18).

222. Schwartz, *Imperialism and Jewish Society*, 111. "In fact, the Babatha papyri may now suggest that even this view requires revision, for one of the striking facts about Babatha and company is that they apparently made almost no use of local judges but brought even trivial cases to the Roman governor" (112). For a similar view of the Greek documents of the archives, see Hannah M. Cotton, "The Rabbis and the Documents," in Goodman, *Jews in a Graeco-Roman World*, 167–79. "Babatha..., as well

Beyond the loss of the integrative political and cultural role of the temple and its representatives, the change of legal status, and the defeat vis-á-vis rival civic claims in cities within and surrounding Judea, the impact of death, enslavement, and dislocation may still have been felt in the first decades after the war, primarily in Judea but also to a lesser extent in Idumea and Perea, the Galilee and the Golan, even if economic recovery was well under way. Those who fled would have resettled not only in Galilee and the Golan but also in Greek coastal cities of Palestine and Phoenicia, and some in towns and villages of southern Syria where there were large numbers of Jews. Moreover, an understandable disaffection as a consequence of the failed revolt was surely to be expected. Even though

---

as her opponents, were in the habit of approaching this [Roman] court on their own initiative.... Another reason could be the need to deposit the deeds in a public archive, similar to what we know to have been the case in Egypt ...; having been registered there, these documents could later be produced in court as evidence" (169). On the question of local judicial authority in the border area of Judea and Arabia at this time, an area of Jewish population described by Cotton as "representative of Jewish society as a whole" (172), it is proposed (in another article) that the Aramaic documents that are not translations may be accounted for not as an issue of the operation of local courts but as a question of choice between the effectiveness and advantages of Roman courts and the convenience in time and expense of turning to private arbitration. An arbiter's verdict would have social and moral force, but not legal backing and could not be enforced (Cotton, "Jewish Jurisdiction under Roman Rule: Prolegomena," in *Zwischen den Reichen: Neues Testament und Römische Herrschaft*, ed. Michael Labahn and Jürgen Zangenberg, TANZ 36 [Tübingen: Francke, 2002], 18). "Whatever courts we hear about in the rabbinic sources, I suggest, may have been no more than forms of private arbitration, not backed by the powers that be, i.e. the Roman authorities of the province" (20); on provincial arbitration, see also Lapin, *Rabbis as Romans*, 98–125. Jacobine G. Oudshoorn, *The Relationship between Roman and Local Law in the Babatha and Salome Komaise Archives: General Analysis and Three Case Studies on Law of Succession, Guardianship and Marriage*, STDJ 69 (Leiden: Brill, 2007), has shown that one cannot equate the language of the documents with the system of law that is operative. She bases her analysis of the private law attested in the documents on a distinction between the procedural formal level and the substantive level of law. Perhaps most controversial is her identification of the documents as representative of a system of Jewish law rather than what was more likely customary Jewish and/ or Nabatean practice. For reviews of the book, see Judith Evans Grubbs, *RBL* (2009), http://tinyurl.com/SBL4520b; Friedrich Avemarie, *JSJ* 40 (2009): 126–27; John S. Kloppenborg, *DSD* 19 (2012): 235–36; and the full-length study, Bernard S. Jackson and Daniela Piattelli, "A Recent Study of the Babatha and Salome Komaise Archives," *Review of Rabbinic Judaism* 13 (2010): 88–125.

it is impossible to know how widespread the disaffection was in the first decades after 70, it is reasonable to include it among the consequences of the war in thinking about the last quarter of the first century.[223] No amount of self-blame, acceptance of divine anger and withdrawal heavenward, expectation of future rectification, or comparison with other respected peoples defeated by enemies could conceal what the destruction of Jerusalem, the end of temple sacrifice, the Flavian victory, monuments and coins, the increased influence of Greek civic polities in the region, and the imposition of the Jewish tax set in public view for questioning: were the ancestral stories, practices, and social formations that distinguished Jews from others still conceivable on a larger cosmic canvas, that is, were they supported by a powerful and reliable god?[224] It is not because such

---

223. As possible evidence of such disaffection, Seth Schwartz refers to those who may be the historical types represented in Martial's burlesque of "crypto-Jewish actors, poets, and deracinated urban debauchees," those represented by the arguments against the law and Moses's tyranny in Zambrias's speech on freedom in Josephus, *Ant.* 4.8.5 §§145–149, the Jews especially affected in Suetonius's reference to Domitian's harsh exactment of the Jewish tax, the scoffers who forsake the covenant in 2 Bar. 41:3, and those Jewish men referenced in t. Shabb. 15 [16].9 who underwent epispasm and were recircumcised in the time of Bar Kohkba (*Imperialism and Jewish Society*, 109–10 with n. 14). To these may be added the tannaitic texts that voice denials on the themes of God's existence, presence, providence, and power (see Adiel Schremer, "'The Lord Has Forsaken the Land': Radical Explanations of the Military and Political Defeat of the Jews in Tannaitic Literature," *JJS* 59 [2008]: 183–200; and Schremer, "Where Is Their God? Destruction, Defeat, and Identity," in *Brothers Estranged: Heresy, Christianity, and Jewish Identity in Late Antiquity* [Oxford: Oxford University Press, 2010], 25–48). For a general treatment of the phenomenon of apostasy and defection among Jews and Christians in late antiquity, see Stephen G. Wilson, *Leaving the Fold: Apostates and Defectors in Antiquity* (Minneapolis: Fortress, 2004).

224. While I remain largely persuaded by Seth Schwartz's revisionist account of the impact of successive regimes of imperialism on Jewish society over the long span of time covered in *Imperialism and Jewish Society*, I am not arguing that the destruction of the temple in 70 was obviously a watershed event, a judgment which depends on the particular framework and on the question, with respect to what and to whom? This is perhaps the most obvious conclusion to be drawn from the collection of papers under the title, *Was 70 CE a Watershed in Jewish History?* I do reject the view that distance from the temple of itself produced ways of identifying as Jews that marginalized the significance of the temple and sacrifice in Jerusalem, or gave priority to types of Jewish practice that would have reduced or even eliminated the impact of 70 on Jews of the diaspora. This view is represented in the volume in a particularly trenchant way in the paper by Michael Tuval, "Doing without the Temple: Paradigms in Judaic

Literature of the Diaspora," 181–239, which seems to me suspiciously like Eusebius in rabbinic dress: "Preparation for Torah without Temple and Sacrifice" (see Tuval, *From Jerusalem Priest to Roman Jew: On Josephus and the Paradigms of Ancient Judaism*, WUNT 357 [Tübingen: Mohr Siebeck, 2013]. For assessments that differ from Tuval on the same issue, see in the same division of the book the papers by Ori Schwarz, "Place beyond Place: On Artifacts, Religious Technologies, and the Mediation of Sacred Place," 115–26, and Jutta Leonhardt-Balzer, "Priests and Priesthood in Philo: Could He Have Done without Them?," 127–53. One can easily arrive at misleading conclusions by isolating diaspora authored texts that focus on institutions, practices and forms of divine-human reciprocity other than temple and sacrifice, while attributing nothing more than a matter of minimal loyalty to evidence outside these texts of the variety of ways in which Jews of the diaspora participated in temple and sacrifice in Jerusalem even from a distance. The frequency of a practice is not the only kind of criterion for evaluating the goods inherent in a practice, for the very reason that such a criterion may only reflect circumstance rather than relative value. If distance made all the difference, there would be no reason to distinguish diaspora Jews from those of the Roman province of Judea, since, excepting those living in Jerusalem and its immediate surroundings in the territory of Judea, most Jews lived too far from the temple to be present with any regularity. For evidence of the centrality of the temple and festivals for diaspora Jews, see Margaret Williams, *The Jews among the Greeks and Romans: A Sourcebook* (Baltimore: John Hopkins University Press, 1998), 59–64, 67–72. Temple and sacrifice in Jerusalem must have been important to diaspora Jews before 70, for it provided a rationale for drawing lines at participation in civic cults, while hopefully demonstrating at the same time that Jews were not themselves paradigms of impiety. Vespasian must have thought that Jerusalem and the temple occupied a central place for diaspora Jews, since he taxed all of them after the war, even if it was simply because they supported annually with funds and gifts a temple that had been the center of the revolt against Rome. We should not draw conclusions about the importance of temple and sacrifice in Jerusalem simply because certain diaspora authors developed paradigms of Jewish life from portions of scripture in which the temple and sacrifice in Jerusalem were not central. As a matter of religious practice, sacrificing animals at the altar of a particular temple did not provide much opportunity for Jews to differentiate themselves from others. Certainly there were other religious practices besides animal sacrifice and other religious specialists besides priests that provided stronger impetus and clearer focus for cultural comparison and competition between Jews and their neighbors in diaspora environments. When Philo wants to show the support of Caesar Augustus for the rights of Jews in Rome, he refers to the emperor's approval of Jews meeting each sabbath in houses of prayer for training in their ancestral philosophy and his approval of collecting funds from first fruits sent to Jerusalem by those who would offer the sacrifices (*Legat.* 156). The distinction is not between what was central to the religious life of Roman Jews and what had only political significance for them, as if such a distinction were relevant, but between different kinds of Jewish practice: discursive practices in the house of prayer (teachings) and nondiscursive practices in Jerusalem (sacrifice); see Stanley K. Stowers, "Does Pauline Christianity Resemble a Hellenistic Philosophy?," in Cameron and Miller, *Redescribing Paul and*

questioning arises only in events of disaster that it focuses attention when
they occur, but because such events place in high profile the risks of everyday human interaction with divine beings in individual and collective life.
For purposes of a judgment regarding the situation in the Roman province
of Judea and its surroundings for a generation that overlapped the war
and Flavian rule, it would not be a question of "Judaism shattered" or an
atmosphere of doom and gloom as justifiable generalizations but rather a
recognition of significant political, economic, and social change, of new
challenges to cultural work, and, surely symbolically, of public shame, thus
raising the stakes on tests of loyalty, on the marking of social boundaries,
on claims of authority and authenticity, and on demonstrations of power
and accumulation of symbolic capital invested in the reputation of the god
among competitors in a particular cultural field. For most inhabitants of
the region life would return much as usual, at least with respect to relations involving ordinary business and private affairs, including for many
Jews religious household practices. But the disaffected and indifferent, on
the one hand, and those not at all pacified and reconciled to Roman rule
in Jerusalem and the land of Israel, on the other, could also serve as a
reminder to inhabitants of the region of what was at stake. So, we need
to set in appropriate context and perspective questions of interaction and
rivalry among the vocal and literate agents of competing affiliations claiming authoritative versions of scriptural interpretation and directives for the
people. There is no reason to suppose that affiliations of Pharisees, Essenes,
and Sadducees simply ceased immediately after 70. However, it is inappropriate to suppose that the interaction and conflict of followers of Jesus in
Galilee or in southern Syria with those claiming other affiliations would

---

the Corinthians, 222–26. I am also not arguing that Jews were stunned into silence in
the wake of the destruction of the temple, or bereft of precedent, traditional resources,
and thoughtful reflection in response to the consequences of a failed revolt. The premise of this paper is the opposite. The importance of the sixth century BCE destruction
as precedent is obvious. The case for significant continuity of thought on legal, philosophical, and theological issues linking Josephus, the Pharisees, and the later rabbis
has been made by Klawans, Josephus and the Theologies of Ancient Judaism. Klawans's
demonstration of this continuity and linkage on ideas of fate and free will, legal theory,
martyrdom and suicide is impressive. Continuity of ideas on theodicy is not as significant, since they are overdetermined by the biblical, particularly Deuteronomic,
precedent. However, the continuity of ideas among religious specialists is not by itself
a measure of societal change in the wake of 70. Nor is it necessarily an index for assessing disaffection as a consequence of military defeat.

have registered for many Jewish villagers or urban residents as a conflict of real authority in the affairs of a network of villages or an urban center. The rhetorical intensity of conflict with scribes and Pharisees in Mark, and particularly in Matthew, are just as likely to have been matters of self-representation than reflections of actual intense interaction and rivalry. The rivalry may have been staged in some measure because competing claims and practices were imagined as an arena of engagement for overcoming or escaping the social and political stigma of a defeated people.[225]

The social world depicted in the archives from the Dead Sea should also be in view, because they show us a set of relations among Semitic inhabitants of the border areas of Judea and Nabatea/Roman Arabia that can probably be extrapolated to other border regions of the province of Judea after the war. Though the documents are considerably more distant in time from the first revolt than the Gospel of Mark, they were written shortly before the outbreak of the Bar Kokhba revolt near the center of where the war was fought. Nevertheless, as Anthony Saldarini remarks,

> The documents do not distinguish, exclude, or polemicize against outsiders. The signatories and principals interact easily with whoever lives in the area. The tensions with gentiles, disputes with Jewish or gentile Christians, and avoidance of idolaters we see elsewhere in Jewish literature have no effect here. Neither the destruction of the temple and Jerusalem, the war of fifty or sixty years previously, the apocalyptic hopes of some groups, nor the reconstructive efforts of the early rabbis receives any notice. These admittedly limited and narrowly focused documents reflect the lives of prosperous Jews living in and around the boundaries of the traditional land of Israel in peace with their neighbors, following traditional Jewish and local ways of life, and cooperating with the government.[226]

---

225. Choi, *Jewish Leadership in Roman Palestine*, leaves basically unanswered the question of the social influence of learned leadership without political authority after the destruction of the temple (189). While it may be the case that there was an even greater variety of claims to leadership than before 70, it cannot be the case that Roman rule through city and village councils, through *coloniae*, and through the military had political, economic, and juridical impact but no consequence for the social influence of variously affiliated and nonaffiliated religious specialists, even if the latter took rhetorical and practical advantage of their distance from the circles of Jerusalem elite that had been decimated in the defeat.

226. Anthony J. Saldarini, "The Social World of Christian Jews and Jewish Christians," in *Religious and Ethnic Communities in Later Roman Palestine*, ed. Hayim

As Saldarini points out, Babatha and company "suggests a context for the instructional, apologetic, and polemical literature of early Jews and Christians in Israel and its neighborhood.... Arguments about how Jewish a region was seem irrelevant in the face of these documents."[227] We would do well to bring to mind Babatha and company, people of some wealth though not elites, when considering some kinds of potential clientele for competing programs of "mission," clientele for the religious expertise of freelance entrepreneurs, for the services of exemplars of wisdom, moral rectitude and ritual piety—and yet, to see Babatha and company also as potential recruits and perhaps participants in the Bar Kokhba revolt. It is unlikely that expectations or at least the hope that Jerusalem and the temple would soon be rebuilt were extinguished after 70, as they are more likely to have been after 135. Despite the counter indications of Flavian policy, it was still possible to think that Rome's noninterference in the practices of established Jewish institutions in the diaspora would soon lead to some rebuilding and autonomy for the temple and city through the remnants of a priestly aristocracy. A Josephus in Rome as a "reluctant provincial" may not be all that distant in sensibilities from those in the next generation who at least partly in response to the failure of these hopes to materialize led and fought in the Bar Kokhba war.[228]

The locations in view in this paper for the composition of Mark, whether they be border areas of Galilee and southern Syria, or farther

---

Lapin, Studies and Texts in Jewish History and Culture 5 (Bethesda, MD: University of Maryland, 1998), 141.

227. Ibid., 142. Compare these observations of Saldarini for the border area of Judea/Nabatea with the observations of Smith and the kinds of questions he proposes would have been up for discussion and debate in another border region, the Phoenician coast ("The Markan Site," 118–20). While I am focusing in this paper on the consequences of a geopolitical event occurring at a time of the emergence of a new imperial dynasty, on the loss of Judean political and cultural influence in southern Syria and increased Roman pressure to integrate provincial populations of the region in Greek civic polities, this is not intended to exclude as unproductive for a redescription of the Markan site situations of consequence arising from interactions of more stable relations of the long term among the peoples of the southern Levant; see above, 232 with n. 52. On *ex eventu* prophecy as a phenomenon of the ancient Near East *longue durée*, see above (Neujahr), n. 87, n. 167, and 284 with n. 174. On Sib. Or. 4, see Smith, "The Markan Site," 125, and below, nn. 256 and 261.

228. See James S. McLaren, "A Reluctant Provincial: Josephus and the Roman Empire in *Jewish War*," in *The Gospel of Matthew in Its Roman Imperial Context*, ed. John Riches and David C. Sim, JSNTSup 276 (London: T&T Clark, 2005), 34–48.

north in Syria, or one of the cities of the Phoenician coast, or a city of the Decapolis, also comprise a region where there existed longer memories of Hasmonean aggression against Greek cities and still fresh memories of outbreaks of violence and mutual fears and suspicions evoked by the prospects of war and its consequences, fears and suspicions which may not have abated by the 80s, even with a return to more typical patterns of social and economic intercourse. If we postulate a close circle of literate friends and their network, include some other kinds of religious specialists practicing in the name of Jesus, and imagine some wider forums of interest in readings, debate, ritual practices within associations and other kinds of family or gender-based and neighborhood social formations, among their numbers and among their associates might be refugees from the war, not just Judeans and Syrians but Galileans, Itureans, Nabateans, Samaritans or Idumeans, possibly some who fought on different sides in the war; descendants of families incorporated in the Hasmonean expansion, that is, people self-identified in some ways and for some purposes as Jews but without having abandoned markers of other ethnic identities; individuals unimpressed by ethnic distinctions, while much more sensible of markers of status as Greeks through language, cultural identification, and civic performance, or as Jews through knowledge of the scriptures in Greek; men and women impressed with the reputation of Jewish prophets and their skills of teaching and healing, and their appeal to a continuous tradition and its written sources, in spite of or perhaps even because of what had happened; people who may have agreed in hindsight that the revolt in Judea had revealed a failed polity, some still chafing at the threat posed by Judeans to established patterns of regional stability, others aggrieved at the outcome, and therefore people who brought different interests and assessments of their situation in relation to Roman imperial projects and their Greek urban polity networks.[229] We should assume a range of reasons for interest and attachment to the teachings, works, and fate of a Galilean prophet and exorcist, a divinely authorized broker of an announced divine rule breaking into the world, a figure of power and suffering in his own time, presented by Mark in a time of the exertion of Judean military power against Rome and the costs and consequences that followed.

229. See above, n. 218 (Andrade, *Syrian Identity*); above, nn. 171 and 216 (Andrade, "Ambiguity, Violence and Community in the Cities of Judaea and Syria").

8. Responses to the Destruction:
Apocalypses, Related Writings, and Josephus

The apocalyptic and related writings from the late first and early second centuries CE must be considered in any account of Jewish responses in a postdestruction setting. Several studies of one or more of these writings raise issues pertinent to our discussion. In arguing against the view that 3 Baruch was a Christian document in its origin, Daniel Harlow calls attention to the distinctively Jewish perspective of the prologue with its lament over the destruction of Jerusalem similar to passages in 4 Ezra, 2 Baruch, 4 Baruch, and rabbinic writings, expressions of mourning over the fate of Jerusalem which do not have "the remotest analogies in early Christian literature."[230] "The *restoration* of Jerusalem surfaces as an object of Christian hope only in connection with the millennial reign of Christ. Not even Christian chiliasts envisioned a restoration of the Temple and a revival of the sacrificial cult."[231] Harlow summarizes the approach of Christian literature for the first four centuries as a spiritualizing of Jerusalem and temple imagery and an apologetic claim that the destruction of city and temple reveals God's rejection of the Jews.[232] As a general consideration in arguments about the origins of 3 Baruch, I would agree with Harlow's judgment, although the Q logion, Luke 13:34–35, even as a judgment oracle, includes an element of lament, while the passages of lament that are cited by Harlow as parallels to 3 Bar 1:2 also recognize God's judgment in the event.[233] The deepest grievance is that God has used as the instrument of judgment the enemy that boasts of its victory. Furthermore, expressions of grief over the destruction of the city and temple or their absence can be misleading if we take the difference to be determinative of the kinds of cultural work being done. As Harlow and others have shown, 3 Baruch appears to be utterly unconcerned about any sort of restoration of Jerusalem or heavenly temple. Moreover, the reception of divine mysteries promised to Baruch after his lament is contingent on his ceasing to irritate God by concerning himself with the salvation of Jerusalem. Baruch

---

230. Daniel C. Harlow, *The Greek Apocalypse of Baruch (3 Baruch) in Hellenistic Judaism and Early Christianity*, SVTP 12 (Leiden: Brill, 1996), 90–91.

231. Ibid., 94–95, emphasis original.

232. Ibid., 96–108.

233. Harlow, 92–93, cites 4 Ezra 3:28; 5:28–30; 2 Bar. 3:5–6; 5:1; 7:2; 4 Bar. 1:6–7; 4:7–9.

agrees and never speaks about it again (1:3–8). At the end of the study Harlow concludes that 3 Baruch is not merely escapist literature. This Hellenistic Jewish writing never shows Baruch attaining the vision of God. The mysteries are those of a cosmic and ethical order revealed to exist for all individuals in the world and after death.[234] One could read 3 Baruch as a kind of Jewish theodicy, though it never makes reference to the law or even to any particular ethical injunctions. Apart from the protagonist Baruch and the opening lament, this ascent apocalypse gives little reason to suppose that the God whose cosmic and ethical order is revealed is in any particular way the God of Israel or that the circles in which this writing circulated were people who really needed to stop worrying about the fate of Jerusalem and the temple. Indeed, if the opening lament could become a basis for a Christian supersessionist reading, it seems to have already been an invitation for Jews to abandon any lingering attachment to the symbols associated with a people's recent humiliation.[235]

Harlow makes the point that the retribution scheme of 3 Baruch brings together the traditional Deuteronomic view of earthly retribution and the apocalyptic view of a personal afterlife.[236] Matthias Henze has made a better case for the joining of Deuteronomic and apocalyptic perspectives in his study of 2 Baruch, because the latter writing, unlike 3 Baruch, affirms the continuing centrality of the Deuteronomic view of the law. "[Second Baruch] incorporates into one program various … traditions that previously were kept in segregation, chief among them the *Deuteronomic promise* of a prosperous life for those keeping the Mosaic Torah and the *apocalyptic promise* that the current, corrupt world would soon give way to a new, incorruptible reality in which Israel would be restored and the righteous would live under the throne in the expanses of paradise."[237] This observation bears on two other matters of emphasis

---

234. Ibid., 206–12.

235. This last point responds to Harlow's final sentence: "How ironic that, when Jewish *3 Baruch* became Christian *3 Baruch*, the work's underlying universalism was transformed into an arrogant supersessionism" (212). Admittedly, this response to Harlow depends on reading Jewish 3 Baruch as an expression of disaffection in the wake of an event perceived as cosmic disruption rather than as a form of cultural persistence. For further consideration, see below, n. 261.

236. Ibid., 208.

237. Matthias Henze, *Jewish Apocalypticism in Late First Century Israel: Reading Second Baruch in Context*, TSAJ 142 (Tübingen: Mohr Siebeck, 2011), 372, emphasis original.

in Henze's study, namely, that 2 Baruch draws on a variety of streams of apocalyptic and other traditions of Second Temple Judaism, demonstrating that the political divide of 70 was not necessarily an intellectual divide and that the milieu of the writing is not sectarian.[238] Henze's observation that Deuteronomic and apocalyptic traditions are linked in 2 Baruch can be compared to Schwartz's discussion of covenantal and mythic systems in *Imperialism and Jewish Society*. However, what Henze sees as the innovation of 2 Baruch, Schwartz sees as different ideological axes which are typically juxtaposed in the literature of the Second Temple.

> The repeated juxtaposition of the covenant and the myth in ancient Jewish writing indicates that though the systems are logically incongruous, they did not for the most part generate social division. That is, the literary evidence provides no grounds for speaking of an "apocalyptic Judaism," or even "apocalyptic conventicles".... Apocalyptic Judaism's opposite number, "covenantal Judaism," may have existed but is marginal in the literature.... Thus, by the first century, if not earlier, the myth was a more or less fully naturalized part of the ideology of Judaism.[239]

Nonetheless, these ideological axes required the cultivation of different scribal skills and could be supported by different practices. Moreover, "the myth retained its *potential* to generate separate social organization."[240] Henze's point is precisely that this is not the case with 2 Baruch. Unlike 4 Ezra, "the book does not consider itself to be part of an esoteric corpus of texts that is distinct from—and, indeed, superior to—what will become 'the canon.'"[241] Schwartz sees the successful incorporation of the myth into the mainstream ideology of the covenant "as an aspect of centralization, of the rise in post-Maccabean Palestine of an integrated Judaism, controlled from Jerusalem by mediators of the Temple and Torah."[242] Henze describes the author of 2 Baruch around the end of the first century CE as one who "was not writing for a small circle of the chosen but intended his

---

238. These matters are presented in brief (ibid., 8–14) and in a more focused discussion of 2 Baruch as nonsectarian (231–40).

239. Schwartz, *Imperialism and Jewish Society*, 81.

240. Ibid., 87, emphasis original.

241. Henze, *Jewish Apocalypticism*, 240.

242. Schwartz, *Imperialism and Jewish Society*, 86.

apocalyptic program to become normative for post-70 Judaism in the land of Israel and beyond."[243]

Henze's proposal should be questioned, if it is intended as a description of the actual social setting and program one can imagine for the literary project of 2 Baruch. In post-70 Palestine, what centralized institution could have given the authorization necessary for such a program, and what Roman approved elite could have provided the backing? A more realistic assessment would posit subelite scribes whose teachings are respected in a network of villages or among families in a particular urban center with access to a synagogue or local association to promote their teaching program and perhaps to establish some connections abroad. The rhetorical stance of 2 Baruch, while perhaps not an expression of sectarian mentality, is not thereby a reflection of widespread influence or authority. It is more likely to reflect an awareness that religious fragmentation is particularly problematic where the reality of disaffection is prominent in a time of political and cultural loss.[244] If we take seriously Baruch's promise

---

243. Henze, *Jewish Apocalypticism*, 240.

244. For similar claims about the anti-sectarian mentality of the sages of Yavneh after 70, although based on the acceptance of different halakhic rulings in the Mishnah, see Shaye J. D. Cohen, "The Significance of Yavneh: Pharisees, Rabbis, and the End of Jewish Sectarianism," *HUCA* 55 (1984): 27–53; repr. in *The Significance of Yavneh and Other Essays in Jewish Hellenism*, TSAJ 136 (Tübingen: Mohr Siebeck, 2010), 44–70. But adherence to the torah of Moses without prioritizing particular commandments or entering into debate over their interpretation (2 Baruch), and citing different rulings without deciding between them (Mishnah) may have the same rhetorical function of presenting one's own program as broadly based and normative against other options. For evidence of continuing sectarian debate on practices of purity in literary sources, including tannaitic sources, and archaeological evidence after 70 of the continuing use of stone vessels and *miqva'ot* among some of the Jewish population of Palestine, see Jodi Magness, "Sectarianism Before and After 70 CE," in Schwartz and Weiss, *Was 70 CE a Watershed?*, 69–89. Magness summarizes the findings of the recent excavations at Shu'afat, some four kilometers north of Jerusalem, the only site thus far discovered in the vicinity of Jerusalem dating between the two revolts (70–135). Among the finds are *miqva'ot*, hand-carved stone vessels, Roman-style bath houses, and pottery manufactured in the kiln works of the Tenth Legion in Jerusalem. "The evidence of a relatively prosperous Romanized lifestyle combined with Jewish purity observance suggests that this was a settlement of elite families including priests who remained as close to Jerusalem as possible after 70, perhaps awaiting the rebuilding of the Temple" (85–86 with notes). On the Essenes after 70, see Joshua Ezra Burns, "Essene Sectarianism and Social Differentiation in Judaea after 70 C.E.," *HTR* 99 (2006): 247–74; on sectarianism, see above, nn. 101 and 103.

that there would be qualified teachers when he is gone, we should take even more seriously the people's fear about its future (46:1–7; 77:11–17). Proselytes were welcome, of course, but not enough to turn a blind eye to apostates (41:1–6). Henze's own point that the historical apocalypses of the late first century show more continuity with the traditions of the past than prospects for the future is certainly the case.[245] The threat of an imminent judgment even worse than what had already befallen was perhaps not all that attractive under the circumstances, and the promise of a radical transformation and special protection soon to be realized may have had limited appeal in the face of an increasing Romanization of the province, or with those who could not make their peace with Roman rule. We can no longer estimate the influence of torah-oriented apocalypses on a wider Palestinian society, let alone across diasporas, by appeal in particular instances to the continuity of ideas across the divide of 70, or by appeal to the centrality of torah among the rabbis of second-and third-century Palestine.

Henze summarizes the close affinities he sees between 2 Baruch and the Gospel of Matthew. Both writings connect the advent of the messiah to the Babylonian captivity, present their protagonist as a new Moses, and feature the centrality of torah for the post-70 community. But there is also a notable distinction between the two documents. Henze calls attention to the absence of specific laws in 2 Baruch, or materials advocating particular interpretations of the commandments, or the presence of a discourse of polemics in contrast to Matthew in which all of these are present to a high degree.[246] Henze implies that Matthew is a more sectarian document, or at least that it is written in a context of ongoing conflict with those adhering to the teachings of other scribes and Pharisees. This may be the case and has long been an assumption of many studies of the Gospel of Matthew. But again I would suggest, first, that in a post-70 setting in regions of Palestine and Syria, such disputes were conducted in contexts of very particular and limited social networks in contrast to having the political support of Roman authorized native councils in wider networks of villages or in an urban center. The legal prestige of pre-70 Pharisees was more likely to have been diminished rather than enhanced by the destruction of Jerusalem and the loss of the temple and its administration. Second, Matthew's polemics may be evidence at some point of significant interaction over

---

245. Henze, *Jewish Apocalypticism*, 10–13.
246. Ibid., 341–47.

related but increasingly disparate programs. What seems to me at least as likely is that leading teachers in Matthean circles faced accusations that their enthusiasm for attracting gentiles was highly inimical to maintaining adequate boundaries of Jewish social formation, considering the actuality and threat of disaffection from Jewish forms of identification in the wake of the destruction. What we see in Matthew then are polemical addresses aimed at competitors, and rhetorical demonstrations formulated in the interests of a self-definition that answers to their own recognition of abandonment of Jewish practices in some circles of followers of Jesus, as well as in wider Jewish circles in the wake of the destruction. It may be the case that such subelite scribal and teaching circles found it useful to imagine that "the survival of the Jewish community without the temple and its related political institutions" was at stake.[247] In the case of the Gospel of Mark, I am proposing that the plot of the gospel story, its dual narrative, was also constructed with a sensibility of collective humiliation and an awareness of the new conditions of an early post-70 time.

In *Jewish Reactions to the Destruction of Jerusalem in A.D. 70*, Kenneth Jones has argued that the post-70 Jewish apocalypses and related pseudepigrapha have been underemployed as a quite unique set of documents for the Roman historian, considering that they offer what is so lacking of evidence of provincial attitudes toward Rome, namely, native provincial sources that are not expressions of elite advantage in cooperation with Rome in local provincial environments. The lack of literary evidence of pre-Roman native cultures of the eastern provinces of the empire is well known, and Greece is a special case because of a greater measure of Roman respect for the culture and autonomy of the Greek polis as well as the dominance of the Greek kingdoms in the region where Greek had become the language of administration and culture. In addition to their value as a prime example of native attitudes toward Rome expressed in their own cultural idiom, these texts shed some light on what is often supposed about Rome-provincial relations. The attitudes of most local elites were shaped more by consideration of the advantages and limits of cultivating ties with Rome for positioning in their own societies than by empire wide considerations or ambitions. As an example, Jones discusses Plutarch's advice to

---

247. Ibid., 339, citing Anthony J. Saldarini, *Matthew's Christian-Jewish Community*, CSJH (Chicago: University of Chicago Press, 1994), 4–5.

the local politician, Menemachus, of the Greek city of Sardis (*Preac. ger. rei publ.* 16a–19f [813c–816a]). Jones summarizes:

> The main role of the city politician is to steer a middle course, encouraging the city's obedience to its masters while preventing its enslavement.... The way to do so is to promote concord among the citizens and refrain from getting Roman officials too often involved in local affairs; indeed, the Romans themselves would prefer not to play the master. Plutarch does, moreover, stress the importance of Roman patronage, which is indispensable as a support for one's career and a means for benefitting one's city.[248]

Jones's study of seven texts, 4 Ezra, 2 Baruch, 3 Baruch, 4 Baruch, Sib. Or. 4, Sib. Or. 5, and Apocalypse of Abraham, is not intended to suggest that their responses to the destruction of Jerusalem are the same. Nevertheless, he has categorized their responses as nonaccommodating to Rome in comparison with the accommodating responses of Josephus and the Herodians, especially Agrippa II. This division works to an extent. The writers of these apocalypses and pseudepigrapha are not writing under Roman patronage and probably never gave support to a Roman general. They are not writing in a Greek historiographical tradition, though the Sibylline tradition is Greek. They are not likely to belong to Josephus's class, nor do they present speeches to the effect that God has changed to the Roman side.[249] Yet, even in a document such as 4 Baruch, highlighted by Jones as an example of rejecting the way in which Josephus uses the figure of Jeremiah to counsel accommodation with Rome, the notion of resistance is one of cultural separation and not political or military resistance.[250] It is precisely with respect to cultural separation that what I find striking is not how different but how similar the writers of these documents are to Josephus. Jones seems to acknowledge as much in his conclusion when he notes that with the exception of 4 Ezra and Sib. Or. 5, far from being preoccupied with the wider problem of Roman imperialism, "the authors of these works seek to locate themselves within the empire and hold fast to their traditions at a time when many were likely to have questioned them.

---

248. Kenneth R. Jones, *Jewish Reactions to the Destruction of Jerusalem in A.D. 70: Apocalypses and Related Pseudepigrapha*, JSJSup 151 (Leiden: Brill, 2011), 10. Jones returns to this text in the conclusion of the study.

249. Ibid., 18–26.

250. Ibid., 158–71.

It should be stressed that Josephus accords with this point of view. In suggesting a *modus vivendi* with Rome his attention is trained inwards."[251] But on the next page Jones concludes, "The testimony of the works examined in the present thesis … suggests that even a stance against accommodation might have more impact in internal power struggles. That is to say, the rejection of accommodation is also the shunning of accommodationists. When separatism is the aim, those pursuing a policy of accommodation can be seen as greater enemies than the outsiders being accommodated."[252]

The thesis is valid, but I do not think Josephus fits this category of accommodation, even if it may have seemed so to the writers of these texts. Josephus's pro-Roman stance is hedged in all sorts of ways. The eschatological visions found in several of these texts bringing Roman power to an end and restoring Israel is likely what Josephus also understood about the temporary dominance of Rome in the prophecies of Daniel and Balaam (*Ant.* 10.10.4 §207; 4.6.4, 6 §§112–117, 126–130; cf. *Ag. Ap.* 2.4 §41). Josephus's theme of divine favor now residing with Rome is qualified by the entire argument of the *Judean War* that the disaster occurred because of God's decision to withdraw divine protection as a consequence of civil strife and the sins of the rebels. Josephus's discussion of Roman order and the discipline of Roman troops to demonstrate the futility of resistance (*Ant.* 3.4.1–6.2 §§70–109) is hardly on stage in his description of the fighting in Galilee or in Titus's command of his troops in Jerusalem. Josephus's claim that he gave his account of the war to Vespasian and Titus and that Titus ordered it to be published as the official version of the war has serious problems. He may have given parts to read as he did with Agrippa II, but some sort of imperial imprimatur is unlikely. Josephus makes these claims only in writings written after the death of both emperors not in the *Judean War*, and the context is the attempt to put the account of Justus of Tiberias in a bad light for his failure to write while the principals were still living (*Ag. Ap.* 1.8, 9 §§44–46, 50; *Life* 357–366). This is more likely evidence of Josephus's need to defend the accuracy of his work than evidence of the connection of his work with the Flavian family.[253] Moreover, between Josephus and the writers of the documents

---

251. Ibid., 277–78.

252. Ibid., 279.

253. I am dependent in this paragraph on the argumentation of McLaren. For more detail on these matters and further evidence that Josephus was not a happy accommodationist of Roman power but a realist about its reality, see James S.

under consideration in Jones's study, we can be sure that the only one to have opposed Roman rule at the level of responsibility for the defense of Galilee was Josephus.[254]

If Josephus was writing his *Judean War* in part for remnants of a Judean elite in the remaining towns of Judea as Jones suggests,[255] the message would have been much the same as the message of the nonaccommodationists of the documents in Jones's study. True, Josephus may have given more credence to an eventual change in Roman policy, but, as noted above, the legitimacy of Rome to rule in Palestine is hardly unqualified, even if adapted to the exigencies of his situation in Rome. Moreover, the rejection of political and military solutions in Jones's documents is also a form of accommodation of Roman rule in the present. Josephus would not have been encouraging a remnant Jewish elite to look for a solution for Judea in Parthian political and military activity against Rome, anymore than the author of Sib. Or. 4 does.[256] What difference would their

---

McLaren, "A Reluctant Provincial"; and see, McLaren, "The *Jewish War* as a Response to the Crisis of Flavian Propaganda," in *Ancient Jewish and Christian Texts as Crisis Management Literature: Thematic Studies from the Centre for Early Christian Studies*, ed. David C. Sim and Pauline Allen, LNTS 445 (London: T&T Clark, 2012), 9–28.

254. For the reasons why it is important to give privilege to what Josephus actually did over the commentary he provides as an interpretation of his actions, see above, n. 96, esp. McLaren, "Delving into the Dark Side."

255. Jones, *Jewish Reactions to the Destruction of Jerusalem*, 22 n. 47.

256. Ibid., 173–207. Unlike many of other scholars, Jones has made a case for the unity of the composition of Sib. Or. 4, the Roman material being seen as integral to the historical scheme of the *ex eventu* prophecy composed in Judea in the early 80s after the eruption of Mt.Vesuvius in 79 CE (178–95; most scholars opt for a location in Syria or the Jordan Valley). The Sibyl adopts a Greek historiographical tradition highlighting the long historical struggle of East and West. "It would seem that our Jewish author composed *Sibylline Oracle* 4 to oppose a tendency among his co-religionists who sought a political solution to their humiliation by Rome. The value of the Greek historiographical convention of a struggle between East and West for propaganda purposes is illustrated by its employment in support of Antiochus III and the Seleucids as they faced the increasing involvement of Rome in eastern affairs.... It is entirely likely that Jews also picked up this theme and refashioned it to fit their own hopes for revenge on the imperial aggressor.... Persia would be an eminently suitable symbolic figure on which to fashion hope. It was Persia, after all, that had liberated the Jews from Babylon. Nor is the use of Persia entirely symbolic, for memories of Persia combined with the reports of Nero returning from the East perhaps reflect the hopes of certain Jews that Parthia might serve as a possible candidate for the position of liberator as had happened once before in Judean history" (195–96).

resentment have made?[257] But in these postdestruction conditions, neither would Josephus have indulged in the irony of advising an individual of the local elite along the lines of Plutarch's advice to Menemachus, to remember, first, that "he is a free man ruling a free people and, second, that he is a subject even while he governs."[258] If Josephus harbored the hope that Flavian policy could change and that his defense of his own class would help toward that end, it was not simply his own sense of self-importance or the interests of his class that drove this self-deception but the assessment of a "reluctant provincial," a Jerusalem priest in Rome, saying in effect that this side of the collapse of Roman dominion, the support of Rome for a mediating Judean priestly elite in a restored temple in Jerusalem was still necessary for a vital Jewish society, including the well being of a widespread Jewish diaspora.[259] It was not to be. Flavian resentment was undoubtedly

---

257. This is not to say, of course, that resentment did not exist or that Josephus did not address it.

258. Jones, *Jewish Reactions to the Destruction of Jerusalem*, 10, citing *Prec. ger. rei publ.* 17 (813e).

259. For what appears to be the very opposite thinking of Josephus from what I am suggesting after some two decades of living as a diaspora Jew in Rome, see Daniel R. Schwartz, "Josephus on the Jewish Constitutions and Community," *Scripta Classica Israelica* 7 (1983–1984): 30–52. In this article, Schwartz deals with the complicated question of Josephus's sources, influences, and seemingly inconsistent positions on types of constitutions and their relationship to high-priestly leadership in *Antiquities*, and seeks to demonstrate that Josephus is distinguishing a continuous high-priestly *prostasia* that had ruling authority over the people during the long periods of biblical history that witnessed changing constitutions. "The *Sitz-im-Leben* of the idea of high-priestly *protasia*, in the sense of leadership and rule, is in fact to be found in the world of the Hellenistic and Roman associations (*thiasos, synodos, politeuma, collegium*, etc.)." Summarizing his findings, Schwartz concludes, "The notion of high-priestly *prostasia* indicates a model of Jewish existence based upon the circumstances of Jewish communities in the Diaspora, and it is probable that the notion originated among Jews of the Diaspora who viewed the high priest as the *prostatēs* of the entire people, in the image of their local community leaders. It thus appears likely that Josephus, in considering how to portray, in *AJ*, Jewish history in such a way as to legitimize Jewish existence even after Jewish political life had ended (note *BJ*'s focus on the destruction of the Jewish *polis*, Jerusalem), chose to portray the people via the nonpolitical category which guaranteed its right to continued existence in the Roman world" (46, 48–49). The conclusions of Schwartz are valid up to a point. It can hardly be the case that Josephus took no notice of Jewish life in diaspora by the time he was writing the *Antiquities*. He surely had to have thought about the grounds on which the continued existence of Jewish populations in the homeland and diaspora could

directed toward the failure of the Judean ruling class, and even Josephus's *apologia* could not hide that it had failed to keep the peace. So, Jones's reading of 4 Baruch to the effect that accommodation of Rome would not endear the remnant Judean elite to Rome is also correct.[260] But the readers

---

be secured at a time when there was no city or temple. In *Ant.* 13, he implies that Galileans, Pereans, and Samaritans were already *Ioudaioi* prior to the Hasmonean conquests, perhaps, as Seth Schwartz has suggested, because of the dangers a post-70 situation posed to an obligation to practice Jewish laws and customs (Schwartz, "The 'Judaism' of Samaria and Galilee in Josephus's Version of the Letter of Demetrius I to Jonathan [*Antiquities* 13.48–57]," *HTR* 82 [1989]: 377–90). Most of all, the apologia of high-priestly rule qualifies as ancestral tradition. It supports Josephus's apologia for his own class with respect to the war, and seeks to garner Roman protection for the ancestral practices of Jews in diaspora by showing that a Jewish state organized by a constitution was changing and temporary, while leadership of the Jewish people in a nonthreatening (to Roman hegemony) decentralized body of local Jewish communities is what Jewish history teaches as its permanent basis. All of this works—as an apologia and as an endorsement of Josephus's prophetic gifts of what was to come. He may have thought this way as he wrote in the 80s and 90s, given also the contingencies of his life in Rome. But even if one concedes the plausibility of the distinction Schwartz is proposing, surely the burden of this distinction between hereditary community leaders and changing constitutions is its endorsement of high-priestly rule. One dare not think about the actual implementation of this apologia. Calling the leaders of local *collegia* priests is one thing; actually putting Josephus and his hereditary class over local Jewish groups is quite another. And where would the serving high priest over the entire people be located? Josephus's references to the temple, its layout, symbolism, and administration in the present tense are not merely literary conceits. Yet, for the present time, there was no alternative to the end of the reciprocity of God and people through daily and festival sacrifice offered by priests in the temple in Jerusalem other than to engage in protecting other practices of reciprocity and securing the integrity of other kinds of social formations. Nonetheless, in my judgment, Josephus in the 80s and 90s is still a priest of the Jerusalem temple who fought for the protection and independence of that temple, its city and territory. He is not a Jewish priest living in third-century Rome. It is one thing to recognize that the loss of the political and religious function of the temple and the mediatorial role of a Judean elite—not just for Judea but occasionally for Jews of the diaspora as well—and the increased Roman presence created conditions in the province of Judea more like those of the diaspora. It is another thing to suppose that in the last decades of the first century no sort of restoration of the temple and the remnants of a Judean elite could any longer be imagined, let alone that anyone would want to, for not much had been lost. For conclusions supporting and developing those of Schwartz, see Tuval, *From Jerusalem Priest to Roman Jew*; see above, n. 224.

260. Jones, *Jewish Reactions to the Destruction of Jerusalem*, 166. However, this

of Josephus's *Antiquities* and the readers of the apocalyptic and pseudepi-graphic writings of the late first and early second centuries, though differ-ent, would have received similar messages promoting varied strategies of cultural persistence.[261]

---

situation was at least as much a matter of current Flavian interests in the legitimation of the dynasty and provincialization of the region as it was the failure of the Judean ruling class; see above, n. 203.

261. Admittedly, these messages may not adequately describe the underlying concerns of documents such as 3 Baruch and Sib. Or. 4. There is no apparent relation of the individualized ethical concerns of these documents to torah as the foundation of the biblical covenant. But there is also a strong individualizing and universalizing of the application of torah in 2 Baruch. I would explain this in the same general way I would explain why there is so little evidence in these documents of expectation of an earthly restoration of Jerusalem and the temple cult. I do not think this rests on the loss of such a hope at the time of writing, but on an assessment that overcoming the sources of disaffection in the present circumstances can only be achieved by letting go the object of mourning and by renegotiating the ground of divine promises and an ordered universe in terms less vulnerable to sacrilege and empirical disconfirma-tion. In some instances this may have been aided by drawing on widely circulating Greco-Roman moral and philosophical teachings. The Gospel of Mark is doing some-thing similar in mystifying the identity of Jesus and the locus of the kingdom of God. The political function of the temple and its administration had failed. The religious function of temple priests in Jerusalem had ceased. In such circumstances it is predict-able that circles that cultivated apocalyptic imaginations, speculations, and solutions in the past would return to them after the disaster. For an example of negotiating the failure of law and covenant associated with the biblical Ezra by reinventing the figure of Ezra in 4 Ezra, see John J. Collins, "Enoch and Ezra," in *Fourth Ezra and Second Baruch*, ed. Matthias Henze and Gabriele Boccaccini with the collaboration of Jason M. Zurawski, JSJSup 164 (Leiden: Brill, 2013), 83–97. For a psychoanalytic approach to mourning and collective trauma in Ezekiel, 4 Ezra, 2 Baruch, and 3 Baruch, see Dereck Daschke, *City of Ruins: Mourning the Destruction of Jerusalem through Jewish Apocalypse*, BibInt 99 (Leiden: Brill, 2010); see above, n. 187 and n. 189 with reference to Alexander, "Theory of Cultural Trauma"). However, one should not wax too elo-quent over the fact that the same moral criteria are applied equally to Jews and gentiles as qualification for inclusion in the category of the pious in a document such as Sib. Or. 4. (Jones, *Jewish Reactions to the Destruction of Jerusalem*, 204). First, descrip-tions of impious behavior target what Jews often thought characteristic of non-Jewish cultures (vv. 30–34). More important, if one had to reject all temples and sacrifice (vv. 27–30) in order to qualify for inclusion, how many non-Jews could qualify? The eschatological drama at the end of the book clearly portrays a time when wickedness so overwhelms piety that God destroys the entire earth with fire. So at the resurrection and judgment that follows, one fully expects that the pious who enjoy the renewed

The importance of the central issue raised in Jones's study should be acknowledged. The real choices of provincials were not the dichotomies of resistance or Romanization, as the rebellions of the thoroughly Romanized Gallic Julii show, but the ambivalence of attraction to the status markers of accommodation and anxiety over the erosion of the traditional markers of identity.[262] But what I believe a reasonable assessment of the evidence of second-and third-century Jewish Palestine also shows, and which is consistent with a reading of the archaeological and epigraphic evidence of Jewish communities in cities of the diaspora, is that a message heavily weighted toward social separation and rejection of new conditions promoting social integration of provincial populations was not the dominant voice among Jews, who continued in other ways to identify themselves and to be identified as Jews—which is not to say it was no voice at all. As Schwartz has noted, the weight it did carry may have had more to do with the limits of the permeability of the cultural center in local environments than the inherent attractiveness of the alternative. Nevertheless, for Josephus and for the readers of the documents under consideration in Jones's study, as later for the rabbis and other Jewish subcultures, what is important is that these responses kept alive nativist cultural options different from the culture of the wider society. In some similar, but also in some

---

earth are few, very few, and the impious who receive their due in Gehenna are many, very many. Jones and others are probably correct in their judgment that vv. 29–30 intend a rejection of all animal sacrifice, including in Jerusalem where of course it was no longer practiced, at least not in the temple. This rejection is surprising nonetheless in a document from the early 80s written in Judea or a neighboring region. Considering that the writer is making use of a Greek prophetess to present the oracles, one might suppose that the rejection of bloody sacrifices is not a rejection of bloodless sacrifices, which was arguably the practice of some in Pythagorean and Orphic traditions and would not be inconsistent with washing in perennial rivers and other signs of repentance (vv. 165–170), though admittedly the distinction is not made in the document. Jones also points out that God's retribution on the Romans by means of the Vesuvius eruption is not specifically linked to their destruction of the temple but to the destruction of the tribe of the pious (vv. 130–137). However, the immediate context of this retribution is not the last days of the earth but the sack of the temple by Pompey (on Jones's reading of vv. 115–118) and the destruction of the temple in 70 (vv. 125–127). Could readers have avoided the assumption that the tribe of the pious must have included some who had perished defending the temple?

262. Jones, *Jewish Reactions to the Destruction of Jerusalem*, 280. In support of this perspective for consideration of early Christianity, see the essays in Brodd and Reed, *Rome and Religion*.

different ways, the gospel story as represented in the Gospel of Mark is among these nativist cultural options.[263]

9. The *Fiscus Iudaicus* and the Parting of the Ways?

Roman officials did need connections with local representatives of Jews. It stands to reason that they would have need of the cooperation of individuals in positions of responsibility in Jewish communal institutions such as synagogues and associations in order to collect taxes, in particular, the newly imposed Jewish tax under the auspices of the *fiscus Iudaicus*. This poll tax was imposed on all Jews empire wide immediately after the war and would probably have made use of registers of those adult males who had formerly paid the temple tax. However, since it was now additional members of households who were liable for the tax, a registration of Jews for payment of the tax would be required.[264] While liability for the tax was obviously associated with the Judean revolt and created an orientation to Rome, it also overrode differences among Jews, at least as a matter of status as Roman subjects. It was an identity marker, a form of self-and collective identification in the obvious sense that Jews had to register as Jews.[265] We can assume that penalties would be enforced by Rome for nonpayment, and we know that Domitian was accused of exacting the tax with excessive harshness and that some policy change with respect to the *fiscus* is advertised by the inscription, FISCI IVDAICI CALVMNIA SVBLATA, on coins issued in Rome by Nerva in the years, 96–97. It is not hard to imagine that this was a distressing tax for many, certainly because

---

263. "Thus, the Jewish core [the rabbis and their circles of adherents] was not very important sociopolitically … but functioned quite significantly in providing for Jews a cultural option radically different from the Greco-Roman norm" (Schwartz, *Imperialism and Jewish Society*, 105). I would want to qualify this conclusion by observing that the rabbis nonetheless belonged to a Greco-Roman urbanized Palestine; see Lapin, *Rabbis as Romans*. For a similar qualification on the wider cultural milieu to which the writer of the Gospel of Mark belonged, see below, n. 353.

264. See above, 314 with n. 220.

265. "This [the tax] meant that now, for the first time, Jews had to be registered as such" (Jörg Frey, "Temple and Identity in Early Christianity and in the Johannine Community: Reflections on the 'Parting of the Ways,'" in Schwartz and Weiss, *Was 70 CE a Watershed?*" 501). "Once personal status was involved the individual became responsible to the state and had to accept the consequences of his identity as defined by the state" (Geiger, "The Jew and the Other," 145).

of the increased financial burden, but also as a reminder of a failed revolt in which most Jews had not participated, and the one consequence in which all Jews were suppose to participate. Did followers of Jesus pay the tax and, if so, which followers? One would think that the answer to this question would have some implications for boundary formation between "Christians" and Jews. Registering to pay the tax may have been a matter that was unavoidable for most, but for some it is likely to have been a matter of internal debate, having significant implications as a mark of public self-identification both as a Jew and as a subject of Rome. While it is easy enough to raise questions about who registered, about how the tax was collected, what Domitian's harsh exaction and Nerva's "reform" were all about, and the likely effect of the *fiscus* on the fluidity or the stabilizing of boundaries between "Christians" and Jews, it is harder to answer any of these questions. There are only a few texts which refer directly to the *fiscus Iudaicus.* Not a single passage in the New Testament is indisputably identified as a reference to this tax or obviously associated with its payment or nonpayment. One could take the absence of explicit reference in the New Testament writings as evidence that most followers of Jesus were not affected by the tax. Contrariwise, one might suppose that for many there was no avoiding payment, and so the tax was not a matter evoking debate or significant conflict. But it is also easy to think of reasons to avoid referring to the tax directly.[266] Alternatively, one can read the few sources for how they might shed light on matters of boundary formation between "Christians" and Jews and apply these insights to the reading of some New Testament texts. This is the strategy of a monograph on the subject by Marius Heemstra, *The Fiscus Judaicus and the Parting of the Ways.* In the preface, Heemstra states the main purpose for writing his thesis: "to try and convince other scholars of the relevance of this Roman *fiscus* for early Jewish and Christian history, including their mutual relationship in the last decades of the first century and beyond."[267]

---

266. Rome expected payment of taxes. If it was not always clear who was liable and followers of Jesus were not registering, it is unlikely that the literature would advertise this in a way that could be easily identified. At the same time, one can hardly deny the significance of registering as a public acknowledgment of Jewish self-identification and of submission to Rome.

267. Marius Heemstra, *The Fiscus Judaicus and the Parting of the Ways*, WUNT 277 (Tübingen: Mohr Siebeck, 2010), vii. The book is a slightly revised version of his

The thesis of Heemstra's study is that Nerva's reform of the *fiscus Iuda-icus* entailed a change in the Roman definition of who was a Jew from what had been an ethnic definition when the tax was first imposed by Vespasian to a cultural or religious definition as a result of Nerva's reform. It was the abuses that resulted from Domitian's harsh exaction of the tax that had forced the issue. Under Domitian, prosecution for tax evasion divided Jewish and gentile Christians. But with Nerva's reform, Jewish Christians were no longer liable for the tax. However, as a consequence they were now subject to prosecution as atheists along with gentile Christians, and at least by the second decade of the second century both could be prosecuted for the crime of confessing that they were Christians. Parallel to Nerva's reform was a growing Jewish interest in distancing their own communities from Jewish Christians, if not always for religious reasons, then clearly for the political liabilities entailed in too close an association with Christian missionary efforts requiring gentiles to renounce their idolatry and become "absolute monotheists." By the end of the first century Jewish Christians were viewed by Jews as heretics and by Romans as atheists. These parallel Roman and mainstream Jewish judgments, the one a result of Nerva's reform, the other the result of perceived endangerment of the Jewish right to practice Judaism, created a situation that was decisive for "the parting of the ways" between Judaism and Christianity as separate religions. Chapters 4–7 of Heemstra's study develop arguments for the dating of the texts of 1 Peter, Revelation, Hebrews, and the Gospel of John and for the relevance of the *fiscus Iudaicus* to the interpretation of prominent features in these texts, as well as the relevance of the rabbinic *birkat ha-minim* to the social context of the Gospel of John. Heemstra's argument for identifying passages in these New Testament texts with Domitian's harsh exaction of the tax and with Nerva's reform depends on his correlation of later rabbinic texts and later Christian texts (especially on the disputed issue of Domitian's persecution of Christians) with his reading of the Roman evidence on the Jewish tax and on purportedly related issues in the reigns of Domitian and Nerva. Since Heemstra must continually refer back to his construal of this Roman evidence in chapters 2–3 in order to establish the plausibility of his thesis and his interpretation of the New

---

PhD thesis for the University of Gröningen. Below I present Heemstra's thesis using his own descriptive registers and terminology.

Testament texts, I will cite these Roman texts and two pertinent passages from Josephus and focus first on Heemstra's reading of them.[268]

Claudius's edict "to the rest of the world" in the year 41 CE:

> It will therefore be fit to permit the Jews, who are in the entire world under us, to keep their ancient customs without being hindered to do so. And I do charge them also to use this my kindness to them with moderation, and not to show a contempt of the religious observances of other nations, but to keep their own laws only. (Josephus, *Ant.* 19.5.3 §290)

The introduction of the Jewish tax under Vespasian:

> He [Vespasian] also laid a tribute upon the Jews wheresoever they were, and enjoined every one of them to bring two drachmai every year into the Capitol, as they used to pay the same to the temple at Jerusalem. (Josephus, *J.W.* 7.6.6 §218)

> Thus was Jerusalem destroyed on the very day of Saturn, the day which even now the Jews reverence most. From that time forth it was ordered that the Jews who continued to observe their ancestral customs should pay an annual tribute of two drachmai to Jupiter Capitoline. (Cassius Dio, *Hist. Rom.* 65.7.2)

Domitian's harsh administration of the *fiscus Iudaicus*:

> Reduced to financial straits by the cost of his buildings and shows, as well as by the additions which he [Domitian] had made to the pay of the soldiers, he tried to lighten the military expenses by diminishing the number of his troops; but perceiving that in this way he exposed himself to the attacks of the barbarians, and nevertheless had difficulty in easing his burdens, he had no hesitation in resorting to every sort of robbery. The property of the living and the dead was seized everywhere on any charge brought by any accuser. It was enough to allege any action or word derogatory to the majesty of the prince. Estates of those in no way connected with him were confiscated, if but one man came forward to declare that he had heard from the deceased during his lifetime that Caesar was his heir. Besides other taxes, that on the Jews was levied with

---

268. Following Heemstra, I cite the translations of the LCL edition of these texts unless otherwise indicated.

the utmost rigour, and those were prosecuted who without publicly acknowledging that faith yet lived as Jews, as well as those who concealed their origin and did not pay the tribute levied upon their people. I recall being present in my youth when the person of a man ninety years old was examined before the procurator and a very crowded court, to see whether he was circumcised. (Suetonius, *Dom.* 12.1–2)[269]

Charges of *atheotēs* and *asebeia* under Domitian and Nerva's counter measures:

And the same year Domitian slew, along with many others, Flavius Clemens the consul, although he was a cousin and had to wife Flavia Domitilla, who was also a relative of the emperor's. The charge brought against them both was that of atheism, a charge on which many others who drifted into Jewish ways were condemned. Some of these were put to death, and the rest were at least deprived of their property. Domitilla was merely banished to Pandateria. (Cassius Dio, *Hist. Rom.* 67.14.1–2)[270]

Nerva also released all who were on trial for *asebeia* and restored the exiles; moreover, he put to death all the slaves and the freedmen who had conspired against their masters and allowed that class of persons to lodge no complaint whatever against their masters; and no persons were permitted to accuse anybody of *maiestas* [Lat. trans. for Gr. *asebeia*, Earnest Cary, LCL] or of a Jewish life [Heemstra's alteration of "adopting the Jewish mode of life"]. (Cassius Dio, *Hist. Rom.* 68.1.2)

The passage from Suetonius's biography of Domitian refers to those prosecuted under this emperor's levying of the Jewish tax "very harshly" (*acerbissime*): "those who without publicly acknowledging it [*qui vel improfessi*] lived a Jewish life" (*Iudaicam viverent vitam*), "and those who concealed their origin [*vel dissimulata origine*] and did not pay the tribute levied upon their people" (*imposita genti tributa non pependissent*). Heemstra takes this description to refer to two distinct classes of people in the eyes of the Romans prosecuted for two different crimes: (1) non-Jews living a Jewish life *improfessi* and (2) tax evading Jews, who if convicted would have their property confiscated and presumably would be regis-

---

269. Suetonius writing during the reign of Hadrian, 117–138 CE.
270. Cassius Dio writing in the first half of the third century, as excerpted by the Byzantine monk Xiphilinus in the eleventh century, for his narrative of the year 95 CE.

tered for the payment of the tax in subsequent years.[271] Heemstra limits the charge of tax evasion to those who *dissimulata origine* and supposes that those living a Jewish life *improfessi* could not be convicted of tax evasion. According to Heemstra, under Domitian liability for the tax was still determined on the basis of an ethnic definition of a Jew. The first class of people to whom Suetonius refers are non-Jews. The crime for which they can be convicted is "atheism," in which case they, like the Jewish tax evaders, have their property confiscated, but they may also be put to death.[272] It seems unlikely that one would construe the biographer's statement in this way based only on the passage cited above. First, the passage in its entirety makes reference only to the confiscation of property based on accusations brought by informers (*delatores*) but does not refer to execution. Second, why would anyone be convicted of any other crime than tax evasion in cases prosecuted in connection with Domitian's harsh exaction of the tax?

Heemstra's reading of Suetonius depends on his bringing to its interpretation the passages from Cassius Dio cited above. The passage about the fate of Flavius Clemens and Flavia Domitilla speaks of charges of atheism, "a charge on which many others who drifted into Jewish ways were condemned. Some of these were put to death, and the rest were at least deprived of their property." The passage about Nerva's counter measures to Domitian says that "no persons were permitted to accuse anybody of *asebeia* or of a Jewish life." Heemstra has construed the clause in Suetonius, *improfessi Iudaicum viverent vitam*, in light of similar terminologies and their contexts in two of the passages cited above from Cassius Dio (ἐς τὰ τῶν Ἰουδαίων ἤθη ἐξοκέλλοντες [*Hist. Rom.* 67.14.1–2] and Ἰουδαϊκὸς βίος [*Hist. Rom.* 68.1.2]).[273] Heemstra also interprets Suetonius's recollection of a ninety-year-old man examined before a crowded court to see if he was circumcised as a test that all males accused of tax evasion had to undergo in court. "If the inspection led to the conclusion that some of the accused were not circumcised, they could still be suspected of 'living a Jewish life'

---

271. Heemstra makes a connection between theft of the "sacred monies" collected for Jerusalem before 70, which was punished by confiscation of property according to Josephus's report of the edict of Augustus (*Ant.* 16.6.2 §§163–164), and the Jewish tax now collected for *Jupiter Capitolinus*. "From this moment on evasion of this tax by Jews was in all likelihood treated in the same manner" (22–23). In any case, confiscation of property is central to the passage in Suetonius.

272. Heemstra, *Fiscus Judaicus*, 29.

273. Ibid., 27–29.

and one may assume that a second test followed to prove or disprove this."[274] Heemstra appeals to the later examination of Christians by Pliny in the reign of Trajan, to passages from the book of Revelation and to Eusebius's reference to Christians persecuted under Domitian, concluding that this second test was offering sacrifice to determine whether the accused should be convicted on a charge of atheism.[275] "If this test turned out to be positive [by refusing to sacrifice], the accused would also face the confiscation of his property and (possibly) execution after conviction."[276]

There are two obvious implications of this reading of the Suetonius passage. The first is that one must imagine that accusations by informers brought to the attention of officials of the *fiscus Iudaicus* anywhere across the empire would entail examining the genitals of every male, presumably the heads of households. (Heemstra does not say what would happen in the case of women who were the heads of households and accused by informers.) It would not help to acknowledge before a court that one was circumcised. An examination would have to be conducted, because if the examination disconfirmed circumcision a different charge would follow and a test of sacrifice applied to determine one's guilt or innocence on a charge of "living a Jewish life *improfessus*," that is, a charge of "atheism," or "drifting into Jewish ways," or "a Jewish life."[277] The second implication is that Domitian was using the *fiscus Iudaicus* just as much (or more?) to

---

274. Ibid., 29.

275. Ibid., 29–31.

276. Ibid., 29.

277. Heemstra states that it is not known for sure whether the tests were used in all cases but thinks that the need for clear legal distinctions in a court makes it likely that they were generally used (ibid., 32). But the uncertainty arises in the first place because of his interpretation of the clauses referring to those prosecuted in the Suetonius passage. The issue is whether Suetonius's recollection of a particular instance in a court where he happened to be present in his youth should be read as a test applied in order to make a legal distinction between victims of the *fiscus* as to the relevant charges and the possibly different punishments following conviction. To say that a court could not make the necessary legal distinctions without these tests is to say that the tests were to be applied. Heemstra points to Heb 10:32–34, which refers to earlier days when some were publicly exposed (θεατριζόμενοι) and had their property plundered, as a plausible reference to the *fiscus Iudaicus* and to the court test of circumcision and conviction of Jewish Christians. He argues that Hebrews is addressed exclusively to Jewish Christians and should be dated to the end of Nerva's brief reign (98). The earlier days referred to in Heb 10:32–34 would therefore be a reference to the situation under Domitian (ibid. 135–36).

uncover non-Jews living a Jewish life, who could then be charged as atheists, as he was to uncover Jewish tax evaders.[278] The former cases would
also increase the revenue of the *fiscus*, since the property of such persons
would be confiscated. Again, Heemstra's argument that Domitian was
using the *fiscus* as an instrument to expose atheists and have some of them
executed can hardly be based on the passage from Suetonius. It depends
entirely on the passages cited above from Cassius Dio.

According to Heemstra the first class of victims, those convicted of
atheism if they did not sacrifice, included "Godfearers" and other sympathizers with Judaism and gentile Christians as a distinct class of sympathizers with Judaism. The second class of victims, those who were circumcised and convicted of tax evasion, included Jews who evaded the
tax because they opposed it in principle, along with proselytes, apostate
Jews, circumcised non-Jews, and Jewish Christians.[279] Heemstra believes
that by the end of Domitian's reign gentile Christians were already being
convicted of atheism, unless they renounced their faith by offering the
required sacrifice.[280] Jewish Christians, however, were being drawn back

---

278. Heemstra attributes the motivation for this to Domitian's assumption of the
title *censor perpetuus* in 85 which gave him a general supervision over conduct and
morals. Heemstra dates the beginning of the harsh exaction of the tax to this same
year on the basis of Cassius Dio (*Hist. Rom.* 67.4.3–5), who makes a "direct connection between the assumption of the censorship by Domitian and the first prosecutions
in Rome for financial motives" (ibid., 26). However, the connection made by Cassius
Dio is not confirmed by Suetonius, who presents a list of actions taken by Domitian
as censor to correct public morals none of which have to do with charges of atheism
(*Dom.* 8.3–5). Nor are they related by Suetonius to Domitian's later financial straits
and greed, which are presented as belonging to a subsequent change of behavior in the
course of his reign (9.3–10.1).

279. Ibid., 64; for his discussion of each group of victims, 32–63. It can be assumed
the *delatores* would usually target the wealthy in order to gain some portion of the
confiscated property of their victims (ibid., 33 with n. 31), referencing L. A. Thompson, "Domitian and the Jewish Tax," *Historia* 31 (1982): 342.

280. Heemstra believes this view is corroborated by the evidence in Pliny's letter
to Trajan (*Ep.* 10.96) about those who had ceased to be Christians as much as 25 years
earlier (thus, late 80s or early 90s), showing that such tests had resulted in some gentile
Christians offering sacrifice at this time in order to avoid the confiscation of property
and possibly execution (130, 156), as well as by passages in Revelation (Rev 13:9–10,
15; 20:4) dated by Heemstra to the end of Domitian's reign distinguishing the punishment of captivity suffered by Jewish Christians from the punishment of execution
suffered by gentile Christians (119–20).

to synagogues at this time, because in addition to the confiscation of their property they would now be registered in the synagogues for future payment of the tax. "[This] could have been blocked by either of two situations: their own unwillingness to do so or the unwillingness of the synagogues to accept them."[281]

For Heemstra, the most decisive factor in creating the historical dynamics for Judaism and Christianity to become separate religions is the concomitance of Nerva's reform of the *fiscus Iudaicus* and Jewish concerns and pressures at the end of the first century. Nerva's reform had as its consequence a Roman definition of Jewish identity now based on a religious rather than an ethnic criterion, so that Jewish Christians could no longer be prosecuted for tax evasion. But this also meant that Jewish Christians could now be accused apart from the *fiscus* of the same crime as their gentile Christian counterparts, that is, of atheism. This linking of Jewish and gentile Christians in a similar situation of exposure to Roman prosecution was particularly effective in creating the separation of religious communities because there was a parallel Roman and Jewish concern to support it. The Roman concern was the Christian mission making "illicit atheists" of non-Jews who were compelled to renounce family and native cults and become "absolute monotheists." The Jewish concern, in addition to boundary issues based on religious differences, was the danger of being associated with Jewish Christians who belonged to mixed groups formed by such mission practices, and therefore being seen to be in violation of the warning expressed by the emperor Claudius not to show contempt for the religious observances of other nations as a condition of retaining the right as Jews to be "licit atheists" (Josesphus, *Ant.* 19.5.3 §290).[282]

The Latin inscription on the coins issued under Nerva is unusual and difficult to interpret with precision.[283] Since it was issued in Rome twice

---

281. Ibid., 65–66. Heemstra discusses these hypothetical situations at length in his chapter on the Gospel of John in connection with the rabbinic *birkat ha-minim*.

282. This paragraph summarizes the major conclusion of chapter 3 of Heemstra's study, 67–84. Heemstra's use of the labels "illicit" and "licit" atheists is reminiscent of Tertullian's reference to Jewish practices as constituting a *religio licita*; on this, see below, n. 300.

283. For a discussion of each word in the inscription and possible interpretations of the inscription, see Martin Goodman, "The Meaning of *'Fisci Iudaici Calumnia Sublata'* on the Coinage of Nerva," in *Studies in Josephus and the Varieties of Ancient Judaism: Louis H. Feldman Jubilee Volume*, ed. Shaye J. D. Cohen and Joshua J. Schwartz, AGJU 67 (Leiden: Brill, 2007), 81–89.

in 96 and again in 97, it must have been a message Nerva thought important to advertise in dissociating his policies from the hated Domitian, and
one can suppose that it referred to a situation known to people in Rome.[284]
Heemstra proposes that the word *calumnia,* "wrongful accusation," should
be taken in a strict singular sense according to its grammatical form and
referred to the wrongful accusation of "living a Jewish life." Thus, the
removal of the wrongful accusation pertains only to non-Jews. Indeed, on
this interpretation the inscription on the coin does not make any reference
to the prosecution of tax evasion![285] The point that Heemstra is making
about the singular form of *calumnia,* namely, that it cannot refer to the
many accusations made by *delatores* but only to the single accusation of
living a Jewish life, does not hold up in my view. Such a wrongful accusation came to the courts by way of information supplied by *delatores.* The
same would be the case if we suppose that the wrongful accusation is that
of tax evasion. The grammatical form conveys the sense that cases based
on accusations made by informers encouraged by Domitian constitute
a single accusation insofar as the victims were wrongfully accused. Key
phrases in the passage from Suetonius, such as "resorting to every sort
of robbery" and "any charge brought by any accuser," highlight the role of
informers and the confiscation of property to increase depleted revenues
as the context of the statements concerning Domitian's harsh exaction of
the Jewish tax.[286]

---

284. "Contemporaries will have been expected to pick up the precise meaning of
this imagery and wording without difficulty, in a similar fashion to public appreciation
of the messages of advertisements nowadays" (ibid., 82–83).

285. Heemstra, *Fiscus Judaicus,* 71–72. I am skeptical of attempts to interpret the
coin inscription in ways that have nothing to do with an abuse related to what a *fiscus*
would do, viz., collect taxes, and therefore nothing to do with Suetonius's statement
about Domitian's harsh exaction of the tax.

286. Goodman, *"Fisci Iudaici Calumnia,"* 85–86, has also insisted on the significance of the singular for interpretation of the inscription, arguing that the singular
makes implausible the more usual interpretation that referred *calumnia* to the accusations brought by informers to the *fiscus Iudaicus.* Goodman believes the false or
malicious accusation was that of Jewish disloyalty to Rome which was the ground
for the imposition of the tax as war reparations under Vespasian. Nerva's reform was
to remove the false accusation of disloyalty and thus to abolish the *fiscus Iudaicus*
altogether. I do not think the more usual interpretation of the inscription referring to
Domitian's harsh exaction of the tax is made implausible by the singular grammatical form of *calumnia.* To suppose that such a meaning would imply that henceforth
any accusation of tax evasion brought by the *fiscus Iudaicus,* even in a case where

Heemstra's interpretation of the coin inscription depends again on his bringing to the passage from Suetonius the information in Cassius Dio's comment that under Nerva "no persons were permitted to accuse anybody of *asebeia* or of a Jewish life" (*Hist. Rom.* 68.1.2). The accusation of living a Jewish life was a *calumnia* because it was made in the context of the wrong institution, the *fiscus Iudaicus*.[287] The removal of the wrongful accusation would have benefitted those non-Jews who had some association with Jews and/or with Jewish practices but who did not leave their own ancestral traditions. This would not apply to gentile Christians who did leave their ancestral traditions. Roman officials would now find more

---

one was registered for the tax and did not pay it, would now be ignored is to completely discount Goodman's own recognition that those who designed the coin had reason to suppose that the inscription would be understood because people in Rome were familiar with the situation to which the *calumnia* referred (above, n. 284). Goodman's understanding of Nerva's reform as the abolition of the tax was first suggested in "*Fiscus Iudaicus* and Gentile Attitudes to Judaism," 176–77. There Goodman suggested that Trajan had reason to follow Flavian precedent and reinstate the tax (see above, 307, and Goodman, *Rome and Jerusalem*, 448–52). Goodman had earlier taken the view that it was Jews who had given up ancestral practices who benefitted from Nerva's reform, because only Jews who continued to observe their ancestral customs as stated by Cassius Dio (*Hist. Rom.* 65.7.2) would henceforth be liable for the Jewish tax (Goodman, "Nerva, the *Fiscus Judaicus* and Jewish Identity," *JRS* 79 [1989]: 40–44). Goodman's more recent position means, first, that there would be no direct connection between the description by Suetonius of the harsh exaction of the tax under Domitian and the coin issued by Nerva. Second, the statement by Cassius Dio could only be referred to his own time and not to Nerva's reform (as acknowledged by Goodman in "*Fisci Iudaici Calumnia*," 89 n. 29). Third, on the more recent position one would have to imagine that Nerva was prepared to revoke a tax that had been imposed by the imperial authority of Vespasian, not merely rectify the abuses of Domitian's reign. (Heemstra refers to the lack of any statistical significance to be drawn from the absence of any tax receipt from Edfu in Egypt during the brief sixteen month reign of Nerva [*Fiscus Judaicus*, 19, 74].)

287. Heemstra states, "Looking at these accusations, tax evasion is a crime that one would expect to be prosecuted by a *fiscus*, so this could not be considered to be a *calumnia*. It could be argued, though, that prosecuting non-Jews who were accused of living a Jewish life (and the atheism that was allegedly part of that according to Cassius Dio), was formally outside the jurisdiction of the *fiscus* officials, who should have limited themselves to collecting tax from Jews" (*Fiscus Judaicus*, 70). Again, this conclusion is not supported by the passage in Suetonius. The phrase, "*Iudaicus fiscus acerbissime actus est*," does not give any indication that the *fiscus* was prosecuting cases outside its jurisdiction as an institution for the collection of taxes.

efficient ways of exposing their atheism than by means of the *fiscus Iuda-icus*. However, since Heemstra's proposal for interpreting the coin inscription pertains only to non-Jews who may have adopted some Jewish practices, why should one suppose there was a change from ethnic origin to religious practices in determining liability for the tax that emerged from Nerva's reform? This is a crucial element of Heemstra's argument, because he sees it as the basis on which Jewish Christians are exposed to charges of atheism. Again, he appeals to one of the passages of Cassius Dio cited above: "From that time forth [the day of the destruction of the temple] it was ordered that the Jews who continued to observe their ancestral customs should pay an annual tribute of two drachmai to Jupiter Capitoline" (*Hist. Rom.* 65.7.2). The supposition is that the Roman historian has backdated to the time of the introduction of the tax under Vespasian what was actually a consequence of Nerva's reform.[288] Those who would have benefitted were those who no longer identified themselves as Jews.[289] The implication drawn by Heemstra from the text of Cassius Dio for the fate of Jewish Christians is that they too no longer were viewed as Jews by Roman officials and thus not liable for the tax. That being the case, they were now exposed in a similar way to accusations of atheism, as gentile Christians were already during the reign of Domitian. Not only apostate Jews, "but also Jewish Christians could be set apart from Judaism in this way. Many Jewish Christians did not meet the criterion of remaining 'faithful to the customs of their forefathers' in Roman (and Jewish) eyes."[290]

---

288. Ibid., 80 n. 50, citing Goodman's earlier position ("Nerva, the *Fiscus Judaicus* and Jewish Identity," 41).

289. Heemstra, *Fiscus Judaicus*, 80, 83. It is contradictory to argue on the one hand that tax evasion could not be a *calumnia* when prosecuted by a *fiscus* (see above, n. 287) and to acknowledge on the other hand that Nerva's reform released Jews by birth who no longer lived as Jews from liability for payment of the tax. If the release was part of Nerva's reform, it presupposes that such Jews had been falsely prosecuted on a charge of tax evasion by the *fiscus* under Domitian. Moreover, on what grounds can it be claimed that people in Rome, or even the Roman officials of the *fiscus*, knew this consequence of the reform in the time of Nerva, if the inscription on the coinage does not presuppose some reference to it? Late first-century Romans would not have been reading the text of the third-century historian.

290. Ibid., 80. It should now be clear just how consequential this aspect of Nerva's reform is for Heemstra's thesis regarding the crucial effect of the *fiscus Iudaicus* in creating the circumstances that led to the parting of the ways between Judaism and Christianity. And this is the case, despite the fact that according to Heemstra

In my judgment, Heemstra has misconstrued the passage in Suetonius on the collection of the Jewish tax under Domitian by reading it to refer to two different classes of people charged with two different crimes, one having nothing to do with tax evasion and punishable in some cases by execution in addition to confiscation of property, with guilt determined by the application of two different tests in the courts. With respect to the test of sacrifice, not even the passages from Cassius Dio (*Hist. Rom.* 67.14.1–2; 68.1.2), which are the basis for Heemstra's reading of Suetonius, make any mention of the application of such a test. It is obvious that Heemstra gets this notion from Pliny's letter to Trajan (ca. 111–112) in connection with the examination of Christians and from passages in the book of Revelation.[291] The test of circumcision is hardly another test, since on Heemstra's reading it would be applied to all males accused before the court in order to determine whether a prosecution should proceed on the charge of tax evasion or of atheism, and only in the latter case would the test of sacrifice be administered. This reading seems to me an over generalizing and legalizing of Suetonius's recollection of an incident in his youth, which is not to say that it is simply a one-off. In context, the rhetorical effect of recounting the incident shows the extent to which a *fiscus* court could go in prosecuting tax evasion, not least because the old man, age ninety, presumably was no longer liable for payment of the tax.[292] I find more plausible the view that the passage from Suetonius and the two from Cassius Dio should be distinguished as descriptions relating to two distinct situations and motivations, the former attesting Domitian's determination to increase revenues and personal wealth, including through the collection of taxes, the latter witnessing to Domitian's fanatical concern to rid himself of

---

the inscription on the coinage of Nerva, the only direct evidence we have of Nerva's reform of the *fiscus* as it operated under Domitian, makes no reference to this aspect of Nerva's reform.

291. Ibid., 30–32.

292. The evidence of the Edfu tax receipts from Egypt suggests that the age limit for liability was 62. Heemstra's resolution is consistent with his reading. The test had to be applied in case the old man was not circumcised, in which case he could be prosecuted by the *fiscus* court for atheism which had no age limit (ibid., 36–37, n. 42). I would suggest instead that the extent to which *delatores* were being encouraged to supply information of tax evasion resulted even in the lifting of an age limit for liability. Alternatively, it may be that in this instance the issue of liability was with respect to other members of the family where there was not another male figure still living.

political enemies through exile or execution.[293] Despite similar references to a Jewish life and Jewish ways, to *maiestas* and confiscation of property, the passages from Cassius Dio make no mention at all of punishments in the context of the collection of the Jewish tax and Suetonius makes no mention of executions. It is more natural to assume that courts prosecuted cases brought by a *fiscus* for tax evasion and therefore that those accused of living a Jewish life *improfessi* were prosecuted for tax evasion like those accused of concealing their origins. The phrase "(and) did not pay the tribute levied upon their people" (*imposita genti tributa non pependissent*) follows in the clause referring to those who concealed their origin not because only those were judged liable for payment of the tax but because "origin" and "*gens*" form a natural association. After all, the tax was in fact levied on the Jewish people. The most obvious and significant connection between the description of the biographer and the accounts of the historian is that increasing revenues and getting rid of political enemies alike depended on encouraging informers to provide the information and accusations.[294] Being accused of atheism, or of drifting into Jewish ways or of a Jewish life were charges most likely to be prosecuted in a particular political climate.[295] In such a climate Goodman may be right that drifting

---

293. Goodman, "*Fiscus Iudaicus* and Gentile Attitudes to Judaism," 174: "According to Suetonius, accusations were encouraged by Domitian out of greed, while, according to Dio, the condemnation of Flavius Clemens was on political grounds." I would add that the passages from Dio appear to refer to imperial circles or at least to Rome, while the abuses associated with the collection of the Jewish tax were not likely to be limited to Rome. It is true that according to Cassius Dio there is a connection between murder and exile and confiscation of property for financial motives in Domitian's reign in the years 84 and 85 (*Hist. Rom.* 67.4.5). However, the two passages in Cassius Dio that are central for Heemstra's interpretation of the actions of the *fiscus* in Suetonius have reference to the years 95 and 96.

294. Domitian was evidently well known for having put to death slaves who informed against their masters in order to cover his own crime of encouraging such information. Cassius Dio refers to this in his account at the very beginning of Domitian's reign (*Hist. Rom* 67.1.3–4). This practice of destroying informers must have changed in the course of his reign; otherwise, it is hard to account for Nerva's action as reported later by Cassius Dio (68.1.2); cf. Suetonius, *Dom.* 9.3–10.1; see above, n. 278.

295. Goodman, "*Fiscus Iudaicus* and Gentile Attitudes to Judaism," 174. Heemstra sees a connection between Nerva's refusal to permit an accusation of *asebeia* or a Jewish life (Cassius Dio, *Hist. Rom.* 68.1.2) and Suetonius's reference to "an action or word derogatory to the majesty of the prince" (*factum dictumve adversus maiestatem*

into Jewish ways is less likely to be evidence of Roman attraction to Jewish practices than a suitable label for accusations of disloyalty to the regime, or even a suitable label for symbolic expressions of opposition to the regime by political opponents of Domitian.[296]

The passage cited from Suetonius highlights accusations of informers made on the flimsiest of grounds and severity in collecting the Jewish tax. The two clauses referring to those who were prosecuted in the collection of the Jewish tax can be interpreted in a number of ways, but for that very reason it seems to me unwise to focus on a classification of victims under each of the clauses. Suetonius has given a general description of two kinds of accusations brought against those prosecuted in the courts for tax evasion. I would make two observations regarding the accusations. First, since the goal was to increase revenues, we should suppose that Suetonius calls attention to the collection of the Jewish tax in particular, because it went beyond the normal measures or capacity of Roman administration to determine liability and uncover tax evaders. This is probably what Suetonius means when he says that the Jewish tax was levied *acerbissime*. Second, with respect to both of the accusations, we are dealing with people who did not identify themselves publicly as Jews and did not register to pay the tax. It is reasonable to think that many of the victims were not registered because they did not consider themselves to be Jews, and so did not identify themselves as Jews in society or before the court. Indeed, people without an axe to grind and not involved in these sorts of prosecutions under Domitian may not have been inclined to identify many of the accused as Jews. Of course, we can assume some of the victims were deliberately hiding their practices or origins in order to avoid paying the tax, but the victims are described according to two kinds of accusations made against them in the court and not according to any defense they may or may not have been allowed to present. Domitian

---

principis; *Dom.* 12.1). However, unlike the passages from Cassius Dio on Domitian's actions and Nerva's counter measures, the passage from Suetonius makes no mention of executions or exiles. Though the passage in Cassius Dio describing Nerva's counter measures can be taken as part of his reform of the policies of Domitian, it should not for that reason be identified with an inscription referring to ending an abuse of the *fiscus Iudaicus*.

296. Ibid., 174–75. "Since 'Jewish ways' could include anything from indolence on Saturdays to aversion to pork …, it could be easy to make the accusation, and hard to disprove its validity" (174).

resorted to inducements to *delatores* in return for flimsy evidence leading to charges. If the victims were generally people without any reasonable grounds for not being registered and paying the tax, Nerva would have had no *calumnia* to remove, unless of course Goodman's more recent proposal that Nerva abolished the tax altogether is correct, a proposal I find very unlikely, not least because it would have announced in Rome that the Flavians had been wrong from the start to take the Judean revolt as evidence of disloyalty to Rome. Roman officials were in a position to know that mere associations with Jews or a private interest in some Jewish belief or practice did not amount to or require a public act of identification as a Jew. They were also in a position to know that sometimes individuals ceased to identify with the community of their birth and no longer live according to ancestral custom, which was not particularly troublesome as long as they were not Romans and did not create a public fuss.[297] But all this could be brushed aside in a situation of abuse. Like Heemstra, some have thought that those accused of living a Jewish life could only have been gentiles. Others have argued that both accusations could only have targeted Jews.[298] The weakness of both views is that they presuppose

---

297. "It may be assumed that Romans accepted the right of ethnic Jews like other people to assimilate into the Roman citizen community or other peregrine communities so long as they gave up their peculiar customs, and Domitian's behaviour was an affront to this attitude" (Goodman, "Nerva, the *Fiscus Judaicus* and Jewish Identity," 41).

298. Goodman writes, "In Suetonius' discussion of Domitian's exaction of the Jewish tax, those who *improfessi Iudaicam viverent vitam* could quite well be native Jews who lived a Jewish life secretly, contrasted by Suetonius with native Jews who practiced openly but hoped to avoid the tax by denying their origins. Such a reading makes better sense of the nature of the tax as described by Suetonius for, if the tribute was levied on the Jewish people (*inposita genti*), it would be peculiar for non-Jews to be required to pay just for behaving like Jews" ("The *Fiscus Iudaicus* and Gentile Attitudes to Judaism," 169). I am not persuaded by this reasoning. I do not think the coins issued by Nerva three times in Rome with their inscription would have occurred if only Jews were affected. It seems to me more likely that the inscription is an advertisement meant especially for the majority community, because the *fiscus* had targeted members of that community in Rome and it was widely known, a point also made by John D. Grainger, *Nerva and the Roman Succession Crisis of AD 96–99* (London: Routledge, 2003), 53. It is fair to say that Domitian was doing something worse than "peculiar," something that was an "affront" (see above, n. 297). The idea that Domitian would be giving legal status as Jews in some cases to Romans targeted by the *fiscus* is probably the wrong conclusion to draw regarding such victims. Suetonius speaks

Domitian announced publicly in advance of prosecutions a change in the criteria of liability for payment of the tax, or expected informers to operate within the parameters of information that representatives of the Jews could themselves supply or verify.

Heemstra's thesis depends not only on his reading of Suetonius and on his interpretation of the coin inscription and Nerva's reform. The situation for Jewish Christians was also abetted by Jewish efforts to distinguish their own groups and practices from those of Jewish Christians.[299] On this construction one sees Jewish interests and actions as a major factor in providing the conditions for the perfect storm, exposing Jewish Christians as "illicit atheists" in the same way as gentile Christians earlier, and distinguishing both from the Jewish communities of the empire. Summarizing his chapter on the *birkat ha-minim*, the *fiscus Iudaicus*, and the Gospel of John, Heemstra concludes:

---

of seizure and confiscation of property on the flimsiest of accusations. Having been charged with evading payment of the Jewish tax and having had their property confiscated, Roman victims would surely have been "allowed" to "come to their senses," "see the error of their ways," and "repent of their practices," and hence not have been made to register for future payments of the tax.

299. Heemstra first makes this case in his chapter on Nerva's reform on the basis of information found in the Acts of Thomas and in talmudic and midrashic sources. Objections based on the nature and late date of these sources are not enough to dissuade Heemstra of their general relevance and their correlation with rabbinic efforts at the end of Domitian's reign to persuade Roman officials of the difference between Jewish groups (and those sympathetic to Judaism) and Jewish Christians and their missionary efforts among gentiles (*Fiscus Judaicus*, 75–79). But it is particularly in his chapter on the *birkat ha-minim* and the Gospel of John that Heemstra makes his case for rabbinic efforts to dissociate mainstream Judaism from Jewish Christians (159–89). It is in the midst of this chapter devoted to constructing an argument on the much disputed issue of the dating and relevance of the *birkat ha-minim*, identifying its earliest version and targets, and showing that it was intended to exclude "Jewish Christians and apostate Jews from the 'community of Israel' by mainstream Judaism around the year 90" (188), that Heemstra acknowledges in a footnote the possibility that the authority of the sages of Yavneh may not have been so pervasive. No matter. "The problems surrounding Jewish Christians were probably felt to be so urgent throughout the diaspora that it does not seem necessary that this particular issue required a strong central rabbinic leadership" (174 n. 62). But this does not prevent Heemstra from concluding with other Johannine scholars that the Gospel of John is responding to a situation provoked in part by the rabbinic *birkat ha-minim*.

After having been labeled "heretics" by other Jews around the year 90 [*birkat ha-minim*], Jewish Christians subsequently lost their legal status as Jews in the year 96, when Nerva came to power and reformed the *fiscus Judaicus*. After that reform they were no longer regarded as Jews by the Romans, which meant that from a Roman perspective they would now be regarded as illegal "atheists".... Therefore, after the year 96 Jewish Christians could no longer officially lay claim to the label "Jew" on the basis of the newly adapted Roman definition of this term in the context of the *fiscus Judaicus*, which changed from an ethnic term to a religious one.... The "enigmatic" use of the word "Jew" or "the Jews" by John is probably the strongest argument for dating this gospel after the year 96 (probably around 100). John was writing at a moment when Jewish Christians had lost their "Jewishness": they were no longer officially Jews under Roman law.... On the basis of this evidence it may safely be concluded that the decisive separation between Judaism as we know it today and Christianity as we know it today, took place at the end of the first century, as the combined result of a decision by representatives of mainstream Judaism (exclusion of Jewish Christians, who were members of mixed Christian communities, from the "congregation of Israelites") and the Roman redefinition of the taxpayers to the *fiscus Judaicus*, excluding these same Jewish Christians.[300]

---

300. Ibid., 187, 189. Heemstra repeatedly uses the label "licit atheists" to refer to Jews in contrast to Christians whom he labels "illicit atheists," referring to gentile Christians under Domitian and to Jewish Christians after Nerva's reform. He seems to consider the difference to be a matter of law and state policy, but this is not at all so clear. When Tertullian in the third century refers to the status of Jewish religious practices in the empire as a *religio licita* (*Apol.* 21.1), he is probably not intending the expression as a reference to legal status but as a way of calling attention to the position of Christians who could be prosecuted as Christians, and whose practices were illegal in that sense. "Scholars have tended to interpret Tertullian's comment more positively than the context warrants.... But Tertullian never implies that the legality of Judaism was a matter of state policy. On the contrary, Judaism is legal only in the sense that no one has bothered to declare it illegal, unlike Christianity" (Schwartz, *Imperialism and Jewish Society*, 189). The right of Jews to live according to their ancestral traditions was a matter requiring imperial sanction from time to time. This is why appeals to different emperors were made during the Republic and early Principate in circumstances in which Jews were in dispute and conflict with elements of their larger host communities. Schwartz discusses whether the state sanctioned "traditional privileges of the Jews," for which there is considerable evidence prior to the destruction of the temple, continued in the second and third centuries. There is some evidence in Antoninus Pius's permission to Jews to circumcise their sons when it was forbidden to others and in the Emperors Severus and Caracalla's permission to Jews to acquire

It would not be long before the crime of atheism would become the crime of confessing to be a Christian, nor much longer before both Jewish and gentile Christians, that is, the mainstream Christian Church, saw itself as the true Israel.[301]

---

honors by fulfilling only those liturgies imposed on them "as do not harm their *super-stitio*" (in the jurists, Modestinus and Ulpian, see Justinian, *Edict.* 48.8.11 and 50.2.3.3 respectively; for text, see Theodor Mommsen, Paul Krueger, and Alan Watson, eds., *The Digest of Justinian* [Philadelphia: University of Pennsylvania Press, 1985], 4:821, 909; for commentary, see Amnon Linder, ed. and trans., *The Jews in Roman Imperial Legislation* [Detroit: Wayne State University Press, 1987], 99–107. What is striking, Schwartz observes, is how little evidence there is of Jewish appeal to imperial sanction after the destruction of the temple to uphold traditional exemptions or of conflict over the matter in comparison to earlier periods. Perhaps such exemptions were widely recognized and rarely generated conflict, though Schwartz thinks it more likely that "Jews themselves were disinclined to press their privileges" (Schwartz, *Imperialism and Jewish Society*, 190). Vespasian's imposition of the Jewish tax was not in any *legal* sense a condition for the right of Jews to observe traditional customs and sacred rites (contra Heemstra, *Fiscus Judaicus*, 7). If the tax could seem to be a substitute form of demonstrating a loyal disposition to Rome to replace sacrifices which were no longer offered in the temple of Jerusalem on behalf of the emperor and the Roman people, it was in fact imposed on an entire people across the empire in the wake of Rome's crushing of a rebellion confined to a limited area. In a practical sense, to be sure, the failure of large numbers of Jews to pay the tax would have had negative repercussions for Jews, because it would have been viewed as a further act of rebellion. Commenting on Tertullian's remark that the Jewish tax was a fine for the right to observe their religious practices, Goodman writes, "The incentive to make such a declaration [of Jewish identity] was presumably the freedom to carry on religious practices without odium, what Tertullian described, rather enviously, as '*vectigalis libertas*' (*Apol.* 18), freedom of worship bought at the price of the Jewish tax" ("Nerva, the *Fiscus Judaicus* and Jewish Identity," 42). It is safe to assume that those whom Tertullian regarded as Christians in his own day were not paying the Jewish tax. By that time a connection may have been made between payment of the tax and the right to observe Jewish practices. But it would have been a matter of state policy only in the practical sense that widespread failure to pay the tax would have brought Roman reprisals.

301. "From now on the issue was about being the real continuation of the history of Israel, which can already be detected in the Revelation of John, the Letter to the Hebrews and the Gospel of John on the Jewish Christian side, and in the *birkat ha-minim* on the side of mainstream Judaism.... The distinction between Jewish and non-Jewish Christians probably disappeared relatively quickly after the year 96 and the claim to be *verus Israel*, initially made by Jewish Christians for themselves, became the claim of all Christians and Christianity in general from the second century onwards" (Heemstra, *Fiscus Judaicus*, 210).

10. The *Fiscus Iudaicus* and Narratives of Victimization, Freedom, and Escape

The problem I have with Heemstra's reading of the Roman evidence on the *fiscus Iudaicus* and Nerva's reform does not amount to a demonstration that writings such as 1 Peter, Revelation, Hebrews, and the Gospel of John have nothing to do with the administration of the *fiscus* under Domitian or the counter measures and reform undertaken by Nerva. However, to the extent that Heemstra's judgments are dependent on his construal of the Roman evidence, the case for interpreting texts in these New Testament writings in connection with the tax is weakened. Heemstra's reading of the Roman evidence is not the only problem I have with the way in which he has constructed an argument to demonstrate his thesis. His use of terms as though they referenced legal concepts, his definitions and generalizations in some cases, his conception of the process of Christian formation in the first two centuries which appears to be presupposed, the lack of considered reflection on the difference between discursive formations and social reality, and the assumption that there were no alternatives for Christians other than apostasy or exposure to prosecution and execution[302] are larger issues with the argument of the monograph. At bottom, Heemstra's approach to texts is over confident that the crucial moment of a social history is available in a fairly transparent way in texts ranging across centuries in date and across a range of genres, if only the evidence is properly correlated and focused on the moment, as though such a moment necessarily occurred.

Most problematic of all, Heemstra's account of the parting of the ways of Judaism and Christianity is a story of the victimization of Christians by the coalescing of Roman and Jewish interests. Consider, for example, Heemstra's two-step formulation of the Johannine author's likely perception of the situation: "(1) Jesus was handed over by Jewish authorities to be executed by the Romans; and (2) John may have felt that in his days Jewish Christians had been 'handed over' to the Roman authorities by mainstream Judaism, which could lead to their being persecuted and

---

302. For an example of opposition to this normative assumption, see the discussion of arguments for the option of participation in the culture and cults of the cities of Asia Minor presupposed by the polemic of the book of Revelation in Warren Carter, "Roman Imperial Power: A New Testament Perspective," in Brodd and Reed, *Rome and Religion*, 137–51, esp. 142–48.

executed as well."[303] Here and elsewhere the transparency of texts witnesses to a unidirectional social history that runs from the fate of Jesus
to the fate of his disciples, and on to the fate of gentile Christians in the
harsh administration of the *fiscus Iudaicus* under Domitian, and finally to
the crucial moment of exposure of Jewish Christians to a similar fate in
the coalescing of Roman actions under Nerva and the actions of "mainstream Judaism" to distance itself from Jewish Christians. Heemstra uses
the crucial verb, "hand over," "betray," though he does not appear to see
the irony that according to this formulation the crucial moment for the
separation of Judaism and Christianity as religions is a moment that replicates the long- entrenched reading of the gospel story. Heemstra's thesis is
a story of victimization, the exposure and victimization of Christians, and,
as the gospel story has it, the agents are Jews and Romans, conceivably
in collaboration, but at least on paths that coalesce.[304] True, the motivation for this victimization from the Jewish side is not seen by Heemstra to
be exclusively, and perhaps not predominantly, theological but political.[305]

---

303. Heemstra, *Fiscus Judaicus*, 186. Heemstra (106 n. 2) does reference books by
Adela Yarbro Collins, L. L. Thompson, Warren Carter, and P. B. Duff that argue against
a situation of current persecution. These views have not convinced Heemstra.

304. These coalescing paths are even more pronounced in Heemstra's contribution, "The *Fiscus Judaicus*: Its Social and Legal Impact and a Possible Relation with
Josephus' Antiquities," in Tomson and Schwartz, *Jews and Christians in the First and
Second Centuries*, 327–47, where he attempts to make the case that the wording of
Claudius's edict in 41, as it appears in Josephus, *Ant.* 19.5.3 §290, that Jews have the
right to practice their ancestral customs but are admonished "not to show contempt
of the religious observances of other nations," contributed to Nerva's reform of the
abuses of Domitian in collecting the Jewish tax and brought about the change of definition of liability from an ethnic definition of Jew to a religious definition (according
to Heemstra's interpretation of Cassius Dio, *Hist. Rom.* 65.7.2). Heemstra thinks that
Nerva as a senator opposing the autocratic rule of Domitian was a good candidate for
belonging to Josephus's audience, and that Josephus and Nerva would have agreed that
Jewish Christians did hold religious observances of other nations in contempt, did not
continue to observe Jewish customs, and therefore were not to be legitimized by being
allowed to pay the Jewish tax (342–45).

305. I would not deny the political dimensions and motivations of occasional
Jewish actions taken against followers of Jesus. In the case of the apostle Paul it is likely
that punishment *at the hands of Jews* was a consequence of political considerations of
synagogue authorities regarding the potential danger of Roman reprisals on account
of Paul's activities. But as a general consideration this should not be exaggerated. Most
followers of Jesus did not see themselves as the apostle to the gentiles, or cultivate a
wide field of influence, or nurture relations with groups one claimed to have founded,

Moreover, Heemstra is clear that the pressure on Christians would very likely have resulted in significant numbers returning to the communities of their birth. Finally, it is not that Heemstra attributes no agency to Christians but that, apart from the adoption by gentile Christians of "exclusive monotheism" (another much over generalized label), such agency tends to be limited to responses to victimization.[306]

I do not believe that Roman assumptions about who was liable for the payment of the Jewish tax would at any time in the first century have prevented followers of Jesus from registering to pay it, even if under Domitian's harsh exaction there were followers of Jesus who had not been registered but found themselves compelled to pay it. The ordinary and necessary interest in defining legal liability for the payment of a tax did not necessarily amount to a capacity to determine who actually registered. In registering to pay the Jewish tax, individuals and households were identifying themselves publicly as Jews, but that is a different matter, for the real question is, who was registered? This question was answered for many Jewish households largely on the basis of affiliations, because collection of the tax, or at least information leading to payment of the tax, would have required the cooperation of the Jews themselves, whether we are thinking of individuals to whom the collection of the tax was farmed out, or we are talking about village authorities in particular toparchies, magistrates and council members in the cities of Palestine, or officials of synagogues and other associations in the Greco-Roman cities of the diaspora whose

or target competitors, in other words, engage in Paul's activities; see above, 299–300 with nn. 194 and 195.

306. Heemstra makes several observations in his monograph that require my registering a caveat to this judgment. Believing that Jewish Christians paid the temple tax, Heemstra ponders their considerations when the Jewish tax was first imposed: "With the introduction of the Jewish tax by Vespasian one may wonder whether they were also registered or if this was a moment at which they could back out (e.g., in cities where some kind of drifting apart from the synagogue had already taken place), also because this was actually a Roman punitive measure for the benefit of a pagan god and no longer a Jewish institution" (*Fiscus Judaicus*, 63). A similar calculation is at least broached in connection with Domitian's targeting of unregistered Jewish Christians (ibid., 65–66; see above, 342–43). And Heemstra also suggests that Rev 2:9 and 3:9 is polemic aimed at Jews who pay the tax (125). Unfortunately, in developing his thesis, Heemstra overlooks the responsibility of followers of Jesus for their own calculations and decisions regarding payment of the tax and focuses exclusively on an outcome determined by Roman and "mainstream" Jewish interests.

services were needed for identifying Jewish families. Those Jews directly involved in assessment or in collecting the tax were of course responsible to the Roman official, most likely a procurator or his assistants.[307] Registration directly with the responsible Roman agent without any Jewish mediation was surely also possible.[308] Failure to pay the tax would have brought sanctions internally within communities for fear of Roman reprisals and would often have ended in severe penalties to the individuals involved.

A change from ethnic to cultural criteria for determining liability runs counter to normal assumptions and seems to me an unnecessary proposal to account for Nerva's actions to end the abuses under Domitian. It is more reasonable to suppose that the typical notion of who belonged to a people was based on the assumption of a correlation of birth and cultural practices. It did not usually matter, even for the collection of taxes, that concepts of family, ancestry, homeland, custom and rites, or even reputations, among other identifiers as ordinary markers of a people, were all disputable and hardly resulted in a set of firm rather than quite blurry boundaries, or that the long term survival of a people depended on mechanisms for adopting others into the group. Ordinary assumptions were adequate for the collection of taxes, as long as it was clear that the principals were serious about collecting them, that the cooperation of local representatives could be expected, that sanctions were severe enough to discourage evasion, and that there were no other factors in play, such as attempting to increase revenues beyond previous years by attracting and empowering informers to bring accusations of tax evasion, and by intentionally obscuring or overriding ordinary assumptions in order to increase the numbers of those who could be held liable. What changed with Nerva was ending the basis on which Domitian had sought to increase revenues: the

---

307. For the provinces of Judea and Arabia from the evidence of the Babatha archive, see Hannah M. Cotton and Werner Eck, "Roman Officials in Judaea and Arabia and Civil Jurisdiction," in *Law in the Documents of the Judaean Desert*, ed. Ranon Katzoff and David Schaps, JSJSup 96 (Leiden: Brill, 2005), 23–44, esp. 29–33. The jurisdiction of imperial procurators of equestrian rank was not delegated by the governor (29).

308. Although the example of Babatha comes from the province of Arabia, ca. 127, and concerns the registration of her orchards, it is still instructive to note that there is no role indicated for magistrates of the *polis* in her census return. She registers the orchards directly with the Roman governor, which does not mean that it was not another Roman official authorized to act in his stead (ibid., 33).

accusations of *delatores*, which probably meant simply a return to procedures for collecting the tax when it was first imposed by Vespasian.[309]

Followers of Jesus who were Jews by birth could have been registered as part of a village population where Jews constituted a majority, or
through continued relations with synagogues and other Jewish corporate
bodies, or as members of households registering directly with the Roman
official responsible. For that matter, they could have organized their own
lists through house churches and other associations. I do not say that there
is direct evidence that any of this happened, but why should the *fiscus* have
rejected the revenue?[310] Indeed, followers of Jesus who were not Jews by
birth could have registered on the grounds that they had become "Godfearers" or a kind of proselyte.[311] If Cassius Dio's observation that the tax
was imposed on Jews who continued to observe their ancestral customs
did have some particular reference to Nerva's reform of abuses under
Domitian (that is, not requiring payment of the tax from those who did
not publicly identify themselves as Jews), there is no reason to suppose
that the Roman historian's observation that those of alien race who zeal-
ously observe their customs are also called Ἰουδαῖος (*Hist. Rom.* 37.17.1)
only came to be recognized in the third century. Nor is it really conceivable that Roman officials saw themselves as the arbiters of which people
of alien race were truly the zealous practitioners of the ancestral customs

---

309. Cf. Schwartz, *Imperialism and Jewish Society*, 187–88. It could be objected
that if this is the case, there is no reason to associate Nerva's reform with the statement
of Cassius Dio (*Hist. Rom.* 65.7.2) regarding the imposition of the tax on those who
continued to observe their ancestral customs. But this objection ignores the difference between a reform of the abuses under Domitian and a change in the definition
of Jewishness.

310. Paul Foster remarks on Matt 17:24–27, arguing for reference to the *fiscus*
rather than the temple tax, "The Roman tax collectors were not interested in the nice-
ties of theological distinctions. The more they raised, the more they profited personally" (Foster, "Vespasian, Nerva, Jesus," 314; on Matt 17:24–27, see below, 363–68).

311. I am not using "Godfearer" and "proselyte" as technical terms whose distinctions Roman officials kept track of, but simply suggesting that the *fiscus Iudaicus*
had no reason to reject households that identified with the Jewish people precisely by
registering to pay the tax. The real impediment to registering to pay the tax for those
who were not Jews by birth was the necessity of registering all the eligible members of
a household. Where one's own actions and affiliations had created tension and division
in a household, registering all the members would hardly have been met with cooperation. However, this should also be kept in view with respect to those who had become
proselytes or in some way associated with Jewish corporate bodies.

of the Jews or that they kept records of which of these among the males were zealous enough to be circumcised, all others not being deemed zealous enough to qualify. Paying the tax was mandatory for those on whom the tax had been imposed, but it was also voluntary because normally only those registered paid it.[312]

I am not discounting the communal interests that Jewish corporate bodies may have sought to protect by distancing their members and adherents from followers of Jesus where the recruitment activities of the latter among other perergrine or native groups was seen as creating a situation or potential for public disturbances. Nor would I discount a measure of protection afforded one's activities by virtue of a public record of payment of the Jewish tax. But these factors are easily blown out of proportion. Jews were not immune to some of the same suspicions. What about their own proselytes? Tacitus expresses his animus toward those who adopt the practice of circumcision and take as their first lesson to despise the gods, disown their country, and set at nought ancestry and family (*Hist.* 5.5.2). Let's be clear. Whatever advantage payment of the tax afforded for the protection of Jewish practices, it was hardly a financial boon to Jewish households and anything but a badge of honor. It is hardly unimaginable to think that during Domitian's harsh collection of the tax some informers could have been Jews who accused followers of Jesus out of spite.[313] Failure to pay the tax compromised a commitment to the well being of Jewish

312. Commenting that registration was also not strictly a matter of Jewish affiliation, Goodman observes, "It would in any case be difficult to decide *which* Jewish community in a town had the right to define its members, for there is no reason to believe that rabbinic authority in the definition of Jewishness was widely accepted even in Palestine at so early a date, let alone in the diaspora. The only alternative, it seems to me, must be that Jews were taxed if, and only if, they declared themselves as Jews" ("Nerva, the *Fiscus Judaicus* and Jewish Identity," 41–42, emphasis original). Whether the opposite holds that all those who did not register to pay the tax were thereby saying that in their own eyes they were no longer Jews, it should hold that by registering to pay the tax followers of Jesus were demonstrating publicly that they identified themselves as Jews.

313. Heemstra thinks this improbable, but it is because he thinks Jews everywhere were motivated only by desire to keep Christians at as much of a distance as possible (*Fiscus Judaicus*, 125). He has not considered the opposite scenario: Jews threatening followers of Jesus through social pressure and informing if they did not register and pay the tax, precisely because evading payment could bring reprisals to Jewish representatives responsible to Roman authorities for seeing to it that all Jews were registered.

communities, for serious default in payment would bring Roman reprisals. However, payment of the tax was no guarantee against Roman intervention in one's practices, either for followers of Jesus or for the vast majority of Jews who were not, especially if these practices resulted in public controversy and disturbances. When Rome sought to crack down on religious specialists operating independently, it was not the followers of Jesus alone who were the target. The difference that being a follower of Jesus made with respect to prospects of Roman intervention and prosecution was a difference arising principally from the greater propensity to engage in activities of attraction and recruitment that resulted in the breakdown of expected social roles, and thus an enhanced potential for creating division in families and public disturbances. The illegality of being a Christian is a particular example of Roman intervention in unauthorized practices.[314]

---

314. I have taken the position that trouble with Roman authorities was mostly occasioned by activities of followers of Jesus that encouraged abandonment of family, native customs and sacred rites. But I have also pointed out that these would have been Roman responses to complaints and public disturbances emerging in local situations where it was not a question of a Roman policy to track down Christians in particular, but a broader Roman concern with the activities of unregulated religious specialists and a vested interest in giving heed to the complaints of local elites and native populations (see my discussion of persecution in Mark and more generally, above, 292–302 with notes). This seems to me still to be the situation in the correspondence between Pliny, Roman governor of Bithynia in northern Asia Minor, and the Emperor Trajan, ca. 112 (Pliny, *Ep.* 10.96–97). Pliny writes for guidance or, perhaps more accurately, for confirmation from Trajan. He acknowledges that he has sent some who are Roman citizens to Rome and has executed others because these, questioned as Christians and having been warned of capital punishment and given ample opportunity to recant, seemed to Pliny to deserve punishment for their implacable obstinacy in refusing to sacrifice to the images and renounce Christ, whatever the crime might be to which they have confessed in being Christians. However, he also acknowledges to Trajan that once having dealt with the question of those brought before him as Christians, the result was the spread of the charge, including many names found in an anonymous pamphlet, and a great variety of cases to judge. Pliny emphasizes that despite the spread of the contagion, his practice of allowing Christians to recant is working to check the problem, which is already evident by the temples once again being frequented and the sacred rites performed. Trajan confirms that Pliny has taken the right approach. A Roman governor cannot simply ignore charges brought before him, but neither should Christians be sought out by Roman officials, and anonymous pamphlets should carry no weight in establishing charges. Trajan confirms Pliny's practice of allowing Christians to recant, emphasizing that no matter what the evidence establishing the person as a Christian in the past, recantation suffices to pardon the person. The evidence from

this correspondence suggests to me that the circumstances and the risks for Christians of persecution by Roman authorities was about the same from the time of Nero to the early second century, and probably beyond to the middle of the third century (Rives, *Religion in the Roman Empire*, 196–200). Followers of Jesus could be isolated and serve as scapegoats under conditions of public stress. They could be informed against, and with enough of a public disturbance Roman officials would respond. But the Roman interest was usually to maintain the status quo, to satisfy local concerns and defuse the situation, not to seek and root out Christians as a policy directed at a uniquely targeted group. Such local concerns and public disturbances are not likely to have popped out of the blue just because followers of Jesus were known to live in their midst, but because of a perception of their growing numbers and influence in a locale, or because they were implicated in a crackdown on independent religious specialists. My reading of the significance of the Pliny-Trajan correspondence will appear quite different from the significance attributed to it by John M. G. Barclay, "'Jews' and 'Christians' in the Eyes of Roman Authors c. 100 CE," in Tomson and Schwartz, *Jews and Christians in the First and Second Centuries*, 313–26, but part of the reason is that we are asking different questions. I am asking about the underlying causes and circumstances in the few known cases of Roman examination and execution of followers of Jesus without focusing on the significance of the label "Christian" itself in Roman sources. Barclay is examining the connotations and relationship between the labels "Jew" and "Christian" in Roman sources in the early part of the second century, there being no Roman references to the latter label in sources before the end of the first century. With reference to his interest, Barclay is correct that the labels belong to different categories and have virtually no relationship. The one is clearly an ethnic label in these sources; the other has political connotations and connotations of criminality and is in no sense an ethnic term in the Roman sources. Barclay acknowledges that the Roman evidence does not correspond well to "the complex social interactions between ordinary Jews, Christ-believing Jews and Christ-believing non-Jews in the first and second centuries," but "as far as the Romans were concerned—both influential opinion-formers and the general public—'Christians' were in a quite different category from 'Jews'" (326). This conclusion is hardly surprising, given that the only settings in which the label "Christian" is used in Roman sources of this period are Nero's scapegoating and Pliny's examination. Epictetus refers to "Galileans" not "Christians." In these two settings ethnic identity was irrelevant and making observations that might indicate the ethnicity of those accused would only complicate the proceedings. Consequently, the comparison Barclay makes between how to cause damage to a "Jew" by accusing the person of tax evasion and how to cause damage to a "Christian" by using the label to call the attention of a Roman authority to the person is truly a comparison of apples and oranges (ibid., 321–25). But the term "Christian" is not widely in evidence in this period, at least as a self-designation. I would not take Tacitus's writing that the crowds were calling the victims "Christians" in the setting of Nero's persecution as evidence of ordinary Romans' knowledge or use of the term at the time (the account given by Suetonius has quite different implications, see above, n. 193). I would also be very cautious about concluding from the evidence of the Pliny-Trajan correspondence that the name itself was illegal or tantamount to a criminal charge, though the label

Whether followers of Jesus paid the Jewish tax would seem to me to have depended much more on what was done when the tax was first imposed by Vespasian than on anything that transpired during the reigns of Domitian and Nerva. This judgment is based on the simple calculation that it would be more difficult to be dropped from the tax-lists once members of a household were registered than it would to be added to them. But I do not believe there is any evidence that gives a secure answer to the question whether followers of Jesus registered in significant numbers from the start. Those most active among the followers of Jesus were likely to be on the move, perhaps conveniently also when tax collectors came around. One can certainly think of reasons they may have had to resist registering, at least in circumstances that did not make registering virtually unavoidable or too risky to avoid. There was of course avoidance of the financial burden, surely an incentive not to be minimized, but beyond that one can imagine a benefit to self-and collective esteem by resisting identification as Jews in this particular way, as Roman subjects defeated and punished, aggressors against regional neighbors, paying the tax imposed on a rebellious people. Moreover, paying the tax could have been resisted on the grounds that it was a sign of collaboration with the enemies of the God of Israel, especially where it was known that the revenues went for the rebuilding of the temple of Jupiter in Rome. These considerations do not amount to evidence about what was or was not done by followers of Jesus with respect to the payment of the tax, but they at least give reason to ask how such matters were discursively manipulated. Evidence of rhetorical aims and discourse centered on the payment of tax, and matters bearing on processes of identity formation may be the more appropriate focus in

---

probably carried connotations of political subversion for Pliny. Counter indications are that "Christians" should not be sought out by Roman officials, that the accuser must face the accused, and Pliny's observation to Trajan that the temples are being frequented again and sacred rites are being performed, even if, as may be the case, Pliny is referring to those accused who have "repented." These indications suggest that the charges that came with the label "Christian" had to do with circumstances in which public controversy had arisen over the failure of the accused to fulfill expected familial, social, and political roles. Moreover, there is overlap in the circumstances in which both Jews and Christians could be targeted by Roman officials having to do with a larger category of unauthorized religious specialists in which the question of ethnic identity was also irrelevant with respect to the grounds for punishment (see above, nn. 191–92).

approaching the one New Testament text with the strongest claim to have this tax in view, Matt 17:24–27.

I must stipulate at the start that I view the pericope to be concerned with ordinary expectations regarding the payment of a tax and not with other kinds of object lessons having nothing to do with the payment of taxes.[315] In its literary context, payment of the *didrachmon* tax inquired about by the collectors would refer to the Jerusalem temple tax.[316] This may be an indication that there was a pre-Matthean version of the narrative, but as it now stands in Matthew, neither the identity of the agents who question Peter nor what the tax supports is specified.[317] One can suppose that Peter's response that his teacher does pay the tax in view is the response that is expected. However, Jesus's subsequent rhetorical query and Peter's response, followed by Jesus's instruction to Peter, can hardly be intended merely to reaffirm the response that Peter gives to the collectors. Jesus's rhetorical question refers to "the kings of the earth" and to "toll or tribute" (τέλη ἤ κῆνσον), clearly references to Roman taxes, collected from "others" not from "their own children," as Peter appropriately responds. I do not believe that these references can be taken as parabolic sayings similar to king parables, where the implied analogy would be that the kings of the earth are to their children as God is to the children of God, signifying that God too does not tax the children, and therefore that the followers of Jesus are not obligated to pay the tax, though God will provide for it in order not to give offence.[318] But if this sort of analogy is not appropriate in this context, the rhetorical question and the further

315. In agreement with Warren Carter, "Paying the Tax to Rome as Subversive Praxis: Matthew 17:24–27," *JSNT* 22 (2000): 3–31; and Edward J. Carter, "Toll and Tribute: A Political Reading of Matthew 17:24–27," *JSNT* 25 (2003): 413–31.

316. The half-shekel tax was also known by its Greek equivalent, *duo drachmas* or *didrachmon*. Since the amount per head was the same in the case of the tax imposed by Vespasian, it was also known by these Greek equivalents, or by the Roman equivalent, *duo dēnarii* (see below, n. 341). The plural form in v. 24, *didrachma*, is probably related to the fact that the collectors in querying Peter refer to "your (pl.) teacher."

317. Foster, "Vespasian, Nerva, Jesus," 313–14.

318. In my judgment Warren Carter is correct that reference to "the kings of the earth" must be understood to refer to kings or political regimes in opposition to God's sovereignty, and that "their sons" from whom taxes are not collected refers to the ruler's immediate physical offspring. The passage (vv. 25–26) does not really work as allegory ("Paying the Tax to Rome," 20–25). A fuller discussion of these verses as parable is found in Carter, "Toll and Tribute," 419–21, who also rejects this interpretation.

instruction given by Jesus cannot refer to the half-shekel temple tax. Even if we posit a post-70 Matthean circle that thought the temple tax had been imposed by the temple priests but not by God, there would be only one appropriate analogy between the Jerusalem temple tax and the Jewish tax imposed by Rome, that is, that both were expected to be paid, the one by Peter and Jesus, the other by the circles addressed by the Gospel of Matthew.[319] For the readers of Matthew, the "tax switch" may be signaled in the narrative by the fact that Jesus is not present when the collectors make their inquiry. When he returns home he needs no report from Peter about the inquiry, but initiates reflection on it by addressing a rhetorical question to Peter, including reference to Roman tolls and tribute, which signals a different *didrachmon* tax.

The opening phrase of verse 27, ἵνα δὲ μὴ σκανδαλίσωμεν αὐτούς, presents three problems: (1) the translation of the connective, (2) the meaning of the verb, and (3) the referent of the pronoun. The particle connective should not be taken in a strong contrastive sense, "however" (RSV and NRSV), which is only appropriate on a parabolic interpretation of verses 25b–26 (implying that Jesus and his disciples are exempt from the tax), but in a loose connective sense, "and."[320] The verb is usually translated "offend," "scandalize." Edward Carter objects to this translation on the ground that it is not the meaning of the verb in the active voice, which is usually rendered "cause to sin" or "lead astray" in Matthew, in contrast to the passive voice, "to be offended," in Matt 15:12.[321] This translation is

---

319. I agree with Edward Carter's contention that it is inappropriate to exclude an imperial context for interpreting Matt 17:24–27 on the grounds that the Jerusalem temple tax is religious and the post-70 Roman tax is political ("Toll and Tribute," 416). But this should not imply that the same political interpretation of the passage would work as well for the former as for the latter. To suppose that the Jerusalem temple was as Roman an institution as the *fiscus Iudaicus*, and therefore that the tax paid to the Jerusalem temple was as much a symbol of subjugation to Rome as the tax paid to the temple of Jupiter in Rome, is as simplistic as the alternative Carter correctly rejects. Reference to the kings of the earth imposing taxes on their subjects while exempting their children (ἄρα γε ἐλεύθεροί εἰσιν οἱ υἱοί) will simply not work in application to the Jerusalem temple tax as it does for the Roman tax, unless one assumes the parabolic interpretation that Carter rejects. It is of course possible that there is an implicit connection with Roman power. The Jerusalem temple proved to be subject to Roman power as much as those upon whom the *fiscus Iudaicus* was imposed.

320. Ibid., 423–24; and Carter, "Paying the Tax to Rome," 26 n. 116.

321. Carter, "Toll and Tribute," 424–25 with n. 45.

convincing if one takes the pronoun to refer to Jesus's disciples, as Carter suggests.[322] But this referent seems much less cogent than assuming the pronoun refers back to its closest antecedents, "the kings of earth" and "their offspring," which makes the translation "offend" or "scandalize" still preferable, the implication being that not paying the tax would provoke their retaliation.

Warren Carter acknowledges that the disciples pay the tax in order to survive, but while this is an important reality it does not convey God's opposition, an expectation triggered by reference to "the kings of the earth." According to Carter, this opposition is implied in Jesus's instruction to Peter to cast for the fish, open its mouth, find the *statēr*, and pay the tax for the two of them.[323] The instruction concerns the ultimate sovereignty of God not only over the fish of the sea but over the tax itself: "The tax too falls within the sphere of God's sovereignty. The story does not promise to provide every disciple with the tax by this means.... Rather, it reframes the significance of paying the tax, offering those who pay it a new context and perspective, that of God's sovereignty."[324] By the time Carter has fully underscored that here too we must see "God laugh[ing] at the kings of the earth by refusing to let their claim of domination, signified by the tax, go uncontested,"[325] we may have forgotten that the explicit reason Jesus gives for paying the tax is in order not to offend the rulers, not to provoke their retaliation. The title of the essay, "Paying the Tax to Rome as Subversive Praxis," comes to full view:

> Paying the tax, then, is no longer for the disciples of Jesus an action defined by Rome, no longer an action that acknowledges the all-controlling power of the (Roman) kings of the earth and the oppressive sovereignty of the empire.... That is to say, paying the tax becomes a subversive not a subjugating act, a defiant act which relativizes and undermines what the tax is supposed to reinforce: Rome's absolute power and control of its subject's reality. The act of paying gives the empire what it demands but not on its terms.[326]

---

322. Ibid., 425–26.
323. Carter, "Paying the Tax to Rome," 27.
324. Ibid., 28.
325. Ibid., 29.
326. Ibid., 28–29.

On the contrary, paying the tax to Rome cannot be a subversive praxis on Carter's interpretation of Matt 17:24–27, because the difference between not provoking Roman retaliation, which underscores subjection to Rome and a realistic fear of Roman power, and highlighting God's ultimate sovereignty over the kings of the earth is precisely a distinction between conditions compelling behavior in the world and a world view represented as undetermined by these conditions, a distinction between what is to be done and why, and what, nevertheless, can be thought. I agree with Carter's interpretation of this passage insofar as it says to Matthean circles that followers of Jesus resist a self-definition and world view that is circumscribed by Roman imposition of the tax. But payment of the tax itself remains an act of subjection to Rome. It is a matter of rectifying in thought what cannot be changed, given the constraints of the situation in the world as depicted in the text. It demonstrates that followers of Jesus can behave exactly as expected in a shared political environment, and at the same time can distinguish themselves from others behaving exactly the same way.[327] Nonetheless, I would still hesitate to draw a firm conclusion from this text about the actual payment of the *fiscus Iudaicus* in Matthean circles. On Carter's interpretation, the narrative only makes its point on the supposition that paying the tax is expected and cannot be reasonably avoided. This should not be taken as a simple reflection of behavior in Matthean circles, or of the actual social and political constraints operating in these circles. It is a narrative constraint designed to bring home to the readers the distinction described above. The fact that the coin for the tax is found by God's provision can certainly inspire a reading that refers the paying of the tax to God's sovereignty and not to the actions of the followers of Jesus, which in practice may have meant, pay it if you must, avoid it if you can. The account in fact does not narrate Peter's acting on Jesus's instructions.

E. J. Carter does not interpret the text as an instance of subversive praxis, but his interpretation also depends on a distinction between behavior and self-representation. "Here…, Jesus, by his reported action of paying the tax, is acknowledging that he and his followers are *mixed up* in the

---

327. Cf. Dunning, *Aliens and Sojourners*, 12, commenting on 1 Peter: "What is non-negotiable for 1 Peter is that these Christians ought to understand themselves in some fundamental way as outsiders…. But what sort of outsiders? These are not aliens who withdraw from Roman society and Mediterranean urban life for the desert or the caves. Rather, they are aliens who submit to Roman governors and honor the emperor."

world of secular political sovereignty, but by the unlikely and miraculous source of the coin, the message is conveyed that he is not *compromised* by it.... Jesus, then, does pay the tax, but only by breaking out beyond the normal boundaries within which political power is exercised."[328] This interpretation, if not inspired by Luther's "two kingdoms" theory, is shown by Carter to be congruent with it. The Christian is in the world and voluntarily serves the world, yet his position is always that of a stranger. "Such service does no harm to him, and he suffers no loss by it, but the world benefits greatly."[329] This notion of simultaneous immersion in and transcendence of the political realm would surely distinguish late first-century Christians from Jews, which it is undoubtedly intended to do, for I cannot imagine many Jews having the thought that in paying the tax to Rome they were serving and benefitting the world, and yet were suffering no loss themselves. One must wonder whether such a notion trumps the political realm of empire without revealing its own complicity or implicating its own duplicity. One can find a similar sort of distinction between behavior and self-representation in those interpretations of Matt 17:24–27 that depend upon a parabolic reading that likens the kings of the earth and their offspring to God and the children of God. As regards their status as the children of God, Jesus and his disciples are "free," that is, exempt from paying the tax, whether it is the Jerusalem temple tax or the Roman *fiscus Iudaicus*. Payment of the tax is not a particularly pressing matter, either because it is voluntary, and, in a Pauline sense, indifferent with respect to the status of the believer and community in Christ,[330] or because, while Jesus and Peter as Jews must pay, "the 'sons' [Christians] of the [Matthean] community are not bound by the rules imposed upon the defeated Jewish

328. Carter, "Toll and Tribute," 426–27, emphasis original.

329. Ibid., 429.

330. See Mikael Tellbe, "The Temple Tax as a Pre-70 CE Identity Marker," in *The Formation of the Early Church*, ed. Jostein Ådna, WUNT 183 (Tübingen: Mohr Siebeck, 2005), 19–44. By taking "voluntary" in this Pauline sense as though it necessarily represented an actual social consensus, Tellbe ignores the possibility that such differences of behavior were a serious source of conflict among followers of Jesus. Commenting on the designation "free ones" in 1 Pet 2:16 and Matt 17:26, which admittedly could be coincidental, Tellbe concludes, "In any case, the term ἐλεύθεροι in Matt 17:24–27 and its only occurrence in the Petrine tradition of 1 Pet 2:16 display the same idea, namely the fundamental freedom of the believer not only from civic duties but also from Jewish cultic obligations" (41).

nation."[331] It would seem then on these interpretations of Matt 17:24–27 that whether one pays the temple tax or does not, one is not "really" a Jew; whether one pays the Jewish tax or does not, one is not "really" a subject of Rome. The difference can be taken as a discursive practice.

I have concluded that Heemstra's account of the significance of the *fiscus Iudaicus* presents what is essentially a narrative of the victimization of Christians by Romans and Jews and have countered that followers of Jesus would not have been prevented from registering to pay the tax. In such circumstances, followers of Jesus who avoided registering to pay the tax made a decision to reject an act of Jewish identification imposed by Rome. I have also questioned the idea that without the cover of payment of the tax such followers were left unprotected from prosecution by Roman officials, a matter that looms large in Heemstra's account but needs far more nuance than it is given. Interpretations of Matt 17:24–27 present narratives of resistance, transcendence and freedom, whether it is freedom from obligation to pay the temple tax or freedom from loss of status and subjection to Rome while paying the Jewish tax. I am not saying these narratives have nothing to support them but that they occlude another narrative, a narrative of exemption and escape from conditions imposed on Jews because Roman power and policy defined the conditions of submission in which Jewish life could persist. There is something inauthentic about narratives of victimization and freedom that fail to recognize the interests of self-distancing from the consequences of political and cultural loss projected in a narrative of exemption and escape.

There is another question about the payment of taxes found in the Synoptic Gospels triple tradition (Mark 12: 13–17 // Matt 22:15–22 // Luke 20:20–25). In the course of his teaching in the temple, Jesus is asked whether it is lawful to pay taxes to the emperor. The question is intended to trap him into a response that presumably will bring him into disrepute

---

331. B. D. Chilton, "A Coin of Three Realms (Matthew 17.24–27)," in *The Bible in Three Dimensions: Essays in Celebration of Forty Years of Biblical Studies in the University of Sheffield*, ed. David J. A. Clines, Stephen E. Fowl, and Stanley E. Porter, JSOTSup 87 (Sheffield: JSOT Press, 1990), 279). "Within the Judaic realm, a set of parables releases Jews from the necessity of paying the half-shekel; within the Matthaean realm, a miracle assures that the imperial tax is paid by Peter within his status as a Jew, not as a Christian" (280). Clearly, for Chilton, "the sons" in the parable who are free are not Jews but Christians, at least in what he calls the Matthean realm. As Jews they are obligated; as Christians they are free.

with the populace or mark him as one who rejects Roman hegemony in Judea. Jesus's clever response, which implicates his interlocutors and the Jerusalem populace in Roman hegemony by producing a *dēnarius* with the image and inscription of the emperor, springs the trap and resets it for his interlocutors. A question about the temple tax rather than Roman taxes might have been expected here in the setting of the temple but may have been made impertinent by Jesus's prior action against "the proximity of economic exchange and reciprocal, sacrificial exchange."[332] In any case, as Fabian Udoh has argued convincingly in my judgment, the scene as it is presented in the Synoptic tradition tells us nothing about taxes paid to Rome during Jesus's time and cannot be a reminiscence of an event in the life of Jesus, whether the historical Jesus was ever addressed about taxes paid to Rome or uttered the saying, or something like it, in Mark 12:17 and its parallels.[333] The scene has been taken as evidence that Jews in Judea paid a poll tax (supposedly indicated by κῆνσον in Mark 12:14 // Matt 22:17; cf. Matt 17:25). "This view, namely, that the Gospel passages provide evidence that 'under Tiberius' the Jews paid 'a poll tax,' which had been introduced in Judea through the census of 6 C.E. has become an orthodoxy among ancient historians and New Testament scholars alike."[334]

Udoh rejects this view in a discussion of two features of the texts: the phrase—literally—"to pay a *census*" and Jesus's call for a *dēnarius*.[335] Udoh

---

332. See Ullucci, *Rejection of Animal Sacrifice*, 82; see above, n. 175.

333. Fabian E. Udoh, *To Caesar What Is Caesar's: Tribute, Taxes, and Imperial Administration in Early Roman Palestine (63 B.C.E.–70 C.E.)*, BJS 343 (Providence, RI: Brown Judaic Studies, 2005), 223–38.

334. Ibid., 223–24. "A population census—a registration of persons in a household (κατ'οἰκίαν ἀπογραφή)—is necessary for the imposition of a poll tax. The format of the census in 6 CE and Babatha's census return constitute *prima facie* rebuttals of the view that the inhabitants of Judea paid a *tributum capitis*—the poll tax—before 70 C.E." (223). This judgment is based on the author's discussion of Roman censuses in the early Empire and comparison of the census in 6 CE and the census return of Babatha in 127 CE (207–18).

335. Udoh discusses and rejects three pieces of evidence to which appeal is made to show that Jews paid a poll tax prior to 70 CE. (1) Appian's statement in *Syr.* 11.8.50, which Udoh argues should be understood as the tax imposed by Vespasian. "If Pompey had imposed a poll tax upon the Jews in 63 B.C.E. it would have been upon those Jews living in Palestine, whom he conquered, not on 'all Jews,' as Appian writes, a phrase reminiscent of Vespasian's levy" (ibid., 20–21); (2) the gospel passages; (3) reference to the *tributum capitis* in Syria by the jurist Ulpian, which could include Judea, and the statement by the jurist Paul about Vespasian's exemption of the

points out that neither the Latin word, *census,* nor its Greek transliteration ever means "tax" or "tribute," and therefore that χῆνσος in Mark and Matthew is not interchangeable with Luke's use of φόρος (20:22). The meaning of *kēnsos* here too is clearly "census" or "assessment."

> The view that the word χῆνσος in Mark 12:14, Matt 22:17, 19 and 17:25 means "tax" is, therefore, surmised from the supposition that Roman provincial censuses since Augustus were an assessment *for the purpose of taxation.* The terms χῆνσος and φόρος in the Gospel passages contain no further information beyond this supposition. They are only vague recollections of the fact that there once had been a census in Judea, leading to Roman taxation. These terms and the "reminiscence" from which they arise tell us nothing specific about Roman taxation in Jewish Palestine in the second and third decades of the first century C.E.[336]

Regarding Jesus's call to be shown a *dēnarius,* Udoh points out that the identification of the coin with an issue of Tiberius's coins simply assumes what the passage is supposed to prove. Udoh appeals to the methodology and conclusions of the numismatic survey of coin finds in Jerusalem by Donald Ariel:[337]

> Counting surface, excavation, and hoard finds in Jerusalem, Ariel identified seven Roman coins dated before 67/68 C.E. Of the seven coins, one (no. 54) is a silver denarius of Augustus (dated 2 B.C.E.–11 C.E.), one (no. 61) is a gold *Aureus* of Tiberius (dated 14–37 C.E.), and only one (no. 60) is a silver denarius of Tiberius (dated 14–37 C.E.). This coin was minted in Rome. Two other facts emerge from Ariel's study. First, Roman silver tetradrachms and denarii were found in Jerusalem in significant numbers only after 69 C.E., especially after the reign of Ves-

---

colonists in Caesarea from payment of the *tributum capitis,* which could imply that it was in force in the region at the time of the exemption (Justinian, *Edict.* 50.15.3 and 50.15.8.7 respectively). Udoh questions the meaning and dating of these statements: "Scholars have yet to determine what *tributum capitis* means for both Paul and Ulpian and at what time, before the third century, this tax was introduced into different parts of Syria" (237). Only for Egypt is there evidence in the region before 70 CE of a poll tax paid in cash and a land tax (238); see Josephus, *J.W.* 2.16.4 §§385–386.

336. Udoh, *To Caesar,* 227–28, emphasis original.

337. Donald T. Ariel, "A Survey of Coin Finds in Jerusalem (Until the End of Byzantine Period)," *LASBF* 32 (1982): 273–326.

pasian. Second, in the period before 69 C.E., there was, on the contrary, a continued preponderance of Tyrian silver coins.[338]

The questions and answers of these Synoptic passages are only possible for the time of Jesus on the assumption that one would have found in the purse of the man in the street in Jerusalem Roman imperial coins with the image and inscription of the emperor. Udoh finds this assumption implausible as well as the claim that Jews paid a Roman poll tax prior to 70 CE.[339] "The first mention of a *per capita* tribute paid by the Jews in Judea in the early Roman period is the temple tax, converted by Vespasian into a head tax imposed upon all Jews after the fall of Jerusalem in 70 C.E."[340]

A post-70 dating of the Gospel of Mark means that there was a census, a registration for the purpose of paying a *per capita* tribute, in much more recent memory of the author than a census in the time of Quirinius in 6 CE, which would have been an assessment for the registration of property and not a head tax in any case. The author of Mark is obviously aware that neither Jesus nor his interlocutors in the scene can have in view the tax imposed by Vespasian. Nevertheless, in a post-70 setting, the saying of Jesus would have a particular resonance with regard to a registration for payment of a Roman tax that was not a distant memory but a tax currently collected from Jews. This tax could be paid in Roman coins, a *dēnarius* being equivalent in value to an Attic *drachma*.[341] But unlike Matt 17, the

---

338. Udoh, *To Caesar*, 233–34. On the *Isfiya* Hoard, Udoh writes, "Whenever it was (in the second half of the first century C.E., or afterwards) that the coins ... might have been hidden away, the proportion of the Roman denarii to Tyrian coins in the hoard is significant. It contained about 4,400 Tyrian coins to 160 Roman denarii, of which about 30 were of Tiberius. The finds from Qumran reveal a similar proportion. Tyrian coins also represent the largest percentage of all the coins found in the Upper Galilee ... and in Sepphoris. Ariel concludes from his analysis of the coinage in Jerusalem that the Roman denarius did not become current in Jerusalem until after 70 C.E., although some Roman coins did circulate in the region.... Tyrian shekels and half-shekels formed the basis of the silver currency of the entire region throughout the period before the Jewish Revolt in 66 C.E." (235–36).

339. Ibid, 233.

340. Ibid., 238. This chapter is part of Udoh's larger thesis that the combination of Roman and Jewish taxation in the late Second Temple period was not particularly excessive, as many have argued in assessing taxation as a major factor of discontent and cause of the revolt in 66 CE.

341. In the Egyptian sources this tax is referred to in three ways: (1) Ἰουδαϊκὸν τέλεσμα ("Jewish tax"); (2) τιμὴ δηναρίων δύο Ἰουδαίων ("the price of two *denarii* of the

question here is not whether Jesus and his disciples pay a certain tax, and Jesus's response is not addressed to his disciples but to interlocutors who represent Judean and Galilean religious and political authority.[342] His response is surely not intended to bring comfort. Rather, as noted above, it is intended to spring the trap set for him and reset it for his opponents. The end of the temple regime is already in view at this point in Mark. In a post-70 setting, the trap reset for his opponents is that the things that once were given to God by the Jewish nation (contributions to the temple) are now the things that are given to Caesar (the Jewish tax). Whether it is "right" to pay taxes to Caesar is ironic in a post-70 historical setting, unless you were planning another revolt. The saying Jesus gives in response to his interlocutor's acknowledgment of the emperor's head and title on the coin is neither a prudent recommendation nor a hidden provocation; it is a riddle-like response, spoken in the temple court with both bite and humor, an ironic pronouncement of judgment intended to shame opponents, a judgment from which those who follow Jesus are exempt. They are exempt not because the scene can tell us whether Markan circles did or did not pay the Jewish tax imposed by Vespasian, but because, even if they did pay it, they

---

Jews," which may indicate that the Latin name for the tax was *duo denarii Iudaeorum*); (3) ἀπαρχαί ("first fruits"). Referring to the view of Sherman Leroy Wallace, *Taxation in Egypt from Augustus to Diocletian* (Princeton: Princeton University Press; London: Oxford University Press, 1938), 176, Heemstra believes the term "first fruits" has to do with the temple of Onias, which was closed a few years after the temple in Jerusalem was destroyed. "This could very well explain the appearance of the ἀπαρχαί in these documents in the fifth year of Vespasian. In this explanation the one Egyptian drachma that was added to the tax had previously been paid to the temple of Onias by Egyptian Jews and thus became part of the Jewish tax in Egypt after this temple ceased to exist" (*Fiscus Judaicus*, 15). In Greek, Josephus and Cassius Dio refer to the charge for the tax as δύο δραχμὰς and δίδραχμον respectively. Incigneri, *Gospel to the Romans*, 194–202, who believes that the tax question in Mark directly reflects an issue facing Jewish Christians in Rome in mid-71 CE, precisely when the Gospel of Mark was written in his view, and coinciding with the first year the tax was collected, points to Mark's reference to the Roman coin as further evidence that the author intends the scene to address Christians in Rome (200).

342. For this reason among others, I am not persuaded by Incigneri's reading: "Thus, it was really Mark's readers who were asking, 'Should *we* pay or not?'—a question Mark places in the mouth of Jesus' opponents (12:15). Mark gives comfort through Jesus' answer: paying Roman coin to a Roman emperor for his Roman Temple does not conflict with the duty to give to God the 'things of God'" (*Gospel to the Romans*, 200, emphasis original).

are exempt from the judgment implied in the saying of Jesus, which is not addressed to them but to the opponents of Jesus who seek to take his life.

11. Conclusion: The Social Logic of Mark's Dual Narrative

The death of Jesus in Mark is presented as a model for emulation. This is clear from the pattern of passion predictions followed each time by the discipleship theme in chapters 8–10. Thus, Jesus's death will be a noble death. It will also be a death that is beneficial for others, which comes to expression in Mark 10:45 and 14:24.[343] The question whether these statements

---

343. Mack, *Myth of Innocence*, 276–78. Jesus's death in Mark as a model for emulation and as a death for others are concepts that should be held together rather than isolated from each other, certainly in the context of Mark 8–10, and particularly with reference to Jesus's teaching in Mark 10:42–45. What has been difficult to resolve and the subject of a long history of debate is the meaning and significance of the climactic "ransom" clause in 10:45b and its relationship to Mark 14:24. For an intratextual reading that rejects an expiatory interpretation of either text, arguing for liberation from the oppression of human tyrants and superhuman enemies of God, see Sharyn Dowd and Elizabeth Struthers Malbon, "The Significance of Jesus' Death in Mark: Narrative Context and Authorial Audience," *JBL* 125 (2006): 271–97. In an article responding in part to Dowd and Malbon, Adela Yarbro Collins, "Mark's Interpretation of the Death of Jesus," *JBL* 128 (2009): 545–50, argues on the basis of Exod 30:11–16 and first to third century CE "confessional" inscriptions from Asia Minor that expiation and propitiation to God for offenses committed is as good an interpretation of *lutron* in Mark 10:45b as liberation from demonic powers; and further, she argues that even if the words in Mark 14:24, "my blood of the covenant," refer to covenant renewal, the expression, "blood poured out," is used in connection with sin offerings in LXX Leviticus. Therefore, Collins avers, Matthew's addition of the words, "for the forgiveness of sins" (26:28), should be taken as a correct inference from the Markan version of the saying (549–50). But the appeal to the pouring out of blood in LXX Lev 4:7b, 18b, 20b, 25b does not support the identification Collins proposes. First, the manipulation of blood in these texts (poured out at the base of the altar) is only one element of the ritual and should not be singled out as though the ritual were effective as a sin offering on the grounds of blood manipulation alone. In fact, in some instances, expiation is effected without the manipulation of blood (Lev 5:11–13). Second, the sins expiated in these rituals are unintentional (Lev 4:2). Third, the pouring out of blood is not identified anywhere else in the New Testament with sacrifice but rather with violent death (Matt 23:35, Luke 22:20; Acts 22:20; Rom 3:15; Rev 16:6), which is obviously in view in the supper text. Finally, if the supper text does the work of bringing meaning and order out of the chaos of Jesus's death for the reader and/or in the context of ritual, it does so by linking acts of consumption to the death of Jesus rather than acts of expiation. Consequently, Matthew's addition, "for the forgiveness of sins,"

are dependent on kerygmatic expressions in Paul's letters is not an issue I can take up here, except to note what I take to have been established: neither Mark's passion predictions nor the passion narrative can be derived from the so-called pre-Pauline kerygma.[344] Nor am I directly concerned with the question whether there were earlier oral or written narrative formulations of the death of Jesus. Since the Gospel of Mark undoubtedly drew on some kinds of teachings and actions attributed to Jesus, and since it is reasonable to suppose that valorizing the death of Jesus was a project

---

should not be taken as a signal that Jesus's violent death amounts to an identification with the pouring out of blood in animal sacrifice. Nor is it likely that the sins which are forgiven in Matt 26:28 are thought to be those that are unintentional. Returning to Mark 10:45, I would conclude that if ransom from sin and thus an exchange with God is also in view, and not only ransom from oppression and an exchange with demonic powers, then it is not Mark 14:24 that can make the case. Lawrence Wills appears to want to accommodate the position of Malbon and Dowd and the position of Collins by emphasizing "the *range* of negatives that sacrifice resolves: ... sin, disorder, impurity, estrangement, or abandonment." But this formulation excludes the position of Malbon and Dowd by presupposing that an identification with expiatory rituals of animal sacrifice is primary in the two Markan texts. Without this presupposition, one can agree with the conclusion, "Mark may not have been as concerned with the distinction among the kinds of estrangement as we are" (Lawrence M. Wills, "The Death of the Hero and the Violent Death of Jesus," in *Religion and Violence: The Biblical Heritage*, ed. David A. Bernat and Jonathan Klawans [Sheffield: Sheffield Phoenix, 2007], 94–95, emphasis original).

344. Mack, *Myth of Innocence*, 278–81. The whole issue of the "Christ cult" is reconsidered in Mack, "Rereading the Christ Myth: Paul's Gospel and the Christ Cult Question," in Cameron and Miller, *Redescribing Paul and the Corinthians*, 35–73. For a carefully argued paper against the common position that the Pauline epistles articulate a sacrificial theology based on biblical ideas about sacrifice and atonement, a paper on which I have drawn in the preceding note, see Aaron Glaim, "Sin and 'Sin-Sacrifices' in the Pauline Epistles," (paper presented at the Annual Meeting of the Society of Biblical Literature, Baltimore, 24 November 2013, for the Society of Biblical Literature Redescribing Early Christianity Seminar). Glaim concludes, "There is vastly insufficient linguistic and conceptual grounds to support the assertion that Paul understood Jesus' death as a sin-sacrifice" (32). Glaim also rejects the identification of sin sacrifices in the relevant biblical data (Lev 4:1–35; 5:1–13; Num 15:22–36) with the punitive notion of vicarious substitutionary sacrifice. He maintains that "expiatory sacrifices are instruments of reciprocity rather than victims of vicarious substitutionary punishment" (28). Transference of sin is not accomplished by the laying on of hands on the animal, since this same procedure is present in "gift" sacrifices which have no expiatory function. Such transference is present only in the case of the scapegoat of Yom Kippur, which has an expiatory function without being a sacrifice or punitive (25–28).

requiring more than a single effort (Q itself attests this),[345] it is possible
that some features present in Mark 14–16 are related to earlier efforts to
identify and construct appropriate memory places for the death of Jesus.[346]
However, this is not to say that Mark's passion narrative is developed from
a pre-Markan version of it. Attempts to demonstrate that it is seem to me
more dependent on the imagined historicity of the narrative than on a
compelling literary demonstration.[347]

---

345. See above, 268–70 with n. 150. Since Q 14:27 concerns the cost of discipleship, the death of Jesus may also be in view as a model for emulation there. But unlike
Mark, where both the identity of Jesus and the death of Jesus are central to the narrative, the sayings of Q, insofar as they construct a narrative world, are more concerned
to locate the person and fate of Jesus in the collective context of the reward of the
righteous, the persecution and vindication of the children of wisdom, and the fate of
the prophets. The person and message of Jesus in Q are central to the ethos of the kingdom. But as John Kloppenborg has concluded, "The particular connection between
Jesus and his message that is found in Q^1 is not so much a matter of christological
claim … as it is a matter of the emulation of a specific ethos and practice associated
with the kingdom of God" (*Excavating Q*, 394).

346. See Kathleen E. Corley, *Maranatha: Women's Funerary Rituals and Christian
Origins* (Minneapolis: Fortress, 2010). For Jesus traditions organized not as build-
ing blocks of Christian origins but as exempla of common themes and techniques of
Jewish storytelling, see Wire, *Holy Lives, Holy Deaths*.

347. Cf. Mack, *Myth of Innocence*, part 3, Narratives of the Passion: ch. 9, "The
Entanglements of History and Myth"; ch. 10, "The Narrative Designs"; ch. 11, "The
Compositional Process," 249–312. Before pursuing his own analysis of the passion
narrative in terms of its development of Markan themes, Mack cites Werner Kelber's
concluding essay, "From Passion Narrative to Gospel," in Kelber, *The Passion Narrative
in Mark*, 157–58: "'Thematically, it is difficult to identify a major non-Markan thrust
or theme in Mark 14–16, let alone extrapolate a coherent pre-Markan source'" (263).
"'The issue … is not why Jesus' passion demanded an early pre-Markan connected
narrative form, because it did not, but the issue is why Mark created the Gospel whole
in its present form'" (264). Nor do I think that classifying the passion narrative as an
example of the genre of the death of famous persons (A. Y. Collins) or as a cult narrative of the death of the hero (Wills) makes the case for a pre-Markan narrative of
the passion of Jesus. Both Collins and Wills do make strong cases for the presence of
features in Mark characteristic of the genre, esp. the conflict between the hero and the
people and the hero and the god (see Collins, "The Genre of the Passion Narrative,"
3–28, and Collins, "Finding Meaning in the Death of Jesus," *JR* 78 [1998]: 175–96, esp.
191–93; Wills, *Quest of the Historical Gospel*, and Wills, "Death of the Hero"). But when
Collins acknowledges that Jesus did not qualify either in his own time or in Mark's,
remaining obscure in the eyes of the general public, she saves the day by introducing
the death of messianic pretenders (messiahs to their followers) as a subtype of the

genre τελευτή. The evidence she cites from the activities and deaths of royal claimants reported in Josephus hardly qualify as evidence of such a subtype, not only because important features are lacking but because we do not have narratives of their deaths from the perspective of protagonists. One would hardly qualify the remarks of Josephus or Tacitus on the death of Jesus as a subtype of the genre τελευτή or *exitus illustrium virorum* from the point of view of antagonists. To the extent that Mark's Gospel has been influenced by this genre, it is the writer's narrative that makes his death an example of the death of famous persons. However, Josephus's material on royal claimants could qualify as "historical reports," and Collins makes a point of noting every scene in her putative pre-Markan passion narrative can qualify as "historical report," the caveat that this does not necessarily amount to reliability notwithstanding. Morever, on her construction the pre-Markan passion narrative has as its climax the omen of the tearing asunder of the temple veil, even though omens are hardly characteristic of the genre ("Genre of the Passion Narrative," 13–18). The main difficulty for me in Wills's identification of the gospel narratives with cult narratives of the death of the hero is not the localization of hero cults at a tomb or the absence of clear reference to such in the narrative itself. It is the problem of interpreting evidence for the vindication of Jesus as tantamount to evidence of a reconciliation between the hero and his people. Such reconciliation strikes me as exactly what is not present in a typical form in any of the gospel narratives, whether pre-Markan, Mark, Matthew, or John, and including reconstruction of an earlier version of the Gospel of Peter ("Death of the Hero," 97–99). Arthur Dewey classifies his reconstruction of an early version of the Gospel of Peter as the story of the just one rather than the death of the hero. He labels the people's fear at the signs of judgment accompanying Jesus's death and their sudden recognition of his innocence as the element of "reaction/acclamation" in the story of the just one rather than reconciliation between hero and people (Arthur J. Dewey, "The Passion Narrative of the Gospel of Peter: Redaction and Interpretation," *Forum* NS 1 [1998]: 53–69). The vindication of Jesus here is linked to the theme of judgment not the theme of reconciliation of the hero and his people, let alone reconciliation through cult. Yet, the very fact that the people, Jews, carry out the crucifixion may be an influence from the genre of the death of the hero. If so, it is not necessarily evidence of an early version of the passion of Jesus but more likely evidence of the tendency of gospel narratives increasingly from earlier to later instances to exculpate Romans and inculpate Jews in the death of Jesus. Discussing the applicability of the genre of martyrdom, Van Henten sums up his explanation for the passion narratives' deviations from Jewish martyrdoms by recognizing the presence of features from other genres. His conclusion seems to me a fair estimate of the situation: "Ultimately, whether one wants to see the Jewish martyrdoms, the suffering righteous pattern or the Graeco-Roman τελευτή reports as the basic skeleton of the passion narratives, remains a matter of taste, because the passion narratives are obviously not the elaboration of a single literary genre" (Jan Willem van Henten, "Jewish Martyrdom and Jesus' Death," in *Deutungen des Todes Jesu im Neuen Testament*, ed. Jörg Frey and Jens Schröter, WUNT 181 [Tübingen: Mohr Siebeck, 2005], 167). I would suggest that one reason for this is that the Gospel of Mark is not merely a passion narrative; Mark 14–16 take up and continue characterizations and themes from earlier portions of the narrative.

Jesus's death in Mark, however, is not only a model for emulation and a death for the benefit of others. Linked to the destruction of the temple, the death of Jesus is associated with an event of geopolitical significance. With the destruction of the temple the Jews lost their geopolitical center and what was arguably the apex of a hierarchy of religious practices. Judgment on Jerusalem and the temple is also forecasted in Q in connection with the death of Jesus, but as a climax to a collective history rather than an event of unique disclosure (Q 11:49–51; 13:34–35 // Matt 23:34–39). In Mark, the death of Jesus is singled out by being plotted in a story of persecution. In its connection with the death of John the Baptist and the expectation of the return of the prophet Elijah (Mark 9:9–13), it is clear that the death of Jesus is not merely the consequence of human rejection and human abandonment but discloses a mysterious divine purpose at odds with human expectations (8:33) to which Jesus must himself submit (14:36), even to the extent of divine abandonment (15:34).[348] In contrast, the death of Jesus in Q belongs to a pattern of expectation.[349] Whatever the composers of Q may have thought about the death of Jesus in particular, it is never hinted that his fate is puzzling or anomalous.

Miller is certainly correct that Mark's empty tomb story exhibits typical features of translation stories. But when he also concludes that Mark elevates his hero-sage "by *interpretatio graeca et romana* … to the rank of the classical Mediterranean demigod," he isolates this description, as though it has no other resonance in Mark.[350] The hero-sage has disappeared/been translated/raptured in order to play an eschatological role, as is true for such figures of Jewish lore as Elijah (2 Kgs 2:12; Mal 4:5–6; Mark 9:9–13), Enoch (1 En. 70–71), Baruch (2 Bar. 13:3; 25:1; 76:2), and Ezra (4 Ezra 14:9, 50 [Syriac]). So, the significance of the empty tomb as a translation story (or the saying about the bridegroom being taken away in Mark 2:20) cannot be fully evaluated for its resonance apart from the identification of Jesus with the Son of Man of Dan 7:13–14 in Mark 13:26 and 14:62, even if that resonance includes familiarity with translations

---

348. On divine abandonment of Jesus to Roman execution and the temple to Roman destruction, see below, 390–92 with n. 379.

349. That Mark has also drawn on this pattern of expectation in the Deuteronomistic tradition of the fate of the prophets is seen in the parable of the Tenants (Mark 12:1–9).

350. Miller, "Mark's Empty Tomb," 776, and above, 239.

and postmortem roles of heroes such as Heracles and Romulus.[351] Neither can one accept without qualification Miller's characterization of the Jesus figure of Mark's Gospel as a "literary-cultural *evocatio sacrorum*, an instrument functioning to delineate and extract the best of a failed religious civilization," a figure representing opposition to an exaggerated but also postured cultural separatism that Miller believes provoked the revolt

---

351. Of course, the above examples from Jewish lore are not *postmortem* translations. In his comparative study of ideas of deity in the ancient Mediterranean world, Litwa describes the gospel narratives of Jesus's resurrection as examples of postmortem "corporeal immortalization" and shows that stories of Asclepius, Heracles, and Romulus belong to the same category, which is not to say that there are no differences (*Iesus Deus*, 156–68, 170–71, 173). There is enough "ambiguity that one should probably categorize the immortalizations of Heracles and Romulus as post-*mortal* rather than post-*mortem*" (171). Litwa maintains that immortalized life is deified life in Mediterranean culture. "To be sure, Jews and Christians did not use the precise vocabulary of deification to speak of Jesus' corporeal immortalization, reception of worship, or ascent. But the lack of shared vocabulary does not undercut shared concepts" (178). Whatever competitive disadvantage Jesus's divinity might have had as a figure of recent times and relatively unknown could be compensated by the fact that his divinity, like that of the God of Israel, was exclusive; he did not belong to a family of gods (see 173). Litwa argues for a form of Jewish deification in his earlier volume, *We Are Being Transformed: Deification in Paul's Soteriology*, BZNW 187 (Berlin: de Gruyter, 2012), 86–116. Daniel A. Smith, *The Post-Mortem Vindication of Jesus in the Sayings Gospel Q*, LNTS 338 (London: T&T Clark, 2006), has argued that a postmortem translation and eschatological role is in view in Q 13:35b. This implies that Jesus is identified in Q with the "Coming One" of LXX Ps 117:26 and the apocalyptic figure of the Son of Man, though not necessarily with the Son of Man of Dan 7:13–14 (see Kloppenborg, *Excavating Q*, 391–93). While disappearance-assumption may be an early formulation of the vindication of Jesus independent of resurrection-appearance traditions (on the relations of these traditions and the early history of Easter, see Smith, *Revisiting the Empty Tomb*), the fact that Q 13:35b follows an oracle announcing the desolation of the temple (v. 35a) argues for a post-destruction dating of this oracle in my judgment. It should be considered together with arguments for a postdestruction dating of the Q apocalyptic sayings that stress the sudden and unanticipated event of judgment (Q 17:24, 26–27, 30, 34–35; see above, 288–89 with nn. 179–80), forceful entry into a house (Q 12:39–40; cf. Matt 24:43–44; Gos. Thom. 21, 103; Mark 3:27; Gos. Thom. 35, 98), parables featuring the departure and return of a master as warnings to insiders (Q 12:42–46 = Matt 24:45–51 and Q 19:12–26, excluding vv. 12b, 14, 15a, // Matt 25:14–29), and the parable concluding the Markan farewell discourse (Mark 13:33–37; cf. Matt 24:42 and Luke 21:34–36).

against Rome.[352] Rather, like the Gospel of Matthew, the writings of Josephus, and the Jewish apocalypses and related writings after the war, the Gospel of Mark must be seen as an expression of a nativist Jewish cultural persistence.[353] In the wake of the war Mark's local Levantine environment is likely to have included both disaffected Jews and relieved Near Easterners of various ethnicities, some of whom surely would have concluded that the road ahead in the region thankfully signals the end of Judean political influence with its own civic-cultic performance in a wider Levantine civilization. It must have included Jews, probably the majority, who drew lessons from the defeat that compelled accommodation to Roman subjection and encouraged integration in the wider local environment, while motivating others to adopt tactics of determined social separation. Unlike the writers of the late first-century Jewish apocalypses, Mark does not mourn the destruction of the temple. Unlike Josephus, he does not seek to recoup either for Judea or for diaspora a polity that had failed or defend the reputation of the remnant of Judean elite to which Josephus himself belonged. Nonetheless, Mark's narrative project reconfigures in its plot and central subject the perception and reality of the loss of Jewish political and cultural capital, especially in competition with ethnic neighbors in urban centers of the Roman province of Syria, while at the same time attempting to immunize and exempt the kingdom of the God of Israel, an alternative symbol of social cohesion and power, from its consequences.

---

352. Miller, "Mark's Empty Tomb," 771; see the discussion above, 246–49 with nn. 94, 96–97.

353. I intend a contrast with Richard Miller's notion of the Jesus of Mark as a figure of opposition to a postured cultural separatism and failed religious civilization. For Miller, this may simply be a particular way of arguing that the Gospel of Mark represents a cultural shift from Judean-Hellenistic Palestinian to non-Judean Greco-Roman Mediterranean, a conception that strikes me as still rooted in cultures as distinct entities in the world (see above, 229 with n. 48). However, I allow that "nativist Jewish" in this instance is an identification that is also encompassed by a wider Syrian Levantine cultural milieu. It is not a question of an essentialist concept of indigenous and foreign but of a perspective marking difference and struggle against being overwhelmed by the pressures and institutions of a wider society (see above, n. 177, and Smith, "The Markan Site," 102–4), sometimes precisely by acknowledging and taking advantage of relations with proximate others (Mark 7:24–30; 9:38–41). I have in view something that could be correlated with what I think Smith intends by "Mark's Levantine Judean association" ("The Markan Site," 118).

Mark's Jesus bursts on the scene in Galilee announcing that the kingdom of God has drawn near (1:14–15) and acting to cleanse the land and its surroundings of demons and Romans (5:1–20). Without believing that Mark has written the gospel with the intention of making transparent in the narrative a project for his own time or that Jesus as a figure of the past is merely a literary conceit, one can point out that acting to cleanse the land and rid it of Roman occupiers, while Jesus himself enters Jerusalem to occupy the Jewish political and cultural center, is more ironic and potentially more blasphemous in a postdestruction world than before the end of the temple's time. It is more ironic because there is no longer a Jewish center to occupy or from which opposition to Jesus and his followers can emerge. It is more blasphemous because such actions can be construed not merely as the madness of prophets but as claims to divine authority seeming to mock the penumbra of weakness of the God of the Jews in a postdestruction time of political and cultural loss. Such readings are tacitly allowed in the interest of vindication (2:7; 3:21, 28–30; 14:64).

Mark's narrative portrays the trials of Jesus as travesties of justice. This is as true of Jesus before Pilate as it is of the night time gathering and judgment of the Jewish council. The scene before Pilate, far from intending a Roman apology, hardly conceals its mocking of Roman justice in the provinces. Andrew Simmonds goes farther. He views the scene in both Mark and Matthew as Roman mime.[354] It portrays Caesar and the crowd at the Roman games. Set in Jerusalem with a Jewish mob, it mimes the release of a prisoner at Roman festivals and Caesar at the gladiatorial games calling for the crowd's decision regarding the fate of the winner and loser. "For Caesar, the absolute worst outcome financially was that, to spite him, the crowd would seek to have popular winners freed and popular losers condemned. That is precisely the stereotypical situation presented in Mark and Matthew."[355] The scene "presents a classic, universal, and timeless trope of subaltern-dominant discourse.... The narratives are disguised to contain hidden messages ... lest the subalterns be subjected to punishment."[356] The narrative skewers Roman justice; it is not anti-Jewish. Rather, it portrays Jews acting badly as Romans, a parody of foreigners.[357] The template

---

354. Andrew Simmonds, "Mark's and Matthew's *Sub Rosa* Message in the Scene of Pilate and the Crowd," *JBL* 131 (2012): 733–54.

355. Ibid., 746.

356. Ibid., 733.

357. Ibid., 733–38.

is the book of Esther and the characters are stereotypes. "Both Mark and Esther contain what appear to be unacceptable outrages. Esther is essentially a courtesan who uses sex to get her way.... In Mark, the crowd is willing to condemn Jesus in order to beat Pilate, and the supremely powerful, yet pathetically weak Pilate cannot manage to stop it." Yet, even though a foreign portrayal, "Mark's presentation is too unstable: having Esther/the crowd choose Haman/Barabbas certainly paints a travesty, but it is too great a travesty.... The foreignness of the story is not enough to contain the travesty."[358] According to Simmonds, the Markan version of the scene is resolved in a psychologically more complicated way by the writer of Matthew, who employs the literary genre of *peripeteia*, rabbinic law, and a technique similar to a Freudian slip. "Pilate's performance of the Jewish hand-washing ritual is a farce that ironically results in the crowd acclaiming Jesus by providentially accepting Jesus' same-day offer of his blood."[359]

Imagining Mark 15: 6–15 to be mocking Roman justice by casting a trial scene set in Jerusalem as a subaltern mimicking of Roman amnesty and gladiatorial games is surely more compelling than supposing the scene presents a credible historical memory or is reminiscent of a "paschal privilege." But labeling the discourse according to the binary opposition "subaltern-dominant" does not seem to me to come off, at least not in the universalizing way that Simmonds contends.[360] There is another set of stereotypical characters in the scene carried over from the hearing before the Judean council. They do not figure in Simmonds account of the scene. The chief priests are the ones who have already called for the death verdict against Jesus, and they are the ones who incite the crowd to ask for Barabbas after Pilate has put the fate of Jesus to their decision. It is not that the chief priests cannot be assimilated to the scene as a parody of foreigners. One might think of senatorial enemies of the emperor inciting the crowd. The problem is that the narrative of Mark as a whole cannot accommodate this role for the chief priests, especially in a scene that directly follows their calling for Jesus's death. The scene can be perceived as a parody of Roman justice and a mocking of Roman power. But it is at the same time a parody of Jews behaving like Roman foreigners, by no means a unique instance of this polemical technique among Jews, as Simmonds himself has noted.[361]

358. Ibid., 747.
359. Ibid., 753–54, 733.
360. Ibid., 733.
361. Ibid., 741–42.

It is for this reason that the foreignness cannot contain the travesty, and not only because the crowd has chosen Barabbas instead of Jesus.[362]

---

362. Jennifer K. Berenson Maclean reads the scene as a scapegoat ritual ("Barabbas, the Scapegoat Ritual, and the Development of the Passion Narrative," *HTR* 100 [2007]: 309–34). The analogy is simple: "Two goats (men) are brought before the people: one is killed, the other released. This connection would be obvious were it not for the assumption, in concert with long-standing Christian tradition, that Jesus was the scapegoat" (313). Maclean argues that the earlier Christian tradition identified Jesus with the immolated goat of the Yom Kippur ritual and resolves the question of why so little was ever said about Barabbas in ancient Christian tradition. There was little to be left to the imagination about one who was thought to have been released in order to be sent into the wilderness to perish. But Maclean also wants to demonstrate that the scene in Mark and Matthew is more plausible in a literary sense (not in the sense of historical memory) when imagined in analogy to "curative exit rites" (313, a category whose label she borrows from Richard E. DeMaris, "Jesus Jettisoned," in *The New Testament in Its Ritual World*, ed. Richard E. DeMaris [London: Routledge, 2008], 91–111). I do not dispute the category label, nor that both the *pharmakos* ritual and the biblical scapegoat ritual belong to the category of curative exit rites. But the claim that this analogy makes the scene in Mark and Matthew a more plausible literary piece I find problematic. I do not think the identity of ritual function in such curative exit rites overcomes the difficulty. Yes, features of *pharmakos* ritual could be identified in the passion narrative of both gospels by their readers. But chief priests, elders, and a crowd in Jerusalem symbolically acting out a ritual of the Day of Atonement with human subjects? Unless of course the scene is taken as a parody of Jews behaving like foreigners. I do not see that Maclean's interpretation leaves room for this sort of farce. Later Christian reflections on the death of Jesus in connection with this scene are a different matter, for in these later contexts it is not literary plausibility that is required but material to be exploited in the search for typological correlations. The invention of a Roman custom of releasing one prisoner at each festival in Jerusalem hardly seems like an inducement to readers to see in Jesus and Barabbas the two goats of Yom Kippur. Rather, the confusions that emerge later over which of the goats is represented by Jesus would seem to confirm that the typologies originate in reading back into the narrative. Moreover, Maclean's interpretation of the scene in Mark not only involves reading in different registers but betrays conflicting motivations and goals in the characters (322–24). Do those in the crowd demand of Pilate that he make good on the custom because they want to work their violence on a scapegoat, or because they want to free their favorite (Mark 11:18; 12:17, 37)? Do the chief priests incite the crowd because they want Jesus dead, or because they fear that the crowd left on its own will spoil the ritual by freeing Jesus? Does Pilate ask what to do with Jesus because he is not in on the ritual and does not know that the other prisoner must be killed, or because he recognizes that it is out of envy that the chief priests have brought Jesus to him for execution? It is true that the scene in Matthew highlights comparison of Jesus and Barabbas. However, Maclean's preferred reading in which Pilate's hand washing

I do not deny that the scene can be read with a view to public and hidden transcripts. But for the projected readers, who are the dominant and who the subaltern? Or better, which dominants and which subalterns are in view? Taking the scene as public transcript with Jewish subalterns acting badly as Jews resulting in a miscarriage of justice does not conceal the patent weakness of Roman authority represented by Pilate. How the story may have worked as public transcript would depend in any case on one's location and place in a hierarchical order. For Roman senators or for native elites, for example, neither the miscarriage nor the weakness would necessarily be regarded as damning Rome where a prefect of the equestrian order was in charge. Josephus made Roman subelites in Judea his target. As hidden transcript, the scene may skewer Roman justice by mimicking the behavior of Romans at the gladiatorial games, but not without polemics also aimed at the Jewish actors in the scene. True, some Pharisees might have no problem with the thought of the chief priests and a mob at Passover acting as Romans, but not the Pharisees in the Gospel of Mark. Here, the humor and the contempt cannot be disentangled. Here, Jerusalem justice is no better than Roman justice. Read post-70, the scene as Simmonds describes it is not just humorous and contemptuous but riddled with ironies: Jews acting as Romans rather than as subjects of Rome. A Jerusalem priestly establishment acting as Roman elite knowing how to get the underclass to undermine Caesar's best interests. A Jewish insurrectionist as gladiatorial victor with the non-militant king of the Jews submitting. To act at once as Romans and defeat the empire! If only the Jews had been as clever as the scene imagines. A travesty indeed! Yet the scene is also bitter and quite transparent. As Mark saw things, the king of the Jews was no earthbound king. As for the ruling class of Judea, whether as collaborators with Rome or as revolutionaries against Rome, it was not vindicated. In both cases the polity was that of a fragmented ruling class and as such it no longer existed; in both cases, the populace of Jerusalem had become a site of contestation and had to be incited, manipulated, and suffer the consequences. After the war, it was not difficult to think these things.

---

is performed with respect to Barabbas and the people's oath anticipates the violence they will work on Barabbas as the scapegoat hardly accords with the way Matthew has developed the scene (324–30). Most of all, Maclean's reading eliminates the ironies of the scene.

As noted, Simmonds finds the Matthean version much more rabbinic in legal subtlety and more complex psychologically in resolving Mark's crowd making the wrong choice. Pilate's washing his hands of innocent blood is a Roman pretending to act as a Jew and botching it. The blood that is relevant to the setting is not the innocent blood with which the hand washing over the heifer of Deut 21 is concerned, but the apotropaic blood of the Passover lambs protecting the people and the covenant blood offered by Jesus (Matt 26:28; Exod 24:8) to which the Roman Pilate cannot be partner.[363] The crowd, however, is a partner—not the crowd mimicking a Roman crowd that asks for the winner to spite Caesar—but the crowd "suppressing their fondness for him" [Jesus], yet betraying their subconscious affinity with him by taking his blood on themselves and their children (Matt 27:25). "The crowd's oath is meant [for the intended audience] as a miraculous acceptance, confirmation, and corroboration of Jesus' offer of his blood."[364] There is a problem with this reading of Matt 27:25. If it is like a Freudian slip, a return of the repressed, one wonders whether those who are only subliminally conscious of its true meaning include the author and readers, for the much more obvious connection of "the blood on us and on our children" of the oath in 27:25 is "all the innocent blood shed upon the earth from the blood of Abel to the blood of Zechariah" that is to come "on you," that is, "on this generation," in the judgment oracle of 23:35–36. This culminating judgment is the destruction of Jerusalem and the temple.

For Catherine Sider Hamilton the blood referred to in the crowd's oath is the innocent blood that pollutes the land, the blood of the righteous Abel and Zechariah, unexpiated blood, as recounted in the story of the murder of Zechariah in 2 Chron 24:20–22 and elaborated in later Jewish legend, as the cause of the destruction of the temple 250 years later by the Babylonian general Nebuzaradan.[365] It is also the blood of Jesus "poured out" (ἐκχυννόμενον) in Matt 26:28, echoing the blood of all the righteous "poured out" (ἐκχυννόμενον) in Matt 23:35 as its climax. His is the "innocent" (ἀθῷος) blood which both Judas (Matt 27:4) and Pilate acknowledge (Matt 27:19, 24), requiring an avenging from which not only Pilate (Matt 27:24) but also the chief priests and elders claim immunity (Matt 27:4).

363. Simmonds, "*Sub Rosa* Message," 748–53.
364. Ibid., 754.
365. Catherine Sider Hamilton, " 'His Blood Be upon Us': Innocent Blood and the Death of Jesus in Matthew," *CBQ* 70 (2008): 82–100.

But there cannot be immunity, not because the ritual Pilate invokes is the wrong ritual but because none will suffice. "It is not just a matter of recompense. Too much blood has been shed, and the land is utterly defiled. There is no help for it, no partial expiation by ritual or sacrifice. Only destruction and a new beginning will do."[366] Hamilton sees Matthew's hope of new beginning not in Matt 27:25 but in the omen of Matt 27:52–53: the opening of the tombs and the raising of the bodies of the saints, which accompany the tearing of the temple curtain and the earthquake, and which culminate in the entrance of the saints into Jerusalem and their appearance to many after Jesus's resurrection. I am not as convinced as Hamilton of the hopefulness of this omen for the people of Jerusalem. The portent seems truly uncanny. Talk about pollution! While the symbolism of Ezek 37 may be pertinent, and postponing the entry and appearances until the resurrection of Jesus is probably significant, it should not be forgotten that the associations of resurrection with eschatology are as much about judgment as about redemption and vindication (see, for example, Matt 12:41–42).

But there is a deeper issue. It is the idea that "judgment and forgiveness coincide" and correlating this with the Jewish legend of the murder of Zechariah. "What is new is the claim that the history of the land and covenant people, the history both of bloodshed and pollution and of sacrifice and purification comes to its climax and end in Jesus.... As the covenant people take defilement upon themselves, the covenant is made again in the blood of Jesus. As the temple is destroyed, the temple cult is fulfilled in Jesus, *in the blood poured out for many for the forgiveness of sins.*"[367] Hamilton sees in Matthew's resurrection of the saints something akin to Nebuzaradan's conversion to torah in later Jewish legend after he has failed to purge the blood of Zechariah's murder with either animal blood or human blood. (The conversion of the Babylonian general to torah seems to me more akin to the soldier's response at the cross in Mark 15:39, a typical martyrological theme). On the theme of innocent blood the analogy between the Jewish legend and the Gospel of Matthew is not altogether apt. As Hamilton herself comments, "Jesus' blood, as Matthew describes it, is poured out not only for the destruction of the covenant people and the temple but for their restoration."[368] The death of Jesus is seen as the one death that is necessary in a history of violence to bring on purgation,

---

366. Ibid., 95.
367. Ibid., 99–100, emphasis original.
368. Ibid.

386MILLER

burning, destruction, and at the same time to effect forgiveness of sins and resurrection. Being put to death by his own people, Jesus belongs to the prophets and/or to the hero in conflict with his people. Crucified by Rome and shedding his blood for many for the forgiveness of sins, the same Jesus is a martyr, but who benefits—disciples? dead saints? Israel? gentiles? Christians? Hamilton is convinced that Matthew is thoroughly Jewish in his rendering of the theme of innocent blood and the death of Jesus.[369] But with Jesus's death as the summation of a history both of violence and of redemption, it is a zero sum game. For just this reason, sectarian styled intercommunal polemics more than anti-colonial intra-Jewish solidarity must be assumed.[370] Indeed, a sign—the opening of the tombs and raising the bodies of the saints—that may have been promising to some would surely have been galling to others. What was an omen of traditional hope to some would have appeared to be a rend(er)ing beyond the pale to others.[371] Hamilton's concluding observation that the destruc-

369. Ibid., 99–100.

370. On this issue, see the essays in Shelly Matthews and E. Leigh Gibson, eds., *Violence in the New Testament* (London: T&T Clark, 2005), and the afterword by David Frankfurter.

371. On the same theme, see Ra'anan S. Boustan, "Confounding Blood: Jewish Narratives of Sacrifice and Violence in Late Antiquity," in Knust and Várhelyi, *Ancient Mediterranean Sacrifice*, 265–86. Boustan treats the Jewish legend of the unavenged blood of the Zechariah of 2 Chron 24 in what is undoubtedly its more appropriate Roman-Byzantine setting in the late fourth to sixth centuries (the Talmuds and the midrash, Lamentations Rabbati), which is not to deny that Matt 23 itself represents a much earlier attestation of a development beyond the brief account in 2 Chronicles. (Reading the Lives of the Prophets for first century traditions on Zechariah is contested by David Satran, who regards the collection as a whole to be Byzantine Christian; see Satran, *Biblical Prophets in Byzantine Palestine: Reassessing the Lives of the Prophets*, SVTP 11 [Leiden: Brill, 1995]; Anna Maria Schwemer defends an early date around the turn of the era; see Schwemer, *Studien zu den frühjüdischen Prophetenlegenden Vitae Prophetarum*, 2 vols. [Tübingen: Mohr Siebeck, 1995], 1: 65–71.) Boustan compares the rabbinic retelling of the murder of Zechariah with the late antique martyrology known as The Story of the Ten Martyrs. He argues that "these particular Jewish texts ... neither bear out Girard's hypothesis of a universal scapegoat mechanism nor encode any putative psychological discomfort with sacrificial violence. Rather, both texts index the pervasive concern among late-antique Jews with the meaning and function of the blood of the murdered righteous, which intensified as the theorization of martyrdom as sacrifice was employed to secure Christian hegemony" ("Confounding Blood," 280). The Story of the Ten Martyrs adopts and competes with Christian views of martyrdom. The Zechariah legend "rejects the equation

tion of the Jerusalem temple brought about a shift in the locus of divine authority for Josephus and for the rabbis as much as for followers of Jesus is true in a sense.[372] The Jerusalem temple was no longer the physical site and functioning institution of annual pilgrimage, the organizing center of much Jewish practice in diaspora, and the authorized site of the continual practice of animal sacrifice, the obvious reason for the end of that practice for Jews and followers of Jesus, including gentiles, alike.[373] But this conclusion can be overdrawn. What is notable is how strong a hold the "thinking of the temple" and the meaning of sacrifice had as a site of contestation among Jews and Christians and between Jews and Christians in late antiquity.[374] In rabbinic circles there was no simple shift from temple to torah with respect to concerns of cultural persistence or for the construction of Jewish identity. Indeed, in the synagogues of late antiquity (fourth to seventh centuries) the experience of the temple exceeded what it would have been for most Jews prior to the destruction of the temple.[375]

A striking feature of Mark's Gospel is the overloading of attributes and roles on the figure of Jesus. One sees this in Q as well, the collective construction of some of the attributes and roles notwithstanding: John's stron-

---

of sacrifice and murder, thereby deflating the discursive power of martyrdom that had so captivated many Jews and Christians in late antiquity.... The two narratives thus reflect the diversity of approaches to the phenomenon of sacrifice among late-antique Jews, a heterogeneity that is likewise attested in early Christian writings" (ibid.). What one does not see in these Jewish stories, however, is a handling of the theme of the blood of the murdered righteous in both ways in a single narrative focused on a single death. They convey entirely different sensibilities.

372. Hamilton, "Innocent Blood," 100.

373. Ullucci, *Rejection of Animal Sacrifice*, 134–35.

374. Ibid., 65–118; and see Jonathan Klawans, *Purity, Sacrifice, and the Temple*. I have taken the metaphor from Schmidt, *How the Temple Thinks* (see above, n. 56).

375. To cite only a few studies in support of this observation, see Ra'anan S. Boustan, "The Dislocation of the Temple Vessels: Mobile Sanctity and Rabbinic Rhetorics of Space," in *Jewish Studies at the Crossroads of Anthropology and History: Authority, Diaspora, Tradition*, ed. Ra'anan S. Boustan, Oren Kosansky, and Marina Rustow, Jewish Culture and Contexts (Philadelphia: University of Pennsylvania Press, 2011), 135–46; and in the same volume, Michael D. Swartz, "Judaism and the Idea of Ancient Ritual Theory," 294–317; Swartz, "Liturgy, Poetry, and the Persistence of Sacrifice," in Schwartz and Weiss, *Was 70 CE a Watershed?*, 393–412; Steven D. Fraade, "The Temple as a Marker of Jewish Identity before and after 70 CE: The Role of the Holy Vessels in Rabbinic Memory and Imagination," in Levine and Schwartz, *Jewish Identities in Antiquity*, 237–65; and Klawans, *Purity, Sacrifice, and the Temple*.

ger one, wisdom's confidant, the last of the prophets whose violent death brings the avenging of all the righteous blood to climax, the one not seen but vindicated by God, the blessed one whose eschatological appearance will be greeted with praise, the Son of Man whose day comes unanticipated. The attributes and roles of Jesus are enhanced, singularized, plotted, and projected in the Gospel of Mark, in particular in the narrative designs associated with the titles, Christ, Son of God, and Son of Man:[376] the teacher with a new teaching of power and authority, the holy man as warrior, the hero in conflict with his people, the prophet of the kingdom at hand, the servant of the Lord, the persecuted righteous one, the martyr, the king of the kingdom to come, the Son of Man of the eschaton—all in the same narrative, collapsing the boundaries of power and purity in a single figure—it is too much![377] One is never quite sure whether to read Mark as a parody of the human hero apotheosized or as an apocalypse of the divine hero humiliated, not the only choices of course, but also not resolved by the writer's penchant for obscurity, ambiguity, irony, and mystery. And so, if the Christ is David's Lord, it is apparently not because of Jesus's messianic office but because of the mystery of Jesus's divinity (Mark 12:35–37). And if the Jesus of Mark's Gospel clearly exhibits features of a Moses-and-Elijah-like figure, his status and authority are declared to exceed theirs at the baptism and on the mountain (Mark 1:11; 9:7). And yet, this overloading of attributes and roles, these declarations of authority and status exceeding prophets and kings of old, do nothing to relieve the fear, doubt, and uncertainty that is pervasive in the story world to the very end. Like the warning in the parable that closes Jesus's discourse in Mark 13, one does not know.[378]

---

376. Mack, *Myth of Innocence*, 288–90.

377. It is too much not as mythmaking but considering the historical chronotype of the narrative and a figure of the recent past.

378. See Douglas W. Geyer, *Fear, Anomaly, and Uncertainty in the Gospel of Mark*, ATLA 47 (Lanham, MD: Scarecrow, 2002). Against a rich background of comparative ancient Mediterranean and Levantine materials, mostly Greek and Roman with some biblical and early Jewish materials as well, Geyer takes us through the elements of fear, anomaly, and uncertainty in the scenes composing Mark 4:35–6:53. I highlight a few of his general observations on individual scenes: The frightful cosmogonic terrors of the sea are stilled by Jesus, but the disciples who are saved from drowning offer no thanksgiving and are questioned and left less secure after the rescue than before (106–10). "From the restless dead to the realm of organized military opposition" (140), Jesus and those with him are impervious to the greatest sources of opposition, demonic and

military, yet he is finally invited to leave. Frightening encounters with death and disease dissipate like so much mist, but "when a terrorizing and dangerous enemy is vanquished, what are people to do with its new conqueror?" (198). If Herod Antipas fears vengeance in the rumors about Jesus because of the execution of John the Baptist, why should we not expect vengeance in view of the utterly degrading and causeless death of Jesus? (215, 270). In a scene depicting Jesus's power over matters of eschatological fullness and benefaction, "standard expectations of food are met, but the public aspect of benefaction is sidestepped" (233). Walking over and through the water is a manifestation of kingly and imperial power, but to the disciples Jesus is a *phantasma* (6:49), a frightful figure from the world of the dead (242–43, 252). Each scene examined begs a score of questions, none of which are raised let alone answered (and see the summary paragraph, 270–71). The scene at the tomb and the "young man's" announcement and directive to the women does not answer them either. Theology, Geyer wants us to see, esp. with insights drawn from his own work with veterans suffering from PTSD mentioned in the preface, can only begin alongside that recognition (269–74). The strength of Geyer's analysis in literary perspective is the range of comparative cultural material he is able to bring to bear in delineating the affective aspects of the anomalous and fantastic in Mark's narrative. The materials of this section of Mark are also related to biblical motifs associated with Moses and Elijah which have been described as variants of a common Levantine hero-monster mythological plot by Donald B. Redford, *Egypt, Canaan, and Israel in Ancient Times* (Princeton: Princeton University Press, 1992), 43–48.

In light of Geyer's work it is possible to view the overloading of attributes and roles on the figure of Jesus as a cumulative effect of Markan techniques of representing Jesus as a counterintuitive figure. Without ignoring the work of other scholars on the literary phenomena of the fantastic in biblical narrative (for example, the work of George Aichele and Tina Pippin), the study of Laura Feldt, *The Fantastic in Religious Narrative from the Exodus to Elisha*, Bible World (Sheffield: Equinox, 2012), seems to me most helpful for what is still a desideratum in the study of Mark: a detailed study of the generation and effects of the phantasms of this gospel, and not only because of the play of intertextuality and mimesis in the production of Mark's narrative, or because it shares with these biblical narratives a set of fantastic events set in a chronotype of the everyday experiential world. Building on advances in cognitive science and in anthropology and cultural studies on the biological bases and cultural dispositions of representations of counterintuitive events, objects, and persons, Feldt develops the theoretical work of Renate Lachmann on the fantastic as a mode of expression, a discourse of alterity rather than a genre, to produce a literary study of the strategies, status, effects, and functions of the fantastic in a wide-ranging set of Hebrew Bible narratives (see ch. 2, "Fantasy and Religious Narrative: Theory and Strategy"). In general, fantastic effects depend upon "the elicitation of ambiguity," "uncertainty or a withdrawal of cognitive guarantees," and "mutability," whether anthropological, cultural, or ontological (58–59). The functions are compensatory, ludistic, and speculative (63–64). Feldt draws particular attention to the significance of ambivalence as a cumulative effect of this mode of expression in religious narratives: the interest is never only the formation of cultural memory but creating a space for counter-cultural memory too;

Abandonment is a motif common to Josephus's account of the temple and its defenders and to Mark's account of Jesus and the disciples. The God who is present in the temple is also the God who attests Jesus's divine sonship and the God who abandons both the Son of God (Mark 14:36; 15:34) and the temple of God (Q 13:35a; Mark 13:14; 15:37–38) to the Roman

---

the goal is never only the securing of a stable identity and social cohesion by way of a myth of origins but reflection on the troubling of identity and the grounds of social cohesion as well (242–54).

On the comparison of counterintuitive and imaginative entities and the implications for the study of religion with early Christian literature as a case in point, see the essay by William E. Arnal and Russell T. McCutcheon, "The Origins of Christianity Within, and Without, 'Religion': A Case Study," in *The Sacred is the Profane: The Political Nature of "Religion"* (Oxford: Oxford University Press, 2013), 134–70. Like Feldt, the authors also take account of results in cognitive science, along with critique and redirection in application to particular cultural phenomena. In formulating a typology not of counterintuitive agents in a technical sense but of imaginative entities more broadly, they argue that the treatment of religion as an object of study in its own right differentiates too sharply its counterintuitive entities from their closely related and more mundane entities of the human imagination. What differentiates these entities is not the qualities of the entities themselves but the differential treatment of their representations in discourse, "a [universal] tendency to treat those imaginary entities with *different degrees of seriousness*" (156, emphasis original). Thus, in addition to the insight of cognitive scientists regarding the necessarily tentative, hypothetical nature of minimally counterintuitive entities, e.g., gods, spirits, angels, devils, their oddness in some respects making them serviceable and memorable, there is the need to recognize that such entities constitute an interstitial category "between entities treated as wholly real (and thus as active social agents in themselves) and entities treated as fictitious (and thus more as mental or social *tools*, to be used more or less at will" (157, emphasis original). Among the social and cognitive ends of this interstitial class are the representation of sociality itself, the half-imaginary half-real nature of these nonobvious beings, "invest [ing] society with an inherently subjunctive character" (159), their capacity to focus thought on difficult and abstract features of the social world generating scrutiny and speculation (160), and their promotion of social deference, the giving over of a portion of one's will for the sake of belonging. "The odder, the less verifiable, the more counterintuitive the entity in question might be, the more the treatment of that entity as real becomes an extravagant display of submission to the social body that has asserted its reality" (162). With respect to representations of divine authority and their human nonrecognition in Mark, one can suggest in connection with the interstitial category proposed by Arnal and McCutcheon that the overloading of attributes and roles on the figure of Jesus is emblematic of such extravagant display required of the disciple of Jesus in believing and following.

imperial power.[379] In this respect, the death of Jesus and the destruction of the temple are *parallel* events, and identifying with the humiliation suffered by Jesus in his death is as inescapable for would-be followers of Jesus as identifying with the humiliation suffered in the destruction of the city and temple for Jews, however various the ways of going on despite humiliation and loss. As parallel events in Mark, mystified and rationalized by divine abandonment, there must be a recognition at some level by followers of Jesus and by those mourning the temple alike of a commonality in the commemoration of loss (Mark 2:20). The way of the cross and the fate of the temple are both roads out of Jerusalem, for followers of Jesus who took flight at his arrest as well as for those who sought to escape the city before the Roman siege. Associating the death of Jesus with an event affecting the fate of the temple, city, people, and land gives epic proportion to that single death, linking it at once to sacred history and to the realities of imperial power. A story of the fate of Jesus could now be written as a story entailed in that history, and therefore it too would exhibit a contest

---

379. God's abandonment of Jesus and the temple to their fate does not mean of course that the same traditions or background are presupposed in both. Deuteronomic and prophetic themes are obvious in the case of the temple. Nonetheless, it is significant that the abandonment of Jesus and the temple are joined climactically at the scene of Jesus's death (Mark 15:33–38). Self-indictment and condemnation are as much a strategy of control as appeal to an unalterable divine plan. With respect to divine abandonment of Jesus (Mark 15:34), whether one thinks directly of the words of Ps 22:1 and the suffering righteous, or invokes the ambivalent and antagonistic god/hero relationship (Collins, "Finding Meaning in the Death of Jesus," 192; Wills, "The Death of the Hero," 91), or appeals to the presence of conflicting logics (Dowd and Malbon, "Jesus' Death in Mark," 288–89, n. 49; Ira Brent Driggers, *Following God through Mark: Theological Tension in the Second Gospel* [Louisville: Westminster John Knox, 2007], 82–83), or conflicting mythologies (John K. Riches, "Conflicting Mythologies: Mythical Narrative in the Gospel of Mark," *JSNT* 84 [2001]: 29–50), or remembers the fate of the "chosen one" in biblical stories (Jon D. Levenson, *The Death and Resurrection of the Beloved Son: The Transformation of Child Sacrifice in Judaism and Christianity* (New Haven: Yale University Press, 1993), 143–69, 201–3, 226–32)— abandonment and death are not the end of the story. But I take the vindication of Jesus, his resurrection/translation, his drinking again of the fruit of the vine in the kingdom of God, his return as the Son of Man at the end of the age to gather his elect, to be strategies in a more utopian mode analogous to those flights of fancy and magical practices described by Weitzman to preserve under increasing cultural constraint something of the survival of the temple and its cult by relocating objects or transferring qualities—that is, strategies of cultural persistence and expressions of hope (see above, 283–86).

for legitimate control of city and temple and elaboration of the humiliation and Roman execution to follow. One did not have to have any direct experience of the war or have read accounts to have felt some sort of haunting of the course of the war in the plotted course of the Markan narrative, if not its map, an affect perhaps simply of talk about the war and how it went: with success and high promise at first, only to fall apart internally and end in destruction in Jerusalem.[380] In any case, exhibiting the death of Jesus and the destruction of the temple as parallel events of divine abandonment is not the only way Mark related the death of Jesus to the end of the temple's time; they are also related antagonistically. The persecution plot of the passion of Jesus in the Gospel of Mark serves as a *substitute* story of loss, humiliation, and death, a story which in time would inhibit identification with the destruction of city and temple as an event of "Christian" history. The outcome for city and temple could have been averted. Instead, the disaster was the inevitable climax of a history of rejection of God's messengers (Mark 12: 1–9). The rejection and execution of Jesus exposed the failure and corruption of the Jerusalem elite and sealed the fate of the city and

---

380. My suggestion here is more about what some first readers of Mark may have sensed than about the writer's deliberate construction and is admittedly far less daring than Gabriella Gelardini's reading of Mark's narrative as the writer's detailed construction of the gospel as a war report, written in 71 in Rome in the wake of the Flavian triumph, presupposing Mark's thorough familiarity with Josephus's war account, at least with what he had first composed in Aramaic ("Cult's Death in Scripture: The Destruction of Jerusalem's Temple Remembered by Josephus and Mark," in Thatcher, *Memory and Identity*, 89–112). Given the extent of this knowledge in Gelardini's description of Mark's Gospel, "keying" Jesus's movements to the movements of the Roman generals, Jesus's situation in Galilee and Jerusalem to the situations of Josephus in Galilee and the priest, Ananus, in Jerusalem, Jesus's entry into Jerusalem to the Roman triumph and his death to the Jewish obloquy (100–109), we must imagine the writer, like Josephus, to be a native Aramaic speaker and also assume a very close relationship between the early Aramaic version of the *Judean War* and the subsequent Greek version, a questionable assumption. The Greek version is usually dated to the years 75–79, with the possible exception of book 7. "Keying" and "framing," are concepts drawn from the work of sociologist Barry Schwartz and are understood as mnemonic rather than rhetorical strategies, the former associating the present with the past, the latter utilizing what is keyed into as an interpretive frame in the present. In that case, given the temporal setting of Mark's Gospel, figures and events of the war should be understood as keyed into Mark's life of Jesus, whose prophecy then serves as a frame for interpreting the destruction of the temple, as Schwartz points out in remarking on Gelardini's essay (318), rather than the reverse.

temple long before the Roman legions did their work. There was no occult mystery in divine abandonment of the temple and city, nothing to mourn. Memorialization of the death of Jesus would in time institute a counter-memory. However, the legacy of this story is not exclusively the function of a later history. The different characterizations of the death of Jesus, as the beginning of the end of the temple's time and as a noble death for the benefit of others, are significant in this respect, in particular because these characterizations are present in the absence of a scene of reconciliation between the hero and some collective representation of his people.[381]

---

381. See above, n. 347. I have avoided identifying the situation of Markan composition with the experience of trauma; see Maia Kotrosits and Hal Taussig, *Re-reading the Gospel of Mark Amidst Loss and Trauma* (New York: Palgrave MacMillan, 2013). This is partly because of the difficulty of defining trauma; see above, n. 105 (Kelber), n. 187, n. 189 (Alexander), n. 261 (Daschke), and n. 378 (Geyer). It seems to me that in a literary sense trauma might be located not in what Mark's Gospel accomplishes but in what it does not accomplish (following David Janzen, *The Violent Gift: Trauma's Subversion of the Deuteronomistic History's Narrative*, LHBOTS 561 [New York: Bloomsbury T&T Clark, 2012]). Gelardini regards Jesus's sacrifice in Mark to have purged Judean war guilt and renewed the covenant with Israel, and his resurrection to have destabilized the Roman memory by anticipating the return of the Son of Man to fight a just war against God's enemies ("Cult's Death in Scripture," 108–9). However more satisfying theologically and aesthetically such a narrative might be, both "a *theologia gloriae* as well as a *theologia crucis*" (ibid., 102), there is no indication in Mark's narrative that the war was unjust rather than that the outcome was sealed proleptically in the rejection of Jesus by the Jerusalem elite. With respect to Jesus's death as "a ransom for many" (10:45) and as an act of covenant renewal (14:24), besides the untenable equation of violent death with expiation in animal sacrifice (see above, nn. 343–44), one cannot avoid the question to whom these benefits apply in Mark's Gospel. The last scene in Mark in which the crowds are present is not the entry into Jerusalem or the scenes in the temple, but the scene before Pilate in which the crowds are stirred up by the chief priests and call for the releasing of Barabbas and the crucifying of Jesus (15:11–13), and those who revile him at the cross (15:29). If the return to Galilee implies some sort of renewal, it concerns the disciples and not the people collectively. Given the many features in Mark characteristic of a genre of subversive biography in which the hero's own people are agents of his death, one has reason to expect some sort of scene of reconciliation between the hero and his people. Insofar as the return of the Son of Man implies judgment as well as vindication of the elect, the judgment is directed not at Rome in particular but at those among the crowds and disciples who are ashamed of Jesus (8:38) and among the Jerusalem elite who condemn him as deserving death (14:62–64). This is not to deny that there are features in Mark of colonial mimicry, including the use of the term *euangelion* as a reference to Jesus's proclamation and possibly to Mark's narrative as well (ibid.). I also

Mark's dual narrative was not only intended to project a different ending to a biblical epic that had in view the building of a temple, though this is surely in the picture, or to appeal to certain readers attracted to the deeds of power and vindication of a marginal Jewish figure whose proclamation of divine rule survived the war, some perhaps with considerable antipathy toward a people who had brought their fate on themselves by following leaders who had threatened regional stability. As a substitute story of humiliation and vindication, the beginning of the gospel of Jesus Christ is a story of leaving, evoking the fantasy of exemption and escape from self-identification as Jews subject to Rome, insofar as the latter were defined as Roman subjects by the circumstances of loss and humiliation that followed upon the failure of a Judean ruling class to achieve either a continuing accommodation of Roman imperial power or greater freedom from Rome. From the lookout of some locale of the southern Levant ca. 80–85 CE, the claim that the figure of Jesus in Mark serves as "a literary-cultural *evocatio sacrorum*," does make sense—the Son of God called out to move on to a "place" not circumscribed by an understanding of the times imposed by Roman victory.[382] Among the features of this literary project

---

agree with Gelardini's conclusion in not thinking "Josephus or Mark believed he had replaced the temple with a memorial construction" (ibid., 110). But in literary terms one might suggest that trauma is present where the discipleship theme appears to be unfinished, where reconciliation with his own people is not forthcoming, where the temple's destruction and the people's obloquy are not mourned in Mark's nativist project. Fasting when the bridegroom is taken away (Mark 2:20) may have suggested a substitute occasion for mourning to that of mourning over the destruction of the temple, even as it suggests a more significant change of behavior for disciples of Jesus than for disciples of the Pharisees and John's disciples, and another way in which the death of Jesus and the destruction of the temple can be seen as parallel events. For other recent major studies of trauma in the biblical field, besides those referred to above, see David M. Carr, *Holy Resilience: The Bible's Traumatic Origins* (New Haven: Yale University Press, 2014) and Eve-Marie Becker, Jan Dochhorn, and Else K. Holt, eds., *Trauma and Traumatization in Individual and Collective Dimensions: Insights from Biblical Studies and Beyond*, Studia Aarhusiana Neotestamentica 2 (Göttingen: Vandenhoeck & Ruprecht, 2014).

382. As I see it, Mark's narrative is more a story of leaving than of homecoming. Leaving is everywhere, for that is what Jesus mostly does, not just as a matter of a change of scene or of life on the road but conspicuously and incomprehensibly, which given the magnitude of his benefactions is not the consequence you would expect, or, given the call of disciples, not a program you would expect to end in flight. Yes, there is the promise of great reward a hundredfold in this life—"houses, brothers and

are the generation of narrative through mimetic writing, the overloading

---

sisters, mothers and children, and fields ..." (10:30), but why should anyone believe it? What we see in Mark's story are the disciples leaving family, but very little hint of gaining new ones. On the road on their own they do what Jesus authorizes them to do; however, as to what can be expected as a consequence, they get instruction about what to do when leaving rejected. Yes, the failure of the disciples, the movement toward abandonment and social dissolution can highlight for the reader the importance and value, the fragility and difficulty, of identity formation and social cohesion through their mirror images in the story. But it *is* a story of leaving. A point in the narrative where the boundary between the narrative world and the writer's world is breached is also about leaving. "Let the reader understand" (13:14) is a directive to take note that the destruction of the temple is to be understood as an occasion of frightful pollution and desecration requiring flight from Judea. The two anonymous characters at the arrest of Jesus (14:47, 51) belong to the company of the disciples, insofar as they too flee (14:50–51). They differ, however, because, unlike the disciples, both can be understood to attempt to come to the aid of Jesus. Therefore, both are potentially at greater risk from "police" and must have their identities protected, as Theissen, *Gospels in Context*, 186–87, has suggested. Even though Theissen believes that the details of Jesus's arrest are historical, he acknowledges that it really makes no difference if they are legendary, because the anonymity of the characters remains equally intelligible in the transmission of such stories (188–89). Nothing would change if the scene is essentially Markan composition. Contrariwise, it is absolutely essential that the women at the crucifixion and at the tomb be identified. They are *the* witnesses to the death of Jesus and the empty tomb. They do not merely happen to be there. They are there as followers of Jesus (15:41), even if the one Mary can be identified only through one or more sons, presuming the sons are better known (15:40, 47). Similarly with a certain Simon of Cyrene, a passerby coming in from the country, who is compelled to carry Jesus's cross. Despite the fact that he is given an identification by place of origin, he is also identified through his sons, Alexander and Rufus (15:21), who are not further described. Mentioning them here in this way implies that they must be well known. But to whom? To Mark's readers? But I would point out that it is not necessary to assume that Alexander and Rufus were in fact well known to Mark's readers, because naming them in this way still performs the literary function of assuring the reader that the scene with Simon of Cyrene is attested by his better known sons. If Alexander and Rufus as the sons of this Simon were in fact so well known to Mark's readers, he would not have had to mention them at all. Nonetheless, there could certainly be readers, such as the writers of Matthew and Luke, who assumed the sons were well known in Mark's circle, but were not known in their own more immediate circle, and therefore dropped them. This literary technique of attestation neatly conveys the idea that attestation is necessarily a generational affair and not simply a matter of an "origin" to which no one has access. So, if the witness to Simon of Cyrene is through his better known sons, why stay in Jerusalem? As we say, there is no there there, no Simon of Cyrene, no Alexander and Rufus, no women at the tomb, no body of Jesus, no temple.

of titles, attributes, and roles heightening interest in the counterintuitive figure of the protagonist, the crossing of territorial and social boundaries, the teaching of practices critical of the broader society, and a measure of accommodation untroubled by the blurring of ethnic identities.[383] With regard to the possible social effects of the narrative, in addition to accruing cultural capital in a network of writers, other religious specialists practicing their varied kinds of expertise in the name of Jesus (Mark 6:7–13; 9:38–41) could claim the prestige and pedigree of a written account of the gospel of Jesus Christ from prophetic call to death and vindication, not only to better retail their expertise but possibly in the interest of connecting to literate circles, with the intended result of attracting broader forums of practice and debate, and, for some, as an influence for promoting social formations of discipleship exemplifying the virtues of believing and following. Mark's literary project could also have contributed to processes of social alienation, as indicated above, especially in connection with efforts of self-representation seeking escape from identification as Jews perceived as a threat to regional stability and subjected to Rome in consequence of a failed Judean revolt. It has been the aim of this paper to contextualize this social distancing in a time of recovery from local conflicts in the region of southern Syria in the wake of the Roman-Judean war, while also conceptualizing Mark's literary project as a strategy of native Jewish cultural persistence. In such a time and setting, I have imagined that the writer of Mark could identify with aggrievement in the region over perceived Judean aggression and threatened territorial expansion but not without deep ambivalence in the outcome. To his own literate circle, the writer contributed a narrative which accounted for what was lost by reference to a figure of divine status whose reputation survived the disaster, whose relative obscurity was accounted for as misrecognition occasioned by a mysterious divine purpose, and whose humiliation and suffering authenticated his place in a time of political, cultural, and symbolic loss.

Mark's final scene at the tomb may have elevated Jesus to the rank of the classical Mediterranean demigod, but there is no celebration or cult, and no hint of reconciliation of the hero with his people, though reconciliation with failed disciples is surely a consideration. Conceivably, reference to seeing Jesus in Galilee is a tacit acknowledgment of the existence of tra-

---

383. On demonstrating that Mark's Gospel is a fusion of teaching and biography composed without access to prior narrative traditions stemming from followers of Jesus, see Arnal, "Mark, War, and Creative Imagination."

ditions claiming appearances of Jesus in Galilee (Mark 9:2–8). Mark clearly
has no interest in narrating these, either in Jerusalem or Galilee, perhaps
because he is skeptical about claims to authority that appeal to postas-
sumption or postresurrection appearances. The response of the women
to the prospect of Jesus going ahead of them to Galilee, especially since it
echoes the language describing the disciples' reaction on the road to Jerusalem (Mark 10:32), might very well be, "Who would want to 'return to
Galilee' to see Jesus again?"[384] So, the return to Galilee is a risk that is itself
in danger of not being confronted because of the story's emphatic telling
of the flight and silence of the women (16:8). Contrariwise, given its high
quotient of indeterminacy, indirection, uncertainty, anomaly, and fantasy,
its cultivation of mysteries and obscurities, the Gospel of Mark is assured
of bringing its *readers* back to Galilee, generating interest and effort to
follow, perhaps in imitation of ancient books, and guaranteeing that
"'Christianity's' foundational gesture is not to be found in Jesus, but in the
story of Jesus."[385] If the unnamed woman's anointing of Jesus beforehand
for burial is a mitzva done for Jesus and a reminder of the poor (14:6–8),
it is also tantamount to an apotropaic rite deflecting vengeance (proper
burial of the dead). As an act that will memorialize her not in monument
but in word (14:9), its telling wherever the gospel is proclaimed necessarily entails that her memorial belongs to Mark's story of Jesus, lest her good
deed be misunderstood.

The destruction of the temple presented an opportunity to imagine
Jesus in the framework of an event of political, social, and cultural conse-

---

384. This is actually the question posed by Geyer and is clearly congruent with
his reading of the topoi, cultural sensibilities, cognitive and emotional effects of the
Gospel of Mark. "The women are perhaps the clearest thinkers" (*Fear, Anomaly, and
Uncertainty*, 271).

385. William E. Arnal, "What Branches Grow Out of This Stony Rubbish? Christian Origins and the Study of Religion," *SR* 39 (2010): 557, emphasis original. For a
similar emphasis on what Mark's Gospel initiated, albeit not as "'Christianity's' foundational gesture" but with reference to the emergence of a Christian book culture, see
Eve-Marie Becker, "The Reception of 'Mark' in the 1st and 2nd Centuries C.E. and Its
Significance for Genre Studies," in Becker and Runesson, *Mark and Matthew II*, 15–36;
Keith, "Early Christian Book Culture" (see above, n. 33); Keith, "Prolegomena on the
Textualization of Mark's Gospel" (see above, n. 34). On the place of middling scribes
in the emergence of a Christian book culture, see John Kloppenborg, "Literate Media
in Early Christ Groups: The Creation of a Christian Book Culture," *JECS* 22 (2014):
21–59.

quence for the people of Israel and for the reading of biblical epic. But it also presented a problem, because it threatened the plausibility and tangibility of any figured representation of the reign of the God of Israel soon to be established in the world. This has little if anything to do with how or where one lined up as a follower of Jesus on the independent Judean state established from 66–70. It was a question rather of the loss of a canopy of symbolic and practical authority, an encompassing system of classification, in terms of which, and even in opposition to which, kingdom discourse and agency could be constructed. Were it not an opportunity and a problem, Mark's narrative would not announce itself as good news, nor plot the entanglements of the death of Jesus with an event of a generation later. As a fantasy of exemption and escape from the demonstration of Roman power and the consequences of a failed revolt, Jesus is the figure one rides out of Jerusalem.[386] The escape announces the risen Jesus's return to the Galilee where he began to teach and act on behalf of the advent of the kingdom, a beginning that had occasioned the crossing of boundaries of identification and practice, of surveillance and refuge, of centers and margins of civilization[387]—crossings which were occasions for application of the arts of cultural persistence, in this case by diffusion, requiring some bleeding across certain boundaries of Jewish practice, possibly a tactic of the weak and unrecognized, an imagination of ruling otherwise, a potential regime of truth for keeping the enemy out.[388] Think of these Galilean beginnings.

---

386. One is reminded of another story of escape from Jerusalem, the classical rabbinic story of the founding of a school at Yavneh (Avot R. Nat. A 4.6; B 6; Solomon Schechter, ed., *Aboth de Rabbi Nathan* [New York: Philipp Feldheim, 1967], 23, 19; b. Git. 56a–b; Lam. Rab. 1:5 (31). In both stories there is preparation for burial, by anointing for burial in the one and by carrying the feigned dead body in a coffin in the other, both acts not being what they seem. In the one the sage-hero though alive plays dead; in the other the sage-hero though dead is declared to be alive. Of course, the rabbinic story of Yohanan ben Zakkai's escape has a much closer relationship to Josephus's narrative of his own escape at Jotapata, since both escapes depend on a prophetic message delivered to Vespasian announcing his impending exaltation to emperor. On Josephus's treatment of abhorrent suicide and noble death as a tactic of cultural persistence, taking account of Flavian sensibilities to the resistance of martyrs and the coherence of Roman and Jewish values on noble death, see Weitzman's ch. 7, "Playing Dead," in *Surviving Sacrilege*; cf. Klawans, *Josephus and Theologies of Judaism*, 115–36. For Josephus, the best martyrs are the kind who do not get killed (Steven Weitzman, "Josephus on How to Survive Martyrdom," *JJS* 55 [2004]: 230–45).

387. See above, 232–33 with nn. 55–56 (Stewart).

388. Weitzman, *Surviving Sacrilege*, 158–61.

If prestigious origins is one way to address problems of social anonymity, and there is no temple, no mother city, no "big tradition," no world ruler that has ever been more yours than theirs; and moreover, if you knew of no special ideological position taken by followers of Jesus in the terrible war and no particular threat to followers of Jesus as such arising from the war, you might find it all the more necessary now to claim that you do indeed have a public persona, that you engage hostile powers, and that the costs of belonging to God's kingdom are even greater than defending the temple. The writer stakes such a claim by narrating the beginning of the uniquely authorized Son of God who does battle with unclean spirits, trumps the authorities by teaching with authority, is persecuted and martyred in the temple city—then recapitulates the pattern in a farewell address by the protagonist in response to questions concerning the time and circumstances of the destruction of that same temple city. As the story of the good news about Jesus begins with preparing the way for his cosmic war to *expel* demons, so it will end with his angels coming to *gather* the elect. This return to Galilee beyond the plotted time of the narrative, though itself in serious question within plotted time, invokes a time of wider horizons (13:10, 26–27; 14:9). Galilee is now as good a place as any from which to imagine a beginning.

Mark, War, and Creative Imagination

William E. Arnal

Ancient Theories and Modern Myths of Christian Origins

The Gospel according to Mark, arguably, laid the framework for most subsequent understandings of Jesus and of the "movement" he allegedly insti-
gated.[1] The predominant "ancient myth" with which our "modern theories" are struggling is thus precisely the one laid down by Mark. It receives
fuller elaboration and extension forward in time in Luke-Acts, which in its
turn offers a basis for Eusebius's even more ambitious conceptualization.[2]
But the narrative *mode* and the substantive implications of that mode—the
view, in short, that Jesus is understood best in terms of his activity and
particularly in terms of a series of sequential and distinctive events—is
something we encounter for the first time in the Markan gospel.[3] Mark
also provides the ancient theory that stands behind the modern scholarly

---

1. Burton L. Mack, *Who Wrote the New Testament? The Making of the Christian
Myth* (HarperSanFrancisco, 1995), 152: "Ever after, Christians would imagine Mark's
fiction as history." See also Mack, *A Myth of Innocence: Mark and Christian Origins*
(Philadelphia: Fortress, 1988; repr. with new preface, Minneapolis: Fortress, 2006),
353 n. 14: "It was Mark's fiction of a fantastic infringement on human history that created Christianity's charter.... Mark's theory of Jesus' authority and the end of Second
Temple Judaism might be regarded only as a little pretention hardly worth a modern
smile but for its legacy. Since Mark's view became the canonical theory, however, the
fiction deserves a thorough analysis."

2. We can speak, therefore, of the Lukan-Eusebian conception of the church. This
conception, however, is simply an extension of the model or paradigm already established in the Markan gospel. Nowhere is this more clear than Luke's adoption of the
Markan narrative as the framework for the first volume of his own "history."

3. This narrative mode even affects how Jesus's "teaching" is conceptualized. On
this matter, see further below.

myth of the historical Jesus. Mark's vast influence is thus apparent not only in nearly all subsequent Christian portrayals but also, and most problematically, in the limits of our modern critical imaginations of the birth of the Christian movement. This influence is perhaps most stunningly illustrated in the highly acclaimed work of E. P. Sanders on the historical Jesus.[4]

Sanders's reconstruction begins from the premise that "there are several facts about Jesus's career …which can be known beyond doubt."[5] These "indisputable facts" include the following:[6]

1. Jesus was baptized by John the Baptist;
2. Jesus was a Galilean who preached and healed;
3. Jesus called disciples and spoke of there being twelve;
4. Jesus confined his activity to Israel;
5. Jesus engaged in a controversy about the temple;
6. Jesus was crucified outside Jerusalem by the Roman authorities;
7. After his death Jesus's followers continued as an identifiable movement;
8. At least some Jews persecuted at least parts of the new movement.

Excepting item four, this list could be read as a summary of the plot line of the Gospel of Mark, beginning with baptism, following a preaching and healing mission, calling a circle of twelve disciples, attacking the temple, and being crucified. Items seven and eight, referring as they do to events subsequent to the Markan story's terminus, are not recounted as narrative in Mark, but they are strongly implied (compare with Mark 13:9–13). Even item four may, arguably, be derived from Mark's characterization.[7]

---

4. See especially E. P. Sanders, *The Historical Figure of Jesus* (London: Allen Lane; London: Penguin, 1993); Sanders, *Jesus and Judaism* (Philadelphia: Fortress, 1985).

5. Sanders, *Jesus and Judaism*, 10–11.

6. The list is taken, almost verbatim, from Sanders, *Jesus and Judaism*, 11.

7. While Mark's Jesus appears to roam throughout "gentile territory" (see, e.g., David Rhoads and Donald Michie, *Mark as Story: An Introduction to the Narrative of a Gospel* [Philadelphia: Fortress, 1982], 69–70), it is by no means clear that these travels necessarily imply any sort of "mission to the gentiles." Indeed, Jesus's response to the Syro-Phoenician woman in 7:27 suggests that even in "the region of Tyre" Jesus intends to address himself only to Jews. For doubts about the extent of Jesus's contact with gentiles in Mark, see, e.g., Werner Georg Kümmel et al., *Introduction to the New Testament*, trans. A. J. Mattill, 14th rev. ed. (Nashville: Abingdon, 1966), 64–65; Willi

In his later work, *The Historical Figure of Jesus*, Sanders is no less confident: "There are no substantial doubts about the general course of Jesus' life."[8] Here Sanders's list provides even more detail, again, most of its substance and sequence drawn from the Markan characterization of Jesus's *bios*:

> Jesus ... spent his childhood and early adult years in Nazareth, a Galilean village; he was baptized by John the Baptist; he called disciples; he taught in the towns, villages and countryside of Galilee (apparently not the cities); he preached "the kingdom of God"; about the year 30 he went to Jerusalem for Passover; he created a disturbance in the Temple area; he had a final meal with the disciples; he was arrested and interrogated by Jewish authorities, specifically the high priest; he was executed on the orders of the Roman prefect, Pontius Pilate ... his disciples at first fled.[9]

What we have, once again, is not so much a critical reconstruction as a paraphrase of Mark's plotline. The problem is not so much that Sanders has used Mark as a source for his reconstruction of the historical Jesus; such a procedure would be perfectly understandable. Rather, Sanders exemplifies the way that some historical Jesus scholars are unable to think in terms other than the Markan narrative scheme, so much so that Mark's tendentious and obviously redactional plotline is, for Sanders, translated wholesale into "indisputable" and "undoubted" evidence of what really happened.[10]

The reason for Mark's massive influence on subsequent (especially ancient) Christian portrayals is something of a mystery, and it is a question

---

Marxsen, *Mark the Evangelist: Studies on the Redaction History of the Gospel*, trans. James Boyce et al. (Nashville: Abingdon, 1969), 66–70; Norman Perrin and Dennis C. Duling, *The New Testament: An Introduction*, 2nd ed. (New York: Harcourt Brace Jovanovich, 1982), 243.

8. Sanders, *Historical Figure of Jesus*, 10.

9. Ibid., 10–11.

10. That Mark's narrative outline is questionable is a fact known since the form critics (see, e.g., Martin Dibelius, *From Tradition to Gospel*, trans. Bertram Lee Woolf [New York: Scribner's, 1934], 218–19; Rudolf Bultmann, *The History of the Synoptic Tradition*, trans. John Marsh, rev. ed. [New York: Harper & Row, 1963], 3, 329, 332), probably since William Wrede (cf. Albert Schweitzer, *The Quest of the Historical Jesus: A Critical Study of Its Progress from Reimarus to Wrede*, trans. William Montgomery [New York: Macmillan, 1968], 330–37), and certainly since Julius Wellhausen (see Bultmann, *History of the Synoptic Tradition*, 2).

I leave to others. The reasons for Mark's influence on modern scholarship are easier to determine. Most obviously, the Markan narrative pattern is accepted and taken for granted by so many modern scholars simply because of the force of almost two millennia of conceiving Jesus in precisely, and only, this fashion. Less obvious but, I think, as important is the congeniality of the narrative mode for historians. The discipline of history itself is often conceived (intentionally or otherwise) as an exercise in narrativization.[11] As Peter Gay notes, "Historical narration without analysis is trivial, historical analysis without narration is incomplete."[12] The process of translation from an already-narrativized Mark to a history is a much simpler process than making narrative sense, effectively from scratch, of the fragmented and isolated individual traditions about Jesus that circumstance has preserved for us.[13] Put differently, narrative provides a convenient interpretive context that makes historical sense of fragmentary data. Sanders admits that this is a factor in his approach when he complains that the sayings tradition "must still be placed in a meaningful context" and that "historical reconstruction requires that data be fitted into a context."[14] He is quite correct, of course; what is less clear is that the wholesale adoption of the Markan narrative outline is the best way to accomplish this contextualization.

---

11. See, e.g., Hayden White, *The Content of the Form: Narrative Discourse and Historical Representation* (Baltimore: Johns Hopkins University Press, 1987), ix–x: "Since its invention by Herodotus, traditional historiography has featured predominantly the belief that history itself consists of a congeries of lived stories, individual and collective, and that the principal task of historians is to uncover these stories and retell them in a narrative, the truth of which would reside in the correspondence of the story told to the story lived by real people in the past."

12. Peter Gay, *Style in History* (New York: Basic Books, 1974), 189.

13. This probably also accounts for the perverse tendency in much modern scholarship to use Acts as a source for Pauline biography even when it is conceded that it is an unreliable source (note the observation of Jerome Murphy-O'Connor, *Paul: A Critical Life* [Oxford: Oxford University Press, 1997], vi: "J. Knox ... laid down the methodological principle, 'A fact only suggested in the letters has a status which even the most unequivocal statement of Acts, if not otherwise supported, cannot confer....' Recent lives of Paul [e.g., Fitzmyer, Baslez, Légasse] all pay lip-service to this principle, but in practice they not only permit Luke to exercise decisive control over the presentation of Paul's career, but fail to recognize the problems of extracting historical data from the Acts of the Apostles"). This is done even when we have, in fact, excellent primary sources for Paul, i.e., his own letters. But the letters have no sequence or narrative in and of themselves, and so require an act of translation which Acts provides ready-made.

14. Sanders, *Jesus and Judaism*, 16, 17.

From Sayings to Biographical Episodes

In order to get a handle on Mark's "ancient theory" of Christian origins, it is important to be clear about just how creative a product his "gospel" really is. I will not belabor the egregiously nonhistorical character of Mark's story;[15] the whole issue of the historical Jesus is of little relevance to us.[16] Instead, I want to focus on the *process* by which Mark invented his narrative story of Jesus. The most striking feature of this process, to my mind, and one apparently dictated (in part) by the nature of his access to information about Jesus, is Mark's transformation of sayings traditions

---

15. As I have stated elsewhere ("A Parting of the Ways? Scholarly Identities and a Peculiar Species of Ancient Mediterranean Religion," in *Identity and Interaction in the Ancient Mediterranean: Jews, Christians, and Others; Essays in Honour of Stephen G. Wilson*, ed. Zeba Crook and Philip Harland, New Testament Monographs 18 [Sheffield: Sheffield Phoenix, 2007], 265–66): "Mark is a text that includes a cast of characters comprising, *inter alia*, God, a son of God, angels, the devil, demons, holy spirits, evil spirits, and what seem to be the ghosts of Moses and Elijah. It is a story that features miraculous healings and exorcisms, as well as walking on water, feeding thousands of people with a handful of loaves and fishes (twice), face-to-face conversations between people who lived centuries apart, spooky prognostications, the sky tearing apart, trees withering at Jesus' command, a sun darkening in the middle of the day, and a temple curtain miraculously tearing itself in half. In the few places where Mark does discuss specific and genuinely historical figures about whom we have outside information, he does so in a way that runs exactly counter to what we otherwise know to be true." I have criticized Sanders's reliance on his "indisputable facts" about Jesus some time ago in "Major Episodes in the Biography of Jesus: Methodological Observations on the Historicity of the Narrative Tradition," *TJT* 13 (1997): 201–26, drawing particular attention to the nonhistorical character of Mark's baptism account, his story of the "temple tantrum," and his account of Jesus's death, all included among Sanders's "facts." In the discussion below, I rely on this article for my conclusions about these specific episodes. Those interested in a more detailed discussion of these particular points should consult that article.

16. See Burton L. Mack, "The Historical Jesus Hoopla," in *The Christian Myth: Origins, Logic, and Legacy* (New York: Continuum, 2001), 25–40: "It is the relationship of the Christ of the gospel story to the cultures that pattern our social constructions that needs to be addressed" (39); and "The place to start is with the observation that the New Testament texts are not only inadequate for a Jesus quest, they are data for an entirely different phenomenon. They are not the mistaken and embellished memories of the historical person, but the myths of origin imagined by early Christians seriously engaged in their social experiments. They are data for early Christian mythmaking" (40).

into narrative. That Mark has done so in a general way—that is to say, he has presented us with a narrative that at least in part consists of strung-together "sayings" material[17]—is no news.[18] But, interestingly enough, on a microcosmic scale, Mark proceeds in essentially the same way. The biographical episodes out of which he constructs his gospel, and which provide him with the sequence of unique events on which his chronology hangs (namely and especially the baptism, the "cleansing" of the temple, and the passion narrative),[19] appear to have been formed, by the author of Mark, on the basis of motifs already present in the sayings tradition. Mark has, in effect, taken sayings and transformed them into narratives.

The Axe Is Laid to the Root of the Fig Tree

A minor, but clear, example of this process occurs in Mark's odd narrative about the fig tree that Jesus cursed on the way from Bethany to Jerusalem in a fit of hungry pique (Mark 11:12–14, 20–21). As it stands in Mark, the story serves as a sort of commentary on the "temple tantrum" episode that it encloses (11:15–19),[20] presumably in order to evoke the typically Markan motif of Israel's failures and to serve as an *ex eventu* foreshadowing of the destruction of the temple.[21] The story in Mark also becomes yet another occasion for the disciples to marvel at Jesus (11:21), as well as a context to which Mark can append some evidently traditional sayings on faith (see Q 17:6; Gos. Thom. 48; 1 Cor 13:2; and further, Q 11:9–13 and John 15:7).

---

17. Particularly if one classifies the Markan apophthegms as sayings, rather than narrative material. On this problem of classification, see Bultmann, *History of the Synoptic Tradition*, 11.

18. So also Mack, *Myth of Innocence*, 54 n.1: "In 1919, Karl Ludwig Schmidt … show[ed] that the gospel was composed of small units of events about which the author had no precise information, and that the overall plan for connecting them together in a single narrative was not an historical memory, but the author's own construction."

19. Mack, *Myth of Innocence*, 54–55, 283–87, refers to these episodes as "framework stories."

20. So, e.g., Rhoads and Michie, *Mark as Story*, 51; Richard A. Horsley, *Hearing the Whole Story: The Politics of Plot in Mark's Gospel* (Louisville: Westminster John Knox, 2001), 72.

21. So, e.g., Mack, *Myth of Innocence,* 243; Frank W. Beare, *The Earliest Records of Jesus* (New York: Abingdon, 1962), 206; Horsley, *Hearing the Whole Story*, 72. Cf. John P. Meier, *A Marginal Jew: Rethinking the Historical Jesus*, 4 vols. (New York: Doubleday, 1991–2009), 2:886–88, 892.

But these latter are not the only traditional sayings that intersect with this episode. The motif of trees (and of fig trees, specifically) and the character of their fruit is already present—and multiply attested—in the sayings tradition. Q 6:43–44 reads: "No healthy tree bears bad fruit, nor does an unhealthy tree bear good fruit. For from the fruit the tree is known. Are figs picked from thorns, or grapes from thistles?" (compare with Gos. Thom. 45). At the secondary stage of Q's development, this saying has been reconfigured in order to harness it to this later redaction's polemical interests, and it has been placed in the mouth of John the Baptist: "Even now the axe is laid to the root of the trees; every tree, therefore, that does not bear good fruit is cut down and thrown into the fire" (Q[2] 3:9; cf. Matt 7:19).[22] The destruction of trees failing to bear fruit is also attested in Matt 15:13–14, Gos. Thom. 40, and comes to fullest expression in the "parable" (again, I suspect, secondarily developed from some version of the saying in Q 6:43–44) that appears in Luke 13:6–9:

> Then he told them this parable: A man had a fig tree planted in his vineyard; and he came looking for fruit on it and found none. So he said to the gardener, "See here! For three years I have come looking for fruit on this tree, and still I find none. Cut it down! Why should it be wasting the soil?" He replied, "Sir, let it alone for one more year, until I dig around it and put manure on it. If it bears fruit next year, well and good; but if not, you can cut it down." (NRSV)

A whole tradition history (or sequence of "performances") of this sayings motif can be sketched as follows: (1) an original sapiential observation about trees being known by their fruit (see Q 6:43–44a);[23] (2) various more specific applications of this saying to human behaviors (see Q 6:45); (3) modification of the application to a more specifically retributory orientation with attention to what becomes of trees failing to bear good fruit

---

22. On the secondary character of this formulation and its direct derivation from the earlier material in Q[1], see my article on John's preaching: "Redactional Fabrication and Group Legitimation: The Baptist's Preaching in Q 3:7–9, 16–17," in *Conflict and Invention: Literary, Rhetorical, and Social Studies on the Sayings Gospel Q*, ed. John S. Kloppenborg (Valley Forge, PA: Trinity Press International, 1995), 165–80.

23. I am not even marginally interested in whether this saying ultimately goes back to the historical Jesus, and the question at any rate has no bearing on this discussion of the subsequent history of the motif.

(see Q 3:9; Gos. Thom. 40; Matt 7:19; 15:13–14);[24] (4) narrativization of these judgmental sayings into *stories* about what happens to unproductive trees or plants (see Luke 13:6–9).[25]

My suggestion, then, is that the New Testament judgment sayings that threaten those trees failing to bear (good) fruit are ultimately secondary textual developments from an original and more neutral saying about trees being known by their fruits.[26] A case could be made that the most striking examples of this development appear in texts to which Mark did not have access.[27] Nonetheless, the development runs across a sufficient range of sources for us to be sanguine in concluding that Mark could have—even probably did—have access to some version of it. Moreover, the developmental trajectory is quite clear, and Mark's narrative in 11:12–14, 20–21 fits right into it, as its final stage; it is no longer a story *by* Jesus but one *about* him. Several commentators have already suggested, in fact,

---

24. This also appears to be the point at which apocalyptic imagery comes to be associated with the saying, particularly in references to the burning of such trees. This is yet another example of the tradition-historically *secondary* character of apocalypticism in ancient Christianity: apocalyptic motifs appear to be developed out of material that was originally nonapocalyptic. Typically, this data is ignored by the "pan-apocalyptic" school of Christian origins (e.g., Bart D. Ehrman, *Jesus: Apocalyptic Prophet of the New Millennium* [Oxford: Oxford University Press, 1999]).

25. Note, too, that this reconstruction is supported by the sequence of the texts in which the relevant sayings appear. That is, we move from isolated sayings behind Q^1, to Q^1 "redaction," to Q^2 and Thomas, to special Lukan material. So the relative procession of the texts in which the sayings appear tends to conform, more or less, to the tradition-historical sequence here suggested. To put this slightly differently, the sequence or development is clearly *textual*, not a nondevelopmental array of distinct oral "performances."

26. This is almost certainly the case with Q 3:9, where a direct knowledge of the source-saying can be demonstrated for the author of the secondary saying. That is, the author/redactor of 3:9 (in Q^2), obviously, had access to and knew the material in 6:43–44 (from Q^1). See the note on 3:9, above.

27. Namely, Q^2 and special Lukan material. I have never been convinced that Mark had access to the written Q document at *any* stage of its development. By contrast, see Mack, *Myth of Innocence*, 324 n. 4; and, at greater length, Harry T. Fleddermann, *Q: A Reconstruction and Commentary* (BTS; Leuven; Paris; Dudley, MA: Peeters, 2005), 180–83; Fleddermann, *Mark and Q: A Study of the Overlap Texts* (Leuven: Leuven University Press; Leuven: Peeters, 1995). I do think a case can be made, however, for Mark's literary dependence on the Gospel of Thomas. See Stevan Davies, "On Mark's Use of the Gospel of Thomas," *Neot* 30 (1996): 307–34.

that Mark's account is a transformation of the parable of the fig tree into a "story of fact" about Jesus.[28]

Whether Mark's source for this story is the specific "parable" recounted by Luke, or, as I think is more likely, *some* version of the saying on unproductive trees, is immaterial. What is clear, I think, is that Mark has created a narrative by transforming a motif securely embedded in the sayings tradition into an activity undertaken by Jesus. Here, Jesus's behavior is something like an "acted parable"—he makes his point by acting out a part, rather than simply by speaking.[29] He thus manifests and interprets his teaching in his own person, at the same time eclipsing that teaching by making it increasingly self-referential. It is worth noting what this implies about Mark's narrative sources. If this reconstruction is correct, then at least for this story, Mark actually required *no* narrative source, *no* extant tradition in which Jesus acted in any way whatsoever toward any tree whatsoever, *no* fragmentary "reminiscence" from an earlier passion narrative or an earlier version of the temple episode. Rather, Mark has sayings traditions about Jesus the teacher, which he transforms into narrative embodiments of the behavior of Jesus the son of God.

I Will Destroy This House

Even Sanders does not appear to make the cursing of the fig tree an "undisputable fact" about Jesus. But the basic technique used here by Mark occurs in much more significant Markan narratives, including those cited as indisputably historical by Sanders. Indeed, the centerpiece of Sanders's analysis of the historical Jesus, the attack on the temple

---

28. See, e.g., Vincent Taylor, *The Gospel according to St. Mark* (London: MacMillan, 1963), 459: "Probably the best explanation of the narrative is that the parable of the Fig Tree in Lk. xiii.6–9, or a similar parable, has been transformed into a story of fact"; and Beare, *Earliest Records of Jesus*, 206: "The same symbolism lies behind the parable of the Barren Fig Tree (Luke xiii.6–9), and it is not unlikely that the miracle-story is a secondary form of the parable."

29. Which in Mark is apparently a point about the destruction of Jerusalem being a function of God's judgment. It is striking that of all the applications given to the original observation about trees and fruit (first, in Q^1, to human behavior in general; then, in Q^2, to failure to "repent"; then, in the Lukan "parable," to the timetable of the apocalypse; and finally, in the Markan narrative, to the destruction of the temple in 70 CE), this one is the most historically specific. This specificity also tends to support the sequence I have argued for here.

recounted in Mark 11:15–19 (bracketed by the fig-tree episode!), happens to be one such narrative.

The story, generally assumed to be an actual event in the life of the historical Jesus[30]— presumably because of its conformity to the Christian supposition that Jesus's mission was to free Judaism from a mindless legalism, and, more reasonably, because it offers a way to account for Jesus's death[31]—has almost nothing to commend it as historical. It is singly attested,[32] appearing only in Mark and in a dependent form in the Gospel of John (2:13–17);[33] it is intrinsically unrealistic,[34] and it fits all too well with Mark's redactional interests and plot development as an indictment

---

30. See the survey in Robert J. Miller, "Historical Method and the Deeds of Jesus: The Test Case of the Temple Demonstration," *Forum* 8 (1992): 5–30, 36, esp. 6–22. See also Taylor, *Gospel according to St. Mark*, 461; Ehrman, *Jesus: Apocalyptic Prophet*, 211–12; Günther Bornkamm, *Jesus of Nazareth*, trans. Irene and Fraser McLuskey with James M. Robinson (New York: Harper & Row, 1960), 158; Robert W. Funk, Roy W. Hoover, and the Jesus Seminar, *The Five Gospels: The Search for the Authentic Words of Jesus* (New York: MacMillan, 1993), 97–98, 174–76; Craig A. Evans, "Jesus' Action in the Temple and Evidence of Corruption in the First-Century Temple," *Society of Biblical Literature 1989 Seminar Papers*, ed. David J. Lull, SBLSP 28 (Atlanta: Scholars Press, 1989), 522–39; and Evans, "Jesus' Action in the Temple: Cleansing or Portent of Destruction?," *CBQ* 51 (1989): 237–70; Peter Richardson, "Why Turn the Tables? Jesus' Protest in the Temple Precincts," *Society of Biblical Literature 1992 Seminar Papers*, ed. Eugene H. Lovering, Jr. SBLSP 31 (Atlanta: Scholars Press, 1992), 507–23; Morton Smith, *Jesus the Magician* (New York: Harper & Row, 1978), 36.

31. So Sanders, *Jesus and Judaism*, 301–6. See also Marcus J. Borg, *Jesus, A New Vision: Spirit, Culture, and the Life of Discipleship* (San Francisco: Harper & Row, 1987), 176; Borg, *Conflict, Holiness, and Politics in the Teaching of Jesus* (Lewiston, NY: Mellen, 1984), 171–77. For a thoroughgoing critique of Borg's reconstruction, see Ron Cameron, review of *Jesus, A New Vision: Spirit, Culture, and the Life of Discipleship*, by Marcus J. Borg, *TJT* 6 (1990): 119–23.

32. Against John Dominic Crossan, *The Historical Jesus: The Life of a Mediterranean Jewish Peasant* (San Francisco: HarperSanFrancisco, 1992), 358, who argues for multiple attestation on the basis of Thomas 71; and Sanders, *Jesus and Judaism*, 61 ("the conflict over the temple seems deeply implanted in the tradition"); and cf. Ehrman, *Jesus: Apocalyptic Prophet*, 212. There is no question that *sayings* about the temple are well-attested in the tradition; what is at issue is whether a narrative of Jesus's *action* in the temple is multiply attested. In fact, it is not.

33. I am assuming here and throughout that the Gospel of John is literarily dependent on the Gospel of Mark, and therefore cannot provide multiple attestation for parallel Markan episodes. This is not to deny that John has access to sources apart from Mark (e.g., miracle catenae). On Johannine dependence on Mark, see, e.g., Mack, *Myth of Innocence*, 357 and elsewhere; Perrin and Duling, *New Testament:*

of the temple and a foreshadowing of its destruction. These factors and others lead Burton Mack to conclude that:

> The temple act cannot be historical. If one deletes from the story those themes essential to the Markan plots, there is nothing left over for historical reminiscence. The anti-temple theme is clearly Markan and the reasons for it can be explained. The lack of any evidence for an anti-temple attitude in the Jesus and Christ traditions prior to Mark fits with the incredible lack of incidence in the story itself. Nothing happens. Even the chief priests overhear his "instruction" and do nothing. The conclusion must be that the temple act is a Markan fabrication.[35]

Interestingly, when Jesus is on trial in the Gospel of Mark, the charge brought against him does *not* refer to any action against the temple, but it *does* refer to a *saying* against the temple: "I will destroy this temple that

---

An Introduction, 334; (apparently) D. Moody Smith, "John and the Synoptics: Some Dimensions of the Problem," *NTS* 26 (1980): 425–44; John Dominic Crossan, "Commentary and History," *JR* 75 (1995): 250; and especially Frans Neirynck, "John and the Synoptics: 1975–1990," in *John and the Synoptics*, ed. Adelbert Denaux (Leuven: Leuven University Press, 1992), 3–62. David Seeley, "Jesus' Temple Act," *CBQ* 55 (1993): 263–83, esp. 272–73, regards the Johannine version of the episode as a direct literary development from the account in Mark. By contrast, in favor of Johannine independence of the Synoptic Gospels, see, e.g., Robert Fortna, "Jesus and Peter at the High Priest's House: A Test Case for the Relation Between Mark's and John's Gospels," *NTS* 24 (1977–1978): 371–83; Barnabas Lindars, "John and the Synoptic Gospels: A Test Case," *NTS* 27 (1981): 287–94.

34. In this story, Jesus performs an overtly seditious and violent act in the very center of elite control, and not only walks away from it, but first sits down and teaches for a while. On the unrealistic nature of both Markan and Johannine versions, see especially Seeley, "Jesus' Temple Act," 265–71. So also Irving M. Zeitlin, *Jesus and the Judaism of His Time* (Oxford: Polity, 1988), 150, citing Martin Hengel, *Was Jesus a Revolutionist?*, trans. William Klassen (Philadelphia: Fortress, 1971), 17–18; and, ironically, Sanders, *Jesus and Judaism*, 270. Seeley in particular points out that it is difficult to find any historical circumstance against which this protest might possibly have been directed. A valiant effort to do so is, however, provided by Richardson, "Why Turn the Tables?"

35. Mack, *Myth of Innocence*, 291–92. For more extended arguments against the historicity of this episode, see also Seeley, "Jesus' Temple Act"; Robert J. Miller, "Historical Method and the Deeds of Jesus"; Miller, "The (A)Historicity of Jesus' Temple Demonstration: A Test Case in Methodology," *Society of Biblical Literature 1991 Seminar Papers*, ed. Eugene H. Lovering, Jr., SBLSP 30 (Atlanta: Scholars Press, 1991), 235–52.

is made with hands, and in three days I will build another, not made with hands" (14:58; cf. 15:29). While Mark refers to the testimony accusing Jesus of uttering this statement as false (14:57: τινες ... ἐψευδομαρτύρουν), the gospel *does* present Jesus as verbally predicting the temple's destruction quite explicitly in 13:2, and indeed as linking this destruction to the apocalyptic scenarios offered throughout chapter 13. It is further clear that, while Mark does not recount Jesus speaking precisely the words in 14:58, he nonetheless regards this "prediction" as accurate,[36] referring as it does (1) to the destruction of the temple predicted also in 13:2 and having been accomplished in Mark's own time; and (2) to the resurrection of Jesus after three days, not recounted, but certainly affirmed (8:31; 9:31; 10:34; 16:6) in the Gospel of Mark. So even as ψευδομαρτυρία, Mark deems these sentiments, and possibly even their attribution to Jesus, to be fundamentally accurate: Jesus *spoke* against the temple, and in spite of Mark's own presentation of an action against the temple, he claims that this *speech* is why Jesus died. Moreover, a version of the saying "falsely" attributed to Jesus is also present in the Gospel of Thomas: "I will destroy this house, and no one will be able to rebuild it" (71).

My point here is not that Jesus himself actually said any such thing. Rather, it is that, regardless of their provenance, sayings about the temple are present in the tradition, and even Mark seems inadvertently to acknowledge their priority to any action associated with the temple. Non-narrative traditions, as exemplified by Q and the Gospel of Thomas, are willing to present the temple as a locus for corruption and sin (Q 11:51), and perhaps even to predict its destruction (Gos. Thom. 71) or at least its desuetude (Q 13:34–35).[37] What Mark has done, then, as with the fig tree, is to cast Jesus

---

36. Perhaps ironically, as is the case with the accusation that Jesus is "king of the Jews": his opponents are made to tell the truth inadvertently in their lies and mockery.

37. It strikes me as unlikely that saying 71, in the context of the Gospel of Thomas, is really intended to refer to the Temple (see Stevan Davies, *The Gospel of Thomas, Annotated and Explained* [Woodstock, VT: Skylight Paths, 2002], 94). More likely, "this house" is intended as a reference to the body. But its original referent is more plausibly the temple, and in any case, Mark's adaptation of what appears to be the same saying in the accusation against Jesus (14:58, 15:29) shows that *he*, at any rate, interpreted the saying this way, in whatever form he found it.

We are on more solid ground with Q 13:34–35, which can only refer to the Jerusalem temple. I cannot concur with Mack's interpretation of this saying as a post-70 lament over the destruction of the Temple deriving from Q's third layer of redaction (Burton L. Mack, *The Lost Gospel: The Book of Q and Christian Origins* [San Francisco:

in terms of action that embodies what Mark, at least, regards to have been his teaching. That teaching, predictably enough, is drawn from the sayings traditions to which Mark has access, whatever those traditions may be. So, once again, the teacher who has become the son of God must, necessarily, *behave* like a son of God, enacting his own divine pronouncements.[38]

A Prophet? Yes, and More Than a Prophet

The complexity of the role of John the Baptist in the Jesus tradition is enormous, and it remains an unsolved problem. Yet most scholars are convinced that much of the gospel material on John is bedrock evidence for a historical person. The Q version of John's apocalyptic preaching, for instance—even though it is singly attested, fails to conform to John's message as recounted in other sources (such as Mark and Josephus), but fits perfectly with the ideological and even stylistic tendencies of the Q^2 text in

HarperSanFrancisco, 1993], 174–75). The classification of this material as Q^3 depends upon a *thematic* approach to stratification, which is a retrograde step from Kloppenborg's *literary* methodology (see John S. Kloppenborg, *The Formation of Q* [Philadelphia: Fortress, 1987], esp. 95–101), on which Mack's stratification of Q is largely based (see *Lost Gospel*, 36–38). One must therefore prefer Kloppenborg's conclusions that Q 13:34–35 belongs to the Q^2 stage of the document's development, and perhaps (likely?) thus predates the Jewish War. (I myself would claim that even Q^3 predates the War: Q^3 4:9 shows no awareness of the temple's destruction, nor even a negative attitude toward it.) More to the point, while the saying does rather unequivocally refer to the temple, it is not at all clear that it refers to the temple's *destruction*. The saying refers to God's *abandonment* (ἰδοὺ ἀφίεται ὑμῖν ὁ οἶκος ὑμῶν) of Jerusalem and its "house," not their destruction.

    38. This tendency is already attested, albeit in germinal form, in Q^3. Here, in the temptation narrative (Q 4:1–13), Jesus is not merely engaging in an exegetical debate with ὁ διάβολος, but is being asked to *act out* the consequences of this exegesis. The devil does not ask him, for instance, whether it is appropriate to turn bread into stones, but to *do* so. Moreover, this activity is explicitly linked to Jesus's status as a "son of God" (εἰ υἱὸς εἶ τοῦ θεοῦ…). So even Q, in the successive development of its redactional layers, attests to this tendency. I am strongly disinclined to attribute this tendency to a wholly *generic* trajectory from sayings to narrative. Rather, in Q as elsewhere, the generic shift seems to be coordinated with an attribution to Jesus of greater and greater status. The more that behavior emanating from Jesus's purported teaching comes to signify an important element of identity for those who adopt or at least transmit it, the more necessary it is to inflate Jesus's status as itself an authorization for this behavior. But the more this is done, the more interest shifts to how a "Christ," or "son of man," or "son of God" behaves.

which it appears—is normally regarded as a fair summary of John's actual message.[39] So also is the case with Jesus's supposed baptism by John. Sanders is not the only one who cannot conceive of Jesus's career without this foundational event.[40] That Jesus would, or could, have been baptized by John is viewed as inherently plausible and as a good way to account for John's ubiquity in the tradition.[41] In addition, the baptism account, especially in its Matthean and Lukan versions, shows a strong sense of embarrassment at the subordination of Jesus to John and at the way the event appears to imply Jesus's sinfulness.[42] Some have even claimed that the event is multiply attested, appearing in the Gospel of John and, possibly, in Q.[43]

39. For a discussion of the historicity of this "preaching" and an argument that it is, with the exception of Q 3:16 (which has a Markan parallel), in fact a Q^2 redactional composition, see my "Redactional Fabrication and Group Legitimation." For a survey and discussion of scholarly arguments for the historicity of this material, see especially ibid., 176–77 nn. 3–4, 6.

40. See, e.g., Bornkamm, *Jesus of Nazareth*, 49; Crossan, *Historical Jesus*, 234; Stevan Davies, *Jesus the Healer: Possession, Trance, and the Origins of Christianity* (New York: Continuum, 1995), 52–53; Elisabeth Schüssler Fiorenza, *In Memory of Her: A Feminist Theological Reconstruction of Christian Origins* (New York: Crossroad, 1983), 118; Meier, *A Marginal Jew*, 2:100; James M. Robinson, "Building Blocks in the Social History of Q," in *Reimagining Christian Origins: A Colloquium Honoring Burton L. Mack*, ed. Elizabeth A. Castelli and Hal Taussig (Valley Forge, PA: Trinity Press International, 1996), 91; Sanders, *Jesus and Judaism*, 370 n. 1; Sanders, *Historical Figure of Jesus*, 93–94; Smith, *Jesus the Magician*, 8, 40–42; W. Barnes Tatum, *John the Baptist and Jesus: A Report of the Jesus Seminar* (Sonoma, CA: Polebridge, 1994), 148; Taylor, *Gospel according to St. Mark*, 158–59; Geza Vermes, *Jesus the Jew: A Historian's Reading of the Gospels* (London: Collins, 1973), 31.

41. On this ubiquity serving as evidence for an *historical* link to Jesus, see Walter Wink, *John the Baptist in the Gospel Tradition* (Cambridge: Cambridge University Press, 1968), 18–19, 23–26, 107–13.

42. So, e.g., James H. Charlesworth, *Jesus within Judaism: New Light from Exciting Archaeological Discoveries* (Garden City, NY: Doubleday, 1988), 14–15; Crossan, *Historical Jesus*, 232–34; Joseph A. Fitzmyer, *The Gospel according to Luke I–IX*, AB 28 (Garden City, NY: Doubleday, 1981), 479–83; Meier, *A Marginal Jew*, 2:101–3; Sanders, *Historical Figure of Jesus*, 93–94; Tatum, *John the Baptist and Jesus*, 148–49; Taylor, *Gospel according to St. Mark*, 156–57, 159. See also the summary of this argument offered by Morton S. Enslin, "John and Jesus," *ZNW* 66 (1975): 8–9.

43. On Johannine attestation of the baptism, see e.g. Meier, *A Marginal Jew*, 1:44–52 and 2:103–5; Tatum, *John the Baptist and Jesus*, 149. On the existence of a baptism account in Q, thus providing multiple independent attestation (by most accounts)

Not one of these arguments stands up to scrutiny. Again, because my focus here is Mark and not the historical Jesus, this is not the place for a detailed discussion of the problem. Here it will have to suffice to assert that, in fact, the story as we have it is *not* even marginally plausible,[44] is *not* multiply attested,[45] and is not particularly embarrassing, at least not

---

alongside Mark, see e.g. Meier, *A Marginal Jew*, 2:103; T. W. Manson, *The Teaching of Jesus: Studies in Its Form and Content* (Cambridge: Cambridge University Press, 1963), 32 n.1; James M. Robinson, "The Sayings Gospel Q," in *The Four Gospels 1992: Festschrift Frans Neirynck*, ed. Frans van Segbroeck et al., BETL 100, 3 vols. (Leuven: Leuven University Press, 1992), 1:382–85; Robinson, "Building Blocks in the Social History of Q," 91–92, 108–9, nn. 20–21 (and literature cited there); Tatum, *John the Baptist and Jesus*, 149. Crossan, *Historical Jesus*, 438, asserts even wider independent attestation, citing Gospel of the Hebrews (2) and Ign. *Eph.* 18.2d alongside synoptic and dependent accounts.

44. I claim elsewhere ("Major Episodes in the Biography of Jesus," 204) that: "the story as we have it is completely implausible. We are not here told by Mark simply that Jesus was baptized by John, but (a) that John was sent to prepare the way; (b) that John preached the coming of the Messiah; (c) that Jesus appeared to John immediately after this prediction; (d) that when Jesus came out of the water the sky was 'ripped apart' (*schizomenos*); (e) that the spirit descended as a dove and lighted on him; and (f) that he heard a voice from heaven proclaiming him God's beloved son. All six of these details are plainly theologically tendentious; the last three are supernatural." This argument requires some qualification, of course; I have to agree with Davies (*Jesus the Healer*, 17) that the presence of supernatural or otherwise implausible details cannot be used to prove that the event in question did not happen; these details may be regarded, precisely, as *embellishments* (cf. Bultmann, *History of the Synoptic Tradition*, 247–48; Bultmann, *Theology of the New Testament*, trans. Kendrick Grobel, 2 vols [New York: Charles Scribner's Sons, 1951–1955], 1:26–27; Dibelius, *From Tradition to Gospel*, 271–72, 274). My point is simply that the narrative itself, as we have it, is not credible.

45. As I assert above, I do not regard John to be independent of Mark, and so cannot see his version of the baptism story as independent attestation of the event. Strangely enough, John does not actually recount this event at all. In John 1:32–33 he has the descent of the spirit as a pigeon onto Jesus and asserts that this is evidence that Jesus is God's son, but this takes place as Jesus is walking around (1:29: βλέπει τὸν Ἰησοῦν ἐρχόμενον πρὸς αὐτόν; 1:36: ἐμβλέψας τῷ Ἰησοῦ περιπατοῦντι), not as, or after, he is baptized. Of course, the natural explanation for this is that John, like Matthew and Luke, was "embarrassed" by the story, and so used its theophanic details while omitting the baptism itself. This may be so, but the fact remains that we cannot deduce multiple attestation from a source that does not actually attest to the event. If John is independent evidence of anything, it is that the supernatural "embellishments" are key to the story. But the issue is moot, from my perspective: John *did* know a story of Jesus's baptism—from Mark.

to Mark.[46] More importantly, the story shows very strong literary and the-

---

The issue of a Q baptism is much more complex and has been forcefully debated. Those who assert that Q did contain an account of Jesus's baptism regard it as another case (cf., e.g., Q 10:1–16 // Mark 6:7–13) in which Mark/Q overlap of similar material may obscure Q's original extent. The evidence that this is the case with the baptism is primarily found in a series of three "minor agreements" between Matthew and Luke against Mark in this episode. Secondarily, it is supported by the claim that some establishment of Jesus's status as "son of God" must be offered prior to the temptation account, which assumes this status. See, among others, Meier, *A Marginal Jew*, 2:103, and especially Robinson, "The Sayings Gospel Q," 382–85; Robinson, "Building Blocks in the Social History of Q," 91–92, 108–9. The latter argument is nonsensical: Q requires no narrative establishment of its *other* christological titles, and in any case the temptation account *itself* establishes Jesus's status as a "son of God." The baptism is actually made superfluous by the temptation, rather than required by it. The alleged minor agreements between Matthew and Luke in this account are not particularly close, and all are explicable as independent redactional alterations. Moreover, the baptism account would be the only pericope in Q to be established on the basis of minor agreements. It is not only an idiosyncratic reconstruction, but also a *dangerous* one: once the door is open to reconstructing Q on the basis of, or as an explanation of, minor agreements, which are so extensive throughout the synoptic tradition, Q rapidly expands to become an Ur-Matthew. This, of course, eliminates the rationale for Q altogether. Against a Q baptism, see Ron Cameron, "'What Have You Come Out to See?' Characterizations of John and Jesus in the Gospels," *Semeia* 49 (1990): 36–37; Crossan, *Historical Jesus*, 233; John S. Kloppenborg, *Q Parallels: Synopsis, Critical Notes, and Concordance* (Sonoma, CA: Polebridge, 1988), 16; Kloppenborg, *Formation of Q*, 84–85 and n. 157; and Frans Neirynck, "The Minor Agreements and Q," in *The Gospel behind the Gospels: Current Studies on Q*, ed. Ronald A. Piper (Leiden: Brill, 1995), 65–67.

The kerygmatic formulations of Acts cannot be cited as independent attestation (cf. Bultmann, *History of the Synoptic Tradition*, 247 n. 2), since the author of Acts was, of course, very well acquainted with Mark. Thomas has no account of Jesus's baptism by John nor makes any reference to it.

46. This is a point often missed by those who claim the account embarrassing: obviously *Mark* did not find it especially so. The story in fact presents Jesus as engaging in behavior that certainly marked some segments of the later Christian movement (i.e., baptism), and thus serving as a model and originary point for this behavior. Moreover, the account serves to link Jesus to what appears to have been a broad and popular "revival movement" (cf. Josephus, *Ant.* 18.5.2 §§116–119); it is thus no more "embarrassing" than Jesus's visits to the temple for festivals in the various canonical gospels. Finally, Josephus's testimony makes it clear that John the Baptist was an extraordinarily popular and well-known figure. The *invention* of various types of association between him and Jesus, therefore, can only have served, initially, to *increase* Jesus's prestige. Similarly, Enslin, "John and Jesus," 9–10. The perception that the event

matic links with the rest of Mark's Gospel,[47] particularly the transfiguration (9:2–13) and the death on the cross (15:33–39). In all three episodes,
Mark is commenting on Jesus's identity, and in all three Jesus is explicitly
identified as a "son of God." This in itself is an interesting pattern. So far as
I can tell, the designation υἱὸς τοῦ θεοῦ appears rather infrequently in Mark,
especially when compared with designations such as υἱὸς τοῦ ἀνθρώπου. It
occurs (or is implied, as in God himself referring to Jesus as τὸν υἱόν μου)
in the three key episodes of Jesus's baptism, transfiguration, and death.[48]
Arguably, it also occurs in Mark's incipit: "The Gospel of Jesus Christ, a
son of God."[49] That each episode is critically important for Mark, occur-

---

decreased Jesus's status, or implied his sinfulness, apparently only developed gradually,
as later writers (Matthew, Luke, John) had the opportunity to reflect on Mark's story,
and as Jesus's uniquely high status came more to be taken for granted. An excellent
discussion of the applicability (or lack thereof) of the "embarrassment" criterion to
Jesus's baptism in Mark can be found in Richard E. DeMaris, "The Baptism of Jesus:
A Ritual-Critical Approach," in *The Social Setting of Jesus and the Gospels*, ed. Wolfgang Stegemann, Bruce J. Malina, and Gerd Theissen (Minneapolis: Fortress, 2002),
142–43.

47. So also especially Leif Vaage, "Bird-Watching at the Baptism of Jesus: Early
Christian Myth-Making in Mark 1:9–11," in Castelli and Taussig, *Reimagining Christian Origins*, 285–86. Both Vaage and Mack (*Myth of Innocence*, 54; *The Lost Gospel*,
155) argue on this basis, as I do here, that Mark's baptism account is in fact a Markan
invention. See also DeMaris, "The Baptism of Jesus," 138–44, for a sympathetic summary of the arguments against the historicity of Mark's account of the baptism.

48. The term, implied or explicit, does occur elsewhere but only infrequently. In
addition to its key biographical usages at Mark's introduction/baptism (1:11), mid-
point/transfiguration (9:7), and death/conclusion (15:39), always from someone other
than Jesus himself (and two of three times directly from God), the attribution is also
applied to Jesus twice by demons (3:11; 5:7; cf. also the demonic designation υἱὲ Δαυίδ,
twice in 10:47–48), once by his opponents as a question/accusation (14:61), and once,
implicitly, by Jesus himself (13:32: οὐδεὶς οἶδεν, οὐδὲ οἱ ἄγγελοι ἐν οὐρανῷ οὐδὲ ὁ υἱός, εἰ
μὴ ὁ πατήρ).

49. The text is not secure: some manuscripts omit the designation υἱοῦ θεοῦ. On
the originality of this phrase, see Ronald F. Hock, "Social Experience and the Beginning of the Gospel of Mark," in Castelli and Taussig, *Reimagining Christian Origins*,
325 n. 47; Robert H. Gundry, *Mark: A Commentary on His Apology for the Cross*
(Grand Rapids: Eerdmans, 1993), 33. Cf. Vincent Taylor, *The Text of the New Testament: A Short Introduction* (New York: St. Martin's, 1961), 82. The phrase υἱοῦ θεοῦ,
however, is bracketed in UBS[3] and NA[27], and a strong case against it is made by Bart
D. Ehrman, *The Orthodox Corruption of Scripture: The Effect of Early Christological
Controversies on the Text of the New Testament* (New York: Oxford University Press,
1993), 72–75. My own inclination is to regard the arguments for retention as most per-

ring at a key moment in the narrative, makes Mark's consistent choice of the term υἱὸς (τοῦ) θεοῦ in each instance—and its general avoidance elsewhere—stand out.

Moreover, this designation is not the only feature that links these episodes. Various scholars have suggested a linkage between the *tearing* (σχιζομένους τοὺς οὐρανοὺς) of the sky at Jesus's baptism and the tearing (τὸ καταπέτασμα τοῦ ναοῦ ἐσχίσθη εἰς δύο) of the temple veil at Jesus's death.[50] The linkage is underscored and supported by Mark's unusual word choice in 1:10 to describe an opening of the heavens as a "tearing." Discomfort with Mark's usage here not only dictated the "minor agreement" reflected in Matthew's and Luke's common replacement of the verb to the more usual ἀνοίγω (Matt 3:16: ἠνεῴχθησαν; Luke 3:21: ἀνεῳχθῆναι) or the scribal corruption of the text of Mark in some manuscripts to reflect this more ordinary wording.[51] But it has even influenced the English translations of Mark, which render σχιζομένους here as "open" (for example, Mark 1:10, RSV: "he saw the heavens opened"). David Ulansey has lent additional support to a linkage between the tearing of the temple veil and the tearing of the sky at Jesus's baptism by drawing attention to Josephus's description of the *outer* veil of the temple in *J. W.* 5.5.4 §212–214: "On this tapestry was portrayed a panorama of the heavens."[52] Ulansey concludes that:

---

suasive. See especially the conclusions of Alexander Globe, "The Caesarean Omission of the Phrase 'Son of God' in Mark 1:1," *HTR* 75 (1982): 218: "Five types of evidence point to the genuineness of the phrase "Son of God" in Mark 1:1. First, the textual witness to the longer reading is impressively varied in terms of text type and geographical distribution, from the second century on. By contrast, the shorter variant is attested by only a handful of Caesarean and Western witnesses, mainly from the third to the fifth centuries. Second, the limited attestation of the shorter text suggests that it originated as a scribal omission by *homoioteleuton*, which never gained wide currency. Third, the grammatical form of the Greek phrase υἱοῦ θεοῦ, without articles, suggests Markan rather than scribal authorship. Fourth, the phrase 'Son of God' summarizes an important theme of Mark's gospel. Lastly, the literary form of the entire first verse parallels other superscriptions found in Mark's most important model, the LXX translation of Old Testament scripture."

50. For a listing, see David Ulansey, "The Heavenly Veil Torn: Mark's Cosmic *Inclusio*," *JBL* 110 (1991): 123 n.1.

51. The text reads ἠνύγμενους, e.g., in codex Bezae (D), and such a reading is also implied in some old Latin and Georgian versions.

52. On the debate over whether the curtain in question is intended by Mark to refer to the inner (before the *sanctum sanctorum*) or outer (before the front doors of the temple) curtain of the temple, see Ulansey, "The Heavenly Veil Torn," 124. While

Upon encountering Mark's statement that "the veil of the temple was torn in two from top to bottom," any of his readers who had ever seen the temple or heard it described would instantly have seen in their mind's eye an image of *the heavens being torn* and would immediately have been reminded of Mark's earlier description of the heavens being torn at the baptism. This can hardly be a coincidence: the symbolic parallel is so striking that Mark must have consciously intended it.[53]

One can go further than Ulansey has on this point, while buttressing his basic insight. The story of Jesus's death is replete with apocalyptic allusions,[54] most particularly to the discourse in Mark 13 but in other respects as well. As Jesus is crucified, the sun is blotted out (15:33; compare with 13:24), the temple is destroyed symbolically (15:38; compare with 13:2; 14:58),[55] and Elijah is invoked (15:35; compare with 9:4, 11–13). Thus the invocation of a tearing of the sky here, in the form of a curtain embroidered with a depiction of the heavens, works well for Mark's agenda, not only forming an *inclusio* with the baptism account, but also echoing Jesus's apocalyptic words in 13:25—"and the stars will be falling from the heaven, and the powers in the heavens will be shaken"—and thus investing the crucifixion of Jesus with an apocalyptic significance, a foreshadowing of the judgment it evokes as its consequence.

The features shared by the baptism and the death on the cross are not limited to the tearing of the heavens and the identification of Jesus as God's son. In addition, the two episodes have in common: (1) references

---

LSJ (s.v. καταπέτασμα) claims that καταπέτασμα refers properly to the inner veil, with κάλυμμα designating the outer curtain, it is quite explicit in Josephus's description that the outer curtain is meant, and the word used by Josephus for this curtain is, indeed, καταπέτασμα.

53. Ulansey, "Heavenly Veil Torn," 125.

54. See Mack, *Myth of Innocence*, 296: "The narrative structure [of the account of the crucifixion in Mark] is clearly that of an apocalyptic event of six hours duration divided into halves by darkness over the land for the second three hours. The times are given together with the events that occurred: third hour (9:00 AM), crucifixion; sixth hour (noon), darkness over the land; ninth hour (3:00 PM), cry, exhalation, rending of the temple's curtain. The symmetry of threes is obvious, as is the correlation of the crucifixion events with those transpiring in the natural and institutional orders of things."

55. For this interpretation of Mark 15:38, see, e.g., Johannes Schreiber, *Theologie des Vertrauens: Eine redaktionsgeschichtliche Untersuchung des Markusevangeliums* (Hamburg: Furche-Verlag, 1967), 34–41, 66–82.

to speaking;[56] (2) references to descent;[57] (3) references or allusions to the figure of Elijah;[58] and (4) references to spirit, with Jesus receiving the spirit (τὸ πνεῦμα, 1:10) at the moment of his baptism and expelling it (ἐξέπνευσεν, 15:37, 39) at the moment of his death.[59] Indeed, not only are these features shared by the two episodes, but both have the same overarching *sequence* of these elements. The overall pattern common to both stories thus includes a detailed series of verbal correspondences, sequences and motifs, and overall structure. The overall symmetry of the two texts—each representing a critical moment in the story of Jesus's activity, essentially its beginning and its ending—is quite striking. The following chart represents an attempt to clarify the extent of this parallelism:

---

56. In the declaration of Jesus to be Son of God, spoken by God in 1:11 and the centurion in 15:39. Note also that at Mark 1:11 there is a φωνή … ἐκ τῶν οὐρανῶν; at Mark 15:37 there is a φωνὴν μεγάλην. Indeed, the parallelism extends beyond this: John the Baptist, at Mark 1:3, is presented in terms of his φωνὴ βοῶντος (βοάω), followed by the scriptural quotation/allusion that John "shouts" (Mark 1:3; cf. Isa 40:3—of course, here the shouting is itself part of the quotation). At Jesus's crucifixion, prior to his death-cry, Jesus follows the same pattern, "shouting" with a "great voice" (Mark 15:34: ἐβόησεν ὁ Ἰησοῦς φωνῇ μεγάλῃ, the content of which shout is also comprised by a scriptural quotation/allusion (Mark 15:34, cf. Ps 22:1). Thus, with respect to voices and shouts, both pericopes contain the same overarching pattern. See further below.

It may be notable, too, that elsewhere in Mark, those who cry out φωνῇ μεγάλῃ include the unclean spirits, who are among those few (God, Jesus himself, the centurion) who recognize Jesus's identity as a son of God; see Mark 1:26 and especially 5:7.

57. In Mark 1:10 the spirit *descends*; in 15:38 the temple curtain is torn *from top to bottom*.

58. In the form of John the Baptist in 1:9, an identification emphasized by Mark's description of John's clothing and deportment in 1:6 and his allusion to Mal 3:1 in 1:2 (cf. Mal 4:5). This identification of John with Elijah is confirmed by Jesus's words in Mark 9:11–13.

59. So Ulansey, "Heavenly Veil Torn," 123. Cf. S. Motyer, "The Rending of the Veil: A Markan Pentecost," *NTS* 33 (1987): 155. Note that Sharyn Dowd and Elizabeth Struthers Malbon, "The Significance of Jesus' Death in Mark: Narrative Context and Authorial Audience," *JBL* 125 (2006): 273–74, highlight Mark's scriptural and textual rationale for this linkage, thus adding further confirmation to these claims, i.e., that the identification of Jesus as "my beloved son" at the baptism is intended to evoke God's words to Abraham about Isaac in Gen 22:2. This observation not only underscores the extent to which Mark links the baptism with Jesus's death, but also assumes the same kind of detailed, allusive, intertextual mode of composition for Mark that I am arguing in this paper.

Item	Introduction/Baptism (1:1–11)	Conclusion/Death (15:33–39)
shouting voice (βοάω+ φωνή)	1:3: John is a φωνὴ βοῶντος in the wilderness.	15:34a: At the ninth hour, ἐβόησεν ὁ Ἰησοῦς φωνῇ μεγάλῃ.
scriptural quotation as content of "shouting"	1:2–3: The φωνὴ βοῶντος is embedded in the quotation itself; Isa 40:3 (LXX): "A voice of one shouting in the desert, 'Make ready.'"	15:34b: Jesus cries out from Ps 22:1a: "My God, my God, why have you forsaken me?"
allusion to Elijah ★	1:6: John as Elijah: allusion to 2 Kgs 1:8 in John's ζώνην δερματίνην.[60]	15:35–36: ἴδε Ἠλίαν φωνεῖ.
tearing (sky) (σχίζω)	1:10b: εἶδεν σχιζομένους τοὺς οὐρανοὺς.	15:38: τὸ καταπέτασμα τοῦ ναοῦ ἐσχίσθη.
ascent/ descent (ἀνα … κατά)	1:10a,c: Jesus is ἀναβαίνων from the water, and the spirit καταβαῖνον on him.	15:38 The temple curtain is torn ἄνωθεν ἕως κάτω.
receipt/loss of spirit/breath (πνευ-)	1:10c: Descent of τὸ πνεῦμα onto Jesus.	15:37 (and 15:39): Jesus breathes his last/expires: ἐξέπνευσεν.
a second reference to a φωνή	1:11: A voice (φωνή) comes from heaven.	15:37: Jesus cries out a second time, offering a φωνὴν μεγάλην.
Jesus identified as son of God	1:11: Voice from heaven says to Jesus, σὺ εἶ ὁ υἱός μου.	15:39: Centurion says of Jesus, οὗτος ὁ ἄνθρωπος υἱὸς θεοῦ ἦν.
demonstrative appendix	1:12–13: Temptation narrative.	16:1–8: Empty tomb.

If this outline is convincing,[61] we are left with four options, only one of which, in my opinion, is ultimately persuasive. The first option is that

---

60. For Mark 1:6 as an allusion to Elijah, see Taylor, *Gospel according to St. Mark*, 156: "The reference to the girdle is probably intended to recall the description of Elijah in 4 Kgdms. i. 8,7 Ἀνὴρ δασὺς καὶ ζώνην δερματίνην περιεζωσμένος τὴν ὀσφὺν αὐτοῦ." See also C. E. B. Cranfield, *The Gospel according to St Mark* (Cambridge: Cambridge University Press, 1966), 47: "Zech. xiii.4 is evidence that the 'hairy mantle' was the sign of a prophet in Israel. The description of John here is no doubt meant to suggest the identification with Elijah (cf. II Kgs i.8)."

61. Note that Vernon K. Robbins, "Last Meal: Preparation, Betrayal, and Absence," in *The Passion in Mark: Studies on Mark 14–16*, ed. Werner H. Kelber (Philadelphia: Fortress, 1976), 23, finds similarly detailed parallel structures in Mark: in his example,

Mark is using the same source for both stories, a source which constructed the stories according to this common pattern. The second is that one or both stories are traditional and that Mark has modified them extensively to create this pattern. The third is that one of the two stories was traditional in essentially the form in which it appears and that Mark patterned the other story after it. Fourth and finally, the similar structures may suggest that both stories were composed by Mark, both therefore reflecting his stylistic, compositional, and ideological proclivities. This last option is supported, I think, not only by the key position that each story occupies in Mark's narrative, but also by the very strong "fit" each story has with Mark's literary/mythic agenda. Both episodes—again, marking the opening and closing of Jesus's career as presented in Mark—quite densely cluster Mark's favorite motifs (especially the motifs of divine sonship, of Elijah, and of celestial turmoil; also those of Jesus's suffering and of the destruction of the temple, at *least* in the death scene[62]). If indeed we are dealing here with a "source," it is a source so close to Mark's own literary patterns and ideological orientation as to be an *Ur-Markus*. I would just as soon conclude that our *Ur-Markus* here is Mark itself.

Nor are these the only two Markan stories that contain such features. The transfiguration (Mark 9:2–13) has the same cluster of motifs, if not so densely crafted. Like both baptism and death, albeit less obviously, the story occurs at a significant point in Mark's narrative, coming immediately after Jesus's first "passion prediction" and immediately prior to his departure from Galilee toward Jerusalem. The episode shares with both baptism and death episodes an identification of Jesus as the son of God—here, as in the baptism, offered by God himself, and coming from the sky (9:7: καὶ ἐγένετο φωνὴ ἐκ τῆς νεφέλης· οὗτός ἐστιν ὁ υἱός μου ὁ ἀγαπητός; cf. the almost identical 1:11: καὶ φωνὴ ἐγένετο ἐκ τῶν οὐρανῶν· σὺ εἶ ὁ υἱός μου ὁ

---

between the preparation for Jesus's entry to Jerusalem (Mark 11:1–6) and the preparations for the Last Supper (Mark 11:13–16).

62. Though I think a case could be made for both motifs being implicit at the baptism scene as well. The destruction of the temple, as claimed above, may be foreshadowed by the skies tearing, which Mark links to the tearing of the temple veil. And Mark *appears* to associate baptism with suffering and death (cf. Paul for a similar association), as suggested by Mark 10:38: "But Jesus said to them, 'You do not know what you are asking. Are you able to drink the cup that I drink, or to be baptized with the baptism with which I am baptized?'" This question is followed up a few lines later (10:45) with the assertion that the "Son of Man came ... to give his life as a ransom for many."

ἀγαπητός). Here also, as with baptism and death scenes, Elijah makes an appearance (9:4); and afterwards this appearance becomes the occasion for reflection on Elijah's identity and eschatological role (9:11–13), a discussion reinforcing Elijah's identity with John ("Elijah has come, and they did to him whatever they pleased"), and thus also introducing a mutually reinforcing association between John, Elijah, and eschatological consummation, an association already implied in the Baptist's introduction in 1:2–3. The way verse 9:13 also reminds the reader of how John met his humiliating and cruel death (as recounted in Mark 6:17–29) provides yet another chain of mutually reinforcing linkages or literary echoes: it foreshadows Jesus's own death and thus reinforces the connection between suffering, scriptural prediction, and eschatological consummation. The story thus acts as a pivot in which motifs from the first half of Mark's narrative (particularly those associated with John and Elijah) and from the latter half are drawn together and shown to relate to one another. Of course, the transfiguration contains celestial imagery of its own: the cloud that overshadows them (9:7), which in its turn reminds one of the splitting sky from the baptism (1:10) and the darkened sun from the death scene (15:33), all of which finds clearest expression in the apocalyptic discourse of chapter 13: "*the sun will be darkened*, and the moon will not give its light, and the stars will be falling from heaven, and *the powers in the heavens will be shaken*. And then they will see the Son of Man coming in *clouds*" (13:24–26).[63] Finally, it is notable that the transfiguration episode shares with the death scene the same interest in the numbers six and three. Just as Jesus's death is described, rather gratuitously, in terms of the third and sixth hours, the transfiguration occurs "after *six* days" (9:2), and as it occurs Peter offers to make *three* booths (9:5).[64] Even the ascent (ἀνά-) and

---

63. That the apocalyptic consummation predicted straightforwardly in chapter thirteen is indeed intended to be alluded to here is confirmed by fact that the story opens with the assertion that "There are some standing here who will not taste death before they see that the kingdom of God has come with power" (9:1). It seems most natural to regard the transfiguration, therefore, as precisely and literally a fulfillment of that prediction.

64. Both of these figures in the transfiguration story are much more gratuitous and much less "natural" than the notice of the times of day given in the crucifixion story, although the latter also seem to serve more a symbolic than a strictly narrative function (see Mack's comments, quoted above, n. 54). One must therefore conclude that these numeric references are deliberate and that they have some symbolic force (cf. also the likely symbolic use of numbers in Mark's twice-repeated miraculous feed-

descent (κατά-) motif appears: Jesus takes his disciples *up* the mountain (9:2: <u>ἀναφέρει</u> αὐτοὺς εἰς ὄρος) at the opening of the story, and *down* the mountain at its conclusion (9:9: <u>κατα</u>βαινόντων αὐτῶν ἐκ τοῦ ὄρους).

The point here is simply that the literary features of Mark's story of Jesus's baptism by John are so densely and thoroughly Markan, and so closely interwoven with two other key episodes in Mark's Gospel, that—scholarly inertia notwithstanding—it is difficult to draw any conclusion *except* that Mark composed the story himself, and essentially from scratch. This is of course precisely what we might expect: a more heavy-handed redactional contribution at the most narratively significant junctures of the author's story. Thus it is precisely at the unique (and singly attested) moments in which Mark's actual chronological and connected narrative of Jesus develops—what Mack calls framework stories—that we would be most likely to, and in fact do, encounter Mark at his most creative. Far from being a source of "indisputable facts" about the historical Jesus, Mark's framework stories, including the baptism, are instead excellent examples of Mark's own mythmaking in its purest and its most sophisticated form.

As with the temple tantrum and the cursing of the fig tree, the ultimate "source" of Mark's story of the baptism—aside, of course, from Mark's own imagination and agenda—is to be found in the sayings tradition and, more specifically, in a reinterpretation of sayings material in light of subsequent events. In the case of the temple tantrum, Jesus is made to *enact* his own traditional teaching.[65] This move is stimulated not only by the inflation of Jesus's authority but also by the actual destruction of the temple in Mark's recent past, an event which put a different cast on traditional say-

---

ing stories [6:44: twelve baskets; 8:8: seven baskets; to which he again draws explicit attention in 8:19–21], and, most obviously of all, in his insistence on *twelve* disciples), perhaps related to apocalyptic scenarios, perhaps linked to the repeated insistence on Jesus's resurrection on the *third* day. I suspect that the fact that the transfiguration occurs six days after an apocalyptic prediction (i.e., in 9:1), that the sun is darkened at the sixth hour, and so on, would allow someone with the time, inclination, and imagination to do so, to actually get at *why* Mark is introducing these numeric references and what he is using them to convey. For my purposes here, however, I am simply trying to show the extent of the literary and thematic linkages between widely separated episodes in Mark, and so, after noting these numeric correspondences, can confess my bewilderment as to what they actually signify.

65. Again, I insist that this teaching need not be traced back to the historical Jesus. The point is only that it was available to Mark *as* Jesus-tradition at the time his gospel was composed.

ings of Jesus about the temple. In the case of the baptism, the "subsequent event" is the practice of baptism itself, which Mark does *appear* to allude to (10:39). The traditional sayings material reinterpreted and narrativized in light of this "new" practice is that which—again, multiply attested among a range of independent sources and appearing in a variety of forms—presents Jesus as commenting on John and/or comparing himself to John.

Perhaps the most enigmatic of these sayings is the peculiar isolated saying that both praises John and simultaneously excludes him from the kingdom of God, occurring in both Q (7:28) and in the Gospel of Thomas (46).[66] But more important for our purposes are those sayings associated with the Jesus-tradition that cast John as a precursor figure. Two such sayings are multiply attested and, since they appear in Mark, were obviously available to him. One is the saying attributed to *John* that a stronger/coming one will appear after him.[67] Obviously, simply by placing such a saying in the mouth of John, he is cast as a precursor figure. It is not at all clear *to what or whom* he serves as a precursor, but in a context in which Jesus is honored in some fashion or another, it is likely to be quickly taken

---

66. The Gospel of Thomas version reads: "Jesus said, 'From Adam to John the Baptist, among those born of women, no one is so much greater than John the Baptist that his eyes should not be averted [or: broken]. But I have said that whoever among you becomes a child will recognize the kingdom and will become greater than John.'"

67. Mark 1:7–8 and Q 3:16. In the material where Mark and Q strictly parallel one another (i.e., leaving aside the additional materials in Q 3:7–9), Mark's and Q's versions appear to differ in two key ways. By virtue of fairly slight alterations in syntax, Q manages to cast the figure for whom John stands as a precursor as ὁ ἐρχόμενος; Mark presents this figure as ὁ ἰσχυρότερός. In my view, the Markan wording is likely to be the more original here: Q uses ὁ ἐρχόμενος in key locations elsewhere (7:19: John's question, σὺ εἶ ὁ ἐρχόμενος; and 13:35: εὐλογημένος ὁ ἐρχόμενος) as something of a "christological" title, and so seems likely to have altered the original wording to fit with this usage elsewhere in the document. See now the brilliant discussion in Daniel A. Smith, *The Postmortem Vindication of Jesus in the Sayings Gospel Q*, LNTS 338 (London: T&T Clark, 2006), 112–16 and throughout. The other key difference is in the description of the nature of this figure's baptism: Is it "with holy spirit" (so Mark 1:8, ἐν πνεύματι ἁγίῳ) or "with holy spirit/wind *and fire*" (so Q 3:16, ἐν πνεύματι ἁγίῳ καὶ πυρί)? Again, my inclination here is to regard Q's wording as secondary. Q's version fits with the additional material tacked on to John's speech in Q 3:17, where the metaphor of *threshing* is used of the coming figure, invoking wind (πνεῦμα) to separate chaff from wheat, and fire to consume the chaff. Thus I see the addition of "and fire" in Q 3:16 as a secondary effort to conform the saying to the threshing metaphor that follows. See my comments in "Redactional Fabrication and Group Legitimation," 169–74.

for granted that the figure in question is Jesus. All that is required, then, for this saying—predating both Q and Mark[68]—to imply in itself both that John was a precursor to Jesus and that his significant activity revolves around baptism is the simple attribution of the saying to John ("John said …") and its circulation among followers of Jesus. Beyond the simplest *chreia* form, no narrative at all is required.[69]

The second important traditional item is the application to John, in one way or another, of the odd mixed quotation of Mal 3:1 and Exod 23:20: "Behold I send my messenger before your face, who will prepare your way before you."[70] It is notable that while Q and Mark frame this quotation differently, they agree not only in its wording but in its application to John and even in the use of γέγραπται to introduce the quotation. For Q, this is a saying, attributed to Jesus, about John the Baptist. In Mark, it is an authorial description of John. It is entirely unclear to me which of these two forms, if either, is more original, and in any case it hardly matters.[71] The point is that the assertion that this composite quotation applies to John the Baptist serves again to cast John in the role of precursor independent of any actual narration of such a role.

Once again, a tradition-historical trajectory can be constructed here, though, as always, without prejudice to the question whether that trajectory need be rooted in or traced to the historical Jesus at all. Individual and rather enigmatic sayings attributed to Jesus in the sayings tradition refer to John in various ways, although without necessarily implying any contact between the two men, nor, explicitly, any precursor role on John's part. Such sayings include especially Q 7:28/Gos. Thom. 46 ("Among those born of women none is greater than John. Yet the least significant in God's

---

68. On the assumption that the two are independent of one another.

69. Both Mark 1:7–8 and Q 3:16 attribute this saying directly to John. Note that both versions of the saying imply in and of themselves, without need for further narrative elaboration (beyond the attribution to John), that John serves as a precursor to someone or something. Thus the role of John as a precursor is already established in this doubly attested saying, quite apart from any narrative context. Note also that the saying—again, in itself and without any need for narrative illustration—links John to the act of baptism.

70. Q 7:27 and Mark 1:2. The quotations are verbatim identical, except for Q's addition of "before you" (ἔμπροσθέν σου) at the very end of the quotation, absent in Mark.

71. Each version, it appears to me, is dictated by the genre of work in which it appears. Q, as a collection of Jesus's sayings, makes the attribution a saying of Jesus; Mark, as a narrative, makes the attribution as part of a narrative introduction to John.

kingdom is more than he"[72]) and the singly attested Q 16:16 ("The law and the prophets were until John. From then on the kingdom of God is violated and the violent plunder it"). Both sayings do roughly the same thing: they praise John as an extraordinary or unique figure, and then go on to relativize him vis-à-vis the kingdom of God. This serves two functions. Its main intention, it seems to me, is to inflate the prestige of the βασιλεία attributed to Jesus, both by *associating* it with John and by claiming for it an even higher (or "more unique") status. But in addition, the sayings isolate John as a pivotal figure in some (unspecified, implicit) way, somehow betwixt the past, on the one hand ("among those born of women," "the law and the prophets"), and the *novum* implied by the kingdom, on the other.

It is thus easy for me to imagine the formation of sayings like these (whether by Jesus or others) as myth-making efforts to support the social formation identified as the βασιλεία τοῦ θεοῦ, asserting its novelty over against the past and simultaneously establishing a kind of pedigree by association with John the Baptist.[73] But the nature of the sayings, in turn, offers its own impulsion to view John as a turning point, a pivot. And this view, in turn, requires clarification. "How was John a turning point?" ancient authors might well have asked. "Well, he was a precursor: this is he about whom it was written...." Clarifying John's initially rationalizing role in terms of a specified function as a precursor to Jesus (which specification, in fact, accomplished the inflation of Jesus's authority and his pedigree even more effectively than the earlier sayings about John) is supported by appeal to authority: either the authority of scripture, which is applied to John (whether as an exegetical assertion or as a claim attributed to Jesus) or the authority of John's own self-understanding, so that now John speaks directly to the double-edged motif of his own simultaneous

---

72. The Gospel of Thomas version differs somewhat, but the basic point appears to be similar to that of Q.

73. This scenario can be imagined with or without any input from the historical Jesus. At the popular level, John appears to have been a well-known, prominent, prestigious figure in Galilee (see Josephus, *Ant.* 18.5.2 §§116–119). Thus it would make sense for Jesus to have compared his own agenda (whatever it was) to John's work as a known touchstone and basis for comparison. But it makes at least as much sense for early tradents of Jesus's sayings to have made the comparison to John as a way of anchoring or inflating the authority of Jesus and his message. What is important here is that the motivation to appeal to John is comprehensible enough without any need for actual contact between Jesus and John, nor indeed any Christian contact with "disciples" of John the Baptist.

authority and relativization over against Jesus: "I baptize you with water, but the stronger one...."

The next stage in the trajectory is the creation, emendation, or new attribution of sayings in such a way as to further retrench or clarify the relationship between Jesus and John. This is not a significant feature in Mark, but does occur quite prominently in Q.[74] The redaction of Q essentially invents John's apocalyptic speech in Q 3:7–9, and amplifies the traditional baptist saying in Q 3:16 (and its parallel in Mark 1:8) by the addition of verse 17, making of a single saying a more extended "speech."[75] The speech of course serves to amplify what the initial saying already suggested: that John's preaching is *like* that of Jesus,[76] and that nonetheless Jesus somehow outdoes John.[77] Q also has created a cluster of John-related sayings (7:19–

---

74. But see Mark 6:14–15 (narrative); 9:11–13 (sayings).

75. For this argument, see Arnal, "Redactional Fabrication and Group Legitimation."

76. The apocalyptic motifs scattered throughout John's speech in Q 3:7–9, 16–17 cohere perfectly with the Q[2] version of Jesus's message. Even among those who doubt that the historical Jesus was an apocalyptist, and view Q's redaction as essentially having invented this orientation, it is still often assumed that John the Baptist was an apocalyptist (see especially James M. Robinson, "The Q Trajectory: Between John and Matthew Via Jesus," in *The Sayings Gospel Q*, ed. Christof Heil and Joseph Verheyden [Leuven: Leuven University Press, 2005], 285–307), and essentially *only* on the basis of the unquestioned historicity of Q 3:7–9, 16–17. Yet this material is singly attested, and neither the Gospel of Mark nor the Gospel of Thomas nor in fact Josephus presents an image of John as an apocalyptic preacher. It makes *much* more sense—especially once we have taken the step of viewing Q[2]'s apocalypticism as a rationalizing strategy—to see this redactional version of an apocalyptic John as a further effort to link him to Jesus, and to further justify this "new" presentation of an apocalyptic Jesus, as well as to clarify and define exactly how John's preaching of a "coming/stronger one" fits into an apocalyptic scenario. For a similar (if not identical) understanding of John's instrumental role in Q, see Burton Mack, *Lost Gospel*, 149, 152–58, especially 152–53: "How to reconcile wisdom and apocalyptic teachings, how to recharacterize Jesus' role, and how to rethink the kingdom of God in terms of epic-apocalyptic history were the challenges now confronting [the Q[2] people]. The authors solved this problem at the beginning of their book of instructions by introducing the figure of a prophet of doom and letting this prophet and Jesus exchange views about each other. By carefully constructing that exchange, the authors prepared their readers for the complex role Jesus would later have to assume. John must have been a known personage, or the stories about Jesus and John would not have worked their magic."

77. All the more so, now that the "coming one" of John's proclamation is associated with an apocalyptic "thresher."

35)—bringing together originally independent material,[78] and no doubt embellishing it somewhat—which operates as a unit to endorse and further Q's interests in both polemic and (relatedly) self-rationalization.[79] In the process, Q redaction has also taken some traditional material that may *not* have originally been applied to John at all and used it to characterize John. This appears to have been done with the sayings material embodying Jesus's rhetorical question, "What did you go out into the wilderness to see? A reed shaken by the wind?" In Q, the immediate context makes this saying of Jesus refer to John; but in the Gospel of Thomas, where the saying is presented as an isolated unit, the natural conclusion is that Jesus is speaking about himself. Since I would regard the contextualization of the saying as a secondary development, it makes most sense to conclude that this saying was not originally about John: Q[2]'s redaction has created this connection.

What of Mark's place in this trajectory?[80] For our purposes all that really matters is that John the Baptist was already present in the Jesus tradition, as a figure whose relationship to Jesus was a subject of rationalizing speculation and whose role had especially come to be conceived as that of a precursor. Mark apparently did not have access to the apocalypticized John of Q, and so he establishes his own manner of fitting John into an apocalyptic schema by identifying him with Elijah, who "must come first" (Mark 9:11–12), rather than by turning him into an apocalyptic preacher. As elsewhere, then, Mark narrativizes a motif already established in the tradition via sayings material. He does this first by opening his chronological account of Jesus with John, thus using narrative sequence to establish John as operating *prior* to Jesus[81] and introducing John with reference

---

78. At the very least the material behind Q 7:24–26, 7:27, and 7:28, all of which appears in some form or another in other, independent, texts (namely, Gos. Thom. 78; Mark 1:2; and Gos. Thom. 46).

79. See especially Kloppenborg, *Formation of Q*, 115–17, 121.

80. Note that the trajectory continues *after* Mark as well. In later developments, John's role, and especially the story of his baptism of Jesus, becomes something of an embarrassment, dealt with variously by Matthew, Luke, and John. (It is worth stressing that this embarrassment is *not* an issue in Mark; it is a later development, a reaction *to* Mark.) Both Luke and John also, in different ways, exaggerate the periodization implied by John's role as precursor.

81. This is another tendentious motif taken for granted as historically accurate in spite of a lack of credible evidence. Josephus discusses John in connection with Aretas's defeat of Antipas's armies (*Ant.* 18.5.1-2 §§109–116), which apparently

to his fulfillment of scripture (1:2–3). In addition, by describing John in terms meant to evoke Elijah (1:6), especially after quoting from Malachi, which appears to be a source for the claim that "Elijah must come first" (Mal 4:5), Mark places John quite firmly within an apocalyptic scenario in which his appearance serves to presage the end-times.

But, as I have said elsewhere:

> The choice to begin the narrative with John as the precursor thus dictates that somehow Mark will have to establish Jesus' messianic status *in connection with John* if he is to maintain that Jesus' entire earthly ministry is a ministry of the son of God. A baptism and subsequent "adoption" and revelation is a suitable means for accomplishing this aim.[82]

In other words, Mark, having narrativized John's role as precursor, is essentially forced by his own narrative logic somehow to present John as the one who initially establishes Jesus's identity as son of God.[83] Since the sayings tradition already identifies John's activity as baptism ("I baptize you with water …"), it makes perfect sense to present such a baptism as the initiation of Jesus's work as the son of God.[84] What Mark appears to have

---

occurred around 36 CE. Josephus's discussion implies—at least if read without the gospels in mind—that Antipas's military defeat followed quickly upon his execution of John (which in its turn is presented as though occurring almost immediately after his arrest). This would place John's arrest and execution about six years *after* the date normally given for Jesus's death. I continue to find remarkable the extent to which the strongly *invested* portrayal of John in the canonical gospels (and Q) has acted as the determinative lens through which Josephus's description is read.

82. Arnal, "Major Episodes in the Biography of Jesus," 205, emphasis added.

83. The author of the Gospel of John is stuck with the same narrative logic, and, while now leery of presenting Jesus as having been baptized by John, cannibalizes Mark's baptism theophany, *sans* baptism, in order to retain the image of John as a critical precursor for Jesus. John serves simply to witness the descent of the spirit on Jesus (John 1:32–34), and to attest explicitly that Jesus is the one he has been predicting. Interestingly, Luke does something similar by retrojecting John's role in identifying Jesus from the baptism (at which point John has essentially disappeared) to an *in utero* celebration of Jesus's (likewise *in utero*) appearance (Luke 1:41).

84. So much sense, in fact, that almost 2000 years later many scholars are still unable to uncouple Jesus's designation as "son of God" from a baptism scene. This is most notable in the scholarly claims that Q originally had a baptism account partly on the grounds that the temptation narrative (Q 4:1–13) requires such a scene to establish Jesus's identity as a son of God (on which argument, and its weaknesses, see Kloppenborg, *Formation of Q*, 84–85; Kloppenborg, *Q Parallels*, 16; and see n. 45 above).

done, once again, is to *narrativize the sayings tradition*; that is, he has created a narrative—the baptism account—in which a motif that had simply been *asserted* in the sayings tradition—that is, that John was a precursor to Jesus—is now, via story, *shown* to be true. Mark is again composing narrative enactments of sayings.

Whoever Does Not Bear the Cross as I Do

A more extreme illustration of Mark's compositional techniques, and especially his reliance on motifs already present in the sayings tradition (or other nonnarrative forms), may be found in the passion narrative. Here my skepticism reaches its limits; I am not prepared to argue that the historical Jesus was not crucified.[85] We therefore have in Mark's passion narrative, unlike in the baptism or "cleansing" of the temple, an account of something that (probably) actually happened. Yet even here, where Mark appears to be "based on a true story," the same compositional patterns and techniques occur that we have already seen at work in more genuinely fictitious anecdotes. While Mark did not "make up" Jesus's crucifixion, he has in fact composed the passion narrative as it appears in his gospel, and has done so in the same predictable manner as in other instances: by narrativizing themes appearing in the sayings tradition, by turning scriptural prooftexts into events,[86] by recasting rituals as episodes in Jesus's life, and even perhaps by (somewhat shamelessly) importing events and characters from his own time into the story of Jesus.[87] Mark's passion is just as much a result of mythmaking as any of his less historically grounded inventions.

---

85. Or, to put it differently, if there was a historical Jesus at all, he *was* crucified; if the character who served as the object of ancient Christian mythmaking (Jesus) was not crucified, there is no historical Jesus. *That* Jesus was crucified is about as multiply attested a claim as one can imagine, appearing not only in Paul and the four canonical gospels, but even, apparently, in texts such as Q and Thomas, which have little significant theological investment in this claim.

86. Cf. my discussion, above, of Mark's presentation of John the Baptist as being to some degree motivated by a narrative presentation/demonstration of scriptural prooftexts, which were (according to the tradition) "about" John, and by an apparently exegetically based apocalyptic schematization in which Elijah precedes the end times. For another analysis of its scripturally allusive character, see Dowd and Malbon, "The Significance of Jesus' Death in Mark."

87. Note that all of these techniques—even this last one (for which I am tempted to invent some monstrous word like "anachronization")—have already been estab-

Here is not the place to review the massive amount of scholarly work that has been done on the passion and on the extent to which Mark composed the narrative himself or made use of existing sources.[88] Suffice it to note that the older form-critical view—that the centrality of the passion to the supposed kerygma (the proclamation of Jesus's death and resurrection) required an extended narrative of Jesus's final days and execution from the very beginning of the Christian movement[89]—has been called into question in more recent decades, both by the observation that some ancient Christian writings lack any interest in the kerygma[90] and by studies that have made a strong case on literary grounds for Markan composi-

---

lished in my discussion of Mark's composition of the fig tree, temple, and baptism accounts. In the case of "anachronization," the precedent is Mark's use of the actual destruction of the temple, more or less in his own time, as part of his basis for the "temple tantrum" episode.

88. Several massive studies exist, with significantly divergent conclusions. See, e.g., Eta Linnemann, *Studien zur Passionsgeschichte* (Göttingen: Vandenhoeck & Ruprecht, 1970); Werner H. Kelber, ed., *Passion in Mark: Studies on Mark 14–16* (Philadelphia: Fortress, 1976); John Dominic Crossan, *The Cross That Spoke: The Origins of the Passion Narrative* (San Francisco: Harper & Row, 1988); Crossan, *Who Killed Jesus?* (San Francisco: HarperSanFrancisco, 1995); Raymond E. Brown, *The Death of the Messiah: From Gethsemane to the Grave; A Commentary on the Passion Narratives in the Four Gospels* (New York: Doubleday, 1994); and of course the discussion of the passion in Mack, *Myth of Innocence*, 247–312.

89. See, e.g., Dibelius, *From Tradition to Gospel*, especially 23, 178–79; Rudolf Bultmann, "The Study of the Synoptic Gospels," in *Form Criticism: Two Essays on New Testament Research*, by Rudolf Bultmann and Karl Kundsin, trans. Frederick C. Grant, Harper Torchbooks (New York: Harper, 1962), 65.

90. Most notably and obviously, Q and the Gospel of Thomas. But it is also noteworthy that little or no kerygmatic orientation may be found in most of the typical units of oral tradition that have been gathered together in our written sources. The controversy stories, the healing miracles, the parables, and so on do not appear to evince any interest in Jesus's death and resurrection, unless and until such an interest is read into them.

It is also worth noting that even where an interest in the kerygma *can* be demonstrated, it is unclear that such an interest requires any extended narrative of the events in question. Paul, despite his substantial interest in Jesus's death and resurrection, seems content, at least in his *letters*, to state simply *that* these events occurred, and not *how* they occurred. While it may be that such a story was taken for granted in Paul's correspondence, the fact that he fails to refer to it should give us pause in assuming any *necessary* connection between kerygmatic interests and an actual narrative of the passion.

tion of the passion.[91] The latter are especially noteworthy for our purposes. The literary evidence derived from Mark itself suggests that the classical form-critics were simply wrong: the passion narrative in Mark is a Markan composition, not a pre-Markan narrative unit.[92] Kelber's conclusions are worth quoting at length, if only to avoid reinventing this particular wheel:

> *Mk 14–16 constitutes a theologically inseparable and homogeneous part of the Gospel whole.*... The very term Passion Narrative may therefore not adequately reflect the nature of Mk 14–16, if the latter is viewed as the culmination of *all major Mkan theological themes.*... [There is] a very intense redactional activity in Mk 14–16. The Evangelist ... takes a tradition of Jesus' words about bread and cup and develops it into a Last Meal scene; he adds the largely redactional section dealing with Jesus' prediction of Peter's denial and the return to Galilee; he composes the three stage Gethsemane narrative out of a lamenting Jesus saying or prayer; he creates Jesus' trial (including Jesus' words of confession) before the San-

---

91. E.g., Linnemann, *Studien zur Passionsgeschichte*; Kelber, *Passion in Mark*; Mack, *Myth of Innocence*, 288–312. By contrast, and unsurprisingly, many scholars still regard at least the outline of the passion narrative as essentially factual. Thus, for instance, E. P. Sanders, while skeptical of some of the details embedded in the passion narratives as they appear in the canonical gospels (see *Jesus and Judaism*, 297–301), nonetheless regards as historical some form of "triumphal entry," Judas's betrayal, and a Jewish trial, formal or otherwise (*Jesus and Judaism*, 306–9; cf. *Historical Figure of Jesus*, 252–75). Similarly, Borg, *Jesus: A New Vision*, 176–84, 187 n. 22; Schüssler Fiorenza, *In Memory of Her*, 138–39; Vermes, *Jesus the Jew*, 36–37.

Happily, the Jesus Seminar prints nearly all of the Markan passion in black or gray, and draws the following general conclusions about Jesus's death: "There was a person named Jesus, who was executed by the authorities during the prefecture of Pontius Pilate (26–36 CE)" (red). "The disciples of Jesus fled when Jesus was arrested" (pink). "The assertion that the Romans were innocent of Jesus' death and the Jews were responsible is pure Christian propaganda" (red). "The underlying structure of the passion story was suggested by prophetic scriptures taken from the Greek Bible (the Septuagint)" (red). So Robert W. Funk and the Jesus Seminar, *The Acts of Jesus: What Did Jesus Really Do?* (San Francisco: HarperSanFrancisco, 1998), 133, cf. 132–61.

92. One might alternatively say that this literary evidence shows that the form-critics were *right*: ancient Christian tradition circulated in small units, and the only exception that the form critics were willing to grant to this "rule" turned out not to be an exception, after all. See, e.g., the comment of Werner H. Kelber, "Conclusion: From Passion Narrative to Gospel," in *The Passion in Mark*, 158: "The theological and literary conclusions derived from these studies on Mk 14–16 show that the Mkan Passion Narrative does *not* constitute the exception to the form critical canons which govern the formation of the Synoptic tradition" (emphasis original).

hedrin out of a story about Jesus' presentation before Jewish officials; he expands a short story of Peter's denial into a lengthy, three-stage account and intercalates it into the newly created trial narrative; he rewrites a crucifixion tradition; and he composes the Empty Tomb story as a fitting conclusion to his Gospel. Mkan vocabulary, Mkan stylistic features, and Mkan compositional techniques further corroborate the impression of the overall Mkan literary character of Mk 14–16…. It is amiss to consider the Passion section of the Gospel as a *literary* unit set apart from the remainder of the Gospel. The issue is not why Jesus' Passion demanded an early pre-Mkan connected narrative form, because it did not, but the issue is why Mk created the Gospel whole in its present form.[93]

Part of the reason I quote this extract at such length is because of its programmatic call to explain "why Mk created the Gospel whole in its present form," rather than (merely) deferring the issue by hypothesizing a pre-Markan passion narrative. But it is also because here Kelber, drawing on the work of the other scholars who contribute to this book on the passion, hypothesizes several instances in the passion narrative of precisely the phenomenon I have been pointing to: the creation of narrative out of sayings material. The two instances he cites are not as clear-cut, perhaps, as the instances I have discussed above,[94] but they still merit some consid-

---

93. Kelber, "Conclusion: From Passion Narrative to Gospel," 157–58, emphasis added.

94. In at least some measure, this is because the sayings out of which these narratives are supposed by Kelber to have been constructed are no longer extant *as* independent sayings. Thus, e.g., while we encounter sayings in Q which depict John as precursor without a narrative, the supposed "lament" of Jesus on which the Gethsemane story may depend appears nowhere (at least, nowhere that I can see) in the tradition. (For an alternative view of the sayings material out of which this story was composed, see below.) Likewise, the Markan "Last Supper" tradition has a Pauline parallel in 1 Cor 11:23–25, but, Kelber's claims notwithstanding, this is, arguably, more than simply "a tradition of Jesus' words about bread and cup"; the "words" are given a narrative frame by Paul, and one that accords, more or less, with the Markan plot-line. It is true, of course, that Paul's "tradition" (ὃ καὶ παρέδωκα) is basically a *chreia*, a form associated generally with the sayings tradition. The distinctive feature here, however, is that the *chreia* frame sets the saying at a unique chronological moment in Jesus's life, indeed the same moment at which Mark places it: the night of his arrest. One could of course claim (and in fact I would claim) that Mark has here, as is his wont, constructed a story from a *chreia*, and hence, at least technically, has narrativized sayings tradition. This particular *chreia*, however, *is* distinctive insofar as the narrative frame functions mainly as a chronological marker.

eration. The passion as a whole serves as an excellent example of Mark's techniques for composing narrative, in this case, a narrative that represents the culmination and the essence of his entire story. It is important to linger somewhat over this example, if for no other reason than that within New Testament scholarship, when it comes to the passion narrative, there remains a strong tendency in the opposite direction: to evaluate and interpret sayings material from the perspective of the "facts" of Jesus's last days in Jerusalem.[95]

First, then, the units Kelber notes as narrative expansions of sayings do indeed strike me as additional examples of the Markan tendency to construct stories from sayings material, although there is room for disagreement on the details. In the case of the Gethsemane story, for instance, it strikes me as superfluous to posit a no-longer-extant "lament" around which the story was built, when we have sayings tradition ready at hand in Mark itself that might have served such a function. I refer to the parable that concludes Mark's apocalyptic discourse in chapter 13, the story of the doorkeeper (13:34–36). The tale, for which Mark himself provides an explicit (and contemporizing!) interpretation—"And what I say to you, I say to all: Keep awake" (13:37)—occurs at the climactic moment of the

---

95. Perhaps most egregious is Arland J. Hultgren's claim (*The Rise of Normative Christianity* [Minneapolis: Fortress, 1994], 33) that the Q saying about followers of Jesus needing to "bear (βαστάζει/λαμβάνει) the cross" (Q 14:27) shows awareness of and deliberately alludes to either Jesus's or Simon of Cyrene's carrying of the cross to the place of execution (as per Mark 15:21–22). Hultgren also claims (*The Rise of Normative Christianity*, 33–34) that Q 13:35 ("you will not see me until ... you say, 'Blessed is he who comes in the name of the Lord'") alludes to the triumphal entry as recounted in Mark 11:9. (For a rejoinder, see John S. Kloppenborg, *Excavating Q: The History and Setting of the Sayings Gospel* [Edinburgh: T&T Clark 2000; Minneapolis: Fortress, 2000], 370.) More than one scholar links 1 Cor 11:23–26 to the Markan passion sequence (particularly Mark 14:22–25) or something akin to it (see, e.g., the comments of Gundry, *Mark: A Commentary on His Apology*, 829); indeed, the typical translation of 1 Cor 11:23 as "on the night when he was *betrayed*" (so, e.g., NRSV) shows a tendency to read Paul's comments in light of the canonical gospel narrative, with its focus on Judas Iscariot as ὁ παραδιδούς (cf. Mark 14:42). Paul uses here the verb παραδίδωμι, without specification or indeed any reference to Judas, to mean "handed over," as in "arrested." The verb is used in exactly the same sense by Mark himself, without any necessary reference to *betrayal*, in describing the arrest of John the Baptist: μετὰ δὲ τὸ παραδοθῆναι τὸν Ἰωάννην... (Mark 1:14). The implication of betrayal, and thus of the existence of Judas, is supplied by an intertextual harmonization, which illegitimately reads (earlier) Pauline material in light of the (later) gospel narratives.

little apocalypse, and it is the very last teaching of Jesus prior to the passion narrative proper. The metaphor of sleep and wakefulness used here corresponds in detail to the exchange between Jesus and his three disciples in Gethsemane.

The details of wording are strikingly similar. In Mark 13:34–37, the imperative, γρηγορεῖτε, is used twice, once within the parable (13:35), and once in its concluding, contemporizing application (13:37). The verb used in the parable for sleeping, καθεύδω, is given as part of a longer phrase, μὴ ἐλθὼν ... εὕρῃ ὑμᾶς καθεύδοντας (13:36). The wording here about what to avoid thus takes the form of a combination of ἔρχομαι with εὑρίσκω, followed by a participial form of καθεύδω. The wording about what to do in lieu of this, γρηγορεῖτε, is expressed as an imperative. We find almost exactly the same phrasing used in the Gethsemane story in Mark 14:32–42. There, as we would expect in Mark, the disciples evince exactly the same behavior Jesus has so emphatically warned against in the apocalyptic speech: they fall asleep (καθεύδω, four times: twice in 14:37, and once each in 14:40, 41). It is not simply that they are sleeping, but that Jesus (= the Son of Man = the master on a journey [cf. 13:27, 32, 34]), coming (ἔρχομαι), finds (εὑρίσκω) them sleeping (in participial form: καθεύδοντας): this descriptive format, from the doorkeeper parable, appears not once but twice in this story: καὶ ἔρχεται καὶ εὑρίσκει αὐτοὺς καθεύδοντας (14:37); καὶ πάλιν ἐλθὼν εὗρεν αὐτοὺς καθεύδοντας (14:40).[96] (Jesus finds them sleeping a third time, but the event is described via direct discourse in this case; still, even here, ἔρχομαι and καθεύδω are the verbs used.)[97] And Jesus's command to them in this story is identical to his advice in the parable: "stay awake," "wake up" (γρηγορεῖτε, in the imperative, twice: 14:34, 14:38).[98]

Kelber notes that at least in the latter part of the Gethsemane story, the emphasis is *not* on Jesus's "temptation" to avoid death but on the odious behavior of Peter, James, and John; the whole point of the story is the

---

96. Cf. also Kelber, "The Hour of the Son of Man and the Temptation of the Disciples (Mark 14:32–42)," in *The Passion in Mark*, 48.

97. It may be worth noting that the remaining uses of καθεύδω in Mark, i.e., 4:27, 38; 5:39, do not appear to have the same moral or symbolic payload as the instances in the doorkeeper parable and the Gethsemane story; these three other instances at least *appear* to refer to literal sleep, with no moral opprobrium implied.

98. Kelber, "Hour of the Son of Man," 48, notes that "*Grēgorein* is restricted in Mk to the parable of the doorkeeper (13:34, 35, 37) and to the Gethsemane scene (14:34, 37, 38)."

"recurrent and incorrigible blindness of the disciples."[99] As Kelber points out, Jesus's rebuke to them in 14:41–42 represents his last words to any of the disciples.[100] From this moment forward in the story, the disciples and Jesus go their separate ways, never again to be reunited. Kelber also notes that the disciples' behavior is in direct contravention of the advice given by Jesus at the close of chapter 13: stay awake.[101] Finally, Kelber draws attention to the triadic structure of the story but views this structure as consisting of two triadic parts: a first, from 14:32–36, which focuses on Jesus's lament, and a second, from 14:37–42, which focuses on the failure of the disciples.[102] While there is certainly a triadic structure to the story, it seems more likely to me to be a simple one that bridges the entirety of the scene, namely the three-fold repetition of injunction-prayer-sleep-rebuke. Regardless, it is clear that the thrice-repeated failure of the disciples here finds both parallel and contrast in other Markan triads: three misunderstood passion predictions (8:31; 9:31; 10:33–34); three Petrine denials of Jesus (14:66–72); and Jesus's three "hours" on the cross (15:25–37).[103]

The parable in Mark 13:34–35 is traditional sayings material, albeit not necessarily in its original form. A fairly close parallel appears in Q 12:42–46; looser parallels are also present in the parable of the talents (Q 19:12–26) and in the extensive tradition of "robber" sayings and parables (e.g., Gos. Thom. 21, 35, 98, 103; Mark 3:27; Q 11:21–22; Q 12:39–40).[104]

---

99. Ibid., 50; cf. 47–50, especially 47: "What should be noted first is a shifting of the spotlight away from Jesus. His continued prayers are mere encores of the initial prayer, and his terror-stricken soul is no longer the issue. Nor is the tripartite drama staged to act out Jesus's inner development.… On the contrary, the spotlight in 14:37–42 is on the disciples."

100. Ibid., 49.

101. Ibid., 48–49.

102. Ibid., 43–50. See especially 44 and n. 7, 47 and n. 11.

103. Ibid., 53. Note that the actual amount of time that Jesus spends on the cross is six hours, not three. What Kelber means here is that three *moments* are distinguished by Mark during the crucifixion, each signified by a use of ὥρα: the moment ("hour") of crucifixion (15:25), the moment of darkness (15:33), and the moment of abandonment and death (15:34–37). On Mark's fondness for triads, see, among others, T. A. Burkill, *New Light on the Earliest Gospel: Seven Markan Studies* (Ithaca, NY: Cornell University Press, 1972), 248, 256–58.

104. I am inclined to view the "robber" sayings in the tradition not only as parallels to, but perhaps even as the ultimate basis for, Mark's version of the doorkeeper parable and the various parallels discussed here. In spite of their lack of obvious and extensive similarity, Mark's tendency (and, apparently, the tendency of the tradition as

By contrast, the Gethsemane story, including any appeal by Jesus to God (or any "lament"), appears only in Mark, and it is riddled with Markan redactional characteristics.[105] One *need* not hypothesize—and it certainly cannot be proven—that Mark composed the entire story in all its details out of the doorkeeper parable and that parable alone. The foregoing discussion, however, allows us to conclude at least that the *Markan form* of the Gethsemane story is indeed Markan, and that its basis was the doorkeeper parable, garnished by Mark's own redactional and exegetical proclivities, and served up as a narrative.[106] If one deletes those aspects of this Markan form of the story that are surely Markan—namely: (1) the presence of a three-fold "inner circle" of disciples (compare with Mark 9:2); (2) the motif of the disciples' failures; (3) the entire theme of repeated sleeping and waking; (4) the loaded use of "the hour" in the narrative notice in 14:35;[107] (5) the redundant narrative paraphrase (14:35) of the following

---

a whole) is to recast older materials in such a way that God or Jesus are represented by figures of high social standing. Thus, most notably, the original form of the parable of the tenants (Gos. Thom. 65) appears to identify the tenants as the protagonists, whereas Mark reconfigures the parable to make the landowner the protagonist (Mark 12:1–12). (See William E. Arnal, "The Parable of the Tenants and the Class Consciousness of the Peasantry," in *Text and Artifact in the Religions of Mediterranean Antiquity: Essays in Honour of Peter Richardson*, ed. Stephen G. Wilson and Michel Desjardins [Waterloo, ON: Wilfrid Laurier University Press, 2000], 135–57.) I am therefore assuming that the original form of the robber parable is best represented by such sayings as Gos. Thom. 35, in which the robber is the protagonist, and that the version which appears in Gos. Thom. 103 represents a later development. Mark's story would thus be a version of a parable about watchfulness and preparation, but told from the perspective of a wealthy householder, a more fitting representative, at least to Mark's mind, of the Son of Man. Obviously, this particular cluster of sayings (robbers, strong men, absentee landlords) has an extensive and complicated history. A brilliant comparison of the Markan and Q versions of the "strong man" sayings is offered by Michael L. Humphries, *Christian Origins and the Language of the Kingdom of God* (Carbondale, IL: Southern Illinois University Press, 1999).

105. So also Mack, *Myth of Innocence*, 306–7.

106. John R. Donahue, "Temple, Trial, and Royal Christology (Mark 14:53–65)," in *The Passion in Mark*, 76–77, argues that the story is a Markan creation in its entirety, based at least in part on the story of the conspiracy against David in 2 Sam 15–17, 20.

107. "The hour" is here used in distinctively Markan fashion to signify the event of Jesus's being "handed over" and crucified, and it links this event to the predicted coming of the Son of Man. So Kelber, "Hour of the Son of Man," 44–46; and cf. especially Mark 13:11, 32; 14:41. Mark uses the word ὥρα nine times, three of which appear in this story (vv. 35, 37, 41). Outside of the apocalyptic discourse and the passion

direct discourse (14:36); (6) the triadic structure of the entire scene—then all that remains is a notice that Jesus prayed to God: "Abba, Father, for you all things are possible; remove this cup from me; yet, not what I want, but what you want" (14:36). In other words, all that survives is a *chreia*. Even there, suspiciously Markan features are present: the fraught metaphoric reference to the "cup" (ποτήριον: compare with Mark 10:38–39; 14:23); and the logic of "not what I want but what you want" may depend for its cogency (and poignancy) on the narrative contrast offered here between Jesus's own attitude and the deportment of his would-be followers. I also note that Jesus's *foreknowledge* of his death is a distinctively Markan emphasis, and it is implied in this saying.[108]

Thus, two different possibilities present themselves here. First, and at the very least, it is possible that Kelber is correct and that Mark has transformed a *chreia* about Jesus lamenting his sufferings into a narrative account contrasting Jesus with his own disciples. To this conclusion, we must add a stronger emphasis on the formative role played by the door-keeper parable in the construction of this narrative. The second possibility, of course, is that Mark created the story in its *entirety* with no direct sources whatsoever, as a narrative exemplification of the doorkeeper parable. While I am inclined to adopt the second conclusion as better evidenced and as dealing better with the thoroughly Markan features of all aspects of the Gethsemane account,[109] what is especially notable about these two options is that, however else they may differ, they both suggest the same compositional procedure on Mark's part. Once again, Mark appears to be using essentially noncontextual sayings material to construct a narrative.

---

narrative, the term occurs three times, all of them literal references to time (as are the references to the "hours" during which Jesus is crucified in 15:25, 33–34).

108. In its present form. If the original *chreia* contained a narrative notice indicating that Jesus was *currently* suffering—e.g., if this is a traditional word uttered on the cross—obviously foreknowledge is not required.

109. With a single exception: the identification of "Gethsemane" as the location of the scene. This detail appears to have no identifiable provenance. Note, however, that Mack (*Myth of Innocence*, 297 n. 2) observes that "every event in the passion narrative has been located somewhere as specifically as possible in relation to Jerusalem and the temple." On the significance of this observation, see further below.

I also note that one *can* find a "tradition," with no explicit narrative context, of Jesus lamenting and pleading with God in Heb 5:7; what is unclear is whether this material is related to the Gethsemane account in Mark, and if so, how.

The other element of the passion narrative that Kelber claims may be a development from a saying is the Markan account of the Lord's Supper (Mark 14:22–25). Here the problem is the specificity of the Pauline account, which not only traces Paul's own agenda for the Lord's Supper (κυριακὸν δεῖπνον) to words of Jesus but to Jesus's actions as well, and chronologically specified actions at that: ὁ κύριος Ἰησοῦς ἐν τῇ νυκτὶ ᾗ παρεδίδετο ἔλαβεν ἄρτον ... (1 Cor 11:23–26).[110] Of course, the material that Paul presents as a tradition (ὁ κύριος Ἰησοῦς ἐν τῇ νυκτὶ ᾗ παρεδίδετο ἔλαβεν ἄρτον) is still technically a *chreia*, there being no formal requirement that a *chreia*'s narrative frame *not* refer to a chronologically identifiable moment (indeed, many such could be cited); only that the saying with its frame be free-standing. Paul's account does meet this requirement. Mark has woven the *chreia* into a more extended presentation of Jesus's last days, including his account of Judas as betrayer (14:10–11, 17–21),[111] his redactional depiction of the preparations for the Passover meal (14:12–16),[112] and his summary prooftexts and predictions (14:26–31), as well as the chronology of

---

110. As Mack notes (*Myth of Innocence*, 298), "The core unit [of the meal cluster] is the breaking of the bread and the distribution of the cup. *This unit is the only story in the entire passion narrative for which a pre-Markan tradition can be established.* It is therefore a text of great significance for understanding the composition of the passion account" (emphasis added). Note that, of course, while Paul's account indicates a pre-existing version of the words about bread and wine, it does not guarantee that Paul's wording perfectly represents the "original" phrasing of that tradition. There is every reason to imagine that Paul has made his own modifications.

111. It is conceivable that the Judas story, too, is a Markan construct suggested by a combination of Mark's theme of the disciples' failures and the traditional wording of the bread and cup *chreia* as ἐν τῇ νυκτὶ ᾗ παρεδίδετο, with Mark viewing παραδίδωμι as implying betrayal (which it can, but need not, mean: see its various New Testament uses and LSJ, s.v. παραδίδωμι). Since this is a technical term that Mark uses elsewhere for the passion as a whole (e.g., especially 9:31; 10:33; cf. 13:9, 12), it is easy to see how the idea of *betrayal* may have suggested itself to Mark. The gospel's very first (and only, prior to the passion) reference to Judas (3:19) identifies him as ὃς καὶ παρέδωκεν αὐτόν (cf. 14:42). Mack, *Myth of Innocence*, 304, suggests precisely the same thing: "The story of Judas' betrayal is a Markan fiction.... Mark played with the double meaning of *paradidonai* as 'arrest' and 'handing over' (betrayal) through the entire gospel story." See as well Mack's comments in ibid., 299, and 299–300 n. 4.

112. Note here the intercalation of this story into the middle of the Judas narrative, as well as the use of the extensive parallelism of this scene with that of Jesus's preparations for the "triumphal entry" (11:1–6). On this parallelism, see especially Robbins, "Last Meal: Preparation, Betrayal, and Absence," 23–24, though, oddly, Robbins concludes that "the particular features of the story—the man carrying the jar of

the passion as a whole. What was originally a free-standing and essentially unembellished *chreia* now becomes a plot-unit in a larger story.[113]

In *Myth of Innocence*, Mack pays careful attention to the function of the "original" *chreia* and the way its function is changed by Mark.[114] In Pauline usage of the account, Mack sees "the etiological myth of the Hellenistic cult meal."[115] Mack has since revised his views considerably, both rejecting the terminology and conceptualization of a pre-Pauline "Christ cult,"[116] and, in addition, rethinking the analysis of Paul's citation of the supper tradition in 1 Cor 11:23–26, noting in particular that Paul does not seem to cite this tradition as an event to be replicated.[117] What remains constant in Mack's perspective is the linking of the "original" meal tradition to a (modified) martyr myth, presenting Jesus in terms of martyrdom for the sake of the group (fictive or otherwise) itself (still reflected in the wording of 1 Cor 11:24: "this is my body for you" [τὸ σῶμα τὸ ὑπὲρ ὑμῶν], in spite of Paul's shifts in emphasis).[118] Paul uses the account as "a myth of origins that grounds an association practice already in place and suggests that the major markers of the common meal as process (taking bread,

---

water, the formula 'The Teacher says…' and the large upper room—point to tradition" (24). He does not indicate *why* these features "point to tradition."

113. On the extent to which Mark has altered the wording of Jesus's statement(s) over the bread and cup, see especially Robbins, "Last Meal: Preparation, Betrayal, and Absence." The complicated issue of the "original" wording of the saying can be set-aside for the moment. For various views, see, e.g., Gundry, *Mark: A Commentary on His Apology*, 829–34; Mack, *Myth of Innocence*, 298; Robert F. O'Toole, "Last Supper," *ABD* 4:234–41; Robbins, "Last Meal: Preparation, Betrayal, and Absence," 34–38.

114. Mack, *Myth of Innocence*, 298–304.

115. Ibid., 304.

116. Because of the misleading freight associated with the terms "cult" and "ritual"; because of the linear and almost-teleological implication that "Christianity" unfolded in a step-by-step development from Jesus the teacher; and because of the general lack of utility found for the concept in our redescriptive efforts. See now Burton L. Mack, "Rereading the Christ Myth: Paul's Gospel and the Christ Cult Question," in *Redescribing Paul and the Corinthians*, ed. Ron Cameron and Merrill P. Miller, ECL 5 (Atlanta: Society of Biblical Literature, 2011), 65–72.

117. See especially Mack, "Rereading the Christ Myth," 54: "It is not at all clear that Paul thought the Lord's meal scenario called for mimetic behavior of any kind, much less its replication by a 'worshipping community' as customarily assumed."

118. See both Mack, *Myth of Innocence*, 114–20; but now especially Mack, "Rereading the Christ Myth," 54–57, in which Jesus's foundational role as a *teacher* continues to be emphasized.

drinking wine) could be used as 'reminders' for the martyr's death of Jesus their founder-teacher and patron."[119]

Mack suggests that this original martyrological narrative function is also the focus of Mark's account. Mack must be at least partly correct in this. It is certainly the case that Mark shows no interest in any etiological potential this traditional *chreia* might have. Mark's "historicizing" interests are most transparent in his elaboration of the activity taking place around the cup (Mark 14:23): "Then he took a cup, and after giving thanks *he gave it to them, and all of them drank from it*."[120] Even such a minor and subtle change has the effect of shifting attention from the word to the activity, and hence this emphasizes Jesus's participation in an actual meal with his actual, contemporary disciples.[121] The observation that "all of them drank" from the cup, it has been noted, underscores the perfidy of Judas.[122] Jesus has just predicted his betrayal at the hands of one of his own disciples, and has underscored that this person is sharing his food (14:18, 20). The notice that *all* of the disciples (πάντες), including Judas, likewise share from the cup (14:23), thus, symmetrically, emphasizes that the betrayal of Jesus is coming from within his circle of intimates and that the betrayer has treacherously shared table communion with Jesus (see similarly, Judas's kiss in Mark 14:45).

---

119. Mack, "Rereading the Christ Myth," 56.

120. Contrast the Pauline wording (1 Cor 11:25): "In the same way he took the cup also, after supper, saying...." Note the similar Markan alteration of the bread-breaking: unlike Paul (1 Cor 11:23–24), he once again specifies that Jesus not only broke the bread, but that he gave it to the disciples (Mark 14:22). Gundry (*Mark: A Commentary on His Apology*, 832) notes: "Instead of inserting an unparalleled command to take the cup as he inserted an unparalleled command to take the bread, or a command to drink from it (as in Matt 26:26 and by implication in the command, 'Keep on doing this...,' in 1 Cor 11:24; Luke 22:19; cf. the command to eat in Matt 26:26; Mark 14:22 v. l.; 1 Cor 11:24 v. l.), Mark now inserts an unparalleled statement that 'they all drank from it.' Narrative obliterates liturgy."

121. Note that the Pauline version of the tradition, while taking it for granted that his audience participates in the meal *now*, nowhere actually specifies that Jesus himself was eating *with* anyone, or speaking *to* anyone, much less a circle of disciples. The situation is exactly reversed in Mark's account.

122. See especially Gundry, *Mark: A Commentary on His Apology*, 830, 832; cf. Mack, *Myth of Innocence*, 301. Kelber, "Hour of the Son of Man," 51 n. 21, notes that the perfidy being underscored here is not limited to Judas: just as "they all" (πάντες) drink from the cup (14:23), so "they all" (πάντες) abandon him shortly thereafter (14:40).

The transformation of the "Lord's Supper" into the "Last Supper" implies a shift of interest from (notionally) shared practices (as in Paul) to Jesus's martyrdom and the mythological ramifications thereof. The event is singular: no command is made to repeat it (contrast with 1 Cor 11:24–26; Luke 22:19). Mark does something very similar in his treatments of baptism and communal drinking in 10:39, which become not habitual practices of Jesus's followers but metaphors for Jesus's own suffering—metaphors that are in fact concretized also, as distinct and unique events in Jesus's life (baptism in 1:19; also perhaps in 14:3–9, as anointing for burial; and the cup in 14:36). Likewise, Mark has transformed *refrigeria* meals celebrating Jesus's death in association with the Passover into Passover-allusive miracle stories unique to Jesus's life but *anticipatory* of his death in Mark's miraculous feeding accounts (6:35–44; 8:1–9). The treatment here is akin to that of the anticipatory transfiguration (9:2–8) or the anticipatory anointing (14:3–9). What we see in all this—baptism, cup, bread, large meals with Passover allusions, anointing, transfiguration—is Mark's consistent tendency to transform distinctive postmortem practices and beliefs associated with Jesus into unique biographical episodes by retrojecting them back into Jesus's lifetime.[123]

In sum, Mark's account of the Last Supper is certainly a narrative expansion of a traditional, pre-Pauline, *chreia* originally serving as an etiology for a common meal (itself an etiology for the movement Paul envisions, in terms of Christ's death *for* the group). It is the exception that proves the rule: Mark has used a critically important episode to construct a more extended narrative about Jesus, a narrative that itself serves to interpret and lay the groundwork for the entire passion as Mark construes it.[124] But if the Pauline form of the tradition is to be relied upon, this key narrative only existed, prior to Mark, in the form of a *chreia*. The centrality of this episode for Mark, and its availability to him as a sayings unit amenable to and suggestive of a major narrative expansion, may have been precisely the model that inspired him (along with a problematic dearth of

---

123. For contrasting assessments of these stories and their relationship to Eucharistic imagery, see, on the one hand, Robert M. Fowler, *Loaves and Fishes: The Function of the Feeding Stories in the Gospel of Mark* (Chico, CA: Scholars Press, 1981), and, on the other hand, e.g., Elizabeth Struthers Malbon, *Narrative Space and Mythic Meaning in Mark* (San Francisco: Harper & Row, 1986), 79.

124. So also Mack, *Myth of Innocence*, 299.

actual narrative tradition about Jesus) to mine the more extensive sayings tradition for narrative fodder.

Mark's treatment of this unit, alongside his treatment of Jesus's baptism, may tell us something very important about the orientation and provenance of this gospel. Mark's origins are *not* to be found among tradents of "Christian rituals," which Mark treats as comments on Jesus's life rather than as etiologies; *nor* among among currents that maintained a focus on Jesus's teaching, since this teaching is reduced to vacuous self-reference.[125] Ritual in Mark does not find its meaning in reference to (ostensive) group practice, as with Paul, but it is simply mined as a source of "information" about Jesus's own actions.

In addition to the two episodes in the Markan passion that Kelber views as expansions of sayings material, others may be cited as well. For instance, the story of the triumphal entry (Mark 11:1–10) appears to be the Markan terminus of a familiar progression from sayings tradition, to exegesis and prooftext, to narrative. While the story itself is, predictably, singly attested, a version of the scriptural quotation that serves as the story's core[126] appears in Q 13:35: ἰδοὺ ἀφίεται ὑμῖν ὁ οἶκος ὑμῶν. λέγω δὲ

---

125. Jesus is most definitely a teacher in Mark (he is addressed as διδάσκαλε no less than ten times in Mark [4:38; 9:17, 38; 10:17, 20, 35; 12:14, 19, 32; 13:1]; and the author describes his activity frequently as "teaching" [e.g., 1:21–22; 2:13; 4:1–2; 6:2, 6, 34; 8:31; 9:31; 10:1; 11:17; 12:35]), but almost all of his teaching refers only to how important Jesus himself is (note the designation of Jesus's first two passion predictions as "teaching"). The character of Jesus's teaching in Mark as vacuous self-reference is most obvious in Mark's interpretation of the parable of the sower (4:3–8 and 4:14–20), where the whole point of the "teaching" seems to be the reception of Jesus's teaching! It is also evident in Jesus's parable of the vineyard (12:1–12), which is merely a prediction of Jesus's own fate. The bizarrely circular and self-referential character of Jesus's teaching as presented by Mark is emphasized by Mack, *Myth of Innocence*, 169–71, especially 171: "Mark did not wish to portray Jesus addressing his generation publicly with instruction about the kingdom of God as if his world could have accepted it and changed. What Jesus says in Mark's Gospel is not instruction to those within the story at all. What Jesus says in the story functioned as pronouncement, a sign of his imperious authority, a behavior that triggered and sealed a predetermined fate of ultimate consequence both for the Christian community and for the opponents of Jesus. What Jesus said then is instructive only for the reader in Mark's own time."

126. As with the temple episode, nothing much happens in this account. Jesus rides into town on a donkey, and the story culminates with the expression of the crowds recognizing in Jesus "the one who comes in the name of the Lord" (Mark 11:9; Ps 118:25–26 MT, with ὡσαννά [diff. Ps 117:25 LXX, εὐόδωσον δή for Hebrew *hôšîʿâ*

ὑμῖν, οὐ μὴ ἴδητέ με ἕως ἥξει ὅτε εἴπητε· <u>εὐλογημένος ὁ ἐρχόμενος ἐν ὀνόματι</u> <u>κυρίου</u>. Several aspects of the Markan story are presaged in the Q version of the saying: (1) the quotation itself, word for word identical in LXX, Mark, and Q; (2) the application of the quotation to Jesus (in Q by being placed in Jesus's mouth, in Mark by being said to and about Jesus; compare this with the similarly divergent treatment of the "prepare the way" quotation vis-à-vis John the Baptist); (3) this acclamation of Jesus is made by other people as a kind of confession (as opposed to being proclaimed directly, by the author, or by individual disciples, or by Jesus, or by God; in Q this identification is effected implicitly by Jesus's directing of his comments to a [more or less unspecified] plural "you" [Q 13:35: λέγω δὲ ὑμῖν], while in Mark those who acknowledge Jesus are πολλοί and ἄλλοι [11:8]); and (4) the people in question are, oddly enough, the people of Jerusalem (a point effected in Q by directing the lament to Jerusalem in 13:34 and effected by Mark in setting the event around Jesus's entry to Jerusalem).

This detailed correspondence, and the different uses of common features in the two texts, lends ammunition to those who claim a literary connection between Mark and Q. I would argue, by contrast, that both are drawing on a common body of exegetical reflection in which a particular scriptural text is construed in terms of an acclamation of Jesus by the people of Jerusalem, either future and anticipated (as in Q) or past and rather ironic (as in Mark).[127] In the case of Q, the current form of the material appears to have been redactionally formulated, with the exegetical statement about Jesus appended to a Sophia-oracle and formulated in terms of Q[2]'s deuteronomistic polemic,[128] and then folded into a larger Q[2]

---

nā']). Aside from the ὡσαννά, however, the Markan wording is identical to that in LXX Ps 117:26: εὐλογημένος ὁ ἐρχόμενος ἐν ὀνόματι κυρίου.

127. It is hard to see Mark's story as anything but ironic in light of the fact that these same crowds, apparently, are those who only a few days later are clamoring for Jesus's death (15:11–15). I note that this observation is further fuel for the claim that Mark used Q, insofar as Q's usage of the prooftext is (redactionally) polemical, and Mark himself has harnessed the same text, implicitly, to a rather negative point about the people of Jerusalem as well. Note how, once again, Mark has taken a postmortem or anticipated future event associated with Jesus and has retrojected it into Jesus's life story.

128. See Kloppenborg, Formation of Q, 228. If I am correct that Mark and Q are here drawing independently on a common tradition, then it may be the prior association of this prooftext acclamation with Jerusalem that inspired the Q[2] redactor to attach this text to the oracle of Sophia in Q 13:34.

construction (Q 13:24–30, 34–35; 14:16–24, 26–27; 17:33; 14:34–35) built around a handful of sapiential Q¹ fragments (Q 13:24; 14:26, 27; 17:33; 14:34–35).[129] In particular, wisdom sayings about the narrow door (13:24), the cost of discipleship (14:26, 27; 17:33), and salt (14:34–35) now become moments in an explicitly polemical discourse about the fate of "this generation." The older sayings tradition forms a platform upon which the exegetical speculation of 13:35 can rest and serve deuteronomistic ends.

In Mark, this supposed exegetical saying of Jesus becomes the basis for a narrative, one which, like Q's usage of the saying, has negative overtones. Unlike the Q version, Mark's version is now presented as something people actually said, as opposed to something people *should* have said, and *will* say in the eschatological future. Several of the aspects of Mark's narrative can be derived from the tradition: the connection with Jerusalem, the acclamation of the people, and the quotation itself.[130] The elements *not* already present in this tradition are the spreading of the cloaks in Mark 11:7–8, the cutting of the leafy branches (στιβάδας) in 11:8, and of course the colt upon which Jesus rides.[131] The branches, however, are suggested by the immediate context of the quotation from Ps 118, where it is specified that, as part of the rejoicing for he who comes in the name of the Lord, one should "bind the festal procession with branches" (118:27).[132] Further exegetical reflections, spinning off from the triumphal entry motif apparent in the latter part of Ps 118 (especially 118:15–27), may have suggested the similar pronouncements of Zech 9:9, reinforced by this text's explicit address to the people of Jerusalem: "Rejoice greatly, O daughter of Zion! Shout aloud, O daughter of Jerusalem! Lo, your king comes to you; trium-

---

129. Kloppenborg, *Formation of Q*, 223–37, 345; and for a more recent, and thorough, analysis of the development of Q 13:34–35, see Smith, *The Post-Mortem Vindication of Jesus*, 31–48, 94–122.

130. This observation, and indeed, the suppositions which follow, remains valid even if Q *is* Mark's source for this saying. In either case, as with most of the examples discussed so far, Mark is using sayings and exegetical traditions—whether oral or written—as a basis for constructing essentially imaginary narratives.

131. The animal is referred to as a πῶλον, which NRSV translates "colt." See BAGD³, s.v. πῶλον; LSJ, s.v. πῶλον; and, for discussion, Gundry, *Mark: A Commentary on His Apology*, 625–26.

132. Mark's awareness of the source of the "he who comes" quotation should be assumed, since Mark adds ὡσαννά to the Q version of the saying; since he shows awareness of this particular Psalm elsewhere (i.e., in Mark 12:10–11, quoting verbatim LXX Ps117:22–23/Ps 118:22–23); and since in general his use of the Psalms is extensive.

phant and victorious is he, humble and riding on an ass, on a colt, the foal of an ass."[133] This material provides us with the source of the colt.[134] We can view Mark's story of the triumphal entry as a rather attractive instance of his practice of generating narratives not simply from sayings traditions, but also, in detail, from exegetical meditations thereon.

Exegetical meditation as a source for stories about Jesus is also famously apparent in Mark's account of Jesus's actual crucifixion, particularly in the extent to which narrative details of the crucifixion are derived

---

133. We can conclude Markan knowledge of this text, since he alludes to it elsewhere. (1) In Mark 6:34, Jesus is said to have "compassion on them [the crowds who followed him] because they were like sheep, without a shepherd." Zech 10:2 asserts that, "The people wander like sheep; they are afflicted for want of a shepherd" (cf. also Ezekiel 34:1–31). Both the texts from Zechariah and Ezekiel use the image of the shepherdless sheep to launch a criticism against the "shepherds." While Mark does not explicitly quote this additional material, the allusion to it is obviously in line with his polemical interests. (2) In Mark 14:27, Zech 13:7 is quoted outright (albeit in a slightly modified form): "I will strike the shepherd, and the sheep will be scattered." (Howard Clark Kee, *Community of the New Age: Studies in Mark's Gospel* [Philadelphia: Westminster, 1977], 46, identifies Zech 13:7 LXX as the source of this quotation.) (3) Even more strikingly, Zech 9 adopts the peculiar phraseology, normally attributed to Exod 24:8 (so Gundry, *Mark: A Commentary on His Apology*, 841), of "the blood of my covenant" (Zech 9:11), and unlike the reference in Exodus, where the "blood of the covenant" is splashed onto stones, this same chapter in Zechariah refers to the *drinking* of blood: "They shall drink their blood like wine" (Zech 9:15 NRSV). It is difficult, at least for me, not to see a procedure here in which Mark takes whole segments from his scriptures, meditates on them, and scatters references and allusions to them through various points in his story of Jesus. Dale C. Allison Jr., *The End of the Ages Has Come: An Early Interpretation of the Passion and Resurrection of Jesus* (Philadelphia: Fortress, 1985), 33, asserts that: "The scriptural background of Mark 11:1–16:8 (excluding chap. 13) consists primarily of three blocks of material: the Psalms (especially 22, 41–43, 61, 69, 109, 118); Deutero-Isaiah; *and Zechariah 9–14*" (emphasis added). See his useful discussion (ibid., 33–36) of the extensive use made of Zechariah by Mark and Mark's theological agenda in so doing, as well as his table of Markan allusions to this text (ibid., 34). On the use of Zechariah more generally, see, e.g., C. H. Dodd, *The Old Testament in the New* (Philadelphia: Fortress, 1963), 17–18.

134. Mark's apparent use of the text of Zechariah elsewhere, and his construction of this story out of an exegetical pastiche, suggests that Matthew's direct quotation of the relevant text, as well as his bizarre alteration of the story to accord more mechanically (if ridiculously) to the prooftext, represents a *recognition* on Matthew's part of Mark's allusion, rather than being Matthew's *creation* of an allusion out of a narrative detail (Matt 21:1–9). In short, Matthew makes explicit what Mark clearly already intended.

directly from Ps 22.[135] As Mack states, after one subtracts Markan redactional motifs and allusions to Ps 22, "there is nothing left over except information about the name of the place, Golgotha."[136] One can go further: the whole fabric of the final hours of Jesus in Mark is a pastiche of various scriptural texts, and while Ps 22 has pride of place, we might also note allusions to Isa 53:7 (consider Mark 14:61; 15:4–5),[137] Ps 69:21 (and Prov

---

135. Again we see, as was especially apparent with the triumphal entry but also in Mark's baptism account and elsewhere, the combination of overt quotation with allusive echoes, in some cases from the same text. In the case of the crucifixion, the direct quotation (albeit in Aramaic, corrected to Hebrew by Matthew and deleted altogether by Luke) of Ps 22 occurs in Jesus's cry of dereliction on the cross: "My God, my God, why have you forsaken me?" (Mark 15:34/Ps 22:1). The mocking and taunts of witnesses to the crucifixion, including details of the sarcastic exhortation that Jesus save himself and that those involved were shaking their heads (Mark 15:29–32), derives from Ps 22:6–8: "I am … scorned by others, and despised by the people. All who see me mock at me; they make mouths at me, they shake their heads; 'Commit your cause to the Lord; let him deliver—let him rescue the one in whom he delights'" (NRSV; for the head-shaking, see also Ps 109:25). The division of Jesus's clothes and casting lots for them in Mark 15:24 is again quite exactly dictated in Ps 22:18: "They stare and gloat over me; they divide my clothes among themselves, and for my clothing they cast lots" (NRSV).

136. Mack, *Myth of Innocence*, 296. He adds that even this is a Markan narrative device with symbolic overtones.

137. Isaiah 52–53 seems generally to have had an impact on Mark's conception of Jesus's passion. It is possible that other specific allusions to this text may be found in Mark, though they are not as obvious as the allusion to Isaiah 53:7. Two in particular stand out. (1) Isaiah 53:12, "and he was numbered with the transgressors," may be hinted at by the Barabbas episode in Mark 15:6–15 as well as, more clearly, by Mark's explicit notice that Jesus was crucified alongside bandits (δύο λῃστάς) in 15:27. It is interesting that Mark 15:28, omitted from most critical texts as a later gloss, draws out this allusion explicitly, following the notice about the robbers with a direct quotation of Isaiah 53:12, introduced by καὶ ἐπληρώθη ἡ γραφὴ ἡ λέγουσα... (and cf. Luke 22:37, for a slightly different application). The omission of the verse is extraordinarily well-attested (א, A, B, C, D, X, Y, etc.), and I am not trying to claim this verse as original to Mark (see also Bruce M. Metzger, *A Textual Commentary on the Greek New Testament*, 2nd ed. [New York: United Bible Societies, 1994], 99; and cf. Adela Yarbro Collins, *The Beginning of the Gospel: Probings of Mark in Context* [Eugene, OR: Wipf & Stock, 2001], 113; Gundry, *Mark: A Commentary on His Apology*, 960; and numerous others). My point, rather, is that, just as Matthew recognized and made explicit Mark's allusion to Zech 9:9 in Mark's description of Jesus riding on a colt, so an ancient glossator recognized and proceeded to make explicit an allusion to 53:12 here. (2) Isaiah 53:9 states that, "They made his grave with the wicked, and with a rich man in his death."

31:6?—compare with Mark 15:23, 36), Amos 8:9 (see Mark 15:33), and possibly Joel 3:15 (see Mark 15:33).[138] None of this is new, of course, but the dominant scholarly tendency has been to see Mark as a preserver of traditions.[139] Hence, the massive prooftexting so obvious in the latter parts of the passion narrative is either regarded as post hoc scriptural applications or embellishments to events that actually happened,[140] or as pre-Markan Christian exegetical traditions taken up into Mark's story,[141] or worse still as genuine actions of the historical Jesus deliberately intended to evoke scripture.[142] Setting aside the traditional scholarly use of Mark

---

While Mark does not characterize Joseph of Arimathea as "wicked," he does appear to be a wealthy man, since he "was a respected member of the council" (Mark 15:43) and since he owned a rock-cut tomb. It is thus possible that Mark's assertion that Jesus was buried in the tomb of a man at least implied to be wealthy (Mark 15:42–46) is intended to allude to Isaiah 53:9.

138. Various other allusions abound in other segments of the passion narrative. See, e.g., George W. E. Nickelsburg, "Passion Narratives," *ABD* 5:172–75.

139. Even while redaction criticism emphasizes Mark's creativity as an author, the extent of that creativity is often compromised in the interests of retaining the possibility of using Mark—"creative author" or not—as a *source* for "Jesus traditions." Hence the "indisputable facts" of Sanders, with which I opened this paper, constitute a summary of the Markan plot, requiring, of course, that Mark's redactional creativity must be restricted to quite minor points.

140. The idea, that is, that Jesus actually was crucified alongside two criminals, and this was rationalized in terms of a selective reading of scripture. See, e.g., Bultmann, *History of the Synoptic Tradition*, 281; implicitly, Sanders, *Jesus and Judaism*, 99–100, in his critique of Vielhauer's hypothesis that scriptural allusions generated the invention of the Judas story; Cranfield, *Gospel according to St. Mark*, 455, on the division of Jesus's clothes in Mark 15:24, and 456, on the mockery of passers-by in Mark 15:29. Taylor, *Gospel according to St. Mark*, 589, also regards the division of Jesus's clothes as a genuinely historical event which *called to mind* Ps 22:19, rather than being *motivated* by it.

141. E.g., Linnemann, *Studien zur Passionsgeschichte*, 157–58, 169; Meier, *Marginal Jew*, 1:266.

142. See, e.g., Joachim Jeremias, *Jesus' Promise to the Nations,* trans. S. H. Hooke, SBT 24 (London: SCM Press, 1958; repr., Philadelphia: Fortress, 1982), 52, where it is argued that Jesus's (historical) entry into Jerusalem on an ass was deliberately intended by him to evoke Zech 9:9, and, moreover, by implication, to evoke also the following verse, which in Jeremias's estimation promises salvation to the gentiles. Similarly, Sanders, *Historical Figure of Jesus*, 274, regarding Mark 15:34/Ps 22:1: "My guess is that Jesus' cry was his own reminiscence of the psalm, not just a motif inserted by the early Christians." Also credulous about the historical Jesus's actual quotation of Psalm 22:1 on the cross are Charlesworth, *Jesus within Judaism*, 144; Cranfield, *Gospel according*

(and other gospel texts) as windows onto the historical Jesus, and bearing in mind Mark's procedure in other places in the gospel, we should instead see in this extensive prooftexting the *source* of Mark's imagination of the death of Jesus. As George Nickelsburg says:

> While, from the point of view of genre, the pattern of persecution and vindication reflects the Jewish stories mentioned above, Mark's Passion narrative also sounds this double motif through allusions to canonical psalms about the suffering and exaltation of the righteous one. Noteworthy are: 14:18 (Ps 41:9); 14:34 (Ps 42:5, 11; 43:5); 15:24, 29, 34 (Ps 22:18, 7, 1); 15:23, 36 (Ps 69:21). Although scripture is not cited in any of these cases (contrast, e.g., 14:27), *the wording of the psalms is narrativized* in a way that was typical of Jewish stories.[143]

As with the baptism account and the triumphal entry, so here also we have a progression from sayings tradition to exegetical analysis of that tradition to, finally, narrative.[144] In the case of the death on the cross the original

---

to *St. Mark*, 458; Taylor, *Gospel according to St. Mark*, 594; and others. See the bizarre discussion of the historical Jesus's supposed consciousness of "fulfilling" scripture in R. V. G. Tasker, *The Old Testament in the New Testament* (Grand Rapids: Eerdmans, 1968), 15–23.

143. Nickelsburg, "Passion Narratives," 173, emphasis added.

144. Crossan, *Historical Jesus*, 376, suggests a similar process, with specific reference to the passion narratives: "The process developed, in other words, over these primary steps. First, the *historical passion*, composed of minimal knowledge, was known only in the general terms recorded by, say, Josephus or Tacitus. Next, the *prophetic passion*, composed of multiple and discrete biblical allusions and seen most clearly in a work like the *Epistle of Barnabas*, developed biblical applications over, under, around, and through that open framework. Finally, those multiple and discrete exercises were combined into the *passion narrative* as a single sequential story" (emphasis original).

Crossan's conclusions are not identical to my own either regarding specific texts (and the sequences and sources of those texts' evolution), or with respect to his positing a pre-Markan origin to many of the scriptural allusions that appear in Mark's passion. But he is worth quoting on this point because he *does*, I think, correctly identify as a general tendency of the tradition the movement (1) from scanty "historical" information (2) to exegetical traditions of various sorts (3) to, finally, comprehensive narrative which fuses the two into a single and coherent whole.

I note in passing that Nickelsburg (cf. the long quotation above), Mack, and others have established that the generic model used by Mark is that of the wisdom story of the righteous one who nobly suffers death and persecution for his cause. I am

sayings tradition is obscured, but the basic Markan procedure of spinning narrative out of exegetical prooftexts is evident once again.

Indeed it is possible to trace *some* minor reference to crucifixion back to the sayings tradition, that is, the triply attested saying that followers of Jesus must be willing to take up the cross, which appears in Q (14:27) and the Gospel of Thomas (55), as well as in Mark (8:34–35).[145] It is striking that this cross saying appears in two texts—Q and the Gospel of Thomas—which show neither narrative nor conceptual interest in Jesus's crucifixion at all and for which the saying is used to offer Jesus as an implicit model for a willingness to endure humiliating or unpleasant duties in the service of wisdom.[146] Taken on its own, the saying focuses not on crucifixion itself but on the shameful pre-execution process of carrying the crossbar to the place of execution. Thus, as I say elsewhere regarding this material (and so can dispense with spelling out in detail here):

> Probably the best reading of the Q saying [14:27], in a document that shows knowledge of some form of persecution, is that the saying inevitably conjures up the image of Jesus' death, rendering the metaphor that much more potent. It allows one to imagine the burdensome humiliation implied in the saying precisely as a way of imitating Jesus. Its primary meaning, however, relies more on everyday knowledge (how execution by crucifixion took place) and the experiences of the people transmitting the saying (public humiliation) than on the specific awareness of how Jesus met his death…. The broadly mimetic thrust of the material suggests that no such narrative [of Jesus' death] would be regarded as interesting by the Q people. The interpretation of Q is such that it would relativize Jesus' death: the death is rationalized by placing it in the context of a whole sequence of other deaths—past (the prophets and John the Baptist, in the later material) and future (the Q people, in both earlier and later material)—thereby rendering it devoid of unique significance.

---

taking this conclusion for granted and focusing instead on determining whence the details and episodes of Mark's story, not its overarching generic logic.

145. For varying assessments and interpretations of this saying, see, e.g., Crossan, *Historical Jesus*, 353; Funk, *Five Gospels*, 78–79; Hultgren, *Rise of Normative Christianity*, 33; and especially David Seeley, "Blessings and Boundaries: Interpretations of Jesus' Death in Q," *Semeia* 55 (1991): 131–46, and "Jesus' Death in Q," *NTS* 38 (1992): 222–34. Several of these authors mention the parallel use of cross imagery in Epictetus, *Diatr.* 2.2.20.

146. This is particularly true of its usage in Q. See my comments in "Major Episodes in the Biography of Jesus," 210–13.

The important thing about Jesus' death is not that it was unique, but that it was just another instance of a predictable and common, if regrettable, occurrence. Explicit mention of Jesus' death, never mind a sequential narrative of its specific circumstances, is no more required than would be a narrative of John's death (which we find, interestingly enough, in Mark 6:17–29). The case with *Thomas* is less clear, but similar. The death of Jesus is known. It is taken up as a mimetic ideal, perhaps metaphorically (much the same way that *Thomas* turns persecution into an internal phenomenon in saying 69), but it is neither the center of interest nor is it conceived to have any unique salvific import. The death of Jesus thus crops up as a multiply attested element in the image of Jesus the teacher, where reference to it is placed in his mouth as a way of underscoring what is involved in truly adhering to his words.[147]

Thus I conclude that:

> One can by no means deny that the crucifixion really happened. What one can deny is that there is any solid evidence that would make the *narrative portrayal* of this event predate the multiply attested sayings noted here. The details of Jesus' crucifixion, and the narrative of it, seem to have been cobbled together from a number of sayings that reflected on the significance of Jesus' death (or at least took it for granted), from biblical proof-texts, and from Mark's literary imagination.[148]

More interestingly, and finally, Mark may have supplemented the sayings, exegesis, and imagination that constitute his "sources" for the passion with yet another technique: the deliberate and self-conscious anachronistic retrojection onto the past of important events of the present. This has already been noted to some degree in the observation that Mark retrojects what may be contemporary ritual practices (*whose* ritual practices, precisely, remains difficult to determine) onto Jesus's lifetime as episodes like the baptism and the Last Supper. It is also apparent in his rendering of the "cleansing" of the temple as a foreshadowing of and symbolic allusion to the actual destruction of the temple that took place in Mark's own recent past. To these examples one might also add Mark's references to Pharisaic debates with Jesus as anachronistic retrojections of postwar circumstances[149] and Rudolf Bultmann's hypothesis that Mark's

---

147. Ibid., 212, 213.
148. Ibid., 215, emphasis added.
149. Famously, Mark 2:18–22 and 2:23–28 deal with the *disciples'* behavior, not

transfiguration (9:2–8) was originally a resurrection appearance story cast back into Jesus's lifetime.[150] More controversially, one may also argue that "the Twelve" as they appear in Mark could be a retrojection as well. References to "the Twelve" as an inner group of Jesus's disciples during his lifetime appear for the first time only in Mark, and their subsequent appearance in gospel texts is probably indebted to Mark.[151] Independent texts that deal with Jesus's disciples, such as the Gospel of Thomas, do not show awareness of a circle of twelve such disciples. Other texts, such as Q, fail to refer to Jesus's disciples as a specific group, and they use twelve only as a symbolic reference to Israel.[152] Paul, however, does mention "the Twelve" in 1 Cor 15:5: after his death, Jesus "appeared to Cephas, then to the Twelve." It is this reference that makes me think Mark is doing more here than his usual spinning of stories out of sayings material (such as Q 22:28, 30). In addition, I think, he has taken an actual, historical (and significant) group of twelve whose import was that they claimed to have had a vision of Jesus resurrected,[153] and he has retrojected that central import

---

that of Jesus, and thus appear to be obvious instances of the retrojection onto Jesus's life of concerns that arose later, among groups of his followers. The issue of the presence and standing of Pharisees in Galilee prior to 70 CE is complex and controversial. See, among others, Shaye J. D. Cohen, "Were Pharisees and Rabbis the Leaders of Communal Prayer and Torah Study in Antiquity? The Evidence of the New Testament, Josephus, and the Early Church Fathers," in *Evolution of the Synagogue: Problems and Progress*, ed. Howard Clark Kee and Lynn H. Cohick (Harrisburg, PA: Trinity Press International, 1999), 89–105. See also the comments of Richard A. Horsley, *Archaeology, History, and Society in Galilee: The Social Context of Jesus and the Rabbis* (Harrisburg, PA: Trinity Press International, 1996), 31, 33–34, 151–53.

150. As noted above. See Bultmann, *History of the Synoptic Tradition*, 259–61. I should note that the massive parallelism, discussed to some degree above, between the transfiguration and the other two key Markan episodes of baptism and death on the cross suggests extensive Markan redactional emendation of whatever tradition might lurk behind this account.

151. For an argument against the historicity of "the Twelve" as Jesus's disciples, see Heinz O. Guenther, *The Footprints of Jesus' Twelve in Early Christian Traditions: A Study in the Meaning of Religious Symbolism* (New York: Lang, 1984).

152. See Q 22:28, 30: "You who have followed me … will sit on thrones judging the twelve tribes of Israel." (Cf. Jas 1:1 for a similar usage. It is notable that, outside of the canonical gospels and Acts, Rev 21:14 *does* refer to "twelve apostles.") Once again, note that there appears to be a precedent in the sayings tradition for Mark's narrative conceptions, though in the case of the Twelve the issue is complicated by Paul's reference (see immediately below).

153. While this reference is usually read in light of the gospel presentation of

back into the life of Jesus by making them his inner circle of disciples. If so, we would have yet another example of anachronistic retrojection as an actual *compositional technique* on Mark's part.

If such a technique be granted, its most striking manifestation might—tentatively, hypothetically, and with all due caution—be found in the passion narrative itself, especially in its account of Jesus's trials. Such a claim has been put forward recently by Theodore Weeden.[154] Weeden refers to the *massive* similarities between Mark's story of a man named Jesus and Josephus's story, set more than thirty years later, of another man named Jesus.[155] Josephus's account is worth quoting in full:

> But a further portent was even more alarming. Four years before the war, when the city was enjoying profound peace and prosperity, there came to the feast at which it is the custom of all Jews to erect tabernacles to God, one Jesus, son of Ananias, a rude peasant, who, standing in the temple, suddenly began to cry out, "A voice from the east, a voice from the west, a voice from the four winds; a voice against Jerusalem and the sanctuary, a voice against the bridegroom and the bride, a voice against all the people." Day and night he went about all the alleys with this cry on his lips. Some of the leading citizens, incensed at these ill-omened

---

"twelve disciples," Paul's wording, taken on its own, only suggests a known group of persons to whom Jesus "appeared." Moreover, Paul's language implies a distinction between Cephas/Peter and "the Twelve," suggesting (again, if Paul is read in isolation, and without interference from familiar gospel presentations) that Peter is *not* a member of this group, flying in the face of the canonical gospels' portrayal. One might also note that if the story of Judas as betrayer is to be taken seriously (which in fact I think it should *not* be), a reference to the disciples who witness Jesus's resurrection should in fact include only "the eleven" (see, e.g., Matt 28:16).

154. See Theodore J. Weeden Sr., "The Two Jesuses, Jesus of Jerusalem and Jesus of Nazareth: Provocative Parallels and Imaginative Imitation," *Forum* NS 6 (2003): 133–341.

155. This story's similarities to the account of Jesus's trials has been noted by others. For instance, Craig A. Evans, *Jesus and His Contemporaries: Comparative Studies* (Leiden: Brill, 2001), 361, notes a whole series of specific parallels between the two Jesuses, but he uses those parallels *not* to suggest any relationship between the two stories, but to affirm the essential historicity of the gospels' trial accounts, seeing the parallels as a function of a common understanding of routine judicial practices. The parallels have also been noted by, among others, Paula Fredriksen, *Jesus of Nazareth, King of the Jews: A Jewish Life and the Emergence of Christianity* (New York: Knopf, 1999), 228; and Richard A. Horsley, *Jesus and the Spiral of Violence: Popular Jewish Resistance in Roman Palestine* (Minneapolis: Fortress, 1992), 300–304.

words, arrested the fellow and severely chastised him. But he, without a word on his own behalf or for the private ear of those who smote him, only continued the cries as before. Thereupon, the magistrates, supposing, as was indeed the case, that the man was under some supernatural impulse, brought him before the Roman governor; there, although flayed to the bone with scourges, he neither sued for mercy nor shed a tear, but, merely introducing the most mournful of variations into his ejaculation, responded to each stroke with "Woe to Jerusalem!" When Albinus, the governor, asked him who and whence he was and why he uttered these cries, he answered him never a word, but unceasingly reiterated his dirge over the city, until Albinus pronounced him a maniac and let him go. During the whole period up to the outbreak of the war he neither approached nor was seen talking to any of the citizens, but daily, like a prayer that he had conned, repeated his lament, "Woe to Jerusalem!" He neither cursed any of those who beat him from day to day, nor blessed those who offered him food: to all men that melancholy presage was his one reply. His cries were loudest at the festivals. So for seven years and five months he continued his wail, his voice never flagging nor his strength exhausted, until in the siege, having seen his presage verified, he found his rest. For, while going his round and shouting in piercing tones from the wall, "Woe once more to the city and to the people and to the temple," as he added a last word, "and woe to me also," a stone hurled from a *ballista* struck and killed him on the spot. So with these ominous words still upon his lips he passed away. Reflecting on these things one will find that God has a care for men, and by all kinds of premonitory signs shows His people the way of salvation, while they owe their destruction to folly and calamities of their own choosing. (Josephus, *J. W.* 6.5.3–4 §§300–310 [LCL: Thackeray])

Noting no less than twenty-three significant parallel motifs as well as common details of wording between the accounts,[156] Weeden explores a variety of potential explanations, ranging from pure coincidence to various kinds of literary dependency. In the end, following the conceptual and methodological framework set out by Dennis MacDonald,[157] Weeden asserts that Mark, like other ancient authors, is deliberately using a *hypotext*, with which he assumes his audience will be familiar, to construct his

---

156. Strikingly, Weeden also notes that the vast majority of these common motifs occur in exactly the same *order* in Josephus and Mark.

157. See Dennis R. MacDonald, *The Homeric Epics and the Gospel of Mark* (New Haven: Yale University Press, 2000), especially 2–14.

story of Jesus's last days, and even, in some cases, details about Jesus that are presented in other portions of his gospel.[158] The hypotext in question, Weeden asserts, may be an *oral* account of the actions and death of Jesus son of Ananias as a portent of the temple's destruction, which circulated after the war, and which was brought to Mark's own context (which Weeden believes is Caesarea Philippi) by postwar refugees, troop movements, and/or military celebrations in the regions around Galilee. Josephus is dependent on the same orally circulating story.

If Weeden is right, then our knowledge of Markan compositional technique vis-à-vis the passion narrative is that much more comprehensive. Mark has used a well-known and orally circulating event from his own time—an event viewed, significantly, as an omen of destruction against the temple—and anachronistically retrojected it thirty or forty years into the past. He has done so in part to provide himself with substance and details for Jesus's last days: the annoyance caused by his antitemple activities, his initial trial by the Jewish authorities, his audience before the Roman procurator, his silence in the face of interrogation, the procurator's lack of interest in the case, the scourging, and so on. But he also does so, according to Weeden, with the full knowledge that auditors of his tale will *recognize* the source of his hypotext, and they will view his composition as an elaboration or commentary thereupon. Mark has taken contemporary, common, non-"Christian" traditions from his broader environment and has modified them in full view of his audience.

In Sum: Mark's Techniques

In addition to the more traditional redaction-critical model of Mark's authorship as consisting predominantly in the selection, ordering, and especially modification of Jesus-traditions available to him, the foregoing

---

158. Such as the notice that people think Jesus is deranged (Mark 3:21: ἐξέστη), parallel to Albinus's conviction that Jesus son of Ananias is deranged (μανίαν); or again, the use of LXX Jer 7:11 in Mark 11:17 (conflated with Isaiah 56:7), and the use of Jer 7:34 as the source of Jesus son of Ananias's condemnation of the temple. These observations are Weeden's, not mine. In his published work on this topic, however, Weeden vacillates on the source of this account: initially the story derives, in both Mark and Josephus, from an actual event, transmitted orally. Subsequently, he argues that Mark's version is derived from Josephus, and that Josephus composed the account with Jeremiah in mind. Of these two options, I have chosen to adhere to the former view.

discussion suggests that we also view Mark's authorship as consisting of straightforward composition of material for which there is *no* direct warrant in the tradition. As one might expect, the materials with the highest claim to having been composed in this fashion are precisely those which are most critical for Mark's generic formulation as a *bios* of Jesus: the framework stories, the unique biographical episodes which are the *sine qua non* of any "life" of Jesus.[159] But we can say more about Mark's creation of these episodes than that he simply composed them *de novo*. In fact, he did no such thing. These new traditions about Jesus were constructed, at least in part, according to a limited number of quite specific and comprehensible techniques, which built upon and played with "prepositioned elements." The elements in question were: (1) sayings tradition, which may or may not have gone back to Jesus;[160] (2) the written scriptures, especially the Psalms and Prophets, most often, apparently, in their LXX form;[161] and (3) events of Mark's own time, both internal and external to the various Jesus movements.[162]

---

159. Hence the spectacle of the most compelling historical Jesus studies, e.g., Sanders's, being based on the positively worst (i.e., least historical) episodes in the tradition: the *need* for those episodes to stand if we are to write a biography of Jesus at all.

160. This qualification is offered not only to address the certainty that some of the sayings material that Mark borrowed from Jesus-tradition does not actually go back to the historical Jesus. It also allows for the possibility that Mark ascribed sayings to Jesus that *existed* prior to Mark but were not *attributed to Jesus* prior to Mark. In other words, there is no particular reason to think that Mark would have balked at taking unattributed sayings, or sayings attributed to figures other than Jesus, and put them in Jesus's mouth.

161. On this point see especially Kee, *Community of the New Age*, 46–47. On the one hand, Kee notes a whole series of Markan texts (11:9, 17a, 17b; 12:10–11, 29, 31, 33c, 36; 13:4a, 7b, 19, 22; 14:27, 34, 38, 62; 15:32; 16:8) in which the point of the quotation or allusion to scripture rides on the details of the LXX's wording. On the other hand, he notes that Mark's freedom with scriptural texts, evidenced also in his tendency to merge or blend together widely separated passages, extends to his choice of which version to cite: "The version of the text employed is chosen so freely that the critic cannot ascertain whether the quotation is based on the Hebrew or Greek recensions, or on some deviant or corrupt text" (47).

162. There is no reason to regard these as the only "prepositioned elements" in question or these compositional techniques as the only ones Mark has employed. They are simply the ones that I happen to have noticed and that I regard as being of interest. I also note that my paper has not focused on the many instances in which Mark *is* using actual traditions about Jesus as direct source material, e.g., the miracle catenae, sayings traditions used as such, controversy stories, healing and exorcism accounts,

All of these compositional techniques are remarkable, not only for their failure to provide any actual historical evidence for Jesus's biography, but also for the way in which they underscore and confirm Mack's conclusions that Mark is not only a highly creative author, but a highly literate and literary one as well.[163] Mack's characterization of Mark as an author bears repeating:

> It is now possible to emphasize that Mark's accomplishment was an authorial, intellectual achievement.... Mark's Gospel stands at the intersection of many streams of cultural, literary, and social history. It was created by effort, intellectual effort, and it is marked by conscious authorial intention. Mark was a scholar. A reader of texts and a writer of texts.... Mark's Gospel was not the product of divine revelation. It was not a pious transmission of revered tradition. It was composed at a desk in a scholar's study, lined with texts and open to discourse with other intellectuals.[164]

Mark thus appears not in the guise of a well-intentioned purveyor of tradition but rather as someone self-consciously constructing information, and doing so on the basis of no real information at all. This argument need not be restricted to the texts and events discussed at some length above; it could probably be shown to apply also to stories such as the call of the Twelve, the empty tomb, and others. In terms of the basic outline of Mark's Gospel, and the unique events of Jesus's life ("framework stories"), Mark appears to have no legitimate sources at all. Everything he knows about Jesus's biography, instead, is taken from sayings material,

---

and so on. I do not mean to deny the existence of such sources; they are simply not my focus here.

163. See especially Mack, *Myth of Innocence*, 321–23 and n. 3.

164. Ibid., 321–323. Horsley, *Hearing the Whole Story*, 283 n. 1 (and cf. 232), asserts that these conclusions show Mack constructing Mark in his own image. But Horsley's disposition of the evidence for Mark's use of texts is far less satisfactory than Mack's (or Kee's). For Horsley, Mark's blending of texts and apparent reliance on different versions of scriptural materials is in fact evidence for his literary *incompetence* and the *orality* of his sources. Not only does this explanation actually fail to account for the extent to which Mark uses and relies on literary allusion, it is also rather disconfirmed by my observations that Mark *constructs* stories, in part, out of scriptural material. If this is so, then we cannot appeal to layers of "tradition" or multiple sources to account for Mark's multiple scriptural references and his freedom in the versions he chooses to cite; this multiplicity comes from Mark himself.

from scripture, and from the exigencies of Mark's own time. Moreover, this approach is itself determined by the exigencies of Mark's genre. As I say elsewhere, "The actual gospel genre creates both a theological and a literary predisposition to biography.... This consideration raises the question of whether we can trust narrative gospels to represent Jesus accurately in those instances in which the information they provide is crucial to their formulation as a genre."[165]

As a result, the creative aspects of Mark's endeavor become that much more pronounced. He has not simply used existing material to compose a new genre for talking about Jesus; he has actually adopted this genre in *spite* of the fact that he has such slender resources for it. Why on earth does Mark adopt a genre that practically compels him to adopt such a demanding approach?

In this connection, it may be worthwhile to consider the peculiarly circular nature of Mark's characterization of Jesus as a teacher and of Jesus's message. On the one hand, it is clear that Mark *does* regard Jesus as a teacher.[166] His mission is described and characterized in terms of "teaching" (or "preaching" to) both the crowds and his disciples.[167] The private time he spends with his disciples is employed in the service of explication of teaching (see Mark 4:10–34) and in correcting the disciples' misunderstandings of God's plan (see 8:27–33). Significant events become occasions for significant teaching.[168] Mark even at times conceptualizes Jesus's *actions* as teaching. Thus, for instance, the point of the healing of the paralytic (2:8–12) is apparently to provide a demonstration of the forgiveness of sins initially offered to the man (2:5); again, the demonstration in the temple (11:15–17) is presented as concurrent with and supplemental to Jesus "teaching and saying" (11:17). In Mark, Jesus's actions illustrate and reinforce his teaching.

---

165. Arnal, "Major Episodes in the Biography of Jesus," 221 n. 35.

166. Hence the name of Vernon K. Robbins's rhetorical study of Mark: *Jesus the Teacher: A Socio-Rhetorical Interpretation of Mark* (Philadelphia: Fortress, 1984).

167. Jesus "teaches" (διδάσκω) at Mark 1:21, 22; 2:13; 4:1, 2; 6:2, 6, 34; 8:31; 9:31; 10:1; 11:17; 12:14, 35; 14:49; he "preaches/proclaims" (κηρύσσω) at Mark 1:14, 38, 39; and he is referred to as "teacher" (διδάσκαλος) at Mark 4:38; 5:35; 9:17, 38; 10:17, 20, 35; 12:14, 19, 32; 13:1; 14:14.

168. E.g., 8:14–21, with reference to the feeding miracles, and 9:9–13, with reference to the transfiguration.

At the same time, the content of Jesus's teaching in Mark is curiously empty. Mark provides little ethical instruction emanating from Jesus, nor again many practical rules for the conduct of groups of followers[169]—doubtless the reason Matthew and Luke saw fit to supplement Mark by the inclusion of Q material, which could be used to "flesh out" and lend needed substance to the image of Jesus the teacher. In Mark, the teaching of Jesus, curiously, is almost entirely about Jesus himself, specifically his identity, authority, and fate. Jesus's "teaching" is simply that he himself is God's Son, the Son of Man, and the Christ, and that this identity both infuses him with authority and simultaneously dictates the path of suffering he must undergo. Thus, even while the events of the gospel are exemplars of Jesus's teaching, all of his teaching in turn refers to the events of the gospel's account. The circular and vacuous nature of the resultant picture of Jesus as teacher is most striking in Mark's interpretation of the parable of the sower (4:1–20), precisely the location in which Mark most fleshes

---

169. There are a few exceptions to this general characterization. Jesus is presented in Mark as offering teaching on proper dining company (2:15–17), on fasting (2:18–20), on Sabbath observance (2:23–28, 3:1–6), on purity issues related to food (7:1–23), on marriage (10:2–12), and on paying taxes (12:13–17). These examples, however, strike me as exceptions that prove the rule. Every single one of them is offered in the context of a controversy story with one or another of the religious authorities. Their main purpose, then, is not to communicate doctrine but to show off Jesus for the authoritative and witty teacher that he is, at the expense of his interlocutors. The point behind such forms—whether in their original form or in terms of their usage in Mark—is thus primarily, at least, *that* Jesus is an effective and exceptional teacher, and not the communication of that teaching's content. Secondarily, of course, the subject matters of the controversies tell us something about the concerns that actuated their original composition. Obviously, matters of religiocultural practice are under debate among Jews, with the Jewish tradents of Jesus-materials perceived by "outsiders" (that is, other Jews who are not interested in Jesus-traditions) to be abandoning appropriate markers of their (shared) cultural identity. The Jesus people thus formulate these controversies, *not*, however, to teach proper practice on the matters under debate (dining company, fasting, etc.), but to justify current practice as emanating from a "great" teacher. In these accounts, Jesus the teacher does not really teach but simply establishes and retrenches his own authority. I assume that the composition of these stories is pre-Markan and that Mark has adopted and adapted the stories in the service of their primary function to undergird the authority of Jesus. On the controversy stories and their rhetorical function, see especially Mack, *Myth of Innocence*, 94–96, 198–99, 203–4. See also, for slightly different conclusions, Vernon K. Robbins, "Plucking Grain on the Sabbath," in *Patterns of Persuasion in the Gospels*, ed. Burton L. Mack and Vernon. K. Robbins (Sonoma, CA: Polebridge, 1989), 123–29.

out this characterization of Jesus. Here we encounter a Jesus who teaches in "parables" which, as it turns out, are allegories which themselves refer to Jesus — and his teaching! The parabolic teaching of Jesus turns out to be about the character of the reception of the teaching of Jesus. If we take Mark at his word, then, Jesus's teaching consists primarily in stressing how important Jesus's teaching is.[170] Since, in fact, a great deal of this teaching refers to Jesus's own fate, the circularity and vacuity of the material in chapter 4 is somewhat mitigated by the content of the rest of the gospel. But it remains true that, in Mark, while Jesus is presented as a teacher, the substance of his teaching remains mainly his own identity and authority. His role as a teacher thus points to an identity *other* than a teacher (Son of God, Son of Man, and so forth).

Something similar occurs in Mark's use of the term "gospel" (εὐαγγέλιον). The (numerically) predominant use of the term in Mark appears to retain the Pauline sense of gospel as "the message about Jesus."[171] This usage occurs in Mark 8:35, 10:29, 13:10, and 14:9.[172] On the other hand, the presentation of Jesus having his own "gospel" and proclaiming it also appears in Mark, and it is used as the opening characterization of Jesus's mission: "Now after John was arrested, Jesus came to Galilee, proclaiming [κηρύσσων] the good news of God [τὸ εὐαγγέλιον τοῦ θεοῦ], and saying, 'The time is fulfilled, and the kingdom of God has come near; repent, and believe in the good news [τῷ εὐαγγελίῳ]' " (Mark 1:14–15). Mark combines and conflates the two usages in his third type of deployment of the word, in the incipit to his gospel: "beginning of the good news (gospel) of Jesus Christ, the Son of God" (1:1), a usage both descriptive and, in consequence and by implication, generic (that is, referring to the text of Mark itself).[173]

---

170. On this strange circularity, see especially Burton L. Mack, "Teaching in Parables: Elaboration in Mark 4:1–34," in *Patterns of Persuasion in the Gospels*, 143–60.

171. So also Helmut Koester, *Ancient Christian Gospels: Their History and Development* (London: SCM; Philadelphia: Trinity Press International, 1990), 11, 13.

172. The first two instances refer to sacrifice "for the sake of the gospel" (ἕνεκεν ἐμοῦ καὶ τοῦ εὐαγγελίου); the latter two refer to the future (from Jesus's perspective) proclamation of the gospel (using κηρύσσω). We are thus dealing with a concept that may be larger than the book that Mark has written or any narrative of Jesus's life.

173. The usage of the term εὐαγγέλιον in Mark has been the subject of various investigations and commentary. Famously, see Marxsen, *Mark the Evangelist*, 117–50. See also, among others, Collins *Beginning of the Gospel*, 36–38; Gundry, *Mark: A Commentary on His Apology*, 32–33; Howard Clark Kee, *Jesus in History: An Approach to the Study of the Gospels* (New York: Harcourt, Brace & World, 1970), 119–23; Mack,

Logically, Mark views Jesus, the authoritative teacher, as having no higher object of his teaching than he himself. Thus his message, and the message about him, turn out to be identical.[174] How better, then, to characterize his own literary production by a fusion of these two senses, as, ambiguously, the message *of*, and *about*, Jesus?[175] As Willi Marxsen says:

> For Mark Jesus is the subject and object of the gospel. He achieves this declaration by viewing the earthly Jesus and the Exalted Lord as one. Paul does the same. For him also the Risen or Exalted Lord is always the Crucified One, and vice versa. What is unique in Mark, however, is that he describes the "Crucified One" of Paul's theology not by appropriating the term, but by using the tradition of the earthly Jesus which is now proclaimed by the Exalted Lord. This gives the Gospel its peculiar concept of re-presentation. Christ himself is the gospel.[176]

Myth of Innocence, 205; Theodore J. Weeden Sr., *Mark: Traditions in Conflict* (Philadelphia: Fortress, 1971), 82–85. The assertion that Mark's use of εὐαγγέλιον in 1:1 is not intended as a generic designation of the type of writing which follows (so, e.g., Koester, *Ancient Christian Gospels*, 13–14; Gundry, *Mark: A Commentary on His Apology*, 33) is probably true but somewhat misleading. The term *is* offered by Mark as a characterization of the story which follows, not because that story is, generically, a "gospel," but because Mark has so fused the conceptions of Jesus's life and the "good news" *about* Jesus.

174. This is saying a little bit more than the old form-critical chestnut that "the *bearer* of the message was drawn into it and became its essential *content. The proclaimer became the proclaimed*" (Bultmann, *Theology of The New Testament*, 1:33, emphasis original). Bultmann is expressing a change in the orientation and substance of the message over time. Mark, by contrast, is suggesting, with considerable tension and subtlety, that the substance of the message never did change, and that the proclamation offered by Jesus was, simultaneously, the proclamation about Jesus.

175. Hence Gundry's puzzlement (*Mark: A Commentary on His Apology*, 29) whether we find in Mark 1:1 an objective or subjective genitive is fitting. For Mark, Jesus is both the subject and object of the εὐαγγελίου Ἰησοῦ Χριστοῦ.

176. Marxsen, *Mark The Evangelist*, 148. See also Mack, *Myth of Innocence*, 205: "Jesus announces the 'gospel of Jesus Christ, the son of God,' that Mark has written (Mark 1:1). Jesus's authority is such that he can proclaim his own appearance as the beginning of the gospel." Weeden, *Mark: Traditions in Conflict*, 82, following Marxsen, notes that in Mark 8:35, 10:29, and 13:9–10, "for the sake of the gospel" is contiguous with "for my [Jesus's] sake," and concludes that "in Mark's mind Jesus and the gospel are synonymous."

Mark is really not interested in teaching *or* cult, and he anchors his ideology in neither of these two potential uses of Jesus-oriented teaching predating his work, even though he is more than willing to pillage such traditions and practices for his own purposes. His focus, rather, is on Jesus as a transformative epic character, a focus that directly and necessarily dictated his own generic innovations. Mark does not appear to be deeply rooted in any identifiable "Christian community" formation at all.[177]

We may gain some important insights into the ways in which the fusion of Jesus's teaching with the "gospel" about Jesus dictated, to some degree, Mark's generic choices, by examining one special instance of this fusion, the parable of the tenants (Mark 12:1–12). This parable, in my view, provides us a blueprint of Mark's construction of his gospel and, along the way, also suggests some details about his understanding and treatment of earlier traditions. It represents both a nexus of teaching and biography and, in its self-referential character, seems to embody the whole gospel in miniature.

From Sayings to *Bios*: The Tenants

For Mark, the genre of Jesus's own teaching is, more or less exclusively, the παραβολή: Jesus "did not speak to them *except* in parables" (4:34: χωρὶς δὲ παραβολῆς)" (4:34). Yet for all their purported significance, parables, however defined, do not appear all that frequently in Mark.[178] The extensive body of parables—conceived as short fictitious narratives making a surprising or counter-intuitive point—that we find in special Lukan material[179] and in the Gospel of Thomas[180] are absent from Mark; even the example-

---

177. See now the important critique of appeals to "community" offered by Stanley K. Stowers, "The Concept of 'Community' and the History of Early Christianity," *MTSR* 23 (2011): 238–56.

178. It is not relevant to my present purposes whether Mark's generic designation is accurate or whether it corresponds to the modern scholarly (re)definition of the parable form. Mack addresses the latter question: "The issue is not whether parables as a genre exist. The issue is whether Mark's statement that Jesus taught ἐν παραβολαῖς refers to parables as modern scholars define them, or to parables and other imagistic sayings in their rhetorical function as comparisons" ("Teaching in Parables," 146).

179. E.g., the good Samaritan (Luke 10:30–37) or the dishonest manager (Luke 16:1–9).

180. E.g., the woman with the broken jug (Gos. Thom. 97) or the assassin (Gos. Thom. 98).

stories typical of Q[181] are mostly lacking in Mark. In terms of those types of narratives normally identified as "parables" in modern scholarship, outside of his cluster of parables in chapter 4,[182] Mark appears to include only the parables of the tenants (12:1–12) and of the doorkeeper (13:33–37). More to the point, even the *term* "parable," identified by Mark himself as characterizing Jesus's teaching, is, outside of chapter 4, only employed in four places: (1) "he spoke to them in parables" (3:23) is offered to describe the *comparison* Jesus offers of Satan divided against himself with a kingdom or house similarly divided (3:24–26); (2) Jesus's teaching that "there is nothing outside a person that by going in can defile, but the things that come out are what defile" (7:15) is described as a parable (7:17); (3) the parable of the tenants (12:1–12) is opened with the notice that Jesus "began to speak to them in parables" and is concluded with the realization, among Jesus's listeners, "that he had told this parable against them" (12:12); (4) Jesus exhorts his followers to "learn from the parable/comparison of the fig tree" (ἀπὸ δὲ τῆς συκῆς μάθετε τὴν παραβολήν, 13:28), which is then followed by a description of its blossoming in the appropriate season.

The most prominent exception to Mark's general failure, outside of chapter 4, to actually reproduce the "parabolic" teaching of Jesus, is found in the parable of the tenants. Here we find both the relatively rare terminology of "parable," not once but twice (12:1, 12), and the generic shape of a somewhat extended story.[183] The point of the parable of the tenants in Mark is quite clear: it is not a simple comparison, not an example offered to illustrate a basic point, but rather, like the sower, is meant by Mark to be interpreted allegorically.

---

181. E.g., the example of the house built on rock (Q 6:47–49), or the parable of the great supper (Q 14:16–24).

182. Mark 4:1–34—including the parable of the sower, the parable of the seed growing secretly, and the parable of the mustard seed—all seed parables.

183. Mack is certainly correct to understand Mark's conception of a parable in terms of the rhetorical function of comparison, as Mark's own use of the term in 3:23, 7:17, and 13:28 indicates. At the same time, when Mark decides, in chapter four, to present us with a compendium of Jesus's parabolic teachings, all three "parables" take the form of a *story*—even the seed growing secretly, which could have been presented in the same terse form as the later "parable" of the fig tree but which instead introduces an extraneous character who acts upon these seeds. It seems incontestable that Mark regards "parable" to mean simply a comparison. At the same time, as evinced in chapter four, he also appears to regard Jesus's "parabolic" teaching as better exemplified by the more extended stories that are capable of allegorization.

Mark has signaled this quite clearly in several ways. First, he has "prepared the ground" for his readers and predisposed them toward this mode of reading such stories in his treatment of the sower in chapter 4. Here Jesus is not presented simply as offering a reading of this particular story but explicitly as giving a paradigm for interpreting his parabolic teaching in general: "Do you not understand this parable? Then how will you understand *all the parables*?" (Mark 4:13). Second, the internal characteristics of this parable as it appears in Mark practically beg for an allegorical reading. The figures of vineyard, master, and son are resonant images, especially in light of Mark's use of "son" language to characterize Jesus and the traditional use of vineyard imagery to characterize Israel. Lest the reader miss this latter connection, Mark makes a point of incorporating detailed allusion to the allegory of the vineyard from Isa 5:1–10 LXX into the introduction of the story (especially the echo of Isa 5:2 in Mark 12:1). These features lead Mack—against those who seek a nonallegorical original of this story—to question whether it is even possible to imagine "a situation in which listeners would not have been tempted to pick up on allusive suggestions to other stories and histories at all."[184] Third, Mark helps to direct his readers' interpretation of the story by having Jesus conclude it with a direct scriptural quotation: "The stone that the builders rejected has become the cornerstone; this was the Lord's doing, and it was amazing in our eyes" (Mark 12:10–12 quoting Ps 118:22–23). Such a text, used as a concluding summation of the story, focuses the reader's attention on the motif of the son's rejection in the parable, and hence on the applicability of the story to Jesus's fate. Fourth and finally, lest all of these signals fail to produce their desired hermeneutical effect, Mark concludes the episode by offering the narrative notice that the chief priests, scribes, and elders (see Mark 11:27) "realized that he had told this parable against them" (12:12).

Mark does not overtly explicate this parable because he does not need to. His various hints make it perfectly clear that the parable of the tenants is to be understood as an allegorical synopsis of his view of Jesus and especially the placement of the Jesus-story within the broader context of Israel's epic. That epic is now reduced to a prelude and foreshadowing of the coming of Jesus, which in its turn becomes the culmination of the whole story. That story is understood as the familiar deuteronomistic one of Israel's rejection of God's call and consequent divine punishment. Now

---

184. Mack, *Myth of Innocence*, 169 n. 24.

it is refigured as a story of escalating stakes, in which greater effort on God's part (as the landlord seeking his rent) leads to greater disobedience on Israel's part (as the tenants seeking to avoid payment by mistreating the landlord's messengers), culminating in murder on one side and total destruction on the other. The killing of Jesus is the pinnacle of disobedience, the final straw, an indication that no "rent" may be expected from Israel whatsoever and thus that the only possible divine rejoinder is disenfranchisement and apocalyptic destruction.

Unlike Mark's other "parables," which only touch on one or another aspect of the gospel, the tenants serves as a summary of the entire basic story, incorporating the whole sweep of epic and gospel in a single brief account. The extent to which this is so is illustrated nicely in a remarkable essay by Ron Hock on the opening sequence of the Gospel of Mark.[185] Hock correlates the advent of John the Baptist to "prepare the way" for Jesus in Mark to the social pattern of an absentee landlord's visit to his tenants:

> The reason I take seriously the sequential ordering of John and Jesus [at the opening of Mark] derives from a similar emphasis on sequence which is involved in an important social event in traditional, or agrarian, societies—the visit of the absentee landlord to his country properties.[186]

Hock notes that other ancient texts describe this same pattern as part of an expected and normal sequence of events. As appears in, for instance, Longus's *Daphnis and Chloe*, the householder's visit is preceded first by servants, then by his son and heir, and finally himself, in a sequence which coordinates the passage of time with an increase in status, by way of preparation for the final appearance of "the most powerful person of all, the householder, the one who will inspect and judge the slaves and tenants who work on his estate, punishing them for their shortcomings or rewarding them for their accomplishments."[187] As a result, we should view the sequencing of John and Jesus in the opening of Mark not as a *Heilsgeschichte* conception, but as a statement about the relative status of Jesus and John: the point is not that John is a *prophet*, but that he is a *slave*. This observation, in turn, sheds light on Mark's christological agenda in identifying Jesus as the "*Son* of God":

---

185. Hock, "Social Experience and the Beginning of the Gospel of Mark."
186. Ibid., 316.
187. Ibid., 319.

But the conventions of the visit of the householder do make it clear why Jesus *follows* John—his status as son puts him farther along the sequence than that occupied by a slave-messenger like John. What is more important, it also makes clear why Jesus is identified as the Son of God at all (rather than by some other title), a role which, incidentally, is not inherent in, say, the expectations regarding the return of Elijah. Astylos, the son of Dionysophanes, however, represents the last step in bridging the gap between the lowly peasants in the *chora* and the powerful householder in the *polis*. The role of Son of God for Jesus thus becomes an especially appropriate and important one.[188]

Specifically, Hock notes, characterizing Jesus as son of God, with the model of householder visits in the background, connotes a three-fold specification of Jesus's role: (1) his power, (2) his mediating role, and (3) the imminence of the householder's arrival.

For my purposes, these observations allow for some striking conclusions. For there is in Mark, as Hock is quite aware, a story that focuses very specifically on this typical social sequence: the parable of the tenants. Hock's observations thus buttress and flesh out the assertion that the parable of the tenants serves as something of a model, not only for Mark's Gospel narrative, but for the way that narrative is used to modify, rethink, and comment on the broader epic sweep of Israel's history. The composition of Mark's Gospel is reflected in the parable of the tenants, not only in the simple notice of the son's advent and death, but even in the preparation for the son's visit represented by John the Baptist. The opening of the gospel with the Baptist preparing the way is, in this sense, dictated by the model of the tenants parable as a précis of Mark's view (and reconfiguration) of epic history. More than this: what the gospel implies, but does not directly *narrate*, is as important for understanding Jesus's role (and the epic as a whole) as is the story of Jesus himself. For Mark this implied material basically contextualizes Jesus within the epic, viewing the prophets as, analogous to John, anticipating the visit of Jesus, and viewing the visit of the householder, the apocalyptic manifestation of God himself, as likewise implied as the conclusion to the epic. Mark, refraining from actually narrating these events, nonetheless builds them into his story in scriptural quotations and allusions, on the one hand, and in apocalyptic predictions and foreshadowings, on the other. What is striking about the parable

---

188. Ibid., 320.

of the tenants, with this in mind, is that unlike his gospel as a whole, the tenants parable *does* directly narrate this additional material as well: the building of the vineyard and the initial requests for rent, on the one hand, and the final appearance and vengeance of the householder, on the other. The parable of the tenants thus serves as a full-blown conceptual template for Mark's use of a narrative of Jesus to thoroughly reconfigure the whole range of epic history.

This conclusion in turn lends an interesting twist to the observation that Mark constructs his narrative episodes, at least in part, out of prior sayings material and, at times, scriptural prooftexts. The parable of the tenants not only predates Mark, but it had an "original" form that was not allegorical or related to Israel's epic at all. As I have argued elsewhere,[189] saying 65 in the Gospel of Thomas attests to a nonallegorical version of the tenants, one that seems more likely to be "primitive" or "original" than the version reproduced in Mark. The version in Gospel of Thomas:

> is wholly lacking in the details that make the story so susceptible to allegorization in Mark: the description of the owner's labor in constructing the vineyard; the innocuous presentation of the owner's motivations (indeed, the version in *Thomas* stresses the owner's intent to exploit his tenants—he lets out the vineyard "so that *they* might work it, and *he* might collect its rent"); the multiple servants; the description of the son as "beloved"; the detail that the body was thrown out of the vineyard; and even the question as to the reaction or retaliation of the vineyard's owner.... Especially the failure of the version in *Thomas* to conclude the parable with the question about the master's subsequent action shows that *Thomas* is uninterested in allegorizing the story.[190]

Mack, however, is quite correct to ask how such a parable might originally have been read, if *not* allegorically.[191] The answer, I argue, may be found in a hint G. E. M. de Ste. Croix drops about the role of (some of) the Aesopic fables as the sole remaining sources we have for self-consciousness of the

---

189. Arnal, "The Parable of the Tenants."
190. Ibid., 140–41.
191. Mack, *Myth of Innocence*, 169 n. 24.

slave underclass of antiquity.[192] Like some of the Aesopic fables,[193] and like a handful of other parables in the Jesus tradition,[194] the parable of the tenants in Thomas assumes an antagonistic relationship between social superiors and inferiors, and it describes with some relish the (isolated and likely temporary) victory of the latter over the former.[195]

Such a story is in itself—even if it does not describe a realistic scenario or prescribe actual rebellious action—one of the "weapons of the weak" described so well by James C. Scott.[196] Setting aside the question of whether such parables, with such an intent, go back to the historical Jesus and setting aside the Gospel of Thomas's particular use of this parable as part of a cluster excoriating wealth as incompatible with proper mental discipline, what I am suggesting here is that it *is* possible to imagine a form and context in which this parable would *not* be read allegorically, or as having anything to do with the Israelite epic. And indeed, its form and usage in Thomas demonstrates not only that the parable could be read nonallegorically, but that it was, and in a more original form than

---

192. G. E. M. de Ste. Croix, *The Class Struggle in the Ancient Greek World: From the Archaic Age to the Arab Conquests* (London: Duckworth, 1981), 444. In support of this view, Ste. Croix cites Phaedrus (*Fab.* 3.prol.) as claiming that "the slave, being liable to punishment for any offense, since he dared not say outright what he wished to say, projected his personal sentiments into fables and eluded censure under the guise of jesting with made-up stories."

193. E.g., Phaedrus, *Fab.* 3.2, 3.7, 4.6; 1.28 is worth quoting in its entirety: "However lofty in station men may be, they should, nevertheless, be apprehensive of lowly persons; for shrewdness may learn a lesson and find the way open to revenge. One day an eagle carried off a fox's cubs and put them in her nest as food for her fledglings to tear. The mother fox followed her and began to entreat her not to bring so great a grief upon her, a pitiable sufferer. The eagle regarded her with contempt, feeling safe from attack in her high place. The fox then snatched a firebrand from an altar and ringed the tree with fire, mixing a potion of grief for her foe which threatened the loss of her own brood. The eagle, in order to rescue her young from the danger of death, turned suppliant and restored to the fox her young ones unharmed" (Perry, LCL).

194. E.g., the parables of the dishonest steward (Luke 16:1–8) and the unjust judge (Luke 18:2–5).

195. See my more extensive comments in "The Parable of the Tenants," 151–54.

196. The classic work is James C. Scott, *Weapons of the Weak: Everyday Forms of Peasant Resistance* (New Haven: Yale University Press, 1985); but for a useful summary, see the excerpt, Scott, "Weapons of the Weak: Everyday Struggle, Meaning and Deeds," in *Peasants and Peasant Societies: Selected Readings*, 2nd ed., ed. Teodor Shanin; (Oxford: Blackwell, 1987), 343–45.

Mark has it. This in turn might suggest that Mark inherited this parable from the sayings tradition associated with Jesus[197] and lent it its allegorical color himself, rather than, as Mack asserts, only making explicit what was already implicit in the story itself.

John S. Kloppenborg has commented on this same parable, likewise comparing the versions in the Gospel of Thomas and in the Gospel of Mark, and his conclusions tend to support the claim that the Gospel of Thomas preserves an original form of the saying, and that, therefore, the original parable could have existed in a nonallegorical form.[198] What Kloppenborg focuses on is the allusion to Isaiah 5:1–7 in Mark's description of the preparation of the vineyard (12:1–2) and the relationship of this description to actual viticultural practices of the time. What he discovers, in the end, is that

> Mark's version of the parable is fundamentally incoherent, mixing a waged-ἀμπελουργικὰ ἔργα with a crop-share rental agreement. This incoherence exists, of course, precisely because of the allusions to Isaiah 5:1–7. As many commentators have pointed out, however, Mark's version of Isaiah is dependent on the LXX rather than the Hebrew text.... It is important to recognize that as long as the Isaian story is present intertextually within Mark 12:1–9 (10–12), the narrative resists realistic reading; it can only be read allegorically. The version of the parable in the *Gospel of Thomas* (65), by contrast, lacks any allusion to Isaiah 5:1–7, and, more importantly, presupposes a coherent scenario of the lease of an existing vineyard for crop shares.[199]

This suggests that the elements of the story that militate most strongly for an allegorical reading also make the story unrealistic, while their excision leaves us with an account that accords well with what we can know about the actual ancient practices of vineyard leases. The allusions to Isa 5 are not

197. Again, I want to stress that in saying that this parable existed as Jesus-tradition prior to Mark, I am by no means arguing that it is an "authentic" teaching of the historical Jesus.

198. John S. Kloppenborg, "Isaiah 5:1–7, the Parable of the Tenants and Vineyard Leases on Papyrus," in *Text and Artifact in the Religions of Mediterranean Antiquity*, 111–34.

199. Ibid., 130–31. See also the much more extensive treatment in John S. Kloppenborg, *The Tenants in the Vineyard: Ideology, Economics, and Agrarian Conflict in Jewish Palestine*, WUNT 195 (Tübingen: Mohr Siebeck, 2006).

original to the parable but represent a Markan addition to and transformation of a story originally lacking in allegorical elements.

The reason I have pursued the question of an "original" version of the tenants parable is that the existence of such a tradition may shed some light on a remarkable aspect of Mark's procedure. If Thomas preserves an earlier and *non*allegorical version of this parable, and if it was the author of Mark who allegorized the parable, largely by creating an intertextual reference to Isaiah 5,[200] then two interesting conclusions about Mark may follow. The first is simply that Mark has, once again, sought out and made use of scriptural associations (associations that *he* has made) to alter the meaning of—indeed, to create a *new* meaning for—a unit from the sayings tradition that had a quite different sense prior to Mark's intervention. Second, and more interestingly, Mark's rereading of this prior sayings material may have served as a template for the entire narrative shape of both his gospel and his even broader conception of the role of the Jesus-story within the epic of Israel. In other words, the argument can be made that just as Mark has used units of sayings traditions to construct discrete narratives, essentially wholesale, likewise his entire narrative *conception* was formulated on the basis of a unit of sayings tradition, that is, the parable of the tenants. The fact that the model provided by this parable extends not simply to Jesus's death (and the threat of subsequent retribution) but, as Hock shows, to the characterization of John the Baptist as a forerunner, lends support to this claim, forcing a revision of the assumption that the allegorization of the parable *followed from* Mark's narrative scheme, rather than, as I am suggesting, generated that scheme. If this is so, then the question of the *rationale* for Mark's novel movement to narrative presentation of Jesus becomes rather less pressing, even less interesting. Mark offers us a repeated pattern throughout his gospel: (1) prior sayings tradition, (2) interpreted in terms of scriptural associations, (3) transformed into narrative. If Mark has done this with the parable of the tenants, the explanation for his application of a novel literary genre to Jesus is the rather disappointing one that he did so because his reading of the parable of the tenants suggested such a portrayal.[201]

---

200. Such a claim is plausible in itself, in light of Mark's tendency to read parables allegorically, as discussed above, and in light of Mark's strong and distinctive tendency to (re)interpret his material in light of intertextual allusions to and quotations of scripture.

201. I cannot help but note that the question of Mark's generic choice, as it stands,

Some Tentative Conclusions and Suggestions

The natural tack to take at this point would be to explore how it is that the compositional procedures described in the foregoing pages inform us about—and mesh with—the immediate context of Mark's composition. I have offered something of a narrative so far, a narrative about *how* Mark was composed, but, alas, it is a sketch that really says nothing much at all about *why* Mark was composed. In this respect, Mark is a hard nut to crack. I am aware of no New Testament writing (with the possible exception of Hebrews) that so strenuously resists our usual procedure of positing a (usually "Christian") *community* and making inferences about the author's agenda in terms of interaction with that community.[202] Mark is clearly, as Mack asserts, the work of a scholar, an intellectual. Unfortunately, it may be that very intellectual bent that obscures the real social foundation of his work. The problem is not that Mark provides us with no clues about his context; it is that he provides us with so little data about the existence of a discrete "Christian" group—the omnipresent "community"—which is

---

is rendered pressing because of the lack of continuity between it and the generic possibilities explored by Jesus traditions prior to Mark's time. It is precisely the radical break that Mark effects in the consistency with which earlier materials seemed *not* to show interest in the biography of Jesus—a break highlighted by my comments so far—that renders Mark's selection of genre puzzling. But to highlight this puzzle is to persist in viewing these developments in terms of the trajectories internal to a unified movement. Once we cease to think in terms of such internal developments, Mark's choice of genre is not remarkable at all; it is just a fact, no more puzzling in itself than the *absence* of examples of this genre prior to Mark. The differences between Mark and his predecessors are probably to be explained in the differences between what Mark, broadly speaking, was up to, and what earlier writings and traditions were intended to accomplish, broadly speaking. There is nothing particularly mysterious about this, especially if we concede Mark's social discontinuity with, e.g., the people responsible for Q.

In some contrast, however, note the comments of Werner H. Kelber, *The Kingdom in Mark: A New Place and a New Time* (Philadelphia: Fortress, 1974), 138–39: "The gospel [of Mark] is not the logical end-product of the prehistory of its individual building blocks … the earliest known Christian gospel is thus not the natural or expected stage in Christian literary history, but the unexpected, yet willed product in a time of crisis. The new gospel form, this utter novelty of the Markan voice, presupposes, negatively speaking, discontinuity with and possibly distrust of the proven literary models of the past. Some dislocation has occurred which required a new perspective on life."

202. Again, see Stowers, "Concept of 'Community.'"

affected by this context and to which he is, more or less particularly and uniquely, directing his writing. In this respect, Mark resists the kind of approach that seems to work with, for example, Q, because Mark resists precise geographical localization; and, all the more, Mark resists the sort of inferences that we can apply to Paul's letters, which explicitly indicate a specific "community" audience.[203] The narrative genre in itself frustrates such approaches; it also, more interestingly, may be itself a direct *symptom* of Mark's social discontinuity with such formations.

As a result, reconstructing the why behind the composition of Mark will, in my view, necessarily require a focus on the intellectual problems solved by Mark, rather than the role of Mark in a distinct group whose essential characteristics can be recovered by us. Indeed, Mark provides so little information about his audience that we cannot even be sure that he has *any* discrete group in mind. It is in this respect that I somewhat part company with Mack in his reconstruction in *Myth of Innocence*, and, indeed, with the attempt by this seminar to answer the question *why* Mark broke in so many ways from prior modes of expression for presenting Jesus. Mark, as I see it, is simply not easily amenable to explanation in terms of precise intra-"Christian" developments.

It is for this reason that I am more sympathetic to an approach to Mark that was hinted at by Smith's paper in this volume, in which a certain broad historical context, to which Mark was somehow reacting, becomes an occasion for the bricolage of motifs in the gospel itself.[204] The primary issue in analyzing such bricolage is *not* that the building materials were transformed from one kind of use to another, nor even where the materials came from, but rather how and why the author used the various cultural-mythic fragments at his disposal to build the edifice he did. And the answer to that question will be found in whatever "situational incongruity" the edifice seems to address, again, regardless of what

---

203. But see Stowers's observations in "Concept of 'Community,'" to the effect that Paul's indications of "community" among his auditors is more prescriptive than descriptive.

204. Jonathan Z. Smith, "The Markan Site" (in this volume). By "broad historical context," I mean the relevant set of "external" circumstances that appear to have motivated the shape of the composition in question. Obviously, what those circumstances might be is a matter for debate. Smith's paper focused on Levantine ethnic identities, but other options are of course possible, either in addition to ethnic questions or as a substitute focus of concern.

transformations the original building materials may have suffered in the process. Thus, it is precisely by focusing on the literary features of Mark as a finished and integral product that, I think, we will make the most progress in answering the question why he composed a gospel, indeed, this particular gospel.[205] Moreover, since at least part of the agenda of this seminar is to show the Christian myth for what it is—a myth—attempting to show that Mark came together as an imaginative narrative rather than as any form of "reminiscence" or "biographical tradition" is in itself a step forward, even if we are left without answers to some of the questions we might have wanted to ask.

Since Mark appears not to have an intra-Jesus-movement "situational incongruity" in mind—or at least does not provide us with enough data to reconstruct that incongruity—and since, by contrast, he does lay very heavy emphasis on the circumstances of the Jewish War and the fallout subsequent to the war, our best chances of eventually making some sense of this gospel rest in looking at the answers his narrative provides to the questions raised by the war. But this approach, even if we eschew positing any particular "community" behind the gospel, requires some assumptions about Mark's immediate context. These matters are sufficiently complex that an adequate treatment of them would require as much verbiage again as I have already indulged in. Neither time nor space permits. So I will conclude by laying out a few simple suggestions about the directions that I happen to think might be most profitable for unraveling the twisted skein of Mark's complex project, without attempting to defend those suggestions in detail.

I note first that a number of things can be said with considerable certainty about Mark's context. Not only the "little apocalypse," but the incredibly important and suggestive role played in this text by imagery of the Jerusalem temple's destruction—and especially the way in which Jesus's

---

205. I want to be clear that, in saying this, I am not trying to revive or defend the ahistorical "literary-critical" approach that was so trendy and strident in the 1980s, whose proponents sometimes claimed that, in terms of theoretical considerations, a consideration of the literary features of any ancient Christian text, to the exclusion of historical factors, was the only possible, and only desirable, approach. In saying that Mark resists any identification with an identifiable community of Jesus-people, I still insist that Mark requires historical contextualization; it is just that such a contextualization will probably not be able to describe any distinctively "Christian" features of Mark's context.

death is linked so thoroughly, if allusively, to such imagery—make it quite clear that Mark is writing in the aftermath of the Jewish War[206] and that the events of the war or immediate postwar period provide the immediate context for his gospel. Trivially, this means that we can be fairly certain that Mark was composed sometime in the early to mid-70s CE, and in some region affected more or less directly by the events of the war. Such a claim, however, does not by itself allow further and more precise geographical specification, either of the textual provenance of the Gospel of Mark or of the author's background.[207] Such general features of Mark as his highly literary character, combined with an interest in the war, do not allow for such precise conclusions as, for example, a location in Tyre. Facility with texts, especially "biblical" (that is, the LXX) texts as is the case with Mark, cannot plausibly be restricted to one city or even one geographical region.

My own conviction is that Mark's context and setting—including both his own ethnic background or place of origin *and* the locale in which he wrote—is, as I suggested above, perhaps best approached by looking to the gospel's literary features. Here I have in mind the fascinating structural studies of Elizabeth Struthers Malbon, especially her brief article on the presentation of Galilee and Jerusalem in the Gospel of Mark.[208] Malbon argues that:

> The fundamental opposition, chaos versus order, is manifest in the Marcan narrative by the opposition, sea versus land, which is "replaced" by the opposition, foreign land versus Jewish homeland.... Jewish

---

206. As noted above, some scholars find the references to the war itself sufficiently compelling to conclude that Mark was written after the commencement of hostilities but, oddly, believe the gospel to have been written *prior* to the destruction of the temple. Such a view makes rather incomprehensible the centrality the temple evidently holds for Mark's narrative, including the very strong relationship Mark suggests between Jesus's death and the temple's destruction. On this linkage see now John S. Kloppenborg, "*Evocatio Deorum* and the Date of Mark," *JBL* 124 (2005): 419–50.

207. I make this distinction advisedly, not only because I intend to make something of it below, but also because, as we saw in Smith, "The Markan Site"—specifically the discussion of Tyrian groups in Italy—ethnicity and location can and do intersect in interesting ways, and identity can (and must) be a synthesis of both factors. Thus where the Gospel of Mark was written is not the same question as the background of the person who composed it.

208. Elizabeth Struthers Malbon, "Galilee and Jerusalem: History and Literature in Marcan Interpretation," *CBQ* 44 (1982): 242–55. See also Malbon, *Narrative Space and Mythic Meaning*.

homeland is narrativized in Mark as Galilee and Judea. The narrative manifestations of foreign land include Idumea, beyond the Jordan, Tyre and Sidon, the country of the Gerasenes, the Decapolis.... The "foreignness," as it were, of these cities and areas is more crucial in Mark than their precise location or Jesus' exact itinerary in reaching them. Narrative signs such as the swine in the country of the Gerasenes (5:11–13) or the conversation with the Syrophoenician woman about the children's crumbs for the dogs (7:26–29) signal the strange, foreign, Gentile nature of these places as opposed to the familiarity of the Jewish homeland of Galilee, with its synagogues (1:21 ff., 1:39; 3:1; 6:2), and Judea, with its temple.... The opposition, foreign land versus Jewish homeland, which "replaces" the opposition, sea versus land, in the "logical" or "mythological" order underlying Mark's narrative is in turn "replaced" by the opposition, Judea versus Galilee.... The Marcan narrative ... reverses the expected associations of Galilee and Judea.... Judea is linked with the chaos-pole of the fundamental opposition, and Galilee with order. At the level of the opposition Galilee versus Judea movement toward the mediation of chaos and order is implied in the Marcan exchange of connotations between the two regions. When Galilee, supposedly chaotic, connotes a new order, and Judea, supposedly orderly, represents chaos, the fundamental opposition is severely weakened.[209]

My impression is that Malbon is embracing the structuralist "prison-house of language" in quite rigid fashion here, construing any given mythic *topoi* as mere instantiations of a desire to rectify fundamental oppositions, particularly that of chaos and order. Moreover, at least in the comments quoted above, she does not stress the extent to which Mark offers Jesus as himself the mediation between all of the polarities or oppositions in the gospel: as lord of the sea as well as land, as lord of gentiles as well as Jews. But if we set aside the rather abstract theoretical agenda she is promoting, and any specific exegetical quibbles, what emerges from her analysis is the quite substantive conclusion that *Mark is engaged in redefining Jewish space*. More than this, the distinctive or surprising feature of this redefinition is *the inversion of the expected valences of Judea versus Galilee as instances of Jewish territory*.

Once we set aside Malbon's apparent distaste for historical analysis,[210] we are in a position to note the remarkable convergence in Mark of con-

---

209. Malbon, "Galilee and Jerusalem," 252, 253.

210. See ibid., 255: "In *interpreting* such a text [as Mark], an historical approach is inadequate, a literary approach promising" (emphasis original). It is for this reason

cerns associated with the Jewish War with concerns about the redefinition—effected by Jesus—of the parameters and valences of "home" space.[211] We may also note that Mark shows as strong an interest in *describing* the very specific features of Jerusalem—its topography, its suburbs, its named places, even its architecture—as he does the regions around Galilee; and, of course, Jerusalem carries as much symbolic weight as does the oft-noted figurative significance of Galilee.[212] It is particularly the intimate knowledge of the environs of Jerusalem that Mark is at pains to demonstrate that seems odd.[213] If Mark preserves accurate traditions of the actual last days of Jesus, the presence in the text of such gratuitous notices as Jesus's staying in Bethany (14:3), or the location of the post-prandial perambulations of Jesus and the Twelve as the Mount of Olives (14:26), or the name of the garden in which Jesus subsequently went to pray (14:32),[214] may perhaps be accounted for as reminiscences (albeit oddly circumstantial ones); indeed, the verisimilitude created by such detail has doubtless contributed to the credulity with which the passion narrative has often been received. But once we have dispensed with such an approach—once we

---

that Malbon rejects Kelber's suggestion that this odd portrayal of Jerusalem and Galilee reflects polemics between a Jerusalem-based community of Christians and a Galilee-based community (254). Her criticisms of this hypothesis are well-placed, I think, but too quickly reject the possibility of inferring *anything* about Mark's historical circumstances from this opposition. I should clarify here that I am somewhat in agreement with Malbon's basic assertions; one must first and primarily understand Mark's settings, characters, actions, and so forth as *literary* features of a *text*, and most categorically not as real events, settings, and the like. But I balk at Malbon's refusal, in this article, to coordinate this literary agenda with a set of actual historical circumstances.

211. That is, the spaces that Malbon describes as "Jewish homeland," Judea and Galilee. I am a little reluctant to use her terminology because it somewhat begs the question of the actual ethnicity of the people involved and of how radical a redefinition is intended by Mark. To describe the territorial division as "home" versus "foreign" thus seems safer.

212. Especially as per Marxsen, *Mark the Evangelist*, 83–92.

213. I am quite deliberately avoiding the claim that Mark *actually* shows knowledge of Jerusalem; rather, he takes pains to display such knowledge, accurate or not.

214. See the discussion, above, of the Gethsemane episode, in which the actual name of the garden is just about the only feature of the story that cannot be explained in terms of Markan redaction. I note in that discussion that Mack argues for a symbolic import to the place names in the passion; this claim makes some sense for "Golgotha" (every site of execution should have as atmospheric a name), but it is difficult to explain what symbolic import "Gethsemane" could have.

concede, that is, that the passion narrative, *including* its constituent units, is essentially the literary invention of Mark—this explanation is no longer available to us, and we are forced to attempt to account for these details in terms of an authorial agenda.

The problem is exacerbated and underscored by another peculiarity of Mark's references to Jerusalem. There is only one place in the entire gospel in which the author appears to be referring to real individuals who are contemporary with, and known to, the author himself. The occasion for this reference, interestingly enough, is in the midst of the passion narrative, in Jerusalem, when an otherwise-unknown person is forced to carry Jesus's cross. Mark offers us an odd description of this figure: "They compelled a passer-by, who was coming in from the country, to carry his cross; it was Simon of Cyrene, the father of Alexander and Rufus" (15:21). Two things are especially notable about this characterization of Simon. The first and most obvious is that describing this person as "the father of Alexander and Rufus" without further specification of *their* identities suggests very strongly that these two characters are people known to Mark's target audience and most likely are themselves members of that audience. This in turn is striking because it implies that *the only known members of Mark's audience are (former) Jerusalemites*. While Simon is described as a Cyrenian (Κυρηναῖον), the description offered by Mark of his "coming in from the country/field" (ἐρχόμενον ἀπ᾽ ἀγροῦ) makes it clear that he lives in the environs of Jerusalem, and either owns or works land just outside of the city. At least *some* members of Mark's audience—indeed, the only members we actually know about—are, or rather were once, Jerusalemites.

The second thing worth noting about this characterization is that although it is quite clear that Simon lives in or around Jerusalem, and is, presumably, a Jew, he is identified in terms of another, different, ethnic or locational affiliation: he is from Cyrene. Josephus indicates that Cyrene had a large Jewish population, one significant enough to spearhead revolts, and to constitute its own separate category of citizenship.[215] Acts 6:9 refers to the presence in Jerusalem of "those who belonged to the synagogue of the Freedmen (as it was called), Cyrenians, Alexandrians, and others of those from Cilicia and Asia." These ethnically distinct, and yet Jewish, individu-

---

215. See Josephus, *Ag. Ap.* 2.44; *Ant.* 14.7.2 §§114–118; cf. also Emil Schürer, *A History of the Jewish People in the Time of Jesus Christ*, div. 1.2, trans. John MacPherson (New York: Scribner's Sons, 1891), 280–87, on the Jewish revolt of 115 CE in Cyrenaica.

als appear to have had a somewhat marginal or at least separate existence in Jerusalem, as attested by the existence of their own synagogue, and, perhaps, by the association of that synagogue with freedmen (Λιβερτίνων).[216] The important thing here is that, regardless of Simon of Cyrene's actual, historical, relationship to the "synagogue of the freedmen,"[217] both his own designation in terms of regional extraction and the notion that "non-Judean Judeans/Jews" had their own synagogue are suggestive. These details allow us to posit the quite unremarkable notion that within Jerusalem, prior to the war, there were groups of people whose *ethnic* affiliation was marginal, straddling both Jewish identity and "foreign" connections of one sort or another. More remarkable is the suggestion—offered here tentatively—that the Markan audience, including the author himself, was constituted of such persons.[218]

Observing that Mark was certainly written after the war, and that it shows a striking interest in the geography and ethnic relations of Galilee and Phoenicia, alongside what we know of the devastation caused by the

---

216. Note, however, the suggestion, made as early as the sixteenth century, that the original text be read as Λιβυστίνων, that is, "Libyans" (see BAGD³, s.v. Λιβερτῖνος). Such a suggestion has the virtue of making for a more sensible overall characterization of this group, but it appears to have no manuscript support whatsoever (aside from the Armenian Vulgate text), and so Metzger (*Textual Commentary on the Greek New Testament*, 297) concludes that "there is no compelling reason to depart from the text of the Greek witnesses."

217. And as usual, I am speaking here without prejudice to the actual historical existence of Simon *or* of the "synagogue of the freedmen." I do in fact assume Simon actually existed, because otherwise the reference to his sons makes little sense. I would like to think that Acts' reference to the "synagogue of the freedmen" also is based on an accurate tradition, but unfortunately cannot do so with confidence, because (1) the reference meshes too well with the author's agenda, and (2) Acts in general appears to me to contain *very* few reliable historical data.

218. Another unexplained character with whom Jesus interacts in Jerusalem is "Simon the leper" (Mark 14:3), obviously, given the description, yet another marginal person within a Jerusalem context. The alienation or marginality I am attributing to the Markan group is *not* to be understood in terms of economic deprivation. Mark shows in several places an apparently knee-jerk tendency to identify with the class of owners, landlords, and the like, over against any strong identification with peasants and day-laborers. He is sympathetic to *social* outcasts, the unclean, the lepers, the ethnically questionable, and even to the Roman (foreign) ruling class, but he seems to lack the kind of economic radicalism that may mark earlier phases of the Jesus-tradition.

war and the essential destruction of Jerusalem in the war's final moments, I am not by any means suggesting that the gospel was actually written in or around Judea. Instead, I am interested in the possibility that Mark was written by and for a collection of doubly displaced persons: ethnically self-identified as "Jews/Judeans," having returned to Jerusalem from their actual homelands to a kind of second-class status, only to be displaced northward to Syria-Galilee by the events of the war (and one may include in this region Phoenicia).[219] If this is so, we might find here an explanation for Mark's *use* of Jesus, and even his *narrative* use of Jesus, as a mechanism for reconfiguring, experimenting with, and commenting on ethnic identity, as well as the narrative's inversion of the valence of Galilee over against Judea as a "homeland," and finally the extensive fashion in which the war and the destruction of the temple are themselves refigured as essentially appropriate, divinely ordained, even positive events, easily assimilated to the Israelite epic, by virtue of being presented as retribution for actions taken against Jesus in the past. In short, exile has become an occasion for rethinking (and perhaps even retrenching) a "Jewish" identity that was

---

219. Marxsen (*Mark the Evangelist*, 106–7, emphasis original), suggests, on the basis of similar concerns (especially the treatment of Jerusalem in Mark), a similar, albeit more "traditional" view: "Mark's use of the term 'Galilee' compels us to ask whether or not it implies a community in Galilee, or whether a movement *toward* Galilee was in the offing. Even the passion narrative with its Jerusalem locale takes on this new orientation. We believe that the reason for the communities' sojourn in Galilee, or the reason for their journey to Galilee might be seen in the fact that the Parousia was expected there. This makes clear the problem of locale. We now take up the question of time. Is there, at any period known to us, a situation in the primitive community to which these observations might correspond? The scope is quite limited, and our knowledge of the time is very scanty. But we are at once reminded of the period after A.D. 66, of the primitive community's flight from Jerusalem to Pella. This exodus would not only have been related to the political events, but to a heightened expectation of the Parousia as well." I am offering a rather different view, for different reasons, most particularly in that I am not relying on the dubious Pella tradition, nor assuming that earliest Christianity was any kind of monolithic "primitive community," nor again that Mark was interested in any abstract notion that the parousia would occur in Galilee. I mention Marxsen's view here simply because he appears to affirm an ultimately Jerusalemite origin for the Markan Christians for reasons similar to my own. Such a notion allows us to have our cake and eat it too, leaving intact a south-Syrian provenance for Mark while simultaneously accounting for his interest in and (apparent) information about Jerusalem.

severely compromised from the beginning.[220] The war has destroyed the city and temple that helped constitute a "homeland," but a homeland from which the Markan auditors were denied unequivocal status. The war has also resulted in the movement of such people from a strange homeland to a location that Mark now attempts to turn into a home in a strange land. The "situational incongruity" of the war and particularly the destruction of the temple serve as what Smith would call "an occasion for thought," in this case, thought about the nature of an already-troubled ethnic identity. The narrative of the people for whom Mark is writing, a narrative of violent displacement, is inverted in value, justified, and explained, by virtue of another narrative, the story of a Son of God who, like Mark, traveled as a stranger to a Jerusalem that should have been home, was mistreated, and subsequently—as a consequence of staggering Roman violence—was returned to his true home and so resumed his true identity.

Referring to the wistful descriptions of "civilized" Massachusetts as "English" offered by Mary Rowlandson, a colonist abducted in 1675 by Narragansetts, Benedict Anderson offers the following comments:

> She sees before her "English Cattle," an "English Path," and "deserted English fields," though she has never been within three thousand miles of England. These are not pluckings from the Cotswolds or the Downs— real places, as it were—but acts of imagination that would never have occurred to a young minister's wife in seventeenth-century Gloucestershire or Surrey. They are, in a way, getting ready to be "English" exactly because they are in Massachusetts, not in England, and are so because they bear for Mary the traces of her "English" people's agricultural labors. But we can also guess that up till the point of her abduction she had thought matter-of-factly about cattle as cattle and fields as fields. Her "nationalizing" moment comes when, in the power of the Narragansetts,

---

220. Hence Mark's polemic against the "authorized" Jewish leadership. The handful of places in the gospel in which the text provides asides and "explanations" of Jewish customs are not, in my opinion, original to the text. Koester, *Ancient Christian Gospels*, 275–84, offers solid literary reasons for concluding that canonical Mark may not perfectly represent the original text. In particular, his reasoning would allow us to exclude, on literary grounds, 2:27, 7:3–4, and 7:19b from the original text of Mark. All of these are texts that—in my view, misleadingly—imply that Mark was written for a gentile audience. Note also the insistence of Dowd and Malbon, "The Significance of Jesus' Death in Mark," especially 271, 280–81, that Mark presents Jesus as a mechanism for release from bondage, as a ransom for captives, and not as an atonement for sin.

she is torn out of the quotidian and—right in the very midst of her native Massachusetts—finds herself in fearful exile.[221]

We need not place too much emphasis on Anderson's opposition between the quotidian and the harrowing circumstances of Rowlandson's abduction; indeed, I am suggesting that Mark's exile as such was not especially "fearful," even if caused by the horrors of war. More to the point is the way in which Anderson draws our attention to the identity-creating function of exile.[222] Like Mark as I have reconstructed him, Rowlandson (whether as a literary or real character) is a double-exile, twice removed from her "native" England, a colonial *and* a kidnapping victim. From this vantage-point, she constructs her actual home, from which she is being taken, as ideally "English," which it clearly is not.

Perhaps Mark is doing something similar—for somewhat similar reasons—with his Jesus-narrative, constructing Galilee as "Judean," which it clearly is not, but which it becomes, for Mark, by virtue of Jesus's sufferings. The point, then, the ultimate explanation for Mark's choice of the narrative mode to discuss Jesus, and his wildly inventive portrayal of Jesus's life, may have very little to do with Jesus or with developments within or among changing groups of Jesus people. Rather, Mark may be using the figure of Jesus to comment on the war, the destruction of the temple, the Israelite epic tradition, and his own ethnic identity. Indeed, Mark may be using the Jesus-traditions to revel in the inversionary effects of the war. The war has become the occasion for new thoughts, thoughts congenial to this author, and Jesus has served as a mechanism for expressing these thoughts.

---

221. Benedict Anderson, "Exodus," *Critical Inquiry* 20 (1994): 314–15. I owe thanks to Willi Braun for drawing my attention to this article.

222. This, indeed, is the main point of the article. Anderson's interest is especially in the alienating effects of modern capitalism, a point that obviously does not apply to Mark's context. I am using his article for ends quite unrelated to those he intended.

Q and the "Big Bang" Theory of Christian Origins*

Robyn Faith Walsh

Introduction

Our earliest writings about Jesus are artifacts not only of the ancient Mediterranean but also of eighteenth-, nineteenth-, and twentieth-century thought.[1] Others, such as Wilfred Cantwell Smith, have made similar claims, noting that scholars of (so-called) Christian origins should approach their source material "not merely as a set of ancient documents or even as a first- and second-century product but as a third-century and twelfth-century and nineteenth-century and contemporary agent."[2] This call for attention to hermeneutics and the inheritances of reception history presents a conceptual paradox. We are trained in the field to position these writings in their "original" context, that is, to identify the people, practices, and social formations that produced them. Yet, we cannot get at "origins" or do history so long as we obscure the influence subsequent centuries of compilation, translation, and scholarship have had on our methods, the starting points of our analyses, and the questions that we ask. We must put a mirror to our approaches in order to evaluate what we may be incorrectly taking for granted about our subject matter. For

---

* I would like to thank Stanley Stowers, Merrill Miller, Jaswinder Bolina, and Justin Ritzinger for their helpful comments on this piece.

1. Jonathan Z. Smith raises this same issue in the case of the J and Q sources in *On Teaching Religion* (New York: Oxford University Press, 2013), 30.

2. Wilfred Cantwell Smith, "The Study of Religion and the Study of the Bible," *JAAR* 39 (1971): 134; Jonathan Z. Smith, *On Teaching Religion*, 30. Also see Jonathan Z. Smith, "On the Origin of Origins," in *Drudgery Divine: On the Comparison of Early Christianities and the Religions of Late Antiquity*, Jordan Lectures in Comparative Religion 14 (London: School of Oriental and African Studies, University of London; Chicago: University of Chicago Press, 1990), 1–35.

materials like the hypothetical sayings-source Q or the canonical gospels, this includes questioning why we tend to assume the authors of these texts are affiliated with any kind of insular Christian "association" or "community"; acknowledging that these writers were not *sui generis* and participated in practices that were both practical and plausible for the literate specialists of the period; and reconsidering whether there has been sufficient justification for dating any writings about Jesus before the Jewish War.

This study attempts to treat ancient writings about Jesus as one would any other piece of Greco-Roman literature, setting aside prejudgments as to dating, precise location, audience, or social setting. Following Cantwell Smith, I simultaneously examine certain moments in the history of interpretation that have influenced the field in idiosyncratic ways. My goal is to demonstrate not only how we might approach these historical documents differently but also how some of our usual starting points and assumptions are informed by intellectual concerns belonging to subsequent centuries that are quite separate from the "original" social context of ancient Christianity. While the primary subject of this volume is Mark, my observations in this piece are applicable to the study of early Christian writers and writings more generally. Moreover, as a case study, Q is particularly compelling because it is not a first-century "Palestinian artifact," but quite literally an artifact of the late eighteenth and early nineteenth centuries.[3] Reexamining the circumstances of its "discovery" as well as what scholars have posited about its setting, composition, and dating, offers key insights into what is often presupposed about the social landscape of ancient Christianity more broadly. In this respect a (re)analysis of Q is also directly applicable to other writings about Jesus, like Mark.

By way of example, certain traditional approaches to the social context of Q claim it was written before the Jewish War by communities of Jesus followers, scribes, or redactor(s) invested in documenting the teachings of Jesus. This description is necessarily based on scant evidence and, arguably, informed by scholarly imagination about origins of early Christianity. This scholarly imagination generally includes the ideas that the early Jesus movement grew rapidly, that it was wide-ranging, well-established institutionally, and that it was more or less cohesive within a generation of Jesus's death. This perspective has been called the "Big Bang" theory

---

3. Smith, *On Teaching Religion*, 30.

of Christian origins.[4] Different early Christian texts have contributed to the myth of the early Christian Big Bang, but it reaches its apex with the origin story and details of the miraculous founding and growth of the Jesus movement as described in Acts.[5] Yet, previous to Acts, our earliest literature about Jesus is taciturn on the subject of the movement's historical development. Even our earliest source material, Paul, reveals a smattering of *ekklēsiai* oftentimes demonstrating little sense of unity, with Paul invoking the language of "group" in an attempt to evoke it. The quintessential example in the gospels is Mark, whose original ending is cast in mystery and silence, leaving a reader wondering how the Jesus movement developed at all. Thus, strong ideas in early Christian writings about certain kinds of social formations—an ideal Israel, communities of disciples, *ekklēsiai*— are as best we can tell literary constructions and not necessarily reliable historical data.[6] Nonetheless, these literary constructions continue to influence what we regard as thinkable about the social environments of those writing about Jesus. Elsewhere in this volume, Burton

---

4. Scholars who have used this terminology include N. T. Wright, *The New Testament and the People of God*, vol. 1 of *Christian Origins and the Question of God* (Minneapolis: Fortress, 1992), 452; Burton L. Mack, "On Redescribing Christian Origins," *MTSR* 8 (1996): 247; Edward W. Klink, *The Audience of the Gospels: The Origin and Function of the Gospels in Early Christianity* (New York: Continuum, 2010), 32; John S. Kloppenborg, "Greco-Roman Thiasoi, the Ekklēsia at Corinth, and Conflict Management," in *Redescribing Paul and the Corinthians,* ed. Ron Cameron and Merrill P. Miller, ECL 5 (Atlanta: Society of Biblical Literature, 2011), 189.

5. The origin story of Acts is adapted and perpetuated by the Pastoral Epistles, Irenaeus, and others. Later leaders within the church would construct a similar kind of "miraculous founding" using stories of violence and martyrdom against early Christians. Tales of the Great Persecution were a mechanism for reconsidering (and amplifying) the role of "the Church" within its own early history. Moreover, self-styled historians such as Eusebius, claiming to rely on eyewitness accounts, chronicled the unjust persecution of emperors and other leaders, mobs and rogue citizens against early Christians in order to herald the bravery, virtue, and obedience of these martyrs. Implicit in these stories was the message that the audience should act in kind. For a recent study on these issues, see Candida Moss, *The Myth of Persecution: How Early Christians Invented a Story of Martyrdom* (New York: HarperCollins, 2013).

6. I am influenced here by the sociologist Rogers Brubaker who cautions that emic categories are often unreliable: "We must … take vernacular categories and participant's understandings seriously, for they are partly constitutive of our objects of study. But we should not uncritically adopt the engaged *categories of ethnopolitical practice* as our *categories of social analysis*" (Rogers Brubaker, *Ethnicity without Groups* [Cambridge; London: Harvard University Press, 2004], 10, emphasis original).

Mack notes that the field commonly looks "for and at a setting mainly through windows provided by the text."[7] To whatever extent these early writings about Jesus and the Jesus movement are myths that Christianity tells about itself and its founding, scholars must be careful not to reinscribe these myths as history.

Nevertheless, it remains the case that the early Christian Big Bang has been codified in various ways throughout later centuries of interpretation. Drawing in part on the social landscapes described by various "Christian" texts, some scholars posit that there are bounded communities encoded in writings like the gospels (such as the Markan community, the Matthean community, and so forth).[8] This interpretive position is unique among fields that study ancient history. To borrow a phrase from Stanley Stowers, "Classicists do not approach Vergil's or Philodemus's writings as the products and mirrors of Vergil's or Philodemus's communities."[9] Recent work on this issue in early Christian studies points to the continuing influence of Romanticism, with its view of the author as an embodiment of the unifying, inspirational *Geist* speaking for the *Volk*. Certain lines of Romantic thought also understood religious literature like the Hebrew Bible (and, later, the New Testament) as expressions of folk speech that "grew organically from people, cultures and communities."[10] I will address the influence of Romanticism in more detail in what follows. When held in tension with the uncritical adaptation of Christianity's own myth of origins, identifying Romanticism's place in the history of New

---

7. Burton Mack, "The Spyglass and Kaleidoscope: From a Levantine Coign of Vantage," 182, in this volume.

8. The possible exceptions to this claim are certain lines of nineteenth-century Homeric Analyst-Unitarian scholarship. The Analyst debate was itself couched in Romantic ideas about oral traditions and national ethos. Some examples include Ulrich von Wilamowitz-Moellendorff, *Homerische Untersuchungen* (Berlin: Weidmann, 1884), and Karl Lachmann, who attempted to trace the 'stemma' (genealogy) of the narrative strands of Homer, comparing the *Iliad* to the German *Nibelungenlied*. See Karl Lachmann, *Betrachtungen über Homers Ilias, mit Zusätzen von M. Haupt* (Berlin: Reimer, 1847).

9. Stanley K. Stowers, "The Concept of 'Community' and the History of Early Christianity," *MTSR* 23 (2011): 247. Of course an author like Vergil is recognized as belonging to a social network of Augustan-era poets like Horace, Ovid, Propertius, and Tibullus that one might term a "community" of a sort. This is precisely the kind of alternative social formation that I seek to identify for the gospel writers.

10. Stowers, "Concept of 'Community,'" 239.

Testament scholarship brings potential clarity to the roots of this "community approach" and why it may be misleading. It also signals that new approaches are sorely needed.

One place to begin a new historical analysis without the baggage of later models of interpretation is by looking at Mediterranean and West Asian literary practices in the Roman imperial period. For example, with literacy the purview of so few, we know that those with enough training to produce their own writings often circulated works within networks of fellow writers and associated literate specialists.[11] The goal of this exchange was to solicit comments, critique, and discussion from social peers, making this a formative network of fellow, elite cultural producers (adapting terminology from Pierre Bourdieu). If we accept this as normal activity among writers in antiquity, why would it not be the same for the writers of Jesus material? Proposing a literary network such as this does not rely on assumptions about social context but utilizes known historical data. While it is possible that these writers were also associated with some kind of social group that we might call a religious community, that would not be taken for granted. By shifting our focus away from talk of communities and back onto the activities and choices of the writer as (usually) he observes the literary conventions, tropes, and possible *comparanda* in the text fosters new discussions about a variety of issues. Among them is the issue of when these texts were written.

Considering the literary interests and conventions evident in their works, I propose that the canonical gospel writers, and even Q, demonstrate an engagement with first century political events that place these texts after the Jewish War. These writings chronicle the teachings and life of a notable Judean figure whose wonderworking and Deuteronomistic viewpoint had particular purchase after the destruction of the temple. Among the options for why such a creative exercise may have been necessary is that it addressed the cultural, social, and religious uncertainties left in the wake of the war and temple destruction. In Q, for example, both Jesus and John the Baptist offer an alternative to the dominant temple system. That is, through their teachings, each arguably exemplify what Jonathan Z. Smith refers to as "heroes-that-succeeded"—figures who

---

11. For example, William A. Johnson, "Pliny and the Construction of Reading Communities," in *Readers and Reading Culture in the High Roman Empire: A Study of Elite Communities,* Classical Culture and Society (New York: Oxford University Press, 2010), 32–62.

managed to recognize and remain outside of the confines of an ill-fated, dominant social order.[12] In the face of a disrupted cosmic order, writers like Q overcame a perceived ritual and social ambiguity by searching for a new center for symbolic-social meaning. Another contributor to this volume, William Arnal, has suggested Mark takes a similar approach with his emphasis on the Judean War and its subsequent "fallout."[13] Mark's writing brings to the fore the realities of dislocation and exile as "opportunities for reimagining identity, nation, and location." In other words, Mark's treatment of Jesus becomes a means to "revel in the inversionary effects of the War" as an "occasion for new thoughts."[14] Barry Crawford's introduction to this volume and Merrill Miller's discussion of the work of Richard C. Miller also recognize a situation of "cultural-political upheaval" in the aftermath of the conflict.[15]

By extending this line of analysis to Q and placing all of our Jesus writings after the war, we not only attend to the literary interests expressed by these authors, but we also avoid the uncritical acceptance of the myth that the first century experienced a spontaneous, cohesive, diverse, and multiple Big Bang of Christian activity. This approach also respects the parameters set by available historical evidence—that is, we have no firm documentation of any material about Jesus's life and teachings before the war, save Paul. In what follows, I begin with a fuller overview of the Big Bang theory of Christian origins and its influence on the field. This is followed by an examination of the role that Romantic thinking has played in codifying the Big Bang approach. The second half of this piece will turn to our historical evidence for writing practices in antiquity and demonstrate how a renewed focus on these authors as literate specialists might lead to new insights about what motivated their writings and why.

---

12. Jonathan Z. Smith, *Map Is Not Territory: Studies in the History of Religions*, SJLA 23 (Leiden: Brill, 1978; Chicago: Chicago University Press, 1993), 139.

13. William E. Arnal, "The Gospel of Mark as Reflection on Exile and Identity," in *Introducing Religion: Essays in Honor of Jonathan Z. Smith*, ed. Willi Braun and Russell T. McCutcheon (London: Equinox, 2008), 59, emphasis original.

14. Ibid., 60.

15. Merrill Miller, "The Social Logic of the Gospel of Mark: Cultural Persistence and Social Escape in a Postwar Time," 240, in this volume; Richard C. Miller, "Mark's Empty Tomb and Other Translation Fables in Classical Antiquity," *JBL* 129 (2010): 759–76.

The Big Bang Theory of Christian Origins

The New Testament, the product of a codifying process that begins in the second century, constructs a myth of origins for Christianity that continues to be immensely influential in both theological and secular scholarly circles. The contours of this account are familiar: following Jesus's death, the disciples established the first church and an apostolic mission of teaching and conversion spread the movement rapidly throughout the empire, culminating in the founding and development of the so-called early churches. Acts informs a great deal of this perspective, with the continual invocation of groupist rhetoric in Paul's letters seemingly supporting the narrative in Acts if read anachronistically.[16] The notion that the practices, interpretive innovations, teachings, and literature of what comes to be known as Christianity emanated from an identifiable, powerful genesis is central to the idea of the early Christian Big Bang. Implicit to this theory is the premise that Christianity as a social phenomenon materialized in a manner otherwise unprecedented for a new religious movement.[17] Certainly, in order for there to have been thousands converted or "turned" in a single day, as claimed by Acts 21:20, the projected rate of growth of the movement would have to have been nothing short of miraculous.[18]

In terms of the texts that document this Big Bang, it is a standard claim among scholars of early Christianity that a "community" is the proper social context for imagining their composition. Usually, the writer is described as belonging to a discrete community of Christians that possesses its own particular theological outlook. As such, the author, the proverbial voice of this group, has developed his thinking within a very specific environment and, therefore, writes his gospel (or other Jesus material) reflecting—either indirectly or, as is more regularly thought, directly—the

---

16. Stowers, "Concept of 'Community,'" 243. Acts brings this full story together. Paul's letters and Matthew are centrally "organized" by Acts in order to produce this narrative.

17. I borrow the concept of "new religious movements" from Rodney Stark's work on Mormonism. See Rodney Stark, *The Rise of Mormonism*, ed. Reid L. Neilson (New York: Columbia University Press, 2005). For a comprehensive guide on the history of scholarship on so-called NRMs, see James Lewis, ed., *The Oxford Handbook of New Religious Movements* (New York: Oxford University Press, 2008).

18. Keith Hopkins, "Christian Number and its Implications," *JECS* 6 (1998): 185–226.

interests and holdings of that community.[19] The result is an approach that accepts communities as a fundamental and axiomatic element of the compositional fabric of early Christian literature. Moreover, these writings are understood to reflect not only the collective perspectives of these communities, but also to document strands of Jesus tradition that have been faithfully passed on by generation after generation of early Christians.[20]

Through artifacts such as the gospels, letters, and figureheads like Paul and Peter, the compilers and redactors of the second century pulled together what were at times disparate writings into a collective narrative aimed at legitimizing a particular view of Christian history.[21] In other words, these actors sought to develop a myth of Christian origins that was sufficiently unifying and novel so as to be worthy of place among the panoply of already established Mediterranean intellectual and religious traditions. To fail to recognize these efforts as the strategic maneuvers of later "inventors" and myth-makers—to believe Christianity's own myth of origins— is to begin our analyses from a limiting perspective that uncritically accepts the early stages of the Jesus movement as a recognizable something called "Christianity." Mark, and especially Q, have become the essential link for "instant-aging" Christianity—dating these writings as early as possible creates a foundation from which to claim continuity and coherence out of what was otherwise an amorphous history that was far from linear.[22]

It is important to pause at this juncture in order to be clear that there are two distinct-but-related observations I am making about how tradi-

---

19. Stowers, "Concept of 'Community,' " 245–46.

20. For example, John G. Gager, in some of his earlier work, viewed the gospels as products of disenfranchised early Christian "converts," as evidenced by the more egalitarian sayings of the gospels and claims that much of the Jesus material in the gospels "span[s] several generations and thus cover[s] the time of the initial apocalyptic excitement as well as the first phases of consolidation [of the church]"; see John G. Gager, *Kingdom and Community: The Social World of Early Christianity* (Englewood Cliffs, NJ: Prentice-Hall, 1975), 20–37, here 35.

21. For more on this, see William E. Arnal, "The Collection and Synthesis of 'Tradition' and the Second-Century Invention of Christianity," *MTSR* 23 (2011), 193–215.

22. The full quotation: "The past is convertible to social power in the present—hence the variety of 'instant-aging' maneuvers familiar to us from the early Christian groups we study. 'Strategic tinkering with the past' is a ubiquitous cross-cultural social rationalizing and formation device" (Willi Braun, "Socio-Mythic Invention, Graeco-Roman Schools, and the Sayings Gospel Q," *MTSR* 11 [1999]: 220).

tion is invented for early Christianity and how the concept of community becomes a normative social construction. While the activities and interests of the second century inform the way we have come to read the writings of the New Testament and other early Christian literature, this does not mean that we are unable to say anything concrete about the first century and the social context of the authors of these texts. However, it does require that we disaggregate our approach from the model of insular or solitary *religious* community that continues to be so influential in our thinking. This model remains dominant in part because of the acceptance of the Big Bang I have described above but also because of later approaches within the academy. Upon reflection, the concept of community employed by early historical-critical scholarship, in many respects, mirrors coeval, German Romantic ideas on folk speech, oral traditions, and communal authorship.

Romanticism and Community

In order to understand the roots of Romantic influence on the study of early Christian writings, it is useful to examine the Romantic idea of the solitary "genius" and the role of the author in the production of literature.[23] The concept of "genius" or "the genius" in Romanticism is not, as we might imagine in contemporary understanding, a theoretical or conceptual extension of reason. Following Immanuel Kant, it is a form of unconscious expression of literary or other artistic meaning that transgresses stric-

---

23. See Andrew Bennett, "Expressivity: the Romantic," in *Literary Theory and Criticism: An Oxford Guide*, ed. Patricia Waugh (Oxford: Oxford University Press, 2006), 48–58: "Inasmuch as Barthes's declaration of the death of the author may be said to be directed against the Romantic-expressive model of authorship, we might conclude, it is misdirected. What Barthes's attack overlooks or misrepresents are precisely the complexities and self-contradictions that energize Romantic poetic theory. The expressive theory of the author as articulated by writers of the Romantic period interrogates the subjectivity and self-consciousness of the author; it interrogates problems of language, representation, and textuality; it interrogates questions of authorial intention, volition, and agency. And despite the importance of the provocation of his essay, it is, in a sense, Barthes himself who closes down these questions by promoting a reductive version of expressive authorship in order to argue against it, and indeed to argue for a notion of the author that is already at work in the Romantic theory of authorship itself" (57).

tures of convention, while still remaining aesthetically successful.[24] Kant referred to genius as the "innate mental predisposition (*ingenium*) *through which* nature gives the rule to art." [25] Kant thereby establishes a symbiotic, and tautological, relationship between the artist and nature itself.

Romantic thinkers like August Wilhelm and Friedrich Schlegel would add to this doctrine a Romantic theory of literature. Friedrich Schlegel in particular brought to bear the autonomous activity of the poet, with "poetry" (Poesie) functioning as an act of continuous creativity or imagination that subsumes all other past expressions of literary genius into its process of achieving "perfect totality."[26] For Schlegel, poetry is an expression of "a progressive universal poetry [Poesie ist eine progressive Universalpoesie].... Only it can, like the epic, become a mirror of the whole surrounding world, a picture of the age."[27] Poetry was an expression of its immediate milieu. However, to be clear, this was not to suggest that the poet was engaged in articulating stages within a grand narrative of history. The linear progression of history was an Enlightenment position rejected by the Romantics, who instead understood historical development as a continuous, cyclical processes of birth, growth, and decay. Past "organic forms" of history could inform present understandings and artistic productions (for example, the dramas of the ancient Greeks or the poetry of the ancient Israelites), but each culture was uniquely expressed within its epoch, informed by its own particular historical circumstances.

---

24. Immanuel Kant, *Critique of the Power of Judgment*, ed. Paul Guyer, trans. Paul Guyer and Eric Matthews (New York: Cambridge University Press, 2000), 317–18. Also see Andrew Bowie, "Romanticism and Music," in *The Cambridge Companion to German Romanticism*, ed. Nicholas Saul (Cambridge: Cambridge University Press, 2009), 250.

25. Kant, *Critique of the Power of Judgment*, §46 (186, emphasis original). On genius as "nature's favorite" see §49 (191).

26. Jürgen Klein, "Genius, Ingenium, Imagination: Aesthetic Theories of Production from the Renaissance to Romanticism," in *The Romantic Imagination: Literature and Art in England and Germany*, ed. Frederick Burwick and Jürgen Klein (Amsterdam: Rodopi, 1996), 59. Also see Gregory Moore, introduction to *Shakespeare*, by Johann Gottfried Herder, ed. and trans. Gregory Moore (Princeton: Princeton University Press, 2008), xxi: "the genius was a second Creator, a Promethean figure who imitated not the ancients or other writers but only nature ... the genius created instinctively, promiscuously, with God-given powers."

27. August Wilhelm Schlegel and Friedrich Schlegel, "Fragmente," in vol. 1.2 of *Athenaeum: Eine Zeitschrift* (Berlin: Fr. Vieweg, 1798; repr. Berlin: Rütten & Loening, 1960), 28–30 (frag. 116).

The period in which ideas about the genius were being discussed was known as the *Geniezeit*—the "age of the genius"— and would give rise to significant innovations in political theory, ethics, and epistemology. It also provided the foundation for a shift in theories of language that willingly abandoned the dominance of French neoclassicism and the German *Kanzleistil* of the previous generations in favor of identifying literary figures representative of a less elite and unifying "*Deutsch*." The late eighteenth and early nineteenth centuries in Germany had seen the "Lilliputian statelets" and other relatively autonomous regions of that geographical expanse coalesce into the Holy Roman Empire of the German Nation, albeit without any cohesive political, economic, or cultural keystones.[28] It therefore fell to the Romantic thinkers, like Johann Gottfried Herder, to establish an invented tradition for Germany—one that demonstrated continuity between the present amalgamated culture and a conceptually unified past.[29] In attempting to reclaim this past, the search for German heritage extended beyond the borders of what constituted Germany, and past "the old fault line dividing Latin from Germanic Europe."[30]

Among the individual geniuses identified by *Sturm und Drang* and Romantic movements, William Shakespeare stands out as a seemingly peculiar choice to represent the language of unified Germany. However, his treatment by men like Herder is instructive for understanding why the individual ancient author I am attempting to redescribe in this project is not commensurate with the Romantic genius. Locating German heritage—the language and art of the people, the non-elites—entailed looking to poets and geniuses like Shakespeare who were unencumbered by the *délicatesse* of the French and, as such, better represented the unmediated spirit of the German people. Shortly before the Romantic movement, Heinrich von Gerstenberg, for instance, imagined Shakespeare presenting "living pictures of moral Nature"; later, Herder would herald him as a craftsman of *Volkspoesie* (popular poetry), along with the likes of Homer, the poets of the Hebrew Bible, and Ossian.[31] For example, Herder avers that in Shakespeare:

---

28. I follow much of Moore's account of German history in the following section (see Moore, introduction to *Shakespeare*, viii–x).

29. For more on later German nation-building and invented tradition, see William Arnal, "Collection and Synthesis of 'Tradition,'" 199–200.

30. Moore, introduction to *Shakespeare*, xi.

31. See Heinrich Wilhelm von Gerstenberg, *Briefe über merkwürdigkeiten der*

The *whole* world [die *ganze* Welt] is only body to this great mind: *all* scenes of nature limbs on this body [*alle* Auftritte der Natur an diesem Körper Glieder], as *all* characters and modes of thought traits to this mind [wie *alle* Charaktere und Denkarten zu diesem Geiste Züge]—and the *whole* [*Ganze*] may be named as that giant god of Spinoza "*Pan! Universum!*"[32]

For Herder, through Shakespeare there is not only an expression of artistic genius but also a synthesis of history in the manner in which he is able to pull together disparate characters, plots, languages, and circumstances into an organic whole.[33] Elsewhere Herder would claim that "the proper subject of the historical sciences is the life of communities and not the exploits of individuals.... Great poets expressed the mind and experience of their societies."[34] Indeed, the anti-Enlightenment notion of society—and religion—as a unified organism, animated by its own particular Spirit (Geist) was widespread in the Romantic period.[35]

Therefore, in Romantic thought Shakespeare was a genius representative of his broader cultural milieu. Like Sophocles before him, he reflected the social life and customs of his epoch.[36] But, crucially, that social life was

---

Litteratur (Leipzig: Hansen, 1766; repr., Hildesheim; New York: Olms, 1971) quoted from Moore, introduction to *Shakespeare*, xvi. Also see Moore, introduction to *Shakespeare*, xvii–xx.

32. Johann Gottfried von Herder, "Über Shakespeare," in *Herders Werke in fünf Bünden* (Ann Arbor: University of Michigan Library, 1903), 5:225–26. Herder's reference to Baruch Spinoza in this passage is likely in respect to the latter's monist philosophy, but it may also signal the *Pantheismusstreit* controversy between Friedrich Heinrich Jacobi and Gotthold Lessing.

33. Herder, *Shakespeare*, 30: "He took history as he found it, and with his creative spirit he combined the most diverse material into a wondrous whole."

34. Isaiah Berlin, *Three Critics of the Enlightenment: Vico, Hamann, Herder*, ed. Henry Hardy, 2nd ed. with a new foreword (Princeton: Princeton University Press, 2000), 211.

35. Ibid., 213: "The spirit of a nation or culture had been central not only to Vico and Montesquieu, but to the famous publicist Friedrich Karl von Moser, whom Herder read and knew, to Bodmer and Breitinger, to Hamann and to Zimmermann. Bolingsbroke had spoken of the division of men into nationalities as being deeply rooted in Nature herself."

36. Herder would also call Shakespeare "Sophocles' brother" in these discussions. See Herder, *Shakespeare*, 49. Robert Edward Norton explains: "In the Shakespeare essay [Herder] triumphantly displayed the one basic modus operandi that united the otherwise apparently so dissimilar playwrights.... Sophocles and Shake-

not expressed through the oppressive literary scruples of his period. It was expressed through the plain speech of the people. In his introduction to a translation of Herder's treatment of Shakespeare in *Von deutscher Art und Kunst* (*On German Character and Art*), Gregory Moore explains:

> Although Sophocles and Shakespeare may be outwardly dissimilar, they have a spiritual kinship that all geniuses share: they are true not only to nature ... but also to the culture from which they emerged.... Both are mouthpieces of the collective soul of the nation, expressing its thoughts and sentiments, manners and morals; in each case their art is a development of indigenous species of expression.[37]

German and English alike could unify under the cultural banner of the genius of Shakespeare, insofar as his work expressed the spirit of the common people, the *Volksgeist*, and their unique experiences and culture. By the later Romantic period, the institutionalization of *Germanistik* and protonationalist projects like that of the Grimm brothers would increasingly look to the *Volkspoesie* and language of the German people for evidence of their shared history. Yet the author-genius continued to function as the inspired mouthpiece of the people and their collective experience of their environment.[38]

---

speare were literally worlds apart in every other respect but in their representative fidelity to nature" (Robert Edward Norton, "The Ideal of a Philosophical History of Aesthetics: The Diverse Unity of Nature," in *Herder's Aesthetics and the European Enlightenment* [Ithaca, NY: Cornell University Press, 1991], 79–80). Interestingly, in his "Demythologizing: Controversial Slogan and Theological Focus," Rudolf Bultmann cites Shakespeare (*Tempest* IV, 1) and Sophocles (*Ajax* 125–126) as examples of "mythical eschatology," thereby maintaining the comparison generations later; see Rudolf Bultmann, "Demythologizing: Controversial Slogan and Theological Focus," in *Rudolf Bultmann: Interpreting Faith for the Modern Era*, ed. Roger A. Johnson, The Making of Modern Theology: Nineteenth and Twentieth-Century Texts (Minneapolis: Fortress, 1991), 295.

37. Moore, introduction to *Shakespeare*, xxx.

38. Herder would not live to see Napoleon Bonaparte conquer Austria and Prussia (1805); however, the civic reforms and rebellions that would follow stoked the protoliberal nationalism articulated by Herder, with the abolishment of serfdoms and the rise of the peasant class. See Hans-Joachim Hahn, "Germany: Historical Survey," in *Encyclopedia of the Romantic Era, 1760–1850*, ed. Christopher John Murray (New York: Fitzroy Dearborn, 2004), 418–21.

The Romantic Genius acting as a spokesperson for his kinsmen is a model for understanding the production of literature that shares a great deal with the kinds of approaches in early Christian studies that focus on the author as a redactor of sayings, teachings, and other materials deemed essential or representative of his community. Again, this community is traditionally envisioned as a religious group of some stripe, unified by their shared "mind and practice."[39] Stowers, reflecting on the concept of community as it pertains to its use in the field, notes that nineteenth-century ideas of *Gemeinschaft* (community) and *Gesellschaft* (society) were often associated with notions of "an essential and totalizing identity and commitment" akin to the idea of conversion.[40] This is the same kind of wholesale turning of allegiance augured in passages like Acts 4:23: "The great number of those who believed were of one heart and one mind." Thus, sociological approaches to nineteenth-century Europe dovetail conceptually with traditional descriptions of the social environment of early Christian writers that emphasize religious groups to the exclusion of other potential associations.

It would be an oversimplification, however, to say that when scholars in the field of New Testament and early Christian studies use the word "community" they are consciously engaging the paradigms of the Romantics. Likewise, not all scholarship on the social world of the early Christians has engaged in discourse about communities, or if they have, some have recognized that the model is problematic.[41] Yet, it remains the case that the study of early Christianity largely persists in making appeals to con-

---

39. Stowers, "Concept of 'Community,'" 238–39: "The range of meanings that has been important for scholarship on ancient Christianity, however, has a different history not only in Christian thought, but also in European and American social and political thought. This is the idea of community as a deep social and mental coherence, a commonality in mind and practice. Although Enlightenment traditions sometimes approached the idea as in the French Revolution's fraternity in 'liberty, equality and fraternity,' it has been the anti-Enlightenment and Romantic traditions that have featured community in this sense."

40. Stowers, "Concept of 'Community,'" 239. Stowers cites the late nineteenth-century work of Ferdinand Tönnies, "with his dualism between *Gemeinschaft* (community) and *Gesellschaft* (society), the former supposedly based upon the essential will (*Wesenwille*) of the participant."

41. For instance, see John G. Gager, *Kingdom and Community*; Abraham J. Malherbe, *Social Aspects of Early Christianity* (Baton Rouge: Louisiana State University Press, 1977).

cepts of community that are at best ill-defined or, more usually, myopically focused on religious groups that reinscribe Acts' myth of origins in some measure.[42] Moreover, much like the author-genius Shakespeare speaking for the "illiterate, low-liv'd" Elizabethan, the early Christian writer is often imagined within a coterie of illiterate fellow Christians.[43] This model for ancient authorship agitates against what we know about the practices of those with sufficient education and training to produce and circulate writings in the ancient Mediterranean world.

The Romantic ideal of the author-genius is incommensurable with ancient writers in three fundamental and interrelated respects. First, the literary practices of ancient authors were not the "pure" and unmediated activities of a poet inspired by creative Nature to express the *Geist* of the people. Ancient writers possessed rich and complex reasons for composing their works as active agents, and their productions should not be understood as the expression of the totalizing "mind and experience" of their social groups, class, or other immediate communities.[44] Second, this is not to say that authors are not engaging certain canons of literature, literary traditions, or attempting to represent particular kinds of discourses in their writing. On the contrary, these authors are self-consciously choosing and crafting their referents and source materials in a rational way. Speaking of Romantic, aesthetic values as they pertain to ancient literature, Tim Whitmarsh notes that Greek literary culture of the imperial period was for some time viewed by scholars as an "embarrassing epilogue" given that its writers' were perceived as failing to embody the Romantic "obsession" with "originality" and "inspiration" characteristic of the author-genius. Writers like those of the Second Sophistic, however, were prized in their milieu precisely for their ability to participate in the creative imitation of other texts or the "intertextual refashioning of earlier literary works."[45] Skill was judged by the author's ability to consciously select the traditions that they wished to emulate and their ability to play the game, as it were,

---

42. Stowers, "Concept of 'Community,'" 239–49.

43. Bettina Boecker, "Groundlings, Gallants, Grocers: Shakespeare's Elizabethan Audience and the Political Agendas of Shakespeare Criticism," in *Shakespeare and European Politics*, ed. Dirk Delabastita, Jozef De Vos, and Paul J. C. M. Franssen, foreword by Ton Hoenselaars (Newark: University of Delaware Press, 2008), 221–22.

44. Berlin, *Three Critics of the Enlightenment*, 211.

45. Tim Whitmarsh, *The Second Sophistic* (New York: Cambridge University Press, 2005), 1.

of participating in that literary culture. It was not judged by the extent to which the author, propelled forward by the *Geist* of the age and their own aesthetic talents, could faithfully represent the *Volk*.

Lastly, it is misleading to associate writers exclusively with nonelites in an attempt to say something about the "common traditions and common memories" of the *Volk*.[46] Writers may reflect certain discernable aspects of the language, culture, politics, and concerns of their milieu, but they are not unvarnished mirrors of the imagined experiences, traditions, and needs of unique groups or other categories of people. For example, and relevant to the last point above, a study of literary culture in antiquity demonstrates that it is the author's critical writing "circle" of fellow elite cultural producers that is the most immediate and formative social context for the production of literature.[47] There is no compelling reason to think that the writers of early Christian literature should be situated in a different environment.

One reason for the persistence of community language in the field is, arguably, its Romantic ties to ideas about religion. One prominent figure in the history of biblical interpretation whose work continues to influence early Christian scholarship is Herder. Herder is widely considered the originator of the notion of the *Volkgeist*—the spirit of the German people and nation.[48] His major contributions to post-Enlightenment and theological lines of thinking were in his critiques of language and history. Consider-

46. Berlin, *Three Critics of the Enlightenment*, 234.

47. See, for example, William A. Johnson, "Pliny and the Construction of Reading Communities," 52. Speaking of the literary communities of elite authors like Pliny, Johnson states: "The community is characterized by a reciprocity that mutually recognizes common values, 'of which the most important is the rhetorical mastery of language,'" citing Florence Dupont, "*Recitatio* and the Space of Public Discourse," in *The Roman Cultural Revolution*, ed. Thomas Habinek and Alessandro Schiesaro (Cambridge: Cambridge University Press, 1997), 54.

48. Coincidentally, Herder's proto-nationalistic positions would have "fateful consequences for the twentieth century" (James C. Livingston, *The Enlightenment and the Nineteenth Century*, vol. 1 of *Modern Christian Thought*, 2nd ed. [Minneapolis: Fortress, 2006], 73). By the end of his life, however, Herder himself rejected nationalism. Isaiah Berlin explains: "He believed in kinship, social solidarity, *Volkstum*, nationhood, but to the end of his life he detested and denounced every form of centralization, coercion and conquest, which were embodied and symbolized both for him, and for his teacher Hamann, in the accursed State. Nature creates nations, not States [through language]. The State is an instrument of happiness for a group, not for men as such" (Berlin, *Three Critics of the Enlightenment*, 224–25).

ing language to be the "foundation of human consciousness"—and not, contra Hamann, principally of divine origin or, contra Rousseau, a human invention—his construction of the circle of language and thought in many ways prefigured Wittgenstein's "language-game," viewing language as "a series of developing revelations" of the human race.[49] Again, to be clear, this is not to say that he held that language signaled a progression of history *per se*. Rather, each epoch of history—each "cultural phase"— was its own unique expression of what Herder termed *Humanität* (humanity).[50]

Herder's view of language had particular implications for his theories of religion. Each religion is embedded in a certain culture and is unique to that context:

> Who has noticed how *inexpressible* the *individuality* of one human being is.… How different and particular all things are to an individual because they are seen by the eyes, measured by the soul, and felt by the heart of *that* individual? As disparate as heat is from cold, and as one pole is from another, so diverse are the various religions.

For Herder, "like nations and cultures, religions are singular, living organisms." That said, while maintaining that each religious tradition is its own unique and valuable representation of a given culture, he still viewed Christianity as "the true conviction about God and human beings … nothing but the pure dew of heaven for all nations."[51]

In his *First Dialogue concerning National Religion* (1802), Herder constructs a conversation between two friends in which one friend asks the other "Would you be annoyed if I hold Christianity to be the religion *of all religions,* of all people?" This then leads to an extended discourse on language as that which shapes the "corporate soul" and that those "who are ashamed of their nation and language destroy not only their religion but

---

49. Livingston, *Enlightenment and the Nineteenth Century*, 74.

50. Herder's student, J. W. von Goethe, would describe this theory as a case of nature evolving from "an unknown centre" moving toward "an unknown boundary"; see Johann Wolfgang von Goethe, *Naturwissenschaftliche Schriften 1*, vol 13 of *Goethes Werke*, ed. Erich Trunz, 14 vols., Hamburger Ausgabe (Munich: Beck, 1981), 35.

51. Cited from Livingston, *Enlightenment and the Nineteenth Century*, 74. The Tübingen philosopher Carl August Eschenmayer would put an even finer point on the matter: the highest expression of *Geist* in human history is found not in art, contra F. W. J. Schelling, but in the early stages of Christianity's development out of the dregs of antiquity.

the bond that ties their people together."[52] Following Hamann, he would equate "linguistic petrifaction" with a valley full of corpses "which only 'a prophet' (such as Socrates, St Paul, Luther, and perhaps himself) could cover with flesh."[53] For Herder, the poetic language of biblical texts was the "mother tongue of the human race" and, in this poetry, "the spiritual genius of a whole people is found."[54]

In keeping with the predominant viewpoints of the emerging historical-critical discipline, Herder could not deny that human hands were at work on the composition of the Bible. He acknowledged that biblical texts revealed human "nature and language ... according to their weaknesses and within the limitations of their ideas." In other words, biblical poetry carried threads of the culture within which it was composed, expressing "a developing divine revelation" that ultimately grows not from autonomous authors alone but through the language of the people.[55] By studying the poetry and other writings of biblical authors, as well as Homer and Ossian, Herder proposed that one could know the "modes of thinking and feeling" of the *Volk*, including "how they were educated, what scenes they looked upon, what were the objects of their affection and passion ... their dances, and their music."[56]

Perhaps Herder's best illustration of the association between nature and language comes in his *On the Spirit of Hebrew Poetry* (1782–1783).[57]

---

52. Cited from Livingston, *Enlightenment and the Nineteenth Century*, 75.

53. Berlin, *Three Critics of the Enlightenment*, 240.

54. Livingston, *Enlightenment and the Nineteenth Century*, 76.

55. Ibid., 77.

56. Johann Gottfried von Herder, *On the Spirit of Hebrew Poetry*, trans. James Marsh, 2 vols. (Burlington, VT: Edward Smith, 1833), 28.

57. Herder's enthusiasm for the Hebrew poets (the *Naturmenschen*) should not be conflated with his views on eighteenth- and early-nineteenth century Judaism. Although he embraced the historical, national character and language of the Hebrew people represented by the scriptures, he was also adamant that epochs remain conceptually segregated and in essence that the modern Jew had little relationship to the heralded and more authentic Hebrew poetry and law. For instance, he held that the "nature of the soul is determined by the natural landscape" and, given the desert terrain of their God-given land, the Jews were "a decrepit corpse." Moreover, he maintained a view of Jews as superstitious and power hungry, the latter a precursor to the fear of *Weltjudentum* and the former evident in the stagnation of natural science and historiography. See Anders Gerdmar, *Roots of Theological Anti-Semitism: German Biblical Interpretation and the Jews, from Herder and Semler to Kittel and Bultmann* (Leiden: Brill, 2009), 59.

In this two-volume work, he equates the sensory metaphors used by the Hebrew poets to the pure and childlike nature of their "savage nation."[58] "Savage" is not intended to be pejorative in this case but a reflection of the simplicity of the *Volk* and their closeness to nature. Herder explains: "The more savage, that is, the more alive and freedom-loving a people is (for that is the simple meaning of the word), the more savage, that is, alive, free, sensuous, lyrically active, its songs must be, if it has songs."[59] This is the framework through which Herder begins his investigation, opening with a celebration of the music he envisages accompanied the Hebrew poets:

> The rattling of the ancient cymbals and kettle-drums, in short the whole music-band of [that] savage nation … is still ringing in my ears. I still see David dancing before the Ark of the covenant, or the prophets summoning a player, that they may feel his inspirations.

Correspondingly, he posits that the first stage of this poetry was chiefly oral. It is the unmediated expression of *Geist* among the *Volk* and the "simplest [form] by which the human soul expressed its thoughts."[60] He goes on to describe the work of these poets as "imperfect," "uncertain and far-fetched," and full of "parallelisms" so monotonous they are an "everlasting tautology." [61] He also suggests "with the Hebrew the verb is almost the whole of the language," offering the caveat that "for this beggarly race of herdsmen, from what sources could they form a language?"[62] However, like with the concept of the "savage," these observations are not designed to be detractions. The language expressed by these poets is the "living language of Canaan … during the period of its greatest beauty and purity … before it was corrupted by the introduction of the Chaldee [and the] Greek."[63] Its active verbs and sensory metaphors combined "form and feeling"; unlike Homer, the words "creak and hiss" and, in its earliest stages, show no signs of having "passed through a refining process."[64]

---

58. Herder, *On the Spirit of Hebrew Poetry*, 26.

59. Cited from Berlin, *Three Critics of the Enlightenment*, 242.

60. Herder, *On the Spirit of Hebrew Poetry*, 46. Also see 94: "All sensuous tribes have a knowledge of that nature, to which their poetry relates; nay, they have a more living, and for their purpose a better knowledge of it."

61. Ibid., 26.

62. Ibid., 31.

63. Ibid., 32.

64. Ibid., 168. Likewise, just as Herder considered the language of the Hebrews

Eventually these oral traditions would be recorded as *Volkspoesie*, experiencing the "refining process" of being converted into literature. Therefore, while Hebrew poetry was embedded in the language of its *Volk*, Herder was also aware that it passed through the "weaving of the book according to later disposition"—that is, it passed through the hands of redactors.[65] Naturally, this would result in a certain amount of degradation of the "purer" forms of the original *Poesie*. However, an enterprising analyst could recover elements of the pretextual oral/folk traditions of the "nation" represented by the text.

Herder's model for an oral tradition behind the development of literature would go on to inform Romantic folklorists like Wilhelm and Jacob Grimm. However, his methods would also indirectly influence later form criticism (*Formgeschichte*) and redaction criticism (*Redaktionsgeschichte*) in the field of New Testament studies, as well as members of the history of religions school (*religionsgeschichtliche Schule*) among them Hermann Gunkel and Johannes Weiss. For form critics, early Christian communities possessed oral and/or small collections of written texts, preserving Jesus's teachings as well as elements of their own collective, yet unique, folk interpretations and interpolations. In this construction of history, the notion of an autonomous writer was absent. Authorship was fundamentally communal. Certain scholars would take these principles and associate the notion of communal *Geist* with the posited informal folk literature of the Christian communities, for which the gospel writer was a mere redactor of collected, communal materials.

Similarly, many notable early Christianity and New Testament scholars saw in this proposed folk literature a window onto the preliterary, oral traditions of early Christian communities. Bultmann, for instance, proposed that one could demonstrate through "critical investigation ... that the whole tradition about Jesus which appears in the three synoptic gospels is composed of a series of layers which can on the whole be clearly distinguished." He maintained that it could be "easily proved" that "many sayings originated in the church itself; others were modified by the church," if one parsed the essential content from the "Aramaic tradition of the oldest Palestinian community" from the material of the manifestly

---

more simplistic and closer to an "unbiased and uncorrupted" state of nature, he considered the cognitive functions and morals of this *Volk* to be similarly "childlike."

65. Willi Thomas, *Herders Beitrag zum Verstehen des Alten Testaments*, Beitrag zur Geschichte der Biblischen Hermeneutik 8 (Tübingen: Mohr Siebeck, 1971), 66.

distinct Greek, "Hellenistic Christian community" of the later gospel writers and their fellow Christians.[66] This Hellenistic brand of Christianity was seen as imbued with Platonism, Stoicism, pneumatology, and other elements that helped to make it palatable to its gentile audience.[67] These interpretive moves would have monumental influence on interpretations of Q as well, as Bultmann proposed that the supposed sayings-source was "a primary source from which we can reconstruct a picture of the primitive community in which the *Logia* [the sayings] arose."[68] Again, the significance of this shift in methodology was that the group was now largely considered the primary actor in the course of authorship, not necessarily the autonomous author. That is to say, the idea of a writer of the gospels or Q was rarely discussed in early Christian literature outside of references to a representative scribe, a redactor, or the like. The idea of collective authorship became the norm or, at the very least, scholars began speaking in terms of the "community" or "communities" that produced these materials and not necessarily individual writers or interpreters.

Redaction criticism entered into this schema with the notion of a redactor compiling disparate remnants from past Christian communities into a text that reflected not only elements of an authentic, more originary Christian past, but the redactor's present social setting, their *Sitz im Leben*. This move found scholars reflecting on the theology of the redactor: how their thought "was created or developed within a particular community, the theology that defined and differentiated the community from other communities." The stories about Jesus's life chosen by the redactor were also mined for information on precisely how they were representative of

---

66. Rudolf Bultmann, "Jesus and the Eschatological Kingdom," in *Rudolf Bultmann: Interpreting Faith for the Modern Era*, 97.

67. Rudolf Bultmann, "Primitive Christianity as a Syncretistic Phenomenon," in *Primitive Christianity in Its Contemporary Setting*, trans. Reginald H. Fuller (New York: Meridian Books, 1956; New York: The World Publishing Company, 1956), 176: "On other occasions the Christian missionaries went direct to the Gentile population, and then, in the first instance, to the lower classes in the cities. There were probably churches of Gentiles only.... Christianity found itself in a new spiritual environment: The Gospel had to be preached in terms intelligible to Hellenistic audiences and their mental outlook, while at the same time the audience themselves were bound to interpret the gospel message in their own way, in light of their own spiritual needs. Hence the growth of divers types of Christianity."

68. Rudolf Bultmann, "The New Approach to the Synoptic Problem," *JR* 6 (1926): 341.

the "issues and needs of a particular community."[69] Once again, the poet—the author-genius—was the voice of the community.

For some the "community-writer" perspective is simply cited in kinship with the idea that authors are embedded within particular social or cultural contexts (*Sitze im Leben*), or that their writings are socially constructed products; however, it is rare to find a study that does not deem the author's presumed *Christian community* to be the most immediate, formative, and relevant social framework. Consequently, this Christian community is theorized in lieu of other kinds of possible social contexts or environments. Some progress has been made in recent years in the field as the social sciences have added to the conversation questions about the social organization of the early Christian communities—were they egalitarian, sectarian, patriarchal, for instance—but the community has remained the starting point of analysis. As Stowers has noted, on the whole, this has been an extremely limiting approach to early Christian literature and one that has allowed "normative theological concepts [to parade] as descriptive and explanatory social concepts."[70]

It is important to note that in this overview of Romanticism's influences on the field, I am not attempting to revive the author-genius or the Romantic-expressive model of authorship. Nor am I going so far as to engage in structuralist lines of thought that would attribute the authorship to "innumerable centres of culture."[71] I am instead proposing a rich and dynamic social context for ancient writers and other literate experts based on historical evidence of their activities. Understanding now how Romantic ideas may have skewed our analyses in a way that is largely ahistorical, a redescription of early Christian writers must begin with what we know about ancient literate specialists.

Early Christian Writers as Literate Specialists

The best way for us to reconstruct ancient writing and literary practices is to examine what writers themselves tell us about their activities. For example, while not intended to faithfully represent a gathering of literary elite, Athenaeus's "The Sophists at Dinner" nonetheless offers a descriptive

69. Stowers, "Concept of 'Community,'" 241.
70. Ibid., 245–46.
71. Roland Barthes, "The Death of the Author," in *Image-Music-Text*, trans. Stephen Heath (New York: Macmillan, 1977), 146.

and amusing illustration of what some of these social networks may have looked like.[72] Comprised of a series of vignettes, Athenaeus's piece combines verse and prose satire, philosophical reflection, and biography with lexica of literary works, authors, sayings, and other sundry items, in the sympotic style of Plato.[73] It is an ecclectic storehouse of a variety of familiar literary genres and figures. Beyond the various delicacies, recipes, and drinking cups his diners discuss, Athenaeus's food-talk is also an occasion for exploring the moral constitutions—the virtues and vices—of a variety of noteworthy figures. For example, at one point, the diners discuss the unfortunate end of one Philoxenus, who chokes on an octopus. The gluttony of Philoxenus is well attested elsewhere in ancient literature, including in the fragments of Aristotle and Theophilus.[74] He is among a number of character-types favored by *bios*-writers, who looked to subversive figures to explore "discourse on excess and temperament."[75] Philoxenus's example also engages the theme of ignoble death found in biographical writings

---

72. One reason I have chosen this example of literate activity is that it demonstrates that the relationship between literacy and class or status is a complicated subject in antiquity. A slave, for example, could have a certain level of literacy in order to serve the needs of a household, but lack access to traditional signifiers of elevated social status. This is a subject I cannot tackle adequately in this piece, but it will feature in my forthcoming research.

73. In addition to his reliance on Plato and Lucian's *Symposium* and *Lexiphanes* and Plutarch's *Table Talk*, Athenaeus employs a version of prose and verse satire popularized by Menippus the Cynic. For more on his possible literary influences, see Derek Krueger, "The Bawdy and Society: The Shamelessness of Diogenes in Roman Imperial Culture," in *The Cynics: The Cynic Movement in Antiquity and Its Legacy*, ed. Robert Bracht Branham and Marie-Odile Goulet-Cazé (Berkeley: University of California Press, 1996), 222–39; Ronald F. Hock, "A Dog in the Manger: The Cynic Cynulcus among Athenaeus's Deipnosophists," in *Greeks, Romans, and Christians: Essays in Honor of Abraham J. Malherbe*, ed. David Balch, Everett Ferguson, and Wayne Meeks (Minneapolis: Fortress, 1990), 20–37; Christian Jacob, *The Web of Athenaeus*, ed. Scott Fitzgerald Johnson, trans. Arietta Papaconstantinou, Center for Hellenic Studies (Cambridge: Harvard University Press, 2013).

74. See Pauline LeVen, "Reading the Octopus: Authorship, Intertexts, and a Hellenistic Anecdote (Machon Fr. 9 Gow)," *AJP* 134 (2013): 30; Aristotle, fr. 83; Theophilus, *FHG* 4:6. Also see Athenaeus, *Deipn.* 8.341d, who cites Machon's account of Philoxenus desiring "a four-foot long throat so as to be able to enjoy food and drink all at the same time."

75. Elsewhere I characterize the gospels and Q as a type of ancient biography that I also call "subversive." See David Konstan and Robyn Faith Walsh, "Civic and Subversive Biography in Antiquity," *Writing Biography in Greece and Rome: Narra-*

like Diogenes Laertius, whose philosophers often come to unceremonious ends. Such episodes recall Plutarch's preface to the *Life of Alexander*: "It is not Histories I am writing, but Lives; and in the most illustrious deeds there is not always a manifestation of virtue and vice, no, a slight thing like a phrase or joke often makes a greater revelation of character" (*Alex.* 2–3 [LCL: Perrin]). Certain biographical subjects are a useful foil for considering dominant ethical principles, even in the breach.

Athenaeus's "Sophists at Dinner" is a fine example of a writer producing a piece of literature informed by his educational training and in conversation with other writers, storytellers, and literary works. Moreover Athenaeus, although featuring a number of different types of *chreiae*, writes within an expected genre—that is, what he produces makes reference to known and established literary conventions.[76] He does not craft an unprecedented or *sui generis* piece of literature. His points of reference and literary aims are intelligible and represent his social location as an author exchanging ideas with members of his intellectual circle. In short, his composition offers a window into the practices of writers and writing culture of the imperial period.

Athenaeus's dinner guests also offer a sense of how literature was consumed. The personal libraries of the sophists recall Philodemus's library at Herculaneum or the caches of book collectors and "bibliomaniacs" like Trimalchio.[77] Ulpian speaks of his quest for rare volumes from booksell-

---

tive Technique and Fictionalization, ed. Koen De Temmerman and Kristoffel Demoen (New York: Cambridge University Press, 2016).

76. The term "genre" is a modern designation. The ancients did not possess the same taxonomies that contemporary scholarship identifies for academic purposes. That said, ancient readers were aware that there were distinguishing features between kinds of literature (e.g., the novel, letter writing), even if they did not always use the same categories. When I use the term, I am indicating that writers conformed to certain literary conventions. While writers were perfectly capable of innovating, there are still certain rhetorical standards and training that are reflected in the works they produce. Also see Jennifer Eyl, "Why Thekla Does Not See Paul: Visual Perception and the Displacement of Erōs in the *Acts of Paul and Thekla*," in *The Ancient Novel and the Early Christian and Jewish Narrative: Fictional Intersections*, ed. Marília P. Futre Pinheiro, Judith Perkins, and Richard Pervo (Groningen: Barkhuis Publishing & Groningen University Library, 2012), 3 n. 1.

77. See Jacob, *Web of Athenaeus*, 56–57, esp. n. 7; Athenaeus, *Deipn.* 13.556b, 7.276a; Petronius, *Satyr.* 48.4; Seneca, *Tranq.* 9.4–7; Lucian, *The Ignorant Book-Collector*; Pliny the Younger, *Ep.* 1.8, 2.17.

ers in Rome in a manner reminiscent of the characters in *Attic Nights* who frequent bookshops and encounter there "true and fake scholars … reading out loud and discussing textual criticism and interpretation of difficult texts."[78] The Sophists are also able to recite certain quotations from memory, although only if the excerpt is relatively fresh in their minds and not something read long ago.[79] Sometimes, with help, a forgotten text could be recalled, albeit not always properly.[80] Even among "living libraries" like Porphyry, they were understood to have reached a "culminating point of *paideia*, at the summit of grammar and rhetoric" within their literary circles.[81] Training received in *paideia* to memorize and critique classical authors like Homer, Hesiod, other poets, and philosophers was also known to serve a writer well when composing their own literature. Philo of Alexandria, for instance, while clearly knowledgable of the Hebrew scriptures, also indicates his knowledge of the Homeric epics, citing the *Iliad* and using a number of Homeric expressions in his writings.[82]

The portrait painted by Athenaeus, coupled with knowledge of literary culture from the likes of Philo, Pliny the Younger, and Quintilian, reveal that writing was a specialist's activity.[83] While one might be trained in certain scribal practices or memorization techniques, the ability to produce literature according to accepted standards required an advanced rhetorical education.[84] Moreover, a writer's most immediate and formative social

---

78. Jacob, *Web of Athenaeus*, 59. Aulus Gellius, *Noct. Att.* 5.41, 13.31, 18.4.

79. Athenaeus, *Deipn.*, 3.126b; 8.359d–e.

80. Jacob, *Web of Athenaeus*, 76; Athenaeus, *Deipn.* 3.83a–c.

81. Jacob, *Web of Athenaeus*, 79: Longinus "embodies Alexandria's erudition and critical authority, and his works fill the libraries of others." Eunapius, *Lives of the Sophists*, 455.

82. Philo, *Contempl.* 17; *Abr.* 10; *Conf.* 170; *Fug.* 31; *Somn.* 2:53, 2:275. Also see Maren R. Niehoff, *Jewish Exegesis and Homeric Scholarship in Alexandria* (New York: Cambridge University Press, 2011), 2–3: "Other anonymous exegetes in Alexandria explicitly compared the biblical story of the Tower of Babel to a similar enterprise of the sons of Aloeidae recorded in the Odyssey (*Conf.* 4–5). Such references are not at all surprising given the known acculturation of Alexandrian Jews. They not only spoke and wrote in Greek but quickly read even their Scriptures only in the Greek translation. Homer's epics, which constituted the most important pillar of Greek education in Hellenistic Egypt, were obviously familiar to them" (3).

83. See n. 72 above.

84. Seneca, for example, speaks of a Calvisius Sabinus "who had bought high priced slaves trained to be living books: each one had learned one classical author by heart—Homer, Hesiod, or the Lyrics—and had the suitable quotations ready at

network was his circle of fellow writers and literary critics—an interconnected network of professional authors and literate consumers with particular kinds of intellectual knowledge and skill. I referred to such groups
earlier as networks of elite literate and specialized cultural producers.
These networks could consist of close friends and teachers, such as the
ones described by Pliny; a group of writers supported by the same patron,
like the Augustan poets; or activities performed within certain philosophical schools, such as writing commentaries.[85] Writings produced within
these networks could circulate outside of their immediate social group
to associated literate writers or other audiences, as Athenaeus's account
of booksellers attests. However, literature was ultimately a product of an
author's education, training, and range of literary and other interests, as
well as the feedback received from social peers.[86]

In his work on reading culture in the Roman Empire, William A.
Johnson refers to these close-knit literary networks as "*amici*" who circulated writings for critique and then gathered to recite, discuss, promote, or reject new works and would-be authors, and to "elicit advance
criticism so that the author could revise his work for publication."[87] Pliny
describes his own literary circle as a group of *amici* or "friends dedicated
to the literary enterprise ... characterized by a reciprocity that recognizes
common values, 'of which the most important is the rhetorical mastery of

---

the disposal of their forgetful master during the banquet conversations" (Seneca, *Ep.*
3.27.5; quoted in Jacob, *Web of Athenaeus*, 79). This kind of training in memorization
does not necessarily mean that Calvisius Sabinus's slaves would also be in a position to
produce literature, but it does not exclude the possibility. Being a slave also does not
necessarily exclude one from participating in literary networks of exchange.

85. William A. Johnson, "Pliny and the Construction of Reading Communities,"
33: "Pliny also had luminary literary connections. Quintilian was his teacher.... He
counted among his *amici* Tacitus ... and Suetonius ... and Martial; he was less familiar
but well acquainted with Silius Italicus ... of the previous generation. He does not
mention Plutarch directly, but they shared two close consular friends." Also see David
Armstrong, Jeffrey Fish, Patricia A. Johnson, and Marilyn B. Skinner, eds., *Vergil,
Philodemus and the Augustans* (Austin: University of Texas Press, 2004); Elaine Fantham, *Roman Literary Culture: From Cicero to Apuleius* (Baltimore: Johns Hopkins
University Press, 1996); H. Gregory Snyder, *Teachers and Texts in the Ancient World:
Philosophers, Jews and Christians* (New York: Routledge, 2000).

86. Stowers, "Concept of 'Community,'" 247.

87. Johnson, "Pliny and the Construction of Reading Communities," 52. Johnson
is citing the work of Roland Mayer, *Tacitus: Dialogus de oratoribus* (New York: Cambridge University Press, 2001), 92 on Tacitus, *Dial.* 2.1.

language.'"[88] In his essay in this volume, Miller makes a similar assessment when he notes that "Mark's project points to circles of friends and collaborators that included a network of readers who were consumers precisely of writings and wanted and were able to consult written texts for comparison, reference, and interpretation."[89]

Therefore, based on our knowledge of ancient writers and writing culture, I believe we can provide a redescription for first-century literature about Jesus that recognizes the author as an elite cultural producer. Rather than posit that an author's reputed religious community is the most influential social group for the production of these materials, ancient authors were engaged in an intellectual practice that makes their literary circle of *amici*—fellow writers—a significant and formative social network, and the one with whom the author shares, following Pliny, significant and reciprocal "common values."[90] To be clear, this is not to deny that when an author explores subjects concerning the gods and associated practices, ethics, and so on that they are not potentially involved with what we might term a religious group of some sort. But this association, and the degree to which it is instrumental, must be demonstrated. Our understanding of an author's social environment should not be limited to the subjects explored in his or her writings, as it is quite possible for an author to be engaged in an ideological exercise of group-making, "ethnicity-making" or "religion-making" that is a reflection of their aspirations or imagination, and not reality.[91] That is, so-called "religious" topics are no more determinative of an author's network of social engagement than any other discourse. As I have discussed, to limit our studies to such a narrow field of analysis

---

88. Johnson, "Pliny and the Construction of Reading Communities," 52. Johnson is summarizing Pliny, citing Florence Dupont, "*Recitatio* and the Space of Public Discourse." Also see Craig A. Williams, "Love and Friendship: Authors and Texts," in *Reading Roman Friendship* (New York: Cambridge University Press, 2012), 174–258, particularly the sections on the letters of Cicero and Fronto.

89. Miller, "Social Logic of the Gospel of Mark," 221–22.

90. Stowers notes that these social networks may have contained members who were not personally known to one another: "Indeed, the most important social formations for these individuals as writers may have been other writers and associated networks that taught high literacy, interpreted and circulated writings, mostly people whom they had never known" (Stowers, "Concept of 'Community,'" 247).

91. Stanley K. Stowers, "The Ontology of Religion," in *Introducing Religion: Essays in Honor of Jonathan Z. Smith*, ed. Willi Braun and Russell T. McCutcheon (London: Equinox, 2008), 446.

risks uncritically accepting the writer's own ideological categories as an accurate reflection of his or her social world or allowing our own assumptions to determine what we regard as thinkable. What is determinative, however, is the author's "field"—the practices that we know are plausible, given the writer's historical and social location.

Bourdieu's notion of habitus is instructive on this latter point. Habitus signifies an unconscious socialization that takes place among agents that drives them to the internalization of the various conditions (social, economic, and so forth) that comprise their "field" or sphere of social and cultural existence. Another way to describe habitus might be to say that people act in ways that are both practical and plausible given their social location and context. Bourdieu focuses his theorization on these actions in terms of practices: "The practices of the members of the same group or, in a differentiated society, the same class, are always more and better harmonized than the agents know or wish."[92] More than an amorphous designation of "culture" on a broad scale, Bourdieu situates agents according to their relative power and cultural capital within specific fields of activity. Elsewhere, he describes habitus as a set of practices that are "internalized and converted into a disposition that generates meaningful practices and meaning-giving perceptions."[93] Rather than attributing something like authorship to a broad and amorphous concept like culture, Bourdieu's pillars of habitus and field allow for a "socialized subjectivity" which unites structures with agents.[94]

The implications of Bourdieu's theorization for understanding the ancient world are that it allows for authors to engage in literary practices that are normal for their historical circumstances and social location. This means that authors participate in particular standards and practices that are dictated by their levels of education, social class, and background, as well as established methods for the composition and circulation of their texts. In other words, they are rational agents who make decisions in and about their writings based on knowledge of certain literary conventions, relevant bodies of literature, and the kinds of issues being actively dis-

92. Pierre Bourdieu, *The Logic of Practice*, trans. Richard Nice (Stanford, CA: Stanford University Press, 1990), 59.

93. Pierre Bourdieu, *Distinction: A Social Critique of the Judgment of Taste*, trans. Richard Nice (Cambridge: Harvard University Press, 1996), 170.

94. Pierre Bourdieu and Loïc Wacquant, *An Invitation to Reflexive Sociology* (Chicago: University of Chicago Press, 1992), 126.

cussed within their historical field. Moreover, contra the Romantics, they do not produce literature that is inspired by the *Geist* and communal mind of an ill-defined social body. Their historical processes, literary fields, and social networks can be described and analyzed.

It is also important to note that a writer like Pliny represents truly elite literary culture and is not necessarily representative of the activities of all Roman-era writers. While in some cases a leisure activity, certainly not all authors were able to luxuriate in the "mastery of language" like members of Roman high society. The modest skills of the author of the Gospel of Mark or the Latin *Apollonius King of Tyre*, for instance, demonstrates that there were varying degrees to which a writer possessed expertise. However, with functional literacy so limited, the processes of training and intellectual development, as well as the nature of social exchange involved in the production and circulation of writings, likely followed along a similar trajectory in other literary and social subfields. Therefore, it follows that authors like the gospel writers and the author(s) of Q were constrained by the same practical aspects of writing ancient literature as any other writer in the ancient world—that is, they required the same relative levels of education, necessary training, and associated social networks. They possessed a certain habitus and composed their writings under the same plausible and practical conditions as other writers within the field of literary production in antiquity.

In order to account for the distinctions in skill level between authors who represent dominant literary registers like Vergil and a writer like Mark, one would simply have to look to the degree to which the author in question felt obligated to adhere to the conventions and standards set by the literary field. Vergil, for instance, has a wealthy patron who demands deference and is charged with producing an epic that meets certain literary expectations (for instance, meter). Although some scholars suggest that the *Aeneid* subverts Augustan Rome in subtle ways, Vergil is unable to break with tradition to such a degree that he can write truly subversive literature.[95] His characters, form, and approach ultimately conform to expectation.

---

95. For a review of recent literature on the question of Vergil's "resistance" or "subversion" of Augustan Rome, see Kenneth Haynes, "Classic Vergil," in *A Companion to Vergil's Aeneid and Its Tradition*, ed. Joseph Farrell and Michael C. J. Putnam (Malden, MA: Wiley-Blackwell, 2010), 421–33.

Writers like Mark and Q, on the other hand, are bound by certain literary conventions, but they have the ability to innovate more substantially. Thus, while some scholars maintain that the gospels are a literary anomaly without clear precedent, I argue that they are a play on the civic biographical tradition.[96] Elsewhere I have called the gospel genre "subversive biography"—a type of *bios* that emphasizes the capabilities of a figure perceived to be outside of the dominant culture in some measure.[97] For example, instead of a chronicle of the military pursuits of a great general, we have in the *Life of Aesop* the tale of a wily and often bombastic slave or a resourceful and clever leader who is something of an antihero in the *Alexander Romance*. I place writings about Jesus within this same trajectory, which alternatively emphasize his wisdom, ready-wit, and wonderworking as a strategy for demonstrating authority and gaining advantage when faced with challenges from more powerful figures. Locating these writers within a field of literary production that makes sense for their milieu dismantles the kinds of Romantic-inspired frameworks that have myopically sought the early Christian "peasant *Volk*" or the gospel writers as their literate spokesmen. While scholars might disagree about the proper *comparanda* or genre placement for writings like the gospels and Q, treating them as proper Greco-Roman literature demonstrates that they fit intelligibly within a broader scope of literary development in antiquity.

---

96. Some examples include Adela Yarbro Collins, *Is Mark's Gospel a Life of Jesus? The Question of Genre* (Milwaukee: Marquette University Press, 1990), to be discussed. Also see Helmut Koester, *Ancient Christian Gospels: Their History and Development* (London: SCM; Philadelphia: Trinity Press International, 1990), 24–25: "In the second half of the 2d century certain documents came to be called 'gospels.' But it is not evident why the term 'gospel'—once the technical term for the early Christian missionary preaching—became the title for a particular type of literature. Explanations for this change have been closely associated with the attempt to define the special genre of the gospel literature. Most commonly accepted, in one form or another, is the thesis developed by Karl Ludwig Schmidt and Julius Schniewind. It states that the gospels, specifically the four Gospels of the New Testament canon, are representatives of a literary genre *sui generis* which cannot be related to other developments in the history of literature in antiquity.... [According to Schmidt, Rudolf Bultmann and Martin Dibelius] the genre of the gospels cannot be determined on the basis of a comparison with the products of literary culture. Rather, they must be understood as collections and publications of traditions in the form of 'casual literature' (*Klienliteratur*) according to the needs of a developing religious community."

97. See Konstan and Walsh, "Civic and Subversive Biography in Antiquity."

Finally, to clarify, while the writing of literature was limited to a relatively small segment of society, this does not mean that people who were unable to read and write were likewise unable to participate in literary culture in some measure. For instance, nonspecialists could attend public recitations or engage in debate over the interpretation of a particular text that was read out loud to them. Moreover, those with a very basic rhetorical training would likely have sufficient ability to interrogate a piece of writing, a theatrical performance, or a speech. Certain writings may have also lent themselves to different kinds of reception, depending on their place within the hierarchy of literary production. David Konstan in his work on the "Active Reader" suggests that in the second and third centuries "there arose, in response to a sharp increase in popular literacy, a new kind of text…. This new literature was addressed to middle levels of society, as opposed to the elite that formed the readership for earlier texts," including items such as cooking manuals, riddles, binding spells, "narratives of pagan martyrs and much Christian material," or romantic novels like Chariton's *Callirhoe*.[98] Konstan explains that these texts did not elicit the same *scholia* as Homer or the *Aeneid*, but readers likely approached them with the same "interrogative relationship to the text for which we have found evidence in Plutarch, Synesius, and other sources."[99] In other words, this literature may not have been ranked among the classics, but it was engaged in the same manner as the poetry and prose encountered in *paideia*.

However, possessing enough popular literacy to interrogate a text, write a receipt, create a *defixiones*, or draft a bill of divorce is not the same thing as writing literature. Authorship remained a specialist's activity that required significant training and rhetorical skill. While they may fall short of the literary prowess of a Homer, Vergil, or Hesiod, authors of the romantic novels or second-century hagiographies were producing literature in a particular social and historical context in which the normal conditions for authorship still applied. Konstan notes that "the expansion of

---

98. David Konstan, "The Active Reader and the Ancient Novel," in *Readers and Writers in the Ancient Novel*, ed. Michael Paschalis, Stelios Panayotakis, and Gareth Schmeling (Eelde: Barkhuis; Groningen: Barkhuis Publishing and Groningen University Library, 2009), 6. On the writing style of the gospel and Paul, see also Paul M. Robertson, *Paul's Letters and Contemporary Greco-Roman Literature: Theorizing a New Taxonomy*, NovTSup 167 (Leiden: Brill, 2016).

99. Konstan, "Active Reader and the Ancient Novel," 7.

literacy thus gave rise to two reading publics with distinct levels of cultural competence, and the texts they read differed accordingly in content, style, and organization."[100] While geared to a less "elite" audience, this literature was not therefore a product *of* or produced *by* this new population of readers. It was designed to appeal to a field of consumers for the purposes of entertainment and edification, as well as to engage those for whom participation in literate practices, including the interpretation and circulation of writings, conferred certain kinds of social capital.

So, in light of all of this, what might we be able to say about the social world of a writer of stories about Jesus?

Given his interest in the interpretation of Judean literature, perhaps he is a Judean himself, who has read, among other things, a good deal of Greco-Roman literature (for example, Homer, some philosophy, and *bioi*). His ability to read and write at this relatively high level indicates that he has received a Greek education and possesses both a specialist's knowledge of texts and an awareness of current issues being discussed among other cultural producers, such as the significance of the destruction of the Judean temple. He is also interested in certain kinds of esoteric materials: riddles, teachings, signs, and wonder workings. He is outside of the dominant cultural field; he is not Vergil. But he has enough skill, means, and training to try his hand at a creative piece of writing. Perhaps he is aware of Pythagoras's *Golden Verses*. Perhaps he is aware of the civic biographical tradition of distinguished statesmen, philosophers, and other leaders. Perhaps he wants to engage that literary genre, offering a *bios* or a collection of sayings of another notable figure and philosopher who came to an untimely end. Here is he faced with a problem, however. Jesus was not a member of the dominant leadership or aristocracy.

Thinking about what source material for which we have concrete evidence in the early stages of the Jesus movement, perhaps our author has among his collected texts some of the letters of Paul. There he finds talk of Jesus as "Christ," a divine lineage of Abraham, and an active principle of God's *pneuma* binding people "in Christ." Perhaps he finds through his own research or through exchanges of ideas and texts within his literary network one or two other lives of Jesus, a collection of some of Jesus's reputed teachings, or he simply refers to some traditional Judean religious

---

100. Ibid., 6.

texts. He then begins to write his text engaging a certain set of issues that are important to him. Those issues might include esoteric teachings or food laws. For Mark, perhaps this is why his reputed messiah went unrecognized. Later, for writers like Matthew and Luke, it would be Stoic ethics or constructing a new, divine genealogy that subverts the one continually being reified by the Roman imperial family. This writer may be aware of other Jesus people. He may even hold identification with a particular group which shares a common interest in Jesus, the writings of Paul, certain related religious practices, and so on. However, this group alone does not dictate the content of his writings. Instead, he is engaged in a writing practice that views other literature and fellow writers as chiefly formative. He exchanges his text among these other writers for comment, critique, and discussion. Some within this network begin to make copies of his writing for circulation. The issues he addresses attract a variety of different kinds of readers, such as those interested in subversive biographies more generally or in examples of Judean figures who offered teachings that were not centered on the temple cult.

This latter point brings me back to the possibility that our dating of Q has been too influenced by a Romantic desire to locate the earliest "folk speech" and not on historical data. Is it possible that Jesus provided a useful foil, like Philoxenus, for an ongoing conversation about the state of Judaism after the fall of the temple? This scenario puts Q in more direct conversation with literary networks, including Mark and the other synoptic gospels, and opens up new possibilities for considering the social world of the Jesus movement and the production of its literature.

Dating Q Postwar

As John Kloppenborg notes in *Excavating Q*, scholars have long been divided on the issue of Q's dating; however, dates as early as the late 30s CE[101] to, more usually, 50/60 CE have been regularly proposed on the basis of Q's supposed failure to adequately announce "the Temple's ruin or

---

101. See John S. Kloppenborg, *Excavating Q: The History and Setting of the Sayings Gospel* (Edinburgh: T&T Clark. Repr., Minneapolis: Fortress, 2000), 82, in which he reviews the work of Gerd Theissen who dates Q shortly after 40 CE on the basis of the story of Jesus's temptation in Q 4:1–13 as a response to Caligula's "attack on Jewish monotheism."

abandonment and the relative absence of overt signs of imminent war,"[102] despite passages like Q 13:34–35 ("Jerusalem, Jerusalem … Behold, your house is forsaken!"), which are generally attributed to later additions to Q of a more apocalyptic or eschatological character.[103] Of note, the proposal that there are later, end-time elements added to the Q document has roots not only in the question of dating but also in the debate over the apocalyptic and political interests of Jesus and his early followers.[104] This long-standing debate—was Jesus apocalyptic or not—is significant in that it often corresponds to different approaches to Q. Because Q is a hypothetical document, it has allowed an inordinate amount of flexibility for

---

102. Kloppenborg, *Excavating Q*, 87. It should be noted that scholars have also looked to a pre-70 CE date for Q because it is generally presumed that, if it was used by Matthew, it had to have been "in circulation" at least a generation before the Judean War. I have not found a source that gives a sufficient explanation for why this time frame must be the case, particularly given what we know about literary networks. Oddly, perceived parallels between the Gospel of Thomas and the first letter of Clement (namely, wisdom and prophetic sayings) have also been cited as a rationale for dating Q to before the war, despite the fact that the Gospel of Thomas and Clement are routinely dated to the late first and early second centuries. See Koester, *Ancient Christian Gospels*, 137.

103. Kloppenborg, *Excavating Q*, 87. Another justification Kloppenborg raises for dating Q to around 50 concerns Q's "silence" on the matter of Jesus's resurrection: "Under what conditions would such a silence be intelligible?… Since in real letters … one normally does not discuss matters of common knowledge but only issues that are new or under dispute, it is likely that Paul's use of Christ's resurrection as an analogy for the resurrection of the believer in 1 Corinthians 15 was a 'new' issue in the 50s [the approximate date of that letter].… Hence … the *terminus ad quem* for Q was ca. 50 C.E.; every year after that, Q's silence about Jesus's resurrection would be increasingly difficult to explain." I caution that the absence of a concern for the resurrection in Q is not necessarily in itself data.

104. I use both terms here recognizing that scholars define "apocalyptic" differently in these debates. Crossan, Mack, and Vermès, for instance, emphasize that the term signals an imminent eschatology and is not inherently "political." Scholars such as E. P. Sanders, Paula Fredriksen, and Richard A. Horsley, by contrast, connect the concept of apocalypticism to social and historical tensions. Fredriksen explains: "The nature of the apocalyptic is political.… Its message of an impending new order at least implies a condemnation of the present one" (Paula Fredriksen, *From Jesus to Christ: The Origins of the New Testament Images of Jesus* [New Haven: Yale University Press, 2008], 124–125). Also see Edith M. Humphrey, "Will the Reader Understand? Apocalypse as Veil or Vision in Recent Historical-Jesus Research," in *Whose Historical Jesus?*, ed. William E. Arnal and Michel Desjardins, SCJ 7 (Waterloo, ON: Wilfred Laurier University Press, 1997), 215–37.

scholars to construct claims about its composition to fit their preferred paradigm. That is, if one believes the earliest Christians or the historical Jesus were not apocalyptic, any language that appears to signal an end-time scenario can be attributed to a later "redactor."[105] However, not all scholars have accepted the premise that the so-called layers of Q have such clearly defined boundaries or that attempting to delineate Q's stages of development or editorial stitchery is even a fruitful endeavor.

While not universal in studies of Q, among those who maintain that Q contains various stages of composition and redaction, there has also been a tendency to view the social circumstances of Q's development in such a way that Q's layers represent distinct communities of Jesus follow-ers. German Romanticism may influence this kind of search for earlier (and sometimes even earlier) layers of Q, largely unconsciously. Much like the efforts of the Brothers Grimm to reclaim a unified Germanic past through the oral stories of the common people or nation (*Volk*), scholars of early Christianity interested in trying to understand the social roots of the Jesus movement have often treated the gospels and Q as a window into the collective outlooks of diverse groups of early Jesus people. Bult-mann, for instance, proposed that Q's logia "are a primary source from which we can reconstruct a picture of the primitive community in which the Logia arose."[106] In Bultmann's estimation, by using form-critical techniques, one could identify "Q's formation diachronically in terms of tradition history and corresponding community development," includ-ing the oral prehistory of the text.[107] In treating Q and the gospels more or less like folk literature, we have preserved an approach to these writ-ings that focuses on using a given text to reconstruct (usually nonliterate) implied audiences or communities and their stories, teachings, and other forms of oral exchange. Writings are mined for evidence of oral teach-ings or other sayings that may have been significant to the gospel author's presumed group of fellow Christians. Again, we know that writing was a

---

105. The divisive "apocalyptic" or "not apocalyptic" debate in the field is complex and involves a detailed history of scholarship that is beyond the scope of this pres-ent study. A future version of this project will include more on this issue. See Bart D. Ehrman, *Jesus, Apocalyptic Prophet of the New Millennium* (Oxford: Oxford University Press, 1999), esp. 132–33.

106. Rudolf Bultmann, "New Approach to the Synoptic Problem," 341.

107. Alan Kirk, *The Composition of the Sayings Source: Genre, Synchrony, and Wisdom Redaction in Q*, NovTSup 91 (Leiden: Brill, 1998), 6.

specialist's activity and that ancient authors circulated their works within literary networks of fellow writers. Yet, focusing exclusively on attempting to reconstruct hypothesized (usually oral) traditions within texts like Q has denied the primacy and influence of an author's fellow writers. As such, this approach has largely failed to treat writers as rational actors, instead portraying them as mere spokespersons for the oral speech of a vaguely defined community of people.

In my view, there is very little, if any, evidence within Q for concrete social groups. Some scholars have attempted to identify community language in passages like Q 12:33–34 and Q 16:13, which focus on issues of wealth and ethics:

> For where your treasure is, there will also be your heart. (Q 12:33–34)

> No one can serve two masters; for a person will either hate the one and love the other, or be devoted to the one and despise the other. You cannot serve God and mammon. (Q 16:13)

There have been notable studies that have viewed these passages as focused on "the hoarding activities of the elite," suggesting that the message behind them is that the "Q folk" (an interesting turn of phrase that is often repeated) are "not of the urban classes in which the Jesus movement eventually spread, but the villages and towns of the Galilee, where God's actions and reign had everything to do with the basics of life."[108] Other studies have suggested that these passages "circulated not among urbanites, but among the rural poor, not in the Gentile cities of the east, but in the towns of Jewish Galilee."[109] Yet, the concrete social process through which this material was circulated among these "folk" or how "this utopian

---

108. John S. Kloppenborg, *Q: The Earliest Gospel: An Introduction to the Original Stories and Sayings of Jesus* (Louisville: Westminster John Knox, 2008), 97.

109. Ibid., 96–97, emphasis original. Kloppenborg suggests that "texts such as Q were composed to function more like musical script for performance than a textbook to be read" and that "oral-scribal interactions" account for the transmission of Q to other gospel writers (ix).

The Q passages cited above are from Kloppenborg's translation. I also rely on James M. Robinson, Paul Hoffmann, and John S. Kloppenborg, eds., *The Critical Edition of Q: Synopsis Including the Gospels of Matthew and Luke, Mark and Thomas with English, German, and French Translations of Q and Thomas*, Hermeneia Supplements (Minneapolis: Fortress 2000).

vision was eventually effaced by the editing of Matthew and Luke" is not adequately explained.[110]

One theory for the transmission and circulation of Q has been the itinerancy hypothesis—that is, Q's internal "rhetoric of uprootedness" and implied social upheaval.[111] Gerd Theissen, for instance, proposes, "the ethical radicalism of the sayings transmitted to us [in Q] is the radicalism of itinerants" who lived under extreme stress.[112] Theissen's reading of Q was influenced, at least in part, by an itinerancy thesis within the field that extends back to Adolf von Harnack's work on the Didache and his belief that the text offered a set of regulations for wandering and impoverished prophets who travelled from Christian community to Christian community, seeking shelter, food, money, and other goods.[113] This imagined class of "professionally homeless preachers of the Christian message" is first encountered with the "missionary journeys on the part of Jesus' disciples … the wandering of Jesus himself, and Acts and Paul's letters."[114] In other words, it derives from Christianity's own myth of origins and maps the

---

110. Kloppenborg, *Q: The Earliest Gospel*, 96.

111. William E. Arnal, *Jesus and the Village Scribes: Galilean Conflicts and the Setting of Q* (Minneapolis: Fortress, 2001), 157.

112. Gerd Theissen, "The Wandering Radicals: Light Shed by Sociology of Literature on the Early Transmission of the Jesus Sayings," in *Social Reality and the Early Christians: Theology, Ethics, and the World of the New Testament*, trans. Margaret Kohl (Minneapolis: Fortress, 1992), 40. Theissen even goes so far as to suggest that Jesus himself did not intend to establish communities of Christians but to establish a band of "travelling apostles, prophets and disciples who moved from place to place and could rely on small groups of sympathizers in these places." Later Theissen describes these "sympathizers" or, as he also calls them "sedentary sympathizers," in terms that resemble a "community" of Christians, using the Essenes as a comparable example to what he has in mind in terms of their eventual hierarchical construction, leadership, etc. He also suggests that these "sympathizers" are banded together by Hellenistic "community organizers" like Paul; however, he continues to see the activities of the itinerants and the "community organizers" as fundamentally distinct. See further Gerd Theissen, *Sociology of Early Palestinian Christianity*, trans. John Bowden (Philadelphia: Fortress, 1978), 8, 18–21, 115.

113. Adolf von Harnack, *Die Lehre der zwölf Apostel*, TUGAL 2 (Leipzig: Hinrichs, 1884), 1–2. Arnal also identifies the Harnack thesis as a foundation for work on Q. See Arnal, *Jesus and the Village Scribes*, 14–18.

114. Arnal, *Jesus and the Village Scribes*, 13. Arnal does not hold the same strong association to Cynic-like wandering charismatics, as does Theissen. He does away with the strict itinerancy hypothesis and suggests instead that the travel implied by "itinerancy," following Kloppenborg, should be imagined more like a morning walk

same kind of explosive beginnings implicated by the Big Bang paradigm. While these studies attempt to give some idea of the kind of social formation that may have acted as a delivery system for Q, and other Christian materials for that matter, they fail to explain the concrete processes by which the messages and teachings of these itinerant charismatics and preachers would have been received and understood, why they would be appealing in the first place, and how they then instituted or added to the supposed existing communities they encountered, among a host of other practical concerns.[115]

Allied to the itinerancy theory is the proposal that Q was composed by Galilean village scribes, informed by the wisdom of "itinerant preachers" or "wandering radicals" tasked with disseminating the teachings of Jesus. Resembling something of a Rube Goldberg Machine of social exchange, the basis of this historical reconstruction is, again, the idea that Jesus and his immediate followers were itinerant prophets and preachers. These Cynic-like wise men traveled the countryside of Galilee and beyond, repeating Jesus's teachings and dispersing the "oral life of these traditions" to communities of Q proto-Christians who wrote them down.[116] Recognizing that such activity requires a degree of literary skill, some scholars suggest that Q was written by multiple "persons who are educated ... but do not occupy the pinnacle of learning antiquity had to offer."[117] Considering Q to be a "very, very old composition" and belonging to a period in which Jesus is "perceived to be a figure from ... the recent past," its composition is often placed in Galilee.[118] Assuming that a community must be involved but also recognizing that the author or authors of Q must be literary specialists of some kind, one social network that has been considered for its composition is Galilean village scribes.

---

around the Sea of Galilee, than travel across long distances; see Arnal, *Jesus and the Village Scribes*, 71, 94.

115. See Stowers, "Concept of 'Community,'" 253.

116. Arnal, *Jesus and the Village Scribes*, 170. Arnal explains: "Theissen identifies itinerants as the formative factor behind the earliest Jesus movement. Jesus himself, Theissen claims, did not intend to found communities but to call into being a movement of wandering charismatics: 'travelling apostles,' prophets and disciples who moved from place to place and could rely on small groups of sympathizers in these places" (24).

117. Ibid., 170.

118. Ibid., 172.

The following quotation appears in the work of both Kloppenborg and Arnal and describes this social network:

> In accord with scribal values, the Sayings Gospel places a premium upon both clarity of perception, especially when it comes to matters of guidance (Q 6:40, 41–42), and good speech, the characteristic mark of good thinking (Q 6:45). Guidance and moral example are also the subjects of the sayings on judging (Q 6:37–38), scandal (Q 17:1–2), and forgiveness (Q 17:3b–4). This reflects the self-consciously "public" character of the scribal pursuit: although the scribe necessarily requires leisure not at the disposal of the peasant or hand-worker, the scribe's responsibility is ultimately to the public and public approbation in the form of honour and fame crowns the sage's achievement.[119]

"A network of villages" in which the scribes worked and lived with the "Q people" has also been proposed.[120]

This social process for Q resembles many details of the mystified Big Bang for Christian origins, including miraculous and cohesive communities of "primitive Christians" seeking a literate representative to help them record their folk speech. Talk of the stratified and developing oral traditions of these communities also conjures associations with Romantic thinkers and the idea of a developing inspirational *Geist* among the *Volk*. Moreover, more research is required to determine whether this depiction of scribal culture and training conforms to what we know about so-called village scribes. While scribes could be hired to write an inscription, send a letter, or use their access to literary materials to help copy or produce a piece of writing like a contract, they did not necessarily possess the training, skill, and literacy necessary to write an original composition at the level of sophistication evident in Q.[121] Catherine Hezser in her work on Jewish literacy, for example, suggests:

> The writings of Josephus confirm the impression already gained from the gospels that before 70 C.E. the majority of scribes continued to be

---

119. John S. Kloppenborg, "Literary Convention, Self-Evidence and the Social History of the Q People," *Semeia* 55 (1991): 83. Cited from Arnal, *Jesus and the Village Scribes*, 170–71.

120. Arnal, *Jesus and the Village Scribes*, 172.

121. Catherine Hezser, *Jewish Literacy in Roman Palestine*, TSAJ 81 (Tübingen: Mohr Siebeck, 2001), 37.

either Temple personnel or employed in the government administration.... Village scribes are only mentioned once, at the time of Salome and Herod, as an example for a very lowly and undesirable profession.... The scribe was probably a person who could read and write and knew the social and legal formalities well enough to write letters, contracts, and petitions. Although the village scribe shared the knowledge of writing with the Temple and royal scribes, he differed from them enormously with regard to his expertise, tasks, remuneration, and status.[122]

In light of our current historical data for the literary abilities of village scribes, I suggest that it is unlikely that an interrelated network of disparate Galilean scribes was responsible for the production of Q. I believe it is possible to read Q as the writing of an individual author without the need for wandering charismatics, multiple redactions, or communities.[123]

A New View of Q

To locate the author of Q, the first step is to examine his literary choices. Of these features, the most prominent is the depiction of both Jesus and John the Baptist as teacher-types. Not only is Q exclusively focused on *chreiae*, it also conspicuously lacks what some might anticipate as taken-for-granted details about the teaching activity of Jesus—accounts of miracles, healings, exorcisms, or even a few words about his death and resurrection. Unlike Paul, this content is not essential to Q's strategic project and interests. As for the figure of John, he performs Jesus's baptism and provides the well-known logion on the "One to Come" (Q 3:16b–17), as well as a number of other *chreiae*. As with Jesus, Q lacks any specific details of John's eventual imprisonment or death. In short, Q's paramount concern is for the teachings of these men.

Because this is a hypothetical document, it is difficult to pinpoint whether Q was indeed a sayings-source, biography, philosophical text, or the like. Therefore, a more immediately useful question is what kind of sociocultural/historical situation might foster the kind of material

---

122. Ibid., 119–20.

123. Interestingly, Arnal notes early on in his work that the itinerancy hypothesis advanced by scholars like Theissen and Adolf von Harnack closely resembles the "concerns of the Age of Progress" and "wandering radicalism (*Wanderradikalismus*)" prominent in Germany in the period between the World Wars. See Arnal, *Jesus and the Village Scribes*, 19–20.

found in Q. With talk of a coming wrath (Q 3:7b–9), the destruction of houses built on sand (Q 6:46–49), a fallen Jerusalem (Q 13:34–35), and slain prophets and wise men (Q 11:49–51), one possibility is a disrupted cosmic order.

Smith's discussion of "cosmic paranoia" in "The Influence of Symbols on Social Change" is useful for considering how a writer might negotiate the topic of significant social and religious upheaval. Smith explains that human beings must continually cope with the reality that nonobvious beings and other cosmic powers are not solely benevolent forces—"guarantors of order, the guardians of a good cosmic and human destiny."[124] Rather, they can be hostile aggressors with the ability to oppress through manipulation of the mortal world. This potential for upheaval is what creates a sense of paranoia. Paranoia also stems from the realization that any disruption in the equilibrium of cosmic order forces a dramatic shift in the ways in which human beings understand their position not only in the cosmos more generally, but in related sociocultural dynamics as well.

Smith ultimately links his observations about paranoia to the notion of place, insofar as it has implications for identifying the limits and bounds of various (cosmic) ties. He states: "The question of the character of the place on which one stands is *the* fundamental symbolic and social question. Once an individual or culture has expressed its vision of its place, a whole language of symbols and social structures will follow."[125] For Smith "*social change is preeminently symbol or symbolic change*," dictating that one adopt a new symbolic universe in order to continue to realize the parameters of the cosmic order and one's "place" within it. [126]

This overview of Smith's work should suffice to illustrate his theoretical model's applicability to Q. Q's Jesus and John are concerned with issues of repentance, judgment, and recognition. In the course of this teaching activity, great resistance is brought to bear against those who fail to recognize God properly and the prophets, those who do not exhibit thoroughgoing faith, and those, like the Pharisees and "exegetes of the Law," who impose themselves between the people and the correct worship of God (Q 11:39a, 42, 39b, 41–48, 52). These emphases are essential for identifying what constitutes a proper relationship with God in the course of negotiat-

---

124. Jonathan Z. Smith, *Map Is Not Territory: Studies in the History of Religions*, SJLA 23 (Leiden: Brill, 1998; Chicago: University of Chicago Press, 1978), 138.
125. Ibid., 141.
126. Ibid., 143, emphasis original.

ing one's (new) place in the cosmic order. Consequently, teaching *logia* like the so-called beatitudes in Q may be guidelines for reimagining how this goal was to be accomplished. The figures of Jesus and John thus become mechanisms for this activity—namely, the process of reconsidering one's place within, in this case, Judean practices and philosophy. They represent, in the words of Smith, a symbolic turn.

The kind of negotiation taking place through the figures of Jesus and John in Q may also suggest a rupture in the cosmic and social order. It makes a great deal of sense that this rupture is the result of war and temple destruction and not a social situation more difficult to assess like the stresses associated with itinerant preaching. With the temple now destroyed, cultural producers like the author of Q may have been seeking new symbols of Judean practice and philosophy. Jesus and John are two prewar prophetic figures who managed to thrive, at least relatively, without explicit ties to a corrupt temple system or cult. As Smith notes in the course of his argument, in the face of what are perceived to be oppressive social or cosmic elements, "man is no longer defined by the degree to which he harmonizes himself and his society to the cosmic patterns of order, but rather by the degree to which he can escape the patterns." Through the teaching *logia* highlighted by Q, it is evident that Jesus and John know these "escape routes."[127]

Thus, the interest in Jesus and John as teachers in Q and, for that matter, the narrative gospels, may represent the challenge of how to envision Judaism in light of the sociocultural upheaval of the war and temple destruction. The elevation of these particular figures is a strategy that explores pressing social and religious questions through a creative reflection on two well-known subversive figures who did not rely on established Judean institutions. To borrow a phrase from Arnal's work on Mark, the author of Q "may ... be using the figure of Jesus to comment on the Jewish War, the destruction of the Temple, and his own ... identity.... The War has become the occasion for new thoughts—thoughts congenial to this author—and Jesus has served as a mechanism for expressing these thoughts."[128]

Finally, Arnal's observations on Mark also raise another crucial issue in regard to the so-called "biographical details" that Q and the other gospel writers provide in their works, which may also have some rele-

---

127. Ibid., 139.
128. Arnal, "Gospel of Mark as Reflection on Exile and Identity," 60.

vance for reconsidering Q's date of composition. As noted briefly above, the prime evidence used by scholars to justify labeling Q as a pre-70 work is the fact that sayings collections are the earliest literary form of Jesus material recorded and handed down by proto-Christians. Marvin Meyer, Helmut Koester, and Gerd Theissen, for instance, maintain that sayings-sources like Q and the Gospel of Thomas lack features typical of later, more developed material, such as the "use of parables without allegorical amplification" or explicit references to the Hebrew Bible and, therefore, are indicative of a nascent or "primitive" stage of the Jesus-movement when these positions are still taking shape within communities.[129] Put differently, the theology expressed in these sayings collections is often considered grossly underdeveloped when compared to other narrative sources like the Synoptics.

While I agree that there are clear differences between sayings-source materials and narrative gospels, I nonetheless find it compelling that what these writings do share in common is an interest in a teaching figure like Jesus and, in a more limited sense, the small biographical details of his life.[130] This is a phenomenon largely missing from the extant work of our only secure pre-70 material, the letters of Paul. Therefore, I find it tempting to suppose that the emergence of gospel material on these teachings and, in some cases, the travels, births, and deaths of Jesus and John are a product of a kind of post-70 reimagining of how exempla from the teachings and lives of these figures can serve a variety of strategic purposes. Again, in the case of Q, this purpose was to act as a site for the negotiation of a new cosmic order in the wake of the destruction of the temple.

---

129. Marvin Meyer, "Albert Schweitzer and the Image of Jesus in the Gospel of Thomas," in *Jesus Then and Now: Images of Jesus in History and Christology*, ed. Marvin Meyer and Charles Hughes (Harrisburg, PA: Trinity Press International, 2001), 73.

130. Scholarship often makes the claim that Q does not contain any significant biographical details of Jesus's life. This largely appears to be a complaint among those interested in retrieving information about the historical Jesus from what is considered our most "primitive" source on the early Jesus movement. However, we see that Q wants us to know that these men were teachers, that their logia have similar thematic elements, and, in the case of John the Baptist in particular, that we are provided with information that suggests he is an ascetic of some kind and, conversely, that Jesus is not. While this short list may not satisfy the historical Jesus scholars, it is nonetheless a small window into what one might call the *bioi* of these figures.

Conclusion

The writers of early stories about Jesus depict him as divinely authorized through his birthright, teachings, and wonderworking as a son of God—a powerful figure, even if a social underdog. At times he is portrayed as a riddler and purveyor of esoteric knowledge, at other points an ethical teacher and miracle-worker. Unlike the notable statesmen, poets, and philosophers that populated civic biographies, Jesus's extraordinary wit and otherworldly superpowers revealed his authority and status. The accounts of healings, resurrections, miraculous mass conversions, and angelically abetted prison breaks in Acts offer a similarly remarkable account of the origins and the development of the social movement later known as Christianity. Incorporating such astonishing events into these narratives functioned as a strategic means of legitimization. Miraculous Big Bang beginnings and notable figures communicate a demand to be taken seriously. When laying claim to a storied past, only "august roots" will do.[131]

Literature was also a means for creating coherence out of what was otherwise an amorphous history that was far from linear. Establishing an origin story for the Jesus movement created a foundation from which to claim continuity.[132] In other words, literature like the gospels and Acts invented a tradition. A stark example of this is Acts' treatment of Paul as the miracle-working apostle to the gentiles and authoritative founder of a number of early Christian "churches." Paul as figurehead and martyr would carry through later writers like the authors of the pastoral epistles, the Acts of Paul, Marcion, and Irenaeus, despite the fact Paul's own letters reveal that his activity stood on far more contested ground. Moreover, the "churches" and other communities described in Acts became a model for understanding social networks in the first century, including the authors of the gospels and related writings.

Analyzing Odysseus's speech on the art of poetry, Bruce Lincoln usefully suggests that the "ideological justification and idealized self-representation" embedded in the speech's meta reflection is "a myth about myth: a story poetry tells about itself as a means to define, defend ... romanticize

---

131. William E. Arnal, "Collection and Synthesis," 199: "Even modern groups seeking to define themselves and their identity in the *present* do so by inventing or laying claim to an ancestral identity which unifies, identifies, and gives them august (or respectable, or congenial) roots."

132. For Willi Braun's reflections on this issue, see above, n. 22.

... legitimate, exaggerate, mystify, modify and advance its own position."[133] The concept of "myth" is multivalent; however Hesiod's meaning of *mythos* is instructive: "an assertive discourse of power and authority ... to be believed."[134]

Whether from the pen of the Romantics or Acts' portrait of the first century, *mythos* on the history of early Christianity is ideologically freighted. If the gospels and Acts are myths that Christianity tells about itself, scholars must be careful not to reinscribe these myths as history. Or, as Lincoln states in his epilogue: "If myth is ideology in narrative form, then scholarship is myth with footnotes."[135]

With Lincoln's cautions about scholarship in mind, even if one wishes to argue that Paul's mission and travel add support to the itinerancy model that has been associated with Q, Paul's evident struggle to establish cohesive communities is instructive for considering how feasible such a model would be for establishing the kinds of expansive growth and stable formations imagined by Acts. Mark's Gospel is of little help for those seeking language about communities and community construction. Mark's Jesus is an elusive, ornery figure. A purveyor of esoteric teachings, Jesus does little to inculcate community. If anything, his continual insistence on secrecy and silence would suggest otherwise, as for example, in 8:30, "And he sternly ordered them not to tell anyone about him." Moreover, Jesus's own disciples are unable to comprehend who he is on the basis of his wonderworking or nearly any of his teachings. This so-called "Messi-

---

133. Odysseus's speech is directed at Demodocus: "Truly it is a good thing to have heard a poet / Such as this, resembling the gods in voice. / For I say there is no more gracious end / Than when joy holds the entire people, / And banqueters throughout the halls listen to a poet, / Sitting in rows, and the tables beside are filled / With bread and meat, and the wine-steward, drawing wine / From the mixing bowl carries it about and pours it into cups. / This seems to me the fairest of things" (*Od.* 9:3–11). For the translation, see Bruce Lincoln, *Theorizing Myth: Narrative, Ideology, and Scholarship* (Chicago: University of Chicago Press, 1999), 21. For a more in-depth examination on ancient discourses on poetry, see Peter T. Struck, "The Genealogy of the Symbolic," in *Birth of the Symbol: Ancient Readers at the Limits of Their Texts* (Princeton: Princeton University Press, 2004), 1–20. Struck also addresses the influence of Romanticism on contemporary understanding of poetry and allegory in "The Symbol Among the Romantics," a section of "Epilogue: Symbol Traces: Post-Proclean Theories," in *Birth of the Symbol*, 272–76.

134. Bruce Lincoln, *Theorizing Myth*, 17.

135. Ibid., 209.

anic Secret" has been a source of conflict for many looking to uncover the Markan community behind the text. Tying the messianic secret to questions of Christology, representative scholarship on the question of Mark's community has focused on the ways in which "the gospel grew out of a christological conflict within the church" as Mark attempted to "correct what it considered to be the dangerous or false Christology.... Mark's Christology is a Christology of the cross and is closely related to the title 'Son of Man.'"[136] Studies along these lines have offered little justification for considering Mark to be enmeshed in a christological orthodoxy/heresy debate within a presumed community of fellow Christians. Notably, such concerns are more characteristic of later debates among church leaders in the second century and beyond.

Unlike Mark, Matthew does have a Jesus that calls for a worldwide mission (28:18–20). Matthew is also concerned with *ekklēsia* (16:18; 18:17) and, in fact, Matthew's choice of the word *ekklēsia* over *synagōgē* is often cited by scholars as evidence of the "Matthean Christians" wanting "to 'differentiate' themselves from Jewish groups."[137] A similar argument is brought to bear with Matt 21:43 ("the kingdom of God will be ... given to a people [*ethnē*] that produces the first fruits of the kingdom"), with some proposing that Matthew wishes to mark the followers of Jesus as the new Israel. Among other first-century writers, the term *ethnē/ethnos* is firmly recognized to be in reference to ethnic Judeans and similar groups; for example, Strabo (ca. 63 BCE–24 CE), who identifies the Jews as one among four *ethnē* in Palestine, as well as Josephus (ca. 37–95 CE) and Philo (ca. 20 BCE–50 CE) who use the category in reference to the Jewish people.[138] Studies of the term more broadly recognize that it does not intend

---

136. Adam Winn, *The Purpose of Mark's Gospel: An Early Christian Response to Roman Imperial Propaganda* (Tübingen: Mohr Siebeck, 2008), 12. In this chapter, Winn is drawing on the work of a number of notable early Christian scholars and their positions on Mark, including William Wrede, Rudolf Bultmann, and Ludwig Bieler. See William Wrede, *The Messianic Secret*, trans. J. C. G. Greig (Cambridge; London: Clarke, 1971); Rudolf Bultmann, *Theology of the New Testament*, trans. Kendrick Grobel, 2 vols. (New York: Scribner's Sons, 1951–1955); Ludwig Bieler, *Theios Aner: Das Bild des "Göttlichen Menschen" in Spätantike und Frühchristentum* (Vienna: Höfels, 1935).

137. Richard S. Ascough, "Matthew and Community Formation," in *The Gospel of Matthew in Current Study: Studies in Memory of William G. Thompson S. J.*, ed. David E. Aune (Grand Rapids: Eerdmans, 2001), 113.

138. Strabo, *Geogr.* 16.2, 2; Philo, *Fug.* 185; *Mut.* 35, 191; *Abr.* 276; *Spec.* 1.190,

to designate a new ethnic group or nation, but it can refer to "a variety of specialized groups such as guilds and trade associations." To suppose that Matthew is talking about issues pertaining to orthodoxy and heresy or a divide between Judaism and the rise of a new, "truer" Israel is reading later theological debates back onto the text. *Ethnē* also has precedent in speaking of idealized communities. Plato, for instance, uses *ethnē* in *Resp.* 421c to speak of various groups within his utopian city.[139]

In short, Matthew does not require a religious community to speak of questions of *ekklēsia* or an ideal Israel. Among the source material at Matthew's disposal are the LXX, possibly Q, Paul, and Mark. It is evident that one of Matthew's prime objectives is to take Mark and clarify the mysteries presented by his obfuscating Jesus through an interpretation of Jewish scripture. Two recent studies on Matthew have also noted that the Jesus in this gospel can be read through a Stoic lens.[140] Matthew's Jesus is a teacher of ethics, reexamining Judean law and engaging in the same kind of intellectual interpretive practices we see among other Judean writers like Philo or Paul. It is also quite possible that Matthew could get his ideas about *ekklēsia* from his knowledge of Paul.[141] None of this literary activity requires the primacy of a Matthean community. In fact, given the

---

2.263; *Opif.* 28; *Mos.* 1.2.12; *Legat.* 83, 102, 141, 145. Cited from Nicola Denzey Lewis, "The Limits of Ethnic Categories," in *Handbook of Early Christianity: Social Science Approaches*, ed. Anthony J. Blasi, Paul-André Turcotte, and Jean Duhaime (Walnut Creek, CA: AltaMira, 2002), 496.

139. Anthony J. Saldarini, "Reading Matthew without Anti-Semitism," in *The Gospel of Matthew in Current Study: Studies in Memory of William G. Thompson S. J.*, ed. David E. Aune (Grand Rapids: Eerdmans, 2001), 172.

140. Erin Roberts, "Anger, Emotion, and Desire in the Gospel of Matthew" (PhD diss., Brown University, 2010); Stanley Stowers, "Jesus as Teacher and Stoic Ethics in the Gospel of Matthew," in *Stoicism in Early Christianity*, ed. Troels Engberg-Pedersen, Tuomus Rasimus, and Ismo Dundenberg (Peabody, MA: Hendrickson, 2010), 59–76. Interestingly, the observation that the gospels and Paul had parallels with philosophical movements of the first century was made very early on in historical critical reviews of this literature, albeit in the context of citing the imposition of those paradigms on the original "primitive Jewish Christian eschatology" of the Jerusalem church. See, for example, Rudolf Bultmann, *Primitive Christianity*, 177: "Christian missionary preaching was not only the proclamation of Christ, but, when addressed to a Gentile audience, a preaching of monotheism as well. For this, not only arguments derived from the Old Testament, but the natural theology of Stoicism was pressed into service."

141. See Stowers, "Concept of 'Community,'" 253.

tautological nature of arguments that attempt to read Matthew's language as a mirror onto his fellow Christians (that is, studies that use Matthew's language to reconstruct an imagined community and then interpret Matthew through the lens of that community), reevaluating Matthew in terms of the literary precedents for terms like *ekklēsia* and *ethnē* weigh in favor of reading his communal references as rhetorical sign-posts and not as literal communities-behind-the-text.[142]

The same observations about Acts that I have made throughout this study also apply to Luke. Luke's communal language is wrapped up with its presentation of a larger myth of origins. Luke presents Jesus as a figure akin in particular ways to other Greco-Roman literature, like Augustan epic, which has occasionally given scholars pause. As Stowers observes about Luke-Acts, in behaving "more like a normal Hellenstic author ... the idea of something that suggested communal authorship was exposed for its oddness."[143] Marianne Palmer Bonz, for instance, notes the parallels

---

142. Again, this does not preclude the existence of some kind of "religious" group among Matthew's social network. I simply question the primacy of any such group over other formative associations, like other writers. Dwight N. Peterson makes a similar argument concerning the dubious nature of assuming that all potential "communal" references within a text are in reference to a concrete fellowship of Christians, stating that the method overall is aimed at establishing a "means of attaining interpretive control ... in order [for the scholar] to achieve desired results" from the text in question. Peterson enumerates several of, what he calls, "unjustified assumptions which are entailed within the drive to construct communities behind documents." Of these critiques, three are particularly striking and, in my view, relevant to the broader study of the Synoptic gospels and Q: first, that "community constructors" assume to be able to understand an author's psychology, "as if one can reconstruct the intention of an author when one has no information about who the author was, or what that author wrote, other than that abstracted from the document one is reading," cautioning that the "intentionality of a document is not the basis of interpretation, but the result"; second, he denies that one can assume to know the condition of the audience of the gospels and, furthermore, that this audience is "somehow constitutive of the meaning of the text"; third, he proposes that the exercise of attempting to retrieve the historical Markan community, for example, "obscures the interests of the reader of Mark behind a screen of alleged historical 'objectivity.' " This then allows the interpreter to impose on the text any number of sociohistorical reconstructions, utilizing preferred methodological devices in order to achieve desired interpretive results. He rightly likens this method to a house of cards that "has the potential to be quite beautiful and complex ... but all one needs to do is to turn on a fan." See Peterson, *The Origins of Mark: The Markan Community in Current Debate*, BibInt 48 (Leiden: Brill, 2000), 156–61.

143. Stowers, "Concept of 'Community,' " 240.

between Luke-Acts and the *Aeneid*'s efforts to bring "the Augustan present directly into contact with the heroic past." Vergil's epic "incorporated a complex synthesis of patriotic, moral, and religious themes in its mythologizing history of archaic Roman origins and of the divine prophecies that would read their eschatological fulfillment in the Golden Age of Augustan rule."[144] The same themes of genealogy, eschatological fulfillment, cosmic destiny, and mythologizing of origins takes place in Luke-Acts and, for that matter, Paul. Bonz also identifies a number of epic poems penned by "Hellenized Jewish" writers as precedent: the fragments of an epic poem and tragedy recorded by first-century CE historian Alexander Polyhistor, preserved by Eusebius; the second-century BCE Alexandrian Philo's *On Jerusalem*; Theodotus's *On the Jews* (second century BCE); and Ezekiel's *The Exagoge of Exodus*.[145] While not in meter, Luke-Acts nonetheless can be situated within an established genre of foundational epic. And unlike Luke-Acts, these other epics are identified with a specific author and not imagined to be the products of a Vergilian or Philonic community.

The Gospel of John presents a dynamic and complex set of discussions about social formations, including references to "true worshippers" (4:23), Samaritans (8:48, 52), Pharisees (7:45–48; 12:42) and the synagogue (9:22; 16:2; 20:19). Scholarship on the imagined Johannine community represented by these polemics has linked it to "Paul's Jewish-Christian opponents in Corinth," "the emergence of motifs that had a later flowering in Gnosticism," or "inner-community controversy ... in a period after the conflict with the synagogue had begun to subside."[146] Of the four canonical gospels, John is the gospel least associated with offering an account of the historical Jesus given its more cryptic and difficult teachings. Yet,

---

144. Marianne Palmer Bonz, *The Past as Legacy: Luke-Acts and Ancient Epic* (Minneapolis: Fortress, 2000), 23–24. It is important to note that, although Bonz recognizes these parallels, she continues to subscribe to the Big Bang understandings of Christianity's social development. Interestingly, however, she remains aware of the implausibility of that social model, even if she does not address it directly. Phrases like: "[Christianity's] proclamation had met with a surprising degree of success" and "Equally as stunning as the rapid success of the Christian mission among Gentiles, however, was the finality of the rupture of the church with its religious past" are found throughout her monograph (Bonz, *Past as Legacy*, 25).

145. Bonz, *Past as Legacy*, 27–29.

146. Robert Kysar, "The Contribution of D. Moody Smith to Johannine Scholarship," in *Exploring the Gospel of John: In Honor of D. Moody Smith*, ed. R. Alan Culpepper and C. Clifton Black (Louisville: Westminster John Knox, 1996), 4.

because of its strong presentation of group, it is almost always associated with the historical circumstances of its supposed community, perhaps because it is otherwise difficult to understand. The vast and complex literature on this gospel is beyond the scope of this study; however, it is notable that John's discussion of social formations does *not* lend itself to a sense of a worldwide movement or Big Bang. John has no mission and ends with the risen Jesus appearing to the disciples on several different occasions and John concluding: "But there are also many other things that Jesus did; if every one of them were written down, I suppose that the world itself could not contain the books that would be written" (John 21:25). In this respect, John explicitly situates itself with the activities of ancient writers, not with a mythic Big Bang of Christian communities.

Returning once more to Lincoln, he also notes that, much like with religious communities, it is common for those studying myths to associate them with "specific, ethnically and linguistically defined populations" and that this orientation

> takes for granted that nations, "cultures," and/or *Völker* (depending on the speaker's discourse) are primordial, bounded, unproblematic entities and that myth is the equally primordial voice, essence and heritage of that group. Myth and group are understood to be linked in a symbiotic relation of co-production, each one being simultaneously producer and product of the other.[147]

He recognizes that this instinctual treatment of myth in contemporary scholarship has roots in the anti-Enlightenment elevation of *völkisch* and the national reclamation projects of men like Herder and the Brothers Grimm. These Romantic era projects possessed a strong political element, aimed at generating a sense of national identification; however, in the process, "they misrecognized and misrepresented" the myths they selected as "the reinstation of something ancient, eternal, and authentic." Romantic studies on the *Volksgeist* of the German people, James Macpherson's *Ossian*, or Herder's meditations on Shakespeare or the *Geist* evidenced in the Hebrew scriptures were what Lincoln terms "myth about myth." Lincoln cautions that it "is not always the case that myths are the product and reflection of a people who tells stories in which they effectively narrative themselves.... Myths are stories in which some people narrate others, and

---

147. Lincoln, *Theorizing Myth*, 210.

at times the existence of those others is itself the product of mythic discourse." On Herder specifically, Lincoln observes that he has been "highly influential well beyond romantic and nationalist circles and arises whenever myths and peoples are understood as mutually—and unproblematically—constitutive." [148] While only a first step, I hope this study has offered a reasonable alternative to these traditional approaches, the community model, and its ties to mythic constructions.

---

148. Ibid., 211.

Ancient Myths and Modern Theories of Christian Origins: The Consultation (1995–1997) and Seminar (1998–2003) in Retrospect with Attention to Successor Groups* and a Recommendation

Barry S. Crawford and Merrill P. Miller

A Social Theory of Religion

In the introduction to *Redescribing Christian Origins*, the editors of the volume stated that the purpose of the project was both historical and theoretical: to redescribe the beginnings of Christianity and contribute to the construction of a social theory of religion.[1] At the outset of these

---

* "Successor groups" here refers to program units of the Society of Biblical Literature organized subsequent to the final year of the Ancient Myths and Modern Theories of Christian Origins Consultation and Seminar and continuing to focus on the redescription of early Christianity: the Redescribing Early Christianity Group (2007–2012, Barry Crawford and Christopher Matthews, cochairs) and the current Redescribing Early Christianity Seminar (2013–present, William Arnal and Erin Roberts, cochairs). Referring to them as "successor groups" is not meant to imply that they should be viewed merely as continuations or extensions of the older seminar. Reference to "Early Christianity" in the titles of these program units rather than to "Christian Origins" is certainly better, not only in dropping a term that is more appropriate as a mythic rather than historical category, but in extending the time frame beyond some of the earliest Jesus and Christ texts (the first-century time frame is in fact what was intended in referring to "Christian origins" in the older seminar and in the title of its first published volume). More substantively, the change also eliminates the older disciplinary dichotomy of New Testament studies and patristics. Reference to "Christianity" is of course not without its own problems.

1. "The purpose of a Seminar devoted to Ancient Myths and Modern Theories of Christian Origins is ... to contribute both historiographically to a redescription of Christian beginnings and imaginatively to the construction of a general theory of reli-

retrospective remarks, it still requires emphasis in stating that the program of the consultation and seminar was conceived from the beginning
as a project of the field of religion and cannot be appropriately understood
and evaluated apart from this location of both its historical and theoretical
aims. Problematizing the historiography of Christian origins was seen to

---

gion" (Ron Cameron and Merrill P. Miller, "Introduction: Ancient Myths and Modern
Theories of Christian Origins," in *Redescribing Christian Origins*, ed. Ron Cameron
and Merrill P. Miller, SymS 28 [Atlanta: Society of Biblical Literature, 2004], 13). For
convenience here and throughout, we often refer to this volume as vol. 1; to Ron Cameron and Merrill P. Miller, eds., *Redescribing Paul and the Corinthians*, ECL 5 (Atlanta:
Society of Biblical Literature, 2011) as vol. 2; and to the current volume as vol. 3. The
introduction to vol. 1 discussed the papers presented in the three years of the consultation (1995–1997), the program, planning, and rationale of the consultation and
seminar, and introduced the work of Burton Mack and Jonathan Z. Smith. The papers
of the first year of the consultation were published in the journal *Method and Theory
in the Study of Religion* 8 (1996), and two from the third year of the consultation were
published in volume 11 (1999) of the same journal; for a listing, see Cameron and
Miller, *Redescribing Christian Origins*, 33 n. 1. Mack's paper in the 1996 issue of the
journal, "On Redescribing Christian Origins," is republished in *Theory and Method
in the Study of Religion: Twenty Five Years On*, ed. Aaron W. Hughes, MTSRSup 1
(Leiden; Boston: Brill, 2013), 177–99. The paper is introduced by Sarah E. Rollens,
"The Rewards of Redescription: An Assessment of Burton Mack's Influence on the
Study of Christian Origins," in *Theory and Method in the Study of Religion*, 171–76.
The papers published in vol. 1 covered the third year of the consultation (Part 1: Alter-
nate Beginnings: The Sayings Gospel Q and the *Gospel of Thomas*, [1997]) and the first
two years of the seminar (Part 2: A Jesus School in Jerusalem? [1998]) and (Part 3: A
Pre-Pauline *Christos* Association, [1999]). The papers of vol. 1 were written by William E. Arnal, Willi Braun, Ron Cameron, Barry Crawford, Arthur J. Dewey, Burton L.
Mack, Luther H. Martin, Christopher R. Matthews, and Merrill P. Miller. Metareflections (part 4) were written by Arnal and Braun, Mack, Martin, Jonathan Z. Smith, and
Stanley K. Stowers, and the Introduction and Conclusion were written by Cameron
and Miller. The papers of vol. 2 were written by Arnal, Richard S. Ascough, John S.
Kloppenborg, Mack, Smith, Stowers, with the Introduction and Conclusion written
by Cameron and Miller. For Mack's discussion and observations on the first two years
of the seminar (1998–1999), see "Annex: The Christian Origins Project" in *The Christian Myth: Origins, Logic, and Legacy* (New York: Continuum, 2001), 201–16. For the
relationship of the seminar to Mack's *A Myth of Innocence: Mark and Christian Origins*
(Philadelphia: Fortress, 1988; repr. with new preface, Minneapolis: Fortress, 2006),
including his rethinking of some earlier positions, see his preface to the reprinting
of the volume. For an excellent summary of the argument of vol. 1, responding to
reviews, see Ron Cameron, "Redescribing Christian Origins," *Annali di storia dell'
esegesi* 25 (2008): 35–54.

be inseparable from challenging the theory of religion, which continues to be presupposed and to support the dominant historical paradigm, characterized in short as the Lukan-Eusebian model of Christian origins.[2]

The agreement of Burton Mack and Jonathan Z. Smith not merely to support a proposal to the Society of Biblical Literature for a consultation to be followed by a seminar aimed at the redescription of Christian origins, but their participation in both units from inception to the final sessions of the seminar was tied directly to a recognition that the historical task of redescription would also take place as a generalizing discourse of the field of religion. Smith himself has characterized the seminar as "a group that has been remarkably persistent in practicing both specialized historical knowledge and generalizing discourse."[3] The older seminar's successor

---

2. Writing in the conclusion of vol. 1, Cameron and Miller reiterate, "The possibility of a redescription of Christian origins is rooted in a different theory of religion. We have introduced another frame of reference and set of categories and have begun to construct a new map of Christian beginnings [concluding the first published volume of a] 'project of describing biblical traditions as ordinary components of religion resulting from equally ordinary processes of social formation'" (Ron Cameron and Merrill P. Miller, "Conclusion: Redescribing Christian Origins," in Cameron and Miller, *Redescribing Christian Origins,* 516; the quotation is from Jonathan Z. Smith, "Social Formations of Early Christianity: A Response to Ron Cameron and Burton Mack," *MTSR* 8 [1996]: 277).

3. Smith, "When the Chips Are Down," in *Relating Religion: Essays in the Study of Religion* (Chicago: University of Chicago Press, 2004), 33 n. 3. There Smith also notes the relationship of the essay to his writing of an intellectual autobiography not intended for publication addressed to several colleagues in the seminar and to his writing of a paper for the seminar's sessions at the Annual Meeting in Toronto in 2002, "Conjectures on Conjunctures and Other Matters: Three Essays" (in this volume). On establishing a discourse, Cameron and Miller wrote in the Introduction to vol. 1: "We have wanted to see if members of the Seminar can engage each other, take positions, present analyses, and make responses on matters of substance, without assuming that there was an essential bond that existed and a continuous development that led from the historical Jesus to the gospel story of his appearance, death, and resurrection, and from there to the Jerusalem church in Acts and the apostle Paul and his mission." Arguing for the necessity of making a complete break with the dominant paradigm and canonical narrative framework of Christian origins, "We are endeavoring to forge a discourse about religious origins that neither imagines the 'religious' as a *sui generis* category, and thus, in the final analysis, as an unfathomable mystery, nor regards 'origins' as a cipher for dramatic encounters with supernatural agents or forces.... We are disposed to translate the insider language of a religious community into the ordinary constraints and imaginative horizons of human thought, into the human social inter-

program units of the Society of Biblical Literature, the group and currently the seminar, have continued to function as projects of redescription and as programs reflexively situated in the field of religion. One instantiation of this location is the number of programs of the North American Association for the Study of Religion (NAASR) at annual meetings, which feature themes of mutual interest to both the leadership of the Association and to the leadership and many participants of the Society of Biblical Literature successor groups.[4] An especially important example is Stanley Stowers's proposal for a comprehensive revisioning of the data of early Christianity in his 2009 NAASR address.[5]

The significance of this reflexive location of the seminar is underlined in an essay by William Arnal on the different principles and goals that obtain in much of the field of biblical studies from those that obtain where comparability and generalizable explanations of religious phenomena are the raison d'être of the field.

Even just the *implicitly* comparative environment of a standard university Religious Studies department may have a latent salutary effect on biblical studies in two ways, one methodological and one theoretical. At the methodological level, the simple presence of comparable instances goes

---

ests to which the labor of the creation and maintenance, contestation and change of human societies might be reduced" (Cameron and Miller, "Introduction," 22).

4. Examples of the themes of such programs sponsored by NAASR at annual meetings are: The Bible in the Study of Religion (New Orleans, 2009); Early Christianity as Graeco-Roman Religion (Chicago, 2012); Historical-Critical Reflection on Formulating the Category of "Religion" (a joint session with the AAR Philosophy of Religion Section, Chicago, 2012); Revisiting "Community" in Early Christianity: Problems and Prospects (Baltimore, 2013); Conceptual Issues in New Testament Scholarship (San Diego, 2014). The Society for Ancient Mediterranean Religions has also explored themes of mutual interest: Divination in Ancient Mediterranean Religions (a joint session with the SBL Greco-Roman Religion Section, Chicago, 2012); Shared Lives, Different Religions? The Roman Empire in the First Two Centuries (Baltimore, 2013); Rethinking Conversion in Graeco-Roman Antiquity (a joint session with the SBL Greco-Roman Religions Section, San Diego, 2014). A session cosponsored by the Society of Biblical Literature Redescribing Early Christianity Group and the Society of Biblical Literature Greco-Roman Religions Section on the theme, The Nineteenth-Century Making of Ancient Religion (Atlanta, 2010), should also be noted.

5. Stowers, "The History of Ancient Christianity as the Study of Religion" (paper presented at the Annual Meeting of the Society of Biblical Literature, New Orleans, 22 November 2009). For more on Stowers's proposal, see below, 569–71.

some way to removing the shroud of uniqueness from Christianity....
[At the theoretical level] it may force us to acknowledge the implicit
theory of religion undergirding most New Testament work. Aside from
Burton Mack and the limited body of work inspired by his efforts, New
Testament scholars have been enormously reluctant to engage theories
of religion. We do, it seems, happily embrace the newest literary theories,
postmodernism, postcolonial theory, queer theory, abstract philosophical critiques of dogmatic 'naturalism' or Enlightenment secularism, and
so on. But when it comes to *religion*, which is, after all, the ostensible
subject matter of much New Testament scholarship, there seems to be an
entrenched reluctance to participate in theoretical discussion.[6]

On Mythmaking and Social Formation

The scholarship of Mack and Smith was recognized as foundational for the
conception of our project by all members of the seminar. By the time of

---

6. William E. Arnal, "A Parting of the Ways? Scholarly Identities and a Peculiar
Species of Ancient Mediterranean Religion," in *Identity and Interaction in the Ancient
Mediterranean: Jews, Christians and Others; Essays in Honour of Stephen G. Wilson*,
ed. Zeba A. Crook and Philip A. Harland, New Testament Monographs 18 (Sheffield:
Sheffield Phoenix, 2007), 268–69, emphasis original. The implicit theory of religion
in most New Testament scholarship is individualistic and idealist and its goals are
primarily exegetical and hermeneutic, "even when using techniques drawn from history, anthropology, sociology, and semiotic theory" (ibid., 269, 274). Arnal observes
that the major review of the seminar's initial publication, James D. G. Dunn, review of
Redescribing Christian Origins, ed. Ron Cameron and Merrill P. Miller, *JBL* 124 (2005):
760–64, is "a trivial, but quite illustrative" example of the gulf that separates two different scholarly agenda, and its "'chilling' effect on novelty in the field" (Arnal, "Parting of the Ways," 272). The seminar was undertaken "to attempt a re-reading of the
first century of 'Christianity,' with a view to cobbling together a model of the origins
of Christianity in terms that might be equally suitable to describing *non*-Christian
religious phenomena, and quite explicitly *without* any apologetic agenda" (ibid., 272–
73, emphasis original). Citing Dunn's conclusion, and regarding his views as "utterly
unsympathetic to, even contemptuous of" the goals of the seminar (the last line of
Dunn's review is, "Sorry, guys, I find your description much more problematic than
Acts" [Dunn, "Review of *Redescribing Christian Origins*," 764]) leads Arnal to the conclusion that "since the Seminar treated religion as a social construct, correspondingly
rejected a heuristic of 'experience,' did not presume unity within the Jesus movements,
and actually talked about social mechanisms behind the texts—all, I note, among the
stated *intentions* of the seminar—one should instead prefer to explain Christianity
in terms of the progress of the Holy Spirit and the miraculous deeds of the apostles"
(Arnal, "Parting of the Ways," 273, emphasis original).

our first consultation in 1995, Mack had already published three volumes linking myth and history in early Christianity from the earliest texts to the formation of the Christian Bible in the fourth century.[7] The categories fundamental to these volumes increasingly were paired as mythmaking and social formation, which became the operative categories for application and testing on the social-textual sites chosen for redescription in the consultation and seminar. "Redescription" was recognized as a key concept in the work of Smith and related to other concepts marking persistent preoccupations in his essays and books.[8] As stated by Ron Cameron and Merrill Miller in their introduction to *Redescribing Paul and the Corinthians*, "Redescription is a form of explanation that privileges difference and involves comparison and translation, category formation and rectification, definition and theory."[9]

In the conclusion of *Redescribing Christian Origins*, the editors presented an assessment of the progress of the project in terms of three sets of consequential vocabulary displacements, a "defamiliarizing endeavor, in

---

7. Mack, *Myth of Innocence* in 1988; Mack, *The Lost Gospel: The Book of Q and Christian Origins* (San Francisco: HarperSanFrancisco, 1993); and Mack, *Who Wrote the New Testament? The Making of the Christian Myth* (San Francisco: HarperSanFrancisco, 1995).

8. Smith explains in "When the Chips Are Down," 29, that he first introduced the term in the essay, "Sacred Persistence: Toward a Redescription of Canon," in vol. 1 of *Approaches to Ancient Judaism: Theory and Practice*, ed. William S. Green, BJS 1 (Missoula, MT: Scholars Press, 1978), 11–28; repr. and rev. in *Imagining Religion: From Babylon to Jonestown*, CSHJ (Chicago: University of Chicago Press, 1982), 36–52. He was drawing on Max Black's and Mary Hesse's comparisons of metaphors and scientific models; see Black, *Models and Metaphors: Studies in Language and Philosophy* (Ithaca, NY: Cornell University Press, 1962), esp. 236–38, and Hesse, *Models and Analogies in Science* (Notre Dame: University of Notre Dame Press, 1966), esp. 164–65. "Comparison does not necessarily tell us how things 'are' … like models and metaphors, comparison tells us how things might be conceived, how they might be 'redescribed'" ("When the Chips Are Down," 24). He adds further: "As I used the term, it expressed a central goal, the redescription of classical categories in the study of religion to the end that these be 'rectified'" (ibid., 29). In Smith's later writings, "redescription" became "the replacement term for older usages such as 'map,' 'model,' 'paradigm,' and the ways in which a set of intellectual operations, ranging from definition to explanation, may be understood as modes of redescription" (ibid., 25).

9. Cameron and Miller, "Introducing Paul and the Corinthians," 1.

one sense of its original, literary-critical usage as a radical alteration of the habitual terms of description, [as] part of an exercise in 'redescription.'"[10]

(1) Terms bearing on theory of religion displacing the traditional theological nomenclature of Christian origins:

- "attraction" instead of "belief"
- "social interest" instead of "individual transformation"
- "social experimentation" instead of "religious experience"
- "social logic" instead of "tradition history"
- "social location" instead of "*Sitz-im-Leben*"
- "reflexivity" instead of "hermeneutic"

(2) Terms of descriptive generalization derived from our redescriptions:
- "homeland" and "diaspora" instead of "origins" and "mission"
- "ethnographic" instead of "messianic"
- "christos" instead of "the Messiah"
- "ethnicity" instead of "personal salvation"
- "epic" and "epic revision" instead of "eschatology" and "eschatological persuasion"

(3) Terms of generalization as operating categories displacing terms too parochial to serve as such, either historiographically or comparatively:
- "mythmaking" instead of "the *kerygma*"
- "*social formation*" instead of "the church"[11]

But at the same time that seminar members agreed that Mack's categories of mythmaking and social formation had put the study of early Christianity on new intellectual foundations and that our vocabulary displacements had accomplished the critical task of problematizing the dominant paradigm of Christian origins,[12] it was also recognized that

---

10. Cameron and Miller, "Conclusion: Redescribing Christian Origins." They cite Smith's metareflection, "*Dayyeinu*," in Cameron and Miller, *Redescribing Christian Origins*, 484.

11. List is from Cameron and Miller, "Conclusion," 503, 506, 511.

12. This is corroborated in Part 4: Metareflections. Arnal and Braun commented, "We offer them [the theses] as our reflections on the Seminar's deliberations, which, and this must be said without reservation, have successfully disrupted, perhaps even displaced, the standard 'Lukan-Eusebian' model of Christianity's historical begin-

the work of redescription had only begun[13] and that our collaborative efforts had raised issues both of method and theory that remained unresolved.[14] Indeed, differences within the seminar with respect both to matters of strategy and of theory were focused precisely on mythmaking and

---

nings" ("Social Formation and Mythmaking: Theses on Key Terms," in Cameron and Miller, *Redescribing Christian Origins*, 459). In his metareflection, Mack wrote, "We have succeeded in charting the terrain differently than it looked before…. And a wonderful discourse is in the making, for we have learned to listen to each other with great care as attempts are made to talk about Christian beginnings without recourse to the usual mystifications" ("Remarkable," in Cameron and Miller, *Redescribing Christian Origins*, 470). Smith agreed: "The topography of earliest Christianities has been decisively altered, dis-placed, re-placed" (*"Dayyeinu,"* 484).

13. Smith called for a second sense of defamiliarization as redescription, which resulted from a mode of comparison necessary to rectify generalizing categories. He pointed to the seminar's undertheorized usages of "ethnic identity" and "epic traditions" (*"Dayyeinu,"* 484–86 with notes). Mack recognized that the redescriptions achieved in the work of the seminar fell short of explanation to account for generative moments of mythmaking and social formation ("Remarkable," 472).

14. While Smith noted that the discourse developing in the seminar exemplified "a sense of urgency with respect to theory, and a concomitant willingness to see the Christian data not as ends in themselves, but rather as exempla of broader theoretical and methodological issues in the imagination of culture and religion" (*"Dayyeinu,"* 486), Luther Martin, in his metareflection, observed a divide among seminar members between prioritizing the redescription of early Christian sites and prioritizing sites that held the most promise for a broader application of method and theory in the study of religion (Martin, "Redescribing Christian Origins: Historiography or Exegesis?," in Cameron and Miller, *Redescribing Christian Origins*, 475). Moreover, Martin maintained that "the redescription proposed by the Seminar remained as undertheorized as the 'analytical' categories employed" (477). Stowers, in his metareflection, held that options regarding social theory had not been clarified in the seminar. He offered a brief account of the theoretical advantages of a social ontology based in practice theory over social ontologies based in individualisms or in social structuralisms. One advantage he cited was that practice theory was more amenable to correlation with neo-Darwinian accounts of human evolution. He also applied the neo-Darwinian idea of *exaptation* to the problem of historical continuity and discontinuity, likening the differences between an earlier Jesus group's references to the "anointed" Jesus and Paul's references to Christ to the differences between the use of a stone as a lintel in building practices and the later use of that same stone after the building collapsed as an anchor in sailing practices. Thus, there would be no continuity of intentionality in the uses of *christos* in the practices of the Jesus group and in the practices of Paul (Stowers, "Mythmaking, Social Formation, and Varieties of Social Theory," in Cameron and Miller, *Redescribing Christian Origins*, 489–95).

social formation as the categorical terms being applied and tested, and especially on the question of their relationship. In their metareflection, Arnal and Willi Braun explained that the purpose of the theses was not "to cajole the Seminar into accepting a single theory about 'social formation' and 'mythmaking' and the nexus between them…. Rather, we sought to bring into the open the evident differences in the assumptions at work among us about this nexus by articulating as sharply as possible our own assumptions."[15] Smith, noting that the dominant "metaquestion" to have emerged in the seminar was specifying the nexus between mythmaking and social formation, offered a caution regarding the classic Marxist distinction between infrastructure and superstructure, as well as a caution regarding the seminar's tendency to construct site redescriptions on the assumption of the congruency of mythmaking and social formation: "The challenge, here, will be to avoid formulations which see the one as the dependent variable of the other, or which see the one as congruent to the other. Such formulations introduce insufficient difference. The task, as Marshall Sahlins has consistently reiterated, is to provide an adequate account of myth both as 'reproduction' and as 'transformation,' to provide both an adequate 'sociological theory of symbolization' and an adequate 'symbolic theory of society.'"[16]

On Different Strategies of Redescription

Clearly, there were underlying differences among members of the seminar in matters of social theory, and even different views of the project's rationale had surfaced. Nevertheless, in retrospect, the internal issues associated with the seminar's first published volume can also be viewed as amounting to different strategies of redescription. In part, this is because the seminar continued to focus on the historical task, though there was

---

15. Arnal and Braun, "Theses on Key Terms," 460.

16. Smith, "Dayyeinu," 486 with nn. 9–10. The "nexus" question continued to be a focus of attention in vol. 2 in the discussion of Smith's paper "Re: Corinthians," in Cameron and Miller, *Redescribing Paul and the Corinthians*, 17–34, esp. 28 with n. 38, particularly the possibility that Sahlins's category, "structures of conjuncture" and the mechanisms of "reproduction" and "transformation," could be helpful in clarifying the question. This interest eventually led to the request that Smith engage Sahlins, esp. in relation to our question. The result is Smith's essay, "Conjectures on Conjunctures" in this volume.

some experimentation with forming a separate track to focus on social theory.[17] The initial debate concerning the way forward for the third year of the seminar (2000) was whether to take up the pre-Pauline traditions, that is, the meal text (1 Cor 11:23–26) and the so-called Christ *kerygma* (1 Cor 15:3–5), in order to relocate and redescribe them before going on to Paul and the Corinthians. We settled on something of a compromise. The seminar would turn directly to Paul and the Corinthians, but Mack would also take up the pre-Pauline traditions for redescription.

The issue had been drawn in Mack's response to the seeming uneasiness of the seminar to work with hypothetical sites and to take their description in the first two years of the seminar any further than we did, and it can be seen in Braun's response to Mack as well.[18] Mack's concern was leaving first-century texts and sites crucial to the dominant picture of Christian origins without redescription in our terms. So, he reminded the seminar, "You already know that I can't imagine moving to Corinth without redescribing the (hypothetical) social situations and the social logics of the several Jesus myths and rituals that Paul's letter document…. I can't jump from the Jesus movements to Paul's spin on these myths and rituals without asking about the changes in social formation, issues, and thinking that must have occurred to generate them."[19] Mack acknowledged that working in the second century would be easier and that the map would be more colorful but would never "render a critique of the traditional notion of Christian origins."[20] Braun responded, "Why can't you jump?"[21] More pointedly,

> Personally, I think the desire to "rectify the categories" of the fathers and contemporary brothers and sisters on *their* sites is doomed to failure anyway…. They have too many offspring who are singing the same song too loudly…. My view is that we move our broadcast to the other end of

17. For reference, see Mack, *The Christian Myth*, 215. And see Arnal's reflections on the place of theory in the context of the seminar's historical project in "On Smith, On Myth, On Mark," 145–48, in this volume.

18. This exchange is published in vol. 1: Mack, "Backbay Jazz and Blues," in Cameron and Miller, *Redescribing Christian Origins*, 421–31; Braun, "Smoke Signals from the North: A Reply to Burton Mack's 'Backbay Jazz and Blues,'" in Cameron and Miller, *Redescribing Christian Origins*, 433–42.

19. Mack, "Backbay Jazz and Blues," 423.

20. Ibid., 426.

21. Braun, "Smoke Signals from the North," 438.

the frequency dial so that our tune will not get confused with the overlay and static of the Christian superstation.... Rather, it is precisely by trivializing ... those sites that are especially sacred in the old, old story that we will clarify what we are up to. The fact that *they* (our predecessors in the field) have set the itinerary for our project is unfortunate and more driven by our polemical desires to mute our fathers than required by *our* emerging social theories.[22]

Mack's strategy, and the strategy in the planning of the seminar, was *to remap the territory* of first-century texts and sites in order to displace the gospel story, or some paraphrase of it, as the explanation for Christian beginnings. An alternative strategy would be *to stake out a different territory for mapping*, a strategy clearly expressed in the theme of the first two years of the Society of Biblical Literature Redescribing Early Christianity Group (2007–2008): The Second Century's Invention of the First.[23] From this angle, the concern is understandable that the seminar in its redescription of first-century sites was in danger of inadvertently presenting a developing myth as constituting the beginnings of Christianity, an untenable idealism, and repeating the historical teleology of the dominant paradigm in a different key. However, without diminishing the issue, it is worth noting that the public response to the publication of *Redescribing Christian Origins* did not pick up on this contention within the seminar, but rather they reacted to what was perceived as an untenable fragmentation of the linked ideological and historical foundations of the Christian religion. Moreover, the importance of "the second century's invention of the first" is not in trivializing first-century texts and sites, in the sense of ignoring them, but in providing an alternative strategy for their redescription.[24]

---

22. Ibid., 441, emphasis original.

23. We should be clear that the issues of the Mack-Braun exchange in vol. 1 cannot be reduced simply to differences in the data and strategies of redescription. In that volume, Cameron and Miller explicitly denied that this was the case (see "Issues and Commentary," in Cameron and Miller, *Redescribing Christian Origins*, esp. 455–56). But in retrospect it does seem important to register that certain facets of the debate have actually had their most significant effect on vol. 2 and on the current volume as matters of differing strategies of redescription.

24. Arnal presents a similar view in a paper first written for a session of the Society of Biblical Literature Redescribing Early Christianity Group on the theme, The Second Century's Invention of the First (paper presented at the Annual Meeting of the

On Rectifications

Mythmaking and social formation not only served as primary tools for redescription and grounds for conversation about differences of strategy and theory. The categories were refined in the course of the seminar. In fact it can be said that the rectification of these categories and the relationship between them demonstrate what has been learned in the course of the seminar. The internal debate that had ensued at the yearly sessions of the seminar published in *Redescribing Christian Origins* had been taken seriously. The suspicion that the seminar may only be presenting a different version of the historical teleology of the dominant paradigm, or proposing a developing myth as explanation for early Christian social formation, or identifying processes of social formation with bounded groups formed and maintained by a collective Christian identity are matters that are addressed in *Redescribing Paul and the Corinthians*, not least in the paper by Mack on the pre-Pauline traditions in that volume.[25]

Society of Biblical Literature, San Diego, 17 November 2007): "If we want ... to understand this myth [the Lukan-Eusebian myth of Christian origins], to trace its development, and ultimately to replace it with something more historically suitable, we will need to pay more attention to the ways in which our first-century artifacts have been appropriated by a more or less coherent and self-conscious *second-century* movement known as 'Christianity.' In the process, we may find additional grounds for liberating older texts such as Q, Thomas, Mark, Matthew, and the (authentic) letters of Paul from the conceptual framework that is imposed every time we identify these objects as 'Christian'" (18, emphasis original). A briefer statement to this effect appears in the published version of the paper, William E. Arnal, "The Collection and Synthesis of 'Tradition' and the Second-Century Invention of Christianity," *MTSR* 23 (2011): 212–13. Here, Arnal also calls attention to the fact that the concept of "Christianity" fosters the illusion of commonality and unity of first-century textual artifacts and accounts for why the work of Burton Mack and the essays in *Redescribing Christian Origins* appear to many intrinsically implausible: "One encounters again and again the criticism that such work has atomized ancient Christianity and needlessly proliferated independent 'communities' with their own distinctive theologies" (212). First-Century textual artifacts are in fact among the data that continue to be taken up for redescription in the programs of the Society of Biblical Literature successor groups, and categories prominent in descriptions of first-century data continue to be rectified.

25. Mack, "Rereading the Christ Myth: Paul's Gospel and the Christ Cult Question," in Cameron and Miller, *Redescribing Paul and the Corinthians*, 35–73. Describing the import of Mack's paper in the introduction to the volume, Cameron and Miller wrote, "Mack's paper underlines the importance of the concerns that made the Corinthian site attractive in the first place and has put to rest, we think, any suspi-

Arnal and Braun had made the case that analytical priority should be given to social contexts over discursive formations, including mythmaking.[26] So, as mentioned, the seminar turned to Paul and the Corinthians rather than devoting a year to the pre-Pauline "traditions." Here, at last, was a site where we could draw on more detailed social data than was true of the hypothetical sites of a Jerusalem school and a pre-Pauline *christos* association from the previous years of the seminar. Precisely where more social data was available, the categories of mythmaking and social formation and their nexus proved to be more complicated than our use of these categories as analytical tools in the first two years of the seminar. On the question of nexus, our conception of a necessary relationship between mythmaking and social formation had been too causal and mirror-like. The work on Paul and the Corinthians and Smith's "Conjectures on Conjunctures" in this volume has led to a relation that is more complex, more associative than causal.[27] In systemic terms, mythmaking

---

cion about 'connecting all the dots on the "Christian" map' [the phrase is from Braun, "Smoke Signals from the North," 440] by establishing a linear sequence of myths as a generative cause. On the contrary. Not only has Mack shown that an earlier martyr myth cannot account for Paul's Christ myth; he also argues that Paul's gospel does not account for Corinthian social formation or contribute much to it" (Cameron and Miller, "Introducing Paul and the Corinthians," 8). The editors conclude, "The principle contribution of Mack's paper ... is to have thoroughly problematized the notion of a pre-Pauline Christ cult and the historical work generated by that notion. In the Bultmannian tradition, it has served as a bridge between Jesus and Paul, making it possible to ring the changes without giving up the primitive Christian church as a historical datum, the unique 'eschatological community' at the foundations of the Christian religion" (9). Arnal has also called attention to Mack's paper as a revision of the chapter on the congregations of the Christ in *Myth of Innocence*, enumerating the reasons for and implications of the revision: "because of the misleading freight associated with the terms 'cult' and 'ritual'; because of the linear and almost-teleological implication that 'Christianity' unfolded in a step-by-step development from Jesus the teacher; and because of the general lack of utility found for the concept in our redescriptive efforts" ("Mark, War, and Creative Imagination," 441 n. 116, in this volume).

26. In Arnal and Braun, "Theses on Key Terms."

27. In "Conjectures on Conjunctures," Smith writes, "Given what I have said above with respect to an attempt to rectify explanation in terms of translation, when I use the term 'nexus' it is in its classical sense of 'association,' 'interwoven,' 'bound together' ... and not in its later nineteenth-century causal sense. That is to say, while there may be necessary relations, these are not necessarily causal ones" (59). He continues, "What is in common to both of my cautions with respect to formulating the nexus between social formation and mythmaking [see above, 543] is a rejection of

and social formation cannot be viewed as a single set of systems. The data of 1 Corinthians was more amenable to translation by a double set of systems.[28] Our discussions and published results also brought home still more clearly that "beginnings" can only be grasped in historical terms as interventions in already existing social formations rather than as dramatic, unique disclosures giving rise to unique social formations. Because this is the case, the rhetoric of exclusive identity and bounded group, for example Paul's Corinthians in Christ, must be distinguished from a far more variable social reality on the ground. Texts that appeal to teachings, practices, and the fate of Jesus and his relationship to God do

---

the notion of the myth as mirror: whether that which is reflected be expressed as social situation (as some functionalisms as well as the seminar has sometimes formulated it), infrastructure (as in some materialisms), or as divine archtypes (as in Mircea Eliade). Clearly my own interest in tension, in incongruency, would resist a replication model" (59–60).

28. "As an effort to relate mythmaking and social formation, our work demonstrates that the relationship is complex, first, because mythmaking and social formation are already intertwined from both sides of the encounter between Paul and the Corinthians and, second, because this double set of differences is reproduced and transformed in the course of the encounter. Thus, though mythmaking and social formation are linked, the implication is that one is not simply a reflection, or cause, of the other.... It also means that a site for redescription does not have to constitute a single social formation, as though it consisted in some firmly bounded corporate entity. The larger import for redescribing Christian origins is that the existence of Jesus-or Christ-centered myths ... does not necessarily presuppose Jesus-or Christ-centered collective identities or bounded groups as their formative social contexts.... What Paul achieved at Corinth was not the establishment of an alternative community founded on the Christ myth and unified through Paul's moral and ritual instructions, but the attraction of a certain cadre of followers" (Cameron and Miller, "Introducing Paul and the Corinthians," 15). In the concluding essay of the volume, Cameron and Miller suggest some further implications of this position: "*Social formation* throughout most of the century may point less to bonded groups of Jesus people, kingdom of God people, or Christ people than to forums of discourse and debate about authority and rule, to settings for the display of wisdom and the cultivation of virtue, and to places for constructing social charters to guide responses to changed circumstances and imagine alternative forms of social cohesion. In such forums, settings, and places the teachings of Jesus (or of Jesus-*christos*), the works of Jesus, the wisdom of Jesus, and the faith, person, and destiny of Jesus could be found to be of interest among still largely other-identified groups," for example, "by gender, household, civic and ethnic identity, by status, particular agendas, intellectual interests, and cultural fields" (Cameron and Miller, "Redescribing Paul and the Corinthians," in Cameron and Miller, *Redescribing Paul and the Corinthians*, 302).

not of themselves make a Christian social identity. Moreover, the term "Christian," barely present in first-century data, becomes by sleight-of-hand a tacit expression of an historical teleology, of theological, ideological, and social unity, even when we know better. It is therefore problematic to imagine these texts as the singular products of practices belonging to an entity that cannot be shown to have yet taken form.[29]

Stowers's demonstration of the problematic concept of "community" and its effect on Christian origins study has clearly influenced papers in the present volume.[30] Smith's reference to Mark's Levantine Judean association is intended precisely to get away from standard reified conceptions of Christian community.[31] None of the papers of the volume assume or appeal to a Markan Christian community as the context or explanation for the Gospel of Mark.[32] It was already clear in the planning stages that the

---

29. For summary statements in this volume on the rectification of mythmaking and social formation as analytical tools for redescription, see esp. Mack, "Cartwheels: Or On Not Staying Upside Down Too Long," 130–33; and Mack, "The Spyglass and Kaleidoscope: From a Levantine Coign of Vantage." In "Spyglass and Kaleidoscope," Mack writes: "Smith's cautions about the many ways in which changing situations and interests impinge upon the mechanisms of transformation/rectification and reproduction/experimental application finally bring us to a thorough reconsideration of the situational context for imagining the processes of social formation and mythmaking. Instead of assuming dramatic events at the social level or shocking ideas at the level of myth that 'trigger' the processes of mythmaking and social formation, we now have "*'situational incongruity*' as it presents itself to thought" (203, citing "Conjectures on Conjunctures," 69, emphasis original).

30. Stanley K. Stowers, "The Concept of 'Community' and the History of Early Christianity," *MTSR* 23 (2011): 238–56. We call attention to the fact that Stowers's observations on the problematic of community in historical work on Christian origins had already appeared in our vol. 2 and played a significant role in the drawing of conclusions for that volume (see Stowers, "Kinds of Myth, Meals, and Power: Paul and the Corinthians," in Cameron and Miller, *Redescribing Paul and the Corinthians*, 108–10). Though it will seem surprising because the volume did not appear until 2011, the conclusions of the volume were fully written up by July, 2006, with only a few updates of bibliographical references added in the intervening years.

31. Smith, "The Markan Site," 118 (in this volume).

32. Mack, "The Spyglass and Kaleidoscope," has in view something on the order of a Jesus school-like formation dealing with the fallout of the war in a more urban, imperially conscious Levantine multicultural situation. Arnal, "Mark, War, and Creative Imagination" (in the last section of his paper) and Miller, "The Social Logic of the Gospel of Mark," albeit in different ways, set Mark in a situation of displacement, responding to ethnic marginalization as Jews after the war. Walsh ("Q and the "Big Bang" Theory") presents Q as a product of a network of producers and consumers of

Gospel of Mark would present us with a quite different challenge than Paul and the Corinthians, where Smith's paper, "Re: Corinthians," had found illuminating analogies in Eytan Bercovitch's "social multiplicity" and in Sahlins's "structures of conjuncture."[33] The Markan site would not present us with a situation of first contact of radically different cultures as in the Cook-Hawaiian encounter, although both Sahlins and Smith have argued that the dynamics of "reproduction" and "transformation" apply also to more typical intracultural situations focused on "incidents" rather than on "events."[34] Smith took up the challenge to prioritize social analysis and to redescribe the Markan context by describing a larger social landscape in a longer time-frame of relations among ethnically related peoples of the Levant, a permanent contact zone of successive empires and Semitic peoples, while bracketing the political and military context of the Roman-Judean war, though he does not ignore ethnic conflict and violence often associated with the antecedents of the war. The papers of Arnal, Mack, Miller, and Robyn Faith Walsh (on Q), however, do take account of the war and the post-70 fallout. The justification is based not only on the possibility of making inferences about a social situation from the data of Mark's Gospel and Q. It is also based on the observations of Nicholas Thomas about the effects of a more developed colonial take over and administration on the constraints of native responses in comparison to the situation of recent intrusion described by Sahlins in the Cook-Hawaiian affair, that is, supposing these effects can be translated to an ancient Levantine social world subsequent to the first Roman-Judean war.[35] While Smith's paper has in view more typical and recurrent situations that also produce occasions

---

writings, not a religious formation, taking rhetorical and social advantage of the "successful hero" in a utopian sense, outside the locative, mainstream upheaval, in a time of major symbol change in the wake of the war.

33. Eytan Bercovitch, "The Altar of Sin: Social Multiplicity and Christian Conversion among a New Guinea People," in *Religion and Cultural Studies*, ed. Susan L. Mizruchi (Princeton: Princeton University Press, 2001), 211–35; Marshall Sahlins, *Historical Metaphors and Mythical Realities: Structure in the Early History of the Sandwich Islands Kingdom*, Association for Social Anthropology in Oceania Special Publications 1 (Ann Arbor: University of Michigan Press, 1981).

34. Smith, "Conjectures on Conjunctures," 30–32. For a more detailed discussion of moving from Sahlins's "conjuncture" to Smith's "situation of incongruity," see Mack, "Cartwheels," 127–30.

35. Nicholas Thomas, "Histories Structured and Unstructured," in *Out of Time: History and Evolution in Anthropological Discourse*, 2nd ed. (Ann Arbor: University

for the perception of incongruity and efforts at rectification in thought, other papers have applied Smith's categories of incongruity, experimental application, and rectification in a context of major disruption.[36]

So, having accounted for the rectifications, exposed as myth and not history the "big bang" theory of Christian origins, and presented a more plausible account of some of the earliest textual data of what was to become Christian canonical literature, are we—at last!—ready to bring to closure the Consultation and Seminar on Ancient Myths and Modern Theories of Christian Origins? Not if the implication is bringing to closure long past midnight a seminar whose final session occurred in November 2003. Rather, as indicated above, we are reporting on what we think we have learned in the course of the consultation and seminar, setting the current volume in the context of the papers published in two previous volumes (2004, 2011), taking account of continuing work in the successor groups (2007–2012, 2013–) and making a recommendation looking ahead.[37] Nor is the point to trumpet the success of the project that was undertaken. In fact, Walsh is telling us in "Q and the 'Big Bang' Theory of Christian Origins" (in this volume) that the older seminar has not avoided the big bang, even if it does not show up at the first moment. We too have been caught in the enormous expansion and acceleration of that first moment.[38]

---

of Michigan Press, 1996), 102–16; see Smith's discussion of the writings of Nicholas Thomas in "The Markan Site," 99–101 with nn. 1–3.

36. This is the case particularly with the papers by Arnal ("Mark, War, and Creative Imagination," 472–82, on double exile), Miller ("The Social Logic of the Gospel of Mark," esp. 302–21 on the situation of the Roman province of Judea post-70 as more akin to diaspora politically, legally and, increasingly, culturally; and on Jews as Roman subjects in the fallout of the war and its wider Roman and regional reverberations), and Walsh ("Q and the 'Big Bang' Theory," esp. 522–25, on Q and cosmic paranoia in the wake of the destruction of the temple). Mack's paper, "The Spyglass and Kaleidoscope," draws heavily on Smith's papers to "tone down" the atmosphere of apocalyptic crisis so much assumed in interpretation of Mark's Gospel (181–96), but it does acknowledge the central importance of the writer's coming to terms with the disorientation in the wake of the destruction of the temple (196–205). Given some very important shared assumptions and commonalities in our redescription of the Markan site and gospel, the papers in this volume present a range and diversity of tasks, positions, arguments, and outcomes.

37. See below, 567–73.

38. We certainly intended to avoid it, by drawing on Mack's exposure and critique of the treatment of diversity in early Christianity as a family tree arrangement or root and branches model (*Myth of Innocence*, 321 n. 3).

Walsh's paper, a recent addition to the volume, is not an afterthought, our failing even to pay attention to the fact that she was writing on Q and not Mark. First, it is obvious she is not writing only on Q but on the gospels as well, insofar as her argument that Q is an artifact of a field, or rather subfield, of literate culture producers, the product of a writer in a network of other writers and readers, is applicable to the gospels. Indeed, Q is probably the tougher case to make.[39] Second, in the context of this volume,

---

39. In her paper for an SBL-NAASR session on the theme, Revisiting "Community" in Early Christianity: Problems and Prospects, Sarah Rollens takes a somewhat different approach to the argument that Q is not the product of a community, defending the view that it is the product of a network of "middling" village scribes and their repeated attention to the text over a period of time ("The Kingdom of God Is Among You: The Scholarly Fixation on a Q Community" [paper presented at the Annual Meeting of the Society of Biblical Literature, Baltimore, 24 November 2013]). While Rollens is clear that the "group mentality" apparent in the document is in fact an ideological construction of the scribes and not of peasant villages, she does think of the text as aimed at promoting social interests and a social movement, thus presumably intending to engage a wider circle than only a network of the text producers and readers, whether successful or not. On her account, attention to the text is intended to promote social activism. See also Sarah E. Rollens, "The Identity of Q in the First Century: Reproducing a Theological Narrative," in *Failure and Nerve in the Academic Study of Religion: Essays in Honor of Donald Wiebe*, ed. William E. Arnal, Willi Braun, and Russell T. McCutcheon (Sheffield: Equinox, 2012), 177–91. Her broader work on Q is published in Sarah E. Rollens, *Framing Social Criticism in the Jesus Movement*, WUNT 374 (Tübingen: Mohr Siebeck, 2014). On Q and bureaucratic village scribes, see most recently, Giovanni Battista Bazzana, *Kingdom of Bureaucracy: The Political Theology of Village Scribes in the Sayings Gospel Q*, BETL 274 (Leuven: Peeters, 2015). Other issues can be raised from the angle of a broader typology of unauthorized or freelance religious specialists; see Heidi Wendt, *At the Temple Gates: The Religion of Freelance Experts in the Roman Empire* (New York: Oxford University Press, 2016). The broader class is not limited to literates capable of producing literature. What difference does this make in imagining circles, circumstances, and practices in which social formation could take place, for example, with reference to Jesus as an imagined source of ethnic-identified expertise, without positing bounded communities of like-minded people all equally and in the same way devoted to Jesus? A somewhat different set of enabling conditions for types of social formation are also imagined when a typology of religious experts is related to the ease or difficulty of the transmission of religious ideas in light of insights from a cognitive theory of religion. See, for example, Luther Martin, "Historiography or Exegesis"; and Daniel Ullucci, "Toward a Typology of Religious Experts in the Ancient Mediterranean," in *"The One Who Sows Bountifully:" Essays in Honor of Stanley K. Stowers*, ed. Caroline Johnson Hodge et al., BJS 356 (Providence, RI: Brown Judaic Studies, 2013), 89–103, both of whom draw on the

Walsh's paper, drawing on the preparation of her Brown University PhD dissertation for publication and several papers presented at annual meetings of the Society of Biblical Literature, represents not only her research on the Romantic heritage of conceptualities and methodologies of biblical historical criticism and her development and application to Q and the gospels of proposals in the work of Stowers. Her paper exemplifies as well the possibilities for the redescription of first-century textual data from the strategic position of the second century's invention of the first. Third, her paper illustrates how much can be done with few elaborated sources, instantiated in detail in the case of the Gospel of Mark in Arnal's "Mark, War, and Creative Imagination." Finally, and most important for the considerations of the editors, Walsh's paper guaranteed that we could not, and would not want to, wrap up this volume and the older seminar under the banner of achieving a new, if incomplete, map of Christian beginnings in the first century. This is so, not only because after a decade there is not enough response to our published volumes within the field to benefit for the purpose of such a presentation, but also because the implications of Walsh's paper question whether our literary data present us with any pre-70 territory to map, that is, with data for constructing a social history of the beginnings of a Jesus movement. In regard to Paul's authentic letters as evidence, it was precisely in our work on Paul and the Corinthians that Stowers and others pointed out the necessity of conceiving the Corinthians addressed in Paul's letter as actually consisting of "social fractions,"[40] and we began to see with greater clarity the problem of constructing intersections of mythmaking and social formation by supposing that they mirror each other. Looking back on our first published volume, constructing such intersections, particularly by inferring the factors accounting for social formation from changes of *mythologoumena*, becomes even more problematic for pre-70 sites of Jesus "traditions" dependent on conceptions and settings of a supposed early Jesus movement and on methods of textual analysis that Walsh is arguing have led us astray.

---

cognitive research of Harvey Whitehouse, who divides the mnemonic support necessary for successful transmission of nonintuitive religious ideas into "imagistic" and "doctrinal" types. Martin suggests the charismatic practices of the Corinthians and the "aphorisms" and "picturesque images" ascribed to Jesus in Q conform better to nondoctrinal imagistic groups (Martin, "Historiography or Exegesis," 480).

40. For the particular terminology, see Stowers, "Kinds of Myth, Meals, and Power," 109 with n. 11.

However, this should not be taken as a withdrawal of what we continue to think makes better social sense of texts in hypothetical social sites. An example would be the altogether unremarkable "Mr. *Christos*" of our volume 1 pre-Pauline *christos* association site, as he was lovingly dubbed by some in the seminar.[41] Even though on longer look it has become clear that we cannot construct some precise stage of a social history of a Jesus movement from this "first use" of the term or relate it to a continuous social history by comparing it to later uses, it is not for that reason devoid of all connection with a situation. It is not a "demythologized" social idea replacing a genuine counterfactual myth.[42] It is an example of myth-making in the sense of myth as a strategy for dealing with a situation of incongruity,[43] a clever strategy at that, making use of an epic term of divine authorization in a way that makes the honorific not one of function within an institutional context of leadership, that is, not so much a matter of role but of identification linked *exclusively* to the name of Jesus, for a figure who has none of the bona fides associated with its more typical use—and who surely has none of the bona fides associated with honorifics linked to the name of the reigning emperor. If one takes this queerness and chutzpah in connection with other ways in which a situation can be inferred as much from the typicality of the resources that are lacking for recognition, then one is not dealing simply with ideational content but with a characteristic of the "situatedness" of their practices, however different the particular practices may be. To elaborate a bit. Mack writes, "Most of the peculiarities of early Christian myths and social formations can be viewed as attempts to enhance and define the importance of a school tradition that did *not* have features of identification common for other peoples, associations, and societies of the time."[44] Arnal sees something similar with the Gospel of Thomas: "*Thomas* seems to envision a social formation of philosophers without patrons, in which a learned practice is cultivated absent the normal social location and conditions for such a practice."[45] Even if the

---

41. The full discussion of this site is found in part 3 of Cameron and Miller, *Redescribing Christian Origins*.

42. Martin, "Historiography or Exegesis," 478 with n. 11.

43. Smith, "When the Chips Are Down," 18, 48 n. 63; "Conjectures on Conjectures," 60 n. 105, 69 n. 118.

44. Mack, "Cartwheels," 139–40, emphasis original.

45. William Arnal, "Blessed Are the Solitary: Textual Practices and the Mirage of a *Thomas* 'Community,'" in Hodge et al., *"The One Who Sows Bountifully,"* 280.

social formation here is not "preponderantly defined by a commitment to Jesus,"[46] the repeated appeal to Jesus in texts exhibiting these generic sorts of abnormalities is itself a mark of commonality, though not marking a situation that is unprecedented. Despite the emphasis on practice in the Gospel of Thomas and not on ideological content, identity formation is necessarily associated with a message, "an assertion of the reader's status, grounded in a nonearthly, and therefore, nonethnic, nonpolitical, nonlocal identity."[47] To return to *Christos*, Mark seems not quite sure how he wants to use the term, but he knows how he does not want to use it. Like the composers of the sayings of the Gospel of Thomas, the author of Mark also deliberately cultivates mysteries and obscurities around an obscure figure of the recent past, engaging readers in interpretation, in imitation of ancient books.

Another example, a pre-Pauline martyr myth, is a different case, though equally difficult to locate within the context of a social history. Different because one does not have to make a bunch of jumps to see how it can be adopted as a strategy for promoting social significance. Finally, we recall that the papers of the third year of our consultation on Q and the Gospel of Thomas, which was in fact the first year of the itinerary envisioned by the seminar, did not focus on the dating of these documents, though a pre-70 date for the main recension of Q was taken for granted. The focus was on a wider range of phenomena in the Greco-Roman world for comparison and on the practices discernible from the documents. The strategy of beginning with these texts was not particularly a matter of date either, as though the point were to argue that these texts were earlier than anything else. As stated, it was an attempt to gain a cognitive advantage for our redescription by saying, in effect, "Well, we don't have to start *there*" (with the historical Jesus or in Jerusalem). Is it not the case that Walsh is taking cognitive advantage of saying to us, in effect, "Well, we don't have to start *there*" (in some pre-70 oral traditions, or even in some pre-70 composition of village scribes). True, in planning the seminar's first two years, the itinerary was then to move to the prominent early sites of the dominant paradigm. Why? In part, because we were confident that showing we could make better social sense of these sites would attract wider attention in the guild. We were wrong.

---

46. Ibid., 281.
47. Ibid., 280.

On Differences of Social Theory and Historical Analysis

There is agreement between Smith and Sahlins in "Conjectures on Con-junctures" and between Smith and other members of the seminar that ulti-mately the classical Marxist distinction of infrastructure and superstruc-ture does not distinguish different realities, the one ideal and the other material. But apart from this reduction, wherein "lies the highest natural-ism, in which Claude Lévi-Strauss joins Karl Marx and Émile Durkheim by his own method of uniting mind and nature,"[48] there are differences of social theory that impinge on historical analysis in privileging one or the other side of this "highest naturalism." This privileging is clearly present in statements of Arnal and Braun[49] and in statements of Mack,[50] Smith, and

---

48. Marshall Sahlins, *Culture and Practical Reason* (Chicago : University of Chi-cago Press, 1976), 122.

49. "As Braun and I wrote ["Theses on Key Terms," 465]: 'It is probably an idealist fallacy to regard ideas and discourse as something other than a component (analyti-cally speaking) of the material framework in which they operate.... There need not be anything idealist about ideas, in which case any dichotomy between ideas and material forces is itself idealist! But *for our purposes here, and as a corrective*, it is worth view-ing those material social manifestations that present themselves as nonmaterial to be effects, if only for the sake of conceptual clarity.' My insistence on the causal priority of 'material' to 'ideal' phenomena—offered in the face of my own recognition of the artificiality of the distinction—was in part a function of the conviction that the tradi-tional picture of Christian origins relies upon an implicit idealist theory of history and that, to whatever extent we persisted in adhering to such a perspective, it would be that much harder to escape from the confines of the traditional view in any decisive way" (Arnal, "On Smith, On Myth, On Mark," 147 n. 4, emphasis added). While the posi-tion stated here is presented as much a matter of strategic as of theoretical concern, it does bear on social and historical analysis. The issue goes back to the consultation on Q and the Gospel of Thomas; see Arnal, "Why Q Failed: From Ideological Project to Group Formation," in Cameron and Miller, *Redescribing Christian Origins*, 84–87; in the same volume, see Miller, "Discussion and Reflections," 133–35. While Arnal acknowledges that the Smith/Sahlins model of historical change does not merely con-cern the alteration of mythic structures but the whole structure of social praxis, he is nonetheless suspicious of the "*potential*" to reduce the model to an idealist reading of historical change by implying that change "only happens automatically or acciden-tally." On the contrary, "Conceptual structures do not simply render things intelligible. They also infuse them with value; they are *interested*.... Is it not then equally important to view structural change in terms of the dynamics of opposition inherent to any given social structure? Should we not insist on the conscious *rhetorical* alteration of struc-

Sahlins.[51] It can be expressed as a relation of encompassment, as Smith

---

ture, for advantage, for exploitation and repression, for resistance and revolt, alongside the *communicative* alteration of structure to incorporate 'accidental' change?" ("On Smith, On Myth, On Mark," 159, emphasis original). For a similar suspicion about Sahlins's notion of the "indissoluble synthesis" between system and event, see Thomas, *Out of Time*, 108–9.

50. When Mack calls attention to Smith's anthropology as radically social and thoroughly rational or intellectualist, and writes, "Because that is so, I have had no trouble thinking that social formations and practices are human intellectualist (linguistic) products, just as mythmaking and discursive practices are" ("Remarkable," 473), he is not in our estimation merely repeating the reduction from the other side but making a statement that bears on social theory and historical analysis. More basic to Mack's theorizing social interests is "organizing their life in common" than "struggling against each other" (the phrases are from Smith's epigraph from Lucien Sebag, *Marxisme et Structuralisme* [Paris: Payot, 1964] in "Conjectures on Conjunctures," 17), though it should also be noted that Mack's theorizing of social interests also finds problematic the reification of "intelligibility" in concepts such as "the human mind" and the social "unconscious" (see Mack, "Cartwheels," 133). His privileging of language is also related to his making more of precursor moments in mythmaking and of the evidence of mutual recognition. Thus, Mack adds, "To acknowledge connections with precursor moments in a myth's history of reconfigurations is not only honest but necessary. It does not mean that one has to think of this 'development' as a continuous unfolding of the implicit significance of an originary moment.... The link to previous configurations is always only one of many factors in social interest, social formation, cultural context, and ideological position taking that impinge upon a new moment of mythmaking" (Mack, "Backbay Jazz and Blues," 426–27). In "The Spyglass and Kaleidoscope," 196–202, Mack does sketch a picture of an internal social history largely on the basis of Markan sources and Q, linking a prewar Jesus school in Galilee to a postwar Markan association in the Levant "that cultivates the teachings of Jesus" (ibid., 205). However, he also thinks of Mark's "myth of origin" as "an author's occasional piece" and recognizes that "the notion of myth as a shared story of importance for a group's common identity has shifted in order to make room for intellectual experimentation, discussion, and disagreement, as well as time lags that can introduce both deletions and revisions" (ibid., 205). And more decisive than the precursor teachings being cultivated in accounting for Mark's narrative project are the competitive challenges of the postwar situation, "of multiple incongruities without a temple 'there' in Jerusalem any more, but with a 'king' capable of being compared imaginatively to the divine king of the new city (or even imperium) they were now to call their home" (ibid., 205). Mack's most extensive discussion of social theory can be found in "Explaining Religion: A Theory of Social Interests," and in "Explaining Christian Mythmaking: A Theory of Social Logic," in *The Christian Myth*, 83–99 and 101–25, respectively.

51. Smith refers to privileging language and thought over praxis. In a note on his formulation of "situational incongruity," besides giving a nod to the influence of

affirms, citing Sahlins's position on the "venerable conflict" in Anglo-Saxon anthropology:

> whether the cultural order is to be conceived as the codification of man's actual purposeful and pragmatic action; or whether, conversely, human action in the world is to be understood as mediated by the cultural design, which gives order at once to practical experience, customary practice, and the relationship between the two. The difference is not trivial, nor will it be resolved by the happy academic conclusion that the answer lies somewhere in between, or even on both sides (i.e., dialectically).... The opposition therefore cannot be compromised ... the relation can only be an encompassment.[52]

Ricoeur, he writes, "From one point of view, my formulation, 'perception of incogruity gives rise to thought,' may be thought of as a neo-Kantian rewriting of the Marxist linkage between the perception of contradiction and (revolutionary) action—characteristically privileging thought over praxis" ("When the Chips Are Down," 46 n. 58). Other indications of this privileging are the influence of Neo-Kantian thinkers in distancing himself from certain forms of materialist thought, as well as the rectifying of "explanation" in terms of "translation," instead of limiting explanation to causality (see "Conjectures on Conjunctures," 55–57 with n. 99 and p. 59). Smith suggests the "ways in which Sahlins modified a mode of structuralism to be more responsible to the historical while not relaxing a commitment to the analytical priority of structure" (ibid., 30).

52. Smith, "Conjectures on Conjunctures," 64 n. 111, citing Sahlins, *Culture and Practical Reason*, 55. Smith continues citing Sahlins, now on the latter's translation of Lévi-Strauss's conceptual scheme: "This scheme is the very *organization* of material production; analyzing it, we are in the economic base itself. Its presence there dissolves the classic antinomies of infrastructure and superstructure, the one considered 'material' the other 'conceptual.' Of course, it does not dissolve the 'material' as such. But the so-called material causes must be, *in that capacity*, the product of a symbolic system" (Smith, "Conjectures on Conjunctures," citing *Culture and Practical Reason*, 56–57, emphasis original). Smith follows with his own assessment: "Within one understanding of Marxism, there would be no strain with respect to both Lévi-Strauss's and Sahlins's translation of the relations of infrastructure/superstructure (if 'intellectual' be substituted for 'symbolic'). I would compare these quotations ... to one of Adler's persistent themes: 'Economic phenomena are never "material" in the materialist sense, but have precisely a "mental" character.' I am well aware that others would sharply disagree" ("Conjectures on Conjunctures" 64 n. 111; Smith's quotation is from Adler, *Soziologie des Marxismus*, 3 vols. [Vienna: Europa Verlag, 1965], 1:118, which he suggests comparing to similar sentiments in Adler, *Marx als Denker: Zum 25 Todesjahre von Karl Marx* [Berlin: Buchhandlung Vorwärts, 1908], 8).

This venerable conflict might be regarded as an expression of a post-Cartesian dualism, which has been rejected in contemporary practice theory. Stowers has spelled out (mostly in publications outside the seminar) his own advocacy for a broad pragmatic tradition of philosophy and social theory developed in recent versions of practice theory. Nonetheless, the resolution depends on a human intentionality that is preconceptual and on an encompassment of language and meaning in socially organized practices. In his essay, "The Ontology of Religion," Stowers writes, "I am … convinced by theorists who argue that meaning does not derive from differences, but rather that meaningful differences derive from socially organized human activities, practices.[53] Practices involve linguistic aspects, but language is dependent on the practical understanding and normativity implicit in practices."[54] Pointing to Heidegger's *Being and Time*, Stowers continues:

> The lasting contribution, from the first part of that book, is the persuasive non-Cartesian account of human cognition and human life. He tried to show that "the present at hand" (the *Vorhanden*) is a precipitate of the "ready at hand" (the *Zuhanden*) that is basic. The latter is a kind of preconceptual intentionality that structures human activity with social significance and thus normativity. It is, in Heidegger's jargon, a how-to-use "tools." "Tools" or "equipment" are things that have been given significance by the roles that they play in social practices. The implicit normativity in practices is thus socially instituted and the basis for language.[55]

---

53. Here Stowers references the work of Theodore Schatzki, *The Site of the Social: A Philosophical Account of the Constitution of Social Life and Social Change* (University Park: Pennsylvania State University Press, 2002), 55–58.

54. Stanley Stowers, "The Ontology of Religion," in *Introducing Religion: Essays in Honor of Jonathan Z. Smith*, ed. Willi Braun and Russell T. McCutcheon (London: Equinox, 2008), 437.

55. Ibid., 438–39. According to Stowers, thinkers such as John Dewey, Martin Heidegger, Ludwig Wittgenstein, Theodore Schatzki, and Robert Brandom, among others, "ought to be set into sharp contrast with the neo-Saussurian tradition of discourse ontology" (ibid., 437). Representatives of the latter include the early Foucault, the social ontology of Giles Deleuze and Felix Guatteri, the neo-Marxist and practice-centered theory of Ernesto Laclau and Chantel Mouffe, and the thought of Judith Butler. These discourse theorists are regarded by Stowers "among the best in the highly Cartesian tradition that wants to undermine the tradition without abandoning its basic assumptions" (ibid., 436). For an account of the Cartesian tradition of subjec-

In another essay, Stowers also addresses Smith's prioritizing of language:

> The mode of analysis illustrated in Smith's taxonomy belongs in the tra-
> dition of Ferdinand de Saussure's linguistic theory and of his heirs such
> as Levi-Strauss. The analysis works with the idea of meaningful differ-
> ence. Meaning is the result of placing something in a larger set or system
> of categories. This approach has had spectacular successes in identifying
> the patterns of meaning in particular areas of a culture or in, say, describ-
> ing abstractly how a culture viewed the cosmos or kinship, but it does
> not help very much in understanding either people's active participation
> in the world or people's values. By the latter, I mean proportional value,
> why people value one thing to a greater degree than another.[56]

But Stowers acknowledges that it is not an either/or: "Theorists like
Bourdieu who have attempted a theory of practice have usually incorporated structuralist elements. Smith has also been influenced by Bourdieu
and others who stress activity.[57] It may be correct that to classify is an act
of power but it takes more than schemes of classification to understand
the strategic and open-ended quality of human practices. I believe that
the structures of thought/language/culture that scholars find ultimately
derive from patterns of human activity, from practices."[58] He adds, "This
is the case, even though these patterns of activity are mediated by language and mind."[59]

---

tivity and the post-Cartesian attempts to overcome it, see Stowers, "Paul as a Hero of
Subjectivity," in *Paul and the Philosophers*, ed. Ward Blanton and Hent de Vries (New
York: Fordham University Press, 2013), 159–74.

56. Stanley K. Stowers, "Theorizing the Religion of Ancient Households and
Families," in *Household and Family Religion in Antiquity*, ed. John Bodel and Saul M.
Olyan (Oxford: Blackwell, 2008), 13.

57. Cf. Smith, "When the Chips Are Down," 53 n. 85: "Influenced by Marx, Heidegger, and later by Bourdieu, the notion of activity was, for me, a crucial element
in critiquing what has been termed above 'conservative' approaches to the study of
religion, whether these latter focus on human passivity in the face of the sacred or
passivity before the 'phenomenon.'"

58. Stowers, "Theorizing the Religion," 13.

59. Ibid., 19 n. 40. Maintaining practice to be more basic than language in ontolo-
gizing the social does not of course put Smith in an idealist camp. Nor does Smith's
"structuralism" lead to his treating culture, society, or religion as holistic entities or
organic totalities, especially in light of his preference for polythetic classification (see
Smith, "Fences and Neighbors: Some Contours of Early Judaism," in *Imagining Religion*, 1–18). Nor does Smith's preoccupation with classification reduce to essences,

On Some Fundamental Agreements

While differences of strategy and theory surfaced in the course of our consultation and seminar, and these are matters of some consequence, they did not derail the work of redescription, for two reasons in particular. The most explicit statement of the first reason is presented by Arnal in his opening response to Smith's theory paper in this volume. Rather than theory in the abstract, or sometimes in the field almost as a quest for consensus to some higher truth, a kind of secular theology, Arnal argues that

> theory should operate (in general) as something of a tool, either a way of achieving some sort of handle on a problematic array of data or as a framework for relating diverse phenomena and indicating how those phenomena should be treated. Specifically for the purposes of this seminar, theory … should give us whatever intellectual leverage we need to produce a picture, or set of pictures, of the earliest Jesus people that differs substantially from the Lukan-Eusebian mythic presentation still taken for granted by most scholarship today.[60]

Stowers himself noting that biological morphology undertakes grouping without admitting of essences ("The Concepts of 'Religion', 'Political Religion' and the Study of Nazism," *Journal of Contemporary History* 42 [2007]: 14). Smith also eschews "a conservative, ideological element" characteristic of replication models of myth, rejecting this, "whether it be expressed through phenomenological descriptions of repetition, functionalist descriptions of feedback mechanisms, or structuralist descriptions of mediation" ("Conjectures on Conjunctures," 60 n. 105). Note Smith's discussion of Sahlins's shift from a Saussurean to a Peircean understanding of signs, from the position of the sign in structure to the indexical sign, the sign in action, and, in particular, the question of evaluating actions: "In the colonial system named 'conjuncture' by Sahlins, how do 'signs in action' enable resistance as a mode of response different from both reproduction and transformation? A rebellion, a revolution is not the same as a 'cultural performance', understood as a 'semiotics of identity'" (ibid., 53). Smith has addressed pointed questions to Sahlins's translation of the dynamics of conjuncture/reproduction, transformation/action into both a "materialist discourse" and into a "linguistic discourse" without being "uncomfortable with Sahlins's position" (ibid., 53–54; for the entire discussion of Sahlins's two examples, 51–54 with notes).

60. Arnal, "On Smith, On Myth, On Mark," 146; cf. Smith's remarks on the work of the seminar, "We have at times seemed impatient to move directly from a mode of redescription that 'rectifies the names' to an overarching cultural theory at the expense of clarifying this middle range" [referring to generic conceptualization and generalization where consensual progress is more likely] ("*Dayyeinu*," 485–86). Smith points to examples in the seminar of undertheorized middle range concepts, such as "ethnic

562 CRAWFORD AND MILLER

The second reason is the commitment of members of the seminar to an intellectualist approach to the study of religion, a thoroughgoing naturalism, and to a rational, cognitivist epistemology in developing historical hypotheses, particularly as both are brought together in Smith's program of comparison, which has been central in the work of the seminar from the beginning.[61] This has meant a considered rejection of Romantic traditions of historical study and symbolic-expressive approaches to language and epistemology.[62] It is important to emphasize this orientation,

---

identity" and "epic revision," understood in too self-evident a fashion in discussions found in vol. 1. Both concepts are important in papers of the present volume, and we think have been better theorized. Moreover, Smith's reference to current anthropological debate around questions of time as a measure of value and legitimation residing in duration is at the heart of Sahlins's effort to bring ethnology and history into relation (ibid., 486 with nn. 8–10). Nicholas Thomas's *Out of Time* is a critical response to efforts, including those of Sahlins, to achieve an historical anthropology (see ch. 9, "The Look of Events," 117–22, and the afterword to the 2nd ed., 123–26).

61. Especially in vol. 2, a number of the papers demonstrated the usefulness of the distant analogies presented in Smith's "Re: Corinthians," while also addressing issues left unanswered. And as already indicated, the conclusions drawn in vol. 2, particularly with respect to "community" and "identity," and "social formation" and "mythmaking," have been central for redescription of the Markan site and an estimation of Mark's narrative project in the present volume.

62. See Smith, "Preface," in *Relating Religion*, xi, with reference to "wider inquiries … in Renaissance and Enlightenment anthropology and linguistics, especially as a foil against Romantic theories of cultural production"; Smith, "When the Chips Are Down," 4, where Smith lists five foundational principles learned from reading the work of Cassirer, the first of which is "symbols are not expressive, they are a mode of thought"; in the same essay, by 1959, finding the Romantic ontology and epistemology of phenomenologists and historians of religion "profoundly nonanthropological and antihistorical and … at its base, in curious ways, disturbingly nonrational. Neither Marx nor Kant could be satisfied" (7); and in "Conjectures on Conjunctures," 57, reference to his "overarching interest in interpreting cultural data in terms of thought and language, and an abiding suspicion of arguments from 'experience.'" See Stowers, "Concepts of 'Religion,'" 12: "There have been two major ways of theorizing religion in the modern era widely known as the symbolist or expressive-symbolist and the rational-cognitivist or intellectualist approaches. In my view and the view of many others, the latter has justified itself as the best approach for the human sciences and the former is a failure with a dark legacy…. The rational-cognitivist approach stresses that religious language is not unique or autonomous, but is ordinary language with ordinary propositional content." Attributing a lack of interest in social theory in recent religious studies to a "naive idealism" and "linguistic idealism," Stowers remarks, "It is often assumed that the word 'theory' means Anglo-American readings/appropriations

particularly in light of what is the most extensive and useful published review of the Mack-Smith project and seminar publications (volumes 1 and 2), Hal Taussig's major review essay of ours and other "Christian origins" projects.[63] While the work of the seminar presupposes a critique of positivistic modes of historiography, unlike Taussig—and others in the field, for that matter—we do not think that Mack or Smith, or most other members of the seminar, share the same sense of epistemological crisis in legitimating and carrying out historical projects concerned with the beginnings and early history of Christianity, though the widely influential and salutary effects of postmodernist and poststructuralist critiques of a naive realism and false objectivity in historical study would hardly be denied.[64] However, we would certainly agree with Taussig's concluding

---

of post-structuralist and post-colonialist writers … and related writing in English-speaking literature departments and in 'culture studies.' My point is not that these areas have not made contributions, but that social theory has often been reduced to theory of the subject, text, or discourse" ("Ontology of Religion," 435). Similarly, Stowers, "Theorizing the Religion of Ancient Households," 7, and Smith, "Bible and Religion," in *Relating Religion*, 206. Affirming the productive and necessary structure of disciplinary and interdisciplinary approaches to the academic study of history in the contemporary university, but not the justification for all the alternatives, Stowers writes, "In fact, I think that both positivistic history and history shaped by post-structuralism and post modernism are versions of the same representationalist epistemological stances that unnecessarily lead to mirror dead ends in untenable kinds of realism and idealism" ("History of Ancient Christianity as the Study of Religion," 5), adding, on the study of religion, "In my estimation, the only approach to the study of religion—meaning inquiry about religion rather than the production of religion or the defense of religion—that has proven productive comes from so-called intellectualist approaches and cognitive approaches" (5).

63. Hal Taussig, "The End of Christian Origins? Where to Turn at the Intersection of Subjectivity and Historical Craft," *RBL* 13 (2011): 1–45. Besides our own, Taussig reviews the projects of Elisabeth Schüssler Fiorenza, Judith Lieu, Karen King, Bart Ehrman, N. T. Wright, The Weststar Institute, The Helsinki Collegium, and takes note of "Counterimperial" New Testament criticism and reconstruction in the overlapping work of Richard Horsley, Brigitte Kahl, Warren Carter, and colleagues. Taussig refers several times to Elizabeth A. Castelli's and his co-written essay, "Drawing Large and Startling Figures: Reimagining Christian Origins by Painting like Picasso," in *Reimagining Christian Origins: A Colloquium Honoring Burton L. Mack*, ed. Elizabeth A. Castelli and Hal Taussig (Valley Forge, PA: Trinity Press International, 1996), 3–20, and notes his participation in our seminar.

64. Although Taussig himself does not call for the end of "Christian origins" projects, it is clear that this call by some postmodern- and poststructuralist-oriented

perspective, when stepping back from the "intersection": "Such perspective does catch sight of massive sociocultural and religious enterprises fully invested in the old master narrative of how Christianity began," and further, that "future large-scale and critically formulated pictures of Christian beginnings may remain a relational strategy for challenging the totalizing master narrative."[65]

Taussig makes clear his own theoretical and methodological orientations in reviewing each of the projects in the first part of the essay.[66] The second part of the review features a close alignment of subjectivity and epistemology as the frame for evaluating the various projects.[67] It is not always clear what Taussig intends by "subjectivity" for purposes of evaluating the projects. Is it a philosophical concept and problematic of the post-Cartesian subject; an interdisciplinary concern in the human sciences with agency and identity in contemporary political, psychological, and cultural studies (he does refer to the journal, *Subjectivity*[68]); or a critique of a presumed objectivity in constructions of history? Be that

---

scholars of early Christianity sets up for Taussig the problematic of the current intersection (Taussig, "End of Christian Origins," 1–2 with n. 1). Relevant to the issues raised by Taussig is Ian Brown, "Epistemology and the Production of History: 'History' as a Discipline and Object in the Study of Early Jesus People" (paper presented at the Annual Meeting of the Society of Biblical Literature, San Diego, 24 November 2014, for a NAASR session on the theme, Conceptual Issues in New Testament Scholarship). Similar to the conclusions of Brown's paper, the editors of *Redescribing Paul and the Corinthians*, 302, conclude by emphasizing the conceptual difficulty and intellectual labor required to avoid anachronism in drawing a map of beginnings, a time frame in which it is particularly tempting to cheat: "Such labor is quite a challenge. As a 'theoretically informed practice,' [quotation from Luther H. Martin, "History, Historiography, and Christian Origins: The Jerusalem Community," in Cameron and Miller, *Redescribing Christian Origins*, 264] historiography is a critical method of selection and classification, construction and redescription, explanation and interpretation, and making comparative judgments. The labor of such an imagination is thus a work of argumentation, of making matters consequential, of making them complicated—for 'the historian's task is to complicate'" [quotation from Jonathan Z. Smith, "The Influence of Symbols upon Social Change: A Place on Which to Stand," in *Map Is Not Territory: Studies in the History of Religions*, SJLA 23 (Leiden: Brill, 1978; repr., Chicago: University of Chicago Press, 1993), 129; and Smith, "Map Is Not Territory," in *Map Is Not Territory*, 209]."

65. Taussig, "End of Christian Origins," 45.
66. Ibid., 2–4 with notes, and 4–28.
67. Ibid., 28–43.
68. Ibid., 30 n. 88.

as it may, in applying his criteria, Taussig does not always take sufficient account of a project or a participant's own methodological and theoretical position.[69] For example, while recognizing that Smith's mode of analogical comparison, illustrated in "Re: Corinthians," works across difference, "taking cognitive advantage of the resultant mutual distortion," Taussig's judgment that this demonstrates "a subtle and conscionable subjectivity within historical craft," may say something about Smith's recognition of historical knowledge as a corrigible construction of human thinking.[70] But what is not commented on is what is important for understanding Smith's historical method: the "mutual distortion" is an advantage for gaining historical knowledge, that is, not necessarily how things are but how they may be redescribed, and the place of this mode of comparison in Smith's thoroughly intellectualist anthropology and post-Kantian epistemology. Similarly, Taussig's concern to uncover where "each project pretend[s] an objectivity"[71] may mistake a confidence about the possibilities of redrawing the map of Christian origins, an intentionally generalizing discourse and determination to report results, and an acceptance of the costs and entailments of a theory for a false objectivity in the construction of historical knowledge.[72] Again, not everyone who recognizes that objects of

---

69. Let it be said, however, that Taussig has brought together for review an array of differing projects conducted in terms of very different issues and concerns, as well as on different assumptions and theoretical grounds.

70. Ibid., 37.

71. Ibid., 42.

72. According to Taussig, "The passion of Mack's contemporary commentary and the playfulness of Smith provide similar caveats to the rather steady objectivist tone of the SBL Seminar and its publications" (ibid., 42–43). We were ourselves more conscious of internal debate within the seminar, though, to be fair, Taussig has not missed this (ibid., 38). Smith concluded his metareflection, "*Dayyeinu*," in vol. 1 on this note: "If these challenges be addressed by the Seminar in a way that clarifies fundamental assumptions, that acknowledges and respects a given theory's intellectual costs and entailments, but results in reaching no final consensus—*dayyeinu*" (486–87). With respect to the "anguished subjectivity" of Mack's contemporary commentary (Taussig, "End of Christian Origins," 37), in the context of his more recent project and books on the formation of a Christian mentality and mythic grammar and its persistence into the twentieth and twenty first centuries, anyone familiar with Mack's responses to reviews of his work at annual meeting sessions of the Society of Biblical Literature Ideological Criticism Section (New Orleans, 2009; Chicago, 2012) will know that he is keenly aware of a current academic climate that rejects grand narratives, the postmodern fascination with the problem of the autonomous subject, and the consequences

historical knowledge are not simply out there or given but are constructed, situated, and corrigible is equally compelled by the notion of a postmodern crisis of historical knowledge.[73]

---

for his own mode of theorizing a social anthropology. But this postmodern intellectual climate and the current appeal of "learn[ing] to live and work with fragments" (Taussig, "End of Christian Origins," 43) is also seen by Mack as part of what accounts for an inability to articulate a thoroughgoing critique of US discourse and practice or imagine a comprehensive picture of a sustainable social world. His most recent books are *Myth and the Christian Nation: A Social Theory of Religion*, Religion in Culture: Studies in Social Context and Construction (London: Equinox, 2008); *Christian Mentality: The Entanglements of Power, Violence, and Fear*, Religion in Culture: Studies in Social Context and Construction (London: Equinox, 2011); and *The Rise and Fall of the Christian Myth: Restoring Our Democratic Ideals* (New Haven: Yale University Press, 2017). On "strong historical-critical loyalties in Mack-Smith" and vulnerability "to speaking from above as objective authorities" (Taussig, "End of Christian Origins," 42), see Arnal's reflexive statement on the historical location and natural bias of the seminar project in "On Smith, On Myth, On Mark," 148–51. At the same time, one can hardly ignore the rich history of debate and contestation, and not just hardened consensus, that comes out of these loyalties. To the point, the paper by Walsh in this volume is a critique of the Romantic heritage of historical-critical scholarship, applied in particular to Q; but the problem as she sees it is not with the objectivist pretensions of historical criticism but with scholarship that is not historical-critical enough. In her judgment, the data do not support widely-held views of the production, date, and circles of the provenance of Q.

73. On the significance and characterization of Smith's "Re: Corinthians" in the context of vol. 2, Taussig remarks, "But the Seminar volume's paean to Smith's essay misses both Smith's own clear deconstructive irony in comparing first-century Corinth to twentieth-century Papua New Guinea and the complex task of recalibrating Paul's place in early Christianity" ("End of Christian Origins," 12). Whatever the shortcomings of the volume's editors or the possibilities of doing something more useful, Smith's essay is not an exercise in deconstructive irony but an exercise in redescription. What is ironic is to miss how productive Smith's analogy was for other papers in the volume as well, because what might be brought to light in the ancient context for "some" Corinthians might not be illuminating for others, where the mutual distortion of a distant analogy opens a different set of questions and leads to a quite different set of insights. As a colloborative project, the volume was actually organized around the recognition of different "social fractions" among the Corinthians. More important, Smith's "distancing" from the projects in which he participates is not a function of his epistemology or of deconstructive irony but of his self-description as a generalist in the field of religion. "As one who claims to be a generalist, I determined early on, at Chicago, that this entailed doing work in relation to the agenda of others.... The question has always been what generalizing or comparative perspective could be brought to issues and to data stipulated as representing their interests. Thus my work represents less of a coher-

Nonetheless, Taussig has recognized, and even highlighted, strengths of the seminar on his own terms: "The Mack-Smith collegia have come closer to such intersubjective epistemological address than any other effort." This judgment is based on "the astounding partnership of Mack and Smith that brings together a leading New Testament scholar and the dean of the history of religions of the last two decades; and the assembling of a strong body of diverse biblical scholars in the three levels of the SBL project [consultation, seminar, and group] for well over a decade."[74] Taussig begins his discussion by noting that "this project represents the most published and written work on Christian origins by a single effort in the past thirty years."[75] He has also included the Society of Biblical Literature Redescribing Early Christianity Group in some of his assessments and writes, "It is not yet clear how much this Group represents continuation of earlier interests, departure from the basics of social formation/mythmaking, and/or projects complementary to the earlier Seminar and volumes."[76] These several comments and assessments are of interest to the editors of this volume in providing a lead for our own sense of the intersection—though not the crisis—of the older seminar and the successor groups, which includes the current Redescription of Early Christianity Seminar (2013–present).

A Recommendation

The Society of Biblical Literature successor groups have organized and conducted their sessions at the annual meetings in ways that are quite different from the operation of the older seminar. The programs are organized and the themes change, mostly from year to year and usually with a different theme for each session. Some of the leadership, the interests and theoretical commitments, and of course the focus on "redescription" of early Christianity as a project within the broader field of religious studies, are closely related to the older seminar.[77] But the successor groups have

---

ent system than it does a series of continuing foci, hence 'Preoccupations'" ("When the Chips Are Down," 11).

74. Taussig, "End of Christian Origins," 38.

75. Ibid., 6.

76. Ibid., 13.

77. On programs of mutual interest organized by NAASR, see 538 with n. 4 above. It is worth noting that increasingly at the annual meetings one sees sessions

also expanded the temporal scope of the project, adopted some different strategies of redescription, given more attention to cognitive science,[78] and reconsidered certain concepts as descriptive categories,[79] while problematizing other standard methods and categories of historical-critical study.[80] What is most obvious, the successor groups have been able to engage the contributions of a wider range of scholars and perspectives than the older seminar, including several whose projects are treated in Taussig's review.[81] Our retrospective remarks in this concluding piece have been intended to take note of continuity, overlap, and feedback between the older seminar and the successor groups, which, to be sure, is easier to discern and partly attributable to the extended time of publication of the seminar materials beyond the dates of the seminar sessions, a not entirely regrettable circumstance for this purpose. But by comparison to the successor groups, certain limitations of the older seminar are obvious. The narrower temporal scope eliminated some scholars whom we had invited to participate; others found themselves uncomfortable with the theoretical assumptions and methodological commitments of the seminar, which were made quite

---

jointly sponsored by American Academy of Religion and Society of Biblical Literature program units.

78. For example, the session of the Redescribing Early Christianity Seminar on the theme, Evolutionary and Cognitive Approaches to Early Christianity at the Annual Meeting in San Diego, 2014. The potential of the cognitive science of religion for the redescription of early Christianity was already represented by some members of the older seminar.

79. For example, the session of the Redescribing Early Christianity Group on the theme, Experience as a Descriptive Category in the Study of Early Christianity at the Annual Meeting in New Orleans, 2009, not exactly a reconsideration one would have expected in the context of the older seminar.

80. Rectification of Categories for the Study of Early Christianity, the theme of a session of the Society of Biblical Literature redescribing Group at the Annual Meeting in Atlanta, 2010; and Disaggregating the Concept of Community, the theme of a session of the same Group in San Francisco, 2011. The current Society of Biblical Literature Seminar took up the theme, Redescribing the Problem and Concept of Sin, at the Annual Meeting in Baltimore, 2013.

81. A paper by Karen King and responses by Judith Lieu and Elizabeth Castelli were featured in a session of the Society of Biblical Literature Group at the Annual Meeting in Chicago, 2012, on the theme, Redescribing the Discourses of Sacrifice and Martyrdom in Early Christian Cultural Formation. Members of the Helsinki Collegium presented papers in the current Society of Biblical Literature Seminar in San Diego, 2014; see above, n. 78.

explicit. Some recognized that participation demanded a sustained commitment over a period of years that could not be coordinated with their own scholarly projects.

But the limitations of scope and participation also serve to highlight comparative strengths of the older seminar. It was conceived as a collaborative research project, though obviously meeting only in two sessions once a year could not be optimal for the purpose. The project began with an assessment of the potential and problematic of much New Testament scholarship in the first year of the consultation. It aimed at testing a hypothesis, which was not simply to extend the work of Mack but to test whether his categories of mythmaking and social formation could serve the interests of redescribing the major social-textual sites of the dominant paradigm of Christian origins. The seminar also aimed at constructing a discourse that could translate specialized research into a generalist's commitment to the study of religion. The sustained participation and guidance of Mack and Smith, as well as the sustained commitment and repeated contributions of other members of the seminar, were advantages in keeping track over the years of what we were doing and where we differed. The seminar was sufficiently experimental to allow scholars "to try things out" without producing publishable papers for the sessions. But the seminar was also committed to evaluating and publishing its work as a collaborative project. The editors of the publications were given the assignment of writing up the "so what?" of the volumes as collaborative efforts, while being responsible to the individual contributions. These assignments were carried out with care, whether the judgments of the editors were in every case acceptable to the contributors, and even if the conclusions as a collaborative project were for the most part ignored in reviews.

So, the older seminar and successor groups have some differing strengths and limitations. We call attention to them because there has been a proposal for the study of early Christianity as religion that we think merits a sustained collaborative application and testing more comparable to the conception, organization, and goals of the older seminar than to the more diverse program and participation of the successor groups, which does not lend itself as well to an accounting of debate, assessment, and results in publications. We have reference to the proposal of Stowers presented in its most programmatic form in his paper, "The History of Ancient Christianity as the Study of Religion." It is precisely a proposal to normalize the study of early Christianity in the university by conjoining the craft of the historian and the academic study of religion, classifying ancient Judaism and Christianity reflexively as examples of ancient Mediterranean and West Asian religion.[82] The proposal formulates an attainable goal for the project. This programmatic paper is by no means the only place where the lineaments of the project are found. Stowers proposes a polythetic definition of religion, which distinguishes religious practices from other forms of cultural practice. He presents a typology of ancient Mediterranean and West Asian religious practices that is viable without being rigid, spells out a social ontology grounded in a theory of practice and a methodology of disaggregating social wholes in favor of more careful tracking of normal social processes.[83]

We have already remarked on the influence of Stowers's proposals on the older seminar, including the current volume, as well as his proposals for the successor groups, not only in the form of his own contributions but even more substantially in the contributions of his former students. But we are suggesting that his proposals constitute a major project which is better served by a collaborative and more sustained application, testing, critique, and accounting of results in publication than is feasible in the

---

82. The oddity of the classification of early Christianity has been remarked on by William Arnal, who points to the section on history in the very useful volume edited by Sarah Iles Johnston, ed., *Religions of the Ancient World: A Guide* (Cambridge; London: Harvard University Press, 2004). The histories are organized entirely by region with the exception of Early Christianity, giving the impression of the latter as "a separate, free-standing entity, engaged with, but not to be confused with, the cultures of the Mediterranean world." The observation appears in the printed version of Arnal, "The King Lecture" (an Annual Lecture sponsored by the Department of Philosophy, Washburn University, Topeka, KS, 24 April 2013), 1–2.

83. In his programmatic paper delivered at the NAASR session, Stowers carefully distinguishes criteria for what constitutes *religious practice*, a type of human activity, from criteria for defining what constitutes *a religion*, a set of social formations ("History of Ancient Christianity as the Study of Religion," 10–11). Stowers's typology of religious practices is presented in more detail in "Theorizing the Religion of Ancient Households" and in "The Religion of Plant and Animal Offerings Versus the Religion of Meanings, Essences, and Textual Mysteries," in *Ancient Mediterranean Sacrifice: Images, Acts, Meanings*, ed. Jennifer Wright Knust and Zsuzsanna Várhelyi (Oxford: Oxford University Press, 2011), 35–56. For Stowers's rejection of the Romantic tradition of theorizing religion, see esp. "Concepts of 'Religion'" and "Paul as a Hero of Subjectivity," and for social ontology and practice theory, esp., "Ontology of Religion." Responses to Stowers's proposals and to his examples of the study of early Christianity as the study of religion can be found in many of the papers in Hodge et al., *"The One Who Sows Bountifully."*

format of the current Society of Biblical Literature Seminar or in individual research projects. We should be clear that we assume that there
would be considerable cross-fertilization between such a collaborative
project and the current seminar. We should be equally clear that in no
way are we suggesting that the greater range of themes and issues and the
more diverse participation characteristic of the successor groups should
be discontinued. On the contrary, we think participation should be open,
especially to younger scholars and to a variety of theoretical approaches
where these can be considered on grounds of contributing to the historical
task of redescription. As an example, we point to an unpublished paper by
Maia Kotrosits, "Diaspora Theory and the End of 'Early Christianity' and
'Early Christian Identity,' " presented at a session of the current seminar.[84]
Whatever one might want to ask about the relationship of Kotrosits's theoretical orientations to social and practice theory as it has more typically
been articulated and debated in the older seminar and in the successor
groups, there is no question about the contribution of the paper to historical issues of "early Christianity" concerned with problematizing a notion
of Christian identity formation. As noted earlier, these issues are in play
in the conclusions of volume 2 and in the papers in this volume, and they
have been given further emphasis and scope in sessions of the successor
groups. But Kotrosits goes further, not only in questioning the descriptive
usefulness of the term and its role in promoting an untenable historical
teleology, but in presenting an alternative with better prospects for engaging the texture and intertextuality of this early literature. "I want to suggest
that without the term 'Christian' as the implicit and primary descriptor for
New Testament and affiliated literature, one of the historical possibilities
that materializes is an expanded archive of ancient diaspora social formations around the entity of 'Israel.' "[85] Kotrosits does not mean by this "diasporic Israel" primarily a separation from homeland but the construction
of homeland out of circumstances of trauma and loss and the experiences
and contestations over belonging and not belonging as a consequence, that
is, a diasporic imaginary.[86]

---

84. Maia Kotrosits, "Diaspora Theory and the End of 'Early Christianity' and
'Early Christian Identity'" (paper delivered at the Annual Meeting of the Society of
Biblical Literature, San Diego, 23 November 2014). The theme of the session was
Social and Practice Theory in the Redescription of Early Christianity.

85. Ibid., 3.

86. Ibid., 4–5. For her published work of broader scope and theory, see Maia

If this recommendation seems to many in our field still to be a benighted love affair with "origins," and not yet fully enlightened by the obstacles to "big picture" historical ventures, nor yet fully cognizant of the "real" subject and context of our redescriptions (or our reimaginings)—Taussig is correct to point out that failing to dislodge the dominant Lukan-Eusebian paradigm of Christian origins does not mean that everyone in the guild is enamored of it; some have given up on that historical project as unviable or uninteresting or perhaps have come to recognize that there are other things to do in biblical studies.[87] Well then, we also have our critics close by: Russ McCutcheon chides us, asking "Why do you seek the living among the dead?";[88] Mack points us away from the

---

Kotrosits, *Rethinking Early Christian Identity: Affect, Violence, and Belonging* (Minneapolis: Fortress Press, 2015). In connection with Kotrosits's proposals, it is worth noting what Burton Mack wrote concerning a possible Jesus school in Jerusalem: "The issues raised for Jews by the Jesus legacy had much to do with Jewish identity (I was tempted to say 'belonging to Israel'), little with loyalties or markers pertinent to self-definition as a Jesus school or Christ cult" (and see the entire passage, Mack, "A Jewish Jesus School in Jerusalem?," in Cameron and Miller, *Redescribing Christian Origins*, 257; cf. in the same volume, Merrill P. Miller, "Antioch, Paul, and Jerusalem: Diaspora Myths of Origins in the Homeland," 177–235). What Mack suggested with respect to "the pillars" in Jerusalem he observed more broadly as an underlying commonality of diverse social formations and diverse mythic rationales among Jews in the Greco-Roman world: "The project was to reimagine and reinvent the collective (in this case, 'Israel') in a form appropriate for the larger human horizon of the Greco-Roman age" (*Christian Myth*, 211; a similar observation on the Gospel of Mark as an instance of epic revision appears in Mack, "Cartwheels," 140–42).

87. Taussig reiterates his view of the current epistemological challenge to "big picture" historical ventures in his contribution to the American Academy of Religion Review Essay Roundtable, Review Essay of *A Myth of Innocence: Mark and Christian Origins* by Burton L. Mack, *JAAR* 83 (2015): 851–57. On "the big picture" as cultural criticism, see Mack, *Rise and Fall of the Christian Myth*.

88. The reference is to McCutcheon's paper, "Why Do You Seek the Living among the Dead?" (presented at the Annual Meeting of the Society of Biblical Literature, Baltimore, 25 November 2013) for a session of the current Society of Biblical Literature Seminar on the theme, What Does It Mean to "Explain" Earliest Christianity? The published version of this paper with an introduction and appendix is Russell T. McCutcheon, "Why Do You Seek the Living among the Dead? (Luke 24:5)," in *A Modest Proposal on Method: Essaying the Study of Religion*, MTSRSup 2 (Leiden: Brill, 2015), 119–39. McCutcheon urges us to move from championing the polygenesis of Christian origins, and even from demonstrating the second century's invention of the first, to "a reconsidered approach to origins in general, and attempts to talk about the

earliest literature, as though there were some beginnings of great moment to be found there, to the beginnings that hold particular relevance for his current projects of cultural critique, the world of Constantine as a foundation of medieval Christendom, that is, the time from which Christianity can be thought of as "in charge" of a full-orbed society; and of course there is Smith, whose proposals for biblical studies as "trajectories of traditions, comparisons, ethnographies," a redescription of biblical studies as religious studies, are clearly distanced from any priority let alone fascination with "origins."[89]

---

origins of some coherent thing called Christianity in particular [that] might shift our scholarly attention from those ancient writers and their now-torn manuscripts to the work done by our own hands and our own pens (or better, our laptops and desktop computer) in imagining them to begin with" (123); cf. Jonathan Z. Smith on the contrasting situations of the philosopher and the historian: "There is for him [the historian] no real beginning, but only the plunge which he takes at some arbitrary point to avoid the unhappy alternatives of infinite regress or silence" ("Influence of Symbols upon Social Change," 129); and Marshall Sahlins on "Heraclitus vs. Herodotus": "Such is the flux that one can never step in the same culture twice. Yet unless identity and consistency were symbolically imposed on social practices, as also on rivers, and not only by anthropologists but by the people, there could be no intelligibility or even sanity, let alone a society. So to paraphrase John Barth, reality is a nice place to visit (philosophically), but no one ever lived there" (*Waiting for Foucault, Still*, 4th ed. (Chicago: Prickly Paradigm Press, 2002), 7, cited more fully in Smith, "Conjectures on Conjunctures," 43 n. 67.

89. The reference in particular is to Smith's Society of Biblical Literature Presidential Address, "Religion and Bible," *JBL* 128 (2009): 5–27. Smith has commented on the richness of the archive of the biblical field. "There are few fields within the human sciences that take as part of their normal activities so keen a sense of their own history of scholarship. In most areas, students of religion who seek to describe not only the situation of the phenomenon in question, but also the placement of that phenomenon in *our* discourse, must reconstruct that history for themselves, often lacking even the most rudimentary bibliographical tool.... By contrast, biblical studies has preserved, and constantly rehearses and reconfigures, an unusually thick dossier of the history of its enterprise" (27). Smith then adds, referring to the two essays to which he was responding, "Unfortunately, to use a term employed in both essays, what this history displays is more often a case of 'magic' than of science" ("Social Formations of Early Christianities," 271, emphasis original).

Bibliography

Aberle, David. "A Note on Relative Deprivation Theory as Applied to Millenarian and Other Cult Movements." Pages 209–14 in *Millennial Dreams in Action*. Edited by S. L. Thrupp. The Hague: Mouton, 1962.

Achtemeier, Paul J. "Toward the Isolation of Pre-Markan Miracle Catenae." *JBL* 89 (1970): 265–91.

Adler, Max. *Ausgewählte Schriften*. Edited by A. Pfabigan and N. Leser. Quellen und Studien zur österreichischen Geistesgeschichte im 19. und 20. Jahrhundert 2. Vienna: Österreichischer Bundesverlag, 1981.

———. *Austro-Marxism*. Edited and translated by Tom Bottomore and Patrick Goode. London: Oxford University Press, 1978.

———. *Das Soziologie in Kants Erkenntniskritik: Ein Beitrag zur Auseinandersetzung zwischen Naturalismus und Kritizismus*. Vienna: Verlag der Wiener Volksbuchhandlung, 1924.

———. *Kant und der Marxismus*. Berlin: E. Laub, 1925.

———. *Marx als Denker: Zum 25 Todesjahre von Karl Marx*. Berlin: Buchhandlung Verwärts, 1908.

———. *Soziologie des Marxismus*. 3 vols. Vienna: Europa Verlag, 1964.

Alexander, Jeffrey C. "Toward a Theory of Cultural Trauma." Pages 1–30 in *Cultural Trauma and Collective Identity*, by Jeffrey C. Alexander, Ron Eyerman, Bernard Giessen, Neil J. Smelser, and Piotr Sztompka. Berkeley: University of California Press, 2004.

Allison, Dale C., Jr. *The End of the Ages Has Come: An Early Interpretation of the Passion and Resurrection of Jesus*. Philadelphia: Fortress, 1985.

———. *The Jesus Tradition in Q*. Harrisburg, PA: Trinity Press International, 1997.

Althusser, Louis. "Conjoncture philosophique et recherché philosophique marxiste." Pages 394–415 in vol. 2 of *Écrits philosophiques et politiques*. Edited by F. Matheron. Paris: Stock: IMEC, 1994–1995.

———. "Contradiction and Overdetermination." Pages 87–116 in *For Marx*. Translated by Ben Brewster. London: Allen Lane, 1969. Repr.,

New York: Vintage Books, 1970. Repr., London: NLB, 1977. Repr., London: Verso, 1979.

———. "Le courant souterrain du matérialisme de la rencontre." Pages 539–76 in vol. 1 of *Écrits philosophiques et politiques*. Edited by F. Macheron. Paris: Stock: IMEC, 1994–1995.

———. *For Marx*. Translated by Ben Brewster. London: Allen Lane, 1969. Translation of *Pour Marx*. Théorie 1. Paris: Maspero, 1965.

———. "Ideology and Ideological State Apparatuses: Notes Toward an Investigation." Pages 127–86 in *Lenin and Philosophy and Other Essays*. London: NLB, 1971.

———. "Letter to the Translator." Pages 323–24 in *Reading Capital*, by Louis Althusser and Étienne Balibar. Translated by Ben Brewster. London: NLB, 1970.

———. *Machiavelli and Us*. Edited by F. Matheron. Translation and introduction by Gregory Elliot. London: Verso, 1999. Translation of "Machiavel et nous." Pages 42–161 in vol. 2 of *Écrits philosophiques et politiques*. Edited by F. Matheron. Paris: Stock: IMEC, 1994–1995.

———. "Machiavelli's Solitude." Pages 115–30 in *Machiavelli and Us*. Edited by F. Matheron. Translation and introduction by Gregory Elliot. London: Verso, 1999.

———. "On the Marxist Dialectic." Pages 161–218 in *For Marx*. Translated by Ben Brewster. London: Allen Lane, 1969. Repr., New York: Vintage Books, 1970. Repr., London: NLB, 1977. Repr., London: Verso, 1979.

———. "To My English Readers." Pages 9–16 in *For Marx*. Translated by Ben Brewster. London: Allen Lane, 1969. Repr., New York: Vintage Books, 1970. Repr., London: NLB, 1977. Repr., London: Verso, 1979.

———. *The Spectre of Hegel: Early Writings*. London: Blackwell, 1997; London: Verso, 1997.

Althusser, Louis, and Étienne Balibar. *Reading Capital*. Translated by Ben Brewster. London: NLB, 1970.

Anderson, Andrew Runni. "Heracles and His Successors." *HSCP* 39 (1928): 7–58.

Anderson, Benedict. "Exodus." *Critical Inquiry* 20 (1994): 314–27.

Andrade, Nathanael J. "Ambiguity, Violence, and Community in the Cities of Judaea and Syria." *Historia* 59 (2010): 342–70.

———. *Syrian Identity in the Greco-Roman World*. Cambridge: Cambridge University Press, 2013.

Ariel, Donald T. "A Survey of Coin Finds in Jerusalem (Until the End of Byzantine Period)." *LASBF* 32 (1982): 273–326.

Armstrong, David, Jeffrey Fish, Patricia A. Johnson and Marilyn B. Skinner, eds. *Vergil, Philodemus and the Augustans*. Austin: University of Texas Press, 2004.

Arnal, William E. "Approaches to the Study of Religion: Introducing Graduate Students to Religious Studies." *MTSR* 11 (1999): 107–18.

———. "Black Holes, Theory, and the Study of Religion." *SR* 30 (2001): 209–14.

———. "Blessed Are the Solitary: Textual Practices and the Mirage of a *Thomas* 'Community.'" Pages 271–81 in *"The One Who Sows Bountifully": Essays in Honor of Stanley K. Stowers*. Edited by Caroline Johnson Hodge, Saul M. Olyan, Daniel Ullucci, and Emma Wasserman. BJS 356. Providence, RI: Brown Judaic Studies, 2013.

———. "The Collection and Synthesis of 'Tradition' and the Second-Century Invention of Christianity." Paper presented at the Annual Meeting of the Society of Biblical Literature. San Diego, 17 November 2007. Published with revisions in *MTSR* 23 (2011): 193–215.

———. "Doxa, Heresy, and Self-Construction: The Pauline *Ekklēsiai* and the Boundaries of Urban Identities." Pages 50–101 in *Heresy and Identity in Late Antiquity*. Edited by Eduard Iricinschi and Holger M. Zellentin. TSAJ 119. Tübingen: Mohr Siebeck, 2008.

———. "The Gospel of Mark as Reflection on Exile and Identity." Pages 57–67 in *Introducing Religion: Essays in Honor of Jonathan Z. Smith*. Edited by Willi Braun and Russell T. McCutcheon. London: Equinox, 2008.

———. *Jesus and the Village Scribes: Galilean Conflicts and the Setting of Q*. Minneapolis: Fortress, 2001.

———. "The King Lecture." Annual Lecture of the Department of Philosophy, Washburn University. Topeka, KS, 24 April 2013.

———. "Major Episodes in the Biography of Jesus: Methodological Observations on the Historicity of the Narrative Tradition." *TJT* 13 (1997): 201–26.

———. "The Parable of the Tenants and the Class Consciousness of the Peasantry." Pages 135–57 in *Text and Artifact in the Religions of Mediterranean Antiquity: Essays in Honour of Peter Richardson*. Edited by Stephen G. Wilson and Michel Desjardins. Waterloo, ON: Wilfrid Laurier University Press, 2000.

———. "A Parting of the Ways? *Scholarly* Identities and a Peculiar Species of Ancient Mediterranean Religion." Pages 253–75 in *Identity and Interaction in the Ancient Mediterranean: Jews, Christians and Others;*

Essays in Honour of Stephen G. Wilson. Edited by Zeba A. Crook and Philip A. Harland. New Testament Monographs 18. Sheffield: Sheffield Phoenix, 2007.

———. "Redactional Fabrication and Group Legitimation: The Baptist's Preaching in Q 3:7–9, 16–17." Pages 165–80 in *Conflict and Invention: Literary, Rhetorical, and Social Studies on the Sayings Gospel Q.* Edited by John S. Kloppenborg. Valley Forge, PA: Trinity Press International, 1995.

———. Review Essay Roundtable of *A Myth of Innocence: Mark and Christian Origins* by Burton L. Mack. *JAAR* 83 (2015): 837–41.

———. "What Branches Grow Out of This Stony Rubbish? Christian Origins and the Study of Religion." *SR* 39 (2010): 549–72.

———. "Why Q Failed: From Ideological Project to Group Formation." Pages 67–87 in *Redescribing Christian Origins.* Edited by Ron Cameron and Merrill P. Miller. SymS 28. Atlanta: Society of Biblical Literature, 2004.

Arnal, William E., and Russell T. McCutcheon. "The Origins of Christianity Within, and Without, 'Religion': A Case Study." Pages 134–70 in *The Sacred Is the Profane: The Political Nature of "Religion,"* by William E. Arnal and Russell T. McCutcheon. Oxford: Oxford University Press, 2013.

Arnal, William E., and Willi Braun. "Social Formation and Mythmaking: Theses on Key Terms." Pages 459–67 in *Redescribing Christian Origins.* Edited by Ron Cameron and Merrill P. Miller. SymS 28. Atlanta: Society of Biblical Literature, 2004.

Arnim, Hans von. *Stoicorum Veterum Fragmenta.* Leipzig: Teubner, 1903–1924.

Ascough, Richard S. "Matthew and Community Formation." Pages 96–126 in *The Gospel of Matthew in Current Study: Studies in Memory of William G. Thompson S. J.* Edited by David Aune. Grand Rapids: Eerdmans, 2001.

Aubet, Maria Eugenia. *The Phoenicians and the West: Politics, Colonies, and Trade.* Cambridge: Cambridge University Press, 1993.

Auerbach, Erich. "Figura." *Archivum Romanicum* 22 (1938): 436–89.

Aune, David E. "Genre Theory and the Genre-Function of Mark and Matthew." Pages 145–75 in *Mark and Matthew I: Comparative Readings; Understanding the Earliest Gospels in Their First-Century Settings.* Edited by Eve-Marie Becker and Anders Runesson. WUNT 271. Tübingen: Mohr Siebeck, 2011.

———. "Heracles and Christ: Heracles Imagery in the Christology of Early Christianity." Pages 3–19 in *Greeks, Romans, and Christians: Essays in Honor of Abraham J. Malherbe.* Edited by David L. Balch, Everett Ferguson, and Wayne Meeks. Minneapolis: Fortress, 1990.

———. "Herakles." *DDD*: 402–5.

Aus, Roger David. *"Caught in the Act," Walking on the Sea, and the Release of Barabbas Revisited.* SFSHJ 157. Atlanta: Scholars Press, 1998.

———. *Feeding the Five Thousand: Studies in the Judaic Background of Mk 6:30–44 par. and John 6: 1–15.* Studies in Judaism. Lanham, MD: University Press of America, 2010.

———. *My Name Is "Legion": Palestinian Judaic Traditions in Mark 5:1–20 and Other Gospel Texts.* Studies in Judaism. Lanham, MD: University Press of America, 2003.

———. *The Stilling of the Storm: Studies in Early Palestinian Judaic Tradition.* International Studies in Formative Christianity and Judaism. Binghamton, NY: Global Publications, Binghamton University, 2000.

Avemarie, Friedrich. Review of *The Relationship Between Roman and Local Law in the Babatha and Salome Komaise Archives: General Analysis and Three Case Studies of Succession, Guardianship and Marriage*, by Jacobine G. Oudshoorn. *JSJ* 40 (2009): 126–27.

Avidov, Avi. *Not Reckoned among Nations: The Origins of the So-Called "Jewish Question" in Roman Antiquity.* TSAJ 128. Tübingen: Mohr Siebeck, 2009.

Bailey, Anne M., and Josep R. Llobera. "The Asiatic Mode of Production, An Annotated Bibliography." *Critique of Anthropology* 2 (1974): 95–107; 4–5 (1975): 165–76.

Baker, Cynthia M. " 'From Every Nation under Heaven': Jewish Ethnicities in the Greco-Roman World." Pages 79–99 in *Prejudice and Christian Beginnings: Investigating Race, Gender, and Ethnicity in Early Christian Studies.* Edited by Laura Nasrallah and Elisabeth Schüssler Fiorenza. Minneapolis: Fortress, 2009.

———. "A Jew by Any Other Name?" *JAJ* 2 (2011): 153–80.

Balibar, Étienne. "Elements for a Theory of Transition." Pages 273–309 in *Reading Capital*, by Louis Althusser and Étienne Balibar. Translated by Ben Brewster. London: NLB, 1970.

———. "L'objet d'Althusser." Pages 81–116 in *Politique et philosophie dans l'oeuvre de Louis Althusser.* Paris: Presses universitaires de France, 1993.

Baltzer, Klaus. *Die Biographie der Propheten.* Neukirchen-Vluyn: Neukirchener Verlag, 1975.

Barclay, John M. G. "Constructing Judean Identity after 70 CE: A Study of Josephus's *Against Apion*." Pages 99–112 in *Identity and Interaction in the Ancient Mediterranean: Jews, Christians and Others; Essays in Honour of Stephen G. Wilson*. Edited by Zeba A. Crook and Philip A. Harland. New Testament Monographs 18. Sheffield: Sheffield Phoenix, 2007.

———. "'Jews' and 'Christians' in the Eyes of Roman Authors c. 100 CE." Pages 313–26 in *Jews and Christians in the First and Second Centuries: How to Write Their History*. CRINT 13. Edited by Peter J. Tomson and Joshua Schwartz. Leiden: Brill, 2014.

———. *Jews in the Mediterranean Diaspora from Alexander to Trajan (323 BCE–117 CE)*. Edinburgh: T&T Clark, 1996.

———. "Judean Historiography in Rome: Josephus and History in *Contra Apionem* Book 1." Pages 29–43 in *Josephus and Jewish History in Flavian Rome and Beyond*. Edited by Joseph Sievers and Gaia Lembi. JSJSup 104. Leiden: Brill, 2005.

Barkun, Michael. *Disaster and the Millennium*. New Haven. Yale University Press, 1974.

Barth, Hans. *Truth and Ideology*. Translated by F. Lilge. Berkeley: University of California Press, 1976.

Barthes, Roland. "The Death of the Author." Pages 142–48 in *Image-Music-Text*. Translated by Stephen Heath. New York: Macmillan, 1977.

Bazzana, Giovanni Battista. *Kingdom of Bureaucracy: The Political Theology of Village Scribes in the Sayings Gospel Q*. BETL 274. Leuven: Peeters, 2015.

Beare, Frank W. *The Earliest Records of Jesus*. New York; Nashville: Abingdon, 1962.

Becker, Eve-Marie. "The Gospel of Mark in the Context of Ancient Historiography." Pages 124–34 in *The Function of Ancient Historiography in Biblical and Cognate Studies*. Edited by Patricia G. Kirkpatrick and Timothy Goltz. LHBOTS 489. New York: T&T Clark, 2008.

———. *Das Markus-Evangelium im Rahmen antiker Historiographie*. WUNT 194. Tübingen: Mohr Siebeck, 2006.

———. "The Reception of 'Mark' in the 1st and 2nd Centuries C.E. and Its Significance for Genre Studies." Pages 15–36 in *Mark and Matthew II: Comparative Readings; Reception History, Cultural Hermeneutics, and Theology*. Edited by Eve-Marie Becker and Anders Runesson. WUNT 304. Tübingen: Mohr Siebeck, 2013.

Becker, Eve-Marie, Jan Dochhorn, and Else K. Holt, eds. *Trauma and Traumatization in Individual and Collective Dimensions: Insights from Biblical Studies and Beyond*. Studia Aarhusiana Neotestamentica 2. Göttingen: Vandenhoeck & Ruprecht, 2014.

Bellwood, Peter. *Man's Conquest of the Pacific: The Prehistory of Southeast Asia and Oceania*. Auckland: Collins, 1978.

Benveniste, Émile. *Problems in General Linguistics*. Translated by M. E. Meek. Coral Gables: University of Miami Press, 1971. Translation of vol. 1 of *Problèmes de linguistique générale*. Paris: Gallimard, 1966–1974.

Bennett, Andrew. "Expressivity: The Romantic." Pages 48–58 in *Literary Theory and Criticism: An Oxford Guide*. Edited by Patricia Waugh. Oxford: Oxford University Press, 2006.

Berchem, Denis van. "Sanctuaires d'Hercule-Melqart: Contribution á l'étude de l'expansion phénicienne en Mediterranée." *Syria* 44 (1967): 73–109.

Bercovitch, Eytan. "The Altar of Sin: Social Multiplicity and Christian Conversion among a New Guinea People." Pages 211–35 in *Religion and Cultural Studies*. Edited by Susan L. Mizruchi. Princeton: Princeton University Press, 2001.

Berg, Paul-Louis van. *Corpus Cultus Deae Syriae*. Études préliminaires aux religions orientales dans l'empire romain 28. Leiden: Brill, 1972–.

Berlin, Andrea. "Jewish Life before the Revolt: The Archaeological Evidence." *JSJ* 36 (2005): 417–70.

Berlin, Isaiah. *Three Critics of the Enlightenment: Vico, Hamann, Herder*. Edited by Henry Hardy. 2nd ed. with a new Foreword. Princeton: Princeton University Press, 2000.

Bickerman, Elias. "Un document relative à la persecution d'Antiochus IV Epiphane." *RHR* 115 (1937): 188–221.

———. *Der Gott der Makkabäer: Untersuchungen über Sinn und Ursprung der Makkabäischen Erhebung*. Berlin: Schocken Verlag, 1937.

———. "Origines Gentium." *CP* 47 (1952): 65–81.

Bieler, Ludwig. *Theios Aner: Das Bild des "Göttlichen Menschen" in Spätantike und Frühchristentum*. Vienna: Höfels, 1935.

Black, Max. "Models and Archetypes." Pages 219–43 in *Models and Metaphors: Studies in Language and Philosophy*. Ithaca, NY: Cornell University Press, 1962.

———. *Models and Metaphors: Studies in Language and Philosophy*. Ithaca, NY: Cornell University Press, 1962.

Boecker, Bettina. "Groundlings, Gallants, Grocers: Shakespeare's Elizabethan Audience and the Political Agendas of Shakespeare Criticism." Pages 220–33 in *Shakespeare and European Politics*. Edited by Dirk Delabastita, Jozef De Vos, and Paul J. C. M. Franssen. Foreword by Ton Hoenselaars. Newark: University of Delaware Press, 2008.

Bonz, Marianne Palmer. *The Past as Legacy: Luke-Acts and Ancient Epic*. Minneapolis: Fortress, 2000.

Borg, Marcus J. *Conflict, Holiness, and Politics in the Teaching of Jesus*. Lewiston, NY: Mellen, 1984.

———. *Jesus, A New Vision: Spirit, Culture, and the Life of Discipleship*. San Francisco: Harper & Row, 1987.

Bornkamm, Günther. *Jesus of Nazareth*. Translated by Irene and Fraser McLuskey with James M. Robinson. New York: Harper & Row, 1960.

Botha, Pieter J. J. "'Publishing' a Gospel: Notes on Historical Constraints to Gospel Criticism." Pages 335–52 in *The Interface of Orality and Writing*. Edited by Annette Weissenrieder and Robert B. Coote. WUNT 260. Tübingen: Mohr Siebeck, 2010.

Boulnois, Luce. *La route de la soie*. Paris: Arthaud, 1963.

Bourdieu, Pierre. *Distinction: A Social Critique of the Judgment of Taste*. Translated by Richard Nice. Cambridge: Harvard University Press, 1996.

———. *The Logic of Practice*. Translated by Richard Nice. Stanford, CA: Stanford University Press, 1990.

———. *Outline of a Theory of Practice*. Cambridge Studies in Social and Cultural Anthropology 16. Translated by Richard Nice. Cambridge: Cambridge University Press, 1972.

Bourdieu, Pierre, and Loïc Wacquant. *An Invitation to Reflexive Sociology*. Chicago: University of Chicago Press, 1992.

Boustan, Ra'anan S. "Confounding Blood: Jewish Narratives of Sacrifice and Violence in Late Antiquity." Pages 265–86 in *Ancient Mediterranean Sacrifice*. Edited by Jennifer Wright Knust and Zsuzsanna Várhelyi. Oxford: Oxford University Press, 2011.

———. "The Dislocation of the Temple Vessels: Mobile Sanctity and Rabbinic Rhetorics of Space." Pages 135–46 in *Jewish Studies at the Crossroads of Anthropology and History: Authority, Diaspora, Tradition*. Edited by Ra'anan S. Boustan, Oren Kosansky, and Marina Rustow. Jewish Culture and Contexts. Philadelphia: University of Pennsylvania Press, 2011.

Bowersock, G. W. "An Arabian Trinity." *HTR* 79 (1986): 17–21.

———. *Hellenism in Late Antiquity*. New York: Cambridge University Press, 1990.

Bowie, Andrew. "Romanticism and Music." Pages 243–56 in *The Cambridge Companion to German Romanticism*. Edited by Nicolas Saul. Cambridge: Cambridge University Press, 2009.

Boyarin, Daniel. *Borderlines: The Partition of Judaeo-Christianity*. Philadelphia: University of Pennsylvania Press, 2004.

———. *The Jewish Gospels: The Story of Jesus Christ*. New York: The New Press, 2012.

Braudel, Fernand. "History and Sociology." Pages 64–82 in *On History*. Translated by S. Matthews. Chicago: University of Chicago Press, 1980.

———. "History and the Social Sciences, The *Longue Durée*." Pages 25–54 in *On History*. Translated by S. Matthews. Chicago: University of Chicago Press, 1980. Translation of "Histoire et sciences sociales: La longue durée." *Annales, Économies, Societés, Civilisations* 13 (1958): 725–53.

———. *The Mediterranean and the Mediterranean World in the Age of Philip II*. Translated by Siân Reynolds. 2nd rev. ed. 2 vols. New York: Harper & Row, 1972.

———. *The Perspective of the World*. Vol. 3 of *Civilization and Capitalism 15th–18th Century*. Translated by Siân Reynolds. New York: Harper & Row, 1984. Translation of *Le Temps du Monde*. Paris: A. Colin, 1979.

———. "Toward a Historical Economics." Pages 83–90 in *On History*. Translated by S. Matthews. Chicago: University of Chicago Press, 1980.

Braun, Willi. "Smoke Signals from the North: A Reply to Burton Mack's 'Backbay Jazz and Blues.'" Pages 433–42 in *Redescribing Christian Origins*. Edited by Ron Cameron and Merrill P. Miller. SymS 28. Atlanta: Society of Biblical Literature, 2004.

———. "Socio-Mythic Invention, Graeco-Roman Schools, and the Sayings Gospel Q." *MTSR* 11 (1999): 210–35.

———. "Worries (On the Way to 'Mark Redivivus'?)." Paper presented at the Annual Meeting of the Society of Biblical Literature. Toronto, 26 November 2002.

Brewster, Ben. "Glossary." Pages 309–23 in *Reading Capital*, by Louis Althusser and Étienne Balibar. Translated by Ben Brewster. London: NLB, 1970.

Brodie, Thomas L. *The Birthing of the New Testament: The Intertextual*

Development of the New Testament Writings. New Testament Monographs 1. Sheffield: Sheffield Phoenix, 2004.

———. "Towards Unraveling the Rhetorical Imitation of Sources in Acts: 2
Kgs 5 as One Component of Acts 8, 9–40." *Bib* 67 (1986): 41–67.

Brown, Ian. "Epistemology and the Production of History: 'History' as a
Discipline and Object in the Study of Early Jesus People." Paper pre-
sented at the Annual Meeting of the Society of Biblical Literature. San
Diego, 24 November 2014.

Brown, Raymond E. *The Death of the Messiah: From Gethsemane to the
Grave; A Commentary on the Passion Narratives in the Four Gospels.*
New York: Doubleday, 1994.

Brubaker, Rogers, *Ethnicity without Groups.* Cambridge: Harvard University Press, 2004.

Brubaker, Rogers, with Frederick Cooper. "Beyond 'Identity.'" Pages 28–63
in *Ethnicity without Groups.* Cambridge: Harvard University Press,
2004.

Brubaker, Rogers, with Mara Loveman and Peter Stamatov. "Ethnicity
as Cognition." Pages 64–87 in *Ethnicity without Groups.* Cambridge:
Harvard University Press, 2004.

Brubaker, Rogers, with Margit Feischmidt. "1848 in 1998: The Politics of
Commemoration in Hungary, Romania, and Slovakia." Pages 161–204
in *Ethnicity without Groups.* Cambridge: Harvard University Press,
2004.

Buchler, Justus, ed. *Philosophical Writings of Peirce.* New York: Dover, 1955.

Bultmann, Rudolf. "Demythologizing: Controversial Slogan and Theological Focus." Pages 288–327 in *Rudolf Bultmann: Interpreting Faith for
the Modern Era.* Edited by Roger A. Johnson. The Making of Modern
Theology: Nineteenth and Twentieth-Century Texts. Minneapolis;
Fortress, 1991.

———. *The History of the Synoptic Tradition.* Translated by John Marsh.
Rev. ed. New York: Harper & Row, 1963.

———. "Jesus and the Eschatological Kingdom." Pages 91–128 in *Rudolf
Bultmann: Interpreting Faith for the Modern Era.* Edited by Roger A.
Johnson. The Making of Modern Theology: Nineteenth and Twenti-
eth-Century Texts. Minneapolis: Fortress, 1991.

———. "The New Approach to the Synoptic Problem." *JR* 6 (1926): 337–62.

———. "Primitive Christianity as a Syncretistic Phenomenon." Pages
175–79 in *Primitive Christianity in Its Contemporary Setting.* Trans-

lated by Reginald H. Fuller. New York: Meridian Books, 1956; New York: World Publishing, 1956.

———. "The Study of the Synoptic Gospels." Pages 11–76 in *Form Criticism: Two Essays on New Testament Research*, by Rudolf Bultmann and Karl Kundsin. Translated by Frederick C. Grant. Harper Torchbooks. New York: Harper, 1962.

———. *Theology of the New Testament.* Translated by Kendrick Grobel. 2 vols. New York: Scribner's Sons, 1951–1955.

Burke, Kenneth. *The Philosophy of Literary Form: Studies in Symbolic Action.* Rev. ed. New York: Vintage Books, 1957.

Burkill, T. A. *New Light on the Earliest Gospel: Seven Markan Studies.* Ithaca, NY: Cornell University Press, 1972.

Burns, Joshua Ezra. "Essene Sectarianism and Social Differentiation in Judaea after 70 C.E." *HTR* 99 (2006): 247–74.

Burridge, R. A. *What Are the Gospels? A Comparison with Graeco-Roman Biography.* 2nd ed. Grand Rapids: Eerdmans, 2004.

Cadwallader, Alan H. *Beyond the Word of a Woman: Recovering the Bodies of the Syrophoenician Women.* Adelaide, Australia: ATF Press, 2008.

Cameron, Ron. "The Anatomy of a Discourse: On 'Eschatology' as a Category for Explaining Christian Origins." *MTSR* 8 (1996): 231–45.

———. "Ancient Myths and Modern Theories of the *Gospel of Thomas* and Christian Origins." Pages 89–108 in *Redescribing Christian Origins.* Edited by Ron Cameron and Merrill P. Miller. SymS 28. Atlanta: Society of Biblical Literature, 2004. Repr., *MTSR* 11 (1999): 236–57.

———. "Introduction to the Papers from the First Year of the Seminar." Pages 151–58 in *Redescribing Christian Origins.* SymS 28. Atlanta: Society of Biblical Literature, 2004.

———. "Redescribing Christian Origins." *Annali di storia dell' esegesi* 25 (2008): 35–54.

———. Review of *Jesus, A New Vision: Spirit, Culture, and the Life of Discipleship*, by Marcus J. Borg. *TJT* 6 (1990): 119–23.

———. "'What Have You Come Out To See?' Characterizations of John and Jesus in the Gospels." *Semeia* 49 (1990): 35–69.

Cameron, Ron, and Merrill P. Miller. "Conclusion: Redescribing Christian Origins." Pages 497–516 in *Redescribing Christian Origins.* Edited by Ron Cameron and Merrill P. Miller. SymS 28. Atlanta: Society of Biblical Literature, 2004.

———. "Introducing Paul and the Corinthians." Pages 1–15 in *Redescrib-*

ing Paul and the Corinthians. Edited by Ron Cameron and Merrill P. Miller. ECL 5. Atlanta: Society of Biblical Literature, 2011.

———. "Introduction: Ancient Myths and Modern Theories of Christian Origins." Pages 1–30 in *Redescribing Christian Origins*. Edited by Ron Cameron and Merrill P. Miller. SymS 28. Atlanta: Society of Biblical Literature, 2004.

———. "Issues and Commentary." Pages 443–56 in *Redescribing Christian Origins*. Edited by Ron Cameron and Merrill P. Miller. SymS 28. Atlanta: Society of Biblical Literature, 2004.

———, eds. *Redescribing Christian Origins*. SymS 28. Atlanta: Society of Biblical Literature, 2004.

———, eds. *Redescribing Paul and the Corinthians*. ECL 5. Atlanta: Society of Biblical Literature, 2011.

———. "Redescribing Paul and the Corinthians." Pages 245–302 in *Redescribing Paul and the Corinthians*. Edited by Ron Cameron and Merrill P. Miller. ECL 5. Atlanta: Society of Biblical Literature, 2011.

Carr, David M. *Holy Resilience: The Bible's Traumatic Origins*. New Haven: Yale University Press, 2014.

Carter, Edward J. "Toll and Tribute: A Political Reading of Matthew 17:24–27." *JSNT* 25 (2003): 413–31.

Carter, Warren. "Matthew: Empire, Synagogues, and Horizontal Violence." Pages 285–308 in *Mark and Matthew I: Comprehensive Readings; Understanding the Earliest Gospels in Their First-Century Settings*. Edited by Eve-Marie Becker and Anders Runesson. Tübingen: Mohr Siebeck, 2011.

———. "Paying the Tax to Rome as Subversive Praxis: Matthew 17:24–27." *JSNT* 22 (2000): 3–31.

———. "Roman Imperial Power: A New Testament Perspective." Pages 137–51 in *Rome and Religion: A Cross-Disciplinary Dialogue on the Imperial Cult*. Edited by Jeffrey Brodd and Jonathan L. Reed. WGRWSup 5. Atlanta: Society of Biblical Literature, 2011.

Cary, George. *The Medieval Alexander*. Edited by D. J. A. Ross. Cambridge: Cambridge University, 1956.

Cassirer, Ernst. *The Logic of the Cultural Sciences: Five Studies*. Translated by S. G. Lofts. Foreword by Donald Phillip Verene. New Haven: Yale University Press, 2000.

———. *The Logic of the Humanities*. Translated by C. S. Howe. New Haven: Yale University Press, 1960. Translation of *Zur Logik des Kulturwissenschaften: Fünf Studien*. Göteborg, 1942.

———. *The Problem of Knowledge: Philosophy, Science and History since Hegel.* Translated by W. H. Woglom and C. W. Hendel. New Haven: Yale University Press, 1950.

———. "Structuralism in Modern Linguistics." *Word: Journal of the Linguistic Circle of New York* 1 (1945): 99–120.

Casson, Lionel. "The Isis and Her Voyage." *TAPA* 81 (1950): 43–56.

Castelli, Elizabeth A., and Hal Taussig. "Drawing Large and Startling Figures: Reimagining Christian Origins by Painting like Picasso." Pages 3–20 in *Reimagining Christian Origins: A Colloquium Honoring Burton L. Mack.* Edited by Elizabeth A. Castelli and and Hal Taussig. Valley Forge, PA: Trinity Press International, 1996.

Certeau, Michel de. "Ethno-graphie, l'oralité, ou l'espace d l'autre: Léry." Pages 215–48 in *L'Écriture de l'histoire.* 2nd ed. Paris: Gallimard, 1993.

———. *The Practice of Everyday Life.* Translated by Steven Rendall. Berkeley: University of California Press, 1984.

———. "Travel Narratives of the French to Brazil: Sixteenth to Eighteenth Centuries." *Representations* 33 (1991): 221–26.

Chancey, Mark A. "The Ethnicities of Galileans." Pages 112–28 in vol. 1 of *Galilee in the Late Second Temple and Mishnaic Periods.* Edited by David A. Fiensy and James Riley Strange. Minneapolis: Fortress, 2014.

Charbonnier, G. *Conversations with Claude Lévi-Strauss.* Translated by John Weightman and Doreen Weightman. London: Cape, 1969.

Charlesworth, James H. *Jesus within Judaism: New Light from Exciting Archaeological Discoveries.* Garden City, NY: Doubleday, 1988.

Charlesworth, Martin Percival. *Trade Routes and Commerce of the Roman Empire.* 2nd ed. Cambridge: Cambridge University Press, 1926.

Chilton, Bruce D. "A Coin of Three Realms (Matthew 17.24–27)." Pages 269–82 in *The Bible in Three Dimensions: Essays in Celebration of Forty Years of Biblical Studies in the University of Sheffield.* Edited by David J. A. Clines, Stephen E. Fowl, and Stanley E. Porter. JSOTSup 87. Sheffield: JSOT Press, 1990.

Choi, Junghwa. *Jewish Leadership in Roman Palestine from 70 CE to 135 CE.* AGJU 83. Leiden: Brill, 2013.

Clastres, Pierre. "De l'un sans multiple." Pages 146–51 in *La société contra l'état.* Paris: Editions de Minuit, 1974.

———. *Le grand parler: Mythes et chants sacrées des Indiens Gurani.* Paris: Editions du Seuil, 1974.

Clifford, James. "Traveling Cultures." Pages 96–116 in *Cultural Studies.* Edited by Lawrence Grossberg, Cary Nelson, and Paula Treichler. New

York: Routledge, 1992. Repr., pages 17–46 in James Clifford, *Routes: Travel and Translation in the Late Twentieth Century*. Cambridge: Harvard University Press, 1997.

Cohen, Shaye J. D. *The Beginnings of Jewishness: Boundaries, Varieties, Uncertainties*. Hellenistic Culture and Society 31. Berkeley: University of California Press, 1999.

———. "The Place of the Rabbi in Jewish Society of the Second Century." Pages 157–73 in *The Galilee in Late Antiquity*. Edited by Lee I. Levine. New York: Jewish Theological Seminary, 1992.

———. "The Rabbi in Second-Century Jewish Society." Pages 922–90 in *The Cambridge History of Judaism: The Early Roman Period*. Edited by William Horbury, W. D. Davies, and John Sturdy. Vol. 3 of *The Cambridge History of Judaism*. Edited by W. D. Davies and Louis Finkelstein. Cambridge: Cambridge University Press, 1999.

———. "The Significance of Yavneh: Pharisees, Rabbis, and the End of Jewish Sectarianism." *HUCA* 55 (1984): 27–53. Repr., pages 44–70 in *The Significance of Yavneh and Other Essays in Jewish Hellenism*, by Shaye J. D. Cohen. TSAJ 136. Tübingen: Mohr Siebeck, 2010.

———. "Were Pharisees and Rabbis the Leaders of Communal Prayer and Torah Study in Antiquity? The Evidence of the New Testament, Josephus, and the Early Church Fathers." Pages 89–105 in *Evolution of the Synagogue: Problems and Progress*. Edited by Howard Clark Kee and Lynn H. Cohick. Harrisburg; PA: Trinity Press International, 1999.

Collart, Paul, and Jacques Vicari. *Le sanctuaire de Baalshamin à Palmyre: Topographie et architecture*. 2 vols. Bibliotheca Helvetica Romana 10. Neuchâtel: Paul Attinger, 1969.

Collins, Adela Yarbro. *The Beginning of the Gospel: Probings of Mark in Context*. Eugene, OR: Wipf & Stock, 2001.

———. "Composition and Performance in Mark 13." Pages 539–60 in *A Wandering Galilean: Essays in Honour of Seán Freyne*. Edited by Zuleika Rodgers with Margaret Daly-Denton and Anne Fitzpatrick McKinley. JSJSup 132. Leiden: Brill, 2009.

———. "Finding Meaning in the Death of Jesus." *JR* 78 (1998): 175–96.

———. "The Genre of the Passion Narrative." *ST* 47 (1993): 3–28.

———. *Is Mark's Gospel a Life of Jesus? The Question of Genre*. Milwaukee: Marquette University Press, 1990.

———. *Mark: A Commentary*. Hermeneia. Minneapolis: Fortress, 2007.

———. "Mark's Interpretation of the Death of Jesus." *JBL* 128 (2009): 545–50.

———. "Messianic Secret and the Gospel of Mark: Secrecy in Jewish Apocalypticism, the Hellenistic Mystery Religions, and Magic." Pages 11–30 in *Rending the Veil: Concealment and Secrecy in the History of Religions*. Edited by Elliot R. Wolfson. Chappaqua, NY: Seven Bridges Press, 1999.

Collins, John J. "Enoch and Ezra." Pages 83–97 in *Fourth Ezra and Second Baruch*. Edited by Matthias Henze and Gabriele Boccaccini with the collaboration of Jason M. Zurawski. JSJSup 164. Leiden: Brill, 2013.

Collins, Marilyn F. "The Hidden Vessels in Samaritan Traditions." *JSJ* 3 (1972): 97–116.

Collins, Steven. "Categories, Concepts or Predicaments? Remarks on Mauss's Use of Philosophical Terminology." Pages 46–82 in *The Category of the Person: Anthropology, Philosophy, History*. Edited by Michael Carrithers, Steven Collins, and Steven Lukes. Cambridge: Cambridge University Press, 1985.

Colpe, Carston. "Hypsistos." *KlPauly* 2:1291–92.

Comfort, Howard. "Terra Sigillata at Arikamedu." Pages 134–50 in *Rome and India: The Ancient Sea Trade*. Edited by V. Begley and R. D. de Puma. Madison, WI: University of Wisconsin Press, 1991.

Cook, James. *The Voyage of the Resolution and Adventure 1772–1775*. Vol. 2 of *The Journals of Captain James Cook*. Edited by J. C. Beaglehole and R. A. Skelton. Cambridge: The Hakluyt Society at the University Press, 1955–1974.

Coote, Robert B. "Scripture and the Writer of Mark." Pages 363–78 in *The Interface of Orality and Writing*. Edited by Annette Weissenrieder and Robert B. Coote. WUNT 260. Mohr Siebeck, 2010.

Corley, Kathleen E. *Maranatha: Women's Funerary Rituals and Christian Origins*. Minneapolis: Fortress, 2010.

Cotton, Hannah M. "Jewish Jurisdiction under Roman Rule: Prolegomena." Pages 13–28 in *Zwischen den Reichen: Neues Testament und Römische Herrschaft*. Edited by Michael Labahn and Jürgen Zangenberg. TANZ 36. Tübingen: Francke, 2002.

———. "The Rabbis and the Documents." Pages 167–79 in *Jews in a Graeco-Roman World*. Edited by Martin Goodman. Oxford: Oxford University Press, 1998.

Cotton, Hannah M., and Werner Eck. "Roman Officials in Judaea and Arabia and Civil Jurisdiction." Pages 23–44 in *Law in the Documents of the Judaean Desert*. Edited by Ranon Katzoff and David Schaps. JSJSup 96. Leiden: Brill, 2005.

Cournot, Antoine Augustin. *Exposition de la théorie des chances et des probabilités*. Paris: L. Hachette, 1843.

Cranfield, C. E. B. *The Gospel according to St Mark*. Cambridge: Cambridge University Press, 1966.

Crook, Zeba. Review of *The Gospel to the Romans: The Setting and Rhetoric of Mark's Gospel*, by Brian J. Incigneri, and *The Purpose of the Gospel of Mark in its Historical and Social Context*, by H. N. Roskam. *RBL* (2006): http://tinyurl.com/SBL4520a.

Crossan, John Dominic. "Commentary and History." *JR* 75 (1995): 247–53.

———. *The Cross That Spoke: The Origins of the Passion Narrative*. San Francisco: Harper & Row, 1988.

———. *The Historical Jesus: The Life of a Mediterranean Jewish Peasant*. San Francisco: HarperSanFransisco, 1992.

———. *Who Killed Jesus?* San Francisco: HarperSanFrancisco, 1995.

Crossley, James G. *The Date of Mark's Gospel: Insights from the Law in Earliest Christianity*. JSNTSup 266. London: T&T Clark, 2004.

Cumont, Franz. ""Ὕψιστος." PW 9:444–50.

———. *The Oriental Religions in Roman Paganism*. New York: Dover, 1956.

Curtius, Ernst Robert. *European Literature and the Latin Middle Ages*. Translated W. R. Trask. Princeton: Bollingen Foundation, 1953.

Daschke, Dereck. *City of Ruins: Mourning the Destruction of Jerusalem through Jewish Apocalypse*. BibInt 99. Leiden: Brill, 2010.

Davies, Stevan. *The Gospel of Thomas, Annotated and Explained*. Woodstock, VT: Skylight Paths, 2002.

———. *Jesus the Healer: Possession, Trance, and the Origins of Christianity*. New York: Continuum, 1995.

———. "On Mark's Use of the Gospel of Thomas." *Neot* 30 (1996): 307–34.

DeMaris, Richard E. "The Baptism of Jesus: A Ritual-Critical Approach." Pages 137–57 in *The Social Setting of Jesus and the Gospels*. Edited by Wolfgang Stegemann, Bruce J. Malina, and Gerd Theissen. Minneapolis: Fortress, 2002.

———. "Jesus Jettisoned." Pages 91–111 in *The New Testament in Its Ritual World*. Edited by Richard E. DeMaris. London: Routledge, 2008.

Dening, Greg. *Islands and Beaches: Discourse on a Silent Land, Marquesas 1774–1880*. Honolulu: University of Hawaii Press, 1980.

Dentith, Simon: *Parody*. London: Routledge, 2000.

Derichs, Wilhelm. "Herakles, Vorbild des Herrschers in der Antike." PhD diss., University of Cologne, 1951.

Destutt de Tracy, Antoine Louis Claude. *Élements d'idéologie*. Parts 2–5 of *Projet d'éléments d'idéologie à l'usage des écoles centrales de la République française*. Paris: Pierre Didot, 1801–1815.

Detienne, Marcel. *Comparer l'incomparable*. Paris: Éditions du Seuil, 2000.

Dewey, Arthur J. "The Locus of Death: Social Memory and the Passion Narratives." Pages 119–28 in *Memory, Tradition, and Text: Uses of the Past in Early Christianity*. Edited by Alan Kirk and Tom Thatcher. SemeiaSt 52. Atlanta: Society of Biblical Literature, 2005.

———. "The Passion Narrative of the Gospel of Peter: Redaction and Interpretation." *Forum* NS 1 (1998): 53–69.

Dewey, Joanna. "The Gospel of Mark as Oral Hermeneutic." Pages 71–87 in *Jesus, the Voice, and the Text: Beyond the Oral and the Written Gospel*. Edited by Tom Thatcher. Waco, TX: Baylor University Press, 2008.

De Wilde, Éliane, and Philippe Roberts-Jones, eds. *Le dictionnaire des peintres belges du XIVe siècle à nos jours*. Brussels: La Renaissance du Livre, 1995.

Dibelius, Martin. *From Tradition to Gospel*. Translated by Bertram Lee Woolf. New York: Scribner's Sons, 1934.

Djurfeldt, Gören, and Staffan Lindberg. *Behind Poverty: The Social Formation in a Tamil Village*. Scandinavian Institute of Asian Studies Monograph Series 22. London: Curzon, 1975.

Dodd, C. H. *The Old Testament in the New*. Philadelphia: Fortress, 1963.

Donahue, John R. "Temple, Trial, and Royal Christology (Mark 14:53–65)." Pages 61–79 in *The Passion in Mark: Studies on Mark 14–16*. Edited by Werner H. Kelber. Philadelphia: Fortress, 1976.

Donham, Donald L. *History, Power, Ideology: Central Issues in Marxism and Anthropology*. Rev. ed. Berkeley: University of California Press, 1999.

Dowd, Sharyn, and Elizabeth Struthers Malbon, "The Significance of Jesus' Death in Mark: Narrative Context and Authorial Audience." *JBL* 125 (2006): 271–97.

Downey, Glanville. *A History of Antioch in Syria: From Seleucus to the Arab Conquest*. Princeton: Princeton University Press, 1961.

Downey, Susan B. *The Heracles Sculpture*. Final Report 3.1.1 of *The Excavations at Dura-Europos Conducted by Yale University and the French Academy of Inscriptions and Letters*. Edited by C. Bradford Welles. New Haven: Dura-Europos Publications, 1969.

Driesch, Hans. *Die Biologie als selbständige Grundwissenschaft: Eine kritische Studie*. Leipzig: W. Engelmann, 1893.

———. *The Science and Philosophy of the Organism.* 2nd ed. London: Black, 1928.

Driggers, Ira Brent. *Following God through Mark: Theological Tension in the Second Gospel.* Louisville: Westminster John Knox, 2007.

Dronsch, Kristina, and Annette Weissenrieder. "A Theory of the Message for New Testament Writings or Communicating the Words of Jesus: From Angelos to Euangelion." Pages 205–35 in *The Interface of Orality and Writing.* Edited by Annette Weissenrieder and Robert B. Coote. WUNT 260. Tübingen: Mohr Siebeck, 2010.

Duby, Georges. *L'histoire continue.* Paris: Odile Jacob, 1991.

Dumézil, Georges. *Mythe et épopée.* 4 vols. Paris: Gallimard, 1968–1973.

Dunn, James D. G. Review of *Redescribing Christian Origins*, edited by Ron Cameron and Merrill P. Miller. *JBL* 124 (2005): 760–64.

Dunning, Benjamin H. *Aliens and Sojourners: Self as Other in Early Christianity.* Philadelphia: University of Pennsylvania Press, 2009.

Dupont, Florence. "*Recitatio* and the Space of Public Discourse." Pages 44–59 in *The Roman Cultural Revolution.* Edited by Thomas Habinek and Alessandro Schiesaro. Cambridge: Cambridge University Press, 1997.

Duran, Nicole Wilkinson. *The Power of Disorder: Ritual Elements in Mark's Passion Narrative.* LNTS 378. London: T&T Clark, 2008.

Durkheim, Émile. *The Elementary Forms of Religious Life.* Translated by K. E. Fields. New York: Free Press, 1995.

Duthoy, Robert. *The Taurobolium: Its Evolution and Terminology.* EPRO 10. Leiden: Brill, 1959.

Dyson, Stephen L. "Native Revolts in the Roman World." *Historia* 20 (1971): 239–74.

Eco, Umberto. *Foucault's Pendulum.* Translated from the Italian by William Weaver. New York: Harcourt Brace Jovanovich, 1989.

Eggan, Fred. "Social Anthropology and the Method of Controlled Comparison." *American Anthropologist* NS 56 (1964): 743–63.

Ehrman, Bart D. *Jesus: Apocalyptic Prophet of the New Millennium.* Oxford: Oxford University Press, 1999.

———. *The Orthodox Corruption of Scripture: The Effect of Early Christological Controversies on the Text of the New Testament.* New York; Oxford: Oxford University Press, 1993.

Eliav, Yaron. "The Matrix of Ancient Judaism." *Proof* 24 (2004): 116–28.

Engler, Rudolf. *Edition critique du "Cours de linguistique générale" de F. de Saussure.* Wiesbaden: Otto Harrassowitz, 1967.

———. *Lexique de la terminologie Saussurienne*. Utrecht: Het Spectrum, 1968.

Enslin, Morton S. "John and Jesus." *ZNW* 66 (1975): 1–18.

Esler, Philip S. "God's Honour and Rome's Triumph: Responses to the Fall of Jerusalem in 70 CE in Three Jewish Apocalypses." Pages 239–58 in *Modeling Early Christianity*. Edited by Philip S. Esler. London: Routledge, 1995.

Evans, Craig A. "Jesus' Action in the Temple and Evidence of Corruption in the First-Century Temple." Pages 522–39 in *Society of Biblical Literature 1989 Seminar Papers*. Edited by David J. Lull. SBLSP 28. Atlanta: Scholars Press, 1989.

———. "Jesus' Action in the Temple: Cleansing or Portent of Destruction?" *CBQ* 51 (1989): 237–70.

———. *Jesus and His Contemporaries: Comparative Studies*. Leiden: Brill, 2001.

Evans-Pritchard, E. E. "Anthropology and History." Pages 172–91 in *Social Anthropology and Other Essays*. Glencoe, IL: Free Press, 1962.

———. "Social Anthropology: Past and Present." Pages 139–54 in *Social Anthropology and Other Essays*. Glencoe, IL: Free Press, 1962.

Eyl, Jennifer. "Why Thekla Does Not See Paul: Visual Perception and the Displacement of Erōs in the *Acts of Paul and Thekla*." Pages 3–19 in *The Ancient Novel and the Early Christian and Jewish Narrative: Fictional Intersections*. Edited by Marília P. Futre Pinheiro, Judith Perkins, and Richard Pervo. Groningen: Barkhuis Publishing & Groningen University Library, 2012.

Fabian, Johannes. *Time and the Other: How Anthropology Makes Its Object*. New York: Columbia University Press, 1983.

Fantham, Elaine. *Roman Literary Culture: From Cicero to Apuleius*. Baltimore: John Hopkins University Press, 1996.

Feldt, Laura. *The Fantastic in Religious Narrative from the Exodus to Elisha*. Bible World. Sheffield: Equinox, 2012.

Ferguson, John. "China and Rome." *ANRW* 9.2:581–603.

Fine, Steven. *This Holy Place: On the Sanctity of the Synagogue during the Greco-Roman Period*. Notre Dame: University of Notre Dame Press, 1997.

Fitzmyer, Joseph A. *The Gospel according to Luke I–IX*. AB 28. Garden City, NY: Doubleday, 1981.

Fleddermann, Harry T. *Mark and Q: A Study of the Overlap Texts*. Leuven: Leuven University Press; Leuven: Peeters, 1995.

———. *Q: A Reconstruction and Commentary*. BTS. Leuven; Paris; Dudley, MA: Peeters, 2005.

Flynn, Thomas R. "Mediated Reciprocity and the Genius of the Third." Pages 345–70 in *The Philosophy of Jean-Paul Sartre*. Edited by P. A. Schilpp. The Library of Living Philosophers 16. La Salle, IL: Open Court, 1981.

Fornander, Abraham. *An Account of the Polynesian Race, Its Origin and Migrations and the Ancient History of the Hawaiian People to the Times of Kamchamcha I*. 3 vols. London: Trübner & Co., Ludgate Hill, 1878–1880. Repr., Rutland, VT; Tokyo: Charles E. Tuttle, 1969.

Fortna, Robert. "Jesus and Peter at the High Priest's House: A Test Case for the Relation Between Mark's and John's Gospels." *NTS* 24 (1977–1978): 371–383.

Foss, Martin. *Symbol and Metaphor in Human Experience*. Princeton: Princeton University Press, 1949.

Foster, Paul. "Vespasian, Nerva, Jesus, and the *Fiscus Judaicus*." Pages 303–20 in *Israel's God and Rebecca's Children: Christology and Community in Early Judaism and Christianity; Essays in Honor of Larry W. Hurtado and Alan F. Segal*. Edited by David B. Capes, April D. DeConick, Helen K. Bond, and Troy A. Miller. Waco, TX: Baylor University Press, 2007.

Foucault, Michel. "Distance, Aspect, Origin." Pages 97–108 in *The Tel Quel Reader*. Edited and translated by Patrick Ffrench and Roland-François Lack. London: Routledge, 1998.

———. *Discipline and Punish: The Birth of the Prison*. Translated by Alan Sheridan. New York: Pantheon, 1977.

Fowler, Robert M. *Loaves and Fishes: The Function of the Feeding Stories in the Gospel of Mark*. Chico, CA: Scholars Press, 1981.

Fraade, Steven D. "The Temple as a Marker of Jewish Identity before and after 70 CE: The Role of the Holy Vessels in Rabbinic Memory and Imagination." Pages 237–65 in *Jewish Identities in Antiquity: Studies in Memory of Menahem Stern*. Edited by Lee I. Levine and Daniel R. Schwartz. Tübingen: Mohr Siebeck, 2009.

France, R. T. *Jesus and the Old Testament: His Application of Old Testament Passages to Himself and His Mission*. Downers Grove, IL: InterVarsity Press, 1971.

Frankfurter, David. "Beyond 'Jewish Christianity': Continuing Religious Sub-Cultures of the Second and Third Centuries and Their Documents." Pages 131–43 in *The Ways That Never Parted: Jews and Chris-

tians in Late Antiquity and the Early Middle Ages. Edited by Adam H. Becker and Annette Yoshiko Reed. Minneapolis: Fortress, 2007.

Fredriksen, Paula. *From Jesus to Christ: The Origins of the New Testament Images of Jesus.* New Haven: Yale University Press, 2008.

———. "Gospel Chronologies, the Scene in the Temple, and the Crucifixion of Jesus." Pages 246–82 in *Redefining First-Century Jewish and Christian Identities: Essays in Honor of Ed Parish Sanders.* Edited by Fabian E. Udoh with Susannah Heschel, Mark Chancey, and Gregory Tatum. Christianity and Judaism in Antiquity Series 16. Notre Dame: University of Notre Dame Press, 2008.

———. *Jesus of Nazareth, King of the Jews: A Jewish Life and the Emergence of Christianity.* New York: Knopf, 1999.

Frey, Jörg. "Temple and Identity in Early Christianity and in the Johannine Community: Reflections on the 'Parting of the Ways.'" Pages 447–507 in *Was 70 CE a Watershed in Jewish History? On Jews and Judaism Before and After the Destruction of the Temple.* Edited by Daniel R. Schwartz and Zeev Weiss in collaboration with Ruth A. Clements. AGJU 78. Leiden: Brill, 2012.

Funk, Robert W., and the Jesus Seminar. *The Acts of Jesus: What Did Jesus Really Do?* San Francisco: HarperSanFrancisco, 1998.

Funk, Robert W., Roy W. Hoover, and the Jesus Seminar. *The Five Gospels: The Search for the Authentic Words of Jesus.* New York: MacMillan, 1993.

Furstenberg, Yair. "Defilement Penetrating the Body: A New Understanding of Contamination in Mark 7:15." *NTS* 54 (2008): 176–200.

Gager, John G. *Kingdom and Community: The Social World of Early Christianity.* Englewood Cliffs, NJ: Prentice-Hall, 1975.

Gaster, Moses. *The Exempla of the Rabbis: Being a Collection of Exempla, Apologues, and Tales Culled from Hebrew Manuscripts and Rare Hebrew Books.* London: Asia Publishing, 1924. Repr., New York: Ktav, 1968.

Gay, Peter. *Style in History.* New York: Basic Books, 1974.

Geiger, Joseph. "The Jew and the Other: Doubtful and Multiple Identities in the Roman Empire." Pages 136–46 in *Jewish Identities in Antiquity: Studies in Memory of Menahem Stern.* Edited by Lee I. Levine and Daniel R. Schwartz. Tübingen: Mohr Siebeck, 2009.

———. "Language, Culture and Identity in Ancient Palestine." Pages 233–46 in *Greek Romans and Roman Greeks: Studies in Cultural Intervention.* Edited by Erik Nis Ostenfeld. Aarhus Studies in Mediterranean Antiquity 3. Aarhus: Aarhus University Press, 2002.

Gelardini, Gabriella. "Cult's Death in Scripture: The Destruction of Jerusalem's Temple Remembered by Josephus and Mark." Pages 89–112 in *Memory and Identity in Ancient Judaism and Early Christianity: A Conversation with Barry Schwartz.* SemeiaSt 78. Atlanta: SBL Press, 2014.

Gerdmar, Anders. *Roots of Theological Anti-Semitism: German Biblical Interpretation and the Jews, from Herder and Semler to Kittel and Bultmann.* Leiden: Brill, 2009.

Gerstenberg, Heinrich Wilhelm von. *Briefe über Merkwürdigkeiten der Litteratur.* Leipzig: J. F. Hansen, 1766. Repr., Hildesheim; New York: Olms, 1971.

Geyer, Douglas W. *Fear, Anomaly, and Uncertainty in the Gospel of Mark.* ATLA 47. Lanham, MD: Scarecrow, 2002.

Glaim, Aaron. "Sin and 'Sin-Sacrifices' in the Pauline Epistles." Paper presented at the Annual Meeting of the Society of Biblical Literature. Baltimore, 24 November 2013.

Globe, Alexander. "The Caesarean Omission of the Phrase 'Son of God' in Mark 1:1." *HTR* 75 (1982): 209–18.

Glueck, Nelson. *Deities and Dolphins: The Story of the Nabataeans.* London: Cassell, 1965.

Godel, Robert. *Les sources manuscrites du cours de linguistique générale de F. de Saussure.* Geneva: Droz, 1957; Paris: Minard, 1957.

Godelier, Maurice. *Rationality and Irrationality in Economics.* Translated by B. Pearce. New York: Monthly Review, 1972; London: NLB, 1972. Translation of *Rationalité et irrationalité en économie.* Économie et socialism. Paris: Maspero, 1966.

Godlove, Terry F, Jr. "Is 'Space' a Concept? Kant, Durkheim and French Neo-Kantianism." *Journal of the History of the Behavioral Sciences* 32 (1966): 441–55.

———. *Religion, Interpretation and Diversity of Belief: The Framework Model from Kant to Durkheim to Davidson.* Cambridge: Cambridge University Press, 1989.

Goethe, Johann Wolfgang von. *Naturwissenschftliche Schriften 1.* Vol. 13 of *Goethes Werke.* Edited by Erich Trunz. 14 vols. Hamburger Ausgabe. Munich: Beck, 1981.

Goldman, Irving. *Ancient Polynesian Society.* Chicago: University of Chicago Press, 1970.

Goodblatt, David. *The Monarchic Principle: Studies in Jewish Self-Government in Antiquity.* Tübingen: Mohr Siebeck, 1994.

Goodenough, Erwin R. *Jewish Symbols in the Greco-Roman Period.* 13 vols. Bollingen Series 37. New York: Pantheon, 1953–1968.

———. *Symbolism in the Dura Synagogue.* Vols. 9–11 in *Jewish Symbols in the Greco-Roman Period.* Bollingen Series 37. New York: Pantheon, 1964.

Goodman, Martin. "Current Scholarship on the First Revolt." Pages 15–24 in *The First Jewish Revolt: Archaeology, History, and Ideology.* Edited by Andrea Berlin and J. Andrew Overman. London: Routledge, 2002.

———. "The *Fiscus Iudaicus* and Gentile Attitudes to Judaism in Flavian Rome." Pages 167–77 in *Flavius Josephus and Flavian Rome.* Edited by Jonathan Edmondson, Steve Mason, and James B. Rives. Oxford: Oxford University Press, 2005.

———. "Jews, Greeks, Romans." Pages 3–14 in *Jews in a Graeco-Roman World.* Edited by Martin Goodman. Oxford: Oxford University Press, 1998.

———. "The Meaning of '*Fisci Iudaici Calumnia Sublata*' on the Coinage of Nerva." Pages 81–89 in *Studies in Josephus and the Varieties of Ancient Judaism: Louis H. Feldman Jubilee Volume.* Edited by Shaye J. D. Cohen and Joshua J. Schwartz. AGJU 67. Leiden: Brill, 2007.

———. *Mission and Conversion: Proselytizing in the Religious History of the Roman Empire.* Oxford: Clarendon, 1994.

———. "Nerva, the *Fiscus Judaicus* and Jewish Identity." *JRS* 79 (1989): 40–44.

———. "Opponents of Rome: Jews and Others." Pages 222–38 in *Images of Empire.* Edited by Loveday Alexander. JSOTSup 122. Sheffield: JSOT Press, 1991.

———. "The Persecution of Paul by Diaspora Jews." Pages 145–52 in *Judaism in the Roman World: Collected Essays.* AGJU 66. Leiden: Brill, 2007.

———. "Religious Variety and the Temple in the Late Second Temple Period and its Aftermath." *JJS* 60 (2009): 202–13.

———. *Rome and Jerusalem: The Clash of Ancient Civilizations.* New York: Knopf, 2007.

———. *The Ruling Class of Judaea: The Origins of the Jewish Revolt Against Rome A.D. 66–70.* Cambridge: Cambridge University Press, 1987.

———. "Sadducees and Essenes after 70 CE." Pages 347–56 in *Crossing the Boundaries: Essays in Biblical Interpretation in Honour of Michael D. Goulder.* Edited by Stanley. E. Porter, Paul Joyce, and David E. Orton. Leiden: Brill, 1994. Repr., pages 153–62 in *Judaism in the Roman World: Collected Essays.* AGJU 66. Leiden: Brill, 2007.

———. *State and Society in Roman Galilee, A.D. 132–212*. 2nd ed. London; Portland, OR: Vallentine Mitchell, 2000.

———. "The Temple in First-Century Judaism." Pages 47–58 in *Judaism in the Roman World: Collected Essays*. AGJU 66. Leiden: Brill, 2007.

Goppelt, Leonhard. *Typos: Die typologische Deutung des Alten Testaments in Neuen*. BFCT 2/43. Gütersloh: Bertelsmann, 1939. Repr., Darmstadt: Wissenschaftliche Buchgesellschaft, 1973.

———. "τύπος, κτλ." *TDNT* 8:246–59.

Gould, Stephen Jay. *The Structure of Evolutionary Theory*. Cambridge: Harvard University Press, 2002.

Grainger, John D. *Nerva and the Roman Succession Crisis of AD 96–99*. London: Routledge, 2003.

Gregg, Robert C., and Dan Urman. *Jews, Pagans, and Christians in the Golan Heights: Greek and Other Inscriptions of the Roman and Byzantine Eras*. SFSHJ 140. Atlanta: Scholars Press, 1996.

Greimas, Algirdas Julien. *Dictionnaire de l'ancien français jusqu'au milieu du XIVe siècle*. 2nd ed. Paris: Larousse, 1968.

Greimas, Algirdas Julien, and Joseph Courtés. *Semiotics and Language: An Analytical Dictionary*. Translated by Larry Crist et al. Advances in Semiotics. Bloomington: Indiana University Press, 1982.

Grimaldi, William M. A. *Aristotle: Rhetoric I; A Commentary*. New York: Fordham University Press, 1980.

Grubbs, Judith Evans. Review of *The Relationship Between Roman and Local Law in the Babatha and Salome Komaise Archives: General Analysis and Three Case Studies of Succession, Guardianship and Marriage*, by Jacobine G. Oudshoorn. *RBL* (2009): http://tinyurl.com/SBL4520b.

Gruen, Erich S. *Heritage and Hellenism: The Reinvention of Jewish Tradition*. Berkeley: University of California Press, 1998.

Guenther, Heinz O. *The Footprints of Jesus' Twelve in Early Christian Traditions: A Study in the Meaning of Religious Symbolism*. New York: Peter Lang, 1984.

Gundry, Robert H. *Mark: A Commentary on His Apology for the Cross*. Grand Rapids: Eerdmans, 1993.

Gustaffson, Gabriella. *Evocatio Deorum: Historical and Mythical Interpretations of Ritualised Conquests in the Expansion of Ancient Rome*. Acta Universitatis Upsaliensis Historia Religionum 16. Uppsala: Uppsala University, 2000.

Haenchen, Ernst. *The Acts of the Apostles: A Commentary*. Translated by Bernard Noble and Gerald Shinn, under the supervision of Hugh

Anderson, and revised by R. McL. Wilson. Philadelphia: Westminster, 1971.

Hahn, Hans-Joachim. "Germany: Historical Survey." Pages 418–21 in *Encyclopedia of the Romantic Era, 1760–1850*. Edited by Christopher John Murray. New York: Fitzroy Dearborn, 2004.

Hall, Robert G. "Josephus, *Contra Apionem* and Historical Inquiry in the Roman Rhetorical Schools." Pages 229–49 in *Josephus' Contra Apionem: Studies in Its Character and Context with a Latin Concordance to the Portion Missing in Greek*. Edited by Louis H. Feldman and John R. Levison. AGJU 34. Leiden: Brill, 1996.

Hamilton, Catherine Sider. "'His Blood Be upon Us': Innocent Blood and the Death of Jesus in Matthew." *CBQ* 70 (2008): 82–100.

Harlow, Daniel C. *The Greek Apocalypse of Baruch (3 Baruch) in Hellenistic Judaism and Early Christianity*. SVTP 12. Leiden: Brill, 1996.

Harnack, Adolf von. *Die Lehre der zwölf Apostel*. TUGAL 2. Leipzig: Hinrichs, 1884.

Harpe, Jean de la. *De l'ordre et du hazard: Le réalisme critique d'Antoine Augustin Cournot*. Mémoires de l'Université de Neuchâtel 9. Neuchâtel: Université de Neuchâtel, 1936.

Harris, Zellig S. *A Grammar of the Phoenician Language*. AOS 8. New Haven: American Oriental Society, 1936.

Hatina, Thomas R. *In Search of a Context: The Function of Scripture in Mark's Narrative*. JSNTSup 232, SSEJC 8. London: Sheffield Academic, 2002.

Hawthorne, Jeremy. *A Concise Glossary of Contemporary Literary Theory*. 2nd ed. London: Edward Arnold, 1994.

Haynes, Kenneth. "Classic Vergil." Pages 421–33 in *A Companion to Vergil's Aeneid and its Tradition*. Edited by Joseph Farrell and Michael C. J. Putnam. Malden, MA: Wiley-Blackwell, 2010.

Heemstra, Marius. *The Fiscus Judaicus and the Parting of the Ways*. WUNT 277. Tübingen: Mohr Siebeck, 2010.

———. "The *Fiscus Judaicus*: Its Social and Legal Impact and a Possible Relation with Josephus' Antiquities." Pages 327–47 in *Jews and Christians in the First and Second Centuries: How to Write Their History*. CRINT 13. Edited by Peter J. Tomson and Joshua Schwartz. Leiden: Brill, 2014.

Hénaff, Marcel. *Claude Lévi-Strauss and the Making of Structural Anthropology*. Translated by Mary Baker. Minneapolis: University of Minnesota Press, 1998.

Hengel, Martin. *Judaism and Hellenism: Studies in Their Encounter in Palestine during the Hellenistic Period.* Translated by John Bowden. 2 vols. Philadelphia: Fortress, 1974.

———. *Was Jesus a Revolutionist?* Translated by William Klassen. Philadelphia: Fortress, 1971.

Henze, Matthias. *Jewish Apocalypticism in Late First Century Israel: Reading Second Baruch in Context.* TSAJ 142. Tübingen: Mohr Siebeck, 2011.

Herder, Johann Gottfried von. "Über Shakespeare." Pages 208–31 in vol. 5 of *Herders Werke in fünf Bünden.* Ann Arbor: University of Michigan Library, 1903.

———. *On the Spirit of Hebrew Poetry.* Translated by James Marsh. 2 vols. Burlington, VT: Edward Smith, 1833.

Hesse, Mary. "The Explanatory Function of Metaphor." Pages 157–77 in *Models and Analogies in Science.* Notre Dame: University of Notre Dame Press, 1966.

———. *Models and Analogies in Science.* Notre Dame: University of Notre Dame Press, 1966.

Hezser, Catherine. *Jewish Literacy in Roman Palestine.* TSAJ 81. Tübingen: Mohr Siebeck, 2001.

———. *The Social Structure of the Rabbinic Movement in Roman Palestine.* TSAJ 66. Tübingen: Mohr Siebeck, 1997.

Hocart, Arthur Maurice. *Kings and Councillors: An Essay in the Comparative Anatomy of Human Society.* Cairo: P. Barbey, 1936. Repr., edited by R. Needham. Chicago: University of Chicago Press, 1970.

———. *The Northern States of Fiji.* Royal Anthropological Institute of Great Britain and Ireland, Occasional Publication, 11. London: Royal Anthropological Institute of Great Britain and Ireland, 1952.

Hock, Ronald F. "A Dog in the Manger: The Cynic Cynulcus among Athenaeus's Deipnosophists." Pages 20–37 in *Greeks, Romans, and Christians: Essays in Honor of Abraham J. Malherbe.* Edited by David Balch, Everett Ferguson, and Wayne Meeks. Minneapolis: Fortress, 1990.

———. "Social Experience and the Beginning of the Gospel of Mark." Pages 311–26 in *Reimagining Christian Origins: A Colloquium Honoring Burton L. Mack.* Edited by Elizabeth A Castelli and Hal Taussig. Valley Forge, PA: Trinity Press International, 1996.

Hock, Ronald F., J. Bradley Chance, and Judith Perkins, eds. *Ancient Fiction and Early Christian Narrative.* SymS 6. Atlanta: Scholars Press, 1998.

Hodge, Caroline Johnson. *If Sons, Then Heirs: A Study of Kinship and Ethnicity in the Letters of Paul.* New York: Oxford University Press, 2007.

Hodge, Caroline Johnson, Saul M. Olyan, Daniel Ullucci, and Emma Wasserman, eds. *"The One Who Sows Bountifully": Essays in Honor of Stanley K. Stowers.* BJS 356. Providence, RI: Brown Judaic Studies, 2013.

Hoïstad, Ragnar. *Cynic Hero and Cynic King: Studies in the Cynic Conception of Man.* Lund: Bloms, 1948.

Holladay, Carl R., ed. *Historians.* Vol. 1 of *Fragments from Hellenistic Jewish Authors.* SBLTT 20. Chico, CA: Scholars Press, 1983.

———. *Poets.* Vol. 2 of *Fragments from Hellenistic Jewish Authors.* SBLTT 30. Atlanta: Scholars Press, 1989.

Hopkins, Keith. "Christian Number and its Implications." *JECS* 6 (1998): 185–226.

Horman, John. *A Common Written Greek Source for Mark and Thomas.* SCJ 20. Waterloo, ON: Wilfrid Laurier University Press, 2011.

Horrell, David G. "The Label Χριστιανός: 1 Peter 4:16 and the Formation of Christian Identity." *JBL* 126 (2007): 362–67.

Horsley, Richard A. *Archaeology, History, and Society in Galilee: The Social Context of Jesus and the Rabbis.* Harrisburg, PA: Trinity Press International, 1996.

———. *Hearing the Whole Story: The Politics of Plot in Mark's Gospel.* Louisville: Westminster John Knox, 2001.

———. *Jesus and the Spiral of Violence: Popular Jewish Resistance in Roman Palestine.* Minneapolis: Fortress Press, 1992.

Howard, Alan. "Cannibal Chiefs and the Charter for Rebellion in Rotuman Myth." *Pacific Studies* 10 (1986): 1–27.

Hudson, Geoffrey Francis. *Europe and China: A Survey of Their Relations from the Earliest Times to 1800.* London: E. Arnold, 1931.

Hultgren, Arland J. *The Rise of Normative Christianity.* Minneapolis: Fortress, 1994.

Humphrey, Edith M. "Will the Reader Understand? Apocalypse as Veil or Vision in Recent Historical-Jesus Research." Pages 215–37 in *Whose Historical Jesus?* Edited by William E. Arnal and Michel Desjardins. SCJ 7. Waterloo, ON: Wilfred Laurier University Press, 1997.

Humphries, Michael L. *Christian Origins and the Language of the Kingdom of God.* Carbondale, IL: Southern Illinois University Press, 1999.

Huntingford, G. W. B., ed. and trans. *Periplus of the Erythraean Sea.* London: The Hakluyt Society, 1980.

Imbert, Gaston. *Des Mouvements de longue durée Kondratieff.* Aix-en-Provence: Pensée université, 1959.

Incigneri, Brian J. *The Gospel to the Romans: The Setting and Rhetoric of Mark's Gospel.* BibInt 65. Leiden: Brill, 2004.

Irwin, Geoffrey. "The Colonization of the Pacific: Chronological, Navigational and Social Issues." *Journal of the Polynesian Society* 107 (1998): 111–44.

———. *The Prehistoric Exploration and Colonization of the Pacific.* Cambridge: Cambridge University Press, 1992.

Jackson, Bernard S., and Daniela Piattelli. "A Recent Study of the Babatha and Salome Komaise Archives." *Review of Rabbinic Judaism* 13 (2010): 88–125.

Jacob, Christian. *The Web of Athenaeus.* Edited by Scott Fitzgerald Johnson. Translated by Arietta Papaconstantinou. Center for Hellenic Studies. Cambridge: Harvard University Press, 2013.

Janzen, David. *The Violent Gift: Trauma's Subversion of the Deuteronomistic History's Narrative.* LHBOTS 561. New York: T&T Clark, 2012.

Jensen, Adolf E. *Myth and Cult among Primitive Peoples.* Chicago: University of Chicago Press, 1963.

Jeremias, Joachim. *Jesus' Promise to the Nations.* Translated by S. H. Hooke. SBT 24. London: SCM, 1958. Repr., Philadelphia: Fortress 1982.

Johnson, William A. "Pliny and the Construction of Reading Communities." Pages 32–62 in *Readers and Reading Culture in the High Roman Empire: A Study of Elite Communities.* Classical Culture and Society. New York: Oxford University Press, 2010.

Johnston, Sarah Iles, ed. *Religions of the Ancient World: A Guide.* Cambridge: Harvard University Press, 2004.

Jones, Kenneth R. *Jewish Reactions to the Destruction of Jerusalem in A.D. 70: Apocalypses and Related Pseudepigrapha.* JSJSup 151. Leiden: Brill, 2011.

Josephus. *The Jewish War.* Translated by H. St. J. Thackeray. Vol. 3. LCL 210. Cambridge: Harvard University Press, 1928.

Justinus, Marcus Juniamus. *Epitoma historiarum Philippicarum Pompei Trogi: Accedunt prologi in Pompeium Trogum.* Edited by Franz Rühl and Otto Seel. 2nd ed. BSGRT. Stuttgart: Teubner, 1972.

Kant, Immanuel. *Critique of the Power of Judgment.* Edited by Paul Guyer. Translated by Paul Guyer and Eric Matthews. New York: Cambridge University Press, 2000.

———. "Von den verschiedenen Racen der Menschen." Pages 427–43 in vol. 2 of *Gesammelte Schriften*. Berlin: G. Reimer, 1902–1983.

Katzenstein, H. Jacob. *The History of Tyre: From the Beginning of the Second Millenium B.C.E. until the Fall of the Neo-Babylonian Empire in 538 B.C.E.* Jerusalem: Schocken Institute for Jewish Research, 1973.

Kazen, Thomas. *Issues of Impurity in Early Judaism*. ConBNT 45. Winona Lake, IN: Eisenbrauns, 2010.

———. *Jesus and Purity Halakhah: Was Jesus Indifferent to Purity?* Rev. ed. ConBNT 38. Winona Lake, IN: Eisenbrauns, 2010.

Kee, Howard Clark. *Community of the New Age: Studies in Mark's Gospel*. Philadelphia: Westminster, 1977.

———. *Jesus in History: An Approach to the Study of the Gospels*. New York: Harcourt, Brace, & World, 1970.

Keith, Chris. "Early Christian Book Culture and the Emergence of the First Written Gospel." Pages 22–39 in *Mark, Manuscripts, and Monotheism: Essays in Honor of Larry W. Hurtado*. Edited by Chris Keith and Dieter T. Roth. LNTS 528. London: Bloomsbury, 2015.

———. *Jesus's Literacy: Scribal Culture and the Teacher from Galilee*. LNTS 413. London: T&T Clark, 2011.

———. "Prolegomena on the Textualization of Mark's Gospel: Manuscript Culture, the Extended Situation, and the Emergence of the Written Gospel." Pages 161–86 in *Memory and Identity in Ancient Judaism and Early Christianity: A Conversation with Barry Schwartz*. Edited by Tom Thatcher. SemeiaSt 78. Atlanta: SBL Press, 2014.

Kelber, Werner H. "Conclusion: From Passion Narrative to Gospel." Pages 153–80 in *The Passion in Mark: Studies on Mark 14–16*. Edited by Werner H. Kelber. Philadelphia: Fortress, 1976.

———. "The Hour of the Son of Man and the Temptation of the Disciples (Mark 14:32–42)." Pages 41–60 in *The Passion in Mark: Studies on Mark 14–16*. Edited by Werner H. Kelber. Philadelphia: Fortress, 1976.

———. *The Kingdom in Mark: A New Place and a New Time*. Philadelphia: Fortress, 1974.

———. "Memory and Violence, or: Genealogies of Remembering (In Memory of Edith Wyschogrod)." Pages 333–66 in *Imprints, Voiceprints, and Footprints of Memory: Collected Essays of Werner H. Kelber*. RBS 74. Atlanta: Society of Biblical Literature, 2013.

———. "The Oral and Written Gospel: Fourteen Years Afterward." Pages 167–86 in *Imprints, Voiceprints, and Footprints of Memory: Collected*

Essays of Werner H. Kelber. RBS 74. Atlanta: Society of Biblical Literature, 2013.

———. "The Oral-Scribal-Memorial Arts of Communication in Early Christianity." Pages 235–62 in *Jesus, the Voice, and the Text: Beyond the Oral and the Written Gospel*. Edited by Tom Thatcher. Waco, TX: Baylor University Press, 2008.

———, ed. *The Passion in Mark: Studies on Mark 14–16*. Philadelphia: Fortress, 1976.

———. "The Works of Memory: Christian Origins as Mnemohistory." Pages 265–96 in *Imprints, Voiceprints, and Footprints of Memory: Collected Essays of Werner H. Kelber*. RBS 74. Atlanta: Society of Biblical Literature, 2013.

Kippenberg, Hans Gerhard. *Garizim und Synagoge: Traditionsgeschichtliche Untersuchung zur samaritanischen Religion der aramäischen Periode*. RVV 30. Berlin: de Gruyter, 1971.

Kirch, Patrick Vinton. *The Archaeology of History*. Vol. 2 of *Anahulu: The Anthropology of History in the Kingdom of Hawaii*, by Patrick Vinton Kirch and Marshall Sahlins. Chicago: University of Chicago Press, 1992.

———. *On the Road of the Winds: An Archaeological History of the Pacific Islands before European Contact*. Berkeley: University of California Press, 2000.

Kirk, Alan. *The Composition of the Sayings Source: Genre, Synchrony, and Wisdom Redaction in Q*. NovTSup 9. Leiden: Brill, 1998.

———. "Social and Cultural Memory." Pages 1–24 in *Memory, Tradition, and Text: Uses of the Past in Early Christianity*. Edited by Alan Kirk and Tom Thatcher. SemeiaSt 52. Atlanta: Society of Biblical Literature, 2005.

Kirk, Alan, and Tom Thatcher, eds. *Memory, Tradition, and Text: Uses of the Past in Early Christianity*. SemeiaSt 52. Atlanta: Society of Biblical Literature, 2005.

Klawans, Jonathan. *Impurity and Sin in Ancient Judaism*. Oxford: Oxford University Press, 2000.

———. *Josephus and the Theologies of Ancient Judaism*. Oxford: Oxford University Press, 2012.

———. *Purity, Sacrifice, and the Temple: Symbolism and Supersessionism in the Study of Ancient Judaism*. Oxford: Oxford University Press, 2006.

Klein, Jürgen. "Genius, Ingenium, Imagination: Aesthetic Theories of Production from the Renaissance to Romanticism." Pages 19–62 in *The*

Romantic Imagination: Literature and Art in England and Germany. Edited by Frederick Burwich and Jürgen Klein. Amsterdam: Rodopi, 1996.

Klein, Kerwin Lee. "On the Emergence of Memory in Historical Discourse." *Representations* 69 (2000): 127–50.

Klink, Edward W. *The Audience of the Gospels: The Origin and Function of the Gospels in Early Christianity.* New York: Continuum, 2010.

Kloppenborg, John S. "Critical Histories and Theories of Religion: A Response to Burton Mack and Ron Cameron." *MTSR* 8 (1996): 279–89.

———. "*Evocatio deorum* and the Date of Mark." *JBL* 124 (2005): 419–50.

———. *Excavating Q: The History and Setting of the Sayings Gospel.* Edinburgh: T&T Clark; Minneapolis: Fortress, 2000.

———. *The Formation of Q.* Philadelphia: Fortress, 1987.

———. "Greco-Roman Thiasoi, the Ekklēsia at Corinth, and Conflict Management." Pages 187–218 in *Redescribing Paul and the Corinthians,* ed. Ron Cameron and Merrill P. Miller. ECL 5. Atlanta: Society of Biblical Literature, 2011.

———. "Isaiah 5:1–7, the Parable of the Tenants and Vineyard Leases on Papyrus." Pages 111–34 in *Text and Artifact in the Religions of Mediterranean Antiquity: Essays in Honour of Peter Richardson.* Edited by Stephen G. Wilson and Michel Desjardins. Waterloo, ON: Wilfrid Laurier University Press, 2000.

———. "Literary Convention, Self-Evidence and the Social History of the Q People." *Semeia* 55 (1991): 77–102.

———. "Literate Media in Early Christ Groups: The Creation of a Christian Book Culture." *JECS* 22 (2014): 21–59.

———. "Q, Bethsaida, Khorazin and Capernaum." Pages 61–90 in *Q in Context II: Social Setting and Archeological Background of the Sayings Source.* Edited by Markus Tiwald. BBB 173. Göttingen: V&R Unipress; Bonn: Bonn University Press, 2015.

———. *Q Parallels: Synopsis, Critical Notes, and Concordance.* Sonoma, CA: Polebridge, 1988.

———. *Q: The Earliest Gospel; An Introduction to the Original Stories and Sayings of Jesus.* Louisville: Westminster John Knox, 2008.

———. Review of *The Relationship Between Roman and Local Law in the Babatha and Salome Komaise Archives: General Analysis and Three Case Studies of Succession, Guardianship and Marriage,* by Jacobine G. Oudshoorn. *DSD* 19 (2012): 235–36.

———. *The Tenants in the Vineyard: Ideology, Economics, and Agrarian Conflict in Jewish Palestine.* WUNT 195. Tübingen: Mohr Siebeck, 2006.

Koester, Helmut. *Ancient Christian Gospels: Their History and Development.* London: SCM; Philadelphia: Trinity Press International, 1990.

Köhnke, Klaus Christian. *Entstehung und Aufstieg des Neukantianismus: Die deutsche Universitätsphilosophie zwischen Idealismus und Positivismus.* Frankfurt: Suhrkamp, 1986.

Konstan, David. "The Active Reader and the Ancient Novel." Pages 1–17 in *Readers and Writers in the Ancient Novel.* Edited by Michael Paschalis, Stelios Panayotakis, and Gareth Schmeling. Eelde: Barkhuis; Groningen: Groningen University Library, 2009.

Konstan, David, and Robyn Faith Walsh. "Civic and Subversive Biography in Antiquity." Pages 26–43 in *Writing Biography in Greece and Rome: Narrative Technique and Fictionalization.* Edited by Koen De Temmerman and Kristoffel Demoen. New York: Cambridge University Press, 2016.

Kornhardt, Hildegard. "Exemplum: Eine bedeutungsgeschichtliche Studie." PhD diss., Göttingen, 1936.

Korshin, Paul J. *Typologies in England, 1650–1820.* Princeton: Princeton University Press, 1982.

Kotansky, Roy D. "Jesus and Heracles in Cádiz (τὰ Γάδειρα): Death, Myth, and Monsters at the 'Straits of Gibraltar' (Mark 4:35–5:43)." Pages 160–229 in *Ancient and Modern Perspectives on the Bible and Culture: Essays in Honor of Hans Dieter Betz.* Edited by Adela Yarbro Collins. Scholars Press Homage Series 22. Atlanta: Scholars Press, 1998.

Kotrosits, Maia. "Diaspora Theory and the End of 'Early Christianity' and 'Early Christian Identity.'" Paper delivered at the Annual Meeting of the Society of Biblical Literature. San Diego, 23 November 2014.

———. *Rethinking Early Christian Identity: Affect, Violence, and Belonging.* Minneapolis: Fortress, 2015.

Kotrosits, Maia, and Hal Taussig. *Re-reading the Gospel of Mark Amidst Loss and Trauma.* New York: Palgrave MacMillan, 2013.

Krader, Lawrence. "The Ethnological Notebooks of Karl Marx: A Commentary." Pages 153–71 in *Toward a Marxist Anthropology: Problems and Perspectives.* Edited by S. Diamond. World Anthropology. The Hague: Mouton, 1979.

———, ed. *The Ethnological Notebooks of Karl Marx: Studies of Morgan, Phear, Maine, Lubbock.* Quellen und Untersuchungen zur Geschichte der deutschen und österreichischen Arbeitrbewegung NS 3. Assen: Van Gorcum, 1972.

Kraeling, Carl H. *The Synagogue: The Excavations at Dura-Europos Conducted by the Yale University and the French Academy of Inscriptions and Letters.* Final Report 8.1. New Haven: Yale University Press, 1956.

Kristeva, Julia. *Strangers to Ourselves.* Translated by Leon S. Roudiez. New York: Columbia University Press, 1991.

Krueger, Derek. "The Bawdy and Society: The Shamelessness of Diogenes in Roman Imperial Culture." Pages 222–39 in *The Cynics: The Cynic Movement in Antiquity and Its Legacy.* Edited by Robert Bracht Branham and Marie-Odile Goulet-Cazé. Berkeley: University of California Press, 1996.

Kuan, J. K. "Third Kingdoms 5.1 and Israelite-Tyrian Relations during the Reign of Solomon." *JSOT* 46 (1990): 31–46.

Kümmel, Werner Georg, *Introduction to the New Testament.* Translated by A. J. Mattill. 14th rev. ed. Nashville: Abingdon, 1966.

Kysar, Robert. "The Contribution of D. Moody Smith to Johannine Scholarship." Pages 3–17 in *Exploring the Gospel of John: In Honor of D. Moody Smith.* Edited by R. Alan Culpepper and C. Clifton Black. Louisville: Westminster John Knox, 1996.

Lachmann, Karl. *Betrachtungen über Homers Ilias, mit Zusätzen von M. Haupt.* Berlin: Reimer, 1847.

Lapin, Hayim. "Post-70 Judaism in Judea and the Near East." Pages 116–37 in *The Cambridge History of Religions in the Ancient World: From the Hellenistic Age to Late Antiquity.* Edited by William Adler. Vol. 2 of *The Cambridge History of Religions in the Ancient World.* Edited by Michelle Renee Salzman. Cambridge: Cambridge University Press, 2013.

———. *Rabbis as Romans: The Rabbinic Movement in Palestine 100–400 C.E.* Oxford: Oxford University Press, 2012.

Last, Richard. "The Social Relationships of Gospel Writers: New Insights from Inscriptions Commending Greek Historiographers." *JSNT* 37 (2015): 223–52.

Le Goff, Jacques. "L'historien et l'homme quotidian." Pages 213–37 in *L'Historien entre l'ethnologue et le futurologue.* Edited by Dominique Moïsi et al. Le savoir historique 4. Paris: Mouton, 1972.

Lenin, Vladimir Il'ich. "Letters from Afar: First Letter; The First Stage of the First Revolution." Pages 1–10 in vol. 2 of *Selected Works.* 2nd rev. ed. Moscow: Progress, 1967.

———. "Letters on Tactics." Pages 16–37 in *The April Theses*. Moscow: Foreign Languages Publishing House, 1951.

Leonhardt-Balzer, Jutta. "Priests and Priesthood in Philo: Could He Have Done without Them?" Pages 127–53 of *Was 70 CE a Watershed in Jewish History? On Jews and Judaism before and after the Destruction of the Second Temple*. Edited by Daniel R. Schwartz and Zeev Weiss in collaboration with Ruth A. Clements. AGJU 78. Leiden: Brill, 2012.

Léry, Jean de. *History of a Voyage to the Land of Brazil*. Latin American Literature and Culture 6. Translated by J. Whatley. Berkeley: University of California Press, 1990. Translation of *Histoire d'un voyage en la terre du Brésil*. La Rochelle: Antoine Chuppin, 1578.

Lesser, Alexander. "Social Fields and the Evolution of Society." *Southwestern Journal of Anthropology* 17 (1961): 40–48.

LeVen, Pauline. "Reading the Octopus: Authorship, Intertexts, and a Hellenistic Anecdote (Machon Fr. 9 Gow)." *AJP* 134 (2013): 23–35.

Levenson, Jon D. *The Death and Resurrection of the Beloved Son: The Transformation of Child Sacrifice in Judaism and Christianity*. New Haven: Yale University Press, 1993.

Levine, Andrew, and Erik Olin Wright. "Rationality and Class Struggle." Pages 17–47 in *Marxist Theory*. Edited by Alex Callinicos. Oxford Readings in Politics and Government. Oxford: Oxford University Press, 1989.

Levine, Lee I. *Caesarea under Roman Rule*. SJLA 7. Leiden: Brill, 1975.

Lévi-Strauss, Claude. "L'Analyse structurale en linguistique et en anthropologie." *Word: Journal of the Linguistic Circle of New York* 1 (1945): 33–53.

———. *Anthropology and Myth: Lectures, 1951–1982*. Translated by R. Willis. Oxford: Blackwell, 1987.

———. "Asdiwal Revisited (1972–3)." Pages 96–101 in *Anthropology and Myth: Lectures, 1951–1982*. Translated by R. Willis. Oxford: Blackwell, 1987.

———. "Four Winnebago Myths: A Structural Sketch." Pages 351–62 in *Culture in History: Essays in Honor of Paul Radin*. Edited by Stanley Diamond. New York: Columbia University Press, 1960. Repr., pages 198–210 in vol. 2 of *Structural Anthropology*. Translated by Monique Layton. New York: Basic Books, 1963.

———. *From Honey to Ashes*. Vol. 2 of *Introduction to a Science of Mythology*. Translated by John Weightman and Doreen Weightman. New York: Harper & Row, 1973.

——. "From Mythical Possibility to Social Existence." Pages 157–75 in *The View from Afar*. Translated by Joachim Neugroschel and Phoebe Hoss. New York: Basic Books, 1985. Translation of "De la possibilité mythique à l'existence sociale." *Le Débat* 19 (1982): 96–120.

——. "How Myths Die." Pages 256–68 in vol. 2 of *Structural Anthropology*. Translated by Monique Layton. New York: Basic Books, 1963.

——. *Introduction to a Science of Mythology*. 4 vols. Translated by John Weightman and Doreen Weightman. New York: Harper & Row; London: Jonathan Cape Limited, 1968–1981.

——. *Mythologiques*. 4 vols. Paris: Plon, 1964–1971.

——. *Naked Man*. Translated by John Weightman and Doreen Weightman. New York: Harper & Row, 1981.

——. *The Origin of Table Manners*. Vol. 3 of *Mythologiques*. Translated by John Weightman and Doreen Weightman. Chicago: University of Chicago Press; New York: Harper & Row, 1978

——. *La pensée sauvage*. Paris: Plon, 1962.

——. "Postscript to Chapter XV ['Social Structure']." Pages 324–45 in vol. 1 of *Structural Anthropology*. Translated by Claire Jacobson and Brooke Grundfest Schoepf. New York: Basic Books, 1963.

——. Preface to *Six Lectures on Sound and Meaning*, by Roman Jakobson. Translated by J. Mepham. Cambridge: MIT Press, 1978.

——. *The Raw and the Cooked*. Vol. 1 of *Mythologiques*. Translated by John Weightman and Doreen Weightman. New York: Harper & Row, 1969.

——. "Relations of Symmetry Between Rituals and Myth of Neighboring Peoples." Pages 238–55 in vol. 2 of *Structural Anthropology*. Translated by Monique Layton. New York: Basic Books, 1963.

——. "The Ritual Hunting of Eagles (1951–2)." Pages 217–20 in *Anthropology and Myth: Lectures, 1951–1982*. Translated by R. Willis. Oxford: Blackwell, 1987.

——. *The Savage Mind*. The Nature of Human Society Series. Translated by John Weightman and Doreen Weightman. Chicago: University of Chicago Press, 1966.

——. "The Scope of Anthropology." Pages 3–32 in vol. 2 of *Structural Anthropology*. Translated by Monique Layton. New York: Basic Books, 1963.

——. "The Story of Asdiwal." Pages 146–97 in vol. 2 of *Structural Anthropology*. Translated by Monique Layton. New York: Basic Books, 1963. Translation of *La Geste d'Asdiwal*. Paris: Imprimerie Nationale, 1958.

———. *The Story of Lynx*. Translated by C. Tihanyi. Chicago: University of Chicago Press, 1995.

———. *Structural Anthropology*. Translated by Monique Layton. 2 vols. New York: Basic Books, 1963.

———. "The Structural Study of Myth." Pages 206–31 in *Structural Anthropology*. 2 vols. New York: Basic Books, 1963.

Lévi-Strauss, Claude, and Didier Eribon. *Conversations with Claude Lévi-Strauss*. Translated by P. Wissing. Chicago: University of Chicago Press, 1991. Translation of *Des prés et de loin*. Paris: O. Jacob, 1988.

Levitt, Cyril H., and William Shaffir. *The Riot at Christie Pits*. Toronto: Lester & Orpen Dennys, 1987.

Lewis, James R., ed. *The Oxford Handbook of New Religious Movements*. New York: Oxford University Press, 2008.

Lewis, Naphtali, and Meyer Reinhold, eds. *The Empire*. Vol. 2 of *Roman Civilization: Selected Readings*. Records of Civilization, Sources and Studies 45. New York: Columbia University Press, 1955.

Lewis, Nicola Denzey. "The Limits of Ethnic Categories." Pages 489–507 in *Handbook of Early Christianity: Social Science Approaches*. Edited by Anthony J. Blasi, Paul-André Turcotte, and Jean Duhaime. Walnut Creek, CA: AltaMira, 2002.

Lincoln, Bruce. *Theorizing Myth: Narrative, Ideology, and Scholarship*. Chicago: University of Chicago Press, 1999.

Lindars, Barnabas. "John and the Synoptic Gospels: A Test Case." *NTS* 27 (1981): 287–94.

Linder, Amnon. *The Jews in Roman Imperial Legislation*. Detroit: Wayne State University Press, 1987.

Linnemann, Eta. *Studien zur Passionsgeschichte*. Göttingen: Vandenhoeck & Ruprecht, 1970.

Littman, Enno, et al. *Greek and Latin Inscriptions in Syria: Div. 3, Sect. A; Southern Syria*. Publications of the Princeton University Archaeological Expeditions to Syria in 1904–1905 and 1909. Leiden: Brill, 1907–1921.

Litwa, M. David. *Iesus Deus: The Early Christian Depiction of Jesus as a Mediterranean God*. Minneapolis: Fortress, 2014.

———. *We Are Being Transformed: Deification in Paul's Soteriology*. BZNW 187. Berlin: de Gruyter, 2012.

Liverani, Mario. *Israel's History and the History of Israel*. Translated by Chiara Peri and Philip R. Davies. Bible World. London: Equinox, 2005.

Livingston, James C. *The Enlightenment and the Nineteenth Century*. Vol. 1 of *Modern Christian Thought*. 2nd ed. Minneapolis: Fortress, 2006.

Luomanen, Petri. "From Mark and Q to Matthew: An Experiment in Evolutionary Analysis." Pages 37–73 in *Mark and Matthew II: Comparative Readings; Reception History, Cultural Hermeneutics, and Theology*. Edited by Eve-Marie Becker and Anders Runesson. WUNT 304. Tübingen: Mohr Siebeck, 2013.

MacDonald, Dennis R. *The Homeric Epics and the Gospel of Mark*. New Haven: Yale University Press, 2000.

———. *Two Shipwrecked Gospels: The Logoi of Jesus and Papias' Exposition of Logia about the Lord*. ECL 8. Atlanta: Society of Biblical Literature, 2012.

MacDonald, John. *The Theology of the Samaritans*. NTL. London: SCM, 1964.

MacGillivray, Erlend D. "Re-evaluating Patronage and Reciprocity in Antiquity and New Testament Studies." *JGRChJ* 6 (2009) 37–81.

Macherey, Pierre. "A propos de la rupture." *La Nouvelle Critique* (1965): 136–40.

———. "A propos du processus d'exposition du 'Capital': Le travail des concepts." Pages 213–56 in *Lire le Capital*, by Louis Althusser, Jacques Rancière and Pierre Macherey. 2 vols. Théorie 2–3. Paris: F. Maspero, 1965. Pages 201–44 in *Lire le Capital*. Edited by É. Balibar and P. Bravo Gala. 3rd ed. Quadrige 186. Paris: PUF, 1996.

———. "Lenin, Critic of Tolstoy: The Image in the Mirror." Pages 105–35 in *A Theory of Literary Production*. Translated by Geoffrey Wall. London; Boston: Routledge & Kegan Paul, 1978.

———. *A Theory of Literary Production*. Translated by Geoffrey Wall. London: Routledge & Kegan Paul, 1978.

Machon. *The Fragments*. Edited by A. S. F. Gow with introduction and commentary. Cambridge Classical Texts and Commentaries 1. Cambridge: Cambridge University Press, 2004.

Mack, Burton L. "Annex: The Christian Origins Project." Pages 203–16 in *The Christian Myth: Origins, Logic, Legacy*. New York; London: Continuum, 2001.

———. "Backbay Jazz and Blues." Pages 421–31 in *Redescribing Christian Origins*. Edited by Ron Cameron and Merrill P. Miller. SymS 28. Atlanta: Society of Biblical Literature, 2004.

———. *Christian Mentality: The Entanglements of Power, Violence, and*

Fear. Religion in Culture: Studies in Social Contest and Construction. London: Equinox, 2011.

——. *The Christian Myth: Origins, Logic, and Legacy.* New York: Continuum, 2001.

——. "Explaining Christian Mythmaking: A Theory of Social Logic." Pages 101–25 in *The Christian Myth: Origins, Logic, Legacy.* New York: Continuum, 2001.

——. "Explaining Religion: A Theory of Social Interests." Pages 83–99 in *The Christian Myth: Origins, Logic, Legacy.* New York: Continuum, 2001.

——. "Heady Stuff." Paper presented at the Ancient Myths and Modern Theories of Christian Origins Seminar. December 2001.

——. "The Historical Jesus Hoopla." Pages 25–40 in *The Christian Myth: Origins, Logic, and Legacy.* New York: Continuum, 2001.

——. "A Jewish Jesus School in Jerusalem?" Pages 253–62 in *Redescribing Christian Origins.* Edited by Ron Cameron and Merrill P. Miller. SymS 28. Atlanta: Society of Biblical Literature, 2004.

——. *The Lost Gospel: The Book of Q and Christian Origins.* San Francisco: HarperSanFrancisco, 1993.

——. *Myth and the Christian Nation: A Social Theory of Religion.* Religion in Culture: Studies in Social Contest and Construction. London: Equinox, 2008.

——. "A Myth of Innocence at Sea." *Continuum* 1 (1991): 140–57.

——. *A Myth of Innocence: Mark and Christian Origins.* Philadelphia: Fortress, 1988. Repr., Minneapolis: Fortress, 2006.

——. "On Redescribing Christian Origins." *MTSR* 8 (1996): 247–69. Repr. as pages 177–99 in *Theory and Method in the Study of Religion: Twenty Five Years On.* Edited by Aaron W. Hughes. MTSRSup 1. Leiden; Boston, 2013. Repr. with revisions as pages 59–80 in *The Christian Myth: Origins, Logic, and Legacy.* New York: Continuum, 2001.

——. "Q and the Gospel of Mark: Revising Christian Origins." *Semeia* 55 (1991): 15–39.

——. "Remarkable." Pages 469–74 in *Redescribing Christian Origins.* Edited by Ron Cameron and Merrill P. Miller. SymS 28. Atlanta: Society of Biblical Literature, 2004.

——. "Rereading the Christ Myth: Paul's Gospel and the Christ Cult Question." Pages 35–73 in *Redescribing Paul and the Corinthians.*

Edited by Ron Cameron and Merrill P. Miller. ECL 5. Atlanta: Society of Biblical Literature, 2011.

———. *The Rise and Fall of the Christian Myth: Restoring Our Democratic Ideals.* New Haven: Yale University Press, 2017.

———. "Teaching in Parables: Elaboration in Mark 4:1–34." Pages 143–60 in *Patterns of Persuasion in the Gospels,* by Burton L. Mack and Vernon K. Robbins. Sonoma, CA: Polebridge, 1989.

———. *Who Wrote the New Testament? The Making of the Christian Myth.* San Francisco: HarperSanFrancisco, 1995.

Maclean, Jennifer K. Berenson. "Barabbas, the Scapegoat Ritual, and the Development of the Passion Narrative." *HTR* 100 (2007): 309–44.

MacMullen, Ramsey. *Paganism in the Roman Empire.* New Haven: Yale University Press, 1981.

Magness, Jodi. "The Arch of Titus at Rome and the Fate of the God of Israel." *JJS* 59 (2008): 201–17.

———. "Sectarianism before and after 70 CE." Pages 69–89 in *Was 70 CE a Watershed in Jewish History? On Jews and Judaism Before and After the Destruction of the Temple.* Edited by Daniel R. Schwartz and Zeev Weiss in collaboration with Ruth A. Clements. AGJU 78. Leiden: Brill, 2012.

Malaise, Michel. *Les conditions de penetration et de diffusion des cultes égyptiens en Italie.* EPRO 22. Leiden: Brill, 1972.

———. *Inventaire préliminaire des documents égyptiens découverts en Italie.* EPRO 21. Leiden: Brill, 1972.

Malbon, Elizabeth Struthers. "Galilee and Jerusalem: History and Literature in Marcan Interpretation." *CBQ* 44 (1982): 242–55.

———. *Mark's Jesus: Characterization as Narrative Christology.* Waco, TX: Baylor University Press, 2009.

———. *Narrative Space and Mythic Meaning in Mark.* San Francisco: Harper & Row, 1986.

Malherbe, Abraham J. *Social Aspects of Early Christianity.* Baton Rouge: Louisiana State University Press, 1977.

Manson, T. W. *The Teaching of Jesus: Studies in its Form and Content.* Cambridge: Cambridge University Press, 1963.

Marcus, Joel. *Mark 1–8: A New Translation with Introduction and Commentary.* AB 27. New Haven: Yale University Press, 2000.

———. "The Jewish War and the Sitz-im-Leben of Mark." *JBL* 111 (1992): 441–62.

Marti, B. M. "L'Hercule sur l'Oeta." *Revue des études latines* 27 (1949): 189–210.

Martin, Luther H. "History, Historiography, and Christian Origins: The Jerusalem Community." Pages 263–73 in *Redescribing Christian Origins*. Edited by Ron Cameron and Merrill P. Miller. SymS 28. Atlanta: Society of Biblical Literature, 2004.

———. "Redescribing Christian Origins: Historiography or Exegesis?" Pages 475–81 in *Redescribing Christian Origins*. Edited by Ron Cameron and Merrill P. Miller. SymS 28. Atlanta: Society of Biblical Literature, 2004.

Marx, Karl. *Capital: A Critique of Political Economy*. Edited by Friedrich Engels. Translated by Samuel Moore and Edward Aveling. Revised and amplified by E. Untermann. 3 vols. New York: Modern Library, 1906.

———. *A Contribution to the Critique of Political Economy*. Edited by M. Dobb. Translated by S. W. Ryanzanskaya. Moscow: Progress Publishers, 1970.

———. "Formen die der Kapitalistischen Produktion vorhergehen." Pages 375–413 in *Grundrisse der Kritik der Politischen Ökonomie*. Berlin: Dietz Verlag, 1953.

———. *Grundrisse der Kritik der Politischen Ökonomie*. Berlin Dietz, 1953.

———. *Pre-capitalist Economic Formations*. Edited by E. J. Hobsbawm. Translated by J. Cohen. New York: International Publishers, 1965.

———. *The Process of Capitalist Production*. Vol. 1 of *Capital: A Critique of Political Economy*. Edited by Friedrich Engels. Translated by Samuel Moore and Edward Aveling. Revised and amplified by E. Untermann. New York: Modern Library, 1906.

———. *The Process of Capitalist Production as a Whole*. Vol. 3 of *Capital: A Critique of Political Economy*. Edited by Friedrich Engels. Translated by Samuel Moore and Edward Aveling. Moscow: Foreign Languages Publishing House, 1962.

———. "The Reproduction and Circulation of the Aggregate Social Capital." Pages 351–523 in *The Process of Circulation of Capital*. Vol. 2 of *Capital: A Critique of Political Economy*. Edited by Friedrich Engels. Translated by Samuel Moore and Edward Aveling. Moscow: Foreign Languages Publishing House, 1961.

Marx, Karl, and Friedrich Engels. *Collected Works*. 50 vols. Translated by Richard Dixon et al. New York: International Publishers, 1975–2004.

———. *The German Ideology*. Vol. 5 of *Collected Works*. Edited by David Riazanov. Moscow: Marx-Engels Institute, 1932.

———. *Selected Correspondence.* Edited by S. Ryazanskaya. Translated by I. Lasker. 2nd ed. Moscow: Progress Publishers, 1965.

Marxsen, Willi. *Mark the Evangelist: Studies on the Redaction History of the Gospel.* Translated by James Boyce et al. Nashville; New York: Abingdon, 1969.

Mason, Steve. *A History of the Jewish War, A.D. 66–74.* New York: Cambridge University Press, 2016.

———. "Jews, Judaeans, Judaizing, Judaism: Problems of Categorization in Ancient History." *JSJ* 38 (2007): 457–512.

———. "Josephus, Daniel and the Flavian House." Pages 161–91 in *Josephus and the History of the Greco-Roman Period: Essays in Memory of Morton Smith.* Edited by Fausto Parente and Joseph Sievers. Leiden: Brill, 1994.

———, ed. *Life of Josephus.* Vol. 9 of *Flavius Josephus: Translation and Commentary.* Edited by Steve Mason. Leiden: Brill, 2001.

———. "Why Did Judaeans Go to War with Rome in 66–67 CE? Realist-Regional Perspectives." Pages 126–206 in *Jews and Christians in the First and Second Centuries: How to Write Their History.* Edited by Peter J. Tomson and Joshua Schwartz. CRINT 13. Leiden: Brill, 2014.

Matheron, François. Introduction to *Écrits philosophiques et politiques,* by Louis Althusser. Edited by F. Matheron. Paris: Stock: IMEC, 1994–1995.

———. "Presentation." Pages 7–22 in *Écrits philosophiques et politiques,* by Louis Althusser. Edited by F. Matheron. Paris: Stock: IMEC, 1994–1995.

Matthews, Shelly. *Perfect Martyr: The Stoning of Stephen and the Construction of Christian Identity.* Oxford: Oxford University Press, 2010.

Matthews, Shelly, and E. Leigh Gibson, eds. *Violence in the New Testament.* London: T&T Clark, 2005.

McCague, James. *The Second Rebellion: The Story of the New York City Draft Riots of 1863.* New York: Dial, 1968.

McCutcheon, Russell T. "Why Do You Seek the Living among the Dead?" Paper presented at the Annual Meeting of the Society of Biblical Literature. Baltimore, 25 November 2013.

———. "Why Do You Seek the Living among the Dead? (Luke 24:5)." Pages 119–39 in *A Modest Proposal on Method: Essaying the Study of Religion.* MTSRSup 2. Leiden: Brill, 2015.

McLaren, James S. "Constructing Judaean History in the Diaspora: Josephus's Accounts of Judas." Pages 90–108 in *Negotiating Diaspora:*

Jewish Strategies in the Roman Empire. Edited by John M. G. Barclay. LSTS 45. London: T&T Clark, 2004.

———. "Delving into the Dark Side: Josephus' Foresight as Hindsight." Pages 49–67 in *Making History: Josephus and Historical Method.* Edited by Zuleika Rodgers. JSJSup 110. Leiden: Brill, 2007.

———. "Going to War against Rome: The Motivation of the Jewish Rebels." Pages 129–53 in *The Jewish Revolt against Rome: Interdisciplinary Perspectives.* Edited by Mladen Popović. JSJSup 154. Leiden: Brill, 2011.

———. "The *Jewish War* as a Response to the Crisis of Flavian Propaganda." Pages 9–28 in *Ancient Jewish and Christian Texts as Crisis Management Literature: Thematic Studies from the Centre for Early Christian Studies.* Edited by David C. Sim and Pauline Allen. LNTS 445. London: T&T Clark, 2012.

———. "A Reluctant Provincial: Josephus and the Roman Empire in *Jewish War.*" Pages 34–48 in *The Gospel of Matthew in Its Roman Imperial Context.* Edited by John Riches and David C. Sim. JSNTSup 276. London: T&T Clark, 2005.

———. "Searching for Rome and the Imperial Cult in Galilee: Reassessing Galilee-Rome Relations (63 B.C.E. to 70 C.E.)." Pages 111–36 in *Rome and Religion: A Cross-Disciplinary Dialogue on the Imperial Cult.* Edited by Jeffrey Brodd and Jonathan L. Reed. WGRWSup 5. Atlanta: Society of Biblical Literature, 2011.

———. *Turbulent Times? Josephus and Scholarship on Judaea in the First Century CE.* JSPSup 29. Sheffield: Sheffield Academic, 1998.

Meeks, Wayne A. "Corinthian Christians as Artificial Aliens." Pages 129–38 in *Paul Beyond the Judaism/Hellenism Divide.* Edited by Troels Engberg-Pedersen. Louisville: Westminster John Knox, 2001.

———. *The Prophet-King: Moses Traditions and the Johannine Christology.* NovTSup 14. Leiden: Brill, 1967.

Meier, John P. *A Marginal Jew: Rethinking the Historical Jesus.* 4 vols. New York: Doubleday, 1991–2009.

Meillassoux, Claude. "From Reproduction to Production: A Marxist Approach to Economic Anthropology." *Economy and Society* 1 (1972): 93–105.

———. *Maidens, Meal and Money: Capitalism and the Domestic Economy.* Cambridge: Cambridge University Press, 1981.

Métraux, Alfred. *La religion des Tupinamba et ses rapports avec celles des autres tribus tupi-guarani.* Bibliothèque de l'école des hautes études, Sciences religieuses 45. Paris: E. Leroux, 1928.

———. "The Tupinamba." Pages 95–134 in *The Tropical Forest Tribes*. Vol. 3 of *Handbook of South American Indians*. Edited by J. H. Steward. Washington, DC: Smithsonian Institution, Bureau of American Ethnology, Bulletin 143, 1946–1949.

———. "Twin Heroes in South American Mythology." *Journal of American Folklore* 59 (1946): 114–23.

Metzger, Bruce M. *A Textual Commentary on the Greek New Testament*. 2nd ed. New York: United Bible Societies, 1994.

Meyer, Marvin. "Albert Schweitzer and the Image of Jesus in the Gospel of Thomas." Pages 72–90 in *Jesus Then and Now: Images of Jesus in History and Christology*. Edited by Marvin Meyer and Charles Hughes. Harrisburg, PA: Trinity Press International, 2001.

Meyer, R. "Die Figurendarstellung in der Kunst der späthellenistischen Zeit." *Jud* 5 (1949): 1–40.

Millar, Fergus. "Last Year in Jerusalem: Monuments of the Jewish War in Rome." Pages 101–28 in *Flavius Josephus and Flavian Rome*. Edited by Jonathan Edmondson, Steve Mason, and James B. Rives. Oxford: Oxford University Press, 2005.

———. *The Roman Near East, 31 BC–AD 337*. Cambridge: Harvard University Press, 1993.

———. "Transformations of Judaism and Graeco-Roman Rule: Responses to Seth Schwartz's *Imperialism and Jewish Society*." *JJS* 57 (2006): 139–58.

Miller, Merrill P. "The Anointed Jesus." Pages 375–415 in *Redescribing Christian Origins*. Edited by Ron Cameron and Merrill P. Miller. SymS 28. Atlanta: Society of Biblical Literature, 2004.

———. "Antioch, Paul, and Jerusalem: Diaspora Myths of Origins in the Homeland." Pages 177–235 in *Redescribing Christian Origins*. Edited by Ron Cameron and Merrill P. Miller. SymS 28. Atlanta: Society of Biblical Literature, 2004.

———. "'Beginning from Jerusalem …': Re-examining Canon and Consensus." *Journal of Higher Criticism* 2 (1995): 3–30.

———. "Discussion and Reflections." Pages 133–38 in *Redescribing Christian Origins*. Edited by Ron Cameron and Merrill P. Miller. SymS 28. Atlanta: Society of Biblical Literature, 2004.

———. "Introduction to Selected Papers from the Third Consultation on Christian Origins." *MTSR* 11 (1999): 207–9.

———. "Introduction to the Consultation on Christian Origins." *MTSR* 8 (1996): 229–30.

——. "The Problem of the Origins of a Messianic Conception of Jesus." Pages 301–35 in *Redescribing Christian Origins*. Edited by Ron Cameron and Merrill P. Miller. SymS 28. Atlanta: Society of Biblical Literature, 2004.

Miller, Richard C. "Mark's Empty Tomb and Other Translation Fables in Classical Antiquity." *JBL* 129 (2010): 759–76.

Miller, Robert J. "The (A)Historicity of Jesus' Temple Demonstration: A Test Case in Methodology." Pages 235–52 in *Society of Biblical Literature 1991 Seminar Papers*. Edited by Eugene H. Lovering, Jr. SBLSP 30. Atlanta: Scholars Press, 1991.

——. "Historical Method and the Deeds of Jesus: The Test Case of the Temple Demonstration." *Forum* 8 (1992): 5–30.

Miller, Stuart S. "Review Essay: Roman Imperialism, Jewish Self-Definition, and Rabbinic Society: Belayche's *Iudaea-Palaestina*, Schwartz's *Imperialism and Jewish Society*, and Boyarin's *Border Lines* Reconsidered." *AJSR* 31 (2007): 329–62.

——. "Roman Imperialism, Jewish Self-Definition, and Rabbinic Society." *AJSR* 31 (2007): 336–50.

——. *Sages and Commoners in Late Antique 'Erez Israel: A Philological Inquiry into Local Traditions in Talmud Yerushalmi*. TSAJ 111. Tübingen: Mohr Siebeck, 2006.

Miner, Earl Roy, ed. *Literary Uses of Typology: From the Late Middle Ages to the Present*. Princeton: Princeton University Press, 1977.

Mommsen, Theodor, Paul Krueger, and Alan Watson, eds. *The Digest of Justinian*. 4 vols. Philadelphia: University of Pennsylvania Press, 1985.

Moore, Gregory. Introduction to *Shakespeare*, by Johann Gottfried Herder. Edited and translated by Gregory Moore. Princeton: Princeton University Press, 2008.

Moreland, Milton. "The Galilean Response to Earliest Christianity: A Cross-Cultural Study of the Subsistence Ethic." Pages 37–48 in *Religion and Society in Roman Palestine: Old Questions, New Approaches*. Edited by Douglas R. Edwards. London: Routledge, 2004.

——. "The Inhabitants of Galilee in the Hellenistic and Early Roman Periods: Probes into the Archaeological and Literary Evidence." Pages 133–59 in *Religion, Ethnicity, and Identity in Ancient Galilee*. Edited by Jürgen Zangenberg, Harold W. Attridge, and Dale Martin. WUNT 210. Tübingen: Mohr Siebeck, 2007.

——. "The Jesus Movement in the Villages of Roman Galilee: Archaeology, Q, and Modern Anthropological Theory." Pages 159–80 in *Oral*

Performance, Popular Tradition, and Hidden Transcript in Q. Edited by Richard A. Horsley. SemeiaSt 60. Atlanta: Society of Biblical Literature, 2006.

Morris, Brian. *Anthropological Studies of Religion.* Cambridge: Cambridge University Press, 1987.

Mosher, Joseph A. *The Exemplum in the Early Religious and Didactic Literature in England.* New York: Columbia University Press, 1911.

Moss, Candida. *The Myth of Persecution: How Early Christians Invented a Story of Martyrdom.* New York: HarperCollins, 2013.

Motyer, S. "The Rending of the Veil: A Markan Pentecost." *NTS* 33 (1987): 155–57.

Moxnes, Halvor. "Identity in Jesus' Galilee: From Ethnicity to Locative Intersectionality." *BibInt* 18 (2010): 390–416.

Murphy-O'Connor, Jerome. *Paul: A Critical Life.* Oxford: Oxford University Press, 1997.

Murray, Gilbert. "Heracles 'The Best of Men.'" Pages 106–26 in *Greek Studies.* Oxford: Clarendon Press, 1946.

Myllykoski, Matti. "The Social History of Q and the Jewish War." Pages 143–99 in *Symbols and Strata: Essays on the Sayings Gospel Q.* Edited by Risto Uro. Publications of the Finnish Exegetical Society 65. Helsinki: The Finnish Exegetical Society; Göttingen: Vandenhoeck & Ruprecht, 1996.

Neirynck, Frans. "John and the Synoptics: 1975–1990." Pages 3–62 in *John and the Synoptics.* Edited by Adelbert Denaux. Louvain: Leuven University Press, 1992.

———. "The Minor Agreements and Q." Pages 49–72 in *The Gospel Behind the Gospels: Current Studies on Q.* Edited by Ronald A. Piper. Leiden: Brill, 1995.

Neujahr, Matthew. *Predicting the Past in the Ancient Near East: Mantic Historiography in Ancient Mesopotamia, Judah, and the Mediterranean World.* BJS 354. Providence, RI: Brown Judaic Studies, 2012.

Neusner, Jacob. *Fellowship in Judaism: The First Century and Today.* London: Valentine, Mitchell, 1963.

———. *From Politics to Piety: The Emergence of Pharisaic Judaism.* Englewood Cliffs, NJ: Prentice-Hall, 1973.

Nickelsburg, George W. E. "The Genre and Function of the Markan Passion Narrative." *HTR* 73 (1980): 154–84.

———. "Passion Narratives." *ABD* 5:172–75.

———. *Resurrection, Immortality and Eternal Life in Intertestamental Judaism*. HTS 26. Cambridge: Harvard University Press, 1972.

Niehoff, Maren R. *Jewish Exegesis and Homeric Scholarship in Alexandria.* New York: Cambridge University Press, 2011.

Niehr, Herbert. "The Rise of YHWH in Judahite and Israelite Religion: Methodological and Religio-Historical Aspects." Pages 45–72 in *The Triumph of Elohim: From Yahwisms to Judaisms.* Edited by D. V. Edelman. Grand Rapids: Eerdmans, 1996.

Nock, Arthur Darby. *Conversion: The Old and New in Religion from Alexander the Great to Augustine of Hippo.* Oxford: Oxford University Press, 1933.

———. "Religious Symbols and Symbolism II." Pages 895–907 in vol. 2 of *Arthur Darby Nock: Essays on Religion and the Ancient World.* 2 vols. Edited by Zeph Stewart. Oxford: Clarendon, 1972.

Norton, Robert Edward. "The Ideal of a Philosophical History of Aesthetics: The Diverse Unity of Nature." Pages 51–81 in *Herder's Aesthetics and the European Enlightenment.* Ithaca, NY: Cornell University Press, 1991.

Obeyesekere, Gananath. *The Apotheosis of Captain Cook: European Mythmaking in the Pacific.* Princeton: Princeton University Press, 1992.

Olick, Jeffrey K. "Products, Processes, and Practices: A Non-reificatory Approach to Collective Memory." *BTB* 36 (2006): 5–14.

O'Toole, Robert F. "Last Supper." *ABD* 4:234–41.

Oudshoorn, Jacobine G. *The Relationship between Roman and Local Law in the Babatha and Salome Komaise Archives: General Analysis and Three Case Studies on Law of Succession, Guardianship and Marriage.* STDJ 69. Leiden: Brill, 2007.

Paget, James Carleton. "After 70 and All That: A Response to Martin Goodman's *Rome and Jerusalem.*" *JSNT* 31 (2009): 339–65.

Palestine Archaeological Museum. *Gallery Book: Persian, Hellenistic, Roman, and Byzantine Periods.* Jerusalem: Palestine Archaeological Museum, 1943.

Parish, Peter J. *The American Civil War.* New York: Holmes & Meier, 1975.

Pasto, James. "The Origin, Expansion and Impact of the Hasmoneans in Light of Comparative Ethnographic Studies (and Outside of Its Nineteenth-Century Context)." Pages 166–201 in *Second Temple Studies III: Studies in Politics, Class and Material Culture.* Edited by Philip R. Davies and John M. Halligan. JSOTSup 340. London: Sheffield Academic Press, 2002.

Peirce, Charles S. *Collected Papers.* Edited by Charles Hartshorne and Paul Weiss. 8 vols. Cambridge: Harvard University Press, 1931–1958.

Penner, Hans H. *Impasse and Resolution: A Critique of the Study of Religion.* Toronto Studies in Religion 8. New York: Lang, 1989.

———, ed. *Teaching Lévi-Strauss.* Teaching Religious Studies 1. Atlanta: Scholars Press, 1998.

Perrin, Norman, and Dennis C. Duling. *The New Testament: An Introduction.* 2nd ed. New York: Harcourt Brace Jovanovich, 1982.

Pervo, Richard I. "A Nihilist Fabula: Introducing the *Life of Aesop.*" Pages 77–120 in *Ancient Fiction and Early Christian Narrative.* Edited by Ronald F. Hock, J. Bradley Chance, and Judith Perkins. SymS 6. Atlanta: Scholars Press, 1998.

Peters, J. Durham. *Speaking into the Air: A History of the Idea of Communication.* Chicago: University of Chicago Press, 1999.

Peters, John P., and Hermann Thiersch. *The Painted Tombs in the Necropolis of Marissa.* Edited by S. A. Cook. London: Committee of the Palestine Exploration Fund, 1905.

Peterson, Dwight N. *The Origins of Mark: The Markan Community in Current Debate.* BibInt 48. Leiden: Brill, 2000.

Pettazzoni, Raffaele. "La confession des péchés en Syrie aux époques préchrétiennes." Pages 197–202 in vol. 1 of *Mélanges syriens offerts à Monsier René Dussaud.* Bibliothèque archèologique et historique 30. Paris: Geuthner, 1939.

Pfister, R. Friedrich. "Herakles und Christus." *AR* 34 (1937): 42–60.

Phear, John B. *The Aryan Village in India and Ceylon.* London: Macmillan, 1880.

Piper, Ronald A. *Wisdom in the Q-Tradition: The Aphoristic Teaching of Jesus.* Cambridge: Cambridge University Press, 1989.

Plassart, André. *Les sanctuaires et les cultes du Mont Cynthe.* Exploration archéologique de Délos 11. Paris: E. de Boccard, 1928.

Plutarch. *Lives VII: Demosthenes and Cicero; Alexander and Caesar.* Translated by Bernadotte Perrin. LCL. Cambridge: Harvard University Press, 1919.

Poirier, John C. "Why Did the Pharisees Wash Their Hands?" *JJS* 47 (1996): 217–33.

Poole, Brian. "Bakhtin and Cassirer: The Philosophical Origins of Bakhtin's Carnival Messianism." *The South Atlantic Quarterly* 97 (1998): 537–78.

Powell, Mark Allan. "Narrative Criticism: The Emergence of a Prominent Reading Strategy." Pages 19–43 in *Mark as Story: Retrospect and Pros-*

pect. Edited by Kelly R. Iverson and Christopher W. Skinner. RBS 65. Atlanta: Society of Biblical Literature, 2011.

Pritchard, James B. *Recovering Sarepta, A Phoenician City: Excavations at Sarafand, Lebanon, 1969–1974 by the University Museum of the University of Pennsylvania.* Princeton: Princeton University Press, 1978.

Puma, Richard Daniel de. "The Roman Bronzes from Kolhapur." Pages 82–112 in *Rome and India: The Ancient Sea Trade.* Edited by V. Begley and R. D. de Puma. Madison, WI: University of Wisconsin Press, 1991.

Quentin, Patrick. *Les origines de l'idéologie.* Paris: Economica, 1987.

Rajak, Tessa. "The Greek Bible Translations among Jews in the Second Century CE." Pages 321–32 in *Jewish Identities in Antiquity: Studies in Memory of Menahem Stern.* Edited by Lee I. Levine and Daniel R. Schwartz. TSAJ 130. Tübingen: Mohr Siebeck, 2009.

———. *Josephus: The Historian and His Society.* London: Duckworth, 1983.

Rashke, M. G. "New Studies in Roman Commerce." *ANRW* 9.2:604–1361.

Redford, Donald B. *Egypt, Canaan, and Israel in Ancient Times.* Princeton: Princeton University Press, 1992.

Reed, Annette Yoshiko. "Rabbis, 'Jewish Christians', and Other Late Antique Jews: Reflections of the Fate of Judaism(s) after 70 C.E." Pages 323–46 in *The Changing Face of Judaism, Christianity, and Other Greco-Roman Religions in Antiquity.* Edited by Ian H. Henderson and Gerbern S. Oegema with the assistance of Sara Parks Ricker. Studien zu den Jüdischen Schriften aus hellenistisch-römischer Zeit 2. Gütersloh: Gütersloher Verlagshaus, 2006.

Rhoads, David M. *Israel in Revolution 6–74 C.E.: A Political History Based on the Writings of Josephus.* Philadelphia: Fortress, 1976.

Rhoads, David, and Donald Michie. *Mark as Story: An Introduction to the Narrative of a Gospel.* Philadelphia: Fortress, 1982.

Richards, William A. *Difference and Distance in Post-Pauline Christianity: An Epistolary Analysis of the Pastorals.* StBibLit 44. New York: Lang, 2002.

Richardson, Peter. "Why Turn the Tables? Jesus' Protest in the Temple Precincts." Pages 507–23 in *Society of Biblical Literature 1992 Seminar Papers.* Edited by Eugene H. Lovering Jr. SBLSP 31. Atlanta: Scholars Press, 1992.

Riches, John K. "Conflicting Mythologies: Mythical Narrative in the Gospel of Mark." *JSNT* 84 (2001): 29–50.

Ricoeur, Paul. *Finitude et culpabilité: La symbolique du mal.* Vol. 2.2 of *Philosophie de la volonté.* Philosophie de l'esprit. Paris: Aubier, 1960.

———. *The Rule of Metaphor*. Translated by R. Czerny, K. McLaughlin, and J. Costello. Toronto: University of Toronto Press, 1977. Translation of *La métaphore vive*. Paris: Seuil, 1975.

Rives, James B. "Flavian Religious Policy and the Destruction of the Jerusalem Temple." Pages 145–66 in *Flavius Josephus and Flavian Rome*. Edited by Jonathan Edmonson, Steve Mason, and James B. Rives. Oxford: Oxford University Press, 2005.

———. *Religion in the Roman Empire*. Blackwell Ancient Religions. Malden, MA: Blackwell, 2007.

Robbins, Vernon K. *Jesus the Teacher: A Socio-rhetorical Interpretation of Mark*. Philadelphia: Fortress, 1984.

———. "Last Meal: Preparation, Betrayal, and Absence." Pages 21–40 in *The Passion in Mark: Studies on Mark 14–16*. Edited by Werner H. Kelber. Philadelphia: Fortress, 1976.

———. "Plucking Grain on the Sabbath." Pages 107–41 in *Patterns of Persuasion in the* Gospels. Edited by Burton L. Mack and Vernon K. Robbins. Sonoma, CA: Polebridge, 1989.

Roberts, Erin. "Anger, Emotion, and Desire in the Gospel of Matthew." PhD diss., Brown University, 2010.

Robertson, Paul M. *Paul's Letters and Contemporary Greco-Roman Literature: Theorizing a New Taxonomy*. NovTSup 167. Leiden: Brill, 2016.

Robinson, James M. "Building Blocks in the Social History of Q." Pages 87–112 in *Reimagining Christian Origins: A Colloquium Honoring Burton L. Mack*. Edited by Elizabeth A. Castelli and Hal Taussig. Valley Forge, PA. Trinity Press International, 1996.

———. "The Q Trajectory: between John and Matthew Via Jesus." Pages 285–307 in *The Sayings Gospel Q*. Edited by Christof Heil and Joseph Verheyden. Leuven: Leuven University Press, 2005.

———. "The Sayings Gospel Q." Pages 361–88 in *The Four Gospels 1992: Festschrift Frans Neirynck*. Edited by Frans van Segbroeck, Christopher. M. Tuckett, Gilbert van Belle, and Joseph Verheyden. BETL 100. 3 vols. Louvain: Leuven University Press, 1992.

Robinson, James M., Paul Hoffmann, and John S. Kloppenborg, eds. *The Critical Edition of Q: Synopsis Including the Gospels of Matthew and Luke, Mark and Thomas with English, German, and French Translations of Q and Thomas*. Hermeneia Supplements. Minneapolis: Fortress, 2000.

Rollens, Sarah E. *Framing Social Criticism in the Jesus Movement*. WUNT 374. Tübingen: Mohr Siebeck, 2014.

———. "The Identity of Q in the First Century: Reproducing a Theological Narrative." Pages 177–91 in *Failure and Nerve in the Academic Study of Religion: Essays in Honor of Donald Wiebe*. Edited by William E. Arnal, Willi Braun, and Russell T. McCutcheon. Sheffield: Equinox, 2012.

———. "Inventing Tradition in Thessalonica: The Appropriation of the Past in 1 Thessalonians 2:14–16." *BTB* 46 (2016): 123–32.

———. "The Kingdom of God Is Among You: The Scholarly Fixation on a Q Community." Paper presented at the Annual Meeting of the Society of Biblical Literature. Baltimore, 24 November 2013.

———. "The Rewards of Redescription: An Assessment of Burton Mack's Influence on the Study of Christian Origins." Pages 171–76 in *Theory and Method in the Study of Religion: Twenty Five Years On*. Edited by Aaron W. Hughes. MTSRSup 1. Leiden; Boston: Brill, 2013.

Rorty, Richard. *Philosophy and the Mirror of Nature*. Princeton: Princeton University Press, 1979.

Rose, Herbert Jennings. "Heracles and the Gospels." *HTR* 31 (1938): 113–42.

Roskam, Hendrika Nicoline. *The Purpose of the Gospel of Mark in Its Historical and Social Context*. NovTSup 114. Leiden: Brill, 2004.

Roth, Wolfgang. *Hebrew Gospel: Cracking the Code of Mark*. Oak Park, IL: Meyer-Stone Books, 1988.

Rowland, Christopher. "The Parting of the Ways: The Evidence of Jewish and Christian Apocalyptic and Mystical Material." Pages 213–37 in *Jews and Christians: The Parting of the Ways A.D. 70 to 135; The Second Durham-Tübingen Research Symposium on Earliest Christianity and Judaism (Durham, September, 1989)*. Edited by James D. G. Dunn. Grand Rapids: Eerdmans, 1999.

Runesson, Anders. "Was There a Christian Mission before the Fourth Century? Problematizing Common Ideas about Early Christianity and the Beginnings of Modern Mission." Pages 205–47 in *The Making of Christianity: Conflicts, Contacts, and Constructions; Essays in Honor of Bengt Holmberg*. Edited by Magnus Zetterholm and Samuel Byrskog. CB 47. Winona Lake, IN: Eisenbrauns, 2012.

Safrai, Zeev. *The Economy of Roman Palestine*. London: Routledge, 1994.

Sahlins, Marshall. *Apologies to Thucydides: Understanding History as Culture and Vice Versa*. Chicago: University of Chicago Press, 2004.

———. "The Apotheosis of Captain Cook." *Kroeber Anthropological Society Papers* 53–54 (1979): 1–31.

———. *The Apotheosis of Captain Cook: European Mythmaking in the Pacific*. Princeton: Princeton University Press, 1992.

———. "Captain Cook at Hawaii." *Journal of the Polynesian Society* 98 (1989): 371–423.

———. "Captain James Cook; Or The Dying God." Pages 104–35 in *Islands of History*. Chicago: University of Chicago Press, 1985.

———. "Cery Cery Fuckabede." *American Ethnologist* 20 (1993): 848–67.

———. "Colors and Cultures." Pages 139–62 in *Culture in Practice: Selected Essays*. New York: Zone Books, 2000.

———. "Comment." *Current Anthropology* 17 (1976): 298–300.

———. "Comments." *Current Anthropology* 38 (1997): 272–76.

———. *Culture and Practical Reason*. Chicago: University of Chicago Press, 1976.

———. "Culture and the Environment: The Study of Cultural Ecology." Pages 215–31 in *Horizons of Anthropology*. Edited by S. Tax. Chicago: Aldine, 1964.

———. "Culture as Protein and Profit," review of *Cannibals and Kings*, by Marvin Harris. *New York Review of Books*, 23 November 1978, 45–53.

———. *Culture in Practice: Selected Essays*. New York: Zone Books, 2000.

———. "Deserted Islands of History: A Reply to Jonathan Friedman." *Critique of Anthropology* 8 (1988): 41–51.

———. "Differentiation by Adaptation in Polynesian Societies." *Journal of the Polynesian Society* 66 (1957): 291–300.

———. "The Domestic Mode of Production." Pages 41–148 in *Stone Age Economics*. Chicago: Aldine-Atherton, 1972.

———. "Economic Anthropology and Anthropological Economics." *Social Science Information* 8 (1969): 13–33.

———. "The Economics of Develop-Man in the Pacific." *Res* 21 (1992): 13–25.

———. "Esoteric Efflorescence on Easter Island." *American Anthropologist* 57 (1955): 1045–52.

———. "Evolution: Specific and General." Pages 12–44 in *Evolution and Culture*. Edited by Marshall Sahlins and E. R. Service. Ann Arbor: University of Michigan Press, 1960.

———. "Hierarchy and Humanity in Polynesia." Pages 195–217 in *Transformations of Polynesian Culture*. Edited by A. Hooper and J. Huntsman. Auckland: Polynesian Society, 1985.

———. *Historical Ethnography*. Vol. 1 of *Anahulu: The Anthropology of His-*

tory in the Kingdom of Hawaii, by Patrick Vinton Kirch and Marshall Sahlins. Chicago: University of Chicago Press, 1992.

———. *Historical Metaphors and Mythical Realities: Structure in the Early History of the Sandwich Islands Kingdom.* Association for Social Anthropology in Oceania Special Publications 1. Ann Arbor: University of Michigan Press, 1981.

———. *How "Natives" Think: About Captain Cook, for Example.* Chicago: University of Chicago Press, 1995.

———. "The Iconization of Elián Gonzalez: The Making of National History by Family Melodrama." *Criterion: A Publication of the University of Chicago Divinity School* 42 (2003): 2–13.

———. *Islands of History.* Chicago: University of Chicago Press, 1985.

———. "Land Use and Extended Family in Moala, Fiji." *American Anthropologist* 59 (1957): 449–63.

———. *Moala: Culture and Nature on a Fijian Island.* Ann Arbor: University of Michigan Press, 1962.

———. "On the Delphic Writings of Claude Lévi-Strauss." *Scientific American* 214 (1966): 131–36.

———. "On the Ideology and Composition of Descent Groups." *Man* 65 (1965): 104–7.

———. "The Political Economy of Grandeur in Hawaii from 1810 to 1830." Pages 26–56 in *Culture through Time: Anthropological Approaches.* Edited by E. Ohnuki-Tierney. Stanford, CA: Stanford University Press, 1990.

———. "Political Power and the Economy in Primitive Society." Pages 390–415 in *Essays in the Science of Culture in Honor of Leslie White.* Edited by G. E. Dole and R. L. Carneiro. New York: Crowell, 1960.

———. "Poor Man, Rich Man, Big-Man, Chief: Political Types in Melanesia and Polynesia." *Comparative Studies in Society and History* 5 (1963): 285–303. Repr., pages 71–93 in *Culture in Practice.* New York: Zone Books, 2000.

———. "Production, Distribution and Power in a Primitive Society." Pages 495–500 in *Selected Papers of the Fifth International Congress of Anthropological and Ethnological Societies.* Edited by A. F. C. Wallace. Philadelphia: University of Pennsylvania Press, 1960.

———. "Raw Women, Cooked Men, and Other 'Great Things' of the Fiji Islands." Pages 72–93 in *The Ethnography of Cannibalism.* Edited by P. Brown and D. Tuzin. Washington, DC: Society for Psychological Anthropology, 1983.

———. "Remarks on Social Structure in Southeast Asia." *Journal of the Polynesian Society* 72 (1963): 39–50.

———. "The Return of the Event, Again: With Reflections on the Beginnings of the Great Fijian War of 1843 to 1855 between the Kingdoms of Bau and Rewa." Pages 293–351 in *Culture in Practice: Selected Essays.* New York: Zone Books, 2000.

———. "The Segmentary Lineage: An Organization of Predatory Expansion." *American Anthropologist* 63 (1961): 322–45.

———. "The Social Life of Monkeys, Apes, and Primitive Men." Pages 186–99 in vol. 2 of *Readings in Anthropology.* Edited by M. H. Fried. New York: Crowell, 1959.

———. *Social Stratification in Polynesia.* Monographs of the American Ethnological Society 29. Seattle: University of Washington Press, 1958.

———. "The State of Art in Social/Cultural Anthropology: Search for an Object." Pages 14–32 in *Perspectives on Anthropology.* Edited by Anthony F. C. Wallace, John Lawrence Angel, and Richard Fox. Special Publications of the American Anthropological Association 10. Washington, DC: American Anthropological Association, 1977.

———. *Stone Age Economics.* Chicago: Aldine-Atherton, 1972.

———. *Tribesmen.* Foundations of Modern Anthropology Series. Englewood Cliffs, NJ: Prentice-Hall, 1968.

———. "Two or Three Things That I Know about Culture." *Journal of Royal Anthropological Institute* NS 5 (1999): 399–421.

———. *The Use and Abuse of Biology: An Anthropological Critique of Sociobiology.* Ann Arbor: University of Michigan Press, 1976.

———. *Waiting for Foucault, Still.* 4th ed. Chicago: Prickly Paradigm, 2002.

———. "War in the Fiji Islands: The Force of Custom, and the Custom of Force." Pages 299–328 in *International Ethics in the Nuclear Age.* Edited by R. J. Myers. Ethics and Foreign Policy Series 4. Lanham, MD: University Press of America, 1987.

Sahlins, Marshall, and Dorothy B. Barrière, eds. "William Richards on Hawaiian Culture and Political Conditions of the Islands in 1841." *Hawaiian Journal of History* 7 (1973): 18–40.

Saldarini, Anthony J. *Matthew's Christian-Jewish Community.* CSJH. Chicago: University of Chicago Press, 1994.

———. "Reading Matthew without Anti-Semitism." Pages 166–84 in *The Gospel of Matthew in Current Study: Studies in Memory of William G. Thompson S. J.* Edited by David E. Aune. Grand Rapids: Eerdmans, 2001.

———. "The Social World of Christian Jews and Jewish Christians." Pages 115–54 in *Religious and Ethnic Communities in Later Roman Palestine.* Edited by Hayim Lapin. Studies and Texts in Jewish History and Culture 5. Bethesda, MD: University of Maryland Press, 1998.

Sanders, E. P. *The Historical Figure of Jesus.* London: Allen Lane; London: Penguin, 1993.

———. *Jesus and Judaism.* Philadelphia: Fortress, 1985.

Sartre, Jean-Paul. *L'être et le néant: Essai d'ontologie phénoménologique.* Paris: Gallimard, 1943.

———. "From Individual Praxis to the Practico-Inert." Pages 79–341 in *Theory of Practical Ensembles.* Vol. 1 of *Critique of Dialectical Reason.* Rev. ed. Edited by Jonathan Rée. Translated by Alan Sheridan-Smith. London: Verso; London: New Left Books, 1976.

———. *L'Idiot de la famille.* 3 vols. Paris: Gallimard, 1971–1973.

———. *The Intelligibility of History.* Vol. 2 of the *Critique of Dialectical Reason.* Edited by Arlette Elkaïm-Sartre. Translated by Quintin Hoare. New York: Verso, 1991.

———. "Qu'est-ce que la littérature?" Pages 55–330 in *Situations II: Qu'est-ce que littérature?* Paris: Gallimard, 1948. Rev. and enl. by Arlette Elkaïm-Sartre. Pages 9–267 in *Situations III: Littérature et engagement.* Paris: Gallimard, 2013.

———. *Search for a Method.* Translated by Hazel E. Barnes. New York: Vintage Books, 1968. Translation of *Questions de méthode,* the prefatory essay in vol. 1 of *Critique de la raison dialectique.* Paris: Gallimard, 1960.

———. *Théorie des ensembles pratiques.* Vol. 1 of *Critique de la raison dialectique, précédé de questions de méthode.* Bibliothèque des idées. Paris: Gallimard, 1960.

———. *Theory of Practical Ensembles.* Vol. 1 of *Critique of Dialectical Reason.* Edited by Jonathan Rée. Translated by Alan Sheridan-Smith. Rev. ed. New York: Verso, 1976

Sasson, Jack. "Circumcision in the Ancient Near East." *JBL* 85 (1966): 473–76.

Satlow, Michael L. "A History of the Jews or Judaism: On Seth Schwartz's *Imperialism and Jewish Society. 200 B.C.E. to 640 C.E.*" *JQR* 95 (2005): 151–62.

———. "Jew or Judaean?" Pages 165–75 in *"The One Who Sows Bountifully": Essays in Honor of Stanley K. Stowers.* Edited by Caroline Johnson Hodge, Saul M. Olyan, Daniel Ullucci, and Emma Wasserman. BJS 356. Providence, RI: Brown Judaic Studies, 2013.

Satran, David. *Biblical Prophets in Byzantine Palestine: Reassessing the Lives of the Prophets*. SVTP 11. Leiden: Brill, 1995.

Saussure, Ferdinand de. *Course in General Linguistics*. Edited by C. Bally, A. Sechehaye, and A. Riedlinger. Translated by R. Harris. La Salle, IL: Open Court, 1986. Translation of *Cours de linguistique générale*. Edited by T. de Mauro. Paris: Payot, 1984.

Schatzki, Theodore. *The Site of the Social: A Philosophical Account of the Constitution of Social Life and Social Change*. University Park, PA: Pennsylvania State University Press, 2002.

Schechter, Solomon, ed. *Aboth de Rabbi Nathan*. New York: Philipp Feldheim, 1967.

Schilling, Robert. "L'Hercule romain et la réforme religieuse d'Auguste." *RevPhil* 16 (1942): 31–57.

Schlegel, August Wilhelm, and Friedrich Schlegel. "Fragmente." Pages 28–30 (frag. 116) in vol. 1.2 of *Athenaeum: Eine Zeitschrift*. Berlin: Fr. Vieweg, 1798. Repr., Berlin: Rütten & Loening, 1960.

Schmidt, Francis. *How the Temple Thinks: Identity and Social Cohesion in Ancient Judaism*. Translated by J. Edward Crowley. BibSem 78. Sheffield: Sheffield Academic Press, 2001.

Schreiber, Johannes. *Theologie des Vertrauens: Eine redaktionsgeschichtliche Untersuchung des Markusevangeliums*. Hamburg: Furche-Verlag, 1967.

Schremer, Adiel. "'The Lord Has Forsaken the Land': Radical Explanations of the Military and Political Defeat of the Jews in Tannaitic Literature." *JJS* 59 (2008): 183–200.

———. "The Religious Orientation of Non-Rabbis in Second-Century Palestine: A Rabbinic Perspective." Pages 319–41 in *"Follow the Wise": Studies in Jewish History and Culture in Honor of Lee I. Levine*. Edited by Zeev Weiss, Oded Irshai, Jodi Magness, and Seth Schwartz. Winona Lake, IN: Eisenbrauns, 2010.

———. "Where Is Their God? Destruction, Defeat, and Identity." Pages 25–48 in *Brothers Estranged: Heresy, Christianity, and Jewish Identity in Late Antiquity*. Oxford: Oxford University Press, 2010.

Schudson, Michael. "The Present in the Past versus the Past in the Present." *Communication* 11 (1989): 105–13.

Schumacher, Helmut, and Norbert Trautz. "Bibliographie zur Valenz und Dependenz." Pages 317–43 in *Untersuchungen zur Verbvalenz: Eine*

Dokumentation über die arbeit an einem deutschen Valenzlexikon. Edited by Helmut Schumacher. Tübingen: Narr, 1976.

Schürer, Emil. *A History of the Jewish People in the Time of Jesus Christ.* Translated by John MacPherson. Div. 1.2. New York: Scribner's Sons, 1891.

———. *The History of the Jewish People in the Age of Jesus Christ (175 B.C.– A.D. 135).* Revised and edited by Geza Vermes, Fergus Millar, and Martin Goodman. 2 vols. Edinburgh: T&T Clark, 1973–1979.

Schüssler Fiorenza, Elisabeth. *In Memory of Her: A Feminist Theological Reconstruction of Christian Origins.* New York: Crossroad, 1983.

Schwartz, Barry. "Christian Origins: Historical Truth and Social Memory." Pages 43–56 in *Memory, Tradition, and Text: Uses of the Past in Early Christianity.* Edited by Alan Kirk and Tom Thatcher. SemeiaSt 52. Atlanta: Society of Biblical Literature, 2005.

———. "Harvest." Pages 313–37 in *Memory and Identity in Ancient Judaism and Early Christianity: A Conversation with Barry Schwartz.* Edited by Tom Thatcher. SemeiaSt 78. Atlanta: SBL Press, 2014.

———. "Where There's Smoke, There's Fire." Pages 7–37 in *Memory and Identity in Ancient Judaism and Early Christianity: A Conversation with Barry Schwartz.* Edited by Tom Thatcher. SemeiaSt 78. Atlanta: SBL Press, 2014.

Schwartz, Daniel R. "Herodians and *Ioudaioi* in Flavian Rome." Pages 63–78 in *Flavius Josephus and Flavian Rome.* Edited by Jonathan Edmondson, Steve Mason, and James B. Rives. Oxford: Oxford University Press, 2005.

———. "Introduction: Was 70 CE a Watershed in Jewish History? Three Stages of Modern Scholarship, and a Renewed Effort." Pages 1–19 in *Was 70 CE a Watershed in Jewish History? On Jews and Judaism before and after the Destruction of the Second Temple.* Edited by Daniel R. Schwartz and Zeev Weiss in collaboration with Ruth A. Clements. AGJU 78. Leiden: Brill, 2012.

———. "Josephus on the Jewish Constitutions and Community." *Scripta Classica Israelica* 7 (1983–84): 30–52.

———. "On Sacrifice by Gentiles in the Temple of Jerusalem." Pages 102–16 in *Studies in the Jewish Background of Christianity.* Tübingen: Mohr Siebeck, 1992.

Schwartz, Joshua. "Yavne Revisited: Jewish 'Survival' in the Wake of the War of Destruction." Pages 238–52 in *Jews and Christians in the First and Second Centuries: How to Write Their History.* Edited by Peter J. Tomson and Joshua Schwartz. CRINT 13. Leiden: Brill, 2014.

Schwartz, Seth. "The Hellenization of Jerusalem and Shechem." Pages 37–45 in *Jews in a Graeco-Roman World.* Edited by Martin Goodman. Oxford: Oxford University Press, 1998.

———. "How Many Judaisms Were There? A Critique of Neusner and Smith on Definition and Mason and Boyarin on Categorization." *JAJ* 2 (2011): 208–38.

———. *Imperialism and Jewish Society, 200 B.C.E. to 640 C.E.* Princeton: Princeton University Press, 2001.

———. "The 'Judaism' of Samaria and Galilee in Josephus's Version of the Letter of Demetrius I to Jonathan (*Antiquities* 13.48–57)." *HTR* 82 (1989): 377–90.

———. "*Sunt Lachrymae Rerum*," review of *Rome and Jerusalem*, by Martin Goodman. *JQR* 99 (2009): 56–64.

———. *Were the Jews a Mediterranean Society? Reciprocity and Solidarity in Ancient Judaism.* Princeton: Princeton University Press, 2010.

Schwarz, Ori. "Place beyond Place: On Artifacts, Religious Technologies, and the Mediation of the Sacred." Pages 115–26 of *Was 70 CE a Watershed in Jewish History? On Jews and Judaism before and after the Destruction of the Second Temple.* Edited by Daniel R. Schwartz and Zeev Weiss in collaboration with Ruth A. Clements. AGJU 78. Leiden: Brill, 2012.

Schweitzer, Albert. *The Quest of the Historical Jesus: A Critical Study of Its Progress from Reimarus to Wrede.* Translated by William Montgomery. New York: Macmillan, 1968.

Schwemer, Anna Maria. *Studien zu den frühjüdischen Prophetenlegenden Vitae Prophetarum.* 2 vols. Tübingen: Mohr Siebeck, 1995.

Scott, James C. *Weapons of the Weak: Everyday Forms of Peasant Resistance.* New Haven: Yale University Press, 1985.

———. "Weapons of the Weak: Everyday Struggle, Meaning and Deeds." Pages 343–45 in *Peasants and Peasant Societies: Selected Readings.* 2nd ed. Edited by Teodor Shanin. Oxford; New York: Blackwell, 1987.

Sebag, Lucien. *Marxisme et Structuralisme.* Paris: Payot, 1964.

Seeley, David. "Blessings and Boundaries: Interpretations of Jesus' Death in Q." *Semeia* 55 (1991): 131–46.

———. "Jesus' Death in Q." *NTS* 38 (1992): 222–34.

———. "Jesus' Temple Act." *CBQ* 55 (1993): 263–83.

——. *The Noble Death: Graeco-Roman Martyrology and Paul's Concept of Salvation*. JSNTSup 28. Sheffield: Sheffield Academic, 1990.

Seyrig, Henri. "Antiquités syriennes 83: Les grands dieux de Tyr á l'époque grecque et romaine." *Syria* 40 (1963): 19–28.

——. "Heracles-Nergal." *Syria* 24 (1944): 62–80.

Shiner, Whitney. "Creating Plot in Episodic Narratives: *The Life of Aesop* and the Gospel of Mark." Pages 155–76 in *Ancient Fiction and Early Christian Narrative*. Edited by Ronald F. Hock, J. Bradley Chance, and Judith Perkins. SymS 6. Atlanta: Scholars Press, 1998.

Simmonds, Andrew. "Mark's and Matthew's *Sub Rosa* Message in the Scene of Pilate and the Crowd." *JBL* 131 (2012): 733–54.

Simon, Marcel. *Hercule et le Christianisme*. Paris: Les Belles Lettres, 1955.

Singer, Milton. *Man's Glassy Essence: Explorations in Semiotic Anthropology*. Bloomington: Indiana University Press, 1984.

Smith, D. Moody. "John and the Synoptics: Some Dimensions of the Problem." *NTS* 26 (1980): 425–44.

Smith, Daniel A. *The Post-mortem Vindication of Jesus in the Sayings of Q*. LNTS 338. London: T&T Clark, 2006.

——. *Revisiting the Empty Tomb: The Early History of Easter*. Minneapolis: Fortress, 2010.

Smith, Jonathan Z. "Acknowledgments: Morphology and History in Mircea Eliade's *Patterns in Comparative Religion* (1949–1999), Part 1: The Work and Its Contexts." *HR* 39 (2000): 315–31. Repr. as pages 61–79 in *Relating Religion: Essays in the Study of Religion*. Chicago: University of Chicago Press, 2004.

——. "Acknowledgments: Morphology and History in Mircea Eliade's *Patterns in Comparative Religion* (1949–1999), Part 2: The Texture of the Work." *HR* 39 (2000): 332–51. Repr. as pages 80–100 in *Relating Religion: Essays in the Study of Religion*. Chicago: University of Chicago Press, 2004.

——. "*Adde Parvum Parvo Magnus Acervus Erit*." *HR* 11 (1971): 67–90. Repr. as pages 240–64 in *Map Is Not Territory: Studies in the History of Religions*. SJLA 23. Leiden: Brill, 1978; Chicago: University of Chicago Press, 1993.

——. "The Bare Facts of Ritual." *HR* 20 (1980): 112–27. Repr. as pages 53–65 in *Imagining Religion: From Babylon to Jonestown*. Chicago: CSHJ. University of Chicago Press, 1982.

——. "Bible and Religion." *BCSSR* 29 (2000): 97–93. Repr. as pages 197–

214 in *Relating Religion: Essays in the Study of Religion*. Chicago: University of Chicago Press, 2004.

———. "Close Encounters of Diverse Kinds." Pages 3–21 in *Religion and Cultural* Studies, ed. S. L. Mizruchi. Princeton: Princeton University Press, 2001. Repr. as pages 303–22 in *Relating Religion: Essays in the Study of Religion*. Chicago: University of Chicago Press, 2004.

———. "*Dayyeinu*." Pages 483–87 in *Redescribing Christian Origins*. Edited by Ron Cameron and Merrill P. Miller. SymS 28. Atlanta: Society of Biblical Literature, 2004.

———. "Differential Equations: On Constructing the Other." Pages 230–50 in *Relating Religion: Essays in the Study of Religion*. Chicago: University of Chicago Press, 2004.

———. "The Domestication of Sacrifice." Pages 191–205 in *Violent Origins: Walter Burkert, René Girard, and Jonathan Z. Smith on Ritual Killing and Cultural Formation*. Edited by Robert G. Hamerton-Kelly. Stanford, CA: Stanford University Press, 1987. Repr. as pages 145–59 in *Relating Religion: Essays in the Study of Religion*. Chicago: University of Chicago Press, 2004.

———. *Drudgery Divine: On the Comparison of Early Christianities and the Religions of Late Antiquity*. Jordan Lectures in Comparative Religion 14. London: School of Oriental and African Studies, University of London, 1990; Chicago: University of Chicago Press, 1990.

———. "The 'End' of Comparison: Redescription and Rectification." Pages 237–41 in *A Magic Still Dwells: Comparative Religion in the Postmodern Age*. Edited by Kimberley C. Patton and Benjamin C. Ray. Berkeley: University of California Press, 2000.

———. "Fences and Neighbors: Some Contours of Early Judaism." Pages 1–18 in *Imagining Religion: From Babylon to Jonestown*. CHSJ. Chicago: University of Chicago Press, 1982.

———. "Good News Is No News: Aretalogy and Gospel." Pages 21–38 in *Christianity, Judaism and Other Greco-Roman Cults: Studies for Morton Smith at Sixty*. Edited by Jacob Neusner. 4 vols. SJLA 12. Leiden: Brill, 1975. Repr. as pages 190–207 in *Map Is Not Territory: Studies in the History of Religions*. SJLA 23. Leiden: Brill, 1978; Chicago: University of Chicago Press, 1993.

———. "Here, There, and Anywhere." Pages 21–36 in *Prayer, Magic, and the Stars in the Ancient and Late Antique World*. Edited by Scott B. Noegel, Joel Walker, and Brannon M. Wheeler. Magic in History 8.

University Park: Pennsylvania State University Press, 2003. Repr. as pages 323–39 in *Relating Religion: Essays in the Study of Religion*. Chicago: University of Chicago Press, 2004.

———. *Imagining Religion: From Babylon to Jonestown*. CSHJ. Chicago: University of Chicago Press, 1982.

———. "In Comparison a Magic Dwells." Pages 19–35 in *Imagining Religion: From Babylon to Jonestown*. CSHJ. Chicago: University of Chicago Press, 1982.

———. "The Influence of Symbols upon Social Change: A Place on Which to Stand." *Worship* 44 (1970): 457–74. Repr. as pages 129–46 in *Map Is Not Territory: Studies in the History of Religions*. SJLA 23. Leiden: Brill, 1978; Chicago: University of Chicago Press, 1993.

———. *Map Is Not Territory: Studies in the History of Religions*. SJLA 23. Leiden: Brill, 1998; Chicago: University of Chicago Press, 1993.

———. "Map Is Not Territory." Pages 289–309 in *Map Is Not Territory: Studies in the History of Religions*. SJLA 23. Leiden: Brill, 1978; Chicago: University of Chicago Press, 1993.

———. "No Need to Travel to the Indies: Judaism and the Study of Religion." Pages 215–26 in *Take Judaism, for Example: Studies toward the Comparison of Religions*. Edited by Jacob Neusner. CSHJ. Chicago: University of Chicago Press, 1983.

———. *On Teaching Religion*. New York: Oxford University Press, 2013.

———. "On the Origin of Origins." Pages 1–35 in *Drudgery Divine: On the Comparison of Early Christianities and the Religions of Late Antiquity*. Jordan Lectures in Comparative Religion 14. London: School of Oriental and African Studies, University of London; Chicago: University of Chicago Press, 1990.

———. "A Pearl of Great Price and a Cargo of Yams: A Study in Situational Incongruity." *HR* 16 (1976): 1–19. Repr. as pages 90–101 in *Imagining Religion: From Babylon to Jonestown*. CSHJ. Chicago: University of Chicago Press, 1982.

———. Preface to *Relating Religion: Essays in the Study of Religion*. Chicago: University of Chicago Press, 2004.

———. "Re: Corinthians." Pages 340–61 in *Relating Religion: Essays in the Study of Religion*. Chicago: University of Chicago Press, 2004. Repr. as pages 17–34 in *Redescribing Paul and the Corinthians*. Edited by Ron Cameron and Merrill P. Miller. ECL 5. Atlanta: Society of Biblical Literature, 2011.

———. *Relating Religion: Essays in the Study of Religion.* Chicago: University of Chicago Press, 2004.

———. "Religion and Bible." *JBL* 128 (2009): 5–27.

———. "Religion Up and Down, Out and In." Pages 3–10 in *Sacred Time, Sacred Place: Archaeology and the Religion of Israel.* Edited by B. M. Gittlen. Winona Lake, IN: Eisenbrauns, 2002.

———. "Sacred Persistence: Toward a Redescription of Canon." Pages 11–28 in vol. 1 of *Approaches to Ancient Judaism: Theory and Practice.* Edited by William S. Green. BJS 1. Missoula, MT: Scholars Press, 1978. Repr. and rev. as pages 36–52 in *Imagining Religion: From Babylon to Jonestown.* CSHJ. Chicago: University of Chicago Press, 1982.

———. "Scriptures and Histories (An Essay in Honor of Wilfred Cantwell Smith)." *MTSR* 4 (1992): 97–105.

———. "A Slip in Time Saves Nine: Prestigious Origins Again." Pages 67–76 in *Chronotypes: The Construction of Time.* Edited by J. Bender and D. E. Wellbery. Stanford, CA: Stanford University Press, 1991.

———. "Social Formations of Early Christianities: A Response to Ron Cameron and Burton Mack." *MTSR* 8 (1996): 271–78.

———. *To Take Place: Toward Theory in Ritual.* CSHJ. Chicago: University of Chicago Press, 1987.

———. "A Twice-Told Tale: The History of the History of Religions' History." *Numen* 48 (2001): 131–46. Repr. as pages 362–74 in *Relating Religion: Essays in the Study of Religion.* Chicago: University of Chicago Press, 2004.

———. "The Unknown God: Myth in History." *HR* 16 (1976): 1–19. Repr. and rev. as pages 66–89 in *Imagining Religion: From Babylon to Jonestown.* Chicago: CSHJ. University of Chicago Press, 1982.

———. "What a Difference a Difference Makes." Pages 3–48 in *"To See Ourselves as Others See Us": Christians, Jews, "Others" in Late* Antiquity. Edited by J. Neusner and E. S. Frerichs. Scholars Press Studies in the Humanities. Chico, CA: Scholars Press, 1985. Repr. as pages 251–302 in *Relating Religion: Essays in the Study of Religion.* Chicago: University of Chicago Press, 2004.

———. "When the Chips Are Down." Pages 1–60 in *Relating Religion: Essays in the Study of Religion.* Chicago: University of Chicago Press, 2004.

———. "Wisdom and Apocalyptic." Pages 131–56 in *Religious Syncretism in Antiquity: Essays in Conversation with Geo Widengren.* Edited by B. A. Pearson. Series on Formative Contemporary Thinkers 1. Missoula, MT: Scholars Press, 1975. Repr. as pages 67–87 in *Map Is Not Terri-*

tory: Studies in the History of Religions. SJLA 23. Leiden: Brill, 1978; Chicago: University of Chicago Press, 1993.

Smith, Morton. *Jesus the Magician.* New York: Harper & Row, 1978.

———. *Palestinian Parties and Politics that Shaped the Old Testament.* 2nd ed. London: SCM, 1987.

Smith, Wilfred Cantwell. "The Study of Religion and the Study of the Bible." *JAAR* 39 (1971): 131–40.

Snowden, Frank Martin, Jr. *Blacks in Antiquity: Ethiopians in the Greco-Roman Experience.* Cambridge: Harvard University Press, 1970.

Snyder, H. Gregory. *Teachers and Texts in the Ancient World: Philosophers, Jews and Christians.* New York: Routledge, 2000.

Sourdel, Dominique. *Les cultes du Hauran à l'époque romaine.* Institut Français d'Archéologie de Beyrouth, Bibliothèque archéologique et historique 53. Paris: Geuthner, 1952.

Spriggs, Matthew. "Pacific Archaeologies: Contested Ground in the Construction of Pacific History." *Journal of Pacific History* 34 (1999): 109–21.

Stalin, Joseph. *Anarchism or Socialism?* Moscow: Foreign Languages Publishing House, 1950.

———. *Foundations of Leninism: Lectures Delivered at the Sverdlow University in the Beginning of April 1924; A New Translation.* London: Lawrence & Wishart, 1924.

———, ed. *History of the Communist Party of the Soviet Union, Bolsheviks: Short Course.* New York: International Publishers, 1939.

———, ed. *History of the Soviet Union, Bolsheviks: Short Course.* New York: International Publishers, 1939.

———. *On Lenin.* Moscow: Foreign Languages Publishing House, 1950.

———. *The Road to Power.* New York: International Publishers, 1937.

Stanner, W. E. H. "The Dreaming." Pages 158–67 in *Reader in Comparative Religion: An Anthropological Approach.* Edited by William A. Lessa and Evan Z. Vogt. New York: Harper & Row, 1965.

Starcky, Jean. "Autour d'une dédicace palmyrénienne à Sadrafa et à Du'anat." *Syria* 26 (1949): 43–85.

Stark, Rodney. *The Rise of Mormonism.* Edited by Reid L. Neilson. New York: Columbia University Press, 2005.

Starner, Rob. *Kingdom of Power, Power of Kingdom: The Opposing World Views of Mark and Chariton.* Eugene, OR: Pickwick, 2011.

Ste. Croix, G. E. M. de. *The Class Struggle in the Ancient Greek World: From the Archaic Age to the Arab Conquests.* London: Duckworth, 1981.

Stern, Menachem, ed. *Greek and Latin Authors on Jews and Judaism*. 3 vols. Jerusalem: Israel Academy of Sciences and Humanities, 1974–1984.

Stewart, Eric C. *Gathered around Jesus: An Alternative Spatial Practice in the Gospel of Mark*. Cambridge, UK: James Clarke & Co., 2009.

Stowers, Stanley K. "The Concept of 'Community' and the History of Early Christianity." *MTSR* 23 (2011): 238–56.

———. "The Concepts of 'Religion', 'Political Religion' and the Study of Nazism." *Journal of Contemporary History* 42 (2007): 9–24.

———. "Does Pauline Christianity Resemble a Hellenistic Philosophy?" Pages 81–102 in *Paul Beyond the Judaism/Hellenism Divide*. Edited by Troels Engberg-Pedersen. Louisville: Westminster John Knox, 2001. Repr. as pages 219–43 in *Redescribing Paul and the Corinthians*. Edited by Ron Cameron and Merrill P. Miller. ECL 5. Atlanta: Society of Biblical Literature, 2011.

———. "The History of Ancient Christianity as the Study of Religion." Paper presented at the Annual Meeting of the Society of Biblical Literature. New Orleans, 22 November 2009.

———. "Jesus as Teacher and Stoic Ethics in the Gospel of Matthew." Pages 59–76 in *Stoicism in Early Christianity*. Edited by Troels Engberg-Pedersen, Tuomas Rasimus, and Ismo Dundenberg. Peabody, MA: Hendrickson, 2010.

———. "Kinds of Myth, Meals, and Power: Paul and the Corinthians." Pages 105–49 in *Redescribing Paul and the Corinthians*. Edited by Ron Cameron and Merrill P. Miller. ECL 5. Atlanta: Society of Biblical Literature, 2011.

———. "Mythmaking, Social Formation, and the Varieties of Social Theory." Pages 489–95 in *Redescribing Christian Origins*. Edited by Ron Cameron and Merrill P. Miller. SymS 28. Atlanta: Society of Biblical Literature, 2004.

———. "The Ontology of Religion." Pages 434–49 in *Introducing Religion: Essays in Honor of Jonathan Z. Smith*. Edited by Willi Braun and Russell T. McCutcheon. London: Equinox, 2008.

———. "Paul as a Hero of Subjectivity." Pages 159–74 in *Paul and the Philosophers*. Edited by Ward Blanton and Hent de Vries. New York: Fordham University Press, 2013.

———. "The Religion of Plant and Animal Offerings Versus the Religion of Meanings, Essences, and Textual Mysteries." Pages 35–56 in *Ancient Mediterranean Sacrifice: Images, Acts, Meanings*. Edited by Jennifer

Wright Knust and Zsuzsanna Várhelyi. Oxford: Oxford University Press, 2011.

———. "Theorizing the Religion of Ancient Households and Families." Pages 5–19 in *Household and Family Religion in Antiquity*. Edited by John Bodel and Saul M. Olyan. Oxford: Blackwell, 2008.

Strong, George Templeton. *The Civil War 1860–1865*. Vol. 3 of *The Diary of George Templeton Strong*. Edited by Allan Nevins and Milton Halsey Thomas. New York: Octagon Books, 1974.

Struck, Peter T. "The Genealogy of the Symbolic." Pages 1–20 in *Birth of the Symbol: Ancient Readers at the Limits of Their Texts*. Princeton: Princeton University Press, 2004.

———. "Epilogue: Symbol Traces: Post-Proclean Theories." Pages 254–77 in *Birth of the Symbol: Ancient Readers at the Limits of Their Texts*. Princeton: Princeton University Press, 2004.

Swartz, Michael D. "Judaism and the Idea of Ancient Ritual Theory." Pages 294–317 in *Jewish Studies at the Crossroads of Anthropology and History: Authority, Diaspora, Tradition*. Edited by Ra'anan S. Boustan, Oren Kosansky, and Marina Rustow. Jewish Culture and Contexts. Philadelphia: University of Pennsylvania Press, 2011.

———. "Liturgy, Poetry, and the Persistence of Sacrifice." Pages 393–412 in *Was 70 CE a Watershed in Jewish History? On Jews and Judaism before and after the Destruction of the Temple*. Edited by Daniel R. Schwartz and Zeev Weiss in collaboration with Ruth A. Clements. AGJU 78. Leiden: Brill, 2012.

Tacitus. *Dialogus de oratoribus*. Edited by Roland Mayer. New York: Cambridge University Press, 2001.

Tambiah, Stanley. *Culture, Thought and Social Action: An Anthropological Perspective*. Cambridge: Harvard University Press, 1985.

Tasker, R. V. G. *The Old Testament in the New Testament*. Grand Rapids: Eerdmans, 1968.

Tate, Allen. *On the Limits of Poetry*. New York: Swallow Press/William Morrow, 1948.

———. "Tension in Poetry." *The Southern Review* (1938): 101–15. Repr. as pages 56–71 in *Essays of Four Decades*. Wilmington, DE: ISI Books, 1999.

Tatum, W. Barnes. *John the Baptist and Jesus: A Report of the Jesus Seminar*. Sonoma, CA: Polebridge, 1994.

Taussig, Hal. "Dealing under the Table: Ritual Negotiation of Woman's Power in the Syro-Phoenician Woman Pericope." Pages 264–79 in *Rei-*

magining Christian Origins: A Colloquium Honoring Burton L. Mack. Edited by Elizabeth A. Castelli and Hal Taussig. Valley Forge, PA: Trinity Press International, 1996.

———. "The End of Christian Origins? Where to Turn at the Intersection of Subjectivity and Historical Craft." *RBL* 13 (2011): 1–45.

———. Review Essay Roundtable of *A Myth of Innocence: Mark and Christian Origins* by Burton L. Mack. *JAAR* 83 (2015): 851–57.

Taylor, Joan E. *The Essenes, the Scrolls, and the Dead Sea.* Oxford: Oxford University Press, 2012.

Taylor, Vincent. *The Gospel according to St. Mark.* London: MacMillan, 1963.

———. *The Text of the New Testament: A Short Introduction.* New York: St. Martin's, 1961.

Teixidor, Javier. *The Pagan God: Popular Religion in the Greco-Roman Near East.* Princeton: Princeton University Press, 1977.

Tellbe, Mikael. "The Temple Tax as a Pre-70 Identity Marker." Pages 19–44 in *The Formation of the Early Church.* Edited by Jostein Ådna. WUNT 183. Tübingen: Mohr Siebeck, 2005.

Tesnière, Lucien. *Éléments de syntaxe structurale.* Paris: Klincksieck, 1959.

———. *Esquisse d'une syntaxe structurale.* Paris: Klincksieck, 1953.

Theissen, Gerd. "Die pragmatische Bedeutung der Geheimnismotive im Markusevangelium: Ein wissenssoziologischer Versuch." Pages 225–45 in *Secrecy and Concealment: Studies in the History of Mediterranean and Near Eastern Religions.* Edited by Hans G. Kippenberg and Guy G. Stroumsa. SHR 65. Leiden: Brill, 1995.

———. *The Gospels in Context: Social and Political History in the Synoptic Tradition.* Translated by Linda M. Maloney. Minneapolis: Fortress, 1991.

———. *The New Testament: A Literary History.* Translated by Linda M. Maloney. Minneapolis: Fortress, 2012.

———. *The Religion of the Earliest Churches: Creating a Symbolic World.* Translated by John Bowden. Minneapolis: Fortress, 1999.

———. *Sociology of Early Palestinian Christianity.* Translated by John Bowden. Philadelphia: Fortress, 1978.

———. "The Wandering Radicals: Light Shed by Sociology of Literature on the Early Transmission of the Jesus Sayings." Pages 33–59 in *Social Reality and the Early Christians: Theology, Ethics, and the World of the New Testament.* Translated by Margaret Kohl. Minneapolis: Fortress, 1992.

Thevet, André. *La cosmographe du Roy, de deux voyages par luy faits aux Indes Australes, et Occidentales*. Paris: Pierre L'Huillier et Guillaume Chaudière, 1575.

———. *Les singularitez de la France Antartique, autremont nommée Amerique*. Paris: Heritiers de Maurice de la Porte, 1557.

Thiessen, Matthew. *Contesting Conversion: Genealogy, Circumcision, and Identity in Ancient Judaism and Christianity*. Oxford: Oxford University Press, 2011.

Thomas, Nicholas. "Against Ethnography." *Cultural Anthropology* 6 (1991): 306–22.

———. *Colonialism's Culture: Anthropology, Travel, and Government*. Princeton: Princeton University Press, 1994.

———. *Entangled Objects: Exchange, Material Culture, and Colonialism in the Pacific*. Cambridge: Harvard University Press, 1991.

———. "Historical Anthropology and the Politics of Critique." *Pacific Studies* 15 (1992): 142–58.

———. "Histories Structured and Unstructured." Pages 102–16 in *Out of Time: History and Evolution in Anthropological Discourse*. 2nd ed. Ann Arbor: University of Michigan Press, 1996.

———. *In Oceania: Visions, Artifacts, Histories*. Durham, NC: Duke University Press, 1997.

———. "The Inversion of Tradition." *American Ethnologist* 19 (1992): 213–32.

———. "The Look of Events" and the Afterword to the Second Edition. Pages 117–26 in *Out of Time: History and Evolution in Anthropological Discourse*. 2nd ed. Ann Arbor: University of Michigan Press, 1996.

———. *Marquesan Societies: Inequality and Political Transformation in Eastern Polynesia*. Oxford: Clarendon, 1990.

———. *Out of Time: History and Evolution in Anthropological Discourse*. Cambridge Studies in Social Anthropology 67. Cambridge: Cambridge University Press, 1989. 2nd ed. Ann Arbor: University of Michigan Press, 1996.

———. "Partial Texts: Representation, Colonialism and Agency in Pacific History." *Journal of Pacific History* 25 (1990): 139–58.

———. "Substantivization and Anthropological Discourse: The Transformation of Practices into Institutions in Neotraditional Pacific Societies." Pages 64–85 in *History and Tradition in Melanesian Anthropology*. Edited by James G. Carrier. Studies in Melanesian Anthropology 10. Berkeley: University of California Press, 1992.

Thompson, D'Arcy Wentworth. *On Growth and Form*. New Ed. Cambridge: Cambridge University Press, 1942.

Thompson, L. A. "Domitian and the Jewish Tax." *Historia* 31 (1982): 329–42.

Thrum, Thomas G., ed. *The Fornander Collection of Hawaiian Antiquities and Folk-Lore*. Memoirs of the Bernice Pauahi Bishop Museum 4–6. Honolulu: Bishop Museum Press, 1916–1920.

Tolbert, Mary Ann. *Sowing the Gospel: Mark's World in Literary-Historical Perspective*. Minneapolis: Fortress, 1989.

Tondriau, J. "Héracles, Héraclides et autres émules du héros." *Annali di Instituto Lombardo. Scienza e lettere* 83 (1950): 397–406.

Torrence, Robin, and Anne Clarke. "Negotiating Difference: Practice Makes Theory for Contemporary Archaeology in Oceania." Pages 1–31 in *The Archeology of Difference: Negotiating Cross-Cultural Engagements in Oceania*. Edited by Robin Torrence and Anne Clarke. One World Archaeology 35. London: Routledge, 2000.

Torrey, C. C. "The Exiled God of Sarepta." *Berytus* 9 (1948–1949): 45–49.

Toynbee, Arnold J. *The Study of History*. 12 vols. London: Oxford University Press, 1934–1961.

Tran, V. Tam Tinh. *Le culte des divinités en Campanie en dehors de Pompei, de stables et d'Herculanum*. EPRO 27. Leiden: Brill, 1972.

Trocmé, Étienne. *Le 'livre des Actes' et l'histoire*. Études d'histoire et de philosophie religieuses 45. Paris: Presses Universitaires de France, 1957.

Tuval, Michael. "Doing without the Temple: Paradigms in Judaic Literature of the Diaspora." Pages 181–239 of *Was 70 CE a Watershed in Jewish History? On Jews and Judaism before and after the Destruction of the Second Temple*. Edited by Daniel R. Schwartz and Zeev Weiss in collaboration with Ruth A. Clements. AGJU 78. Leiden: Brill, 2012.

———. *From Jerusalem Priest to Roman Jew: On Josephus and the Paradigms of Ancient Judaism*. WUNT 357. Tübingen: Mohr Siebeck, 2013.

Udoh, Fabian E. *To Caesar What Is Caesar's: Tribute, Taxes, and Imperial Administration in Early Roman Palestine (63 B.C.E.–70 C.E.)*. BJS 343. Providence, RI: Brown Judaic Studies, 2005.

Ulansey, David. "The Heavenly Veil Torn: Mark's Cosmic *Inclusio*." *JBL* 110 (1991): 123–25.

Ullucci, Daniel C. *The Christian Rejection of Animal Sacrifice*. Oxford: Oxford University Press, 2012.

———. "Toward a Typology of Religious Experts in the Ancient Mediterranean." Pages 89–103 in *"The One Who Sows Bountifully": Essays in*

Honor of Stanley K. Stowers. Edited by Caroline Johnson Hodge, Saul M. Olyan, Daniel Ullucci, and Emma Wasserman. BJS 356. Providence, RI: Brown Judaic Studies, 2013.

Uro, Risto. "Washing the Outside of the Cup: *Gos. Thom.* 89 and Synoptic Parallels." Pages 303–22 in *From Quest to Q: Festschrift James M. Robinson.* Edited by Jón Ma. Ásgeirsson, Kristina de Troyer, and Marvin W. Meyer. BETL 146. Leuven: Leuven University Press, 2000.

Uttley, W. V. *A History of Kitchener, Ontario.* Waterloo, ON: Chronicle, 1937.

Vaage, Leif. "Bird-Watching at the Baptism of Jesus: Early Christian Myth-Making in Mark 1:9–11." Pages 280–94 in *Reimagining Christian Origins: A Colloquium Honoring Burton L. Mack.* Edited by Elizabeth A. Castelli and Hal Taussig. Valley Forge, PA: Trinity Press International, 1996.

Valeri, Valerio. *Kingship and Sacrifice: Ritual and Society in Ancient Hawaii.* Translated by P. Wissing. Chicago: University of Chicago Press, 1985.

———. "The Transformation of a Transformation: A Structural Essay on an Aspect of Hawaiian History, 1809 to 1819." Pages 101–64 in *Clio in Oceania: Toward a Historical Anthropology.* Edited by Aletta Biersack. Washington, DC: Smithsonian Institution Press, 1991.

Van Henten, Jan Willem. "Jewish Martyrdom and Jesus' Death." Pages 139–68 in *Deutungen des Todes Jesu im Neuen Testament.* Edited by Jörg Frey and Jens Schröter. WUNT 181. Tübingen: Mohr Siebeck, 2005.

Vermes, Geza. *Jesus the Jew: A Historian's Reading of the Gospels.* London: Collins, 1973.

Vines, Michael E. *The Problem of Markan Genre: The Gospel of Mark and the Jewish Novel.* AcBib 3. Atlanta: Society of Biblical Literature, 2002.

Vorländer, Karl. *Kant und Marx: Ein Beitrag zur Philosophie des Sozialismus.* Tübingen: Mohr, 1911.

Wacholder, Ben Zion. *Eupolemus: A Study of Judaeo-Greek Literature.* Cincinnati: Hebrew Union College-Jewish Institute of Religion, 1975.

Waddington, William Henry. *Inscriptions grecques et latines de Syrie.* Paris: Firmin-Dodot, 1847–1870; repr. Rome: "L'Erma" di Bretschneider, 1968.

Wallace, Sherman Leroy. *Taxation in Egypt from Augustus to Diocletian.* Princeton: Princeton University Press; London: Oxford University Press, 1938.

Watson, Burton. *Hsün Tzu: Basic Writings*. New York: Columbia University Press, 1963.

Watson, David F. *Honor among Christians: The Cultural Key to the Messianic Secret*. Minneapolis: Fortress, 2010.

———. "The *Life of Aesop* and the Gospel of Mark: Two Ancient Approaches to Elite Values." *JBL* 129 (2010): 699–716.

Weeden, Theodore J., Sr. *Mark: Traditions in Conflict*. Philadelphia: Fortress, 1971.

———. "Two Jesuses, Jesus of Jerusalem and Jesus of Nazareth: Provocative Parallels and Imaginative Imitation." *Forum* NS 6 (2003): 135–341.

Weisler, Marshall I., ed. *Prehistoric Long-Distance Interaction in Oceania: An Interdisciplinary Approach*. New Zealand Archaeological Association Monograph 21. Auckland: New Zealand Archaeological Association, 1997.

Weitzman, Steven. "Josephus on How to Survive Martyrdom." *JJS* 55 (2004): 230–45.

———. "On the Political Relevance of Antiquity: A Response to David Goodblatt's *Elements of Ancient Jewish Nationalism*." *Jewish Social Studies: History, Culture, Society* 14 (2008): 165–72.

———. *Surviving Sacrilege: Cultural Persistence in Jewish Antiquity*. Cambridge: Harvard University Press, 2005.

Welles, Charles Bradford, Robert O. Fink, and J. Frank Gilliam, eds. *The Parchments and Papyri: The Excavations at Dura Europos Conducted by Yale University and the French Academy of Inscriptions and Letters*. Final Report 5.1. New Haven: Yale University Press, 1959.

Wellhausen, Julius. *Kritische Analyse der Apostelgeschichte*. Abhandlungen der königlichen Gesellschaft der Wissenschaften zu Göttingen. Philologisch-historische Klasse, NS 15/2. Berlin: Weidmann, 1914.

Welter, Jean Thiébaut. *L'Exemplum dans la littérature religieuse et didactique du moyen âge*. Paris: Occitania, 1927.

Wendt, Heidi. *At the Temple Gates: The Religion of Freelance Experts in the Roman Empire*. Oxford: Oxford University Press, 2016.

———. "*Ea Superstione*: Christian Martyrdom and the Religion of Freelance Experts." *JRS* 105 (2015): 1–20.

———. "'Entrusted with the Oracles of God': The Fate of the Judean Writings in Flavian Rome." Pages 101–09 in *A Most Reliable Witness: Essays in Honor of Ross Shepard Kraemer*. Edited by Susan Ashbrook Harvey, Nathaniel DesRosiers, Shira L. Lander, Jacqueline Z. Pastis, and Daniel Ullucci. BJS 358. Providence: RI: Brown Judaic Studies, 2015.

——. "*Interpres Legum*: Judean Diviners in the Early Roman Empire." Paper presented at the Annual Meeting of the Society of Biblical Literature. Chicago, 19 November 2012.

——. "*Iudaica Romana*: A Rereading of Judean Expulsions from Rome." *JAJ* 6 (2015): 97–126.

Wheeler, R. E. M., A. Ghosh, and K. Deva. "Arikamedu: An Indo-Roman Trading Station on the East Coast of India." *Ancient India* 2 (1946): 17–124.

White, Hayden. *The Content of the Form: Narrative Discourse and Historical Representation*. Baltimore; London: Johns Hopkins University Press, 1987.

White, L. Michael. *Building God's House in the Roman World: Architectural Adaptation among Pagans, Jews, and Christians*. Vol. 1 of *The Social Origins of Christian Architecture*. HTS 42. Valley Forge, PA: Trinity Press International, 1990.

Whitmarsh, Tim. *The Second Sophistic*. New York: Cambridge University Press, 2005.

Whitney, William Dwight, and Benjamin Eli Smith. *The Century Dictionary and Cyclopedia*. 12 vols. New York: The Century Company, 1911.

Wilamowitz-Moellendorff, Ulrich von. *Homerische Untersuchungen*. Berlin: Weidmann, 1884.

Wilde, Eliane de, and Philippe Roberts-Jones. *Le dictionnaire des peintres belges du XIVe siècle à nos jours*. Brussels: La Renaissance du Livre, 1995.

Wilford, John Noble. "Under Centuries of Sand, a Trading Hub." *New York Times*, July 9, 2002, sec. D: 1 and 9.

Will, Ernest. "Cultes et salles de banquet dans les cultes de la Grèce et de l'Empire romain." Pages 393–402 in *De l'Euphrate au Rhin: Aspects de l'hellenisation et de la romanisation du Proche-Orient*. Beirut: Institut Français D'Archéologie du Proche-Orient, 1995.

Willi, Thomas. *Herders Beitrag zum Verstehen des Alten Testaments*. Beitrag zur Geschichte der Biblischen Hermeneutik 8. Tübingen: Mohr Siebeck, 1971.

Williams, Craig A. "Love and Friendship: Authors and Texts." Pages 174–258 in *Reading Roman Friendship*. New York: Cambridge University Press, 2012.

Williams, Margaret. *The Jews among the Greeks and Romans: A Sourcebook*. Baltimore: John Hopkins University Press, 1998.

Williams, Raymond. *Keywords: A Vocabulary of Culture and Society.* Oxford: Oxford University Press, 1976.

Wills, Lawrence M. "The Death of the Hero and the Violent Death of Jesus." Pages 79–99 in *Religion and Violence: The Biblical Heritage.* Edited by David A. Bernat and Jonathan Klawans. Sheffield: Sheffield Phoenix, 2007.

———. *The Jewish Novel in the Ancient World.* Ithaca, NY: Cornell University Press, 1995.

———. *The Quest of the Historical Gospel: Mark, John, and the Origins of the Gospel Genre.* London: Routledge, 1997.

Wilson, Stephen G. *Leaving the Fold: Apostates and Defectors in Antiquity.* Minneapolis: Fortress, 2004.

Wink, Walter. *John the Baptist in the Gospel Tradition.* Cambridge: Cambridge University Press, 1968.

Winn, Adam. *Mark and the Elijah-Elisha Narrative: Considering the Practice of Greco-Roman Imitation in the Search for Markan Source Material.* Eugene, OR: Pickwick, 2010.

———. *The Purpose of Mark's Gospel: An Early Christian Response to Roman Imperial Propaganda.* Tübingen: Mohr Siebeck, 2008.

Wire, Antoinette. *The Case for Mark Composed in Performance.* Biblical Performance Criticism 3. Eugene, OR: Cascade, 2011.

———. *Holy Lives, Holy Deaths: A Close Hearing of Early Jewish Storytellers.* SBLStBL 1. Atlanta: Society of Biblical Literature, 2002.

———. "Mark: News as Tradition." Pages 52–70 in *The Interface of Orality and Writing.* Edited by Annette Weissenrieder and Robert B. Coote. WUNT 260. Tübingen: Mohr Siebeck, 2010.

Wolf, Eric R. *Europe and the People without History.* Berkeley: University of California Press, 1982.

Woolf, Greg. "Provincial Revolts in the Early Roman Empire." Pages 27–44 in *The Jewish Revolt against Rome: Interdisciplinary Perspectives.* Edited by Mladen Popović. JSJSup 154. Leiden: Brill, 2011.

Wrede, William. *The Messianic Secret.* Translated by J. C. G. Greig. Cambridge: James Clarke & Co., 1971.

Wright, N. T. *The New Testament and the People of God.* Vol. 1 of *Christian Origins and the Question of God.* Minneapolis: Fortress, 1992.

Yadin, Yigael. *The Finds from the Bar-Kokhba Period in the Cave of Letters.* Jerusalem: Israel Exploration Society, 1963.

Zeitlin, Irving M. *Jesus and the Judaism of His Time.* Oxford: Polity, 1988.

Zumthor, P. "Topique et tradition." *Poétique* 2 (1971): 354–65.

CONTRIBUTORS

William E. Arnal is Professor and Head of the Department of Religious Studies at the University of Regina in Saskatchewan, Canada. A Past President of the North American Association for the Study of Religion, his many publications include *Jesus and the Village Scribes*, *The Symbolic Jesus*, and *The Sacred Is the Profane* (with Russell McCutcheon). He is currently cochair (with Erin Roberts) of the Society of Biblical Literature Seminar on Redescribing Early Christianity (2013–), a successor group of the original Society of Biblical Literature Ancient Myths and Modern Theories of Christian Origins Seminar.

Barry S. Crawford is Professor of Religious Studies at Washburn University in Topeka, Kansas. His publications focus on Christian origins, especially the formation and development of early Jesus traditions and the letters of Paul. A member of the original Society of Biblical Literature Ancient Myths and Modern Theories of Christian Origins Consultation and Seminar, he served as cochair (with Christopher R. Matthews) of the first of the Seminar's successor program units, Redescribing Early Christianity (2007–2012).

Burton L. Mack is John Wesley Professor in Early Christianity, Emeritus, at the Claremont School of Theology and Graduate University, Claremont, California. His many publications on Christian beginnings, especially *A Myth of Innocence: Mark and Christian Origins*, led to the formation of the original Society of Biblical Literature Consultation and Seminar on Ancient Myths and Modern Theories of Christian Origins and to their Society of Biblical Literature successor groups. He is currently researching the underlying Christian mythic grammar and social logic of contemporary American culture.

Christopher R. Matthews is Research Professor of New Testament at Boston College, School of Theology and Ministry. He is editor of *New Testament Abstracts* and Editor-in-Chief of Oxford Bibliographies: Biblical Studies. A contributor to the revised fourth edition of *The New Oxford Annotated Bible with the Apocrypha*, he was also cochair (with Barry Crawford) of the Society of Biblical Literature Redescribing Early Christianity Group (2007–2012), the first successor program unit of the original Society of Biblical Literature Ancient Myths and Modern Theories of Christian Origins Seminar.

Merrill P. Miller is Professor Emeritus of Religious Studies at the University of North Carolina at Pembroke. He has written articles in the areas of New Testament, Hebrew Bible, Early Judaism, and Rabbinics. He was cochair (with Ron Cameron) of the original Ancient Myths and Modern Theories of Christian Origins Consultation (1995–1997) and Seminar (1998–2003), and coeditor (with Ron Cameron) of *Redescribing Christian Origins* and *Redescribing Paul and the Corinthians*, the previous two volumes of seminar papers, to which he contributed several key essays.

Jonathan Z. Smith is Emeritus Robert O. Anderson Distinguished Professor of the Humanities in the College and the Committee on the Ancient Mediterranean World at the University of Chicago. A leading authority on method and theory in the study of religion, his publications include *Map Is Not Territory: Studies in the History of Religions*, *Imagining Religion: From Babylon to Jonestown*, *Drugery Divine: On the Comparison of Early Christianities and the Religions of Late Antiquity*, *Relating Religion: Essays in the Study of Religion*, and *On Teaching Religion*. His methodological categories provided the template for much of the work of the original Society of Biblical Literature Consultation and Seminar on Ancient Myths and Modern Theories of Christian Origins.

Robyn Faith Walsh is Assistant Professor of New Testament and Early Christianity at the University of Miami. Her research interests include the letters of Paul, the history of the interpretation of the Synoptic problem, Greco-Roman archaeology, and cognitive science. She is currently working on a number of articles and a monograph on the influence of Romanticism on the field of early Christian studies and authorship practices in antiquity. She is also Regional Editor for the Database of Religious History Project.

Index of Ancient Texts

Hebrew Bible/Old Testament		20	438
Genesis		**1 Kings**	
10:15	116	16:31	123
22:2	420	17:8–16	123, 179
34:14–18	115	17:8–24	179
37–50	269	17:17–24	123
		18	179
Exodus		18:20–40	123
23:20	426		
24:8	384, 447	**2 Kings**	
		1:8	421
Leviticus		2	179
4:1–35	374	2:12	377
4:2	373	4:18–37	179
4:7b LXX	373	5:1–27	123, 179
4:18b LXX	373		
4:20b LXX	373	**2 Chronicles**	
4:25b LXX	373	24:20–22	384
5:1–13	374		
5:11–13	373	**Psalms**	
		22	447, 448
Numbers		22:1	391, 420, 448, 449, 450
15:22–36	374	22:1a	421
25:3	109	22:6–8	448
25:5	109	22:7	450
25:18	109	22:18	448, 450
31:16	109	22:19	449
		41–43	447
Deuteronomy		41:9	450
3:9	116	42:5	450
21	384	42:11	450
		43:5	450
2 Samuel		61	447
15–17	438	69	447

Psalms (*cont.*)

69:21	448, 450
109	447
109:25	448
117:22–23 LXX	446
117:25 LXX	373
117:26 LXX	373, 445
118	446, 447
118:15–27	446
118:22–23	446, 450
118:25–26	444
118:27	446

Proverbs

31:6	448–449

Isaiah

5	471
5:1–7	11, 470
5:1–10 LXX	465
5:2 LXX	465
23	117
23:2 LXX	116
40:3	420
40:3 LXX	421
53:7	448
53:9	448, 449
53:12	448
56:7	284, 456
69:19b	268

Jeremiah

7:11 LXX	456
7:34	456
9:24–25	117
12:7a LXX	265

Ezekiel

26–28	117
27:12–24	117
32:30	117
34:1–31	447
37	385

Daniel

3	269
6	269
7	263, 290
7:13	287
7:13–14	377, 378
7:22	287
9	279
9:27	277, 279
11:31	277
12:1 LXX	279
12:11	277

Hosea

6:6	236

Joel

3:15	449

Amos

8:9	449

Malachi

3:1	420, 426
4:5	420, 430
4:5–6	377

Zechariah

9	447
9:9	446, 448, 449
9:11	447
9:15	447
13:4	421
13:7	447
13:7 LXX	447

Deuterocanonical and
Pseudepigraphical Works

2 Baruch

3:5–6	322
5:1	322
7:2	322
13:3	377
25:1	377

41:1–6	326
41:3	316
46:1–7	326
76:2	377
77:11–17	326

3 Baruch
1:2	322
1:3–8	323

4 Baruch
1:6–7	322
4:7–9	322

1 Enoch
62:3–5	287
70–71	377

4 Ezra
3:28	322
5:4–5	291
5:28–30	322
14:09	377
14:50	377

1 Maccabees
1:29–32	279
1:54	277, 279
1:59	279
2:28	279

2 Maccabees
2:21	210
4:18–20	118
6:02	118
7	269
8:01	210
14:38	210

3 Maccabees
1:9–15	280

4 Maccabees
4:26	210

Assumption of Moses
10:1–10	291

Sibylline Oracles, Book 4 330
1–48	125
8–11	125
24–30	125
27–30	333
29–30	334
30–34	333
102–192	125
115–116	125
115–118	334
115–119	125
125–127	125, 334
130–137	334
165–170	334

Testament of Levi
18	141

Wisdom of Solomon
2	269
4–5	269
5:2	287

New Testament

Sayings Gospel Q
3:7–9	407, 425, 428
3:7b–9	523
3:9	407, 408
3:16	414, 425, 426, 428
3:16–17	407, 428
3:16b–17	522
3:17	425, 428
4:1–13	413, 430, 515
4:9	413
6:22–23	268
6:37–38	521
6:40	521
6:41–42	521
6:43–44a	407
6:43–44	407, 408
6:45	407, 521

Sayings Gospel Q (cont.)

6:46–49	523
6:47–49	464
7:19	425
7:19–53	428–429
7:24–26	429
7:27	426, 429
7:28	425, 426, 429
10:1–16	416
10:13–15	123
11:9–13	406
11:21–22	437
11:39–41	237
11:39a	523
11:39b	523
11:41–48	523
11:42	523
11:49–51	268, 377, 523
11:51	412
11:52	523
12:33–34	518
12:39–40	378, 437
12:42–46	378, 437
13:24	446
13:24–30	446
13:34	445
13:34–35	264, 268, 322, 377, 412, 413, 425, 446, 516, 523
13:35	435, 444, 445, 446
13:35a	259, 265, 266, 378, 390
13:35b	378
14:16–24	446, 464
14:26	446
14:26–27	446
14:27	268, 375, 435, 446, 451
14:34–35	446
16:13	518
16:16	427
17	288
17:1–2	521
17:3b–4	521
17:6	406
17:24	288, 378
17:26–27	288, 378
17:30	288, 378
17:33	446
17:34–35	288, 378
19:12–26	378, 437
22:28	453
22:30	453

Matthew

3:16	418
7:19	407, 408
12:41–42	385
15:11	237
15:12	364
15:13–14	407, 408
15:21	116, 121
15:21–28	121
15:22	116, 122, 231
15:22b–24	122
15:26	122
15:28a	122
16:18	528
17	371
17:24–27	364, 366, 367, 368, 358, 363
17:25	369, 370
17:25–26	363
17:25b–26	364
17:26	367
17:27	364
18:17	528
21:1–9	447
21:43	528
22:7	152
22:15–22	368
22:17	369, 370
22:19	370
23	386
23:25–26	237
23:34–39	268, 377
23:35	373, 384
23:35–36	384
24	288
24:2	278
24:3	292
24:14	278
24:15–20	278
24:37–42	288

24:42	378	2:7	380
24:43–44	378	2:8–12	459
24:45–51	378	2:13	444, 459
25:14–29	378	2:15–17	460
26:26	442	2:18–20	460
26:59–61	274	2:18–22	452
26:28	373, 374, 384	2:20	377, 391, 394
27:4	384	2:23–28	452, 460
27:19	384	2:27	481
27:24	384	3:1	476
27:25	384, 385	3:1–6	460
27:52–52	385	3:6	267
28:16	454	3:7–8	179, 230, 231
28:18–20	528	3:11	417
		3:19	440
Mark		3:21	380, 456
1:1	418, 461, 462	3:23	464
1:1–11	421	3:24–26	464
1:2	420, 426, 429	3:27	378, 437
1:2–3	421, 423, 430	3:28–30	380
1:3	420, 421	4:1	459
1:6	420, 421, 430	4:1–2	444
1:7–8	425, 426	4:1–20	292, 460
1:8	425, 428	4:1–34	461, 464
1:9	420	4:2	459
1:9–11	10, 267	4:3–8	444
1:10	268, 418, 420, 423	4:3–9	285
1:10a	421	4:10–34	459
1:10b	421	4:13	220, 465
1:10c	421	4:14–20	285, 444
1:11	388, 417, 420, 421, 422	4:27	436
1:12–13	421	4:34	463
1:14	435, 459	4:35–6:53	388
1:14–15	380, 461	4:37–38	233
1:19	443	4:38	444, 459
1:21	459, 476	5:1–20	380
1:21–22	444	5:2–5	233
1:21–28	267	5:7	417, 420
1:22	459	5:11–13	476
1:26	420	5:21–23	121
1:33	462	5:35–43	121
1:38	459	5:35	459
1:39	459, 476	6:2	444, 459, 476
2:1–6:6	187	6:5	231
2:5	459	6:6	444, 459

Mark (cont.)

6:7–13	396, 416
6:14–15	428
6:17–29	423, 452
6:34	444, 447, 459
6:35–44	443
6:44	424
6:49	389
7	178, 235
7:1–5	234
7:1–8	234
7:1–23	237, 292, 460
7:1–30	230
7:2–3	236
7:3	230, 236
7:3–4	234, 236, 481
7:5	236
7:6–13	237
7:12–23	234
7:14–23	234
7:15	234, 235, 236, 237, 464
7:17	464
7:19	237, 238
7:19a	237
7:19b	230, 234, 236, 237, 481
7:21–23	208
7:24	116, 121, 179
7:24–30	4, 6, 121, 163, 170, 172, 186, 379
7:25c	122
7:26	116, 122
7:26–29	476
7:27	116, 121, 122, 170, 179, 232, 402
7:31–37	232
8–10	270
8:1–9	443
8:8	424
8:10	232
8:12	286, 287
8:14–21	459
8:22–9:29	232
8:27–33	459
8:31	244, 290, 412, 437, 444, 459
8:33	377
8:34–35	451

8:35	461, 462
8:38	286, 287, 393
8:38–9:1	290
9:1	290, 423, 424
9:2	423, 424, 438
9:2–8	290, 397, 443, 453
9:2–13	417, 422
9:4	419, 423
9:5	423
9:7	388, 417, 422, 423
9:9	424
9:9–13	377, 459
9:11–12	429
9:11–13	419, 420, 423, 428
9:13	423
9:14–29	292
9:17	444, 459
9:19	286
9:19–21	424
9:31	412, 437, 440, 444, 459
9:38	444, 459
9:38–40	297
9:38–41	379, 396
9:41	297
10:1	444, 459
10:1–12	292
10:2–12	460
10:17	444, 459
10:20	444, 459
10:29	461, 462
10:30	395
10:32	397
10:33	440
10:33–34	437
10:34	412
10:35	444, 459
10:38	422
10:38–39	439
10:39	425, 443
10:42–44	232
10:42–45	373
10:45	373, 374, 393, 422
10:45b	373
10:47–48	417
11:1–6	422, 440

11:1–10	10, 444	13:1	444, 459
11:1–12	10	13:1–2	258, 291
11:1–16:8	447	13:1–4	276
11:7–8	446	13:1–2ab	258
11:8	445, 446	13:2	258, 259, 266, 267, 272, 412, 419
11:9	435, 444, 457	13:2bc	258
11:12–14	10, 406, 408	13:3	291
11:12–21	266	13:4a	457
11:13–16	422	13:5–23	286
11:15–16	285	13:5–31	289, 291
11:15–17	459	13:6	276
11:15–18	267	13:7	244
11:15–19	10, 266, 406, 410	13:7b	457
11:17	284, 285, 444, 456, 459	13:7–8	276
11:17a	284, 457	13:9	194, 440
11:17b	278, 457	13:9–13	271, 272, 276, 292, 302, 402
11:18	382	13:10	278, 290, 399, 461, 462
11:20–21	10, 406, 408	13:11	438
11:21	406	13:12	440
11:27	465	13:13a	284, 295
11:27–34	266	13:14	254, 277, 279, 390, 395
12:1	464, 465	13:14–18	278
12:1–9	392, 470	13:14–20	278, 279
12:1–12	266, 272, 290, 438, 444, 463, 464, 465, 470	13:14–23	276
		13:15–16	279
12:9	267	13:19	279, 286, 457
12:10–11	446, 457	13:20	244
12:10–12	470	13:21–23	289
12:12	464, 465	13:22	457
12:13–17	368, 460	13:23	287
12:14	369, 370, 444, 459	13:24	286, 419
12:15	372	13:24–26	423
12:17	369, 382	13:24–27	276, 290, 291, 292
12:19	444, 459	13:25	419
12:29	457	13:26	286, 287, 377
12:31	457	13:26–27	287, 399
12:32	444, 459	13:27	287, 436
12:33c	457	13:28	464
12:35	444, 459	13:28–29	276, 286, 287
12:35–37	388	13:30	276, 286, 288, 289
12:36	457	13:32	288, 289, 417, 436, 438
12:37	382	13:32–35	291
13	9, 199, 245, 255, 256, 276, 277, 284, 288, 289, 292, 388, 412, 419, 423, 437	13:32–37	276, 289, 291, 292
		13:33–37	378, 464
		13:34	436

Mark (cont.)

13:34–35	437
13:34–36	287, 435
13:34–37	436
13:35	436
13:36	436
13:37	292, 435, 436
14–16	375, 376, 433, 434
14:3	477, 479
14:3–9	443
14:6–8	397
14:9	397, 399, 461
14:10–11	440
14:12–16	440
14:14	459
14:17–21	440
14:18	442, 450
14:20	442
14:22	442
14:22–25	10, 435, 440
14:23	439, 442
14:24	373, 374, 393
14:26	477
14:26–31	440
14:27	447, 450, 457
14:32	477
14:32–36	437
14:32–42	10, 292, 436
14:32–50	233
14:34	436, 450, 457
14:35	438
14:36	244, 377, 390, 439, 443
14:37	436, 438
14:37–42	437
14:38	275, 436, 457
14:40	436, 442
14:41	436, 438
14:41–42	437
14:42	435
14:43–52	292
14:45	442
14:47	395
14:49	244, 459
14:50–51	395
14:51	395

14:55	271
14:57	412
14:57–59	289
14:58	257, 259, 272, 274, 412, 419
14:61	448
14:61–62	292
14:62	270, 287, 377, 457
14:62–64	393
14:64	380
14:66–72	292, 437
15:4–5	448
15:6–15	381, 448
15:11–13	393
15:11–15	445
15:21	478, 395
15:21–22	435
15:23	449, 450
15:24	448, 449, 450
15:25	437, 439
15:25–37	437
15:27	448
15:28	448
15:29	257, 393, 412, 450
15:29–30	270, 274
15:29–32	448
15:31–32	270
15:32	457
15:33	266, 419, 423, 437, 449
15:33–34	439
15:33–39	417, 421
15:34	377, 390, 391, 420, 448, 449, 450, 449
15:34–37	437
15:34a	421
15:34b	421
15:35	419
15:35–36	421
15:36	449, 450
15:37	420, 421
15:37–38	390, 391
15:38	266, 267, 268, 272, 419, 420, 421
15:38–39	270
15:39	267, 385, 417, 420, 421
15:41	395

15:40	395	8:52	531
15:42–46	449	9:22	531
15:43	449	12:42	531
15:47	395	15:7	406
16:1–8	292, 421	16:2	531
16:6	412	19:6	273
16:8	397, 457	19:10	274
		19:11	275
Luke		20:19	531
3:21	418	21:25	532
4:16–30	123		
4:25–27	123, 179, 180	Acts	
10:30–37	463	4:23	496
11:39–41	237	6:13–14a	273
11:41	237	6:14a	274
13:3–9	408	8:26–40	179
13:6–9	407, 409	8:40	178
13:34–35	322	9:32–10:48	178
16:1–8	469	10:1–11:18	179
16:1–9	463	20:21	489
17	288	21:8	179
18:2–5	469	22:20	373
19:43–44	279	28:13–14	105
19:43–44a	259	28:14	105
20:20–25	368		
20:22	370	Romans	
21:20	152	3:15	373
21:20–24	278, 279	14:20	237
21:24	152		
21:34–36	378	1 Corinthians	
22:19	442, 443	8	301
22:20	373	8:7–12	238
22:37	448	10:14–22	301
		11:23	435
John		11:23–24	442
1:29	415	11:23–25	434
1:32–33	415	11:23–26	435, 440, 441, 544
1:32–34	430	11:24	441, 442
1:36	415	11:24–26	443
2:13–17	410	11:25	442
2:18–22	275	13:2	406
4:20	114	15	516
4:23	531	15:3–5	544
7:45–48	531	15:5	453
8:48	531	16:12	155

2 Corinthians
  11:24   299

1 Thessalonians
  4:15–17   291

2 Timothy
  4:13   155

Hebrews
  5:7   439
  10:32–34   341

James
  1:1   453

1 Peter
  2:11–12   298
  2:14   299
  2:14–16   299
  2:16   367

Revelation
  2:9   356
  3:9   356
  11:12   287
  13:9–10   342
  13:15   342
  16:6   373
  20:4   342
  21:14   453

Rabbinic Works

m. Avodah Zarah
  3.4   124

Avot of Rabbi Nathan
  A 4.6; B 6   398

b. Gittin
  56a–b   398

m. Hallah
  4.11   101

t. Ketubbot
  12.6   102

Lamentations Rabbah
  1:5 (31)   398

t. Shabbat
  15 [16].9   316

Early Christian Literature

Acts of Peter
  5–6   105

Augustine, *Expositio quarumdam quaestionum in epistula ad Romanos*
  13   122

Eusebius, *Preparatio evangelica*
  9.16.417C   116

Gospel of Thomas
  14.5   237
  21   378, 437
  35   378, 437, 438
  40   407, 408
  45   407
  46   425, 425, 429
  48   406
  55   451
  65   438, 468, 470
  69   452
  71   274, 410, 412
  78   429
  89   237
  97   463
  98   378, 437, 463
  103   378, 437, 438

Ignatius, *To The Ephesians*
  18.2d   415

Tertullian, *Apologeticus*
  18   353
  21.1   352

Greek and Latin Texts

Appian, *Syriaca*
11.8.50   369

Athenaeus, *Deipnosophistae*
3.83a–c   507
3.126b   507
7.276a   506
8.37   103
8.341d   505
8.346c–e   103
8.359d–e   507
13.556b   506
34c–e   103

Aulus Gellius, *Attic Nights*
5.41   507
13.31   507
18.4   507

Dio Cassius, *Historia Romana*
5.5.2   359
37.17.1   358
54.7.6   124
65.5.2–4   262
65.7.2   314, 338, 345, 346, 353, 358
67.1.3–4   348
67.4.3–5   342
67.4.5   348
67.14.1–2   339, 340, 347
68.1.2   339, 340, 345, 347, 348
80.11.1   117

Diodorus Siculus, *Bibliotheca historica*
1.28   116
2.4.2–6   103
17.4.3   111
20.14.1–2   111

Epictetus, *Diatribai*
2.2.20   451

Eunapius, *Vitae sophistarum*
455   507

Herodian, *Historia*
5.6.9   117

Herodotus, *Historiae*
1.105   103
2.44   110
2.104   117

Homer, *The Odyssey*
9:3–11   527

Josephus, *Against Apion*
1.7–8 §§37–38   243
1.8 §42–43   249
1.8 §§44–46   329
1.9 §50   329
1.17–18 §§107–127   118
1.22 §§169–171   117
2.4 §§38–39   313
2.4 §44   478
2.15 §148   249
2.17 §§164–165   248
2.22 §§184–187   248
2.24 §§193–194   249
2.29 §§209–210   249
2.34 §236   249
2.37 §258   249
2.38 §272   249
2.39 §277   249
2.37 §261   249
2.37–38 §§255–270   249

Josephus, *Jewish Antiquities*
1.7.2 §§159–160   116
3.4.1 §§70–109   329
4.6.4 §§112–117   329
4.6.6 §§126–130   329
4.8.5 §§145–149   316
8.2.6–9 §§50–60   118
8.4.6–8 §§127–154   118
8.5.3 §146   110
8.10.3 §262   117
9.14.3 §288   115
10.10.4 §207   329
11.1.3 §§12–18   249

Josephus, Jewish Antiquities (cont.)

11.5.1 §§123–130	249
11.7.2 §302	115
11.8.4 §§322–324	115
12.1.1 §10	114
12.2.5 §§40–84	249
12.3.1 §§121–124	307, 313
12.5.5 §257	115
12.5.5 §§257–264	115
12.5.5 §258	115
12.5.5 §260	115
12.5.5 §261	114
13.2.1–3 §§48–57	332
13.3.4 §74	114
13.9.1 §§255–256	115
13.9.1 §§257–258	116
14.4.4 §§71–72	280
14.7.1 §§105–109	281
14.7.2 §§114–118	478
16.6.2 §§163–164	340
17.6.2–3 §§149–157	114
17.10.2 §264	281
17.12.1–2 §§324–338	119
17.21.1 §328	105
18.2.2 §§29–30	114
18.3.1 §§55–59	114
18.4.1 §§85–87	125
18.4.1 §§85–97	114–115
18.4.3 §§90–95	281
18.5.1–2 §§109–116	429
18.5.2 §§116–119	416, 427
18.7.2 §248	105
18.8.1–8 §§257–309	281
19.5.3 §290	338, 343, 355
20.1.1–2 §§6–14	281
20.2.4 §§41–42	238
20.6.1–3 §§119–136	114
20.8.7 §§173–178	102
20.9.1 §§200–202	273

Josephus, Jewish War/Judean War

1.2.6 §§62–63	115
1.7.6 §§152–153	280
1.8.8 §179	281
1.33.2–4 §§648–655	114

2.3.3 §50	281
2.7.1 §§101–110	119
2.7.1 §104	105
2.9.2–3 §§169–174	114
2.9.2–4 §§169–177	281
2.10.1–5 §§184–203	281
2.12.1 §§224–227	121
2.12.3–7 §§232–246	114
2.13.7 §§266–270	121
2.14.4–5 §§284–292	121
2.16.4 §§385–386	370
2.13.7 §§266–270	102
2.14.4–5 §§284–292	102
2.17.2–10 §§408–456	247
2.18.1 §§457–458	102
2.18.1–5 §§457–480	250
2.18.2 §463	250
2.18.3 §§466–468	164
2.18.5 §§477–479	121
2.19.5–20.1 §§533–556	247
2.20.2 §§559–560	118
2.20.2 §§559–561	164
2.20.2 §§560–561	250
2.20.4 §§566–568	247
2.21.8–10 §§632–646	102
2.22.1 §651	248
3.3.5 §58	250
3.7.32 §§307–315	115
3.9.7–8 §§445–461	102
4.3.10 §§182–183	277
4.5.2 §§320–321	248
5.5.4 §§212–214	418
5.9.3 §362	263
5.9.4 §412	258
5.13.3 §§541–542	263
6	264, 265
6.2.2 §§113–115	305
6.4.2 §241	281
6.5.2 §§285–286	262
6.5.2–3 §§285–288	263
6.5.2–4 §§285–315	263
6.5.3 §§288–300	262
6.5.3 §300	262
6.5.3 §§300–309	259, 263
6.5.3–4 §§300–310	454–455

6.5.4 §§310–315	263	Marinus, *Vita Procli*	
6.5.4 §§312–315	263	19	120
6.6.1 §316	277		
6.9.3 §421	262	Nonnus, *Dionysiaca*	
6.10.1 §439	115	40.311–580	110
7.1.1 §1	258	40.369–410	110
7.2–3 §§36–37	121	40.411–580	110
7.3.1 §39	121		
7.3.3 §43	250	Pausanias, *Graeciae descriptio*	
7.3.3 §45	250	7.5.5–9	110
7.3.3 §50	250		
7.3.4 §§54–62	250	Petronius, *Satyricon*	
7.5.1 §96	121	48.4	506
7.5.2 §109	250		
7.5.2 §§100–111	121, 307	Phaedrus, *Fabulae*	
7.5.2 §§110–111	250, 313	1.28	469
7.5.4–6 §§123–157	302	3.2	469
7.[5.5 §]150	304	3.7	469
7.6.6 § 218	314, 338	4.6	469
Josephus, *Vita/The Life*		Philo, *De Abrahamo*	
3 §16	105	10	207
4–5 §§17–23	247	276	528
6 §25	250		
6 §§25–27	164	Philo, *De confusione linguarum*	
17–22 §§87–107	102	4–5	507
53–55 §§271–286	102	170	507
65 §§340–345	102		
65 §348	248	Philo, *De Fuga et inventione*	
65 §§357–366	329	31	507
		185	528
Justinian, *Edicta*			
48.8.11	353	Philo, *De mutatione nominum*	
50.15.8.7	370	35	528
50.2.3.3	353		
		Philo, *De opificio mundi*	
Lucian, *De Syria dea*		28	529
45	103		
		Philo, *De providentia*	
Lucian, *Philopseudes*		2.64	103
16	121		
		Philo, *De somniis*	
Lucretius, *De rerum natura*		2.53	507
2.21–293	82	3.275	507

Philo, *De specialibus legibus*
1.190 528
2.263 529

Philo, *De vita contempliva*
17 507

Philo, *De vita Mosis*
1.2.12 529

Philo, *In Flaccum*
27 105

Philo, *Legatio ad Gaium*
78–79 110
81 110
83 529
90–93 110
102 529
141 529
145 529
156 317
185 105
200–373 281

Philo, *Questiones et solutiones in Genesin*
3.48 117

Plato, *Respublica*
421c 529

Pliny the Younger, *Epistulae*
1.7 506
2.17 506
10.96 342
10.96–97 298, 360

Plutarch, *Alexander*
2–3 506

Plutarch, *Praecepta gerendae rei publicae*
16a–19f [813c–816a] 328

Porphyry, *De abstinentia*
1.14 117

2.61 103

Seneca, *De tranquillitate animi*
9.4–7 506

Seneca, *Epistulae morales*
3.27.5 508

Silius Italicus, *Punica*
3.21–26 117

Strabo, *Geographica*
2 528
16.2 528
16.2.34 116
17.1.7 106

Suetonius, *Domitianus*
8.3–5 342
9.3–10.1 342, 348
12.1 349
12.1–2 339

Suetonius, *Nero*
16.2 299

Tacitus, *Annales*
15.44 299

Tacitus, *Dialogus de oratoribus*
2.1 508

Tacitus, *Historiae*
5.5.2 359
5.13 263

Inscriptions and Papyri

Corpus Inscriptionum Latinarum
3.4789 118
3.10393 110
3.79545 118
5.4242 117
6.8750–8751 118
6.30931 118

10.1554	107, 109
10.1576	107
10.1579	107
10.1590	119
10.1596	107
10.1598	107
10.1601	108
10.1634	107
10.696	119

Corpus Papyrorum Judaicarum
2.160–226	314
2.241	314
2.460	314

Inscriptiones Graecae
12(8).9	108
12(8).186	108

Inscriptiones graecae ad res romanas
419	108
1.412	109
3.1045	118
3.1533	118

Inscriptiones Latinae Selectae
4289	106
4291	107

Kanaanäische und aramäische Inschriften
14	109
47	109
60	109, 110

Orientis Graeci Inscriptiones Selectae
494	108
591	119
593	102
594	107
595	109

Index of Modern Authors

Aberle, David 68

Achtemeier, Paul J. 121, 123

Adler, Max 55, 64, 238, 558

Alexander, Jeffrey C. 293, 298, 333, 393

Allison, Dale C. 447

Althusser, Louis 23, 24, 76–85, 87, 130

Anderson, Andrew Runni 119

Anderson, Benedict 481–82

Andrade, Nathanael J. 207, 217–19, 231, 282, 301, 310, 312, 321

Ariel, Donald T. 370–71

Armstrong, David 508

Arnal, William E. 5–6, 10–12, 14–16, 146–47, 160, 169, 170, 174–76, 181, 226, 259, 267, 299–301, 390, 396–97, 401, 405, 428, 430, 438, 459, 468, 488, 490, 493, 516, 519–22, 524, 526, 535–36, 538–39, 541, 543–47, 549–54, 556, 561, 566, 570

Arnim, Hans von 103

Ascough, Richard S. 528, 536

Aubet, Maria Eugenia 117

Auerbach, Erich 44

Aune, David E. 119, 120, 242, 528, 529

Aus, Roger David 241

Avemarie, Friedrich 315

Avidov, Avi 312–13

Bailey, Anne M. 88

Baker, Cynthia M. 8, 209–10, 213

Balibar, Étienne 24, 76, 79–81, 85, 87

Baltzer, Klaus 242

Barclay, John M. G. 103, 139, 209, 243–44, 248, 361

Barkun, Michael 68

Barrière, Dorothy B. 19

Barth, Hans 65

Barthes, Roland 491, 504

Bazzana, Giovanni Battista 552

Beare, Frank W. 406, 409

Becker, Eve-Marie 227, 242–43, 307, 394, 397

Bellwood, Peter 35

Benveniste, Émile 67

Bennett, Andrew 491

Berchem, Denis van 117

Bercovitch, Eytan 131–32, 136, 550

Berg, Paul-Louis van 103, 116

Berlin, Andrea 248, 252

Berlin, Isaiah 494, 497–98, 500–501

Bickerman, Elias 114–15

Bieler, Ludwig 528

Black, Max 60, 540

Boecker, Bettina 497

Bonz, Marianne Palmer 530–31

Borg, Marcus J. 410, 433

Bornkamm, Günther 410, 414

Botha, Pieter J. J. 221

Boulnois, Luce 106

Bourdieu, Pierre 213–14, 295, 300, 487, 510, 560

Boustan, Ra'anan S. 386–87

Bowersock, G. W. 113, 120

Bowie, Andrew 492

Boyarin, Daniel 211–12, 235, 251–52

Braudel, Fernand 23–24, 41, 74–76, 81, 83–84

Braun, Willi 127, 147–48, 160, 482, 488, 490, 509, 526, 536, 541, 543–45, 547, 552, 556, 559

Brewster, Ben 24, 77

Brodie, Thomas L. 179, 241
Brown, Ian 564
Brown, Raymond E. 432
Brubaker, Rogers 207, 213–15, 217, 227, 485
Buchler, Justus 53
Bultmann, Rudolf 403, 406, 415–16, 432, 449, 452–53, 462, 495, 500, 502–3, 512, 517, 528–29, 547
Burke, Kenneth 61, 69–70
Burkill, T. A. 437
Burns, Joshua Ezra 325
Burridge, R. A. 241
Cadwallader, Alan H. 230, 231
Cameron, Ron 2–3, 20–21, 30, 58, 128–29, 147, 160, 186, 189, 197–98, 224–26, 274–75, 317, 374, 410, 416, 441, 485, 536–49, 554, 556, 564, 572
Carr, David M. 394
Carter, Edward J. 363–67
Carter, Warren 307, 354–55, 363–66, 563
Cary, George 44
Cassirer, Ernst 55–56, 73, 94, 562
Casson, Lionel 106
Castelli, Elizabeth A. 11, 231, 414, 417, 563, 568
Certeau, Michel de 47, 48, 228
Chance, J. Bradley 242
Chancey, Mark A. 216
Charbonnier, G. 25
Charlesworth, James H. 414, 449
Charlesworth, Martin Percival 105
Chilton, Bruce D. 368
Choi, Junjhwa 250–51, 253, 305, 319
Clarke, Anne, 23
Clastres, Pierre 48
Clifford, James 35
Cohen, Shaye J. D. 87, 102, 111–12, 121, 136, 210–11, 251, 325, 343, 453
Collart, Paul 119
Collins, Adela Yarbro 233, 243–45, 267–69, 291, 355, 373–76, 391, 448, 461, 512
Collins, John J. 333
Collins, Marilyn F. 125

Collins, Steven 56
Colpe, Carston 111
Comfort, Howard 106
Cook, James 19–20, 30, 40–41, 45–46, 83–84, 86, 91, 100–101, 128, 157, 204, 550
Cooper, Fredrick 214, 217
Coote, Robert B. 220–23
Corley, Kathleen E. 375
Cotton, Hannah M. 314–315, 357
Cournot, Antoine Augustin 81–82
Courtés, Joseph 83
Cranfield, C. E. B. 421, 449
Crawford, Barry S. 488, 535–36
Crook, Zeba 209, 255, 405, 539
Crossan, John Dominic 410–11, 414–16, 432, 450–51, 516
Crossley, James G. 236
Cumont, Franz 109–11
Curtius, Ernst Robert 44
Daschke, Dereck 333, 393
Davies, Stevan 408, 412, 414–15
DeMaris, Richard E. 382, 417
Dening, Greg 35
Dentith, Simon 242
Derichs, Wilhelm 119
Destutt de Tracy, Antoine Louis Claude 65, 66
Detienne, Marcel 18
Deva, K. 106
Dewey, Arthur J. 226, 376, 536
Dewey, Joanna 221
De Wilde, Éliane 74
Dibelius, Martin 245, 403, 415, 432, 512
Djurfeldt, Gören 90–91
Dochhorn, Jan 394
Dodd, C. H. 447
Donahue, John R. 438
Donham, Donald L. 88
Dowd, Sharyn 373–74, 391, 420, 431, 481
Downey, Glanville 125
Downey, Susan B. 110
Driesch, Hans 56
Driggers, Ira Brent 391

Dronsch, Kristina 223
Duby,Georges 74
Duling, Dennis C. 403, 410
Dumézil, Georges 37
Dunn, James D. G. 245, 539
Dunning, Benjamin H. 295, 305, 366
Dupont, Florence 498, 509
Duran, Nicole Wilkenson 268, 295–96
Durkheim, Émile 55–57, 63, 133, 224, 293, 556
Duthoy, Robert 107
Dyson, Stephen L. 303
Eck, Werner 357
Eco, Umberto 169
Eggan, Fred 19
Ehrman, Bart D. 408, 410, 417, 517, 563
Eliav, Yaron 310–11
Engels, Friedrich 65–66, 82, 86, 89–90
Engler, Rudolf 49, 50
Enslin, Morton S. 414, 416
Eribon, Didier 93–94
Esler, Philip S. 304
Evans, Craig A. 410, 454
Evans-Pritchard, E. E. 18
Eyl, Jennifer 506
Fabian, Johannes 17
Fantham, Elaine 508
Feischmidt, Margit 227
Feldt, Laura 389–90
Ferguson, John 106
Fine, Steven 283
Fink, Robert O. 119
Fish, Jeffrey 508
Fitzmyer, Joseph A. 404, 414
Fleddermann, Harry T. 408
Flynn, Thomas R. 52
Fornander, Abraham 36–37
Fortna, Robert 411
Foss, Martin 57
Foster, Paul 308, 358, 363,
Foucault, Michel 42–43, 59, 169, 559, 573
Fowler, Robert M. 443
Fraade, Steven D. 387
France, R. T. 291

Frankfurter, David 312, 386
Fredriksen, Paula 274, 454, 516
Frey, Jörg 335, 376
Funk, Robert W. 410, 433, 451
Furstenberg, Yair 235–36
Gager, John G. 490, 496
Gaster, Moses 44
Gay, Peter 404
Geiger, Joseph 216, 231, 335
Gelardini, Gabriella 392–94
Gerdmar, Anders 500
Gerstenberg, Heinrich Wilhelm von 493
Geyer, Douglas 388–89, 393, 397
Ghosh, A. 106
Gibson, E. Leigh 386
Gilliam, J. Frank 119
Glaim, Aaron 374
Globe, Alexander 418
Glueck, Nelson 106
Godel, Robert 49
Godelier, Maurice 41, 70, 76, 86, 90–92
Godlove, Terry F., Jr. 56–57
Goethe, Johann Wolfgang von 55–56, 93, 95, 499
Goldman, Irving 36–37
Goodblatt, David 250, 260
Goodenough, Erwin R. 102, 123
Goodman, Martin 102, 247–52, 262, 285, 299, 303–7, 314, 343–46, 348, 350, 353, 359
Goppelt, Leonhard 44
Gould, Stephen Jay 93
Grainger, John D. 350
Gregg, Robert C. 120
Greimas, Algirdas Julien 83
Grimaldi, William M. A. 44
Grubbs, Judith Evans 315
Gruen, Erich S. 118
Guenther, Heinz O. 453
Gundry, Robert H. 417, 435, 441–42, 446–48, 461–62
Gustaffson, Gabriella 246
Haenchen, Ernst 179
Hahn, Hans-Joachim 495
Hall, Robert G. 244

Hamilton, Catherine Sider 384–87
Harlow, Daniel C. 322–23
Harnack, Adolf von 519, 522
Harpe, Jean de la 82
Harris Zellig S. 122
Hatina, Thomas R. 290–91
Hawthorne, Jeremy 76
Haynes, Kenneth 511
Heemstra, Marius 336–48, 350–56, 359, 368, 372
Hénaff, Marcel 63, 133–34
Hengel, Martin 115, 124, 411
Henze, Matthias 323–26, 333
Herder, Johann Gottfried von 492–95, 498–502, 532–33
Hesse, Mary 60, 540
Hezser, Catherine 251, 521
Hocart, Arthur Maurice 27, 36
Hock, Ronald F. 11, 242, 417, 466–67, 471, 505, 549
Hodge, Caroline Johnson 8, 191–92, 208, 552, 554, 570
Hoffmann, Paul 518
Hoïstad, Ragnar 119
Holladay, Carl R. 115–16, 118
Holt, Else K. 394
Hoover, Roy W. 410
Hopkins, Keith 489
Horman, John 238
Horrell, David G. 298
Horsley, Richard A. 226, 406, 453–54, 458, 516, 563
Howard, Alan 101
Hudson, Geoffrey Francis 106
Hultgren, Arland J. 435, 451
Humphrey, Edith M. 516
Humphries, Michael L. 438
Huntingford, G. W. B. 106
Imbert, Gaston 75
Incigneri, Brian J. 255, 294, 372
Irwin, Geoffrey 35
Jackson, Bernard S. 315
Jacob, Christian 505–8
Janzan, David 393
Jensen, Adolf E. 60, 71–72, 201

Jeremias, Joachim 449
Johnson, Patricia A. 508
Johnson, William A. 487, 498, 508–9
Johnston, Sarah Iles 570
Jones, Kenneth R. 327–34
Kant, Immanuel 50, 55–57, 96, 491–92, 558, 562, 565
Katzenstein, H. Jacob 118
Kazen, Thomas 234–36
Kee, Howard Clark 447, 453, 457–58, 461
Keith, Chris 221, 223, 227, 397
Kelber, Werner H. 221–23, 225–26, 256–57, 269, 375, 393, 421, 432, 433–40, 442, 444, 472, 477
Kippenberg, Hans Gerhard 115, 245
Kirch, Patrick Vinton 20, 23, 35
Kirk, Alan 225–27, 517
Klawans, Jonathan 234, 253, 263, 285, 318, 374, 387, 398
Klein, Jürgen 492
Klein, Kerwin Lee 227
Klink, Edward W. 485
Kloppenborg, John S. 9, 120, 153, 226, 246, 258–59, 263, 265–67, 269, 278, 315, 375, 378, 397, 407, 413, 416, 429–30, 435, 445–46, 470, 475, 485, 515–16, 518–19, 521, 536
Koester, Helmut 461–62, 481, 512, 516, 525
Köhnke, Klaus Christian 55
Konstan, David 505, 512–13
Kornhardt, Hildegard 44
Korshin, Paul 44
Kotansky, Roy D. 233
Kotrosits, Maia 393, 571–72
Krader, Lawrence 90
Kraeling, Carl H. 123
Kristeva, Julia 295
Krueger, Derek 505
Krueger, Paul 353
Kuan, J. K. 117
Kümmel, Werner Georg 402
Kundsin, Karl 432
Kysar, Robert 531

Lachmann, Karl 486
Lapin, Hayim 238, 251, 311, 315, 320, 335
Last, Richard 225, 296
Le Goff, Jacques 22
Lenin, Vladimir Il'ich 65, 77–80, 82, 87
Leonhardt-Balzer, Jutta 317
Léry, Jean de 47
Lesser, Alexander 23
LeVen, Pauline 505
Levenson, Jon D. 391
Levine, Andrew 88
Levine, Lee 102, 231, 247, 251, 311, 387
Lévi-Strauss, Claude 17, 20, 23, 25–30, 35–36, 38–40, 46, 48, 50, 52, 55, 61–64, 66, 67–69, 89, 92–98, 130, 133–34, 141–42, 148, 152, 154, 156–57, 176–77, 201, 556, 558, 560
Levitt, Cyril H. 165–66
Lewis, James R. 489
Lewis, Naphtali 109
Lewis, Nicola Denzy 529
Lincoln, Bruce 526–27, 532–33
Lindars, Barnabas 411
Lindberg, Staffan 90, 91
Linder, Amnon 353
Linnemann, Eta 432–33, 449
Littman, Enno 120
Litwa, M. David 290, 378
Liverani, Mario 186
Livingston, James C. 498–500
Llobera, Josep R. 88
Loveman, Mara 214
Luomanen, Petri 226
MacDonald, Dennis R. 229, 241, 264, 455
MacDonald, John 125
MacGillivray, Erland D. 312
Macherey, Pierre 65, 79, 82
Mack, Burton L 2, 5–8, 11–12, 14–15, 58, 72, 120, 127, 137, 146, 160, 169–70, 172–74, 176–78, 187, 192, 194–98, 216, 218, 231, 237, 265, 267, 270, 273, 373–75, 388, 405–6, 408, 410–14, 417, 419, 423–24, 428, 432–33, 438–44,

448, 450, 458, 460, 461–65, 468, 470, 472–73, 477, 485–86, 516, 536–37, 539–42, 544–47, 549–51, 554, 556–57, 563, 565–67, 569, 572
Maclean, Jennifer K. Berenson 382–83
MacMullen, Ramsey 118
Magee, David, Jr. 120
Magness, Jodi 304, 306, 325
Malaise, Michel 106
Malbon, Elizabeth, Struthers 220, 291, 373–74, 391, 420, 431, 443, 475–77, 481
Malherbe, Abraham J. 120, 496, 505
Manson, T. W. 415
Marcus, Joel 255, 277–78
Marti, B. M. 119
Martin, Luther H. 536, 542, 552–54, 564
Marx, Karl 17, 20, 24, 34, 40–42, 55–56, 64–66, 70, 73, 76–82, 85–90, 92, 129, 148–49, 159, 226, 403, 461, 543, 556–60, 562
Marxsen, Willi 402–3, 461–62, 477, 480
Mason, Steve 8, 210–12, 218, 248, 261, 263, 282, 302
Matheron, François 77, 79, 81–82
Matthews, Shelly 273, 386
McCague, James 167
McCutcheon, Russell T. 390, 488, 509, 552, 559, 572
McLaren, James S. 185, 248, 260–61, 281, 320, 329–30
Meeks, Wayne A 120, 125, 300, 505
Meier, John P. 406, 414–16, 449
Meillassoux, Claude 87–88
Métraux, Alfred 48
Metzger, Bruce M. 448, 479
Meyer, Marvin 237, 525
Meyer, R. 114
Michie, Donald 402, 406
Millar, Fergus 102–3, 109, 122, 252–53, 302–3, 310–11
Miller, Merrill P. 2, 3, 5, 7–10, 14–15, 20–21, 30, 127–129, 135, 139, 147, 160, 181, 186, 189, 197–98, 202,

224–26, 274–75, 317, 374, 441, 483, 485, 488, 509, 536–51, 554, 556, 564, 572

Miller, Richard C. 239–40, 246–47, 249, 254, 267, 377–79, 488

Miller, Robert J 410–11

Miller, Stuart S. 251–52, 310–11

Miner, Earl Roy 44

Mommsen, Theodor 353

Moore, Gregory 492–95

Moreland, Milton 216, 226

Morris, Brian 151

Mosher, Joseph A. 44

Moss, Candida 485

Motyer, S. 420

Moxnes, Halvor 215

Murphy-O'Connor, Jerome 404

Murray, Gilbert 119

Myllykoski, Matti 288–89

Neirynck, Frans 411, 415–16

Neujahr, Matthew 245, 280, 284, 320

Neusner, Jacob 58, 71–72, 119, 211–12

Nickelsburg, George W. E. 268–70, 272, 449–50

Niehoff, Maren R. 507

Niehr, Herbert 117

Nock, Arthur Darby 105, 118

Norton, Robert Edward 494–95

Obeyesekere, Gananath 91

Olick, Jeffrey K. 226

Olyan, Saul M. 560, 601

O'Toole, Robert F. 441

Oudshoorn, Jacobine G. 315

Paget, James Carleton 304–5, 307, 309

Parish, Peter J. 167–68

Pasto, James 210, 212, 232

Peirce, Charles S. 51, 53–54, 561

Penner, Hans H. 63–64

Perkins, Judith 242, 506

Perrin, Norman 403, 410

Pervo, Richard I. 242–44, 506

Peters, J. Durham 223

Peters, John P. 102

Peterson, Dwight N. 530

Pettazzoni, Raffaele 118

Pfister, R. Friedrich 119

Phear, John B. 90

Piattelli, Daniela 315

Piper, Ronald A. 416

Plassart, André 117

Poirier, John C. 234–35

Poole, Brian 56

Powell, Mark Allen 219

Pritchard, James B. 107

Puma, Richard Daniel de 105

Quentin, Patrick 65

Rajak, Tessa 247, 263

Rashke, M. G. 106

Redford, Donald B. 389

Reed, Annette Yoshiko 312

Reinhold, Meyer 109

Rhoads, David M. 260, 402, 406

Richards, William A. 19, 155

Richardson, Peter 410–11, 438

Riches, John K. 320, 391

Ricoeur, Paul 60, 558

Rives, James B. 299, 302, 308–10, 314, 361

Robbins, Vernon K. 241, 421, 440–41, 459–60

Roberts, Erin 529, 535

Roberts-Jones, Philippe 74

Robertson, Paul M. 513

Robinson, James M. 237, 410, 414–16, 428, 518

Rollens, Sarah E. 299, 536, 552

Rorty, Richard 65

Rose, Herbert Jennings 119

Roskam, Hendrika Nicoline 255, 294

Roth, Wolfgang 241

Rowland, Christopher 245

Runesson, Anders 227, 242, 285, 307, 397

Safrai, Zeev 120

Sahlins, Marshall 3–5, 18–21, 23–24, 26–38, 42–43, 45–46, 48–49, 51, 53–54, 63–64, 74, 83–86, 88, 91–92, 101, 129–30, 157–61, 171, 204, 543, 550, 556, 558, 561–62

Saldarini, Anthony J. 319–20, 327, 529

Sanders, E. P.   274, 402–5, 409–11, 414, 433, 449, 457, 516

Sartre, Jean-Paul   33–34, 52, 69, 158

Sasson, Jack M.   117

Satlow, Michael L.   8, 208, 310–12

Satran, David   386

Saussure, Ferdinand de   25, 40, 45–46, 49, 50–51, 53, 55, 63, 560–61

Schatzki, Theodore   559

Schechter, Solomon   398

Schilling, Robert   119

Schlegel, August Wilhelm   492

Schlegel, Friedrich   492

Schmidt, Francis   233, 387

Schreiber, Johannes   419

Schremer, Adiel   310, 316

Schudson, Michael   227

Schumacher, Helmut   82

Schürer, Emil   102–3, 111, 116, 120, 478

Schüssler Fiorenza, Elisabeth   213, 414, 433, 563

Schwartz, Barry   223, 227, 392

Schwartz, Daniel R.   231, 247, 252, 285, 305, 325, 331, 335, 387

Schwartz, Joshua   218, 252, 343, 355, 361,

Schwartz, Seth   211–13, 215, 232, 250–53, 304, 310–12, 314, 316, 324, 332, 334–35, 352–53, 358

Schwarz, Ori   317

Schweitzer, Albert   403, 525

Schwemer, Anna Maria   386

Scott, James C.   469

Sebag, Lucien   17, 148, 557

Seeley, David   198, 411, 451

Seyrig, Henri   110, 111

Shaffir, William   165–66

Shiner, Whitney   242

Simmonds, Andrew   380–81, 383–84

Simon, Marcel   119

Singer, Milton   54

Skinner, Marilyn B.   508

Smith, Benjamin Eli   74

Smith D. Moody   411, 531

Smith, Daniel A.   240, 378, 425

Smith, Jonathan Z.   2–8, 13–15, 20–21, 27, 30–31, 37, 43, 50, 54, 58–60, 63, 68–73, 95–96, 113, 127–137, 139–40, 142–43, 145–48, 150–56, 158–63, 169–89, 192–195, 198, 200–205, 211–13, 218, 222, 226, 228–32, 241, 283–84, 286, 320, 379, 473, 475, 481, 483–84, 487–88, 509, 523–24, 536–37, 539–44, 547, 549, 550–51, 554, 556–67, 569, 573

Smith, Morton   71, 115, 263, 410, 414

Smith, Wilfred Cantwell   113, 483

Snowden, Frank Martin   105

Snyder, H. Gregory   508

Sourdel, Dominique   120

Spriggs, Matthew   35

Stalin, Joseph   80, 81

Stamatov, Peter   214

Stanner, W. E. H.   70

Starcky, Jean   118

Stark, Rodney   489

Starner, Rob   242

Ste. Croix, G. E. M. de   468–69

Stern, Menachem   116, 231, 247

Stewart, Eric C.   207, 232–33, 398

Stowers, Stanley K.   8, 12, 15, 191, 208, 215, 224–25, 296, 317, 463, 472–73, 483, 486, 489–90, 496–97, 504, 508–9, 520, 529–30, 536, 538, 542, 549, 552–53, 559, 560–63, 569–70

Strong, George Templeton   167, 168

Struck, Peter T.   527

Stuart, Duane Reed   120

Swartz, Michael D.   387

Tambiah, Stanley   283

Tasker, R. V. G.   450

Tate, Allen   57

Tatum, W. Barnes   414–15

Taussig, Hal   11, 231, 393, 414, 417, 563–568, 572

Taylor, Joan E.   253, 266

Taylor, Vincent   409–10, 414, 417, 421, 449–50

Teixidor, Javier   111, 119

Tellbe, Mikael 367
Tesnière, Lucien 73, 82, 83
Thatcher, Tom 221, 223, 225–27, 392
Theissen, Gerd 230–31, 242, 245, 254–55, 257, 278, 291, 395, 417, 515, 519–20, 522, 525
Thevet, André 47–48
Thiersch, Hermann 102
Thiessen, Matthew 213
Thomas, Nicholas 4, 14, 99–101, 120, 129, 204, 229, 232, 550–51, 557, 562
Thompson, D'Arcy Wentworth 93–95
Thompson, L. L. 342, 355
Thrum, Thomas G. 36
Tolbert, Mary Ann 242
Tondriau, J. 119
Torrence, Robin 23
Torrey, C. C. 107–8
Toynbee, Arnold J. 104
Tran, V. Tam Tinh 105–9
Trautz, Norbert 82
Trocmé, Étienne 179
Tuval, Michael 316–17, 332
Udoh, Fabian E. 274, 369–71
Ulansey, David 267, 418–20
Ullucci, Daniel C. 285, 369, 387, 552, 601
Urman, Dan 120
Uro, Risto 237–38, 288
Uttley, , W. V. 164–65
Vaage, Leif 417
Valeri, Valerio 45
Van Henten, Jan Willem 376
Vermes, Geza 102, 414, 433, 516
Vicari, Jaques 119
Vines, Michael E. 243–44
Vorländer, Karl 55
Wacholder, Ben Zion 118
Wacquant, Loïc 510
Waddington, William Henry 120
Wallace, Sherman Leroy 372
Walsh, Robyn Faith 3, 11–12, 14–15, 224–25, 296, 505, 512, 549–53, 555, 566
Wasserman, Emma 577, 601

Watson, Alan 353
Watson, Burton 72
Watson, David F. 243, 245
Weeden, Theodore J., Sr. 263–67, 270–73, 454–56, 462
Weisler, Marshall I. 35
Weissenrieder, Annette 220–21, 223
Weitzman, Steven 228–30, 249, 260, 280–81, 283–84, 391, 398
Welles, Charles Bradford 110, 119
Wellhausen, Julius 178, 403
Welter, Jean Thiébaut 44
Wendt, Heidi 216, 294, 296–99, 304, 552
Wheeler, R. E. M. 106
White, Hayden 404
White, L. Michael 105
Whitmarsh, Tim 497
Whitney, William Dwight 74
Wilamowitz-Moellendorf, Ulrich von 486
Wilde, Eliane de 74
Wilford, John Noble 106
Will, Ernest 119
Willi, Thomas 502
Williams, Craig A. 509
Williams, Margaret 317
Williams, Raymond 65
Wills, Lawrence M. 241–43, 374–76, 391
Wilson, Stephen G. 209, 316, 405, 438, 539
Wink, Walter 414
Winn, Adam 241, 528
Wire, Antoinette 220, 375
Wolf, Eric R. 22–23, 229
Woolf, Greg 303
Wrede, William 403, 528
Wright, Erik Olin 88
Wright, N. T. 485, 563
Yadin, Yigael 106
Zeitlin, Irving M. 411
Zumthor, P. 40

Index of Subjects

abandonment motif, 9, 268 n. 148, 377, 390–392

abomination of desolation, 277, 278 n. 165, 279

Aesopic fables, 242 n. 81, 244, 468–69, 512

agency
emphasized over structure, 211–12
Sahlins's formulation on, 32–34
in tax payments, 356

Agrippa II, 255 n. 104, 264, 305, 328

Albinus, 455

Alexander (son of Simon of Cyrene), 395 n. 382, 478

Alexandria (Egypt), 507 n. 82

anachronistic retrojections, 431 n. 87, 452–56

analogical comparison (Smith's program), 58, 130, 562

Analyst-Unitarian scholarship, 486 n. 8

animal sacrifice, 284 n. 175, 317 n. 224, 334 n. 261, 374 n. 344, 387

antagonistic events, 392–393

anthropology
comparative method, 19 n. 6
relation between history and, 17–18
reproduction in, 88–90
theoretical revisions in, 22–23
"venerable conflict" in, 558–59

antidraft riots (Civil War), 166–68

Antioch, 106 n. 8, 250 n. 99

Antiochus Epiphanies, 115, 277

apocalyptic traditions
associated with tree motifs, 408 n. 24
functions of, 194–96

apocalyptic traditions (cont.)
in John the Baptist's speeches, 428 n. 76
in the Levant, 124–25
in Mark's Gospel, 195–96, 244–46
as responses to destruction, 322–34
in the transfiguration scene, 423
variant usages of term, 516 n. 104

Apologies to Thucydides (Sahlins), 32–34

appearance traditions, 378 n. 351, 385, 396–97, 453

Arabia (Roman province), 315 n. 222, 319–20, 357 n. 308

Arch of Titus, 281 n. 169, 302–3

arrest of Jesus, 267 n. 143, 271–73, 395 n. 382, 435 n. 95

ascension/descension motif, 420 n. 57, 421, 423–24

Asdiwal myth, 62 n. 106

Ashkelon, 103 n. 4

Atbalmin Christians, 131–32

atheism, 337, 339, 340–43, 351–53

attestation (literary technique), 395 n. 382

audience (Gospel of Mark), 219–22, 240–41, 276–77, 293–96, 472–73, 478–82

audience (Q), 518–19

author/genius (Romantic), 491–97

authors (ancient Mediterranean)
contrasted with Romantic "genius," 497–98
and nonspecialist participation, 513–14
role of literary networks, 487, 504–8
training of, 507–8

authors (ancient Mediterranean) (cont.)
varying skill levels, 511
authors (early Christian)
assumptions about, 484, 518, 530 n.
142
book culture, 221 n. 33, 223, 397 n.
385
form criticism's views of, 502–3
Gospel of Mark, 220 n. 31, 221 n. 33,
458–59, 511–12
influence of communities on, 487,
489–91, 496–97
proposed social world of, 514–15
of Q, 484, 511–12, 520–22, 552 n. 39
role of literary networks, 487, 509–14
Baal (deity), 109 n. 16, 111, 118
Baal-Melqart (deity), 108, 185
Babatha, 314 n. 222, 320, 357 n. 308, 369
n. 334
baptism of Jesus
associated with suffering, 422 n. 62
debated embarrassment in, 414, 416
n. 46
debated plausibility of, 414–16
and Jesus's divine status, 430 n. 84
in John's Gospel, 415 n. 45
parallels to Jesus's death, 267 n. 145,
417–22
in Q, 416 n. 45
sources for Markan version, 424–25
Barabbas, 381–82, 448 n. 137
Bar Kokhba revolt, 319–20
behavioral incongruities, 31, 366–67
Being and Time (Heidegger), 559
biblical studies, 538–39, 573, 573 n. 89.
See also religious studies
"Big Bang" theory (Christian origins),
484–86. *See also* Christian origins
impact on legitimization, 526
overview of, 489–91
role of communities in, 521
biological morphology, 56 n. 99, 93–95
bios genre
combined with martyr myth, 7–8,
199, 201–2

bios genre (cont.)
framework stories for, 457
and the gospels, 459, 512
of Greco-Roman authors, 505–6
reasons for writing, 196–202
birkat ha-minim, 337, 343 n. 282, 351 n.
299
blood, 373 n. 343, 384–87. *See also* sacrifices
Bororo myths, 97–98
burial of Jesus, 397, 449 n. 137
Caesar Augustus, 317 n. 224, 380
Caesarea, 102 n. 4, 178–80, 282 n. 171
Caligula, 254 n. 104, 278, 281
calumnia (wrongful accusation), 344–45,
346 n. 289, 350
Canaan, 115, 116 n. 24, 122
Capital (Marx), 86–87, 88–90, 92
Caracalla, 352 n. 300
censuses, 357 n. 308, 369–71
Cestius Gallus, 250 n. 99
chirographs, 221, 222 n. 34
chreia (pronouncement stories), 186–87,
197, 440–44
Christianity
assumptions on early communities in,
224–25
"Christian" label, 297–300
Hellenistic brand of, 503
illusion of unity in, 546 n. 24
Mark's Gospel's influence on, 161
reasons for spread of, 297 n. 191
separation from Judaism, 335–37,
343, 352–53, 354–55
and social memory studies, 225–28
under Tertullian, 352 n. 300
as the "true Israel," 353
Christian origins
and the Atbalmins, 131–32
"big bang" theory of, 484–86, 489–91,
521, 526
idealism of traditional view, 148 n. 4
itinerancy hypothesis in, 519–20
Lukan-Eusebian model of, 1, 401 n. 2,
537, 546 n. 24, 572

Christian origins (cont.)
  in Luke's Gospel, 530–31
  New Testament construction of, 489–91
  role of theory in studying, 146–47
  Seminar's approach to, 1–2, 13–14, 149–50, 160–61, 535–39, 572 n. 88
Christie Pits riots, 165–66
christological motif, 138, 197, 270–74, 528, 554, 555
circumcision, 117, 340–42, 347, 359
Civil War (American), 166–68
civil wars (68-69 CE), 302
classification systems. *See also* societies; structure
  Fijian example, 27–30, 159–60
  intrinsic nature of, 157 n. 22
  Lévi-Strauss's clan division example, 25–27
  myths rationalizing, 149
  status hierarchies in, 233 n. 56
Claudius, 338, 343, 355 n. 304
client-king system, 177, 253 n. 103, 305, 313 n. 219, 314
coins
  Isfiya hoard, 370–71
  issued under Nerva, 335, 343–47, 350 n. 298
  Iudaea capta, 303, 313
  and the Roman-Judean war, 260 n. 114
  Tyrian, 282 n. 171, 371 n. 338
cold societies, 25 n. 20, 39
collective memories, 225–28
colonialism
  contrasted to Markan situation, 3–4
  inversion as response to, 100 n. 3, 232 n. 53
  in the Levant, 104–5
  power relations, 99–101
  resistance as response to, 101 n. 3
Colosseum, 302
communicative (unconscious) myths, 5–6, 61, 63–68, 153–55, 159–60, 174–77

communities
  associating myths with, 532–33
  assumptions in constructing, 530 n. 142
  and the "big bang" origin theory, 521
  evidence within Q for, 517–22
  in form criticism, 502–3
  in John's Gospel, 531–32
  in the Levant, 111–12
  in Mark's Gospel, 472–73, 527–28, 549
  Marx's writings on Indian, 88–90
  in Matthew's Gospel, 529–30
  problems as analytical term, 208, 215–16, 224–25, 549
  in redaction criticism, 503–4
  role in Christian literature, 489–91, 496–97, 515
  Romantic views of, 486–87, 494–96
comparative method, 19 n. 6
conjunctural agency, 33
conjunctures. *See also* situational incongruity
  Althusser's notion of, 76–82, 84–85
  applicability to Markan situation, 30–34, 129, 204
  Braudel's conception of, 74–76, 83–84
  broader context for, 22–23
  genealogy of term, 23–25
  Lenin's notion of, 77–80
  marking intercultural events, 171–73
  meanings of, 73–74
  Pacific Island examples of, 36–38
  replaced by "situational incongruity," 69
  Sahlins's formulation of, 40–42, 83–86
  Seminar's work as, 150
  Tesnière's notion of, 82–83
conscious (rhetorical) myths, 5–6, 61, 68, 153–55, 159–60, 174–77
constructivism, 213–14
Consultation, SBL (1995–1997)
  fundamental agreements in, 561–63
  general procedures for, 2–3
  primary purposes of, 1–2

Consultation, SBL (1995–1997) (*cont.*)
  as religious studies project, 536–37
  results of, 551
controversy stories, 432 n. 90, 460 n. 169
Cook-Hawaiian example, 30, 40 n. 65, 45–46, 100, 101 n. 3, 204, 550
Copper Scroll, 283
cosmic paranoia, 523–25
counterintuitive entities, 390 n. 378
covenantal system, 324, 373 n. 343, 385
Crassus (governor of Syria), 280–81
crisis/response model, 68 n. 116, 137–38, 163–68
cross saying, 451–52
crucifixion. *See* death of Jesus
cultural materialism, 22–23
cultural persistence
  defined, 286 n. 177
  following the Roman-Judean war, 275, 283–86
  and imperialism, 228–230
  Mark's Gospel as, 9–10, 284–86, 379–80
  strategies for, 333–35, 398
  vindication of Jesus as, 391 n. 379
Culture and Practical Reason (Sahlins), 40 n. 65, 42 n. 67
Culture in Practice (Sahlins), 19 n. 6
cultures. *See also* societies
  diversity in the Levant, 232
  historical change processes in, 24 n. 19, 30–34, 573 n. 88
  relations between, 22–23
  relation to myth, 61–62
  in Roman colonialism, 3–4
curative exit rites, 382 n. 362
currency. *See* coins
Cyrene, 478–79
Damascus, 116 n. 24, 250 n. 99
Daphnis and Chloe (Longus), 466
dating of Mark, 296 n. 189, 490
  ca. 80–85 CE, 9, 207, 254–62, 277, 289
  early- to mid-70s CE, 475
  end of first century, 193
  postwar, 487–88

dating of Q, 378 n. 351, 412 n. 37, 484, 487–88, 490, 515–16, 525
death of Jesus. *See also* passion narrative
  apocalyptic allusions in, 419
  as beneficial to others, 373, 393
  legacy of story of, 393
  links to baptism account, 267 n. 145, 417–22
  links to temple's destruction, 9–10, 256–57, 266–75, 377–78, 391–94, 397–99, 474–75
  Markan narrativization of, 431–35
  as model for emulation, 373
  multiple attestations of, 431 n. 85
  political significance of, 274 n. 161
  ransom clause, 373 n. 343
  sources for account of, 447–51
  symmetry of threes in, 419 n. 54, 423, 437 n. 103
"death of the hero" genre, 375 n. 347, 377–78
Decapolis, 103 n. 4, 230 n. 50, 476
delatores (informers), 340, 344–45, 348–51, 358, 359
Delos, 111–12, 136
dependency grammar, 82–83
descension/ascension motif, 420 n. 57, 421, 423–24
devotio, 258–59, 263
diachrony, 25, 39, 50–51, 154 n. 16
diaspora
  difficulties distinguishing, 103 n. 4
  expanse of, 309 n. 215
  high priestly *protasia*, 331 n. 259
  impacts of Roman-Judean war on, 307 n. 212, 313–18, 320–21, 332 n. 259
  religious patterns in, 111–12
  value of homeland, 139–40, 571
dietary laws, 103 n. 4, 117, 119 n. 30, 234–38
dining rooms (Syrian temples), 118 n. 30
discipleship, 293–294, 396
disciples of Jesus. *See also* followers of Jesus
  comprehending Jesus, 527–28

disciples of Jesus (cont.)
    fears experienced by, 388 n. 378
    in the Gethsemane story, 435–39
    Jesus as teacher to, 459–60
    leaving motif in stories of, 394 n. 382
    in the Lord's Supper account, 442–43
    in Matthean tax narrative, 363–67
    and the messianic secret, 245 n. 89
    as retrojection, 453–54
    and the temple destruction prophecy, 275–76
divine abandonment motif, 9, 268 n. 148, 377, 390–92
"Domestic Mode of Production, The" (Sahlins), 85
Domitian, 303, 337, 338–42, 344–52, 357–58
doorkeeper parable, 287–92, 291 n. 183, 435–39, 466
doxa, 300 n. 195
draft riots (American Civil War), 166–68
Drudgery Divine (Smith), 58
Dura, 119 n. 30, 123
Edfu (Egypt), 314 n. 220, 345 n. 286, 347 n. 292
Egypt, 314 n. 220, 347 n. 292, 372 n. 341, 507 n. 82
ekphrasis (rhetorical device), 280 n. 169
Eleazar b. Simon, 277 n. 164
Elijah, 123, 179, 241, 377, 389 n. 378, 420, 421, 423
Elisha, 123, 179, 241
empty tomb narrative, 239, 377–78, 395 n. 382, 396–97
enargeia (rhetorical device), 280 n. 169
epic of Israel, 141, 176, 465–68, 471
epics (genre), 197, 244, 531, 562 n. 60
Essenes, 251 n. 101, 253 n. 103, 318, 519 n. 112
Esther, 381
ethnic identity
    addressed in Mark's Gospel, 192–93, 230 n. 50
    and the *fiscus Iudaicus,* 337, 340, 343, 346

ethnic identity (cont.)
    and groupism, 213–15
    impact of conflict on, 163–68
    irrelevance to Roman prosecution, 361 n. 314
    and Judaism, 211 n. 6, 212 n. 10
    in the Levant, 135–36, 183–85, 232
    Mark's narrativization of, 478–82
    methods of marking differences, 135–36
    as negotiable, 187
    Paul's "Jew/gentile" division, 192
    problems as analytical term, 208–12
    purity codes as markers of, 191
    redefined in religious terms, 111–12, 136
    relation to location, 475 n. 207
    and the Roman-Judean war, 282 n. 171
    in the Syro-Phoenician woman narrative, 121–23
    in translating *Ioudaios/Ioudaioi,* 208–10
    in Tyre, 183–85
Europe and the People without History (Wolf), 22–23
events
    Lévi-Strauss's formulations on, 25–27
    and practico-inert, 158 n. 25
    relation to myths, 152–153
    relation to structure, 25–30, 156–58, 161
    Sahlins's reconception of, 32–34, 156–57
evocatio deorum, 246, 258–59, 263
evocatio sacrorum, 378, 394
Excavating Q (Kloppenborg), 515–16
"exemplary figure," 44
exemption narratives
    of followers of Jesus, 372–73
    following failed revolt, 9–10, 379, 394–96
    Mark's plot as example of, 229–30, 398
    and Roman power, 368
ex eventu prophecy, 279 n. 167, 284, 330 n. 256

experimental application. *See also* reproduction
  contextualization of term, 71 n. 119
  in the Levant, 172, 174
  replacing "reproduction," 69, 70 n. 119
  Seminar's work in, 14
  and situational context, 203
expiation, 373 n. 343, 374 n. 344
fantastic motif, 389 n. 378
fear motif, 388 n. 378
fig tree
  Jesus cursing, 266–67, 406, 408–9
  parable of, 287–92, 407–9
Fijian case study, 27–30, 35–38, 40 n. 65, 84–85, 101 n. 3, 159–60
fire (Antioch), 250 n. 99
fire (Rome), 299 n. 193
First Dialogue concerning National Religion (Herder), 499–500
fiscus Iudaicus (Jewish tax)
  age limits for, 314, 347 n. 292
  analysis of Heemstra's thesis, 354–56, 368
  collection of, 356–57
  compared to the temple tax, 308 n. 212, 313–14
  Domitian's harsh exaction of, 337, 338–42, 344, 357–58
  in Egyptian sources, 371 n. 341
  identity based on, 335–37, 353 n. 300
  introduction of, 306, 338
  Matthean tax narrative, 363–68
  Nerva's reform of, 335, 337, 339, 340, 343–46, 348 n. 295, 352, 355 n. 304, 357–58
  political significance of, 353 n. 300, 364 n. 319
  projects financed by, 302
  reasons for, 335–36
  registration for, 335–36, 356–59, 362
  sources for data on, 314 n. 220
  tax evasion, 337, 339–45, 346 n. 289, 347–49, 357, 359–60
fish avoidance, 103 n. 4

followers of Jesus, 215–16. *See also* disciples of Jesus
  and the "Christian" label, 297–300
  conflicts with other affiliations, 318–19
  and the *fiscus Iudaicus,* 336, 358–59, 362, 367
  impact of Jesus's death on, 391
  in the itinerancy hypothesis, 519–20
  Jewish persecution of, 355 n. 305
  and the kingdom of God, 284
  persecution of, 292–94, 296–302, 360 n. 314
  portrayed in Matthew, 528–30
  Roman Empire's interest in, 294 n. 188, 360
  vagueness of label, 216 n. 22
food laws, 103 n. 4, 117, 119 n. 30, 234–38
For Marx (Althusser), 78–79
form criticism, 224, 432–33, 502–3, 517
"Foundations of Leninism" (Stalin), 80
"Four Winnebago Myths" (Lévi-Strauss), 61–63
framework theory, 57–58, 65 n. 112
fruit motif, 407–9
Galilee
  impact of defeat on, 315
  Markan interest in, 139, 189–90, 475–77, 479–80
  postwar Roman rule of, 255 n. 104
  relation to Jerusalem, 189
  as setting for *bios*-martyr myth, 199–200
  social situation of, 139, 173–74
gentile Christians, 136, 337, 342–46, 351–53, 402 n. 7, 503 n. 67. *See also* followers of Jesus
"gentile mission," 179, 191–92, 230 n. 50, 232
Gerasenes, 476
Gethsemane story, 435–39, 477 n. 214
Golan, 232, 315
Gonzalez, Elián, 33
gospel (genre), 459. *See also* literature (early Christian)

Greece, 112, 217 n. 25, 327–328
groupism, 213–215
Grundrisse (Marx), 87–88
habitus, 510–511
Hadrian, 307, 310
hand washing (purity practice), 234–238
  Pilate's performance of, 381, 384–385
Hawaiian example, 30, 35–38, 40 n. 65, 45–46, 100, 204, 550
"healing of the paralytic" narrative, 459
Heracles/Herakles, 110, 118, 185, 198–199, 378 n. 351
Herder, Johann Gottfried, 493–495, 498–502
heresy, 300 n. 195
Herod Antipas, 389 n. 378, 429 n. 81
hero-sage narratives, 242 n. 81, 375 n. 347, 377–378
Historical Ethnography (Sahlins), 32, 37 n. 58
Historical Figure of Jesus, The (Sanders), 403
Historical Metaphors and Mythical Realities (Sahlins), 24 n. 19, 41 n. 65, 42 n. 67, 84
historiography, 243 n. 83, 330 n. 256, 404 n. 11, 564 n. 64
  and mantic practices, 244 n. 87, 266, 279 n. 167, 284 n. 174
history
  Braudel's divisions of, 74–76
  idealist views of, 158–159, 563 n. 62
  narrative mode in, 404
  relation between anthropology and, 17–18
  Romantic theories of, 492, 494–495, 498–499
  tensions between structure and, 25–30, 39, 157–158
  traditional historiographic view of, 404 n. 11
"History and the Social Sciences" (Braudel), 75–76
hot societies, 25 n. 20

"householder on journey" parable, 287–292, 291 n. 183, 435–439, 466
human sacrifice, 37 n. 58
hypotexts, 455–456
idealism, 147 n. 4, 158–159, 556 n. 49
identity
  and alienation, 295 n. 188, 301 n. 195
  defined through the past, 526 n. 131
  ethnicity and location synthesized in, 475 n. 207
  and the *fiscus Iudaicus,* 335–337, 357–359, 362
  formation of, 362
  impact of exile on, 480–482
  impact of labels on, 215 n. 20
  in the Levant, 111–112, 217 n. 25
  logic of, 44–46
  methods of marking, 135–136
  and persecution, 298 n. 192
  problems as analytical term, 213–215
  in the Roman Empire, 282 n. 171, 312 n. 218
  and trauma, 295 n. 189
Idumea, 102 n. 4, 116 n. 24, 189, 315, 476
ignoble death theme, 505–506
imperialism, 104–105, 104 n. 5, 111–112, 228–230. See also colonialism; Roman Empire
incidents (happenings), 121 n. 36
  marking intracultural events, 129, 171–173
  relation between structures and, 32–34, 156–158, 161
incongruity, 60 n. 105. See also situational incongruity
indexical signs, 53 n. 96
indigenous cultures, 35–38, 99–101, 104–105
informers *(delatores),* 340, 344–345, 348–351, 358, 359
infrastructures/superstructures, 64 n. 111, 87, 90–91, 148 n. 4, 556
integration, 211–212, 232 n. 52, 309–310, 312 nn. 218–219, 350 n. 297
intellectualism, 151–156, 176, 562 n. 62

inversion strategies, 100 n. 3, 232 n. 53

Ioudaios/Ioudaioi translation, 208–11, 232 n. 52. *See also* Jewish collective identity

Isfiya hoard, 371 n. 338

itinerancy hypothesis, 519–20, 527

Iudaea capta coins, 303, 313

Izates of Adiabene, 238 n. 69

James (brother of Jesus), 273 n. 160, 297

Jeremiah, 263 n. 120, 264–66

Jerusalem. *See also* Roman-Judean war; temple (Jerusalem)
  axis with Galilee, 7, 183, 188, 232
  destruction of, 338, 392–93
  following destruction of, 307–10
  place in Levantine situation, 189–90
  role in the diaspora, 317 n. 224, 475–82
  Roman siege of, 261–62
  Seleucid-Maccabean conflict, 279
  as setting for *bios*-martyr myth, 199–200
  writings following destruction of, 322–24

Jesus. *See also* baptism of Jesus; death of Jesus; passion narrative
  addressing sacrifice, 284 n. 175
  apocalyptic interests of, 516–17
  attributes and roles of, 387–89, 389 n. 378
  burial of, 397, 449 n. 137
  compared to Herakles, 198–99
  cursing the fig tree, 266–67, 406, 408–9
  divine status of, 257 n. 106, 378 n. 351, 413 n. 38, 416 n. 45, 417–18, 421, 466–67
  fear in scenes of, 388 n. 378
  John the Baptist as precursor to, 425–31, 466–67
  as model of persecution, 271–73, 377
  parable of the fig tree, 287–92, 407–9
  parallels to Jesus ben Hananiah, 263–66, 454 n. 155
  portrayed in John's Gospel, 531–32

Jesus (*cont.*)
  portrayed in Mark's Gospel, 140–42, 153, 196–197
  portrayed in Matthew's Gospel, 528–29
  portrayed in Q, 268–69, 375 n. 345
  prophecy of Son of Man's coming, 286–92
  prophecy of temple destruction, 257 n. 106, 258–59, 267, 275–78, 291–92
  and the purity system, 190–91, 233 n. 56, 235 n. 61
  reasons for Mark's use of, 153, 253–54, 321, 480, 482
  Sanders's historical "facts" of, 402–3
  spatial range of activity, 231–33
  as synonymous with the gospel, 462–63
  and the Syro-Phoenician woman, 186–187
  taxation addressed by, 363–67, 368–73
  as teacher, 444 n. 125, 459–63, 522–25
  temple disruption scene, 266–67, 285 n. 175, 409–13, 424–25, 452
  temptation of, 413 n. 38, 416 n. 45
  transfiguration of, 290 n. 182, 417–18, 422–24, 443, 453
  use of parables, 463–71
  woman's anointing of, 397

Jesus ben Hananiah (Jesus-Ananias), 259, 262–66, 270, 273, 454–56, 454 n. 155

Jesus movements. *See also* Christianity; followers of Jesus
  creating identification, 139–40
  early stages of, 489–90, 525
  and itinerancy theory, 520 n. 116
  and Jewish identity, 572 n. 86
  kingdom of God focus of, 177–78, 200
  Mark's use of, 196–97, 457–59
  origin story development, 201–2, 526–27
  parallels to Seminar, 149–51
  in a postwar setting, 199–200

Jesus movements (*cont.*)
    reacting to external happenings, 160–61
    role of Mark's Gospel in, 201–2, 401–2
    role of theory in studying, 146–47
    scholarly imagination on, 484–86
    significance of synagogues to, 193–94
    in a southern Syria location, 189–90, 204
Jewish Christians. *See also* followers of Jesus
    and the *fiscus Iudaicus,* 337, 342–46, 351–53, 355 n. 304, 356 n. 306, 358–59
    labeling of, 361 n. 314
    religious identity of, 136, 337, 343–46
    separation from Jewish communities, 351–53
Jewish collective identity
    in the diaspora, 334, 479–82
    and the *fiscus Iudaicus,* 314, 335–37, 343, 358–59
    impact of exile on, 480–82
    impact of religious practice on, 309–10
    Paul's threat to, 300 n. 194
    problems as analytical term, 208–10
    in the Roman Empire, 350
    Schwartz's formulations of, 311 n. 218
Jewish Reactions (Jones), 327
Jewish Revolt. *See* Judean Revolt (66 CE)
Jewish War. *See* Roman-Judean war
John the Baptist. *See also* baptism of Jesus
    complexity of role, 413–14
    death of, 274 n. 161, 430 n. 81
    debated apocalyptism of, 413–14, 428 n. 76
    identified with Elijah, 420 n. 58, 421, 423
    and the parable of the tenants, 466–67
    popularity of, 416 n. 46
    as a precursor figure, 425–31, 466–67
    "shouting" references, 420 n. 56, 421
    teaching of, 522–25
    tree/fruit sayings of, 407

Joseph of Arimathea, 449 n. 137, 454–56
Judaism
    boundary making, 212 n. 10
    covenant/myth juxtaposed in, 324–25
    following the war, 251 n. 101, 304–10, 311 n. 218, 318–19, 524
    as a religion, 210–12
    separation from Christianity, 335–37, 343, 352–53, 354–55
    under Tertullian, 352 n. 300
Judas Iscariot, 435 n. 95, 440 n. 111, 442, 454 n. 153
Judea
    consequences of defeat, 302–10, 313–18
    ethnic relations in, 319–21
    following the war, 318–19
    in the Levantine picture, 185–86
    portrayed in Mark, 199–200, 476
    relations between Samaria and, 114–16
    Roman rule of, 219 n. 29, 252 n. 102, 255 n. 104, 305 n. 203, 315 n. 222
Judean elite ruling class
    end of Roman support for, 310 n. 216
    following the war, 261 n. 116, 305–6, 330–32
    Josephus's portrayals of, 247–49, 260 n. 114, 332 n. 259
    Mark's portrayals of, 287, 383
Judean revolt (66 CE). *See also* Roman-Judean war
    consequences of, 219 n. 29, 253 n. 103, 302–10
    and the *fiscus Iudaicus,* 336
    Josephus's version of, 247–49
    underlying causes, 281–82, 304 n. 200
Jupiter Capitoline, temple of, 302, 307, 338
Justus of Tiberias, 329
Kant, Immanuel, 491–92
kerygma, 195, 269, 374, 432–33. *See also* apocalyptic traditions
kingdom of God, 177–78, 200, 284, 427
king parables, 363

Kingship and Sacrifice (Valeri), 45 n. 74
kinship systems, 90–91
Kitchener, Ontario, 164–65
language. *See also* linguistics
  in the Levant, 116
  and mythmaking, 557 n. 50
  privileged over praxis, 557 n. 51
  relation to practices, 559–60
  Romantic theories of, 493–95, 498–502
  in Sahlins's formulations, 49–53
  Saussure's chess analogy, 46, 49–51
  unconscious/conscious frames, 5–6, 153–54
Last Supper narrative, 440–44
"leaving" motif, 394 n. 382
legal systems, 253 n. 103, 314, 380–83
Lenin, Vladimir, 77–80
Levant. *See also* Syria
  apocalyptic traditions in, 124–25
  contested nature of, 102–5
  ethnic conflict in, 114–20, 122
  ethnic identities in, 135–36, 183–84, 232
  New Testament portrayals of, 123
  political history of, 177–78
  as potential Markan setting, 136–37, 139, 181–82, 187–90, 192–93, 379
  religion in, 105–12, 184–85
  sociocultural situation in, 139, 171–74, 184–86
Life of Aesop, 242 n. 81, 244, 468–69, 512
linguistics. *See also* language
  structuralism in, 94 n. 203
  unconscious character of, 153–54
literary-critical approach, 474 n. 205
literary networks, 487, 498, 505–8, 518
  of early Christian authors, 509–14
literature
  form criticism, 502–3
  legitimizing myth through, 526–33
  redaction criticism, 503–4
  Romantic theories of, 491–97
literature (early Christian)
  authorship of, 484, 509–14
  gospel genre of, 459, 512

literature (early Christian) (cont.)
  innovation of, 512
  "instant-aging" maneuvers, 490 n. 22
  Jesus movements described in, 485–86
  Markan influence on, 402–4
  non-mythic aspects of, 155–56
  post-destruction period, 322–334
  production of, 511–12, 514–15
  role of communities in, 484, 489–91, 496–97
  scholarly approaches to, 483–88
  social world of authors, 514–15
  term "gospel" used in, 461–62, 512 n. 96
literature (Greco-Roman)
  audiences of, 513–14
  categories in, 506 n. 76
  consumption of, 506–8
  contrasted to Romantic literature, 497–98
  gospels as, 239–46, 512
  nonspecialist participation in, 513–14
  production of, 504–8
  rhetorical devices in, 280 n. 169
  varying skill levels of writers, 511
literature (Jewish)
  impact of Roman-Judean war on, 304 n. 201
  postdestruction, 322–34
Lord's Supper narrative, 440–44
mantic practices, 244 n. 87, 266, 279 n. 167, 284 n. 174
Marisa (Idumea), 102 n. 4
martyr myths
  blood motif in, 385–86
  combined with *bios,* 7–8, 199
  in the Greco-Roman world, 197–99
  and the Lord's Supper accounts, 441–43
  in the passion narrative, 376 n. 347, 386
  and religious specialists, 297 n. 191
  as sacrifice, 386 n. 371
Marxism, 34, 64 n. 111, 65 n. 112, 78, 80–81, 86–92

Mattathias, 279

Mediterranean and the Mediterranean World, The (Braudel), 74–75, 76

Melqart (deity), 108, 110, 185

memory, 225–28, 389 n. 378

Menemachus, 328, 331

messianic secret, 245 n. 89, 527–28

metonymy, 283–84

mimetic literature, 241, 264–65, 380–83

miracle stories (genre), 187, 197

morphology, 56 n. 99, 93–95

Muslim identity, 166

mythmaking

  addressing situational incongruities, 201, 473–74, 554

  avoiding dependency/congruency formulations, 20, 59–60, 131

  categorical rectification of, 540–43, 546–49

  conscious/unconscious frames, 66–68, 176–177

  defined, 3

  in early Christian literature, 405 n. 16, 490–91

  function of quotidian notices in, 155 n. 17

  intelligibility of, 149–50

  in Mark's framework stories, 424

  in Mark's passion narrative, 141–42, 431–35

  nexus between social formation and, 3, 59–60, 67–68, 132–33, 156–61

  precursor moments in, 557 n. 50

  responding to external incidents, 161

  sayings traditions used in, 427

  of the Seminar, 149–51

  Seminar's approach to, 202–5

Myth of Innocence, A (Mack), 2–3, 12, 120, 137–38, 441, 473

Mythologiques (Lévi-Strauss), 96–98

myths

  communities associated with, 532–33

  conscious-unconscious functions of, 5–6, 61, 63–68, 153–55, 159–60, 175–77

myths (cont.)

  creating identification through, 139–40

  as experimental application, 71 n. 119

  and ideology, 64–65, 526–33

  incongruity in, 60 n. 105

  intellectualist approaches to, 151–56

  juxtaposed to covenant system, 324

  Lévi-Strauss's formulation of, 26–27, 39–40, 64 n. 111, 96–98

  of martyrdom, 201–2, 441–43

  as a "mirror," 59–60, 132

  modern theories as, 149–50

  Pacific Island examples, 27–30, 35–38, 41 n. 65

  rationality of, 148–50

  rectification through, 72 n. 120

  relations between, 62–63, 152–53, 161, 162

  relation to culture/society, 61–62

  relation to events, 152–53

  relation to reality, 62 n. 106, 152–53

  relation to situations, 69 n. 118, 154–55, 174–77

NAASR. *See* North American Association for the Study of Religion

Nabatea, 319–20

Naked Man, The (Lévi-Strauss), 93–95

narratives

  determining audiences for, 473

  in history discipline, 404

  in Mark's Gospel, 401

  pronoun usage in, 67 n. 115

  reasons for Mark's use, 482

  sayings transformed into, 405–6, 409

nature (Romantic conceptions of), 492 n. 26, 500–501

Nebuzaradan, 384, 385

Neo-Kantianism, 55–57

Nero, 297, 299 n. 193, 303, 361 n. 314

Nerva, 307, 335, 337, 339, 340, 343–46, 348 n. 295, 350, 352, 355 n. 304, 357–58

New Testament literature. *See also* literature (early Christian)

  myth of origins in, 489–491

New Testament literature (cont.)
 referencing the *fiscus Iudaicus,* 336
 religious theory in scholarship of, 539
noble death motif, 373, 393, 505–6. *See also* martyr myths
North American Association for the Study of Religion, 538
numeric symbolism, 419 n. 54, 423, 437
Odysseus, 526, 527 n. 133
On German Character and Art (Moore), 495
On Growth and Form (Thompson), 93–95
Onias, temple of, 306, 372 n. 341
On the Spirit of Hebrew Poetry (Herder), 500–501
oral traditions, 220–24, 501–2, 517–18
orthodoxy, 300 n. 195
Out of Time (Thomas), 4, 99–101
Pacific Island societies, 28–29, 35–38, 41 n. 65, 45–46, 85, 100–101
Palestine, 311 n. 218, 315, 325–27. *See also* Judea
parables
 circularity of, 461
 as comparisons, 464 n. 183
 householder on journey, 287–92, 291 n. 183, 435–39, 466
 Jesus teaching through, 463–71
 "robber" sayings, 437 n. 104
 seed parables, 464 nn. 182–83
 of the sower, 460–61
 of the tenants, 377 n. 349, 438 n. 104, 463, 464–71
parody, 242 n. 79
passion narrative. *See also* death of Jesus
 anachronistic retrojection in, 454–56
 arrest of Jesus, 267 n. 143, 271–73, 395 n. 382, 435 n. 95
 betrayal theme in, 435 n. 95, 440 n. 111, 442
 burial of Jesus, 397, 449 n. 137
 christological motif in, 270–74
 debates on historicity of, 433 n. 91
 developmental process, 450 n. 144

passion narrative (cont.)
 empty tomb narrative, 239, 377–78, 395 n. 382, 396–97
 Gethsemane story, 435–39, 477 n. 214
 Last Supper narrative, 440–44
 Markan narrativization of, 431–35, 477–81
 martyrdom theme in, 376 n. 347
 Pauline parallels to, 434–35 nn. 94–95
 place names in, 477 n. 214
 pre-Markan versions, 269 n. 150, 270, 375 n. 347
 rectifying situational incongruity, 256 n. 105, 481
 resurrection of Jesus, 378 n. 351, 516 n. 103
 ritual elements in, 295 n. 189
 sources for, 374–75, 448 n. 137, 449–51
 as substitute story, 9–10, 392–93
 temple motif in, 270–75
 trial of Jesus, 270–75, 380–87, 411–12, 454–56
 triumphal entry scene, 440 n. 112, 444–47, 449 n. 142
 as a wisdom tale, 264–65, 269 n. 149
Paul
 Acts as biography source for, 404 n. 13
 apocalyptic scenarios of, 195
 Christian origins described by, 178, 489
 Christ myth of, 138, 198
 disrupting Roman imperial hegemony, 300 n. 195
 establishing communities, 527
 on food offered to idols, 238 n. 68
 gentile mission of, 136, 191–92
 interest in the passion narrative, 432 n. 90
 Jesus movement described by, 485
 Lord's Supper account, 440–43
 passion narrative parallels, 434–35 nn. 94–95
 persecution of, 299–300, 355 n. 305
 portrayed in Acts, 526

Paul (*cont.*)
    in Puteoli, 105 n. 6
    referencing the disciples, 453–54
    and sin sacrifices, 374 n. 344
Perea, 315, 332
persecution, 9
    and the "Christian" label, 297–300,
        361 n. 314
    evidence of, 255 n. 104
    and the *fiscus Iudaicus,* 337, 368
    of followers of Jesus, 292–94, 296–302
    Heemstra's formulation of, 354–56
    of independent religious specialists,
        298 n. 192, 360 n. 314
    Jesus as model of, 271–73, 377, 392
    Jesus's prophecy of, 275, 292–302
    under Nero, 299 n. 193
    of Paul, 299–300, 355 n. 305
    reasons for, 301 n. 195
    role in Christianity, 485 n. 5
Persia, 330 n. 256
Peter (disciple), 178–79, 297, 363–67, 454
    n. 153
Pharisees. *See also* priests
    antagonistic role of, 190–91, 192–93
    and followers of Jesus, 200
    following the war, 124, 251 n. 101, 253
        n. 103, 318–19, 326
    Jesus's debates with, 190, 192–93, 452
    Mark's portrayals of, 140–41, 383
    as problematic in Mark, 124, 188–89
    and purity practices, 119 n. 30, 190–
        91, 192–93, 234–38
    Taylor's views of, 253 n. 103
Philip, 178–79
Phoenicia, 116 n. 24. *See also* Syria
    impact of Judean defeat on, 315
    Markan interest in, 479–80
    as possible Markan site, 173, 218 n. 27
Pilate, 114, 273–74, 274 n. 161, 275, 281,
    380, 381, 384–85
poetry, 492, 500–502
Pompey (emperor), 369 n. 335
"Poor Man, Rich Man, Big-Man, Chief"
    (Sahlins), 19 n. 6

pork avoidance, 117
Port-Royal grammarian tradition, 83
practice theory, 542 n. 14, 559–60
practices (social)
    changing nature of, 573 n. 88
    as crucial element, 31
    and *habitus,* 510–11
    relation between praxis and, 34–35
    in Sahlins's Fijian example, 29
    situating Mark through, 187–88
    Stowers's formulations of, 559–60
    structure of the conjuncture in, 24 n.
        19
"practico-inert" concept, 51–52, 158 n. 25
praxis
    conceptual schemes structuring, 151–
        52
    language privileged over, 557 n. 51
    myth's role in, 156, 159
    and the practico-inert, 52 n. 92
    relation between practices and, 34–35
    transformation as, 51–52
presentism, 17–18
priests. *See also* Judean elite ruling class;
        Pharisees
    antagonistic role of, 190–91
    in the diaspora, 331 n. 259
    following the war, 305–6
    at Jesus's trial, 381–83
pronouncement stories (*chreia*), 186–87,
    197, 440–44
purity practices. *See also* religious prac-
        tices; sacrifices
    as ethnic marker, 191
    hand washing, 234–38
    impact of temple's destruction on, 124
    inner *versus* outer, 237 n. 64
    and the Shu'afat site, 325 n. 244
    spaces embodying system, 233 n. 56
    and the temple system, 190–91
Puteoli, 105–11
quotidian notices, 155 n. 17
rabbinic movement, 235, 251 n. 101, 335
    n. 263
ransom clause, 373 n. 343

rational-cognitivist approach, 562 n. 62
recantation, 360 n. 314
rectification. *See also* transformation
  contextualization of term, 72 n. 120
  in Markan context, 162, 174
  replacing "transformation," 72
  of Seminar's approach, 130–34, 546–55
  of terminology, 177
redaction criticism, 224, 503–4
Redescribing Christian Origins (Cameron and Miller), 2, 535–36, 537 nn. 2–3, 539 n. 6, 540–41, 545, 546, 563–67
Redescribing Paul and the Corinthians (Cameron and Miller), 2, 536 n. 1, 540, 546–49, 562 n. 61, 563–67
redescription, 542 nn. 13–14
  defined, 540
  different strategies of, 543–45
  vocabulary displacement, 540–41
religion. *See also* Christianity; Judaism; religious studies
  counterintuitive entities in, 390 n. 378
  disembedding of, 211 n. 6
  diversities within similar traditions, 113–14
  feasting associated with, 118 n. 30
  impact of trade on, 110–11
  incongruity in, 60 n. 105
  and Jewish identity, 208–12
  in the Levant, 105–12, 118–19, 184–85
  locative deities, 109 n. 16
  Roman recognition of, 304–10
  Romantic conceptions of, 498–502
Religions of the Ancient World (Johnston), 570 n. 82
religious identity. *See also* Jewish collective identity
  and the *fiscus Iudaicus,* 337, 343, 346
  and *Ioudaioi* translations, 208–10
  shifts from ethnic to, 111–12, 136
religious practices. *See also* purity practices; sacrifices
  dietary laws, 103 n. 4, 117, 119 n. 30, 234–38

religious practices (cont.)
  and the *fiscus Iudaicus,* 359–60
  following the war, 307–10, 311 n. 218, 316 n. 224
  in the Levant, 105–12
  Stowers's typology of, 570
  under Tertullian, 352 n. 300
religious specialists
  effects of Mark's Gospel on, 396
  and followers of Jesus, 216
  impact of the war on, 319 n. 225
  Roman regulation of, 294 n. 188, 296 n. 191, 298 n. 192, 360–61
religious studies
  proposals for, 569–73
  relevance of, 150 n. 6
  role of theory in, 145–47
  Seminar's approach to, 1–2, 536–39, 562–63
  terminology for redescription in, 541
reproduction
  anthropological sense of, 88–90
  as crucial element, 31
  and history, 158–59
  Lévi-Strauss's formulation of, 39–40
  in Marxist discourse, 86–92
  meanings of, 86
  Pacific Island examples, 28–29, 36–38, 85
  relation between transformation and, 20, 159 n. 27
  relation to myth, 63
  replaced by "experimental application," 69
  role of tension in, 157–158
  Sahlins's formulation of, 24 n. 19, 40–46, 48, 51 n. 88, 88, 91–92, 157–59
  in the Syro-Phoenician woman narrative, 174
  Thomas's formulation of, 99–101
resurrection, 385–86
resurrection of Jesus, 378 n. 351, 516 n. 103
"Return of the Event, Again, The" (Sahlins), 32

rhetorical (conscious) myths, 5–6, 61, 68, 153–55, 159–60, 174–77

"robber" sayings, 437 n. 104

Roman Empire. *See also* fiscus Iudaicus (Jewish tax)

  atheism prosecuted in, 339–43

  censuses in, 357 n. 308, 369–71

  "Christian" label in, 297–300, 361 n. 314

  civic-political imperial policy, 217–18

  colonialism of, 3–4

  direct rule policies, 252 n. 102, 305 n. 203, 313 n. 219, 314, 319 n. 225

  eliminating client-king system, 253 n. 103, 313 n. 219

  illegality of Christianity in, 352 n. 300, 360

  imperial hegemony structure, 300 n. 195

  integration policy, 312 nn. 218–19

  interest in followers of Jesus, 294 n. 188

  Jewish integration into, 219 n. 29, 309–10, 314

  justice system, 253 n. 103, 273 n. 160, 380–83

  patronage system, 312 n. 219

  policies on Judaism, 352 n. 300

  poll taxes of, 369–72

  postwar monument building, 302–3

  proselytizing mission of, 285 n. 176

  provincial attitudes toward, 327–34

  regulating religious specialists, 296 n. 191, 298 n. 192, 360 n. 314

  religious relations within, 111–12

  response to Judean revolt, 302–10

  violating sanctity of temple, 280–82

Roman-Judean war

  consequences of defeat, 302–10, 313–18

  cultural persistence following, 275

  and dating of Mark, 254–62, 276–77

  disaffection following, 249 n. 97, 315–18, 327, 332 n. 261

  ethnic crises following, 163–64

Roman-Judean war (*cont.*)

  impacts on followers of Jesus, 292–93

  impacts on the diaspora, 320–21, 480–82

  Jewish tax imposed following, 335–36

  Josephus's version of, 247–49

  Levantine social environment following, 379

  Mark's Gospel as response to, 204–5, 223 n. 34, 246–54, 393 n. 381, 474–75, 479–82

  parallels to Jesus's death, 392–93

  Q as response to, 288–89, 524–25

  reasons for, 260–61 nn. 114–15, 280–82, 303–4

  siege of Jerusalem, 261–62

Romanticism

  "author/genius" in, 486–87, 491–97

  conceptions of religion, 498–502

  contrasted to ancient literature, 497–98

  impact on approaches to Q, 517

  influence of, 224, 486–87

  Seminar's rejection of, 562

  theories of language, 498–502

  treatment of myths in, 532–33

Rowlandson, Mary, 481

Rufus (son of Simon of Cyrene), 395 n. 382, 478

Russian Revolution (1917), 77–80

sacrifices. *See also* religious practices

  and atheism charges, 341, 347

  blood motif, 373 n. 343, 384–87

  death of Jesus as, 373 n. 343–74 n. 344, 384–87

  in the diaspora, 317 n. 224

  following the war, 306–9, 316 n. 224

  and Jesus's temple act, 285 n. 175

  martyrdom as, 386 n. 371

  Valeri on decomposition, 45 n. 74

Sadducees, 251 n. 101, 253 n. 103, 318

Samaria, 114–16, 189, 282 n. 171

Sanhedrin, 270–72, 273 n. 160, 287

Sarepta, god of, 107–8, 109–10

Savage Mind, The (Lévi-Strauss), 25 n. 20, 38–39, 48, 62, 64 n. 111

sayings traditions
  attributed to Jesus, 457 n. 160
  as baptism scene source, 424–25
  contextualization of, 404
  and the crucifixion, 450–52
  dating of, 525
  developmental sequence of, 408 n. 25
  and the Gethsemane story, 435–39
  Jesus's temple actions in, 410 n. 32
  John the Baptist as precursor in, 425–31
  and the Lord's Supper account, 440–44
  Markan narrativization of, 400, 405–6, 409, 429–31, 434–35, 439, 446 n. 130, 450–52, 457–59, 471
  as Markan source, 424–25, 447
  in Mark's passion narrative, 431–35
  parable of the tenants, 468–71
  "robber" sayings, 437 n. 104
  trees motif in, 406–9
  and the triumphal entry, 444–47
scapegoat rituals, 382 n. 362
Schlegel, Friedrich, 492
scribes, 43, 325, 520–22, 552 n. 39
Search for a Method (Sartre), 33–34
secrecy motif, 245 n. 89
seed parables, 464 nn. 182–83
Seminar, SBL (1998–2003)
  agenda discussion questions for, 142–43
  approach of, 13–14, 537 n. 3
  category formation issues, 129–30, 546–49
  comparison to successor groups, 567–69
  differences among, 15, 542–45, 563 n. 72
  fundamental agreements in, 15, 561–63
  general procedures for, 2–3
  goals of, 147, 150, 539 n. 6, 569
  limitations of, 568–69
  located in religious studies, 536–39
  mythmaking of, 149–51

Seminar, SBL (1998–2003) (cont.)
  potential idealism in, 147 n. 4
  purposes of, 1–2, 535 n. 1, 537 n. 3
  results of, 542–43, 551
  role of theory in, 146–48, 150, 561
  and Stowers's proposal, 569–71
  strengths of, 569
  Taussig's review of, 563–67
  vocabulary displacements of, 540–41
Severus (emperor), 352 n. 300
Shakespeare, William, 493–95
Shechem, 115 n. 24
shepherd/sheep metaphors, 447 n. 133
Shu'afat, 325 n. 244
Sidon, 102 n. 4, 115 n. 24, 231 n. 51, 476
signs, 49–53, 63 n. 108, 95
silk industry, 106 n. 8
Simon of Cyrene, 395 n. 382, 478–79
Simon the leper, 479 n. 218
situational incongruity
  approach to studying, 162
  contextualization of term, 69 n. 118
  crisis setting accounting for, 168
  following the Roman-Judean war, 222 n. 34, 474, 481, 557 n. 50
  in Mark's Levantine Judean association, 136–37
  mythmaking addressing, 61 n. 105, 71 n. 119, 132–33, 473–74, 554
  passion narrative rectifying, 257 n. 105
  replacing "conjuncture," 69
  Seminar's approach to, 203–5
  Seminar's work as, 149, 150
  Smith's formulation of, 557 n. 51
  in the Syro-Phoenician woman narrative, 172
situations (social)
  behind Q's writing, 522–25
  intracultural-intercultural boundaries, 170–73
  relation to myths, 154–55, 174–77
  Seminar's approach to, 128
  "site" redescribed as, 131
slaves, 339, 348 n. 294, 469 n. 192, 505 n. 72, 507 n. 84

social classes
  antagonistic relations between, 469
  and literacy, 505 n. 72
  Mark's treatment of, 479 n. 218
social escape narratives
  of followers of Jesus, 396
  following failed revolt, 9–10, 379, 394–96
  Mark's plot as example of, 230, 398
  and Roman power, 368
  of Yohanan ben Zakkai, 398 n. 386
social formations. *See also* communities
  Althusser's understanding of, 81
  among followers of Jesus, 215–16, 396, 548 n. 28
  anthropological interest in, 88–89
  avoiding dependency/congruency formulations, 20, 59–60, 131
  categorical rectification of, 540–43, 546–49
  creating identification through, 139–40
  defined, 3
  in early Christian literature, 485–86, 520, 531–32, 554–55
  enabling conditions for, 552 n. 39
  Heemstra's approach to, 354
  impact of the war on, 285–86, 316–19
  maintaining boundaries, 327
  nexus between mythmaking and, 3, 59–60, 67–68, 132–33, 156–61
  problematic labels in, 215–16
  reflected in the Seminar, 150–51
  sayings traditions supporting, 427
  Seminar's approach to, 202–5
  and social memory studies, 225–28
  of writers, 486 n. 9
social interests, 133–34, 175–76, 557 n. 50
social memory studies, 225–28
social theory
  differences of, 556–60
  in religious studies, 562 n. 62
  Seminar's approaches in, 543–45
  space in, 233 n. 56

societies
  Brubaker's theoretical model, 213–17
  classification division examples, 25–30
  "hot" *versus* "cool," 25 n. 20
  imperialism's impact on, 212
  relations between, 22–23
  relation to myth, 61–62, 157–59
  reproduction in tribal, 87–88
  role of counterintuitive entities in, 390 n. 378
  social logic structuring, 133–34
Sophocles, 494–95
sources (Gospel of Mark), 264–66, 278, 408 n. 27, 409, 422, 446 n. 130, 458–59
  sayings traditions, 424–25, 447
  scriptures, 447–51, 457 n. 160
sources (Q), 264–66
sower, parable of, 460–61
Stalin, Joseph, 80
Stephen, 273 n. 160, 297
stereotypic reproduction, 29, 39, 40 n. 65, 90, 91–92
"stilling the sea" narrative, 388 n. 378
Story of the Ten Martyrs, 386 n. 371
structure
  agency emphasized over, 211–12
  alteration of, 556 n. 49
  Braudel's aligning with the *longue durée,* 75–76
  of language, 94 n. 203, 153–54
  relation between incidents and, 32–34, 156–58, 161
  relation to events, 156–58, 161
  of systems, 95–96
  tension between history and, 25–30
structure of the conjuncture. *See also* conjunctures
  in Braudel, 83–84
  genealogy of term, 23–25
  in the Hawaiian-Cook example, 40 n. 65
  Sahlins's use of, 83–84, 85–86
  trade/exchange example, 24 n. 19
  and transformation, 42 n. 67
subjectivity (Taussig's concept), 564–65

successor groups (SBL), 1, 535, 545, 569–71

  agreements among, 13–14

  comparisons to older seminar, 567–69

  location in religious studies, 537–38

  Taussig's assessment of, 567

superstructures/infrastructures, 64 n. 111, 87, 90–91, 148 n. 4, 556

synagogue of the Freedmen, 478–79

synagogues, 140–41, 188–89, 193–94, 343

synchrony, 25, 39, 50–51, 154 n. 16

Syria

  Andrade's study on, 217–18

  apocalyptic traditions in, 124–25

  as a "contact zone," 112

  geographical definition, 102 n. 4

  geopolitical history of, 104 n. 5

  impact of Judean revolt on, 315

  as potential Markan site, 102, 173, 189–90, 218 n. 29, 379

  relations to Jerusalem, 189–90

  religious feasting in, 118 n. 30

  religious patterns in, 112

  under Roman rule, 217–18, 311 n. 218

Syria Phoenicia

  geographical definition, 102 n. 4

  Pharisees in, 124

  as potential Markan site, 173

  religious feasting in, 118 n. 30

  religious relations in, 118–19

Syro-Phoenician woman narrative

  as double *chreia,* 186–87

  ethnic identity in, 121–23, 187, 230 n. 50

  intracultural-intercultural situations in, 170–73

  Markan plot of, 186–87

  Matthean redaction, 121–22, 231 n. 50

systemic agency, 33

taxes. *See also fiscus Iudaicus* (Jewish tax); temple tax (Jerusalem)

  addressed by Jesus, 368–73

  Matthean tax narrative, 363–67

  payment as subjection, 366

  payment as subversive praxis, 365–66

taxes (cont.)

  poll taxes, 369–71

  and Roman censuses, 369–71

temple (Jerusalem)

  as civic cult, 308–10

  desecration of, 277–82

  following the war, 302

  Jesus's cleansing of, 266–67, 285 n. 175, 409–13, 424–25, 452

  links to Jesus's baptism, 418–19, 422

  purity codes defined by, 190–91, 233 n. 56

  reasons for Mark's use of, 140–41, 188–89

  Roman violations of, 280–82

  significance to Jesus movements, 139, 194, 199–200

temple destruction (Jerusalem). *See also* Roman-Judean war

  apocalyptic traditions responding to, 124–125, 195, 322–335

  consequences for Jerusalem cult, 308–10, 387

  cultural persistence following, 283–84, 333 n. 261, 387

  and dating Mark's Gospel, 254–62, 289

  disaffection following, 249 n. 97, 316–317, 327, 332 n. 261

  impact on purity practices, 124, 387

  Jesus's prophecy of, 257 n. 106, 258–59, 275–78, 291–92, 412

  Josephus's version of, 247–49, 332 n. 259

  linked to Jesus's death, 9–10, 256–57, 266–75, 377–78, 391–94, 397–99, 474–75

  Markan portrayals of, 140–41, 152 n. 10, 294 n. 188

  possible reasons for, 195, 310 n. 216

  Q written in response to, 524–25

  significance to Jesus movements, 200–202

  as situational incongruity, 481

  and Son of Man prophecies, 289–91

temple destruction (cont.)
  symbolism of curtain tearing, 266–68
temple of Jupiter Capitoline, 302, 338
temple of Onias, 306, 372 n. 341
Temple of Peace, 246, 302
temple tax (Jerusalem)
  compared to the *fiscus Iudaicus,* 308
    n. 212, 313–14
  evasion consequences, 340 n. 271
  Matthean narrative, 363–68
  names of, 363 n. 316
  political significance of, 364 n. 319
temptation narrative, 413 n. 38, 416 n. 45
tenants, parable of, 263, 264–71, 377 n.
  349, 438 n. 104
Tenth Legion, 306, 325 n. 244
Theandrites/Theandrios, 113, 120 n. 32
theory
  impact of presentism on, 17–18
  impact on legitimization, 526
  role in religious studies, 145–47
  as a tool, 146, 561
Titus, 121 n. 38, 250 n. 99, 261 n. 116,
  262, 281, 302–3, 308, 329
Toronto, Canada, 165–66
trade, 106 n. 8, 106 n. 10, 110–11
traditionsbruch, 222 n. 34, 256 n. 105
Trajan, 307, 310, 341, 342 n. 280, 345 n.
  286, 347, 360 n. 314
transfiguration account, 290 n. 182, 417–
  18, 422–24, 443, 453
transformation. *See also* rectification
  as crucial element, 31
  in the Levant, 171–74
  Lévi-Strauss's formulation of, 39–40,
    48, 66–67, 93–98
  in Mark's passion narrative, 443
  morphological understandings of, 93–
    95
  Pacific Island examples of, 29, 36–38,
    45–46, 85, 100
  as a process of translation, 95–98
  relation between reproduction and,
    20, 159 n. 27
  relation to myth, 63

transformation (cont.)
  replaced by "rectification," 72
  role in history, 158–59
  Sahlins's formulations of, 24 n. 19, 29,
    41 n. 65, 42, 47–54, 92, 98, 157–58
  of sayings material into narrative,
    405–6, 409, 471
  Thomas's formulation of, 99–101
translation fables, 239, 377–78
trauma, 255–56 nn. 104–5, 295 n. 189,
  393 n. 381
tree motif, 406–9
trial of Jesus narrative, 270–75, 380–87
  anachronistic retrojection in, 454–56
  charges against, 411–12
  Matthean version, 380–81, 384–86
  sacrifice theme in, 384–87
  as a scapegoat ritual, 382 n. 362
tribulation, 279, 286–87
triumphal entry narrative, 440 n. 112,
  444–47, 449 n. 142
Tsimshian, 62 n. 106, 66–67
Tupi tribe, 47 n. 80, 97
"two kingdoms" theory, 367
Tyre. *See also* Levant; Syria
  Greek Syro-Phoenician texts con-
    cerning, 107–11
  in the Hebrew Bible, 117 n. 27
  multiethnic markers in, 183–85
  portrayed in Mark, 476
  in the silk trade, 106 n. 8
  sociopolitical setting, 181–82, 183–85
unconscious (communicative) myths,
  5–6, 61, 63–68, 153–55, 159–60, 174–
  77
Vergil, 486, 511
Vespasian, 302, 309, 317 n. 224, 329, 338,
  353 n. 300, 369 n. 335
Vesuvius, Mount, 330 n. 256, 334 n. 261
vineyard imagery, 11, 465, 470
Waiting for Foucault (Sahlins), 43 n. 67
"When the Chips Are Down" (Smith), 2
  n. 2, 537 n. 3
wisdom tales (genre), 264, 265, 268–69,
  268 n. 149, 446, 450 n. 144

women, 231 n. 50, 395 n. 382, 397
wrongful accusation *(calumnia)*, 344–45,
    346 n. 289, 350
Xiphilinus (Byzantine monk), 339 n. 270
Yom Kippur, 374 n. 344, 382 n. 362
Zakkai, Yohanan ben, 398 n. 386
Zechariah, 384, 385, 386 n. 371, 447 nn.
    133–34

Lightning Source UK Ltd.
Milton Keynes UK
UKHW010745240519
343261UK00001B/161/P